A Standard History

OF

OKLAHOMA

An Authentic Narrative of its Development from the Date of the First European Exploration down to the Present Time, including Accounts of the Indian Tribes, both Civilized and Wild, of the Cattle Range, of the Land Openings and the Achievements of the most Recent Period

BY

JOSEPH B. THOBURN

Assisted by a Board of Advisory Editors

VOLUME V

ILLUSTRATED

THE AMERICAN HISTORICAL SOCIETY
CHICAGO AND NEW YORK
1916

1535239

HISTORY OF OKLAHOMA

ROY M. JOHNSON. An aggressive and strenuous young business man of Ardmore, Carter County, Roy M. Johnson had the foresight and good judgment to profit largely through his associations with industrial and financial enterprises in Oklahoma. He was best known for a number of years as head of the principal republican newspaper in Southern Oklahoma, but the chief objects of his attention are now banking and the oil industry in his section of the state. He is an alert and progressive young man of affairs, and has discovered and accepted many opportunities for disinterested public service.

He was born at Cashton, Monroe County, Wisconsin, July 11, 1881. His parental grandfather was born and reared in Norway, and on coming to the United States in 1850 settled in Illinois, but later became a pioneer settler in Wisconsin. He finally established his home near Cambridge, Dane County, that state, where, as a prosperous farmer, he spent the remainder of his life. Mr. Johnson's maternal grandfather was Dr. John B. Skinner, whose ancestors had come to America in early colonial times. He was an early country physician in Wisconsin, went from that state as a soldier of the Union during the Civil war, and was member of a regiment of Wisconsin cavalry until incapacitated by sunstroke, from the effects of which he never fully recovered. He was a resident of Cashton at the time of his death in 1880.

Prof. O. Andrew Johnson, father of the Ardmore business man, was born in Illinois in 1851 and was a child when taken to Dane County, Wisconsin. While growing up he acquired a liberal education in schools and colleges, and is a man of high scholarship who has been an influential figure in educational affairs and also in the Seventh Day Adventist Church. His home was in Wisconsin until 1882, when he removed with his family to Fort Calhoun, Nebraska, where he continued his evangelic labors for a decade. In 1892 he became a member of the faculty of Union College at Lincoln, Nebraska, but in 1894 returned to Wisconsin and served three years as president of the Adventist Conference of that state. In 1897 he resumed his professorship in Union College, where he remained until 1900, and then went to Norway, the land of his ancestors, and became president of the Norwegian Adventist Conference. In 1908 he resigned from that position and has since held the chair of Bible History in Walla Walla College, the Adventist institution in Walla Walla, Washington. He is one of the most distinguished representatives of the religious organization of the Seventh Day Adventists, and his wife was also a devout and zealous member of the same body. Professor Johnson married in Wisconsin Miss Sarah M. Skinner, who was born in Illinois in 1851. She died at Walla Walla, Washington, in May, 1915. Roy M. Johnson is the older of their two sons, while Harry Lynn, who is becoming distinguished in the field of mechanical inventions, is now president of the Johnson Automatic Machinery Company of Battle Creek, Michigan.

It was in the public schools of Nebraska that Roy M. Johnson acquired his early training, followed by a course in Union College, where he was graduated A. B. in 1899. In the meantime he had also been a student for three years in Milton College at Milton, Wisconsin. Mr. Johnson learned the printer's trade at Battle Creek, Michigan, where he lived from 1900 to 1903, except the summer of 1902 spent with his parents in Norway. For four years, 1903-07, he followed his trade at Beaumont, Texas, employed alternately in the offices of the two daily papers of that city.

In 1907, the year Oklahoma became a state, Mr. Johnson established his home at Ardmore and founded the Ardmore Statesman. In a short time he had made this one of the model weekly papers of the state and was its editor and publisher until the spring of 1915, when he sold the plant and business to Edward L. Gregory of Lawton. The Statesman has been an effective exponent of the republican party, and under Mr. Johnson's control it became the official republican organ for a large part of Southern Oklahoma, and in fact was the only important republican paper in the South Central section of the state.

Practically from the time he established his home at Ardmore Mr. Johnson was convinced that the city was the center of what would ultimately prove a great petroleum oil district. His confidence was one of action, and several years ago he mortgaged his newspaper plant for $2,000 and with some progressive associates leased a tract of land in the Healdton District. Their activities brought in the now celebrated field, which, though only one third developed, gives a yield of 100,000 barrels a day. Mr. Johnson's individual holdings in this field are valued at approximately over half a million dollars.

He is now president of the Crystal Oil Company, a heavy stockholder in the Bess Tucker Oil Company, the Vernon Collins Oil Company, and the Scivally Petroleum Company, as well as a stockholder in several developing companies. His judicious investments have also extended to farm land, and he is the owner of a large amount of that class of property in Carter County. His largest income is from his royalties in his oil properties in the Healdton fields. He is a director of the Guaranty State Bank of Ardmore and a stockholder in several other banking institutions in Southern Oklahoma.

It was as a sincere and straightforward republican that Mr. Johnson became so successful in making the Ardmore Statesman a leading organ of his party in the new state. For a number of years he has been a man of prominence and influence among Oklahoma republicans, is a member of the Republican State Central Committee from Carter County and in 1914 served as president of the Republican Press Association of Oklahoma. There has been less of personal ambition than of broad civic loyalty in his work as a partisan and citizen, and his name might be justly linked with all the important movements and enterprises for the good of his section of the state. He is one of the directors of the Ardmore Chamber of Commerce, a member of the Dornick Hills Country Club, the Chickasaw Lake Club, the Ardmore Rod and Gun Club, and he and his wife are members of the Presbyterian Church of Ardmore, of which he is a deacon.

For a number of years he has been actively interested in fraternal work, especially in the various branches of the Masonic Order. His affiliations are with Ardmore Lodge No. 31, A. F. & A. M.; Ardmore Chapter No. 11, R. A. M.; Ardmore Council No. 11, R. & S. M.;

Ardmore Commandery No. 9, K. T.; Indian Consistory No. 2, Scottish Rite at McAlester, and Indian Temple of the Nobles of the Mystic Shrine at Oklahoma City. He is also a member of the Ardmore Lodge of the Benevolent and Protective Order of Elks, the Knights of Pythias and the Woodmen of the World.

On April 22, 1913, at Dallas, Texas, he married Miss Odessa Otey, of Huntsville, Texas. Her parents died while she was a young girl, and before her marriage she was a popular teacher in the Ardmore schools. They have one son, Otey, born July 14, 1914.

WILLIAM H. MITCHELL. One of the most important municipal positions of the City of Guthrie is that of commissioner of public safety and chief of police, offices which at this time are being capably filled by William H. Mitchell. He is one of the strong figures of the day who are boldly standing for political reform, and none of the officials of Guthrie has a better record or a more appreciative audience. Mr. Mitchell was born March 29, 1863, at Salem, Massachusetts, and is a son of Robert P. and Margaret H. (Costello) Mitchell.

Robert P. Mitchell was born in Ireland, in 1831, and came to America with his brother, James Mitchell, in 1841, taking up his residence at Salem, which continued to be his home until his death in 1913. He was a good business man and for many years carried on operations in grain, and through honorable business methods and straightforward transactions won a firmly established place in the esteem and confidence of those among whom his fortunes were cast. Mr. Mitchell was married in 1853 to Miss Margaret H. Costello, a native of England, born in 1831, who died in 1910. They became the parents of three daughters and four sons, namely: Lizzie K., who is single and resides at Salem; Charles H., who is deceased; William H.; Mrs. Rachael Park, who is deceased; Emma, who died unmarried; and George M., who has also passed away.

William H. Mitchell was reared in the City of Salem, where his education was secured in the public schools. After graduating from the high school in 1876 he started to work for his father in the grain business and continued to be so occupied until 1884, thus gaining experience that was to prove invaluable to him in later years. In the year mentioned he went to Worcester, Massachusetts, where he accepted a position as a traveling salesman and went on the road as the representative of wholesale tea and coffee houses. In 1887 he came to the West, locating in Kansas, and in the following year engaged in the retail grocery business at Winfield, an enterprise which he conducted for two years. In 1889 he participated in the original opening of Oklahoma, when he located at Guthrie, and here engaged in the real estate business. At the time of the opening of the Sac and Fox reservations, in 1892, he secured a claim on Bear Creek, in Logan County, a property which he still owns. In 1893-4 he served capably and energetically as deputy sheriff of Logan County, and at the outbreak of the Spanish-American war he enlisted in Troop K, First United States Volunteer Cavalry, the famous "Rough Riders" under Col. Theodore Roosevelt. He was with that regiment in all its engagements and movements in Cuba, including the battle of San Juan Hill, where he was in the thickest of the fight. While he was never seriously wounded, on one occasion he had a narrow escape, having the heel of one of his boots shot off. He was intensely loyal to his regiment, his country and his comrades, was one of the most cheerful and faithful members of his troop, and did a great deal of helpful work in caring for the sick and wounded. Mr. Mitchell was mustered out of the United States service at Montauk Point, New York, from whence he went to his boyhood home at Salem and there remained two years with his parents. In 1901-2 he was with Col. W. F. Cody ("Buffalo Bill") as sergeant of rough riders, touring the United States, and in 1903 joined the police department of Guthrie. In this department his executive ability, his detective powers and his fearless performance of every duty devolving upon him won him constant promotion, and in 1906 he was finally made chief of the police department, an office in which he capably served until 1912. In 1915, under the commission form of government, he was elected commissioner of public safety, the prerogatives of which office include police, streets and alleys, public buildings and lighting of streets.

As to the movements directly concerned with the civic reform of Guthrie, he has been one of the city's most helpful men. He has always been an enthusiastic worker for good roads, and many substantial improvements have made their appearance under his administration, including the inauguration and installation of a modern "white way" system. He was the promoter of the plan also to utilize the labor of the city prisoners in the improvement of the streets, thus reducing taxes. Elected on the reform platform, he has faithfully fulfilled every promise made during his campaign. Commissioner Mitchell is active in all Masonic bodies of Guthrie, is a thirty-second degree Mason and a member of the finance committee of the Masonic Temple of this city and holds membership also in the Benevolent and Protective Order of Elks. Altogether he is a man who touches and improves life on many sides. As his thorough official requirements have been reinforced by extensive travels, during which he has been a thoughtful student of affairs, he has acquired a depth as well as a breadth of view which is enjoyed by few men now before the people.

Commissioner Mitchell was married at Worcester, Massachusetts, September 20, 1905, to Miss Alice M. Cheney, daughter of Wheelock A. and Lovina (Browning) Cheney. She was born at Salem, Massachusetts, July 8, 1859, and learned the printer's trade there under her father, who was a publisher of that city. Mr. and Mrs. Mitchell have no children.

REV. ROBERT CARR. A lifelong resident of the old Creek Nation, Rev. Robert Carr has found opportunity for usefulness and service to his people both as a farmer and for many years as a preacher. He is one of the old timers well worthy of the distinction of historical record.

He was born west of Fort Gibson on the Arkansas River in the Creek Nation, about 1845, a son of Thomas and Sally (Russo) Carr. His parents were natives of Alabama and were members of the Creek tribe. Thomas Carr was a well educated man, having been sent to a boarding school in Kentucky. The mother came to Indian Territory first, and she lived in the territory until her death, in 1871. She died about a mile from where her son, Rev. Robert, now lives. The father was a soldier in the Confederate army, and died at one of the refugee camps about 1863. His business was that of stock raiser. Of the two children the son Richard served all through the Civil war, and died in 1867.

Robert Carr during his boyhood attended the Asbury Mission School, and learned to read, but after the school was broken up at the beginning of the war he had no further education. In a business way he has found employment for his energies and accumulated a considerable estate by farming and stock raising. Since the close of the war he has had his home in what is now Hughes County, and his 110 acre homestead adjoins the little city of Wetumka on the southeast. Until Wetumka was founded, in 1900, the nearest town was

Eufaula. All members of Mr. Carr's family have their allotments.

Rev. Robert Carr was for several years sheriff, or light horse captain, in the Creek Nation. In politics he is a democrat. In 1871 he joined the Missionary Baptist Church, and ten years later was ordained as a preacher, and has been active in the work ever since. For many years he traveled as a missionary among his own people and the Cherokees, and served as pastor of local missions.

In 1871 he married Elizabeth Barnette, who was a Creek Indian and was born near Eufaula, April 13, 1855. She has spent practically all her life in this one locality. Her parents were Daniel and Sally Barnette, the former a Creek Indian and the latter possessing half white blood. Mrs. Carr's mother died along the Red River during the war, while her father was a Confederate soldier and died near Fort Smith. Of the three sons and three daughters in the Barnette family two are now living, Louisa Gray, near Wetumka, and Mrs. Carr. Mr. and Mrs. Carr lost three sons in infancy, and their five living daughters are: Mrs. Nettie Frazier, who lives in the same neighborhood as her parents, and has one child; Addie Smith, of Wetumka; Ida McCoy, who lives at Wetumka, and has seven children; Lulu Canard, of Wetumka, and the mother of one child; and Anius Canard, of Wetumka, who has two children.

JAMES C. STEWART. The profession of education has no worthier or more efficient representative in Grady County than James C. Stewart of Rush Springs, superintendent of city schools and a man who has passed practically his entire career in the calling to which he is now devoted. His advance has been steady and consistent and has come as a result of personal merit and close application, inherent and peculiar talent for imparting to others his own broad knowledge, and a deep and comprehensive sympathy that attracts his pupils to him and make easy their control. He has likewise displayed the possession of marked executive ability and in the management of the affairs of his office has shown no little business acumen.

James C. Stewart was born at Russellville, the county seat of Pope County, Arkansas, July 14, 1884, and is a son of T. B. and Margaret (Allen) Stewart. As the name would suggest, the family originated in Scotland, James C. Stewart, the grandfather of James C. of this notice, and for whom he was named, having been a native of Scotia and an emigrant to the United States from the City of Edinburgh. On his arrival in this country the grandfather became a pioneer planter and lumberman in Tennessee and through a long life of industry rose to a place of prominence and financial independence, and died at Franklin, Tennessee, well advanced in years, and standing high in the esteem of his fellow citizens.

T. B. Stewart, father of James C. Stewart, was born at Stephensville, Alabama, in 1852, and as a young man removed to Winchester, Tennessee. In 1881 he removed to Russellville, Arkansas, where he remained until 1886, then going to Pottsville, Arkansas, where he followed his vocations of farmer and lumberman until 1906. In that year he retired from active participation in business and agricultural life and moved to South Pittsburg, Marion County, Tennessee, where he still resides. Mr. Stewart is a deacon in the Baptist Church, and in political matters is a democrat. He married Miss Margaret Allen, who was born at Winchester, Franklin County, Tennessee, in 1853, and she died at Russellville, Arkansas, in 1906. They became the parents of four children, as follows: John, who died at the age of two years; Jack, who married T. B. Lax, superintendent of schools of Mulberry, Arkansas; Minnie, who is the wife of John Dane, a farmer of Russellville; and James C.

As a youth, James C. Stewart attended the public schools of Pottsville, Arkansas, where he was graduated from the high school with the class of 1900. During the next two years, desiring to see something of the country, he traveled extensively from Canada to the Gulf of Mexico in all the states east of the Rocky Mountains, and not only derived much pleasure from his travels, but also an education which could have been gained in no other way, and experience that has proved of immeasureable value to him since that time. For one year, also, he was in the service of the Iron Mountain Railroad. In 1903 Mr. Stewart enrolled as a student at Washita College, Arkansas, and graduated therefrom in 1907. He next spent one year at the University of Chicago, which he left in 1908, and this training was later supplemented by a full course at the Central State Normal School, from which he was graduated in 1914. In the meantime, he had started upon his educational career in 1902, when he began to teach a summer school near Russellville. He rose steadily in his calling from that time on, and in 1907 was appointed principal of Willow Point (Oklahoma) School, two years later being made principal of the high school at Comanche, where he remained two years. In 1910 he received the appointment as superintendent of schools at Loco and retained that office until the fall of 1915, when he was given his present position as superintendent of city schools of Rush Springs. He bears an excellent reputation as an educator, and while a strict disciplinarian has always had the esteem and friendship, as well as the confidence, of his teachers and pupils. Mr. Stewart is a democrat in politics. He belongs to the Baptist Church, and is fraternally affiliated with Loco Camp, Woodmen of the World, in which he is past consul commander, and Loco Lodge No. 361, Independent Order of Odd Fellows, in which he is past grand. He has numerous friends in both orders, as he has also in professional life.

Mr. Stewart was married in 1908, at England, Lonoke County, Arkansas, to Miss Alma Swain, daughter of the late J. H. Swain, deceased, who was a merchant, banker and oil man of England, Arkansas. To Mr. and Mrs. Stewart there have come two children: Pearl, born June 8, 1910; and Ruby, born May 5, 1911.

HON. J. L. MCKEOWN, as an expert accountant, has been prominently identified with various departments of the government of the State of Oklahoma and retired from the office of financial secretary of the Oklahoma Agricultural and Mechanical College at Stillwater, Payne County, when he was elected a representative of that county in the fifth general assembly of the State Legislature. Entering the Legislature with an experience of a number of years as an expert accountant in the service of the state, both as a member of the official staff of the state examiner and inspector and as financial secretary of the state board of agriculture, Mr. McKeown came to his new duties specially well equipped, particularly for the service assigned to him in connection with committee work, in which capacity he became one of the influential members of the house of representatives in the legislative session of 1914-15.

Mr. McKeown was born in Wisconsin in the year 1873, and is a son of Patrick and Julia McKeown. His father, a native of Ireland, came to America when a young man and for many years was a successful representative of the great basic industries of agriculture and stock-growing—first in Wisconsin and later in Missouri. He whose name initiates this article was a child at the time of the family removal to Missouri, where he received his preliminary educational discipline in the public schools. In 1899 he was graduated in the Missouri State Normal School at Warrensburg, and he then turned his attention to the pedagogic profession, of which he was for five years one of the successful and popular representatives, as a teacher in the public schools of Missouri. Later he completed a thorough course in scientific accounting, in the Spaulding Business College in Kansas City, that state, and for the ensuing five years he gave his attention to work as an expert accountant, a portion of the time through assignment to important special work in Oklahoma Territory. When the state government was organized in 1907, Mr. McKeown assisted in planning and executing the first work of the office of state examiner and inspector, and upon his retiring from this department he entered the service of the state board of agriculture, by which he was assigned to the position of financial secretary at the Oklahoma Agricultural and Mechanical College at Stillwater, a post of which he continued the efficient and valued incumbent until his election to the lower house of the State Legislature, in 1914. Prior to his election to this office Mr. McKeown had accomplished valuable service for the state through his interposition and investigation as an expert accountant, and it is specially worthy of note that he effected in this capacity the discovery of the issuing of fraudulent state warrants to the amount of $37,000, this discovery having resulted in the prosecution and conviction of a trusted attache of the office of the state auditor.

In the fifth Legislature Mr. McKeown was assigned to the following named committees of the house of representatives: appropriation, education, general agriculture, banks and banking, initiative and referendum, manufacturing and commerce, and oil and gas. He was specially concerned in legislation affecting the oil and gas industries and that pertaining to the State Agricultural and Mechanical College with which he had been actively identified. He took an active interest in the preparation, championship and enactment of the noteworthy oil conservation bill, especially by reason of the fact that he is personally interested in the oil industry, as an operator in the celebrated Cushing field, a part of which is in the county of which he is a representative. He is secretary of the Cimarron River Oil and Gas Company and vice president of the Cimarron Oil Company, both of which have valuable producing wells in the Cushing field of Oklahoma. Mr. McKeown was joint author of the admirable good roads measure that was passed by the Fifth Legislature, this being considered one of the most important passed at that session in touching the interests of the rural communities of the state. He was joint author also of measures fixing proper penalties for the desertion of wives and children by recalcitrant husbands and fathers. Mr. McKeown was zealous in the supporting of adequate appropriations for the Oklahoma Agricultural & Mechanical College in his home City of Stillwater, one of these appropriations having been for the replacing of buildings that had been destroyed by fire and the loss of which seriously crippled the work of the college.

The political allegiance of Mr. McKeown is given to the democratic party; he is affiliated with Guthrie Lodge No. 426, Benevolent and Protective Order of Elks, in the City of Guthrie and also with the Modern Woodmen of America. In addition to his interests in the oil and gas industry he is a stockholder of the Employes Building & Loan Association of Guthrie.

In 1906 was solemnized the marriage of Mr. McKeown to Miss Effie Lovell, of Guthrie, this state; they have no children. Mr. McKeown has two brothers and two sisters: James is a farmer near Eldorado Springs, Missouri; William T. is engaged in the practice of law in the City of Kalispell, Montana, and is one of the representative members of the bar of that section of the Treasure State; Mrs. A. J. Clark resides in Portland, Oregon, where her husband is foreman of the repair shops of the Oregon Railroad & Navigation Company; and Miss Kate McKeown is a resident of Kansas City, Missouri.

WALTER WALLACE HOUSEWRIGHT. Since his arrival at Devol, Oklahoma, September 28, 1908, at which time he opened the Farmers State Bank, Walter Wallace Housewright has been intimately identified with the interests, business and financial, of this thriving and energetic little city of Cotton County. In the capacity of cashier of the institution mentioned, he has become well and widely known in banking circles, as a citizen he has been a factor in fostering and bringing to a successful conclusion several movements which have meant much to his community, and in social affairs he has taken an active part.

Mr. Housewright was born at Wylie, Collin County, Texas, October 22, 1888, and is a son of William and Henrietta (Wallace) Housewright. The family originated in Germany and was founded in this country in Mississippi, where, in 1835, was born William Housewright. He was a pioneer of Collin County, whence he went from Mississippi thirty years before the founding of the Town of Wylie, and was engaged practically all of his life as a farmer and stock raiser. During the war between the North and the South, he joined a Texas regiment, and throughout the conflict served ably and bravely under the flag of the Confederacy. He was a member of the Masonic fraternity. Mr. Housewright died at Wylie, Texas, October 20, 1889, aged fifty-four years. Mrs. Housewright, also a native of Mississippi, survives her husband and lives at Wylie. There were eight children in the family, as follows: Panola, who married Charles Anderhub, a farmer, and lives at Wylie; Ponta, deceased, who was the wife of H. R. Riffe, also a farmer at Wylie; Estella, who is the wife of W. W. Combs, engaged in farming in the vicinity of Wylie; W. R., who is engaged in horse dealing and lives at Hot Springs, Arkansas; Ernest, a resident of Wylie, where he is engaged in painting and decorating; Hester, who is unmarried and resides with her mother; Jick, a rural free delivery mail carrier, residing at Wylie; and Walter Wallace, of this review.

Walter Wallace Housewright was given good educational advantages in his youth, attending first the public schools at Wylie, where he was graduated from the high school in 1904, and next going to the Commercial College at Tyler, Texas, where he completed his course in 1905. When only sixteen years of age, he entered the Bank of Temple, Oklahoma, as bookkeeper and stenographer, and rapidly won promotion through the display of unusual ability and fidelity to duty, so that he rose to teller and subsequently to the position of assistant cashier. Mr. Housewright remained at Temple until March, 1908, when he removed to Hot Springs, Arkansas, and for a short time was employed in the Arkansas National Bank. On September 28, 1908, he came to Devol, Oklahoma, opened the bank here, and became cashier of the Farmers State Bank, a position which he has since retained. He has shown marked ability in the discharge of his duties, has risen steadily in favor with the depositors, and has established himself firmly in the confidence of his associates. The Farmers State Bank occupies the first building completed at Devol, at the

LOUIS M. MILLER AND FAMILY ON TIGER CREEK FARM

corner of Wichita Avenue and Mulberry Street, and bears an excellent reputation among the financial institutions of Cotton County. It is capitalized at $10,000, with a surplus of $2,000, and its present officers are: A. J. Emery, president; W. T. Huff, vice president, and W. W. Housewright, cashier.

Mr. Housewright is a democrat, but practically confines his political activities to supporting men and measures which he believes will be beneficial to the interests of his community. His fraternal connections include membership in Devol Lodge No. 420, Ancient Free and Accepted Masons, of which he is past master by service; Devol Chapter, Order of the Eastern Star; Devol Lodge No. 548, Independent Order of Odd Fellows, and the local lodges of the Woodmen of the World and the Modern Woodmen of America. He takes a keen interest in fraternal affairs, and is decidedly popular with his fellow lodge members.

On April 15, 1909, at Temple, Oklahoma, Mr. Housewright was united in marriage with Miss Erma Tipton, daughter of I. W. Tipton, a merchant and rancher of El Paso, Texas. Mr. and Mrs. Housewright have had no children.

REV. LOUIS M. MILLER. One of the most influential representatives of the old Creek Nation, Louis M. Miller has spent his active lifetime in Hughes and Seminole counties and is now a resident of near Holdenville. For many years he has been a prosperous farmer in that community, but in addition to the management of his private affairs has also mingled closely with his own people and has been a leader in public and religious life. He is now pastor of the Indian church in his locality. He was born at Coweta, December 22, 1862, his parents, Daniel and Sophia (Jacobs) Miller, having had their home two and a half miles west of that place. His father was a fullblood Creek and was born in Alabama. His mother was a halfblood Creek, her father, Eli Jacobs, having been a white man. The mother was born in 1823, and came to Indian Territory when ten years of age, and died in 1873. The father passed away about 1872, at the age of sixty-five. They spent their married lives along the Arkansas River near the eastern border of the state, in the Creek Nation. Daniel Miller was a farmer and stock raiser, and also made a good living. During the war he served with the Confederate army in the First Creek Regiment, under Col. D. N. McIntosh. Though a man without education, he had a practical training in those arts which were most useful to a people living in a frontier community, and he was greatly aided by his wife, who was a woman of excellent education. They were members of the Missionary Baptist Church. Mrs. Daniel Miller had three children by a former marriage, and three by her second union, named Louis M., Sam of Sasakwa, and Dora McGirt, the last being now deceased.

Louis M. Miller grew up near Muskogee and Checota, and after the death of his mother came to what is now Hughes County at the age of eleven, and completed his education in boarding schools and in the Asbury Manual Labor School at Eufaula, under Rev. Theodore F. Brewer, who was on the advisory board. He had the regular English course and enjoyed the advantages of the commercial school at Quincy, Illinois. At the age of nineteen he entered the employ of Gov. John F. Brown and the latter's brother, A. J. Brown, at Wewoka, in their store. He was one of their trusted clerks for twelve years, and then spent three years on their ranch, thus giving fifteen years of service to these prominent leaders of the Seminole Nation. Since 1893 Mr. Miller has been an independent farmer.

On March 5, 1893, he married Lily Thomas, who was born a mile and a half north of Wewoka, in Seminole County, in April, 1874. She is a three-quarter-blood Creek, and was educated in the common schools. Since his marriage Mr. Miller has been farming on his present place, situated a mile north and half a mile east of Holdenville, and containing 240 acres, most of it well improved and under cultivation. His enterprise has brought him considerable note as a stock raiser and he raises registered Hampshire hogs.

One of the features of his farm is that a portion of the land is occupied by the Tiger Creek Baptist Church. Mr. Miller was one of the principal builders of this church in 1910 and his brother Sam H. Miller was the first pastor, but for the last two years Louis M. Miller has been its spiritual leader and director. This is one of the important centers of Indian religious life. The services are held every fourth Sunday, and according to the custom that has long prevailed in Indian Territory, the meeting begins on Saturday and holds over until Sunday night, the time being spent in preaching, singing and prayer service, and on each quarter a community service is held. On this occasion the worshipers begin to assemble on Friday and the services continue until Monday morning. These quarterly services are somewhat in the nature of a "camp meeting." Every family brings its supply of provisions and all the features of camp life prevail. At such times preachers come from all over the Seminole and Creek Nation, and while there are easily upwards of two hundred camps some of the meetings frequently bring out as many as a thousand. The whites also come and attend these meetings with their Indian brethren.

Another distinction that belongs to Mr. Miller is that he was the last district judge of the Wewoka District at the time the tribal government was discontinued. At the coming of statehood he was elected a county commissioner of Seminole County, but he did not qualify. His family were all reared as democrats, but he maintains a rather independent attitude and votes for the best man. Mr. and Mrs. Miller have five children: Lizzie, wife of Jackson Hill; Thomas O., Sam H., Jr., James A. and Josie J.

HARRY EMERSON AUSTIN. Among the city officials of Clinton who are contributing to the general welfare by capable and faithful performance of duty, one who is winning the community's gratitude and commendation is Harry Emerson Austin, the young and energetic city clerk. During the short period of his incumbency he has shown an earnest desire to maintain a high standard in his department, one of the most important in the city service.

Mr. Austin was born at Knoxville, Tennessee, September 14, 1890, and is a son of William B. and Corda (Burkhart) Austin, and a member of an old family of Virginia, which was founded in the Old Dominion in Colonial days. His father was born in Knox County, Tennessee, in 1861, and as a young man adopted the vocation of educator, which he pursued for several years at Dandridge, Tennessee. Later, however, he turned his attention to pharmacy, and for more than twenty years was the proprietor of a drug store at Knoxville, where he died in August, 1904. He was a democrat in his political views, a member of the Methodist Episcopal Church, and belonged to the Knights of Pythias. Mrs. Austin, who survives him, makes her home at Knoxville. There were three children in the family, namely: Ethel Louise, who married Earl Sterchi, who is engaged in the furniture business at Knoxville, Tennessee; Harry Emerson; and William, who is engaged in the automobile garage business at Newkirk, Oklahoma.

Harry Emerson Austin received his early education in

the public schools of Knoxville, following which he took a business course at Hill's Business College, Oklahoma City, from which he was graduated in 1912. From February until June of that year he was identified with the Bray Drug Company, of Clinton, and then returned to Knoxville, Tennessee, where he was for thirteen months associated with the Knoxville Outfitting Company. In July, 1913, he returned to Clinton and again entered the employ of the Bray Drug Company, with which concern he continued to be identified until April 15, 1915. In the meantime, on April 6, 1915, he had been elected city clerk of Clinton on the democratic ticket, and since that time he has occupied offices in the City Hall. Mr. Austin is generally popular with his associates and has proved himself a young man whose ambitions and abilities combine to make him one to whom much higher honors will probably come. He is a member of the Methodist Episcopal Church, and is fraternally affiliated with Lodge No. 83, Knights of Pythias, at Clinton.

Mr. Austin was married at Oklahoma City, Oklahoma, to Miss Nora Le Febvre, in June, 1912. Mrs. Austin is a daughter of E. I. Le Febvre, who is a retired agriculturist and resides at Eldorado Springs, Missouri. Mr. and Mrs. Austin have no children.

E. D. McLAUCHLIN. A young attorney, already well established in practice at Blanchard, E. D. McLauchlin was for nearly ten years before entering the law engaged in the mercantile business at Denver, Oklahoma.

He was born December 27, 1885, at Love Station, De Soto County, Mississippi. His father was R. B. McLauchlin, who was born in Mississippi, in 1847, and was left an orphan by the death of his mother when he was seven years of age. His father, who died five years earlier, had emigrated from Scotland to North Carolina. R. B. McLauchlin was reared in Mississippi, and became dependent upon his own resources at an early age. He was married in De Soto County, Mississippi, to Miss S. E. Perry, who is now living with her son, Dr. J. R. McLauchlin, ten miles east of Norman, Oklahoma. In 1889 R. B. McLauchlin moved with his family to Clarendon, Arkansas, and he died there in 1896. For many years he was an active school man, later a farmer, and at the time of his death was serving as county surveyor of Monroe County, Arkansas. He was a democrat, and very active in the Baptist Church, and fraternally was associated with the Knights of Honor. His wife was born in De Soto County, Mississippi, in 1843. Their children were: Emma, deceased, whose husband, Robert Haines, is a music teacher at Clarendon, Arkansas; D. D., who was actively associated with his brother, E. D. McLauchlin, in merchandising until his death; Mattie married Henry Harris and both are now deceased; R. J. lives as a farmer near Paragould, Arkansas; Fannie is the wife of John Hatcher, a farmer near Chickasha, Oklahoma; Sallie, who died at the age of eighteen; Alice, wife of Sam Cooper, a farmer at Paragould, Arkansas; Essie, who died at the age of twenty-four, was the wife of Tom Vaughn, a teacher in the public schools at Cordell, Oklahoma; J. R., a physician and surgeon at Denver, Oklahoma, ten miles east of Norman, who is a graduate M. D. from the Oklahoma State University; and E. D. McLauchlin, the youngest of the ten children.

The last named attended the public schools in Clarendon, Arkansas, and continued his education in Paragould in Greene County, when his mother removed to that town in 1898. When twenty-eight years old he left school and at once engaged in the mercantile business at Denver, Oklahoma, with his brother, D. D., under the firm name of McLauchlin Brothers. His older brother, D. D. McLauchlin, died February 7, 1914. At that time the junior member of the firm sold the business and during 1914-15 was a student of law in the Cumberland University at Lebanon, Tennessee, where he graduated LL. B. in 1915. After four months at Norman, Oklahoma, he took the bar examination and was admitted to practice in June, and on the first day of July opened his office at Blanchard. He has his offices in the court house and his ability has already attracted a profitable practice, especially in civil cases. He has been called upon to act as special county judge and is now city attorney for Blanchard.

In politics he is a democrat and is affiliated with Camp No. 10835 of the Modern Woodmen of America at Franklin, Oklahoma. On January 24, 1910, at Norman, he married Miss Ethel Cohee, whose father, J. K. Cohee, is a retired farmer at Capitol Hill, Oklahoma.

JAMES H. ADAMS, of Dewey, Oklahoma, is one of the prominent young business men of the state, and is naturally proud of his prominent Indian ancestry.

He was born at Fort Gibson, Oklahoma, December 4, 1895, a son of Richard C. and Carrie F. (Meigs) Adams. His father was descended from the famous Captain White Eyes, who was chief of the Delaware Indians in Revolutionary times. His mother is a descendant of the noted John Ross, and also of Colonel Meigs of Revolutionary fame, and another maternal connection was the Bigelow family.

James H. Adams attended school in Washington, D. C., but left school at the age of seven. In 1910 he was employed in the folding room of the national capital, and from 1914 to 1916 was a member of the national guard at Washington, District of Columbia. At his home in Dewey he busies himself largely with oil lands.

A. A. BALDWIN. One of the most progressive and enterprising of the newspapers of Southwest Oklahoma is the Hollis Tribune, which is published at Hollis, the county seat of Harmon County, by A. A. Baldwin, a man of broad and varied business experience and of much journalistic ability. Since taking charge of the editing of this newspaper, in 1914, Mr. Baldwin has built up an excellent circulation, and is now giving his readers a newsy, interesting and well-printed sheet which supports local interests and industries.

Mr. Baldwin is a native of the Hoosier State, and was born at Albion, the county seat of Noble County, Indiana, May 13, 1863, a son of Howard and Lorena (Douglas) Baldwin, and a member of a family of Scotch-Irish extraction which settled in Ohio in the days of the Western Reserve. Howard Baldwin was born in Ohio, in 1837, and as a young man moved to Albion, Indiana, where he completed his preparation for the legal profession and settled down to practice. He had but started on a successful career, and had served as county attorney of Noble County, when he was called by death, in 1870, when only thirty-three years of age. He was one of the influential young democrats of his community and a man universally admired and respected, and was a member of the Masonic fraternity. He was married in Noble County, Indiana, to Miss Lorena Douglas, who was born in 1839, in Illinois, and who still survives him, her home being at Wichita Falls, Texas. There were three children in the family, as follows: Helen, who died at the age of fifteen years; A. A., of this review; and Lucy Edith, who married L. E. Miller, of Alexandria, Texas, where he is the proprietor of a cotton gin and she is serving as postmistress.

A. A. Baldwin was a lad of seven years when his father died, and was fourteen when he accompanied his mother and sisters to Hood County, Texas. His education was limited to the training he could secure in the public schools, for it was necessary that he assist in the support of the family, and when he was only fifteen years old he began his struggle with life by becoming an apprentice to the painter's trade. After mastering that vocation he became a journeyman, and continued to follow painting as an occupation until 1883, at which time he entered a printing office at Granbury, Texas, and there served another apprenticeship, this one of three years. His next location was Alexandria, Texas, where he leased the Alexandria News for one year, and then, in partnership with E. A. Anderson, founded the Blanket Herald, at Blanket, Texas, which they conducted for twelve months. Disposing of his interests in that venture, Mr. Baldwin next went to Erath County, Texas, and for three years was engaged in farming, then entering upon a career in mercantile lines which extended over a long period. For five years Mr. Baldwin was the proprietor of a country grocery store in Galveston County, Texas, and at the end of that time first came to Oklahoma, taking up his residence, in 1903, at Cordell, where for three years he conducted a grocery establishment. He next spent a like period at Gunter, Texas, and in 1909 moved to Higgins, Texas, where he remained for three years. Mr. Baldwin returned to Oklahoma in 1911, and, establishing his home at Hollis, was engaged in carpentering and other work until 1914, when he leased the Hollis Tribune, which he has continued to edit to the present time. This paper, founded in 1910, is a democratic organ of some influence, and circulates in Harmon and the surrounding counties. Its office and plant are located on Main Street, near Broadway, in the business section of the village, and are well equipped not only for the printing of the newspaper, but for all kinds of first-class job work. As a molder of public opinion, the Tribune has contributed its full share in advancing the interests of Hollis, and both in the columns of the paper and personally Mr. Baldwin has warmly supported all movements promising progress and civic welfare. Mr. Baldwin is a stanch democrat, and with his family belongs to the Christian Church. His fraternal connections are with the Independent Order of Odd Fellows and the Knights of Pythias. A man of much experience, he has lived his life amid the scenes that have gone to make up the history of the Southwest, and has learned to view human nature with a broad understanding.

Mr. Baldwin was married December 24, 1889, in Erath County, Texas, to Miss Mamie A. Bass, daughter of B. F. Bass, a farmer of Ranger Lake, New Mexico. Five children have been born to Mr. and Mrs. Baldwin, as follows: Benjamin Ulice, educated at Arlington Heights Training School, Forth Worth, Texas, and now a member of the ministry of the Christian Church, stationed at Shreveport, Louisiana; Edith Amelia, who was deputy register of deeds of Harmon County, at Hollis, until 1915, and is now attending the Oklahoma City Business College; Marguerite, who is a member of the senior class at Hollis High School; Charles Anson, who is a student in the public schools of Hollis; and Fred Allen.

HENRY MEAD HARRIS. Antlers at one time was the seat of a United States Court with jurisdiction over the greater part of the Choctaw Nation. Here such men as Judge Clayton and Judge Thomas C. Humphries presided, and during court sessions many tribes and many nationalities assembled at the seat of justice. During those sessions Antlers was probably the most populated and busiest town of the Choctaw Nation. Here were enacted many historic and many tragic events, growing out of the conflicting interests and the multiplicity of charges against men brought here for trial.

At that time, in 1904, Joseph R. Foltz was clerk of the United States Court, and Henry M. Harris, a young man recently come over from Red River County, Texas, was a deputy. The events of that period are among the most cherished memories of Mr. Harris, who has for a number of years lived in this section of the old Choctaw Nation, and is now deputy county treasurer at Antlers. Other experiences in succeeding years brought him nearer to the scenes of actual and vital history, for he was secretary to Thomas Latham, a United States commissioner stationed at Antlers, during a period when in a few months the number of probate cases filed in his court increased from 200 to 2,100. This increase was due to an Act of Congress providing for the allotment of lands in preparation for statehood. It was a period of great activity for the grafter who sought wrongful possession of Indian property, and his kind was in evidence in all shades of color, nationality and profession. Indian wills were stolen from the records. Indians were robbed boldly on the highway. Every device that scheming minds could conceive for separating the Indian from his property or money was attempted. Such activities as these, however, had a wholesome effect on the welfare of the Indians, since it taught Congress that more stringent laws were necessary for his protection.

Henry Mead Harris was born in Red River County, Texas, in 1886 and was a son of Frank M. and Nannie B. (Parks) Harris. His father, who died in 1898, came from Virginia to Texas in the '80s. He was a civil engineer and did considerable map and plat work all over North Texas, some of it under the direction of the state. Before establishing in Clarksville, Texas, he was engaged for a while in the cattle business in the southern part of the Choctaw Nation. The mother of Mr. Harris now lives in Antlers. In the family are also a daughter and two other sons, Mrs. W. N. John, wife of a physician in Hugo; Max Harris, a dry goods salesman in El Paso; and Roy C. Harris, employed by the railway company at Hugo.

After attending public school in Red River County, Henry M. Harris was a student for one year in the Southwestern University at Georgetown, Texas, and he also attended school for a time in Antlers. His first employment was as clerk in the drug store of J. T. Hackett & Company in Antlers. He then became a deputy clerk of the United States Court, and on retiring from the service of the Government he became timber appraiser for the Guy & Ralph Gray Lumber Company of Cleveland, Ohio, a concern that contemplated establishing lumber mills and railroads in the commercial timber section of the Choctaw Nation. For several months he traveled over the Kiamichi and other mountains in this work. At one time his camp was pitched at Waterhall, an old settlement of the Choctaw Nation which sat beside the military highway. Another time his camp was at the Mullins place, situated on an old Indian camping ground near Daniel spring and beside Jack trail, a rough and narrow highway used by Indians and other early settlers in their journeys to and from Tuskahoma, capital of the Nation. Settlements were few and game plentiful. The guns of the party brought its members plenty of venison and turkey. The scheme of the Gray Company, had it been carried out, would have been a big factor in the development of the northern part of the Choctaw Nation. Antlers would have been the western terminus of the company's railroad lines. One of these lines, headed northeast, would have crossed Little River seven times, had the engineers' preliminary surveys been followed.

At the time of statehood Mr. Harris became clerk in the office of County Judge L. P. Davenport, and later was assistant county clerk. In 1911 he moved to Choctaw County, and became under sheriff under the Lofton administration. Still later he was deputy treasurer of Pushmataha County, and he now has his home at Antlers and is giving most of his time and attention to his duties as deputy county treasurer.

At Antlers in 1905 Mr. Harris married Miss Bessie Eubank. They are the parents of two children: Henry Mead Jr. and James.

HON. CLARENCE EUGENE GANNAWAY. In the life of Clarence Eugene Gannaway, who is now serving his second term as mayor of Clinton, there may be found an illustration of the high awards to be attained through adherence to industry and integrity and the following out of an honorable ambition. Commencing his career as a youth of eighteen years, with only the advantages of a high school education, he has directed his activities so capably and prosecuted them so vigorously that today, still in the prime of life, he finds himself at the head of important business interests in a thriving and prosperous community, and the possessor of the unqualified confidence of the best element of the people.

Mr. Gannaway was born at Unionville, Tennessee, January 14, 1870, a descendant of Irish ancestors who emigrated to America during Colonial days and settled either in Virginia or North Carolina. His father, John A. Gannaway, was born in Rutherford County, Tennessee, in 1824, and passed his entire life in that state, where he followed farming and merchandising, served as justice of the peace, and for a period of thirty years acted as postmaster of the Town of Bellbuckle, Bedford County, where he died in 1911. He was a democrat in politics, steward in the Methodist Episcopal Church and a member of the Masons and Odd Fellows. Mr. Gannaway married Rex Tarpley, a native of Tennessee, who resides at Hot Springs, Arkansas, and they were the parents of eleven children: Emma, who is the widow of the late Dr. W. E. Harrison, a physician, and makes her home at Nashville, Tennessee; Maggie, who is the widow of the late W. A. Winsett, a farmer and merchant, and resides in California; John, an attorney, who died at Victoria, British Columbia; James W., who is a traveling salesman with headquarters at Oklahoma City; Nannie, who is the wife of B. A. Clary, a merchant of Bellbuckle, Tennessee; Cassie, who is the wife of C. H. North, a farmer and trader of Christiana, Tennessee; E. T., who was a mechanic and engineer and died in Texas; Cora, who is the wife of Dr. F. M. Williams, a physician and surgeon of Hot Springs, Arkansas; Clarence Eugene; Horace B., who is in the life insurance business at Oklahoma City; and C. V., who is a member of the board of city commissioners of Teague, Texas.

Clarence Eugene Gannaway received his education in the graded and high schools of Unionville, Tennessee, and upon leaving school at the age of eighteen years, became the organizer and teacher of a brass band, which he instructed in the evenings after he had spent the day in clerking in a store at Statesville. Later he engaged in the same pursuits at Woodbury, Watertown and Pittsburg, Tennessee, and in 1898 came to El Reno and became clerk in a store. A short time later he removed to Enid, where he was employed in a drug store for six months, and at the end of that period secured employment as a traveling salesman for a dry goods house, a capacity in which he traveled throughout Oklahoma until 1904. That year saw Mr. Gannaway's entrance upon the field of banking, at Sayre, Oklahoma, where he remained until 1907, on May 27 of which year he came to Clinton as cashier of the First National Bank. In 1909 he was made vice president of that institution, a position which he still retains, although since October, 1914, he has not been actively engaged at the bank, because of ill health. At this time he is engaged in the farm loan, real estate and insurance business, with offices in the Thurmond Building, Fourth Street and Frisco Avenue. He is the owner of 440 acres of farming land in Custer County, Oklahoma, as well as property in Beckham County, city lots in Oklahoma County, and his residence at Clinton. Mr. Gannaway is an enthusiastic citizen, who has studied his community's situation and incomparable resources, and has unbounded faith in its possibilities of growth and business. He has not feared to venture his own capital in buying lands here or to advise his clients to do so, for while many fortunes have been built up in Oklahoma in commerce, in manufacture, and in corporate control and management, there has been no surer road to fortune than that offered by real estate. While he has pursued with undeviating steadiness of purpose his business transactions, he has not been unmindful of civic duties. In the spring of 1913, as the democratic candidate, he was elected mayor of Clinton, and his first term contributed so greatly to the city's good, that in 1915 he was elected to succeed himself. He is a member and regular attendant of the Methodist Episcopal Church. Mayor Gannaway is prominent in fraternal life, being a member of Clinton Lodge No. 339, Ancient Free and Accepted Masons; Clinton Chapter No. 69, Royal Arch Masons; Sayre Commandery, Knights Templar; India Temple, Ancient Arabic Order Nobles of the Mystic Shrine, Oklahoma City; Clinton Lodge No. 83, Knights of Pythias, of which he is past chancellor commander; Clinton Lodge of the Brotherhood of American Yeomen; and Clinton Chapter, Order of the Eastern Star.

In 1904, at Elk City, Oklahoma, Mr. Gannaway was married to Miss Florence Thurmond, who was born in 1881, in Tarrant County, Texas, only daughter of E. G. and Amanda (Harmon) Thurmond, her father now being a retired banker of Elk City, Oklahoma. Mayor and Mrs. Gannaway are the parents of one daughter: Florence Amanda, who was born August 1, 1912, at Clinton.

OSCAR HOLMES THURMOND. Western Oklahoma contains a great many able men who have adopted finance as the field in which to conduct their activities. That all should be equally successful in such a career would be an impossibility; the high rewards in this field come to but few, and the fortunate must be gifted with qualifications of a diversified character, including not only intelligence, good judgment, prudence, industry, sagacity and integrity, but a thorough understanding of political economy as it affects the great industries of production and distribution, a quick and accurate perception of character, skill in determining the dominant influences that control human action, and a comprehensive knowledge of the principles of finance. Among the financiers of Western Oklahoma few possess these qualities in a greater degree than Oscar Holmes Thurmond, president of the First National Bank, who, with his brothers, E. K., A. L., I. C. and J. P. Thurmond, owns eleven banks in this state.

Mr. Thurmond is a Texas by nativity, born in Tarrant County, sixteen miles northwest of Fort Worth, at Dido, September 26, 1869. The family is of Irish-German descent and in pioneer times was founded in Kentucky, in which state, in 1844, E. G. Thurmond, the father of Oscar H. Thurmond, was born. E. G. Thurmond became one of the early ranchmen of Tarrant County, Texas, where, during the Civil war, he enlisted in the Texas Rangers. In 1885 he removed to Wheeler County, in the Texas Panhandle, where he resided on a ranch for seven years, and in 1892 came to Cheyenne, Roger Mills County, Oklahoma, there purchasing another ranch on which he made his home until 1901. Since that year he has lived at Elk City and is practically retired from business affairs. He is a democrat in politics, and his religious connection is with the Baptist Church. Mr. Thurmond married Miss Amanda Harmon, a native of Tennessee, and they became the parents of six children: Oscar Holmes; A. L., born in 1872, cashier of the First National Bank of Elk City, Oklahoma, a member of the firm of Thurmond Brothers, and a thirty-second degree Mason; E. K., born in 1875, president of the First National Bank of Sayre, Oklahoma, where he resides, and of the First National Bank of Elk City, a member of the firm of Thurmond Brothers and a thirty-second degree Mason; I. C., born in 1878, a banker of Oklahoma City, also a thirty-second degree Mason, and a member of the firm; Florence, born in 1881, who is the wife of Hon. C. E. Gannaway, mayor of Clinton, Oklahoma, and a well known operator in farm loans, real estate and insurance; and J. P., a member of the firm, who lives at Elk City with his parents.

Oscar Holmes Thurmond attended the public schools of Tarrant County and was sixteen years of age when he went with the family to the Panhandle. Subsequently he accompanied his father to the ranch near Cheyenne, and remained there until the spring of 1903, when he went to Erick, Oklahoma, and founded the First State Bank, of which he was first cashier and was later made president, a position which he retains. The Thurmond Brothers began their extensive operations in the field of finance in 1895, when they organized the Bank of Cheyenne, and since that time they have constantly increased their interests in this direction until at present they control the following concerns: First National Bank of Clinton; First National Bank of Elk City; First National Bank of Sayre; State Bank of Strong City; State Bank of Foss; State Bank of Carter; Cordell National Bank, of Cordell; First State Bank of Camargo; State Bank of Hammon; Bank of Cheyenne, and First State Bank of Erick. Oscar H. Thurmond has been president of the First National Bank of Clinton since 1907, but did not come to this city to reside until July 3, 1913. Since that time he has entered actively into business, financial and public life here, and has contributed materially to the development and upbuilding of the community. The Thurmond Brothers own and control in partnership some 13,000 acres of land in Texas and Oklahoma, and in addition to this Oscar H. Thurmond owns personally 550 acres in Custer and Beckham counties. As a financier Mr. Thurmond is quick of perception, intuitive in judgment, rapid in conclusions and generally accurate in his estimate of character. His ability, displayed in the management of the institution of which he is the head, and of his various other interests, is recognized by his brethren of the banking profession, by whom he is held in the greatest confidence. He has taken an unshrinking part in whatever movements have been set on foot for the betterment of his community, and among the positions of honor and dignity which he has been called to fill is that of president of the Clinton Chamber of Commerce, representing in its membership the most important branches of business and the most active industries of the city. In politics a democrat, while a resident of Cheyenne he served as postmaster during President Cleveland's administration, and was alderman for several years while a resident of Erick. He is a deacon in the Baptist Church, and has been liberal in his support of its movements.

In 1903, at Erick, Mr. Thurmond was married to Miss Sallie Longmire, daughter of Mrs. E. J. Longmire, who makes her home with her daughter and son-in-law.

DANIEL R. DIAL of Mangum, dealer in real estate and loans since 1904, when he first came to this city, is one of the best established business men in the community. His business activities extend through Greer, Harrison, Jackson, Beckham, Kiowa and Comanche counties, Oklahoma. He is a son of S. W. Dial, and was born in Miller County, Missouri, on March 6, 1874.

The Dial family is Scotch-Irish in its ancestry, and they were early pioneers in Tennessee, where S. W. Dial was born in 1833. He died at Martha, Oklahoma, in the spring of 1897, and is there buried. When a very young man he went to Miller County, Missouri, where he married and made his home. He was a prominent farmer and stock man there for forty-eight years. In 1883 he went to Anderson County, Kansas, five years later coming to Greer County, Texas (now Oklahoma), and settled on a farm about ten miles south of the Town of Mangum.

Mr. Dial was a republican in his political faith, and he served in the Federal army throughout the Civil war as a member of the Forty-eighth Missouri Volunteer Infantry. He was a lifelong member of the Christian Church, of which he was an elder, as well as a preacher. He married Nancy E. Lovell, who was born in Illinois in 1838, and died in Martha, Oklahoma, in 1897. Five children were born to them: Sheridan, who died in July, 1913, in Bartlesville, Oklahoma, was a banker; Lettie A. married P. W. Myers, a prosperous farmer of Lone Elm, Kansas; Dora R. married M. Harris, a mail carrier in Mangum, where they live; Daniel R., of this review, was the fourth child, and Maggie, the youngest born, lives in Guthrie, Oklahoma, where she is cashier of the Pioneer Telephone Company.

Daniel R. Dial attended the public schools in Anderson County, Kansas, and finished his schooling in Greer County, when he was graduated from the high school in 1890. After that he gave his attention to farming and stock raising in Greer County, Oklahoma, until 1904. In that year he moved to Mangum, giving up his farming activities, and established himself in the real estate and loan business. The success he has enjoyed has been very marked, and mention has already been made of the many counties in which he operates. He has his offices in the Mangum National Bank Building.

Mr. Dial was married in January, 1900, to Miss Eula McAuley, daughter of C. McAuley, a retired farmer of Martha, Oklahoma, now living in Mangum. They have three children: Elmer, a freshman in the Mangum High School, and LeRoy and Wilma, in the grade school of the city.

Mr. Dial is an elder in the Christian Church, in which he has membership with his family, and his politics are those of a republican.

OMER SCHNOEBELEN. An active participant in the life of Mooreland, both business and civic, since his arrival in 1903, Omer Schnoebelen has made himself more and more a necessary factor in the development of this thriving Oklahoma community. As a publisher of the Mooreland Leader he has been foremost in advancing movements of a beneficial character, while in various official capacities he has rendered his fellow citizens signal service, and at present, in the office of postmaster, is handling the Mooreland mail in a manner that is bringing him commendation from all sides.

Mr. Schnoebelen was born February 10, 1884, at Riverside, Iowa, and is a son of Nicholas and Mary (Bouquot) Schnoebelen. His father was born December 8, 1833, in Alsace Lorraine, France (now Germany), and was three years of age when brought to the United States by his parents, the family settling at Riverside, Iowa. There the lad grew to sturdy young manhood, receiving a public school education and learning the trades of blacksmith and mechanic, lines in which he built up a good patronage. In 1865 the lure of the West, with the promise of large fortune, called him and he made his way to Omaha, Nebraska. During the days of the frontier, with its hostile Indians, its outlaws and hold-up men, and various other dangers, he conducted a freighting outfit between Omaha and Denver, Colorado, and in the five years he was so engaged met with numerous thrilling experiences. While so engaged Mr. Schnoebelen was married, in 1868, to Miss Mary Bouquot, who was born August 28, 1844, at Burlington, Iowa, daughter of Joseph and Mary Bouquot, natives of France. Ten children were born to Mr. and Mrs. Schnoebelen: Rose, now a nun in the Order of the St. Vincent de Paul, with mother house at Emmitsburg, Maryland; Crescencia, who is unmarried and resides at Riverside, Iowa, with her parents, a musician of unusual talent; Anna R., who is the wife of Judd Brown of Lincoln, Nebraska; Marcella, who is the wife of George d'Autremont, a Canadian farmer; Omer, of this review; Marietta, who is the wife of Oscar d'Autremont, a merchant of Portland, Oregon; Celestine and Hugh, who are deceased; Clair, who is editor and publisher of the Quinlan Advance of Quinlan, Oklahoma; Lillian, the wife of Bert Tilford, of Waynoka, Oklahoma; and Herman, residing with his parents. With the coming of the railroads to the West, the freighting business began to be unprofitable, and in 1870 Nicholas Schnoebelen disposed of his outfit, returned to his home at Riverside, and there continued to be engaged in the blacksmithing business for many years. He is now living in quiet retirement at that place, enjoying the fruits of his many years of industrious and well-directed labor.

Omer Schnoebelen was educated in the public schools of Riverside, Iowa, and when but sixteen years entered the vocation which he was to make his life work by starting to learn the trade of printer. He was only nineteen years of age when he took up his residence at Mooreland, where, April 18, 1903, he founded the Mooreland Leader, of which he has since been editor and owner. His start was made in a modest way, but when the citizens of this rapidly-growing community saw the young man had come to remain and recognized the worth of the sheet which he was publishing, they began to give him their support, and he was able to enlarge his plant and paper and to give his readers a more advanced newspaper. He now has a plant modern in every respect, his equipment including up-to-date presses, a linotype machine and other machinery for the publishing of a twentieth century paper, while his circulation and advertising have grown by leaps and bounds. Mr. Schnoebelen has never been backward about supporting the movements or men whom he has believed to be beneficial to his community. The paper maintains an independent policy in regard to political affairs, and it is the aim of the editor to not only give his readers all the news in an authentic way, but to publish each side of every question of public importance that may arise.

Personally, Mr. Schnoebelen is a democrat and has been active in county and state politics, frequently attending county, state and congressional conventions as a delegate and giving his stanch support to his party's candidates. He was a member of the first board of trustees after the town was incorporated and has since served as a member of the town council, his services on which have been of an energetic and helpful character. On July 26, 1914, he was appointed by President Wilson to the position of postmaster of Mooreland, and is now acting in that capacity. Mr. Schnoebelen is a member of the Knights of Columbus. While the greater part of his time is devoted to his newspaper, he has at times been interested in outside enterprises, and during 1911 and 1912 was employed as assistant cashier of the Security State Bank of Mooreland.

On January 12, 1904, Mr. Schnoebelen was married to one of Mooreland's young ladies who had served for two years as assistant to the postmaster, Miss Edna Knittel, who was born at Riverside, Iowa, November 17, 1883, a daughter of F. J. and Louise (Kortzborn) Knittel, the former a native of France and the latter of Iowa. They are the parents of three children: Rita, born May 11, 1907; Omer, Jr., born November 5, 1912; and Hugh, born December 13, 1914.

HON. T. J. LEAHY is widely known as a man of high attainments, of profound erudition and practical ability as a lawyer, and as one who has achieved success in his profession. He is one of the most interesting of the prominent characters whose worth and merit have graced the history of Oklahoma as a state and territory, and was one of the two members elected to the Constitutional Convention from the Fifty-sixth District. In that high position he performed particularly notable work as a member of the Committee on Public Service Corporations, as such, making a thorough study and unprejudiced investigation of the great problems in connection with the governmental regulation of public service corporations, giving his best thought and judgment in an effort to arrive at a just solution of this modern and somewhat complex phase of legislation. The constitutional provisions result of this committee's work in the convention are conceded to be of the greatest beneficence to the state.

Mr. Leahy is one of the strong leaders of the bar in Oklahoma. For several years he conducted a large criminal practice, which is still a feature of his legal business, having an established reputation for success in that line. His practice as a whole, however, is of a general nature, extending into several states in addition to the Oklahoma State and Federal courts and the Interior Department. He was chairman of the commission that investigated the status and value of the segregated coal and other mineral lands of the Indian Territory and made recommendations as to the advisability of having the state purchase those lands. He spent much time and labor on the work of this commission, the report of which was submitted to the governor of Oklahoma in 1908. Mr. Leahy was also father of the measure, which was made a part of the Bill of Rights, providing that the right of the state to enter into public enterprise for public purposes should not be denied. The labor unions and laboring element generally were particularly pleased with Mr. Leahy's championship of measures in their interest in the Constitutional Convention. He is democratic in politics.

Mr. Leahy is a member of a family well known in the Osage Nation for many years back, and his cousin, W. T. Leahy, and uncle, Thomas Leahy, stockmen and bankers and residents of Pawhuska, have been prominently identified with various interests in this country since the early eighties. But the Hon. T. J. Leahy is a native son of Kansas, born in Neosho County, in 1868, his parents being natives of Ireland, being early settlers in that state. His father died in 1869, but his mother is still living. Her home is in Pawhuska. Mr. Leahy was reared in Neosho County, Kansas, receiving a common school and normal education. He studied law in both Kansas and Oklahoma and was admitted to the bar in 1892. In that year he settled permanently in Pawhuska, the capital of the Osage Nation, although he had been in the Nation back and forth since 1884. He belongs to the Masonic

Order, and also the Knights of Pythias, of which latter he is past grand chancellor of Oklahoma.

Mr. Leahy married in Pawhuska, Miss Bertha Rogers, who was born and reared there, a member of an old family of part Osage Indian blood, and daughter of Hon. Thomas L. Rogers, whose sketch is found in another page of this volume. Mr. and Mrs. Leahy have four children: Thomas Rogers, Cora Willella, Mabel Ann and Edward Arthur.

STRATTON D. BROOKS. Dr. Brooks has been president of the University of Oklahoma, Norman, since 1912, is a native of Everett, Missouri, where he was born September 10, 1869. At the age of twenty-one he graduated from the Michigan State Normal College, and subsequently the following degrees were conferred upon him: B. Pd., 1892, and M. Pd., 1899, by the Normal College; A. B., by the University of Michigan, 1896; A. M., by Harvard University, 1904; LL. D., Colby University, 1912.

Doctor Brooks served as vice president of the Mt. Pleasant (Michigan) Normal School in 1893; as principal of the high school at Danville, Illinois, in 1890-2, and held a similar position at Adrian, Michigan, in 1896-8, and at LaSalle, Illinois, in 1898-9. In 1899 Doctor Brooks was appointed assistant professor of education and high school inspector of the University of Illinois, and thus continued for three years; served as assistant superintendent of the Boston (Massachusetts) schools in 1902-06, as superintendent of schools at Cleveland, Ohio, from January to March, 1906, and was at the head of the Boston schools in 1906-12. In May of the latter year he was called to the presidency of the University of Oklahoma, which he has since ably filled. He has served as a trustee of the Massachusetts College and is a member of the national council of the National Educational Association and of the fraternity Phi Beta Kappa. Doctor Brooks is also a leading writer in his professional field, being assistant editor of the 'School Review and Journal of Pedagogy, and author of text books on composition, rhetoric, elementary composition and reading.

LAURENCE L. COWLEY. Since 1901 Mr. Cowley has been engaged in the practice of his profession in Oklahoma, and since 1913 he has been one of the representative members of the bar of Okmulgee, in which city he now controls a large and important law business, besides which he is serving as secretary of the board of trustees of the Okmulgee Public Library.

At Columbus, the judicial center of Cherokee County, Kansas, Laurence L. Cowley was born on the 18th of February, 1877, a date that denotes that his parents could claim pioneer honors in the Sunflower State. He is a son of William R. and Florence J. (Smith) Cowley, the former of whom was born in the Borough of Boston, Lincolnshire, England, in 1843, and the latter of whom was born at Oskaloosa, Iowa, in 1848, a member of one of the early pioneer families of that section of the Hawkeye State, where her marriage to Mr. Cowley was solemnized about the year 1868.

William R. Cowley was a lad of about eight years when he accompanied his parents on their immigration to the United States, in 1851, and the family home was established at Hudson, Ohio, in which state he was reared and educated. Prior to attaining to his legal majority he established his residence in Iowa, and in 1871, about three years after his marriage, he removed thence to Kansas and established his residence at Columbus, where soon afterward he entered the legal profession and engaged in active practice, in which he there continued, as one of the leading lawyers and highly honored citizens of Cherokee County, until the time of his death, which occurred on the 13th of July, 1914. He served for thirty-two years as general attorney for the Log-Bell Lumber Company, a large and important corporation. Prior to engaging in the practice of law he had been ordained a clergyman in the Christian Church, and he continued one of its active and zealous members until the close of his long and useful life. His widow, who continued to reside at Columbus until her death, December 30, 1915, was likewise a devoted adherent of this church. Mr. Cowley was a gallant soldier of the Union in the Civil war, in which he first served as a member of the Sixty-fourth Ohio Volunteer Infantry, and later as a member of the Fifteenth Iowa Volunteer Infantry. His service covered a period of about three years, he was promoted to the office of sergeant and he took part in numerous engagements marking the progress of the great conflict through which the integrity of the nation was preserved, a prominent part of his military career having been that in which his regiment accompanied General Sherman on the ever memorable march from Atlanta to the sea. He was an effective and stalwart advocate of the principles and policies of the republican party and was affiliated with the Grand Army of the Republic. Of the six children the eldest is William Frederick, who is engaged in farming and stock raising in Southeastern Kansas; Minnie is the wife of Charles S. Huffman, M. D., who is engaged in the practice of his profession at Columbus, Kansas; Clement Sidney died in childhood, as did also Anna B.; Laurence L., of this review, was the next in order of birth; and Clare J. holds a responsible position in the general offices of the Long-Bell Lumber Company, at Kansas City, Missouri.

In the public schools of his native place Laurence L. Cowley acquired his early education, and from 1892 until 1893 he attended the public schools of Akron, Ohio. He then entered the literary department of the University of Kansas, at Lawrence, in which he was graduated as a member of the class of 1899 and from which he received the degree of Bachelor of Arts. In the law department of the same institution he was graduated in 1901, and soon after receiving his degree of Bachelor of Laws he came to Oklahoma and engaged in practice at Perry, the present judicial center of Noble County. There he continued his successful professional activities until 1913, when he removed to the City of Okmulgee, where he has found a broader field, in which his success has been unequivocal, as shown by his substantial and representative practice and his high reputation for efficiency and versatility as a trial lawyer and as a well fortified counselor. In 1910 he was elected county attorney of Noble County, of which office he continued the incumbent one term, comprising two years. He also served as referee in bankruptcy in Noble County, prior to the admission of Oklahoma to statehood. He is unwavering in his allegiance to the republican party and has given yeoman service in support of its cause. He is a member of the official board of the Christian Church at Okmulgee, in which Mrs. Cowley also is a zealous worker, and he is affiliated with the Masonic fraternity and the Knights of Pythias, besides which he is actively identified with the Okmulgee County Bar Association and the Oklahoma State Bar Association.

On the 10th of June, 1903, was solemnized the marriage of Mr. Cowley to Miss Gertrude M. Chapman, who likewise was born and reared in Kansas: they have no children.

SAM R. HAWKS, JR. Since his arrival at Clinton, in 1908, there have been few activities, commercial, civic or political, that have not been participated in by Sam R. Hawks, Jr. He has contributed to the upbuilding of the city by the erection of the Grace Hotel, has encouraged its business interests as secretary of the Chamber of Commerce, and has been known in the journalistic field as part owner of the Clinton News and the Clinton Chronicle, and since 1913 has capably served in the capacity of postmaster, a position which he won fairly, both because of merit and his loyalty to and hard work in the interests of the democratic party in Custer County.

Mr. Hawks was born at Lebanon, Tennessee, March 8, 1882, a descendant of Scotch ancestors, who came to Virginia in Colonial days. His father, Sam R. Hawks, Sr., was born near Lebanon, Tennessee, in 1855, and for a number of years was general manager for the Cedar City Mills, an ice and light plant, but in 1911 came to Clinton, Oklahoma. After a short stay he removed to Amarillo, Texas, and is now manager for the State of New Mexico of the Red Star Milling Company, a large and well known Kansas concern. Mr. Hawks is a democrat, belongs to the Knights of Pythias, and is a member of the Christian Church. He married a native of Lebanon, Tennessee, Miss Carrie Smith, and they are the parents of five children: H. C., who is engaged in the grain and milling business and in farming at Lebanon; Sam R., Jr.; Miss Lou Kate, who lives with her parents; Virginia, who is the wife of K. C. Alexander, a cotton buyer of Clinton, Oklahoma; and Miss Christine, who lives with her parents.

Sam R. Hawks, Jr., attended the public and high schools of Lebanon, Tennessee, and after his graduation from the latter, in 1897, at once became identified with the milling and grain business, with which he was connected until 1908, in June of which year he came to Clinton. Here his first venture was the erection of the Grace Hotel, without a doubt one of the best hostelries in Western Oklahoma, of which he is still the owner, although he has never conducted it personally. In 1909 he became secretary of the Clinton Chamber of Commerce, this time bought a half interest in the Clinton News a position which he held for two years, and during and the Clinton Chronicle, in which newspapers he is still interested. In September, 1913, he received the appointment as postmaster of Clinton from President Wilson. Mr. Hawks was one of the original Wilson men of Oklahoma in 1912, being the manager of the campaign in his district, and also took an active interest in the campaign of Senator Owens, his ability as a political manager having been demonstrated by the large votes which his candidates received in his district. He has attended state and county conventions of his party since 1908, and has been a faithful and tireless worker in the cause of democracy, so that his appointment to the postmastership came as a reward for service cheerfully given and capably rendered. That he is well fitted for the position has been shown by the entirely efficient manner in which he has conducted the affairs of the mail service during his incumbency. He belongs to Lotus Lodge No. 20, Knights of Pythias, of Lebanon, Tennessee, of which he is past prelate, and to the Oklahoma State Press Association, and with his family holds membership in the Christian Church.

Mr. Hawks was married at Lebanon, in 1907, to Miss Frances Jones, daughter of J. L. Jones, engaged in the plumbing and tinning business at Lebanon. Three children have been born to this union: Catherine, Preston and Jim Woodrow, the first-named of whom has started to attend the public schools.

PEARL A. LITTLE first became identified with Oklahoma as a member of a painting crew operating in various districts of Western Oklahoma, and for nearly fifteen years has had his home at Frederick. Largely by private study and practical experience Mr. Little has made himself an expert civil engineer, and for a number of years has served as county surveyor and city engineer of Frederick and has a substantial private practice in the profession. Born in Ralls County, Missouri, August 24, 1879, Pearl A. Little is a son of John W. and Mary (McAllister) Little. The Little and McAllister families moved to Missouri from Kentucky and John W. Little was also born in Ralls County, Missouri, in 1856, and died there in 1889. He was a farmer and stock raiser and was accidentally killed by a horse while running cattle. His church was the Catholic, and he took a prominent part in local affairs as a democrat, and belonged to the Grange, and also to a local organization known as the Wheel. His wife, Mary McAllister, was born in Missouri, and now resides at Quincy, Illinois. Pearl A. was the oldest of their six children. Roy, the next in age, is a street railway conductor at Quincy, Illinois; Alice is the wife of Chris Schrand, a cigar manufacturer at Quincy; Lambert, a farmer in Ralls County, Missouri; Annie lives with her mother; and Mary died when nine months of age.

In 1889 Mr. Little's mother removed from Ralls County to Monroe County, Missouri, and in 1890 to Shelby County, and his education came from attendance at the schools of all those places. He received the equivalent of a high school education, and in June, 1897, was graduated from St. Francis College, at Quincy, Illinois, with a diploma as Master of Accounts. During the next year he kept books for John J. Rogers, proprietor of a department store at Monroe City, Missouri, and then engaged in different lines of occupation up to 1900. Going to Pratt, Kansas, he found work on a farm until the fall of the year and then joined a painting crew working in Kansas, and in December, 1900, came with that organization to Enid, Oklahoma. On March 15, 1901, he went to Kingfisher, Oklahoma, and on November 24, 1901, arrived at Frederick, which has been his home practically ever since. Up to July, 1906, Mr. Little continued his work as a painter, and then took a review course in engineering covering the freshman and sophomore years in the Agricultural and Mechanical College at Stillwater. Returning to Frederick in 1908, he began practice as a surveyor and engineer and since that time has performed the duties of city engineer, though he was not regularly put under bond for the office until 1914. In 1911 he became county surveyor of Tillman County and has been regularly returned to that office without opposition. On September 17-18, 1915, he successfully passed a civil service examination given by the highway department of Oklahoma for engineers who wished to practice as county engineers in Oklahoma. Since then he has been appointed county engineer for Tillman, Harmon and Jackson Counties.

Mr. Little is a democrat, and a member of the Catholic Church. On November 25, 1903, at Lawton, Oklahoma, he married Miss Lillie McClellan, whose father, George R. McClellan, is a farmer at Del Norte, Colorado. Their home has been blessed with the birth of six children: Catherine, who attends a parochial school at Quincy, Illinois; Paul, Lawrence and Alice, in the public schools at Frederick; and Rita and Annie, who are not yet of school age.

FRED H. CLARK, M. D. For twelve years Doctor Clark has given his services as a widely experienced and capable physician and surgeon to the community of El Reno.

Doctor Clark is one of the best known figures in medical circles of the Southwest, and is a man of broad range of experience and activities in the world.

Fred H. Clark was born on a farm near Vernon, Michigan, May 15, 1864, a son of Jesse and Eliza Jane (Pratt) Clark. Like many successful men in the profession he considers himself fortunate to have spent his early youth in the environment of the country. While living on a Michigan farm he attended the common schools, and in 1885 was graduated from the high school at Owosso, Michigan, where he afterwards held the position of teacher in the city schools two years and for a like period had a commercial position. The following ten years of his life were devoted to work as secretary of Young Men's Christian Associations, largely in Michigan, though his last service in this capacity was at Kansas City, Missouri.

In Kansas City Doctor Clark pursued his studies in medicine at the University Medical College, and was graduated M. D. in 1900. In order that his equipment might be brought up to the highest grade of efficiency and tested by association with men of eminence he has subsequently taken post-graduate work in Chicago three times and once in New York City. For about three years Doctor Clark was engaged in practice in Kansas City, then came to Oklahoma and spent about a year at Minco and since the fall of 1903 has been located at El Reno.

The wide scope of his professional interests is indicated by his membership in the following organizations: The Canadian County and Oklahoma Medical societies, the American Medical Association, the Southwest Medical Society of the Southwest, the Rock Island Railway Surgeons, the Central Oklahoma, the Western Oklahoma and Missouri River Medical associations, the Mississippi Valley Medical Association, and the Association of American Railway Surgeons. Doctor Clark is consulting surgeon for the Rock Island Railway. He is secretary of the Southwest Medical Society of the Southwest, and the official organ of that society, known as the Southwest Journal of Medicine and Surgery, has been owned and published by Doctor Clark for the past three years.

Doctor Clark is a Knight Templar Mason and a member of the Temple of the Mystic Shrine, belongs to the Baptist Church and in politics is a republican. In 1887 he married for his first wife Miss Rose Johnson, who died in 1897, leaving one daughter. In 1899 Doctor Clark married Miss Elizabeth Phillips, who is the mother of one daughter. For the past eleven years Doctor Clark has been connected with the state military service in the medical department, with the rank of major and has charge of the field hospitals.

PETER W. HUDSON. One of the younger men in the official life of Eastern Oklahoma, Peter W. Hudson is now court clerk of Pushmataha County, with home at Antlers. He is a native of Indian Territory and his people have been closely identified with the educational and official and business life of that section for many years.

To erect a state government and keep it in operation during the period of its infancy is necessarily expensive. In Oklahoma the actual expenses of state government proper have not been exorbitant. However, every county and municipality paid the price for their individuality as entities of the larger state government. Hence, for a few years taxes were unusually high. Every campaign of every character conducted since 1907 has in one way or another involved the principle and issue of economy. The candidate who has convinced the people that he would maintain efficiency at the lowest possible cost has won in a majority of campaigns. Usually these candidates have found it quite a difficult thing to make good a pledge of economy, so heavy and numerous have been demands for public improvement.

Among those who kept the faith was Peter W. Hudson. It is probable that no other county court clerk in Oklahoma up to 1915 had conducted his office without any expense of assistance. It has required long hours of arduous work and much candle power of night. District Court dockets have been heavy and the duties of the clerk onerous, but Mr. Hudson inaugurated and strictly followed a system whereby at the end of a session his records were written and ready for the approval of the District Court before the judge was ready to depart for another court center. The saving to Pushmataha County has been considerable, and this has been an important reason why Mr. Hudson has been in office ever since the year of statehood. After Frank Trigger, the first elected district clerk of Pushmataha County, had been in office about a month he died and the county commissioners appointed Peter W. Hudson to fill the vacancy. The following year he was elected to the office, on the democratic ticket, without opposition. He was re-elected in 1910 and again in 1912. The legislature then passed an act consolidating certain county offices and the duties of clerk of the County Court and those of the clerk of the District Court were imposed on an official designated as court clerk. In 1914 Mr. Hudson was elected to that office.

Even before statehood he had clerical experience as clerk in the Choctaw Legislature. He held the position five years under the administration of Principal Chief McCurtain. He was in that position during the McCurtain-Hunter contest at Tuskahoma, and kept the minutes of the meeting held under the shade of trees or in a hotel while the Hunter faction was in possession of the council house. Meantime he was also in the employ as clerk of W. H. Isherwood, a merchant at Tuskahoma, and did some work for his uncle Peter J. Hudson, who was at that time superintendent of the Choctaw Female Academy at Tuskahoma.

Peter W. Hudson was born August 29, 1877, and is a son of Washington and Frances (Bohannan) Hudson. His father, who was born at Eagletown in Indian Territory, was a farmer and merchant during most of his life, and died in 1897. Washington Hudson's brother Daniel was a Confederate soldier and for sixteen years served as sheriff of Eagle County in the Choctaw Nation. James Hudson, the maternal grandfather of Peter W. Hudson, was a Presbyterian minister, was educated in English, and his labors among the Indians were directed by the missionary board of the Presbyterian Church. Other children in the family of Washington and Frances Hudson were: Roy, a farmer at Eagletown; George, a student in Jones Academy; Mrs. Byington, Mrs. Jefferson and Mrs. Lewis, all of them wives of farmers at Haworth.

Peter W. Hudson was educated in the neighborhood schools near his birthplace at Eagletown, and spent five years in Spencer Academy. While in the academy he was a classmate of Gabe Parker, who later became commissioner to the Five Civilized Tribes. In 1901 Mr. Hudson married at Tuskahoma Miss Myrtle Campbell. Their three children are named Lillian Thelma, Dorothy and Peter W., Jr. Mr. Hudson is a member of the Methodist Episcopal Church South. Fraternally his associations are with the Woodmen of the World, the Independent Order of Odd Fellows and the Masonic Order, and he is senior warden of the Blue Lodge, a member of the Royal Arch Chapter at Hugo and the Knight Templar Commandery and the Mystic Shrine at Muskogee.

JOHN SHERTZER. During the past ten years the firm Shertzer Bros. have been among the largest operators and producers in the Dewey oil district. Both these brothers are experienced oil men, having become identified with the practical details of the business back in Ohio, where they served their apprenticeship during the high tide of oil production in that state.

John Shertzer, the older of the two brothers, was born in Bedford County, Pennsylvania, December 25, 1869, a son of William and Samantha (Studebaker) Shertzer, both natives of Pennsylvania and of old Pennsylvania Dutch stock. The family lived in Pennsylvania until 1877, and then removed to Gibsonburg, Ohio, where the mother died in 1910 at the age of fifty-four. The father is now living at Bartlesville, having come to that city about three years ago. He was engaged in the business of lime manufacturing until 1885 and has since been an oil well contractor and producer. John Shertzer was the oldest of five children, the others being: C. P. Shertzer, the junior member of the firm of Shertzer Bros.; Effie, wife of Raymond Pryor of Lake View, Ohio; Elsie, wife of James Neely of Lima, Ohio; and Ollie, wife of A. C. White, who is general manager of the American Express Company at Cleveland, Ohio.

John Shertzer was about eight years of age when the family removed to Ohio, and grew up in Gibsonburg and gained a common school education. At the age of twenty he first became connected with the oil business as a contractor and producer. For five years he was engaged in the manufacturing and retailing of shoes at St. Louis. His experience as an oil man extends to the California fields, where he spent one year, then returned to Ohio and was a contractor at Gibsonburg two years, spent two years at Chanute, Kansas, and in 1905 located at Dewey. For the past ten years he has been recognized as one of the leading oil producers in Northern Oklahoma. As a contractor he put down the first well in the Weber pool, and altogether has sunk about 600 wells in this district, partly as an independent operator and partly on contract. For the past seven years he has been a member of the firm of Shertzer Bros., and their interests extend to about sixty wells in the Bartlesville District.

John Shertzer is a republican, while his brother and business associate is a democrat. He is a member of the Benevolent and Protective Order of Elks at Freemont, Ohio. In 1907 Mr. John Shertzer married Pearl Damon of Dundee, Michigan. They have one child, Lillian Joyce.

C. P. Shertzer, the younger member of the firm of Shertzer Bros., was born in Bedford County, Pennsylvania, September 4, 1872, and as a boy learned the lime business with his father. His first practical experience in the oil industry came at the age of seventeen, and for about two years he dressed tools with his father. He did his first contracting at Lima, Ohio, and for about four years was in the employ of other parties, but since then has mainly been independent. For a time he was in the Indiana oil fields, and in November, 1904, located at Chanute, Kansas, and eighteen months later at Dewey. Shertzer Bros. now produce about 3,000 barrels of oil a month, and have a number of small farms around Dewey. C. P. Shertzer served on the city council of Dewey three years, and has been a trustee in the Methodist Episcopal Church since locating in that town. He is also a member of the Masonic fraternity. In 1899 he married Miss Inez Brinkerhoff, who was born in Ohio, a daughter of Nelson Brinkerhoff. Their three children are Boyd, Frances and Charles.

CHARLES ELMER GRADY. The entire career of Charles Elmer Grady has been devoted to educational work, a field for which he is singularly equipped and for which he has had a most thorough and comprehensive training. When he assumed the duties of his present office, that of superintendent of city schools of Clinton, he brought to their discharge an enthusiasm for his calling, ripe experience gained in several important and laborious positions, and energetic and progressive methods that have had a very beneficial effect upon the school system here. Superintendent Grady was born in Crittenden County, Kentucky, May 2, 1879, and is a son of R. N. and Margaret (Everle) Grady. The family, as the name would indicate, is of Irish origin, and the first paternal ancestor in America settled in Fauquier County, Virginia, during the days of the Colonies.

R. N. Grady was born near Lexington, Kentucky, in 1845, and when the Civil war came on gave his support to the Union cause, enlisting in the Fifteenth Kentucky Cavalry, with which organization he served for three years. At the close of the war he resumed his operations as a farmer, stock raiser and merchant in Crittenden County, and continued to be so engaged during the remainder of his life, with the exception of ten or twelve years passed in Clark County, Indiana. He died in the faith of the Methodist Episcopal Church, of which he was a steward, in 1907. Mrs. Grady, who was born near Louisville, Kentucky, in 1847, died in Crittenden County, Kentucky, in 1898. Their children were as follows: Mary, who is the wife of W. R. Sullivan, in the real estate and insurance business at Waco, Texas; Mattie, the wife of Ira Robinson, a farmer residing in Crittenden County, Kentucky; Anna, who married J. D. Crider, a farmer of Mississippi County, Missouri; Nellie, who married W. D. Cain, a merchant, and resides at Charleston, Missouri; Charles Elmer; Ruth, who married J. N. Swansey, engaged in the livery business at Sturgis, Kentucky; A. L., a liveryman, residing at Kansas City, Missouri; Clarence, a prosperous merchant at Weston, Crittenden County, Kentucky; the old home town; and Lester, a graduate of the University of Kentucky, class of 1915, degree of Bachelor of Arts.

The public schools of Marion, Crittenden County, Kentucky, furnished the foundation for the training which was to fit Charles E. Grady for educational work, and subsequently he went to the Northern Indiana Normal School, at Valparaiso, which he left in 1906. Two years later he was graduated from the University of Indiana, with the degree of Bachelor of Arts, and in 1910 was given the master's degree by that institution. He holds membership in the Phi Delta Kappa Greek letter college fraternity, which he joined while attending the university. In 1910 Mr. Grady was appointed superintendent of schools at Iowa Park, Texas, and during 1911 and 1912 was president of the Western College, Cordell, Oklahoma. In 1913 and 1914 he was superintendent of schools at Granite, Oklahoma, and in the fall of 1915 came to Clinton as superintendent of city schools, an office in which he has charge of three schoolhouses, with twenty-two teachers and 1,000 scholars. In this, one of the most difficult of the learned professions, Superintendent Grady has won material success and position solely through the exercise of his own industry and native abilities. A born educator, with the happy faculty of being able to impart his own knowledge to others, he is also possessed of no small degree of executive ability, so necessary in such a position as he holds. He is a democrat, although not a politician, and with his family belongs to the Presbyterian Church. He is well and popularly known in fraternal circles, belonging to Clinton Lodge No. 339, Ancient Free and Accepted Masons; Clinton Lodge of Odd Fellows; the Brotherhood of American Yeomen; the Woodmen of the World, and the Columbian Woodmen.

In 1909, at Duckhill, Mississippi, Mr. Grady was united in marriage with Miss Winnie Lee Rose, daughter of the late James L. Rose, who was a merchant. Mr. and Mrs. Grady have two children: Charles Elmer, Jr., born January 13, 1910, and Robert L., born August 26, 1914.

DAVID D. DAVISSON. With twenty-five years of Oklahoma residence to his credit, David D. Davisson has well earned the privilege of retirement and comfort and ease, and is now living somewhat quietly with an ample competence for his declining years at Carnegie.

In the years preceding the original opening of Oklahoma Territory Mr. Davisson was one of the men most prominent in the political and civic affairs of the original Canadian County. He is an Oklahoma eighty-niner, and made the run on that eventful day, April 22, 1889. He found his claim in the old Downs Township, which at that time was part of Canadian County. Until he retired a few years ago Mr. Davisson was a practical farmer and has derived most of his prosperity from his work as an agriculturist.

As a democrat he was very active in the organization of Canadian County, and in 1890 was elected county clerk, being the first man to hold that office by popular election. He remained in office two years, and in 1893 was elected superintendent of Canadian County, a position he also held two years, and in that time did much in behalf of the establishment of the schools and development of the first schools established in that section of the state. At a later date Mr. Davisson served as deputy county clerk of Kingfisher County, and for a time was principal of the Banner School at Guthrie.

In 1901 Mr. Davisson participated in another grand opening, when the Kiowa and Comanche reservations were given over to actual settlers, but he subsequently located in Caddo County, where he still has extensive holdings.

David D. Davisson was born January 21, 1851, at Centerville, West Virginia, a son of Dr. D. D. Davisson, who was born in the same state. Mr. Davisson completed his early education in old St. Vincent College of Wheeling, West Virginia, and for twenty years altogether was a successful teacher, following his profession in Missouri, Kansas and Oklahoma.

In 1881, at McPherson, Kansas, he married Miss Sarah C. Horton. She was born in New York City in 1855. They have one son, Gilbert Horton, born November 26, 1885, at Pratt, Kansas. This son, who now lives on his father's original Oklahoma homestead in Kingfisher County, married Miss Mary Johnson, and has one child, DeLon.

DR. KIAH RIX RONE. The Rones of Kentucky are well known to natives of that state, and men of the name have been history makers in the Blue Grass region through several successive generations. The family is of remote English ancestry, as is a good deal of the best blood in the land, and the first American representatives of the name settled in Virginia on coming from England, one branch continuing there and another, the one with which we are directly concerned in this review, locating in Kentucky. The Rones are closely connected by ties of blood with the well known family of Randolphs, whose deeds have shed a bright light over pages of American history through many years.

Dr. K. R. Rone, of Vici, Oklahoma, was born in Warren County, Kentucky, on June 28, 1865, and he is the son of J. B. Rone, born in Butler County, Kentucky, in 1824. The latter died in Warren County, Kentucky, in 1895. All his life he had been a successful farmer and stockman in his native state, and he was a man of prominence in his chosen field of activity. He was a member of the Methodist Episcopal Church, South, and was a deacon and a member of its official board through many years. He was also a member of the Masonic fraternity, a democrat in politics, and a man esteemed of all who shared in his acquaintance. He married Elizabeth McGinnis, a Warren County girl, born there in 1833, and she died in her native community in 1897, the mother of two children. The first born was Kiah Rix Rone of this review, and the second was J. B., a graduate of the Louisville Medical College in Kentucky and now a practicing physician and surgeon in Oklahoma City.

Dr. K. R. Rone attended Ogden College for two years and was graduated from Vanderbilt University in Nashville, Tennessee, in the class of 1889, at that time receiving the degree M. D. He followed his training there with a post-graduate course in the New York Polyclinic in physical diagnosis and surgery, spending the year 1890 there, and in later years he took postgraduate work in the Chicago Polyclinic and in the Mayo Brothers' Institution at Rochester, Minnesota. His Chicago training he took in 1895 and his work under the celebrated Mayo brothers he took in 1914. While there he was elected president of the Mayo's Surgical Club, of which he is a life member.

In 1889 Doctor Rone began the practice of his profession in his native county. He continued there, enjoying a good deal of prosperity in his work, until 1893 when he moved to Logan County, Kentucky, in search of a wider field. He spent seven years there and in 1900 came to Oklahoma City, in which city he conducted a general practice up to March 1, 1911, when he located in Vici, and here he has since conducted a large general practice. He has, in recent years, been making something of a specialty of surgery, but in a community like Vici deems it best to conduct a general rather than a special practice. He has enjoyed a generous measure of success in all the years of his practice, and especially has he prospered in recent years.

While practicing in Oklahoma City Doctor Rone for two years held the chair of instructor in genital, urinary and rectal diseases, in the Oklahoma City College. He gave up the post in order that he might have more time for the demands of his practice. At present Doctor Rone is local surgeon for the Wichita Falls & Northwestern Railroad. He is president of the Dewey County Medical Society, and is also a member of the State, American and Southwestern Medical associations. While a practicing physician in Logan County, Kentucky, Doctor Rone was county health officer, as well as city physician of Russellville.

In 1895 Doctor Rone was married, in Warren County, Kentucky, to Miss Minnie Taylor, daughter of William Taylor, a well known farming man there, now deceased. Five children have blessed the home of Doctor and Mrs. Rone. Lucille, the eldest, married Claude Taylor, cashier of the German State Bank at Elk City, Oklahoma. Caryee is an instructor in dancing at Medicine Park, Oklahoma. Guthrie is a druggist, located in California. The two youngest children, Martrie and Jack, are students in the local high school, and are bright and promising young people, popular in school circles and with many friends throughout the town.

ROBERT C. MCCREERY, M. D., F. A. C. S. In the difficult field of surgery, the importance of which is daily being brought forcibly to mind by the achievements of its devotees in the great struggle now raging in Europe, Dr. Robert C. McCreery has won distinction among Oklahoma practitioners. Since his arrival at Erick, in June, 1909, he has held an increasingly significant position in the life of the community, his fine abilities entitling him to mention among the leading men of the state who are exponents of a profession that must be rated as one of the greatest triumphs of human intellect, energy and resource.

Doctor McCreery belongs to a family which originated in Scotland and was founded in New York in Colonial days, and was born at DeSoto, Jefferson County, Missouri, March 18, 1869, being a son of Charles E. and Plotina (Hollensbeck) McCreery. His father was also a native of that county, where he passed a long and successful career as a farmer and raiser of livestock, and died March 17, 1913, in the faith of the Baptist Church, in which he was a deacon for many years and an active worker throughout his life. During the Civil war he fought as a Union soldier in the Sixth Regiment, Missouri Volunteer Infantry, and was once wounded in action. Mrs. McCreery, who was likewise born in Jefferson County, died there in 1895, aged fifty-two years. She was the mother of the following children: Laura, who is the wife of W. E. Jones, of Chicago, Illinois, superintendent of a fruit growers' car association; Adelia, who died in 1903 as the wife of G. W. Showers, of Bryan, Texas, general foreman of railroad car service; Dr. Robert C.; Hester, who is the wife of A. M. Lane, a contractor and builder of Sacramento City, California; G. E., a manufacturer of Los Angeles, California; Nellie G., who is the wife of J. J. O'Keefe, of Crystal City, Missouri, a traveling representative for milling products; and Jeannette, the wife of J. E. Hart, of St. Louis, Missouri, holding an important position with the United States Government.

Robert C. McCreery attended the public schools of DeSoto, Missouri, where he was graduated in 1891 from the high school. His medical studies were commenced at the College of Physicians and Surgeons, Chicago, where he spent one year, the following year being passed at the Kansas City University of Medicine. In 1908 he was graduated from the medical department of the University of Arkansas, with the degree of Doctor of Medicine, although prior to this time, from 1903 to 1907, he had been engaged in practice at Kansas City. Until 1909 he carried on his practice at Little Rock, Arkansas, where he was physician for the athletic association of the district, and June 5, 1909, came to Erick, where he has carried on a general practice, although specializing in surgery, a field in which he has taken a commanding position. In 1914 he took a post-graduate course in gynæcological surgery at Tulane University, New Orleans. In 1910 Doctor McCreery founded a hospital, a modern institution, accommodating twenty patients, which is located at No. 120 East Broadway, his offices being in the Erick State Bank Building. He belongs to the Beckham County Medical Society, the Oklahoma Medical Society and the American Medical Association, and is a fellow of the American College of Surgeons. A democrat in politics, he has served as health officer at Erick, and has taken an interest in all beneficial civic, educational and moral movements. With his family, he attends the Baptist Church, of which he is a member, and at present is superintendent of the Sunday School. Doctor McCreery is also well known in fraternal circles, belonging to the Modern Woodmen of America; Lodge No. 1144, Benevolent and Protective Order of Elks, of Elk City, Oklahoma; Far West Lodge No. 1, Independent Order of Odd Fellows, Little Rock, Arkansas, of which he is past noble grand, and to the Encampment and Canton of Odd Fellowship.

Doctor McCreery was married at DeSoto, Missouri, in 1899, to Miss Nannie J. Gowan, daughter of the late Capt. Reason E. Gowan, who was a captain in the Union army during the Civil war, and for many years a Missouri farmer. Two children have been born to Doctor and Mrs. McCreery: Glenn A., who married S. J. Harrell, engaged in farming at Liberal, Kansas; and Robert W., who is attending the Erick public schools.

PORTER N. MCCALLUM. In spite of what the great majority of individuals would consider a most discouraging handicap, Porter N. McCallum, of Devol, Oklahoma, has attained a most desirable and satisfying success. Only one possessed of energy, perseverance and determination could have saved himself from total failure, but Mr. McCallum has so directed his energies that he now occupies an established place among business men of his community, and is well known for a number of large transactions in real estate.

Porter N. McCallum was born in the City of Dallas, Texas, August 21, 1881, and is a son of J. N. and Maggie (Porter) McCallum, natives of Tennessee. The father, now a resident of Devol, was born in 1852, and in 1880 removed from his native state to Texas, settling first at Dallas, moving to Denton in 1894, and in 1907 coming to Devol. In his early years he learned the trade of painter and gradually developed into a contractor in that line, also following for a number of years the business of railroad surveying. At the present time he is county weigher of Cotton County. In political matters Mr. McCallum is a staunch democrat. He and Mrs. McCallum are members of the Presbyterian Church, in which he is an elder. They have been the parents of two children: Porter N., of this notice; and J. D., who is the proprietor of a cigar store at Oklahoma City, Oklahoma.

The public schools at Denton, Texas, furnished Porter N. McCallum with his education, and when he left the high school in 1899 he became a telegraph operator for the Texas & Pacific Railroad. Later he took a position as brakeman with the same road, and held this employment until 1901, in which year, while in the performance of his duties, he slipped and fell beneath two cars, one of which passed over him and severed his left leg. Thus handicapped, when he had recovered, Mr. McCallum was forced to face life anew, and resolutely set about to learn the business of paper hanging, and followed that vocation at Denton until 1907, at that time accompanying his parents to Devol. He continued to carry on the same line of business here until 1912, when he established himself in business as a real estate dealer, and has so continued to the present time. Mr. McCallum has an interest in several properties, and now owns his own residence on Wichita Avenue. He received an indemnity from the railroad company on whose line he was injured.

Like his father Mr. McCallum is a strong democrat, and has taken something more than a passing interest in political affairs, as he is now chairman of the Democratic County Committee of Cotton County and is accounted to possess a wide influence in party circles. He has never allowed partisanship, however, to keep him from aiding in every way the best interests of his community. Mr. McCallum belongs to Camp No. 11,823, of the Modern Woodmen of America, at Devol, and is very popular with his fellow members. He also holds membership in the Devol Commercial Club, and co-operates loyally in the movements of this public-spirited organization.

Mr. McCallum was married in 1902, at Denton, Texas, to Miss Effie Anderson, daughter of the late J. F. Anderson, who was a well-known financier of Denton, owning a chain of banks which included institutions at that place, Ardmore, Durant, and other Oklahoma and Texas points. Mr. and Mrs. McCallum have no children. Mr.

McCallum comes of sturdy old Scotch stock, his grandfather, Neill McCallum, having been born in Scotland. He was eight years of age when brought to the United States by his parents, the family settling first in Virginia and subsequently moving to Tennessee. The grandfather was engaged principally in buying and selling mules, rounded out a long and successful life, and died in 1886, at Pulaski, Tennessee, aged seventy years.

HARRY C. LACY. The progressive and financial standing of a city is indicated as much by the type of business men who conduct its affairs as by its institutions. Harry C. Lacy, cashier of the well known Bank of Hydro, is an astute financier and a citizen whose loyalty to his home community is of the most sincere order. He has been a resident of Hydro since 1901 and has been engaged in the banking business since 1909. He also owns a splendidly improved farm of one-half section, in Caddo County, Oklahoma, and the same is devoted to diversified agriculture.

A native of Des Moines, Iowa, Harry C. Lacy was born January 2, 1870, and he is a son of Henry D. and Lestine (Betts) Lacy. The father was born in Vermont, in 1847, and he is of Irish stock, his father having settled in the Green Mountain state from Ireland about 1835. Prior to the outbreak of the Civil war H. H. Lacy journeyed west to Des Moines, Iowa, and in 1861 he enlisted for service in the Fourth Iowa Volunteer Infantry. He took part in many important conflicts marking the progress of the war and after Lee's surrender was mustered out of service as an officer. He then returned to Des Moines, where he married and where he entered into business as a merchant. Later he removed to Shelby County, Iowa, and turned his attention to farming; thence he removed to Western Kansas. In 1893 he made the run at the opening in Garfield County, Oklahoma, and obtained a fine homestead of 160 acres. He lives on this farm now and has increased it to 320 acres. Much of his attention is given to stock raising. He is a republican, is affiliated with the Masonic fraternity, and in religious faith is a devout member of the Methodist Episcopal Church. Mrs. Lacy, who was born in Pennsylvania, in 1849, is a woman of most gracious personality and she and her husband are held in high esteem by all who know them. They became the parents of eight children, concerning whom the following brief data are here inserted: W. J. is a resident of Detroit, Michigan; Harry C. is the subject of this review; Edith married M. J. Lambert and lives in Wichita, Kansas, at the age of twenty-six years; Louis is a farmer in Idaho; Frank is at home with his parents; Weaver is a railroad man in Minneapolis, Minnesota; Rex is an auctioneer and farmer in Garfield County, Oklahoma, as is also Ray.

Harry C. Lacy attended the public schools of Des Moines, Iowa, until his sixteenth year, when he went to Anthony, Kansas, where he engaged in the livery and bus business for the following four years. In 1893 he came to the Cherokee Strip and secured a claim, and he was engaged in agricultural pursuits until 1901, which year marks his advent in Hydro, where he was engaged in the implement business for the ensuing seven years as a member of the firm of Pope & Lacy. Disposing of his interest in the above concern, he purchased a farm in Cotton County, Oklahoma, and developed the same for one year, when he turned it over to tenants and entered the Bank of Hydro, of which he is now cashier. This bank was established as a state bank in October, 1903, by G. W. Snapp and W. H. Henke, and a new brick building was erected for it on the corner of Main Street and Broadway, in 1910. The official corps of the bank is as follows: F. R. Miller, president; M. E. Scott, vice president; H. C. Lacy, cashier, and A. J. Arbes, assistant cashier. The bank has a capital stock of $10,000 and its surplus and profits amount to $5,000.

Mr. Lacy is a republican in his political allegiance and although not an office seeker he is serving at the present time as city treasurer. His fraternal connections are with Hydro Lodge No. 230, Ancient Free and Accepted Masons, of which he is past master; Valley of Guthrie Consistory No. 1, fourteenth degree; Hydro Chapter, Order of the Eastern Star, and the local lodges of the Modern Woodmen of America and of the Brotherhood of American Yeomen.

In Garfield County, Oklahoma, in December, 1900, was solemnized the marriage of Mr. Lacy and Miss Katy Pope, a daughter of John Pope, who is living retired in Enid, Oklahoma. Mr. and Mrs. Lacy have one son: Perrin, born February 10, 1904, and a pupil in the Hydro public schools.

JUDGE JAMES B. RUTHERFORD. One of Oklahoma's ablest lawyers, and one whose practice had extended over old Indian Territory when the Federal courts for this jurisdiction were maintained at Fort Smith, was the late Judge James B. Rutherford, who died at his home in Sapulpa March 18, 1916. As a criminal lawyer he had few peers, and because of his varied abilities and his active participation in many of the notable cases tried in Eastern Oklahoma from pioneer times down to the present, his record is one of special significance in the history of Oklahoma.

He was born at Fayetteville, Washington County, Arkansas, November 3, 1859, a son of Bayless and Mary (Curtis) Rutherford, both of whom were natives of Tennessee. His father was born in 1815 and was about fifteen years old when his family moved in 1830 from Tennessee to Arkansas Territory, which was not admitted to statehood until about six years later. Bayless E. Rutherford became one of the prosperous agriculturists and stock growers of Arkansas, and was for many years prominent and influential as a citizen in Washington County, where he resided until his death in July, 1900. At that time he was eighty-five years of age and one of the venerable pioneer citizens of Northwestern Arkansas. His widow passed away September, 1913, aged seventy. Of their ten sons and five daughters all reached maturity and most of them are still living.

The fifth among the children in age, James B. Rutherford acquired his early education in the common schools of Arkansas, and made such good use of his advantages that for six years he was a popular teacher in the public schools. At the age of twenty-nine he married Miss Mary Etta King, who was born in the State of Mississippi, a daughter of James K. and Nancy King, who removed to Arkansas when she was a child. Mrs. Rutherford is still living.

A few months after his marriage Judge Rutherford took up the study of law and in 1890 was admitted to the bar of Arkansas. For ten years his practice was largely confined to the Federal courts of Fort Smith, though he also achieved a reputation in the cases which he presented before the various state courts. In September, 1902, with the high prestige he had acquired as a criminal lawyer, he came to Indian Territory and established his home in Claremore, now the county seat of Rogers County. There he continued to practice before the Federal Court of the Territory until Oklahoma was admitted to the Union. Soon after statehood he removed his family to Sapulpa, where he kept his home and office until his death. Judge Rutherford appeared in many of the most important criminal cases tried in old Indian Territory and the new Oklahoma, and his career as a lawyer is this section covered fully a quarter of a century. At the time of his death he was senior member of the well known law firm of Rutherford & Blackmore. It is significant that three of his former partners have served as United States district attorneys.

Judge Rutherford particularly excelled in defense. During his active career he defended more than one hundred murder cases in Arkansas, Indian Territory and Oklahoma, and capital punishment was not inflicted on a single one of his clients, and the extreme sentence imposed was not more than ten years in the penitentiary. He was always a loyal advocate of the republican party, but found his professional duties too exacting to consent to participation in a campaign for any official honors himself. He was a member of the Baptist Church, belonged to the Oklahoma State Bar Association and the Creek County Bar Association, and was affiliated with the Benevolent and Protective Order of Elks. He was widely known in professional, civic and business affairs and acquired some interests in the oil districts of Oklahoma.

Mrs. Rutherford became the mother of eight children: Mamie B., Lona, Ruby, James A., Alden B., Marcus, Dudley, and Mary Aileen. The daughter Mamie is the wife of William Graham of Sapulpa, and Ruby is the wife of Albert Hancock of the same city.

CHARLES H. COFER. Since he did his pioneering work on a homestead after the opening of the Cherokee Strip more than twenty years ago, Charles H. Cofer has been identified with numerous business enterprises in Western Oklahoma, and particularly in Dewey County, and is now best known as president of the Citizens State Bank of Vici.

Though he came to Oklahoma from Missouri, Mr. Cofer was born at Salem, Forsythe County, North Carolina, February 17, 1869, and the Cofer family were in the Carolinas from almost the earliest period of settlement. His father, James Hamilton Cofer, was born in North Carolina in 1830 and died near Conway, Missouri, in 1882. Most of his life was spent in Forsythe County, North Carolina, where he was reared and educated and married, and where he followed farming and stock raising. During the war between the states he served the Confederate cause in a factory for the making of army wagons. In 1876 he removed to Laclede County, Missouri, and lived on a farm near Conway the rest of his life. James H. Cofer married Mary Brown, who was born in Virginia in 1843 and died near Conway, Missouri, in 1881. Their large family of children are briefly noted as follows: William, a rancher in Texas; James Lewis, instructor in a high school at St. Louis; Charles H.; Sallie, wife of W. E. Ernest, a farmer and stock raiser near Fairview, Oklahoma; Vic, who first married Ned Day, a farmer, who died in Niangua, Missouri, and she married for her second husband Mr. Dougherty, a piano dealer, also deceased, her home being now in Houston, Texas; Mellie, who is a dressmaker living in the State of Washington; Nettie, wife of Robert Jamisson, a farmer and stock raiser at Conway, Missouri; Effie, who is married and lives on a farm near Buffalo, Missouri; Alice, wife of H. O. Miller, a merchant in the State of Washington.

Charles H. Cofer was about seven years of age when the family removed to Northeastern Missouri, and he was reared on a farm and gained his early education in the common schools of Laclede County. In 1890 he completed a course in the business college at Springfield, Missouri, and for about a year was employed in a store at Conway. With the opening of the Cherokee Strip in 1893 he removed to Richmond, Woodward County, secured a claim of 160 acres three-quarters of a mile south of Richmond, and spent several years in developing and proving up on that tract of land which he still owns. Since then his interests have taken a much broader scope and he has become one of the most successful business men of Dewey County. He also owns 120 acres 3½ miles south of Mutual, and has an attractive residence at Vici.

After making his home on his homestead until 1898 Mr. Cofer went to Hobart, was a merchant there a year and a half, and then engaged in the drug and general merchandise business at Cestos, in Dewey County, until 1910. In that year he organized the Citizens State Bank at Cestos, became its president, but in 1911 moved the bank to Vici, where it has since been the Citizens State Bank of Vici. He is the president, and the other officers are: David Jones, vice president; W. F. Cuberly, cashier; V. Cuberly, assistant cashier. The capital stock is $10,000, and since its removal to Vici the bank has occupied a home of its own at the corner of Broadway and Main Street.

Mr. Cofer has taken much interest in fraternal organizations. He is past chancellor commander of Cestos Lodge of the Knights of Pythias, and now has membership in the lodge at Vici; belongs to the Vici Lodge of the Independent Order of Odd Fellows; Cestos Camp of the Modern Woodmen of America, and is a member of the Oklahoma Bankers' Association. In politics he is a democrat, is a member of the Methodist Episcopal Church, and at the present time is serving on the Vici School Board.

At Woodward, Oklahoma, in 1905, he married Miss Sallie E. Hayes, daughter of W. H. Hayes, who owns half a section of land near Woodworth. Mr. and Mrs. Cofer are the parents of five children: Thelma, Lewis and Lola, all of them attending the public schools at Vici; and Charles and Imogene.

CHARLES A. WELCH is the present county attorney of Pushmataha County, and in point of continuous practice is one of the oldest lawyers in this section of Oklahoma, having begun practice in the Choctaw Nation about fifteen years ago. His home is at Antlers.

Before the dissolution of tribal government, the seat of the District Court of the First Judicial District of the Choctaw Nation was Red Oak. The facts of its history are fully as interesting as those connected with Alikchi, seat of the Third Judicial District of the nation, though the southern part of the nation boasts of more romance and enlivening legend than does the region surrounding Red Oak. Red Oak was in Gaines County and the seat of district government for several counties. Over the court there presided at one time Noel J. Holson and James Culberson was his clerk.

It was during the Holson administration that Charles A. Welch, who had been born and partly reared in the Chickasaw country, was appointed attorney for the First Judicial District by Principal Chief Gilbert W. Dukes. The appointment was made shortly after Mr. Welch had been admitted to the bar in 1901, before United States Judge H. H. Clayton of the Central District of Indian Territory. During the two years of his service in this office Mr. Welch prosecuted many cases involving misdemeanors and minor crimes and was instrumental in a number of Indians being punished at the whipping tree. At Red Oak the punishment was inflicted beside a tree rather than at the post, and the tree remains yet on the spot bearing evidences of the fulfilling of the law's demands.

The era of many murders in the Indian country had passed at that time and Mr. Welch was not called upon to prosecute any men charged with that crime. But the era in which many white men were accused of murder had not passed, and what Mr. Welch missed in that line as a prosecutor he found abundant later as a private attorney. Between the years 1907 and 1914 he successfully defended seventeen men in LeFlore and Pushmataha counties charged with the crime of murder. Then, in 1914, having been elected prosecuting attorney of Pushmataha County, he reverted to the tactics of his early experience in the law and took up the business of punishing men accused of breaking the law.

Born in old Indian Territory in 1871, Charles A. Welch is a son of W. A. and Alice (Walner) Welch. His father, a native of Alabama, settled in Indian Territory before the Civil war, and is said to have been one of the two first white men to make permanent settlement in the territory. During the war he served as a captain in the Confederate army, and then returned and settled at Rock Springs and engaged in merchandising. Still later his business was removed to Caddo, where he lived for a number of years. He was also engaged in business at Brazil and Talihina in the Choctaw Nation west of Fort Smith. W. A. Welch was a well educated man, a lawyer as well as a merchant, and practiced in the United States courts of old Indian Territory. Early in the '70s he took a conspicuous part in Chickasaw political affairs, holding several offices before intermarried citizens were forbidden to hold office. Alice (Walner) Welch was a daughter of Dr. William Walner, who was a surgeon in the Confederate army. Mrs. Welch was of part Indian blood. Doctor Walner was one of the pioneer settlers at a stage station on the Washita River in the Chickasaw Nation known as Cherokee Town, and there for a number of years lived his son John Walner, a prominent Chickasaw citizen of early days. Besides the county attorney of Pushmataha County, other children of W. A. and Alice Welch are: J. H. Welch, a merchant at Albion; Mrs. T. C. Branham, wife of a physician at Pauls Valley; and Mrs. Walter Davis, wife of a merchant at Sulphur.

The first school attended by Charles A. Welch was at Caddo. It was taught by a Mr. Chapin. One of his schoolmates was Thomas Hunter of Hugo. On leaving school Mr. Welch became a clerk in his father's store at Brazil and later at Talihina, and by business activity he supported himself and family for a number of years. In the meantime he took up the study of law, and in 1901 was admitted to the bar.

At Talihina in 1890 Mr. Welch married Miss Delia Morton. Her father was one of the earliest settlers in the vicinity of Talihina and for many years was a teacher in tribal schools. To their marriage have been born five children: S. E. Welch, a graduate of the class of 1910 in the Law Department of the University of Oklahoma and now his father's law partner; Fitzhugh Lee, Daniel M., Mabel and Ruth. Mr. Welch is an active member of the County and State Bar associations. In Masonry he is affiliated with the Blue Lodge and Chapter at Antlers, the Commandery at Hugo and the Temple of the Mystic Shrine at Muskogee. He is also a member of the Independent Order of Odd Fellows and the Knights of Pythias. His church is the Presbyterian.

REV. A. HUBERT VAN RECHEN. The honored pastor of St. Anthony's Church in the City of Okmulgee has achieved a large and benignant work during the period of his activities as a priest of the Catholic Church in Oklahoma, his initial services having been in the old Indian Territory, as a missionary, and he is one of the distinguished and influential members of the Catholic clergy in the vigorous young commonwealth in which he has found a fruitful field for his zealous and consecrated activities in his noble calling. In the community slight use of his family name is indulged, as he is familiarly and affectionately known as Father Hubert. He has identified himself most fully with the spirit of American institutions and customs but to him consistently remains deep and abiding love for his native land, which now lies prostrate and devastated by the ravages of the great European war that has brought death and desolation of unprecedented horror.

Father Hubert was born at Cruyshantem, a village in East Flanders, Belgium, about seven miles southwest of the ancient City of Ghent, and the date of his nativity was February 25, 1879. As may naturally be inferred, he is a man of high scholarship, but aside from this it is worthy of note that through early associations he gained a thorough knowledge of both the Flemish and French languages, besides which he has perfected himself in the English language. He is a son of Henry and Renilde Elizabeth (deWolf) Van Rechen, the former of whom passed to the life eternal on the 4th of August, 1911, and the latter of whom still retains her home at Cruyshantem. Of the family of four sons and three daughters the subject of this review is the only one who has established a home in America.

Henry Van Rechen was born in East Flanders on the 4th of July, 1845, a scion of one of the old and patrician families of that section of Belgium, and he received the best of educational advantages in his youth. He attended the College of St. Nicholas, in his native country, and thereafter continued his studies for some time in the City of Rome, Italy. He answered the call of Pope Pius IX and served gallantly during the conflict between church and state in Italy. Thereafter he was long an influential figure in connection with public affairs in East Flanders, and, as a remarkable accomplished musician, he served forty-two years as organist of the Catholic Church at Cruyshantem, he having been a most devout communicant of the Catholic Church, as is also his venerable widow. Henry Van Rechen was awarded the title of chevalier of the Order of St. Sylvester and received the medal of bene merenti, besides other honorable decorations, a number of his medals and other evidences of distinction being now in the possession of Father Hubert of this review.

In the parochial schools of his native village Father Hubert acquired his preliminary education, and he was signally favored in having been reared in a home of distinctive culture and ideal associations. Thereafter he continued his studies in turn in St. Mary's College, at Audenaerde, and in the Catholic university, in the City of Louvain, this having been the largest and most important of the many great Catholic educational institutions which so long gave Belgium precedence in the domain of higher education. Father Hubert completed his philosophical courses at St. Nicholas, and his theological at Louvain and there he learned also the English language, in the American College of Louvain, in which he was graduated, as was he also in the great university. On the 13th of July, 1902, he was ordained to the priesthood of the Catholic Church, his reception of the sacerdotal orders having been at the hands of Bishop Maes of Covington, Kentucky, in Louvain. In the following September he came to the United States, and soon after his arrival in New York City he was appointed Indian missionary at Antlers, Indian Territory, the present judicial center of Pushmataha County, Oklahoma. There he continued his earnest and effective services until the following year, and in the meanwhile a goodly number of the missionary Indians were received as communicants of the church. For a time Father Hubert was pastor at Wilburton, the present county seat of Latimer County, and later he was assigned to Poteau, where he effected the erection of a church building. On July 1, 1903, he returned to the pastoral charge at Antlers, where likewise his energy and consecrated zeal found tangible fruitage in the erection of a church edifice, the while he was able also to inspire the devotion which made possible also the erection of churches at Bentley, Atoka County; Boswell, Choctaw County; and Hugo, Choctaw County.

In June, 1910, Father Hubert became the first resident priest of the parish of St. Anthony's Church at Okmulgee, where he has since continued his earnest and devoted labors and where he has succeeded in infusing vitality into both the spiritual and temporal activities of the important parish. With the appreciative and able assistance of Judge Wade, Stanfield District judge, he has erected and properly equipped a rectory, which they donated to the congregation of St. Anthony's Church, the parish having specific incorporation under the laws of the State of Oklahoma since October 21, 1914. The local rectory is conceded to be one of the best in the state. The church edifice has been enlarged and otherwise improved under the administration of Father Hubert, and he is now (1916) bending his energies to accomplishing the erection of a building for the parish school. The parish is one of the most important and vigorous in Oklahoma and its loved pastor not only has the devoted esteem and co-operations of the members of his flock but also the high regard of the entire community, as he is essentially broad-minded, loyal and progressive in his civic attitude and does all in his power to further the best interests of the community in general. Incidentally it may be noted that he has been specially active in the support and advancement of the Oklahoma National Guard, in which he maintains a deep interest.

ROY M. FELTON. Caddo County, Oklahoma, figures as one of the most attractive, progressive and prosperous divisions of the state, justly claiming a high order of citizenship and a spirit of enterprise which is certain to conserve consecutive development and marked advancement in the material upbuilding of this section. The county has been and is signally favored in the class of men who have contributed to its development along financial and agricultural lines, and in the former connection the subject of this review demands recognition as he has been actively engaged in banking operations at Hydro during the greater part of his career thus far. Mr. Felton is cashier of the First National Bank of Hydro, and he has served the city in several positions of trust, namely, as city clerk and member of school board.

Almond D. Felton, grandfather of Roy M. Felton, was born in New York, in 1819, and he died at Ellenburg, New York, in 1899. He conducted an iron foundry in the Adirondack Mountains in his younger days and for sixteen years had served as justice of the peace in Clinton County, New York. He was descended from English stock, his ancestors having settled at Felton's Hill, Massachusetts, in 1627. His son, Marshall A. Felton, was born in Clinton County, New York, in 1849. He came West in 1874 and located in Kansas, where he helped build the canal, and for many years he did freighting from Arkansas City to Fort Sill, Oklahoma. He was at Hennessey, Oklahoma, only a few hours after the murder of Patrick Hennessey by the Indians. Later in life he became a farmer and he died at Ellenburg, New York, in 1898, while on a visit home. He served in the Civil war for one year as a member of the Ninety-second New York Volunteers. He was a member of the Methodist Episcopal Church, in which he was an active office holder, belonged to the Masonic fraternity, and also affiliated with the Grand Army of the Republic. He was a republican in his political allegiance. He married Belle Nichols, born in Illinois, in 1858, and now a resident of Hydro. This union was prolific of the following children: Roy M. is the subject of this sketch; Ralph A. is a resident of Roselle, New Jersey, where he is a member of the Presbyterian Board of Home Missions; O. C. is a rancher in the vicinity of Filer, Idaho; Mary C. is the wife of L. L. Williams, a merchant at Orange, California; and Esther, who was graduated in the Hydro High School in 1915, is now a teacher in Idaho. For her second husband Mrs. Felton married M. M. Klein, a furniture dealer and undertaker at Hydro. They have one child: Margaret, born in October, 1904, and now a pupil in the public schools of Hydro.

Roy M. Felton was born in Arkansas City, Kansas, January 11, 1880. He was graduated in the graded schools of Cowley County, Kansas, and attended the high school at Ponca City, Oklahoma, whither his parents had removed in 1893. He was graduated in Southwestern College, at Winfield, Kansas, in 1902, and then engaged in farming in the vicinity of Hydro for the ensuing two years. He entered the Hydro State Bank in 1904 as assistant cashier and in 1906 was raised to the position of cashier. The Hydro State Bank was established in January, 1902, and was nationalized as the First National Bank of Hydro in 1911. The first bank building was erected in 1904 and it was destroyed by fire in 1910. The present structure was built in the same year and is a fine brick building on Main Street. The officers of the bank are: George B. Pope, mentioned elsewhere in this work, president; W. H. Collins, vice president; Roy M. Felton, cashier; and H. Larson, assistant cashier. The bank has a capital stock of $25,000, a surplus of $3,500 and profits of $2,500.

Mr. Felton's work as bank cashier has been most satisfactory and he is well known as a booster of his home town. He is a republican in politics and has given efficient service as city clerk of Hydro for three terms, and in that capacity brought about many material improvements of great benefit to this community. He is a trustee in the Methodist Episcopal Church and his fraternal affiliations are as follows: Hydro Lodge No. 230, Ancient Free and Accepted Masons, of which he is junior warden; Hydro Chapter, Order of the Eastern Star; and he is an ex-member of the Knights of Pythias.

At Guthrie, Oklahoma, in 1904, was solemnized the marriage of Mr. Felton to Miss Grace Rose, a daughter of the Rev. W. H. Rose, pastor of the First Methodist Episcopal Church at Guthrie. Mr. and Mrs. Felton have two children: Marshall Rose, born August 6, 1905, and William Roy, born October 27, 1907, both of whom are attending school at Hydro.

ROBERT B. THOMAS. The present postmaster at Cache is one of the early settlers in that section of Comanche County, having come soon after the opening of this region to settlement, and has been variously identified with the growth and business activities of the locality.

Mr. Thomas comes from an old and prominent Southern family. The Thomases originally emigrated out of Wales to Virginia, where they lived when Virginia was still a colony, and afterwards became identified with pioneer settlement of Kentucky. Mr. Thomas had two great-grandfathers who were in the Revolutionary war, his great-grandfather Thomas having held the rank of colonel, and on his mother's side his great-grandfather, Colonel

Woolfork, attained a similar rank in the American forces, fighting for independence. The grandfather, William Thomas, a native of Virginia, went to Kentucky at an early date, and was killed while living in Ballard County, when his horse fell on him.

Robert B. Thomas was born in Bardwell, Kentucky, January 1, 1881. His father, Dr. George A. Thomas, was born in Ballard County, Kentucky, February 3, 1844, and early in his career became identified with the Southern armies in the war between the states. For one year he was a member of Polk's Scouts, and for the following three years was in the cavalry under General Forrest. After the war he graduated Doctor of Medicine from the Louisville Medical College, removed to Bardwell in 1871, and was prominent as a physician and also in politics and civic affairs in that locality until his death in 1907. Doctor Thomas married Miss Hannah J. Webb, who was born in Bardwell, Kentucky, January 2, 1856, and is now living at Cache, Oklahoma. Their children are: Herbert, who is in the insurance business at Tyronza, Arkansas; Wallace W., in the ice business at Cache, Oklahoma; Ada, wife of Louis Harrison, a farmer at Bardwell, Kentucky; Robert B.; Bettie, wife of S. B. Ray, a farmer at Cache, Oklahoma; Charles, a railway employe living at Muskogee, Oklahoma; and Luther, an electrician at Cushing, Oklahoma.

As a boy Robert B. Thomas grew up at Bardwell and attended the public schools, graduating from high school in 1900. At the age of twenty-one he came out to Southwestern Oklahoma, and found his permanent location at Cache, where for two years he was a clerk in the Indian trading store for E. M. Harris. In 1904 he became connected with the mercantile enterprise of V. E. Gregg, and also for Mr. Gregg's successor, A. J. Lawrence, and remained in the general store at Cache until June, 1908. The following twelve months were spent at Browning, Missouri, where he was again in the employ of Mr. V. E. Gregg. Returning to Cache in the fall of 1909, he engaged in the general mercantile business for himself until February 12, 1913. Next followed an experience as a traveling salesman representing the Star Clothing Company of Kentucky. This was terminated on September 5, 1914, at which date he received his appointment as postmaster of Cache under the civil service rules. He is now giving practically all his attention to the administration of the office.

Mr. Thomas has been active in local affairs in that part of Comanche County for a number of years. For four years he was township clerk at Cache, and in 1914 was defeated by only a small majority as candidate for the office of county assessor. He is a democrat, and is well known as a party leader in Comanche County, and for six years was democratic township committeeman. He is a fluent public speaker, and was one of the first men of Comanche County to support President Wilson on the stump. His church is the Christian.

Mr. Thomas is especially well known in Odd Fellowship and is now serving as president of the Southwest Odd Fellows Association, an organization for general benefit among the Odd Fellows lodges in Comanche, Cotton, Tillman and Jackson counties. His local affiliation is with Cache Lodge No. 269, Independent Order of Odd Fellows, and at three different times he has attended the grand lodge of the state and the first time was present as a delegate when only twenty-one years of age, being the youngest delegate in the grand lodge. He is a past grand and past grand representative, and a member of the Odd Fellows Encampment.

On June 21, 1914, at El Reno, Oklahoma, Mr. Thomas married Miss Mittie Fronaberger of Lawton, Oklahoma.

JOHN P. MILLER, M. D. Many of the older commonwealths of the Union have contributed to the personnel of the able and representative physicians and surgeons of Oklahoma, and though Doctor Miller claims the historic old State of North Carolina as the place of his nativity he was reared to manhood in Texas, where he received his early education and whence he came to Oklahoma Territory in September, 1892, when he settled at Cheyenne, the present vital metropolis and judicial center of Roger Mills County, where he has been established in the successful practice of his profession during the intervening period of nearly a quarter of a century, and where he holds secure prestige and popularity as one of the leading pioneer physicians and surgeons of this section of the state, even as he has made his influence definitely felt through his activities as a progressive and public-spirited citizen.

Dr. John Powell Miller was born in Madison County, North Carolina, on the 19th of July, 1851, and is a son of Samuel and Jane (Jack) Miller, the former of whom was born in Buncombe County, North Carolina, in 1822, and the latter of whom was born in Greene County, Tennessee, in 1823, both families having been founded in America in the colonial days. Samuel Miller removed with his family to Texas in December, 1862, and there he passed the remainder of his life as a farmer and stock grower. He survived his wife from 1889 to 1907, his death occurring on the 30th of April of the latter year. The mother was summoned to eternal rest on September 28, 1889, both having been consistent members of the Methodist Episcopal Church South, and the father having been a stanch democrat in politics. He was a scion of a sterling family that was founded in Pennsylvania in the colonial era of our nationary history, and the original American progenitors came from Scotland. In the following paragraph is given brief record concerning the children of Samuel and Jane (Jack) Miller.

William Elbert is a retired merchant and resides at Claude, Armstrong County, Texas; Robert T. maintains his home at Floydada, Floyd County, that state, and has large farm and stock interests in that section; Samuel Madison, who likewise was a substantial farmer in Texas, died at the age of fifty years, in Brown County, that state; James Anderson, twin of Samuel M., died in Johnston County, Texas, at the age of seventeen years; Doctor Miller of this sketch was the next in order of birth; Octavia Jane is the wife of James H. Keith, of Cleburne, Texas; Harriet Emily is the wife of Willis M. Armstrong, a prosperous farmer of Brown County, Texas; Rev. Jacob Glance, a clergyman of the Methodist Episcopal Church South, resides at Stamford, Texas; Margaret Cordelia is the wife of John H. Dortch, a retired farmer, and they reside at Dalworth, Texas; Mary Elizabeth, who died at Panhandle City, Texas, in the autumn of 1891, was the wife of Monroe Jack, who still resides in that state, a farmer by vocation; and Catherine Ann is the wife of William C. Dysart, a farmer of Collin County, Texas.

Doctor Miller was a lad of about ten years at the time of the family removal to Texas, where he was reared to manhood on the homestead farm, with the work and management of which he continued to be associated until he had attained to his legal majority. In the meanwhile he profited duly by the advantages of the local schools, and in September, 1872, he entered Mansfield College, in which excellent Texas institution he continued his studies three years. Thereafter he remained on the home farm until 1879, when he engaged in the drug business at Marystown, Johnson County, and incidentally devoted as much time as possible to the study of medicine. His business venture proved successful and in September, 1880, in consonance with his ambitious purpose, he was matriculated in the medical department of Vanderbilt University at Nashville, Tennessee, in which great institution he was graduated as a member of the class of 1883 and from which he received his well earned degree of Doctor of Medicine. He then returned to Johnson County, Texas, where he served his practical novitiate in his profession and where he continued in successful general practice until 1889. He then removed to Claude, Armstrong County, but within a year he established himself at Panhandle City, Carson County, where he remained until the autumn of 1892, when he came to Oklahoma Territory, his permanent home having been established at Cheyenne, county seat of Roger Mills County, in September of that year. He was the pioneer physician of the county, and five years elapsed ere another representative of his profession engaged in practice at Cheyenne. In the earlier years Doctor Miller encountered the most arduous labors and many trials in pursuing his humane mission over a wide area of thinly settled and wild country, but he placed no limitations upon his professional zeal and devotion, so that it is but natural that he is held in the highest popular esteem in the community which he has served faithfully and with marked ability for many years. He has kept in close touch with advances made in medical and surgical science and has given to the people of this section of the state the best that could be offered by a physician and surgeon of distinctive technical talent and of abiding appreciation of the dignity and responsibility of his exacting vocation. He has long controlled a large and representative general practice, and he maintains his well appointed office on Broadway, in the business center of the town. The doctor is the owner of his attractive residence property, likewise on Broadway, and in addition to other local realty he has two valuable farms in Roger Mills County, one comprising 320 and the other 160 acres. During nearly the entire period of his residence at Cheyenne, Doctor Miller has served as health officer of the county, and though he is a stanch democrat in politics he was first appointed to this position, in 1892, by Governor Sea, who was elected territorial governor on the republican ticket. He assisted in the organization of the Roger Mills County Medical Society, was one of the early presidents of the same and still continued one of its appreciative and valued members, besides which he is identified with the Oklahoma State Medical Society and the American Medical Association. Doctor and Mrs. Miller are zealous members of the Methodist Episcopal Church South, in which he has served in official positions for forty years, his service having been in the capacities of steward, trustee, Sunday-school superintendent, etc. He is past master of Cheyenne Lodge, Ancient Free and Accepted Masons; past high priest of Cheyenne Chapter, Royal Arch Masons; and affiliated also with Cheyenne Council, Royal and Select Masters, as well as with the commandery of Knight Templars at Elk City, Beckham County. He holds membership in the Cheyenne Camp of the Woodmen of the World and was formerly in active affiliation with the Independent Order of Odd Fellows.

At Jefferson, Texas, in 1881, was solemnized the marriage of Doctor Miller to Miss Ruth Bockman, daughter of the late Michael Bockman, a substantial farmer of that state. Doctor and Mrs. Miller have two children— Thomas Madden, who holds a responsible executive position with the Collins Investment Company, at Oklahoma City; and Volina, who is the wife of Taylor Lee Miller, a representative dry goods merchant of Cheyenne.

J. R. PEARSON. In the development and improvement of the old Osage country, J. R. Pearson has for thirty-five years supplied the important elements of individual enthusiasm and enterprise. He has spent most of his active career in this part of Oklahoma, and has had unusual opportunities for judging the country and for participating in its affairs, and there is probably no citizen of Pawhuska who is considered more vitally and substantially related with local development than Mr. Pearson.

Born in Andrew County, Missouri, February 29, 1852, he has had a life of varied experience beginning with boyhood. His parents were William Madison and Delilah (Hunter) Pearson. His father was born in Kentucky, but was reared in Missouri, the grandparents having settled as pioneers in the northwestern quarter of that state. Grandfather Nathaniel Pearson died in Northern Kansas at the age of ninety and William M. Pearson passed away May 30, 1912, at the age of eighty-nine, in Maryville, Missouri, and both had spent all their active careers as blacksmiths. Mr. Pearson's mother, who was born in Missouri of a pioneer family, died when her son was four years of age. The latter is now the only one living out of a family of four girls and two boys, and there were also two sons by his father's second marriage.

When he was thirteen years of age J. R. Pearson left home on account of incompatibility with his step-mother, and thenceforth largely made his own way in the world. He lived a few years with his older sisters and then rambled from place to place, paying his way by day or monthly labor, largely engaged in railroad work in different sections of Missouri.

It was in 1878, while still in search of a permanent home, that J. R. Pearson arrived in the Osage country. Here, on July 4, 1878, he married Miss Rosa Denoya, who was born in Washington Territory August 26, 1864. She died at her home in Pawhuska, January 26, 1913, at the age of forty-nine. She had come to Indian Territory with her parents in 1873, and received her education in the government schools. Her parents were Francis and Martha (Tessett) Denoya, her father a full-blooded Frenchman and her mother of part French and part Osage stock. Her mother died at Pawhuska May 23, 1913, in her eighty-fifth year, and it is said that she was the mother, grandmother, great-grandmother, and great-great-grandmother to more children in the Osage tribe than any other living woman. She was twice married, the father of Mrs. Pearson having died about twenty-seven years ago.

In order to support his wife, Mr. Pearson for several years after his marriage worked at wages of fifty cents a day, but soon engaged in ranching and stock raising, and has lived continuously in what is now Osage County with the exception of a few years spent at Cedarvale, Kansas, where he was giving his children the advantages of the local schools. He and each of his children now have allotments of land amounting to 657 acres each, and he is one of the large property holders over Osage County. Besides his land he is a stockholder in the Pawhuska Oil and Gas Company, the largest corporation operating in that industry in Osage County; is also a stockholder in the oil and gas company of which J. W. Stroud is president; is a stockholder in the Citizens National Bank of Pawhuska. For a number of years he has also carried on an individual business as a money lender.

In 1908 Mr. Pearson erected what is considered one of the most attractive homes in Pawhuska, known as Pearson Heights, adjoining the city limits at the southwest corner. The house is itself a commodious and attractive one, and stands on a site that commands an extensive and beautiful view not only of the city, but of a large scope of surrounding country. The house is

HISTORY OF OKLAHOMA

surrounded by 120 acres of well improved land, and that is the center of Mr. Pearson's continued interests in the stock business. He still keeps a large number of horses, and has some especially fine strains represented in this class of stock.

In politics he is a republican. In Masonry he has been through both the York and Scottish Rite branches as far as he could go, and was one of the first men in the Osage country to take the thirty-two degrees of the Scottish Rite Consistory. He is a member of the Consistory at Guthrie and the Temple of the Mystic Shrine at Oklahoma City, and belongs to the various other branches represented at Pawhuska. To Mr. and Mrs. Pearson were born a large family of eleven children: Claude, who died at the age of four years; Cartona, who died at seven years; October, who lives at Pearson Spur in Osage County, and is married and has five children; Della, who died at the age of six years; Madeline, wife of Robert E. Wynn, living in Osage County, and the mother of four children; Cordelia, wife of Frank R. Kent of St. Joseph, Missouri, and the mother of two children; Lillian, wife of J. P. Compehaver of Independence, Kansas, and the mother of one child; Bertha, wife of Grover Badey of Osage County, and the mother of two children; Catherine V., Joseph W. and Rosa V., all living at home with their father.

LUCIEN ALBERT PELLEY. Since 1908 Mr. Pelley has been a resident of Altus, has been an active and successful member of the Jackson County bar for the past four years and even for a longer time has been a very influential figure in the political life of Jackson County.

Born in Casey County, Kentucky, April 25, 1881, he was reared from the age of seven principally on his father's farm in Bates County, Missouri, and while there had the benefit of country schools. He also finished the junior year in the State Normal School at Warrensburg, and subsequently took a business course at Sedalia, Missouri. He has had to pick and choose his own opportunities for the most part, and with an ambition to become a lawyer, went through considerable practice and experience before reaching that goal. Mr. Pelley came to Altus, Oklahoma, in 1908, and during 1909 was deputy county clerk of Jackson County. He finally accumulated a sufficient sum to put him through law school, and in 1911 was graduated LL. B. from the law department of Cumberland University at Lebanon, Tennessee. Returning to Oklahoma, he was admitted to the bar in the same year, and is now well established in his profession, looking after a large and growing civil and criminal practice, and his offices are in the courthouse at Altus.

He represents an old southern family, and his forefathers were prominent farmers and stock breeders in Kentucky. It was his great-great-grandfather who emigrated from England and established this branch of the Pelley family in Virginia, and out of that state his great-grandfather moved into Casey County, Kentucky, where he was numbered among the pioneer settlers. Mr. Pelley's grandfather was widely known over his section of Kentucky as Doc Pelley, was born and reared and spent all his life in Casey County, where he was well known as a stock raiser, and for fifty years owned and operated the largest mill in that section of the state. His death occurred before the Altus attorney was born. The latter's father is Z. T. Pelley, who was born in Casey County, Kentucky, in 1853 and is now in business in Kansas City, Missouri. He moved from Casey County to Bates County, Missouri, in 1888, and since 1912 has lived in Kansas City. His career has been largely that of a farmer and stock raiser, but after selling his place in Bates County, Missouri, he spent several years as a traveling salesman. He is an active member of the Christian Church, and for many years has held some official position in his home church. Z. T. Pelley married Miss Dolly Ermine Mayes, who was born in Casey County, Kentucky, in 1863. Lucien A. is the oldest of their five children. Wilma, the next in age, is the wife of James M. Dillard, who is an attorney and formerly served as county attorney of Jackson County and is now living at Carlsbad, New Mexico. Zula T. is a deputy county clerk of Jackson County, Oklahoma. Carl Estel is a rancher at Craig, Colorado, and the next younger brother, Cecil Alton, is associated with him in that industry.

Lucien A. Pelley is a democrat in politics, is a deacon in the Christian Church at Altus, is a member of Altus Lodge No. 62, Ancient Free and Accepted Masons, and is past grand of Altus Lodge No. 134, Independent Order of Odd Fellows, and is also past chief patriarch of the local encampment of Odd Fellows. He also belongs to Altus Lodge No. 1226 of the Benevolent and Protective Order of Elks. Professionally he is a member of the County and State Bar Association, and takes much interest in the work of the local Commercial Club, and is a member of the large Cumberland Alumni Association found in the State of Oklahoma. As a democrat he is a member of the Young Men's Democratic Club, has regularly attended the County and State Democratic conventions of recent years, and is a candidate for the office of county attorney of Jackson County.

GEORGE B. POPE. A progressive and enterprising citizen of Hydro, Oklahoma, is George B. Pope, who came to this city in 1901 and who has here been engaged in the banking business since 1908. He was elected president of the Hydro State Bank in 1909, and is now president of the First National Bank. He has always manifested a deep and sincere interest in public affairs and is serving his second term as city councilman. The Pope family came originally from Scotland and members of the name were pioneers in Indiana, Missouri and Kansas.

George B. Pope was born at Emporia, Kansas, January 7, 1873, and he is a son of John Pope, whose birth occurred in the vicinity of Indianapolis, Indiana, in 1833. John Pope removed from the Hoosier state to Missouri as a young man and at the outbreak of the Civil war enlisted for service in the Union army as a private in the Fifth Missouri Cavalry. He served for a period of four years, during which time he participated in many important battles marking the progress of the war, at one time he was taken prisoner and was later exchanged. He was a pioneer settler in Emporia, Kansas, after the war, and although he was a contractor and builder by trade he devoted his attention to farming for many years. He helped build the first brick building ever erected at Atchison, Kansas, and he was at Wichita, Kansas, when that city was nothing but an Indian trading post. In 1880 he removed with his family to Caldwell, Kansas, and that was before the railroad was built. He came to Oklahoma in 1893, and took up a homestead in Garfield County. In recent years he has lived retired at Enid, Oklahoma, where he and his devoted wife are held in high esteem by their fellow citizens. At Maryville, Missouri, Mr. Pope was united in marriage to Miss Susan E. Bishop, who was born in Tennessee, in 1843. It is interesting to note that the Bishop family was driven out of Tennessee on account of sympathy with the Union cause during the Civil war. Mr. Bishop hired a yoke of oxen and removed the household goods to Indiana, he and the children being compelled to walk most of the way. Five children were born to Mr. and Mrs. Pope, as follows: Capitola is the wife of J. P. Clapp, a merchant at Hillsdale, Oklahoma; Robert R. is a merchant at Hillsdale; George B. is the subject of this sketch; William is a rural mail carrier at Hillsdale; and Katy is the wife of H. C. Lacy, cashier of the Bank of Hydro.

Under the invigorating discipline of farm life George B. Pope grew to maturity and he attended public school and high school at Caldwell, Kansas. He came to Oklahoma with his parents in 1893 and proved up a claim on the Cherokee Strip. Subsequently he removed to Carrier, this state, and there entered into the general mercantile business, also having charge of the postoffice before the railroad was built. In 1901 he came to Hydro and here was most successfully engaged in the implement business until 1908, when he turned his attention to banking. For one year he served as vice president of the Hydro State Bank, now the First National Bank, and at that time it was capitalized at only $5,000. He was made president of that institution in 1909 and is still serving with the utmost efficiency in that capacity. He is possessed of remarkable business acumen and much of the bank's success is traced to his good judgment. He is a republican in politics and is now serving his second term on the city council. While a resident of Garfield County he was a member of the school board. In a fraternal way Mr. Pope is affiliated with Hydro Lodge No. 230, Ancient Free and Accepted Masons, of which he is past master; Weatherford Chapter, Royal Arch Masons; Weatherford Commandery, Knights Templar; Valley of Guthrie Consistory No. 1, thirty-second degree; India Temple, Ancient Arabic Order Nobles of the Mystic Shrine, at Oklahoma City; Hydro Chapter, Order of the Eastern Star; and Hydro Lodge, Modern Woodmen of America.

Mr. Pope has been twice married. In 1898 he married Miss Zue Carrier, a daughter of S. E. Carrier, a farmer prior to his demise. She died at Eureka Springs, Arkansas, in 1900. For his second wife Mr. Pope married, at Leavenworth, Kansas, Miss Pearl Orr, a daughter of William Orr, now deceased. Mr. and Mrs. Pope have two children: Eugene, born October 24, 1908; and Olive, born December 20, 1910. In religious faith the Popes are devout members of the Methodist Episcopal Church, and they are popular factors in the social life of Hydro.

STERLING PRICE SMITH. As an educator Mr. Smith has unusual qualifications and experience. He is a man of liberal education, was admitted a number of years ago to the Texas bar, though he has practiced very little, is a practical surveyor, and his varied associations with men and affairs are a splendid foundation for his work as superintendent of the city schools of Grandfield.

His father was a Confederate soldier and named his son, who was born near Burleson, Franklin County, Alabama, August 14, 1862, in honor of the great Confederate leader under whom the father was at that time serving. The Smith family came from England, and grandfather Frank Smith was a soldier under Francis Marion in the Revolutionary war. F. M. Smith, father of the Grandfield school superintendent, was born in Georgia in 1828 and died at Garner, Texas, in 1896. The year following his birth, in 1829, his parents removed to Calhoun County, Alabama, and he grew up there and married. He was a farmer by occupation, lived for a number of years in Franklin County, and finally established his home at Garner, Texas. In 1861 he entered the Confederate army with an Alabama regiment, was with Price in his campaign in Mississippi, was with Johnston at Corinth, and after the reorganization of the Confederate army was under the command of Lee in Virginia, and participated in all the battles and campaigns leading up to Appomattox. In politics he was a loyal democrat. The maiden name of his wife was Jane Schencks, who was born in Alabama and now lives in Garner, Texas. To their marriage were born twelve children: Floyd, who died at the age of eight years in Calhoun County, Alabama; Laura, wife of John Williams, a farmer in Franklin County, Alabama; Flora, whose husband is J. M. Sullivan, a farmer at Garner, Texas; Maggie, who married P. M. Inzer, a druggist at Savoy, Texas; W. L., who is a farmer near Mineral Wells, Texas; Sterling P.; Kate, who died after her marriage to Mr. Davis, a farmer now living in Franklin County, Alabama; Fannie, wife of Thomas Hefrin, who is in the employ of the Government at El Paso, Texas; Frank, who died at the age of three years; and Mary and Elizabeth, both of whom died early in childhood; and Dena, wife of Gus Bumgarner, a farmer at Garner.

Sterling Price Smith attended the public schools of Franklin County, Alabama, also the Burleson Academy, and for three terms was in the high school at Honey Grove, Texas. In 1891 he graduated Bachelor of Science from the Central College at Sulphur Springs, Texas, subsequently took two years work in the Texas Christian University at Waco, this university being now at Fort Worth, and was graduated A. M. in 1897. In the meantime he had followed teaching for a number of terms, read law, and in 1899 was admitted to the Texas bar. For four years Mr. Smith was county surveyor of Fannin County, Texas. In 1907 he removed to Mill Creek, Oklahoma, was a teacher there one year, was superintendent of schools at Lindsay one year, principal of ward schools in Paul's Valley for two years and then for one year was principal of schools at Stratford, Oklahoma. Mr. Smith came to Grandfield to take the superintendency of the city schools in 1913. Though Grandfield is a comparatively new town, it has an excellent public school system, and Mr. Smith is at the head of a corps of six teachers and the total enrollment in the schools numbers 310. Mr. Smith has never found any work quite so attractive as school work, and is not only ambitious for the best attainments as a school executive but also for continued advancement in individual scholarship. He was engaged as a teacher for one summer term in the Ada Normal School at Ada, Oklahoma, and has been taking special studies through that institution and received a diploma in 1913. He also spent one summer term in the University of Chicago and is now working on his tenth college credit. He belongs to several of the school associations, is a member of the Methodist Episcopal Church South and was formerly identified with the Independent Order of Odd Fellows and the Knights of Pythias.

On August 25, 1897, Mr. Smith was married at Savoy, Texas, to Miss Frankie Chenoweth, whose father, Thomas Chenoweth, is now a retired property owner at Sabinal, Texas. To their marriage have been born four children: Sterling D., a junior in the high school at Grandfield; Leta Mae, a sophomore in the high school; Elizabeth, in the sixth grade, and Jennie Lou, who is in the fourth grade of the public schools.

A. C. BRADSHAW. It is nearly fifteen years since A. C. Bradshaw came into the western part of Oklahoma Territory and was first known to the people of what is now Roger Mills County as a teacher. He has since extended his interests to various other affairs, has performed much official service and is now proprietor and editor of the Leedey Times at Leedey.

The Bradshaw family to which he belongs came from England to Virginia during colonial times. A. C. Bradshaw himself was born in Adair County, Missouri, December 3, 1874. His father, Joseph R. Bradshaw, was born in Kentucky in 1845 and died in Sullivan County, Missouri, in 1899. From Kentucky he removed to Adair County, Missouri, and though only a boy at the time in 1861 enlisted in the Second Missouri Cavalry, and went through the entire conflict, coming out with a gallant record of military duty well performed. Returning to Adair County, he took up the pursuits of farming and stock raising, and from there in 1890 moved to Sullivan County. As a man who had fought on the Union side during the war he naturally affiliated with the republican party. He was a member of the Missionary Baptist Church. Joseph R. Bradshaw married Mary S. Thornton, who was born in Georgia in 1848, and is still living, her home being with A. C. Bradshaw at Leedey. Their children were: William T., a carpenter and contractor at Wichita Falls, Texas; John, a farmer in Adair County, Missouri; A. C.; Cassie, wife of John I. Starkey, a farmer and stock raiser in Kingman County, Kansas; and Valley E., wife of Albert A. Butler, a clerk in the B. & O. Cash Store at Leedey.

The primary fact in the career of A. C. Bradshaw has been a propelling self effort toward larger accomplishment. As a boy he had to be content with such education as the public schools of Adair County could supply him, but later he paid for a course in the State Normal School at Kirksville for one year in 1896. He then took up teaching in Adair County, and in 1901 arrived in what was then Oklahoma Territory, and was employed for a year as teacher in the public schools at Angora in what later became Roger Mills County. He also homesteaded a claim of 160 acres, proved up on his land, and that is still included among his business assets. The farm is nine miles southwest of Leedey. In the meantime, as he became better acquainted with the people and the people became better acquainted with his capabilities, he was the recipient of various honors and responsibilities of a public nature. In 1905 he was appointed United States commissioner, and held that office until Oklahoma became a state in 1907. In 1906 he was appointed postmaster of Texmo, and held that office until the postoffice was discontinued on August 15, 1915.

His work in the newspaper field began in 1907, when he leased the Texmo Times. He later bought the plant and in June, 1911, removed the paper to Leedy, where it is now known as the Leedey Times, with Mr. Bradshaw as editor and proprietor. It is a republican paper, and has a large circulation throughout Dewey, Custer, Roger Mills, Ellis and other counties. Mr. Bradshaw owns the plant and building in which the paper is published on Broadway. He also owns one of the finest residences of the town, situated on Phillips Street.

In politics Mr. Bradshaw is himself aligned with the republican interests; is a member of the Baptist Church; is affiliated with Leedey Lodge No. 443, Ancient Free and Accepted Masons; is past noble grand in Leedey Lodge No. 369, Independent Order of Odd Fellows; is past consul of Camp No. 15436 of the Modern Woodmen of America at Leedey. As a newspaper man belongs to the Oklahoma State Press Association.

In 1899, in Sullivan County, Missouri, he married Miss Effie Belle Wilkin, daughter of Jacob Wilkin, who is now a resident of Oklahoma, a farmer eight miles southwest of Leedey. Mrs. Bradshaw died April 22, 1915, leaving three children: Raymond Dale, who died at the age of seven years in 1907; Eugene Lyle, a student in the Leedey public schools; and an infant son, Harvey Dean.

S. S. LAWRENCE is the Choctaw tribal attorney at Antlers, an office in which he has given most creditable service during the past two years. He is a bright young lawyer, and most of his practice has been in the southeastern section of Oklahoma.

The office of probate attorney in former Indian nations of Oklahoma has proved its particular value in the fact that the Indians, thousands of whom for years have been victimized by unscrupulous white men, have been taught to counsel with the man the United States Government has placed among them for that purpose. The duties of a probate attorney, an office that was created only a few years ago, were not specifically stated in any statute or department regulations, and when Secretary Franklin K. Lane of the Interior Department distributed its commissions to young lawyers of Oklahoma they were supposed to learn for themselves what was necessary in becoming counsel to the wards of the government over whom they were placed. The office has supplied the needs of that quality in the Indians which once caused them to be denominated children of the forest, the quality of dependence and succor. This is the beginning of the successful administration the probate attorneys should have, for it has acquainted them with every form and character of need the Indian experiences.

The dependence of Choctaw Indians in Pushmataha County, for instance, is exemplified in the character of advice sought of Attorney Lawrence. He recalls that one Indian who once belonged to the Clan of Snakes, wanted to borrow $5 at a bank. The loan was made, on the Indian's unsecured note, and gladly, for he is honest. A few days later this Indian came back to Mr. Lawrence, rather than going to the bank for the information, and inquired when the note would mature. Many Indians ask the attorney where to buy provisions and clothes, and while he probably could not conscientiously make any recommendations of that nature, he is in position to guard the Indian against trading with a merchant whom he knows would make exorbitant charges for his goods. Indians ask the attorney to rent or lease their lands, collect their debts, write their checks, pass upon their legal instruments, etc. It is not obligatory upon an Indian that he consult the attorney regarding mortgages, transfers, notes, etc., yet he is learning that it is best to do so. While the labors of the attorney are burdensome and he has to hear all manner of trivial complaints, requests and tales, he nevertheless is learning the secret of what economists for many years have called the Indian problem. The attainment of this knowledge has convinced Mr. Lawrence that the position of probate attorney should not be a political one.

An example of the reformatory character of the attorney's work is found in the case of Abel Noah, all his life until recently a member of the Clan of Snakes who recognize no government, accept no patents, sell or lease no lands, and receive no pay from the Government. Noah recently was convinced that his attitude toward the Government was wrong, and he consented to sell some of his land, a valuable fertile tract in Bryan County. The sale was executed after some technical reverses had been remedied, and Noah came into possession of $1,600 of good American money. He spent it with spirit and relish, and since that time has been accepting all that other Indians get from the Government. He has seen the light after many years of Snake darkness.

There are about 5,000 Indians in the district assigned Mr. Lawrence, which comprises Pushmataha and Choctaw counties. A part of each week he spends in Hugo. In Antlers he offices with Principal Chief Victor M. Locke, Jr., of the Choctaw Nation, and it is a little matter of interest that the principal chief, whose whole ambition is to be of service to his people, frequently acts as interpreter for the probate attorney. It was Chief Locke who first introduced Mr. Lawrence in the Indian service. On March 18, 1914, Mr. Lawrence was selected and commissioned by Chief Locke as probate attorney for a district of the Choctaw Nation. On July first following he received his commission from the Secretary of the Interior.

Of an old Southern family, S. S. Lawrence was born in Surry County, North Carolina, June 25, 1884, a son of P. W. and C. O. (Gordon) Lawrence. His father, who now at the age of eighty-two lives at Pilot Mountain, North Carolina, is a veteran of the war between the states, and has spent most of his active life as an agriculturist. He lives at the place where he settled more than half a century ago, loved and tenderly revered by the entire community. Other children besides the Antlers attorney are: J. R. Lawrence, a traveling salesman in New York; and Miss Victoria Lawrence, who lives with her parents in North Carolina.

After attending the public schools of his home county, Mr. Lawrence completed a course in law in the University of North Carolina, receiving his LL. B. degree in 1908. On the first of December of that year he began practice at Mount Airy, North Carolina. Then with two or three years of practical experience to his credit, he came to Oklahoma and on August 1, 1911, located in Antlers, where he was making promising progress in the acquirement of a profitable private practice until appointed to his present position as probate attorney.

On August 28, 1912, at Mount Airy, North Carolina, he married Miss Roberta Vance Price, a great-niece of Zeb Vance, who many years ago was a United States senator from North Carolina. Mr. Lawrence is a member of the Presbyterian Church. Fraternally he is a Mason and belongs to the Pushmataha Bar Association. Mrs. Lawrence is a member of the Methodist Episcopal Church, South.

JAMES C. TYE. In several different communities where he has lived, both in Kentucky and Oklahoma, James C. Tye has helped to make history. In fact he has been an energetic factor in affairs for more than half a century. Prior to that he was a gallant soldier in the Civil war and made a record which redounds to his credit and to that of his descendants. Mr. Tye at present is one of the officers in The First National Bank of Bristow. He helped to found that bank and also to found the town. That he is a successful business man goes without saying and there is plenty of evidence to support the statement that he has been as honorable and straightforward in all his relations as he has been prosperous.

Of an old Kentucky family, he was born at Lot, May 25, 1844, a son of Hiram and Rachel (Siles) Tye. His parents were also born in Kentucky, his father in 1814 and his mother in 1817. All their lives were spent on a farm near Lot in Whitley County, where the father died in 1855. The mother survived and was past eighty when called away by death. Hiram Tye was a farmer and stock raiser and bought and shipped a great many hogs in the years before the war. In the family were four daughters and six sons, and one daughter and four sons are now living. Besides James Tye his older brothers John and Henry were also soldiers in the Civil war. John served for three years and Henry for eighteen months. Both James and John enlisted in 1861, John in the Eighth Kentucky Infantry and James in the Seventh Infantry. The brother Henry went out with the 49th Kentucky Regiment.

In the meantime James C. Tye had grown up in his district of Kentucky, had received the rugged discipline of the farm, had attended the common schools after he learned his letters—probably two months, and that when about sixteen years old, and was in the full bloom of early manhood. When seventeen years of age he responded to the call for volunteers to put down the southern rebellion, and on August 20, 1861, was enrolled in Company G of the Seventh Kentucky Infantry. He served until October, 1864, a little more than three years. He was in many of the greatest campaigns which cleared the Mississippi Valley from the Confederate forces. He was in the great campaign around Vicksburg, under Grant and Sherman. For much of the time he had the rank of sergeant, and during the Vicksburg campaign he was detailed as a member of the Pioneer Corps and did part of the heavy work involved in advancing the army over the difficult ground around the mighty fortress over the Mississippi.

After the war Mr. Tye returned to his native village of Lot, and took up farming. He also conducted a Kentucky distillery for about twenty years.

With a good deal of material prosperity to his credit, Mr. Tye came out to Oklahoma in the spring of 1890, not long after the original opening of lands. His first location was seven miles west of Edmond. He engaged in farming there, but soon moved to Chandler, and three years later came into the Creek Nation in 1894. Since then for more than twenty years his activities have identified him with what is now Creek County. He first leased about 700 acres of farm and ranch land and cultivated it to crops and went into the stock business on an extensive scale. When the Town of Bristow was started he came into the village bringing two carloads of lumber, and set up as the first lumber merchant. He soon sold the two carloads of lumber which he brought, and it nearly went into the construction of the pioneer buildings of the town.

Along with other parties he engaged in banking when the first banking facilities were given to Bristow. He was associated with the old Farmers & Merchants Bank, and later was one of the organizers of the First National Bank, in which he has since been vice president. The other officers are J. W. Teter, president, and N. T. Gilbert, cashier. A recent statement shows that the total resources of the First National Bank of Bristow are more than $240,000, a splendid showing for a bank in a town of that size. The capital stock is $25,000, with over $7,000 of surplus and profits. The deposits aggregated about $180,000. Besides his position as a banker Mr. Tye also has some valuable farming interests in Oklahoma. He is also associated with Mr. B. B. Jones in the ownership and control of some oil interests in the Bristow field.

A lifelong democrat, Mr. Tye was quite interested in politics while a resident of Kentucky, but has done little in that direction in Oklahoma. He held some minor offices, though he was never a willing candidate for such honors. He is a member of the Christian Church and affiliates with the Grand Army of the Republic.

On March 23, 1865, he was united in marriage with Elizabeth Brummet. Mrs. Tye was born in Whitley County, Kentucky, not far from the birthplace of her husband, on March 17, 1845, a daughter of George and Jane (Lambdin) Brummet, who spent all their lives along the Cumberland River and were substantial farming people. Five children were born to Mr. and Mrs. Tye: S. Jane, who died at the age of eighteen months; Hiram, who is an attorney practicing law at Williamsburg, Kentucky; John, who died in 1910, and whose widow and two children live at Bristow; George, who died in infancy; and Ortha, wife of J. E. Lurton of

Bristow. Perhaps at the conclusion of this sketch Mrs. Tye should be allowed a little bit of testimony.. She says that she has lived with Mr. Tye for fully half a century and that he measures up to all the standards and qualifications of a truly good man.

HARRY G. JONES. In his varied career as farmer, postmaster and newspaper man Harry G. Jones has met with many interesting experiences and he has manifested a peculiar aptitude for different lines of endeavor. He has been a loyal and public-spirited resident of Hydro since 1901 and since 1906 has been sole proprietor and editor of the Hydro Review, a republican paper with an extensive circulation throughout this section of the state.

Harry G. Jones was born in Smith County, Kansas, October 9, 1879. He is a son of Ora and Melvina (Rhodes) Jones, the former of whom was born in Ohio, in 1835, and the latter in Iowa, in 1840. As a young man Ora Jones removed from the Buckeye state to Iowa, was married there and then went to California, where he enlisted in the Civil war as a Union soldier. His army experience consisted mostly in subduing the Indians, whose uprisings were a sore trial to the Federal forces during the period of civil strife. Mr. Jones retained a deep and abiding interest in his comrades at arms and indicated the same by membership in the Grand Army of the Republic. After the close of the war he located in Smith County, Kansas, arriving there several years before the noted grasshopper year, and he was engaged in farming operations and in stock raising until he retired, in 1903, to Smith Center, where his death occurred in 1908. He was a republican and took an active interest in party affairs. He served on the town board of commissioners for a number of years at Smith Center and was also active on the school board. His cherished and devoted wife, whose maiden name was Melvina Rhodes, survives him and lives at Smith Center, Kansas. They became the parents of the following children: Jennie, married to A. N. Nye, a retired farmer, living at Franklin, Nebraska; Prue married F. H. Houston, a farmer near Wharton, Texas; Clarence E. is station agent for the Missouri Pacific at Anthony, Kansas; Frank and Orin C. are both farmers in Smith County, Kansas; Dolly is the wife of Warner Sanford, a merchant at Blessing, Texas; Harry G. is the subject of this sketch; Carl is a baker at Belleville, Kansas; and May is the wife of Milo Stanley, a farmer in Smith County, Kansas.

To the public schools of his native place Harry G. Jones is indebted for his preliminary educational training. In 1896 he became rural mail carrier at Smith Center and two years later he turned his attention to farming. In 1901 he drew a homestead four miles northeast of Hydro, Oklahoma, and lived on it until 1907. In 1902 he became assistant postmaster at Hydro and for eight months was acting postmaster. He disposed of his farm in 1909 but repurchased it in 1911, and has since conducted it as a stock farm, later buying another eighty-acre tract adjoining the farm. He owns 250 head of hogs in addition to numerous head of cattle and horses. July 1, 1904, he became interested in the Hydro Review, becoming associated with Dr. W. M. Wellman, who founded the paper in October, 1901. Mr. Jones obtained control of this publication in 1905 and the following year bought up the interests belonging to Mrs. Wellman. The paper is republican in its politics and it circulates in Caddo, Blaine and Custer Counties. The offices and plant are located on Main Street and this paper has the distinction of being the only one in the county whose plant has never been mortgaged. In addition to his other numerous interests in this section Mr. Jones owns a number of city lots. He is a republican in politics and for four years he served as a member of the county election board. He is a member of the Methodist Episcopal Church and is affiliated with Hydro Lodge No. 230, Ancient Free and Accepted Masons.

At Hydro, in 1907, Mr. Jones was united in marriage to Miss Irene Smith, a daughter of Mrs. Alberta Smith, of Eaply, Oklahoma. Prior to her marriage Mrs. Jones was a popular and successful teacher in the public schools of Hydro. Mr. and Mrs. Jones have no children.

ROSCOE C. THOMAS. While he first became identified with the Panhandle district of Oklahoma as a homesteader and farmer, Mr. Thomas has for a number of years been best known as a newspaper publisher and is now editor and owner of the Cimarron News at Boise City. He is probably the leading and most influential democrat of this section of the state, and is well known to the leaders of the party all over Oklahoma.

A Tennesseean by birth, Roscoe C. Thomas was born February 22, 1883, on a farm in Wilson County. The house in which he was born was constructed of log timbers, and in the same house his father, Eli, was born October 30, 1839, a son of J. B. and Mary (Wilson) Thomas, who were natives of Virginia and of Welsh origin. Eli Thomas has been a farmer all his life, but is now living retired at Lebanon, Tennessee. During the war between the states he was with the Confederate army as a private in the Second Tennessee Regiment. On October 30, 1869, his thirtieth birthday, Eli Thomas married Miss Eliza Sneed, who was born in Wilson County, Tennessee, January 30, 1846, and her parents were likewise natives of Tennessee. To their marriage were born ten children, eight sons and two daughters, all of them living as follows: Crittenden, born July 30, 1870; Houston, born September 5, 1871; Charles, born January 4, 1873; Ephraim, born August 5, 1875; Arizona, born June 10, 1876; Baxter, born July 20, 1877; Hogan, born March 22, 1879; Gordon, born January 16, 1881; Roscoe C., who is the ninth in order of birth; and Ophelia, born January 4, 1885.

Roscoe C. Thomas was reared in Wilson County, attended the public schools there, and as opportunities were not so abundant in his native state as he imagined they would be in a newer country, he came in 1904 to Oklahoma and spent one year on the famous 101 Ranch in Kay County. In 1905 he located on a homestead in Texas County, but in addition to proving up and cultivating his claim he also operated a real estate office in Guymon. Since then he has been closely identified with the substantial activities of this section of the state. In 1907 he was one of the organizers of the Cimarron Town Company, and was manager of that company until the town failed to realize the sanguine expectations of its founders. In 1908 he removed to Boise City, and in 1910 bought the plant of the Cimarron News at Kenton and removed it to Boise City, where he consolidated it with the Boise City Tribune in 1911. He now has the leading paper in that section, and has a printing plant that is unusually well equipped, having among other facilities a typesetting machine and modern rotary presses.

During 1913-14 Mr. Thomas was a member of the Oklahoma State Board of Agriculture. He is democratic state central committeeman from Cimarron. Fraternally he is affiliated with the Independent Order of Odd Fellows and is a member of the Methodist Episcopal Church.

On June 29, 1910, at Boise City he married Miss

Ruby Allison, who was born June 10, 1885, at Groesbeck, Texas, a daughter of A. B. Allison, who now lives at Boise City, Oklahoma. Mr. and Mrs. Thomas have one child, Roscoe C., Jr., born March 28, 1914.

JOHN G. REID, M. D. A physician and surgeon of broad and successful experience, Dr. John G. Reid in 1914 located in Lincoln County at Fallis, and later in Oklahoma City, where he enjoys the esteem and the practice which indicate the possession of both ability and high personal character. Doctor Reid has spent many years in Oklahoma, having first come to the territory at the opening of the Cherokee Strip in 1893, and after participating in the run he located a claim in that section. He came to Oklahoma from Wellington, Kansas. Doctor Reid is a graduate in medicine from the Northwestern University of Chicago, Illinois, with the class of 1877.

John G. Reid was born at Jacksonville, Illinois, April 8, 1847, and his early life was spent on a farm. His grandfather and father were, respectively, Stephen H., Sr., and Stephen H., Jr. Both were natives of Kentucky and were of Scotch-Irish ancestry. Stephen H. Reid, Jr., grew up in his native state and married there Martha Capps, who became the mother of three children. His second wife was Miss Martha Garrett, who was born in Cheshire, England, of English parentage. Her children were: John G.; Lydia C.; Richard W., who was a lawyer, and is now deceased; George W., of Jacksonville, Illinois; Enoch S., now deceased; and Elijah J., a farmer near Jacksonville, Illinois. The father of these sons died at the age of seventy-six. Politically he was a republican, and before the war was a great friend and admirer of Owen Lovejoy, the great abolitionist. His wife died at the age of sixty-one. She was a member of the Methodist Church, and a woman of admirable temper and excellent qualities of heart and mind.

Dr. John G. Reid was reared on the old farmstead in Illinois, and owing to many circumstances, life in a country community, the turmoil of war times, and other things, he had only a limited educated while growing to manhood. He later secured his education from the proceeds of his own endeavors, studied at home, attended higher schools, and then prepared for a professional career in Chicago. After graduating from medical college his first location was at Woodburn, Illinois, subsequently he practiced in Chicago several years, then located in Texas, and since 1893 has been identified with the Territory and State of Oklahoma. For several years he was in Enid, and in 1901 removed to Hydro, where he conducted his general practice until removing to Fallis, and came in 1916 to Oklahoma City.

Doctor Reid was first married March 20, 1877, in Illinois, to Mary J. Whittier, a niece of the great Quaker poet, John G. Whittier. She was born and educated in New York State, and was a woman of fine culture and education, and died at Welington, Kansas, at the age of fifty-five. She left one daughter, Mrs. Welch. Doctor Reid married his present wife in Kansas, Miss Evelyn Schamell. Mrs. Reid was born in Lincoln, Nebraska, and was educated chiefly in Kansas. Her parents, Peter and Margaret (Bonet) Schamell, were, respectively, German and Irish. Doctor and Mrs. Reid have one son, Cranston, who was born January 25, 1912. Doctor Reid is a member of the Modern' Woodmen of America. Politically he is a prohibitionist; both he and his wife are members of the Methodist Episcopal Church.

LEROY H. KEYS of Bartlesville, is a sterling representative of the old Cherokee Nation. He is a native of the Cherokee Nation, and has spent most of his life in and around the present site of Bartlesville, where his business activities and his civic influence have counted for much in local development. As a farmer, oil man, property owner, he has been known for his successful management of every enterprise he has undertaken. He is a genial gentleman, a wholesome and public spirited citizen and a man whom the Bartlesville community counts as one of its livest and most esteemed citizens.

Born in the Cherokee Nation of Indian Territory, March 16, 1864, he was the only son of Isaac W. and Jane (Ramsey) Keys. His mother died when he was an infant. Both parents were natives of the Southern States, and were part blooded Cherokees. When that tribe was removed west of the Mississippi River during the '30s, Isaac Keys went along, and he and his wife spent the rest of their lives in the new district set aside for the homes of the Indians. The history of the family is thus closely associated with the history of Indian Territory from the very beginning. Isaac Keys was a Southern sympathizer and fought with Gen. Stand Waitie during the Civil war, and most of the family were Confederates, either actively or in sympathy. Isaac Keys was one of sixteen children, and some of them were in both armies, including his brothers George and Judge Riley Keys, who allied themselves with the Northern forces.

Aside from his participation in the struggle between the North and South Isaac Keys devoted most of his life to farming and stock raising. He was honest and honorable, stood high in the community, and his death, in the spring of 1887, marked the passing of one of the worthy old time citizens of what is now Eastern Oklahoma. By his second marriage he had no children, and by a third marriage the three daughters were: Jessie, now deceased, married Sam Jordan and left a daughter Ruby M., who is now living with her grandparents; Nellie, deceased; and Myrtle, who lives at Nowata, Oklahoma. There were also four orphan children reared in the home of Isaac Keys. Three of them were the Cobb boys, William, John and Mack, William having died some years ago, while the other two are prominent in Nowata County. The other orphan reared in the Keys household was Georgia Russell, whom Mr. Leroy Keys has always esteemed as an own sister. She first married James Stokes, and their children were as follows: Floyd, deceased; Olive, who married Tom Mix and has one child, Ruthe; Gretta, who married L. C. Rothe, and they have one child, Russell. After the death of James Stokes she married Walter Brown, and they now reside north of Bartlesville.

With such sterling family associations, it is not surprising that Leroy H. Keys has always been extremely loyal to the country which gave him birth, and his own accomplishments have brought him the highest rank among the influential citizens of Indian blood in Oklahoma. Almost his entire career has been spent in the Cherokee Nation and Oklahoma State, with the exception of four years, 1885-88, in Santa Rosa, California. As a boy he acquired a common school education, and his early life was spent in working on cattle ranches. He has been accustomed to meeting hardships and dangers and has never flinched from the responsibilities of existence. For many years he has been an active and prosperous farmer, and with other members of the family received his allotment of eighty acres, which now constitutes one of the valuable tracts of land in Washington County. For two and a half years, up to April, 1915, he was proprietor of a livery establishment in Bartlesville, but then sold out, and is now giving his attention to his farming interests. There are several oil wells on his property and he has not only shared in the great material wealth of this section of the

Leroy H. Keys

state, but has also helped to create and utilize those abundant resources.

In early times Mr. Keys herded cattle over the present site of Bartlesville as an employe of P. L. Yocum. In 1876 he accompanied his father on a trip to Colorado, from which state they returned in the spring of 1877. That was a journey which he recalls with a great deal of interest, since he saw some buffaloes, then being rapidly dissipated and soon to disappear almost entirely from the great plains, and he also saw a great many antelope. In 1901 Mr. Keys participated in the rush of new settlers into the Kiowa and Comanche country in Southwestern Oklahoma. Though he sold his business as a liveryman he is still owner of the building in which it is conducted and he owns several other pieces of good property in Bartlesville.

Special mention should be made of the handsome home which he built at a cost of $6,000, and is located at 918 Cherokee Avenue, in Bartlesville. It is not only one of the beautiful places of the city from the standpoint of material structure, but it is also a real home in comfort and family associations, and within its walls Mr. Keys finds his chief pleasure. On May 8, 1891, he married Miss Belle Thomas, who was born in Arkansas June 11, 1869, and came to Indian Territory when a young lady. Her father, who was born in Jackson County, Alabama, spent his life as a farmer, and married Miss Lavinia West, who was a native of Crawford County, Arkansas. In the Thomas family were four sons and two daughters, and all of them lived either in or near Bartlesville. Mr. and Mrs. Keys have five children: Albert Leroy, a farmer in Washington County, married Hattie Montgomery. The second child is Pearl. Raymond W. was married in June, 1915, to Miss Jeanette Whiteturkey, and they have an infant daughter named Maxine. Olive M. is still at home with her parents. The other child, Lela J., died at the age of three years.

E. P. CLARK. An atmosphere of romance surrounds the experiences of the hardy pioneers in the several historic land openings of Oklahoma, and it would be a volume of surpassing interest which might select and give record to the many narratives heard from the lips of those early settlers. Numerous little incidents in the life of E. P. Clark, now manager of the Chickasha Milling Company at Verden, make his career an extraordinary one. When he is in the proper mood Mr. Clark can relate experiences that furnish a delightful and refreshing hour to his audience. He lacks only two months of being an Oklahoma Eighty-niner, and was a participant in three Oklahoma openings, those of the Cherokee Strip, the Cheyenne and Arapaho Country and the Kiowa and Comanche district. His travels have been transcontinental in the seeking and establishing of homes, but most of twenty-six years have been spent in Oklahoma.

E. P. Clark was born in Monmouth, Illinois, August 5, 1866, a son of Horace and Jeanette (Coutlet) Clark. On both sides the ancestry goes back before the Revolutionary period in American history. One of the maternal ancestors came to America with Lafayette and fought under that great Frenchman during the war for independence. Horace Clark, the father, died at Medford, Oregon, in 1914, at the age of seventy-six. Mr. E. P. Clark has a half brother, Carl B. Clark, who is an instructor in engineering in a college in New York State.

Mr. Clark's first schooling was in Janesville, Wisconsin, to which place his father removed when the former was a small boy. The next year the family moved to New York and in that state he attended a school at Sandy Creek. The following year was spent in school at Cedar Rapids, Iowa, and his common school education ended at Eldora, Iowa. As a young man he did farming at Anthony, Kansas.

These experiences sum up his career until he came to Oklahoma. Soon after the original Oklahoma opening in 1889, he conceived the idea of growing vegetables for the market in the new country. Buying a supply of garden seeds he dispatched John Freeman from Anthony, Kansas, to Kingfisher, Oklahoma, to put out the first garden. Later, after Mr. Clark had concluded an assignment in a salt plant in Kansas, and with only a few dollars for expenses, he set out on foot for Oklahoma. Settlements were few in the new country and it was wild and much frequented by bad men. His journey first led him to Bluff City and later to the Crisine Ranch, in what was then the Cherokee Strip. At that ranch he rested for a time, and then resumed his journey on foot, arriving in due time at Pond Creek, where he fell in with a man driving an ox team. They were companions for several days in the tedious journey towards the promised land, getting poor and insufficient food all the way. Their destination was Hennessey, and on the day of their arrival Mr. Clark was approached by George Bear, a druggist, who asked him to sign a petition for the removal of the county seat from Kingfisher to Hennessey. Clark protested that he was not a citizen of the territory, having just arrived, but his name went on the petition.

After a few days he reached Kingfisher and found that Freeman had arrived there with his garden seed and was well on the way toward a lucrative income. Mr. Clark's money was all gone and he set about working at odd jobs to pay for his food. Working with him was Amos Ewing, called "Shorty" in those days, who afterwards became one of the leading men in republican politics in the territory and was a member of the recent Fifth Legislature, from Logan County. Mr. Clark dug post-holes and cellars and worked as a section hand until he had saved fifty dollars, which he invested in a bakery at Hennessey. He sold this later and entered the fur trade, which he followed for several years in Oklahoma and Kansas. It is of interest that he was employed for a time in a store belonging to Fred Ehler, who remains one of the picturesque pioneer citizens of Hennessey. Later he entered the milling business under George H. Block, who is another of the interesting characters of the early days and a well known capitalist and lumber-dealer of the present day. With the exception of a short time spent in Lee's Summit, Missouri, Mr. Clark has continued uninterruptedly in the milling business, as salesman and plant manager. He has been manager of the Chickasha Milling Company's plant at Verden about a year. In coming back to Oklahoma in 1914 to take the Verden station of this company, he found luck lurking in numbers of ill reputation. He came out of door No. 13 in the Union Station at Kansas City, took train No. 23 and arrived in his office at Chickasha on Friday the 13th.

Mr. Clark was married twenty-one years ago at Hennessey, to Miss Grace L. Fowler. The half-brother of Mrs. Clark, Harry Fowler, has lived with them as a member of the family, but at the present time is in Alaska. The five children are named Horace, Helen, Henry, Hazel and Herbert. Mr. Clark is affiliated with the Improved Order of Red Men and was formerly a member of the United Commercial Travelers and the Ancient Order of United Workmen. He was a member of the first grand lodge of Red Men in Oklahoma and assisted in its organization. He is a member of the

JOHN LINSY ALLEN. One of the oldest cattlemen in the Panhandle district of Oklahoma is John Linsy Allen, whose home is now at Boise City, Oklahoma, where he is assistant postmaster, his wife, Mrs. Allen, being the chief in that office. Mr. Allen is also a prominent democrat in his section of the state and is widely known among all the cattlemen of that district.

He was born October 21, 1871, in a log house on a farm in Hancock County, Illinois, a son of James T. and Mary M. (Phillips) Allen. His father, who was a son of Ethean Allen, a native of New York and of Scotch ancestry, was also born in Hancock County, Illinois, April 1, 1846, and has been a prominent stockman all his active career. From Illinois he moved to Missouri in 1872, when his son, John, was about one year old, and for eleven years farmed and raised stock in Sullivan County. In 1883 he went to Kansas, continued cattle raising on the open range in Clark County for two years, and then went still further west to Las Animas County, Colorado. There he engaged in the cattle business for eighteen years, and for nine years operated a large ranch in No Man's Land of Oklahoma. In 1914 he retired, and is now living at Lamar, Colorado. In 1868 he married Miss Phillips, a daughter of Brice and Lavina Phillips, who were natives of Pennsylvania. Mrs. Allen was born November 16, 1848, in Allegheny County, Pennsylvania. To their marriage were born five sons, all of whom are still living: Alfred B., born in 1869, is now postmaster at Lobatos, Colorado; John L. is the second son; Crittenden E., born in 1875, is a cattleman in Cimarron County, Oklahoma; Thomas Eldon, born in 1878, is now county judge of Baca County, Colorado; and Charles Alva, born in 1882 is a beet sugar manufacturer at Rocky Ford, Colorado.

John Linsy Allen received his early education in the public schools of Sullivan County, Missouri, and in Las Animas County, Colorado. When only eighteen he took up the life of a cowboy on the open range and was employed by various outfits and also on his own account in Indian Territory, Kansas, Colorado, Wyoming, and Montana for a period of seventeen years. In recent years his operations have been confined to the states of Colorado and Oklahoma, and he is particularly well known in the old No Man's Land of Oklahoma.

In 1910 Mr. Allen was elected a member of the board of county commissioners of Cimarron County and was re-elected in 1912, giving four years of his time and attention to that office. He is very influential in the democratic organization. On February 4, 1915, at Boise City, Oklahoma, he married Miss Adalee Allison, who was born in Texas November 20, 1885. Mrs. Allen completed her education in the University of Chicago and for a number of years prior to her marriage was engaged in teaching. In 1915 she was appointed postmaster of Boise City. Fraternally Mr. Allen is a Knight Templar Mason and also an Odd Fellow.

HERBERT E. SMITH. It is as a lawyer of broad and varied experience that Mr. Smith is chiefly identified with the State of Oklahoma, where he has lived since 1908. His home and offices are in Okmulgee, where he has gained prominence and success as a general attorney, but much of his practice is connected with land, oil and gas interests and litigation.

A Virginian by birth, he is of an old and interesting family of that commonwealth. Born in Petersburg, Virginia, August 22, 1871, he is a son of E. D. T. and Mary Elizabeth (Pace) Smith. His parents were also born in Virginia, and both families were of colonial stock. The great-grandfather Smith came from Scotland and located in Dinwiddie County, Virginia. In the successive generations there have been representatives of the family in every important war in which this country has had a part. Mr. Smith's parents both died in Virginia in 1912, their deaths occurring only twenty days apart. His father was aged ninety and his mother eighty. The father spent most of his active career as a farmer, and at one time served as mayor of his home city of Petersburg. He was a Confederate soldier throughout the Civil war under the command of General William Mahone. He was captured near Norfolk, and was one of the men drawn by lot to be shot by the Federal authorities. He escaped when Lee informed Grant that if Confederate prisoners were put to death he would shoot three Federals for every Confederate so put to death. One of Mr. Smith's most interesting possessions is the diary kept by his father for many years and detailing many of his experiences while a soldier. He escaped from the northern prison in which he was held, and was shot three times while swimming in Chesapeake Bay. All of Mr. Smith's uncles were soldiers in the Civil war, and at three different times the northern and southern armies were engaged in fighting on the old Smith homestead at Petersburg.

Herbert E. Smith was one of seven sons, and his only brother now living is John Edward of Bradentown, Florida. Three members of the Smith family lost their lives during that brief but victorious conflict with Spain.

Reared on a farm, Herbert E. Smith has largely made his own way in the world. He acquired a common school education and at the age of sixteen he went to Rochester, New York, and found employment at various occupations, keeping up his studies in night school. He studied law with Judge J. M. Mullen at Petersburg, Virginia, and was admitted to the bar August 23, 1892, the day following his twenty-first birthday. He practiced law in his native state less than three years and then went to Buffalo, New York, where he was admitted to practice in June, 1895. In 1898 he went to the Island of Porto Rico, where for six years he was engaged in practice as a lawyer and was the first American attorney to open an office on that island. In March, 1905, Mr. Smith went to Washington, D. C., and practiced as member of a law firm of that city until he came to Okmulgee, Oklahoma, on May 24, 1908.

In politics Mr. Smith is a republican. He is a traveler who has seen a great deal of the world, and has practically visited all the important countries of the globe, his travels having been especially extensive in South America and Alaska. He is a man of many interests, and has the genial nature which makes him hosts of friends. In 1901 he married Cora M. Belden, who was born in Chautauqua County, New York, and who is directly related to the Curtis and Van Rensselaer families of old colonial New York stock.

GUY BARTON VAN SANDT, M. D. From the point of continuous practice Doctor Van Sandt is the oldest physician and surgeon at Wewoka. Soon after taking his degree of medicine he located in that little city in Eastern Oklahoma twelve years ago and has since been shown every mark of appreciation and favor in his capacity as a physician and also as a citizen and good worker for community welfare.

He was born at Montrose, Illinois, November 14, 1878, a son of Dr. H. G. and Henrietta F. (Morton) Van Sandt. His grandfather, John Van Sandt, was a native of Kentucky, but was an ardent abolitionist, was connected with the underground railway, and figured in a

notable fugitive slave case. He was convicted before one court of having assisted fugitive slaves to escape to the North, but he carried the case to the Supreme Court, where he was defended by such notable attorneys as Chase and Stone. His character is also preserved in literature, and he is the figure known as Van Trump in Harriet Beecher Stowe's "Uncle Tom's Cabin." Dr. H. G. Van Sandt was born at Glendale, Ohio, in 1843, and served throughout the Civil war, having enlisted in the three months service with the 12th Ohio Regiment, and afterwards going to Illinois and enlisting in Company I of the 125th Illinois Infantry. The greater part of his military service was spent as a scout, and he was detailed with Captain Powell. After the war he took up the practice of medicine in Missouri, remained there four years, then spent two years in the St. Louis Medical College and located permanently at Montrose, Illinois, where he carried on an active practice until his death in 1906. He also took a prominent part in republican politics, was a member of the Masonic Lodge, and affiliated with the Grand Army of the Republic. His wife, Henrietta F. Morton, was born in Iowa in 1849, was reared in Jacksonville, Illinois, coming of a staunch Presbyterian family, and of old Boston and Massachusetts stock. She was married in Jacksonville in 1872, and she is still living, her home being at Montrose, Illinois. Of the eight children, the first three died in infancy. The oldest of those living is Dr. Van Sandt, John Arthur died in 1912; Harrison G. lives at Montrose, Illinois; Vallie V. is the wife of Harry Jenuine at Greenup, Illinois; Leona lives with her mother.

Doctor Van Sandt spent his early youth in Montrose graduated from high school, took a course in Whipple Academy at Jacksonville, Illinois, at Austin College in Effingham, and took the greater part of his medical work in Barnes Medical College of St. Louis, where he was graduated M. D. in 1903.

On January 1, 1904, Doctor Van Zandt began practice at Wewoka, and while he was not the first physician to locate there, he has seen those who were here when he came leave or retire, and thus he is the oldest practitioner and also is a recognized leader in his profession. He is a member of the county and state medical societies and the American Medical Association and belongs to the Railway Surgeons' Association.

On April 9, 1903, Doctor Van Sandt married Miss Lucile M. Cuddy. The marriage ceremony was performed by John D. Vincil, who also gave him his medical diploma. Mr. Vincil was grand secretary of the Masonic Grand Lodge of Missouri. Mrs. Van Sandt was born in Kansas, but was reared chiefly in Oklahoma, being a daughter of Joseph and Emma (Suppiger) Cuddy. They have one son, Max. Doctor Van Sandt is a republican, has served as county chairman, and in Masonry is affiliated with the thirty-second degree Consistory, with the Mystic Shrine and is also a member of the Benevolent and Protective Order of Elks.

GEORGE W. PULLEN. From a primeval landscape that marked sections of the picturesque Cherokee Nation a quarter of a century ago Hon. George W. Pullen, representative of Murray County in the Fifth Legislature of Oklahoma, has evolved a picture that affords an effective presentment of progress, prosperity and culture. This depicture in a material way represents his fine and essentially modern farmstead of 153 acres, two miles distant from the thriving little City of Davis. On the farm the purest of water flows in superabundance from streams and wells, the fertile soil brings forth its increase as one season follows another, and on the estate is to be found one of the finest farm residences in Murray County, this attractive home being situated on a rise of ground and constituting one of the many evidences of peace, comfort, prosperity and appreciative enterprise in developing the splendid natural resources of that favored section of the state, where Mr. Pullen is known and honored as a progressive and public-spirited citizen.

George W. Pullen was born in Lawrence County, Tennesee, on the 20th of February, 1862, and is a son of Jesse and Mary (Atwell) Pullen, both likewise natives of Tennessee, to which state the parents of Jesse Pullen removed in an early day from Virginia. Jesse Pullen was a prosperous farmer of Tennessee and in that state both he and his wife passed their entire lives. He whose name initiates this article passed the period of his boyhood and youth on the home farm and though his early educational advantages were limited to a somewhat irregular attendance in the local schools he early developed a fondness for study and reading, showed ambition in the acquirement of knowledge, and through individual application amply stored his retentive mind with information which well equipped him for the responsibilities and productive activities of later years. He was but thirteen years of age at the time of his father's death and upon his youthful shoulders thus fell heavy responsibilities. He remained on the homestead farm until he was twenty-three years of age, and with all of filial solicitude provided for his widowed mother. At the age noted Mr. Pullen went to Alabama, in which state he remained three years, at the expiration of which he returned to Tennessee. Two years later, in 1892, he numbered himself among the pioneer settlers near Davis, Indian Territory. There he secured a tract of land in a section that was chiefly notable for its unreclaimed stretches of land, covered with sage brush and practically unsettled. Houses were few and widely separated and the population was very small. In the midst of the virgin wilds he erected a primitive dwelling and then essayed the task of developing a farm. That he has brought to bear much energy, discrimination and progressiveness is best demonstrated in the extent and condition of his finely improved landed domain of the present day, and he is known as one of the leading agriculturists and stockgrowers of Murray County, where in recent years he has given special attention to the raising of high-grade Jersey cattle.

Liberal in the support of all measures and enterprises tending to advance the civic and material welfare of his home county, and known as a man of much acumen and judgment, Mr. Pullen naturally became influential in public affairs and his high standing in the community was shown by his election, in November, 1914, as representative of Murray County in the Fifth General Assembly of the State Legislature. He proved a sincere, loyal and valuable working member of the House of Representative, in which he was assigned to the following named committees: Charities and corrections, roads and highways, manufacturing and commerce, and pure food and drugs. In his home county, at Sulphur, is situated the State School for the Deaf, and his interest in the same was shown significantly by his obtaining from the Fifth Legislature appropriations for the institution to the aggregate amount of $159,000, of which the sum of $20,500 is applied for the erection of new buildings. He introduced a bill requiring that the records of county officials be checked or audited every two years, but this bill was killed in the committee room. Another bill which he introduced and which met the same fate, made requirement that teachers in the public schools undergo medical examinations to determine whether or not they were afflicted with tuberculosis. Mr. Pullen was a staunch supporter of measures furthering the good-roads movement and those of importance to rural communities and the conserving of the agricultural industry, the while the cause of education likewise received his earnest support in the Legislature.

In politics Mr. Pullen is arrayed as a stalwart advocate of the principles of the democratic party, and in a fraternal way he is identified with the Woodmen of the World, the Ancient Order of United Workmen and the A. H. T. A., in each of which he has held important offices. He has been specially active and influential in the last named organization, in which he has on three occasions represented his lodge in the state organization of the order and once at the national convention of the same.

In Tennessee the year 1885 recorded the marriage of Mr. Pullen to Miss Amanda A. Kelly, who was there born and reared. They have six children: Cecil Bayard is a progressive young farmer of Murray County; Jesse remains at the parental home and is still attending school; Minnie is the wife of John Springer, a prosperous farmer of Murray County; Miss Pearl is a popular teacher in the public schools at Elmore, Garvin County; and Carrie is attending the public schools.

MISS STELLA C. BAYLESS. What a sphere of activity and usefulness a woman may fill in this twentieth century age finds probably one of its most interesting illustrations in the career of Miss Bayless, one of the present county superintendents of schools in the county. Miss Bayless is as much a pioneer in the new educational movement as her father was a pioneer during the developing years of early Kansas and Oklahoma. She has great physical vitality, all the qualities of courage and fortitude that distinguish the other sex, and has brought a vigor and enthusiasm to her work which makes her easily one of the foremost educators in the state.

She was born in Adams County, Ohio, October 14, 1885, but early in her infancy her parents, H. T. and Flora (Clinger) Bayless, moved to Winfield, Kansas. Her parents were also natives of Adams County, Ohio, where her father was born, September 20, 1845, and her mother, November, 1858. The family lived in that section of Southern Ohio until they moved out to Kansas. However, her father was a Kansas pioneer, having gone to that state in 1866. He hunted buffalo on the plains, and proved up a claim near Winfield. After working his farm for several years he returned to Ohio, but about 1886 he moved his family back to Kansas. On September 16, 1893, he participated in the race into the Cherokee Strip and secured a claim two miles south of Tonkawa. He was one of the five men who organized and laid out the Village of Tonkawa, and suggested that its name be the same as the Indian tribe which occupied some of the land in that locality. Mr. Bayless is now the only survivor of that quintet of town founders. After living at Tonkawa eight years he moved to Noble County, locating near Otoe, five years later went to Bliss, lived there for five years, and then moved to Edmond. His life has been a very active one and on the whole unusually successful. He has some land interests near Phoenix, Arizona, and spends much of his time there. Both he and his wife in their younger years taught school, and there have been several teachers in the different generations of the family. The father is an independent republican, a member of the Baptist Church, and is affiliated with the Independent Order of Odd Fellows. There are four children: Maude, wife of Will Beasley of Charleston, Oklahoma; L. R. and W. P., who lives in Kansas; and Miss Stella.

Miss Bayless lived at home with her parents until she was seventeen years of age. For three years she was a student in the University Preparatory School at Tonkawa, and she also taught school at Bliss. From early girlhood she has indulged her enthusiasm for outdoor life and for many of those activities which are usually considered strictly limited to men. In the summer vacations while she was attending school at Tonkawa she was on a ranch, and almost constantly on horseback. There is nothing which she could not do in the routine of ranch duties except roping a steer. She could ride anything that walked on four feet, and frequently broke the colts and mules. While at Edmond she attended the Central State Normal School for two terms and there secured a state certificate as a teacher.

Her first school was a sod schoolhouse near Tonkawa. She taught for seventeen months at Bliss, for one year at White Eagle and then for a year was traveling representative for the Bufton Book Company and Supply House, of Kansas City. Her territory included the states of Texas, Kansas, Missouri, Oklahoma and Iowa. While with that company she visited over three thousand schools, and the notes which she made of her observations in the different schools have proved valuable to her in her later work as an educator.

Coming to Creek County on June 1, 1911, she taught in this county for three terms prior to her election as county superintendent on November 4, 1914. Miss Bayless gives her restricted suffrage to the support of the republican party. She is a member of the Baptist Church at Edmond, and is affiliated with the Brotherhood of American Yeomen and with the Fraternal Aid and Woman's Relief Corps.

Many pages might be written of her varied and interesting experiences in Oklahoma and elsewhere. While she was teaching at White Eagle she met a herd of buffaloes on a stampede and in the scrimmage her buggy was torn to pieces, and it was with difficulty that she was rescued by some cowboys. While she was traveling for the book house she was driving a team across a ford over the Red River and the horses were swept by the waters and drowned. She has come to know much of Indian life and customs, and has always closely studied tribal institutions. While she was living at Otoe, near the Ponca reservation, she took part in some of the tribal dances, also attended the weddings and funerals of the Otoe and Ponca Indians, and has many interesting relics given her by those tribes.

The element of progressiveness stands out prominently in Miss Bayless' work as an educator. One of the ideals toward which she is working is the consolidation of the rural schools of Creek County, so as to promote greater efficiency and eliminate those schools which under the present system cannot possibly maintain the average standard. She has also done much to develop social centers, has brought about in a number of schools a system for the awarding of credit to the pupils for home work, and has been able to secure much more co-operation between school and home than was ever considered possible. She established the Creek County School News, through whose columns many progressive ideas have been spread into the homes of the people, and this is the first publication of its kind ever attempted in the state. She has not neglected any of those modern agencies for education and enlightenment. She has some interesting experiences to record showing the possibilities of the "Victrola" and the use of lantern slides as a part of her educational program. Since she became superintendent ten men have been engaged as special lecturers in the schools, besides the employment of home talent whenever possible for the same purpose. Miss Bayless has organized the "moonlight" schools in the county, for the purpose of affording instruction and extending the facilities of the schools to people of adult age whose education had previously been neglected. The State of Oklahoma should be proud of this splendid young woman, who has done so much to vitalize school work in Creek County.

GUY W. STACK. Still at an age when most men are just beginning to realize the possibilities of life, Guy W. Stack is the possessor of a substantial business, an enterprise that stands a monument to his energy, capacity and business judgment. When he came to Kenton, Oklahoma, in 1908, his capital was chiefly represented by his ambition and determination; within the short space of seven years he has developed the largest business of its kind in Cimarron County, and is justly considered one of the leading influences in the movements which of recent years have contributed so substantially to this thriving community's growth.

Mr. Stack was born July 10, 1886, on a farm in Barber County, Kansas, and is a son of Charles W. and Sarah Elizabeth (Rose) Stack. His father was born in Iowa, August 25, 1859, a son of Samuel and Sarah Stack, natives of Canada, of English extraction, and was reared on a farm and has been an agriculturist all of his life. When he first removed to Kansas, in 1870, Charles W. Stack settled on Government land in Reno County, where he lived among the pioneer farmers for eight years and carried on farming and stock raising. In 1898 he removed to Barber County, where he resided until 1894, and at that time came to Oklahoma, settling in Lincoln County, where he is now a prosperous farmer and stockman. Mr. Stack is a republican in his political views and a member of the Presbyterian Church, in the work of which he takes an active interest. He was married in 1879, in Reno County, Kansas, to Miss Sarah Elizabeth Rose, who was born December 3, 1860, near Sheridan, Poweshiek County, Iowa, daughter of William and Jane (Ogden) Rose, natives of Ohio. Prior to her marriage Mrs. Stack was engaged in teaching school for ten years in various parts of Iowa and Kansas, and became well and favorably known as an educator. Mr. and Mrs. Stack were the parents of four daughters and two sons, namely: Jessie L., born June 15, 1882; Jennie L., born April 2, 1884; Guy W.; Rose H., born September 13, 1888; Belle M., born January 31, 1889; and Benjamin H., born September 15, 1892.

Guy W. Stack was eight years of age when brought to Oklahoma, and his education was secured in the public schools of Chandler, where he was graduated in the class of 1903 from the high school. Subsequently he attended the Oklahoma Central Normal School, at Edmond, and then for four years was engaged in teaching in the schools of Lincoln County. In 1907 Mr. Stack settled on a homestead in Union County, New Mexico, twelve miles west of Kenton, Oklahoma, and in 1908 was made assistant postmaster at Kenton, and moved to this place where he accepted a position as bookkeeper in a mercantile establishment. In June, 1910, having thoroughly assimilated business methods and conditions, he embarked in the general merchandise business on his own account, and now has a trade which covers the entire community, with a branch house at Texline, Texas. His store at Kenton is the largest in Cimarron County, with a $75,000 stock of general merchandise, lumber and agricultural implements, his annual business approximating $200,000. This enterprise has been built up entirely through his own efforts, and in addition he has extensive and valuable real estate holdings in Cimarron and Lincoln counties, Oklahoma, and in Union County New Mexico. Mr. Stack is one of the leading members of the Kenton Commercial Club. He has the confidence and esteem of his associates in the business world, and is a general favorite in social circles, although his important business interests have practically occupied his time to the exclusion of other affairs.

Mr. Stack was married September 2, 1909, at Chandler, Oklahoma, to Miss Ida M. Bickford, who was born June 5, 1886, in McDonald County, Missouri, daughter of Dennis C. and Mary Jane (Moore) Bickford, natives of Maine. She is a graduate of the Chandler (Oklahoma) High School, class of 1905, and for four years prior to her marriage was a teacher in the public schools of Lincoln County. Mr. and Mrs. Stack are consistent members of the Methodist Episcopal Church.

SOL D. BARNETT. Among the men who made the run for land at the opening of the Cherokee Strip, in 1893, was a young Texan, Sol D. Barnett, who, mounted on a race horse trained by himself, led the run for four miles and staked out a desirable property. However, he was induced to relinquish his property owing to his ignorance of the methods used by unscrupulous persons, and it was not until 1899 that he came to permanently reside in Oklahoma. Since that time Mr. Barnett has been engaged in a number of successful business ventures, and at the present time is the proprietor of a large real estate and loan business at Hollis, and tax assessor of Harmon County, a position which he has held since 1912.

Mr. Barnett was born in Union County, Kentucky, August 18, 1872, and is a son of Dr. J. J. and Mary V. (Roley) Barnett, and a member of a family which came to Virginia in colonial times from Ireland. J. J. Barnett was born in Virginia in 1829 and as a lad removed with his parents to Union County, Kentucky, where he was educated for the medical profession. He was there married to Mary V. Roley, who was born in that county, in 1838, and continued to follow the practice of his calling there until 1880, in which year he moved to Wise County, Texas. In 1893 he went to Ford County, in the same state, and in 1899 located at Mangum, Oklahoma, from whence he finally moved to Blake, Oklahoma, where he passed the last few years of his life in retirement, and died in 1908, Mrs. Barnett surviving him until 1911 and passing away at Hollis. In addition to being a learned and skillful medical practitioner, Doctor Barnett was a minister of the Baptist Church, and followed both callings together for fifty years. He was a highly esteemed citizen in whatever community happened to be his home and won the esteem and regard of his fellow-men by his strict integrity and probity of character. He was a Mason for many years and rose to the thirty-second degree. During the Civil war he enlisted in a Kentucky infantry regiment, in the Confederate army, and served for three years with the rank of captain. Being finally taken a prisoner, he was sent to Johnson Island, and there confined for a year before being exchanged. Dr. J. J. and Mary V. Barnett were the parents of eight children, as follows: Major, who is engaged in farming in Wise County, Texas; J. D., who is deceased; J. J., who is engaged in agricultural operations at Acme, Texas; S. P., a farmer of Wayne County, Tennessee; Clarence L., who followed farming and stockraising and died at Mangum, Oklahoma; H. B., who is engaged in the same pursuits and resides near Mangum; Sol D.; and Molly, who is the wife of W. H. Stewart, of Amarillo, Texas.

Sol D. Barnett was eight years of age when the family removed to Wise County, Texas, and there he enjoyed the advantages of a high school education. In 1892 and 1893 he attended the Fort Worth Business College, and was thus excellently equipped for a business career. Being determined to secure land, he had carefully trained a favorite horse for the run to be made at the opening of the Cherokee Strip, and in September, 1893, as before noted, led the race for four miles and staked out a claim of 160 acres, on Turkey Creek, two miles west and 4½ miles north of Hennessey. Although he had fairly secured his land and had made the run through burning prairie grass, the youth allowed others to convince him that his claims were not substantial, and returned to his Texas home. From 1893 until 1899 he was engaged in the cattle business in Ford County, Texas, and with capital thus gained returned to Oklahoma and settled as a pioneer near Mangum, where he continued his operations in cattle. Subsequently he was elected county assessor of what was then Greer County, Oklahoma, an office in which he acted from 1900 until 1902, when the office was abolished. In the meantime he became interested in the real estate and loan business, which he followed at Mangum until 1903, when he came to Hollis, his present field of activity, and established his business here, his offices being located in the Cross National Bank Building. His business has grown to large proportions and he is justly accounted one of the leading men of his locality in his line.

Always an active democrat, Mr. Barnett has attended the state and county conventions of his party as a delegate, and during the campaign of Gov. Lee Cruce was successful in gaining almost the solid support of Harmon County and Southwestern Oklahoma for the Governor, as campaign manager. In 1912 he was appointed by Governor Cruce as tax assessor of Harmon County, and this appointment was approved by the people as shown when they elected him to that office in 1914. His incumbency has been characterized by straightforward dealings, expeditious handling of the affairs of the assessor's office, and conscientious and capable performance of duty. Mr. Barnett is a supporting member of the Methodist Episcopal Church.

In 1894, in Ford County, Texas, Mr. Barnett was married to Miss Mary C. Adams, daughter of Dr. W. H. Adams, a pioneer of Ford County, Texas, where he is still engaged in the practice of medicine. Five children have been born to Mr. and Mrs. Barnett: Claude, born October 13, 1895, who has finished his junior year at the Hollis High School and is now assisting his father in his business and official duties; Homer, who is a member of the freshman class at the Hollis High School; and Thurston, Louis and Murray Haskell, who are attending the public graded schools.

JUDSON CUNNINGHAM. A native of the Southwest and an effective exemplar of its vital spirit, Mr. Cunningham, the efficient and popular young county clerk of Roger Mills County, is a scion of the fourth generation of the family in America, his paternal great-grandfather, Alexander Cunningham, having immigrated to the United States from Ireland and having established his residence in the State of Tennessee, where Robert Cunningham, father of James Cunningham, was born. He afterwards moved to Alabama, where he became a prosperous agriculturist and where he passed the remainder of his life.

Judson Cunningham was born in Hill County, Texas, on the 20th of March, 1889, and is a son of James F. Cunningham, who was born in Alabama, in 1851, and who as a young man immigrated to Texas, where he became a farmer and stock man and where was solemnized his marriage to Mrs. Mary (Cason) Couble, widow of Paul Couble, who had been engaged in the cattle business in Hood County, that state. In 1892 James F. Cunningham came with his family to the newly organized Oklahoma Territory and became one of the pioneer settlers of Roger Mills County, where he entered claim to a homestead of 160 acres, one and one-half miles northwest of Cheyenne, the present thriving county seat, where he has reclaimed a productive and valuable farm and where he and his wife still maintain their home. He is a staunch advocate of the cause of the democratic party and both he and his wife are zealous members of the Baptist Church, in which he has for a number of years past given devoted and efficient service as a minister. He is one of the well known and highly honored pioneers of this section of the state, is a loyal and progressive citizen and is affiliated with the Masonic fraternity. Of the children the eldest is Pearl, who resides at Cheyenne, the judicial center of Roger Mills County, she being the widow of Orlando R. Bellamy, who was a successful school teacher at the time of his death. Dean, the second child, was a prosperous young farmer of Roger Mills County at the time of his death. He was burned to death when his farm house was destroyed by fire, and was only twenty-two years of age at the time. Grace died at the age of fifteen years. May is the wife of Henry C. Kisar, who is engaged in the hardware business in the State of Colorado. Kenneth is a farmer and stock-raiser in the State of New Mexico. Jesse remains at the parental home and is associated with his father in the work and management of the farm. Judson, of this review, was the next in order of birth. Bertha is the wife of Charles W. McKinney, who is engaged in the furniture business at Butler, Custer County, Oklahoma; and Ray remains at the parental home.

The present county clerk of Roger Mills County was a child of about three years at the time when the family home was here established, and his boyhood and early youth were compassed by the conditions and influences of the pioneer farm, the while he made good use of the advantages afforded in the local schools. In 1911 Mr. Cunningham was graduated in the high school at Cheyenne, and in the following year he had the distinction of being elected county clerk, when twenty-three years of age. The most effective voucher for his personal popularity and his able administration is that afforded in the fact that in 1914 he was re-elected for a second term of two years. He has shown marked fidelity and circumspection in handling the multifarious affairs of his office, the work of which he has thoroughly systematized, and he is one of the valued executive officers of the county that has represented his home from early childhood and to which he is intrinsically loyal, even as he is appreciative of its many natural and acquired advantages. Mr. Cunningham is found arrayed as a stalwart supporter of the principles of the democratic party and is one of its influential representatives in his home county. He is a member of the Baptist Church. In his home city he is affiliated with Cheyenne Lodge No. 237, Independent Order of Odd Fellows, and with the local organizations of the Daughters of Rebekah, the Modern Woodmen of America and the Fraternal Order of Eagles, and in the Independent Order of Odd Fellows he is further identified with Encampment No. 63 at Elk City, Beckham County. His name is still enrolled on the list of eligible young bachelors in Roger Mills County.

WILLIAM T. LEAHY. No name is better known in the Osage Nation district of Oklahoma than that of Leahy. The family was established there more than forty years ago, and William T. Leahy of Pawhuska has lived there since childhood. As a farmer, stock man, capitalist and banker his resources and influence are among the strongest factors in the business affairs of that section. Before statehood he was one of the leading representatives of the Osage people in the handling of their interests both in Indian Territory and at Washington, and since statehood he has been an active figure in political life.

By inheritance Mr. Leahy has an unusual combination of racial stocks. His father was a native Irishman, while his mother was part French and part Osage Indian. William T. Leahy was born at the Old Osage Mission, now the village of St. Paul, in Neosho County, Kansas, July 9, 1869, a son of Thomas and Mary L. (Champaigne) Leahy. His father was born in County Tipperary, Ireland, while his mother was born near the present site of Kansas City, Missouri, a daughter of William and Genevieve (Rivard) Champaigne. Her father was a Frenchman and her mother of the Osage Indian tribe. When Mary Champaigne was an infant she lost her father and her mother subsequently took her out to Sacramento, California, during the excitement following the discovery of gold. They made the trip across the country with four team and wagons, spent six or seven years in the West, and then returned to the Osage Mission in Southeastern Kansas. She lived there until her marriage, in 1868, to Thomas Leahy. After the Indians had given up their lands in Kansas and had removed to the Osage Nation in Indian Territory, Thomas Leahy was located for a time at Fort Riley as a trader and as a dealer in buffalo hides. As a boy in the late '70s during the high tide of the buffalo hide industry, William T. Leahy has seen as many as fifteen hundred buffalo carcasses, the animals having been killed entirely for the sake of their hides. He has also seen around his father's trading post stacks of hides piled as high as it was possible to pile them, and covering an area two or three hundred yards square. In 1875 Thomas Leahy moved his home permanently to Osage County, Indian Territory, and spent the rest of his life in that section. He became prominent as a cattle man, and his death occurred at Los Angeles, California, while visiting in the West, May 10, 1913, at the age of seventy. He had come to America in 1855 in company with his brother Edward, he being then twelve years of age. In Illinois he was bound out to a man named Nugent, who subsequently located near Fort Scott, Kansas, and remained in the employ of that man until nineteen years of age. For some time he was engaged in driving government teams between Fort Scott and Fort Smith, but during the war one of the trains was captured. Thomas Leahy frequently stopped at the old Osage Mission on these trips, and while there became acquainted with Miss Champaigne, and they were subsequently married. Mrs. Thomas Leahy is still living at Pawhuska at the age of sixty-five. They were the parents of three children: Viva, who is the wife of W. S. Conners, now living at San Antonio, Texas; Cora, widow of George Saxton, living at Los Angeles, California; and William T., the only son and the oldest of the family.

William T. Leahy lived with his father until twenty-five, and gained a thorough training not only in the merchandise business, but also as a farmer and stock man. For several years the firm of Leahy & Son was conducted both in the general merchandise business and in stock raising. As a young man Mr. Leahy attended the primary schools at Osage Mission and completed his education in the Southeast Kansas Normal College at Fort Scott. He was sent back to Kansas to get his education while the family were living in Indian Territory. At the age of twenty-five Mr. Leahy started at Pawhuska its first bakery and confectionery store, and was proprietor of that establishment for six or seven years. He then became identified with cattle and horse raising, and still later, banking. He is now interested in four different banks, being vice president of the First National Bank of Pawhuska, vice president of the First National Bank of Foraker, president of the Bank of Bigheart, a state bank, and a director in the Bank of Prue, also a state bank. These institutions are all located in Osage County. Some of the richest oil and gas fields in the Osage Nation have been developed by the Pawhuska Oil & Gas Company, of which Mr. Leahy is vice president, and he holds a similar office in the Pawhuska-Cleveland Gas & Oil Company. At a fine stock ranch and farm two miles north of Pawhuska, he has a thousand acres comprising one of the model estates of Northeastern Oklahoma. In addition he has twenty-one quarter sections of land elsewhere in Osage County. As a stock man he keeps about a thousand head of cattle and has some sixty registered Hereford cows. He gives his personal superintendence to the management of his large farm. In Pawhuska he is half owner in a large store building on Main Street, built at a cost of $14,000, owns a garage building that cost $4,500, and has a number of residences in that city. Mr. Leahy recently completed a home on Main Street that cost $12,000 and represents all the modern ideals of comfort and attractiveness of architectural arrangement and appearance.

A democrat throughout his active political career, Mr. Leahy is one of the energetic and public spirited leaders of his home county and in more recent years of the state. He served for about ten years on the Osage council, and for four year was treasurer of the Osage Nation. He was a member of the committee that drafted the Osage allotment bill and in the interests of his people spent the greater part of three winters in Washington, D. C., advocating the passage of this allotment bill through Congress. The people of Oklahoma will recall how, a few years ago, Mr. Leahy was arrested by the Interior Department on the charge of having attempted to intimidate the Osage council in behalf of some measures which were before it for consideration. Several other well known men were involved in the same charge, but after a trial which went on for six weeks in Oklahoma City before Federal Judge Cottrell and a jury, Mr. Leahy was not only acquitted, but completely exonerated from every particular of the indictment. During the administration of Governor Cruce Mr. Leahy served on the State Board of Agriculture until that body was reduced by the Legislature from ten to five members, and though offered reappointment under Governor Williams, he declined the honor on account of the demands upon his time made by his large private business affairs.

Mr. Leahy is a member of both the State and National Bankers' associations, is a Catholic, in which faith he was reared, a member of the Knights of Columbus, and of the Benevolent and Protective Order of Elks. Having spent most of his life among the Osage people, he has a fluent command of the Osage language. He is a fine type of the successful business man, positive, energetic, a hard worker in everything he undertakes, public spirited and always ready to engage his energies and resources in behalf of some movement that will affect the welfare of the community and the people among whom he lives.

On January 28, 1897, Mr. Leahy married Miss Martha E. Rogers, a daughter of the late Thomas L. Rogers, one of the most prominent characters in the Osage Nation, a sketch of whose career is found on other pages of this publication. Mr. and Mrs. Leahy have two sons: William Timothy, Jr., and Thomas B.

BRUCE LAZZELL KEENAN. For over twenty years Mr. Keenan has been identified with the old Cherokee capital of Tahlequah, and has attained prominence in professional circles as an able and thorough lawyer, has taken a leading part in civic movements, and in numerous ways has contributed to the material welfare of that section of Oklahoma. Mr. Keenan came into the Cherokee Nation from Kansas to take the position of Commissioner of the United States Court at Tahlequah, and when his duties in that position were terminated with statehood he resumed the active private practice of law, in which he has been eminently successful.

Though most of his professional life has been spent in the West Mr. Keenan is a native of West Virginia, having been born on a farm near Morgantown, October 16, 1856. His father, John P. Keenan, was born in Pennsylvania, a son of Hugh Keenan, a native of Ireland. Mr. Keenan's mother was Nancy Lazzell, also a native of West Virginia and of English lineage.

The environment of a West Virginia farm encompassed the youth of Mr. Keenan, and he took from that a hardy constitution and the advantages of home and district school training to the University of West Virginia, from which he was graduated in 1880. Then came a period of school teaching, by which means he earned the money necessary to defray his expenses through law school. In 1885 he was graduated from the law department of his home state university, and soon after completing his law course he came West and located at Wichita, Kansas. Mr. Keenan was engaged in the active practice of law at Wichita until April, 1894, when his appointment to the duties of United States Commissioner caused his removal to Tahlequah. This important office he most creditably filled until statehood, in 1907, and in the past eight years has built up a large and remunerative practice as a lawyer.

In 1890 Judge Keenan married Miss Alice M. Overstreet, who comes of the Indiana family of Overstreets, many of whom have become prominent in business, in professional circles and in politics. Five children have been born to their union, Robert Bruce Keenan, a lawyer at Sapulpa, Oklahoma; Margaret, wife of Chester O. Holly, of Stigler, Oklahoma; Hypatia, wife of Thurman Wyly, of Tahlequah; and Claude and John Kenneth, both at home. In politics Judge Keenan has always upheld the principles and policies of the republican party. He is a Master Mason, and in his personal relations is noted for his unostentatious bearing, has a great many friends gained through more than twenty years of residence in Eastern Oklahoma, and among them is marked with every esteem.

WILLIAM M. EDDY. A resident of Cimarron County since 1897, William M. Eddy has taken an important and helpful part in the development of this section, and particularly of the Town of Kenton. He was the first county treasurer under statehood, from 1900 to 1907 practically had charge of the Kenton Postoffice, and in 1914 was appointed postmaster, which position he holds at this time. Mr. Eddy has also been identified prominently with business affairs, and both in commercial and public life has substantially entrenched himself in the confidence and esteem of the people.

William M. Eddy was born in a log house on a farm in Guadalupe County, Texas, December 4, 1861, and is a son of Lynch T. and Fannie R. (Giles) Eddy. Lynch T. Eddy was born in 1832, on a plantation in Shelby County, Kentucky, a son of William and Sallie Eddy, natives of Kentucky, and members of old and honored families of that state. He removed to Texas in 1858 and settled on a farm in Guadalupe County, where he was residing at the outbreak of the war between the states, and enlisted as a private in a Texas infantry regiment, under the flag of the Confederacy. In 1866 he returned to Kentucky, took up the study of medicine and became a prominent practitioner of Louisville, with a large and representative practice. In 1888 he was chosen a member of a medical board sent to Jacksonville, Florida, to stamp out a serious yellow fever epidemic, and became one of the martyrs to the cause, himself contracting the disease, from which he did not recover. His death occurred in the same year. In 1860, while a resident of Texas, Doctor Eddy was married to Miss Fannie R. Giles, who was born in 1843, in Tennessee, daughter of William T. Giles, a native of that state. Mr. and Mrs. Eddy became the parents of four sons and one daughter: William M.; Cordelia P., born in 1863; Alexander Campbell, born in 1866; Stuart T., born in 1868; and Roy, born in 1870. All the children survive.

William M. Eddy was educated in the public schools of Louisville, Kentucky, and at the age of twenty years began teaching as a profession. Not long thereafter he went to Guadalupe County, Texas, where for four years he divided his time between teaching school and farming, and then turned his attention to mercantile pursuits as salesman in a general store at Waring, Texas. Next, Mr. Eddy had two years of experience in the hotel business, conducting a hostelry at Lockhart, Texas, but in 1897 disposed of his interests in that venture and came to Oklahoma, where he resumed his activities as an educator. After three years of teaching in the public schools of Cimarron County, he once more became a salesman in a store at Kenton, and from 1900 until 1907 served also as assistant postmaster here, a capacity in which he was practically at the head of the office. In 1907 Mr. Eddy was elected county treasurer of Cimarron County, being the first incumbent of that office under statehood, and discharged his duties in an energetic, capable and conscientious manner. At the expiration of his term of office he embarked in the general merchandise business at Kenton, successfully conducting a store until 1914, when he was appointed by President Wilson to his present position as postmaster. He has worked faithfully and energetically to improve the mail service, and his labors have won him the gratitude and regard of his fellow-townsmen. Mr. Eddy is a democrat and one of the influential men in the councils of his party in Cimarron County. He can be depended upon to give his support to all movements which are launched in behalf of the public good, and to give liberally of his time and abilities in advancing education and good citizenship.

Mr. Eddy was married at Waring, Texas, August 8, 1888, to Miss Fannie V. Palmer, who was born January 25, 1864, at Westpoint, Mississippi, daughter of B. T. and Fannie (Cliett) Palmer, natives of Mississippi. For a number of years prior to her marriage Mrs. Eddy was a teacher in the public schools. They are the parents of seven children, as follows: Palmer, born June 20, 1890; Marcellus R., born October 8, 1891; Richard Baxter, born December 2, 1893; Douglass A., born September 20, 1895; Oran, born December 20, 1897; Cordelia P., born January 20, 1900; and Arthur C., born December 4, 1904.

OSCAR A. LAMBERT, M. D. For a number of years Doctor Lambert was the leading physician and had the biggest practice of any doctor in Marietta, Ohio. He has been known less as a physician and more as a leader of enterprise and of big affairs since coming to Oklahoma. In fact, it may be said without disparagement of his other fellow citizens, that Doctor Lambert has been more vitally identified with the growth and upbuilding of Okmulgee as a city than any other person. He has helped accomplish big things for the town, and is a big man for the work, big in heart as well as resources. While successful in business affairs, he is none the less liberal and generous in everything he does. In fact, as has been said, he is the man who meets the stranger within the gates of Okmulgee and makes him like the town before he leaves it.

His has been a many sided career. Like many substantial men, he tried in his earlier years several lines with indifferent success. He found his real vocation when he entered medicine, and from that has passed into the ranks of men of affairs. He was born near Plantsville in Morgan County, Ohio, October 16, 1865, a son of Reece B. and Lydia (Hanson) Lambert. His parents were both of Quaker stock; they held strongly to that religion themselves and they reared Doctor Lambert to the simple belief of the faith. Notwithstanding the aversion of Quakers to warfare, Doctor Lambert has a relative, General Lambert, who distinguished himself in the battle of New Orleans under General Jackson at the close of the War of 1812. The parents were both born in Belmont County, Ohio, were married there, and afterwards went to Morgan County, where they still reside. The father is a retired farmer and lives at Chesterhill, Ohio. During his active career he was noted for his progressiveness, and was always ready and among the first to use the improvements and innovations which came into his rural district.

Doctor Lambert himself was reared as a farmer boy, and among other accomplishments he has a very practical knowledge of agriculture in all its phases. His early education came from public and private schools, he attended Bartlett Academy in his native state, and during three winters he taught school, while the summers were spent in farming. Having pursued a course of law study, he did some "pettifogging," as he calls it, for a time, but never became enrolled among the members of the Ohio bar. For three years he was in the general merchandising business, until stricken with typhoid fever. During his long recuperation from that sickness he determined to take up the study of medicine. In consequence three years were spent in Starling Medical College at Columbus, Ohio, from which he had his degree M. D. in 1894. He was a member of a class of thirty-three, and went out from college with the first honors of his class and with two prizes in addition. After two years of preliminary practice at Chesterhill in his native county he settled at Marietta, the old and historic city on the Ohio River, and for fifteen years lived there, and in that time he enjoyed the largest practice in the town.

At the same time he was active in public affairs. Though reared a republican he became a Bryant democrat and has been affiliated with the democratic party since 1896. While in Ohio he was a candidate for the Legislature and at one time refused the nomination for congress. He was elected mayor of Marietta. Besides handling his large medical practice he organized three industrial companies at Marietta, and became interested in oil fields while there. He also organized the Marietta Journal, and was active in the management of that publication for a time.

It was journalism to which he first turned his attention after coming to Oklahoma. A year before statehood Doctor Lambert located at Okmulgee, and in company with J. J. Maroney bought the Okmulgee Democrat. He retained his interest in that paper until 1915.

Doctor Lambert is president of the Okmulgee Interurban Railroad, and it was due to his management that it became a paying proposition after a long struggle with adversity. His business interests also extend to the holding of some oil properties, and he is developing several leases in the Oklahoma field. Doctor Lambert does little practice now and in fact medicine is only an incident of his busy life. He is a director of the Chamber of Commerce and has been identified with that body ever since it was organized. Anything that concerns Okmulgee and its welfare concerns Doctor Lambert. By common consent he is the vitalizing factor in many of the town's most important affairs. He is a member of the official board of the Methodist Episcopal Church and is superintendent of the largest Sunday school in Okmulgee. Fraternally he is affiliated with the Knights of Pythias, the Independent Order of Odd Fellows and the Modern Woodmen of America.

On December 2, 1889, Doctor Lambert married Carrie E. Lewis. She was born in Ohio but was living in Pennsylvania at the time of her marriage. They had two sons: Ernest C., who is now associated with his father in business affairs; and Harold, who died at the age of nine years.

JOSEPH BOWDEN TIMS. The community of Paden in Okfuskee County will long remember the enterprise and the fine character of the late Joseph Bowden Tims, who died there at his home July 18, 1911. He was the first man to make investments of any importance in that town and surrounding community, and was essentially a business man, thoroughgoing, upright, and with a record for integrity and fair dealing that followed him after death.

He was born at Keechi, Louisiana, September 25, 1866, the youngest of seven children born to Amos and Mary E. (Kinnard) Tims. Both parents were natives of Mississippi, and his father, who was a shoemaker, died at Timpson, Texas. The mother is still living in East Texas. Joseph B. Tims was still an infant when his parents moved into East Texas and located at Nacogdoches, where he grew to manhood. His education came from the common schools, and at the age of sixteen he started out in life on his own account, at that time manifesting the enterprise and self reliance which were always his most striking characteristics.

Going out to West Texas, he had a life of eventful experience, and finally became a lumber merchant at Fort Worth, Texas. He followed business there until the panic of 1908, and in 1909 he moved to the new community of Paden in Okfuskee County, Oklahoma, which was his home for one year only, but in that time he impressed his ability and influence in many ways. He made extensive investments in lands, in stock, and was also the mainspring of mercantile activity. He had acquired extensive holdings in the oil fields, though he did not live to see the land developed in its mineral deposits.

He was a democrat, though always a business man and not a politician. His church was the Christian denomination.

At Weatherford, Texas, June 17, 1896, Mr. Tims married Miss Nancy J. Taylor, who was born near Fayetteville, Arkansas, April 25, 1869. When six months of age she moved to Texas with her parents, Ezekiel E. Taylor and wife, to whom reference is made on other pages, and she grew up in Parker County and lived in that section of the Lone Star State until 1909, when she came with her husband to Paden, Oklahoma. Mrs. Tims, since the death of Mr. Tims, has shown remarkable business judgment and ability in the management of the estate and is thoroughly capable of safeguarding her own interests and in managing and increasing the value of the property left her. She takes an active part in the Order of the Eastern Star and is a member of the Cumberland Presbyterian Church.

Mrs. Tims became the mother of four children: Rita May, who died at Weatherford, Texas, at the age of eight years; Oscar William, Vergil Elbert and Eugene Paul.

WILLARD NEWTON LEWIS. Along with general success has come at least one interesting distinction in the career of Mr. Lewis as an Oklahoma lawyer. In February, 1901, he was appointed city attorney of

Davis, his present home town. He still holds the office, and has been continuously its incumbent for fifteen years. This makes him in point of continuous service the oldest city attorney in the state. He has filled this office so creditably and with so much valuable service to his home town that no other man has been considered for the place so long as Mr. Lewis will consent to remain.

While a member of the legal profession more than twenty years, Mr. Lewis has always been active in the affairs of the Methodist Episcopal Church South and comes of a family that has furnished a number of ministers to that denomination. His people originally came from Wales and settled in Maryland in colonial times, representatives subsequently moving to North Carolina, thence to Alabama, and finally to Mississippi. His grandfather, Rev. Wiley Lewis, was born in North Carolina in 1820 and died in Choctaw County, Mississippi, in 1885. He was a minister of the Methodist Episcopal Church South.

James A. Lewis, father of the Oklahoma attorney, who was born in Alabama in 1835, has for sixty years been an active member of the Methodist Church and for fifty years has filled official positions, such as steward, trustee and superintendent of the Sunday school. He was reared in Chickasaw County, Mississippi, and for many years operated a fine farm of 600 acres eleven miles south of Houston, the county seat of Chickasaw County. He still owns that property but is now living retired in Houston. During the war between the states he was a Confederate soldier for three and a half years. He was in the great Georgia campaign under Gen. Joseph E. Johnston in the sturdy opposition to the advance of Sherman's army. He has for the past half century been a member of the Masonic fraternity. As a democrat he represented his party four times in the State Legislature, was for six years a supervisor of Chickasaw County and spent many years on the County Pension Board. He married Bettie Foster who was born in Alabama in 1837 and died at Houston, Mississippi, in 1913. Their children were: T. W. Lewis, who is now pastor of St. John's Methodist Episcopal Church at Memphis, Tennessee; Nannie, who died in July, 1915, at Jackson, Mississippi, was the wife of F. A. Whitson, a Methodist minister who died at New Albany, Mississippi, in 1899; Willard Newton, who is the third in order of age; E. S. Lewis, pastor of the Methodist Episcopal Church at Oxford, Mississippi; John Silas who was born in 1875, was a general mechanic by trade and died at Houston, Mississippi, in 1908; William Finis, a twin brother of John S., who died in 1882; and Dixie, who is a bookkeeper at Chattanooga, Tennessee.

Willard Newton Lewis was born near Atlanta in Chickasaw County, Mississippi, October 11, 1865, and acquired his early education in the common schools of that county. In 1886 he graduated A. B. from the Mississippi State Normal School at Buena Vista, and in 1894 took his degree in law from the University of Mississippi. Beginning practice at Magnolia, Arkansas, he remained there three years, and this was followed by three years of work in the educational field. In 1897 he taught at Atlanta, Arkansas, one year and taught at Bagwell, Texas, in 1898 and 1899.

Mr. Lewis has lived in Davis, Oklahoma, and been engaged in general civil and criminal practice as a lawyer there since May, 1900. He has served on the school board nine years and exercises considerable influence in the democratic party of Murray County. He is a steward and trustee in the local Methodist Episcopal Church South, has been local lay leader and district lay leader and for the past year and a half has been a lay preacher. He also takes much interest in fraternal matters. He is affiliated with Ivanhoe Lodge No. 116, Knights of Pythias, at Davis, of which he is past chancellor commander, and since 1906 has been a trustee of the Grand Lodge and was formerly grand vice chancellor of the state; is a member of Tyre Lodge No. 42, Ancient Free and Accepted Masons, at Davis; and of Cedar Camp No. 42, Woodmen of the World. Professionally he is a member of the County and State Bar associations and of the Commercial Law League of America.

On December 25, 1893, at Kilmichael, Mississippi, he married Miss Lillie Williams, whose father, R. A. Williams is a farmer at Kilmichael. Mrs. Lewis died in the sanitarium at Ardmore, Oklahoma, April 7, 1905. On December 27, 1909, at Oklahoma City he married Miss Hattie Ruth Collins. Her father was the late Dr. G. H. Collins, a physician and surgeon, and her mother, Mrs. Maud Collins, is still living at Oklahoma City. Mr. Lewis has no children by either marriage.

MONTFERD W. PUGH. One of the men who have assisted in making history in that district of Oklahoma formerly known as No Man's Land is Montferd W. Pugh, now serving in his fourth consecutive term as county judge of Cimarron County, and recognized as a lawyer of very high attainment and with a practice hardly second to any of his professional brethren in that section of the state.

Judge Pugh was born August 28, 1878, on a farm in Perry County, Illinois, a son of Charles E. and Margaret Jane (Peery) Pugh. His father, who was also born in Perry County, Illinois, in 1848, was a son of William and Betsie Pugh, natives of Ohio, who moved to Illinois as pioneer settlers in 1842. Grandfather Pugh died there in 1854, followed a few years later by his wife. Charles E. Pugh spent his active career as a farmer in Perry County, Illinois, where he died March 4, 1890. He was married in 1872 to Miss Peery, who was born in 1852 in Perry County, Illinois, a daughter of James and Elizabeth (Lindsey) Peery, the former a native of Tennessee and the latter of Ohio. Charles E. Pugh and wife were the parents of four children, three sons and one daughter: Bertie, born in 1875 and died in 1880; Dollie, born in 1876 and died in the same year; Montferd W.; and Craig A., born in 1886, now a farmer and stock raiser in Cimarron County, and was married in 1914 to Edith Hanes.

Montferd W. Pugh was educated in the public schools at Tamaroa, Illinois, graduating from high school with the class of 1897. He then took a normal course in the Southern Illinois Normal University at Carbondale, and for four years did some successful work as a teacher in Perry County and at the same time studied law. The years 1901-03 he spent in Valparaiso University at Valparaiso, Indiana, and was graduated in the law department with the class of 1903 and the degree LL. B. Following his admission to the Illinois bar he practiced three years in Pinckneyville in that state and for two years of that time was city attorney.

It was in 1906 that Mr. Pugh came to Oklahoma and his first location was at Texhoma, on the line between Oklahoma and Texas. He filed on a claim of land in Cimarron County and conducted a practice as a lawyer for one year at Texhoma. In February, 1908, he removed to Kenton, which was then the temporary county seat of Cimarron County. In September, 1908, he followed the county seat on its removal to the permanent location at Boise City.

His qualifications and ability as a lawyer were not

long in securing recognition in this part of Oklahoma, and in 1907 he was nominated on the democratic ticket and elected county judge of the newly organized Cimarron County. He was thus the first elected official in that capacity to preside over the county court of Cimarron County. He has since been regularly re-elected and now in his fourth consecutive term. Judge Pugh is a Knight Templar, and is also affiliated with the Independent Order of Odd Fellows.

On October 4, 1904, at St. Louis, Missouri, Judge Pugh married Miss Lora G. Jack. They were married during the year of the Louisiana Purchase Exposition, and the marriage ceremony was performed in the Illinois State Building on the fair grounds at St. Louis. Mrs. Pugh was born November 22, 1881, at Beaucoup, Illinois, a daughter of Samuel C. and Emma (Seibert) Jack, the former a native of Tennessee and the latter of Illinois. Mr. and Mrs. Pugh are members of the Methodist Episcopal Church South. To their marriage have been born three children: DeMotte J., born June 25, 1905, and died August 23, 1905; Paul G., born November 15, 1909; and Jack, born October 15, 1915.

JAMES A. YOUNG, M. D. A physician of many years experience, Doctor Young came to Oklahoma from Iowa, and since 1909 has been in practice at Britton, where he is senior member of the firm of Young & Stewart, physicians and surgeons. Doctor Young is regarded as one of the most expert medical men in Oklahoma County as an obstetrician and in the treatment of diseases of children.

James A. Young was born in Hancock County, Illinois, July 23, 1861, a son of Rev. W. M. and Lydia (Souther) Young. His father was a Baptist minister, and for many years was one of the best known and best loved men in the ministry of that church in the State of Iowa. He died in 1881.

Doctor Young spent his boyhood in Montrose, Iowa, where he attended public schools and there took up the study of medicine in the office of Dr. T. C. Hayes. Subsequently his studies were continued under Dr. John Bencher at Reiner, Missouri, and with that preliminary training he entered the College of Physicians and Surgeons at Keokuk, Iowa, where he was graduated M. D. in 1894. While in medical college he was a special student of obstetrics and diseases of children under Dr. F. B. Dorsey, an eminent authority on those subjects and a member of the faculty of the College of Physicians and Surgeons. For twenty years now Doctor Young, though a general practitioner, has found himself more and more in demand as a specialist in cases involving these subjects. He began practice at Acosta, Clark County, Missouri, but three years later removed to Bonaparte, Iowa, and from that state came to Britton, Oklahoma, in 1909, to join Doctor Stewart in practice.

In 1881 Doctor Young married Miss S. L. Stewart, a sister of his partner in the firm of Young & Stewart. their four children are: Mrs. Lydia Jane Norwood, whose husband is an employe of the Standard Oil Company at Britton; Mrs. Mary E. Scott, wife of another Standard Oil man at Owosso, Oklahoma;; Mrs. Gertrude Staley, wife of a hardware merchant at Oklahoma City; and James A. Young, agent for the Santa Fe Railroad Company at Plainview, Texas.

Doctor Young is a member of the Baptist Church and affiliates with the Camp of the Modern Woodmen of America. In Iowa he was a member of various medical and surgical organizations and since coming to Oklahoma has taken an important part in the development of his community. While his experience and practice has been of the broadest character, he has always been a student, and some years ago spent some time in post-graduate study in the Chicago Clinical Post-graduate School. He is regarded as one of the best informed and most successful practitioners in his part of the state.

B. F. STEWART, M. D. In Oklahoma more than in older states it is not difficult to trace the influence of one or more men in the building of a community. The history of almost every locality in the state is a record of what only a few men have planned and carried out. The statement of this fact serves to emphasize the importance of Doctor Stewart in addition to his regular service as a member of a profession, and at the same time it is not meant to detract from the good that other men of the community have done. One of the great improvements brought to Oklahoma by statehood was the Corporation Commission, which was given authority to regulate the action of public service corporations. Doctor Stewart was one of the leaders of a body of men of Britton who shortly after statehood, through appeal to the commission, procured for the town a modern depot, thus ridding it of a make-shift frontier-town affair. As the little prairie town on a hill immediately north of Oklahoma City began to take on metropolitan ways during the bright period of material prosperity for the entire country, the necessity of better roads and streets was apparent, and Doctor Stewart was among those who fostered a movement looking to highway improvement. His influence has been an important factor since the birth of the Town of Britton in the establishment of modern schools and providing them with modern equipment; in selecting progressive men for town and school board offices; in the erection and maintenance of churches, and in the elevation of health, morals and public welfare.

Dr. B. F. Stewart was born in Iowa in 1869, a son of James and Jane (Payne) Stewart. His father, a native of Scotland, was a mechanic and an early settler of Iowa, and the mother's people, the Paynes, were also early comers to the same state, of English extraction. Doctor Stewart has three brothers and one sister: Mrs. J. A. Young, wife of a physician at Britton who is a partner of Doctor Stewart; William Stewart, a miner in Montana; John L. Stewart, an Iowa farmer; James A. Stewart, farmer, of Missouri, and A. T. Stewart, who lives in British Columbia.

Doctor Stewart was educated in the public schools of Iowa and in 1900 graduated M. D. from the Keokuk Medical College at Keokuk, Iowa. In the summer following his graduation he began the practice of medicine in his native state, but later in the same year moved to Oklahoma locating at Britton. He interrupted his private practice in 1907 to take a post-graduate course in the Chicago Post-Graduate School.

On August 18, 1901, Doctor Stewart married Miss Florence McCollum at Walton, Kansas. Mrs. Stewart had been a teacher for several years in the public schools of Iowa. They have an adopted child, Helen Bell, aged two years. Doctor Stewart is a member of the Methodist Episcopal Church, is affiliated with the Independent Order of Odd Fellows, and as already indicated has been a member of various organizations that sought the betterment of conditions in his home town. He is a successful physician, and has built up a large clientele in the Town of Britton and the community round about. He is a member of the firm of Young & Stewart, and a sketch of his partner in practice is given in preceding sketch.

CHARLES T. C. SCHRADER. The Town of Bristow in Creek County has come into particular prominence as the center of one of the greatest oil districts in the country.

It is comparatively a new town and in ten years' time its progress has been phenomenal. One of the early men of medicine to locate in the community was Dr. Charles T. C. Schrader, whose home has been there almost ten years. Doctor Schrader has proved himself not only a very capable physician, but has made himself a factor in community affairs to a large extent and is one of the very substantial men of that young city.

He is an Indiana man, having been born on a farm near Evansville in that state April 6, 1879. His parents are Charles O. and Margaret (Klippert) Schrader. Both parents were born near the City of Berlin, Germany, the mother on February 29, 1835, and the father in December, 1835. She was brought by her parents to the United States when eight years of age, and grew to young womanhood in New Orleans. The father was fourteen years old when he came to this country, and grew to manhood at Evansville, Indiana. For fully forty years they have lived on one farm in Indiana, and it was on that place that Doctor Schrader was born. The parents are devout Methodists, and in politics the father is a republican. He showed his loyalty to his adopted country by enlisting during the Civil war and serving three years, ten months, being honorably discharged at the close of hostilities. He has for many years been identified with the Grand Army of the Republic. In the family were twelve children, six sons and six daughters, eleven of whom are still living, with Doctor Schrader next to the youngest.

His early life was spent on the old Indiana farm and he lived with his parents until he was seventeen. His early educational advantages were sufficient to qualify him as a teacher and he spent two years in that vocation. He first chose a business career and after a course in bookkeeping at the Bryant & Stratton Business College he spent a year in clerical work, and then took a more definite step by entering the Hospital College of Medicine at Louisville, Kentucky. He remained a student there until awarded his degree M. D. in 1905.

During the first year out of college Doctor Schrader practiced at Evansville, Indiana. In May, 1907, he arrived in Bristow, and here his office and home have been during the succeeding years, and with the growth and development of the town and tributary country his practice has assumed proportions that tax his energies. For seven years of his residence he has served as county physician and is still holding that position. More recently he has become identified with the oil industry and has some valuable holdings in the Bristow district.

For two years he was a member of the Town Council. In politics he is a republican and in Masonry has attained the thirty-second degree of Scottish Rite. In 1907 Doctor Schrader married Miss Dollie Bogle, a native of Kansas. Their three children are named Marjorie, George and Theodore Roosevelt.

FRANK C. RUSSEL. A man of inviolable integrity, of buoyant and optimistic nature and of fine intellectuality, the late Frank C. Russel became one of the pioneer settlers in Garfield County, Oklahoma, at the time when the historic Cherokee Strip was thrown open for settlement in 1893. Here he passed the remainder of his life, a citizen of much prominence and influence in community affairs, and his character and achievement were such that there is all of consistency in offering in this history of the state of his adoption a tribute to his memory.

Mr. Russel was born on a farm in Stewart County, Tennessee, August 13, 1860, and died of paralysis on the 19th of July, 1914, so that his death occurred shortly before the fifty-fourth anniversary of his birth. He was buried in the cemetery at Canton, Kansas. He was a son of John and Mary E. (Sypert) Russel, the former of whom was born in Pennsylvania and the latter in Tennessee. John Russel was proud of being the descendent of a Mayflower passenger. In Tennessee he became a successful planter and representative citizen of Stewart County, where he continued his residence until the early '70s, when he sold his property in that state and removed with his family first to Illinois thence to Kansas, where he became one of the pioneer settlers of McPherson County. He there reclaimed and developed a valuable farm near Canton and lived up to the full tension of the pioneer era in the history of the Sunflower State, and was uniformly esteemed as a citizen of sterling worth and of marked industry and progressiveness. Both he and his wife continued their residence in McPherson County until their death, and their children, five sons and one daughter, are living. He was a stanch Presbyterian worthy of his Puritan fathers, and in politics a republican. His wife was a woman known for her practical Christianity and executive ability, her love and loyalty.

Frank C. Russel acquired his rudimentary education in the schools of his native state and was eleven years of age when he accompanied his parents to the pioneer wilds of Kansas, where he was reared to maturity in McPherson County, and where he continued his studies in the pioneer schools until he had completed the curriculum of the high school at Salina, the county seat of Saline County. For several years thereafter he was a successful and popular teacher in the schools of Central Kansas, where also he continued to be concerned with agricultural pursuits.

In 1893 Mr. Russel was one of those who came to Oklahoma Territory and participated in the opening of the Cherokee Strip or Outlet, which was thrown open to settlement in that year. He entered claim to a tract of land in Garfield County, at a point 3½ miles southwest of the present thriving Town of Hunter, and there he vigorously instituted the homesteading of a farm, the while he became one of the prominent and influential men in the new community, to the civic and material development and progress of which he contributed in generous measure. While improving his farm he also found requisition for his services as a teacher in the pioneer schools of the county. As a man of mature judgment and much public spirit he was naturally called upon to serve in various local offices of trust.

In 1909 Mr. Russel purchased the plant and business of the Hunter Enterprise, a weekly paper published at Hunter. He vitalized this newspaper and made it an effective vehicle through which to exploit and foster the interests of the town and county as well as to further the cause of the democratic party and to direct popular sentiment and action. After continuing as editor and publisher of the Enterprise for two years, impaired health compelled him to abandon this field of enterprise and he sold the property to D. H. Perry.

Mr. Russel was one of the leaders in the councils and campaign activities of the democratic party in Garfield County and served with characteristic ability. He was an earnest and devoted member of the Christian Church, and he was a deacon of the church of this denomination at Hunter at the time of his death. Mr. Russel commanded high place in the confidence and good will of all who knew him and in his death the community mourned the loss of one of its most honored and valued citizens.

On the 13th of May, 1897, in Superior, Nebraska, was solemnized the marriage of Mr. Russel to Miss Anna C. Sypert, who still maintains her home at Hunter, no children having been born to their union. Mrs. Russel was born at Hopkinsville, Kentucky, on the 13th of September, 1870, and is a daughter of Col. Leonidas A.

and Martha D. (Henry) Sypert. After duly availing herself of the advantages of the public schools of her native place she there continued her studies at South Kentucky College. After leaving this institution she was for two years a popular teacher in the schools of that section of the old Blue Grass State. In 1891 she removed to McPherson, Kansas, where for six years she continued her successful work as a teacher in the public schools, in the meantime taking a normal course at McPherson College. In 1897 she came to Oklahoma Territory with her husband where she continued her service as a teacher for a period of five years. When her husband assumed control of the Hunter Enterprise Mrs. Russel became his able coadjuter in the editorial work of the paper, and in this connection her exceptional literary talent, her broad intellectual ken and her definite public spirit gained to her a wide reputation as one of the able representatives of the journalistic profession in Oklahoma. She became an active and valued member of the State Editorial Association, of which she served as a vice president in 1911. She still continues to a certain extent her literary activities and is a popular leader in the representative social activities of her home community, as well as in the work of the Christian Church.

Col. Leonidas A. Sypert, father of Mrs. Russel, was born in Lebanon, Tennessee, on the 15th of December, 1832, and died at Hopkinsville, Kentucky, on the 23d of March, 1892. He acquired a finished education and was a graduate of Lebanon, Tennessee, Law School, soon after becoming a member of the Hopkinsville bar. He represented Kentucky as a gallant soldier and officer of the Confederate service in the Civil war, became an eminent member of the Kentucky bar, and in addition to continuing many years in the active work of his profession he was also prominent and influential in political affairs in his section of the Blue Grass State. In Kentucky was solemnized his marriage to Miss Martha D. Henry, who was born at Hopkinsville, that state, on the 23d of February, 1850, and who was a daughter of Col. William Henry of that place and Martha D. (Cocke) Henry of Mississippi, both members of old and cultured families. Their lineage traces back to stanch Scotch and English origin, both the Henry and Cocke families having been founded in America in the early colonial era of our national history.

WILLIAM M. SPECK is one of the men who helped to place the new town of Dewey on the map as a commercial and industrial center. His home has been there for the past fifteen years, and the town has no citizen of broader interests, of greater public spirit, or one whose energies have gone more effectively into movements which make for real progress.

His career began with his birth at Bedford, Pennsylvania, September 3, 1850. Pennsylvania was also the native state of his parents, Henry and Mary (England) Speck. His father, who was a shoemaker by trade, died in Ohio, March 28, 1893, and the mother passed away at the same place in 1898.

One in a family of ten children, William M. Speck since early boyhood has depended largely upon his own resources and has found his own opportunities in the world. At the age of twenty-one he left Pennsylvania, where he had gained his early education and had learned the trade of shoemaker, and for some years was engaged in the shoemaker's trade and shoe merchandising in Ohio. Subsequently for about two years he conducted a grocery store and also sold musical merchandise. Finally giving up his business interests in Ohio, Mr. Speck located himself with the newer country of Kansas, locating in Sumner County in that state about 1883. In 1884 he moved to Garfield County, Kansas, and secured a preemption homestead claim. At Ravanna, Kansas, he built a hotel and was its proprietor for five years. In 1889 he was elected to the legislature on the republican ticket, and in 1891 was returned for a second term. He helped to organize Garfield County. About 1893 he removed to Topeka, conducted a hotel in that city for a year, and selling out continued his hotel enterprise for four years at Independence, Missouri.

Coming to Dewey, Oklahoma, in 1900, Mr. Speck established the Dewey Hotel and also the Right-Way Hotel at Bartlesville. He proved an energetic booster for both these growing young cities, and also interested himself in the larger political life of the territory, serving as a delegate from Washington County at the national capital in the interests of statehood. For several years Mr. Speck has devoted his time primarily to farming and fruit growing, and has some handsome and valuable property in and about Dewey. In 1914 he was republican candidate for the state senate from Washington and Tulsa counties, and though on the minority party ticket his defeat was accomplished by only forty-eight votes. Mr. Speck is at the present time president of the Washington County Fair Association. He was also one of the promoters of the interurban line between Bartlesville and Dewey, which is one of the pioneer electric transportation lines in the state.

On December 25, Christmas Day, of 1874, Mr. Speck married Miss Christina Levers, a daughter of David and Mary (Kaylor) Levers. Mrs. Speck was one of a family of twelve children. To their marriage have been born three sons. Howard is still single and living at home in Dewey. Lloyd married Miss Grace Hunt of Ossawatomie, Kansas, and their two children are named Glenn and Thomas. Roscoe, who lives in Kansas, married Miss Sadie Clay, and they have a child named Emma. Mr. Speck is affiliated with the Loyal Order of Moose and the Homesteaders, and both he and his wife are members of the Methodist Episcopal Church. While a resident of Ohio, Mr. Speck spent several years in Stark County, and during 1881-2 was chairman of the republican central committee of that Ohio county, the county seat of which is Canton, the old home of President McKinley and wife. Mr. Speck was a personal friend of President McKinley, and during the latter's first campaign for the presidency in 1896 he wrote a personal letter to Mr. Speck, who was at that time living in Kansas.

Mr. Speck is interested in good farming in Washington County and is doing all he can to boost this movement.

OLIN W. MEACHAM. Those individuals who have given their energy, skill, ambitious vigor and enthusiasm in the building up of a community are benefactors of humanity, and their names cannot be held in too high esteem. In every undertaking there must be a logical beginning, and a man who lays the foundation for what afterwards may become a flourishing city must have the courage of his convictions and unlimited confidence in the future of the location which he selects as the scene of his endeavors. One of the best small cities in Eastern Oklahoma is Henryetta in Okmulgee County. The mayor of that little city is Olin W. Meacham. Mr. Meacham was for thirteen years postmaster of the town. He came here attracted by the beauty of the site and the presence of coal deposits nearby, and fifteen years ago was one of the "fathers of Henryetta" and from the day he helped lay out the townsite his keen mind and boundless enthusiasm have kept him looking beyond the narrow horizon of the day and reading the signs of a splendid tomorrow.

By profession he is an old newspaper man and printer, and was identified with early Kansas journalism as well as with some of the first newspapers in the original Oklahoma Territory. It is an interesting fact that he is one of the survivors of the famous group of "Oklahoma boomers" headed by Captain Payne during the '80s. Thus there are many interesting features of Mr. Meacham's career. His most permanent work has without doubt been the building up of Henryetta. He exercised not only enthusiasm but good judgment in promoting this town in the early days. He sold a large number of lots for less than they were worth in order to get people located in the town. The first private residence there was put up by him in 1900, a box house of the simplest character, 20x20 feet. He also constructed the brick flue attached to any house or building, and also had the first plastered house. In the past fifteen years he has built three homes for himself, and now has one of the most attractive residences of the town. He was given the choice of a large stretch of land along the railroad when it was constructed for townsite purposes, and after much investigation chose what is now Henryetta.

An Illinois man, Olin W. Meacham was born near Rushville in Schuyler County March 16, 1858, a son of Ahira Gault and Mary E. (Jewell) Meacham. His father was born at Rochester, New York, in 1836, while the mother was born at Augusta, Maine. They were married at Mount Meacham, Illinois, a postoffice that was named in honor of Mr. Meacham's grandfather, who had located there about 1855. Mr. Meacham's mother died in Schuyler County in 1866 when he was about eight years of age. In 1872 the father took his family out to Kansas, and a number of years later came to Oklahoma in 1890, soon after the opening, and died at Guthrie about 1906. He was a carpenter and contractor nearly all his active career, though he did considerable farming while living in Kansas. During the Civil war period he enlisted in the hundred day service at the first call, and afterwards re-enlisted and remained until the close of the war. He was with a Missouri Regiment of engineers, and did some hard work in digging the canal which cut off Island No. 10 in the Mississippi River, one of the most notable exploits of Grant's army in opening up the river to the Federal invasion of the South. He afterwards took part in many pitched battles, and served as a non-commissioned officer. While living at Leon in Butler County, Kansas, he was in the real estate and loan business and put up the first opera house there. He was a strong prohibitionist and one of the men who lent their influence to the establishment of prohibition in Kansas. In general politics he was a republican, was a member of the Grand Army of the Republic, the Independent Order of Odd Fellows and the Methodist Episcopal Church. In 1869 the father married for his second wife Amelia Wright of Peru, Illinois. By this marriage there were three sons and one daughter, Olin W. Meacham is the only survivor of the first marriage, two children having died in infancy.

In 1874, when eighteen years of age, Olin W. Meacham left home and went to Marion, Kansas. In the meantime he had acquired a common school education. At Marion he was associated with E. W. Hoch, who a few years ago filled the distinguished position of Governor of Kansas. Mr. Hoch at that time had a printing office at Marion, and the two young men "bached" in the little building which served as an office and home. Mr. Meacham besides doing his share of the work around the printing office also performed the cooking, and on Sundays made the little office an impromptu barber shop. There was no regular barber in the town and he shaved most of the men who needed or wanted such service. He was associated with Mr. Hoch for a year and a half and employed his razor to good effect when Hoch celebrated his marriage.

He afterwards went to Augusta, Kansas, and worked on the Southern Kansas Gazette eight years. From there he went to Leon, and in 1881 married Olive L. Chambers, who was born in Missouri and was reared chiefly in Kansas. After his marriage Mr. Meacham returned to Augusta, conducted a paper for some time, later bought the Leon Quill and after selling that property moved to Greensburg in Kiowa County, where he managed the Kiowa County Times 2½ years. Then he was again in Augusta, where he managed the Augusta News, this later becoming the Industrial Advocate, and the plant was afterwards sold and moved to El Dorado, Kansas.

Mr. Meacham came to Oklahoma City in 1890, and was made foreman of the Daily Evening Gazette, being connected with that pioneer newspaper three years. From there he went to Norman to take charge as editor and manager of the Norman Transcript in 1893. He was with that journal three years. In 1896 he went to Shawnee, and with J. E. Queen established the Shawnee Quill. After 2½ years this paper was sold, and Mr. Meacham was then foreman on the Vinita Leader until 1900.

In that year he gave up journalism and associated with G. F. Clarke and Lake Moore chose and laid out the townsite of Henryetta. This town had its practical beginnings in March, 1900, and in September Mr. Meacham was appointed postmaster, succeeding Ed Ray, who had filled the office for about two months. For thirteen years he had full charge of the local postal service, from September, 1900, until July, 1913. When he took charge of the office the mail was kept in a cracker box, but when he left it thirteen years later the office was one feature of a thriving little city, and the fixtures alone were worth $2,500. He left it as a third class office, and in the meantime had given a service which was beyond criticism and which made him many strong personal friends in spite of politics. In fact, though he was a republican and living in a democratic community, a large number of his political opponents petitioned for him to keep the postoffice. From September, 1913, to February, 1914, he was in the banking business at Dewar, Oklahoma, and has also been identified with insurance. For one year after leaving the postoffice he was local editor of the Free Lance, but in 1915 was elected mayor, and is now giving most of his attention to that office. Henryetta's normal political complexion is about 400 democrats to 200 republicans, but he was elected on the republican ticket as mayor by a majority of 103.

Mr. Meacham served as secretary-treasurer of the Henryetta Townsite Company, and was also identified with the Kusa Townsite Company. A number of years ago (1895) he assisted Professor Amos in organizing the State Historical Society. He is a thirty-second degree Mason and Knight of Pythias, also a member of the Modern Woodmen of America, and is an elder in the Christian Church.

Mr. Meacham has two daughters: Bertha I., who is the wife of James Hawes of Henryetta and their children are named Olive Vermelle and James. Mary Vermelle, Mr. Meacham's younger daughter, has been connected with the Henryetta High School for the past eight years, and for four years was its principal.

DELANY G. ROGERS, of Buffalo, Oklahoma, has been an early settler in both the States of Kansas and Oklahoma. In fact, he has lived nearly all his life close to the frontier and in intimate touch with the people and the activities of a new country. Mr. Rogers only recently retired from the office of postmaster at Buffalo, a position he had held for a number of years. His chief vocation in life has been farming and stock raising, and it is the testimony of his friends and neighbors that whatever he does he does well.

His birth occurred in a log house on a farm in Jefferson County, Indiana, on April 6, 1862. His birth occurred while his father was away fighting the battles of the Union in the Civil war. His parents were Gamaliel and Lydia (Lewis) Rogers. His father was born November 17, 1840, in Jefferson County, Indiana, and was still a very young man when the war broke out. He served three years as a private in Company C of the Sixth Indiana Infantry, but with the exception of that service has spent all his active life as a farmer. From Indiana he moved out to Kansas in 1886, locating on government land in Clark County. That was his home for six years, after which he spent two years in Mead County, then returned to Clark County for eight years, and finally moved to Texas County, Missouri, where he still has his home. He has now reached the age of three quarters of a century, and has lived so usefully he can enjoy the comforts of retired existence. In 1858 Gamaliel Rogers married Lydia Lewis who was also born in Jefferson County, Indiana, August 17, 1840. To their marriage were born ten children, four sons and six daughters, namely: Florence, born December 5, 1860, was married in 1880 to Merritt M. Cosby and they now reside at Protection, Kansas; Delany G., who was the second in order of birth; Willis born in 1864 and died in 1885; Jessie, born in 1868, was married in 1888 to Charles Pauley, and they now live at Oklahoma City; John Belle, born in 1870, is now an osteopathic physician at Hastings, Oklahoma, and in 1905 she became the wife of Charles Morrison; Celia, born in 1872, married in 1910 Mr. L. Dees, and they now live at Rosston, Oklahoma; Samuel Nicholas, born in 1874, is a farmer in Harper County, Oklahoma; Tena, born in 1876, was married in 1908 to Charles Sworkey and they now live at Norman, Oklahoma; Pearl, born in 1878 was married in 1905 to William and they live in Beaver County, Oklahoma.

It was on a farm in Jefferson County, Indiana, that Delany G. Rogers spent his early youth. He had the advantages of the local public schools. The discipline of farm work gave him a rugged constitution, and the experience which he has utilized in his own active career. In 1884 he moved out to Clark County, Kansas, and secured a tract of Government land in a district which at that time had very few agricultural and permanent settlers. Mr. Rogers lived in Kansas until 1899, and in the meantime had improved an excellent farm there. In the latter year he moved to old Woodward County, Oklahoma, and again acquired a homestead, situated two miles from the Town of Buffalo. While Mr. Rogers' activities have kept him in town for a number of years, he still owns considerable land and has most of it under improvement.

On February 23, 1907, he was appointed postmaster of Buffalo, and continued the incumbent of the office through two terms until February 23, 1915. He is an active republican, is affiliated with the Independent Order of Odd Fellows and is a member of the Methodist Episcopal Church.

On October 16, 1884, at Taylorsville, Indiana, Mr. Rogers married Miss Isabelle Phillips, daughter of Madison and Mary (Wallace) Phillips. Mrs. Rogers was born June 11, 1860, in Jefferson County, Indiana, and her parents were natives of the same state. It will be recalled that Mr. Rogers left Indiana and went out into the new country of Kansas in 1884. He made that trip as his wedding journey, being accompanied by his young bride, and they journeyed across the country by wagon and team, like some of their pioneer ancestors who had come from a point still further east to the region of the Ohio Valley. Mr. and Mrs. Rogers are the parents of seven children, four sons and three daughters, namely: Ora Lawrence, born August 14, 1885, now the wife of Irwin Baker of Ashland, Kansas; Madison Gamaliel, born May 25, 1888, and still living at Buffalo; Estella Iris, born March 10, 1890, was married in 1908 to Piri Baker, and they now live at Protection, Kansas; Alta Rachel, born February 19, 1892; William McKinley, born May 10, 1894; John, born February 14, 1896; and Edward Taft, born August 20, 1907, died July 20, 1908.

WILLIAM C. PENDERGRAFT, M. D. The most enlightened tenets of medical and surgical science have found expression in the career of Dr. William C. Pendergraft, a general practitioner of Hollis, Harmon County, since 1902, a leading and progressive factor in business and financial circles, and a potent influence in advancing the civic interests of Hollis and the welfare of its people. He was born in Polk County, Missouri, September 22, 1864, and is a son of Joseph A. and Irene (Self) Pendergraft, and a member of a family which, originating in Germany, emigrated to England, came thence to America in colonial days, and from its original settlement in New York went during the pioneer days to Tennessee.

Joseph A. Pendergraft was born in 1838, in Cape Girardeau County, Missouri, and as a young man went to Polk County, in the same state, where he was married and where he subsequently engaged in farming and stockraising. Later he went to Arkansas and continued his agricultural operations until removing to Western Texas, where he lived on a ranch until 1899, and in that year came to Hollis, Oklahoma, and lived a retired life until his death in 1913. While a resident of Missouri, during the war between the states, Mr. Pendergraft enlisted in the Confederate army and served four years under Price and Shelby, and toward the close of the struggle was taken prisoner and confined in a Federal prison until peace was proclaimed. He was a stalwart democrat in his political views, and a lifelong member of the Christian Church, in which he served as elder for many years. He was married in Polk County, Missouri, to Miss Irene Self, who was born in Tennessee, in 1803, and died in Polk County, Missouri, in 1878, and they became the parents of six children, as follows: L. J., who is the widow of J. N. Hofman, a farmer, and resides in New Mexico; L. E., deceased, who was the wife of W. H. Hofman, also deceased, who was a mechanic in the employ of the Frisco Railroad Company for a period of forty years; S. E., who is the wife of R. C. Hodges, a farmer and stockman of Hollis, Oklahoma; J. M., who is an agriculturist of Harmon County; James C., who died in infancy; Mary E., who is the wife of M. C. Dodd and resides on the old homestead in Polk County, Missouri; and Dr. William C., of this review.

William C. Pendergraft received a graded and high school education in his native county, and after some preparation entered the Missouri Medical College, at St. Louis, Missouri, which he attended two years. He next entered the St. Louis College of Physicians and Surgeons, from which he was graduated in 1892, with the degree of Doctor of Medicine, and since that time, in 1915, has taken a post-graduate course at the Chicago Post-Graduate Medical School. Doctor Pendergraft entered upon the practice of his calling at Pleasant Hope, Missouri, where he continued to maintain his office until 1898, in that year going to a larger field at Springfield, in the same state, that being his place of residence until 1901. Coming next to Hollis, Oklahoma, he soon attracted to himself a large and representative practice, and has continued to make this thriving community his field of labor, his offices now being located in the Hollis Drug Company's building on Broadway, corner of Main Street. His practice is broad and general in its lines, and professionally he may be said to belong to the emancipated class whose mind is open to light and who sanction the beliefs of the past only insofar as they are in harmony with the greater progress and enlightenment of the present. In his private practice he has had charge of the welfare of the most representative families of Hollis, and has officiated at the birth of two sets of triplets and one set of quadruplets, the latter born to Mrs. F. M. Keys, of Hollis, June 4, 1915. In this case all four are girls, and it is the only case on record where all four have been of one sex and where all have lived. Aside from his private practice, Doctor Pendergraft is local surgeon for the Missouri, Kansas & Texas Railroad and medical examiner for more than a dozen of the old line life insurance companies. He holds membership in the Harmon County Medical Society, the Oklahoma Medical Society and the American Medical Association, and has been health officer of Hollis since the attainment of statehood. Doctor Pendergraft is one of those men who may be said to have chosen well their vocation. Possessed of a kind, sympathetic nature, a keen sense of discrimination, and a natural taste for the various branches of his honored profession, he has achieved a signal success. In politics he is a democrat, and was a member of the First Oklahoma Legislature. With his family he belongs to the Baptist Church. Doctor Pendergraft's fraternal connections are numerous. He belongs to Hollis Lodge No. 219, Ancient Free and Accepted Masons, in which he has filled all chairs save that of master; Hollis Camp, Independent Order of Odd Fellows, in which he is past grand; Hollis Camp, Woodmen of the World and the Woodmen Circle, of which he is medical examiner; the Modern Woodmen of America, of which he is medical examiner; and the Fraternal Union. He belongs also to the Commercial Club. The Doctor has also taken an active part in business affairs and is vice president of the State National Bank of Hollis and of the Hollis Drug Company, Incorporated.

In 1886, at Pleasant Hope, Missouri, Doctor Pendergraft was married to Miss Lena Mayfield, daughter of the late H. B. Mayfield, a farmer, and to this union there have been born three children: one who died in infancy; Roy L., a senior in the medical department of the Tennessee University; and Glen, who belongs to the freshman class at the Hollis High School.

JUDGE HENRY M. FURMAN, who died at his home in Oklahoma City in April, 1916, was one of the able lawyers and jurists who helped to mold and formulate the early jurisprudence of the state. From statehood until he had to retire on account of ill health he was one of the judges of the Oklahoma Criminal Court of Appeals.

His valuable services to the Oklahoma judiciary had their best appreciation and description in the words of Judge Thomas H. Doyle, presiding judge of the Criminal Court of Appeals, who was associated with Judge Furman as a member of that court from its organization. Judge Doyle has said:

"Judge Henry M. Furman, full of years and full of honor, has passed from life's labors to his eternal rest. He was an extraordinary man and a lawyer and jurist of rare endowments. His professional learning and ability was not the fruit of any advantages in legal education, but was founded on his large experience and inexhaustible diligence. In intellectual power he was a giant, and a logician of the highest order, and he was a consummate master of the rhetorical art.

"No judge ever more clearly realized the wide scope, exalted dignity and consequent responsibility of the judicial office, and no judge could be more scrupulous in inflexible fairness and impartiality. The force of his noble character and powerful mind is demonstrated by the results of his judicial labors. The value of his services and the high character of his contributions to the development of our criminal jurisprudence will grow in appreciation as years go by.

"Many of his opinions are now published as leading cases, and they have given the progressive criminal jurisprudence of Oklahoma an international reputation. I do not think it would be an extravagant statement to say that among the names of the great judges who adorn the annals of American jurisprudence will be found the name of Henry M. Furman.

"Personally Judge Furman was a kindly, genial, warm hearted man, whose devotion to high ideals, capacity for friendship, high minded patriotism and loyalty to duty and honor could be fully appreciated only by those who knew him intimately. The benevolence of his heart was in full accord with his master mind. I can safely say without disparagement to others that no man in public life in Oklahoma was held in higher esteem by the people of the state than Judge Henry M. Furman."

Judge Furman was a resident of Oklahoma twenty years. He was born in the Village of Society Hill, South Carolina, June 20, 1850, a son of Dr. Richard Furman, a Baptist minister, whose father was the founder of Furman University, Greenville, South Carolina. He acquired his primary education in Greenville and Sumter, South Carolina, spent several years working on a farm, and in 1871 came west, spending a year or so in the office of Judge J. L. Whitaker at New Orleans, and in 1872 going to Texas, where he taught school. In 1874 he was admitted to the bar at Brenham. After a brief practice at Comanche, Texas, he located in Bell County, and in 1876 was elected county attorney. This office he resigned the following year and entered upon the practice of his profession at Fort Worth. There he met Miss Frances Virginia Hutcheson, who, in May, 1879, became his wife, and who with their children, Henry Marshall Furman, Jr., and Miss Florence Furman, survive him. Their married life was an uninterrupted period of mutual love and comfort. In 1890 he moved to Denver, Colorado, and there engaged in the practice of law. In 1893 he moved back to Fort Worth. In 1895 he moved to Ardmore, and in 1904 he moved from there to Ada, Indian Territory.

He was the founder of the Masonic Home now located at Darlington, Oklahoma. At the democratic primary preceding the first state election he received the second highest number of votes for the office of United States senator, but in deference to a resolution passed at a previous meeting of the State Democratic Committee that the senators should be elected one from each of the former territories, he waived his right to the nomination. First appointed in 1908, he was twice elected as a judge of the Criminal Court of Appeals of Oklahoma, which position he held at the time of his death, being presiding judge the first four years of his service.

WILLIAM H. CAMPBELL, M. D. For the greater part of twenty years Doctor Campbell has practiced his profession in old Indian Territory and Oklahoma. He is now in the enjoyment of a substantial business at Hickory and has a high standing among Oklahoma medical men.

He was born in Randolph county, Arkansas, November 22, 1872. His great-grandfather was a Scotch-Irishman who came to this country and settled in Tennessee as a pioneer. Doctor Campbell's grandfather was Judge

Campbell, a native of Tennessee, a farmer by occupation, and a Confederate soldier who lost his life during the struggle between the states. He was shot by an enemy who was hiding in the bushes and was at home when his death occurred. John Stone Campbell, father of Doctor Campbell, was born in Illinois, and died from drowning in Eleven Point River near Pocahontas, Randolph County, Arkansas, September 16, 1915, aged sixty-eight years, six months, twenty-five days. He spent practically all his life in Randolph County, Arkansas, as a farmer and stockman, and during the last two years of the Civil war served in the Confederate ranks and in one battle received a bullet through the thigh. For a number of years he was regarded as a power in local democratic politics and was active both in his town and county affairs. His church was the Christian. John S. Campbell married Mrs. Alcy (Hufstedler) McClain. She was born in Tennessee in 1836 and died in Randolph county, Arkansas, on the old homestead in January, 1901. The children of this marriage were: J. W. Campbell, who is a teacher by profession living at Shreveport, Louisiana; Dr. William H.; T. W. Campbell, an attorney at Pocahontas, Arkansas; and J. N. Campbell, a railroad man at Shreveport.

Doctor Campbell acquired a high school education in Randolph County and grew up on his father's farm there until seventeen. He then came with his parents to Erath County, Texas, in 1889, but in 1891 the family returned to Randolph County, Arkansas. While in Erath County Doctor Campbell did some independent farming for himself until 1893, and then re-entered the public schools and remained for a year.

He began his medical studies in the Fort Worth Medical College, now the Fort Worth University, and applied himself industriously to the courses for one year. As an undergraduate he began the practice of medicine in Indian Territory, being located four years at Comanche, at Rush Springs a year and at Healdton for one year. The years 1903 and 1904 he spent in the J. Marion Sims Medical School of St. Louis, where he was graduated M. D. in 1904. Returning to Indian Territory, he practiced at Lone Grove until the beginning of 1907. He then went to New Mexico and practiced in the vicinity of Roosevelt until January, 1910, at which date he came to Oklahoma and located at Pontotoc. There he carried on a drug business in connection with his private practice for three years. After another year at Mill Creek, in February, 1915, he located at Hickory, where he already has a satisfying practice. His offices are in the H. C. Bowen drug store.

While at Lone Grove he served as health officer, and is a member of the Murray County and the Oklahoma State Medical societies and the American Medical Association. At Mill Creek he was a member of the city council. He is a democrat, a member of the Christian Church and affiliated with the Independent Order of Odd Fellows.

While living in Erath County, Texas, in 1892, Doctor Campbell married Mrs. Cordelia (Kennedy) Craig, widow of Frank Craig and daughter of Sabert Kennedy, a Texas farmer, who accidentally shot himself while his daughter Cordelia was an infant. Doctor Campbell and wife have five children: Hallie May, wife of Charles Mosman, who is an oil tank builder and lives at Wilson, Oklahoma; Darrel, wife of W. B. Norman, a farmer near Pontotoc, and they have two children, Delilah and Camilla; Oran, Farris and Jirl D., all of whom are in the public schools at Hickory. Mrs. Campbell had three children by her first husband, Barto, Bertha and Bert Craig. Barto Craig married Miss Anna Holemberg, of Fort Worth, Texas, and they have one child, Jack Craig, Jr.

JESSE WILLIAM BELL. Since he was seventeen years of age Jesse William Bell has found a sphere of usefulness and honorable activity as a citizen in Oklahoma. He prospered as a farmer, and has also been in mercantile activities and is publisher of one of the leading papers of the county, and at the present time is serving as postmaster of LaKemp.

He was born in a log house on a farm in Franklin County, Missouri, April 8, 1881, a son of William Lafayette and Amy Lee (Farrar) Bell, both of whom were natives of the same county. His grandparents were Russell and Elizabeth (Caldwell) Bell. Russell Bell was a Confederate soldier during the Civil war, and was captain of a company in the army commanded by General Sterling Price. William Lafayette Bell was born August 20, 1854, and died in Cleveland County, Oklahoma, September 29, 1902. His life was spent as a farmer, and in 1898 he came to Oklahoma and his closing years were spent in this state. On June 12, 1873, he married Amy Lee Farrar, who was born in Franklin County, Missouri, July 31, 1854, and is now living at LaKemp. Her parents were Jesse P. and Mary (Bullock) Farrar. He was born in Missouri and she in Ohio. William L. Bell and wife were the parents of eleven children, five sons and six daughters, nine of whom are still living: Edward Russell, who was born April 23, 1874, and is now a farmer in Beaver County, was married in 1896 to Susie E. Hethcock; Birtie E., born February 6, 1876, married in 1908 Samuel McGrath and they now live at Seattle, Washington; Mollie Virginia, born July 12, 1878, in Texas, was married in 1895 to Marion F. Hethcock and they live on a farm in Beaver County; the fourth in age is Jesse William; Thomas Franklin was born September 21, 1884, and lives at May, Washington; Minnie Pearl, born May 18, 1886, and was married in 1912 to Bruce Eslick, and they live in Montana; Drusie was born in 1888 and died in 1891; Arthur Lafayette, born March 5, 1891, died January 9, 1916; Ollie Clinton, born November 3, 1893, is now a farmer in Baca County, Colorado; Sylvia Mabel, born September 24, 1897, was married in 1915 to Howard Gordon, who is a farmer in Baca County, Colorado; Girtie Lee was born February 3, 1901, and is now with her mother.

Jesse W. Bell is the type of citizen who makes the best of his opportunities wherever he finds them. His early life was spent on his father's farm in Franklin County, Missouri, and he had a public school education. In 1898 he came to Oklahoma with his parents, and in 1907 he located a tract of government land in Beaver County two miles east of the present Town of LaKemp. He still owns that land and has increased it by considerable other valuable holdings in the country district of the county. In 1912 leaving the farm Mr. Bell engaged in the drug business at the new Town of LaKemp, and in the same year he bought the LaKemp Mirror, of which he was editor and publisher until February, 1915, when he removed the plant to Beaver, the county seat, and changed the name of the paper to the Democrat. It is now published under the incorporated title of the Enterprise Publishing Company, of which Mr. Bell is secretary and treasurer. Mr. Bell was appointed postmaster of LaKemp August 23, 1914, and is giving a very efficient administration of that office. Fraternally he is affiliated with the Masons and with the Modern Woodmen of America, and politically his actions have always been in line with the democratic party. On February 14, 1904, at Tecumseh, Oklahoma, he married Miss Dora May Little, who was born on a farm in Hickory County, North Carolina, August 23, 1887, a daughter of F. P. and Elizabeth (Little) Little, both of whom were natives of North Carolina. The Little family came to Oklahoma in 1901, when Mrs. Bell was about fourteen years of age and located in Pottawatomie County. Mr. and Mrs. Bell have four children: Jesse Charles, born September 13, 1908; Edith Lee, born June 30, 1911; Irl. Clinton, born August 3, 1913; and Thelma Elizabeth, born October 27, 1915.

JOEL SPRING. When Joel Spring died at Hugo February 21, 1908, it was said that no other contemporary had done so much to enrich his community in those elements which make for civic wholesomeness and material prosperity. Such a citizen was an honor to Oklahoma history, and such an account of his character and activities as can be given in this article is but a meager memorial to one whose life left much that was practical in its accomplishment and inspiring in its character.

Nearly twenty-five years before his death Joel Spring, having recently married, engaged in merchandising at Roebuck Lake in what is now Southeastern Oklahoma. From Roebuck Lake he removed to Clear Springs Court Ground, about two miles west of the present Hugo and then the seat of Kiamichi County. After the building of the Frisco Railway through that section of the country he removed his business and his household to Goodland, where for years he conducted one of the largest mercantile establishments in the Indian Territory.

Then in 1902 the new Town of Hugo was established. Mr. Spring, quickly seeing the great promise for the new town, located there as one of its first merchants, and from the first took the position of the most prominent business man and citizen. He at once acquired an interest on the townsite on the east side, erected a large attractive and beautifully furnished residence on an eminence in that part of the city, built a number of the most substantial business houses of the place, and in every practical way showed his unbounded faith in Hugo and its people. And this feeling was heartily reciprocated, for citizens and countrymen trusted in his judgment, integrity and generosity with unbounded faith, placing in his keeping their property and their future with no security other than that of his long-tried character. He became the friend, adviser, banker and father of the entire community, but with all his later affluence and unique standing he cast an affectionate eye over the struggling days of his early life. On the walls of his residence in Hugo was a reproduction from a small photograph of the tiny log cabin in which he commenced married life on the banks of Roebuck Lake, showing the proud nineteen year old husband standing in the yard and his fifteen year old bride in the doorway.

Of his part as a town builder, the editorial expression of the entire community at Hugo found in the columns of a local paper, should be quoted: "As a town builder and developing force he was without a peer in Southern Oklahoma. He was a person of wealth and resource and owned much property in this city. During the past five years he erected seven large brick buildings all of the very best and constructed with a view to permanency, majestically beautiful and an ornament to a city of many thousand people. As are all great men, he was at times subjected to unjust criticism, but when a task was completed no fault could be found with it. He was charitable and liberal, giving freely to the construction and maintenance of the churches and other moral institutions. At one time, several years ago, the Methodist Church was advertised for sale to liquidate its indebtedness, and it was Joel Spring who came to the rescue. He made a large donation and placed the then struggling band upon their feet, and that with only an expression of regret that they had not made him fully conversant with conditions before resorting to such extremities. By spending his money so freely to develop the town he encouraged others to do so; and he was in deed and in truth 'the father of Hugo.' However great it may become in the future will be due to his efforts in its struggling pioneer days. One day, when Hugo shall have become a large city, we wish to stand on one of our principal streets with uncovered heads before an imperishable statue dedicated to the memory of this tireless man who was such a great factor when the town was in its infancy."

From the columns of this paper it is possible to learn some of the particulars regarding the business character and activities of the late Joel Spring. From an examination of the records and from such comments as are still freely passed on his life and influence, the conspicuous attribute of Mr. Spring was undoubtedly character, that part of the human soul which dominates all else and which must stand imperishable while the earthly tabernacle falls. As the artice just referred to says: "In his case it was a steady, honest character that formed the foundation of his success. In the early days he was the only man in this country who owned a safe. In those days many of the settlers were prosperous and had a large amount of ready cash at their command. They were afraid of the banks in the state run by men of whom they knew but little, but they were acquainted with Joel Spring, and knew that every dollar would be conscientiously accounted for; and for years he was not only a merchant but a banker for a large section of country. Men came from Nashoba County, seventy miles away, for the sole purpose of entrusting their savings with him for safe keeping. Many times a large herd of cattle would be sold and the owner knowing but little of the business world would accept nothing but a check payable to Joel Spring. He was the chief adviser of his people on business matters. He had at all times many thousand dollars deposited with him and while he kept a safe reserve in cash, robbers were not unknown and a large amount was kept invested in good security. He was a banker subject to no regulation or inspection, yet no man lost a cent or had cause for uneasiness. Thus his success was to a large extent built upon confidence which the world entertains for only the highest order of manly character.

"In character Joel Spring was of the most manly and lofty type. He enjoyed the full confidence and respect of his fellow men, and we have yet to hear of the man who claimed that Joel Spring ever beat him out of a cent, or that in any instance did he violate that sacred honor which exists between man and man. He was systematic in his work and successful in every undertaking, and had he entered other fields of labor than that of business he would probably have reached the goal of his ambition with the same measure of success."

Born within three miles of where Hugo now stands on February 2, 1863, Joel Spring came of unusual lineage. His grandfather, Christian Spring, was born in Switzerland, of German parentage, was educated in Germany and served a time in the army of that nation. Subsequently he was a commissioned officer in the Army of Napoleon, and after Waterloo emigrated to America, landing at New Orleans, drifting into Mississippi, where he married Susan Bohannan, who was of mingled French and Indian extraction.

Samuel Spring, father of Joel, married Elizabeth LeFlore. She was a representative of that family which for generations furnished the Choctaws with their hereditary chief. One of them was Greenwood LeFlore, author of the celebrated Dancing Rabbit Treaty of 1830. Of Greenwood LeFlore President Jackson said: "There is no greater statesman among any people." Samuel Spring was a Confederate soldier, and died in service in the same year that his son Joel was born. The mother of this future merchant, banker and town builder also died when he was a child.

He grew up principally in the home of his uncle, prominently known in this section of Indian Territory as "Uncle Billie Spring." Uncle Billie sent his nephew at the age of twelve to old Spencer Academy. He soon grew tired of books and the confining discipline of school, ran away to Texas, and finally entered the household of M. E. Savage in the vicinity of Whitewright. He remained there two years, and then crossed the Red River and went back to his uncle's home. He gained his first practical experience in merchandising as clerk for Victor M. Locke, Sr., in the latter's store near the present Town of Antlers. For a time Joel Spring was associated with Uncle Billie Spring in the proprietorship of a small store on Roebuck Lake, and then moved the store to old Rockwall Lake, a short distance south of the present site of Hugo. About that time, on September 28, 1883, Joel Spring married Miss Winnie Gooding, daughter of H. L. Gooding of old Goodland, and granddaughter of Gov. Basil LeFlore, also a prominent member of the LeFlore family just mentioned. Miss Gooding brought to her husband as her marriage portion a small herd of cattle. These were soon sold and the proceeds used to purchase Uncle Billie's interest in the store. This was the commencement of Joel Spring's progressive career as a merchant and business man.

At his death Joel Spring was survived by his widow and seven children. The children are: Joel, born January 24, 1888; Lawrence E., born December 15, 1889; Jesse H., born August 4, 1891; Winnie, born November 20, 1894, and now Mrs. H. S. Griffiths of Hugo; Dewey L., born May 14, 1898; Robert M., born October 27, 1899; and Cicero O., born December 23, 1903.

SAMUEL LEE ARNOLD. The wearisomeness which frequently ensues from the continuous following of one line of endeavor has never been a feature of the career of Samuel Lee Arnold. Gifted with business ability of a diversified character, the present postmaster of Devol, Oklahoma, has at various times followed farming, merchandising and dealing in real estate, and in each connection has made his operations a success. As postmaster, a position which he has held since October 11, 1914, he has discharged his duties capably and faithfully, and there are few more popular officials in Cotton County.

Mr. Arnold is a native son of the Southwest, born at Omen, Smith County, Texas, July 18, 1879, his parents being George M. and Susan (Darnell) Arnold. The Arnold family originated in England, from whence the progenitor of the family in this country emigrated probably before the days of the Revolution, settling in Virginia. From the Old Dominion the family moved to Tennessee, where, in 1826, was born George M. Arnold, who was born and reared on a farm there and engaged in agricultural pursuits. Some time after his first marriage, but prior to the outbreak of the Civil war, he migrated to Texas and bought a farm in Smith County, on which he made numerous improvements and erected buildings. When the trouble between the North and the South culminated in hostilities, he entered the ranks of the Confederacy, in which he served until the close of the struggle. He then returned to his farm and continued to carry on operations until his retirement, when he moved to Omen, and there passed away in August, 1912, aged eighty-six years. He was a member of the Baptist Church, and was affiliated with the Masons, in which he attained the Royal Arch degree. Mr. Arnold's third

Vol. V—4

wife was Susan Darnell, a native of Texas, who died in Smith County, that state, in 1883, and they were the parents of five children, as follows: Beulah, who married Louis Horton, a carpenter and builder of Tyler, Texas; Samuel Lee, of this notice; Sallie, who resides with her half brother, Mitch, in Smith County, Texas, on the old homestead; Harvey, who died at the age of twelve years; and Homer, who died in infancy.

The early education of Samuel Lee Arnold was secured in the district schools of Smith County, Texas, and following some further preparation he entered the University of Oklahoma, in 1900, remaining until June, 1904. He drew a farm of 160 acres, two miles west of Bridgeport, Oklahoma, in Caddo County, while still a college student, and this he proved up in 1901. In the fall of 1904 he turned his attention to mercantile lines, establishing himself in a hardware business at Bridgeport, but after two years disposed of his interests there and moved to the "Big Pasture," in 1907 engaging in real estate transactions at Randlett. That city continued to be his home and the scene of his business labors until 1913, when he came to Devol and became clerk in a hardware store, which position he held until October 11, 1914, when he was appointed postmaster of Devol by Postmaster-General Burleson. The entirely capable and thoroughly courteous manner in which he has discharged his official duties demonstrates his fitness for public service. In politics Mr. Arnold is a democrat, and while a resident of Randlett served in the capacity of justice of the peace. With his family, he attends the Baptist Church. Mr. Arnold is interested in fraternal matters, belonging to Devol Lodge No. 420, Ancient Free and Accepted Masons;. Weatherford Chapter No. 31, Royal Arch Masons; Devol Chapter, Order of the Eastern Star; and the local Lodge of ...e Woodmen of the World.

On December 27, 1907, Mr. Arnold was married at Overton, Texas, to Miss Ida Bagwell, a daughter of B. J. Bagwell, a retired farmer now living at Overton. To this union there have come two children: Wayne, who was born April 19, 1908; and Odell, born December 9, 1911.

JOHN R. GUYER. The romantic and rugged home of the Welsh people, and the land of the ancient Cymri, who from their wild mountain fastnesses for centuries defied the hordes of the foreign invaders, has produced some of the best citizens of which this broad country can boast. Steady, industrious, plodding, in America they have helped to push forward into the new and undeveloped regions, laying substantially the foundation for a better citizenship. John R. Guyer, attorney, of Oklahoma City, while not himself a native of Wales, is a representative of an honored family whose members have been pioneers of Kentucky and Missouri. He was born in the latter state, in 1864, and is a son of Henry S. and Mary A. (Claunch) Guyer.

The Guyer family, while originating in Wales, has for many years been located in America. The grandfather of John R. Guyer, Williamson Guyer, was a pioneer settler of Kentucky, and as early as 1830 migrated to Missouri, at a time when the nearest neighbor of the family was twelve miles away. The grandfather was an agriculturist, and through years of steady industry became the proprietor of a satisfying fortune. Henry S. Guyer was born in Kentucky, and was still a child when taken by his parents to Missouri. There he grew up amid agricultural surroundings, adopted farming as his life work and throughout his active career was engaged in the pursuits of the soil. He was also well known as a public-spirited citizen, and at one time served as a special representative of the Missouri Legislature.

John R. Guyer was educated in the public schools and at Clarksburg College, Clarksburg, Moniteau County, Missouri, and as a youth took up the study of telegraphy, which he mastered. After leaving college he engaged in teaching school for five years, and, following his marriage in 1888, took up telegraphy as a business, being engaged as an operator for the various telegraph companies and the Associated Press. During this period Mr. Guyer somehow found time from his duties to devote to the study of law, and so assiduously did he apply himself thereto that in 1894 he was admitted to practice before the bar of Texas, in which state he was at that time located. For two years thereafter he practiced his profession with some success in Armstrong County, Texas, then moving to Clayton, New Mexico, where he remained until 1910. While a resident of that state Mr. Guyer became actively interested in politics, and in 1899-1900 was a member of the Thirty-third Legislative Assembly of New Mexico and was speaker pro tem of the House of Representatives. Mr. Guyer came to Oklahoma City in 1910, and here has continued to be engaged in a general practice, in which he has met with deserved success. Ever studious, industrious, conscientious and alive to the best interests of all of his clients, thorough in the preparation and complete in the presentation of his cases, fair-minded and honorable in his methods of trial, he is accounted in his professional life in this city as a most capable and successful practitioner, a safe counselor, and a lawyer thoroughly equipped in every department of his calling. Mr. Guyer is a valued member of the various organizations of his profession, and is popular with his fellow members in the lodge and encampment of the Odd Fellows. His religious belief is that of the Cumberland Presbyterian Church. Mr. Guyer maintains offices at No. 518-524 Lee Building.

In 1888 Mr. Guyer was married to a college classmate, Miss Elizabeth Steele, daughter of Judge D. K. Steele, of Clarksburg, Missouri, who was a lieutenant in the Union army during the Civil war and subsequently represented his county three different times in the State Legislature. He was also prominently identified with the Grange movement in its inception in that county. Mr. and Mrs. Guyer have three children: Wendell B., an electrical engineer; Harry L., and Juanita. The family home is at No. 1608 East Tenth Street. Mrs. Guyer's family descended from the Kirkpatricks of Ireland. All were a music loving people, and in the present Guyer family this is well expressed, both Mr. and Mrs. Guyer, as well as their children, being accomplished vocalists and talented instrumentalists.

WILLIAM E. McGUIRE. If "a good name is rather to be chosen than great riches," and if a purposeful life, conforming to high ideals, impresses one's personality upon the society in which he lives to its lasting betterment, then one of Oklahoma's most useful citizens is William E. McGuire of Pawhuska. Mr. McGuire is postmaster at Pawhuska, and his seventeen years of continuous service in that office makes him the oldest postmaster in the state from point of continuity. However, his most important service has been as a teacher. He is not unjustly referred to as "the children's friend," since his greatest enthusiasm and interest have always been in behalf of the younger and growing generation. He taught school for a great many years, was superintendent of schools, has served on school boards and helped to found educational facilities in different parts of Oklahoma, and has also been an almost constant worker in church and Sunday school. Mr. McGuire is one of the old timers in Oklahoma, having first become identified with this section as a teacher in the government Indian schools many years ago and later moving into the Cherokee Strip when it was opened.

A native of Missouri, he was born at Macon, November 28, 1858. He is a brother of former Congressman B. S. McGuire, who for twelve years represented the First Oklahoma District in Congress and is now practicing law at Tulsa. Their parents were Joel and Rachel (Harriman) McGuire. His father was born in St. Clair County, Illinois, in 1832, and his mother in Washington County, Illinois, in 1834. They grew up and were married in their native state, and in 1857 removed to Missouri. During the war Joel McGuire enlisted in a Missouri regiment of the Union army, and served the last three years of the conflict. In 1881 he removed from Missouri to Chautauqua County, Kansas, and died there in 1894. The mother died at the home of her son William in Ponca City, Oklahoma, June 3, 1896. Joel McGuire was a successful farmer and stock raiser, and for a number of years bought, fed and shipped stock, mainly to the St. Louis market. He was active in Grand Army circles, was a member of the Baptist Church, and politically was in the main a republican, though at one time he affiliated with the greenback party and was also active in the Granger movement in Kansas. In the family were ten children, three daughters and seven sons, two of the sons being now deceased.

William E. McGuire lived with his father until the latter removed to Kansas. While at home he attended common schools and also was a student for two years in the State Normal at Kirksville, Missouri. Steadily for fifteen years he gave practically all his time to his work as a teacher. His first two terms were in Missouri, and he also taught in Kansas. In 1884 he was appointed a teacher in the Government Indian school at Pawhuska, and lived in this city when hardly any permanent buildings marked the site, and when wild deer frequently ran across the prairie now intersected by numerous streets and built up with business blocks and homes. After one year Mr. McGuire resigned owing to the incoming Cleveland administration, since at that time the schools were not under the civil service rules. Returning to Kansas he continued teaching there until 1893, and then participated in the opening of the Cherokee Strip, locating at Ponca City. During his first two years there he served as city clerk, but was chiefly active in organizing the local school districts. He was chairman of the board, and by his prompt and energetic work had the first permanent school house built and dedicated on the sixtieth day after the opening. Several years later Mr. McGuire resumed his work as a teacher and was superintendent of the schools at Ponca City, and also conducted teachers' normal during the summer seasons. In 1898 he was appointed postmaster at Pawhuska, and has held that office continuously since April 1st of that year, his present term expiring February 1, 1916. During all this seventeen years of service, which is unique in the records of the postoffice department as affecting Oklahoma, he has conducted the office with a regularity and efficiency like clockwork, has never been the object of any formal complaint from the authorities and has in fact made his administration one of model thoroughness. He has helped introduce all the many improvements in the postal service inaugurated since he became postmaster, including rural delivery, parcel post, and other changes. When he took charge at Pawhuska he found a fourth class office, and it is now an office of the second class, employing nine clerks, with up to date equipment, and with everything in perfect running order.

Ever since he attained his majority Mr. McGuire has been a republican in politics, though his chief concern has been service rather than political honors. He is active in the Methodist Episcopal Church, and since moving to Pawhuska has been continuously superintendent of the

local Sunday school, and is also chairman of the board of trustees of the church. In masonry he is affiliated with the Lodge and with the Royal Arch Chapter, and also belongs to the Independent Order of Odd Fellows and the Knights of Pythias. Mr. McGuire claims all children as his friends, and there are hundreds of young men and young women all over the Southwest who remember with gratefulness his kindly influence while he was their teacher. He assisted in organizing the schools of Pawhuska and was president two years and a member five years of the local board of education, and held that office until the constitution legislated him off the board on account of his relation as a federal official.

While he was superintendent of a school in Chautauqua, Kansas, Mr. McGuire married one of his teachers. July 23, 1888, he married Miss Jennie Slater. She was born at Quincy, Illinois, December 6, 1868. Four children comprise their happy home circle at Pawhuska. Naomi is a student in the music and fine arts department of the State University at Norman. Joseph, the second child, is now in high school. The two youngest are twin brothers, Robert and Rolland, both in high school. These twin boys are so much alike that their teachers have much difficulty in distinguishing them. Along with his many others talents as a useful worker Mr. McGuire combines a taste and training in music, and has identified himself with local choirs for twenty-five years.

JOHN D. APPLEBY. The subject of this sketch was born near Alberton, in Henderson County, Tennessee, on March 6, 1878, being the oldest of eight children, only three of whom are now living. His father, A. R. Appleby, was married to Dona Roberts in 1876, and to this family were born: John D.; William F.; Addie; James A.; Elizabeth; Luther; Mary Beth and Emmons.

John D. Appleby attended the summer schools of his county and when sixteen years old stood the teachers' examination and was granted a certificate to teach school but because of his age did not begin the active teaching of schools until he was seventeen years old. He continued to teach school and go to school until he was twenty-one, at which time he graduated from the Southern Normal University, located at Huntingdon, Tennessee, taking the LL. B., B. S., and B. A. degrees the same year.

After having been admitted to the practice of law, he went to Henderson, Tennessee, where he opened an office and there practiced his chosen profession during the year 1900. Being politically inclined he took a very important part in the McKinley campaign of that year making many speeches throughout that and adjoining counties.

In January, 1901, Mr. Appleby left Henderson, Tennessee, and came to Oklahoma, locating at El Reno, where he resided until the opening of the Kiowa and Comanche countries, when he came to Hobart on August 5, 1901, and where he has since resided. During the time that Mr. Appleby has been in Hobart he has at all times taken a leading part in everything that went for the betterment and upbuilding of his community.

For the time being at least Mr. Appleby has not followed up his chosen profession, but has interested himself in other vocations. He was deputy county clerk for a number of years, and in 1912 was appointed postmaster at Hobart by President Taft, his appointment being a personal one. He served in that capacity until December 7, 1914, at which time he tendered his resignation to take up private business.

On March 4, 1904, Mr. Appleby was married to Miss Madge L. Osterhout, to which union one baby now graces their home, John D. Jr., three years old. Mrs. Appleby is one of those versatile, helpful personages who takes keen delight and pleasure in all the activities of her husband.

Always more or less politically inclined, Mr. Appleby has at all times been found doing what he could for the advancement of the republican party, in an honorable way. He was the campaign manager for Hon. James A. Harris of Wagoner, Oklahoma, for National committeeman, and was successful in having his man elected National committeeman for Oklahoma in what was one of the most stubborn political fights that has ever been waged in the state. On April 22 of this year he was unanimously elected secretary of the State Central Committeee.

JAMES D. OSBORN, JR., M. D. One of the native-born sons of the Southwest who has contributed his ablest efforts to the progress of his community and labored faithfully in its behalf is James D. Osborn, Jr., M. D., who has been engaged in practice at Frederick, Oklahoma, since 1906. He has been remarkably successful in his profession, his skill having won for him a foremost place among the physicians of Tillman County.

Doctor Osborn was born at Cleburne, Texas, December 22, 1878, and is a son of Dr. J. S. Osborn, Sr., and a member of a family which migrated to America from England prior to the Revolutionary war and settled in Virginia. Dr. J. D. Osborn, Sr., was born at Greensboro, Hale County, Alabama, in 1846, and was reared in his native community, where he began the study of medicine. Graduated from the University of Virginia with the degree of Doctor of Medicine, he was engaged in practice for several years in Alabama, but for the past forty years has followed his profession at Cleburne, Texas, and is one of the well known and highly esteemed physicians and surgeons of that part of the Lone Star State. The high regard in which he is held professionally is shown by the fact that he has served in the capacity of president of the Texas State Medical Society, and his standing among his professional brethren in the various other organizations of his calling, while as a citizen he has taken a constant interest in civic affairs and has served as mayor of Cleburne for many years. He has likewise been a member of the Texas State Examining Board, is one of the leading and influential democrats of his locality, and is prominent in the Knights of Pythias and other social and fraternal orders. During the Civil war, Doctor Osborn served as captain of a company under the redoubtable Forrest, of the Confederacy, and was wounded in the shoulder in one of the numerous battles in which he participated. He married Miss Julia Pittman, who was born in Palmyra, Missouri, in 1851, and died at Cleburne, Texas, in 1904, and they became the parents of four children, namely: Dr. E. B., a graduate of the University of Texas, who is engaged in the practice of medicine with his father at Cleburne, Texas; Hattie Lu, who died unmarried in 1895 at the age of twenty-two years; Irene, who married Frank Blair, a wholesale grocer of Wichita Falls, Texas; and Dr. James D., of this notice.

James D. Osborn, Jr., attended the public schools of Cleburne, Texas, and was there graduated from the high school with the class of 1896. He next became a student at the military school at Forney, Texas, where he remained one year, this being followed by two years of attendance at the University of Texas. Doctor Osborn then passed a like period at the University of Louisiana, where he was graduated in 1901 with the degree of Doctor of Medicine, and this has since been supplemented by post-graduate work at the Chicago Eye, Ear, Nose and Throat College, where he prepared himself for specializing in diseases of these organs. He began practice at Oklahoma City, Oklahoma, in 1901 and remained in that city until 1906, when he came to his present field practice, the City of Frederick, where he maintains offices in the McFadden Building, at 214½ Grand Avenue. He carries on a general medical and surgical practice and has been successful in building up an excellent business, and at this time is surgeon for the Frisco and Missouri, Kansas & Texas railroads at Frederick. Doctor Osborn continues as a careful student, keeping fully abreast of his profession in every way, and is a valued member of the Tillman County Medical Society, the Oklahoma Medical Society and the American Medical Association. A democrat in politics, he served Tillman County as its first coroner, but has not been a seeker after public preferment, the exacting demands of his calling having taken his entire time and attention. His religious connection is with the Episcopal Church, and fraternally he belongs to the Praetorians and to Frederick Lodge No. 1217, Benevolent and Protective Order of Elks, of which he is past exalted ruler.

In October, 1902, Doctor Osborn was married at Cleburne, Texas, to Miss May Brown, daughter of John C. Brown, a retired citizen of Texas. One child has been born to this union: Pauline, who is attending the public school.

WILLIAM MASON COTT, M. D. In point of continuous residence and practice Doctor Cott is now one of the oldest physicians and surgeons of Okmulgee County, where he has had his home since 1900. Professionally he stands among the leading physicians in the state, and has accomplished a great deal of service in Okmulgee during the past fifteen years, and has been rewarded proportionately in a business way.

Doctor Cott came to Oklahoma with considerable experience in his profession acquired during his residence in Missouri. He was born in Saline County, Missouri, December 1, 1869, a son of Jackson Washington and Mary Jane (Wilhite) Cott. His father was born at Knightstown, Indiana, January 10, 1829, and the mother was born in Saline County, Missouri, October 7, 1834. The Wilhites were among the pioneer settlers in Saline County. The parents were married in that county in 1856 and they continued to make their residence on one farm there until about ten years ago, when they moved to Okmulgee, where they are now spending their declining years. The father is at this writing eighty-seven years of age. He was a soldier in a Missouri regiment during the Civil war. There were seven sons and three daughters in the family, with Doctor Cott as the sixth in order of age.

His early life was spent on a farm, and his education came from the rural schools supplemented by two years in William Jewell College at Liberty, Missouri. He earned a large part of the money necessary for his own education, and in 1896 graduated M. D. from the St. Louis College of Physicians and Surgeons. Then followed four years of practice in his home state, two years in Cooper County and two years in the Sweet Springs Sanitarium.

He arrived at Okmulgee April 29, 1900, and has since looked after a large general practice and since statehood has been county superintendent of health and county physician. For fourteen years his offices have been in the Bell Building, ever since it was constructed. At this writing he is completing a handsome new country home a mile and a half northeast of the city. In politics he is a democrat, and he was the first secretary of the chamber of commerce at Okmulgee. Fraternally he is a Mason and Shriner, a member of the Elks, and charter member of the Independent Order of Odd Fellows. His church is the Baptist.

On October 9, 1897, Doctor Cott married Mary Louise Wing, who was born in Cooper County, Missouri, daughter of D. Warner Wing. Doctor Cott and wife have three children: Dorsey Wing, Marian Elizabeth and William Warner.

JAMES S. ROSS. During his professional career at Oklahoma City, in the last five years, Mr. Ross has enjoyed a large and growing practice mainly in the field of corporation law, and his associations and connections are those enjoyed by the leaders of the bar. Mr. Ross is a Tennesseean, a descendent of the Scotch clan of Ross, and his father was a successful Tennessee lawyer.

James S. Ross was born at Fort Donelson, Stewart County, Tennessee, in 1878, a son of Ambrose B. and Missouri (Gray) Ross. His father died in 1882 and his mother in 1908. The former was for thirty years connected with various county offices in Stewart County in addition to his practice as a lawyer, and was well known in local affairs.

Educated in the public schools of his native county, Mr. Ross read law in a private office, and was admitted to the Tennessee bar in 1899. After practicing a short time in Tennessee he moved to Paducah, Kentucky, and during the ten years of his residence in that city enjoyed a prosperous business. In 1909 he located in Oklahoma City, where much of his practice is in handling the legal affairs for various corporations, both of Oklahoma and other states. He is a member of the County and State and American Bar associations.

Active in the democratic party, Mr. Ross was one of the candidates in 1912 for the democratic nomination to Congress from his district, but the peculiar conditions that prevailed during the primary campaign put him among the losers.

A member of the Masonic fraternity, he has taken fourteen degrees in the Scottish Rite, and his church home is with the First Christian Church of Oklahoma City. In 1901 Mr. Ross married Miss Emma Halloway, daughter of C. M. Halloway of Tennessee. Their three children are Virginia, James A. and Myra. Mr. Ross resides at 544 West Thirty-second Street, and his offices are in the American National Bank Building.

JUDGE PRESLIE B. COLE. While the present generation of lawyers in Oklahoma will have no difficulty in identifying Judge Cole on account of his long established position as a member of the McAlester bar, there is no question that he deserves the grateful remembrance of a later generation, particularly on account of splendid record while on the District Bench, from which he retired early in 1915 after eight years of capable service as judge. Judge Cole represented the best quality of the judiciary and in his official capacity set some high standards of service for his successors to follow. For fully a quarter of a century he has given all the energy of his nature to a profession which represents to him the dignity and service associated with the law.

He was nearly thirty years of age when admitted to the bar and his earlier career has been one of struggle and hard work to support himself and gain the object of his steadfast ambition. He was born at Turin, Georgia, December 6, 1862, a son of Monroe W. and Nancy (Russell) Cole. His father was born at Danville, Virginia, of German lineage, while the mother was a native of South Carolina and of Scotch-Irish ancestry. Judge Cole's parents were married in Georgia, where they afterwards lived until their death. His father was an architect and building contractor, and during the war between the states he made a fine record as lieutenant of his company.

Reared in Georgia, Preslie B. Cole accepted such

advantages as were presented by the local schools where he spent his boyhood, but most of his liberal and broad education and knowledge of men and affairs have come as a result of his varied experience since leaving school and becoming dependent upon his own resources. When nineteen he left home and undertook to make his own way in the world. From Georgia he removed to Arkansas, and at this stage of his early career was not too proud to accept any honorable means of earning a living. He finally became clerk in a small store at Hackett City, and later developed as a traveling salesman. His headquarters at first were at Fort Smith and later at St. Louis. With this experience back of him he realized that his real talent pointed in another direction and he quietly but determinedly took up the study of law while in Arkansas.

Judge Cole was admitted to the Arkansas bar in 1891, but in the same year moved to Indian Territory and established his home and began practice at McAlester. That city has been his residence ever since, and in a few years his abilities had gained him recognition as one of the leading attorneys of the old territory. His experience and other qualifications made him the logical candidate when Indian Territory became merged with Oklahoma Territory as the new state, for the office of district judge, and he was nominated and elected judge of the Fourth Judicial District. In that office he served eight years, his term ending in January, 1915.

While Judge Cole sat on the District Bench more than 1,000 criminal cases came before him, 100 or more of them being murder trials. It is a supreme tribute to his judicial temperament, his fairness and impartiality, and his sound knowledge of precedence and equity, that in only two instances were his decisions in criminal cases reversed by a higher court. At the same time a great number of civil cases were tried before him, and in that class of cases there resulted not more than half a dozen reversals altogether.

Judge Cole has long been an active democrat, and was a delegate to the National Democratic Convention at Baltimore in 1912, where he served as a member of the committee on credentials. He was an ardent supporter of the candidacy of Champ Clark for president, and served as a member of Clark's advisory committee.

ROBERT H. LOOFBOURROW. Judge Loofbourrow retired from the distinguished office of associate justice of the Supreme Court of Oklahoma on the 1st of January, 1915, after having declined nomination for a second term, and his incumbency of this position fully established his prestige as one of the leading lawyers and jurists of the state within whose borders he has maintained his home since 1890. The judge is a scion of a staunch old Scottish family that is of patrician lineage and that was founded in America prior to the War of the Revolution, the name having been prominently and worthily identified with the civic and industrial development of various of the sovereign commonwealths of the Union. The genealogy is traced back to Lord Loofbourrow, whose descendants immigrated to America in the colonial days and established a home in North Carolina, where they became citizens of marked prominence and influence. Representatives of a later generation became identified with the pioneer history of Kentucky, and from the old Bluegrass State went forth members of a still later generation to become sterling citizens of Ohio. Judge Wade Loofbourrow was long one of the most honored lawyers and jurists at Washington Court House, Fayette County, Ohio, and by his will he devised to that attractive little city, the judicial center of the county, his extensive and well selected law library, which is still maintained as a public law library at that place, the bequest having been the valuable nucleus around which has been gathered one of the best technical libraries of its kind to be claimed by any of the non-metropolitan counties of the Buckeye State. Judge Wade Loofbourrow served on the bench of the Circuit Court and was a lawyer of specially high attainments, so that his great-grandson may consistently be said to have as a natural heritage a predilection for the profession in which he has achieved marked success and distinction.

Judge Robert H. Loofbourrow was born on a farm in Marion County, Illinois, on the 29th of January, 1873, and is a son of Orlando J. and Sarah T. (Wilson) Loofbourrow. The judge was a boy at the time of the family removal to Missouri, and a short time thereafter removal was made to Kansas, where his father became a successful agriculturist and stockgrower and where he remained until 1890, when the family came to Oklahoma Territory and settled in Beaver County. Orlando J. Loofbourrow was born at Washington Court House, Ohio, but was reared and educated in Illinois, and it was his to gain a full quota of pioneer experience in the West. After coming to Oklahoma he became one of the representative exponents of the agricultural and live-stock industries in the territory.

To the public schools of Kansas Judge Loofbourrow is indebted for his early educational discipline, and in preparation for his chosen profession he entered the Iowa College of Law, in the City of Des Moines, from which institution he withdrew prior to graduation. Thereafter he continued the study of law under effective private preceptorship, at Beaver, Oklahoma, where, in 1896, he was admitted to the territorial bar, upon examination before the District Court of Beaver County. He initiated the practice of his profession at Beaver, where he has since continued to maintain his home and where he soon gained place as one of the leading members of the bar of Beaver County, besides proving one of the most loyal and progressive citizens of that section of the present State of Oklahoma. From 1897 to 1899 he served as county attorney, and for the ensuing two years his services continued to be enlisted in the position of assistant county attorney. In 1904 he again became county attorney, and of this office he continued the valued incumbent until the admission of Oklahoma to statehood, in 1907. Higher honors then became his, for under the new state regime he was elected to the bench of the Nineteenth Judicial District. He gave a most able and effective administration and his possession of exceptional judicial acumen gained to him further and distinguished recognition, since, on the 1st of September, 1913, he was appointed associate justice of the Supreme Court of the state, to accept which preferment he retired from the District Court bench. As associate justice of the Supreme Court his earnest and admirable services are now an integral part of the history of that tribunal, from which he retired in January, 1915, owing to his desire to resume the private practice of his profession at Beaver, the judicial center of the county of the same name.

Judge Loofbourrow is a member of the directorate of the Bank of Beaver and is the owner of valuable real estate in his home city and county. In the Masonic fraternity he has attained the eighteenth degree of the Ancient Accepted Scottish Rite, besides which he is affiliated with the Independent Order of Odd Fellows, the Benevolent and Protective Order of Elks, and the Knights of Pythias, in which last mentioned he is past chancellor of Beaver Lodge, No. 7.

On the 16th of May, 1897, was solemnized the marriage of Judge Loofbourrow to Miss Bertha L. Groves, daughter of Ansel Groves, of Beaver, and they have three sons, Harold, Bernard and Hale.

CHARLES A. HOLDEN. Among the men who are winning success at the bar of Western Oklahoma, one who is rapidly coming to the forefront is Charles A. Holden, city attorney of Clinton, and one of the energetic and influential young democrats of Custer County. Mr. Holden was born at Walhalla, Oconee County, South Carolina, September 23, 1887, and is a son of A. P. and Anna P. (Conley) Holden.

The Holden family originated in England, from whence one John Holden came to America about the year 1700 and settled near Williamsburg, Virginia, where he was a planter, a vocation followed by many of the family. Among his descendants were three who fought as soldiers in the Revolutionary war, John Holden, William Holden and Capt. John Holden. The last named was a captain of militia in the patriot army, and, like the others, a planter. The son of Capt. John Holden, also named John, was the great-grandfather of Charles A. Holden, and in 1805 located in the Pendleton District, South Carolina. He passed his life in planting and died in 1856, leaving a family of twelve children. Five of his sons were in one company in the Second Regiment, South Carolina Volunteer Infantry, during the Civil war, and another son was a captain in another regiment under Wade Hampton. The oldest of the twelve children of John Holden was the grandfather of Charles A. Holden. He was born in Pendleton District, South Carolina, in 1813, and followed the family vocation of planting. When he attained his majority he left home and secured a plantation of his own in the vicinity of Pine Mountain, Georgia, and there his death occurred May 31, 1893.

A. P. Holden was born at Pine Mountain, Georgia, in 1860, and about the time of his marriage moved across the state line to Walhalla, South Carolina. There he was engaged as a lumberman until November, 1907, when he came to Cordell, Oklahoma, where his death occurred February 1, 1908. He was a stanch and unswerving democrat and a member of the Masonic fraternity. Mrs. Holden, who survives and resides at Cordell, is a native of Macon County, Georgia. There were three children in the family, as follows: Charles A., of this notice; W. S., who is a merchant and resides at Cordell; and Bessie, who died February 17, 1908, at Cordell, aged sixteen years.

Charles A. Holden received his early education in the public schools of Walhalla, South Carolina, being graduated from the high school there in the class of 1906. The next two years were spent at the University of North Carolina, at Chapel Hill, and three years were then passed at the University of Missouri, at Columbia, where he was graduated in 1911 with the degree of Bachelor of Arts. He was admitted to the bar in that same year and in September began practice at Cordell, Oklahoma, from whence he came to Clinton in July, 1913. This city has continued to be his field of practice, his offices being located in the Welch Building, on Frisco Avenue. He has built up an excellent general practice, being equally at home in all branches of his profession, and is the representative of some large interests. A stanch democrat, he has taken an active part in county and state convention work, having attended every county convention since coming to Oklahoma and being a campaign speaker of note, whose services are always in demand. In 1914 he was the successful candidate of his party for the office of city attorney, a position in which he is rendering his adopted city valuable service. Mr. Holden is a member of the Phi Alpha Delta Greek letter college fraternity, and is generally popular in social circles of the city.

On April 15, 1914, at Pawnee, Oklahoma, Mr. Holden married Miss Jennie B. Berry, daughter of George M. Berry, who was a member of the Oklahoma Constitutional Convention and is now a well known banker of Pawnee.

JAMES R. CALLOWAY, M. D. The pioneer medical practitioner of Paul's Valley is Doctor Calloway, who located in that small village in October, 1889. That, it will be remembered, was only a few months after the original opening of Oklahoma Territory, and at the beginning of the epoch of modern development and civilization in the present state. For more than twenty-five years Doctor Calloway has carried his skill and counsel to hundreds of homes and families in that city and surrounding country. In the early days he underwent all the hardships and privations of a pioneer doctor, traveling for miles to visit his patients, being quite regardless of his own health and comfort in the performance of his professional duties. In later years his practice has become more and more an office practice, and confined to a smaller radius of country. He is a specialist in diseases of children and in that department of the profession is regarded as second to none in this part of the state.

His lifetime has covered a great variety of scenes and experiences. He was born in Denton County of Northern Texas August 22, 1854, and his father, T. H. Calloway, was also a physician and surgeon. Dr. T. H. Calloway was born in Missouri in 1825. It is interesting to note that the famous Daniel Boone had a brother-in-law named Calloway, after whom Calloway County, Missouri, was named. The Calloways were Scotch-Irish people and located in Virginia during colonial times. T. H. Calloway's parents were pioneers in Northern Texas, where he was reared and married. In 1859, when Dr. James R. was five years of age, he moved out to California, and lived in various places of that state and in Oregon. In 1863 he went as one of the first pioneers to Boise City, Idaho, and was in that state for several years during the interesting period following the discovery of the mines in that country. At one time he was a member of the Idaho Legislature, and always took a prominent part in civic and political affairs. In 1872 Dr. T. H. Calloway moved to the eastern part of Indian Territory, but not long afterwards returned to Texas and located near Decatur in Wise County. In 1884 he was again attracted to the Northwest and settled at Caldwell, near Boise City, Canyon County, Idaho, and lived there until his death in 1904. When a very young man he had served with General Price as a soldier in the war with Mexico and was a participant in some of the campaigns in New Mexico. Besides his regular profession as a physician he was a minister of the Christian Church. In politics he was a democrat and a member of the Masonic fraternity. Dr. T. H. Calloway married Mary Allen, who was born in Missouri in 1835 and died at Caldwell, Idaho, in 1894. Their children were: Dr. James R.; William T., a farmer at Namba, Idaho; Ida, wife of Frank Brown, who is a miner and lives in Boise City, Idaho; Melinda O., wife of J. A. Dement, a stock raiser at Caldwell, Idaho; and Mary Allen, who is unmarried and a graduate physician now practicing at Boise.

Dr. James R. Calloway spent his early youth and manhood in Texas, California and Oregon, was about nine years of age when the family removed to Idaho, and in 1872 came with them to Indian Territory and soon afterwards to Decatur, Wise County, Texas. His early experiences were as a farmer and he also did some mining in Colorado. From boyhood he was a student and some of his family called him a book worm. Having access to his father's medical library, he became well grounded in the medical science so far as text-books were concerned

Haward Weber M.D.

before reaching his majority. His father was opposed to the idea of his practicing medicine, and it was not until he came to Paul's Valley in the fall of 1889 that he set up as a regular member of the profession. For a number of years he was an undergraduate practitioner, but finally entered the medical department of the Texas Christian University at Fort Worth, where he was graduated M. D. in 1897. He is properly regarded now as one of the leading physicians in this section of Southern Oklahoma. He was frequently called into consultation by fellow physicians, and his wide experience has given him a thorough post-graduate knowledge of medicine.

Like his father he was a regularly ordained minister of the Christian Church, and between the ages of twenty and fifty preached quite regularly and still fills an occasional pulpit. His offices are in the Bruce Building of Paul's Valley. In territorial days he belonged to the old Chickasaw Medical Society and was the first president of the Washita Valley Medical Society, which afterwards became the Garvin County Medical Society, to which he still belongs. He is a member of the Oklahoma State Society and a member of the American Medical Society. In politics he is an independent democrat and is affiliated with Paul's Valley Lodge No. 196, Independent Order of Odd Fellows, in which he has frequently filled the office of chaplain.

In Texas in 1876 Doctor Calloway married Miss Frances Elizabeth Clemens. Her father was the late Andrew Clemens. To their marriage have been born five children: John R., who is a physician and surgeon, having taken his degree in 1907 in the St. Louis College of Physicians and Surgeons, and is now practicing in Mescalero, New Mexico; Ethel M. is the wife of W. W. Howerton, a farmer at Foster, Oklahoma; Lillian M. is the wife of Francis L. Armstrong, a fire insurance man at Spokane, Washington; Etta Frances, who is still single, was graduated from the Boise City High School, was a teacher for a number of years and is now a stenographer and living at home with her father; Vivienne, also unmarried, is a sophomore in the School of Journalism at the Oklahoma State University at Norman.

JOSEPH LAMAR GRIFFITTS. During the twenty years since his admission to the bar in Tennessee, fifteen of which have been spent in Oklahoma, Joseph L. Griffitts has employed his talent and abilities in such a way as to place him among the front rank of Oklahoma lawyers, and he has the chief practice in his home Town of Buffalo, Harper County.

His birth occurred at Friendsville, Tennessee, July 23, 1864, and he represents old and prominent family stock of that state. His parents were John W. and Mary Elizabeth (Donaldson) Griffitts. His grandfather, Manuel Griffiths, was a native of Virginia, and married a Georgia girl. John W. Griffitts, who was born in Kentucky, June 13, 1831, and died December 18, 1909, spent his active lifetime as a farmer in Tennessee. He was also prominent in local affairs, and for twenty years was a member of the County Court of Loudon County, Tennessee, having filled that office up to the time of his death. He served as an elder in the Presbyterian Church forty years. He was married in 1856 to Mary Elizabeth Donaldson, who was born February 3, 1839, in Tennessee, and died January 16, 1897. She became the mother of eight children, five sons and three daughters: James Henry, who was born July 16, 1857; Nancy Elizabeth, born September 15, 1859, was married in 1886 to Samuel S. Hutsell, and is now a resident at Sweetwater, Tennessee; Thomas Nelson, born September 26, 1861, is a farmer at Lenoir City, Tennessee; Joseph L. was the fourth in age; Stephen Alexander was born January 22, 1866, and died August 18, 1913; Jacob Lafayette, born May 20, 1868, is a minister of the Methodist Episcopal Church South at Cedar Keys, Florida; Lucinda Jane, born July 11, 1875, died November 28, 1903; Nora Blanche was born March 20, 1877, and is still single.

Joseph Lamar Griffitts completed his early education in Maryville College at Maryville, Tennessee. His early life was taken up with varied labors and employments, until he realized his ambition to study law. He read his text books at Loudon, Tennessee, until 1895, and was then admitted to practice in all the courts of the state. From Tennessee he came to Oklahoma in 1900, and began practice at Tonkawa. While there he served as police judge until 1905 and was elected city attorney in 1907. However, in the same year, he resigned that office and moved to Buffalo, and after statehood was elected the first county judge of Harper County. That office he filled with distinction and credit for three years and two months. Since then he has applied all his time and energies to his large private practice at Buffalo. He is a democrat, and is affiliated with the Masonic Order.

At Alva, Oklahoma, February 5, 1909, Judge Griffitts married Miss Grace Pennington. She was born February 11, 1880, in Wabaunsee County, Kansas, a daughter of J. W. and Catherine Pennington, who were natives of Illinois. Mrs. Griffitts prior to her marriage was for four years a teacher in the public schools of Dewey County, Oklahoma. To their union have been born three daughters and one son: Guendolen Grace, Josephine L., Cassius Lamar and Muriel Elaine.

HOWARD WEBER. Probably everyone in Oklahoma and anyone who has any general information on the oil industry of the United States is familiar with the Weber pool in Washington County in the Bartlesville district. The discoverer of this pool and the man who supplied the enterprise and capital for its development has been an honored resident of Bartlesville for the past ten years.

Dr. Howard Weber is a physician, is enrolled in the medical fraternity of Oklahoma, but has never practiced since locating within this state. Since coming here he has been one of the really big men in Oklahoma affairs. A fortune has been amassed through his operations in mining and as an oil producer, and there are few Oklahomans who control a greater volume of resources both in this state and elsewhere. Doctor Weber is also a prominent man in the democratic party of Oklahoma, and is now serving as a member of the State Central Committee.

Considering his great achievements as an oil man it seems fitting that he should have been born in the state of Pennsylvania. Doctor Weber was born in Dempseytown in the Keystone state, October 20, 1862, a son of George K. and Elizabeth (Homan) Weber. Both parents were born in Center County, Pennsylvania, and spent all their lives in their native state. When quite young they moved to Venango County in the western part of Pennsylvania, and George K. Weber died there in February, 1905, at the age of seventy-four. He was a tailor by trade, but later went into general merchandising. A stanch democrat, he was much interested in politics, being a man of simple habits and plain living acquired a substantial competency. The widowed mother, who died February 23, 1916, at the age of eighty, represented people who were among the pioneers of Western Pennsylvania. She was the ninth in a large family of children, and nearly all of them are still living, the youngest more than seventy years old. Doctor Weber was one of ten children, six of whom are still alive.

He went into the world with the equipment of a

liberal education. He had attended Allegheny College at Meadville and in 1887 was graduated in medicine from Long Island Hospital Medicine College. For nearly ten years he applied himself diligently to his chosen work with home at East Hickory, Pennsylvania. With the resources then at his command he started his really great work in developing the natural wealth of the West. In 1896 he went to Colorado, became interested in mining, and in 1897 took part in the great rush to the Alaska gold fields, where he remained about a year, being associated with H. H. Breene of Bartlesville in that field. In July, 1898, he returned to the states, and resumed the practice of medicine at Dempseytown and at Oil City, Pennsylvania.

His interests in the oil industry led him to move to Kansas in 1903, and he also became an investor in the Oklahoma fields. From Independence, Kansas, he moved to Bartlesville in 1905, and has since given all his time to his extensive interests as an oil and gas operator and to his large mining holdings.

As already stated Doctor Weber discovered the famous Weber pool east of Dewey, developed it, and made a large share of his fortune from that locality. He also discovered the shallow sand pool northeast of Dewey, and developed that and several other properties in Washington County. With George B. Harmon, under the name of the Harmon Oil Company, he developed the Huffsteter & Burr leases half a mile south of Kiefer, finally selling his interests in that property for $87,000. He then bought 700 acres east of Delaware, was engaged in development work for a year and sold out to the Prairie Oil and Gas Company for half a million dollars. Doctor Weber still has some extensive holdings and leases in this vicinity.

For a year or more there was a lull in his operations as an oil operator and in that interim he invested heavily in copper mines north of Bisbee, Arizona. In August, 1914, he purchased from former Gov. Charles N. Haskell a half interest in the noted Barney Thlocco lease, and developed it to its output of about eleven thousand barrels per day, and it is still producing over two thousand barrels a day from thirty wells. He also owns 360 acres in the territory covered by the Weber pool, and operates under lease about as much more.

As a democrat, Doctor Weber has taken much interest in politics in every community where he has lived. For the past four years he has been a member of the state central committee, and served as a delegate at large to the Baltimore convention, which named Woodrow Wilson for President. On April 11th, 1916, he was elected a delegate at large to the Democratic National Convention, which convenes at St. Louis, June 14th, 1916, to renominate Woodrow Wilson for the next President by a unanimous vote. He was a member of the finance committee which supplied the funds for the Cruce campaign in Oklahoma, and since taking his place on the state committee the organization has never made any demand upon Washington County which has not been met. While living in Pennsylvania he was chairman of the Forest County Democratic Committee. He has also been appointed a member of the Southern Development Congress.

Doctor Weber is a member of the Benevolent and Protective Order of Elks, and in 1915 took his first degrees in Masonry, and has now gone by rapid succession as far as he can get in the various degrees and orders of that ancient fraternity.

With all his material success Doctor Weber finds his greatest pride in his family and home. In 1885 he married Miss Etta J. Carter, a native of Pennsylvania. They have five children: Dr. H. C., who lives in Bartlesville; Mark U.; Morris Kritzer, who graduated from the Culver Military Academy in Indiana in June, 1916; Savilla, wife of W. C. Raymond; and Sherwell G., who is now a student in the Culver Military Academy. All of the children have their home in Bartlesville and are young people of great promise, and the older ones are already filling useful places in the world.

WILLIAM W. WILSON. In Choctaw County, a place of distinctive prominence and influence is held by William Ward Wilson, who, as a merchant, banker and stockman, has played an important and worthy part in connection with the civic and industrial development of this section of the state and especially of his home town of Fort Towson.

Wherever the United States Government established a frontier military post in the early part of the eighteenth century there abounds history and a certain atmosphere of romance at the present day. Fort Towson, where once were stationed two members of the United States Army who were destined to achieve great distinction, Gen. Ulysses S. Grant and Gen. George B. McClellan, possesses more of historic charm and interest than many other military posts that, like it, have lived and thrived and finally been abandoned. The martial phase of its history can never fail of interest and this interest is enhanced by its later record as a place of importance in the Choctaw Indian Nation. The story of Fort Towson is for another chapter of history, but because its crumbled ruins still mark the place where it was built nearly one hundred years ago, almost within a stone's throw of the modern and vigorous town which perpetuates its name, a reversion to its ancient history puts a breath of charm into the community that "Billy Wilson" founded. On the site of the present Village of Fort Towson Mr. Wilson once herded and fed his cattle, and long before that he killed deer and turkey on the site where substantial brick business buildings now stand. The Town of Fort Towson, not far distant from the site of the old fort, is situated on a tract of land that Wilson and his brother possessed or controlled before the allotment period. This tract was once a part of their cattle range, and they were among the pioneers of the cattle industry in this section of the former Choctaw Nation. When it was made known that Billy Wilson is not yet sixty years old and that he grew to manhood long after the post at Fort Towson had been abandoned, and when it is made known that within a few hundred yards from the post he has seen deer in herds of forty and fifty and wild turkey by the hundreds, some idea is conveyed of the frontier wildness of the landscape at the time when the government here established a military post, nearly a century ago.

The Town of Fort Towson is new and vital. It was established in 1903, at the time when a line of railroad was in process of construction through this section. Prior to its founding Doaksville had been the general trading post of this region, the latter place having been one of the earliest settlements of the Choctaw Nation. The first store in the new town was erected and stocked by the Doaksville Trading Company, which had developed a substantial business at Doaksville, from which older town soon came other merchants to cast in their lot with the ambitious and newer community, the result being that within a comparatively short time Doaksville became little more than a memory. The Wilson brothers eventually purchased the stock and business of the Doaksville Trading Company and about the same time they organized one of the first banking institutions in the new town. Several changes and reorganization have taken place since, and on December 31, 1915, the First National Bank, of which W. W. Wilson, E. H. Wilson and R. D. Wilbor had controlling interests, and the First State Bank, controlled by Ed Leonard and Sam McKinney and T. E. Hopson consolidated and retained the name of the First State Bank. This is a strong institution, with Ed Leonard, president; W. W. Wilson, vice president, and Sam McKinney, cashier. One of the largest and best equipped mercantile establishments of the former Choctaw Nation is the finely equipped general-merchandise store of William W. Wilson and it occupies a substantial brick building of modern design and facilities, so that both the establishment and the business are a distinct contribution to the civic and business prestige of Fort Towson.

That Mr. Wilson should continue to maintain his home in this community and here rise through his own efforts to a position of commanding influence and large success, is the more interesting in view of the fact that he was born at a point but a few miles distant from the fine little town that is now the stage of his important business activities. In a pioneer log house near the old educational institution known as Wheelock Academy, and one-half mile distant from the stone Presbyterian Church that was erected in 1846, by Rev. Alfred Wright, Mr. Wilson was born in the year 1857, and the old log house which was his birthplace is still standing, in a fair state of preservation and as one of the landmarks of this part of the state. In the neighborhood he acquired his first definite educational instruction in the primitive schoolhouse in which Miss Jane Austin was the teacher, she later becoming the wife of the principal chief of the Choctaw Nation, Chief Jackson McCurtain. Mr. Wilson continued to attend the neighborhood schools until he had attained to the age of fourteen years, and his parents then sent him to Spencer Academy, which was then established about ten miles northeast of Fort Towson and which was the first higher educational institution established by the Christian missionaries who have labored faithfully among the Choctaw Indians. The interesting and important history of this old institution has never been properly written and is worthy of the careful study of those who would attempt to prepare adequate record concerning the history of Oklahoma and its early advances along educational lines, long before Indian Territory had lost its original identity. The Civil war caused a cessation in the work of Spencer Academy, but in 1871 it was reopened for the reception of students, under the superintendence of Rev. J. H. Colton, and Mr. Wilson entered the school at the time that it thus resumed operations. Prior to the war it had been a scholastic mecca for many years. Some of the old buildings at Spencer are still standing and are situated on land owned by the heirs of the late Robert Frazier, an Indian citizen of sterling character and excellent repute. After spending four years at the academy Mr. Wilson sought to obtain from the Choctaw Nation an appointment as a student in some eastern school, but his application was rejected, owing to the fact that the nation's quota of students to be given such advantages had already been filled. In his earnest ambition for a higher education he sought the assistance of his uncle, George James, who was one of the leading citizens of the Chickasaw Nation, but through this medium he likewise failed to realize his desires, under which conditions he entered the employ of his uncle, George James, in the cattle business, and here he earned his first money, his employer having paid him $15 a month. The James ranch was near Bloomfield Academy, in the Chickasaw Nation and the range of the James cattle to the north covered a vast era of country in which houses were on the average twenty miles apart.

Within a short time Mr. Wilson engaged in the livestock business on his own account, and for nearly forty years this line of enterprise engrossed the major part of his time and attention, his herds having grazed over large areas of the southern section of the Choctaw Nation. The open range was the common property of the cattle men and hence few fences were needed. Mr. Wilson was one of the pioneers in the cattle industry in this region and to him is due in large measure the credit for the development of this important line of enterprise into one of the profitable and permanent features of industrial activity in this section of Oklahoma. Over this country rode the buyers who came from other states and territories and from other Indian nations, and good prices were usually paid for the cattle. Market cattle that were not sold to such buyers locally were shipped principally to the City of St. Louis, Missouri, and Mr. Wilson made such shipments in an independent way. He still continued to be associated with the cattle industry on a modest scale, the former broad scope of operations having met with gradual curtailment with the elimination of the open range, the allotment and sale of Indian lands and the general settling up of the country by farmers, several of whom may be found to the square mile on the tillable land, and roads having been established along section lines.

Shortly after he attained to the age of twenty-one years Mr. Wilson was elected to a seat in the Choctaw Nation, from Towson County. Later he became a member of the senate, and his service in legislature was under the administration of Chief C. C. Cole and Chief B. F. Smallwood as principal chiefs. In this connection it is interesting to note that the officials of the Choctaw Nation never have been compelled to live at the capital. Until the tribal government was abolished they assembled at the capital each successive year, and ordinarily the members of the legislature and other officials completed the transaction of their business in about thirty days, after which they returned to their homes. Mr. Wilson served two terms as national auditor of the Choctaw Nation and one term as national treasurer. He was frequently importuned to become a candidate for the office of principal chief, but as often declined the honor, by reason of the exactions of his private business affairs and his lack of desire for political office.

Under appointment by Principal Chief Gilbert Dukes, Mr. Wilson became a member of the Choctaw commission that assisted the Dawes Commission in making the supplemental treaty by which the vested rights and property interests of the Choctaws were effectively conserved and protected. The other members of the Choctaw commission were Chief Dukes, C. B. Wade, Simon Lewis and Thomas Ainsworth. The first office to which Mr. Wilson was called in the service of the public was that of circuit clerk of the Apokshonubbi District, under appointment by Circuit Judge Jefferson Gardner. He and his wife hold membership in the Christian Church.

In 1879 Mr. Wilson married Miss Rose Garland, a kinswoman of Crockett Garland, who was once principal chief of the Choctaw Nation. She died in 1882 and is survived by no children. The second wife of Mr. Wilson bore the maiden name of Nannie Carney and she was of Choctaw blood, a relative of Albert Carney, who was a prominent citizen of Savannah, Indian Territory. The one child of this union is a son, Oscar. In 1906 was solemnized the marriage of Mr. Wilson to Miss Ollie Baird, of Paris, Texas, and they have two children, William Ward, Jr., and Ollie Jane.

Mr. and Mrs. Wilson have an attractive home in the Village of Fort Towson and they delight to extend its hospitality to their many friends.

JAMES W. WEBB, M. D. Most punctilious preliminary discipline, natural predilection, deep humanitarian spirit and successful practical experience have given to Doctor Webb distinct precedence as one of the representative physicians and surgeons of Southern Oklahoma, and he controls a large and important general practice which attests his professional skill and his secure place in popular confidence and esteem. He maintains his residence and office in the Village of Berwyn and his practice extends throughout the wide area of country tributary to this thriving town of Carter County.

Dr. James William Webb was born at Winchester, Franklin County, Tennessee, on the 26th of February, 1882, and is a son of James L. and Sallie (Lawson) Webb, both likewise natives of Winchester, where the former was born in 1861 and the latter in 1867. James L. Webb was reared and educated in his native state and there he continued his residence until 1891, when he removed with his family to Texas and purchased a tract of land in Eastland County, where he has since continued successful operations as a farmer and stockgrower, his home being in the Village of Cisco. He is a democrat in politics, a broad-minded and public-spirited citizen, is affiliated with the Masonic fraternity, and is a member of the Methodist Episcopal Church South, as was also his wife, who was summoned to the life eternal in 1903, and who is survived by eight children: Charles is a confectioner and is engaged in business in the City of Wichita, Kansas; Doctor Webb of this review was the next in order of birth; John is a prosperous farmer near Quanah, Texas; Henry, who maintains his residence at Bartlesville, Oklahoma, is a traveling commercial salesman; Mollie remains at the paternal home; Madison is engaged in farming and stockgrowing near Quanah, Texas; and Car and Diona remain with their father and are attending the Cisco High School.

Doctor Webb was about nine years old at the time of the family removal to Texas, and he continued his studies in the public schools at Cisco, that state, until his graduation in the high school in 1899. In consonance with his ambitious purpose and well formulated plans he thereafter attended the medical department of the University of Nashville, Tennessee, where he continued his studies during two terms. He then entered the Memphis Hospital Medical College, in the City of Memphis, that state, and in this excellent institution he was graduated as a member of the class of 1903 and with the degree of Doctor of Medicine.

Soon after his graduation Doctor Webb engaged in the practice of his profession at Cisco, Texas, where he continued his successful work until 1908, when he came to the new State of Oklahoma and established his home at Berwyn, where he has since continued his labors as a physician and surgeon and where his extensive practice is one of representative order. He established also a drug store in the village, and of this he continued the proprietor from 1909 until July, 1915, when he sold the stock and business to his father-in-law, Dr. John O. Gilliam, concerning whom individual mention is made on other pages of this publication. The doctor is actively identified with the Carter County Medical Society and the Oklahoma State Medical Society.

Though inflexible in his allegiance to the democratic party, Doctor Webb has had no time or inclination for the activities of practical politics, but his civic loyalty prompted him to give most efficient service when he was chosen clerk for Carter County of Rod District No. 11. His ancient-craft Masonic affiliation is with Berwyn Lodge No. 59, Ancient Free and Accepted Masons, and in Indian Consistory No. 2, Ancient Accepted Scottish Rite, at McAlester, he has received the thirty-second degree. In Oklahoma City he is affiliated with India Temple, Ancient Arabic Order of the Nobles of the Mystic Shrine, and he holds membership in Berwyn Camp, Woodmen of the World. The doctor is a scion of a family that is of English lineage, the original American progenitors having settled in North Carolina in the Colonial era of our National history.

At Berwyn, in 1908, was solemnized the marriage of Doctor Webb to Miss Lulu Maud Gilliam, daughter of Dr. John O. Gilliam, of whom specific mention is made elsewhere in this volume and who conducts the well equipped drug store at Berwyn. Doctor and Mrs. Webb have three children, whose names and respective years of birth are as follows: Theresa Amelia, 1910; James William, Jr., 1912; and John, 1915.

JOHN O. GILLIAM, M. D. Well may Doctor Gilliam be termed a pioneer of pioneers in what is now the State of Oklahoma, and it has been given him to wield much influence in connection with civic and industrial progress in Carter County, where he established his residence at Berwyn nearly forty years ago and where he became one of the first physicians and most influential citizens of the frontier community. He still maintains his home at Berwyn and here conducts a well appointed drug store, the while he finds it impossible to retire definitely from the practice of his profession, owing to the insistent demand made for his ministrations on the part of families to whom he has long been a guide, counselor and friend. It is specially gratifying to be able to present in this publication a review of the career of Doctor Gilliam, whose life has been one of signal usefulness and deep humanitarian spirit.

Dr. John Overstreet Gilliam was born in Chariton County, Missouri, on the 17th of August, 1849, and is a son of James A. and Martha Ann (Martin) Gilliam, both natives of the historic Old Dominion State and both persons of superior intellectual attainments. James A. Gilliam was born on the old family homestead on the banks of the Appomattox River, in Eastern Virginia, and the year of his nativity was 1820, his death having occurred in Saline County, Missouri, in 1905. He was reared and educated in Virginia, where his marriage was solemnized and where he continued to be identified with agricultural pursuits until his removal to Missouri. In the latter state he became a pioneer of Chariton County, and there he long held precedence as a progressive and successful farmer, planter and stockgrower. He held an appreciable number of slaves and not only raised tobacco but also became a dealer in this product, on an extensive scale. When well advanced in years he removed to Saline County, where he continued to reside until his death. He was an inflexible advocate of the principles of the democratic party, was a Royal Arch Mason and both he and his wife, who died in Chariton County, Missouri, were earnest members of the Methodist Episcopal Church, South. His father, William Gilliam, was a wealthy planter and slaveholder on the Appomattox River in Virginia, where he was specially prominent as a grower of tobacco, and where he continued to reside until his death, which was the result of virtual starvation, owing to his being afflicted with the severest type of dyspepsia. He was a descendant of one of two brothers who came from England and settled in Virginia in the Colonial period of our national history. Anthony Woodson, an uncle of Doctor Gilliam of this review, was a soldier in the War of 1812, and the heavy cannonading incidental to the battle of Norfolk destroyed the drums of both of his ears, so that thereafter he was totally deaf.

As a youth Doctor Gilliam, who was signally favored in being reared in a home of distinctive culture, was afforded the advantages of an academy at Keytesville, the judicial center of his native county, and this discipline was supplemented by his attendance in William Jewell College, in Ray County, Missouri, and Central University, a Missouri institution conducted under the auspices of the Methodist Church. In the latter college his training was advanced to the point that made him eligible for the reception of the degree of Bachelor of Arts, and in the institution he also availed himself of the advantages of the medical department. Leaving college in 1872, Doctor Gilliam thereafter gave his attention to farm work and the reading of medicine until he had gained a thorough training in medicine and surgery and was well equipped for the practical work of the profession which has been dignified and honored by his services.

On the 5th of August, 1876, Doctor Gilliam came to Indian Territory and established his residence at Berwyn, where he engaged in the practice of medicine and also assumed the direction of the Indian school, in which he was a successful and popular teacher. At that time there were nine schools maintained for the Indians in the Chickasaw Nation, and the office of teacher in the same was a position much sought, there being avid competition, owing to the fact that the teacher was paid a salary of $45 a month, which was looked upon as a large emolument under the conditions obtaining at the time. Doctor Gilliam proved his ability and was chosen from a number of competitors, his service as teacher of the Indian school having thereafter continued for a period of three years. Thereafter he gave his attention to the active practice of medicine for a term of twelve years, and in the meanwhile he became the owner of 1,100 acres of land in what is now Carter County. In 1880 he instituted the improvement of this property and established his home on the pioneer ranch, of which he still retains 400 acres, given over to diversified agriculture and the raising of excellent grades of livestock.

In July, 1915, Doctor Gilliam purchased of his son-in-law, Dr. James W. Webb, the drug store at Berwyn, and he now conducts the store, which was established many years ago and is the only one in the village. When Doctor Gilliam retired from the active practice of his profession, nearly a quarter of a century ago, he sold his stock of drugs and medicines to the proprietor of the drug store of which he himself is now the owner, it being interesting to note that certain of his original medicines are still to be found on the shelves of the establishment. Concerning the former owner, Doctor Webb, individual mention is made on other pages of this work.

In politics Doctor Gilliam has always been found strongly aligned as a supporter of the cause of the democratic party, with well fortified convictions concerning matters of economic and governmental policy. He served one year as mayor of Berwyn and in the territorial days he served also as a member of the school board, an office of which he was the incumbent one year. His religious views are in harmony with the tenets of the Methodist Episcopal Church South, which he attends and liberally supports. He is affiliated with Berwyn Lodge No. 59, Ancient Free and Accepted Masons, and served eight years as master of the same. In this time-honored fraternity the doctor has received also the thirty-second degree of the Ancient Accepted Scottish Rite, and is affiliated with Indian Consistory No. 2, at McAlester. He holds membership also in the Berwyn Lodge of the Independent Order of Odd Fellows.

Doctor Gilliam has been thrice married. In 1872, in Chariton County, Missouri, he wedded Miss Lizzie Harper, and she died at Berwyn, Indian Territory, in 1879. Three children were born of this union: Robert, who died at the age of thirty-two years, he having been a prosperous farmer; Mary Pauline, who died at Berwyn June 16, 1915,—her thirty-eighth birthday anniversary; and Alva Edward, who was killed by lightning when he was twenty years of age.

In 1880 Doctor Gilliam married Susan Brushingham, an orphan of part Chickasaw Indian blood, she having been well educated in the schools of Kansas, and her death having occurred in 1891. Concerning the children of this marriage the following brief data are entered: Lizzie is the wife of Frank Tindall, of Durwood, Carter County, in which vicinity he is engaged in farming, having formerly been a merchant. Olivet H. is the wife of Roy Cotner, of Pryor Creek, this state, and her husband is a traveling salesman. Sallie died at the age of eighteen years. John, James and Howard are triplets, John being a prosperous ranchman in Southwestern Texas, James being identified with the cattle business near Marietta, Oklahoma, and Howard being his father's assistant in the drug store at Berwyn.

On the 9th of August, 1892, Doctor Gilliam married Mrs. Nannie (Sigmon) Largen, a daughter of the late Israel Sigmon, who was a farmer in the State of Arkansas, the first husband of Mrs. Gilliam having been Frank Largen, who was a farmer of Carter County, Oklahoma, at the time of his death. Doctor and Mrs. Gilliam have four children,—Mary, Amon, Leslie and Donald. Mary, who has been a popular and successful school teacher, married, in July, 1915, Carson Hatifield, and they maintain their residence at Berwyn.

REV. JOHN REAGAN ABERNATHY. There are two fields in which Rev. Mr. Abernathy, who is a young man of about thirty-six, has attained more than ordinary distinction. He is one of the hard-working, earnest and effective leaders in the Methodist Episcopal Church, South, and in that capacity has traveled over nearly all parts of Oklahoma and has a wide acquaintance. He has turned his ability and talent to great usefulness in the cause of his Master. He is now pastor of the Methodist Episcopal Church, South, at Okmulgee. Rev. Mr. Abernathy is also one of the best known figures in Oklahoma Masonry, and was recently honored with the thirty-third degree of the Scottish Rite, that honor having been conferred upon him at the minimum age of thirty-five.

A native Texan, he was born at Hamilton in that state October 29, 1879, a son of J. E. and Cassandra (McCleary) Abernathy. His parents were born in Giles County, Tennessee, and were partly reared there, but both were educated in Ebenezer College at Springfield, Missouri, where they graduated with the class of 1858. In the following year they were married in Giles County, Tennessee, and they afterwards moved to Texas, where J. E. Abernathy was a farmer and mechanic. His death occurred in 1885 at the age of sixty, and the mother passed away in 1912 at seventy-two. During the war J. E. Abernathy became a Confederate soldier under General Price and was a commissioned officer. For many years in Texas he was a power in church work. He possessed a fine tenor voice, was song leader in many of the meetings which he attended, and his presence was always felt as a stimulating course whether in the small meetings held within doors or the larger assemblages at camp grounds. His wife was also a devout Christian. In their family were five daughters and two sons, and the two sons and two of the daughters are still living.

As a boy Rev. Mr. Abernathy grew up largely at the home of his uncle M. T. Abernathy. He attended public schools both in Texas and in Missouri and graduated at Scarrett College in Neosho, Missouri, in 1900 with the degree Ph. B. In the same year he joined the Southwest Missouri Conference of the Methodist Episcopal Church, South, and has now been active in church work for fifteen years. For the first year he was at Lamar Station, and then for two years was pastor of the Washington Street Church in Kansas City. The next two years, 1903-'04, he spent as a student in Vanderbilt University at Nashville, after which he returned to Missouri and was active in pastoral work until 1908.

On coming to Oklahoma Rev. Mr. Abernathy became pastor of the large church at Guthrie, and remained there until 1914, when he accepted the call to the church at Okmulgee. During the last four years at Guthrie he was also a Masonic lecturer under the auspices of the Scottish Rite bodies, spending about five months of the year at that work in addition to his church duties. It was in October, 1915, at Washington, D. C., that Mr. Abernathy received the thirty-third and highest degree in Scottish Rite Masonry. He has also done some lecture work in the State Chautauquas.

He is a man of many interests and possesses many splendid talents which have made him valued and esteemed in whatever community he has lived. He is now an active member of the chamber of commerce at Okmulgee. In 1907 he married Miss Helen Hinman of Centralia, Missouri. Mrs. Abernathy takes a prominent part in church and club work, especially in the musical side, possessing a well trained voice for singing.

JEAN P. DAY. Few of the vital and progressive cities of Oklahoma have forged so rapidly, and substantially to the front rank as has McAlester, the metropolis and judicial center of Pittsburg County and the center also of one of the finest coal-producing districts in the state. The elements of stability have been in distinct evidence in this splendid advancement and the city is vigorous and prosperous—the stage of large and important commercial and industrial activities and the home of an enterprising and progressive element of citizenship. He whose name initiates this paragraph has secure prestige as one of the able and successful representatives of the legal profession in Pittsburg County and is in control of a substantial and important law business in the City of McAlester, so that he is well entitled to recognition in this publication, as one of the representative members of the bar of this section of the state.

Mr. Day was born in Webster County, Mississippi, on the 31st of January, 1874, and is a son of Jonathan J. and Amanda R. (Pollan) Day, both of whom were born and reared in Mississippi, where the respective families were founded in an early day. In 1889 Jonathan J. Day came with his family to what is now the State of Oklahoma and became a pioneer settler when the original section of the old Indian Territory was thrown open for such settlement, though Oklahoma Territory was not formally created until the following year. He entered claim to a homestead in what is now Oklahoma County, where he instituted the reclamation of a farm and where he and his wife continued to reside until 1903, when they removed to Pittsburg County and established their home in the thriving little City of Hartshorne, where Mrs. Day was summoned to the life eternal in 1914, at the age of sixty-six years. The death of Mr. Day occurred November 13, 1915, he having celebrated his seventieth birthday anniversary in that year. He had the energy and good judgment to profit fully by the advantages afforded to him in Oklahoma and became one of the sterling and honored pioneers of the state to whose civic and industrial development and upbuilding he contributed his quota, practically his entire active career having been marked by close and effective identification with the great basic industry of agriculture.

He was aligned as an unswerving advocate of the principles of the democratic party and during the climacteric period of the Civil war he represented his native state as one of its gallant soldiers who went forth in defense of the cause of the Confederacy. Jonathan J. and Amanda R. (Pollan) Day became the parents of only two children, and the elder is Jean P., whose name introduces this article; Allie is now the wife of Robert M. Boardman and they maintain their home at Decatur, Illinois.

Jean P. Day acquired his early education in his native state and was a lad of fifteen years at the time of the family removal to the wilds of the newly organized Territory of Oklahoma, into which he recalls that he rode in dignified state by the side of his father and mounted on the back of a gray mule which claimed the "dejected havior of the visage" that is common to the animals of this type. Mr. Day found ample demand upon his time and services in connection with the reclamation and other work of the pioneer farm in Oklahoma County, but was not denied opportunities for the proper supplementing of his education. He attended the old Central Normal School of Oklahoma Territory, at Edmond, where he fortified himself admirably for successful work in the pedagogic profession. For several years he was an efficient and popular teacher in the public schools of Oklahoma, and his services in this line included his effective work as principal of the Emerson School in Oklahoma City.

In preparation for the vocation of his choice, Mr. Day began the study of law under the able preceptorship of Hon. Henry H. Howard, of Oklahoma City, and in 1899 he was admitted to the territorial bar. He initiated the practice of his profession at Poteau, Indian Territory, a place that is now the judicial center of LeFlore County, Oklahoma, and there he remained ten years, within which decade he developed a good practice and gained a place as one of the leading members of the bar of that section. In 1909 Mr. Day was appointed to aid in the revision of the code of laws of the recently organized State of Oklahoma, and the result of that revision is the well known Harris-Day Code of Oklahoma Law, issued in 1910. During the time that he was engaged in this important work Mr. Day maintained his residence at Guthrie, the former territorial capital, and in 1910 he removed to the rapidly growing City of McAlester, where he has since continued in the successful general practice of his profession and where he has appeared in much important litigation and as attorney and counselor for many representative corporations and individually influential citizens.

The democratic party has found Mr. Day as one of its resourceful and unfailing supporters in Oklahoma and though he has been influential in the party councils and campaign activities under both the territorial and state regimes he has not been ambitious for public office, but recently he was elevated to the supreme court bench and his friends, both democrats and republicans, joined in a banquet celebrating this honor. Mr. Day was a delegate to the Democratic National Convention in 1908. He has received the thirty-second degree of the Ancient Accepted Scottish Rite of the Masonic fraternity and is affiliated also with the Benevolent & Protective Order of Elks. He is a prominent member of the Pittsburg County Bar Association and holds membership also in the Oklahoma State Bar Association.

The year 1900 recorded the marriage of Mr. Day to Miss Aubie Oates, of Paris, Texas, and they have one child, Doris, who was born in 1901.

LINDSEY L. LONG., M. D. That historic section of Western Oklahoma that was designated as No Man's

Land and organized into Cimarron Territory in a local way prior to the opening of Oklahoma Territory to settlement, has become one of the vital and prosperous sections of the state, and one of the important counties is Beaver, in which Doctor Long controls a large and important practice as a physician and surgeon and has gained precedence as one of the representative members of his profession in Western Oklahoma. He maintains his residence and professional headquarters at Beaver, the county seat, and is one of the progressive and loyal citizens of the town and county.

Dr. Lindsey Lowder Long was born on a farm in Neosho County, Kansas, on the 22d of September, 1875, a date that clearly demonstrates that his parents were numbered among the pioneers of that section of the Sunflower State. He is a son of David and Jeanette (Lowder) Long, the former a native of North Carolina and the latter of Indiana, in which latter state their marriage was solemnized in 1850.

David Long was born in North Carolina on the 15th of October, 1824, and his parents claimed the Old Dominion State of Virginia as the place of their nativity, the respective families having there been founded in the colonial era of our national history. In 1828, when he was a child of about four years, the parents of David Long removed from North Carolina and became pioneer settlers in the wilds of Greene County, Indiana, where they passed the remainder of their lives and where the father reclaimed a farm from the wilderness. In Greene County David was reared under the conditions and influences of the early pioneer days, in the meanwhile availing himself of the advantages of the schools of the locality and period, and in 1850, when about twenty-five years of age, he there wedded Miss Jeanette Lowder, who was born in Lawrence County, that state, on the 2d of July, 1832, a daughter of John R. and Aesah (Hodson) Lowder, pioneers of that county, to which they removed from their native State of North Carolina. After his marriage Mr. Long continued his activities as a farmer in Greene County, Indiana, until 1871, when he removed with his family to Kansas and became one of the pioneer settlers in Neosho County. He purchased a tract of land two miles south of old Osage Mission, and there reclaimed a productive farm. He became one of the substantial and representative citizens of Neosho County and there continued to reside on his fine homestead farm until his death, which occurred on the 7th of March, 1896. His widow survived him by nearly fifteen years and was a resident of Erie, the judicial center of Neosho County, when she, too, was called to the life eternal on the 25th of November, 1910. Concerning their children the following brief data are entered: Rev. Matthew T., who was born October 16, 1851, is a clergyman of the Methodist Episcopal Church and maintains his home in Oklahoma. In 1875 he wedded Miss Etta Noble, and they have four children—Stella, Frederick, Ethel and Ruth—the eldest daughter, Stella, being now the wife of Rufus O. Renfrew, a prominent capitalist and influential citizen of Woodward, Oklahoma, one individually mentioned on other pages of this work. Linda A., who was born November 9, 1853, is the wife of John J. Fields, editor and publisher of the Sentinel Leader at Sentinel, Washita County, Oklahoma. Their marriage was celebrated in 1875, and they have four children—Robert, Cornelius, David and May. Cornelius, the next in order of birth of the children of David and Jeanette (Lowder) Long, was born March 6, 1855, and died on the 13th of the same month. Finley, who was born March 30, 1857, died December 20, 1908. Henry, who was born January 22, 1861, is a leading lawyer in the City of Ottawa, Kansas. John R., born February 23, 1864, is a prosperous farmer of Neosho County, Kansas. Rolla E., who was born April 27, 1869, is superintendent of the city schools of Galena, Kansas. May M., who was born March 28, 1871, is a successful and popular teacher in the public schools of the City of Sherman, Texas, and Doctor Long of this review is the youngest of the nine children.

Passing the days of his childhood and early youth on the homestead farm in Neosho County, Kansas, Doctor Long acquired his preliminary education in the district schools and thereafter attended the public schools of Erie, the county seat, where he was graduated in the high school as a member of the class of 1895. In the meanwhile he had formulated definite plans for his future career, and in the year that marked his completion of his high school course he entered the University Medical College at Kansas City, Missouri, in which institution he was graduated March 19, 1898, with the degree of Doctor of Medicine.

Immediately after his graduation in the medical college Doctor Long came to Oklahoma Territory, and, on the 20th of April of the same year, he opened an office at Alva, judicial center of Woods County, where he continued in the successful practice of his profession during the ensuing eight years. He then took an effective post-graduate course in one of the leading medical institutions of the City of Chicago, and in May, 1906, he established his home at Beaver, Oklahoma, where he has since been engaged in active general practice and where he has secure prestige as the leading representative of his profession in Beaver County. He has served as mayor of Beaver, besides holding other local offices of minor order, and has shown a lively interest in all that touches the welfare and progress of his home town and county. While a resident of Alva he served as a member of the city council and also of the board of education, besides which he did effective service as county health officer of Woods County. He holds membership in the Oklahoma State Medical Society and the American Medical Association, has completed the circles of both York and Scottish Rite Masonry, in the latter of which he has received the thirty-second degree, besides being affiliated with the Ancient Arabic Order of the Nobles of the Mystic Shrine and the Knights of Pythias.

On the 10th of September, 1899, was solemnized the marriage of Doctor Long to Miss Maude Beegle of Alva. She was born in Kingman County, Kansas, on the 13th of March, 1875, and is a daughter of Adam and Elizabeth Jane (Crottzer) Beegle, both natives of Pennsylvania and both honored pioneers of Kansas. Mr. Beegle was born in 1836 and his death occurred June 10, 1908. The mother of Mrs. Long was born in 1832 and was summoned to eternal rest on the 25th of December, 1911. Prior to her marriage Mrs. Long had been a successful and popular teacher, her work in the pedagogic profession having continued for three years after she had completed a course of study in the Colorado State Normal School at Greeley. Doctor and Mrs. Long have one child, Lenore Madge, who was born at Alva, this state, on the 12th of November, 1902.

WILLIAM ELBERT GREEN. Superintendent of the city schools of Noble, Mr. Green is an Oklahoma school man of considerable experience and holds a life teacher's certificate in this state. At Noble he has under his supervision a corps of six teachers, 250 enrolled scholars, and a modern $10,000 school house thoroughly equipped. He took charge of these schools in the fall of 1915.

He was born at Senatobia, Mississippi, July 6, 1893. His ancestors were Scotch-Irish who came to North Carolina in the early days, and there has since been a small admixture of Indian stock. Thomas Walter Green, his father, was born in Senatobia, Mississippi, in 1866, and has spent his active career as a farmer and stock man. He came to Oklahoma and located in the vicinity of Clanmore a number of years ago, but after a time returned to Mississippi, and located permanently in Chandler in 1907, and still resides there. He owns 240 acres, and does diversified farming and raises blooded stock. He has held various township offices, being prominent in local affairs in his locality. He is a democrat and has been a member of the official board of the Christian Church, and affiliates with the Modern Woodmen of America, the Woodmen of the World and the Knights of Pythias. Thomas W. Green married Sallie Eva Hancock, who was born in Independence, Mississippi, in 1871. Their children are: William E.; Mary Elizabeth, wife of Walter E. Ward, a farmer, stockman and grain dealer at Westboro, Missouri; Mattie Pearl, who graduated from the Chandler High School and was a student in the state normal at Edmond and is now a teacher in Chandler; Marvin Presley, a graduate of the Chandler High School and a teacher in Okfuskee County; Lottie Lucile, a junior in the Chandler High School; and Dollie Eula, a sophomore in the high school.

William Elbert Green attended the public schools of Independence, Mississippi, the state normal college at Sherman, Mississippi, and the University of Tennessee. He graduated from the high school at Claremore, Oklahoma, in 1912, and in 1913 completed the course of the Edmond State Normal School and was granted a life teacher's certificate. During 1914 he attended the State University at Norman and has taken courses during the summer time at the university for three years past. The school year of 1914-15 he served as principal in one of the public schools at Ardmore, and he previously served as assistant superintendent of schools of Okfuskee County.

Mr. Green is a democrat, is a member of the Christian Church, and is affiliated with Chandler Lodge No. 19, Independent Order of Odd Fellows, and with the Modern Woodmen of America. He is unmarried.

MRS. BERTA (KEYS) SPOONER. In business circles of Hollis there is no name more highly esteemed than that of Mrs. Berta (Keys) Spooner, owner of the Spooner Hardware Company, and a woman of marked commercial ability. She was born at Decatur, Alabama, a daughter of C. M. and Mary (McDaniel) Keys, and a member of a Scotch-Irish family who were pioneers of Texas. C. M. Keys was born in Alabama in 1850, and in 1879 removed with his family to Cleburne, Johnson County, Texas, where for a number of years he was engaged in farming and raising stock. He now resides at Hollis, practically retired, being the owner of a farm of 160 acres four miles north of Hollis, which is being operated by tenants. Mr. Keys is a member of the Baptist Church, in which he serves as deacon.

Mr. Keys married Miss Mary McDaniel, also a native of Alabama, and they became the parents of twelve children, namely: Cricket, who is the wife of B. A. Copass, of Dallas, Texas, assistant secretary of the Baptist State Missionary Society; Berta; Ernest L., a hardware merchant of Wynnewood, Oklahoma; F. M., who is manager of the Spooner Hardware Company, at Hollis; Wood, who is connected with the hardware business at Hollis; May, who married Rev. W. A. Knight, pastor of the First Baptist Church at Frederick, Oklahoma; J. E., who is associated with his brother, Ernest L., in business; Yater, who married J. D. Pennington, bookkeeper for the Spooner Hardware Company; John, who is the wife of V. A. Grissom, the owner of the City Drug Store at Hollis; Rob, the wife of Elmer Sheppard, engaged in the real estate and insurance business at Ballinger, Texas; Sam, who holds a clerical position at Hollis; and Mott, a sophomore at the William Jewell College, Liberty, Missouri.

Mrs. Spooner accompanied her parents to Cleburne, Texas, in 1879, and there attended the public schools, following which she went to a select school for young ladies and received a high school education. She next studied the millinery art at St. Louis, Missouri, and Dallas, Texas, and was a filler in the millinery trade before her marriage. Mrs. Spooner, since the death of her husband, has been the owner of the Spooner Hardware Company, the policy and activities of which she directs, but also finds time to devote to social, religious and charitable work. She is an active member of the Baptist Church, and at the present time is state treasurer of Oklahoma for the P. E. O. Sisterhood.

In September, 1900, at Waxahatchie, Texas, Berta Keys was united in marriage with Horace Nelson Spooner, Jr., who was born at Peoria, Texas, January 9, 1872, a member of a family which originated in England and whose members were pioneer settlers of Mississippi. Horace Nelson Spooner, Sr., the father of Mr. Spooner, was born in 1843, and during the greater part of his life was engaged in clerical work. He lived for some years at Peoria, Texas, and in 1873 removed to Hillsboro, Texas, where his death occurred in 1905. He was a member of the Methodist Episcopal Church, took an active part in religious work, and was a member of the official board of his congregation for many years. His fraternal affiliation was with the Independent Order of Odd Fellows. Mr. Spooner married Miss Julia A. Foote, a native of Virginia, and she survives him and resides at Ardmore, Oklahoma.

Horace Nelson Spooner, Jr., was sent to Bethel College, Russellville, Kentucky, from which institution he was graduated in 1894, and in that same year entered a hardware store at Hillsboro, Texas, in order to become familiar with the business. There he remained several years, mastering every detail of the trade, and in 1897 went to Whitney, Texas, where he was entrusted with the position of buyer for the W. T. Herrick Hardware Company, a capacity in which he gained experience that was of the greatest value to him in later years. After eight years with that concern, he felt qualified to embark upon a venture of his own, and in January, 1905, came to Hollis, Oklahoma, and established the Spooner Hardware Company, on Broadway, which under his management soon became one of the largest hardware concerns in the State of Oklahoma. The establishment has a floor space of 50 by 100 feet, with a basement of the same dimensions, trade is drawn from all over Harmon and Greer counties, Oklahoma, and Collingsworth County, Texas, and the firm carries a most complete line of shelf and heavy hardware, stoves, implements, etc., all of the latest design and manufacture. Mr. Spooner at the time of his death, which occurred May 19, 1910, was justly accounted one of the foremost among the younger generation of business men in this part of Oklahoma. He had made his own way, unaided, and had gained success solely through his own initiative and resource. At the time of his death he was president of the Hollis Commercial Club, and enjoyed the friendship and confidence of the leading and influential men of the city. His fraternal connections included membership in Hollis Lodge No. 219, Ancient Free and Accepted Masons, and the various degrees up to the thirty-second; he being a member of Consistory No. 1, Valley of Guthrie. He was also a Pythian and an Odd Fellow, and in social circles had many friends who sincerely mourned his death. He was a democrat, but not a politician. Always a faithful member of the Methodist Episcopal Church, he was acting as steward and superintendent of the

Sunday school when called away. Though his presence is gone, he leaves behind him as a monument to his integrity and ability a firmly-established business, and an influence for good citizenship and high ideals that will remain for years after his name has been forgotten.

WILLIAM G. CAPPS. Though not yet thirty-five years of age, for more than ten years William G. Capps has been a resident of Oklahoma, and all that time an effective working force in the successive lines to which he has applied himself, whether in business, in politics and public affairs, or as a banker. He is the leading financier of Mountain Park, where he is now president of the Planters State Bank, and his name as a banker and his financial judgment are respected not alone in his home state but among bankers of national reputation.

The Capps family to which he belongs originated in France, but William G. Capps was born in Yell County, Arkansas, December 25, 1881. His father is Dr. B. F. Capps, still a prominent physician at Bluffton, Arkansas. Doctor Capps was born in Tennessee in 1850, moved from that state to New Orleans and there acquired his education for medicine, began practice at Fort Smith, Arkansas, in 1879 moved to Yell County, in 1887 to Morrillton in the same state, and finally located at Bluffton. He is an active member of the County and State Medical societies and the American Medical Association, is a democrat in politics, belongs to the Methodist Episcopal Church, is a Royal Arch Mason and also a Knight of Pythias. Doctor Capps married Miss H. L. Ward, who was born in Fort Smith, Arkansas, in 1861. Her father was Major John C. Ward, who enlisted from Arkansas at the beginning of the war between the states and became major of the First Arkansas Mounted Infantry. He re-enlisted with his regiment in Colonel John F. Hill's regiment of cavalry, and on August 10, 1861, was wounded on the south side of Bloody Hill at Wilson Creek and died as a result of his wound. He was a native of Virginia and a contractor by profession. Dr. Capps and wife were the parents of five children: William G.; Edwin, who died at Bluffton, Arkansas, at the age of twenty-one; Erick, who is bookkeeper in the Planters State Bank at Mountain Park, Oklahoma; B. F., who died at the age of two years; and Clarence, who is attending the Bluffton High School and lives with his parents.

William G. Capps had a substantial education but has been in practical business ever since he was nineteen years of age. He attended the public schools of Morrillton, Arkansas, finished the high school course there, and in 1898 took a course in a business college at Birmingham, Alabama. His first regular position was as a stenographer for the Doster & Northington Drug Company at Birmingham, with which firm he remained one year. Then after six months at Demopolis, Alabama, he returned to Bluffton, Arkansas, and spent one year in the mercantile business on his own account. Selling out, he was for six months acting secretary of the Fort Smith Commercial Club, and in 1904, at the age of twenty-three, identified himself actively with the Indian Territory portion of the present State of Oklahoma.

For one year he was bookkeeper with the Hayes Mercantile Company at Redland, and in 1905 removed to Muskogee and became advertising agent and afterwards business manager for Governor Haskell's New State Tribune. He held those positions during Haskell's successful campaign for governor of the new state. Governor Haskell then appointed him the chief food and drug inspector of Oklahoma, and he looked after the responsibilities of that newly created state office for two years. In the meantime he had acquired some financial interests in banking in Indian Territory and in 1909 went into the western part of the state and organized the Oklahoma State Bank at Frederick, serving as its cashier two years. In 1911 Mr. Capps organized the Planters State Bank at Mountain Park, and has been its active president since that date. This is one of the substantial institutions for general banking in one of the small but flourishing towns of Southwestern Oklahoma, and has a capital stock of $10,000 and a surplus of $2,000. The vice president is A. N. Trader, the assistant cashier is Edwin Herstein. The bank owns and occupies the building of the old Citizens State Bank on Main Street.

For several years Mr. Capps has furnished considerable correspondence to the newspapers of Kiowa County on various subjects related to banking. His articles have attracted more than local attention, having been quoted by some of the leading newspapers in the United States, and the wide currency of some of his ideas on country banking is well illustrated by the following quotation of a brief article which was published by the Wall Street financial journal in 1914, and subsequently quoted extensively in the financial columns of papers all over the United States. The article, furthermore, well expresses Mr. Capps' belief respecting banking activities and such prominent questions as rural credits. He said: "A country banker promotes the development of his community in proportion that he employs his money through loaning it to farmers for constructive work and improved methods—not for food or for stock feed. Present rural banking methods have resulted in entirely too much money being employed in a way that is not constructive and brings no development whatever, and thereby reduces the bank's ability to loan money for constructive farming. In proportion that a country banker fails to provide money for farm development and constructive farming, in that proportion he injures his best farmers, his community, and first of all injures himself.''

Mr. Capps has organized several banks in Oklahoma and also two wholesale houses, but has sold most of his interests in these establishments. He was for a time vice president and a stockholder in the Farmers State Bank at Quanah, Oklahoma. He has served as a member of the advisory committee of the State Bankers' Association of Oklahoma and was chairman of the Bureau of Agriculture of the Oklahoma Bankers' Development Committee. His thorough training in country banking has made him familiar with all branches of bank work, he has already gained a broad acquaintance with prominent men in the banking world, and those who know him best predict that he is far from having reached the climax in his career.

In politics Mr. Capps is a democrat. He represented the State of Oklahoma at Denver at the Conference of National and State Food and Drug Officials in 1909. He also served as county chairman of the Democratic Central County Committee in Tillman County and as city treasurer of Frederick for two years. He is now president of the board of education at Mountain Park and is always keenly alive to the needs of his home community. He assisted in organizing the Lodge of Elks at Frederick, held the position of esteemed leading knight in the lodge there, and is now a member of Hobart Lodge No. 881, Benevolent and Protective Order of Elks. He is also affiliated with Mountain Park Lodge No. 381, Ancient Free and Accepted Masons, and with Snyder Chapter No. 76, Royal Arch Masons.

At Mountain Park in 1912 Mr. Capps married Miss Lillian Trader, daughter of A. N. Trader, who is a farmer and is also vice president of the Planters State Bank at Mountain Pass. They have one daughter, Marjorie, born August 7, 1913.

DENZIL A. DRAKE. A significantly varied and interesting career has been that of Mr. Drake, who has been a resident of Oklahoma since the year that marked its organization under territorial government, and who is now one of the most liberal and progressive citizens of the Village of Hitchcock, Blaine County, where he is not only engaged in the real estate business but where he is also the senior member of the firm of D. A. Drake & Son, publishers and editors of the Hitchcock Clarion, a weekly paper that has been brought up to high standard under his administration and control and in the directing of the affairs of which he has given new evidence of his versatility.

Mr. Drake has been distinctively one of the world's workers, he has gained varied experience in divers sections of the Union, he has been steadfast and sincere in all of the relations of life, has shown initiative ability and a mastery of expedients in varied fields of endeavor, and in Oklahoma he has found ample scope for the achieving of success and for exerting admirable influence in the furtherance of general civic and material advancement and prosperity.

A due amount of satisfaction is given to Mr. Drake in claiming the fine old Buckeye State as the place of his nativity and as a commonwealth in which the family of which he is a scion was founded in the early pioneer era of its history. He was born in Summit County, Ohio, on the 26th of April, 1859. His paternal great-grandfather was one of three brothers who immigrated to the United States from Wales, and his grandfather became a pioneer of Ohio, besides which he manifested his loyalty to the land of his adoption by serving as a valiant frontier soldier in the War of 1812. Both he and his wife were residents of Summit County, Ohio, at the time of their death, and he had taken well his part in the development of that section of the Buckeye State.

Denzil A. Drake is a son of Jasper B. and Caroline (Hardy) Drake, both natives of Summit County, Ohio, where the former was born in 1814 and the latter in 1819,—dates that clearly indicated that the respective families were early pioneers of that section. Jasper B. Drake and his wife passed the closing years of their long and worthy lives at Ness City, judicial center of Ness County, Kansas, where he died in 1899, and where his widow was summoned to eternal rest in 1904, at the venerable age of eighty-five years, both having been for many years zealous members of the Christian Church, and the entire active career of Mr. Drake having been one of close identification with agricultural industry. Just prior to the outbreak of the Civil war Jasper B. Drake removed with his family to Cedar County, Iowa, where he became a pioneer farmer in the vicinity of the present Town of Durant. In 1866, shortly after the close of the war, he removed to Cass County, Missouri, and later he became a representative farmer of Ness County, Kansas, where he passed the remainder of his long and useful life, the closing period of which was spent in well earned retirement, at Ness City.

He whose name introduces this article, was a child of about four years at the time of the family immigration to Iowa, and there he acquired his rudimentary education in the pioneer rural schools of Cedar County, his studies having later been continued in the little frame school house near his father's farm in Cass County, Missouri. He applied himself to study at home during his youth and through his self-application and broad and varied experiences in later years he has rounded out what may consistently be termed a liberal education. He continued to be associated with his father in farm work until he was sixteen years of age, when he initiated his independent career. This initiation was far from being one of prosaic order, for in 1875, soon after celebrating his sixteenth birthday anniversary, he made his way to California, where he proceeded up the Sacramento Valley and devoted his attention to the selling of books and periodicals, a line of enterprise which he followed during the first years of his residence in the Golden State. During the second year he ''held down'' a comparatively profitable position as collector for the waterworks at Colusa, that state.

Remaining in California about two years, young Drake then returned to Cass County, Missouri, in 1878, and in February of the following year he there took unto himself a wife, who remained his devoted helpmeet until her death, about thirteen years later. After his marriage Mr. Drake removed to Ness County, Kansas, where he took up homestead and timber claims and instituted the reclamation and development of a farm. There he continued to devote his attention to agricultural pursuits and stock raising for a period of five years, within which he perfected his title to his homestead. At the expiration of the interval noted he exchanged his farm and livestock for a stock of goods and engaged in the general merchandise business at Buffalo Park, Gove County, Kansas, where he continued his operations in this line of enterprise from 1884 until 1887, when he again exercised the true Yankee trading proclivity by ''swapping'' his stock of merchandise and the good will of the business for a bunch of cattle. He thereupon returned to Ness County and filed entry on a preemption claim, where he placed his cattle and resumed his activities as a farmer and stock raiser. He remained on this farm one year and proved up on the property. From his farm he removed to the Town of Utica, Ness County, and there established a real estate office. He developed a substantial business in the handling of Kansas land, and at one time owned fully thirty quarter-sections, but depreciation in the prices of land in that section of the Sunflower State led him to dispose of his holdings by his favored method of making exchange of properties, and in 1890, the year that marked the organization of Oklahoma Territory he came to the present Oklahoma County and was a pioneer of the Town of Edmond. He remained only a few months, however, and then returned to Missouri, where he devoted one year to farming, in Jasper County.

Mention has already been made of the fact that Mr. Drake is possessed of marked versatility, and after leaving the Jasper County farm he engaged in work at the stone mason's trade, at Carthage, that state, this trade having been learned by him in earlier years. He resumed work in this line principally for the benefit of his health and after following the same during one summer he removed with his family to the City of Wichita, Kansas, where he engaged in the furniture business until the financial panic of 1897 compelled him to sacrifice the same. From that time forward until 1900 he served as a commercial traveling salesman, handling queensware.

In 1900 Mr. Drake purchased a general store situated five miles southeast of Hitchcock, Blaine County, Oklahoma, and after conducting this rural store one year he removed, in 1901, to Hitchcock, becoming virtually one of the founders of the town, in which he erected the first building and in the same opened the first stock of merchandise. He named his establishment the Pioneer Store, and conducted the same from August, 1901, until the following February, when financial circumstances compelled him to abandon the enterprise. In the same spring, however, he opened the first drug store in the village, and after conducting the same four years he

sold the stock and business and turned his attention to the handling of real estate, in which he has since continued with distinctive success, his operations having been of broad scope and importance and having been potent in furthering the settlement and development of this section of the state.

In October, 1908, Mr. Drake purchased a half interest in the Hitchcock Clarion, and in the following year he acquired the full ownership of this newspaper property and business. As editor and publisher of the Clarion he has made the paper a most effective exponent of local interests and has made it a valuable factor in the directing of popular sentiment and action in the community. In the editing and publishing of the Clarion Mr. Drake has an able coadjutor in the person of his son, Frank, though the latter gives the major part of his time and attention to the Stratford Tribune, at Stratford, Garvin County, of which he is editor and publisher, the business at Hitchcock being conducted under the firm name of D. A. Drake & Son. Mr. Drake was assisted greatly in the movement that resulted in the founding of the Hitchcock Clarion, which dates its inception from March 27, 1908, and, as previously intimated, he soon came into control of the property and business, the paper being independent in politics and having an excellent circulation in Blaine and adjacent counties.

Mr. Drake has been one of the most vital, far-sighted and progressive of the enterprising citizens who have wielded great influence in the development and upbuilding of the town of Hitchcock, and he has served two terms as mayor of the village, besides which he have held the office of justice of the peace eight years. He has served two terms as clerk of the school board, and within his incumbency of this position he was one of the foremost in the movement that brought about the consolidation of six school districts and the erection, at Hitchcock, of a substantial and thoroughly modern building for the accommodation of these combined districts, this action having made possible the bringing of the school work up to a far higher plane of efficiency an was previously maintained, this being one of the first of such consolidated school districts in this part of the state.

Mr. Drake has been a member of the Christian Church since he was a lad of twelve years, and amid "all the changes and chances of this mortal life," his abiding Christian faith has dominated his course and constituted a bulwark of defense and reconciliation. He was one of the founders of the Christian Church at Hitchcock and is earnestly and ably serving the same in the office of elder, his wife likewise being a zealous and valued member. Mr. Drake is affiliated with Watonga Lodge, No. 176, Ancient Free and Accepted Masons, at Watonga, the county seat of Blaine County, and is an appreciative and popular member of the Oklahoma State Press Association.

In February, 1879, at Harrisonville, Cass County, Missouri, Mr. Drake wedded Miss Alma Robertson, whose father, William A. Robertson, was a merchant of that place, though he passed the closing period of his life as a farmer in Oklahoma. Mrs. Drake was summoned to the life eternal in 1892, in Jasper County, Missouri, and she is survived by five children, concerning whom brief mention is here made: Caroline is the wife of William E. Beard and they reside in the City of Claremore, Oklahoma, where Mr. Beard conducts a garage. Hattie is the wife of Ford O. Shoemaker, of Wichita, Kansas. Pearl is the wife of Oscar Burton, a merchant at Caldwell, Kansas. George is engaged in the grocery business at Wichita, Kansas. Florence is the wife of Harry Sumption, who is engaged in the jewelry business in the City of Seattle, Washington.

In February, 1893, was solemnized the marriage of Mr. Drake to Miss Hattie Robertson, a sister of his first wife, and their only child is Frank, who was born in March, 1894, who was graduated in the Watonga High School, and who is associated with his father in the newspaper business at Hitchcock. He is one of the alert, successful and representative young newspaper men of Oklahoma, and has shown marked ability in his chosen field of enterprise.

DR. THOMAS JEFFERSON DODSON is one of the pioneer physicians and surgeons of Mangum, Oklahoma, having come here in 1900. He has been in constant practice here since that time, and has a high standing in the community and among his professional brethren. He is a native son of the state, born in Coriell County, Texas, on September 23, 1862, and his parents were William P. and Rachel G. (Green) Dodson.

William P. Dodson was born in Kentucky in 1824, and died in Paint Rock, Texas, in 1898. From his native state he came to Coriell County, Texas, in 1849, one of the pioneers of that time, and in 1879 he settled in Concho County, Texas, where he passed the remainder of his life. He was a rancher and stock raiser, and was successful and prosperous. During the Civil war he served the South as a frontier guard in Texas. Mr. Dodson was a Methodist and was long a steward in the church. He was a Mason, and was past senior warden of his lodge. His politics were those of a democrat. His wife was a woman of Missouri birth and parentage, born in 1824, and she died in Paint Rock in 1907. They were the parents of a family of nine children. Adeline, the first born, married George Jackson, and lives on their farm in New Mexico; Mary Jane is deceased; she married O. A. Lewis, and he is now a resident of San Angelo, Texas; Jesse P. is a carpenter and builder in Oklahoma; J. F. is a stock farmer at Paint Rock, the old home of the family; Sarah married J. C. Oliver, a Baptist minister of Abilene, Texas; Casana died at the age of ten years; the seventh born child was Thomas Jefferson, subject of this review; Sophronia married Edward Dozier and they live at Paint Rock; he is a stock farmer and has served as county sheriff; Lucy married James Davis and they live in Paint Rock, where Mr. Davis is a farmer.

Dr. Thomas Jefferson Dodson was born and reared on his father's ranch in Coriell County, and in 1879, when he was seventeen years old, the family moved from that place to Paint Rock, Concho County. From then until 1887 he lived at home and in that year he entered Centenary College, Lampasas, Texas, and there completed a three years' course of study. In 1891 he was graduated from the medical department of the University of Tennessee at Nashville, with the degree M. D. In 1891 Doctor Dodson began the practice of his profession at Bartlett, Texas, continuing until 1898, and then he engaged in practice in Sonora, where he remained until October, 1900. It was then that he came to Mangum, since which time he has been engaged in a general medical and surgical practice, barring one year. 1904, which he spent in the Chicago Post Graduate School in further preparation for his work.

Doctor Dodson has his offices in the Elliott Building. He is president of the Grier County Medical Society and is a member of the State and American Medical associations.

The doctor has always been ready and willing to give public service when it was required of him, and he has been health physician of Grier County on the democratic ticket. While practicing in Sonora he served as a member of the local school board, and he is a trustee of the Methodist Episcopal Church of Mangum.

Doctor Dodson is a Mason, and those Masonic bodies with which he is connected are as follows: Mangum Lodge No. 61, Ancient Free and Accepted Masons, of which he is past master; Mangum Chapter No. 35, Royal Arch Masons, in which he served for nine years as high priest; Hobart Commandery, Knights Templar; Mangum Chapter, Order of the Eastern Star, of which he is past patron; India Temple, Ancient Arabic Order of Nobles of the Mystic Shrine, Oklahoma City. He is also a member of the local lodge of the Knights of Pythias and of the Modern Woodmen of America.

Doctor Dodson was married on October 15, 1890, in Sonora, Texas, to Miss Della Pool, of Bartlett, Texas. She died in 1894, leaving two daughters. Daphne, the eldest, is a graduate of the Mangum High School, and also studied music at Baylor University in Belton, Texas, and at Epworth University in Oklahoma City. She is now engaged in teaching music in Mangum. The second child, Fay, died at the age of eleven years. In 1895 Doctor Dodson married Miss Elizabeth Smith, of Bartlett, Texas, a daughter of Benjamin R. Smith, who was a well known farmer there, and who died in 1904. There are two daughters of this marriage: Thelma, a graduate of the Mangum High School in 1915, and Naomi, now a senior in that school.

DANIEL WILLIAM PEERY. In a record of the men who have taken an important part in the upbuilding and development of Oklahoma, it would be almost impossible to avoid extended mention of Daniel William Peery. A member of the First and Second Territorial legislatures, one of the founders of the state, subsequently elected to the State Legislature, the editor and publisher of a newspaper for eight years, and one of the organizers of the City of Carnegie, his name is indissolubly identified with the history of the commonwealth, where he has been prominent in business and political circles from the time of his arrival.

Mr. Peery was born at Edinburg, Grundy County, Missouri, August 16, 1864, and is a son of Dr. Arch and Elizabeth (Kirk) Peery. The family is of Norman origin, the name having been originally spelled Perie, and was founded in the Colony of Virginia in 1717 by the American ancestor, a native of the North of Ireland who located in Augusta County. From that county, William Peery, the great-grandfather of Daniel W. Peery, moved to Tazewell County, Virginia, in 1775, and enlisted from the latter county as a soldier in the American army during the War of the Revolution. As a soldier in the Revolution he served with Gen. Roger Clark in his expedition against old Fort Vincennes and was one of five men who were with General Clark from Tazewell County. His son, George Peery, was born in Tazewell County, from whence he migrated in 1835 as a pioneer to Northern Missouri, where he rounded out a long and active career in the pursuits of farming.

Arch Peery, the father of Daniel William Peery, was born in Tazewell County, Virginia, in 1818, and was a lad when he accompanied his father to Missouri. He grew up amid pioneer surroundings and was reared on the home farm, but was granted good educational advantages, and after thorough preparation enrolled as one of the early students of the old Missouri Medical College, at St. Louis, where he was duly graduated with his degree. He became one of the pioneer physicians and surgeons of Grundy County, Missouri, and for many years practiced at Edinburg, where he died, honored and respected, in 1888. Doctor Peery married Miss Elizabeth Kirk, who was born in Giles County, Virginia, in 1826, a daughter of Maj. Thomas Kirk, of Giles County, who was an officer in the American army during the War of 1812. Mrs. Peery died in Grundy County, Missouri, in 1898, having been the mother of eight children, as follows: Horace J., who at the time of his death at Albany, Missouri, in 1911, was register of deeds and county clerk; Florence H., who is the wife of John H. Peery, a distant relative, of Jamesport, Missouri; Nash A., now a practicing attorney of Portland, Oregon; Dr. T. P., a graduate of the Missouri Medical College, and now engaged in the practice of medicine and surgery in Yuba City, Sutter County, California; Mary C., who has been for thirty-three years a teacher, and for twenty-two years of that time at Portland, Oregon; Arch, who is engaged in farming and resides in the vicinity of Apache, Oklahoma; Daniel William, of this notice; and John T., who is now living on the old homestead farm at Edinburg, near Trenton, Missouri.

Daniel William Peery received his education in the public schools of Grundy County and Grand River College, an institution which had been founded by his family and chartered by the Legislature of Missouri in 1852. He was brought up to farming pursuits, and remained on the homestead until reaching the age of twenty-four years. He came to Oklahoma April 22, 1889, and filed on a homestead of 160 acres a few miles southeast of Oklahoma City. Mr. Peery has been present and assisted at every opening of public land in the state, and has taken part in all the runs, including the opening of the Sac, Fox, and Pottawatomie reservations, September 19, 1891; the opening of Cheyenne and Arapahoe counties, in April, 1892, the Cherokee Strip, September 16, 1893, and the drawing of the Kiowa and Comanche reservations, and in the latter assisted in locating many of the settlers.

On August 6, 1890, Mr. Peery was elected one of five representatives from Oklahoma County to the First Territorial Legislature, and in that capacity assisted in the organization of the great State of Oklahoma. He was sent to the Second Legislature, in 1893, and in that year removed to El Reno, where, with William Clute, he founded the El Reno Globe, a newspaper which became one of the prominent and influential publications of the state, and which he edited until 1901. In that year Mr. Peery came to Carnegie, Caddo County, as agent for the Townsite of Carnegie, a capacity in which he sold the land and helped to found the town. In 1910 he was again elected to the Oklahoma Legislature, representing the counties of Caddo, Canadian and Cleveland. In that body he was known as one of the most active and prominent members, having charge of the bill which located the capital at Oklahoma City, and also taking an active part in educational legislation, in assisting in locating the agricultural college at Stillwater, the university at Norman and the normal school at Edmond. A leading democrat, he was a delegate from the Territory of Oklahoma to the Kansas City National Convention of his party, which nominated William Jennings Bryan for the presidency, and from the State of Oklahoma to the Denver National Convention, which also chose that statesman as the leader of the party. He has been active in state and county democratic conventions, nearly every one of which he has attended since the organization of the state, and over several of which he has presided. In 1911 he became a candidate for Congress from the Northwest District, becoming the seventh candidate in the field, but met with defeat undoubtedly because he only presented his name twenty-six days before the primaries, when the greater number of his friends were already pledged.

At the present time Mr. Peery is a member of the real estate firm of Peery & Crose, his partner, L. P. Crose, being the present mayor of Carnegie. Among the men who, as public servants, have made enviable records for their faithful, earnest and successful efforts in securing beneficial and wise legislation, none is better or more favorably known than is Dan W. Peery. An earnest worker for the advancement of his party's interests, he yet has never allowed his partisanship to interfere with his efforts in the advancement of what he has considered best for the interests of his constituents as a whole. And in every walk of life, whether public or private, the same high principles have been found to govern his actions.

POSETHIA L. SANDERS, M. D. The pioneer physician and surgeon of Carnegie, Oklahoma, Dr. Posethia L. Sanders, has been engaged in practice here since 1903, and has been successful in building up a large and important professional business. Prior to coming to this city, he had secured a thorough and comprehensive training in the line of his calling, and the newly-opened community offered a prolific field for the display of his talents. Doctor Sanders was born in Christian County, Illinois, February 11, 1877, and is a son of F. M. and M. A. (Fultz) Sanders.

The Sanders family originated in Scotland, and from that country the American progenitor came to this country long before the outbreak of the War of the Revolution, settling in the colony of Virginia, from whence the family spread to various of the southern states, and particularly to Kentucky, where the name is well known. Members of the family have been well known in public life, in business, agriculture and the professions, and have always been men and women of substance and standing, honored by and honoring their communities. F. M. Sanders, the father of Doctor Sanders, is a member of the branch of the family which went to Kentucky, and was born in that state in 1838. He received a common school education, and was brought up to agricultural pursuits, so that when he entered upon his career he adopted farming as his vocation. From his native state he removed to Greene County, Illinois, and in 1860 went to Christian County, in the same state, where he settled on a farm. There he continued successfully engaged in farming and stockraising operations for many years, but in 1892 removed to Sumner County, Kansas, where he has since made his home. He continued to be occupied as a tiller of the soil until a few years ago when advancing years caused his retirement and he moved to Wellington, Kansas, where he is living quietly in his comfortable home, enjoying the fruits of his many years of honest toil. Mr. Sanders has been a lifelong democrat, but has been content to remain a farmer, and has not let public life lure him from his home. For many years he has been identified with the Masonic fraternity, and is now a member of the Royal Arch Chapter of that fraternity. Both he and Mrs. Sanders are consistent members of the Baptist Church, in the faith of which their children have been reared. To Mr. and Mrs. Sanders there were born three children: Dr. Posethia L., of this review; Mattie M., who is the wife of L. A. Boory and resides at Wellington, Kansas, where Mr. Boory is engaged in the plumbing and gasfitting business; and Arleigh G., whose death occurred at the age of twelve years.

The early education of Dr. P. L. Sanders was secured in the district schools of Christian County, Illinois, in the vicinity of his father's farm, on which he worked as a lad and youth during the summer months. He was fifteen years of age when the family moved to Sumner County, Kansas, and there he continued his public training, attending both the graded schools and the high school at Mayfield, Kansas. He had always cherished an ambition to engage in the practice of medicine, and to gratify this wish took up the study of the profession at the University of Kansas, where he was duly graduated from the medical department with his diploma and degree, in 1901. His studies did not end there, however, for he has continued to be an assiduous scholar, and has taken several post-graduate courses, including a course in 1906, at the New York Medical School, of the University of New York, and courses in 1911 at the Chicago Polyclinic and the Chicago Post-Graduate School.

At the time of his graduation from the University of Kansas, in 1901, Doctor Sanders embarked in practice at Mayfield, Kansas, where he remained until 1903, at that time coming to Carnegie and opening an office as the pioneer physician and surgeon of the place. Important professional business was soon attracted to him by his undoubted talents, and as the years have passed he has steadily advanced in professional prestige and public favor. His broad and general practice includes every branch of his calling, and in each he is recognized as a thoroughly capable and reliable practitioner. Doctor Sanders maintains well-appointed offices on the second floor of the Cole-Hugill Building. He holds membership in the various organizations and societies of his profession, including the Caddo County Medical Society, the Oklahoma State Medical Society, the Southwestern Medical Society and the American Medical Association. That he is highly esteemed by his professional brethren is shown by the fact that he has served in the capacity of president of the Caddo County organization. Doctor Sanders has various financial and business interests at Carnegie, and is a director in the Benedict Oil Company, of Arizona. His fraternal connections include membership in Carnegie Lodge, Ancient Free and Accepted Masons, the lodges of the Modern Woodmen of America and the Woodmen of the World, at Carnegie, and the Fraternal Mystic Circle, at Mayfield, Kansas. He is a republican in politics, but his only public office has been that of health officer of Carnegie. He is a member of the Methodist Episcopal Church, and a member of the board of trustees of that congregation.

Doctor Sanders was married in June, 1905, at Carnegie, to Miss Ethel Fredregill, daughter of G. W. Fredregill, who was a pioneer hardware merchant of Carnegie, but is now engaged in farming in Caddo County. One child has been born to Doctor and Mrs. Sanders: Vera Bernadine, born in October, 1907, who is now attending the Carnegie public schools.

EUGENE D. POWELL. For a young man of twenty-four years Eugene D. Powell has covered a good deal of ground in the newspaper profession and is now editor and manager of the Times at Altus. He was practically reared in the trade and profession of printer and newspaper man, and consequently knows all the ins and outs of the business, and since taking charge of the Times has succeeded in giving it a considerable impetus to increase circulation and influence.

The Powell family which he represents came originally from England and was settled in Virginia during the colonial days. Eugene D. Powell was born at Wilton, Arkansas, July 2, 1891, a son of Rev. C. M. and Georgia (Walden) Powell. His father, who was born at Mineral Springs, Arkansas, in 1860, is now a resident of Bellevue, Texas. Rev. Mr. Powell was educated in the common schools at his birthplace in Arkansas and studied theology in the Southern Baptist Seminary at Louisville, Kentucky. Since leaving the seminary he has been continuously active in his profession as a Baptist minister, and his duties brought him in 1901 to Stillwell in Indian Territory. From there he moved to Afton in the territory in 1904, subsequently to Eldorado, Oklahoma, and finally to his present place of residence at Bellevue,

Texas, where he is pastor of the Baptist Church. While living at Wilton and also at Stillwell and Afton in Indian Territory he edited the newspapers of those towns in addition to his regular duties as a minister. He is a democrat in politics, and served on the school board at Wilton and was mayor of Afton. His wife, who was born in Arkansas in 1866, died at Winthrop in that state in 1900. She became the mother of eight children: Ruth, wife of Charles Gallegly, of Lockney, Texas; Verda, wife of C. R. Carr, in the lumber business at Texarkana, Texas; Augusta, wife of A. C. Smith, a salesman at Erick, Oklahoma; Doyle, who is a graduate of the Afton High School and also attended Baylor University at Waco, Texas, and is now city editor of the Altus Times; Eugene D.; Mary, who was married in 1911 to Louis T. Tucker, a salesman at Eldorado, Oklahoma; Maude and Doris, both of whom are students in the Baptist College at Decatur, Texas.

Eugene D. Powell received his early education in the public schools at Wilton, Arkansas, and at Stillwell, Indian Territory, and was graduated from the Afton High School in 1905. Later in 1908 he took a business course at the Oklahoma Baptist College in Blackwell. Meantime, in 1900, when only nine years of age, he secured his first instruction in printing and newspaper work under the direction of his father, and from that age has seldom been long absent from a newspaper or printing office. In 1911-'12 he was employed to conduct a paper at Hale Center, Texas, and afterwards for one year was with the Beacon-Times at Idabel, Oklahoma. On September 1, 1913, he came to Altus and was associated with the Altus Times, and during 1915 was editor and business manager of that paper. The Altus Times was established in 1900, is a democratic organ, has a general circulation throughout Jackson and surrounding counties, and lives up to the reputation that Altus has for a live and hustling town and business center. Mr. Powell is himself a democrat and is affiliated with Altus Lodge No. 62, Ancient Free and Accepted Masons, with Altus Lodge No. 134, Independent Order of Odd Fellows; and with Altus Lodge, Benevolent and Protective Order of Elks, No. 1226.

PAUL H. JONES. The ancestral history of this well known citizen of McAlester, Pittsburg County, is one of the most interesting and distinguished order and he is a scion of a family whose name has been prominently linked with the annals of American history from the early colonial era, each successive generation having produced men of sterling character and women of fine personality, while representatives have been found prominent and influential citizens in New England, New York, Maryland, Illinois, Georgia and other states of the Union. Family tradition, amply fortified by records still extant, indicates that the original American progenitor or progenitors of this family of Jones came from England on the historic ship Mayflower, and the lineage is traced back to William Jones, one of the stern Englishmen whose loyalty to principle led him to become a member of the historic company of regicides who made decisive blows in behalf of human independence. Members of the Jones family were numbered among the early settlers of both Massachusetts and Connecticut, and the grandfather of Prince Jones, from whom the subject of this review is a lineal descendant, was a brother of the mother of the celebrated colonial hero, Paul Revere. The mother of George H. Bissell, the distinguished sculptor, was a sister of Prince H. Jones, who was the paternal grandfather of him whose name introduces this article. Judge Samuel D. Lockwood, the first attorney general of Illinois and later an associate justice of the Supreme Court of that state, was a brother of the mother of Prince H. Jones. Abraham Prickett, great-grandfather of Paul H. Jones in the maternal line, was one of the first settlers at Edwardsville, Illinois, became the first mayor of that town, was a member of the committee that framed the constitution of Illinois in 1818, was a member of the first Legislature of that state, and became the founder of the first banking institution at Edwardsville, his son George having been the first white child born in the pioneer village that is now a thriving and beautiful city.

Paul H. Jones, who is numbered among the representative business men of McAlester, Oklahoma, and who served as a member of the State Board of Prison Control until the board was eliminated by legislative enactment in March, 1915, was born in the historic old Town of Edwardsville, Madison County, Illinois, in the year 1874, and is a son of William and Clare (Prickett) Jones. The only other surviving child is Miss Minna Jones, who remains with her parents at Edwardsville, the family home being that in which the mother was born, sixty years ago.

Mr. Jones continued to attend the public schools of his native city until he had completed the curriculum of the high school, and as his father met with severe financial reverses about this time, the youth was denied the advantages of a collegiate education. He initiated his business career by obtaining employment in a bank at Edwardsville, where he continued to be identified with this line of enterprise until 1897, when failing health rendered it imperative for him to seek less sedentary occupation and it behooved him also to find a change of climatic conditions. For a year thereafter he was a cowboy on ranches in Wyoming and Colorado, the ensuing year having been by him devoted to mining in the gold and silver fields of the latter state, and the manual application and free and open life having resulted in his fully regaining his health, with the accumulation of a robustness greater than he had previously enjoyed at any period. Upon his return to the East he established his residence in the City of St. Louis, Missouri, where he was engaged in the coal business during the ensuing four years. In 1902 Mr. Jones made a prospecting trip in Indian Territory, and while on a hunting expedition out from McAlester he became so favorably impressed with the attractions and advantages of the locality that he decided to make permanent location at McAlester. Here he became identified with the brick-manufacturing industry, in connection with which he was for several years general manager of the Choctaw Pressed Brick Company. In the spring of 1915 he severed his association with this corporation and established an independent brokerage business, in which he deals principally in building material, his personal popularity and unsullied business reputation having made the enterprise successful from its initiation.

In politics Mr. Jones is aligned as a staunch supporter of the cause of the republican party, and he has not been permitted to deny his services in public offices of trust during the period of his residence in Oklahoma. Within recent years he served two terms as city clerk of McAlester, and in 1913 he was appointed by Governor Cruce a member of the State Board of Prison Control, a position in which he served with utmost loyalty and circumspection until the abolishment of this department of the governmental service of the state, in March, 1915. This board recommended, upon careful investigation, the issuing of paroles to 385 prisoners in the state penal institutions, and most of these paroles were granted by the governor, only fourteen of the prisoners thus paroled having failed to live up to the conditions and provisions under which they were released.

Mr. Jones is one of the progressive and public-spirited citizens of the vital and ambitious City of McAlester, is an active and valued member of the McAlester Chamber of Commerce; is a member of the board of trustees of All Saints Hospital, maintained in this city under the auspices of the Protestant Episcopal Church; is secretary of the McAlester Golf and Country Club; is senior deacon, in 1915, of McAlester Lodge, No. 196, Ancient Free and Accepted Masons; and is one of the most influential and popular members of McAlester Lodge, No. 533, Benevolent and Protective Order of Elks, of which he has twice served as exalted ruler. Both he and his wife are communicants of the Protestant Episcopal Church.

In 1909 was solemnized the marriage of Mr. Jones to Miss Agnes Stuart, daughter of Judge Charles B. Stuart, of Oklahoma City, who was formerly a law partner of Senator Bailey, who represented Texas in the United States Senate. Under the administration of President Cleveland Judge Stuart served on the bench of the United States Court of the Eastern District of Indian Territory. Mrs. Jones was graduated in a college for young women at Lexington, Kentucky, and she is a leader in the representative social activities of the City of McAlester. Mr. and Mrs. Jones have one child, Halleck Stuart, who was born in 1912.

A scion of honored and influential pioneer families of Illinois, Mr. Jones has maintained a deep interest in the history of his native state and among his most prized possessions are a table, a rocking chair and a straight chair which were there used by the martyred President, Abraham Lincoln, upon whose death these valued memorials became the property of Thomas C. Prickett, a maternal ancestor of Mr. Jones. A few years ago Mr. Jones loaned the table and chairs to the Lincoln Memorial Association. He has in his possession also a letter writter by President Lincoln under date of September 27, 1852, in which Lincoln sought to have the administrator of the Prickett estate correct the title to some town lots that had been transferred to "Billy, the barber," a negro who had shaved Lincoln in Bloomington, Illinois.

C. C. ATWOOD. A flourishing little center of trade and business in Hughes County is named Atwood, a village that was laid out along the M. O. & G. Railroad by members of the Atwood family, and the railroad company named it in honor of C. C. Atwood, who for forty years has been a resident of Indian Territory, the greater part of the time in what is now Hughes County, and has been prominent as a cattle man, banker and citizen.

A native of Texas, he was born in Coryell City, July 4, 1861, a son of Eli and Katy (Trousdale) Atwood. His father was a native of Nashville, Tennessee, and his mother of Springfield, Missouri. The father grew up in Tennessee, but after his marriage in Missouri moved to Texas in 1860 and he and his wife spent the rest of their days there, his business being that of farmer. During the war, though too old for active service, he was a member of the home guard and served as a scout. C. C. Atwood was twelve years of age when his father died and eleven when his mother died. The six children were: C. M. of Belton, Texas; Bettie, deceased wife of Hugh Phillips; Eliza, deceased wife of A. A. Edwards; William, deceased; Matt, deceased; and C. C.

The first fourteen years of his life C. C. Atwood spent in Texas, and while there acquired a common school education. In 1875 he went into the Chickasaw Nation and located near Tishomingo, moved from there to Okmulgee in the Creek Nation, and then in 1881 to Tobucksee County in the Choctaw Nation, and soon afterwards located in the vicinity where he has ever since kept his home and the center of his activities. Throughout this long period of activity he has been a farmer and stock raiser chiefly.

He has seven children, and all of them have allotments in Hughes County. When the M. O. & G. Railroad was built they bought land for a townsite from Mr. Atwood, and that was the origin of the present Village of Atwood.

Mr. Atwood was one of the original stockholders in the City National Bank of Calvin, and he is now a director in the First National Bank of that place and a director in the First State Bank of Atwood. At one time he was president of the City National Bank at Calvin. However, he has given his chief attention and has made his success in farming and stock raising. At one time he grazed very large herds over his own holdings and leased lands. At the present time his landed possessions comprised, with those of his children, several sections of rich land, and about 640 acres are under cultivation. He is a democrat and is an elder in the Church of Christ, of which he has been a member for the past twenty years.

In 1882 Mr. Atwood married Miss Patsy Ann Burris, who was born at old Doaksville in the Choctaw Nation, a daughter of Benjamin and Sally (Nelson) Burris. Both her father and mother were half-blood Choctaws. Mr. and Mrs. Atwood have seven children, all of whom were born at Atwood, and briefly noted as follows: Ottie, wife of R. C. Lee of Parsons, Kansas; Arry, wife of Dr. W. B. Berninger of Atwood; Bennie, of Cordell, Oklahoma; Ollie, wife of R. L. Henley of Atwood; Colman of Atwood; Lizzie, who lives at home; and Ambrose, also at home.

HENRY C. DORROH, M. D. Possessing in generous measure the qualities which make the personally popular as well as financially successful physician, Dr. Henry C. Dorroh has a firmly established reputation at Hammon as an earnest, cautious and painstaking healer of men. He represents a kind of medical practice which is a long way removed from the standards of even a decade ago, his progressive mind rejecting mercilessly dogmas whose only claim is their antiquity, and which have no place in the light and intelligence of modern investigation.

Doctor Dorroh is of Irish descent, his great-grandfather, who spelled his name O'Dorroh, coming from Erin about the time of the Revolutionary war and settling in North Carolina. William W. Dorroh, father of Doctor Dorroh, was born at Fredonia, Kentucky, February 22, 1827, and in 1875 removed to within four miles of Princeton, the county seat of Caldwell County, Kentucky, where he passed the remaining years of his life in the pursuits of farming and stockraising and died in September, 1904. He was a stalwart supporter of the democratic party and with his wife belong to the Baptist Church. Mrs. Dorroh, who bore the maiden name of Mary Easley, was born in 1830, in Virginia, and when nine years of age was taken by her parents to Fredonia, Kentucky, where she received her education and was reared and married. She died at Princeton, Kentucky, in February, 1891, the mother of six children, as follows: Bobbie, who is the wife of Charles W. Guess, a farmer of Princeton; Frankie, who is the wife of J. J. Rorer, a farmer of Fredonia, Kentucky; William T., who is engaged in agricultural pursuits in Caldwell County; Annie, who is the wife of W. T. Hurst, a carpenter and mechanic of Hopkinsville, Kentucky; Dr. Henry C., of this notice; and Doctor Lee, a graduate of the Louisville Hospital College, of Louisville, Kentucky, and now engaged in a medical and surgical practice, a sketch of whose career will be found elsewhere in this work.

Henry C. Dorroh was born at Salem, Livingston County, Kentucky, December 23, 1869, and in the following year was taken by his parents to Caldwell County, where he attended the public schools. He was reared on the home farm, but had no liking for an agricultural career, and on attaining his majority, in 1891, went to Washington, in which state and Oregon he spent the next six years in engineering. His next location was Angels Camp, California, where he was connected with the Utica Gold Mining Company until 1903, and in that year joined the gold-hunters of Alaska, spending 1½ years at Nome in search of the precious yellow metal. Returning to California at the end of that period, for a time he was engaged in engineering at San Francisco, but finally turned his attention to the profession of medicine, and in the fall of 1905 entered the Louisville Hospital College of Medicine, at Louisville, Kentucky, which he attended for two years. During his vacation, in 1907, he returned to California, but in the fall of the same year went back to Louisville and completed his medical course, being graduated with the class of 1910 and receiving the degree of Doctor of Medicine. Shortly thereafter Doctor Dorroh came to Oklahoma and commenced practice at Aledo, Dewey County, but August 15th of the same year changed his field of practice to the Town of Hammon, where he has since continued in the enjoyment of a rapidly growing medical and surgical practice, his offices being located in the Hammon News Building on Broadway. Practicability and simplicity have been the professional efforts and he is a most careful and expert diagnostician as well as a close and inquiring student. In the search for clearer vision and larger usefulness he has allied himself with the various organizations of his vocation, being a member of the American Medical Association, the Oklahoma Medical Society and the Roger Mills Medical Society, of which latter he served one term as treasurer, his service expiring in January, 1915. He is a democrat in politics, but not particularly active in public affairs save as a good citizen and a supporter of progressive and beneficial movements. Fraternally, he is connected with Russell Camp No. 51, Woodmen of the World, and the local camp of the Woodmen's Circle.

Doctor Dorroh was married at Angels Camp, California, in 1904, to Miss Edna Covens, of Chicago, Illinois, and they have one child: Edna May, born April 17, 1913.

WILLIAM C. HUGHES. One of the most fertile counties in Eastern Oklahoma is that of which Holdenville is county seat, and it was created at the time of statehood and was named in honor of William C. Hughes, one of the most striking and influential figures in the Constitutional Convention. Mr. Hughes is an able brilliant lawyer, practiced law in Oklahoma for many years, and is now a resident of St. Joseph, Missouri.

He comes of an old and distinguished Missouri family. He was liberally educated, and from Kansas City he moved to Oklahoma in March, 1901, locating at Oklahoma City. As a lawyer he had soon established a state reputation.

He was elected a member of the Oklahoma Constitutional Convention in 1906 from the Twenty-eighth Conventional District, comprising the business center of Oklahoma City. He was chosen as a democrat and by an overwhelming majority. In the convention he was a prominent candidate for president, and lost that distinction by a very small majority, largely on account of becoming seriously ill. In the constructive work of the convention his was one of the most important individual influences. He was chairman of the Municipal Corporation Committee, and the imprint of his judgment and foresight is upon all the provisions of the organic law affecting this subject. He is author of provisions of the constitution as follows: The provisions giving to the people of the cities the right to make the charters for their government, the rights of the initiative and referendum in city affairs, the right to require by direct vote the granting of franchises; the provisions prohibiting the granting, renewal or extension of franchises without approval by the people by direct vote; the provisions expressly authorizing cities to own and operate their public utilities and providing means by which they may raise money for such purposes; the provisions creating the office of state commissioner and corrections; the provisions prohibiting child labor.

It was as a tribute to his valuable services that Hughes County was named in his honor.

William C. Hughes was born at Georgetown, then the county seat of Pettis County, Missouri, October 24, 1869, a son of Dr. B. F. and Catherine (Kidd) Hughes, and he later lived in Sedalia and Kansas City. His parents were also native Missourians and the grandparents on both sides were pioneers in the state, Grandfather Hughes having come from Virginia and grandfather Kidd from Kentucky. Mr. W. C. Hughes was one in a family of seven children, four of whom are still living. Doctor Hughes, his father, served as surgeon of the Seventh Missouri Cavalry, and also of the Sixth Missouri Cavalry, in the Civil war. He was afterwards a member of the Missouri Constitutional Convention known as the "Drake" Convention, having been elected from Pettis County as an independent, and he ardently fought against the establishment of a military despotism by that convention, which was in a measure a result and consequence of the reconstruction following the war. His name is signed to the ordinance abolishing slavery in Missouri.

On June 14, 1893, W. C. Hughes married Luella Gaines of Clinton, Missouri. They are the parents of four daughters and one son: Jeanette Cameron, Elizabeth, Lucy Briscoe, William C. Jr., and Donna.

JOSEPH W. CHILDERS. When Joseph W. Childers came to Okmulgee in June, 1905, he brought with him the accumulated experience of twenty years as a successful lawyer in the State of Missouri. In the past ten years Mr. Childers has gained prominence as an attorney in the new state and has also taken an active part in local and state politics. The people of Okmulgee County especially appreciate his service as county attorney for four years. He was first elected to that office in 1910, and his first term brought him a vote of renewed confidence in his re-election in 1912. In 1914 Mr. Childers lost the nomination for district judge, his successful opponent being Judge Hughes.

Though most of his life until coming to Oklahoma was spent in Missouri, Joseph W. Childers was born in Monroe County, Iowa, near Blakesburg, August 11, 1859, a son of Isaac and Huldah A. (Tharp) Childers. The Childers family is of Welsh stock, and there had been a number of prominent men of that name in Wales, one of them having served as a member of the parliament and an active supporter of the Gladstone administration. The Tharp family is of Scotch descent. Mr. Childers' father was born in Wood County, West Virginia, December 10, 1819. and his wife in Harrison County in the same state in 1824. They were married in West Virginia in 1841, and in 1850 went out as pioneers to the new State of Iowa, where the father entered a tract of government land in Monroe County. They lived there until 1861, and then moved to Sullivan County in Northern Missouri.

The father was a sturdy and practical farmer and had an honorable career in all its relationships. He died in Missouri August 29, 1891, while his wife passed away April 2, 1887. They became the parents of a large family of fourteen children, two of whom died in infancy. A brief record of the others is as follows: Preston R., who is now seventy-two years of age and lives at Littleton, Colorado, served four years as a Union soldier, having veteranized after his first enlistment, and was with Sherman on the famous march to the sea; Sylvanus W. lives in the State of Oregon; Delia Ann Tipton lives at Nuckols, Nebraska; Mary died at the age of twelve years; Stephen L. is a farmer at Helena, Oklahoma; Addison H. is a contractor at Denver, Colorado; Hulda A. Page lives on the home farm back in Sullivan County, Missouri; W. H. is an attorney at Milan, Missouri; Joseph W. is next in age; Marion V. met an accidental death in 1883; Sherman died at the age of fourteen; and Emma L. Akers lives at Alva, Oklahoma.

Joseph W. Childers grew up on the home farm and remained there until 1879. In the meantime he had attended the district schools, and on leaving home his first experience was as clerk in a store at Milan, Missouri. In 1884 he began the study of law in the office of John P. Butler at Milan, and was admitted to practice May 16, 1886. Continuing to make his home at Milan, he soon built up a promising profitable practice and continued it until his removal to Oklahoma in 1905. In this state in addition to his large private practice he has acquired considerable interests in oil lands. In politics he is a democrat, and is a member of the Presbyterian Church.

On November 15, 1888, he married Lillie M. Graham. She was born at Milan, Missouri, June 29, 1869, a daughter of James S. and Samantha (Swanger) Graham. Mr. Childers has one daughter, Wodenia, wife of Louis B. Bradfield, of Greeley, Colorado.

JOHN WALKER TILLMAN. An able and influential member of the Oklahoma bar, John Walker Tillman, of Pawhuska, has won unmistakable prestige, his scholarly attainments and comprehensive knowledge of law having won him an assured position in the legal fraternity of Osage County. He was born June 16, 1886, in Fayetteville, Washington County, Arkansas, coming from distinguished ancestry, being a son of John N. Tillman, LL. D., and a descendant of the same immigrant ancestor that founded in America the family from which Benjamin R. Tillman, who won distinction as United States senator from South Carolina is descended.

A native of South Carolina, John N. Tillman moved with his parents to Southwestern Missouri in childhood, and during his earlier life received exceptionally good educational advantages. Entering the legal profession, he became prominent as a lawyer, and after his removal to Fayetteville, Arkansas, where he still resides, was one of the leading educators of that state, for seven years serving as president of the University of Arkansas. A lifelong democrat, he has exerted great influence in the councils of his party, and has filled various public offices with ability and fidelity, winning the approbation of his constituents. He was circuit judge for some time, and is now serving his third term as congressman from the Third Congressional District of Arkansas. His wife, whose maiden name was Tumpy Walker, was born, bred, and educated in Benton County, Arkansas. Three children were born of their union, namely: John Walker, the special subject of this sketch; Frederick Allen, of Fayetteville, Arkansas, a lawyer, and his father's secretary; and Kathleen, wife of L. B. Shaver, of Oklahoma City.

After his graduation from the University of Arkansas, John Walker Tillman began the study of law with Messrs. C. B. Wall and Charles H. Brough, and in 1907 was admitted to the Arkansas bar. Beginning the practice of his profession in his home city, he met with most encouraging success as a lawyer, and was soon prominently identified with public affairs, serving two terms as assistant prosecuting attorney, and for two terms being city attorney of Fayetteville. In 1911 Mr. Tillman located at Pawhuska, Oklahoma, and has here gained an excellent position among the leading men of this section of the state. In 1912 he was elected assistant county attorney of Osage County, and after serving two years under C. K. Templeton was elected, on March 3, 1914, county attorney of Osage County, his election being proof of the satisfactory manner in which he performed the duties of his previous office.

Politically Mr. Tillman is a stanch adherent of the democratic party, supporting its principles by voice and vote. He is a member of both the county and the state bar associations, and belongs to two fraternal organizations, the Benevolent and Protective Order of Elks, and the Knights of Pythias.

Mr. Tillman married, in November, 1911, Miss Jennie Walker, a daughter of C. W. W. Walker, a well-known attorney of Fayetteville, Arkansas.

DANIEL P. LOWE. The experienced engineer is able to operate noiselessly and smoothly a complicated machine because he understands the power exerted by every minute inanimate part, and it is often a marvelous accomplishment. It is, likewise, a notable achievement when an executive can control wisely and efficiently a great human organization, because, while the engineer, it is not possible for him to comprehend fully the capacity of its working parts. The office of a county superintendent of schools is one of honorable but heavy responsibility. In his field there is vital work to be done but not always is he able to find the hidden screw or lift the governing lever, as can the engineer, and only through the knowledge and ripened judgment that long experience has brought about can he satisfy both the public and himself when he assumes the duties pertaining to this office. Beckham County, Oklahoma, in Superintendent Daniel P. Lowe has an official thoroughly equipped to still further advance the present high standards of the county's educational system, and his untiring efforts are meeting with general approval.

Daniel P. Lowe was born in Cook County, Texas, January 12, 1870, and is a son of J. D. and M. M. (Tittle) Lowe. The Lowe family is of Scotch-Irish descent, early settlement being made in Virginia, from which section they were pioneers in Texas and later a branch settled in Missouri, and in that state the father of Professor Lowe was born, in 1833. From there, in 1859, he moved to Cook County, Texas, where he married M. M. Tittle, who was born in 1838, and to this union six children were born: Joan, who is the wife of Paris Hodge, who is a farmer in Oklahoma; Daniel P.; Janey, who is the wife of J. F. Walker, a farmer near Orr, Oklahoma; Julia, who was the victim of an accident, died at Forestburg, Texas, in her twenty-second year; T. B., who is a farmer and stockman near Sweetwater, Oklahoma; and W. A., who died at Forestburg, Texas, at the age of twenty-five years.

J. D. Lowe in 1873 removed with his family to Montague County, Texas, and from there, in 1907, came to Sweetwater, Oklahoma, where he yet resides, a retired farmer and stockman. During the war between the states, he served four years in the Confederate army, enlisting from Texas, in Marsh's Regiment, surviving all the hardships and dangers of that time and returned home practically unharmed. He is identified with the democratic party and both he and wife are members of the Christian Church and are people justly held in high esteem.

Daniel P. Lowe began school life in Montague County, Texas, continuing until his graduation from the high school, afterward taking a course in the commercial department of the normal school, some years afterward, in 1905, taking the teacher's course in the Denton Normal School. Beginning educational work in 1897, Mr. Lowe has been almost continuously in this field ever since, in the fall of 1914 coming to Beckham County in his present capacity with eighteen years' of varied educational experience behind him.

At Forestburg, Texas, in 1897, Mr. Lowe had his first teaching experience, remaining there until 1900, after which he taught two years in Fannin County and then two years in Denton County, when he was recalled to Forestburg and taught there for three more years. In 1907, on the day that Oklahoma became a state, he filed on a claim of 160 acres in Beckham County situated ten miles due north of Texola, later proved up and still owns this property, which has become very valuable. In the same year he began teaching in this county and continued until 1912, when he accepted the position of principal of the high schools of Delhi, Oklahoma, where he continued until November 6, 1914, when he was elected county superintendent of the schools of Beckham County, assuming the duties of this office on July 1, 1915, taking up his residence at Sayre, his offices being in the courthouse. Superintendent Lowe has under his care, control and supervision, 72 schools, 130 teachers and 5,000 pupils. In his administration he has proved wise, resourceful and firm and there is great reason for the citizens of this county to be well satisfied with their choice.

At Forestburg, Texas, on December 29, 1900, Mr. Lowe was united in marriage with Miss Josie Wylie, who is a daughter of J. F. Wylie, who is a retired farmer residing in that city. Professor and Mrs. Lowe have two children: Fay, who was born January 30, 1912, and D. P., who was born April 3, 1914, both at Delhi, this state.

Although not particularly active in politics, Mr. Lowe has always been firm in his adherence to the principles of the democratic party. He is quite well known in fraternal life, having membership in Erick Lodge No. 327, Ancient Free and Accepted Masons; Sayre Lodge No. 258, Odd Fellows; and Delhi Camp, Modern Woodmen of America. As a representative educator of the state he is frequently called on for addresses and lectures and is a valued member of both the Beckham County and the Oklahoma State Teachers' associations. Both he and wife are members of the Christian Church.

WILBERT W. BRUNSKILL. A considerable part of the enterprise and energy that have gone into commercial and agricultural development in and about Elgin has been supplied by Wilbert W. Brunskill, president and owner of the Bank of Elgin. Mr. Brunskill is a banker of long experience, having been identified with that business back in Iowa, and is also a large land owner and is identified with several of the most important enterprises at Elgin.

The Brunskills were pioneer settlers in the vicinity of Dubuque, Iowa, where Mr. Brunskill's grandfather, Joseph J., who came from England and first settled in Ohio, located about the time Iowa was admitted to the Union and before any railroads had been constructed to Dubuque. He was identified with the development of the lead mines in that region, and owned some large interests of that kind. He died at Dubuque. It was in Dubuque City that Wilbert W. Brunskill was born April 15, 1877. His father, J. W. Brunskill, who was born at Dubuque in 1848, removed not long after his marriage to Cherokee County, Iowa, where he was a farmer and also in the grain and general merchandise business. In 1884 he removed to Hawarden in Sioux County, Iowa, where he was a hardware, harness and implement dealer, also owned the opera house at the time, and had farming property. In 1902 J. W. Brunskill left Iowa and settled at Bridgewater, South Dakota, on a farm, but since 1907 has been a farmer at Sauk Center, Minnesota. He is a member of the Methodist Episcopal Church and of the Masonic fraternity. His wife was Maria Frost, who was born in Dubuque, Iowa, in 1850, and died at Hawarden in Sioux County of that state in 1892. The children now living are: Nettie E., a resident of Petaluma, California; Wilbert W.; Grace M., of Gray Eagle, Minnesota; and J. William, who is with his father at Sauk Center, Minnesota.

Most of his early schooling Wilbert W. Brunskill acquired in the public schools of Hawarden, Iowa, where he was graduated from the high school with the class of 1894. He had already become connected with the Northwestern State Bank of Hawarden, and was assistant cashier in that institution until 1900. That year he became vice president of the Bank of Chatsworth, Iowa, but in 1906 removed to Elgin, Oklahoma, and for the past ten years has made himself one of the leading factors in the development of that town. On coming to Elgin he bought the Bank of Elgin, but sold out in 1908, and the following six years were spent in other local affairs. In February, 1914, he again acquired the sole ownership of the bank, and both during his former ownership and at present has been president. The Bank of Elgin was established in 1902 as a state bank by J. A. Butler and F. R. Dykeman. Its building, situated on Main Street, was erected in 1902. While Mr. Brunskill is president, the vice president is B. M. Brunskill and the cashier is A. L. Roberts. The bank has a capital stock of $5,000, and surplus of $3,500.

Mr. Brunskill is also secretary and treasurer of the Elgin Farmers Telephone Company, is owner of the Elgin elevator and Elgin flour milling plant, and one of the largest stockholders in the Elgin Bonded Cotton Warehouse Company. His interests as a farmer are extensive, including the supervision of the efforts of a number of tenants who employ his 800 acres situated in Cotton, Comanche and Garfield counties for diversified agriculture. He is a member of the Oklahoma State Bank Association and the Oklahoma Grain Dealers Association, has served on the local school board, and in 1915 was elected mayor of Elgin. In politics he is a republican.

At Lyons, Nebraska, in 1900 Mr. Brunskill married Beatrice Coffin, whose father, L. C. Coffin, is a general merchant and. farmer at Elgin, Oklahoma. Four children have been born to their marriage: Donovan W. is a student in the state university at Norman, where he is specializing in the Spanish language and in music; Hollis W. is in the fourth grade of the Elgin public schools; and the two younger children are Milo S. and James Bonar.

FREDERICK R. DOLSON, M. D. The first physician and surgeon to locate permanently at the new Town of Faxon in Southwestern Oklahoma was Dr. Frederick R. Dolson, who has been identified professionally with that community for the past eight years and has also contributed to the commercial life of the village by establishing and maintaining the only drug store. He is otherwise a factor in public affairs and has a large practice and is one of the most useful members of the community.

Born at New Orleans, Louisiana, November 6, 1869, Doctor Dolson has had a life of varied effectiveness and experience. His early schooling was continued only to about twelve or thirteen years of age, at which time he went out to the great cattle range of Kansas, and for several years pursued the active and exciting life of a cowboy. He became ambitious for a good education and for a work of more permanent usefulness than that of cattle herder, and while in Kansas he attended night schools at Wichita for six years and also completed a three years' course in a preparatory college conducted by the Adventist Church at Battle Creek, Michigan. In 1898 Doctor Dolson completed his medical course in the Tulane University at New Orleans, where he was graduated M. D., and almost immediately after leaving college enlisted for service in the Spanish-American war as a surgeon. He was surgeon on duty at Fort St. Philip at the mouth of the Mississippi two months, was then transferred to the First Army Corps, and sent to Jacksonville, Florida, two months, then to Savannah, Georgia, and finally to Cuba. His service with the army continued for two years. After this experience as an army surgeon Doctor Dolson practiced medicine at Fort Worth, Texas, from 1900 to 1903, removed to Lawton, Oklahoma, in the latter year, and maintained his office in that city up to 1907, in which year he identified himself with the newly established Town of Faxon. Both his business and reputation have been of growing proportions since locating there, and in 1907 he also opened a drug store now the only enterprise of that kind in the village, situated on Main Street.

Doctor Dolson's grandfather emigrated from England and settled near Chatham, Ontario, Canada, where he was a hardware merchant. He also lived in Louisiana for a time, where his son J. A. Dolson was born in 1838. Doctor Dolson's father died at Frankfort, Indiana, in 1880, having removed to that locality from Louisiana. He was a stock broker by trade, and during the war between the states had served 3½ years in a Louisiana regiment in the Confederate army. He was once wounded and taken prisoner. In religion he was a Presbyterian, and was affiliated with the Masonic Order and the Independent Order of Odd Fellows. His wife was Jane Chambers, who was born in Ohio, in 1823, and died at Frankfort, Indiana, in March, 1915. Her children were: Stella, who is the wife of Fred Mash and lives on their farm near Tulsa, Oklahoma; Nettie, who is still living at Frankfort, Indiana; Bessie, who died in 1900 when about twenty-two years of age; John, who is a contractor and builder in California; and Doctor Frederick, the youngest.

Doctor Dolson is a democrat, and for the past seven years has been city treasurer of Faxon. He is affiliated with Faxon Lodge No. 534 of the Independent Order of Odd Fellows, and is also identified with the various medical organizations. At Lawton in 1908 he married Miss Ida Covell, whose father, Winkell Covell, is a resident of St. Louis, Missouri. They have one son, Jack Woodrow, who was born August 27, 1912.

HON. JERRY C. DULANEY. A representative of the type of citizenship which has been the main factor in the upbuilding and development of the newer towns of Oklahoma is found in the person of Hon. Jerry C. Dulaney, mayor of Devol and proprietor of the only drug establishment at this place. Since his arrival here, in 1909, he has identified himself with the best interests of this thriving community, and in his official capacity, in which he has served since 1912, has instituted many reforms and secured numerous advantages which have combined to add to the importance and prestige of his adopted place.

Mayor Dulaney was born February 11, 1864, in Texas, and is a descendant of ancestors who came to America from France prior to the Revolutionary war. From one of the eastern states members of the family migrated as pioneers to Mississippi, where in 1829 was born the father of Jerry C. Dulaney, William Payton Dulaney. The latter, as a young man of twenty years, moved to Texas and engaged in farming, and continued to be so occupied until 1863. In the meantime he had enlisted in the Home Guards, and was made captain of his company, and in the year mentioned was sent out to hold the hostile Indians in check, taking his family with him. He had reached Weatherford, Parker County, Texas, when he met his death, shot by one of his men for an Indian. In December, 1863, Mrs. Dulaney, who had been born in Mississippi in 1830, at once started back toward Corsicana, Navarro County, Texas, with her children, but ere she could reach there, her child, Jerry C., was born, about two months after his father's death. Mrs. Dulaney bore the maiden name of Lucinda White, and survived her husband many years, dying at Devol, Oklahoma, in January, 1915, when in her eighty-third year. She and her husband were the parents of eight children: T. J., who resides in Harper County, Oklahoma, and is engaged in agricultural pursuits; Susie, who married James Chappell, a farmer of the State of New Mexico; J. N., who carries on farming at Temple, Oklahoma; Sarah, who married S. A. Ritchie, and resides at Paris, Texas, Mr. Ritchie being a carpenter and builder; J. W., the proprietor of a cotton gin at Altus, Oklahoma; J. G., who was a merchant at Paducah, Texas; J. D., who is a carpenter and builder of New Mexico; and Jerry C., of this notice.

Jerry C. Dulaney received his education in the public schools of Texas, which he attended, off and on, until he was twenty-one years of age. He was reared to agricultural pursuits, and when he entered upon an independent career started farming in Falls County, Texas, where he remained until 1888. In that year he entered the drug business at Durango, Texas, where he remained three years, subsequently drifting from place to place in Western Texas for two years, and finally coming to Ryan, Oklahoma, where he remained three years as a druggist. Returning to Falls County, for four years he had a pharmacy of his own, and in 1901 returned to Ryan, Oklahoma (then Indian Territory), and conducted a drug store until the opening of the Comanche country in the fall of the same year. At that time he obtained a claim south of Temple, Oklahoma, on which he lived until he had proved it, and in 1907 went to Temple and engaged in the grocery business, remaining something more than a year. In 1909 Mr. Dulaney came to Devol and started a drug store, and this has since continued to be the only establishment of its kind in the city. The business is located on Wichita Avenue, where Mr. Dulaney carries an up-to-date line of drug goods of all descriptions, attractively arranged and moderately priced. He has built up an excellent business through good management and a spirit of progress and enterprise, and is known as one of the substantial merchants of the city. A democrat in his political views, Mr. Dulaney's well known ability caused him to be chosen by his fellow-citizens for the office of mayor, in 1912, and he still retains that office, his administration having been marked by faithful and efficient performance of duty and careful conservation of his city's interests. He is a member of the Methodist Episcopal Church, South, is an active worker in the Devol Commercial Club, and fraternally is affiliated with Lodge No. 548, Independent Order of Odd Fellows, of which he is past grand; and Devol Lodge No. 11,823, Modern Woodmen of America, of which he is past venerable consul.

Mr. Dulaney was married in 1896, in Lee County,

Texas, to Miss Abbie Martin, of Giddings, Texas, daughter of C. M. Martin, who is now a farmer and resides at Devol, Oklahoma. To this union there have been born seven children, as follows: Willie Earl, who died at the age of eighteen months; Ima, who is a freshman at the Devol High School; Ila, who died at the age of eight years; LeRoy, who died at the age of six years; Thelma, who is attending the public schools; and Edna and an infant daughter.

WILLARD R. BLEAKMORE. Prominent among those who are lending dignity and distinction to the bench and bar of the State of Oklahoma is Judge Bleakman, who has served as associate justice of the Supreme Court of this commonwealth, who has been a resident of Oklahoma since 1890 and a representative member of its bar since 1892.

Judge Bleakmore is a scion of an old and honored family of the historic Old Dominion and takes just pride in reverting to that commonwealth as the place of his nativity. He was born in the City of Richmond, Virginia, on the 22d of September, 1872, and is a son of Wylie H. and Mary E. (Goddard) Bleakmore, who now maintain their residence at Ardmore, Oklahoma, where they established their home in 1894 and where the father is a representative merchant and an honored and influential citizen, he having been in able representative of the newspaper fraternity prior to turning his attention to his present line of business enterprise.

He whose name initiates this review was a boy at the time of his parents' removal to the State of Iowa, where he was reared to maturity and where he duly availed himself of the advantages of the public schools. In 1890, when seventeen years of age, Judge Bleakmore came to the Territory of Oklahoma and established his residence in Oklahoma City, where he studied law under effective preceptorship and where he was admitted to the territorial bar in 1892. He was here engaged in the practice of his profession until 1894, when he removed to Ardmore, now the judicial center of Carter County, where he has since maintained his home save for the time that his official duties on the supreme bench have demanded his presence in the capital city of the state. At Ardmore he was engaged in the active general practice of his profession until his elevation to the bench of the Supreme Court, in 1914, and from 1898 to 1910 he was there a member of the representative law firm of Cruce, Cruce & Bleakmore. In 1912 Judge Bleakmore was elected county attorney of Carter County, of which office he continued the incumbent until May 25, 1914, when he was appointed an associate justice of the Supreme Court of the state, to fill out the unexpired term caused by the retirement of Judge Stillwell H. Russell. He continued a zealous, circumspect and valued member of the supreme tribunal of the state until the expiration of the term for which he was appointed, in January, 1915, when he resumed the private practice of his profession at Ardmore, where he retains a substantial and representative clientage.

Judge Bleakmore is prominently identified with the Masonic fraternity, in which, in addition to being affiliated with the lodge, chapter and commandery bodies of the York Rite, he has received the thirty-second degree of the Ancient Accepted Scottish Rite, and holds membership in India Temple of the Ancient Arabic Order of the Nobles of the Mystic Shrine at Guthrie. In his home city he is affiliated with Ardmore Lodge, No. 648, Benevolent and Protective Order of Elks. Both he and his wife are members of the Presbyterian Church of Ardmore, and his political allegiance being indicated by his zealous and effective advocacy of the principles and policies of the democratic party.

In the year 1892 was solemnized the marriage of Judge Bleakmore to Miss Annie Hazen, daughter of Alonzo E. Hazen, of Oklahoma City, and they have four sons, Frank W., Jack K., Robert and Kenneth.

THOMAS LANE, M. D. A worthy and capable representative of the medical fraternity of Oklahoma is found in the person of Dr. Thomas Lane, who since 1899 has been engaged in an ever-increasing practice at El Reno. That measure of resource, energy and broad-mindedness which is required of the professional man of today seem to be an integral part of his equipment, and being an enthusiastic and careful thinker, while he maintains a respect for tradition, he is not afraid of untrod paths, or independent individual effort.

Doctor Lane was born near Springfield, Missouri, August 10, 1858, and is a son of Calvin and Cynthia (Harris) Lane. When he was four years of age his mother died, and only one year later his father passed away, so that he was taken to the home of his grandparents in Illinois, and by them was reared. His literary education was obtained at Mountain Grove (Missouri) Academy and Blackburn University, Carlinville, Illinois, and thus equipped entered upon a career as an educator, but after four years thus spent turned his attention to the study of medicine, for which profession he had had a predilection from boyhood. He subsequently entered the Missouri Medical College, now the medical department of Washington University, St. Louis, from which he was graduated with his degree of Doctor of Medicine in 1886. He at once entered upon the practice of his profession at Mountain Grove, Missouri, and continued there for fourteen years, building up a very satisfying professional business. In 1899, seeking a wider field for his labors, Doctor Lane came to El Reno, Oklahoma, where he has continued as a practitioner to the present time. Doctor Lane's practice is broad and general in its character, he being equally at home in the various departments of his profession. His superior talents and abilities have been demonstrated on numerous occasions, and among his professional brethren he enjoys a high reputation as one who observes the unwritten ethics of the calling. He has kept fully abreast of the various advancements made in medicine and surgery during recent years, and, unlike many others, did not cease his studies when he left college, for he has continued to be an earnest, zealous and painstaking student, and has pursued postgraduate work at various institutions in Chicago, St. Louis and New Orleans. Doctor Lane's professional connections include membership in the Canadian County Medical Society, the Oklahoma State Medical Society and the American Medical Association. In his political views he is a democrat, but confines his public activities to taking a good citizen's interest in matters that affect the welfare of the community. Fraternally he is connected with the Benevolent and Protective Order of Elks, the Ancient Order of United Workmen and the Modern Woodmen of America, and is also a Mason and a past master of his lodge.

In 1884 Doctor Lane was united in marriage with Miss Emma Dora McCuiston and to this union there have been born three children: Gertrude, Ray and Lorraine.

H. M. FREAS. Every community owes a debt of gratitude to the men who protect it from the depredations of the criminal classes. A once popular song contained the line, "A policeman's lot is not a happy one," and it is often the case that the arduous duties of the guardians of the law are faithfully performed without meeting with

an adequate reward or a due measure of appreciation. The latter, however, cannot be said of H. M. Freas, of Pawhuska, Oklahoma, whose services as sheriff of Osage County for the last five years are highly regarded by his fellow citizens. Sheriff Freas was born in Berwick, Columbia County, Pennsylvania, March 15, 1863, and is now therefore in the prime of life. His parents were Jonathan and Susanna (Campbell) Freas, who in 1868 moved to Sterling, Illinois, and later to southeastern Kansas, the father dying at Independence, Montgomery County, that state, in 1909, at the advanced age of eighty-seven years. He was a farmer by occupation, and a veteran of the Civil war, having served as captain of Company G, One Hundred and Fifth Pennsylvania Infantry. A republican in politics, he belonged also to the Grand Army, and was a loyal, patriotic and useful citizen, in short, a good American. His widow is still living and is a resident of Independence. They were the parents of five children, namely: H. M., the subject of this sketch; Sadie, who resides in Waterloo, Iowa; Ella, wife of W. H. Tasker of Tyro, Kansas; Ida, wife of Frank Shudy, of Okmulgee; and Bertha, who married W. H. Harper, and resides with her husband in Independence, Kansas.

H. M. Freas resided in Montgomery County, Kansas, for the first twenty-two years of his life, from early boyhood being engaged in agricultural pursuits. In 1886 he came to Oklahoma, settling in Osage County and buying a farm about three miles east of Pawhuska, on which he still resides, and where he is operating successfully. A democrat in politics, he has long taken an active interest in public affairs, and in 1910 was elected sheriff of Osage County, being re-elected to the same office in 1912 and 1914, so that he is now serving in his third term. Fearless in the discharge of his duty, he has proved his efficiency by sending over seventy men to the penitentiary, many of whom were among the worst criminals in the state. In thus safe-guarding life and property he has made himself a terror to evil doers and has rendered a great service to the county, which his fellow citizens appreciate.

Sheriff Freas was married in 1885 to Miss Pauline Palzin, who was born in Berlin, Germany, in 1862, and emigrated with her parents to Illinois, where he first met her. They have had seven children born to them, namely: Bertha, who is the wife of J. M. Gordon, of Osage County, Oklahoma; Florence, wife of Joe Bowers, of Osage County; Amy, who married Sam Kennedy and resides with her husband in Pawhuska; Bessie; Pauline and H. M. Freas, Jr.

LELAND H. D. COOK. When the City of Okmulgee adopted a new municipal charter of the commission form, the people chose as their first commissioner of finance L. H. D. Cook and during his one term in that office he made a very creditable record and completely reorganized the financial system of the city.

He was able to bring to that office a thorough experience in commercial affairs, acquired largely through the insurance business. Mr. Cook has lived in Okmulgee since 1908, and since then has been in the real estate and insurance business with the exception of the term he served the city government. Among other interests which he represents he is general agent for the United States Fidelity & Guaranty Company of Baltimore. He has also acquired oil interests in the new state and is secretary and treasurer of the John Owen Oil Company of Okmulgee.

L. H. D. Cook was born in Newfield, New York, in Tompkins County, June 27, 1884. His parents, S. Dudley and Anna (McDaniels) Cook were also born at Newfield, New York, but for the last three years have made their home at Rochester in that state. The father is a retired merchant. He was one of the organizers of the Tompkins County Co-operative Fire Insurance Company, said to be the most successful company of its kind in the United States. Mr. Cook's grandfather was Dr. C. C. Cook, a successful physician who was engaged in recruiting and other service during the Civil war. It will be of interest to state that Doctor Cook was a schoolmate and friend of Grover Cleveland, and Mr. Cook of Okmulgee has in his possession some letters written by the former president to his grandfather.

The only child of his parents L. H. D. Cook lived at home until he was fifteen, and his early experiences outside of home were connected with the public schools of Newfield and with his father's store. At the age of fifteen he entered Cornell University, where he became a member of the class of 1904, and remained in college two years. After that for a year he was clerk in a drug store at Corning, New York, and then took up the business which has been his real vocation. He represented the Prudential Life at Corning until 1907, and then went to Syracuse as manager of the Syracuse office for the Security Mutual Life Insurance Company of Binghamton, New York. From there he removed to Okmulgee in 1908.

In politics Mr. Cook is a republican, is a member of the Episcopal Church, and has been especially interested in Masonry. His Blue Lodge affiliations are with King Hiram Lodge No. 784, Ancient Free and Accepted Masons, at Newfield, New York. His grandfather was a charter member of this lodge, and both his father and uncles were members. Mr. Cook is a member of the Royal Arch Chapter and of Commandery No. 25, Knights Templars, at Okmulgee.

In April, 1909, he married Linnie Parker, who was born October 13, 1884, at Clarksburg in Carroll County, Tennessee. She came to Muskogee, Oklahoma, in 1907. They are the parents of two children: Anna Lynn and Dudley Parker.

HARPER WRIGHT, M. D. Many of the new towns in Western Oklahoma are attracting professional men of decidedly superior attainments and training, and the general average of proficiency and ability to be found among the professional men of these new communities is decidedly higher than that which prevailed in the older part of the state in earlier years. An example of these younger leaders in the professional life of Western Oklahoma is Dr. Harper Wright, a physician and surgeon who has recently taken up practice at Grandfield.

Born at Farill, Alabama, November 23, 1887, Harper Wright attended the public schools there, graduated from the Gaylesville High School in Alabama with the class of 1904, in 1907 finished the course of the noted old Webb Preparatory School at Bellbuckle, Tennessee, and in the same year took a business course in Eastman's Business College at Poughkeepsie, New York. In 1913 Doctor Wright was graduated from the Atlanta College of Physicians and Surgeons at Atlanta, Georgia. His thorough training in preparation for the profession also included one year spent as interne at the Erlanger Hospital in Chattanooga, Tennessee, and for six months he was associated with an eminent surgeon, Dr. Raymond Wallace, F. A. C. S., of Chattanooga.

The Wright family came from England to Georgia prior to the Revolution, and was related to the family of General Oglethorpe, the founder and leader of the Georgia colony. Doctor Wright's father was A. R. Wright, who was born at Cave Springs, Georgia, in 1859, and for the past thirty years has been prominently identified with the business community of Farill, Alabama, where he has been a merchant, a farmer and stock raiser, sawmill owner, manufacturer of charcoal, and with practically every enterprise of any importance in that town. He is a democrat and a member of the Baptist Church. He died March 1, 1916. His wife was Effie Stewart, who was born at Atlanta, Georgia, in 1867, and died at Farill, Alabama, in July, 1911. Doctor Wright was the oldest of their children, and the others were: Annie, wife of J. F. McGee, who is assistant to the secretary and treasurer of the Anchor Duck Mills at Rome, Georgia; Gus, who is a farmer at Farill, Alabama; Margaret, wife of Lewis Lilley, of Parrot, Georgia; and Mose, attending the preparatory school at Rome, Georgia.

Doctor Wright was married in September, 1914, at Indianapolis, Indiana, to Ellen C. Gallagher, whose home was formerly in Winona, Minnesota. She is a member of the Catholic Church. Doctor Wright belongs to the Phi Chi Greek letter medical fraternity, is a member of the Baptist Church, and has fraternal affiliations with Lodge No. 91, Benevolent and Protective Order of Elks, at Chattanooga, Tennessee, with Grandfield Lodge No. 378, Ancient Free and Accepted Masons; with Gaylesville Lodge No. 256, Independent Order of Odd Fellows in Alabama; and with Banyan Camp No. 573, Woodmen of the World at Grandfield. He located for practice at Grandfield, Oklahoma, September 23, 1914, and already enjoys a substantial practice and reputation as a physician and surgeon. His offices are in the Tillman County Bank Building.

J. C. FERGUSON, who was one of the early business men to add his enterprise to the City of Pawhuska, has during the last ten years not only developed a successful local industry, but has also exercised much influence on local affairs. Mr. Ferguson is an Ohio man who enjoyed a substantial position as a business man in that state before coming to Oklahoma, and his record has been a continuation and amplification of the work with which he was identified back in his native state.

His birth occurred in Highland County, Ohio, March 19, 1862, a son of Joseph C. and Mary Elizabeth (Gwinett) Ferguson. His father was born in Ohio while his mother was a native of Germany, and came to America with two brothers. She died in 1867 at the age of thirty-two, leaving four children. The father married again, having five children by his second marriage, and died in 1880 at the age of sixty-two. Practically all his life was spent in the vicinity of Cincinnati, and he developed a large business there as blacksmith, and also had a carriage shop, employing a force of from eighteen to thirty men.

It was with this industry that J. C. Ferguson, after gaining his advantages in the public schools, became identified at the age of sixteen. He learned blacksmithing in all its details under his father's direction, and was one of his valuable helpers until twenty-one. At that time he leased from his father the blacksmith department of the business, and conducted it until the death of his father. He then bought the entire business, and continued it successfully until November, 1899, when he sold out.

It was fifteen years ago that Mr. Ferguson came to Oklahoma. His first location was in Garfield County, near Waukomis, where he bought a farm and set up a blacksmithing shop. Later he moved into the town, bought a blacksmithing business, but sold out in 1904 and moved to Pawhuska, which was then a somewhat inconspicuous village. He bought a shop, and soon began to develop a business which is now the chief iron working and repair business of the city, and its facilities have recently been extended to include a general automobile repair and garage. His two sons, Joe W. and Fred L., are now his active partners under the firm name of J. C. Ferguson & Sons. This firm handles the local agency for the Ford and Hudson automobiles, and automobile repairing is now an important part of their business. While all three of the partners are engaged in the business, they also require the services of three blacksmiths and four other men in the garage. They have recently erected a new garage 50 by 100 feet on East Sixth Street. Mr. Ferguson also owns a fruit farm of forty-five acres adjoining the city, though this is operated through a tenant. A republican voter, Mr. Ferguson has never been a politician, but at different times has been honored with positions of responsibility and in such places has always worked with an eye single to the good of the community. While living in Ohio he served eight years as township and school director, and in 1908 was honored with election to the office of mayor of Pawhuska for a term of two years. The citizens desired an efficient business administration, and he gave them one which was marked by a big forward movement in the matter of municipal improvement. His administration witnessed the beginning of effective street paving, an issue of bonds for electric light and waterworks system, and the beginning of construction on these important local utilities, and he also thoroughly cleaned up the city, paying no attention whatever to local politics while engaged in this work. He is a member of the Presbyterian Church and one of its trustees, is affiliated with the various bodies of Masonry, including the thirty-second degree of Scottish Rite, and also with the Knights of Pythias and the Benevolent and Protective Order of Elks.

In 1885 Mr. Ferguson married Miss Mary L. Waddell, who was born in Ohio June 2, 1866, a daughter of Waverly and Naomi Waddell. They have a fine family of eight children: Jessie, wife of J. L. Darby of Pawhuska; Joseph W. and Fred L., both already mentioned as partners of their father; Nell, who is married; Margine, Clifford, Delos and Leone, all at home and several of them in school.

W. LUSK. One of the pioneers of the Town of Morris, Okmulgee County, W. Lusk has been a very energetic factor in local business affairs and has supplied much of the capital and enterprise for the upbuilding of that section.

He was born in Springfield, Missouri, February 5, 1866, a son of Alfred T. and Elizabeth (Bond) Lusk, both of whom were born in Tennessee and came to Missouri in 1835, in childhood, with their respective parents. They married in Missouri and lived in that state on a farm the rest of their days. The father passed away in 1901 at the age of eighty-three and the mother in 1908 at the age of seventy-three. Their four children were: C. D. Lusk of Fort Scott, Kansas; W. Lusk; Isabella, wife of Robert Kimmons at Missouri; and Benjamin, of Missouri.

W. Lusk lived on the Missouri farm with his parents until he was eighteen years of age. Since then he has been in active business, working for himself and others, and was principally identified with the drug business until 1914, when he sold out. He acquired his knowledge of pharmacy in the St. Louis School of Pharmacy, from which he received a diploma in 1886. For a number of years he worked as a drug clerk in Kansas City, Missouri.

It was in 1907 that he came to Morris, Oklahoma, and invested his small capital and started the Morris Drug Company, a business which is still conducted under the same name. Since then his interests have taken on a

much wider scope, and for the past two years he has been in the oil business, having four wells in the district around Boynton. He has been associated with a number of other men in developing this section of the country, and owns himself about 320 acres of farm land in Okmulgee County. It was his money and enterprise that constructed the garage on Main Street, one of the largest buildings in the town, which he sold in 1915. He is now having built an opera house, which will be used for moving picture shows.

Since statehood Mr. Lusk has served as township committeeman of the democratic party and has also been a member of the school board and of the town board the greater part of the time since Oklahoma entered the union. One example of his public spirit was the donation of a portion of the site for the Morris Library. He is affiliated with the Masonic Order, the Independent Order of Odd Fellows and the Fraternal Order of Eagles.

On June 30, 1908, Mr. Lusk married Myrtle M. Grissom of Okmulgee. She was born in Okmulgee, a daughter of J. E. Grissom of that town. They have one daughter, Wynema, who is now four years old.

LEWIS DALE SOUTER. Prominent among the county officials of Osage County is Lewis Dale Souter, of Pawhuska, who is now serving with acceptance as county assessor. A son of George W. Souter, he was born, January 11, 1874, in Pontotoc County, Mississippi, and was there reared to man's estate.

Born in South Carolina in 1837, George W. Souter was brought up in Mississippi, where his parents located when he was a child. He engaged in agricultural pursuits as a young man, in 1890 moving with his family to the northwestern part of Texas, from there coming, in 1896, to Oklahoma. Locating, in Cleveland, he was there engaged in agricultural pursuits until his death, which occurred February 22, 1905. He was a democrat in politics, and during the Civil war served for four years in the Confederate army. Both he and his wife were active members of the Baptist Church, and he was one of the founders of the church of that denomination in Cleveland. His wife, whose maiden name was Saleta Rodgers, was born in Georgia, and died, August 8, 1898, in Cleveland, Oklahoma. Four of their six children are now living, as follows: B. V., of Osage County; Lewis Dale; F. M., of Cleveland; and Jettie E., wife of Dr. Ira Mullins, of Hominy, Oklahoma.

Brought up on the home farm, Lewis Dale Souter was educated in the public schools, and as a boy and youth was trained to habits of industry, becoming skilful in the various branches of agriculture. Coming with the family to Oklahoma, he began life for himself at the age of twenty-four years, engaging in the peaceful and profitable occupation of a farmer, buying land in the vicinity of Cleveland, where he still has title to 160 acres. In 1912 he was elected county assessor of Osage County on the democratic ticket, and displayed such energy and ability in responding to the demands of the office that he was re-elected in 1914.

On December 19, 1907, Mr. Souter was united in marriage with Unie Tocy, who was born in Texas, a daughter of I. S. Tocy. The union of Mr. and Mrs. Souter has been blessed by the birth of six children of whom two have passed to the bright life byond, Dale having died at the age of five years, and Bert when but seven months old. Four are living, namely: Prentiss, Dyke, Iris, and Mullins. Politically Mr. Souter is a steadfast democrat and active in party affairs. Fraternally he belongs to the Ancient Free and Accepted Order of Masons, at Cleveland, Oklahoma. Religiously, he is a member of the Baptist Church, with which he united while living in Mississippi.

CALVIN JONES. The State of Tennessee has contributed a considerable amount of brain and muscle necessary to the building of the new State of Oklahoma. In every county and in nearly every community it is represented. It has sent some of the brightest lawyers and most skilled physicians. The elements of Tennessee progress are contained in the fundamental elements of social and religious life wherever white men have formed communities here. It has been said that many of them cros·ed'the Arkansas line seeking office, and this humorous reference was based on the fact that in many counties in earlier years Tennesseeans were in the majority in office-holding circles. Two generations ago Tennessee sent some of its leading ministers here as missionaries, and in recent years many of the state's leading educators have come from the colleges of Tennessee. It has furnished more ministers to Oklahoma Methodism than any other state, birth and parentage considered. Many of the ablest and most prominent club women in the recent years in Oklahoma came from Tennessee.

A Tennesseean at Hugo is Calvin Jones, one of the city's brightest and most successful young lawyers. He was born at Summerville, Fayette County, in 1883, a son of J. M. and Anna (Moody) Jones. His father, a native of Fayette County, has spent most of his life on the farm, and served through the Civil war as a soldier in the Cavalry Brigade of General Forrest. The paternal grandfather was also named Calvin. He was a native of North Carolina and gained distinction in two fields. As an educator he was once professor in the University of Alabama, and later as a lawyer he became the first chancellor in the district in which he lived in West Tennessee.

After completing his public and high school education, Calvin Jones entered the University of the South at Sewanee, Tennessee, and later the law denartment of the Cumberland University, from which he received his degree LL. B. in 1903. Beginning practice at Summerville, he remained there until 1906, when he located at Grant, a small town near Hugo, and from there moved to Hugo. For two years Mr. Jones was deputy county attorney under Robert K. Warren. In June, 1915, he became junior member of the firm of McDonald & Jones. He is a democrat, a member of the Benevolent and Protective Order of Elks and the Woodmen of the World, and also of the County and State Bar associations.

BART M. WOOLDRIDGE. The kind of western energy, resource and large-mindedness required of the young man who would succeed in the field of finance in these days of strenuous effort and severe competition, seem to be an integral part of the equipment of Bart M. Wooldridge, who since February 1, 1914, has been cashier of the Citizens Bank of Headrick. Notwithstanding his well known caution and respect for conservative measures in banking, he has the progressiveness and courage of the present, and while carefully conserving the interests of the depositors has contributed materially to the growth and development of the institution, the prominence of which adds to the prestige of the community.

Mr. Wooldridge was born in Russell County, Kentucky, September 22, 1877, and is a son of Jesse and Nancy A. (Blankenship) Wooldridge, and a member of a family which came from Ireland to America during colonial times and settled in Virginia. Jesse Wooldridge was born at Jamestown, Russell County, Kentucky, November 3, 1844, and there grew up, was educated, and married, his wife having been born in the Blue Grass State in 1847. In 1869 he went to Northwestern Missouri, where he spent two years, but soon returned to his native state, and remained there engaged in farming and stockraising until 1894, when he again went to Missouri.

After two years he removed to Eddy, McLennan County, Texas, where he continued actively engaged in agricultural pursuits until 1906, and then came to Hollis, where he now makes his home, practically retired. Mr. Wooldridge has been industrious and energetic all his life, and although now over seventy years of age, still takes a keen interest in affairs of an agricultural nature. In political matters he is a democrat, but has not been an office seeker, while his fraternal connection is with the Masons. He has been a lifelong member of the Methodist Episcopal Church, South. Mrs. Wooldridge died in Missouri, in 1896, aged forty-nine years, the mother of six children: Ada, who is the wife of G. D. Mabery, a farmer of Eddy, Texas; Bart M., of this notice; May, who married Bell Sasser and resides on his farm at Memphis, Texas; Mervin H., who is engaged in the hardware business at Hollis, Oklahoma; Everett R., who is engaged in farming in the vicinity of Hollis; and Walter R., who is a banker and resides at the home of his parents. Mr. Wooldridge was married a second time in 1899, when united in marriage at Eddy, Texas, with Mrs. Martha (Shelton) Hix, a native of Tennessee, but a resident of Bruceville, Texas. One child, Thelma, has been born to this union, she being a student in the public schools.

Bart M. Wooldridge was reared on the home farm and secured his education in the public schools of Russell County, Kentucky, being graduated from the high school there in 1894. Until 1898 he remained on the homestead, engaged in assisting his father in its operation, and then turned his attention to educational work and for five years taught in the country schools of McLennan County, Texas. Mr. Wooldridge's advent in Oklahoma took place in 1903, when he located at Martha, and was principal of the school there for two years. While he had gained a reputation as an efficient and popular educator, he was not satisfied with his progress, and in 1907 entered the Altus State Bank, in the capacity of bookkeeper, giving up his teaching work entirely. Through faithful and competent performance of duty he was promoted to the position of assistant cashier and remained with that institution until 1909, when he organized the Martha State Bank, of which he was cashier until January 1, 1914. On February 1, 1914, he came to Headrick to accept the position of cashier of the Citizens Bank, and this he has retained to the present time. This institution was established in 1904, the founder being J. E. Ernst, and in 1912 the present handsome banking house was erected on the corner of Main and Fourth streets. The capital of the bank is $10,000, its officials are W. E. Sanderson, president; J. R. McMahan, vice president, both of Altus; and B. M. Wooldridge, cashier, and it is known as one of the substantial financial concerns of Jackson County. Mr. Wooldridge has thoroughly established himself in the confidence of the people of this community, and his own well-known integrity has done much to attract business to the bank's coffers. He is a director in the Wichita Southern Life Insurance Company of Wichita Falls, Texas.

In political matters Mr. Wooldridge is a democrat, but he has selected his career and has followed it closely, and in it public service has played no part. With his wife he attends the Methodist Episcopal Church, of which both are active members, Mr. Wooldridge being a member of the board of stewards. His fraternal connections are numerous, including membership in Altus Lodge No. 62, Ancient Free and Accepted Masons; Altus Chapter No. 60, Royal Arch Masons; Altus Council; Eldorado Commandery, Knights Templars; Altus Chapter, Order of the Eastern Star; and Altus Lodge of Odd Fellows, and he is also a member of the Oklahoma State Bankers Association.

In September, 1909, at Altus, Oklahoma, Mr. Wooldridge was married to Miss Crowell Ham, daughter of J. R. Ham, of Artesia, New Mexico. They have no children.

JAMES P. THOMPSON. The wild, untamed, uncivilized, romantic West of the old pioneer Indian Territory meets and merges into the modern Oklahoma with its progressive and bettered civilization in the life of Col. James P. Thompson of Woodville. Colonel Thompson has lived in that section of the present state, in what was old Pickens County of Indian Territory, for the past thirty years. Born in the strenuous days before the Civil war, at historic Preston Bend, just south of Red River in Grayson County, Texas, and reared amid the thrilling scenes enacted on a frontier unfettered by the restrictions of law, his life has contained enough incidents to make material for an intensely interesting romance.

Not only by residence but by family relationships and early experiences he has been in many ways identified with old Indian Territory as well as with modern Oklahoma. He was born November 26, 1850. His father was James G. Thompson, who was born in 1802 in North Carolina, moved to Tennessee and then to Alabama, and in the latter state became acquainted with and married Miss Mary McNary, member of a prominent Cherokee Indian family, and herself a quarterblood. In 1831 they accompanied the first emigration of that people to the Cherokee Nation in Indian Territory, locating at Webber's Falls, where James G. Thompson established a general mercantile store which he conducted for about twelve years. At the death of his wife, in 1843, having sold his business in Indian Territory, he moved to the south side of Red River in Grayson County, Texas. There he spent the rest of his life until his death in 1879. He was a member of the Legislature of Texas, when that state seceded from the Union and in the early '50s was county judge of Grayson County. He always had the high esteem and unqualified confidence of the Indians, to whom he was a good and faithful friend, and the people of the Cherokee Nation often solicited him to return and live among them. After his removal to Texas he married Miss Martha J. Caruthers, who was born in Georgia in 1820 and who was of white family, the Caruthers having been among the pioneers of Grayson County, Texas. At one time she owned the townsite of Denison. Her death occurred in 1894. By the second marriage there were eight children, namely: Elizabeth, who married Capt. Tom Randolph, a merchant and very prominent citizen of Sherman, Texas; James P.; Virginia, who married James Potts, a stockman; Arizona, who became the wife of Judge David E. Bryant, formerly a United States district judge, and one of the distinguished citizens of Sherman; Frank P., who is a retired merchant and farmer; Josephine who was drowned when a little girl; Breckenridge, who died in infancy; and Alice, who married Joe Meadows, a farmer and stockman of Grayson County.

Reared on the old farm in Grayson County, Col. James P. Thompson from early boyhood felt the fascination of the wild and free life of the frontier. He attended the common schools of Preston Bend, also Sherman High School, and for a time was a student in Burleson College. It was with difficulty he kept his mind on his studies, since he was by nature too closely akin to the free untrammeled life of the country and scenes among which he had been reared. As a boy before the war he had helped his father haul and sell corn to the United States military post at Fort Washita, Arbuckle, and Cobb. This corn sold at a price as

Col. Jim Thompson

high as $2.25 per bushel. In the years following the war he became an expert in all branches of ranch life. His father had a large horse ranch at Pottsboro, and his cattle ranch, on which frequently ranged 3,500, head, was five miles west of Sherman. Before coming to Indian Territory Colonel Thompson became well known as a stock man all over Northern Texas and after the building of the railroad across Indian Territory he used Denison, Texas, as a shipping point for his stock to the markets at St. Louis and Chicago.

In 1877 Mr. Thompson married Miss Maggie E. Massey, a member of an old Kentucky family that emigrated to Texas in 1848. Mrs. Thompson died in 1883, being survived by two children: Myrtle Lillian and Henry M. The daughter Myrtle is now the wife of Claude R. Howard. His son Henry M. married Miss C. F. Taylor, and their two children are named Ollie Lee and Maggie May.

After the death of his first wife Colonel Thompson married Lucy Juzan, who was a resident of Indian Territory and a descendant of the Chickasaw lineage, being a fourth blood Chickasaw. Her parents were Jackson and Mississippi Juzan. Jackson Juzan belonged to the Choctaw tribe and was born in Tennessee but came to Indian Territory during the '40s, and for many years followed farming in the vicinity of Atoka. He was one of the Choctaw volunteers in the Confederate army during the Civil war, and afterwards was active in the affairs of his nation until his death in 1866. Jackson Juzan married Mississippi Allan, who was of Chickasaw blood. She was born in Mississippi, and came to Indian Territory in 1835. She died in December, 1865. After their marriage Colonel and Mrs. Thompson took up their residence at the present beautiful homestead adjoining the Town of Woodville in July, 1886. No children were born to their union, and Mrs. Thompson died there in April, 1898. It is noteworthy that she was a cousin of Charles Le Flore, who was the father-in-law of former Governor Lee Cruce of the State of Oklahoma.

After locating in Pickens County, Colonel Thompson soon had extensive holdings. His cattle covered many hills and his brand became well and widely known. In one season he marked 1,200 calves. In Woodville he provided for his family the finest house in the town, with all the comforts and furnishings that wealth and culture can suggest. He has now reached the age of sixty-five, but still retains his interest in all that affects his community, and is a partner with his son Henry M. in the cattle business. In many ways his business judgment has been almost infallible, and his prosperity is only an adequate return for his abilities and energy. Colonel Thompson possesses many fine personal qualities, is whole souled and genial and as he knows everybody in his section of the country so everybody knows and honors "Uncle Jim." His loyalty to friends and neighbors has often been tested, and one case in point will illustrate the quality of his friendship. He spent much of his valuable time and $16,000 of his money a few years ago to prove the innocence of Steve Bussell. He belongs to no secret organizations or fraternal societies and finds his greatest enjoyment in the management of his farm and in association with his old and tried friends.

JOHN J. GAYMAN. High personal character and solid attainments as a business man and citizen have given John J. Gayman an important place in Lincoln County, where for the past five years he has held the responsible office of county treasurer. He was first elected to that position in 1910, and his present term expires in June, 1915. Mr. Gayman has been identified with Oklahoma citizenship for many years, and he has exerted his influence in many ways for the benefit of his home and community. In 1905 he served in the Oklahoma Territorial Legislature.

John J. Gayman was born August 27, 1875, on a farm in Indiana, a son of Isaiah Gayman, a native of Ohio. His father was reared in Indiana, became an early settler in Indiana, and enlisted and served for three years in the Union army as a member of the Eighth Indiana Volunteer Infantry. He married Sarah Wilson, who was descended from an Irish family of County Antrim, Ireland. They were the parents of nine children, eight of whom are living, as follows: Mrs. M. Drumm of Columbia, Missouri; Dr. S. E., a successful physician at Agra, Oklahoma; Mrs. L. Johnson, of Monett, Missouri; W. K. of Edmond, Oklahoma; John J.; Mrs. W. A. Moore of Lincoln County; Mark, a student in the University of Oklahoma; and Arthur, in business in Little Rock, Arkansas. Isaiah Gayman brought his family to Lincoln County, Oklahoma, many years ago and died there in 1901. He was a member of the Grand Army of the Republic, and belonged to the Christian Church. His widow is now living at Oklahoma City.

John J. Gayman grew up on a farm, and there developed his physique and gained his first lessons in honest toil. He received a public school education, and from an early age took much interest in republican politics attending as a delegate a number of county and district conventions. His constituents had special reason to be proud of his services as a member of the Legislature. He was connected with the passage of some of the best bills in that term of the Territorial Legislature.

In 1901, in Lincoln County, Mr. Gayman married Miss Grace Newell, who was born in Iowa and was reared and educated in that state and in Kansas, a daughter of J. A. Newell. To this union have been born four children, Ruth, Marion, John H. and Richard N. Mr. Gayman has given much attention to Masonic activities, is a member of the lodge, chapter and Knight Templar Commandery. He and his wife are members of the Presbyterian Church. Mr. Gayman is a man of splendid stature and physical proportions, has a pleasing address, and no one connected with official affairs around the courthouse has more stanch friends.

E. LEE ADAMS has been a resident of Oklahoma for fifteen years or more. In that time his life has been one of service as a teacher, farmer, newspaper man, and as an active and energetic worker in local affairs and local and state politics. He is now editor and owner of The Harper County Democrat at Buffalo, and owns considerable valuable real estate both in Buffalo and in the county.

His birth occurred in Linn County, Missouri, June 21, 1880. He was the only child of Mr. and Mrs. A. A. Dick, his present name being an adopted one. His father went to the Black Hills of Dakota in 1882 and was never heard from afterward. When but five years of age, with his mother, E. Lee Adams left Missouri, and he attended his first school at Harper, Kansas. His early life was one of abject poverty, but his one determination was to secure an education. At the age of fourteen he finished his high school work at Hamilton, North Dakota, but afterwards took a special normal course in the John B. Stetson University at DeLand, Florida. In Florida and also in Oklahoma Mr. Adams followed the profession of teacher in the public schools.

It was during his career as a teacher that in 1898, soon after the outbreak of the Spanish-American war, he enlisted in Company F of the First Florida Volunteer Infantry. He was with that command for a year and after his honorable discharge resumed his place in the schoolroom. In 1901 he moved to Oklahoma, and in 1902 gave up school work to become one of the editors of the Augusta Sun then published at Old Augusta, Oklahoma. After two years, in 1904, he founded the Sun at Dacoma, and a year later moved to his homestead in northwest Harper County, on which he had filed a claim in 1903. He spent two or three years in developing and improving a first class farm, but then answered the old call to newspaper work, and on April 19, 1907, founded The Harper County Democrat at Buffalo, being the first business institution started in the new county seat. He has since owned and edited this very live and enterprising journal and has given it much influence and a very satisfactory circulation through his home and adjoining counties. From absolute poverty he has, in fifteen years, risen to success and influence, all of which he attributes to his own determination and the encouragement and assistance of a good mother.

While an active democrat, Mr. Adams has never sought office, though he has filled the place of chairman and secretary of the County Central Committee and has held a place on the State Committee. Fraternally he is a thirty-second degree Scottish Rite Mason, being affiliated with the Consistory No. 1 at Guthrie, and a Shriner. He is also an Odd Fellow.

On January 1, 1908, in Harper County, Mr. Adams married Miss Minnie E. Torrance, who was born in Kansas December 17, 1888, a daughter of S. A. Torrance, who is now one of the leading farmers in Harper County. Mr. and Mrs. Adams have four children, three daughters and one son: Marion, Maxine, Wilmer and Evelyn.

CHARLES G. NESBITT. In his capacity as editor and proprietor of the Hinton Record Charles G. Nesbitt has a splendid opportunity of voicing the public opinion in regard to general improvements. He has been a resident of Hinton since the fall of 1909 and his citizenship here has ever been characterized by a loyal interest in all matters tending to advance the good of the community.

A native of Nelson, Nebraska, Charles George Nesbitt was born May 9, 1879, and he is a son of J. B. and Evaline (Lee) Nesbitt, both of whom are living, their home being at Watonga, Oklahoma. The father was born in the State of Ohio, in 1840, and as a young man he journeyed west to Iowa. In the latter state was solemnized his marriage and there he continued to reside until 1873, when the family home was established on a claim near Nelson, Nebraska. In 1889 removal was made to Fairfield, Nebraska, but 1891 finds the family again in the old community near Nelson. From 1894 until 1905 the Nesbitts resided at Eldorado Springs, Missouri, and in the latter year came to Oklahoma, settling at Norman and removing thence to Watonga in 1908. Mr. J. B. Nesbitt has devoted much of his active career to work as a contractor and builder. He gave evidence of his loyalty to the cause of the union during the Civil war by enlisting for service in Company B, Twelfth Illinois Volunteer Infantry. He served as a soldier for four years and five months and participated in many important battles marking the progress of the war. He and his wife are devout members of the Baptist Church and to them were born seven children, as follows: E. F. resides at Altus, Oklahoma, where he is manager of the wholesale grocery firm of Williamson-Halsell-Frazier; Walter died at the age of nine years; Paul, whose home is at McAlester, Oklahoma, was a member of the State Legislature in 1915; Lura Rose is the wife of C. E. Harritt, a farmer near Watonga; Maud married Louis Shaw, who is engaged in farming at Fairfield, Nebraska; Charles G. is he whose name forms the caption for this review; and Howard is a newspaper man at Mounds, Oklahoma.

Charles G. Nesbitt was educated in the public schools of Nebraska and lived at home on his father's farm until he had reached his sixteenth year. At that time he went to Eldorado Springs, Missouri, where he was engaged in truck farming until September, 1899, at which time he removed to Watonga, Oklahoma. In February, 1900, in partnership with his brother, Paul, he established the Oklahoma Senator, which they edited for about a year. In the fall of 1980 Mr. Nesbitt was matriculated as a student in the University of Oklahoma and he attended that institution for eighteen months. From January, 1902, until the fall of 1904 he was engaged in newspaper work in Watonga and on the latter date he and his brother Paul took over the Watonga Herald which they owned and edited until 1907. For nine months thereafter Mr. Nesbitt worked in a newspaper office in Oklahoma City and during that time he made up the first sixty editions of the Oklahoma News. In May, 1908, he began to work for Tom Ferguson on the Watonga Republican and in the fall of 1909 he bought the Hinton Record from Henry A. White. This publication was established in 1902; it is independent in politics and has a large circulation in Caddo and neighboring counties. The offices of the Record are on Main Street and the printing machinery and presses are up-to-date in every particular.

Mr. Nesbitt is a democrat in his political allegiance and he is a member of the Methodist Episcopal Church. In October, 1903, at Watonga, Oklahoma, was celebrated his marriage to Miss Lillian Woolverton, a daughter of W. C. Woolverton, a farmer in the vicinity of Abilene, Kansas. Mr. and Mrs. Nesbitt have four children, as follows: J. Wellington, C. Hubert, Norma May and William N., the three former of whom are attending school at Hinton.

M. H. MILLS. In 1909 M. H. Mills was admitted to the bar of the State of Oklahoma, since which time he has been engaged in a general civil and criminal practice in Mangum. In 1912 he formed a partnership with Judge J. L. Carpenter, under whom he had studied while in training for his profession, and together they enjoy a nice practice in the city and county.

Mr. Mills was born at Burleson, Johnson County, Texas, on January 24, 1878. He is a son of W. F. and Cora (Hix) Mills, and is one of their large family of ten children. W. F. Mills was born in Illinois in 1841 and died in Greer County, Oklahoma, in 1898. When he was yet a boy his parents moved from Illinois to Mississippi, and in 1851 they came to Texas, settling at Burleson, Johnson County, and there he continued to live for many years. He married there and his children were all born at Burleson, where he carried on a farming and stock-raising business. Mr. Mills served three years in the Confederacy as a member of a Texas regiment of volunteer infantry, and he was a life-long democrat and a member of the Methodist Episcopal Church, South. In 1890 he moved to Grier County, Texas, now Grier County, Oklahoma, and there homesteaded 160 acres of Government land, which he later increased to 320 acres, and which his wife sold after his death. The land was situated sixteen miles south of Mangum.

In 1869 Mr. Mills married Cora Hix. She was the maternal granddaughter of the Lee family. Her great grandfather was of English birth and ancestry. She was born in Kentucky in 1851 and is now living in Mangum. Their children are here briefly mentioned as follows: Rosa, the first born, died at the age of eighteen years. Mollie married J. B. Roberson and lives in Martin

County, Texas, where Mr. Roberson is engaged in farming. Price lives in Springfield, Colorado, and is a stock raiser. Annie married J. B. Hacker and resides in Hollis, Oklahoma, where Mr. Hacker owns and operates the telephone exchange. The fifth child was M. H. of this review. William lives in Springfield, Colorado, and is a farmer. Alice married J. F. Eddleman, and they have their home at Cleburne, Texas. Walter is a machinist and lives at Marshall, Texas. Mattie married H. E. Galbraith, and lives at Hollis, Oklahoma, where her husband is a manufacturer of soft drinks. Queen married Charles Brock, a machinist of the oil mill at Mangum.

M. H. Mills was raised on his father's farm and attended the schools of Greer County. He was twenty years old when he left home in 1898 for the first time. He went to Montana and worked on cattle ranches and in the mines for four years, and in 1902 returned to Greer County, Oklahoma, and spent a year in work on a farm there. He then entered the Tyler Commercial College in Tyler, Texas, and finished a thorough business course, after which he entered the office of Judge J. L. Carpenter in Mangum and began the study of law. He also read law in the office of G. A. Brown, now a judge of the Supreme Bench, and in several other offices did he get some training. He spent something like five years in study and in 1909 was admitted to practice. For three years he conducted an independent practice, and then, in 1912, joined forces with Judge Carpenter, and they have since worked together under the firm name of Carpenter & Mills. They have their offices in the Mangum National Bank Building.

Mr. Mills is a democrat, a member of the Methodist Episcopal Church, South, and of Lodge No. 1169, Benevolent and Protective Order of Elks.

In 1908 Mr. Mills was married to Miss Edna Derrick, daughter of W. A. Derrick, for many years a minister of the gospel of the Methodist Episcopal Church, South. Reverend Derrick is now an old man and resides in Wheeler County, Texas. Mr. Mills and wife have one child, Frances Byron, born October 10, 1914.

It may be said here that the Mills family is one of the old ones that came to this country from England in early Colonial days, settling in Pennsylvania, where many of the name are to be found today. Jonathan Mills, grandsire of the subject, was born in Illinois, whither a branch of the family had migrated, and he later lived in Mississippi and still later in Texas, where he died in advanced years. He was a farmer and a successful merchant, and like all the family, of the Methodist faith. His wife was a Miss Bond, born in Illinois, and she died in Burleson, Texas.

CHARLES M. COPE. An attorney of wide experience in practice both in this state and in Kentucky, Charles M. Cope formerly served as county attorney of Osage County, has figured prominently in democratic politics in the state, and enjoys a secure and substantial position in his profession at Pawhuska.

A native of Kentucky, he was born in Menifee County February 20, 1872, son of Thomas T. and Ruth Ellen (Tyre) Cope. His parents were also natives of Kentucky, and are now living at Jackson in that state. His father has for more than forty years been a practicing lawyer, and for sixteen years served as county attorney.

The second in a family of seven children, Charles M. Cope spent all his younger career in Kentucky, and from that state came to Pawhuska in 1907. He received most of his literary education in the S. P. Lee Collegiate and Military Institute, from which he was graduated in 1898. His law studies were pursued under the direction of his father, and in March, 1906, he was admitted to the Kentucky bar and practiced for about a year in his native State, serving during that time as attorney for a large coal company.

Since coming to Oklahoma Mr. Cope has found abundant employment for his time and energies in a general practice. For two years he served as county attorney of Osage County, and Governor Cruce appointed him county assessor for one year. In 1914 he was a candidate before the democratic primaries for the office of attorney general of the state, and his candidacy, while unsuccessful, has served to familiarize his name among many remote sections of Oklahoma. Mr. Cope has attained thirty-two degrees in Scottish Rite Masonry, being affiliated with the Consistory at Guthrie, belongs to the Blue Lodge at Hominy, and is also a member of the Benevolent and Protective Order of Elks. On November 4, 1908, he married Miss Edna May Venus, who was born in Texas.

CHARLES O. BLAKE, of El Reno, for the past nine years has been the Chicago, Rock Island & Pacific Railroad attorney for Oklahoma. He is one of the pioneer lawyers of the old Oklahoma, having located in El Reno in 1890, after five years of practice in Southern Kansas. His work and reputation as a lawyer have been fully proportionate to his long experience as a resident in this state.

Born at Blake's Landing, Ohio, October 29, 1860, he is a son of C. B. and Gratia (Fuller) Blake, both natives of Ohio. His father was born on the farm where his father before him was born, and has spent his entire active career as a farmer and stock raiser, and is still living on the old homestead in Ohio. He finished his education in the college at Marietta, Ohio, and at the outbreak of the Civil war organized a company and entered the Federal service, where he continued until mustered out in 1863 for disability. In 1857 he married Miss Fuller, who died May 22, 1915, after nearly sixty years of married companionship. They were the parents of six sons: A. F., an oil operator at Louisville, Kentucky; C. O.; Edward, a farmer in Canadian County, Oklahoma; Clarence, who died at the age of six years; Ernest E., a lawyer at Oklahoma City; and C. B., an oil operator at Louisville, Kentucky.

Charles O. Blake studied law in the Cincinnati Law School, and in 1883 was admitted to practice at Indianapolis, Indiana. He soon afterwards came west and in 1885 located at Coldwater, Kansas, where besides his private practice he was elected on the republican ticket as county attorney of Comanche County.

It was in 1890 that Mr. Blake came to El Reno, and with his brother, Ernest E., established a law office under the firm name of Blake & Blake. In 1900 Mr. Blake became local attorney for the Chicago, Rock Island & Pacific Railway, and in 1907 was appointed attorney for Oklahoma and Indian Territory to represent the interests of the Rock Island Line. He still holds the same office, though his official designation has been changed to correspond to the admission of the two territories as a single state.

During the last quarter century, covering almost the entire political history of old and new Oklahoma, Mr. Blake has been active in republican politics, though he never sought an office for himself. He served as a member of the board of regents of the State Agricultural and Mechanical College and of the Oklahoma State University at different times. Fraternally he is affiliated with the Benevolent and Protective Order of Elks and the Independent Order of Odd Fellows.

On February 18, 1885, he married Miss Cora Bryan, daughter of William H. and Julia Bryan of Gallipolis,

Ohio, but natives of Virginia. Mr. and Mrs. Blake have four children: Bryan T., Marion, Bordwell and Ansel.

HORACE A. SMITH. Since his arrival at Perry, in 1893, Horace A. Smith has been continuously engaged in practice, and during a large portion of this time has served in positions of trust and public responsibility, of a county, civic and judicial nature. As a lawyer he bears a reputation for legal information and acumen, and in the capacity of county attorney of Noble County is serving faithfully the interests of the people who placed their confidence in his integrity and fidelity.

Mr. Smith was born near Waukegan, Lake County, Illinois, January 6, 1858, the son of Charles H. Smith. His father, who served in an Illinois volunteer infantry regiment during the Civil war, was engaged in farming in Illinois for some years and then removed to St. Clair County, Missouri, where he located on new land. In 1881 or 1882 he moved to Eldorado Springs, Cedar County, Missouri, where he is still living in retirement. He is one of the well known and influential citizens of his community and has served as circuit clerk of Cedar County and as a justice of the peace for several years.

The boyhood of Horace A. Smith was passed on a farm in St. Clair County, Missouri, near Appleton City, where he secured his early education in the public schools and Stahl Academy. He had decided upon a career in the law, but lacked the means to secure a university training, and in order to supply this deficit began teaching school while still in his 'teens, thus working his way through college. He attended the University of Missouri, at Columbia, during 1880 and 1881, and received his diploma and was admitted to the bar in the latter year. Mr. Smith at once engaged in practice at Eldorado Springs, Missouri, but in 1885 removed to Coldwater, Kansas, at that time a new town. Two years later he was elected county attorney of Comanche County, Kansas, an office in which he served for two terms, or four years, and during this time he secured some valuable experience in the carrying of the old county bond case to the Supreme Court, as well as in several notorious murder trials.

In 1891 Mr. Smith came from Coldwater, Kansas, to El Reno, Oklahoma, and practiced at the latter place until September 16, 1893, when he made the run for land, and choosing the vicinity of Perry, secured 160 acres southwest of this city. This he proved up as soon as permitted. In the meantime he opened a law office at Perry, where hundreds of attorneys had hung out their shingles, and some remained for several years, but only three of the original lawyers are still here, these being Henry S. Johnston, H. A. Johnson and Mr. Smith. Mr. Smith continued to be engaged in practice until 1901, when he was elected county judge of Noble County, and acted in that capacity during that and the following years under the territorial government. He was mayor of Perry at the time of statehood, and during his administration the city secured the Carnegie Library as well as the valuable city waterworks, and the city's finances were placed upon a substantial basis. In the fall elections of 1914 Mr. Smith was elected county attorney of Noble County, and since assuming the duties of that office, January 1, 1915, has administered its affairs in an expeditious, capable and conscientious manner. He has always been a stanch republican, and at various times has been a delegate to state, county and congressional conventions of his party, where he is in much demand as a speaker. In fraternal affairs Mr. Smith is an Odd Fellow and a Mason, and was one of the organizers of the Odd Fellows Lodge at Ponca City.

On June 6, 1897, Mr. Smith was married in Kay County, Oklahoma, to Miss Mabel A. Dean, of Arkansas City, Kansas, who until the time of her marriage had been a teacher in the public schools. She is well known in social circles of Perry, and a valued and popular member of the Tuesday P. M. Club. Mr. and Mrs. Smith are the parents of one son: Horace Adrian.

OWEN FREDERICK RENEGAR. One of the younger professional men of Cordell is Owen Frederick Renegar, who has been engaged in a general law practice here since he was admitted to the bar in 1913. Mr. Renegar is of Tennessee birth and parentage. He was born near Fayetteville, Lincoln County, Tennessee, on June 23, 1892. The Renegars settled in Virginia and North Carolina in early colonial days, and many of the name will be found in those states today, while at least three generations of them have helped to develop the state in which the subject was born. His father, J. F. Renegar, passed his early life as a stockman and farmer in Lincoln County, and in 1905 came to Oklahoma and settled near Cordell. J. F. Renegar married Elsie Snoddy, the daughter of a prominent Lincoln County farmer and of the union there were four children: Owen F. was the first born; Carrie and Loris are living and Alton, the youngest, died in infancy.

Owen Frederick Renegar attended the country schools of Lincoln County and finished the common school work there. Soon after his parents decided to move West and this seemed to bring somewhat of a stop to school work for Mr. Renegar. He quit school work for about three years and followed the work of a printer in the emulation of Franklin. Soon he began to realize the necessity of a higher education and he entered Cordell Academy and finished high school and did some college work there, and was graduated therefrom. After graduation he taught school for a while and was very successful in that field holding a number of good positions, among them superintendent of Cowden Consolidated School. All the time he was teaching he studied law and higher literary work attending school whenever he could and taking extension work and graduated from Potomac University, Washington, District of Columbia, in the law school and in the arts and sciences departments with the degrees A. B. and LL. B. He was admitted to the bar in 1913, since which time he has conducted a general office practice. He has thus far enjoyed a reasonable measure of success and his future seems well assured.

Mr. Renegar is a democrat and a Christian. He is a member of the Masons, Odd Fellows, and Woodmen of the World. He has already shown himself a leader in politics, and is the organizer and manager of the democratic clubs of the Seventh Congressional District. Mr. Renegar is a member of the Commercial Club of Cordell, and is a member of the County, State and National Bar associations.

Mr. Renegar is a young man filled with the vim and power to accomplish something in this world. He is progressive and believes in the motto: "Load always when the opportunity is right and just; follow never without thorough consideration." He has accepted the call of the world: "Young man, show us what thou canst do."

EMERY W. KING, M. D. In the practice of medicine at Bristow since 1905, Doctor King is now one of the oldest established physicians of that little city. He has an excellent practice and has well and worthily won his place in professional life. He is both a physician and business man and a few years ago was honored by his fellow citizens with the post of mayor.

His birth occurred at Charleston, Coles County, Illinois, December 22, 1879. His parents are John and Susan

(Kelley) King, the former a native of Missouri and the latter of Illinois. They are now living in Charleston, where the father is a retired farmer. He still owns 220 acres of good Illinois land and has been thoroughly prospered in all his undertakings. At different times he has quietly exerted a considerable influence in local politics, though never as a candidate for public office. Both are active members of the Baptist Church.

Doctor King, who is the oldest of six children, spent the first nineteen years of his life on a farm. He had its discipline combined with the instruction of rural schools. In order to secure a more liberal education he attended the Southern Illinois Normal School two years, and was also a student in a private school at Aledo, Illinois. Like many successful professional men he preceded his active career by work as a teacher, and altogether taught three years. Entering the Hospital Medical College at Louisville, Kentucky, he continued his studies there until he earned his M. D. degree in 1905. Soon after graduating Doctor King located at Bristow, which only two or three years before had started its growth, and has been rapidly acquiring a fine practice and lending his aid to every public spirited movement in behalf of the town's welfare. He is a member of the County and State Medical societies and the American Medical Association, and is affiliated with the Knights of Pythias. As a republican he has done much in behalf of local organizations of the party. The only important office he has held was as mayor of Bristow one term. He has three times been a delegate to state conventions of his party.

On December 23, 1905, Doctor King married Gertrude Rice. She was born near Carrollton, in Greene County, Illinois, a daughter of Fisher and Elizabeth (Bradley) Rice, who still live in Greene County. Doctor and Mrs. King have one child, Nadine.

HON. ALONZO McCRORY. It has been frequently observed that politics is America's oldest pastime, and a great many men take as naturally to politics as others do to baseball. Since the pursuit is so well established among the activities of men, it is not surprising that its duties and responsibilities rest so lightly on the shoulders of the majority who are thus employed. That citizenship is a duty as well as a privilege is not so frequently exemplified as to be commonplace. The individual who assumes an earnest attitude for the public welfare has been sufficiently rare at all times. For this reason there is much promise for the future and commendation for what has already been accomplished by such an able young political leader as Alonzo McCrory, who is the present speaker of the House of Representatives in the Fifth Legislature. As a profession Mr. McCrory is a newspaper editor and publisher, with residence at Ringling, in Jefferson County. He has gone into politics actuated by certain ideals and schemes the basis of which is the fundamental principle of service, and there are a great many who predict for him a splendid career as a public leader far beyond what he has already accomplished, creditable though that is in every sense.

Born in Fayette County, Texas, September 10, 1878, Alonzo McCrory was educated in the Texas public schools and was a student in Baylor University at Waco, for two years, 1896-98. He did not complete his college course, but took up a business career, and in 1903 moved to Durant, Oklahoma, and for a time manufactured soda water, extracts, syrups, etc. In 1904 he became bookkeeper in a general mercantile establishment at Comanche, Oklahoma. December 1, 1905, he removed to Cornish, Oklahoma, and continued the mercantile business as secretary of the firm of Bennett & Spragins. He sold out his interest in that business in 1909, and on the 18th of June of that year founded the Cornish News, which he published there until May, 1914. At that date the Town of Cornish was moved bodily to the new site of Ringling, and the newspaper went along, changing its name at the same time to the Ringling News.

Mr. McCrory represented Jefferson County in the Fourth Legislature, having been elected practically without opposition after over 500 representative citizens of the county had signed a petition offering support in the race. He came into the Legislature with an unusual equipment gained both by observation of practical politics and by a close study of politics as a science. He had participated in county and state conventions of the democratic party, and for a time was clerk of the County Court at Cornish. He was president of the first democratic club organized in Cornish after Oklahoma became a state. As a member of the House in the Fourth Legislature Mr. McCrory was chairman of the Judicial and Senatorial Redistricting Committee, and was author of a bill, which never became a law, that provided for decreasing the number of district judges from thirty-one to twenty. When he returned to the House in the Fifth Legislature he was elected speaker after a brief campaign, the other candidates having withdrawn from the contest. He accordingly obtained this much coveted honor without prejudice, and has used his office with one idea to secure the utmost efficiency from the body over which he presides and also to maintain an effective harmony among the members and between the Legislature and the governor. Among important measures that have claimed Speaker McCrory's attention was the one amending the bank guaranty law so that the guaranty system would be on a better and more substantial basis.

Mr. McCrory is a son of A. S. and Clara (Wier) McCrory. His father, a native of Tennessee, was a Confederate soldier under. Gen. Sterling Price. His mother, a native of Mississippi, was of Irish and Dutch descent. Among the father's ancestors were two Irish boys who came to America and participated as soldiers in the Revolution. A. S. McCrory died in 1913, and his widow now lives at Waelder, Gonzales County, Texas. There were seven boys and five girls in the family. A. W. McCrory, the oldest, is a stockman and farmer at Waelder, Texas; Mrs. Sallie Johnson is the wife of a stockman and farmer at Jeddo, Texas; Mrs. Maggie Galloway is the wife of a farmer and stockman at McCaulley, Texas; William is a stock raiser at Flatonia, Texas; Mrs. Katie Miller is the wife of a farmer and stockman at Waelder; Sam Houston, nicknamed "Pug" and who named himself Sam Houston when four years of age, is a teacher and stockman at Flatonia; Mrs. Cora Fike is the wife of the second assistant superintendent of a tramway company at San Antonio; Mrs. Bessie Cowan is the wife of a stockman and farmer at Waelder; Marshall E. is a bookkeeper at Waelder; and Dorsey is a farmer and stockman at Waelder. Speaker McCrory was married July 26, 1902, to Una B. Cochran of Fayette County, Texas. Their four children are Staton, aged twelve; Lucile, aged nine; Claude, aged six; and Harry Lee, aged four. Mr. McCrory is a member of the Ringling Lodge of Woodmen of the World, and is a member of the board of directors of the Cornish Orphans Home, a state institution.

His political career has been primarily characterized by straightforwardness and an absolute integrity in all his relations. At different times he has been offered support in politics during county seat fights and other contests that would have compromised him, and has rejected all such overtures and his success is entirely due to methods eminently fair and above board. He is a fine type of young man with wide experience, unusual executive ability, unassuming, and ambitious only for the good service he can perform.

WILLIAM PENN HICKOK. Worthily in the front rank of his important and difficult profession, William Penn Hickok, of Taloga, has won his own way to his present position. His early years were devoted to widely different vocations, but from youth he was determined upon a career in the law, his success in which has evidenced the fact that he made no mistake in the choice of an occupation. Mr. Hickok was born at Guilford, Nodaway County, Missouri, February 23, 1862, and is a son of James E. and Olive L. (Bowen) Hickok.

The Hickok family is one which dates back to the Plymouth Colony in Massachusetts, where it was founded at an early day by William Hickok, the emigrant ancestor, who came from England. His son, Aaron Hickok, removed from Massachusetts to Connecticut, and the latter's son, James, fought in the Revolutionary army as captain of a company in a Connecticut regiment. James Hickok's son, also names James, went to Vermont, where his son, David Nicholas Hickok, the grandfather of William Penn Hickok, was born in 1806. From that state the grandfather moved to Pennsylvania as a pioneer farmer, fought throughout the Civil war as a Union soldier, was once wounded, and returned to his agricultural operations and finally died at St. Joseph, Missouri, in 1892, to which point he had moved with his family just before the war.

James E. Hickok, father of William Penn Hickok, was born in Bradford County, Pennsylvania, in 1833, and there passed his early years, receiving a common school education and being reared as a farmer. He was married in Pennsylvania, and after marriage moved to Fayette County, Illinois, that community being his home and the scene of his agricultural activities until 1860. In that year he took his family to Nodaway County, Missouri, and in 1869 moved on to Andrew County, in the same state. His next location was Peabody, Kansas, where he resided from 1879 until the spring of 1883. Up to that time Mr. Hickok had been engaged in farming, but on removing to Sumner County, Kansas, he embarked in merchandising and met with more or less success there until his retirement in 1901. Two years later he went to Anthony, Kansas, and there his death occurred in 1905. As a business man Mr. Hickok was straightforward and honorable in his dealings with his fellows. He was a professed Christian and lived his religion every day, being a devout member of the Baptist Church and a member of the board of trustees for many years. His political support was given to the principles and candidates of the republican party. Mr. Hickok married Miss Olive L. Bowen, who was born at Colden, Erie County, New York, in 1839, and she survives and makes her home in Sumner County, Kansas. There were eight children in the family, as follows: James E., who died in Anderson County, Kansas, at the age of twenty-one years; Luella B., who is the wife of W. G. Rupp, a contractor and builder and brick and tile manufacturer of Trinidad, Colorado; William Penn, twin of Luella B.; Charles D., who is engaged in the banking business at Ulysses, Kansas; Esther C., of Argonia, Kansas, widow of J. C. Colin, formerly a school teacher for a long period, superintendent of schools of Sumner County, Kansas, for a number of years, and postmaster at Argonia at the time of his death; Mary A., who died at Oquawka, Illinois, as the wife of James W. Gordon, an attorney of that place; Hadassah, who died in childhood; and Galen R., who is engaged in the real estate and farm loan business at Satanta, Kansas.

William Penn Hickok received his early education in the public schools of Missouri and Kansas, to which latter state he accompanied the family when he was seventeen years of age, graduating from the Peabody High School with the class of 1880. He had been reared as a farmer's son and remained on the home farm until reaching his majority, at which time he turned his attention to mercantile lines, conducting a store at Harper, Kansas, for three years. His next venture was in the line of real estate at Harper, and while thus engaged for three years found the leisure to pursue his legal studies, having decided to follow the law as his life work. In 1889 Mr. Hickok went to Fort Supply, Indian Territory, where he became teacher at the army school, a position which he retained for three years, then participating in the opening, in 1892, of the Cheyenne-Arapaho Reservation for white settlement, when he secured a homestead of 160 acres. He proved up on this land and sold it for a satisfactory consideration in 1897, having in the meanwhile continued to teach school and to devote what time he could to his legal studies. In December, 1898, Mr. Hickok came to Taloga, having been admitted to the bar of the state September 13 preceding, and here has continued to practice in civil and criminal law to the present time. His practice carries him into all of the courts, his admission to practice before the Supreme Court having been granted January 10, 1902, and his clientele is representative of the largest interests in this section of the state. In the fall of 1898 he became the candidate of the democratic party for the office of county attorney of Dewey County, a position which he retained for two terms, or four years, having been re-elected in 1900. He has served also as a member of the town board and the town school board, and at present is the incumbent of the office of town treasurer. Fraternally Mr. Hickok is connected with Taloga Lodge No. 179, Ancient Free and Accepted Masons; Taloga Chapter No. 54, Royal Arch Masons; Taloga Council; Taloga Commandery, Knights Templar; India Temple, Ancient Arabic Order of Nobles of the Mystic Shrine, Oklahoma City, and Consistory No. 1, Valley of Guthrie, having attained the thirty-second degree of Masonry; and with Taloga Lodge, Independent Order of Odd Fellows, of which he is past noble grand, and the Modern Woodmen of America of this city. His professional affiliation is with the Dewey County, Oklahoma State and American Bar associations, while his numerous business connections include the treasurership of the Taloga Oil Company, Inc.

Mr. Hickok was married September 15, 1895, at Taloga, to Miss N. E. Shumate, daughter of the late Balus Shumate, a farmer of the locality of Taloga. Three children have been born to this union, namely: Charles B., a graduate of the class of 1914, Taloga High School, and now a teacher in the public schools of Dewey County; Gordon W., a freshman at Southwestern State Normal School, Weatherford, Oklahoma; and Galen J., who attends the public schools of Weatherford.

JOHN F. KROUTIL. A lad of about ten years at the time when he accompanied his parents on their immigration from Austria to the United States, the career of Mr. Kroutil has shown in a most significant and emphatic way how great are the opportunities afforded in our great republic for the achievement of large and worthy success on the part of a young man who has the will to dare and to do, and who, dependent upon his own exertions, has the energy and self-reliance that make for personal independence and prosperity. Far from the Fatherland, now involved in the most horrible warfare known in the history of the world, Mr. Kroutil pursues the even tenor of his way under the benignant conditions of peace, and has secure status as one of the influential and representative business men of Oklahoma, he

and his elder brother, Frank L., having been residents of Oklahoma since the year the territory was organized and having kept pace with the marvelous advancement that has here been made under the territorial and state regimes. They are now interested principals in what is undoubtedly the most extensive and important enterprise of its kind in the State of Oklahoma, the subject of this sketch being president and his brother secretary and treasurer of the Yukon Mill & Grain Company, at Yukon, Canadian County.

From the status of a young man without more than nominal financial resources, Mr. Kroutil has risen to that of executive head of the largest and most modern flour mills in Oklahoma, the products of which are shipped to many distant states of the Union, as well as into Cuba, and in connection with which has been developed a grain business of extensive volume. The Yukon Mill & Grain Company dates its organization back to the year 1902, and within the intervening period its business has had an almost phenomenal expansion in scope and importance. The original mill purchased by the Kroutil brothers at Yukon was a modest establishment with a daily capacity for the output of only seventy-five barrels, or one carload of flour a day. At the present time the splendid plant, with the best of modern equipment and facilities, has an output capacity of 1,200 barrels a day, the equivalent of twenty carloads. The average daily business has attained to the noteworthy aggregate of nearly $10,000, and the flour and other mill products are of the highest grade. The mill is a substantial brick structure of four stories and of modern design architecturally as well as in the matter of providing the best facilities for the purpose for which it was erected. The mill elevators are of large capacity and the facilities for storage are adequate to meet the demands of the enormous business controlled. From this fine milling plant products are shipped throughout Oklahoma and also into the states of Texas, Arkansas, Louisiana, Mississippi, Alabama, Georgia, North and South Carolina, Tennessee, New York and Connecticut, the substantial and widely disseminated trade affording the most effective voucher for the specially high grade of the products. By the way of the City of New Orleans the company ships flour to Cuba, and this export trade is constantly increasing. In addition to the central elevator at Yukon the company maintain also and own well equipped elevators at Union, Oklahoma, and other points in the state. The officers of the company are as here noted: John F. Kroutil, president and general manager; Anton F. Dobey, vice president; and Frank L. Kroutil, secretary and treasurer. The Kroutil brothers became residents of Oklahoma in 1890, and they have been closely associated in their business activities during the intervening years. The subject of this review acquired at Ponca City, Kay County, this initial experience as a buyer of grain, and there he was soon joined by his elder brother, Frank L., their residence and business operations having there continued for six years. In 1902 they purchased a sawmill at Yukon, and from this nucleus has been developed the fine milling plant of which mention has already been made. In the earlier period of their residence in Canadian County the brothers were associated in the development and management of a farm, but their ambition and progressiveness soon led them into broader fields of industrial enterprise. They came to Oklahoma Territory from David City, Nebraska, in which state they had previously been engaged in agricultural pursuits. They were born near the city of Prague, Austria,—Frank L. in 1872, and John F. on the 16th of May, 1875,—and thus both were boys at the time of the family immigration to America in 1882, the father establishing a home on a farm near David City, Nebraska, where the sons were reared to adult age and were afforded the advantages of the public schools. The parents, Frank and Katherine (Vice) Kroutil, are still living and maintain their residence in Oklahoma, as do also their four sons and one daughter, the latter being the wife of Anton F. Dobey, vice president of the Yukon Mill & Grain Company. He whose name introduces this article has become one of the substantial capitalists of Oklahoma and in addition to being president of the Yukon Mill & Grain Company he is president of the Yukon National Bank. While he has been unflagging in his application to business and has achieved large success, he has had appreciation of the responsibility imposed by such success and is most loyal, liberal and public-spirited in his civic attitude. Though a strong supporter of the cause of the democratic party he is essentially a business man and has had naught of ambition for the honors or emoluments of public office. He and his family are communicants of the Catholic Church, and he is a life member of the Oklahoma City Lodge of the Benevolent and Protective Order of Elks. As a man of large business activities, Mr. Kroutil has formed a wide acquaintanceship in the state of his adoption, is liberal in the support of measures and enterprises advanced for the general good of the community at large, and his honorable, straightforward course, as combined with a genial and buoyant nature, has gained to him hosts of staunch friends.

The maiden name of the first wife of Mr. Kroutil was Leonora Borek, and she is survived by one child, Bernice. A few years after the death of his first wife Mr. Kroutil wedded Miss Mary Fisher, and they have one daughter, Margarette, the family home being one of the most attractive in Yukon and a center of most gracious hospitality.

HENRY H. EDWARDS, city attorney of Mangum, and former member of the state legislature, is a native son of the State of Illinois. He was born in Greene County on September 29, 1878, and is a son of George P. and Jane (Moore) Edwards, both of Illinois birth.

George P. Edwards is a prosperous and well known farmer in Greene County, Illinois, and has his home in the Town of Whitehall at the present time. He was born in 1850 and has passed his days in the county and state of his birth. Five children were born of his marriage to Jane Moore. Henry H. of this review is the eldest. Ward, living in Greene County, has charge of a drainage district on the Illinois River. Walter lives in Humboldt, Iowa. Grover is a locomotive engineer and lives in Centralia, Illinois. Nina married Minor Morrow, a traveling salesman, and they have their home in Whitehall, where her parents live.

Henry H. Edwards attended the common schools of Greene County and was graduated from the Whitehall High School with the class of 1897. He taught for three years in the public schools of the county, and then, in 1900, went to Chicago where he was engaged as an instructor in a business college. For five years he continued in that work, reading law in his spare time, and in 1905 he took a position as a traveling salesman. In 1907 he came to Oklahoma, located in Stigler, and soon after was admitted to the bar. He began the practice of law in Stigler at once and continued in practice there until 1911. He was prominent and popular in the county and in 1910 was elected to the Legislature, serving through 1910 and 1911. He served on several committees during that time, among them the Judiciary, Insurance, Federal Relations, Code and Special Investigations committees. During his incumbency he fathered and introduced three companion bills on road laws, which were passed and entered upon the statute books. In 1911 he resumed the practice of law, locating in Dallas, Texas, and he was there until 1914, coming to Mangum in July of that year. He has since been engaged in general practice. In February, 1915, Mr. Edwards was elected to the office of city attorney for a four year term, and since his election has taken quarters in the city hall.

Mr. Edwards was married in January, 1914, in Calera, Oklahoma, to Miss Bertha Burrow, a daughter of B. B. Burrow, former postmaster of Calera, where he now lives retired. Mr. and Mrs. Edwards have found many warm friends in their new home, and they are prominent in social circles of the community.

T. T. BLAKELY is now secretary and manager of the Chamber of Commerce at Okmulgee. However, he is the type of man who is always larger than any office with which he happens to be connected. Mr. Blakely is a man of unusual parts and talents. Perhaps the dominant quality in his makeup has been enterprise, and he has succeeded not only in doing a large amount of work and business through his individual efforts, but has been peculiarly effective in getting other men to do what he wants them to do.

He was born at Grafton, Massachusetts, April 18, 1873, son of C. J. and Nellie M. (Bacon) Blakely. His father was born in Northern Vermont and his mother in Canada, so their birthplaces were not far apart, being separated by the international boundary line. They grew up and married in that community, and by trade the father was a shoemaker. Eventually he was made foreman of the finishing department in one of the large shoe factories of Grafton, Massachusetts. He later invented a machine which performed an important part in the making of shoes. Leaving the East he finally located at Janesville, Wisconsin, when his son T. T. was two years of age. He established a shoe factory at Janesville and has spent the rest of his days in that city. The mother passed away in 1906 at the age of sixty-two. She was at one time president of the Grand Lodge of the Rebekahs of the State of Wisconsin and the father was also an active lodge man. In their family were five children, three daughters, after whom in age comes T. T. Blakely, and then a younger brother.

Mr. Blakely was reared in Janesville, and finished the high school course there in 1891. At an early age, though he lived in a comfortable home, he found it necessary to do something practical in addition to acquiring knowledge and living the usual routine of boyhood. He paid much of his expenses through high school by carrying laundry. In 1891 he entered the State University at Madison, where he paid his expenses by handling a laundry agency, by collecting bills and running a students' club. In the summer vacations he sold books for three years. In 1895 leaving the university he spent a year as a teacher in Janesville, and then returned to school and completed the literary course in 1896. He also gained some credits in the engineering course.

From 1896 to 1900 Mr. Blakely was principal of the high school at Middleton, Wisconsin, and from 1900 to 1904 was superintendent of schools at Sun Prairie, Wisconsin. During that period he also conducted summer schools for teachers at Janesville and other places in the state. Mr. Blakely has the distinction of having organized the first teachers' association in Dane County, Wisconsin, a county of which Madison, the state capital, is the county seat with 400 teachers connected with the schools. He was elected the first and second president of the association, and filled that office in 1898-99. While engaged in teaching in Wisconsin he spent his summer vacations largely as a book agent, selling students' reference books, the Encyclopedia Britannica and Stoddard's Lectures. Probably few men have had a more successful experience in the book business than Mr. Blakely. Because of his success he received an offer from the E. R. Dumont Publishing Company of Chicago, at $50 per week and expenses, to cover the company's territory in Wisconsin, Missouri, Illinois, Indiana, Ohio and Pennsylvania. He was then sent South, the company paying the expenses of the removal of his family, and he covered the states of Kentucky, Tennessee, North Carolina, South Carolina, Alabama and Georgia. During this time his family resided at Shelby, North Carolina, Spartanburg, South Carolina, Columbus and Dawson, Georgia, and Montgomery, Alabama. He was next sent north to Toronto, Canada, and continued his work as a canvasser all along the lake region, and still later located at Coffeyville, Kansas. For two years his family lived at Mound Valley, Kansas, and he continued his work as a canvasser through Louisiana, Arkansas, Texas and Oklahoma. In that district he covered every town above 5,000 population.

From 1907 to 1912 Mr. Blakely had his residence at Caney, Kansas, having gone there when gas was discovered. He entered the real estate business, and for a time was very successful in that field. When the gas supply gave out he lost all his investments and started all over again. This time he began selling Florida lands, with headquarters at Lakeland, Florida.

In September, 1914, Mr. Blakely was elected secretary of the Chamber of Commerce of Bartlesville, Oklahoma, and after a year accepted a similar position at an advanced salary at Okmulgee, where he is now doing a great deal to vitalize and organize the work of the local chamber of commerce. During his residence at Caney, Kansas, he was elected a member of the city council and also served on the county high school board of Independence, Kansas, having been chosen as a republican. Fraternally he is a Mason and Odd Fellow. Mr. Blakely has great ability as a public speaker and in his long and varied career has been called upon to exercise this talent on many occasions.

In 1898 he married Hattie Louise Ferrin, who was born at Darlington, Wisconsin, and is a graduate in music. Five children have been born to their union, but their daughter Moyne died at the age of eight months. The four sons are: Thurston, Merle, Kenneth and Malcolm. Mr. and Mrs. Blakely are members of the Presbyterian Church at Okmulgee.

HON. ALBERT RENER MUSELLER. One of Oklahoma's lawyers, and one of the assistant editors of this work, whose home is now in Pawhuska, was formerly register of the United States land office at Alva, and his name and influence have been identified in many important ways with the development of this new state where he has lived since 1893.

He was born June 3, 1857, at Clayton, Illinois. His father, Rener R. Museller, was born in the province of Aurich, Germany, and was a subject of the King of Hanover. He emigrated to the United States and became a naturalized citizen before his death which occurred in 1864, when the subject of this sketch was only six years old. He was a gunsmith and blacksmith and he married Malissa Wallace of Winchester, Illinois, who was born in 1837 and still lives at an advanced age in Wichita, Kansas. Malissa Wallace was a daughter of Joseph Wallace, one of the pioneers of Illinois, at whose house in Winchester, Illinois, Stephen A. Douglass lived when he taught his first and only term of village school. The father of Joseph Wallace was Charles Wallace, who

married Peggy Short in Longford County, Ireland, and in 1776 emigrated to Baltimore, Maryland. These Wallaces were Scotch-Irish, and descendants of the Wallaces who left Scotland and settled in Northern Ireland in the seventeenth century.

Albert R. Museller had no inheritance. What he has been able to accomplish in life has been the result of his own effort and ambition. He educated himself and had only the advantages of the common schools of his country, and yet he is a man of liberal education, for which he always says, he is largely indebted to an aunt, Mrs. H. W. Craig, of Vermilion County, Illinois, with whom he lived for several years when a boy.

He taught school in Illinois and Indiana for several years, read law in Lincoln, Illinois, was admitted to the bar of that state and subsequently in Kansas and also Oklahoma.

He resided for several years in Wichita, Kansas, and for four years was judge of the City Court of that city. After coming to Oklahoma, in the year 1893, he was for two years, county judge of Noble County, was county attorney of the same county for two years, and for four years was register of the United States land office at Alva, Oklahoma. He is now engaged in the practice of law in Pawhuska.

In politics he has been identified with the republican party, although in 1912 he supported the progressive ticket nationally. He is a fluent and ready public speaker, and there are not many cities or towns in old Oklahoma in which his voice has not been heard discussing the political issues. He has contributed articles to various magazines, chiefly on games and sports and the aborigines of this country. The Indians have always been of great interest to him. He loves God's out of doors, and there are few plants, birds, insects, trees or flowers with which he is not familiar. His chief recreation is artificial bait casting for bass, in which accomplishment he is an adept. Mr. Museller's ready pen has also contributed many articles to the various papers of his state on agricultural subjects.

Fraternally, he is affiliated with Wahshahsho Lodge No. 110, Ancient Free and Accepted Masons, of Pawhuska, and is a member of the Consistory of Scottish Rite at Guthrie.

On May 6, 1880, at New Holland, Illinois, he and Ida R. Thomas were married. Mrs. Museller is of old New England stock and is a descendant of Gen. Israel Putnam of Revolutionary fame. The Thomases emigrated from Ohio to Illinois in the early years of the nineteenth century. Mr. and Mrs. Museller are the parents of three children. Crete is now the wife of Fred M. Merkle, who is in the Government service at Perea, New Mexico. Leo, the second daughter, is the wife of Hon. John B. Doolin, formerly state fish and game warden of Oklahoma, and their only son, Albert R. Museller, Jr., is occupying a good position with the Southern Pacific Railway at Redwood City, California.

SHAWNEE CARNEGIE LIBRARY. One of the first institutions to mark the growth of Shawnee as a center of culture and liberal education was the Shawnee Carnegie Library. This central city of Oklahoma now has much to be proud of, not only as a commercial metropolis of a large and distinctive territory, but as a city of churches, schools, and the various institutions and organizations that increase the attractiveness and advantages for those who not only seek opportunities to advance in a business way, but the facilities of enlightenment.

The handsome new library building in which the large collection of books are stored and are distributed to the public was erected in 1905 in beautiful Woodland Park, on North Broadway. This building cost $15,768. The library now comprises 10,500 volumes and is steadily growing, not only in additions to the book collection but in a more important degree in the use of the books themselves.

The first librarian was J. C. Holt, who was succeeded by Mrs. J. C. Parker in 1907. Since 1909 the librarian has been Mrs. T. S. Funk. The present library board is made up of the following persons: Mayor F. P. Stearns, president; Judge W. M. Engart, vice president; George E. McKinnis, Otis Weaver, Mrs. W. H. Dodge, Mrs. Agnes Amos and Mrs. George Larch-Miller. Mrs. Funk was secretary of the library board almost from its organization in 1902. The first president of the board was Mrs. J. R. Schloss. Other members who at different times have been especially identified with the work of this organization were: Mr. and Mrs. C. J. Benson, Mrs. Dr. Shive, Mrs. Glen Lehman, Mrs. Henry Beard, Mrs. James Aydelotte, Hon. R. E. Wood, Victor E. Harlow, Paul Cooper and Mrs. Frank Boggs.

MRS. T. S. FUNK. Librarian of the Carnegie Library at Shawnee, Mrs. Trimmier (Sloan) Funk was born at New Albany, Mississippi. The Sloans came originally from Ireland and England and were early settlers in South Carolina. Another branch of her family were the Henrys, who were of Scotch-Irish descent. Mrs. Funk is a great-granddaughter of Nancy Trimmier, whose father was born in a Revolutionary camp. Nancy Trimmier lived in South Carolina near Spartanburg. The Trimmiers were of French origin, and were extensive planters, cotton mill owners, conducted carriage factories, and were prominent in the South in an official way. Mrs. Funk's father was Capt. T. B. Sloan, who was born at Spartanburg, South Carolina, in 1830, but when a boy his parents settled in New Albany, Mississippi. He is still living at New Albany at the age of eighty-five. He received his early education at Spartanburg and New Albany, and in 1861 went into the Confederate army, and at Gettysburg he was wounded and made a prisoner, and remained in the Federal prison on Johnson's Island in Lake Erie until the close of the war. He then settled at New Albany, was married, and became a planter and merchant. He married Mary Henry, who was born in South Carolina in 1840 and died at New Albany, Mississippi, in 1885. Their children were: Georgia A., widow of W. H. Gantt, and she now resides on a plantation in Arkansas; Mrs. T. S. Funk; Minnie Frances, wife of Major W. Stroud, who is a large shipping contractor and at the head of a transfer business at Greenwood, Mississippi; Willie Theodore, wife of W. H. Bone, a planter at New Albany, Mississippi; Compton, whose whereabouts have been unknown for several years; Elizabeth Irma, wife of Frank W. O'Keeffe, connected with a department store at Meridian, Mississippi.

Mrs. Funk received her early education in the public and private schools of Mississippi. She spent some time training for library work in the Carnegie Library at Oklahoma City. In 1886 in New Albany she married Richard Walker Funk. He was born in Wallerville, Mississippi, received a public school education in his native town and at New Albany and in the University at Oxford, Mississippi, and in business became a general merchant and furniture dealer in Mississippi. In 1902 he moved to Shawnee, where he established the Shawnee Furniture Company in partnership with J. B. Armstead. This house was burned out in 1904, and since then Mr. Funk has been connected with the Flemming-Brown Furniture Company at Shawnee. He is a democrat and is a member of the Knights of Pythias. Mr. and Mrs. Funk have two children: Waller Adair, who received a high school education at Shawnee and pursued further training in a school of technology in Chicago and is now superintendent for an electric company in New York City. Louise Trimmier is now a sophomore in the high school at Shawnee.

F. P. STEARNS. For a good many years Shawnee has reposed the administration of its municipal affairs in the hands of Frank P. Stearns. He is one of Oklahoma's very capable mayors. He is one of the old settlers and has lived in Shawnee and has been a witness and participant in its growth and development for more than twenty years.

He was born in Paris, Maine, October 5, 1861. His ancestors came over from England in Governor Winthrop's ship in 1636 and three brothers of the name settled in Waltham, Massachusetts. S. P. Stearns, father of Mayor Stearns, was born at Paris, Maine, in 1829, and has spent all his life in that community as a farmer and banker. Though past eighty-five years of age he is still attending to his duties as a banker. In politics he is a republican and is a member of the Universalist Church. He married Isabelle Partridge, who was born in Paris, Maine, in 1832, and is also still living in advanced years. Their children were: Austin P., a farmer at Paris, Maine; Frank P.; Henry K., a miller at Hebron, Maine; William C., on the old homestead at Paris; Mary, wife of E. C. Park, a lawyer at Bethel, Maine; and Joan, wife of E. S. Kilborn, a retired lumberman, who spends part of the year in Bethel and during the winter resides in Portland, Maine.

Mayor Stearns attended the public schools of his native village, in 1881 graduated from Hebron Academy, and for one year was a student in Colby College. In the meantime he had begun teaching and for a time was principal of the high school at Pine Hill. In 1885, coming West, he located at Abilene, Kansas, and spent two years in the grain and stock business at Chapman. Removing from there to Dighton, Kansas, he became a rancher, handled real estate, and for two terms filled the office of county superintendent of schools.

At the opening of the Cherokee Strip he entered Oklahoma, secured a homestead of 160 acres one mile north of Enid, but after a year sold out and since November 7, 1894, has lived in Shawnee. Since then Mr. Stearns has been identified with many of the business activities of this city. For two years he conducted a general store. He established the first gas plant, but after a year sold out to present Gas Company. To a greater or less extent he has been in the real estate business. He was elected and served three years as city treasurer, and for 4½ years held the office of postmaster, having been appointed at the close of McKinley's administration and remaining in office until 1905. He was secretary of the chamber of commerce a year and its president one year. In the spring of 1906 he was elected mayor, and held that office for two terms, or four years. After being out of office a year he was again selected, this time for a three year term, and is now serving a second three-year term. In politics he is a republican, and is affiliated with Shawnee Lodge No. 657, Benevolent and Protective Order of Elks, with the Maccabees, the Fraternal Order of Eagles, the Modern Woodmen of America, and the Brotherhood of American Yeomen. Mr. Stearns is a director in the Shawnee Building and Loan Company, has served on the board of education, is president of the Provident Association, having been chosen for a second term in that office on November 11, 1915, and is by virtue of his office president of the Carnegie Library Board. Mayor Stearns was largely instrumental in securing the establishment of the splendid hospital at Shawnee and it is recognized as the finest municipal hospital in the state and the only one that is on a paying basis. He is now governor of the hospital board.

In 1893, at Dighton, Kansas, Mayor Stearns married Miss Winifred Arnold, daughter of S. E. Arnold, now of Kansas City. They have two children: Helen, who graduated from Bethany College in June, 1915, and is now taking a special course in music in Kansas City; and Arnold, in the first year of the Shawnee High School.

JUDGE WILLIAM MARSHALL ENGART. A prominent Shawnee attorney and vice president of the Shawnee library board, Judge Engart was born in Boone County, Indiana, October 14, 1849. The Engart family is of Dutch-Irish descent and arrived in Virginia about the time of the Revolutionary war. His father, Absalom Engart, was born in Virginia in 1818 and died in Clinton County, Indiana, in 1886. He came to Boone County, Indiana, about 1845, having been reared and married in his native state. He was a farmer and stock raiser and about 1876 he moved to Clinton County, where he died. Absalom Engart married Elizabeth Brawley, who was born in Virginia in 1820 and died in Clinton County, Indiana, in 1876. Their children were: Diana Johnson, a widow, who lives in Clinton County, Indiana; Marietta, who married J. C. Ghent, a druggist, both being now deceased; Martha, who married John Pauley, a stockman, and they also are deceased; Caroline, who married John Jelf, a carpenter, and both died at Chattanooga, Tennessee; Rush, a farmer, who died at Frankfort, Indiana, and William M.

Judge Engart attended the common schools in Boone County, Indiana, and for a time was a student at Thornton Academy, under John C. Ridpath, the great popular historian. He graduated Bachelor of Science in 1869 from Stockwell University. His early life was spent on his father's farm, and for three terms he was a teacher in the district schools of Boone County. In the meantime he took up the study of law, and also attended the law department of the Indiana University at Bloomington. He was admitted to the Indiana bar in 1873, and has had more than forty years of active experience as a lawyer. His first practice was done at Colfax, Indiana, from 1873 to 1881. Then for a few years, until 1888, he was engaged in farming in Jasper County, Missouri, and from there went to Dallas, Texas, and was in the planing mill business there until 1892, in which year he returned to Indiana.

Judge Engart is an Oklahoma pioneer, having come to the territory in 1893, and after securing admission to the bar practiced at Guthrie for ten years. On January 1, 1904, he removed to Shawnee and has since enjoyed a general civil and criminal practice, his offices being over the State National Bank. He has frequently served as special judge of the district court and in the superior court of Pottawatomie County. He has served as president of the Pottawatomie County Bar Association, and in politics he is affiliated with the socialist party. In Clinton County, Indiana, in 1875, Judge Engart married Mrs. Matie J. (Dean) Long. Her father was a farmer in Carroll County, Indiana. The seven children of their marriage are: Linus M., who is connected with the Royal Typewriter Company and resides at Corpus Christi, Texas; Zoe, wife of A. E. Church, who is in the fire department at Los Angeles, California; Ethel, wife of R. C. Raglan, also with the fire department at Los Angeles; Grace, wife of Joe Hawkins, proprietor of a restaurant in Shawnee; Blanche, wife of N. L. Hardin, connected with the Pacific Railway at Los Angeles; C. R.,

+Rt. Rev. Theo Meerschaert
Bp of Oklahoma

with the L. C. Smith Typewriting Company at Shawnee; and Gertrude, a stenographer at Shreveport, Louisiana.

BISHOP THEOPHILE MEERSCHAERT was born August 24, 1847, in the Village of Russignies, about an hour's walk from the City of Renaix, in the Belgian Province of East Flanders. His father was of that sturdy stock which has played so great a part in the history of Northern Europe; the stock which was first to declare its independence of feudalism to build up the great manufacturing and commercial cities of the middle ages—Ghent, Bruges, Lille, Audenarde and Ypres—cities of the guilds, the Christian prototypes of our modern trades unions; cities which sent forth their armies of tradesmen and mechanics, who, under the walls of Courtrai, in 1302, humbled the pride of Philip the Fair and his courtiers in the battle of the Golden Spurs. His mother was of that other race of Belgium, Walloon, whose ancestors Caesar, in the introduction to his History of the Gallic Wars, declares, "Of all these, the bravest are the Belgians."

He was the eighth of ten children, a family of only average size in that country even now. His earliest instruction was received in the public school of his native village, as at that time the public schools of Belgium were all Catholic. In 1859, at the age of twelve years, his vocation to the priesthood must have been already marked, for he entered the then recently founded diocesan College of Renaix. Here the child studied each day from 8 A. M. to 6 P. M., making the journey of three miles to and from home on foot. His first great sorrow came during the first college year, on May 28, 1860, when his mother died after an illness of only a few hours. His eldest sister, Victorine, who had intended to enter the convent, at once took her mother's place in the care of the growing family, remaining for their sake in, but not of, the world, an humble heroine of simple devotion to duty. She, whom the Bishop loves to call his second mother, died December 23, 1914, on the forty-second anniversary of his ordination to the priesthood.

When the College of Renaix, which was then far from its present rank as it now includes, besides a complete classical course, a famous school of weaving and other manual training, could take him no further in his studies, the young Theophile entered the diocesan College of Audenarde in October, 1864, whence he was graduated in August, 1868. While there, he devoted his leisure to the Society of St. Vincent de Paul, and found in its work a suitable outlet for his zeal and charity toward the sick and poor. He was successively secretary and president of the local conference, and obtained from the first the rare privilege of being allowed to visit the sick at the hospital, which he did each week for four years.

The time was now at hand to begin his immediate training for the priesthood, and as he was resolved to be a missionary in America, young Mr. Meerschaert entered the American college at Louvain in October, 1868. Here he had as professors the famous Dupont and Monsignor Cartuyvels, long the beloved vice-rector of Louvain University. On June 10, 1870, he received minor orders; took the irrevocable step to subdeaconship, December 17, 1870; was ordained deacon June 3, 1871, and priest, December 23, 1871; remaining, however, as a student in the American college until July, 1872.

It may not come amiss to notice here an incident of his seminary days that will serve to shed some light upon his later life. A neighbor in his village, who lived alone, had died. Victorine, his sister, invited the young seminarian to come with her and prepare the body for burial. The man had been dead nearly twenty-four hours when they arrived. It was summer, and although he took hold bravely enough, the flesh was weaker than the spirit. As she saw him about to faint, Victorine cried out, "Shame on you: Is that the kind of man who wants to be a missionary?" The lesson was never forgotten and served to buoy him up through many a sickening ordeal in after years.

Now came the second great trial, the parting from home and friends. To those who go abroad for a visit or for recreation, there is little in this; yet even then there is frequently a reluctance at the last moment that causes emotion. For those who leave home for a longer period to study in preparing for life work, the trial is greater; yet even here there is great hope of return to live at home; and the knowledge that one's life is not being torn up by the roots to be transplanted in an alien soil. But when we definitely leave behind all that is dear, and know that if we ever do return it will be only as a visitor; when we go forth to face what difficulties we know not, and to give ourselves for strangers who may not appreciate or welcome our sacrifice; to labor among people whose language, whose customs, whose very outlook upon life is foreign and perhaps repugnant to our own; and when we know that after all we need not go; that friends without number would gladly bid us stay; ah then, there is something to give up! The Belgian loves his home and native land. This is abundantly shown by the fact that although it is the most densely populated land upon the face of the globe, and conditions of life are correspondingly hard, yet the number of its emigrants is negligible. If our young missionary, then, shed a few tears at parting, can we find it in our hearts to blame him? Especially since through it all, like so many of his brave countrymen, his purpose, never faltered, nor took one backward look on what it left behind. On September 26, 1872, Father Meerschaert left Russignies. He arrived in New York October 13th. His first sea voyage was a long one, but was thoroughly enjoyed by the young missionary, who was from the first an excellent sailor. He did not tarry long to enjoy what to him must have been a new world full of wonders, but proceeded as rapidly as circumstances and the then slow and arduous means of transportation would permit, to report for duty to Bishop Elder of Natchez, Mississippi, afterwards Archbishop of Cincinnati.

The young priest was blessed in his bishop. A man whose combined learning and true holiness with greatness of mind and soul and the simplicity of an apostle, Bishop Elder was in deed as in word a pattern to his flock. His angelic pity for the poor and suffering, and his heroism during the repeated visitations of his war-scarred diocese by the yellow fever, made him loved by both priests and people.

On November 16, 1872, Father Meerschaert, after a few weeks at the bishop's house, was sent to his first charge. No doubt he felt quite flattered to think he was at once to be a pastor. This feeling, however, promptly subsided after his first visit to his missions. His parish consisted of the missions of Jordan River, Pearl River and Wolf River, in Hancock and Harrison counties, along the sea coast. Although invited to make his headquarters with a neighboring pastor in a well established parish, he reserved this privilege for one week in three months, and lived the rest of the time as best he could in his own poor missions.

The first visit was not very encouraging. It was sixty miles through the pine woods and swamps to his destination, and the trip was made in a little cart. Six or seven miles out, while fording a stream, his valise fell out into the water. To add to his discomfort a norther came up and it began to sleet and freeze. Father Meerschaert was afraid that his aged driver would be ill, so, although he himself was wet through from the rescue of the precious valise, he wrapped the old man in his cassock. They walked and drove alternately for twenty-five miles, and at 3 o'clock in the afternoon arrived at the residence of a Catholic family, a one-room house, where they sat down to a dinner of rice and cabbage. It is safe to say that was the best rice and cabbage the young priest had ever tasted. The aged driver was ill, and there was not much room to spare, so Father Meerschaert walked three miles to the home of a relative of his host to spend the night. There he found a family of ten, again in a one-room house. The evening meal was sweet potatoes, served alone. The missionary had not yet learned to like them, so he concluded to wait for the second course. But there was no second course! His bed was in the corn crib upon a husk tick with one quilt for covering. Old sacks were hung before the cracks in the corn crib to keep out the wind. On this bed he lay down, fully dressed and tried to pray himself to sleep, while the wind howled through the pines, and the latter kept up a continual crashing as they rid themselves of their accumulated burden of encrusted sleet. The next morning he set up a portable altar between the beds in the house, and thus celebrated his first Holy Mass as pastor in his new missions. As his feet were badly swollen from the previous day's trip, he decided to return on horseback. The saddle was not well girded and when he attempted to mount, it promptly turned under the horse. Finally he got it securely fastened and rode off. Being yet but an inexperienced horseman he got his horse into a hole at the Wolf River ford, and was plunged into the icy water to the hips. Before he could dry his clothes or obtain food he had to ride through the cold three miles further to a farmhouse.

It will readily be seen from these incidents, that his people were desperately poor. They were people of some education and refinement but had lost all their wealth in the Civil war, then comparatively recent. For the most part Catholics, they were sadly in need of instruction. Many full grown and even old persons among them had never made their first Confession or Communion, and knew next to nothing of their religion. Added to this was a certain spirit of hostility toward the church, and this spirit it was the task of the young missionary to eradicate.

During the first winter he called his people to a week's encampment at a central point. Here each day was begun with Mass, followed by a solid forenoon's instruction on the catechism, the prayers, the ceremonies of the church, etc. At noon a recess for lunch, and all afternoon was again devoted to study and instruction. Confession began Thursday, and Sunday morning nearly a hundred, ranging from sixteen to seventy years, made their first Holy Communion. All received confirmation at the hands of Bishop Elder at Bay St. Louis, February 2, 1873.

Father Meerschaert was changed to Ocean Springs in August, 1874, and had been in his new parish not quite a year when yellow fever broke out. The first cases occurred in the latter part of June, but the epidemic reached its greatest virulence in September and October. From the first outbreak the young pastor was in the thick of the danger. He did not confine himself to spiritual ministrations, but busied himself with nursing the sick, Catholics and non-Catholics alike, sitting up with them every alternate night, as a rule, and by word and example heartening the people to care for their own afflicted ones, instead of fleeing in panic to a place of safety, and leaving husbands, wives or children to die without consolation, as was so often the case in other communities. Finally, on the last Friday in October, after having spent the whole night by the bedside of a dying German, he was called by a Protestant old lady, one of those who thought Catholics so bad that they would not even sell vegetables to the priest, but who said in calling him: "Mr. Priest, my neighbor is sick and wants you. She is a Catholic and I know you will do her good." It was three miles in the country and the transportation was apostolic; that is, on foot. After he had given the sacraments to the dying girl, "Mr. Priest," said the old lady, "you are sick, too?" "No," replied Father Meerschaert, "Only a bad cold." "But you look bad; perhaps you are afraid?" "Well, hardly, after nursing the sick for eight weeks." "Well, if you take the fever, send for me; I will come and nurse you." The following day, Saturday, she came after Mr. Priest to come and bury the dead girl, and on Sunday, during Mass the premonitary symptoms appeared. After Mass came the chill; and a non-Catholic, whose daughter was being instructed for first communion, put the priest to bed. On Tuesday he suffered a relapse, and for a week his life was despaired of, as he had even the black vomit, considered a sure sign of death. The next day, though still unable to sit up, he was brought six miles into the country in a spring wagon, supported by a man on each side, to give the last sacraments to the little girl he had been instructing for first holy communion, the daughter of the man who had put him to bed. He was brought back home, arriving at half past one in the morning. The girl died the same morning at nine.

In 1878, while on his first visit to Europe, he learned that the yellow fever had again broken out in Mississippi, and hurried back to his flock. This epidemic was worse than the preceding one and out of twenty-six priests, six died with the fever, and thirteen sisters. During this second epidemic, Father Meerschaert had to attend, not only his parishioners, but those of Biloxi, and Pascagoula as well, as the pastors of both these places were down with fever.

In June, 1879, Father Leduc, then pastor of Bay St. Louis, was sent away on sick leave, and Father Meerschaert was sent to replace him until his return. In November, 1880, he was appointed to Natchez, where he remained until his appointment as Vicar Apostolic of the Indian Territory. In Natchez he continued the same course which had so endeared him to the people in his former parishes. No one, whether Protestant, Catholic, Jew or atheist ever fell ill, without being visited by Father Meerschaert and no one who was not glad to call him friend. After the coming of Bishop Janssens, afterwards Archbishop of New Orleans, in May, 1881, Father Meerschaert became acting vicar general, and after the death of Father Grignon in April, 1887, he received the title. Bishop Janssens was promoted to New Orleans August 6, 1888, and Father Meerschaert was designated Administrator of the Diocese of Natchez until the coming of the new bishop. Bishop Heslin arrived in Natchez June 23, 1889, and appointed Father Meerschaert again vicar general.

On April 20, 1891, Archbishop Janssens received a cablegram that Father Meerschaert was selected as Vicar Apostolic of the Indian Territory. The news reached Natchez the same night at 3:30, but as Father Meerschaert was out visiting the sick, he did not receive it until 6 o'clock in the morning. The announcement was made in Consistory on May 7, 1891, and on June 11th, the bulls appointing him Bishop of Sidyma and Vicar Apostolic of the Indian Territory were issued. The new bishop-elect made his retreat preparatory to consecration at Jefferson College in New Orleans, from August 27th to September 3d. His consecration took place in the cathedral at Natchez, September 8, 1891. The consecrator was his dear friend, Archbishop Janssens, assisted by Bishops Fitzgerald of Little Rock, and Heslin of Natchez.

The consecration of the new bishop was most appropriately the grandest church function witnessed in Natchez up to that time, or even since. Prelates, priests and people vied with one another to do honor to the man, who, after many years of arduous labor among the people of Mississippi, was now called by the voice of the Supreme Pastor to a greater but no less trying field. Among the testimonials of regard received by Bishop Meerschaert on this occasion were, a purse of $700, full pontifical robes, crozier, mitres, pectoral cross and chain, chalices, etc. On the evening of his consecration he was tendered a public reception by the citizens of Natchez, and on the following evening, by the colored people. While they could not but rejoice at the honor bestowed upon one so dear to them, still their hearts were saddened at the thought that these honors signalized their separation from one whom they all, irrespective of religion, had grown accustomed to call "Father."

Our Bishop's first Holy Mass in his new vicariate was celebrated in the convent at Purcell in the early morning of September 19, 1891. He arrived at Guthrie, the place designated by the Congregation of the Propaganda as his residence, the same day, and was met at the station by Governor Steele, numerous officials of Oklahoma Territory, and other prominent citizens.

Let us now glance briefly at the conditions existing in the new vicariate, comprising what is now the State of Oklahoma, but at that time known as Oklahoma and Indian Territory. Truly a beautiful land, but still slumbering in the ignorance of childhood regarding the bounteous material resources hidden within its breast, and having as yet no idea of the greatness a few short years would bring. Vast reaches of its area were as yet forbidden to the settler. The only inhabited portion of Oklahoma Territory comprised the counties of Logan, Kingfisher, Oklahoma, and Canadian, with a part of Lincoln, Pottowatomie, and Cleveland. The population of this territory was less than 6,000 souls. The Indian Territory with its five civilized tribes and some smaller tribal governments, together with a comparatively small number of whites and negroes, numbered less than 200,000. Of railroads, there were only what are now known as the main lines of the M. K. & T., the Santa Fe, and the north and south line of the Rock Island, the latter terminating at El Reno. In the Indian Territory there were no laws but the tribal governments, and this portion of the future state was largely a refuge to the lawless of other states. There were but sixteen priests, all told; and nearly half of them were but more than fully occupied with the labors and trials incident to the solid foundation and upbuilding of College and Indian School at Sacred Heart. The number of secular priests was three. The total number of baptisms the first year was 347, of marriages, 52, and of burials, 78; while the total Catholic population, white, Indian and colored, was 7,994, and the total number of children in the Catholic College and schools was 766.

One of our bishop's first cares was to visit and confirm in every part of his vicariate. Though he was then, as he has been ever since, received with honor, loyalty, and the affection which those who know him best understand so well, yet the physical labor of traversing so great an area largely by wagon, fording streams, braving storms, and enduring the hardships inseparable from travel in a new, wild country, was always great. He had now, however, to concern himself more and more with the spiritual burdens and financial responsibilities of his position. He has traveled a great deal, both in and out of the state; and has always made good use of his travels, especially his trips to Europe, to obtain young and zealous priests and has employed the donations of the charitably disposed to assist those laboring in the poorer missions, as well as to provide for the education of those who desire to devote their lives to missionary work, and who would otherwise be prevented by lack of means. He has always made his house a home for priests, and many a weary missionary, coming to see the bishop after months of discouragement and almost hopeless, has received refreshment, both material and spiritual, and after a short rest has departed with courage renewed for his field of labor.

On August 23, 1905, the vicariate was erected in the Diocese of Oklahoma with the Episcopal See at Oklahoma City. Since that time, as before, its growth has been steady, even during the reaction which followed the early boom days. By way of comparison with the statistics given for the first year of our bishop's presence here we see that in 1915 there were in the diocese 71 secular and 34 regular priests, 64 churches, with residence priests, 84 missions with churches, 127 stations, and 4 chapels. Besides these there are 12 Brothers of the Sacred Heart in Muskogee, and in the diocese 320 members of religious sisterhoods. There are 15 ecclesiastical students, 3 colleges for boys, Sacred Heart, Muskogee, and the Catholic University in Shawnee; 238 college students, two academies for young ladies, with 190 boarders, 2 hospitals, St. Anthony's in Oklahoma City and St. Mary's Infirmary in McAlester; St. Joseph's Orphanage at Oklahoma City, with 70 orphans; 39 schools for white, 8 for Indian, and 2 for colored children with a total of 4,972 pupils and a total of 5,152 young people under Catholic care. There were during the year 1,620 baptisms, of whom 201 were converts; 387 marriages and 365 burials, and the Catholic population was 40,633.

It must not, however, be imagined that everything has been easy sailing in the diocese during all these years. The bishop has had his trials, and they have been both many and heavy. The one thing that has sustained him when everything looked darkest has been his spirit of prayer. He has always enjoyed to a very high degree the love and loyalty of both his priests and his people, and forscoth the hope and prayer of all is—

"May he be still our Bishop and our Father for many years to come."

LEONIDAS HORTON MCCONNELL, M. D. The arrival of Dr. Leonidas Horton McConnell at Elmer was coincident with the opening of the village. At that time he was but recently graduated from his medical college, and he was forced to pass through the period of hard struggle to gain a foothold that all young physicians must experience; but his abilities and knowledge of his calling soon made themselves felt, and since that time he has attracted to himself an excellent practice and established himself firmly in the confidence and esteem of the people.

Doctor McConnell was born at Maryville, Blount County, Tennessee, November 29, 1871, and is a son of J. R. B. and Sarah (King) McConnell. The branch of the family of which he is a member originated in Scotland and the original emigrant located in Virginia, probably prior to the War of the Revolution. J. R. B. McConnell was born in 1840, also at Maryville, where he was engaged in farming at the time of the outbreak of the Civil war, and enlisted in a Tennessee infantry regiment in the Union Army, with which he served until the declaration of peace. He continued to be a resident of Tennessee until 1902, in which year he came to Oklahoma, locating at Guymon, the county seat of Texas County, where his death occurred in 1907. Mrs. McConnell, who was born in Knox County, Tennessee, in 1845, died at Maryville, that state, in 1885. They were the parents of nine children, as follows: Moses, who was a farmer and died at Maryville, Tennessee, in his thirty-second year; Jennie, who resides at Guymon, Oklahoma; Dr. Leonidas Horton; Josephen, who married John Nuchals, and died in 1907; Annie, who married Clell Ballinger, a carpenter and builder of Guymon; Elizabeth, who is the widow of M. G. Wylie, an attorney, and resides at Guymon; Adelia, who is the wife of John Curtis, a merchant at Guymon; John, who is the editor of a newspaper at that place; and Olive, who died at Carlsbad, New Mexico, as the wife of R. R. Cline, a mechanic.

Leonidas H. McConnell grew up on his father's Tennessee farm. He attended the schools of Maryville, where he was graduated from the high school in 1893, and Maryville College, where he pursued a full course of three years. Following this, he spent three years in teaching school in Blount County, and in the meantime applied himself to the study of medicine, which he had decided upon as his life profession. In 1898 he matriculated at the Chattanooga (Tennessee) Medical College, where he was graduated in 1901, with the degree of Doctor of Medicine. Between medical school courses he taught public school to make the next medical school year. While a member of Maryville College he was active in college literary circles and a member of the Athenian Literary Society. After a short period of practice in his native state, July 11, 1901, Doctor McConnell came to Oklahoma, first taking up his residence at Yelldell, near the present Town of Elmer, and when the latter town was founded, in the same year, transferred his residence and professional headquarters to this place. Here Doctor McConnell has carried on a broad and general medical and surgical practice, being equally at home in both branches. He has kept in close touch with the professional brotherhood, belonging to the organizations of his calling. His well-appointed offices are located on Main Street, in the Elmer Drug Store. Doctor McConnell is a republican in national affairs, but in local matters is disposed to hold views of a rather independent nature, preferring to use his own judgment in the selection of candidates for office. He is somewhat interested in fraternal work, being a member of Yelldell Lodge No. 196, Ancient Free and Accepted Masons, Elmer Chapter of the Order of the Eastern Star, and Elmer Camp, Woodmen of the World, and has many friends in each. He has always been known as a public-spirited citizen who can be depended upon to give his energetic support to movements of a progressive and advantageous nature.

On May 12, 1911, at Elmer, Doctor McConnell was united in marriage with Miss Kate McCabe, daughter of the late Barney McCabe, retired, of Litchfield, Kentucky, who died in 1914. Doctor and Mrs. McConnell are the parents of one son: Henry Lee, born at Elmer, January 7, 1914.

DUDLEY B. PHILLIPS. The genial, popular and efficient cashier of the First National Bank of Yukon is recognized as one of the representative executives in connection with financial affairs in Canadian County and is well entitled to consideration in this history of Oklahoma, within whose borders he has maintained his home since 1889, the year that marked the opening of the territory to settlement. Mr. Phillips has been identified with the First National Bank of Yukon for nearly a score of years, and has had much influence in its development into one of the substantial and important financial institutions of Canadian County, the while his character and services have given him inviolable place in popular confidence and good will.

Though a representative of one of the honored pioneer families of Oklahoma, Mr. Phillips claims the fine old Bluegrass state as the place of his nativity, and there also were born his parents, John B. and Martha A. F. (Lain) Phillips, who emigrated thence to Oklahoma in 1889 and settled on a farm six miles southeast of the present thriving little City of Yukon. There the father continued to reside until his death, in 1897, at the age of seventy years, his wife surviving him by a number of years, and the names of both meriting enduring place on the roll of the sterling pioneers who initiated and carried forward the civic and industrial development of a now vigorous and opulent young commonwealth.

Dudley B. Phillips was born in Hancock County, Kentucky, on the 8th of March, 1867, and in the schools of his native state he received meager advantages. He preceded his parents to the West, as he came to Kansas in 1884, when seventeen years of age, and he remained in the Sunflower state until the opening of Oklahoma to settlement, in 1889, when he came to the new territory and established his residence in Canadian County, where his parents located in the same year. Thereafter he was for a few terms a representative of the pedagogic profession in this county, as a teacher in rural districts, and in the furtherance of his own education he attended for a time the University of Oklahoma.

In 1898 Mr. Phillips assumed the position of bookkeeper in the Bank of Yukon, and soon afterward he was advanced to the position of assistant cashier, of which he continued in tenure until he was made cashier of the institution in 1900. The Bank of Yukon was converted into the First National Bank in 1902. Prior to entering the banking business he had been identified with agricultural pursuits in Oklahoma, but in his present vocation he has found opportunity and scope for most effective service and has become known as an able financier of marked discrimination and progressiveness.

Vitally interested in all that touches the general welfare of his home community, county and state, Mr. Phillips is loyal and public-spirited, and though never troubled with aught of ambition for the honors or emoluments of political office he accords unwavering allegiance to the democratic party. He is a Master Mason, and is a member of the Baptist Church of Yukon, of the Sunday school of which he has served as superintendent for more than seventeen years—covering virtually the entire period of his residence in Yukon.

In 1899 was solemnized the marriage of Mr. Phillips to Miss Clara Artt, who was born in Iowa and whose father, Jefferson Artt, was a sterling pioneer of Canadian County, Oklahoma. Mr. and Mrs. Phillips have six children: Lucille, Daniel Artt, Dudley Bernard, Dorace, George Dayton and Jean Lewis.

J. S. BARHAM. During the dozen years he has been a resident of Oklahoma, J. S. Barham has become one of the leading men of Seminole County, has been engaged in merchandising, in the management of stock and ranch interests, has served as a member of the Legislature, and is now postmaster of Wewoka.

A native of Tennessee, he was born at Satillo June 8, 1867, a son of William I. and Tennessee C. (Hawk) Barham. Both parents were born in the same locality of Tennessee and the father died there in 1871 at the age of thirty-five. He was a tanner by trade and also a general merchant, and three of his brothers were in active service in the Confederate Army under the noted cavalry leader, Forrest. These brothers were Samuel J., Newsom and A. P. Mr. Barham's mother is still living, having spent most of her life at the old home in Tennessee, but is now residing at Grayson, Louisiana.

Her five children were: Mollie N., now deceased; Newsom R., who for the past twelve years has served as district judge at Lexington, Tennessee; Samuel J., deceased; J. S.; and Rena, wife of A. B. Mitchell, of Grayson, Louisiana.

J. S. Barham grew up in Tennessee and lived in that state until about 1903. He had limited opportunities to gain an education, but made the best of them, and at the age of sixteen began a business career as a mercantile clerk. From 1898 to 1904 he was purchasing agent for the Ayer & Lord Company of Chicago, buying up timber for the manufacture of ties and other kindred material. He was also for four years postmaster at Parsons, Tennessee.

Since November, 1904, Mr. Barham has been a resident of Oklahoma. For a time he was a merchant at Coalgate, but in April, 1905, moved to Konawa, in Seminole County, was in the land and loan business there until moving to Wewoka in 1908. From 1908 to December 31, 1910, he served as under sheriff of Seminole County and then resumed the real estate and loan business during 1911-12. Again he filled the office of under sheriff until July 27, 1913, and then accepted appointment as postmaster of Wewoka, an office in which he has rendered valuable service to the community. While Mr. Barham has also had some experience in handling the affairs of a postoffice back in Tennessee, it is noteworthy that his mother was for some time in charge of the postoffice at Satillo, Tennessee, and Mr. Barham's sister, Mollie, was also postmaster of the same town. Among other business interests Mr. Barham is closely identified with agriculture in Seminole County, and has about 600 acres under cultivation.

He has always been a democrat, and was chairman of the first democratic campaign committee in Seminole County. From 1911 to 1913 he represented Seminole and Pontotoc counties in the State Legislature, and thus in addition to handling his private affairs successfully he has rendered public service to his county and home community and also to the state at large. Mr. Barham is a Mason, having attained thirty-two degrees in the Scottish Rite, is a Knight of Pythias and a member of the Woodmen of the World. In 1898 he married Miss Eula Corine Payne at Iuka, Mississippi. To their marriage have been born six children: Hugh Payne, Anna Irene (who died in infancy), Willie Tina, Lewis, Newsom, and J. S., Jr.

CHARLES WILLIAMS. One of the enterprising and progressive business men of the younger generation at Hooker, Texas County, Hon. Charles Williams, who is here conducting a substantial enterprise through his well established general insurance agency, and he has otherwise been prominently identified with local interests, is broad-gauged and public-spirited, and that he enjoys unalloyed popularity is fully vouched for in his election as representative of Texas and Cimarron counties in the Fifth General Assembly of the Oklahoma Legislature. Mr. Williams has reason to take pride in the fact that he was born and reared within the present State of Oklahoma, his parents having been numbered among the pioneer settlers in Indian Territory, and though the conditions of time and place placed certain limitations on the advantages afforded to Charles Williams in his boyhood and youth, he imbibed deeply of the progressive spirit of the West, early learned the value of self-reliant purpose, developed definite ambition, and thus was able to make good all handicaps and to press forward to the goal of worthy achievement. He is a young man of strong mentality, and well fortified opinions, and as a member of the Legislature of his native state he has acquitted himself with credit and no little distinction.

Mr. Williams was born in that part of Indian Territory that is now Bryan County, Oklahoma, and the year of his nativity was 1884. He is a son of Cicero B. H. and Nancy (Swagger) Williams, the former of whom was born in Mississippi and the latter in Virginia, both families having been founded in the South several generations ago. Cicero B. H. Williams was a youth when he accompanied his parents to Texas, in 1869, his father having thus become a pioneer of the Lone Star State, where he established his residence within a few years after the close of his service as a loyal soldier of the Confederacy in the Civil war. Cicero B. H. Williams continued his residence in Texas until the early '80s, when he became a pioneer settler in Indian Territory, where he engaged in farming and stock growing. He has been successful in his association with these lines of industrial enterprise in Oklahoma and he and his wife reside on their well improved homestead farm near Hooker, Texas County, being well known in this section of the state and being honored as sterling pioneer citizens who have done their part in accelerating the civic and industrial development of Oklahoma.

The rudimentary educational advantages afforded to Hon. Charles Williams and the other children of the family were necessarily somewhat primitive, as the pioneer facilities in what is now Oklahoma were meager. In what is now Garvin County he pursued his studies in a little log schoolhouse, the equipment of which was on a parity with those in the older states of the Union three generations ago, and the school was maintained on the subscription plan. Mr. Williams made good account of himself in his initial application to scholastic lore, and later he was able to extend his education by broader advantages and by personal application in an independent way, so that he has become a young man of excellent information and mature judgment. Concerning the other surviving children of the family it may be stated that Mrs. Benjamin D. Mills resides on a farm near Hooker, her husband being a progressive agriculturist and a successful teacher; Henry is now a resident of Richards, Colorado; William likewise maintains his home at that place; and the younger of the two sisters is the wife of Michael C. Young, a successful farmer near Hooker, Texas County, this state.

In the early youth of Mr. Williams the family home was maintained for fifteen years at Elmore, not far distant from Pauls Valley, the present judicial center of Garvin County, and after leaving the public schools Mr. Williams completed an effective course in the Indianola Business College at Ardmore, Carter County. In 1904 he accompanied his parents on their removal to Texas County, where he has since maintained his residence and where his circle of friends is limited only by that of his acquaintances.

In 1905-6, the only period of absence from his native state, Mr. Williams was employed as freight and ticket agent for the Atchison, Topeka and Santa Fe Railroad, at Hartland, Kansas, and in 1907 he settled on a farm near Hooker, Texas County, Oklahoma. He still owns this homestead, has made good improvements on the same and has continued to be identified with farming in a limited way. In 1913 Mr. Williams was appointed deputy court clerk at Hooker, and of this position he continued the incumbent until his election to the lower house of the Oklahoma Legislature, in the following year. In the campaign for representative of Texas and Cimarron counties in the Legislature Mr. Williams made an effective canvass and his popularity was shown in his receiving at the polls a plurality 250 greater than his representative district accorded to the state ticket in general.

In the Fifth Legislature Mr. Williams was assigned to the following named House committees: Labor and arbitration, insurance, county and township government, state and school lands, public roads and highways, and that on levees, drains, ditches and irrigation. He was specially interested in legislation for good roads, a measure which he had made an issue in his campaign, and he was a supporter of the movement looking to the abolishing of the office of county judge. He introduced a few bills but in the main his ideas and policies were embodied in bills that were introduced by other members of the house, and he earnestly devoted himself to the furtherance of legislative measures in harmony with his convictions and his campaign pledges.

The political allegiance of Mr. Williams is given to the democratic party; he is affiliated with Hooker Lodge No. 366, Ancient Free and Accepted Masons, in his home village, and in the Scottish Rite of Masonry is identified with the consistory in the Valley of Guthrie. He is master of ceremonies of the Oklahoma State organization of the Brotherhood of American Yeomen, besides being secretary of his Masonic lodge. He is secretary of the Hooker Commercial Club and has been active in the promotion of its progressive policies, notably the obtaining of better freight rates and passenger service for Hooker in connection with railway transportation. Both he and his wife hold membership in the Christian Church.

On the 14th of January, 1914, was solemnized the marriage of Mr. Williams to Miss Catharine Hiebert of Hooker.

MAURICE E. BIVENS. The present mayor of Vici, Oklahoma, is a man who has been engaged in the mercantile business in this region for the past fifteen years. It was not until the year 1911, however, that he established a place of business in this town, and when the enterprise at Vici was well under way Mr. Bivens withdrew from his mercantile activities in the towns of Seiling and Cestos, since which time he has confined his interests to the upbuilding of the business here. Mr. Bivens has been successful in the field of merchandising to which he has devoted himself, and his present place of business is a center for trading in hardware, implements and furniture. As one of Vici's leading business men he is well entitled to the prominence he has won, and as mayor of the town he is rightfully regarded as the first man in the community.

Maurice E. Bivens was born in Madison County, Illinois, on November 11, 1874, and he is the son of Charles N. and Martha (McGilvery) Bivens. The father was of Scotch-Irish parentage and the mother Scotch, Welsh and English. Charles N. Bivens was born in Madison County, Illinois, in 1843, and he died in Denver, Colorado, in 1888. He spent his life in Madison County up to the year 1880, when he went to Denver, unaccompanied by his wife, but in 1884 the family joined him and located in Burden, Cowley County, Kansas, where Mrs. Bivens yet lives. Mr. Bivens went to Denver in search of health, and died there in 1888. While resident in Madison County and Denver he served as a policeman, and while in Denver he also conducted a cigar factory for some time. He was a veteran of the Civil war, and served in Company K, Eightieth Illinois Volunteer Infantry for three years. He saw much of the less attractive side of war, and was in action in many important engagements of the long conflict. Mr. Bivens was a church member all his life, and was identified with a number of the more prominent fraternal organizations.

In Illinois he was married to Martha McGilvery, who was born in that state in 1850. She was the daughter of Martin McGilvery, who immigrated from Scotland in young manhood and settled in Madison County, where he spent the remainder of his life as a farmer and stockman. He was a man of many sterling qualities, and he was a leader in his community as long as he lived. Coming into Illinois in its pioneer days he did his full share in shaping the destinies of Madison County, and his influence on that section of the state is felt today in the progressive spirit that has ever marked its life.

To Charles N. and Martha (McGilvery) Bivens were born five children, two of whom, daughters, died in infancy. Laura May, the eldest, married John Burchell, a farmer, and she now lives in Oklahoma City, Oklahoma. The second child was Maurice E., of this review. Arthur, the youngest, lives on his homestead farm in the vicinity of Cestos, Oklahoma, and is a prosperous farmer.

After the death of Mr. Bivens in 1888 his widow married Edmond E. Rhodes, a Kentuckian, and two children have been born to them, H. Ray Rhodes, who is associated in business with his half brother, Maurice E. Bivens, the subject, and Mabel, who died in infancy.

Mr. Bivens as a boy had such educational advantages as usually fall to the lot of a country boy, and it might be said that he had no actual schooling after he was sixteen years old. However, he has in a larger sense gone to school all his life, for it is in the great school of experience that he has had his best training. After he left his books he applied himself to farming in Cowley County, Kansas, where the family then resided, and he was there until the latter part of 1897, when he came to Dewey County, Oklahoma, and filed on a homestead claim of 160 acres near the Town of Cestos. He lived on that place until 1900, when he proved title thereto. Mr. Bivens still owns the land, which is steadily increasing in value, and which lies three miles east and a half mile south of Cestos.

In 1901 Mr. Bivens engaged in the mercantile business in the Town of Cestos with a Mr. Ingle as his business partner. They prospered, as the result of good management and a natural tact for the economical administration of a small business house, both men being fortunate in their possession of that invaluable quality, and as time went on they established branch houses in Seiling and Vici. They broadened their lines from time to time, until they carried very complete stocks in hardware, farm implements and furniture. The Vici branch was established in 1911, and the growth of the business at this point broadened so rapidly that Mr. Bivens decided to discontinue the stores at Cestos and Seiling, so that the Vici establishment is the only one now controlled by Mr. Bivens. The firm is called M. E. Bivens & Company, and besides himself it includes his mother and his half-brother, H. R. Rhodes.

This enterprise is undeniably one of the most successful in the county, and it draws its patronage from the counties of Dewey, Ellis and Woodward. Splendid business principles have been the rock on which the house has made its stand, and its growth has been sure and steady. The house has the confidence of the public and its patronage follows as a natural sequence.

In 1912 Mr. Bivens became mayor of Vici and he is still serving in that office. He has proved himself a capable and wide-minded citizen, equipped in every way to guide the actions of the city council, and in his administration of local affairs he has made an excellent record for himself. The same sturdy qualities that have spelled success for him in his business career have entered largely into his work as mayor of Vici, and the

results have been creditable to him and invaluable to the city.

Mr. Bivens is a socialist in the matter of his politics, and he is a member of the Christian Church. He has long served the local church as deacon and elder, and while at Cestos he was superintendent of the Sunday school for four successive terms. He is a Mason, with Ancient Free and Accepted Masonic affiliations, and a member of Cestos Lodge No. 80, Independent Order of Odd Fellows. Other business connections are with the Home Investment Company and the Aetna Insurance Company, in both of which he is a stockholder.

In June, 1904, Mr. Bivens was married to Miss Esther Gates, daughter of G. W. Gates, now living retired in Orange, California. They were married* in Seiling, then the home of the Gates family. Three children have been born to them. Martha Euleta was born November 26, 1905; Arthur Lewis on September 5, 1907, and Randall Ray on August 5, 1909. All three attend the Vici High School, and they are popular and prominent young people in their circles. The family is prominent socially in Vici, and have many friends.

ELIJAH B. SHOTWELL. A man of marked technical and practical ability, Mr. Shotwell is now giving most effective service as county farm demonstrator of Okmulgee County, and maintains his home at Okmulgee, the judicial center and metropolis of the county. He may consistently be termed a pioneer of Oklahoma, where he established his home in the former Sac and Fox Indian country soon after it was thrown open to white settlement, and he has thus been actively identified with the civic and industrial activities of this favored commonwealth since 1892. He has been more than ordinarily influential in connection with the furthering of educational work in Oklahoma, as he has served as county superintendent of schools in both Lincoln and Okmulgee counties, in which fields he achieved splendid results.

Mr. Shotwell was born near St. Thomas, Province of Ontario, Canada, on the 28th of January, 1857, but was a lad of fifteen years at the time of his parents' removal to the State of Kansas, where he was reared to maturity and maintained his home until his removal to Oklahoma Territory. He is a son of William and Martha E. (Taylor) Shotwell, both of whom were born and reared in the Province of Ontario, the former's father, Smith Shotwell, having been a native of the State of New Jersey, whence he removed to Ontario, Canada, where he passed the residue of his life as a substantial farmer. In 1872 William Shotwell removed with his family to Kansas and became one of the pioneers of McPherson County, where he entered claim to land and reclaimed and improved a productive farm, this homestead having continued to be his place of residence until his death and his widow having passed the closing period of her life in the home of her son W. C. Shotwell, near Cushing, Payne County, Oklahoma. Of the children six attained to years of maturity, namely: Samuel, who is now a resident of Hawards, California; Smith, who resides at Crescent, Oregon; Emily, who is the wife of Elijah Prior, of Riverside, California; Elijah B., who is the immediate subject of this sketch; Whitson, who is a progressive farmer near Cushing, Oklahoma; and Letitia A., who is the wife of Jenas G. Scott, of Salem, Texas.

He whose name introduces this article acquired his earlier education in the schools of his native county in Ontario and, as before stated, was about fifteen years old at the time of the family removal to Kansas, where he was reared to maturity on the pioneer farm in McPherson County and in the meanwhile supplemented his education by attending the public schools of the locality. He continued to be associated with the work of his father's farm and teaching school winters until he had attained to his legal majority, and thereafter he conducted individual operations as a farmer and teacher in the Sunflower State until 1892, when he came to Oklahoma Territory and became one of the pioneer settlers in what is now Lincoln County. He secured a tract of land from the Government and developed the same into one of the productive and valuable farms of Lincoln County. There he continued to reside until 1901, when he was elected county superintendent of schools and removed to Chandler, the county seat, where he continued as the energetic and efficient incumbent of this position for a period of four years. Soon after his retirement from office he removed to Okmulgee, in July, 1905, and here he engaged in the abstract business, to which he continued to give his attention until September, 1907, when he was elected the first county superintendent of schools of Okmulgee County under the new regime of state government. With characteristic vigor and circumspection he defined and organized the work of the schools of the county, and in his two terms of service in this important office he brought the schools up to a specially high standard of efficiency, as gauged by the conditions and influences that obtained at that period in the history of the county. Since July, 1913, he has given equally commendable and valuable service in his present office, that of county farm demonstrator, a position to which he was appointed by the director of the extension work conducted in connection with the Oklahoma Agricultural and Mechanical College and the United States Department of Agriculture. He has proved himself unmistakably the right man in the right place, has carefully timed his visitations in all sections of the county, and both by instruction along scientific lines and by exemplification of practical order has done much to raise the standards of agricultural and live stock industry in Okmulgee County, where, as a matter of course, he has gained a very wide acquaintanceship and a host of valued and appreciative friends.

Mr. Shotwell is aligned as a staunch and effective supporter of the cause of the democratic party and is a birthright member of the Society of Friends, but as there is no church of this denomination at Okmulgee he attends and supports the local Methodist Episcopal Church, South. He is affiliated with the Okmulgee Lodge A. H. T. A. and also with the lodge of the Knights of Pythias.

In 1878 was solemnized the marriage of Mr. Shotwell to Miss Carrie Pilgrim, who was born in Iowa but who was reared principally in Kansas, where her parents established their residence in 1874. She was a daughter of Philip and Amelia Pilgrim, both of whom were born in Germany. The supreme loss and bereavement in the life of Mr. Shotwell came to him when his devoted wife was summoned to eternal rest, on the 29th of April, 1915, and her memory is revered by all who came within the sphere of her gracious influence. She was active in church and social life after coming to Oklahoma and for two years she had charge of the work and instruction of the Girls' Canning Clubs of Okmulgee County. In conclusion is entered brief record concerning the children of Mr. and Mrs. Shotwell: James T. is one of the progressive farmers near Cushing, Payne County; Orlando has the active supervision and control of the old homestead farm upon which his parents established their residence when they came to Oklahoma, in 1892; Earl is manager of the cotton-seed oil mill at Chandler, Lincoln County, Oklahoma.

THOMAS C. SHACKLETT. Coming to Oklahoma Territory with his parents when a lad of nine years, the present postmaster of Yukon, Canadian County, has here found ample opportunity for worthy achievement and has proved himself one of the world's productive workers, the while his present official position vouches for the estimate placed upon him in the community in which he maintains his home.

Born in Meade County, Kentucky, on the 5th day of November, 1880, Mr. Shacklett is a son of Jesse S. and Susan M. (Easton) Shacklett. When he was five years old, in 1885, his parents removed from the old Bluegrass state to Southwestern Kansas, and from the latter state they came to Oklahoma in 1889, thus becoming pioneers of the new territory when it was thrown open to settlement. The family home was established in the old town of Frisco, Canadian County, and later removal was made to Yukon, a new village in the same county, where the father conducted a hotel for some time, his death having there occurred in 1910 and his widow still maintaining her home in this now thriving little city, in which her son is postmaster. In earlier years Jesse S. Shacklett devoted his attention to agricultural pursuits, and thus the boyhood days of the postmaster of Yukon were principally compassed by the conditions and influences of the farm, in Kansas and Oklahoma. He made good use of the advantages afforded him in the public schools of Canadian County, within whose borders he has been a resident since he was nine years old, and here he followed various vocations until his appointment to the office of postmaster of Yukon, his commission having been given in April, 1914, and his administration, careful and efficient, having gained to him the approval of the community. In politics, as may be inferred, he is a staunch supporter of the cause of the democratic party, and in a fraternal way he is affiliated with the Woodmen of the World. The maiden name of his wife was Orie McComas, and they have no children.

GEORGE A. MCDONALD. Every progressive city now has its chamber of commerce, or an organization of similar purposes though perhaps under a different name. The chamber of commerce at Shawnee is a particularly virile and efficient body, and is made up of practically all the high class and responsible business men and professional men of the city. In that one organization are represented the best resources and the best ideas and ideals of the city.

It is as secretary of the Shawnee Chamber of Commerce, an office he has held for the past five years, that George A. McDonald has performed his most important service in that city. Mr. McDonald is himself a business man and has had a considerable breadth and depth of experience, though he is still young. He has lived in Oklahoma ten years, and for a time was connected with railroading in this state.

The McDonald stock of which he is a representative came from Scotland to Virginia before the Revolutionary war. His great-grandfather, William McDonald, was a Virginia planter. The grandfather, James McDonald, was born in Virginia and spent his life as a farmer and planter in that state. Mr. George A. McDonald of Shawnee was born in Springfield, Ohio, October 21, 1875.

His father, Samuel McDonald, was born at Romney, in Hampshire County, West Virginia, or Old Virginia as it was then, in 1842. His birthplace was afterwards the scene of one of the important battles in the Civil war. Samuel McDonald was reared in West Virginia, went in young manhood to Springfield, Ohio, where he married, and he lived in that locality the rest of his days, passing away in 1895. By occupation he was a farmer, was a democrat in politics, and took a very active part in the work of the Methodist Episcopal Church, in which he served as a steward, trustee and deacon. During the war between the states his only participation in military affairs was as a member of the Home Guard in West Virginia. Samuel McDonald married Emily Collier. She was born in Springfield, Ohio, and is now living in Yellow Springs in that state. To their marriage were born the following children: James R., a tinsmith living at Purcell, Oklahoma; Edith O., wife of D. F. Hupman, a farmer at Springfield, Ohio; Harry E., who is in the real estate business but has no settled location or permanent residence; Thomas F., a farmer at Urbana, Ohio; George A.; Lewis Clark, a carpenter and builder at Middletown, Kentucky.

The country schools of Clark County, Ohio, gave George A. McDonald his first advantages, and he also had the benefit of some college training, having finished the sophomore year in Antioch College in 1897. His early years had been spent on his father's farm, and he enjoyed much of the wholesome and rugged discipline of country life. He taught school in Jefferson County, Kentucky, as principal of rural schools two years, but soon found school teaching unsatisfactory. After taking a course in telegraphy he was employed as telegraph operator on the L. & N. Railroad at Louisville, and remained in the service of that railroad company until January 1, 1906.

That was the date when he became identified with Shawnee. For the first two years he was a clerk with the Rock Island Railroad offices in Shawnee. Going into business for himself, Mr. McDonald was one of the successful grocery merchants of the city until 1911. In that year he was elected secretary of the chamber of commerce, and has since given practically all his time and attention to the duties of this office. He is also secretary of the Provident Association, secretary of the Pottawatomie County Fair Association, and a stockholder in the Fidelity Building and Loan Association. His offices are in the Convention Hall Building.

In politics he is a democrat. Like his father, he takes much interest in the First Methodist Episcopal Church of Shawnee and is a steward. He is affiliated with Shawnee Lodge No. 107, Ancient Free and Accepted Masons, and with Shawnee Chapter No. 32, Royal Arch Masons.

In 1903, at Middletown, Kentucky, he married Miss Lucy E. Mitchell, daughter of Robert S. Mitchell. They have one son, Samuel Vance, who was born November 5, 1905, and is now a student in the public schools of Shawnee.

BIRT ARTHUR WAGNER. During the past fifteen years Mr. Wagner has played an important part in the public affairs of Woodward and Ellis counties. He is now filling the office of court clerk of Ellis County and has his home at Arnett. Mr. Wagner is one of the genial and popular citizens of Ellis County, a man of undoubted integrity, and exercises both competence and honesty in all his public and private dealings.

He was born January 8, 1877, on a farm in Nemaha County, Kansas, a son of Arthur H. and Cynthia (Peaver) Wagner. The Wagners came originally from Germany. His paternal grandfather was George Wagner, a native of Germany. Arthur H. Wagner was born March 12, 1853, in Putnam County, Ohio, and has spent all his active career as a farmer and merchant. In 1874 he moved out to Kansas and became an early settler on a farm in Nemaha County, close to the northern line of the state. He lived there and cultivated the soil until 1892, and then went to Kansas City, Kansas, where he engaged in business eight years. In 1900 he

came to Oklahoma and set up in business at Woodward, and in 1901 moved to Shattuck, where he was likewise one of the first merchants. In 1902 he was appointed postmaster of Shattuck and held that position seven years. Arthur H. Wagner was married in Union County, Ohio, October 8, 1874, to Miss Cynthia Peaver. Her father was John Peaver, who married a Miss Poling, and both were born in Virginia. Mrs. Wagner was born May 14, 1854, in Union County, Ohio, and she died at Kansas City, Kansas, October 21, 1915. She was a very active member of the Methodist Episcopal Church and was devoted to church and home and children. She was the mother of seven, five sons and two daughters, namely: Harry, born August 27, 1875; Birt A.; John Peaver, born September 17, 1878; Elsie, born July 9, 1879; Grace, born August 25, 1881; George, born August 12, 1883; Roy Foster, born August 12, 1885.

The early training of Birt A. Wagner was acquired in the public schools of his native county and in Kansas City, Kansas. After leaving school he served an apprenticeship at the baker's trade, and that was his regular work for five years. Not long after his father came to Oklahoma he followed on January 1, 1901, and was soon taking an active part in local affairs in Woodward County. He served two years as deputy county clerk of that county. On coming to the state he had taken up a claim in Woodward County near Shattuck, and he is thus to be considered among those who have helped to develop the land in this new state. For a few years he also was assistant postmaster under his father at Shattuck and for one year carried mail on a rural route.

On the organization of Ellis County he was soon active in its affairs, and served as deputy county clerk in 1910-11-12. During 1914-15 he was clerk of the Shattuck branch of the Ellis County Court at Shattuck. In November, 1914, he was elected on the republican ticket court clerk of Ellis County and is now giving all his time and attention to those responsibilities. Fraternally Mr. Wagner is a Mason.

On January 18, 1908, at Shattuck, Oklahoma, he married Miss Kathryn Lee Ewing. She was born March 4, 1881, in Buchanan County, Missouri, a daughter of William J. and Cassie (Patton) Ewing, the former a native of Virginia and the latter of Missouri. Mrs. Wagner in addition to the training of the public schools attended the Synodical College at Fulton, Missouri, graduating with the class of 1902. She was an active member of the Presbyterian Church. Her death occurred April 6, 1910, at Shattuck. She is survived by one child, Charles Edward, who was born February 11, 1910.

CHARLES W. SHANNON, A. M., is known as a prominent figure in educational and scientific circles in Oklahoma. He has been an able and popular instructor in geology at the University of Oklahoma, and is now director of the Oklahoma Geological Survey, with office in the library building of the university at Norman, Cleveland County.

Mr. Shannon is a scion of one of the sterling pioneer families of the fine old Hoosier State, of which he himself is a native son. He was born in Tipton County, Indiana, on the 3d of August, 1879, and is a son of Alexander and Elizabeth J. (Foster) Shannon, both of whom were born and reared in that county. Alexander Shannon passed virtually his entire active life as one of the representative agriculturists in the vicinity of Tipton, the county seat. He was born in the year 1855, and died at Brazil in 1910. Elizabeth J. Shannon was born in 1858 and died in 1906. Both Mr. and Mrs. Shannon were devoted members of the United Presbyterian Church, in which he served as deacon and trustee. Of the children, C. W. Shannon of this review is the eldest; Herbert died in babyhood; James Vinton wedded Miss Grace Poling of Bloomington, Indiana, and both are now missionary teachers in a school maintained under the auspices of the Presbyterian Church on the Island of Hainan, China.

The lineage of the Shannon family traces back to staunch Scotch-Irish origin and the original American representatives settled in Virginia in the colonial era of our national history.

Mr. Shannon acquired his early education in the public schools of his native state, where he was graduated in the high school at Tipton as a member of the class of 1900. During the ensuing spring and summer he was a student in the University of Indiana at Bloomington. For three years he was retained as teacher in the Bryan School in Tipton County. During this time he continued his studies in the university by attending the spring and summer sessions. He finally completed a full academic course in the university, in which he was graduated as a member of the class of 1906, and from which he received at that time the degree of Bachelor of Arts. The following year he received the degree of Master of Arts from his alma mater. He has since taken effective post-graduate studies in the University of Indiana, specializing in geology and other branches of science.

In 1902, at Bloomington, Indiana, was solemnized the marriage of Mr. Shannon to Miss Mary E. Pinkerton, who was born and reared in Indiana, and who is a daughter of the late Charles Pinkerton, a representative merchant at Muncie for many years prior to his death.

From 1907 to 1911 Mr. Shannon was teacher of science in the high school at Brazil, Indiana. During this time he was also in the employ of the Indiana State Geological Survey, in connection with which he covered and made specific reports from seventeen different counties.

In September, 1911, Mr. Shannon came to Norman, Oklahoma, and assumed the position of field geologist for the Oklahoma Geological Survey. He served a few weeks in this capacity and was then appointed instructor in geology at the University of Oklahoma. After teaching one semester he resumed his position in connection with the Geological Survey of which he has been the director since January, 1914. His work in this office has been carried forward with utmost efficiency and discrimination, and will prove of enduring value to the state from both a scientific and a utilitarian standpoint.

Mr. Shannon is a valued and influential member of the Oklahoma Academy of Science, of which he served three years as president. He is also a member of the Indiana Chapter of the Sigma Xi fraternity, a national scientific organization whose membership is confined to those college students and graduates who have achieved independent scientific research work. He is a democrat in his political allegiance, and is a member of the board of education of Norman. Both he and his wife are zealous members of the Presbyterian Church, in which he was a teacher of the Young Woman's Christian Association class of the Sunday School until January 1, 1916, when he was elected supervising superintendent of the Sunday School. He also serves as one of the trustees of the church.

Mr. and Mrs. Shannon are prominent and popular factors in the leading social activities of Norman, the principal educational center of the state, and both are specially appreciative and loyal as citizens of this vigorous young commonwealth. They have two children,—

Vol. V—7

Gayle L., who was born May 1, 1906, and Viola Ruth, who was born November 19, 1914.

CALVIN E. BRADLEY, M. D. The medical profession of Kiowa County, Oklahoma, is capably represented at Mountain View by Dr. Calvin E. Bradley, who although one of the younger members of the profession has made a substantial reputation for himself in professional circles as well as in the confidence of the people of his community. Born in Phelps County, Missouri, April 16, 1885, he comes honestly by his predilection for his calling, being the son and grandson of physicians and the bearer of a name which has been honored in medicine and surgery.

On the paternal side, Doctor Bradley is a grandson of the founder of the family in the United States, Dr. Calvin Bradley, a native of England, who emigrated to the United States, first settled in North Carolina and subsequently moved to Georgia, where he was engaged in the practice of his profession for many years, and where his death occurred. Doctor Bradley's maternal great-grandfather Burns was the emigrant of the family from Scotland. Dr. W. A. Bradley, the father of Dr. Calvin E. Bradley, was born in North Carolina, in 1852, and from his native state removed to Georgia, subsequently going, in 1880, to Phelps County, Missouri, where he was married. He was a graduate of the Southern Medical College, one of the distinguished institutions of Atlanta, Georgia, and after eight years of practice in Phelps County, moved his family in 1888 to Houston, Texas County, Missouri, where he continued to be engaged in practice until his death, in 1911. He was an able and thorough practitioner and held a substantial place in the ranks of his calling. A democrat in politics, he filled various local offices within the gift of his fellow townsmen, while his fraternal connection was with the Independent Order of Odd Fellows. Doctor Bradley married Miss Elizabeth Burns, who was born in 1865, in Missouri, and died at Houston, that state, in 1888, daughter of Dr. Edward Burns, who for many years was a physician and surgeon of Newburg, Missouri, where his death occurred. Two children were born to Dr. W. A. and Elizabeth Bradley: Calvin E., of this review; and Kate, who became the wife of C. F. Peake, and resides in Texas County, Missouri, where Mr. Peake is county superintendent of schools.

Calvin E. Bradley received his early education in the public schools of Houston, Missouri, where he was graduated from the high school with the class of 1901. He received his early medical training under the able preceptorship of his father, and enrolled as a student at Barnes Medical College, St. Louis, Missouri, where he was graduated with the class of 1905, receiving the degree of Doctor of Medicine. Doctor Bradley began active practice at Newburg, Phelps County, Missouri, where his paternal grandfather had been well known as a practitioner for years, but in 1908 removed to Memphis, Tennessee, where he remained during that and the following year. In 1909 he went to Dewey, Oklahoma, where he gave up professional work for a time to engage in the oil and drug business, but in 1912 came to Mountain View and resumed practice, and has continued to the present time in a constantly growing general medical and surgical business. He occupies well-appointed offices in the Reynolds Building on Main Street, where he has every appliance and instrument for diagnosis and treatment of diseases. Doctor Bradley keeps in close touch with every advancement made in medical or surgical work and is a close student of the science, besides holding membership in the organizations of his calling. He has been an active democrat, but his only public service has been that of coroner, an office which he filled while a resident of Phelps County, Missouri. He is popular in fraternal circles, and is a member of the local bodies of the Independent Order of Odd Fellows and the Knights of Pythias.

Doctor Bradley was married February 4, 1916, to Miss Louise Stinson, daughter of Mr. and Mrs. A. E. Stinson, of Mountain View, Oklahoma.

PATRICK J. KELLY. The intellectual alertness, vigor and circumspection of Mr. Kelly make him a specially effective and valued executive in the responsible office of which he is the popular incumbent, that of cashier of the Yukon National Bank, in the progressive little City of Yukon, Canadian County, and his unqualified hold upon the confidence and good will of the people of this favored section of the state is indicated by the fact that he served six years as county clerk of Canadian County, his residence in Oklahoma dating from the year 1892, when he came to the newly organized territory from the State of Iowa.

Mr. Kelly was born in Chariton County, Missouri, on the 3rd of July, 1863, and is a son of Patrick and Rose (Barrett) Kelly, both natives of Ireland and both residents of Iowa for many years prior to their death. Patrick Kelly was identified with the great basic industry of agriculture during virtually his entire active career in America. He was a farmer in Missouri until 1881, when he removed with his family to Iowa, where he continued his activities as an agriculturist and stock grower and achieved a due measure of independence and prosperity, both he and his wife having been devout communicants of the Catholic Church, and having lived lives of distinctive usefulness and honor. He whose name introduces this article is indebted to the public schools of Missouri for his early educational discipline and was eighteen years of age at the time of the family removal to Iowa, in which state he taught several terms of district school.

In 1892 Mr. Kelly left the Hawkeye state and came to Oklahoma Territory, where he filed entry to a claim of land in Canadian County. He perfected his title to this property, but eventually disposed of the same. In 1899 he assumed the position of deputy in the office of the county clerk of Canadian County, and he retained this post at El Reno, the county seat, until he was elected county clerk, in the autumn of 1904, this advancement having been a well justified reward for his former effective service. He assumed office in January, 1905, and after serving six years he retired from office on the 1st of January, 1911, his long and efficient tenure of this important position having been terminated only a short time when, on the 1st of March, 1911, he was chosen cashier of the First National Bank of El Reno. He retained this position until July 1, 1912, when he assumed the duties of his present office, that of cashier of the Yukon National Bank, his careful and progressive administration having been a potent force in the developing of the substantial business of this institution, which bases its operations on a capital stock of $25,000.

The political views of Mr. Kelly are shown by the staunch support which he accords to the cause of the democratic party; he and his wife are communicants of the Catholic Church, and he is affiliated with the Benevolent and Protective Order of Elks, the Knights of Columbus, and the Modern Woodmen of America.

In the year 1912 was solemnized the marriage of Mr. Kelly to Miss Agnes Fitzgerald, who likewise was born and reared in Missouri, and both are popular figures in the representative social activities of their home community.

WILLIAM MARSHALL GALLAHER, M. D. A specialist in the medical profession at Shawnee since 1909, whose practice is confined to diseases of the eye, ear, nose and throat, Doctor Gallaher has not only been a valuable professional man to this city, but has fitted in with all departments of civic progress, and has been especially enthusiastic as a worker in behalf of school improvement. He is now secretary of the board of education.

Born in Roane County, Tennessee, March 1, 1877, Doctor Gallaher is a member of a branch of a family that came originally from Ireland and first settled in Pennsylvania about Revolutionary times. From Pennsylvania one branch of the family moved to Tennessee, and another to Missouri. Doctor Gallaher's father, D. H. Gallaher, was born in Knox County, Tennessee, in 1836, and died in Roane County in 1904. His entire active career was spent as a farmer and stock raiser. For two years he was a soldier on the Southern side of the Civil war, and was wounded during the Shenandoah Valley campaign. In politics he was a democrat, was a member of the Cumberland Presbyterian Church and of the Masonic fraternity. He married Mattie Owen, who was born in Tennessee and still resides on the old homestead in Roane County. Their children were: Lucy, wife of S. R. Stegall, a feed and grain merchant at Chattanooga, Tennessee; Albert, who died in 1880; Daisy, who married C. W. Lackey, a physician and surgeon in Texas, and both are now deceased; R. O., who is county engineer of Knox County, with home at Knoxville, Tennessee; Mayme, who is a music teacher and makes her home with her mother in Tennessee; G. H., a farmer and stockman in Roane County; Dr. William Marshall; Sally, wife of R. O. Wheeler, a farmer and stockman in Ellis County, Oklahoma; and Mattie, wife of Elmer Sineknecht, a mine operator at Oliver Springs, Tennessee.

Doctor Gallaher acquired a liberal education. He was reared on a farm, attended public schools in his native Roane County, graduated from Roane College in 1897, and from there entered Chattanooga Medical College, where he graduated M. D. with the class of 1900. In the fifteen years of his active practice Doctor Gallaher has extended his studies both privately and by attendance at some of the leading institutions of the country. In 1907 and in 1908 he took post-graduate work in the Polyclinic of Tulane University at New Orleans, specializing in eye, ear, nose and throat. He spent portions of the year 1909 and 1915 in the Chicago Eye, Ear, Nose and Throat Infirmary.

He did his first practice near Texarkana, Arkansas, and was engaged in general practice there until 1909. In March, 1909, he came to Shawnee, and in this larger field has confined himself entirely to his specialty in the treatment of eye, ear, nose and throat. His offices are in the Mammoth Building. He is a member of the State and County Medical societies and is a Fellow in the American Medical Association.

Fraternally he is affiliated with Shawnee Lodge No. 107, Ancient Free and Accepted Masons; Shawnee Chapter No. 32, Royal Arch Masons; Shawnee Commandery No. 36, Knights Templar; Indian Temple of the Nobles of the Mystic Shrine at Oklahoma City; and the Shawnee organization of the Woodmen of the World. He is a member of the Presbyterian Church, U. S., and is a member of the Shawnee Chamber of Commerce.

In July, 1902, in Roane County, Tennessee, Doctor Gallaher married Miss Fannie B. Smith. Her father, M. L. Smith, is farmer in Knox County, Tennessee. To their marriage have been born three children: Clinton, now in the public schools at Shawnee; Paul Clark and Mary Lee.

SHAWNEE PUBLIC SCHOOLS. In laying the foundation and building the great State of Oklahoma the citizenship have kept in mind the fact that future growth would be impossible without establishing good schools. No man, with or without a family, would want to buy property and live in any community stripped of schools and churches. In view of these facts the people of Oklahoma have spared no means in securing the best educational opportunities. This condition is especially true with the City of Shawnee. It is, indeed, fitting that the fourth city of Oklahoma (not in general resources, but in school population), a city located in one of the richest regions of the state, should have the best possible school system which can be devised by human minds and hearts.

Shawnee has not only been generous in the construction of buildings but the good people of the city have voted three extra levies for maintenance within the last six years. In equipment the Shawnee public school buildings are second to none in the state. Of the nine buildings, all except one are built of brick and are equipped with all modern conveniences, such as lavatories, electric lights, etc.

As a matter of information and proof of the steady growth of Shawnee public schools, a few statistics are here given. The total enrollment for the past four years is as follows:

1912-1913 2,805
1913-1914 2,947
1914-1915 2,961
1915-1916 3,400

The total number of teachers employed, including three substitutes, is 84, of which 15 are men and 69 are women. The total number of employees for the schools, including the secretary to the superintendent and clerk of the board of education, is 97. The average salary of the grade teacher is $57.95 per month; the minimum salary is $40.00; the maximum salary, $65.00. The maximum salary for the primary grades is $76.50. The estimate for maintenance of the schools in 1914-15 was $70,385. The total valuation of Shawnee School District is $7,772,226.56.

Recesses twice daily were inaugurated in all the schools in 1914-15. The cultivation of school gardens has recently been instituted. The study of agriculture has been added to the course in the elementary grades within the last year. Four of the war schools have recently installed $80.00 Victrolas, the moneys being raised through the efforts of the teachers and children. A $1,000 Everett Concert Grand piano has been placed in the high school recently. This will cost the district nothing. One of the ward schools has been equipped with modern playground equipment.

The value of the high school building and equipment is $123,000. Twenty-one teachers are employed. The high school has experienced a wonderful gain, as indicated in the enrollment below:

1910-1911 276
1911-1912 332
1912-1913 374
1913-1914 425
1914-1915 480
1915-1916 547

The increase in the graduating classes for the past four years is as follows:

1911-1912 43
1912-1913 63
1913-1914 64
1914-1915 79
1915-1916 93

At the beginning of the 1915-1916 school year the entire system was reorganized. The length of the daily recitation was increased from forty-five minutes to seventy minutes, each period being planned for thirty-five minutes recitation on the previous day's lesson and thirty-five minutes carefully supervised study on the advanced lesson. One of the primary objects of this plan is to teach the pupil how to study, and so prevent a very common waste of time in more or less aimless groping for a method of study.

Below is given a list of the special department in the high school showing cost:

Commercial	$1,500.00
Domestic Science	1,900.00
Manual Training	2,500.00
Agriculture	600.00
Chemical Department	2,000.00
Physics Department	2,000.00
Biology Department	400.00
Gymnasium	1,500.00

Each of the above departments is being strengthened every year.

There are organized in the high school: One first class orchestra; four literary societies—two girls and two boys; one German Club; one Girls' Glee Club; a school paper is published—the Caldron.

With the already high state of improvement and efficiency and with the support of the progressive citizenship of Shawnee, the school authorities anticipate wonderful advancement in Shawnee public schools for the coming years.

RANDOLPH BROOKS FORREST. One of the senior lawyers of Western Oklahoma is Randolph Brooks Forrest of El Reno, who became identified with the Oklahoma bar about four years after the opening of the original Oklahoma Territory, and his prestige and influence as a lawyer and citizen have been increasing in proportion to the length of his years of residence. Mr. Forrest is now serving as county judge of Canadian County, where he has had his home since coming to Oklahoma in 1893.

Randolph Brooks Forrest is an Ohio man by birth, having been born in that interesting section of Southern Ohio along the Ohio River at Portsmouth October 20, 1850. His parents, Joseph H. and Vancaline (Vance) Forrest were natives of Ohio, but their respective parents were Virginians who were among the pioneers in Southern Ohio, having located there in 1809. His paternal great-grandfather, Zachariah Forrest, was an officer in the Revolutionary army, from Maryland; his grandfather, Archibald Forrest, was a soldier in the War of 1812, from Ohio; his uncle, Elza Forrest, was killed in the battle of Beuna Vista in Mexico, and his own father served in the war of the states for the Union. In 1851, when Judge Forrest was about a year old, his parents removed to Illinois, finally locating on a farm in Logan County. His father was a farmer by pursuit and reared his family on a farm.

Judge Forrest had his education from Illinois country schools, followed by a course in the high school at Atlanta, Illinois, and two years in the Illinois Normal University at Normal. His early ambition was directed to the law, and he took up the study of Blackstone while teaching school, a vocation which held him for three years. At the age of twenty-three Judge Forrest was editor of the Logan County Journal, which he published at Lincoln for one year. He then sold the paper, and in June, 1876, successfully passed the examination before the Illinois Supreme Court and was admitted to the Illinois Bar. Judge Forrest has had a long and interesting experience as a lawyer, both in the Middle West and in the Northwest and Southwest. He practiced at Lincoln, Illinois, for several years, and in 1880 was elected state's attorney of Logan County, an office he held four years, and which gave him a splendid training as an advocate. During the winter of 1884-85, Mr. Forrest removed from Illinois to Minneapolis, Minnesota, and was successfully identified with the bar of the flour metropolis of the Northwest until 1893. In the latter year he came to Oklahoma and located at El Reno. Of his work as a lawyer it is hardly necessary to speak except to state that he is regarded as a lawyer of thorough ability, broad knowledge of jurisprudence, and with a most successful record in the handling of litigation. His public and political career is a matter of interest and reflects some of the interesting political history of Oklahoma. In the early days he practiced as an attorney over nearly all of Western Oklahoma Territory, gained a wide acquaintance, and in 1898 the democrats of Western Oklahoma favored his candidacy as territorial delegate to Congress. However, the heavier vote of the eastern part of Oklahoma gave the nomination to another candidate. The Western Oklahoma democrats again preferred him as their candidate for Congress in 1900, but he declined to run because of the fusion of democrats and populists in the convention. Two years later he was again an unsuccessful candidate for the nomination. Judge Forrest is an Oklahoman who deserves credit for his participation in the statehood movement in all its phases for more than ten years before statehood became an actuality. In 1895 he was chosen a delegate to the statehood convention of that year. From the first he espoused the cause of "single statehood," that is one state for the two territories of Oklahoma and Indian Territory. He sat as a delegate in the statehood convention of 1901, and for a third time was a delegate in 1902. In both these conventions he was chairman of the committee on resolutions. In 1904, because of his convictions in favor of single statehood, Mr. Forrest supported for re-election to Congress Mr. McGuire, a republican and the author of the then pending single statehood bill in Congress. In the same campaign Judge Forrest supported the local democratic ticket, and always before and always since has been a loyal and vigorous advocate of the man and measures of the democratic political party. Since his residence in Oklahoma he has been a delegate to every democratic county and territorial and state convention. It will be recalled that there was much division of public sentiment with respect to the question whether Oklahoma and Indian Territory should go into the Union as one or two states, and Judge Forrest's attitude on statehood led to his defeat as a candidate from this county to the constitutional convention which in 1907 perfected the first organic law for the new state. In the primary election of 1912 Mr. Forrest was an unsuccessful candidate for nomination to Congress from his district. One of the chief planks in his platform during that campaign was the advocacy of the conservation of surface water.

In 1913-14 Mr. Forrest served as assistant county attorney of Canadian County, and in 1914 was elected county judge, and is now giving his time and attention to a capable administration of Canadian County's affairs. His election to the office of county judge is somewhat of a vindication of his course in political affairs. Fraternally Judge Forrest is affiliated with the Independent Order of Odd Fellows, and the Benevolent and Protective Order of Elks. He was married in Illinois in 1872 to Miss Mary Randolph. They are the parents of two daughters and one son.

Judge Forrest is a man of broad intellectual interests, and is the author of a small book of verse on current topics, which has been well received.

W. T. BERENTZ. Bartlesville has one of its most forceful business men in the person of W. T. Berentz, who is president of the Berentz Hardware Company and is also proprietor of a furniture and undertaking establishment. A number of years Mr. Berentz saw a crop of wheat cut from the site of the city where he now makes his home and where his business activities have been concentrated for nearly fifteen years. He has helped in an important way in making Bartlesville the center of trade and industry for a large surrounding territory, and has identified himself in a public-spirited fashion with all local movements for upbuilding and improvements.

A resident of this section of Oklahoma for twenty-five years, W. T. Berentz was born in Danville, Illinois, February 21, 1867, a son of Jeremiah and Emma (Olmstead) Berentz. His father was born in Ohio. From Illinois the family emigrated to Kansas and took up a homestead in Labette County in 1869. W. T. Berentz at that time was about two years of age, and his youthful recollections concern themselves largely with the pioneer conditions found in Southeastern Kansas during the late '60s and '70s. His father died in October, 1913, at the age of seventy-one, and the mother passed away May 5, 1905, at the age of sixty-three. Jeremiah Berentz served for more than forty-eight months with the Twelfth Illinois Volunteer Infantry during the Civil war. After his three-year term had expired he veteranized and continued until the close of the mighty struggle between the North and the South. He was a member of the Presbyterian Church and a republican in politics. W. T. Berentz was the oldest of four children, and the second, Myra, died at the age of twelve years, and two daughters, Maude and Mabel, twins, who were born in 1875, are now living in Los Angeles, California.

W. T. Berentz grew up in Kansas, received his education from country schools, and for the greater part of the time up to 1897 lived with his parents. In the spring of 1890 the entire family had moved from Kansas to Indian Territory, and the son operated a ranch here up to 1901. In 1897 his parents went back to Kansas, but Mr. Berentz has lived continuously in Northeastern Oklahoma for the past twenty-five years. In 1901 he became a merchant in the new Town of Bartlesville, and at that time started in the hardware, furniture and undertaking business associated with R. H. Muzzy under the name Berentz & Muzzy. In 1907 he bought out his partner's interest and in 1914 organized a stock company known as the Berentz Hardware Company, Incorporated, of which he is president. In the meantime the furniture and undertaking had been separated and has been conducted under the individual name of Mr. Berentz. He owns the building where he first started in business on Second Street, but his present large store is located on Johnstone Avenue. He is also interested with J. P. Goveran in the buggy and implement business. For a number of years he was also identified with the manufacture of brick at Bartlesville.

As a citizen Mr. Berentz has served as a member of the city school board for the past six years, and was re-elected in the spring of 1915 to the same office. He is well known in Masonry, being a member of the Lodge, Chapter, Commandery, the Scottish Rite Consistory and the Mystic Shrine, and is also affiliated with the Benevolent and Protective Order of Elks. In January, 1903, Mr. Berentz married Miss Florence Forrester, who was born in Illinois, a daughter of William Forrester. To their marriage have been born two sons: Russell and Robert.

J. W. STROUD. The founder of one of the thriving towns of Lincoln County is now a wealthy and prominent citizen of Pawhuska, in Osage County, with which locality he has been identified practically throughout the period of its greatest development. J. W. Stroud is an Oklahoma Eighty-niner, a man who came into the original territory with capital and business experience, and by his shrewd judgment, foresight and enterprise has not only lifted himself above the plane of modern success, but at the same time has assisted several localities to grow and prosper. He is one of the men whose names should be permanently linked with the history of Oklahoma during the past twenty-five years.

Born at Springfield, Missouri, August 2, 1859, he is of German parents, L. D. and Priscilla (Schmidt) Stroud. His father was a natural mechanic, handy with all manner of tools, and developed his trade into a business as builder. He helped construct the first buildings of the normal school at Warrensburg, Missouri. He was also a soldier during the Civil war, having served with the Second Missouri Artillery.

The only child of his parents, J. W. Stroud, at the age of fifteen, started out for himself, and is strictly a self-made man. He gained a limited education, but has improved all his opportunities by observation and experience and by industry and economy finally got started in the world along the lines for which he has shown special inclination and ability. He was reared on a farm, but soon developed his instinct as a trader and in 1881 established a small store near the City of Springfield, Missouri, and made that in a few years an important trading center for a large surrounding community.

Mr. Stroud came into Oklahoma in 1889 and soon after the opening was proprietor of a small grocery store on Main Street in Oklahoma City. With the opening of the country east and south of Oklahoma City to settlement, he set up a rough frame shack out on the prairie, put in a stock of goods, and that was the beginning of a settlement which came to be known as Stroud, the actual beginning of whose history was on April 6, 1892. He conducted his store in that locality until 1898, and in the meantime had taken an important part in securing the construction of the Frisco Railroad through Lincoln County, and then moved his store over to the railroad site, and his name was applied to the new Town of Stroud. He was first in all matters of public enterprise there, and that thrifty and prosperous community is well pleased to have his name identified with it. Mr. Stroud conducted a lumber yard at Stroud, was also vice president of the First National Bank, which he helped to organize, and later organized the City State Bank, of which he was president. He finally sold out his interests in both of these institutions, and had also in the meantime acquired a large amount of real estate, both in the city and the surrounding country.

Since January, 1907, Mr. Stroud has made his home and the center of his interests at Pawhuska. Among other important investments he has four brick buildings on Ki-hi-Kah and Sixth streets, and he has also built and occupies a beautiful bungalow home on the hill which is second to none of the Pawhuska residences of that class. Mr. Stroud also owns 1,200 acres in Osage County, and has much of his land under cultivation and improvement.

In 1909 Mr. Stroud drilled two gas wells on the city site of Pawhuska and then turned over the plant to the city at cost. As a result of this public-spirited enterprise the price of gas was at once reduced one-half, and fuel was furnished in abundance to the water and light plants. This act of public spirit made him a great many friends and admirers, and in turn the people of Pawhuska made him mayor of the city for two years.

Politically Mr. Stroud is a republican, was reared in the faith of the German Baptist Church, and in Masonry has attained the thirty-second degree of the Scottish Rite, being affiliated with both the Consistory and the Temple of the Mystic Shrine.

When a poor struggling young man back in Missouri at the age of nineteen Mr. Stroud married Miss Martha Gregg, who was born in that state. To their union were born seven children: Lucas lives in Texas; Priscilla is the wife of Henry Ward of Fairfax, Oklahoma; Samuel also lives in Texas; Alma is the wife of Henry McMillen of Osage County; Charles lives on a farm in Osage County; Maude is the wife of W. H. Spurr, who is cashier of the First National Bank at Seminole, Oklahoma; LeMoyne is now attending law school at Chattanooga, Tennessee. In 1903 Mr. Stroud married for his present wife Ella Fisher, who was born in Nebraska.

Mention has already been made of Mr. Stroud's part in helping to build the Frisco Railroad through Lincoln County. He was one of the active promoters of that line from Sapulpa to Oklahoma City, and not only lent all his influence and resources but assisted in making the survey and in securing the right of way and also conducted a canvass for funds to pay for the construction. He also laid out some of the townsites along the line, and the judgment of railroad builders and civil engineers has confirmed his excellent judgment in locating that line of railroad, which was one of the most considerable factors in the early days in establishing the pre-eminence of Oklahoma City. Since then he has helped in making the surveys of several other railroad lines in the state. In addition to his various other investments Mr. Stroud is president and general manager of the Acacia Oil & Gas Company of Pawhuska, an Oklahoma corporation which is composed entirely of home capitalists and investors.

WILLIAM L. CHAPMAN. As part of the political machinery methods necessary to the establishment of state government in Oklahoma and as an official of that government after it was established in 1907, William L. Chapman, the well known lawyer of Shawnee, has contributed much to the welfare of the state. Equipped with a literary and commercial education he has successfully filled the positions of editor and banker, and a legal training has enabled him to make a success in the law. For six years prior to and subsequent to statehood he was secretary of the Territorial and State Democratic Central committees, serving in that capacity during the campaigns for the election of delegates to the Constitutional Convention, the adoption of the constitution and the election of the first state officials. After statehood he was he first secretary of the Corporation Commission and in that position laid the foundation for a systematic and methodical keeping of the records of that department of state government.

Born in Wingo, Kentucky, October 12, 1867, a son of Thomas and Nannie (Hatchell) Chapman, William L. Chapman having completed the public school course in his native state entered Marvin College at Clinton, Kentucky, from which he was graduated in 1888 with the degree Bachelor of Arts. He holds the degree Ph. D. from Cumberland University at Lebanon, Tennessee, awarded him in 1895. While in Marvin College he swept floors and worked in a chair factory at odd times to pay expenses, and during part of the time helped out his sister who was in the same college. On leaving school he was for ten years a successful teacher in Kentucky, Texas, Arkansas and Oklahoma, was at one time superintendent of city schools at Stephenville, Texas, and at another time president of Willie Halsell College at Vinita, Oklahoma. He is a graduate of Hills Business College at Waco, Texas, having completed the course there as preparation for a clerical position that was waiting him in Oklahoma.

On leaving college work at Vinita Mr. Chapman entered the First National Bank of that city as a clerk and afterwards became assistant cashier. Later he moved to Shawnee, was in the banking business and for four years was editor of the Shawnee Herald. For sixteen years he was a member of the Democratic Territorial and State Central committees and was secretary of that committee during two national campaigns. In these campaigns he was in charge of special trains that toured the state with W. J. Bryan as the speaker. Only a brief summary can be made of his varied public service. At Vinita he was a member of the board of education that established one of the first public schools in Indian Territory. He was city clerk of Norman, Oklahoma, and city treasurer of Shawnee. He resided at Norman when the University of Oklahoma was founded and there became associated with F. S. E. Amos, now of Vinita, who was then a member of the faculty of the university and is an advisory editor of the Standard History of Oklahoma. Mr. Amos accompanied Mr. Chapman to Vinita and became a teacher with him in the Willie Halsell College.

At Columbus, Kentucky, June 5, 1895, Mr. Chapman married Miss Maud Taylor. Mrs. Chapman is a woman of thorough culture as well as a most capable home maker. She graduated with high honors from Marvin College in Kentucky and a year after graduation was given a chair in the faculty of instruction at that institution. To their marriage there are three living children: Merle, aged sixteen, in high school; Marie, aged thirteen, also in high school; and Vernon, aged ten. Mr. Chapman has one sister, two half-sisters and a half-brother: Mrs. Ada Moore, wife of a farmer at Clinton, Kentucky; Mrs. Charles Crawl, wife of a lumber dealer at Eufaula, Oklahoma; Mrs. Ola Painter, whose husband is an oil supply man at Wichita Falls, Texas; and H. M. Myers, who for seven years has been in the auditing department at Muskogee of the Missouri, Oklahoma & Gulf Railway Company. Mr. Chapman is a member of the Masonic and the Knights of Pythias lodges, and of the Methodist Church.

CHARLES W. WILSON. Noted for his sound judgment and keen business sagacity, Charles W. Wilson is regarded as one of the safe and sound financiers of Woodward County, and his connection with the Security State Bank of Mooreland, of which he has been cashier since 1914, has resulted very advantageously to that concern. Mr. Wilson came to the West in his youth, with little to aid him save his ambition and energy and after a number of years spent in Kansas came to Oklahoma in a business capacity in which he displayed qualities that led to his introduction to banking circles.

Born July 3, 1863, on a farm in Lenawee County, Michigan, Mr. Wilson is a son of Charles B. and Rosa M. (Hill) Wilson. His father was born in 1832, at Thomaston, Connecticut, where the family was well and favorably known and where the grandparents were born, and was one year old when taken to Lenawee County, Michigan. There Charles B. Wilson was reared on a pioneer farm, was given an ordinary education and as a young man engaged in teaching school, although later he turned his attention to agricultural pursuits and succeeded to the ownership of the farm which had been proved up by his father. An industrious and enterprising man, his life was passed in the peaceful pursuits of the soil, and his

death occurred on his Michigan farm April 20, 1900. In his community he had an excellent reputation in business circles, while his good citizenship was evidenced on all occasions. In 1857, in Michigan, Mr. Wilson was united in marriage with Miss Rosa M. Hill, who was born in 1837, in Connecticut, daughter of Rollin E. and Millicent (Kasson) Hill, natives of Litchfield County, Connecticut. She was taken as a child to Michigan, where she was reared and educated and prior to her marriage was, like her husband, a teacher in the public schools. Her death occurred February 8, 1884, and thirty years later, in 1914, one of the classrooms of the Methodist Episcopal Church at Morenci, Michigan, was dedicated to her as a memorial to her faithful and devoted work in behalf of that congregation during the early days. Two sons and one daughter were born to Charles B. and Rosa M. Hill, namely: Clarence A., Luella Josephine and Charles W. Clarence A. Wilson of this family was born August 14, 1859, in Lenawee County, Michigan, and was given good educational advantages, being graduated from Valparaiso College, at Valparaiso, Indiana. He took up banking in 1884, when he was elected cashier of the Wakefield State Bank of Morenci, Michigan, a position which he still retains, being one of the best known bankers in that part of the state. He was married in 1904 to Miss Marie Beauchamp, a native of Newport, Kentucky, and they are the parents of two daughters: Charlotte and Millicent. Luella Josephine Wilson was born in Lenawee County, Michigan, February 20, 1861, and early displayed literary talent of more than ordinary order. In addition to being a magazine writer of note, she was secretary of the Writers' Club of Toledo, Ohio, and held that position at the time of her death, April 20, 1912. She married Frank Smith, a native of Ohio, in 1886, and they became the parents of two children: Herbert W. and Dorothy.

Charles W. Wilson was reared on the home farm in Michigan and received his education in the public schools of Lenawee County. At the age of twenty-two years, in 1885, he left home to seek his fortune in the West, his destination being Harper, Kansas, where he secured a position in a flouring mill. During the fifteen years that followed he worked at milling at different points in Southern Kansas, and in various capacities, and became well and favorably known to the people of Barber County, in that state, who, in 1902, elected him to the office of county clerk. The manner in which he discharged his duties during his first term resulted in his election to succeed himself in 1904, and the entire four years of his incumbency were marked by faithful, capable, energetic and conscientious performance of duty. In 1907, 1908 and 1909; Mr. Wilson was assistant cashier of the First National Bank of Kiowa, Kansas, where he gained excellent experience, but in 1911 he transferred his activities to Oklahoma, coming to Mooreland to accept the management of the grain elevator of the Alva Roller Mills, a concern which is being capably managed by George A. Harbaugh, with a large mill at Alva and a chain of grain elevators in Kansas, Oklahoma and Texas. Mr. Wilson soon became known as a business man of unusual capacity and in 1914 was offered and accepted the cashiership of the Security State Bank of Mooreland, of which office he has since been the incumbent. This is one of the sound and conservative financial institutions of Woodward County, established in 1906, whose depositors come from Woodward and the surrounding counties. He has maintained his position as a man of substantial business qualities and exceptional character, and is rapidly becoming one of the most prominent and successful citizens of his locality. Fraternally, Mr. Wilson affiliates with the Masons and the Knights of Pythias, in both of which he has numerous friends. Since attaining his majority he has been an unswerving republican. Mr. Wilson was married October 26, 1892, at Medicine Lodge, Kansas, to Miss Lizzie C. Clark, who was born February 14, 1872, at old Osage Mission, Kansas. Mr. and Mrs. Wilson have had no children. She is a member of the Presbyterian Church and has taken an active interest in its work.

WILLIAM P. HARPER. A resident of Oklahoma City since 1889, Judge Harper has here been engaged in the practice of law since 1891 and he holds secure vantage-place as one of the representative members of the Oklahoma bar. Under the territorial regime he served as judge of probate of Oklahoma County and of this office he was the incumbent also at the time when Oklahoma was admitted to statehood, in 1907. He controls a large and important law business, has been influential in public affairs in the territory and state, and is one of the progressive and liberal citizens of Oklahoma City, where he maintains his well appointed law offices at 207-9 Majestic Building.

Judge William Philip Harper was born at Wheeling, Delaware County, Indiana, on the 18th of February, 1859, and is a son of Charles A. and Mary J. (Wendall) Harper. His father was a lawyer by profession and for a number of years was engaged in the practice of his profession at Muncie, the judicial center of Delaware County, Indiana, and there the subject of this review initiated the study of law under the effective preceptorship of his father, after he had duly profited by the advantages afforded in the public schools of his native state. From 1876 to 1885 Judge Harper was a resident of Clinton County, Indiana, and he then came to the West and passed three years in the State of Kansas. In December, 1899, the year in which Oklahoma Territory was organized and opened to settlement Judge Harper numbered himself among its pioneer settlers, and he has wielded not a little influence in the civic and material development and progress of both territory and state. Upon coming to the territory he established his residence in Oklahoma City, where he resumed the study of law and where he was admitted to the bar in 1891. He here engaged in the practice of his profession and in 1894 he was elected, on the republican ticket, to the office of judge of the Probate Court of Oklahoma County, of which position he continued the efficient and valued incumbent for a term of two years, within which he did much to systematize, solidify and make authoritative the important business of this territorial court of the county. After his retirement from office the judge again engaged in the general practice of his profession, and few lawyers have been more prominently associated with important litigations and legal interests in the state than has he. He retains at the present time a large and representative clientage, is well known to his professional confreres throughout the state, and commands unqualified popular confidence and esteem. In 1902 he was again elected judge of probate, and he continued in the effective administration of the affairs of this office until the admission of Oklahoma to the Union, in 1907, having retained the post during the pending agitation and legislation incident to the creation of the new state. Since that time he has given virtually his undivided attention to his large and important law business, and his name merits enduring place on the roster of the pioneer members of the Oklahoma bar. The judge has continued a stalwart and effective advocate of the principles of the republican party and is one of its influential representatives in Oklahoma.

In the city that has long been his home was solemnized the marriage of Judge Harper to Miss Cora B. Gregory, and she is a popular factor in the representative social activities of Oklahoma City. Judge and Mrs. Harper have three children, Annabel, Wendel and William P., Jr., the family home being an attractive residence owned by the judge at 2204 West Nineteenth Street.

GEORGE A. JOHNS is member of the well known law firm of McCrory & Johns of Okmulgee, and besides a large general practice he is well and favorably known over the county as former county judge.

He was born in Pekin, Illinois, June 14, 1880, son of J. J. and Elizabeth (Weber) Johns. His father was born in Pekin, Illinois, but his mother was a native of Germany, and came to Illinois when a child. She is now living in Chicago. The father died at Quincy, Illinois, in 1896, at the age of forty-six. He was a merchant during all his active career, and had stores at Pekin and Quincy.

One of five children, George A. Johns, remained in the home of his mother until 1908. He finished his education in Northwestern University, where he was graduated in the law department in Chicago in 1906 with the degree LL. B. He was admitted to the Illinois bar in 1906 and practiced law in that state for a year or so.

In 1908 he was admitted to the Oklahoma State Bar, and since then has had his home in Okmulgee. In 1913 he formed a partnership with C. B. McCrory under the firm name of McCrory & Johns.

It was in 1911 that Mr. Johns was elected county judge of Okmulgee County and served in that office with admirable efficiency for two years, one term. In politics he is a republican and a Knight Templar Mason and Shriner. In 1910 he married Florence Collins, who was born in Binghamton, New York, daughter of Daniel Collins. They have one child, Ellen.

THOMAS LOVE LILLARD. An extensive and progressive agriculturist of Osage County, and a prominent citizen of Pawhuska, Thomas Love Lillard is a man of worth and stability, and enjoys the fullest confidence and esteem of the community in which he resides. A native of Kentucky, he was born September 20, 1860, in Boyle County. His father, Thomas Madison Lillard, was for many years engaged in the cattle business, during his earlier life buying and selling in Charleston, South Carolina, and in New York City, his operations being largely confined to those two cities. Subsequently buying land in Kentucky, he devoted the remainder of his years to the raising of stock, and to farming, both he and his wife dying on their Kentucky plantation. To him and his wife, whose maiden name was Mary Bright, eleven children were born.

Remaining on the home place until after the death of his father, Thomas Love Lillard was well trained in the art and science of agriculture, which he selected as his occupation in life. Coming to Oklahoma in 1901, he resided at Ponca five years. In 1906 he located at Pawhuska, where he has since been profitably engaged in general farming, making a specialty of stock growing, in partnership with T. P. Kiger, being widely known as junior member of the enterprising firm of Kiger & Lillard. He is a democrat in his political relations, and both he and his wife are valued members of the Christian Church. Fraternally he belongs to the Benevolent and Protective Order of Elks.

Mr. Lillard married September 20, 1893, Miss Alice Hubble, who was born in Boyle County, Kentucky, March 3, 1865, a daughter of Levi and Martha (Stigall) Hubble, who reared three children, namely: William, who died at the age of twenty-four years; Alice, now Mrs. Lillard; and Laura, wife of George Shelby. Mr. Hubble spent his entire life in Central Kentucky, his death occurring there in 1896. His widow survived him many years, dying in 1915, in Pawhuska, Oklahoma, where she had been a resident for eight years.

Mrs. Lillard is a woman of rare ability and accomplishments, scholarly in her attainments, and possessing a winning personality. As a young lady she received excellent educational advantages, being graduated, in 1882, from Hamilton College, in Lexington, Kentucky, with the degree of Bachelor of Arts, and in 1884 taking a post-graduate course at the same institution. She then taught a year in the Miller School, in Cincinnati, taking charge of the classes in English, after which she established a private school in which she prepared pupils for college. Subsequently she attended to the correspondence and banking business of her father, who was an extensive stock grower and breeder of fine saddle horses, and an able assistant in making Kentucky famous in that line of industry. The family meeting with financial reverses after the death of her father, Miss Hubble again assumed her duties in the school room, and after teaching for a time in Ponca, Oklahoma, accepted a position in the Pawhuska High School, with which she continued two years.

Interested in everything pertaining to the advancement of the educational status of Oklahoma, Mrs. Lillard assisted in the organization of schools, and since Oklahoma assumed the garb of statehood she has been a member of the examining board for teachers in Osage County, a position for which she is amply qualified. In October, 1912, she was appointed county superintendent of the Osage County schools to fill a vacancy caused by the resignation of W. E. Gill, and in November of that year was elected to the same responsible position. Giving such eminent satisfaction in the discharge of her duties during the next two years, Mrs. Lillard was honored with a re-election to the same high office in 1914 for a term that will not expire until July 1, 1917. In the performance of her duties Mrs. Lillard covers an area of 2,300 square miles, some of the schools of which she has the supervision being widely separated. She was elected to her present office on the democratic ticket, and has the distinction of being the first woman to fill the position in Osage County.

Mrs. Lillard is an active worker in the church, and is prominent in club affairs, belonging to both the mother's department and the art department of the Pawhuska Woman's Club.

Mr. and Mrs. Lillard have a fine family of children, three in number, namely: William H., Alice, and Mary Bright, and they have also reared a nephew, William Lillard. Mr. Lillard has in his possession a complete genealogy of the Lillard family, compiled and published in 1890 by his brother, John T. Lillard, an attorney in Bloomington, Illinois.

PROF. HUGH GRAHAM FAUST. To a rapidly increasing number of Oklahoma school men Professor Faust of Shawnee is becoming known for the ability with which he is administering the fine public school system at Shawnee and also for the influential work which he is doing in professional organization. Ever since graduating from college Mr. Faust has been in school work. He has spent about fifteen years in the profession, and is a man of ripe scholarship, of dignified manner, and of splendid character. He is just the man for the heavy responsibilities which he now carries as city superintendent of Shawnee schools.

A Tennesseean by birth, he is a native of Newmarket, Tennessee, where he was born, January 28, 1879. His parents were M. L. and Belle (Parrott) Faust. The Fausts came originally from Germany, but at a very early time in colonial history, having located in Virginia and going across the mountains into Tennessee about the time of the American Revolution. Another branch of ancestors was the Sawyer family and representatives of that name fought on the American side in the war for independence. Some of the Fausts were soldiers in the Federal army during the war between the states, while Mr. Faust's maternal ancestors were found in the Confederate army.

M. L. Faust was born at Newmarket, Tennessee, in 1850, and has spent practically all his life in that community being a substantial farmer and stock raiser. He is also a good citizen and for a considerable term of years has served as a member of the board of education in his home locality. He has taken an especially active part in the affairs of the Presbyterian Church, and served many years on the official board. The mother, whose maiden name was Belle Parrott, was born in Granger County, Tennessee, in 1847. She became the mother of seven children, briefly noted as follows: Edna, wife of Beecher Coxe, a merchant at Newmarket, Tennessee; L. C. Faust, who lives at Newmarket and is engaged in the raising of blooded stock; Professor Hugh Graham; Professor C. J. Faust, who was superintendent of schools in Knox County, Tennessee, and died at Knoxville in 1903; Lynn E., who is an automobile dealer in Hood River, Oregon; Leon, engaged in mercantile business at Hood River, Oregon; and Dr. G. T. Faust, who was graduated from the Louisville Medical College in 1914 and is now practicing medicine at Dorchester, Virginia.

Hugh Graham Faust had the average opportunities and advantages of the country boy. He had an ambition for things beyond the horizon of the farmer's son, and was not satisfied with the education which the public schools in the vicinity of Newmarket could afford him. He afterwards entered one of the oldest and best small colleges in Tennessee, the Carson & Newman College at Jefferson, where he was graduated A. B. with the class of 1906. At different times he has interrupted his work or has accepted the leisure afforded by vacation periods in order to continue his studies in higher institutions. Much of his post-graduate work has been done at the University of Chicago.

It was in 1900 that Mr. Faust did his first practical work as a teacher in the public schools of Jefferson County, Tennessee. He remained there two years, and in 1902 became principal of the Bearden High School in Knox County, Tennessee, remaining there also two years. This was followed by a position as teacher in Jacksboro, Tennessee, where he was principal of the Campbell County High School three years.

On coming to Oklahoma Mr. Faust was superintendent of the city schools at Weatherford for two years, spent another three years as superintendent of schools at Frederick, and in 1914 was called to the heavy responsibilities connected with the superintendency at Shawnee. In 1915 he was re-elected on the basis of his first year's record and for a term of three years.

Other activities should be referred to in this article. During the scholastic year of 1905-06 he was instructor at Greeneville and Tusculum College at Greeneville, Tennessee. After coming to Oklahoma he served one year as president of the Tillman County Teachers Association. During the summers of 1903 and 1904 he took postgraduate work in the University of Tennessee. He is an active member of the Pottawatomie County Teachers Association and in the Oklahoma Educational Association

is chairman of the City Superintendents Division, of which Supt. H. L. Nicholas of Holdenville is secretary. In politics he worked with the democratic party. He is a deacon in the Presbyterian Church, and fraternally is identified with Shawnee Lodge No. 106, Ancient Free and Accepted Masons; Shawnee Chapter No. 32, Royal Arch Masons; Shawnee Commandery No. 36, Knights Templar; and with the Weatherford Lodge of Knights of Pythias, in which he is past chancellor commander. He is a member of the Shawnee Commercial Club, of the Provident Club of Shawnee and belongs to the Fidelity Building & Loan Association. He was a member of the Avis Society of the University of Chicago.

At Chicago in 1909 Professor Faust married Miss Bertha Weiman. Her father was the late Judge Weiman of Grand Rapids, Michigan. Miss Weiman graduated with the degree Bachelor of Arts from the University of Chicago and for several years before her marriage was a successful teacher, being an instructor in one of the high schools in Chicago and in the public schools of Evanston, Illinois.

T. M. BURROW. Among the well known officials of Dewey County, one who has won standing because of ability and faithful service, and popularity by reason of courtesy and fidelity, is T. M. Burrow, clerk of the courts. Prior to his election to his present office, Mr. Burrow was engaged in a variety of pursuits, although his energies were principally devoted to educational work, and the ability which he displayed in this direction was chiefly responsible for bringing him forward as a desirable candidate for public service. During the three years that he has served he has established an excellent record.

Mr. Burrow was born at Bardwell, Carlisle County, Kentucky, January 6, 1882, on a farm, and is a son of T. W. and Melinda (Shelbourne) Burrow. On the paternal side he belongs to a family which settled in North Carolina during colonial days, having come from Scotland, while on the maternal side he is also descended from Scotch ancestors, who settled in New York before the Revolution. His father was born at Lovelaceville, Ballard County, Kentucky, in 1847, and was reared, educated and married there, following which he moved across the line into Carlisle County and settled on a farm eight miles east of Bardwell. There he continued to be engaged in farming and stock-raising during the remaining years of his active life, passing away December 22, 1908. A democrat in his political views, he took a keen, active and intelligent interest in public affairs, and for six years was supervisor of Carlisle County, being the incumbent of that office at the time of his death. He was a strong supporter of the movements of the Baptist Church, held a place on the official board for many years, and led a consistent Christian life. His fraternal connections were with the local lodges of the Masons and the Odd Fellows. Mr. Burrow married Melinda Shelbourne, who was born in the State of New York, in 1843, and who still survives her husband in comfortable old age, being a resident of Paducah, Kentucky, at her home located at No. 821 Adams Street. T. W. and Melinda Burrow were the parents of nine children, as follows: Wilmoth, who is the wife of C. W. Black, a farmer and shipper of stock at Kevil, Kentucky; James, who is an Illinois Central Railway engineer and resides at Paducah, Kentucky; Cora, who is the wife of J. H. Peck, a railroad contractor of Hickman, Kentucky; E. R., who died at Bardwell, Kentucky, aged thirty-six years, as a salesman; Ira O., a farmer residing at Mayfield, Kentucky; Ada, deceased, who married A. D. Lynn, a farmer of Dewey County, Oklahoma; T. M., of this notice; Euphy, who is the wife of N. A. Mabry, a rural mail carrier of

Paducah, Kentucky; and A. W., who died at Bardwell, Kentucky, at the age of sixteen years.

T. M. Burrow was reared on his father's farm until he was fourteen years of age, and during his early boyhood he attended the district schools of Carlisle County. In 1896 the family moved to Bardwell, where he became a pupil in the public schools, and this training was furthered by attendance at the state normal school, Bowling Green, Kentucky, where he remained for two years, or until 1901. In that year he began his business experience as clerk in a clothing store at Fulton, Kentucky, but at the end of eight months became a fireman in the employ of the Illinois Central Railroad. Mr. Burrow remained in that position for about one year, when, acting upon his belief that the West offered better opportunities for the display of his abilities, he came to Rhea, Dewey County, Oklahoma, where he entered upon his career as an educator. During the next nine years he held positions in various parts of the county as principal of schools, and was thus brought favorably before the people. In 1912 he was elected clerk of the district court, holding that office for two years, and November 6, 1914, was elected clerk of the courts for a period of two years, the name of the office having been changed. His offices are in the court house, Taloga. Mr. Burrow has always been a stalwart democrat and since coming to Oklahoma has become influential in the ranks of his party in Dewey County. He has been also an enthusiastic fraternalist, and now belongs to Aledo Lodge No. 415, A. F. & A. M.; Taloga Chapter No. 54, R. A. M., and Taloga Camp, Modern Woodmen of America.

Mr. Burrow was married February 14, 1909, to Miss Ada Vandervort, daughter of Rev. W. S. Vandervort, a preacher of the Methodist Episcopal Church, who is retired and resides at Aledo. They have two children: Myrle, born January 11, and Adele, born October 11, 1913.

MICHAEL H. LYONS. All honor is due to Sergeant Lyons for his loyal and efficient service of thirty years as a member of the United States army, in which he attained to the rank of ordnance sergeant. He gained wide experience in connection with military operations at the various military posts of the West and Southwest, took part in a number of engagements with hostile Indians, was with the reinforcements that arrived on the scene of the historic massacre of General Custer and his gallant soldiers within two days after that disastrous engagement, and otherwise grew familiar with life on the frontier. His service extended into the original Indian Territory, and while still in the army he was one of the pioneers in entering claim to land within the borders of Oklahoma Territory when it was thrown open to settlement, more than a quarter of a century ago, and here he had become a successful agriculturist and stock grower long before his retirement from the military service that so long engrossed his attention and in which he won distinction as a faithful, efficient and valiant soldier and officer. Sergeant Lyons is now an honored and influential citizen of El Reno, the judicial center of Canadian County, and through his distinctive business acumen and well ordered enterprise he has accumulated a substantial competency, so that he may well feel that, with troops of friends about him, his lines are indeed "cast in pleasant places."

Michael H. Lyons was born in Montgomery County, Pennsylvania, on December 25, 1856, and is a son of Patrick and Elizabeth (Hicky) Lyons, both natives of Ireland. The sergeant passed the period of his childhood and early youth at Fort Washington, Pennsylvania, where he acquired his rudimentary education in the parochial and public schools, and he was fifteen years old at the time of the family removal to the City of Philadelphia, where he continued to reside until he had attained to adult age.

In 1876, in Philadelphia, which city was then a point of national interest by reason of being the stage of the great Centennial Exposition, Sergeant Lyons, as a youth of twenty years, enlisted as a private in the United States Army. After a service of about two years he was promoted corporal and later a sergeant, and in 1885 he was advanced to the rank of first sergeant, an office in which he continued to serve eleven years, after which he held the office of ordnance sergeant until the date of his retirement from the army, in January, 1907. The initial military service of Sergeant Lyons was in Dakota Territory, and thence he proceeded with his command into Wyoming, where these forces arrived on the Custer battlefield the second day after the historic massacre. Thereafter he was with his command in Texas and his final service was in what is now the State of Oklahoma. He participated in a number of spirited engagements with hostile Indians, and concerning his admirable record as a member of Troop K, Fifth United States Cavalry, the following statements are self-explanatory and significant, the same having been written as a testimonial at the time when the subject of this review was appointed ordnance sergeant, in 1894, and the author of the commendatory words having been Capt. A. E. Woodson, who later rose to the rank of brigadier general. In recommending Sergeant Lyons for promotion, Captain Woodson wrote as follows: "He was at all times, in the garrison and in the field, an excellent soldier, ever ready when called, quick to respond, a leader of men, cheerful in disposition, and an exemplar to the men of his command."

Though a stickler for discipline and always found at the post of duty, the buoyant and genial nature of Sergeant Lyons won him the high regard of his comrades and superior officers, and to-day he has many friends of high standing in the United States Army, in public life and in business circles,—in fact, it may consistently be said that his circle of friends is limited only by that of his acquaintances. Though he has had no ambition to enter the arena of practical politics and has had no desire for public office, the sergeant has given loyal support to the cause of the republican party and has aided in the election of its candidates, both national and local. Both he and his wife are communicants of the Catholic Church.

In 1885 Sergeant Lyons came with his cavalry command for the first time to old Fort Reno, Indian Territory, a military post near the present thriving City of El Reno, Oklahoma, and while here stationed he was promoted first sergeant. Later he was with his troop in Texas, where they were stationed in turn at Fort Brown and Fort San Antonio, and in 1896 he was sent back to Fort Reno, as ordnance sergeant at this post. Here he continued until the expiration of his service in the army, and since his retirement he has maintained his residence principally in the city of El Reno. While at Fort Reno he was sent by the commander of that garrison to lay off the grounds for the railway station of the Atchison, Topeka & Santa Fe Railroad at Oklahoma City, and this duty he discharged with characteristic efficiency and fidelity.

Within a short time after Oklahoma Territory had been opened for settlement, Sergeant Lyons filed claim to a homestead of 160 acres in Canadian County, and this property he developed into a fine ranch. For twenty-five years, while still in active service a portion of the period in the army, he here devoted attention to the breeding and raising of registered short-horn cattle,

and in this field of enterprise he had met with gratifying success long before he disposed of his interests in the same. His excellent judgment and business sagacity have conspired to bring to him a comfortable fortune since his days of active military service, and he is one of the best known and most popular citizens of Canadian County, with a wide acquaintanceship also in other parts of the state.

In 1885 was solemnized the marriage of Sergeant Lyons to Miss Maggie Cambric, who was born in the City of Toledo, and she has proved a devoted companion and helpmeet during their long years of wedded life, the while she is a popular chatelaine of their attractive home in El Reno, where they delight to welcome their many friends. They have no children. They reside in the Lyons apartment building, a modern building which was erected and is owned by Sergeant Lyons, who has also other valuable city real estate in El Reno.

JAMES J. CAVINESS, M. D. Among the younger generation of professional men of Jackson County, one who is rapidly winning success and position is Dr. James J. Caviness, physician and surgeon, who since 1912 has been engaged in practice at Headrick. During this time his skill in diagnosis and his successful treatment of complicated and long standing cases have created a gratifying demand for his services and laid the foundation of what promises to be a career of exceptional breadth and usefulness.

Doctor Caviness was born at Danville, Yell County, Arkansas, July 13, 1889, and is a son of R. S. and Margaret (Costen) Caviness. The Caviness family is of Scotch-Irish extraction and its members have been pioneers of several states in the Union, notably those of Oklahoma and Texas. R. S. Caviness was born at Paris, the county seat of Lamar County, Texas, in 1860, and was there reared and educated. When still a young man he went to Danville, Arkansas, where he embarked in business as a merchant, and continued to be so occupied successfully until 1904, in which year he returned to Texas and settled at Memphis, where he followed stock raising for four years. Mr. Caviness came to Oklahoma in 1908, when he took up his residence at Eldorado, and since that time has been proprietor of a pharmacy. Mr. Caviness has shown versatility in his business ventures, and in each has won a satisfying measure of success through the exertion of energy and enterprise, good management and foresight. In political matters he is a stanch democrat, and in each of the communities in which he has resided has taken an active part in political and civic matters, although rather as an influence than as a seeker for the honors and emoluments of public office. Throughout his life he has been a member of the Methodist Episcopal Church, in the work of which he has taken a helpful part, and at the present time is a member of the official board of the church at Eldorado. He is well known in Masonry, belonging to Eldorado Lodge, Ancient Free and Accepted Masons; Eldorado Chapter, Royal Arch Masons; Eldorado Commandery, Knights Templar, and Consistory No. 1, Valley of Guthrie, of the thirty-second degree. While residing at Danville, Arkansas, Mr. Caviness was united in marriage with Miss Margaret Costen, who was born in 1870, in Georgia, and they have been the parents of five children, as follows: C. A., who resides at Eldorado, and is associated with his father in the conduct of the drug business; Dr. James J., of this review; Ruth, who is the wife of C. A. Hatch, a practicing attorney at Eldorado; Naomi, who is the wife of Earl Messersmith, proprietor of a general merchandise store at Eldorado; and Baxter, who resides with his parents and is a student in the Eldorado High School.

James J. Caviness received the early part of his education in the public schools of Danville, Arkansas, and when fifteen years of age went with the family to Memphis, Texas, where he completed the studies of the primary grades. He was graduated from the Memphis High School in the class of 1907, and following this began preparing for the medical profession which he had chosen in his youth as his life work. He eventually entered Vanderbilt University, of Nashville, Tennessee, where he pursued a full course of study and was duly graduated from the medical department with the class of 1912, and with his newly acquired degree of Doctor of Medicine settled down to practice at Eldorado, whence the family had moved. After three months of practice at that place, Doctor Caviness decided better opportunities awaited him at Headrick, where he settled September 18, 1912, and where he has since remained in practice, having offices in the Headrick Drug Store. Doctor Caviness is thoroughly at home in all branches of his calling, and carries on a general practice in both medicine and surgery. To a thorough professional equipment, he adds a kindly and sympathetic manner, a genuine liking for his calling and a ready adaptation to its multitudinous and exacting demands. He has never ceased to be a student, passing much of his time in personal research and investigation, and maintaining membership in the Jackson County Medical Society, the Oklahoma State Medical Society and the American Medical Association. While he is a stanch democrat in politics, he has confined his activities in that direction to casting his vote, although always eager to add his name to the list of supporters of any good and progressive movement. Fraternally, the Doctor is affiliated with Headrick Lodge No. 311, Free and Accepted Masons, and Headrick Camp No. 128, Woodmen of the World.

On June 17, 1913, at Nashville, Tennessee, Doctor Caviness was married to Miss Mary Moore, daughter of J. T. Moore, who resides at College Grove, Tennessee, and is a prosperous farmer and stockraiser. One child has been born to this union: James J., Jr. Doctor and Mrs. Caviness are members of the Methodist Episcopal Church and are general favorites in social circles of their home community. Doctor Caviness expects to locate in Altus about July 1, 1916.

MILLARD T. KIRK. Since coming to Oklahoma, in 1906, Millard T. Kirk has taken an active and purposeful participation in the affairs of his adopted community, where his influence has always been exerted in behalf of advancement and progress in business and civic life. For a time he was connected with various mercantile concerns, and also served acceptably in the capacity of postmaster of Bartlesville, but since his retirement from that position has been engaged in general and dairy farming three miles northwest of the city. He is now the owner of a valuable and well-improved property, and is making a decided success of his new venture.

Mr. Kirk is a native son of Kentucky, born at Inez, the county seat of Martin County, July 6, 1876, a son of James D. and Mahala (Canfield) Kirk. His father was born at Wayne, West Virginia, July 31, 1845, and his mother in Greenup County, Kentucky. James D. Kirk moved from his West Virginia home to Kentucky in young manhood, and at the outbreak of the Civil war enlisted in the Thirty-ninth Kentucky Regiment, with which he served with valor and bravery for three years. On his return at the close of hostilities, he became one of the foremost men of the community of Inez, and served as county clerk of Martin County for twenty-six years and as county judge for eight years. He is now living in quiet retirement after a long and useful career. Mr. Kirk is a republican. Mrs. Kirk died in 1880, leaving four children, namely: Willa, who is the wife of Capt. A. Allen, and a resident of Bartlesville; Laura, who is the wife of J. P. H. Tinkaus, of Knoxville, Tennessee; Millard T., of this review; and Jennie, who is the wife of John F. Algeo, of Bartlesville, a merchant.

Millard T. Kirk received his early education in the public schools of Inez, following which he became a student in the University of Kentucky, but left that institution during his junior year, because of poor health. He soon secured a position with the Triple State Natural Gas and Oil Company, of Inez, being connected with that firm for five years, and then established himself in a general merchandise business at Inez, in which he had three years of experience. Subsequently he went to West Virginia in charge of a large mercantile establishment and remained there three years, and in 1906 came to Bartlesville, Oklahoma, with John F. Algeo. He remained with Mr. Algeo as bookkeeper for a short period and then accepted the position of assistant postmaster under William Higgins, retaining that office for five months and then resigning to take a position with H. M. Preston, who is now a resident of Tulsa. Mr. Kirk was appointed postmaster of Bartlesville, January 27, 1911, and served very ably in that office until March 15, 1915, when the change of administration made itself felt by his being succeeded by a democrat. When he left official life, Mr. Kirk established himself on his present farm, located on Butter Creek, three miles north of Bartlesville. Here he has since carried on general farming and dairying, lines in which he has already been so successful that his future prosperity may be safely prophesied. As a business man he has always merited the high esteem in which he has been held by his associates, and his public life has been above reproach. Since attaining his majority Mr. Kirk has been a warm supporter of the principles of the republican party, and he still retains membership in the Methodist Episcopal Church, in the faith of which he was reared. His fraternal connections are with the Blue Lodge, Chapter and Commandery of the Masonic order at Bartlesville, the Shrine at Tulsa, Lodge No. 1060 of the Benevolent and Protective Order of Elks, at Bartlesville, of which he is past exalted ruler, and the Knights of Pythias, in which he is a charter member of Bartlesville Lodge.

Mr. Kirk was married December 5, 1906, to Miss Sarah Cassady, who was born at Inez, Kentucky, a daughter of Philip Cassady, a merchant and cattleman of the Bluegrass State. To this union there have been born five children, namely: Dorothy, Darwin, Elizabeth, Rae and Joseph P.

FRANK R. NOE came to Eastern Oklahoma some months after statehood, and by his activity as a merchant and citizen made himself a very popular and useful factor in Seminole County. Governor Cruce selected him for a local appointment, and he is now filling the office of county treasurer, and is giving the people a systematic and thorough administration of the fiscal affairs of the county government.

Ancestrally Mr. Noe descends from a French line, but they have been identified with America for many generations. Frank R. Noe was born at Pineville, Arkansas, October 19, 1880, a son of Rev. Frank R. and Serena (Matthews) Noe. His father was a native of Springfield, Missouri, and his mother of Arkansas. Rev. Frank R. Noe served all through the Civil war as a corporal in the Confederate Army. After that his active career was spent as a minister of the Methodist Episcopal Church South and he was connected with the White River Conference in Arkansas. He died in 1906, at the age of sixty, highly honored and respected. The mother of Frank R. Noe died when he was two years of age at the age of thirty-five, and he was one of four sons and two daughters. The father married again and had three sons and one daughter by the second marriage.

Frank R. Noe lived with his father until he was twenty years of age, and spent most of his early youth in school. At the age of twenty he went to Memphis, Tennessee, kept a set of books for the William R. Moore wholesale dry goods house for eight years, and in 1907 went out to California, participating in the activities of the mining district for a time, and spending one year in Los Angeles. From there he came to Seminole County, Oklahoma, and for some time was associated in general merchandising business with his brother T. D. Noe, under the firm name of Noe Brothers. He is still a merchant and one of the prospering men of this section. In 1912 Governor Cruce appointed him county assessor of Seminole County, and he was elected to that office in 1913. In 1914 he was chosen county treasurer, and most of his time is now given to the duties of that office.

He has been a democrat since casting his first vote, is affiliated with the Woodmen of the World and the Modern Woodmen of America, and is loyal to the church of his father, the Methodist Episcopal South.

On January 1, 1906, Mr. Noe married Miss Cecil Price of Beebe, Arkansas. She died in 1912, and of her two children Carroll, seven years old, is with his Grandmother Price at Little Rock, Arkansas, while Mildred died in infancy. In December, 1914, at Springfield, Missouri, Mr. Noe married Phyllis Duncan.

ALLEN J. JETER, M. D. Engaged in active general practice as a physician and surgeon, Doctor Jeter now holds precedence and priority as the dean of his profession in the thriving town of Foss, Washita County, where he established his residence in 1902, no other physician who was his contemporary in the early years of practice here being now a citizen of this village, so that he is the veritable pioneer of his profession here, his practice being extensive and of representative order—implying due recognition of his high attainments, effective ministrations and personal popularity.

The original American progenitors of the Jeter family were two brothers who emigrated from Denmark in the colonial era of our national history, one settling in either North or South Carolina and the other in Virginia, the one who figures as the ancestor of Doctor Jeter having been the Carolinian. James Jeter, grandfather of the Doctor, was a soldier in the War of 1812 and participated in the battle of New Orleans, under General Andrew Jackson. He became one of the prominent planters and slaveholders of Louisiana, and in 1862, after the initial activities of the Civil war, he sought refuge in Texas, his death having occurred in Hopkins County, that state, after he had reached venerable age.

Doctor Jeter was born in Union Parish, Louisiana, on the 14th of February, 1862, and, his father being at the time a soldier in the Confederate ranks, the Doctor was taken by his mother and paternal grandfather to the Lone Star State, the removal to Texas having been made to escape the perils and ravages incident to the war. He is a son of Allen W. and Susan (Seale) Jeter, whose marriage was solemnized in Texas, from which state he and his wife returned to Union Parish, Louisiana. He was born at Columbus, Georgia, in 1832, but when he was very small moved with his parents to the State of Louisiana, and was reared and educated in that state, whence, as a young man, he removed to Texas. He was

a resident of Louisiana at the inception of the Civil war and promptly tendered his service in defense of the cause of the Confederate States, his service as a soldier having continued four years—virtually the entire period of the great conflict between the South and the North. In 1865, soon after the close of the war, he established his residence in Van Zandt County, Texas, where he became a prosperous agriculturist and stock-grower. He was preparing to establish his home in New Mexico many years later, and while making a preliminary visit to that state, which was then a territory, his death there occurred, in 1907, after he had passed the psalmist's alotted span of three score years and ten. His widow, who was born in 1840, still maintains her home in Van Zandt County, Texas, she being a devoted member of the Missionary Baptist Church, of which her husband was an active member for many years prior to his demise. Mr. Jeter participated in many engagements during the Civil war, was wounded and taken prisoner, but after his exchange had been effected he resumed his service with his old regiment, his interest in his former comrades being perpetuated in later years through his affiliation with the United Confederate Veterans. He was for many years actively affiliated with the Masonic fraternity.

Of the children of Allen W. and Susan (Seale) Jeter the firstborn is he whose name introduces this article; Sarah Jane is the wife of Thomas G. Hayden, a prosperous farmer and stock-grower of Van Zandt County, Texas; Mary Elizabeth died at the age of one year; Rev. Elias D., a clergyman of the Missionary Baptist Church, is now a resident of Lawton, Oklahoma; Dr. Thomas M., who was graduated in the Fort Worth Medical College, is now engaged in the practice of his profession in the City of Fort Worth, Texas; Minnie is the wife of James M. Gillian, a farmer of Denton County, Texas; Ella and her husband, Wm. Comford, are missionaries in China; Joseph J. is engaged in the drug business at Maybank, Texas; and Dr. Drayton, likewise a physician and surgeon, is engaged in practice at Murkison, Texas. James and William Jeter, son of the first marriage of Allen W. Jeter, are representative agriculturists of Western Texas.

As previously stated, Dr. Allen J. Jeter was an infant when he was taken by his paternal grandfather to Texas, where he attended the public schools of Van Zandt County until he had been graduated in the high school. In consonance with his ambition and well formulated plans for a future career, he finally entered the Memphis Hospital Medical College, in the City of Memphis, Tennessee, and in this institution he was graduated as a member of the class of 1893, with the well earned degree of Doctor of Medicine. His progressiveness in the line of his profession has been manifested in the insistent care he has taken to keep at all times in touch with the advances made in medical and surgical science, and in this connection it should be noted that in 1895 he completed a post-graduate course in the New Orleans Polyclinic, and that in 1904 and 1907 he took effective post-graduate courses in the Illinois Post Graduate Medical School, in the City of Chicago.

From 1893 until 1897 Doctor Jeter was engaged in the practice of his profession in Ellis County, Texas, and from the latter year until 1902 he practiced successfully at Plano, Collin County, that state. In April, 1902, he established his residence at Foss, Oklahoma, where he has since continued his able and unremitting service as a physician and surgeon, with well appointed offices in the Temple Building. He has been one of the loyal and progressive citizens who have contributed to the development and upbuilding of the village along both civic and material lines and he is known and honored as one of the pioneer representatives of his profession in Washita County, his circle of friends being coincident with that of his acquaintances. He has served as village health officer, and he is actively identified with the Washita County Medical Society, the Oklahoma State Medical Society and the Southwestern Medical Society. The Doctor is affiliated with Foss Lodge No. 204, Ancient Free and Accepted Masons, and also with the local lodge of the Knights of Pythias. At Clinton, Custer County, he is the owner of a modern business building, known as the Jeter Building, and in addition to the ownership of his attractive residence property in the western part of Foss he has in his possession a small tract of valuable land near the village. His political allegiance is given unreservedly to the democratic party, and both he and his wife hold membership in the Missionary Baptist Church.

At Allen, Texas, in 1901, was solemnized the marriage of Doctor Jeter to Miss Anna Spradley, daughter of James R. Spradley, who still maintains his home at that place and who is a retired farmer and stockman. Doctor and Mrs. Jeter have one child, James Rolater, born July 3, 1908.

J. S. MAYTUBBY. Few men of the Chickasaw country have had a more picturesque career than J. S. Maytubby, now a farmer-stockman at Wapanucka, but a lawyer by profession, long closely identified with the affairs of the old Chickasaw Nation. Common sense was a usual trait among members of the old Chickasaw Legislature, and oratory is an attribute of the Indian tribe that has been manifested in nearly every family that rose to distinction. But as a rule the leading men were lacking in an English education and many of them were unable to correctly frame bills introduced into the Legislature. It became necessary therefore that the governor select a draftsman for that important duty of framing bills. During an administration of Governor Johnston, Mr. Maytubby was selected for this important post. He was especially qualified for the work, having been educated in the Rock Academy at Wapanucka, Trinity College at Durham, North Carolina, and completed a course in law at the University of Texas. He was assisted by a law committee of the Legislature in the preparation of bills and all measures before introduction had to pass through his hands and the hands of the law committee. This, however, was not the first official distinction of Mr. Maytubby in the Chickasaw Nation, since he filled it after the fortunes of politics has caused his resignation from the office of superintendent of public instruction, which he filled under the administration of Governor S. H. Harris, and after he had served under Governor D. H. Johnston, the successor of Governor Harris, as auditor of public accounts of the Chickasaw Nation.

Mr. Maytubby was born of a fullblood father, Tony Maytubby, and a white mother, Mary Lamb, in what was then Kiamichi County of the Choctaw Nation, in the Village of Goodland on the site of which the present Town of Hugo stands. Both parents died when he was a small child, and he has no recollection of them, neither does he know the year of his birth, but estimates his age as about forty-five. Cast out into the world an orphan, he was taken in charge by officials of the Chickasaw Nation and sent to school at Caddo, Indian Territory, in an educational institution owned and controlled by the Chickasaw Nation. Later he attended Rock Academy, subsequently known as Wapanucka Institute, and while there was a student under Cicero A. Skeen, who is now superintendent of the State Boys Training School at Pauls Valley. In 1892 Mr. Maytubby entered the Trinity College of Durham, North

Carolina, where he was graduated Ph. B. in 1896. In the same fall he entered the University of Texas, and completed his law education there. His career as a practicing lawyer covers less than ten years. In 1897 he began practice at Tishomingo in partnership with S. L. Garrett. Mr. Garrett, who was a first cousin of United States Senator Charles A. Culberson of Texas, was United States Commissioner at Tishomingo during the administration of President Cleveland. Later he became a member of the firm of Wolf, Bleakmore & Maytubby, his partners being Nick Wolf and Willard Bleakmore, the latter now a member of the Oklahoma Supreme Court Commission. In 1905 Mr. Maytubby retired from the practice of law and moved to his farm near Wapanucka, where he has since enjoyed the various interests of country life and has been very successful in the raising of fine horses and in the intensive cultivation of his land.

Mr. Maytubby is a nephew of the noted Peter Maytubby who was a captain in the Confederate army, and who during the days of the Dawes Commission represented the Chickasaw Nation before that body, and subsequently served as an interpreter before the commission. Peter Maytubby was one of the best informed men of the Chickasaw country, and assisted the United States Government in keeping out fraudulent claimants when the first annuity was paid to these Indians. The instruction of Peter Maytubby was a means of giving his nephew a knowledge of many things regarding the history and traditions of the Indians, but the latter owing to the fact that his education was obtained in schools where only English was spoken never learned to speak the tongue of his father.

In 1903 Mr. Maytubby married Miss Theodoshia Kemp of Tishomingo. They have one son, Joel Kemp, now five years of age. Mr. Maytubby has also one sister, Mrs. Mary Correll, wife of a farmer-stockman at Ada, Oklahoma. Mr. Maytubby is a member of the Methodist Church, belongs to the Johnston County Bar Association, is a republican in politics, and has been a leader in public affairs. He has the distinction of having been elected to first mayor of Tishomingo, and his election is the more interesting on account of the fact that he defeated William H. Murray, who was his rival for the office. Mr. Murray is now a member of Congress from Oklahoma. Mr. Maytubby has served as precinct committeeman, as a member of the finance committee of the state organization, and also as a member of the Congressional Committee.

PETER B. FRANCE. Twenty years or more ago Peter B. France was driving over the sparsely settled country of Eastern Oklahoma selling shoes to the retail merchants. For many years prior to that he had been a successful merchant and business man in Missouri. After a time he and James C. Menifee established the second mercantile house in Sapulpa.

His many friends and business associates credit Mr. France with a great deal of the constructive enterprise which has made Sapulpa one of the leading towns of Eastern Oklahoma. It is said that he has erected more buildings and owned more real estate than any other one individual in the city, and in fact has always been a leader in everything that affects the welfare of the community. Few men arrive at the age of three score and ten with so much constructive accomplishment to their credit as Mr. France.

He was born at Sodus in Wayne County, New York, April 5, 1844, a son of John and Elizabeth (Bayze) France. His father was born in Yorkshire, England, and his mother in Lincolnshire, where both were reared and married. His father was a mechanic in the cotton mills in England until he came to the United States, and he also worked at his trade in Wayne County, New York, but finally bought a farm and followed agriculture until he retired. After the death of his wife and after some of his children had gone to Missouri he joined them there, and died there at the age of fifty-nine. He was first a whig and afterwards a republican, but was more interested in church affairs than in politics, being a member of the Methodist denomination. His wife died in New York at the age of forty-two, and she was also a Methodist. There were six children. Thomas B., a Methodist minister, is now living retired at Long Beach, California. John H., who died at Grant City, Missouri, at the age of forty-two, was a Union soldier in the One Hundred and Sixtieth New York Volunteers, was wounded at Port Hudson and was an officer in the Veteran Reserve until the close of the war. In 1866 he established his business enterprise at Grant City, Missouri, was in the furniture trade, and six months later was joined by his younger brother Peter, and after a few years they established a partnership in the merchandise business, and also in the buying and shipping of stock. The third child in the family is Peter B. France. The daughter Mary, who married Dr. J. H. Housser, died at the age of twenty-two. Fannie after her sister's death married Dr. J. H. Housser and she died at the age of thirty-two. Anna C. married J. T. Rothwell, and she is now living at Long Beach, California.

Peter B. France grew up on the old farm in Wayne County, New York, and gained a public school education. In 1866, at the age of twenty-two, he moved out to Grant City, Missouri, and joined his brother John. Grant City at that time was sixty-five miles from the nearest railroad point at St. Joseph. For about two years he was associated with a physician in the drug business and then opened a stock of general merchandise. After about four years his brother John joined him as a partner, and the latter exercised his energies in buying and shipping live stock, while Peter France managed the store. In that comparatively early day there were no banks, and the patrons of their store not only bought goods there but left all their surplus currency for safe keeping. Both brothers were men of absolute integrity and thorough business men in every respect. Consequently their enterprise prospered and was expanded by the addition of four other stores, two located in Iowa and three in Missouri. Mr. Peter France had active supervision of all the stores, and the partners also bought and shipped stock on an extensive scale. After the death of his brother Peter France abandoned the live stock business and in 1888 sold out his mercantile interests in Northwest Missouri, realizing over $50,000. He had loaned money extensively and had done much to build up that section of the country.

In 1888 he moved to Southern Missouri and engaged in merchandising, mining and the reduction of lead and zinc, with headquarters at Aurora. Closing out his business affairs in 1893, he went on the road selling shoes in Missouri, Oklahoma and Indian Territory. It was then that he drove so extensively over Oklahoma and became acquainted with the country. He had a wagon and team and a driver, and sometimes they camped out under the wagon at night. He was very successful as a salesman, and finally established a permanent business at Claremore, but a year later moved his stock to Sapulpa and formed the partnership already mentioned with J. C. Menifee. They conducted this second store for about three years. Mr. France then bought ten acres in what is now the residence part of Sapulpa, dissolved partnership with Mr. Menifee, and began the development, buy-

ing and trading of real estate. He has been the chief factor in building up the real estate interests of Sapulpa, and at the present time is reputed to own property worth fully $100,000. He also built the France Hotel at Sapulpa.

In 1872 Mr. France married Anna V. Lucas, a daughter of Judge B. F. Lucas, a prominent attorney of Pittsburg, Pennsylvania, where Mrs. France was reared and educated and where she lived until her marriage. Mrs. France was a woman of many domestic virtues and much social talent, and founded the chapter of the Eastern Star at Sapulpa, and was also active in church affairs. Her death occurred December 2, 1912. There were three children: Bessie, Alberta and Fannie. The daughter Bessie married V. R. Bryan, and left four children named Curtis, France, Hazel and Vaughn, Jr. Alberta, who died when about twenty-five years of age, as the wife of John Gregory, left one daughter Margaret. Fannie E. is the wife of W. J. Briscoe, a Sapulpa merchant, and has one son named Jackson France Briscoe.

Mr. France has always voted the republican ticket but has had no aspirations for public office, though in his private capacity and as a business man has done a great deal for the public welfare. While living in Grant City, Missouri, he took his degrees in Odd Fellowship and helped organize the lodge of Odd Fellows at Sapulpa. He is active in the Methodist Episcopal Church, as was his wife.

RUFUS R. SEAY. The present editor and proprietor of the Oklahoma Ledger at Sterling has had a long and varied career in the states of Oklahoma and Texas, was one of the early settlers in Pottawatomie County, Oklahoma, more than twenty years ago, and has at different times been a farmer, rancher, preacher and editor. He is one of the strong men of his community, and conducts his paper for the enlightenment of the community.

Born in Van Zandt County, Texas, November 25, 1857, he comes of an old North Carolina family, which was transplanted from Ireland in the early days by his great-grandfather, Austin Seay, who spent the rest of his days in North Carolina. Richard Anderson Seay, father of Rufus R., was born in North Carolina in 1823, went to Georgia in 1827, and in 1849 became one of the pioneers in Anderson County, Texas. In 1851 he removed to Van Zandt County, where he owned an extensive farm, partly in that county and partly across the line in Henderson County, and in 1866 in removing his home from one part of the farm to the other, became a resident of Henderson County. He finally removed to Kaufman County, Texas, in 1897, and died there in 1898. He was a fine type of the early farmer and stock man who developed the resources of those East-central Texas counties. He was a member of the Methodist Episcopal Church, of the Masonic fraternity, and during the war between the states gave several years of service to the Confederate side, serving first in the Sixth Texas Cavalry and later being transferred to other commands. Richard A. Seay married Molsey Ellen Delaney, who was born in Georgia in 1826 and died in Comanche County, Texas, in 1907. The first four of their children, John, Mary, James and Frances, are now deceased; Ann Eliza first married James Cavitt, a farmer, now deceased, and her present husband is John Steele, and they live in Western Texas on a farm; the sixth in age is Rufus R.; Richard Jefferson is a farmer and stockman in Motley County, Texas; Vernon Virginia has been lost track of by his family; Ida is the wife of Leslie Stallings, a grocer at Childress, Texas; Robert is a hotel proprietor in California; Thomas is a civil engineer with home near Marfa, Texas; and George W., the twelfth of the family, is a rancher in New Mexico.

Rufus R. Seay attained his early education in the country schools of Henderson County, Texas. The first eighteen years of his life were spent on his father's farm, following which he was employed at farming and ranching in Erath County, Texas, for a period of eighteen years, which brings his career down to 1893. In that year he moved to Oklahoma and became a resident of Pottawatomie County soon after it was opened to settlement. While there he was a farmer, and was also a minister of the Missionary Baptist Church, with which denomination he has long been identified, and in its ministry has performed a great amount of valuable service. In 1904 Mr. Seay removed to Cement in Caddo County, Oklahoma, and continued farming and preaching there and in that vicinity until August, 1913. At that date he acquired complete ownership of the Oklahoma Ledger at Sterling, the former proprietor having been W. R. Key. The Ledger was established in 1905, is conducted independent in politics, has a circulation in Comanche, Caddo, Grady and neighboring counties, and Mr. Seay has continued it as a wholesome and attractive journal furnishing a good news and advertising service to its patronage and locality. He has also recently purchased the Cement Courier, at Cement, Caddo County, Oklahoma, which he is publishing on the same principle as the Ledger, and which was established in 1902.

Mr. Seay is a democrat in politics, and while living in Pottawatomie County served as a member of the school board. He takes much interest in fraternal affairs and is a past master by service of Cement Lodge No. 297, Ancient Free and Accepted Masons; past grand chaplain of Oklahoma Ancient Free and Accepted Masons; a member of Chickasaw Chapter, Royal Arch Masons; is past grand of Cement Lodge No. 272, Independent Order of Odd Fellows; a member of Purity Lodge No. 113 of the Order of Rebekahs at Sterling; and Cement Camp No. 129 of the Woodmen of the World.

While living in Erath County, Texas, in 1874, Mr. Seay married Miss Dona Smith, who died in that county in 1883. There were three children by this marriage: John Anderson, who is a farmer in Bryan County, Oklahoma; Thomas Newton, a farmer near Gorman, Comanche County, Texas; and Henry Harrison, who died in infancy. In 1884 Mr. Seay was married in Erath County to Nancy Henderson, whose father was the late James Henderson, an Erath County farmer. The home of Mr. and Mrs. Seay has been blessed with the birth of ten children: Nancy Ellen, wife of George S. Bradley, a farmer in Seminole County, Oklahoma; James Richard, who is connected with a cement plant in Grady County, Oklahoma; Oscar Reagan, who lives in Cement; Effie, at home; Ethel, who performs the typing service for her father in the newspaper office; Alice, living at Cement; Lena, at home; Lea, a twin sister of Lena, died in infancy; William Arvel and George, who are still in the public schools at Sterling.

WALTER F. LEARD. Thirty years ago the Choctaw Indians enjoyed a leisure that was not enforced or restrained. It was of the same nature as that which had been the portion of their forefathers and which they believed they had been sent to the Indian Territory to enjoy continuously. It was not a perpetual leisure, for the Indians were fairly prosperous with their herds and with their little patches of maize and vegetables. They had not been contaminated by money, nor was the desire for money a hindrance to their social life. Missionaries had been among them and taught them the Christian religion, with the result that their communal interests advanced to a stage that their forebears had not known. Their idleness was an innate attribute and extravagances were unknown among them. Among their chief pastimes was Indian ball, a game peculiar to the Choctaws and Chickasaws. It was within this period that Walter Fitzgerald was born in the Indian Village of Pocola, County of Skulliville, Choctaw Nation, and his early recollections touch no happier scenes than those pertaining to witnessing and participating in the Indian ball games. He recalls one that took place between teams representing Skulliville and San Boise counties and which was one of the last of the great games between Choctaw counties. The game was played within a few hundred yards of the Leard home and it was attended by several hundred persons, some of whom came from points from forty to fifty miles distant. Elias Thomas, of a well known Choctaw family, was captain of the San Boise team, and Robert Chubby, a Methodist exhorter, was captain of the Skulliville team. J. W. LeFlore, a deputy United States marshal, of Choctaw blood, led the parade in which the Skulliville team indulged before the game began, but this advance exhibition, while it may have excited inspiration, was not sufficient to win the game, for the San Boise team carried away the honors. For a good many years there existed among the people of San Boise County an interesting and innocent feeling of superiority over their neighbors of Skulliville County.

While this incident illustrates, as forcibly as anything can, the pleasures of Choctaw life in that period, its recalling also brings to mind that it was about that time that the Indians experienced their first money contamination. Each member of the tribe was paid the sum of $103 out of the Choctaw funds in the hands of the United States Government. So large an amount of money had never before been in circulation in the Choctaw Nation. Unfortunately for the Indians, this distribution brought into their domain many white men of questionable character and motives. Some of these men brought spirituous and intoxicating liquors, knowing the weakness of the Indian for strong drink, and others came for the purpose of getting hold of as much as possible of the large sums of money which the Indians had received. There are men in the Choctaw Nation who have lived there forty to fifty years and who declare that the retrogression of the Choctaws began with that period. Young bucks bought ponies and saddles, bright blankets, hickory-bark bridles, Winchester rifles and other types of firearms. They decorated their horses and saddles with vividly colored ribbons and rode promiscuously over the wide ranges. They imbibed freely of "bootleg" liquors and many of them became intoxicated for the first time. Their sprees lasted for several days and made beasts of them for the time being.

That these two extremes of life among his people should come within the early recollections of Walter F. Leard is a striking point in Choctaw annals, for he is only of thirty-second degree Choctaw blood and has an unprejudiced comprehension of Indian affairs. His father, James Thomas Leard, had settled in Skulliville County when a youth and had there married Cora McCarty, of the Choctaw tribe. Mrs. Leard is a daughter of Robert S. McCarty, who was a native of Georgia and a pioneer in Texas. At the time of the Mexican troubles in Texas Mr. McCarty came into the Indian Territory, where for several months he was quartered with the United States soldiers at old Fort Towson, one of the early frontier posts. Continuing his residence in the Choctaw Nation for many years, Mr. McCarty was for twenty-seven consecutive years a Sunday school superintendent at Kavanaugh, across the line in the State of Arkansas.

Walter F. Leard was born in the year 1882, and his rudimentary educational training was received in the Pine Log School, on Owl Creek, where his first teacher was Mr. Sinclair, who later became a physician and engaged in the practice of his profession in the Choctaw Nation. Mr. Leard continued to attend the local schools until he had attained to the age of eighteen years, after which he was for one year a student in Spencer Academy. He then entered Jones Academy, under the administration of Superintendent W. B. Butts, who had previously been his instructor in Spencer Academy, though the principal teacher had been Spencer Gabe Parker, who is now commissioner to the Five Civilized Tribes. In Jones Academy Mr. Leard was a schoolmate of W. F. Semple, now an Indian probate attorney under the Department of the Interior, with headquarters at Durant, Bryan County; W. R. McIntosh, now of McAlester, who was mining trustee of the Choctaw Nation under the administration of Principal Chief V. M. Locke, Jr.; and others who have become representative men in business and professional life. After leaving Jones Academy Mr. Leard assumed a position in the office of John D. Benedict, superintendent of education for the Five Civilized Tribes, and there he remained three years. In 1908 he engaged in farming near Durant, where he continued operations one year. In 1909 he entered the employ of the Caylor Lumber Company, and in 1913 he was transferred to the new and thriving Town of Fort Towson, where he has since continued his effective service as manager of the company's extensive business in this section of Choctaw County and where he is a popular and representative factor in business circles and known as a loyal and progressive citizen. He is affiliated with the Masonic fraternity and the Woodmen of the World, and both he and his wife hold membership in the Baptist Church. Mr. Leard's parents are still living and their other children are: Joseph N., who is engaged in the lumber business at San Jose, Texas; Andrew J., who is a prosperous agriculturist and stock grower at McCurtain, Haskell County, Oklahoma; Robert R. and Terry T., who are representative farmers near Hugo, Choctaw County; Mrs. Helen Davis, whose husband is a prominent business man at Stigler, Haskell County; and Miss Laura and Wheeler R. Leard, who remain at the parental home, in Hugo, the judicial center of Choctaw County.

In May, 1907, was solemnized the marriage of Walter F. Leard to Miss Winena Ross, of Durant, her father having been one of the early missionaries among the Choctaw Indians. Mr. and Mrs. Leard are popular factors in the social activities of their home community and are the parents of one son, Ross, who was born in the year 1908.

ELMER HAROLD DODD. The receiving and disbursing of all the public moneys and revenues of a county entails the possession of executive ability of more than ordinary character by the incumbent of the office, but, further than this, he must possess also the absolute confidence of the public, the faith in his integrity and character that may be built up only through a life of probity and honorable dealing. Elmer Harold Dodd, treasurer of Dewey County, has gained his office through the possession of the qualities named. It has been his fortune to have succeeded in public life as he has in business affairs; in each avenue of endeavors his name has been synonymous with straightforward transactions with his fellow men and energetic and well-directed effort.

Mr. Dodd is a Kansan by nativity, born at Burrton,

Harvey County, August 7, 1883, a son of Charles D. and Lucy E. (Lancett) Dodd. His family is an old and honored one, of Scotch-Irish descent, which was founded in America in colonial times and subsequently moved to Indiana, where the great-grandfather of Elmer H. Dodd was a pioneer settler and for many years a farmer. Joseph Dodd, his grandfather, was born in 1826, in Indiana, and there grew to manhood, receiving a common school education and early learning the trade of carpenter. He followed this vocation, in connection with farming, until the opening of the Civil war, when he enlisted in an Indiana volunteer infantry regiment and served therewith four years as a private in the Union army. Returning to Indiana, he continued to be occupied in the same way for several years, when he decided to try his fortunes in the West and accordingly moved to Harvey County, Kansas. He located there on a farm, to the cultivation of which he devoted his attention, although he was engaged also at times as a carpenter, erecting a number of the early structures of that community. His death occurred there in 1914.

Charles D. Dodd was born in Indiana in 1858 and was still a youth when he accompanied his parents to Harvey County, Kansas, where he completed his education, grew up as a farmer boy, and was married. At the time of his marriage, he turned his attention to mercantile lines, establishing himself in the retail furniture business, as a merchant at Burrton. In 1890 he removed to Hutchinson, Kansas, where he became foreman in the salt works, and in 1895 became a pioneer of Dewey County, Oklahoma, where he took up a homestead of 160 acres in Sickle township, a beautiful tract of land which he still owns. When he came to Oklahoma he had practically nothing, his business ventures not having met with a very gratifying success up to that time, but in the field of agriculture he soon began to accumulate a handsome property, and at this time is the owner of 700 acres of land in Dewey and Roger Mills counties. This land is practically all under a state of cultivation and is improved with substantial buildings and modern equipment of all kinds. In 1903 Mr. Dodd again entered the mercantile business, starting a furniture establishment at Thomas, Oklahoma. This he conducted until 1914, when he sold out and came to Roll, his present home. Mr. Dodd bears an excellent reputation in business circles and as a citizen has shown himself capable, energetic and public-spirited. He maintains an independent position in regard to politics, is a devout member of the Methodist Episcopal Church, and is fraternally connected with the Masons. Mr. Dodd was married in Harvey County, Kansas, to Miss Lucy E. Lancett, who was born in 1863, in Indiana, and who is also a member of the Methodist Episcopal Church and active in its work. They have been the parents of six children, as follows: William C., who is engaged in the life insurance business at Thomas, Oklahoma; Elmer Harold, of this notice; Roy, who resides at Oakwood, Oklahoma, and is the proprietor of a hardware business; Ray, twin to Roy, who is a chiropractitioner of Elk City, Oklahoma; Charles, Jr., who resides at Canton, Oklahoma, and is a general merchant; and Bertha, who is the wife of G. W. Ford and resides on the old family homestead farm in Dewey County.

Elmer Harold Dodd attended the public schools of Hutchinson, Kansas, and went to school at Burrton, Kansas, in 1895-6, in April of the latter year coming to his parents' homestead in Dewey County, Oklahoma. There he continued to pursue his studies in the little log school house until he was sixteen years of age, and then, until he was nineteen, devoted his energies to assisting his father in the cultivation and development of the home place. Mr. Dodd was married in 1903, at Kingfisher, Oklahoma, to Miss Grace M. Thrush, daughter of Charles B. Thrush, a pioneer homesteader of Dewey County, Oklahoma, who now resides on his farm near Putnam. Three children have been born to Mr. and Mrs. Dodd: Cecil, born November 16, 1903; Vera, born August 16, 1905; and Carroll, born in November, 1907, all attending the Taloga public schools.

For one year after his marriage, Mr. Dodd continued to be engaged in farming, then turning his attention to railroading. Nine months, in 1905 and 1906, convinced him that he did not care for a career as a railroad man, and he accordingly resigned his position and accepted a clerkship in the grocery store of Ogden Brothers, at Thomas. Later he went to Oakwood, Oklahoma, where he was employed in the general store of E. L. Porter, former county treasurer of Dewey, and in 1908 became manager of Burt Groves' general store. After two years he was made head salesman for Mr. Groves, in the store at Canton, but after one year, in 1911, returned to the pursuits of the soil, being engaged in farming in Harrison Township, Dewey County, for one year. He then resumed his connection with mercantile affairs, being with Keller's Hardware Store at Oakwood for a short time and then again with E. L. Porter, at Oakwood, and in August, 1912, purchased Mr. Porter's interest in the establishment and continued to be engaged in the mercantile business on his own account until selling out in June, 1914. In the fall of that year he was elected county treasurer and assumed charge of the duties of that office July 1, 1915, for a period of two years. A republican in his political views, for a number of years he has been interested in public affairs, having served both on the school board and as a member of the council at Oakwood. With his family he belongs to the Christian Church, where he is a chorister. Mr. Dodd is possessed of much musical talent, and was a member of the first band ever organized in Dewey County, at Butte, Oklahoma, playing at the various county fair in the early days under the leadership of his uncle, Andrew Lancett of Chicago, who now resides at Clinton, Oklahoma, and is a grain buyer. He belongs of the A. H. T. A., and is fraternally affiliated with Oakwood Lodge No. 386, Ancient Free and Accepted Masons, and Putnam Lodge No. 89, Independent Order of Odd Fellows, of which he is past vice grand.

ALVA LUM MCDONALD. Among the men who have lent practical encouragement to agricultural interests, and who have also taken an active part in business affairs and the struggles of the political arena, Alva Lum McDonald has been numbered since 1901. Coming here a stranger, he soon won the esteem and respect of all with whom his business brought him into contact, and from that time to the present his popularity has steadily increased. In addition to farming and stockraising, Mr. McDonald is extensively engaged in the real estate business at El Reno, and has been entrusted with important positions as one of the foremost members of the progressive party in Oklahoma.

A. L. McDonald was born at Curdsville, Daviess County, Kentucky, September 16, 1876, and is a son of Hiram C. and Sarah Catherine (Brogan) McDonald, the former a native of Curdsville, Kentucky, and the latter of the State of Tennessee. The great-grandfather of Mr. McDonald was the founder of the family in America, coming, as the name would suggest, from Scotland, and settling in Virginia. From this source this branch of the family scattered throughout Virginia and Kentucky, in which state the name is still well known. All of Mr. McDonald's male relatives, including his father, served as Confederate soldiers during the Civil war, some of them fighting throughout that struggle with Gen. Joe Wheeler.

The public schools of his native locality on Panther Creek furnished Alva L. McDonald with his early education, and this was subsequently supplemented by attendance at Hartford (Kentucky) College, from which he was graduated in the class of 1894. He no doubt inherited the military spirit which sent his father and others into battle, for when the Spanish-American war came on he offered his services to the volunteer army and was accepted. When that struggle was finished he took part in putting down the Filipino rebellion, and while thus engaged was under the brave General Wheeler, with whom members of the family had fought in the Civil war. He had at first been a member of the Seventh California Volunteers, but after a few months was transferred to the Thirty-first United States Volunteer Infantry, serving in Luzon and Mindanao Islands altogether for thirty-seven months. During the time he was at Mindanao he served ten months as military postmaster.

On his return from the Philippine Islands Mr. McDonald located at El Reno, Oklahoma, where he had drawn a farm at the opening of the Kiowa and Comanche drawing at El Reno in 1901. He resided on this property for two years, and then moved to the city of El Reno and entered actively into the real estate business, buying and selling farm lands principally on his own account.

In 1905 Mr. McDonald was elected a member of the El Reno City Council, and during his two years served as president of that body. During the administration of President Roosevelt, Mr. McDonald was clerk of the Third District Federal Court of Alaska, stationed at Fairbanks, for two years, under Judge Silas H. Reed. From the time that he had come to Oklahoma Mr. McDonald had always been an active republican and a dutiful worker for his party. In 1912 he was a delegate from this state to the Chicago convention, and when the break came, he joined the Roosevelt forces and returned home to do untiring work for the cause of the new progressive party. He was elected chairman of the state committee of the new organization, and prosecuted a vigorous campaign for his ideal candidate, the indomitable Colonel. He served as chairman of the state committee of the progressive party for two years, handing over to his successor the party organization in the state in the best possible shape attainable under the adverse circumstances under which he was compelled to work. These services cost Mr. McDonald many hundred hard-earned dollars.

At El Reno, Oklahoma, November 27 (Thanksgiving Day), 1903, Mr. McDonald was united in marriage with Miss Scottie Belle Barker, daughter of Beverly R. and Eliza (Eaton) Barker, both natives of Virginia. Mrs. McDonald's father and practically all her male relatives were Confederate soldiers during the Civil war. To Mr. and Mrs. McDonald there have been born two children: Vinita Mary, born February 16, 1905; and Alva Ferguson, born December 9, 1906. Mr. McDonald is a member of the local lodge of the Benevolent and Protective Order of Elks, in which he has numerous friends, as he has also in business and public life. Mr. and Mrs. McDonald are consistent members of and active workers in the First Christian Church of El Reno.

ORA O. DAWSON, M. D. Oklahoma is one of the youngest of the commonwealths of the Union and yet its age is sufficient to have enabled it to claim as representative figures in its business and professional ranks not a few ambitious young men who have been reared and educated within its borders. Such an one is Doctor Dawson, who is the only physician and surgeon engaged in practice at Wayne, McClain County, and who has gained secure prestige as one of the able and successful representatives of his profession in this section of the state.

Doctor Dawson is a scion of staunch Scotch ancestry and the family was founded in America in the colonial era of our national history. His grandfather, Thomas Benoni Dawson, was born in Virginia, in 1804, was a gallant soldier in the Mexican war, became one of the pioneer farmers and stock-growers of the State of Iowa, and passed the closing period of his life at Long Beach, California, where he died in 1905, at the remarkable age of somewhat more than 100 years. His ancestors settled in Virginia in an early day, upon their immigration from Scotland, and the name has been worthily linked with the annals of American history during the long intervening years, as one generation has followed another on to the stage of life's activities.

Doctor Dawson was born near Sherman, Texas, on the 26th of March, 1884, and has been a resident of Oklahoma since he was a lad of about eight years. He is a son of William and Lucretia (Moorman) Dawson, the former of whom was born in Iowa, in 1840, and the latter in Ohio, in 1845. William Dawson was reared to manhood in the Hawkeye State, where his early experiences were those gained under the conditions and influences of the early pioneer days. After his marriage he removed to Nebraska, later resided for a time in Kansas, and in 1881 he removed with his family to Grayson County, Texas, near Sherman, where he remained until 1892, when he came to Oklahoma Territory and established his residence at Guthrie. Since 1906 he has maintained his home in the vicinity of Wanette, Pottawatomie County, where he is a prosperous agriculturist and stock raiser. He is a republican in politics and is a veteran of the Civil war, in which he gave valiant service as a member of an Iowa regiment of volunteer infantry. He and his wife have an attractive home in the state of their adoption and are numbered among the sterling pioneer citizens of Oklahoma. Of their children Doctor Dawson of this review is the youngest; Thomas B. is a progressive farmer near Wanette; Ollie, who is deceased, was the wife of John Williams, who is still engaged in farming near Wanette; William W. is a successful agriculturist of the same locality; Charles T. is engaged in the lumber business at Luther, Oklahoma County; LeRoy is a farmer near Wanette; Lucy is the wife of William Van Meter, a farmer near the City of Guthrie; and John is another of the progressive agriculturists of Pottawatomie County.

The rudimentary education of Doctor Dawson was acquired in Texas and, as already noted, he was about eight years of age at the time of the family removal to Oklahoma, where he was enabled to continue his studies in the public schools of the City of Guthrie until he had completed a course in the high school, in which he was graduated in 1906. For a year thereafter he gave his attention to the buying of cotton and he finally entered the medical department of the University of Oklahoma, in which he was graduated as a member of the class of 1912 and from which he received his degree of Doctor of Medicine. He soon afterward established his residence at Wayne, where he has since continued in active general practice and where he has gained distinctive success, besides holding secure place in the confidence and esteem of the community and standing forth as a progressive and public-spirited citizen. The doctor is a member of the Oklahoma State Medical Society and the McClain County Medical Society and of two Greek letter fraternities, Beta Theta Pi and Phi Beta Pi. He is also a member of Wayne Lodge of the Independent Order of Odd Fellows. His political allegiance is given to the republican party, but he has no desire to enter the arena of practical politics, as he deems his profession worthy of his undivided attention. The doctor is still a bachelor.

DR. P. G. MURRAY. Six years ago Dr. P. G. Murray came to Thomas, Oklahoma, and engaged in medical practice. He has been here occupied in a professional way since that time. He came as a young physician, with some more than four years of actual practice behind him, but his record here has been highly creditable to him and to the medical fraternity. He is well established in Thomas and enjoys a pleasing popularity. Doctor Murray was born in Sedgewickville, Missouri, on March 9, 1880, and he is a son of H. J. Murray, born in Bollinger County, Missouri, in 1845. The senior Murray is now a resident of Thomas, having come here in the year 1913, after his retirement from his lifelong business as a farmer and stockman in his native county.

The Murray family is one that has long been established on American soil. It is of Scottish origin, and three brothers, Bennett, William and James, came together to these shores in early Colonial days, settling in North Carolina, where many of the name will be found today. The ancestor of the subject was Bennett Murray, and Doctor Murray has a brother named in his honor.

H. J. Murray was born and reared in Bollinger County, Missouri, and when the war broke out in 1861 he enlisted from his county, serving two years in the Union army. He was taken prisoner, but was exchanged after several months of prison life, and returned to his home to recuperate from the effects of that unfortunate experience. He married Sarah Dunlap, who was born in Perry County, Missouri, in 1849, and they became the parents of a large family of fourteen children, named as follows: Morris, now deceased; Bennett, a merchant, living in Independence, Oklahoma; James, a farmer and teacher, living near Thomas, Oklahoma; Charles, a farmer and teacher, living near Marquard, Missouri; the fifth child died in infancy; Anna married Robert Vance, and they live in Thomas, Oklahoma; Dr. P. G. was the seventh born; Travis lives in Pittsburg, Kansas; Ray, a farmer, lives in Thomas, Oklahoma; John died in infancy; Levi lives in Waurika, Oklahoma, and is a graduate of Barnes Medical College, now in practice in Waurika; Mary married Emil Mabuce, a farmer of Marquard, Missouri; David, a teacher, lives in Thomas with his father; Lew also lives at home.

Doctor Murray attended the public schools in Sedgewickville, Missouri, and he was graduated from the high school there in 1896. He then entered the Marvin Collegiate Institute, in Fredericktown, Missouri, and continued there for two years, after which he engaged in teaching, and for three years thereafter he was employed in the public schools in Bollinger County. In the spring of 1899 he went to Custer County, Oklahoma, where he taught school for a year, and in 1901 he entered Barnes Medical College in St. Louis, from which he was graduated in 1905 with the degree M. D. Since that time Doctor Murray has returned on several occasions for clinics and post-graduate work, supplementary to a very complete medical training, so that he is well equipped for the work he has chosen. Doctor Murray first began practice in Patton, Missouri, and he continued there in practice until April 4, 1909, when he took up his residence in Thomas, Oklahoma, and has here been located ever since, with offices in the B. & H. drug store.

Doctor Murray is a member of the county, state and American Medical societies, and aside from his regular practice he is examining physician for the Pacific Mutual, the Bankers Reserve, the Midland, the Oklahoma National, the Mid-Continent and the Merchants Life Insurance companies. He is also serving in the same capacity the Modern Woodmen of America, the Royal Neighbors and the Brotherhood of American Yeomen. He served the City of Patton in the office of health physician while practicing there, and has given the same service to Thomas. He is a republican. A member of the Methodist Church, Doctor Murray is serving that body as a steward and trustee. His fraternal affiliations are with the Modern Woodmen and the Yeomen, and he is an alumnus of Barnes Medical College. He is a member of the Thomas Chamber of Commerce, and has taken an active part in municipal affairs since identifying himself with the community.

On July 27, 1905, Doctor Murray was married in Yount, Missouri, to Miss Ellen Heitman, daughter of William Heitman, a prominent miller and farmer of Yount. They have two children: David William, born May 8, 1906, and Mary Jane, born August 24, 1907.

THOMAS J. PALMER. Of those who pioneered into the Strip country of Oklahoma in 1893, it is doubtful if there has been a more energetic and influential and useful citizen than Thomas J. Palmer, whose local work has identified him particularly with the Town of Medford in Grant County, but whose influence in politics, in the prohibition movement, and in all movements for uplift and betterment, has helped to make the texture of Oklahoma life what it is today.

It will be recalled that the famous run at the opening of the Cherokee Strip was made on Saturday. On the following Tuesday, September 19th, Thomas J. Palmer arrived from Hutchinson, Kansas. He had since 1887 lived in Kansas, chiefly at Meade. He has had a long and versatile career. For a number of years he lived in Iowa, and went from Mason City in that state to Kansas. During the twenty-two years of his Iowa residence he was a school teacher for six years and the rest of his time an active newspaper man. While it would be impossible to classify Mr. Palmer by any one vocation or line of activity in Medford, he has longest been identified with the newspaper profession in this and other states.

Thomas J. Palmer was born at Port Perry, Canada, February 6, 1847. While both he and his father were natives of Canada, earlier ancestors were from the United States. His great-grandfather was Ebenezer Palmer, said to be a direct descendant of one of the Mayflower Pilgrims of the Plymouth Colony. Ebenezer Palmer seems to have been a frontiersman, and spent much of his life in the then Far West. Stephen Palmer, grandfather of the Oklahoma citizen, was a native of Pennsylvania and went from that state to Canada, where he did some pioneering on his own account in the Canadian woods. Stephen Palmer married Abigail Jones, who was of German descent. Their children were David, Thomas, Henry, Joseph, Elizabeth and Amanda.

Thomas Palmer, father of Thomas J., was also a native of Canada, was a shoemaker by trade, spent his life in that vocation and in the cooperage business. He alone among all the children of Stephen Palmer came to the United States. He located in Iowa, where he farmed and conducted a store, and his death occurred at Whatcheer, Iowa. It was in 1865 that he brought his family to the United States. He was an Adventist in religion and a member of the sect known as "Millerites." Thomas Palmer married Catherine McVay. She also died and is buried at Whatcheer, Iowa. She was a native of Canada, and had in her veins the blood of Irish, German and Scotch, while her husband was both

English and German, so that their children possessed an unusual mingling of those substantial ancestral stocks which have had most to do with the settlement and development of the New World. Thomas and Catherine Palmer were the parents of the following children: Daniel D., who is noted as the founder and originator of the science of chiropractic, and he founded a school for the propagation of the art at Davenport, Iowa, though he died in Los Angeles, California, October 20, 1914, leaving a family of three children: Thomas J. Palmer is the second in age; Lucinda is married and lives at Plattsmouth, Nebraska; Jennie is the wife of H. G. Palmer of Tacoma, Washington; Bartlett D. died at Whatcheer, Iowa; Mrs. Katie Wiles lives in Plattsmouth, Nebraska.

Thomas J. Palmer at the age of five years started to attend school in Canada, and until nearly nine years his only teacher was a man named John Black. He made rapid advance in his studies, and before he was ten years of age was carrying high school work, including the sciences. The health of his father and other causes then kept him out of school for several years, but he finally had another nine months of instruction just before he became a teacher. He was eighteen when he took the Goose Creek School in his home county in Iowa. He had been promised the school by a board of directors before he interviewed them, his qualifications having been introduced to the board by a lawyer friend. He was promised the school on condition that he secured a third grade certificate. He agreed to try for the certificate and rode horseback to the county seat and passed the ordeal of examination in four hours. So well did he acquit himself that he was almost granted a first grade certificate. His clothes were ragged, his trouser linings showed at the knees and coat linings at the elbows, and he might well have been an object of curiosity to all eyes. His exceedingly creditable showing in the examination was the surprise of the superintendent in charge as well as of the board where he taught. He was accepted as the new teacher after an overnight session with one of the board, who "tried him out" and advanced him ten dollars for a new suit of clothes. To put himself in the good graces of the larger boys of the school he spent a week before the opening attending spelling schools and literary societies, and took the lead in all matters in which the senior boys would be interested. In consequence he was "passed" by these larger scholars and endorsed by them in a public motion while on the road home from one of the spelling bees. The fact that Mr. Palmer entered so earnestly and enthusiastically into his task make it hardly necessary to state that he was a very successful teacher. He had the aid of his influential pupils and the patrons of the district, and showed much originality as a teacher. He attracted more than local attention to the various new methods he instituted for arousing interest in the pupils in the various subjects studied. For six years he was a teacher in Iowa and for a similar period in Mercer County, Illinois. While in the latter state he was for three years president of the Mercer County Teachers' Association. While there he explained his plan of teaching spelling to the advanced pupils, and his demonstration so interested President Edwards of the Illinois State University that the latter subsequently prepared and published upon the lines suggested by Mr. Palmer the school text book known as Edwards' Analytical Speller. Mr. Palmer did his last work in the school room in Hardin County, Iowa, just before entering the newspaper field.

Soon after coming from Canada to the United States Mr. Palmer took out his naturalization papers. His first political attitude was that of the independent. Subsequently he became a granger, when that movement was at its height and from that took up the cause of the greenback party. When the republican party adopted the principal planks of the greenback party he united with the older and larger organization. He became a republican also for the reason that the Iowa republicans took up the prohibition movement in the state and directed its influence to the suppression of the liquor traffic. The main policies of the old greenback party were the remonetization of silver, the reissue of greenbacks and the adoption of prohibition. All these principles Mr. Palmer espoused, and when they were adopted by the republican organization he found no difficulty in effecting a partisan change. Mr. Palmer was a personal friend of the late General J. B. Weaver, the eminent Iowa statesman, and has been a close student and observer of political progress in the Middle West for fully forty years.

A number of years ago while living in Iowa Mr. Palmer, in order to express his convictions on some of the burning questions of the hour, prepared an article on some phase of the financial problems and asked a local newspaper to publish it. The request was refused, and Mr. Palmer then determined to have the article expressing his views given to the public if he had to found a newspaper himself. Thus it was that he entered the field where his abilities have given him much prominence in later years. He first took up newspaper work in Greenfield, Iowa, where he founded the Greenback Patriot. His capital when he entered this business was sixty cents, and he walked from the railroad station to Greenfield, which was then without a railroad, because he did not have enough money to hire a conveyance. He had ordered a plant and equipment costing fourteen hundred dollars from the Illinois Type Foundry Company of Chicago, and secured the services of a practical printer to install the new plant. He soon afterwards became the sole proprietor and for some time made his paper a noted organ for greenback doctrines. Later he moved his paper to Muscatine, where he renamed it the Muscatine Patriot and subsequently it was taken to Whatcheer and there was called the Whatcheer Patriot. The policy of the Whatcheer Patriot was largely independent in political matters, but proved a strenuous advocate for the suppression of the liquor traffic. In the face of violent contrary public sentiment, the Patriot led the way and was one of the chief factors in abolishing the thirty-two saloons of Whatcheer. Some of the doctrines which Mr. Palmer espoused in earlier days have already been worked into the general political and social policy of the country, and for others there have been substituted different policies. But prohibition is still a vital question, perhaps more so taking the nation at large than ever before, and hardly anyone could claim to have worked more devotedly for its success during the last thirty years than this Oklahoma man. He early saw that the success of prohibition would be most definitely advanced whenever either of the two larger political parties should endorse the policy. When the republicans in his section of Iowa wrote a prohibition plank into the platform he joined that party, and he made his aid count for a great deal in the results which subsequently brought about the adoption of a local option amendment to the state constitution.

In 1886, having sold his paper and other interests at Whatcheer Mr. Palmer went to Mason City, bought the Republican there, consolidated it with the Express, sold a half interest, and after making considerable profit in the enterprise disposed of his business and went to Meade Center, Kansas. He arrived in that town during the midst of its boom, and left it when the financial crisis came on in 1892. While at Meade Center he conducted the Meade Republican, which he founded and which he published for six years as a republican organ. In 1893 he moved the plant to Hutchinson and for a few months published a daily paper espousing the policies of the republican party and showing an unmitigated enmity to the saloons.

When in September, 1893, the Cherokee Strip was opened for settlement, Mr. Palmer moved his newspaper plant to Medford, and there founded the Medford Patriot. Medford at that time was a town only in name. The depot and small grocery were the meager nucleus of business. He at once erected a building, and soon published the first copy of the oldest paper now in Grant County. Grant County was then called "L" County. He had hardly been here a week before he was using his influence in behalf of political organization and for the extension of his policies in line with the republican party and as a prohibitionist. He soon met some of his old acquaintances from Iowa and Kansas, and he was one of the leaders in moulding republican sentiment and shaping the affairs of the locality. In a county republican convention he suggested the name of Grant for the new county. Up to that time some of the letters of the alphabet had been used to designate the civil divisions in the Cherokee Country. In February, 1898, Mr. Palmer was made postmaster of the Town of Medford. He filled that office for more than eleven years, having succeeded D. L. Cline in the office. While postmaster he was appointed by Judge Burford as United States Court Commissioner. He performed the duties of that office without a bond for five years, and in that time thousands of dollars of public money passed through his hands, and there was never a flaw in his records.

At the incorporation of Medford he was inspector and turned the town to the first officers chosen by ballot without a dollar of indebtedness. For four years he was president of the Board of Education, from the time of the organization of the district. While he was in that office there was not a warrant presented to the school treasurer and endorsed "not paid for want of funds." In every line of advancement in Medford he and his paper, The Patriot, were always in the front leading the way. In a material way he has contributed substantially to the town in the Opera House and a brick store building. For several years he was postmaster, court commissioner, manager of the Opera House and editor of the Patriot all at one time, and probably the busiest and hardest working citizen of Medford.

Soon after coming to Oklahoma Mr. Palmer began attending the state republican conventions and has done much to direct that party in its state campaign. He is personally acquainted with all the men who have served Oklahoma in the time of its greatest development, and from the first issue of his paper to the last he was an unswerving and determined enemy and opponent of the liquor traffic. On March 1, 1910, he sold the Patriot and has since been in the ranks as a private citizen, though his interest in public affairs is in no wise abated. He hopes to live to see national prohibition, but in any case he realizes that such a condition cannot be many years away. Considering the opportunities that surrounded his own early youth Mr. Palmer has had a really remarkable career. From the first he had high moral standards and ideals, and in following them he has probably accomplished work of greatest benefit. As a boy he spent his money for books instead of for tobacco and other pleasures, although at a later date he tried tobacco for three months, only to his disgust.

On April 4, 1871, at Port Perry, Canada, he married Miss Sarah Lazier, daughter of James B. and Hannah (Orser) Lazier. Mrs. Palmer was one of a family of seven children. Three children have been born to their union: May is the wife of George E. Honey, local agent for the Santa Fe Railway at Kingman, Kansas. Clyde N. is a printer at LaGrande, Oregon, and married Miss Rena Aikens. Cora is now Mrs. F. C. Wright of Wakita, Oklahoma. Mrs. Wright was educated in music, graduating from the famous musical college at Lindsborg, Kansas, took private instruction for six years with Ella Bachus Behr of Kansas City, spent two years abroad in Berlin, and another year in New York City. She also taught a year in Wichita College of Music, while pursuing her studies, and after her education was finished she continued as an instructor and leader in musical affairs until her marriage.

MONT Z. SPAHR. In both the paternal and maternal lines Mont Zartman Spahr is a scion of families that were founded in America prior to the war of the Revolution, the lineage of the Spahr family tracing back to sterling Holland Dutch origin and the progenitors of the American branch having left Holland at the time of the religious reformatory movement in that country in the seventeenth century and upon coming to America having settled in the Virginia colony, the maternal ancestors of Mr. Spahr having settled in Pennsylvania about the same time. Edward Spahr, grandfather of him whose name introduces this paragraph, was born in the beautiful Shenandoah Valley of Virginia, in 1778, and he became one of the pioneer settlers in Greene County, Ohio, where he reclaimed and developed a farm and where he continued to reside until his death, which occurred in 1861.

Since 1908 Mr. Spahr has been one of the successful and popular representatives of the pedagogic profession in Oklahoma, and his zeal and ambition are based on thorough academic or literary training, the while his marked ability as an executive has tended greatly to conserve his success in the vocation which he has followed for virtually a quarter of a century. He is now the incumbent of the position of superintendent of the public schools of the village of Foss, Washita County, and has brought the same up to high standard, the while he has personally gained secure vantage-ground as one of the representative figures in educational circles in this section of the state.

Mr. Spahr was born in Greene County, Ohio, on the 5th of November, 1866, and is a son of John E. and Adelia (Zartman) Spahr, the former of whom was likewise a native of Greene County, Ohio, where he was born in 1832, and the latter of whom was born in Pennsylvania, in 1834. Both passed the closing years of their lives in Wayne County, Nebraska, where the mother passed to eternal rest in 1904 and the father in 1909. Of their children the eldest is Frank, who is a prosperous farmer in Wayne County, Nebraska; Annie died in that county, at the age of twenty-six years, she having been the wife of Ora Newton, who is now a merchant in the City of Pasadena, California; Charles is engaged in the live-stock business in Phillips County, Kansas; Mont Z., of this review, was the next child; Wilbur is a retired farmer residing in Wayne County, Nebraska, where Harvey, the next in order of birth, is a progressive and successful agriculturist; and Maude is the wife of Henry W. Perkins, a successful contractor residing at Loveland, California.

John E. Spahr was reared and educated in Greene County, Ohio, where his early experiences were those gained in connection with the work of the home farm. After his marriage he continued his activities as a farmer in his native county until 1876, when he removed with his family to Shelby County, Iowa, in which section of the Hawkeye State he remained until 1881, when he removed to Wayne County, Nebraska, where he purchased a tract of land and where he became a prosperous agriculturist and stock-grower, both he and his wife having there passed the residue of their lives and both having been zealous members of the Methodist Episcopal Church, in which he served for a long period in the office of steward. At the time of the Civil war Mr. Spahr was enrolled as a member of the state militia, or home guard, of Ohio, circumstances having made it impossible for him to go to the front in defense of the cause of the Union, though he did all in his power to further and uphold that cause and to aid the needy families of soldiers. He was a stalwart advocate of the principles of the republican party and his mature judgment and well fortified opinions were such as to equip him well for the prominent part which he took in political and other public affairs in the various communities in which he lived at different stages in his active and useful life.

Mont Z. Spahr was a lad of about ten years at the time of the family removal to Iowa, and the rudimentary education he had gained in the schools of his native county in the old Buckeye State was supplemented by his attending the schools of Iowa, the while he assisted materially in the work and management of the home farm. He remained at the parental home until he had attained to the age of nineteen years, and thereafter he provided the means through which he acquired his higher education and fitted himself for the profession in which he has achieved such distinctive success. In 1891 Mr. Spahr was graduated in the Western Iowa Normal College, at Shenandoah, from which he received the degree of Bachelor of Didactics, at the completion of a two years' course. In the following year he was graduated also in the Nebraska State Normal School at Wayne, and for the four ensuing years he held the office of superintendent or principal of various public schools in Wayne County, that state. In 1896, counting as satisfactory naught but the best possible fortification for his exacting and responsible vocation, Mr. Spahr attended the Central Normal College in the City of Indianapolis, Indiana, and from this admirable institution he received the degrees of Bachelor of Science and Bachelor of Pedagogy. Prior to this Mr. Spahr had served as principal of public schools in the Gulf coast section of Texas, his services in this capacity having been rendered, in turn, at Alvin, Hallettsville and Edna. After his course in the college at Indianapolis he became principal of the public schools of Portales, New Mexico, where he remained thus engaged until 1911, in July of which year he came to Oklahoma and assumed his present position, that of superintendent of the schools at Foss, Washita County. Under his supervision is a corps of five specially competent teachers, who give to him most earnest and effective co-operation, and the enrollment of pupils in the village schools numbers 175.

Mr. Spahr has made himself one of the vigorous and influential factors in the general community life and is enthusiastic in all that pertains to the work of the schools, so that his administration has proved altogether effective and worthy of popular approval. His political allegiance is given to the republican party, he is affiliated with the Foss Lodge No. 204, Ancient Free and Accepted Masons, he is identified with the Oklahoma State Teachers' Association and the National Teachers' Association, and both he and his wife hold membership in the Methodist Episcopal Church, South.

At Alvin, Texas, on the 28th of June, 1899, was solemnized the marriage of Mr. Spahr to Miss Zona Kimmans, who was born in the City of Wheeling, West Virginia, on the 2d of August, 1867, who was educated in Southern Ohio, and who was a successful and popular teacher prior to her marriage, of which no children have been born. William R. Kimmans, father of Mrs. Spahr, was a representative business man at Alvin, Texas, at the time of his death, and his wife also is deceased.

DAVID W. VANN. Among the well known merchants and farmers of Marshall County, one who for fifteen years has assisted in maintaining a high standard in both commercial and agricultural affairs is David W. Vann, of Woodville, a citizen universally respected in his community by reason of his strict business integrity and high order of citizenship. He belongs to a family around which romance and history entwine in the Cherokees and Chickasaws. Gen. Stand Watie, the noted Cherokee general, who displayed such gallant courage in behalf of the Southern Confederacy during the Civil war, and who was known as Degatugo in the Cherokee tongue, was the commander under whom William Vann, the father of David W. Vann, served during the war between the states. At Cabin Creek William Vann helped to take 600 wagons and teams from the Union troops; at Pea Ridge he marched away in defeat without the lead of General McCullough, who was killed. Belle Starr, the noted woman outlaw and desperado was captured and her gang broken up on the Canadian River through the efforts of William Vann, who was at that time sheriff of the Canadian District of the Cherokee Nation. Dick Triplett, another noted Cherokee outlaw, who had escaped the clutches of the law, was captured by Deputy Sheriff Vann after Sheriff Stand Gray had refused to make the arrest because of fear. William Vann replaced Sheriff Gray and the older residents of that section still remember the bravery and absolute fearlessness of this officer who operated in the desperate days following the close of the Civil war.

The Vann family, preceding the war between the North and the South, had been considered wealthy Indians; they had about seventy-five negroes as slaves and cattle whose increase was enough to bring in a splendid yearly income. After the war, their home destroyed, their property gone and their nation devastated, William Vann and his family went South into the land of the Chickasaws. Here he found among the people of his adoption a faithful helpmate in Miss Lottie Willis, sister of Holmes and Britt Willis, and daughter of J. Hamp Willis, who with his brother, Britt, left their Tennessee home to marry among the Indians, Britt uniting with a Choctaw girl and J. Hamp with a Chickasaw girl. Thus the two families of Willis: one Choctaw and one Chickasaw. Gabe E. Parker, of Muskogee, superintendent of Indian Affairs, is the grandson of Britt Willis.

In the spring of 1868, William Vann moved with his Chickasaw wife back to the Cherokee Nation, and it was after this removal that he became sheriff and succeeded in breaking up the many bands of outlaws that infested the Cherokee country. After his service as sheriff, he served for ten years as a member of the Cherokee Council, and when finally defeated in election again returned to the Chickasaw Nation. Here he died March 15, 1911, and his widow died November 21, 1915. Six children were born to William and Lottie (Willis) Vann, all of whom are living: David W., of this review; Ellen, who married a Mr. Graves, a farmer near Wilkinson, Oklahoma (Cherokee Nation); James, who is associated with his brother David W. in the mercantile business at Woodville; Mrs. Georgia Lynch, who is one of the popular and efficient school teachers of Marshall County; Lulu and William reside at home.

David W. Vann was born at Willis, Oklahoma, then the old Chickasaw Nation of the Indian Territory, January 8, 1868. He was educated in the common schools which existed at the time of his boyhood and youth, but the important part of the requirements of that day did not consist of book learning so much as it did of the ability to maintain life. In August, 1891, Mr. Vann was married to Miss Fannie Doyle, of Webber's Falls, Cherokee Nation, and to this union there have been born five children, as follows: Lolo, now deceased; Louis, also deceased; Arthur, who is attending school at Muskogee; Jennie, who is attending school at Denison, Texas; and David P., who lives at home with his parents.

Mr. Vann came to Woodville in 1900, and embarked in the mercantile business, in association with farming. He has been successful in both lines of endeavor, being an energetic, enterprising and industrious man, with modern ideas and methods, who does not neglect his duties as a citizen. His only fraternal connection is with the local camp of the Woodmen of the World.

J. H. VANN. A native son of the Old Cherokee Nation, and a prominent farmer and stock raiser in the community of Woodville in Marshall County, J. H. Vann is one of the solid and substantial citizens of that section of Oklahoma.

He was born at Webber Falls in Canadian District, Cherokee Nation, a son of William and Lottie Vann. As a boy he attended the old Cherokee Male Seminary at Tahlequah, leaving school in his sophomore year, and afterwards took a business course at Muskogee. While there have been some minor experiences of his life, he has spent his years most profitably in farming and stock raising, and he also conducts a general store at Woodville and is one of the principal merchants in that county. He has prospered and has accumulated means that can be translated into sufficient comfort and satisfaction to provide liberally for himself and family.

Mr. Vann is a democrat, is affiliated with the Woodmen of the World and is a member of the Presbyterian Church. At Preston, Texas, near the Red River, on December 6, 1902, he married Miss Laula Gresham. They have a daughter and two sons. The daughter is Cloy Vann, and the sons are John Henry and James Edward Vann.

J. N. MCCALLISTER. The history of the people and country around Bartlesville is an open book of recollections to J. N. McCallister, who has lived in that locality nearly twenty years, and has been not only a close observer but has been drawn into close participation in the events and affairs of a growing city. For the past ten years Mr. McCallister has been the leading undertaker of Washington County and with the aid of his children now conducts an establishment both at Bartlesville and at Dewey.

Born in Cass County, Missouri, August 18, 1871, he is a son of J. N. and M. F. (McKinney) McCallister. His parents were also natives of Missouri, and lived there for several years after their marriage, when they moved to Montgomery County, Kansas, in 1873, and in 1881 went to Greenwood County, Kansas, where they are still living. His father is a retired merchant. He was a farmer up to 1881, and then engaged in merchandising, which was the basis of a successful career until he retired with a competence in 1903. The Bartlesville citizen is one of four children. His sister Maude is the wife of John A. Gill of Selma, Kansas; Bertha is the wife of Carl A. Dixon of Kansas; and Lela is now deceased.

Mr. McCallister grew up in Kansas and lived at home with his parents until he removed to the Cherokee Nation of Indian Territory on February 8, 1897, and this has been his home ever since. In the first spring of his arrival only twenty votes were cast in this community, and there was only a handful of white residents at that time. Up to the age of eighteen Mr. McCallister had attended school and worked for his father, then became a barber, and followed that trade fifteen years. For the past ten years he has given his time to his business as undertaker. Mr. McCallister was elected the first coroner of Washington County under statehood rule, and has the distinction of having performed the first inquest in the new state. He took the oath of office at 3 o'clock in the afternoon and was called upon to hold the inquest at 8 in the evening of the same day. At that inquest he secured the two bullets which had killed the first two men in Washington County after statehood, and has these as relics of that historic occasion. Mr. McCallister held the office of coroner for two years, and was the only one ever to hold that official position in Washington County, since in the meantime the courts had ruled that the constitution had not provided for such an office, and it has consequently not been a distinct subdivision of county functions since that time.

For the past ten years Mr. McCallister has given his entire time to undertaking, although he owns a farm in Washington County and one in Kansas. Since starting at Bartlesville he has established a branch of his business at Dewey. On first engaging in business at Bartlesville he erected a building on Third Street and then traded that for the one he now occupies at the corner of Second and Dewey Avenue. He is also interested in the oil industry.

Mr. McCallister is well known in fraternal circles, having affiliations with the Knights of Pythias, with the Uniform Rank of that order, with the Fraternal Order of Eagles, the Order of Owls, the Modern Woodmen of America, the Woodmen of the World, the W. C., with the Dramatic Order of Khorassan and with the Loyal Order of Moose and several other benevolent and mutual benefit organizations.

In 1891 Mr. McCallister married Miss Maggie Pedigo, who died in May, 1908. Two children survive her. Ernest lives at home and is associated with his father in business at Bartlesville. Daisy is the wife of C. H. Burt, and they manage the Dewey branch of the undertaking firm. Mr. McCallister has made his two children equal partners in the McCallister Undertaking Company. The son received a license as an embalmer when he was sixteen years of age, and that is the youngest age on record for such a distinction. Mr. and Mrs. Burt have one child, Bonita, and when she was born she made the fifth living generation in the family, her two great-great-grandmothers being living at that time.

When Mr. McCallister came to the vicinity of Bartlesville a wheat field covered a portion of the site now occupied by the flourishing city, and all the country south of Third Street was an open range. Among his interesting relics of the past is a photograph taken fifteen years ago showing himself and a party of friends with more than 500 pounds of catfish hauled out of the Caney River at one catch. One of the fish weighed more than sixty-five pounds. These fish were taken out at the dam in the river.

PLUMER W. LUTMAN. Maintaining his residence in the thriving little City of Edmond, Oklahoma County, and prominently concerned in its development and upbuilding, Mr. Lutman has been a resident of this county since 1898, and that he has an impregnable place in popular confidence and esteem needs no further voucher than the statement that he has served consecutively since 1910 as a member of the board of county commissioners of Oklahoma County,—a body whose functions are of the most important order, and involve the expenditure of many thousands of dollars of public funds in the county in which is situated the metropolis and capital city of the state. Mr. Lutman has been closely and successfully concerned with the agricultural and livestock industries during the entire period of his residence in Oklahoma, has been vigorous and progressive as a dealer in real estate, and his influence and co-operation are invariably given in the furtherance of judicious policies of local government and in support of measures and enterprises projected for the general good of the community.

Plumer Wartes Lutman was born in Perry County, Pennsylvania, on the 14th of February, 1866, and is a son of John Miller Lutman and Margaret E. (Comp) Lutman, both of whom were born and reared in the old Keystone State. Mrs. Comp was the daughter of Rev. Andrew Comp. Mr. John M. Lutman removed with his family to Morgan County, Missouri, in 1867, both he and his wife having passed the residue of their lives in that state.

He whose name introduces this article was about one year old at the time of the family immigration to Missouri, and he was reared to adult age in Morgan County, that state, where he continued to attend the public schools until he had completed a course in the high school at Versailles, the county seat. That he made good use of the advantages thus afforded him is evidenced by the fact that after leaving the high school he was for three years a successful and popular teacher in the public schools of Pettis County, Missouri. He then turned his attention to agricultural pursuits, and during the long intervening years he has never severed his allegiance to this great basic industry. He is at the present time the owner of valuable property in Oklahoma, where he has maintained his home from the time of coming to the territory, in 1898. He established his residence that year in the little village of Edmond, and he has been one of the prominent figures in the development of the town into one of the most attractive and prosperous cities of the state, besides having contributed much to the general industrial and civic progress of Oklahoma County. From 1900 until 1909 he served as assistant postmaster at Edmond and in the meanwhile controlled a large and prosperous business in the handling of real estate. In 1910 Mr. Lutman was elected, as a republican, a member of the board of county commissioners, and of this office he has continued the loyal, circumspect and valued incumbent, through re-election in 1912. Concerning his association with this service for his county the following estimate has been given: ''As a member of this important board, Mr. Lutman has distinguished himself as a most proficient and capable official, and his counsel has frequently resulted in saving to the taxpayers of the county large sums of money, through his having prevailed upon his associate members to coincide with his conservative and judicious policies. A successful business man and one of utmost civic loyalty, he has naturally brought to bear in the discharge of his public duties marked efficiency and safe business methods.''

Mr. Lutman is known as a zealous and effective advocate of the principles and policies of the republican party, has attained to the thirty-second degree in the Ancient Accepted Scottish Rite of the time-honored Masonic fraternity, besides which both he and his wife are affiliated with the adjunct organization, the Order of the Eastern Star. In the Independent Order of Odd Fellows he has filled all official chairs in both the subordinate lodge and the encampment. Both he and his wife hold membership in the Presbyterian Church.

At Billings, Noble County, Oklahoma, on the 15th of August, 1900, Mr. Lutman wedded Miss Beulah M. Sears, a daughter of Wiggins W. and Mary (Cushingberry) Sears, both natives of Kentucky, in which state Mrs. Lutman's paternal grandfather was a slaveholder and an extensive breeder of fine horses and mules prior to the Civil war, he having been said to have had the largest number of mules in the Bluegrass State, long famous as a center for the breeding and raising of high-grade stock. Mr. and Mrs. Lutman have no children.

CHARLES G. VANNEST. One of the best known educators in the old Cherokee Strip country of Oklahoma is Charles G. Vannest, now superintendent of the Medford schools, and formerly identified for a number of years with the office of county superintendent of Noble County. He came to this state in 1906, a year before statehood. He is an educator with high ideals and with a keen understanding of conditions and requirements. Much of his work in Oklahoma has been as an organizer and developer. He has laid the foundation for sound and wholesome educational work in Noble County and his name is known among educators all over the state.

A native of Vermilion County, Indiana, Charles G. Vannest was born June 7, 1880. He belongs to what was really the first white family of Vermilion County, a county that lies along the Wabash River in Western Indiana. His great-grandfather was John Vannest, who is given the distinction of having been the first permanent white settler in Vermilion County. He came out to Indiana from Virginia about 1816, and secured a tract of Government land on which the City of Clinton in Vermilion County now stands. He lived there and devoted the rest of his years to farming. His family comprised several sons, one of whom was Samuel Vannest. Samuel Vannest married Amanda Potter, and their lives were spent as farmers in Vermilion County. They have three daughters and three sons: Samuel, Polk, Taylor, Jane, Mary and Serena. The daughter Serena is the wife of J. F. Raine and lives in Kansas.

Taylor Vannest, father of the Oklahoma educator, was also a Vermilion County farmer, where he spent all his life. He died in Clinton in that county in 1913 at the age of seventy-nine. He was a soldier in the Union Army during the Civil war, having gone out with Company D of the Eighty-fifth Indiana Infantry as a private. He was in Sherman's army and after the fall of Atlanta went with that great commander on the march to the sea. The earlier part of the war he was in the western campaign and was wounded in the battle of Pea Ridge, Arkansas. After the war he gave his time with characteristic industry to his work as a farmer, and though an intelligent voter and a republican, he never held an office. He was a member of the Methodist Church. Taylor Vannest married Catherine Henry, who was one of the five children of James and Mary (Tolle) Henry who came from Kentucky. Catherine Henry's brothers served in the Union Army from Kentucky. Mrs. Taylor Vannest died in April, 1915. Her children were: Harry, of Clinton; Claud, of Clinton; Maud, wife of Clint Bennett of Sidel, Illinois; and Charles G. Mrs. Taylor Vannest by a former marriage to William Mitchell had one son, Samuel Mitchell, who died in Indiana.

The boyhood of Charles G. Vannest was spent in the Town of Clinton on the banks of the Wabash River. He attended the local schools, graduating from high school, and then entered the Terre Haute Normal School, where he was graduated in 1900. His first work as a teacher was done in the rural schools of his native county, and afterwards he became one of the instructors in the schools at Clinton. After five years as a teacher he turned his attention to newspaper work and for a year was editor of the Clintonian, a weekly paper at Clinton.

Giving up his connections in his native county, Mr. Vannest came to the Southwest for the purpose of looking up a newspaper location. Instead he was attracted into school work, a turn which has been very beneficial to the country, though perhaps not as remunerative as some other occupations would have been. He was first located at Morrison as principal of the schools. Morrison is in Noble County, and after about two years as principal he was elected county superintendent. Altogether he spent four and a half years in that office. His chief aim in work as superintendent was to secure the proper consolidation of local districts and the correlation of subjects in the curriculum of instruction in the rural schools. His work in that office attracted much attention, and his recognized qualifications caused his nomination by the republicans of the state for the office of state superintendent of public instruction. This was in the campaign of 1912, when the republican party was itself divided, and though Mr. Vannest made a very vigorous campaign there was hardly any chance from the beginning that he would be elected. In July, 1913, Mr. Vannest took his present position as superintendent of schools at Medford, becoming the successor of J. O. Allen. He has always given his active support to the teachers association in Noble County, and while county superintendent he was a member of the State Teachers' Association and of the County Superintendents' Organization. Mr. Vannest has accumulated a great fund of experience as a school man, and he is now engaged in compiling a United States history and a work on civics for use in the common schools.

He cast his first presidential vote in Indiana in 1904 for Roosevelt. While in his native county he took a considerable part in politics and was a member of the county committee and its secretary. He was elected mayor of Perry in April, 1915. Fraternally he is affiliated with the lodge and chapter of Masons and with both the subordinate and encampment branches of the Independent Order of Odd Fellows. His church is the Methodist.

In Indiana on April 13, 1901, Mr. Vannest married Miss Maud Carmichael. Mr. and Mrs. Vannest are not people who take much account of superstitious belief. They were married on Friday the 13th. Mrs. Vannest is a daughter of C. A. and Ruth (Moss) Carmichael, her father having been born in Greene County, Indiana, and was a farmer in Vermilion County, Illinois. Mrs. Vannest is the oldest of six children, and was a successful teacher before her marriage.

CHARLES EDGAR HILL, proprietor and editor of the Granite Enterprise, assumed his present position in 1909. Today no man in Granite is better known or more highly esteemed than he.

Mr. Hill was born in Jackson County, North Carolina, on May 24, 1869, and is a son of Charles D. Hill, born in South Carolina in 1844. The Hills are an Irish family, and they came to Virginia from Ireland among the first emigrants to that state. One of them, a brother of the paternal great-grandfather of the subject, was a colonel in the Revolutionary war, and was killed in action at Kings Mountain.

Charles D. Hill moved to Jackson County, North Carolina, from his native state, South Carolina, in company with his parents when he was a boy in 1852, and in 1870 he went to Macon County, North Carolina, where he lived until 1894, when he went to Grayson County, Texas. In 1906 he moved to Pawnee, Oklahoma, where he remained three years and in 1909 took up his residence in Davenport, Oklahoma, where he now resides and is engaged in the nursery and poultry business. All his previous years had been spent in mining in his various locations, but he is now content with the quiet life he leads in Davenport. Mr. Hill served three years in the Confederate army, enlisting from South Carolina in the First South Carolina Heavy Artillery. He is a member of the Methodist Church and a steward therein. His politics are those of a democrat and he is a member of the Odd Fellows.

Mr. Hill married Miss Jane Crenshaw, who was born in South Carolina in 1847, and eleven children were born to them. Charles Edgar Hill of this review was the first born. Thomas Edward lives in Blackburn, where he is a prosperous farmer. Frank Clifford is a pressman in Marshall, Texas. Jane married W. F. Coombs, of Denison, Texas, where they have a fine farm. Herbert Clinton is a farmer in Davenport, Oklahoma. Walter died at the age of twenty-one years. Sallie married Roy Youwell, and they live on a farm in Whitewright, Texas. Daisey married Charles Barker, a farmer of Iowa. Annie is the wife of Carl Whitman, a druggist at Henryetta, Oklahoma. Christine married H. Isbell, a Blackburn farmer. Felix Grundy is a farmer of Blackburn, and Georgia, the youngest, lives with her parents.

Charles Edgar Hill was reared on his father's farm until he reached the age of eighteen. During that time he entered the printing office of the Highland Enterprise, in North Carolina, and there served a printer's apprenticeship. In 1887 he went to Knox, Tennessee, traveling two years as a salesman, and in 1890 went to Dallas, where he was employed in various printing establishments. He continued there until 1896 when he went to Fort Worth and there assisted in the establishment of the Fort Worth Register, now called the Fort Worth Record, and one of the leading newspapers of the state. Mr. Hill remained there for a year, and in 1907-8-9 was engaged in the job printing business in Fort Worth. In 1909 he came to Granite, Oklahoma, in search of a new field, and he promptly bought out the Granite Enterprise, which he has since owned and operated.

The Enterprise was established in May, 1900, by James Scarborough, and is a democratic paper in political sentiment. The plant is situated on Fourth Street, just off Main Street, and under Mr. Hill's management the equipment has been brought up to a high standard. The Enterprise circulates in Greer and other counties in Oklahoma, as well as in Texas, and has a large certified circulation outside its home state.

Mr. Hill, who is a democrat, was elected by acclamation to the office of mayor of Granite in 1915, for a term of two years. He is a member of the Methodist Episcopal Church, and his fraternal affiliations are with the Masons, Granite Lodge No. 134, Ancient Free and Accepted Masons, and Granite Lodge No. 127, Independent Order of Odd Fellows, of which he is secretary. He is a member of the State Press Association and the Typographical Union.

In 1891 Mr. Hill was married in Arcadia, Louisiana, to Miss Mattie Owen, daughter of Rev. W. D. Owen, a Presbyterian minister, now deceased. She died in Fort Worth, Texas, in 1898, leaving him two children, Cecil and Earl, both employed by the Dallas News, in Dallas, Texas.

Mr. Hill married a second time, when in 1901 Miss Lena Van Vark became his wife in Fort Worth. She is a daughter of Peter Van Vark, a farmer, now deceased.

Five children have been born to them. Ethel is now attending the Oklahoma College for Women, in Chickasha.

Charles and Irene are attending the Granite High School, and the two youngest, Ernest and Albert, are yet in the home.

The Hills own a nice home on West Third Street, and they have a wide circle of friends and acquaintances in the city.

DAISY M. PRATT. Oklahoma is a vigorous young commonwealth of large things, and in nothing has its bigness been more effectively manifested than the merited recognition it has given to its womenfolk in connection with governmental and educational affairs in its various counties. The intellectual attainments and executive ability of Miss Daisy Maud Pratt have thus brought her prominently forward in the domain of practical educational work and have given her the distinction of being chosen to her present office, that of county superintendent of schools for Blaine County, an exalting position in which she is giving a most able and progressive administration.

Miss Pratt is a representative of a sterling pioneer family of the fine old Hoosier State, which she claims as the place of her nativity. On her father's farm in Ripley County, Indiana, she was born on the 19th of May, 1885, and that she has imbibed fully the inspiration and progressive spirit of the great West is not to be held a matter of wonderment, for in the year succeeding that of her birth her parents removed to Kansas, a few years later finding them numbered among the pioneer settlers in what is now the State of Oklahoma. Miss Pratt is a daughter of John Diah and Almira C. (Sheldon) Pratt, the former of whom was born in Prattsburg, Ripley County, Indiana, and the latter in Iowa. Prattsburg was named in honor of the Pratt family. The paternal grandfather of Miss Pratt was a native of Maine and a scion of a sterling colonial family of New England, where the original American progenitors settled upon their emigration from England. The grandfather of Miss Pratt, who was born in Maine March 12, 1808, became a pioneer in Ripley County, Indiana, where he was owner of some large sawmills. He died while a passenger on a Mississippi River packet-boat, which was near the City of New Orleans at the time, he having been about fifty years old at the time of his demise. He was buried at Prattsburg, Indiana. His wife, Nancy Hunter Pratt, survived him by a number of years, and died at Rago, Kingman County, Kansas. His father, Jonathan Pratt, served as a messenger for General Washington in the War of the Revolution.

Miss Pratt's father's grandfather on his mother's side was John Hunter, of Strong, Massachusetts. On April 15, 1805, he was appointed under Caleb Strong, governor of Massachusetts, as ''captain of a company in the Fifth Regiment of the Second Brigade, Eighth Division of the Militia of this commonwealth.'' This paper is signed by John Strong, secretary. This same John Hunter was appointed by Christopher Gore, governor of Massachusetts, as justice of the peace of the County of Somerset, Massachusetts. This appointment was made February 19, 1810. Signed by William Tudor, secretary commonwealth.

The authentic record of this patriotic service makes Miss Pratt eligible for membership in the Society of the Daughters of the American Revolution. The founders of the Pratt family in America were three brothers of the name who came from England in the colonial era of our national history and who became pioneer settlers of Maine, the historic Pine Tree State.

On the maternal side Miss Pratt is a descendant of George Niles Sheldon who came from Canada to York State in 1812. He was a Methodist preacher. His son, Robert Palmer Sheldon, was born in Canada in 1806, and in 1824 he was married to Lucy Amy Marsh. He was also a Methodist preacher, and worked as a missionary among the Indians in Michigan in an early day. In the magnificent new Methodist Episcopal Church at Mount Pleasant, Michigan, one whole window is inscribed to the memory of Rev. Robert P. Sheldon.

The grandfather of Miss Pratt, Ancile Lorenzo Sheldon, was born in Courtland County, New York, January 21, 1826, and lived in Ohio, Indiana, Iowa, Oklahoma and Nebraska. He was married in 1848 to Mary Jane Richardson and they had three children: Harmon Palmer, Almira C. and Wilber Clarence. Mrs. Sheldon died in 1865 and several years after her death Mr. Sheldon was married to Mary R. Sutton. To them two daughters were born, Maud S. and Clara. Mrs. Mary Sutton Sheldon died of typhoid fever, and in 1877 Ancile L. Sheldon married Georgia Edwards of Page County, Iowa, who survived him and is now living in Omaha, Nebraska. Mr. Sheldon was a devout Christian and a devout member of the Methodist Episcopal Church. His early life was spent in farming and in after years he owned and kept a large hotel, and later owned and operated grain elevators. His last days were spent with his daughter, Mrs. Almira Pratt of Darrow, Oklahoma.

John D. Pratt, father of the popular superintendent of schools in Blaine County, Oklahoma, was born in Ripley County, Indiana, in the year 1852. In 1886 he disposed of his farm property in his native state and removed with his family to Kingman County, Kansas, in the second tier of counties above the Oklahoma State line. There he continued his operations as an agriculturist and stock-grower until 1891, when he came to the newly organized Territory of Oklahoma, took part in the ''run'' made by ambitious settlers at the opening of the territory to settlement and obtained a tract of land in Kingfisher County, as at present constituted. He did not, however, perfect his title to this government claim, but in April, 1892, at the Cheyenne and Arapahoe opening, he ''made the run'' into this new district and entered claim to a homestead of 160 acres in the northern part of what is now Blaine County. He improved this property, developed the same into a productive and valuable farm and it is still owned by the family, the place being eligibly situated three miles west of the town of Homestead. He subsequently rented the farm and moved to Homestead. At the time of the platting and upbuilding of the new town of Darow Mr. Pratt removed to the new town, and there he continued to maintain his home until his death, which occured August 7, 1914, his widow still residing in the attractive homestead which he there provided.

Mr. Pratt was a man of strong mentality, broad information and well fortified convictions, the while his life was guided and governed by the highest principles of integrity and honor. He manifested a specially lively interest in public affairs and, after his removal to Oklahoma, did all in his power to further the development and progress of both the territory and the state, was unswerving in his allegiance to the republican party, and was influential in political and other civic affairs. He served many years as a member of the school board and held also the offices of justice of the peace and notary public. He was a republican committeeman for years and delegate to many conventions.

She whose name initiates this review was the fourth in order of birth in a family of seven children, and concerning the others the following brief data are available. Nella, a young woman of gracious person-

I

J. D. Pratt

Daisy M. Pratt

ality and high attainments, died on the 13th of June, 1906, at the age of thirty-two years, she having been the wife of Clifford Drum Thaxton and having served as county superintendent of schools of Blaine County for some time prior to her death. Mr. Thaxton is now superintendent of the schools of Port Hill, Idaho. Lola W., the second daughter, is principal of the Central School of Watonga, the judicial center of Blaine County. Diah Sheldon resides at Duncan, Stephens County, and is one of the representative farmers of that section of Oklahoma. Florence Mabel is the wife of Earl A. Schreffler, a blacksmith at Homestead, Blaine County. Cary A. remains with his widowed mother at Darrow and has the supervision of the old homestead farm. Delphine Almira, a graduate of the Oklahoma State Normal School at Alva, is the wife of Rolla T. Hoberecht, who holds an executive position in the First National Bank at Watonga.

Miss Daisy M. Pratt was about six years of age at the time of the family removal to Oklahoma Territory, and she was reared to adult age in Blaine County, to whose public schools she is indebted for her early educational discipline. Later she attended the Southwestern Oklahoma State Normal School, at Weatherford, and she has continued an ambitious student, has made marked advancement in the higher planes of academic learning, and has proved also a most successful and popular teacher, as well as a strong executive in the directing of educational affairs of important order. In 1901 Miss Pratt served her pedagogic novitiate by serving as teacher in the rural school of District No. 74, Blaine County, and here she brought, through consideration of kindliness, combined with insistent discipline, the best of order and most efficient work in a school that had previously been known for its unruliness. After teaching two terms in this district Miss Pratt taught one year, 1903, in the primary department of the village schools of Homestead, and during the following year she held the position of principal. In 1905-6 she was a valued and popular teacher in the public schools of Watonga, the county seat of Blaine County, where, in her official and private capacity, she now maintains her home. In 1907 she became principal of the schools at Darrow, where she continued her effective labors until 1910, when there came a most gratifying popular recognition of her ability and successful achievement, in that she was elected to her present responsible office of superintendent of schools of Blaine County,—this preferment, in view of her having maintained her home in the county since her childhood, setting at naught the application of the conditions implied in the scriptural aphorism that "a prophet is not without honor save in his own country."

Miss Pratt assumed her official duties as county superintendent of schools in January, 1911, and the best voucher for the admirable way in which she has administered the affairs of the office is that offered by her re-election in November, 1912, and again in November, 1914, so that she is now serving her third consecutive term. Within her jurisdiction are 111 schools; 158 teachers are employed; and the enrollment of pupils shows a total of 5,006. Miss Pratt has made an excellent record as one of the admirably qualified and specially successful county superintendents of Oklahoma and is enthusiastic and active in all matters pertaining to educational work in the state. She holds membership in the Methodist Episcopal Church and is a popular teacher in the Sunday School. In a fraternal way she is affiliated with the Royal Neighbors and the Daughters of Rebekah. She is a popular factor in the social life of her home county, throughout which her circle of friends is virtually coincident with that of her acquaintances.

J. M. HANNA, M. D. In the picturesque and fertile Valley of the Washita in the eastern part of Grady County blossomed the attractive Town of Alex. The community abounds in evidences of prosperity, and one of the chief of these is a public school building that cost $20,000. Matching the rich natural resources has been the character of the men who have been chiefly instrumental in creating these evidences of prosperity, and one who is accounted a leader among them all is Dr. J. M. Hanna, who as a member of the board of education helped to direct the destinies of the community's public education. Doctor Hanna has also been mayor of Alex and president of its live Commercial Club, the activities of which have been instrumental in building excellent highways and attracting men of means to develop the agricultural and industrial resources around the town. It has been well said that there has never been an enterprise in behalf of the community's welfare which Doctor Hanna has not done his best to help along, and particular credit is given him above all other local citizens for the successful basis upon which the public schools of the village now rest. Doctor Hanna has been with the Town of Alex since its beginning, and has given largely of his time, energy and money to make it a wholesome place for good people to live and prosper.

Doctor Hanna was a poor but ambitious lad during the '70s. He completed a common school and academy education at Saltillo, Tennessee, and then worked for the modest salary of $10 a month, out of which he saved enough for a start in medical education. By going to college a while and practicing for a while he completed his medical course, graduating with the degree M. D. from the Memphis Hospital Medical College at Memphis, Tennessee. His first regular schooling in medicine was acquired at the Fort Worth Texas Medical College. After graduating he completed a post-graduate course in the New Orleans Polyclinic. His practice as a regular physician began at Lebanon, Indian Territory, in 1895, and that was his home for twelve years. He moved to Alex in 1907, and there has been a pioneer not only in his profession but in many broad civic activities. His reputation is of the best of a physician, and his practice is among the best of a thrifty class of town and country people.

Dr. J. M. Hanna was born in Tennessee in 1866, a son of Madison C. and Elizabeth (Hawkins) Hanna. His father was a pioneer in the profession of dentistry in that state, but also for many years was well known as a local Methodist preacher and a skilled mechanic. Evidences of his talent in the latter line are indicated in the fact that he perfected some of the types of threshing machines then in use. Doctor Hanna's grandfather was Capt. James Hanna, also a native of Tennessee and a well known figure in his time and generation. Two brothers of Doctor Hanna, Thomas W. and William A., are car builders in the employ of the Iron Mountain Railway Company at Little Rock, Arkansas. Two brothers are deceased: Dr. J. B., who was a practicing physician at Coalgate, Oklahoma, and C. N., who was a merchant at Dallas, Texas. A deceased sister was Miss Leora Beatrice, who died while attending school.

Doctor Hanna was married at Beebe, Arkansas, to Miss Isabel Virginia Scraps. Her grandfather was serving in the English navy at the time of the War of 1812 and being then temporarily a resident of United States, went into hiding in Mexico and changed his name to avoid fighting against the people of this country. Doctor and Mrs. Hanna have five children: Ralph M., who is now twenty-one years of age and is employed by the Ford Motor Car Company at Chickasha; Orin Virginia, Mary Lewis, James O'Neill and Carthell Mott, all at home and attending school.

Doctor Hanna is a member of the Methodist Episcopal Church, South, and fraternally has affiliations with the Masons, the Independent Order of Odd Fellows and the Woodmen of the World. He is a member of the Alex Commercial Club and the Alex Board of Education, is chairman of the Grady County Election Board and is city physician of Alex.

REV. L. W. MARKS. In the little City of Edmond L. W. Marks is distinguished for his work as minister, and also for his successful administration of the municipality in the office of mayor up to April, 1915. Perhaps the most important work by which Mr. Marks will deserve the gratitude of future generations has been that of historical secretary of the State Baptist Convention. The religious activities of the old Indian Territory cannot be passed over without robbing the history of that country of much of the romance that has made it inviting. The minister, of many denominations, was closely identified with the annals of the Five Civilized Tribes. Probably no man of recent years has done more toward revealing the lives of minister-missionaries in that region than Mr. Marks. In his position already named he has for the past eleven years delved into the lives of many early missionaries of the Baptist Church in Oklahoma. From what he brought out he has produced "L. L. Smith of Oklahoma, a Man of God on the Frontier," a little book that has been generally circulated over the state. He has also written, down to the Five Tribes, the most complete account of the Baptist Church in Oklahoma. His source of inspiration for the data of this manuscript was Dr. J. S. Murrow of Atoka, one of the editors of the "Standard History of Oklahoma," who is the dean of living missionaries in Oklahoma. Doctor Murrow furnished the "key" to many an Indian home and many an Indian story and legend in the land of the Five Tribes. Mr. Marks has written of the remarkable careers of Doctor Murrow, Dr. H. F. Bucker and Jesse Bushyhead, a Cherokee leader and preacher, and of John Brown, for thirty years governor of the Seminole Nation. He learned that Bushyhead made settlement at a place called Baptist, near Tahlequah, and that there W. P. Upham of Boston, early in the '40s, published the first newspaper in Indian Territory.

L. W. Marks was born at Canton, Missouri, February 1, 1862, a son of George Edward and Mary J. (Henton) Marks. He has one sister, Mrs. John L. Highbee, wife of a farmer in Lewis County, Missouri. The mother, now at the venerable age of eighty-one years, lives with this daughter. The father of Mr. Marks was a captain in the Confederate army under General Price. A great-uncle, General Martin E. Green, was killed at Vicksburg. The maternal grandparents were among the first settlers on Upper Sugar Creek in Northeast Missouri during the early '30s.

Rev. Mr. Marks was educated in the public schools at Lewis County, Missouri, the LaGrange College at LaGrange, Missouri, the William Jewell College at Liberty, Missouri, and the Southern Baptist Theological Seminary at Louisville, Kentucky, from which he was graduated with the degree Master of Theology. He had entered the Baptist ministry in 1888, and finished his collegiate education after taking up active work as a pastor. For 2½ years he served as pastor of the Baptist Church at Lamar, Missouri, two years at Shelbyville, Missouri, two years at Meadville, Missouri, and for five years had charge of the church at Edmond, Oklahoma. For eleven years he was on the editorial staff of Word and Way of Kansas City, one of the leading Baptist publications in the country, and for ten years has represented that publication in Oklahoma. Besides being historical secretary of the Baptist State Convention, he has held the office of recording secretary and has been president of the board of trustees of the Baptist College at Blackwell, Oklahoma.

In whatever he undertakes Mr. Marks is known as a man of accomplishment, of great energy, and one who worked steadily and vigorously for the upholding of moral principles. Those characteristics followed him during his administration as mayor of Edmond, to which office he was elected on the democratic ticket in 1913. Fraternally he is affiliated with Edmond Lodge No. 37, Ancient Free and Accepted Masons. Mr. Marks was married at Memphis, Missouri, February 19, 1895, to Miss Sadie Freeman. Their ten children are: Zula, Paul Eaton, L. W., Jr., Frances, Nona, Walter, Joy, Marcus Marion, Ferrell and Bertie Lee.

TIERNAY & WALKER. One of the thoroughly reliable, enterprising, progressive and energetic newspapers of Kingfisher County, and one that is wielding a distinct and forceful influence in assisting the wheels of progress and in securing for the people a greater degree of prosperity, is the Hennessey Clipper, which is published at Hennessey by the firm of Tiernay & Walker. This concern, founded in 1913 by Frank G. Tiernay and Miss Mabel Walker, has met with a satisfying degree of success from the start, and in 1914 removed all opposition by purchasing the only other newspaper published at that place.

Frank G. Tiernay, the senior member of the concern, has passed his entire life, with the exception of three years, in connection with printing and journalistic work from the time when, as a lad, he received his introduction to stick and case. He was born April 26, 1874, at Fredonia, Louisa County, Iowa, and is a son of Patrick J. and Julia (Fahey) Tiernay. Patrick J. Tiernay was a native of New York, born in 1824, and was a farmer and mechanic all his life. He lived at various points during the course of a somewhat diversified career, and died in 1898, at Quincy, Illinois. Mr. Tiernay was married in 1859 to Miss Julia Fahey, also a native of New York, born in 1830, who died in 1884. They were the parents of four sons and three daughters: John J., Helen, Mary, William, Anna, Frank G. and Henry, all of whom are still living.

Frank G. Tiernay received his early education in the public schools of Burlington, Iowa, to which city his parents removed when he was a small lad. When he was fifteen years of age he expressed a desire to enter the printing business, and accordingly was taught the trade. From that time forward he worked as a journeyman at various places and with numerous newspapers until 1900, in which year he became editor and part owner of the Herald, at Belle Plaine, Iowa. In 1908 he came to Oklahoma, where he purchased the Press-Democrat, at Hennessey, of which he continued as editor and owner until 1910, that year marking his entrance upon the real estate field. However, the constant call of the craft was not to be denied, and after an experience of three years in realty affairs he returned to journalism in 1913 when he purchased a half-interest in the Hennessey Clipper, in partnership with Miss Mabel Walker, under the firm style of Tiernay & Walker. Mr. Tiernay is personally a democrat, but the paper maintains independent policies, and seeks to give to its readers a fair and unbiased presentation of all matters of interest and importance. Under wise management both subscription and advertising departments a flourishing, and the Clipper is rapidly assuming the proportions of a necessary adjunct. Mr. Tiernay is unmarried.

Like her partner, Miss Mabel Walker, junior member of the firm, learned the printing business when but a child and has been its active devotee throughout the course of her active career. She is also an Iowan by nativity, having been born on a farm in Grundy County, February 14, 1876, a daughter of Rigdon B. and Rachel (Dew) Walker. Rigdon B. Walker was born December 5, 1842, at Rock Island, Illinois, a son of Amos and Mary (Abbott) Walker, natives of Kentucky. Mr. Walker went in young manhood from Illinois to Iowa, where he engaged in farming in Grundy County, later went to Reno County, Kansas, in 1882, and in 1895 came to Oklahoma and bought land seven miles north of Enid, where he continued to farm and raise stock until his death in 1901. When the Civil war came on Mr. Walker was a resident of Illinois, and enlisted in Company C, One Hundred and Second Regiment, Illinois Volunteer Infantry, with which he served two years. He was seriously wounded at the battle of Resaca. After the close of the war, in 1865, he was married at Monmouth, Illinois, to Miss Rachel Dew, who was born in 1840, at Zanesville, Ohio, daughter of Hiram and Bettie (Weston) Dew, natives of the Buckeye State. Six children were born to Mr. and Mrs. Walker: Ransom, Robert, Maude, Mabel, Oliver and Julia, of whom Robert is deceased.

Miss Mabel Walker received the foundation for her education in the public schools of Reno County, Kansas, and was but fourteen years of age when she entered the office of the Sylvia Banner, at Sylvia, Kansas, to learn the printing trade. In 1895 she returned with her parents to Enid, Oklahoma, where she worked as a printer, as she did also later at Chickasha, on newspapers. In 1911 she became editor and manager of the Hennessey Clipper, and in 1913 purchasing it with Mr. Tiernay. In the year following all opposition was removed when the Clipper absorbed the Press-Democrat. Miss Walker is a newspaper woman of marked talent, and, while pre-eminently a business woman, has her full share of the feminine graces, attractions and accomplishments.

JAMES W. NEWTON, M. D. Among the successful professional men of Stephens County, Oklahoma, there is probably no one more perfectly in sympathy with that public spirit which has contributed to the progress of the various communities than Dr. James W. Newton, of Loco. Persevering and energetic in whatever direction his efforts have been turned, material success is not the greatest of his achievements, for he has fairly gained and steadfastly maintained the unqualified esteem and confidence of the people. He was born at Holly Springs, Marshall County, Minnesota, April 10, 1866, and is a son of Dr. James A. and Phoebe (Riggs) Newton.

The Newton family was founded in the United States by the grandfather of Doctor Newton, who brought his wife and children from London, England, to Philadelphia, Pennsylvania, in 1823, and spent the remaining years of his life in that city. James A. Newton was born in the City of London, in 1817, and was six years of age when brought to the United States, his boyhood and youth being passed in Philadelphia. He enjoyed good educational advantages, and when ready to enter upon a career of his own chose medicine as his field of effort and was duly graduated from the Philadelphia Medical College, with the degree of Doctor of Medicine. In the early '60s, Doctor Newton removed with his family to Marshall County, Mississippi, where he practiced for several years at Holly Springs, and in 1863 went to Phelps County, Missouri. For a short time during the Civil war he served in the Confederate army as a regimental surgeon, but was discharged because of disability, and it is probably that his army experiences were the cause of his early death, in 1865. Doctor Newton married Miss Phoebe Riggs, who was born in Tennessee, in 1823, and died in Missouri, in 1907, and of their children, four are still living: A. C., who is a farmer and resides in Northern Arkansas; Dr. James W.; Mary, who married John Clark, a merchant of Missouri; and Ulysses, a farmer, residing in Arkansas.

After attending the graded public school of Phelps County, Missouri, James W. Newton was sent to the academy at Vienna, Missouri, and there pursued a course of study which fitted him for labors in the field of education. Accordingly, he took a teacher's license and during six years was principal of schools in Missouri, Arkansas and Kansas. During this time he had decided to engage in the practice of medicine. In 1900 he came to Oklahoma and located at Duncan, where he passed two months, then coming the first time to Loco, where he remained three and one-half years. During his residence here he pursued a course of study at Barnes Medical College, St. Louis, Missouri, and was graduated in 1903, with the degree of Doctor of Medicine. His first field of practice was the State of Missouri, where he passed two years, and in 1905 went to Fort Smith, Arkansas, and later to Benton County in that state. He took up his permanent residence at Loco, Oklahoma, in 1906, and this city has continued to be his home and field of practice. During the years of his practice, Doctor Newton has made his profession remunerative financially and has won a warm place in the esteem of his patients. He belongs to the Stephens County Medical Society and other organizations of his calling, and is fraternally affiliated with the Royal Arch Chapter of the Masonic Order in Benton County, Arkansas, and the Independent Order of Odd Fellows at Ozark, Missouri. He is a socialist in his political views.

Doctor Newton was married in Benton County, Arkansas; to Miss Mary Johnson, who died in 1888, the mother of one child, William A., who is cashier of the Bank of Rush Springs, Oklahoma. In 1891 Doctor Newton was married a second time, in Benton County, Arkansas, to Miss Loui V. Stanley, daughter of the late George P. Stanley, who was a farmer in the Cherokee Nation, now Oklahoma. Six children have been born to this union: Maude, who is the wife of Jesse Rader, who is engaged in the automobile business at Loco; Percy, who is cashier of the Bank of Loco; Opal, who is a teacher in the public schools of Stephens County and resides with her parents; Nell, who is the wife of Ivan Heath, an oil man of Stephens County; and Lucille and Stanley, who are attending the public schools of Loco.

BEN F. WILLIAMS. Among the present generation of Oklahoma lawyers it is perhaps needless to say that Ben F. Williams of Norman has a record that places him among the leading criminal attorneys of the state. He has served as attorney for the defense in some of the most noted criminal trials held since the admission of Oklahoma to the Union. It was on the strength of his well known qualifications as a lawyer that he was appointed by the Supreme Court as a member of the Bar Commission of Oklahoma. There are eleven members of this commission, two from each Supreme Court District, and one member at large. It is this commission which examines all applicants for admission to the bar, and it sits twice a year in June and December.

Ben F. Williams, who is a son of the late Judge B. F. Williams, who was a prominent lawyer and well known both in Texas and Oklahoma, was born at Granbury, Hood County, Texas, March 21, 1877. His ancestors were of Welsh stock and were colonial pioneers in South Carolina. Judge B. F. Williams was born in Giles County, Tennessee, in 1826, and died at Clinton, Oklahoma, in March, 1912. Reared in Tennessee he went to Mississippi, where he married Miss H. E. Rucker, who was born in that state in 1837 and is still living in venerable years at Clinton, Oklahoma. Not long after his marriage Judge Williams moved to Falls County, Texas, and from there to Hood County. In 1878 he located at Graham City in Young County, which was then on the northwestern frontier of Texas. In 1886 he removed to Henrietta, Texas, and in 1890 identified himself with the early bar of Oklahoma City, and from 1896 until his death was a resident of Norman. He died while on a visit at Clinton, Oklahoma. In the various localities mentioned he enjoyed a large civil practice as a lawyer, and at one time was judge of the District Court of Wichita Falls and Henrietta, Texas. In politics he was a democrat, and his only secret order was the Independent Order of Odd Fellows. In the Methodist Episcopal Church he found opportunities for much service, and held every lay office in the church. He and his wife had the following children: Annie, wife of W. I. Brannon, a merchant at Clinton, Oklahoma; Clara, wife of Rev. Mr. Cameron, a Baptist minister at Clarence, Oklahoma; Mattie, wife of W. M. Newell, an attorney at Norman; Jean, wife of W. E. Forgy, an attorney at Archer City, Texas; Ben F.; Etta, wife of W. R. Barksdale, a merchant at Memphis, Tennessee; Johnnie, wife of H. L. Quiet, who is cashier of the First State Bank of Clinton, Oklahoma; Charlie, twin sister of Johnnie, and wife of William Milterberger, a miller and grain buyer at Clinton, Oklahoma; Lee, who married Doctor Baugaus, a physician and surgeon at Temple, Texas; Kate, twin sister of Lee, who is unmarried and is a teacher now living at Archer City, Texas. Judge Williams by his first marriage had two children: Mrs. Mary Carnahan, wife of a retired farmer at Rogers, Arkansas; and Robert L. H., who was an attorney at Goldthwaite, Texas, but died in a hospital at Temple, Texas.

Ben F. Williams had a public school education in Texas, finishing in a high school at Henrietta, and for three years was a student in the Polytechnic College at Fort Worth. His home has been at Norman since 1897, and in the meantime he had studied law in his father's office and was admitted to the bar in 1899. His offices are in the Hullum Building on East Main Street, and for fifteen years he has given all his time to his large civil and criminal practice.

His services as a criminal lawyer have taken him to all parts of the state. Only a few of the more noteworthy cases in which he has been engaged can be mentioned. He assisted in the defense of James Stevenson, who was charged with the murder of City Marshal Cathey of Pauls Valley; this case was tried in 1908 and resulted in an acquittal of the defendant. He assisted in the defense of Loreno Mathews, who was charged with the murder of her husband, and she was acquitted when tried at Guthrie in 1913. He was chief counsel for John D. Lindsay, former treasurer of Murray County, Oklahoma, who was charged with the murder of Editor Schenk at Sulphur; this case, tried at Norman under a change of venue in 1914, resulted in acquittal. He was chief counsel in the case of State v. Dr. J. H. Colby and Wade Stovall, who were charged with the murder of two school directors in McClain County in 1911. The case was tried at Norman in November, 1913, resulted in acquittal.

Mr. Williams has been a democrat ever since casting his first ballot. He is an active member of the County and State Bar associations, and fraternally is affiliated with Norman Lodge No. 7, Independent Order of Odd Fellows, Norman Camp No. 154, Woodmen of the World, with the Ancient Order of United Workmen at Norman, and with Purcell Lodge No. 1260, Benevolent Protective Order of Elks. He is a stockholder in the Norman State Bank. In September, 1900, at Norman, Mr. Williams married Miss Ninis O. Hullum. Her father is a retired capitalist and banker of Oklahoma City. To their union have been born two daughters: Mildred Lee, born August 28, 1904; and Margaret Lucile, born June 2, 1908.

THOMAS I. TRUSCOTT. The roll of men who have taken an active and helpful part in the development of the various communities of Jackson County would be incomplete did it not contain the name of Thomas I. Truscott, who since his arrival in 1898 has played an important part in the business, financial and civic life of Olustee. When he first came to this community it was as the proprietor of a cotton gin, but soon he entered the grocery business in which he has continued to be engaged, and subsequently became vice president of the First National Bank. In 1913 his worth as a citizen and his capacity for public service were recognized when he was appointed postmaster, an office in which he has efficiently served to the present.

Mr. Truscott is an Illinoisan by nativity, born at the Village of Kane, in the southern part of Greene County, August 12, 1853, a son of J. J. and Eliza (Kirkland) Truscott. His grandfather, Thomas Truscott, came to the United States from England in 1821 and soon settled as an early pioneer in Greene County, Illinois, where he was engaged in farming until the discovery of gold in California, in 1849, when he made the long and dangerous trip across the plains to the gold-fields. He was one of the fortunate miners who secured valuable claims and subsequently passed his life in the West, where he became a prominent capitalist. J. J. Truscott was born in Greene County, Illinois, in 1832, and some years after his marriage there went to Arkansas, continuing to make his home in that state until 1879, when he went to Thorpe Springs, Hood County, Texas, as a pioneer. An attorney by profession, he was engaged in practice at various places in Texas and held a high position in his vocation, being elected county judge of Knox County, Texas, an office in which he served for nine years. After retiring, in 1900, Mr. Truscott came to Olustee, Oklahoma, and in 1911 went to Maud, Oklahoma, where he is now living quietly in his comfortable home. He has been a democrat all his life and has always taken an active part in political and civic affairs, while his fraternal connection is with the Masons. Mrs. Truscott, who was born in Greene County, Illinois, in 1835, died at Thorpe Springs, Texas, in 1874. They were the parents of five children, as follows: Thomas I.; George E., who is engaged in merchandising at Maud, Oklahoma; Addie, of Frederick, Oklahoma, who is the widow of W. W. Rogers, a mechanic; Estella, who is the wife of Hon. D. F. Gaus, an attorney at Seymour, Texas, and a member of the Texas State Senate; and Lucien K., M. D., who is a practicing physician and surgeon of Oklahoma.

Thomas I. Truscott attended school at Kane, Illinois, in Arkansas, and at Thorpe Springs, Texas, and in 1875 was graduated from the Texas Christian University, receiving a diploma in higher mathematics. Following this, for four years, he was principal of a school in Rockwall County, Texas, and at the end of this period bought a school property at Seymour, Baylor County, Texas, which he owned and operated for eight years. His next venture was in the handling of cattle, an enterprise in which he was engaged for eight years in Knox County, Texas, and during this time also taught school, but in 1898 disposed of his Texas interests and came to Olustee, Oklahoma, where he erected a cotton gin. Selling this one year later, he embarked in the grocery business, and from a modest beginning has built up an enterprise that is now considered one of the substantial business concerns of the city. Almost from the time of its inception, Mr. Truscott has been vice president of the First National Bank and has taken a leading part in shaping its policies and directing it to success. When he came to Olustee he interested himself almost immediately in civic affairs, and as a friend of education was made a member of the school board, on which he acted almost continuously until 1913. He also displayed his ability and integrity as a member of the village council for six years, and June 17, 1913, was appointed postmaster of Olustee by President Wilson and has continued to discharge the duties of that position in an expeditious, efficient and courteous manner to the present time. With his family, Mr. Truscott belongs to the Christian Church. He is a member of the lodge and encampment of the Independent Order of Odd Fellows, in which he is deservedly popular. His political beliefs have made him a democrat from the time of attaining his majority.

Mr. Truscott was married in 1883 in Rockwall County, Texas, to Miss Zona Polly, who died at Seymour, Texas, in 1897, the mother of four children, namely: Edith, who is the wife of F. A. Edwards, who is engaged in the insurance business in Texas; Margaret, who is the wife of H. A. Armstrong, of Dallas, Texas, connected with the Holland Magazine; Mida, who is the wife of Miles Bivins, a well-to-do cattleman of Amarillo, Texas; and Gwendoline, who married J. P. Chose, a pharmacist of Helena, Montana. Mr. Truscott was again married, in 1904, at Olustee, Oklahoma, when united with Mrs. Stella (Crockett) Carter, widow of the late T. B. Carter, who was a farmer of Quanah, Texas. Two children have been born to this marriage: Dorothy and Barbara Tom, who are attending the Olustee public schools.

PROFESSOR JOHN DAVIS. The history of educational development in Oklahoma becomes more interesting in proportion to the recital of facts relating to the contributions made by such men as Professor Davis, since the number of individuals who may be counted as pioneers in the school history of Oklahoma is small. It was twenty years ago that Professor Davis began his activities in Oklahoma, becoming superintendent of the Blackwell public schools in 1895. The year after statehood he was called to the Central State Normal School at Edmond, and now for several years has been head of the department of physics and chemistry in that institution. His activities and influence both in and out of the class-room have been an important feature in the remarkable growth of the Central Normal.

John Davis was born in a plain rural Indiana community at Wolcott, March 7, 1867, a son of Joseph W. and Nancy M. (James) Davis. His paternal grandfather was a first cousin of Jefferson Davis, President of the Confederacy, and was born in 1800. The father was a farmer, minister of the Methodist Episcopal Church, and about two years before the birth of Professor Davis had come back from the war with the rank of first lieutenant in an Indiana regiment. Professor Davis has two brothers and four sisters: Reed Davis, a lumber dealer at Grandfield, Oklahoma; Mrs. Harriet Stocks, wife of a farmer at Clinton, Oklahoma; Arthur Davis, agent for the Santa Fe Railway at McPherson, Kansas; Mrs. Josie Erickson, wife of a stockman at Latham, Kansas; Mrs. Cynthia Pitts, whose husband is a music dealer at Lafayette, Indiana; and Mrs. Mary Pierce, who lives with her daughter at Yale, Oregon.

Professor Davis was educated in the public schools of Butler County, Kansas, to which state his parents removed in a covered wagon in 1876. He was afterwards in the Kansas Agricultural College at Manhattan and in the Kansas State Normal at Emporia. His life up to the age of nineteen was spent on a farm, at which time he left home to enter the agricultural college. He worked his way through that school, graduating with the degree Bachelor of Science in 1890. He then took professional work in the Kansas State Normal, graduating in 1892. For several years after that he was principal of several important schools in Kansas, and in 1895 came to Oklahoma and was elected superintendent of schools at Blackwell. In 1899 he became a member of the faculty of the Northwestern State Normal School at Alva, and during the following six years was the successful instructor and guide of hundreds of prospective teachers. Following that for two years he was superintendent of schools at Nowata, and in 1908 took the chair of physics and chemistry in the Central State Normal at Edmond.

Some of the methods employed in his successful work as an instructor have been reduced to book form, under the title, "A Laboratory Course in Physics," which is now in use in the schools of Oklahoma and has been adopted as a text book in twelve other states. An important feature of his work in the Central State Normal School was the development of a school of photography, the attendance upon which has increased in a few years from 80 to 236. In this school are taught the rudiments of the art and the scientific developing and finishing of the pictures. This school does nearly all the photographic work for the Central State Normal. Lantern slides made here are used in advertising the Normal, and Professor Davis is assigned the duty each year of traveling over the state in the interest of the school, using his slides in illustrating the character of the work done there.

Professor Davis was married in Ponca City, Oklahoma, in 1896 to Miss Lily Reed, who since their marriage has been associated with her husband in educational work. She has been critic teacher in the Central State Normal School, and in 1915 taught a public school in Harmon County. They have one daughter, Ruth, aged fourteen, and in 1915 a freshman student in the Central Normal.

Professor Davis is a member of the Presbyterian Church, and is affiliated with the Masonic fraternity and the Order of Yeomen. He is well known in educational circles, is a member of the Oklahoma Educational Association, the Central Oklahoma Educational Association, and the Oklahoma Academy of Science. His motto is hard work. He is devoted to the duties of his position, and spends a great deal of time in advancing the education of students in overflowing classes.

JOHN M. JONES. In point of energy, enterprise and determination, John M. Jones, of Hennessey is probably one of the best known men of Kingfisher County. His career has been a singularly active one, and has been crowned with success in a number of directions. A resident of Hennessey since 1890, he has steadily forged his way to business prominence as president of the Jones Dry Goods Company, is an ex-mayor and present postmaster of the city, and is a leading and influential Mason, belonging to the Guthrie Consistory of the thirty-second degree. The success that has been gained by this sturdy citizen and capable man of affairs has come entirely as the result of his own efforts and in its gaining his activities have ever been characterized by the strictest adherence to honorable business principles.

Mr. Jones was born February 20, 1861, on a farm in the rich agricultural community of Peoria County, Illinois, and is a son of Hugh and Esther (Breed) Jones. Hugh Jones was born in 1806 at Johnstown, Pennsylvania, a son of Malachi and Mary (Addy) Jones, the former a native of Wales and the latter of Scotland. When Hugh Jones was eight years of age the family removed from Pennsylvania to Ohio, and there he was reared and educated and resided until 1835, when he went to Peoria County, Illinois, and settled on United States Government land. There he continued in agricultural pursuits on a large scale during many years. In addition he was a steamboat pilot, was one of the builders of the Ohio Canal, and for a period twenty years' was county judge of Peoria County. In 1858-59 he preempted land in Douglas County, Kansas, but at the outbreak of the Civil war returned to Illinois, where he drilled and organized a company for the Union army, but because of disabilities did not serve actively at the front. He was a Mason, and for forty years was a deacon in the LaMarsh Baptist Church in Peoria County. Mr. Jones died near Canton, in Fulton County, Illinois, May 2, 1878. In 1835, at Canton, Mr. Jones was married to Miss Esther Breed, daughter of Jonas and Grace (Niles) Breed, the former a native of England and the latter of Wales. She was born in 1812, at New London, Connecticut, and died at Joplin, Missouri, in 1895, the mother of four sons and four daughters, as follows: William E. and Hugh, who are deceased; Amos, who is now a ranchman of Kingfisher County, Oklahoma; John M., of this notice; Martha, who is the widow of S. G. Chambers; Barbara, who is the widow of James Northrup; Charity J., who is the wife of W. P. Roy; and Charlotte, who is the wife of John A. Powell.

John M. Jones was educated in the public schools of Peoria County, Illinois, taking a special course at the county normal school, and in 1878 removed to Kansas, where he settled on Government land in Kingman County. However, because of his youth, he failed to make final proof on this property. The journey to Kansas had been made by wagon, with his brother, Amos, and in 1886 Mr. Jones located at Greensburg, Kansas, where he became manager of a loan company. He took an active part in the organization of Kiowa County, Kansas, and became influential in democratic politics, but confined his activities to helping his friends, and was never a seeker after personal preferment. Mr. Jones resided at Greensburg for three years, following which he passed a year in prospecting in Colorado, and in 1890 came to Oklahoma and located at Hennessey, which town had been founded the year before and gave promise, since fulfilled, of becoming an important center of commercial activity. Here Mr. Jones associated himself with the firm of J. H. Crider & Company in general merchandise operations, and three years later became identified with Frederick Ehler, in the Ehler Dry Goods Company. He was a member of the firm and vice president and secretary of the company for thirteen years, or until 1908, when he incorporated the Jones Dry Goods Company, of which he is now president. This enterprise has been developed to large and important proportions and is one of the leading dry goods houses of the county. At Hennessey Mr. Jones continued to manifest an interest in democratic political affairs, and in 1906 was elected mayor of the city, an office which he held during that and the following year, and in which he established a record for helpful, energetic and conscientious service. He is at this time postmaster, to which office he was appointed by President Wilson, November 16, 1914, in recognition of his abilities and integrity, as well as of the service he has rendered the party. He has endeavored faithfully to improve the efficiency of the mail service. Mr. Jones is past master of Coronado Lodge No. 56, Ancient Free and Accepted Masons, and has risen to the thirty-second degree in Masonry, holding membership in the Guthrie Consistory of the Scottish Rite.

On October 20, 1890, at Hennessey, Mr. Jones was united in marriage with Miss Zetta Prince, who was born in 1865, in Illinois, and they have three daughters and one son: Calla, Roy Kohler, Beatrice and Marcie. Roy Kehler Jones was born August 15, 1894, at Hennessey, Oklahoma, and was graduated from the Hennessey High School in the class of 1910. In 1911 he was appointed a cadet at large from Oklahoma to the United States Naval Academy, at Annapolis, Maryland, and was graduated in 1916 with the rank of ensign.

EDWARD W. DOWNS, M. D. The world instinctively pays deference to the man whose success has been worthily achieved and whose prominence is no less the result of an irreproachable life than of natural talents and acquired ability in the field of his chosen labor. Doctor Downs occupies a position of distinction as a representative of the medical profession at Hinton and the best evidence of his capability in his chosen work is the large patronage which is accorded him.

The original progenitor of the Downs family in America was a native of England and he emigrated to this country in the colonial days and settled in Connecticut. Henry Downs, father of the Doctor, was born at Hamden, Connecticut, in 1832, and as a young man he removed to Iowa City, where he was married and whence he went to Tama County, Iowa, there farming until 1866. In that year he located on a farm in Jasper County, Iowa, and there he served as township treasurer and as school director for many years. He was a democrat in his political allegiance and in early manhood he devoted much of his time to work as a stationary engineer. He was summoned to life eternal at Baxter, Iowa, in 1910. His wife, whose maiden name was Lucy Maria Worden, was born at Utica, New York, July 10, 1832, and she now maintains her home at Baxter, Iowa. There were four children born to Mr. and Mrs. Downs, as follows: Edward W. is the subject of this sketch; Harry owns and operates a garage at Baxter, Iowa; Horace is a druggist at Baxter; and Capitola died at the age of four years.

In Tama County, Iowa, just twelve miles north of Toledo, January 22, 1860, occurred the birth of Doctor Downs. He passed his boyhood and youth on his father's farm and received his preliminary educational training in the public schools of Jasper County, Iowa. He was a student in the academy at Newton, Iowa, and in 1879 he began to farm, devoting three years to that occupation. In 1882 he began to study medicine under Doctor Knepper, of Collins, Iowa, and the following year he entered the University of Iowa, in the medical department of which he was graduated in 1885, with the degree of Doctor of Medicine. In 1901 he pursued a post-graduate course in the Chicago Clinical School. Doctor Downs initiated the active practice of his profession at Coon Rapids, Iowa, where he built up a large and lucrative patronage and where he continued to reside until 1905. In that year he purchased a farm forty miles south of Winnipeg, Canada, and there was engaged in agricultural pursuits for one year, at the end of which he disposed of his farm, on which he still holds a mortgage, however, and came to Hinton. Here he has built up a splendid medical practice, being one of the pioneer physicians and surgeons in this vicinity. He is a member of the Caddo County Medical Society, the

Oklahoma State Medical Society and the American Medical Association. He is affiliated with the county and the Iowa State medical societies, likewise, and for years was health officer in Coon Rapids, Iowa. In a fraternal way he is connected with the Iowa State Lodge No. 34, Knights of Pythias, in which he is past chancellor.

Doctor Downs has been twice married. June 29, 1898, at Coon Rapids, Iowa, he married Miss Jessie Fletcher, a daughter of the late Capt. John Fletcher, a pensioned Civil war veteran. Mrs. Downs was a popular and successful teacher in Coon Rapids prior to her marriage and she died in that city in 1902. She is survived by one child: Henry W., born February 1, 1902, a pupil in the Hinton public school. For his second wife Doctor Downs married Mrs. Eliza (Clearwater) Johnson, widow of Christopher Johnson, a jeweler at Coon Rapids, and a daughter of Reuben Clearwater, a retired business man of Spaulding, Nebraska. To this union has been born one child: Iowa Capitola, whose nativity occurred February 10, 1913. Doctor and Mrs. Downs are popular in the social life of Hinton and they command the unqualified confidence and esteem of their fellow citizens.

EDMOND J. GARDNER. "Biography is history teaching by example." Every human life helps to make or reflect the progress and experience of the age. Not only does biography serve to interpret the life of a state, but it also furnishes lessons of inspiration and encouragement for individual appreciation. These points are noted as of special application to the life of Edmond J. Gardner of Valliant. Of the sketches and life histories that appear in this publication there are few that better illustrate the power of an idea and a purpose working steadily in the soul of the individual than can be found in the following paragraphs. The sketch also illustrates many important phases of early history in old Indian Territory, particularly the Choctaw Nation.

In August, 1832, a company of about six hundred persons headed by Col. Thomas LaFlore, assembled at a place near what is now the City of Paulding, Jasper County, Mississippi, to begin a journey of about eight hundred miles to their future home in a new country west of the Territory of Arkansas. It was an unusual exodus. All the inhabitants of the surrounding country were gathered together preparatory to the journey—men, women and children of every age and every degree of social standing. Following the edict of the general government, they were to leave that country forever. Naturally their hearts were sad, and they set out with much weeping and sorrow, sustained only by such comfort as came from the prospect of their future home. Some years prior to this departure the people of the country had become divided into two factions—Christians and anti-Christians. Naturally on assembling the two elements formed themselves into divisions, being drawn together by ties of kinship, friendship and beliefs. This particular company was called a "Christian company" because they favored Christianity. They traveled only on week days, announcing the hour of their daily devotion by blowing a large horn, while the Sabbath was a day of rest and of holding religious services. They traveled by ox wagons, horse wagons, horseback, and about two-thirds walked. The wagons were chiefly used for carrying the necessities for the journey. Many were thinly clad and had no shoes, and as they journeyed westward cold weather came on and they suffered greatly from the cold. About thirty died from exposure and were buried along the roadside near where they died. The roads were new and the many wagons made them almost impassable. While they were favored with reasonably fair weather, the suffering was great, especially among the feeble and children. Several babies were born during the journey. Passing through Jackson and crossing the Mississippi at Vicksburg, they followed a northwest course up Red River, and about the first day of December came to a permanent stop about forty miles across the boundary in the new country. They selected building places and set up a very populous settlement. On the 9th of December, under the leadership of Rev. Alfred Wright, a noted missionary, they organized a church and established a school, naming the place Wheelock.

At the time of the removal from Mississippi to Indian Territory in 1832, the five brothers, Isaac, Jerry, James, Noel and Edmond Gardner, were boys and young men, not more than one of them being married at the time. Their parents had died some years before in Mississippi. These five were all there were at that time of the Gardner name that were Indians by blood.

Jerry died near Wheelock a few years after his arrival, and his descendants and all the Gardners except Noel later moved further west.

Noel Gardner married Henrietta LeFlore, daughter of Colonel Thomas LeFlore. He settled a mile and a half west of Wheelock, cleared up a farm, engaged in farming and stock raising, and was also a minister of the Gospel, assisting in the church and school work at Wheelock as interpreter and native preacher. His possessions consisted of a small farm, cattle, horses, sheep, hogs and a small herd of deer. He died at his home about the year 1860, leaving a widow and three sons, Jefferson, Jerry and James. The widowed mother being an industrious and intelligent woman managed the affairs of the home to good advantage. About two years later Jefferson and James began work in a store for their uncle Michael LeFlore, while Jerry remained on the farm with his mother to oversee the farming and livestock interests.

In 1863 Jefferson moved to Eagletown, and engaged in merchandising, became prosperous and a man of prominence, serving his people in several official capacities and subsequently becoming governor of the Nation. His death occurred in 1906. His brother James was for several years in the merchandise business at Wheelock, but in 1883 moved his business to Bonton on the Red River. He married Miss Ida Lick, and lived on Red River until his death in 1887.

Jerry Gardner married first Rebecca Wilson, whom he divorced, and then married Jinny James, daughter of William James. As already stated he remained on the old homestead. Able to speak the English language very limitedly, he realized the importance of learning it, and he and his wife entered into an agreement when they were married not to speak their native tongue in their home except when absolutely necessary. He did this in order to learn the language, and after he had acquired a fluency in it the habit was so strong that he and his wife continued through their married life to speak it and their children never learned the native tongue.

In the meantime, after the death of their mother in 1871, Jerry Gardner and his two brothers had some of their interests in common, and Jerry remained at the homestead looking after the livestock for all three. That was the condition until 1882, when Jerry bought a small farm on Red River near Bonton, and set up in farming and stock raising for himself. He prospered, accumulated considerable property about him, cleared up a good farm, and in 1886 became sheriff of his county. This was apparently the high tide of his earthly achievements. Thenceforward his was a somewhat downward course. In 1887 his family was visited with an unusual amount of sickness, resulting in the death of two of his children. In 1888 the fullbloods of Towson and Boktuklo Counties armed themselves in bands and threatened extermination of the mixed bloods who were outnumbered several to one. Consequently the mixed bloods fled to Texas on short notice to save their lives, leaving their families and possessions. Jerry Gardner remained in Texas about six months, visiting his family only a few times and then only at night. Sending word to his wife by a friendly hand to meet him at midnight at a lone pine tree that stood a short distance from the home, he would cautiously set out for the trysting place, while his wife, having previously made close watch for any of the hostile bands, would take her babe in arms at about ten o'clock at night and followed by her three sons, make her way through the darkness to the place of meeting and then sit at the roots of the tree in perfect silence. The breaking of a stick would announce his approach, but in order to guard against any possible mistake there was no communication until an exchange of signals was made. Speaking in a low tone, making a few inquiries and giving a few instructions, not being permitted to see the faces of his loved ones, Jerry Gardner would depart into the stillness of the night and would then ride his horse in all haste for Texas, swimming the Red River wherever he reached its banks. Along the south banks the Red River at every crossing was a saloon, and great quantities of "fire water" were smuggled across the river into the Indian country. This only added fuel to the inflamed minds. During the civil war between the full bloods and the half bloods several were killed, including the agitators, before peace was restored. During this time Jerry Gardner suffered not only the privations already mentioned but also incurred considerable material loss. In 1889 he lost his wife, and after that he showed little interest in anything and his misfortunes preyed heavily upon his mind. In 1892 he married Mrs. Ida Gardner, his brother's widow. However, he was never himself again, and he continued to decline in attitude toward life and in his material prosperity until his death in 1898. At that time he had a daughter living by his first marriage, Mrs. Susan Parsons of Millerton. By the second marriage there were two sons and a daughter, Alfred T., Edmond J. and Carrie. Alfred T. married Mattie Bartee and settled on a farm on Red River. Carrie became the wife of George Tyler, a farmer and stock man, and settled at Wheelock.

It was of this family and of this ancestry that Edmond J. Gardner comes. He is a half-blood Choctaw. He was born November 27, 1877, on the old homestead near Wheelock. The first employment that claimed his attention was at the age of four when he was called to "carry the cat to eat the lizards" around the farm fenced by his two brothers who with neighbor boys killed them by bow and arrow. His parents then moved to Red River, near Bonton, where he lived to the age of thirteen in a wild country, feasting on wild meats, listening to the voices of wild animals, and to men too corrupt to live in any other place, with plenty of "fire water." There he absorbed and was saturated with the environments of the time and took up many of the prevalent bad habits.

The writer has seen a photograph of Mr. Gardner at the age of thirteen. It shows a boy with strong face and features, and with some of the wonder at the mystery of life impressed upon his countenance. It was at that time that this child of the back woods became cognizant in a strange and mysterious way of the things of the future, and that change in mental and spiritual attitude subsequently affected his entire life. During the next five years he lived with relatives, friends and others, going to neighborhood schools part of the time and advancing in his studies to the third reader and taking up the study of arithmetic. Though he had a great desire for knowledge and requested to be sent away to school, he was unfortunate in this respect and was never given the privileges he craved. At the age of eighteen, becoming tired of living with other people, he moved into an old house by himself and lived alone. His lonely life was happily interrupted when he met Miss Laura James, and they were married July 5, 1896.

Soon after, being stricken with a desire to see the West, in September of the same year he loaded his belongings, consisting of a little bedding and cooking utensils, in with those of another family, and started West. His first stop was about fifty miles distant. There in a short time he came face to face with starvation. For ten days or more he and his wife ate mush made up only with water and cooked from meal that had been borrowed. At the same time the young wife did a neighbor's washing for a family of four to obtain enough soap to do her own washing one time. Edmond J. earnestly sought work, but the people who gave it to him had no money, and as a last resort he accepted two small steel animal traps for a small job of work, thinking he would set the traps on the creek near his house and catch a coon and in that way get some meat to eat. At the next house for some work he was given a small piece of meat and a gallon of meal. With this he hurried home, cooked it for supper, and that night the little household was one of feasting and joy, though little provision remained for breakfast.

In March, 1897, a friendly neighbor moved them further west and unloaded them in an old house on a river bank. There Edmond Gardner became a fisherman. He took as a partner a boy named Henry James. While they caught fish in quantities they had no way to take them to market. It is an old saying that where there is a will there is a way. Gathering some scrap lumber and making a wheelbarrow, they loaded it with three hundred pounds of fish, and while one pulled the other pushed and thus they traversed eight miles through the black mud to the nearest town. Here the fish had a ready sale at five cents a pound and within two hours they were returning with a supply of provisions and, as Mr. Gardner says, happier than millionaires. This fishing was continued until June, and each week they made one or two trips with their wheelbarrow, both going barefooted during the rainy season of the year. In June Edmond loaded his belongings in with those of another family bound for the West, and after going 100 miles started out again to look for work. Crops were a total failure and no employment was to be had. It seemed that an unseen hand led him to face everything that brings disappointment, discouragements and hardships. Thus in January, 1898, he returned to his old home in Towson County, a wiser, better and a more experienced man. Before taking this trip he did not know the value of a dollar, neither did he understand the vision of his childhood. Now he began to think seriously of the future, and was ready and anxious to undertake some real vocation. At a loss to know what to do or how to start, again and again have the words "you must" flashed before his mind and he could not sit still.

Moving to Clear Creek, he began work in a blacksmith's shop, and in a few months later in a store. In January, 1899, he bought the store on "promises" and was appointed postmaster. This gave him time for study and thought. Recognizing the need of an education, he began collecting school textbooks, studied them assiduously, and his interest and application brought rapid advancement. That was the turning point in his career, and everything thenceforward seemed to change for the better. Out of that experience he evolved some precepts and resolutions. In January, 1900, he resolved "that the leisure hour was the most valuable part of the day," and that "he would never sleep in the daytime unless his health demanded it, for there is too much that need to be done," and that "knowledge and not money shall be my aim." These cardinal principles he has put to a worthy test in his subsequent career. In the same year he was appointed clerk and treasurer of Towson County and served two years. In the meantime merchandising occupied him until 1901, when he sold out and moved to Valliant, his present home, taking up business as a photographer. While his income was small, he laid away 10 per cent to buy books, calling it "the self instruction fund." Thus he acquired books and magazines, but read very little fiction or story books because he thought it too expensive a luxury for a poor man, not in dollars and cents, but in hours and days. Further, the reading of stories caused him to lose interest in more substantial literature.

In 1905 he was elected city clerk and in the same year appointed county clerk. In 1906 he was elected mayor. In the meantime he had gained familiarity with the law and was practicing as senior partner of the law firm of Gardner & Cochran. He soon gave up the law because it did not harmonize with his conscience. In 1909 Mr. Gardner organized the "Puritan Family," a fraternal order. He wrote the ritual of the initiatory degree, which exemplified the struggles of life from beginning to success, pointing out idleness, intemperance and self-importance as the chief stumbling stone; passing to old age with its joys and sorrows and closing with a scene of death and our hope in the resurrection. The purpose of this order was "mutual assistance," its motto, "do something," and the benefits were providing medical aid for the sick. The order was intended for the young people, boys and girls, but it was enjoyed by the old and young alike, the best people of the town becoming members.

In 1910 he was appointed assistant postmaster and served 3½ years. During his leisure hours he invented a complete system of shorthand writing for his own use, which was considered by many as being equal to if not better in some respects than the standard systems. While studying shorthand he discovered and worked out a complete phonetic alphabet for the English language, very different from the common English alphabet in characters used and names for them, consisting of sixty-seven characters, each having only one sound, suitable for type form and a printer's press. In 1915 he invented a small writing machine, small enough to be carried in the pocket, having only five keys and operated entirely with one hand and using his phonetic alphabet; the sounds of the words being made in the same manner as a chord on a musical instrument—by a combination of keys.

While concerning himself with these higher aims and objects, in order to support himself and family, Mr. Gardner learned the trade of watchmaker and jeweler, and is probably the only Indian of his tribe in that location. It is not to be understood that what measure of success he has had was accomplished with ease and magic. On the other hand it was accomplished, as this narrative should show, in the face of many discouragements and difficulties. At times the road seemed steep and toilsome with no reward in sight, and he suffered times of despair. Again, financial necessities would interrupt his real work, and, troubles seemed insurmountable mountains in his path. Having passed the crisis and having taken up the fight anew, all these previous discouragements passed away like snow under a summer sun.

Mr. Gardner is the father of eight children, of whom five are living: Mrs. Lela Shackelford, Bonnie, Susie, Alzara and Lois. The family live in the Town of Valliant. He is a member of the Methodist Church and is fraternally connected with the Masons, Independent Order of Odd Fellows and the Woodmen of the World.

CHARLES M. ROBERTS. Not all the Oklahoma pioneers were successful from a financial and business standpoint. Nearly all of them possessed daring and enterprise, without which qualities they would hardly have ventured into this country. There are a few conspicuous cases of substantial success, however, and one of these is illustrated by Charles M. Roberts of Okmulgee. Mr. Roberts first became identified with what is now the State of Oklahoma in 1888, the year before the original opening. In 1893 he made the run into the Cherokee Strip, starting from the Mickasuckee Mission, where he was employed at that time. He secured a claim but afterwards abandoned it.

His principal operations have been in old Indian Territory, now Eastern Oklahoma. It was on May 30, 1900, that he arrived at Okmulgee. At that time not more than twenty white people were settled on the site of that old Indian town. The railroad had not quite reached here, and in fact he was just ahead of the railroad. For several years he conducted the Frisco Hotel of Okmulgee, but he soon saw larger opportunities in the oil and real estate business and that has been the source of his unqualified success. As an investment and operator in the oil district he is one of the many men who have acquired a fortune. Some of his associates say that Mr. Roberts made $50,000 out of a single oil deal. His interests are chiefly confined to the largest and most productive oil fields in the country at this time, the Cushing field, and he also has some leases and oil property in Okmulgee County.

Charles M. Roberts was born in Berrien County, Michigan, March 8, 1864. His parents were Lowell L. and Lydia C. (Liscomb) Roberts, who were also natives of Michigan. The family lived in that state until Charles was nine years of age and they then moved to Southwestern Missouri, locating in Lawrence County in 1872. In 1886 they went to Wichita, Kansas, and in the spring of 1888 the parents settled at Rogers, Arkansas, where the father died later in the same year at the age of sixty-three. The mother died at Seneca, Missouri, March 5, 1893, aged fifty-eight. Lowell L. Roberts was a carpenter and wagon maker by trade and a very industrious and proficient workman. While living in the North in Michigan he made a great number of sleighs and bob sleds as well as wagons. In the family were four children, Nellie E., wife of Frank Good of Seattle, Washington; Jennie, wife of Lynn Wilks at Winfield, Kansas; Charles M.; Daisy E., wife of H. C. Davis of St. Joseph, Missouri.

Mr. Roberts lived with his parents and followed them in their various removals until about 1888, when he was twenty-four years of age. After he had finished his early education he went into his father's shop and practically grew up in the wagon making trade. That trade furnished him his means of living for a number of years, practically until he came to Okmulgee in 1900. When he first came into what is now Oklahoma in November,

1888, he settled at Muskogee and found outlet for his energies in work at his trade there for 6½ years. During the next 4½ years he lived in Texas, and then returned to Indian Territory and established himself at Okmulgee. Mr. Roberts has given his influence and means to the upbuilding of his home city, and is one of the leading members of the Chamber of Commerce.

In 1888 at Rogers, Arkansas, he married Miss Mary Johnson, who was born in Missouri, but was partly reared in Arkansas. Her father was J. J. Johnson. To their marriage were born three sons, two of whom died in infancy. The son Fred Roscoe, who lives at home, and who was married October 2, 1915, to Miss Sadie Miers of Muskogee has come into considerable prominence as an aviator. In the spring of 1915 he went to Ithaca, New York, and took a practical course in aviation. He has a fine aeroplane of his own, built in the Thomas Brothers factory at a cost of $8,000, and similar to those employed by the European allies for military purposes. The Okmulgee Chamber of Commerce has built for him an aviation field and hangar and he has proved a very skillful flyer and usually practices in his machine or takes it out for exhibition purposes about once a week, and may be seen soaring about in the clouds over Okmulgee every Saturday if the weather permits.

HARRY W. EBY, cashier of the Colony State Bank, Colony, Oklahoma, has been a resident of this state since 1909, when he came to Colony with Messrs. Shaub and Millner, and secured control of the bank with which he has since been identified. The bank was organized in 1903, as a state institution, by W. Montgomery and Doctor Davis, both of Weatherford, and a Mr. Galloway of Colony. The present officers of the bank are P. E. Shaub, president; E. L. Millner, vice president; and Mr. Eby, cashier. The capital stock is $10,000, with a surplus of $2,900. Under the supervision of Mr. Eby the bank has paid a 20 per cent dividend for the past six years, and its surplus has been increased from $1,300 to $2,900. It was at no time a paying investment prior to Mr. Eby's connection with it, and since he came to be connected with it the present fine home of the bank was erected.

Mr. Eby was born in Hannibal, Missouri, on December 5, 1878, and he is a son of Frank Eby, born in New York State, near Rochester, in 1827, and died in Hannibal in 1897.

Frank Eby left his native state in early manhood and went to Rock Island, where he engaged in the mercantile business and was there located for many years. He finally went to Hannibal, where he spent the last years of his life. He was a member of the Methodist Episcopal Church, and a deacon in it, and he helped to organize the church in his home town. He was a Mason and a veteran of the Civil war, having served four years as quartermaster of an Iowa regiment of volunteer infantry. He married Sarah Jane Webb, who was born in Indiana in 1830, and who died in 1906 while on a visit in New Mexico. Harry W. is the only child born to them. Sarah Webb, however, was the second wife of Mr. Eby. His first wife was a Miss Gilman of Bangor, Maine. She died in Saverton, Missouri, leaving him six children. Charles is a railroad contractor and lives in Denver, Colorado, where he is interested officially in the American National Bank. Louis died at St. Charles, Missouri, where he was a merchant for some years. Seth G. lives in Denver, and like his brother, is a railroad contractor. Mary is the wife of a Mr. Colburn, and lives in Mt. Rose, Colorado. Grace, now deceased, was the wife of J. Ross, a merchant of Mt. Rose, Colorado.

Hattie married Van Slingerland and lives in St. Louis, Missouri.

Harry W. Eby attended the public schools in Hannibal, Missouri, and was graduated from the Hannibal Commercial College in 1897. He then engaged in railroad contracting with his brothers, Seth and Charles, and was associated with them until 1906, carrying on their operations through Georgia and Alabama, and coming to Oklahoma in 1900 on a contract for the Frisco, between Sapulpa and Denison, Texas. They finished that contract in 1901 and then came to Weatherford on a contract for the old Choctaw Railroad, now the Rock Island. They built the road bed on this line from Weatherford to where the town of Clinton now stands, finishing the work in 1901, toward the close of the year. The brothers then took a similar contract in Texas for the Frisco, from Sherman to Fort Worth, and they were one year completing that piece of work. Returning to Oklahoma, they carried out a contract with the Choctaw Railroad from Tecumseh to Asher, finishing the work in 1903, and then took a contract with the Rock Island from Chandler to Guthrie, completing the work in February, 1904. Other contract work of a similar nature with the Midland Valley, from Fort Smith to Tulsa, they completed in 1905, after which Harry W. Eby of this review withdrew from association with his brothers and started operations on his own initiative. His first contract was a levee job at the mouth of the Arkansas river, and he finished that work in 1906. In 1907 he was connected with the A. B. & A. R. R. at Atlanta, Georgia, and he then entered the Clovis National Bank at Clovis, New Mexico, as a book-keeper. He was employed there for two years and in August, 1909, he came to Colony, Oklahoma, since which time he has been associated in an official capacity with the Colony State Bank, as has already been stated in detail.

Mr. Eby is a democrat and takes an active part in local politics of that faction. He has served as treasurer of the school board of Colony, and is a member and a deacon in the Presbyterian Church. He is a Mason and is a member of Weatherford Lodge No. 138 Ancient Free and Accepted Masons, Weatherford Chapter No. 31 Royal Arch Masons, and Weatherford Commandery No. 17, Knights Templar.

Mr. Eby is well known in Oklahoma City, and is connected with the Oklahoma City Building and Loan Association there. While in that city he married, in 1901, Miss Lillian Rice, whose father was then postmaster at Weatherford, and who is now living retired in this city. Five children have been born to Mr. and Mrs. Eby: Wesley, born in 1904, attends the public schools, as do also Reginald and Carolina, born in 1906 and 1910, respectively. The two younger children are Frank, born in 1912, and Virginia, in 1914.

FRANK A. DINKLER. An honorable place among the citizens of Hennessey, Oklahoma, is occupied by Frank A. Dinkler, a leading pharmacist of this wide-awake city. For nearly a quarter of a century has Mr. Dinkler been a resident of this community, and by his business energy, integrity and public spirit, has ably contributed to its prosperity and growth. On a number of occasions he has been before the people in positions of importance and his service as a public servant has been alike gratifying to his numerous friends and a credit to his capability and executive power.

Mr. Dinkler was born on a farm near Churchtown, in Washington County, Ohio, November 14, 1863, and is a son of Joseph and Susanna (Walter) Dinkler. Joseph Dinkler was born in Germany in 1835 and was nineteen years of age and an orphan when he came to the United

States. He had secured only an ordinary education in his native land, but was willing and ambitious and ready to accept any honorable employment that would start him on his way to his cherished goal, the winning of his fortune in his adopted country. Soon after his arrival, in 1854, Mr. Dinkler succeeded in securing a position in a Pittsburgh, Pennsylvania, glass factory. He spent some years in various establishments in the famous manufacturing city and finally secured the necessary means to invest in a small farm near Marietta, Ohio, in Washington County. To add to his income he also conducted a small store, and both his farm and his business were subsequently built up to very respectable proportions. In 1877, with his family, Mr. Dinkler removed to Saline County, Kansas, where he took up land from the United States Government. There he continued to be engaged in farming and stock raising until 1893, then changing his residence to Oklahoma, and died at Hennessey, May 30, 1913. Mr. Dinkler was a man of great and tireless industry, thrifty and far-sighted in money matters, and of the strictest integrity. While not a politician or an office seeker, he took an interest in the affairs of his community, and at all times conducted himself as a progressive and public-spirited citizen. He was married August 20, 1861, to Miss Susanna Walter, who was born in Germany in 1842. She was four years of age when brought to the United States by her parents, both of whom were natives of Baden, Germany. Mrs. Dinkler died at Brookville, Kansas, May 12, 1892, in the faith of the Roman Catholic Church, of which her husband was also a communicant. They were the parents of six sons and four daughters, as follows: Mary R., born April 14, 1862, who made the run for land to the Cherokee Strip at the opening in 1893, securing a tract of Government land in Garfield County, Oklahoma, on which she proved up, has been a professional nurse, but has now retired from that vocation and is living quietly at her home at Oklahoma City; Frank A., of this notice; John, born October 15, 1865, who is engaged in agricultural operations in Saline County, Kansas; William Ignatius, born December 23, 1867, who met his death in a mine accident at Seattle, Washington, in 1908; Louisa A., born December 3, 1869, who in 1895 married Fred Eishmann, a farmer of Caddo County, Oklahoma; George E., born January 21, 1872, who died unmarried November 6, 1893; Susanna Rosa, born February 14, 1874, who died as a child March 1, 1880; Joseph A., born March 30, 1876, who is engaged in business as manager of his brother's drug store at Anadarko, Oklahoma; Emma, born August 3, 1878, who was married in 1901 to O. E. Deane, a farmer of Caddo County, Oklahoma; and Frederick P., born February 3, 1881, who is a physician and surgeon now engaged in practice at Fort Cobb, Oklahoma.

Frank A. Dinkler received his public education in the schools of Washington County, Ohio, while growing up on his father's farm, and when fourteen years of age accompanied his parents to Saline County, Kansas, where he was also surrounded by an agricultural atmosphere. He had shown no desire for farming as a vocation, however, his inclination running toward the calling of pharmacist, and accordingly, in the same year as he arrived, he took up the study of his chosen profession. When he had mastered its many details he secured employment and for a number of years lived at various points until 1892, when he came to Hennessey and purchased a drug stock. Since that time he has been successful in building up a large and paying business. He now has an excellent trade and carries a large and up-to-date assortment of goods, selected wisely, arranged tastefully and attractively and priced moderately. Aside from his business Mr. Dinkler has found time to serve his community in offices of public trust, having been mayor for two years and city treasurer for eight years. In both offices he has shown his executive ability and strict integrity. Mr. Dinkler is a director of the First National Bank of Hennessey, owns a well cultivated farm in Caddo County, and considerable property at Anadarko, including the drug store that is being conducted by his brother, Joseph A. Mr. Dinkler and the members of his family are communicants of the Roman Catholic Church.

Mr. Dinkler was married at Augusta, Kansas, May 23, 1906, to Miss Margaret Flanagan, who was born February 18, 1878, in Butler County, Kansas, daughter of Martin and Johanna (Hamilton) Flanagan, the former a native of Ireland and the later of Dubuque, Iowa. One son and one daughter have come to Mr. and Mrs. Dinkler: Clara Johanna, born March 30, 1908; and George Martin, born June 30, 1911, both at Hennessey.

CHARLIE ELLIS THORNTON. Ranking as one of the representative business men of Washita County is Charlie Ellis Thornton, proprietor of an undertaking and furniture establishment at the county seat, Cordell. He is also known as a man who has contributed to the welfare and advancement of the city, and although a comparatively recent addition to the life of Cordell has already strongly entrenched himself in the confidence of its citizens. Mr. Thornton comes of a family which located prior to the Revolution in Georgia, and was born April 8, 1877, at Black Springs, Montgomery County, Arkansas, a son of A. N. and Mary (Sloan) Thornton.

A. N. Thornton was born in Georgia in 1843, and still survives, hale and hearty in spite of his seventy-three years. He has a winter home at Corpus Christi, Texas, while during the summer months he resides at Cordell. Mr. Thornton enlisted for service in the war between the states in 1861, as a member of a Georgia regiment in the Confederate army, and served four years with gallantry and valor. Later he removed to Black Springs, Montgomery County, Arkansas, and in 1891 to Limestone County, Texas, settling near Mexia. After four years he moved to the Panhandle and took up a ranch near Memphis, Texas, where he and his son, Charles E., owned nine sections of land, and although their large and valuable ranch property has been sold, the greater part of Mr. Thornton's interests are still centered at Memphis. Mr. Thornton is a deacon in the Baptist Church. He has been active in democratic politics, and at one time served as justice of the peace. Mr. Thornton married Miss Mary Sloan, also a native of Georgia, and they became the parents of six children, namely: Tommie, who was a carpenter and met his death in 1879, at Black Springs, Arkansas, when he fell from a scaffolding while working on a church belfry; Nettie, who is the wife of S. P. McKinney, an electrician of Amarillo, Texas; Lee M., who owns several farms in the vicinity of Memphis; A. H., who is a school teacher and minister of the Baptist Church, at Cordell; Charlie Ellis, of this notice; and E. K., who was a cattleman and died at Rio, Texas, in 1914.

Charlie E. Thornton secured a graded school education, and was attending the high school at Mexia in 1895, when the family moved to Memphis. Leaving school at that time, he assisted his father in the work of the ranch until 1906, then entering the furniture business at Memphis, where he continued for one year. He next moved to Rowe, Donald County, Texas, and established himself in the general merchandise business, but after one year his store was destroyed by fire. He rebuilt, but soon thereafter disposed of his interests and went to Clarendon, Texas, where he engaged in the grocery business, a successful enterprise with which he was identified until ill health caused him to sell out, in 1909. He next spent one and one-half years at Sulphur, Oklahoma, and April 8, 1911, came to Cordell, where he has since been engaged in the undertaking and furniture business. His store is situated on the west side of the square, the ground floor being 100 by 25 feet; and the second floor 75 by 50 feet, and in addition to a large stock of furniture, is equipped with every known appliance for the dignified and reverent handling of the dead. Mr. Thornton has a patronage which extends into Washita and the surrounding counties, and his business reputation is an excellent one all over this section. Mr. Thornton is a democrat and a member of the Baptist Church. He is an active and enthusiastic member of the Cordell Commercial Club, and is fraternally identified with Cordell Lodge No. 167, Independent Order of Odd Fellows Memphis Lodge No. 729, and Cordell Chapter No. 75, of the Masonic Order; Cordell Chapter No. 206, Order of the Eastern Star; and Cordell Lodge of the Brotherhood of American Yeomen.

On December 11, 1899, in Childress County, Texas, Mr. Thornton was married to Miss Ollie Barnett, daughter of J. A. Barnett, a capitalist of Clarendon, Texas. Two children have been born to this union: Moselle, born in February, 1902, and now a freshman at Cordell High School; and Harry, born in October, 1903, who is attending the Cordell graded schools.

G. M. BARRETT, prosecuting attorney of McCurtain County, went alone on a tour of inspection of the moonshine regions of the old Choctaw Nation in 1911. For a week he traveled, unmolested and practically unquestioned, never suspected, visiting one community after another, making memoranda of the location of the distilleries and charging his memory with the names and physiognomies of the men operating them. Back in his office at Idabel, he marshalled his data, placed some of the names of operators he had obtained upon warrants, and held a conference with Sheriff Tom Graham. The important result was the capitulation of six distilleries, the confiscation of their property, the arrest of a "higher up" in the liquor manufacturing business, the confessions of several others who voluntarily surrendered, and—a brass band. The brass band led a parade of law-abiding citizens of McCurtain County who rejoiced in the clever work of the young Arkansas lawyer whom they had elected prosecuting attorney and in the fact that he had achieved what United States officials had not accomplished in half a century of effort. The brass band was also a feature of the reception given Mr. Barrett, and, piled upon a wagon that featured in the parade, were the kettles and other paraphernalia of the moonshiners.

Mr. Barrett's clue that led to this clever piece of work was secured in Sevier County, Arkansas, where he was reared and where he had known two illicit manufacturers of liquor who had established themselves later in Indian Territory, where settlements were fewer and molestation infrequent. These men were brothers and in his campaigns of the county for office, Mr. Barrett had learned of their location. His lonely journey as a sleuth led him there, and on a public highway he met one of the brothers, but was not recognized.

His route to a still usually was found by an almost unfailing sign, i. e. the stumps of small trees that had been cut for logs to use in the construction of liquor plants. With few exceptions he found the plants far removed from public highways and in almost inaccessible canyons and caves of the wildest section of the Kiamichi Mountains, although one was discovered within 200 yards of the public road which he was traveling.

"Mountain Dew" he found in divers quantities. The most prosperous of operators put their product in barrels and it was hauled to points in Arkansas on the Kansas City Southern. Others put it in kegs and jugs and bottles and delivered it to peddlers who operated in adjoining territory, visiting such settlements in the mountains as Hochatown, Ida, Bethel, Smithville and Alikchi, and at Idabel, Valliant, Garvin and Haworth in the southern part of the county. A few moonshiners raised the crops of corn from which their white liquor was made, while others depended upon the little farmers of the mountain country to sell them corn or to trade it for liquor.

The first moonshiner placed in jail happened to be one of the men whom Mr. Barrett had known in Arkansas and whom he visited in his cell, relating his experience as a detective. The man, in his surprise, confessed to being a moonshiner, whereupon, he and Mr. Barrett agreed that if this man would return to the mountains, advise his fellows of the coup and the predicament they were in, and assist the sheriff in delivering their plants into possession of the county, there would be prosecutions of only the oldest of them in the business, provided all agreed to refrain from re-entering the business. The moonshiner was thereupon released upon his own recognizance. He headed for the mountains and in a few days six plants had been brought in by the sheriff and all the men connected with them had surrendered. The men agreed among themselves who should plead guilty and when they were presented to Mr. Barrett he recommended light sentences. These occurrences happened in 1911. For several years the Kiamichis were tolerably free of the big stills.

G. M. Barrett was born in Dyer County, Tennessee, June 7, 1874, and is a son of John F. and Ulysses Luvisa (Hopper) Barrett. His father, born in North Carolina, ran away from home at the age of fourteen years to join his three brothers who were in the Confederate army, in which he likewise enlisted and was wounded three times, the last wound being received at Appomattox, where General Lee surrendered. Mr. Barrett was taken a prisoner and on account of his wound was not finally released until nearly a year after the war had closed. In the meantime, a negro boy came to the hospital and inquired if a Confederate soldier was there, and, on being introduced to Mr. Barrett, remained with him until after he had rejoined his relatives in Tennessee. When he returned to his former home in North Carolina, after a long and arduous trip on a sore leg, he found that his father had taken his wife and other children and set out for a new home in the West. About the same time, Mrs. Hopper, also widowed by the war, took her two boys and two girls from their home in South Carolina and headed for the West. It happened that the Barrett and Hopper families joined and made the trip together, locating in Middle Tennessee. After much wandering, veteran John F. Barrett found the remnant of his family, and in due time was married to Ulysses Luvisa Hopper. They became the parents of six sons: G. M., Earnest L., a farmer at Corn Hill, Arkansas; John W. and J. E., farmers at Garvin, Oklahoma, and S. S. and C. C., who are teachers. At the close of the war, John F. Barrett settled on an unimproved farm of eighty acres in Arkansas, near Brownstown, where he resided for some years, but finally moved to Garvin, Oklahoma, where he now makes his home.

G. M. Barrett was reared on the home farm, where he remained until he was twenty-one years of age, and at that time started out to secure an education. "I had a yearning for an education," he says, "an ambition to rise in the world and increase the sphere of my usefulness. My father, who desired to help me all he could, furnished me with provisions and I rented a small house where I did my own cooking and cut wood on Saturdays to pay rent. I worked out and went to school until I was able to teach. I then studied law and July 9, 1902, was admitted to practice law in Little River County, Arkansas. I was admitted to practice in the United States courts September 11, 1905." In 1904, while still living in Arkansas, he bought the Little River News, at Ashdown, Arkansas, which he later sold to Charles L. Shinn, of Hale, Missouri.

Mr. Barrett came to Oklahoma in 1905 and located at Garvin, where he engaged in farming and stock raising, as well as in the practice of law. In 1906 he was secretary of the Democratic Central Committee of the 111th District, and on October 6th of that year, called the first primary election ever held in the district, this being for the purpose of nominating a candidate for the Constitutional Convention. The election call was issued by the committee, of which W. L. Ray was president, in session at Garvin, September 8, 1906. In 1907, Mr. Barrett made the race for the democratic nomination for county attorney, in the first statehood campaign, and was defeated by Robert E. Steel by a narrow margin. This campaign had an especially exciting feature in that it stirred certain republicans of the north end of the county, who believed Mr. Barrett would be nominated and who knew what his policy would be with reference to the enforcement of the law. In 1908 Mr. Barrett was appointed county attorney to succeed Robert E. Steel, temporarily suspended, and in a letter, dated September 4th of that year, addressed to William H. Harrison, regarding the appointment, he said in part: "I pray God that when I shall have lived my allotted time out on earth and come to bid farewell to those who know me, I shall have the pleasure of knowing that my life has been of some service and has been appreciated. Next to my family the thing I treasure most is the friendship, well being and happiness of the people among whom I live." During the ten days of his incumbency of that office, Mr. Barrett convicted seven men for murder and one for larceny. This was a record that had not been surpassed in the state, considering the brevity of time and the character of defense made by those he prosecuted.

In the campaign of 1910 Mr. Barrett made a speaking tour of the county in behalf of the celebrated "Grandfather Clause Act," which was given a substantial majority by the county. In that year he came before the people again as candidate for county attorney of McCurtain County, and was elected to that office without opposition in the general election, receiving 1,314 votes, the highest number cast for any county candidate, and the largest vote with one exception cast for any democratic candidate that year in Oklahoma. In 1912 he defeated Jeff D. McLendon for the nomination for the office and was re-elected by a large majority. During his campaign in 1910, he said: "I am no politician and know nothing of politics. I did not come from a family of politicians. But must I be defeated because my father is not a politician, because he honored the plow handles instead of the judge's bench? Must the favored few always hold the positions of honor and trust and the politicians rule our government? Are honesty and integrity qualifications worth anything against political influence?"

Among his first duties after entering the office of county attorney in 1910 were the preferring of charges, involving failure to enforce the law, and Indian misdealings, against the county judge. Conditions relating to Indian transactions had reached an acute stage and Governor Cruce and Governor McCurtain of the Choctaw Nation were appealed to with the result that D. C. McCurtain was assigned to the county as special assistant attorney general to assist in an investigation started by Mr. Barrett. Judge Hill of McAlester, and G. V. McVeigh, an Indian agent, also joined in the investigation. This resulted in the removal from office of the county judge, the return to county of about $74,000 that had been unlawfully taken from the Indians and the deeding back to Indians of lands taken unlawfully. Mr. Barrett is essentially a prohibitionist and he had much to do with the McCurtain County prohibition majority of 245 in the election of 1912 wherein it was sought to substitute local option for statewide prohibition.

No case he was ever engaged in had a more spectacular interest and is likely to be longer remembered in McCurtain County than the Coltrane Case. He took it up long after the deeds of crime had been committed and judgment passed, and in fact his efforts were directed toward a righting of the processes of justice, a reparation to a man who had already served some half a dozen years in the Federal prison at Leavenworth, and a conviction of the real criminal.

Only a brief history of the case can be attempted. In the fall of 1902 Cicero and Sam Coltrane made arrangements to live a few months at the log home of Tom Watson and his rather attractive wife, a few miles from Hochatown. In a short time there was friction between Cicero Coltrane and Watson partly over business matters, partly, it is said, because of the former's attentions to Mrs. Watson. One evening in May, 1903, Cicero left the house, to feed a hog. While near the pen he was shot down with a double barreled gun, one load being of fine shot and the other of buckshot. That night the body was conveyed to a field some distance away and buried.

The next day Sam Coltrane was arrested charged with the murder. While in custody he made a confession that he had killed Cicero, though neither at that time nor at any subsequent time was a strong and impelling motive for the killing given or proven.

Coltrane had his examining trial and was bound over to the United States Court. Suspicion was very strong against Watson also, and the officers arrested him. Later on he was bound over and placed in jail with Sam, but failing to get any testimony that would corroborate Sam's against Watson, and being unable to convict either Watson or Sam without using the testimony of Watson and his wife against Sam, the grand jury dropped the case against Watson and used Watson and his wife as witnesses against Sam. Thus after a number of trials and one or more disagreements, Sam Coltrane was sentenced before the Federal judge of Durant to serve the rest of his natural life in the Federal penitentiary at Leavenworth. He not only protested his innocence of the real crime but kept unceasingly diligent in securing the influence of friends to effect his release from prison and the establishment of his innocence.

It was after his election as county attorney that Mr. Barrett first became identified with the case. He had been in office only a few weeks when an old man named Saunders who lived in the Hochatown neighborhood was murdered in his home and his house burned down on the body. Mr. Barrett conducted an investigation and in the debris of the house found some scraps of letters, which indicated that the letters had been written from the penitentiary at Leavenworth. In the meantime Sam Coltrane having learned of the killing of Saunders, wrote Governor Cruce a synopsis of the killing of Cicero Coltrane, stating that Watson was the man who killed old man Saunders for the purpose of covering up all the facts in reference to the killing of Cicero. While old man Saunders was an important witness against Tom Watson, it was really his son Harry Saunders who had passed the Watson place on the evening of the killing of Cicero Coltrane, and Watson's wife had seen the young man and, though it being about dark had mistaken him for the father. Mr. Barrett soon afterward went to Leavenworth and procured all information he could from Sam Coltrane. After examination of all the information, Mr. Barrett came to the conclusion that Watson was the real murderer, and that he had been led to kill the old man Saunders for the purpose of getting him out of the way as a last remaining witness against him. After Watson had killed Cicero for the protection of himself, he and his wife conspired together to lay it all on Sam Coltrane, and that was an easy matter under the circumstances since Coltrane was a comparative newcomer in the neighborhood and from the first realized that he could never get his word believed against that of Watson, and that his life depended upon his covering up the murder and shielding Watson. It was for this reason that he had consented to a plot outlined by Watson by which it was agreed that the first one arrested for the murder should assume all responsibility for it, while the other would lend his influence in getting the defendant cleared. Sam Coltrane thus fell a guileless victim to the plot, and while he was thus "accessory after the fact" he was not the real murderer.

All this was brought out by Attorney Barrett, who assembled a great volume of evidence and proceeded with characteristic vigor in the prosecution of the case against Watson subsequent to the Saunders murder. In 1912, a few months after Saunders was murdered and his house burned down, Tom Watson was indicted charged with the murder of Cicero Coltrane. Mr. Barrett conducted the prosecution of Watson, and toward the close of 1913 secured his conviction and Watson was subsequently sent to ten years confinement and a thousand dollars fine. In passing, it may be noted that Sam Coltrane has been pardoned and Mr. Barrett recently signed a petition for the pardon of Watson.

Mr. Barrett was united in marriage December 10, 1899, at Brownstown, Arkansas, to Miss Della R. Herndon, daughter of Robert Herndon and granddaughter of an officer in the Confederate army during the Civil war. To this union there has been born one daughter, Ulice, who is now ten years old. Mr. Barrett and his family are members of the Baptist Church. Fraternally, he is affiliated with the local lodges of the Masons, the Independent Order of Odd Fellows and the Woodmen of the World, and his professional connections include membership in the McCurtain County and Oklahoma Bar associations.

GLEN W. DILL. The Dills, father and son, have been prominent in financial and other affairs at Hobart for twelve years, almost from the founding of the city. The late Judge D. S. Dill occupied a position of prominence and influence as a banker and attorney such as few of his contemporaries in Southwestern Oklahoma enjoyed, and since his death many of his financial activities have been assumed by his son Glen W., who now looks after the extensive farm loan business established by his father, and is also one of the largest stock holders and a director in the City National Bank of Hobart.

The late Judge D. S. Dill was born in Ohio in 1858, his ancestors having come originally from Germany, and probably settled in Ohio from North Carolina. At the age of sixteen he went west from Ohio to Nickerson, Kansas, and eventually studied and became a lawyer. In 1887 he removed to Kansas City, Missouri, and in 1890 to Caldwell, Kansas, and at the opening of the Cherokee Strip established his home on a claim at Medford, Oklahoma. In 1903 he removed to Hobart, where he became prominent as one of the early lawyers and bankers and for ten years was an active force in everything connected with the civic and political life of that city and was conspicuous as a town booster. He became president of the City National Bank, and held that position at the time of his death in January, 1913. Judge Dill was a trustee in the Presbyterian Church, was a member of Hobart Lodge No. 198, Ancient Free and Accepted Masons, and was one of the leading democrats of Kiowa County. He married Cora Wolfinger, who was born in Ohio in 1863. Their children are: Glen W.; Todd, who was killed by a fall over a precipice in the Washita Mountains at the age of twenty just before he was ready to graduate from the Hobart High School; Cora Marie is now a freshman in the Hobart High School.

Glen W. Dill was born at Kansas City, Missouri, February 10, 1888, and since early childhood has lived in Oklahoma, having gained his early education in the public schools at Medford, and graduating from the Hobart High School with the class of 1906. In 1907 he took a business course in the Gem City Business College at Quincy, Illinois, and after returning to Hobart spent five years as bookkeeper in the City National Bank. In 1913, following the death of his father, he took charge of the large farm loan business and brokerage interests built up and established by his father in connection with banking, and has carried on this business which represents an extensive clientage throughout Kiowa and surrounding counties. His offices are in the City National Bank Building. In the bank, of which his father was president, he is a director and one of the principal stockholders. Mr. Dill is also secretary and treasurer of the Hobart Ice & Bottling Company, is secretary of the Hobart Mill & Elevator Company, and secretary of the Hobart Building & Loan Association.

In politics he is a democrat, is a trustee in the Presbyterian Church, and is affiliated with Hobart Lodge No. 198, Ancient Free and Accepted Masons, and Hobart Chapter No. 37, Royal Arch Masons. At Hobart in 1910 he married Miss Zelma Vandegrit, a daughter of the late D. E. Vandegrit, who was a real estate broker in Hobart but who died in Oklahoma City.

ALBERT ANDREW WEBER, M. D. Since the year 1908 the health and sanitation of the thriving little community of Bessie, in Washita County, have been under the care of Dr. Albert Andrew Weber, a medical and surgical practitioner who has brought to his practice a most thorough and comprehensive training and devotion and skill of a high order. Doctor Weber was born at Jackson, Jackson County, Michigan, April 29, 1875, and is a son of John and Emma (Gass) Weber.

Albert Weber, the grandfather of Doctor Weber, served his term in the German army in his youth and when he entered upon his career chose the vocation of farming, in which he continued to be engaged throughout his life in the province of Wurtemburg, Germany. His death occurred at Esslingen, when his grandson was still very young, the grandfather being then seventy-four years of age. John Weber was born at Esslingen, Germany, in 1841, and emigrated to the United States in 1867, settling at Detroit, Michigan, where he was engaged in butchering. From Detroit he subsequently moved to Jackson, where he established himself in a wholesale and retail meat business, and with native thrift and industry increased his holdings and enlarged his scope of operation so that his business activities invaded the fields of milling, real estate and banking, in all of which lines he met with unqualified success. He died at Jackson in 1891, aged fifty years, the possessor of a handsome property as well as of the regard and confidence of those among whom he had lived. He was a consistent member of the Lutheran Church, and a democrat in politics, and took a keen and active interest in civic affairs, as well as in the various lodges and fraternities to which he belonged, and which included the Harmonica, the Arbeiter Verein, the Turner Verein, the Maennerchor and the Independent Order of Odd Fellows. Mr. Weber married Miss Emma Gass, who was born in Ohio in 1854, and died at Jackson, Michigan, in 1884, and they became the parents of five children: Emma, who lives at Jackson, Michigan; Albert Andrew, of this review; John, who is a resident of Chicago; Charles, a bookkeeper residing at Jackson, Michigan; and Estella, who is the wife of James Molyneaux, auditor for the Illinois Central Railroad at Chicago.

Albert Andrew Weber attended the public schools of Jackson, Michigan, and in his youth spent three years, from 1888 until 1891, in academic work at Stuttgart, Germany. He was graduated from the Jackson High School in the class of 1894, following which he went to the University of Michigan and was graduated in 1898 with the degree of Bachelor of Science. This was followed by three years of work in the medical department of the same institution, and his senior year was then passed at Rush Medical College, Chicago, where he received his degree of Doctor of Medicine in 1903. To further prepare himself he did hospital work in Chicago at St. Luke's Hospital as well as the Cook County Hospital and continued to practice in that city from June, 1903, until March, 1904. At that time he first came to Perry, Oklahoma, where he was engaged in practice for four years, and in this time was elected county coroner of Noble County, a position in which he was serving up to the time of his resignation, when, in June, 1908, he came to Bessie. Here he has continued in the enjoyment of an excellent practice, attracted by his skill, sympathy and earnest devotion. He carries on a general practice in both medicine and surgery, being the only practitioner at Bessie, and belongs to the Washita County Medical Society, the Oklahoma Medical Society and the American Medical Association. He has continued to be a close and discriminating student, and in 1913 took a post-graduate course at Rush Medical College. Doctor Weber maintains well appointed offices in the O. P. Smith Drug Store, where he has a comprehensive medical library, and surgical equipment for the handling and care of the most difficult and delicate operations. He is a democrat in politics, and in additioon to acting as coroner of Noble County was also a member of the insanity board while there. While reared in the faith of the German Lutheran Church, he attends the Presbyterian Church at Bessie. Fraternally, Doctor Weber belongs to Perry Lodge, Ancient Free and Accepted Masons; Perry Lodge of the Knights of Pythias; Bessie Camp of the Modern Woodmen of America, and the Phi Beta Pi Greek letter medical fraternity.

In 1908, at Perry, Oklahoma, Doctor Weber was married to Miss Frances E. Irwin, daughter of Milton Irwin, deceased, who was a millwright, and one child has been born to this union: Vivian Alberta, born September 17, 1911.

S. E. BELL. When Mr. Bell arrived in Bartlesville in 1903 he found it a village of a few hundred people and just coming into fame as one of the centers of the oil and gas industry. Since that year his own fortunes and energies have been identified with the development of the oil resources, and his holdings and connections give him rank as one of the most prominent men in that industry in Northern Oklahoma.

S. E. Bell, who has spent many years in the old Indian Territory part of Oklahoma, was born at Mendon, Adams County, Illinois, December 29, 1863, a son of John A. and Eliza (Mills) Bell. His father was born in Indiana and his mother in Kentucky, and both were taken to Illinois when children and grew up and married there. The father enlisted at Canton in the spring of 1862 in an Illinois regiment of infantry, and was with the armies of Grant and Sherman until the close of the war. He took part in the Atlanta campaign, then in the march to the sea, and finally reached Washington and marched up Pennsylvania Avenue in the grand review after the close of the war. Soon after the war he removed to Knox County, in Northeastern Missouri, and about 1890 went to Neosho County, Kansas, where his wife died in 1897 at the age of fifty-six. The father is now living at Caney, Kansas, retired. In early life he was a farmer, but for many years was in the hardware business in Missouri and Kansas. He is a member of the Methodist Church and is a stanch republican. He served as mayor and justice of the peace at Cunningham, Missouri, and also as justice of the peace in Neosho County, Kansas, and as police judge at Caney.

S. E. Bell was one of a family of five sons and five daughters, all now living except two sons. His early life was spent at home until the age of seventeen, and his education came from the common schools. In 1883, when about twenty years of age, he went to Neosho County, Kansas, and spent two years as a clerk in a hardware store. For two years following he was in business for himself at Erie, Kansas, and then entered the Indian Territory and was employed for three years in a general store at Fort Gibson. For the next three years he was connected with the old Ann Percival store, a well known establishment in that part of the territory. Mr. Bell finally came out of the Indian Territory and was engaged in the hardware and implement business at Caney, Kansas, until 1903. He then located in Bartlesville, which was then a mere hamlet, and has since made himself a factor in the oil industry, both as an individual operator and in association with others. He is president of the Bell Oil Company, incorporated, and was formerly president of the Lehman-Bell Oil Company. He is now manager of the co-partnership company of Bell, Stratton & Company, operating extensively in Kay County. His holdings as an oil man extend to practically all the better known districts of Northern Oklahoma.

Mr. Bell is a republican, and for two terms served as clerk of the city council at Bartlesville. He is also a Master Mason. In 1892 Mr. Bell married Mrs. Minnie R. Vann. She was born in the Cherokee Nation and has a thirty-second portion of Cherokee Indian blood. Her father, John Cunningham, was a pioneer at old Fort Gibson. By her first marriage her three children were: John C. Vann, of Bartlesville; N. B. Vann, of Arizona; and Fannie, who died at the age of seven years. Mr. and Mrs. Bell have three children of their own: Alfred E., who is associated with his father; Laura P., who is now a student at Chicago, taking courses in domestic science and art preparatory to teaching; and Lorena, who is in the high school at Bartlesville.

JAMES W. PORTER. Though a young man of only thirty years, James W. Porter has for almost ten years of that time been an active factor in banking affairs in Western Oklahoma. He is now vice president of the Cotton Exchange Bank of Leedey, assisted in organizing that and several other institutions in Dewey and other counties and is also vice president of the State Bank of Commerce at Trail and vice president of the Texmo Cotton Exchange Bank at Moorewood.

Born at Newton, Tennessee, December 5, 1885, James W. Porter comes of a family that originated in Ireland and established itself in Alabama during the period of early settlement in that commonwealth. His father, J. W. Porter, who was born at Montgomery, Alabama, in 1839, is now living retired at Shawnee, Oklahoma. From Alabama he went to Rock Island, Illinois, and later to Newton, Tennessee, in 1893 established his home at Cleburne, Texas, and in 1903 went to Shawnee. For many years he was in the hotel business. He served throughout the conflict between the North and the South as a Confederate soldier, going out with an Alabama regiment, was wounded and taken prisoner, but subsequently returned to the ranks after being exchanged. J. W. Porter was married in New York State to Miss Utica Streeter, who was born in Utica, New York, in 1848.

James W. Porter from the age of eight years lived in Cleburne until his father removed to Shawnee. He attended the public schools at Cleburne, and graduated with the high school class in 1903, and from that year until 1906 was laying the foundation of his business career as an employee in a department store at Shawnee. In 1906 he became associated with W. O. Horr and Irving H. Wheatcroft. These gentlemen organized at Ray the Cotton Exchange Bank and similar banks in Texmo, Cheyenne, Crawford and Elk City. In 1911 the bank at Ray was removed to Leedey, and has since been the Cotton Exchange Bank of Leedey. Its present officers are; Irving H. Wheatcroft, president; James W. Porter, vice president; C. R. Flint, cashier. The bank has a capital stock of $15,000 and the present surplus account is $1,500. In 1911 at the corner of Main Street and Broadway a modern and well furnished banking house was constructed, the banking rooms being on the lower floor and offices above. It is a cement block building.

In politics Mr. Porter is a democrat, but has given most of his attention to local affairs, and for two years served as mayor of Leedey. He still has membership in the First Baptist Church at Cleburne, Texas, and is affiliated with Leedey Lodge No. 227 of the Knights of Pythias. At Texmo, Oklahoma, in 1906 he married Miss Velma Horr, daughter of C. A. Horr. Mr. Horr is a resident of Leedey and in the real estate business.

HON. E. E. GLASCO. One of the leading civil and criminal lawyers of the state, Hon. E. E. Glasco, has also won distinction as a public servant, the value of whose labors in the Oklahoma Legislature cannot be overestimated. He was born in White County, Illinois, in 1870, but was reared principally in Wayne County, where his parents, Thomas M. and Martha A. (Burrell) Glasco, resided on a farm. Thomas M. Glasco, a native of Illinois, was but fifteen years of age at the outbreak of the Civil war, but he bravely joined his father in the same company of the Eighty-seventh Regiment, Illinois Volunteer Infantry, and subsequently served four years under the flag of the Union. Mr. Glasco's paternal and maternal grandfathers were natives of South Carolina, and the ancestry of the former has been traced back beyond the days of the Revolution in America. Both parents are living now at Washington, Oklahoma. In the family of Thomas M. and Martha A. Glasco there were three sons and three daughters, as follows: E. E., of this review; E. D., who is a prominent stockman and real estate dealer at Washington, Oklahoma; Clarence, who is a prosperous farmer at Athens, Texas; Mrs. Ada Jackson, who is the wife of a machinist at Athens, Texas; Mrs. Mary E. Smith, who is the wife of a member of the firm of Smith-Glasco Hardware Company, at Blanchard, Oklahoma; and Mrs. Sarah Sapp, who is the wife of an agriculturist and stock dealer of McClain County, Oklahoma.

E. E. Glasco was educated in the public schools of Illinois and the Hayward Collegiate Institute, at Fairfield, Illinois, from which he was graduated in 1892 with the degree of Bachelor of Arts. Following this, he completed a course in the Southern Illinois State Normal School, at Carbondale, Illinois, and for the eight succeeding years was a popular and efficient teacher in the public schools. While in Illinois, Mr. Glasco served two years in the capacity of assessor of Wayne County.

In 1897 Mr. Glasco moved to Athens, Texas, and for three years thereafter continued to follow the vocation of educator. At that time he became interested in journalistic work, founding the Henderson County News at Athens, and this paper soon became involved in a heated campaign involving the liquor question, supporting the side of the prohibitionists and assisting them to victory. The character of officers sought by the prohibitionists were elected, among them being District Judge R. L. Gardner, who still retains his seat on the bench. Following the outcome of this struggle, Mr. Glasco went to Tishomingo, Oklahoma, where he began the practice of law, to which he had devoted much study for several years. He succeeded in building up a good practice, but in 1906 came to Purcell, Oklahoma, and in 1907 was elected the first county judge of McClain County, an office which he acceptably filled for one term.

Mr. Glasco was first elected to the Oklahoma Legislature in 1912 and during that term was made chairman of the Committee on Banks and Banking. He was the author of the banking act passed by that body which remedied defects in the guaranty law and placed the guaranty plan on a more substantial basis, and was joint author of the law prohibiting race track gambling and of a series of bills regulating the loaning of money. In 1914 he defeated the late C. M. McClain, who had been a member of the Constitutional Convention, for the nomination and was re-elected to the Legislature, on a platform pledging an anti-usury law and exemption reforms. His victory was notable in view of the opposition encountered at the hands of bankers and retail merchants who opposed his plan of remedial legislation relating to usury and exemptions. He was made chairman of the Committee on Judiciary No. 1, and a member of the committees on Criminal Jurisprudence, Congressional Redistricting, Revenue and Taxation, Prohibition Enforcement and Banks and Banking. He was the author of a bill preventing usury, and a bill validating insurance policies and requiring insurance companies in case of a total loss of property insured to pay the face amount of the policy. Mr. Glasco was a stanch adherent of measures advocating the interests of labor and the farmers, and in the 1912 Legislature was sternly opposed to the passage of a bill relating to coal miners which, after being passed by the Legislature, was referred to and defeated by the people. He was a candidate for speaker of the House of the Fifth Legislature, but withdrew from the contest and threw his strength to A. McCrory, who was thus elected. Mr. Glasco has been a delegate to every state democratic convention since the acquirement of Oklahoma statehood, being a member of the 1912 convention platform committee, and was a delegate to the democratic national convention at Baltimore in 1912.

Mr. Glasco was married in 1889, while still a resident of Illinois, to Miss Rosa E. Donovan, who died in March, 1907. To this union there were born four children, as follows: Roy, aged twenty-one years, who passed the state bar examination in 1914 and is now employed in the law office of Thompson & Patterson, at Paul's Valley, Oklahoma; Ellen, aged nineteen years, who is a high school graduate and lives at home with her father; Raymond, aged seventeen years, who is employed as a chemist in the plant of the Kansas Chemical Company, at Wichita, Kansas; and Crystal, aged twelve years, who is a student at Purcell High School. In 1908 Mr. Glasco was again married, his second wife having borne the name of Mrs. Mattie Keener. They have one daughter: Evelyn, who is three years of age.

Mr. Glasco and his family are members of the Methodist Episcopal Church. South. Professionally, he is connected with the McClain County Bar Association and the Oklahoma State Bar Association. He is senior member of the law firm of Glasco & Osborn, and is justly accounted one of the leading civil and criminal lawyers of his part of the state.

DILLARD WATTS, M. D. One of the hardest working physicians in Oklahoma is Dr. Dillard Watts of Laverne. It is said that Doctor Watts has a practice extending over three counties and is almost constantly at work answering the calls of his large patronage.

He represents one of the old families of Kansas, and much of his early experience was connected with farming and other lines of business until he could realize his ambitions by entering the medical profession. He was born on a farm in Johnson County, Kansas, March 15, 1869, a son of Josiah and Sarah (Mann) Watts. Josiah Watts was a notable figure in western life in the early days. He was born in 1820 in St. Charles County, Missouri, and was directly related to the family of Daniel Boone, the Boones having been among the pioneers in St. Charles County. Josiah Watts was also of French stock, his great-grandfather having been an officer in the Revolutionary army under General Lafayette, with whom he emigrated to America. Josiah Watts showed his stock by a life of much excitement and adventure in the West. In 1849 he participated in the rush to the West during the gold excitement and spent four years on the Pacific Coast as a prospector and miner. He went out by ox team overland and returned by the Isthmus of Panama. After his return to Missouri he became associated in mercantile business with James Bridger, the famous trapper and Indian fighter, and for a number of years was located at the eastern terminus of the Santa Fe Trail, at what is now Kansas City, He then homesteaded land in Johnson County, Kansas, prior to the Civil war, and the title to that land still remains in the Watts family. He was one of the prominent men of Johnson County, where he died April 30, 1896. In 1858 Josiah Watts married Miss Sarah Mann, who was born March 20, 1838, a daughter of Samuel Mann, a native of Missouri, and she now lives at Stilwater, Kansas. There are seven children, five sons and two daughters, namely: Banaugh, now a physician at Okemah, Oklahoma; Samuel, deceased; Mary, who died in infancy; Ada, widow of Jerry R. Harbeson of Sapulpa, Oklahoma; Robert B., a physician at Wellington, Missouri; Leo, a farmer in Beaver County, Oklahoma.

Dr. Dillard Watts, the youngest of the family, grew up on a farm in Johnson County, gained a public school education, and worked on the farm with his father until he was twenty-one. For the following four years he was in the drug business at Napoleon, Missouri, and after earning and accumulating the necessary means he entered in 1898 the Kansas City Medical College, where he spent two years. He also practiced under a preceptor for two years, and thus by continued hard work and paying his own way finally graduated from medical college with the degree M. D. in the class of 1908. Seeking a permanent location Doctor Watts came to Oklahoma, and practiced at the old Town of Speermore, where he built up much of the practice which he still retains. Speermore was his home until 1914, in which year he moved to Laverne to be near the railroad, and now has his office and residence in that growing little city.

Doctor Watts is a Scottish Rite Mason, belonging to the bodies of that order at Guthrie. In 1896 he married Miss Jessie Hawkins, who was born in Bates County, Missouri, in 1872, and who died January 20, 1899, at Kansas City, Missouri. To their marriage were born two children: Zoe, wife of Philip Doherty, a lumberman at Laverne; and Beulah, who is an elocutionist. On March 29, 1915, Doctor Watts married Emma Garrity, who was born in Riley County, Kansas.

J. C. SHEETS. The wonderful development of the oil and gas industry of Oklahoma during recent years has attracted to this state men of ability, enterprise and progressive spirit from all parts of the country. Among the first to come to the vicinity of Copan was J. C. Sheets, a West Virginian, who has since been active in the promotion and development of some of the leading industries of this part of the state. At the present time he is associated with enterprises of importance and large proportions that have contributed materially to the business prestige of Washington and the surrounding counties.

J. C. Sheets was born at Salmon, West Virginia, November 19, 1876, and is a son of Leander and Alice Starr (Curtis) Sheets. His father was born at New Matamoras, Washington County, Ohio, March 18, 1838, and as a young man went to West Virginia, where he continued to be engaged in agricultural pursuits until his retirement. In his later years he came to Oklahoma, and his death occurred at Copan, in September, 1908. Mrs. Sheets was born at Hockingport, Athens County, Ohio, November 24, 1849, and was about ten years old, in 1860, when taken to West Virginia by her parents. That state continued to be her home until she came to Oklahoma, where she still resides. There were four children in the family: Vaughn L., a graduate of the American Medical College, and now a practicing physician and surgeon of Chicago, Illinois, where he has offices at No. 59 East Madison Street; Earl H., a resident of Muskogee, Oklahoma, and partner in the oil producing firm of Sheets Brothers and various other concerns; J. C., of this review; and Dr. F. C., a graduate of the American Medical College, and now a practicing physician of Oklahoma City.

J. C. Sheets received his education in the public schools of Cameron, West Virginia, and in 1899 became interested in the oil business as a producer, although he had been connected with this industry in one or another capacity since his sixteenth year. In 1902, as one of the first producers of Copan, he came here with his brother, Earl H., and founded the firm of Sheets Brothers, which has steadily grown into one of the largest concerns in this line in Washington County. The firm now operates twelve properties, and since its inception has drilled about 300 wells, the brothers operating farm lands and timber tracts extensively. J. C. Sheets is secretary and treasurer of the Georgia Oil and Gas Company, manager of Sheets & Company, president of the Alamo Oil Company, secretary and treasurer of the Swastika Oil and Gas Company, secretary and treasurer of Sheets Brothers & Jackson and manager of the Collis Oil and Gas Company.

He is known among his associates as one of the shrewdest oil operators in the state, and his judgment is taken as final in regard to gas and oil properties.

Mr. Sheets' contribution to the upbuilding of Copan is a beautiful home, built in 1905, of reenforced concrete, with eight rooms, modern in every particular, and including private sewerage and private water works. He was reared a democrat, but is inclined to vote independently, preferring to use his own judgment in the selection of candidates. At the present time he is serving as treasurer of his school district. He is a thirty-second degree Mason, belonging to the Shrine at Tulsa, the Commandery at Sistersville, West Virginia, of which he is a life member, the Consistory at Guthrie, and the Blue Lodge at Copan. He is also a life member of the Benevolent and Protective Order of Elks, at Independence, Kansas, and holds membership in the local lodges of the Independent Order of Odd Fellows and the Knights of Pythias.

Mr. Sheets was married in 1904, to Miss Millicent E. Holdren, who was born at Independence, Ohio, January 16, 1876, a daughter of H. H. and Harriet E. (Webber) Holdren, natives of the Buckeye State and residents at Newport. To Mr. and Mrs. Sheets there has been born one daughter: Alice Millicent.

HUGH HENRY. There is a picturesque elevation in Okmulgee County known as "the Hugh Henry Hill" which rises 192 feet above the general elevation of the town at its foot. Crowning this hill is the home of Mr. Hugh Henry, who has lived in this one locality for fully forty years. He is a quarter blood Creek Indian, having inherited that ancestry from his mother, and consequently was given an allotment of the lands in this part of the old Creek Nation. For many years Mr. Henry had extensive livestock interests, and is one of the old time cattlemen of Texas and Indian Territory.

That part of the ranch which he called his meadow land up to fifteen years ago is now the site of the thriving little City of Henryetta. The name was given to honor him as the oldest settler, and seldom has a name been better bestowed as a token of honor and respect.

Hugh Henry is one of the picturesque characters still surviving from the early days of old Indian Territory. He grew up on the frontier, and early learned some of the pioneer virtues, to speak the truth, zealously to guard his honor, and to do justice to his fellow men, and to treat all under his roof with due hospitality. In the early days his home was noted for its generous hospitality, and though he lived in the midst of outlawry and violence he was always safe because he treated others as he expected to be treated. His home again and again served as a place of entertainment for United States marshals, outlaws, train robbers, horse thieves, and bootleggers. In fact he has had officers of the law and outlaws in his home at the same time, and many a beef was slaughtered from his herd to provide them food. He made it a rule and it was one thoroughly respected to protect all persons who were his guests, despite their character or vocation, and it was probably due to this custom that he never lost a life or any property by theft.

Hugh Henry was born in the "old stone fort" at Nacogdoches, Texas, that historic building which had been the bulwark of the early Spanish against the Indians and French along the Texas frontier and which was the scene of a bloody battle during one of the early revolutionary uprisings in Eastern Texas. In that historic place he first saw the light of day January 13, 1848. His parents were Woodson D. and Lovisa (Hutton) Henry. His father was a white man and his mother a half-blood Creek Indian. Both were born in Alabama, where they married, and they came to Texas in 1832. Woodson Henry and his wife's father, James Hutton, took thirty families of Indians into Texas in that year, corresponding with the general migration of Indians from the east to the west side of the Mississippi River. Soon after the birth of Hugh Henry his parents moved to the Brazos River in Hill County, Texas, and there the mother died when Hugh was four years of age, leaving a still younger child, Patrick, then only two years old. The six children were: James, Caroline, Parelee, Ezekiah, Hugh and Patrick. Of these Mr. Hugh Henry is the only one still living. After the death of the mother the father carried Hugh and Patrick back to the home of Nancy Hutton, their grandmother, in Smith County, Texas. There Hugh Henry lived until he was nine years of age. His father having in the meantime married again took his two boys home in Cherokee County. Hugh Henry did not like his stepmother, and after two months he ran away and returned to his grandmother. His father followed and carried him back home, where he received a sound thrashing for his disobedience. A few days later his father went to court, and the self reliant youth again made his escape from conditions which he thought intolerable, but this time took an unfamiliar route. He traveled west into Fannin County, Texas, sleeping by the roadside at night. In Fannin County he met a Mr. Cannon, boss of a cattle ranch, and the boy remained on that ranch and had a good home with the Cannons for seven years, receiving only board and clothes for such work as he could do. While there he became an expert in all the arts and practices of the old time range.

He was only thirteen years of age when the war broke out, and in 1863 he joined John Terry's regiment under Captain Glasscock. He was with his command until the close of the war, and to use his own words, "had his last fun at the Mansfield fight in Louisiana."

After the war he started for San Antonio, Texas, and at Lampasas Springs met his old friend and protector, Cannon, for whom he took a herd of cattle north to Dodge City, Kansas, being paid $65.00 a month. This was in 1866. In 1867 he was again in the Rio Grande country, and in the fall of that year started north. On this trip he stopped on the Canadian River and joined his uncle, Watt Grayson. Mr. Henry had many interesting experiences in the early days, and during the two seasons of 1867-68 he was out on the range hunting buffalo. That was just about the beginning of the buffalo hide industry, and Mr. Henry relates that the hunters classified the buffaloes into three divisions. The pelt of the buffalo cows were unfit for commercial purposes, and the leather and fur came chiefly from the bulls. He remained with his uncle, Watt Grayson, as an employe on the cattle ranch until the latter's death in 1875.

That was the year when Mr. Henry located on Coal Creek, near the present site of the City of Henryetta. Here for fourteen years and four months he was associated with Sam and Wash Grayson in the stock industry. When he first started with the Grayson brothers he had only sixty-two head of cattle, but at the end of the fourteen year period had turned off the ranch and sent to market about 36,000 head. He did his first work at wages of $15.00 per month, but was drawing $2,400 a year when he gave up ranching. It was the coming of the railroad and the founding of Henryetta which caused him to abandon ranching.

When Mr. Henry first located in this neighborhood in 1875 his nearest neighbor was six miles away, and

consequently he readily deserves the distinction of being the oldest settler. He still owns 160 acres adjoining the little City of Henryetta, while his children have their allotments nearby. He has a fine home on the hill already mentioned, and for the past fifteen years has devoted his land to farming and general stock raising. The approach of civilization has been viewed not altogether with satisfaction by Mr. Henry, although he recognizes its benefits. It is largely due to his inconsistency with the restricted pursuits and customs of the populous community, and even now he is planning to take his wife and children further west into New Mexico and hunt up an unrestricted cattle range. He is just as vigorous apparently as he was thirty years ago, and he can use a Winchester with all the deadly accuracy which made him noted as a sure shot in days gone by.

The first postoffice established after the railroad was built was called Henry City, and when Henry Beard became prominent in promoting the town caused the change of the name to Henryetta, the latter part, etta, being in honor of Mr. Beard's wife.

Mr. Henry was first married in Texas to Malinda Ann Dickerson, who was born in that state. She died at the old home in Indian Territory in 1883. Of her six children two are now living: James of Payton; and Luella, wife of John Key of Henryetta.

In 1885 Mr. Henry married Arminta Exon, who was born in Warsaw County, Illinois, in March, 1868. When she was four years of age her parents came to Indian Territory, and she grew up in the Creek Nation. To this marriage were born twelve children, nine of whom are still living: Patrick, who lives at Ponca City; Mack; Sam, who died at the age of eight months; Anna May, wife of Stephen Gillam of Henryetta; Woodson, who died at the age of twelve years; Hettie, wife of Ed Burgen, a full-blood Creek Indian of Okmulgee; Hugh, Jr.; Hilibymicko; Muskogee, who died at the age of three weeks; Tsininina, who lives at home; Wynema; and Yahola.

It is noteworthy that Hugh Henry never had a day in school in all his life, though he learned to write his name while riding in the saddle. He appreciates the value of an education, especially in modern times, and is giving his children the best possible advantages. There is a photograph extant showing Hugh Henry in the picturesque garb by which he was familiarly known to all the old timers in this part of Oklahoma. He then wore his hair long, as was the custom, and his locks fell to his waist, some of them being two feet four inches long.

COURTLAND M. FEUQUAY. One of the young men who have made a promising record as a lawyer in the Lincoln County bar is Courtland M. Feuquay, who was admitted to practice three years ago and has already shown some striking ability in the handling of cases entrusted to his charge.

Courtland M. Feuquay was born in Kansas April 15, 1890; and is a son of the late John W. Feuquay, for many years a leading and successful business man of Chandler. He built and owned the Feuquay Block, one of the well known buildings in the central business district. He was born in Parke County, Indiana, and during the Civil war served with an excellent record in the Union army. He had many narrow escapes from danger, was wounded and at one time left on a battlefield as dead. He married Jence C. Holland, who was born in Goldsboro, North Carolina, of a prominent family of that state, a daughter of West Holland. John W. Feuquay died at Chandler at the age of sixty-nine. For many years he was engaged in business as a coal operator. He was also in the government service. His political affiliations were with the democratic party, and he was a member of Chandler Post of the Grand Army of the Republic. Mrs. Feuquay, his mother, is one of the prominent women of Oklahoma, active in club affairs, and a member of the Woman's Relief Corps in Oklahoma and also one of the leaders in the Women's Suffrage movement of the state.

Courtland M. Feuquay, the only child of these parents, received his education in the Chandler High School, received the degrees of B. O. from Epworth University, B. A. from University of Oklahoma and LL. B. from Yale. He is also an alumnus of the University of Virginia. For a man of his years he has seen much of the world and was orator of the day, American Boy Day, at the St. Louis World's Fair in 1904 and at the Jamestown Exposition in 1907. He was associated for two years in the practice of law with Colonel Hoffman at Chandler, and since that time has been in practice for himself. He has shown the results of a studious mind and a fine individual fitness for the profession. Mr. Feuquay is a Scottish Rite Mason of thirty-two degrees, and also affiliates with the Knights of Pythias and the Independent Order of Odd Fellows, and while at college was a member of a Greek letter fraternity.

MILAS LASATER was born in Palo Pinto County, Texas, in the year 1872, and is the eldest of four sons of George M. and Mary S. (Johnston) Lasater.

George M. Lasater, the father, was a pioneer cattleman of Palo Pinto County, his father having been the first county judge after the organization of that county, to which unorganized territory he had removed from Fannin County in the early '50s.

Milas Lasater spent his boyhood on his father's ranch, and attended the public schools of that section of the state. He was for a time in the city schools of Murfreesboro, Tennessee, and lastly continued his studies at DePauw University, Greencastle, Indiana. While prosecuting his own studies, and afterwards, he engaged in teaching school in Indian Territory and Texas. In the year 1893 he withdrew from this work and settled on a ranch near Pauls Valley, the present county seat of Garvin County, Oklahoma. In that locality he conducted trading operations in the live stock business, and engaged in the breeding of pure bred Herefords. He became a stockholder in the First National Bank of Pauls Valley, later cashier and active vice president of that institution, of which he still remains a director and one of its vice presidents. While engaged in the banking business at Pauls Valley he became owner and publisher of the Pauls Valley Democrat.

It was at Pauls Valley that Mr. Lasater had met and wedded Miss Sarah Waite, whose father, Thomas Waite, was a pioneer settler of that section of Indian Territory and whose mother was a member of the Chickasaw tribe of Indians, one of the Five Civilized Tribes. Mrs. Lasater's early education was in the Chickasaw tribal schools, but she spent nine years in the schools at Oberlin, Ohio, graduating from Oberlin College with an A. B. degree. Mrs. Lasater takes an active interest in the public school work of Oklahoma City, and devotes much of her time to the education of their daughters, Corinne and Carol.

Mr. Lasater's material interests in Oklahoma are varied and important, consisting of banking connections and ranching interests that he has maintained for many years, but the major part of his time and attention is given to his executive work as agency supervisor in Oklahoma and Kansas for the Equitable Life Assurance Society of New York.

The following statements were written by one familiar

with the character and services of Mr. Lasater: A citizen by marriage of the Chickasaw Nation of Oklahoma, Mr. Lasater has for many years been a representative leader in the growth and development of that section of the state. In recent years his activities have far transcended local limitations, and his philanthropic spirit has been manifested in divers ways. He is a man of high intellectual attainments, broad views, and distinctive liberality. His public career has covered several years, beginning with membership in the Sequoyah convention that assembled at Muskogee and adopted a constitution for a state proposed for Indian Territory alone. In 1906 he was elected a member of the Constitutional Convention that prepared and adopted the organic constitution on which is based the government of the present State of Oklahoma, combining the two territories, then Indian Territory and Oklahoma Territory.

As a member of the Constitutional Convention of the State of Oklahoma, Mr. Lasater was chairman of the Committee on Revision, Compilation, Style and Arrangement, and as such he edited and prepared for permanent record every paragraph of the constitution. He was a member also of the Committee on County Boundaries, the report of which he prepared, also a member of the Banking Committee, the Committee on Public Institutions, and other special committees created from time to time.

In 1908 Mr. Lasater was appointed by Governor Haskell a member of the first Text-book Commission of the new commonwealth, a position of which he continued the incumbent until a decision held the work of the commission to be not legally effective. Later, when the defect of law was remedied he asked that he be not reappointed a member of this commission. In 1908 also Mr. Lasater received from Governor Haskell appointment to membership on the board of control of the State Training School at Pauls Valley. In this position he aided in the founding of this institution. In 1909 Governor Haskell appointed Mr. Lasater, state insurance commissioner, a position particularly important at that time for it was during this administration that Oklahoma's Insurance Code became operative. Mr. Lasater made a good record in the administration of the affairs of that office.

Wherever he has lived Milas Lasater has been active in the social and club life of the community. At Pauls Valley he served as president of the Commercial Club of that city. He is a life member of the Pauls Valley Lodge of the Ancient Free and Accepted Masons. In the Consistory of the Ancient and Accepted Scottish Rite of Masonry at McAlester he has received the thirty-second degree. He is a Noble of the Mystic Shrine. In college he affiliated with the Delta Kappa Epsilon Greek Letter Fraternity. He is an active and influential member of the Oklahoma Life Underwriters' Association, and in the capital city he is identified with the Oklahoma City Golf and Country Club, the Men's Dinner Club, and the Chamber of Commerce.

Mr. Lasater is a staunch and effective exponent of the principles of the democratic party. He is liberal in his religious views with a deep reverence for the spiritual verities as expressed in the following beautiful words by William Henry Channing, words that he has stated most perfectly represent his creed: "To live content with small means; to seek elegance rather than luxury, and refinement rather than fashion; to be worthy, not respectable, and wealthy, not rich; to study hard, think quietly, talk gently, act frankly; to listen to stars and birds, to babes and sages, with open heart; to bear all cheerfully, do all bravely, await occasions, hurry never; in a word, to let the spiritual, unbidden and unconscious, grow up through the common,—this is my symphony."

HON. TOOMBS H. DAVIDSON. A prominent Muskogee lawyer, and now a member of the state senate from the twenty-seventh senatorial district, Toombs H. Davidson, having lost his father at the age of seven, made his own way in the world, doing farm and railroad work in vacations to earn money sufficient to complete his education. He was elected to the senate at the age of thirty, and was to an extent the political product of a strong organization of young democrats in Oklahoma. For the nomination he defeated two of the strongest and most popular men of Muskogee County. His residence in Oklahoma is coextensive with statehood, and he has gained a gratifying success both in law and politics.

Senator Davidson was born June 4, 1884, at Chepultapec, Blount County, Alabama, a son of William H. and Martha (Hartley) Davidson. His paternal grandfather, a native of South Carolina, served under General Wheeler in the Confederate army, while in private life he was a newspaper editor. Senator Davidson's maternal grandparents were prominent citizens of Alabama, and the Hartleys came to America about the time of the Oglethorpe colony.

Senator Davidson attended public school in Alabama, graduating in 1902 from the high school at Haleyville. His law studies were pursued in the office of an attorney at Haleyville until admission to the bar in 1906. His first experience as a lawyer was in Haleyville, and from there he removed to Stigler, Oklahoma, in 1907. Mr. Davidson was admitted to practice before the Supreme Court of Oklahoma shortly after statehood. In July, 1913, he located in Muskogee, where he now has a promising private practice.

His political record begins in Haskell County, in which he was a delegate to every democratic state convention while living at Stigler, and in 1912 was treasurer of the Haskell County Democratic Campaign Committee. He also filled the offices of city attorney and justice of the peace in Stigler. When Senator Davidson was elected to the senate in 1914 he carried Haskell County by more than 1,000 majority, without making a campaign in that county. While in Haskell County he was a leader in the organization of the Young Men's Democratic Club and president of the local club at Stigler.

His legislative record is highly creditable. He was chairman of the Committee on Private Corporations and a member of committees on Judiciary No. 2, Commerce and Labor, Banks and Banking, Insurance, Public Buildings, Oil and Gas, and Legislative and Judicial Apportionment. He was one of the authors of the popular home ownership bill and assisted in the passage of the rural credits bill. Coming from a city that has made repeated efforts to be officially designated as the seat of a state fair, he was interested in the passage of a state fair bill. Having made his own way in the world by hard manual labor, Senator Davidson has shown sympathy with important measures bearing the approval of the State Federation of Labor, and assisted in the passing of a bill requiring railroad companies to build hospitals for employees in the state, and also a bill establishing working hours for women.

Senator Davidson is unmarried. He is affiliated with the Odd Fellows Lodge at Muskogee and with Lodge No. 179, Knights of Pythias, at Stigler, being a past chancellor. He is the past master of the Masonic Lodge No. 121 at Stigler, and while master was the youngest man in the state in years and Masonic experience to fill that position. His lodge re-elected him master after his removal to Muskogee. In a higher degree with the Scottish Rite he belongs to McAlester Consistory No. 2 at McAlester, and also to Bedouin Temple of the Mystic Shrine of Muskogee. He also belongs to the D. O. K. K. at Muskogee, an order affiliated with the Knights of Pythias. Senator Davidson is a member of the Haskell County Bar Association. He is a lieutenant in the Pickett-Wheeler Camp of Confederate Veterans at Stigler. He and County Judge Crittenden organized the camp and compromised a lively though friendly contest over the name, Crittenden holding out for the name Pickett and Davidson for Wheeler.

HON. J. W. MARSHALL. Among the members of the Oklahoma judiciary there are many whose early training has been secured as teachers, their first introduction to the mysteries and perplexities of the law having been gained in the evening hours after long and exhausting labors in the schoolroom. In this category is found Hon. John Walter Marshall, judge of the County Court of Stephens County, whose first term in this office proved so satisfactory to the people of the county that he was reëlected in 1914 without opposition. Judge Marshall also has the distinction of having a township created for and named after him, i. e., Marshall Township, which includes the City of Duncan, the Judge's place of residence since 1906.

John Walter Marshall was born at Graham, Young County, Texas, November 7, 1874, and is a son of W. H. and Elizabeth (Blocker) (Walker) Marshall. His paternal grandfather, a farmer and minister of the Baptist faith, was born in Virginia and died in Tennessee, while his maternal grandfather, John Blocker, went from Missouri in pioneer days to Parker County, Texas, and there died, after a number of years spent in agricultural pursuits. W. H. Marshall, father of the Judge, was born in 1832, in Tennessee, and from his native state removed to Mississippi, from whence he removed in 1873 to Graham, Young County, Texas, and in 1884 to Nacogdoches County, in the same state. Four years later he went with his family to New Birmingham, Cherokee County, Texas, and in 1894 came to Oklahoma and located at Duncan. Here he resided until 1900, when he made removal to Denton County, Texas, and there lives in quiet retirement. During the period of his active career, Mr. Marshall carried on operations in farming and stockraising, and in the various communities in which he resided took an active and helpful part in civic and public affairs. He was one of the organizers of Young County, Texas, and also served as the first county assessor there. He is a member of the Methodist Episcopal Church. During the Civil war he enlisted in the Confederate army, with which he served for four years, participating in a number of battles and having numerous thrilling experiences. At the sanguine battle of Shiloh he was wounded; at Paducah, Kentucky, had his horse shot under him, and at one time was taken prisoner by the northern troops, but succeeded in making his escape. Mr. Marshall married Mrs. Elizabeth (Blocker) Walker, a widow, daughter of John Blocker. She was born in Arkansas, in 1837, and died at Marlow, Oklahoma, in 1900. There were three children in the family: John Walter, of this notice; Lee, who resides at Duncan and is engaged in farming and stockraising; and Sydney, who died at the age of fourteen years.

John Walter Marshall acquired his preliminary education in the public schools of Young and Nacogdoches counties, Texas, and as a youth learned the trade of printer, which, however, he followed only a short time. He had remained on the home farm assisting his father until he was fourteen years of age, and in 1894 accompanied his parents to Duncan, Oklahoma, where for three years he helped his father cultivate a farm. Securing a teacher's certificate, in 1897 he started teaching in the public schools of Stephens County, and continued for two years, when he turned his knowledge of printing and the newspaper business to account by editing the Marlow Review, a journal with which he was connected one year. He then resumed school teaching as a vocation, and continued to be thus engaged until 1906, in which year he occupied the position of assistant principal of the Duncan High School. In the meanwhile, he had devoted himself to the study of law in his leisure hours, and in 1907 was admitted to practice after successfully passing the state examination. He soon attracted to himself an important and lucrative practice, and has gradually advanced to a leading position at the Stephens County bar. A democrat in his political views, for a number of years he has been active in local affairs, and at the time of statehood campaigned this district in the interests of Hon. J. R. Allen, who was sent to the Oklahoma Legislature. About the same time Marshall Township was created for him and named in his honor, and he became the first justice of the peace, serving as such for two terms. In November, 1912, he was elected county judge of Stephens County, and November 6, 1914, was elected to this office for a second term, without opposition. He has proven an able, impartial and dignified judge, conferring honor upon the locality over which he has jurisdiction and being generally popular with the members of the bench and bar. His offices are in the courthouse. Judge Marshall is a member of the Methodist Episcopal Church. He holds membership in the Duncan Chamber of Commerce and the various organizations of his profession, and is fraternally identified with Mistletoe Lodge No. 17, Ancient Free and Accepted Masons, of which he is past chancellor; Duncan Camp No. 515, Woodmen of the World, of which he is past consul commander; and Camp No. 9680, Modern Woodmen of America, of Duncan.

Judge Marshall was married at Robberson, Garvin County, Oklahoma, to Miss Nettie Vandagriff, daughter of S. J. Vandagriff, a farmer now residing in Comanche County, Oklahoma, and four children have been born to this union: Maude, born April 20, 1902, attending public school; Lois, born March 22, 1903, also a public school student; Blanche, born December 2, 1909, attending public school; and John, born November 2, 1913.

DR. ROSS STATLER CANNON is a physician and surgeon of note and although he has lived at Hydro for only one year to date he has already gained the faith of his fellow men and is rapidly building up a splendid patronage. Prior to coming here he was engaged in professional work at Sterling, Oklahoma, for thirteen years and while there was deputy health officer of Comanche County.

A son of Thomas M. and Kate Wood (Statler) Cannon, Doctor Cannon was born at Neosho, Newton County, Missouri, February 17, 1877. The father was a native of Indiana, where he was born in 1849, and he was summoned to the life eternal in 1880, at which time the doctor was but three years of age. He was a grist and flour miller and removed from the Hoosier State to Neosho, Missouri, in young manhood. In politics he was a republican. Mrs. Cannon was born at Bedford, Pennsylvania, in 1850, and she now maintains her home at Albany, Oregon. After being widowed she taught in the Seneca, Shawnee and Wyandotte Indian Reservation schools and subsequently was superintendent of the Pottawatomie Indian School, north of Topeka, Kansas; of the Ponca Indian School, three miles from Ponca City; and of the Lagoona Schools, at Lagoona, New Mexico. She was engaged in the profession of teaching for fifteen years and was very popular and successful in that line. During her work in the various Indian reservations she collected a remarkable series of Indian photographs which were unfortunately burned in her trunk in the depot fire at Lagoona in 1903. Two children were born to Mr.

and Mrs. Cannon: Ross S. is the subject of this sketch; and Thomas M., Jr. is a resident of Albany, Oregon, where he is a registered druggist and operates a poultry ranch.

Doctor Cannon attended the public schools of Neosho, Missouri, and also those of Cassville and he completed his high-school course in the City of St. Louis, Missouri. In 1898 he was graduated in the St. Louis Medical College, with the degree of Doctor of Medicine. He entered upon his professional practice at Newkirk, in Kay County, Oklahoma, and remained there until 1901. He was coroner of Kay County and also served as medical examiner on the insanity board, and was county physician. In 1901 he located at Sterling, in Comanche County, Oklahoma, and remained there until April, 1914, which date marks this advent at Hydro. He was deputy health officer of Comanche County while a resident of Sterling and there controlled a large and lucrative practice. His offices at Hydro are in the Opera House Building on Main Street. He is a staunch republican in politics and is a member of the Comanche and Kay County Medical Societies and of the Missouri State Medical Society.

In Oklahoma City, Oklahoma, in 1914, Doctor Cannon married Miss Cleo V. Collier, a daughter of R. S. Collier, who is living in retirement at Hydro. Doctor and Mrs. Cannon are both popular in connection with the social activities of Hydro and their home is the scene of many attractive gatherings.

HUSER & HUSER. One of the ablest law firms of Okfuskee County is that of Huser & Huser, both of whom have made a fine record as attorneys and citizens and they now control and handle a large share of the important litigation in the local courts. The firm comprises Judge William A. Huser and his brother, Eugene Huser. They have their offices at Okemah. William A. Huser is a former county judge of Okfuskee County and Eugene Huser is now serving as city attorney.

Judge William A. Huser was born in the geographical center of Spencer County, Indiana, July 12, 1872. His birth occurred on a farm, and just ten miles from the old homestead was the little cemetery where Lincoln's mother, Nancy Hanks Lincoln, was buried, and as a boy he frequently visited her grave. Judge Huser is of old American and Revolutionary stock. Two of his Revolutionary ancestors, Thomas Chancellor and William May, were both buried in Spencer County, Indiana. His great-grandfather, Robert Huser, was also in the Revolutionary war and was buried in Kentucky. Both May and Chancellor were present at the surrender of Cornwallis, at Yorktown, in 1781, at the close of the Revolution.

The parents of these brothers were John Thomas and Martha E. (May) Huser. The former was born in Switzerland County, Indiana, in 1842, and the latter in Spencer County in 1846. John T. Huser grew up in Marion County, Indiana, but spent most of his life in Spencer County, where he died October 22, 1900. The mother died at Okemah, Oklahoma, in 1912. The father spent all his active career as a farmer. The parents had only two sons, Eugene being the older.

Eugene Huser was born in Spencer County, Indiana, August 12, 1867, and continued to reside there until June, 1903, when he moved to Comanche County, Oklahoma, and joined his brother in the practice of law at Okemah in July, 1912. He had a common school education back in Indiana, and after going to Oklahoma studied law in Comanche County, where he was admitted to the bar in 1912. He is an active democrat, a member of the Presbyterian Church, and is affiliated with the Knights of Pythias and the Independent Order of Odd Fellows. In 1889 Eugene Huser married Cora Farris, who was born in Indiana, a daughter of George and Emily Farris. To their marriage have been born seven sons: James Alston, George Thomas, Oliver Stanley, Samuel Jennings, Ellis Alvin, Herbert M. and John Marshall.

William A. Huser spent his early years on the old homestead in Spencer County, Indiana, and besides an education in the local schools he attended the law department of the Indiana State University at Bloomington, and in 1893 was admitted to the Indiana bar at Rockport. He took up practice in his native county, and left a promising business there in 1899 to come to Oklahoma. He established his first home at Hastings, in Comanche County, but at statehood moved to Okfuskee County and engaged in practice with C. B. Connor, under the firm name of Connor & Huser. In 1910 Mr. Huser was elected county judge of Okfuskee County and gave a careful and efficient administration of those duties during 1911-12. In 1912 he was a candidate before the democratic primaries for congressional nomination, but was defeated. Since then he and his brother, Eugene, have been associated as partners.

Judge Huser is democratic member of the state committee from Okfuskee County. He is a member of the American Historical Association, belongs to the Methodist Episcopal Church, is a Knight Templar Mason, and is now Master of Okemah Lodge No. 234, Ancient Free and Accepted Masons. He is also affiliated with the Knights of Pythias.

In 1904 Judge Huser married R. M. Pettit, who was born in Iowa, daughter of C. G. and Jennie Pettit, who now live in Jefferson County, Oklahoma. Judge Huser and wife have two daughters, Margaret and Elaine.

ELMER C. WHEELER. The business enterprise of Elmer C. Wheeler has been an important factor in conserving the property and civic rights of the people of his blood and race in Oklahoma. Mr. Wheeler is descended from two stocks of American Indians, with an important admixture of the French pioneers who first explored and traversed the country west of the Mississippi. He is now the head of a prominent family at Pawhuska in Osage County and is carefully looking after the large interests which are under his supervision as a result of the allotment in severalty of the Indian lands of the Osage Nation.

Mr. Wheeler was born in Thurston County, Nebraska, March 17, 1878, a son of M. P. and Eliza (Loise) Wheeler. His father was born in Wisconsin in 1846, and his mother was born in Nebraska in 1847. These parents were married in Richardson County, Nebraska, and moved from there to the Omaha Indian Reservation, on which they lived until June, 1891, when they came with other members of the tribe to Pawhuska, in Indian Territory. Mr. Wheeler's mother was a daughter of Edward Paul and Mary Jane (Barada) Loise. They belonged to some of the earliest French families in the vicinity of St. Louis. Mr. Wheeler's mother first married Antoine Cabaney, and had one son by that union. Mr. Wheeler's grandfather was half Osage and half French origin, and his grandmother was half French and half Omaha Indian. His grandfather established a trading post at what is now the City of Omaha, where a Frenchman by the name of Edward Sarpy, in the employ of the American Fur Company, had established a post in the early '40s, this enterprise giving the first distinction to the site now occupied by that flourishing city. Mr. Wheeler's grandfather lived at Omaha until a short time before his death, when he went to St. Louis and there fell a victim to the cholera. Mr. Wheeler's

great-grandfather on his mother's side was Mitchell Barada, who was one of the first white men to locate west of the Missouri River. He was with the historic expedition of Lewis and Clarke that explored the Missouri River to its source early in the nineteenth century, and a number of years later he made three trips to California after the discovery of gold, and died in Nebraska. Mr. Wheeler's parents both reside in Osage County, his father being a retired farmer. They had ten children, five of whom died in infancy, and the five now living are: Paul E., of Cleveland, Oklahoma; Elmer C.; Lovania, wife of L. E. Brock, a rancher in Osage County; Anna, wife of Jack Weinrich, a merchant at Pawhuska; and Alma, living with her parents.

Elmer C. Wheeler lived with his parents until his marriage in 1903, though much of his time was spent away from home attending different Indian schools. From 1888 to 1890 he was in the Indian School at Genoa, Nebraska, and then spent three years in the Osage Indian Boarding School. From 1896 to 1897 he was in the Chilocco Indian School and graduated in 1897. During 1899-1900 he was in the Indian Training School at Santa Fe, New Mexico, and took his diploma from that institution in the latter year. After leaving school he spent some time in the employ of the United States Government as an engineer at the ice plant in Pawhuska.

On September 23, 1903, Mr. Wheeler was married to Eva E. Rogers. She comes of the noted Rogers family of Oklahoma, and was born in Osage County August 3, 1877, a daughter of Antoine and Elizabeth (Carpenter) Rogers, who are still living and have their home at Wyana. Mr. and Mrs. Wheeler have one child, Virginia Rogers. They are also rearing five children by Mrs. Wheeler's sister. Their father was Arthur, a son of Judge Thomas L. Rogers, one of the distinguished citizens of Northeastern Oklahoma whose career will be found sketched on other pages of this work. These five orphan children now in the home of Mr. and Mrs. Wheeler are: Joseph L., Ellen Elizabeth, John R., William C. and Isabel Rogers.

In recent years Mr. Wheeler has been busied in supervising the allotment of his family and children, comprising altogether about 6,000 acres. Of this handsome estate about 1,000 acres are already under cultivation as farming land, and the rest is pasture and grazing land. Mr. Wheeler owns two good buildings in Pawhuska, and occupies a substantial home which is the property of his children.

In politics he is a republican, and is prominent in the Masonic order. He is a Knight Templar Mason and is also a thirty-second degree Scottish Rite Mason. His local affiliations are with Wahsahshe Lodge No. 110, Ancient Free and Accepted Masons, Horeb Chapter No. 63, Royal Arch Masons; Omega Council, Royal and Select Masons; Palestine Commandery No. 31, Knights Templar; Oklahoma Consistory of the Scottish Rite; The Temple of the Mystic Shrine at Tulsa. He is a past master of his lodge and past commander of Palestine Commandery. He is also affiliated with the Benevolent and Protective Order of Elks and the Knights of Pythias.

JAMES A. EMBRY. This name has long had significance in the political life of Oklahoma, and one of its bearers is James A. Embry, now serving as circuit clerk of Lincoln County. Mr. Embry is a son of one of the early settlers in Lincoln County, and his own life has been spent in this state from early boyhood, a period of twenty-five years. He has recently been admitted to the bar and prior to his election as district clerk in 1912

Vol. V—10

had made an acceptable record as district clerk of Lincoln County.

James A. Embry was born September 21, 1878, on a farm near Owensburg, Kentucky, son of V. R. Embry, now a resident of Jennings, Oklahoma. His father was a native of Kentucky and of old Kentucky lineage, with many of the characteristic qualities of the Kentucky people. V. R. Embry was reared in Kentucky and when a boy in his teens enlisted for service in a Kentucky regiment in the Union army and saw four years' of active service as a soldier. At the beginning of settlement in Lincoln County, Oklahoma, he came as one of the pioneers and developed a large farm. He subsequently removed to the City of Jennings, and died at Morgantown, Kentucky, in February, 1916. He married Miss E. Bratcher, who died some years ago. She transmitted some of the noble qualities of her heart and mind to her children, who were six in number, as follows: Clinton, of Lincoln County; John, a prominent lawyer of Oklahoma City; James A.; Iverson; Eliza, living in Iowa City, Iowa; and Hannah, of Oklahoma. The parents were both Methodist Church people.

James A. Embry was eleven years of age when his parents located in Lincoln County, and many of his early recollections are associated with the wilderness conditions which then prevailed in this state. He grew up on a farm, and by the wholesome occupations of the country developed a strong physique and a vigorous mentality. He was educated partly in the public schools of Kentucky and partly in the high school at Chandler, and his early life was devoted to farming and stock raising. He was associated with his brother, John Embry, and later took up the study of law with him and was admitted to the bar in 1914.

In 1904 Mr. Embry married Ivy Boatright, a woman of refinement and culture. Mr. and Mrs. Embry have six children: John, Henry, Glen, Dorothy, Ivy and James A., Jr.

Mr. Embry, like his father, has a military record to his credit, having served for twenty months in the Thirty-third United States Infantry during the Spanish-American war. He subsequently served as lieutenant of the National Guard, and in 1916 was elected department commander for Oklahoma of the United States Spanish War Veterans. He and his wife are members of the Methodist Church and he belongs to the Veteran Reserve Corps and is a member of the Masonic Lodge.

WARREN L. THAYER. The first appearance of Warren L. Thayer in Oklahoma was as a harvest man. About fifteen years ago he took up a Government claim in Harper County, and his prosperity and influence has been steadily growing ever since. He is now one of the leading citizens and business men of Laverne.

His birth occurred February 27, 1880, at Union City, Michigan, a son of Robert M. and Frances M. (Blosser) Thayer. His father, who was of Scotch parentage, was born June 17, 1855, at Jackson, Michigan, and was a lumberman until he came to Oklahoma in 1901. In that year he took up a claim in Woodword County and became active in the organization of Ellis and Harper County. He now owns and operates a large stock farm seven miles from May. Robert M. Thayer was married in 1877 and his wife was born November 30, 1854, at Logan, Hocking County, Ohio, a daughter of Abraham and Miriam (Graffis) Blosser, who were natives of Pennsylvania and of Dutch stock. Mrs. Thayer had a college education and is an active member of the Methodist Church. Their children are: Warren L.; Goldie, who was born March 23, 1888, and is now the wife of Bert B. Waltman, a railway official in Denver, Colorado; Pearl Blanche, who was born August 3, 1891, and is now the wife of Bynum Bouse, a rancher at Des Moines, New Mexico; Ernest Blaine, who was born May 7, 1894, and now lives at Laverne, Oklahoma; and Katie Lorena Thayer, who was born July 16, 1896, and is now the wife of W. T. McNeil of Beaver City, Oklahoma.

At the age of seventeen Warren L. Thayer completed a high school course at Knoxville, Tennessee, and at the age of twenty-one graduated A. B. from the Ewing and Jefferson College in Blount County, Tennessee. It was with this education and preliminary experience that he came to Grant County, Oklahoma, and spent his first season in the harvest fields. He also taught school one term. Then in 1901 he settled on his claim of Government land in Woodward County, and by hard work and good judgment has become one of the extensive farmers of that section, having a large tract under cultivation. For one year he was connected with the Spearmore State Bank of Laverne, but is now engaged in a prosperous life insurance business at Laverne. He is also interested in oil properties in Oklahoma and Texas as a promoter and developer, and having read law in the intervals of his business pursuits was admitted to the Oklahoma bar in 1916 and is now prepared to practice his profession. Mr. Thayer is a member of the Masonic Order, the Benevolent and Protective Order of Elks, the Knights of Pythias and the Independent Order of Odd Fellows. Politically he is a republican.

On January 12, 1910, at Coleman, Texas, he married Miss Sallie May Smith, who was born at Alvarado, Texas, January 8, 1887, a daughter of Thomas and Emma (Quinn) Smith, natives of Texas. Mrs. Thayer is a granddaughter of Deaf Smith, a pioneer scout and frontiersman in Texas, a historic character in the Texas Revolution, and his name is indelibly impressed upon Texas geography in Deaf Smith County, which is now the largest county in area in the United States. Mrs. Thayer completed her education in a Texas college. They have three daughters: Helen, born January 19, 1911; Dorothy, born August 24, 1913; and Virginia Pauline, born February 16, 1916.

JOSEPH J. HENKE, M. D. A physician and surgeon splendidly equipped for his work of curing the sick, Dr. Joseph J. Henke has gained prestige throughout Caddo County by reason of his natural talent and acquired ability in the field of his chosen work. His professional career excites the admiration and has won the respect of his contemporaries in a calling in which one has to gain reputation by merit and long hours of patient work.

At Westphalia, in Osage County, Missouri, occurred the birth of Dr. Joseph J. Henke, a son of Henry H. and Mary (Radmacher) Henke, the former of whom was born near Osnabruck, Prussia, in 1848, and the latter at Van Buren, Missouri, in 1853. As a young man the father learned the trade of merchant tailor and located at Westphalia, Missouri, where he is now living retired. He and his wife are the parents of five children, as follows: Joseph J. is the subject of this sketch; William is cashier of the Bank of Erick, at Erick, Oklahoma; Charles is a mechanic and resides with his parents at Westphalia, Missouri; Annie, deceased, was the wife of Henry Eicholz, a well-to-do property owner in St. Louis, Missouri; and Regina is the wife of Andrew Fennewald, a dry-goods merchant at Westphalia.

After completing the prescribed course in the public schools of Westphalia, Doctor Henke pursued a business course at St. Joseph's College, at Teutopolis, Illinois, being graduated in that institution in 1892. For two years thereafter he taught school in Osage County, Missouri, and he then removed to Westphalia, Texas, where he was engaged in teaching for the ensuing four years. In 1898 he was matriculated as a student in the College of Physicians & Surgeons at St. Louis and was graduated therein April 11, 1900, with the degree of Doctor of Medicine. He took a post-graduate course in that institution in 1903 and in 1915 did post-graduate work in the Physicians & Surgeons College of St. Louis, Missouri. Immediately after graduating he was an interne in Jefferson Hospital, St. Louis, for one year, and he then located at Lindsay, Texas, where he practiced for a year. In 1902 he came to Hydro and he has the distinction of being the pioneer physician and surgeon in this place. He controls a general medical and surgical practice and the large patronage given him is the best evidence of the faith bestowed in him by his fellow citizens. His offices are located on Broadway just off Main Street and in connection with his life work he is a valued and appreciative member of the Caddo County Medical Society, the Oklahoma State Medical Society and the American Medical Association. He is a republican in politics and his religious faith coincides with the teachings of the Roman Catholic Church. It is interesting to note that Doctor Henke, with others, established the Bank of Hydro, and was for years a stockholder in that corporation.

October 29, 1901, in Waco, Texas, Doctor Henke married Miss Rose Kleypas, a daughter of Bernard and Bernadine Kleypas, the former of whom is now deceased and the latter of whom resides at Waco, Texas. Bernard Kleypas was an officer in the Franco-Prussian war in 1870. Doctor and Mrs. Henke became the parents of three children, the oldest of whom, Bernard H., died at the age of six months; Mildred B. was born November 17, 1906; and Joseph Reid was born November 15, 1911.

DR. G. F. BORDER, prominent surgeon of Magnum, and mayor of the city, is one of the foremost men of his community. He came here in 1900, and in the same year opened the Border Hospital. It was all inadequate in the beginning to the demands of the place, but today he is the owner and proprietor of one of the finest and best equipped private hospitals to be found anywhere in the country. With accommodations for thirty patients, it is always filled to capacity, though it is exclusively a surgical hospital.

Doctor Border was born in San Augustine, Texas, on December 22, 1873, and is the son of G. F. Border, who was born in England in 1838, and who died in San Augustine, Texas, in 1883. Charles F. Border, grandfather of the subject, was an English emigrant to America, settling in San Augustine, Texas, while others of the same generation came over and settled in Ohio, where their descendants may be found today. G. F. Border, Sr., was a boy when he came to America with his parents, and he was reared in San Augustine, where they settled. While quite young he entered the wholesale hardware business in Galveston, later became the proprietor of a similar establishment, and for many years was thus engaged. He was a major in the Southern army during the Civil war, serving four years in Hood's Brigade. He was severely wounded in the service, and suffered a term of imprisonment. After the war he returned to business pursuits, but he suffered much ill health as a result of his wound, and he finally died from its effects. He was a member of the Masonic fraternity and a democrat. He married Elizabeth Brooks, daughter of Gen. T. G. Brooks, who served in the Civil war and after the war was a merchant in San Augustine. She was born there in 1848, and now makes her home with her son, Doctor Border, who is one of their five children, briefly mentioned as follows: May married S. M. Polk, a mechanic of Mangum. Mattie is the wife of J. M. Burleson, a near relative of Postmaster General

Burleson, and they live in San Augustine, where he is engaged in the cattle business. Dr. G. F. was the third child. C. L. died at San Augustine, and he was sheriff of the county at the time of his death. Cora married E. H. Roberts, and lives in Dallas. Mr. Roberts is deceased. He was a real estate man of Dallas, and his widow is now the owner of a great deal of land in the state. She has two sons,—E. H. and Isaac, both of whom are medical students in Baylor University.

G. F. Border had his early education in the public schools of San Augustine, and was a graduate of the Patron High School, class of 1891. He later attended Center Texas College, and was graduated from the Louisville Medical College in 1895 and from the St. Louis College of Physicians and Surgeons in 1900 with the degree of M. D. Doctor Border began practice in the U. S. Marine Hospital in Atlanta as assistant surgeon before he had his degree, and he has since taken numerous post-graduate courses, among the courses at the Chicago Polyclinic, the New York Polyclinic and with Mayo Brothers at Rochester, Minnesota. In 1899 he practiced medicine in Holland, Texas, and in 1900 he came to Mangum, in the same year opening the Border Hospital. It was a small and unpretentious place then, with a few rooms over the City Drug Store, but the demand for places in the little hospital was so great that in 1907 Doctor Border built his present modern hospital at 224 West Jefferson Street. His is the oldest private hospital in the State of Oklahoma, and it accommodates patients from all over the state, from Texas and from other states. Thirty beds is its capacity, and it is owned and managed exclusively by Doctor Border, whose professional work is confined wholly to the surgical field.

Doctor Border is official surgeon for the Rock Island Railroad and for the M. K. & T. Road. He is health officer for Mangum and has held that office for the past fifteen years.

A democrat, Doctor Border was elected to the office of mayor in 1912, and again in November, 1914, for a term of four years. At the last election he had no opposition. He has a good deal of civic pride, and it has been his ambition to make Mangum the cleanest town in the state. In 1914 the city won the state prize for cleanliness as a result of Doctor Border's efforts. Through his efforts, too, were sanitary drinking fountains placed in the public schools.

Doctor Border is a member of Mangum Lodge No. 61, Ancient Free and Accepted Masons; Mangum Chapter No. 35, Royal Arch Masons, Consistory No. 1, Valley of Guthrie; India Temple, Ancient Arabic Order of Nobles of the Mystic Shrine, Oklahoma City; Mangum Lodge No. 1169, Benevolent and Protective Order of Elks; and he is a member of the County, State and American Medical societies. At one time he was a stockholder in a number of insurance companies. Doctor Border is unmarried.

JAMES L. AUSTIN. A representative member of the bar of Washita County, Senator Austin is engaged in the practice of his profession at Cordell, the attractive and thriving metropolis and judicial center of the county, and there came consistent recognition of his character and ability when, in the fall of 1912, he was elected a member of the State Senate, as representative of the Sixth senatorial district. In both the Fourth and Fifth sessions of the Legislature he proved himself a valuable working member of the Senate and his influence was potent in the furtherance of judicious legislation and in the furtherance of the best interests of the state and its people, the while he has shown himself specially mindful of and loyal to the interests of his specific constituency.

Senator Austin was born at Mount Airy, Sequatchie County, Tennessee, on the 24th of June, 1870, and he is a son of Thomas Jefferson Austin and Sarah Austin, both of whom still maintain their home in the fine Sequatchie Valley of Tennessee, where the paternal grandfather of the senator was a pioneer settler and where numerous representatives of the family still remain. Thomas J. Austin was born and reared in Sequatchie County, and is one of the substantial agriculturists of that section, besides being a grower of high-grade live stock. He is influential in public affairs of local order and is one of the honored citizens of the community that has been his home from the time of his birth. Of the children other than him whose name initiates this review it may be stated that Elijah F. is identified with the oil industry at Duffey, Texas; Mrs. Thomas J. Sutherland and Mrs. Alexander Standefer, reside at Mount Airy, Tennessee, the husband of the former being a farmer and Mr. Standefer being a merchant; Cleveland is a farmer in the vicinity of Mount Airy, and the younger sons, Melvin and Monroe, remain at the parental home.

James L. Austin attended the public schools of his native county a portion of each year until he had attained to the age of eighteen years, when he entered Terrill College, in Lincoln County, Tennessee, in which institution he was graduated in 1896, with the degree of Bachelor of Arts. In the same year he became a teacher in the public schools of Johnson County, Texas, where he remained thus engaged four years. He then came to Washita County, Oklahoma Territory, where he continued his efficient services as a successful and popular teacher in the public schools until the admission of Oklahoma to statehood, in 1907, when he was elected the first district clerk of the county, a position which he retained five years, in the meanwhile having gained secure vantage-ground in popular confidence and esteem and having become well known in that section of the state. In 1912 he was elected from that district a member of the State Senate, for a term of four years, and this term will expire in 1916. While still teaching school Senator Austin had given close attention to the study of law and had admirably fortified himself in the science of jurisprudence, so that he was well equipped when, in 1913, he formed at Cordell a law partnership with Swan C. Burnette and Charles A. Holden, the firm establishing an office at Clinton, Custer County, also. This alliance continued until 1914, and Messrs. Austin and Holden are still associated in the control of a large and important law business in Washita and Custer counties, the while Senator Austin is identified also with the newspaper business, as owner and publisher of the Clinton News.

In the Fourth Legislature Senator Austin was chairman of the committee on fees and salaries and was assigned to other important Senate committees. At this session he was the author of a bill relating to the construction of public highways, and though the bill passed both houses of the Legislature its provisions met with the disapproval of the governor, but was enacted by the Legislature in 1915. Senator Austin was the author also of a proposed constitutional amendment reorganizing the judicial system of the state, and this failed of enactment in 1913, but passed both branches of the Legislature in 1915. One of the distinctive ambitions of Senator Austin in the Fifth Legislature was to bring about the success of these two measures which he had valiantly championed at the preceding session and which he again introduced, but with the desired results. In the Fifth Legislature he was chairman of the committee on revenue and taxation, and held membership also on the committees on ways and means, private corporations, roads and highways, Federal relations, public printing, and drugs and pure foods. He was a consistent supporter of measures projected for the remedying of defects in labor conditions and for the reduction of the expense of government in the state. Senator Austin, as a stalwart and able champion of the principles and policies of the democratic party, had charge of the political campaign activities of four counties when Governor Williams was candidate for the office of chief executive, and he was in full accord with the principles of reform outlined in the democratic platform of and also the recommendations for legislation made by Governor Williams in the vigorous campaign. Senator Austin is a member of the Washita County Bar Association and the Oklahoma State Bar Association, is actively identified with the Commercial Club in his home city of Cordell, is affiliated with the Modern Woodmen of America and the Woodmen of the World, and holds membership in the Baptist Church, both his wife and daughter being members of the Christian Church.

At Mount Airy, Tennessee, in 1895, was solemnized the marriage of Senator Austin to Miss Florence A. Standefer, who was born and reared in that section of the state and whose grandfather, Hon. James Standefer, of English lineage, served as a member of the Tennessee Legislature. Senator Austin and his wife had been schoolmates in Tennessee, and after their marriage both were popular teachers in the schools of Texas and Oklahoma, Mrs. Austin being now a valued member of the corps of teachers in the public schools at Cordell, with great enthusiasm in her work and with reputation for being one of the most efficient primary teachers in the state. Ruby Lee, the only child of Senator and Mrs. Austin, was born in Johnson County, Texas, in 1898, and is a young woman of exceptional talent and accomplishment in music and dramatic expression. She is a member of the class of 1916 in the Cordell Christian College, in her home city, and after her graduation in this institution she will complete her education in music and expression in the celebrated Boston Conservatory of Music. She is a leader and loved personality in her class at the Cordell Christian College, and an active worker in the Christian Church in her home city, she having been a member of the church since she was twelve years of age.

ANDREW B. OLESON. The present mayor of the City of Chandler is one of the pioneer white settlers of Oklahoma Territory, having been identified with this country more than twenty years. Mr. Oleson has been a resident of Chandler for the past twelve years, and as a business man conducts the office of mayor on business principles, with emphasis on efficiency and with an impartial administration for the benefit of all concerned. Mr. Olson came to Oklahoma in 1892 with the tide of home-seekers that made Oklahoma famous in those days. He was first located on the Sac and Fox Reservation.

A. B. Oleson was born in Norway, July 9, 1845, of a family noted for industry, thrift and physical and mental vigor. His parents were Bertel and Angie Oleson, his father dying at the age of seventy-five and his mother still living at ninety-two. His father was a farmer, and there were five sons and five daughters in the family.

Mayor Oleson grew up on a farm, received a wholesome training in body as well as mind, and leaving school at the age of fifteen became a sailor before the mast, and spent five years in sailing about the world. In 1867, at the age of twenty-two, he came to America and located at Madison, Wisconsin, where he was employed in the carpenter's trade. He did some general railroad work and later was a builder and contractor, and in that business laid the foundation for his substantial prosperity. He was in Western Kansas for a time, erected some courthouses and other important buildings, lived in Iowa, later in Princeton, Illinois, and for several years was a building contractor for the Chicago, Burlington & Quincy Railroad. Later he returned to Iowa, and in 1886 located in Kansas, where he did an extensive business as a building contractor. He afterwards took some large contracts from railroads, lived in Pueblo, Colorado, for a time, and in 1892 came to Oklahoma. Since moving to this state he has performed a number of important contracts in building, including courthouses, business blocks, private residences and other structures. He was superintendent of the courthouse here, which was built in 1907. He has been quite successful in his operations and owns 160 acres of land in this county, also his home and three houses in Chandler which he rents, besides city and farm property in other parts of the state.

In 1872 Mr. Oleson married Elizabeth Hildebrand, a native of New Jersey, and she died here in 1913 when sixty-two years of age. To their marriage were born six children, four sons and two daughters. Those still living are: Ben, a business man at Sapulpa, Oklahoma; Harry, of Chandler; Ann, who married Tom Jessem, of Dakota; Edward Charles of Sapulpa, Oklahoma; and Ella, at home. Mr. Oleson has always been a stanch supporter of the republican party. For the past forty years he has been connected with the Independent Order of Odd Fellows, and in whatever relation he has stood with business or with the community has exemplified a thorough integrity and a high degree of public spirit. He is a member of the Lutheran Church.

CHARLES SWINDALL. The bar of the State of Oklahoma claims as one of its leading representatives in Woodward County the well known attorney whose name initiates this paragraph and whose large and important law business extends not only into the various courts of Oklahoma but also into those of the Panhandle of Texas, is wide ramification affording ample voucher for his distinctive ability in his profession and the high estimate placed upon him as a lawyer and citizen.

Mr. Swindall was born at College Mound, Kaufman County, Texas, on the 13th of February, 1876, and is a son of Jonathan W. and Mary E. (Standley) Swindall. His father was born in the City of Macon, Georgia, on the 11th of April, 1831, a son of Andrew and Panina (Ward) Swindall, both natives of Virginia and representatives of families that immigrated to America from England in the Colonial days and that settled in the historic Old Dominion. In 1859, when about twenty-eight years of age, Jonathan W. Swindall removed from Georgia to Texas, but in 1861 he returned to his old home in Georgia, where he remained until the close of the Civil war. He had received excellent educational advantages and after the termination of the great conflict between the states of the North and the South he engaged in teaching school in Louisiana. There he remained until 1872, when he returned to Texas, in which state he continued his labors as a successful and popular representative of the pedagogic profession for nearly a quarter of a century, his retirement from this vocation having occurred in 1895, when he established his home on a farm in Kaufman County, that state. In 1886 he became superintendent of the first high school established at Terrell, Texas, and the total period of his service as a teacher comprised forty-five years. He and his wife still reside on their fine homestead farm, their marriage having been solemnized November 5, 1857. Mrs. Swindall was born near the City of Rome, Georgia, on the 9th of November, 1836, and is a daughter of

Jonathan and Mary (Maddux) Standley, who likewise were natives of Georgia, where they passed their entire lives. Mrs. Swindall was graduated in Andrews Female College, at Cuthbert, Georgia, and her husband acquired his higher education in the famous old University of Virginia, at Charlottesville. They became the parents of four sons and four daughters: Lula F. was born December 25, 1859; Edith A., February 23, 1862; Annie A., February 18, 1865; Standley M., December 12, 1868; Frederick Ward was born December 18, 1870, and died April 20, 1900; Mary Maddux was born June 26, 1873, and died October 18, 1891; William and Charles, twins, were born February 13, 1876, and the death of the former occurred July 20, 1877, the latter being the immediate subject of this review.

On the homestead farm of his father, in Kaufman County, Texas, Charles Swindall was reared to manhood, and in 1895 he was graduated in the high school in the City of Terrell, that county. In the same year he entered Vanderbilt University, in the City of Nashville, Tennessee, and in the law department of this admirable institution he was graduated as a member of the class of 1897 and with the degree of Bachelor of Laws. During his senior year he was vice president of the Philomathian Literary Society of the university.

In the year of his graduation Mr. Swindall came to Oklahoma Territory, and in August of that year he arrived at Woodward with the portentious cash capital of $6. He was forthwith admitted to the territorial bar and gallantly opened an office and prepared to serve his strenuous professional novitiate. During the first six months he supplemented the somewhat precarious income derived from his budding law practice by serving as bookkeeper in a newspaper office. On the 1st of April, 1898, he was appointed county attorney of the adjoining County of Day, and at the ensuing popular election he was chosen the regular incumbent of this office, of which he continued in tenure three years and in which he not only gained valuable experience but also made a record that materially advanced his reputation as an able trial lawyer. Upon retiring from office he returned to Woodward, where he has since continued in active general practice and gained secure vantage-place as one of the representative lawyers of Western Oklahoma. He continues a close and appreciative student and his law library is the largest and best private collection of its kind in this section of the state.

Mr. Swindall is a staunch and effective advocate of the principles and policies of the republican party and is a representative of Woodward County as a member of the Republican State Central Committee. He has completed the circle of York Rite Masonry and has received also the thirty-second degree of the Ancient Accepted Scottish Rite, besides being affiliated with the adjunct organization, the Ancient Arabic Order of the Nobles of the Mystic Shrine. He was the third to be elected worshipful master of Woodward Lodge, No. 189, Ancient Free and Accepted Masons, and in his home city he is identified also with the organizations of the Knights of Pythias, the Benevolent and Protective Order of Elks and the Modern Woodmen of America. Mr. Swindall is a member of the Woodward County Bar Association and the Oklahoma State Bar Association, and in the district of Western Oklahoma he is retained as attorney for the Atchison, Topeka & Santa Fe Railroad Company. He was unanimously selected as a delegate in 1916 to the Republican National Convention at Chicago.

On the 31st of January, 1911, at Guthrie, this state, was solemnized the marriage of Mr. Swindall to Miss Emma E. Endres, who was born at Macomb, McDonough County, Illinois, on the 19th of September, 1886, the marriage ceremony, at the former territorial capital City of Oklahoma, having been performed by Judge Jesse J. Dunn, chief justice of the Supreme Court of the state. Mrs. Swindall is a daughter of Conrad and Martha Endres, who maintain their home in the City of Wichita, Kansas. Mr. and Mrs. Swindall have no children.

THOMAS D. PALMER, M. D. The professional activities of Dr. Thomas D. Palmer have spanned fifteen years of Oklahoma history, during which time he has achieved distinction and material success in his calling. Since his arrival at Elk City, in 1911, he has won the confidence of a large practice, not through any of the methods of the charlatan, but by reason of large professional skill and a devotion to the best ethics and standards of his honored vocation.

Doctor Palmer was born at Plymouth, Illinois, May 31, 1877, and is a son of A. S. and Phoebe (Kennedy) Palmer. The family originated in England, from whence the first American ancestor emigrated during colonial days, and subsequently the family branched out from the original settlement, the direct ancestor of Doctor Palmer taking up his residence in Illinois. In that state, at Plymouth, Hancock County, A. S. Palmer was born in 1851. A farmer and stock raiser throughout his life, he continued to reside at Plymouth until 1900, then moving to Topeka, Kansas, where his death occurred four years later. He was active in the affairs of the Christian Church, being a member of the official board in his own town for many years, and in political and civic matters also took an active participation, holding various offices within the gift of his fellow-citizens, acting as county treasurer of Hancock County, Illinois, for several years, and generally acquitting himself in a commendable manner in all of life's affairs. He was a member of the Masonic fraternity. Mr. Palmer married Miss Phoebe Kennedy, who was born at Plymouth, Illinois, in 1853, and died at Kansas City, Missouri, in 1909, and they became the parents of six children, namely: Dr. Thomas D.; Ida May, who married George Grigson, purchasing agent for the Rock Island Railroad at Kansas City, Missouri; Fluta, who married Otto Ahrens, private secretary to Henry C. Frick, the American coke and steel manufacturer of Pittsburgh, Pennsylvania; Edward, coal weigher for the Rock Island Railroad at Kansas City, Missouri; his twin, Edwin, a linotype machine operator for the Kansas City Star, at Kansas City, Missouri; and Carl, also a linotype operator at Kansas City.

Thomas D. Palmer attended the public schools of Plymouth, Illinois, where he was duly graduated from the high school in the class of 1883. He was reared on his father's farm, where he continued to reside until attaining his majority, but it was not his desire to follow an agricultural career, and in 1896 he entered the Kansas City Medical College and completed his studies there in 1901, being graduated with the degree of Doctor of Medicine. In 1906 he took a post-graduate course at the Chicago College of Physicians and Surgeons, in 1908 at the Chicago Polyclinic, and in 1910 at Fisher's School, Chicago, where he specialized in diseases of the eye, ear, nose and throat. At the time he received his degree, in 1901, Doctor Palmer came to Oklahoma, it being his belief that this state offered an excellent field for the young and ambitious professional man. His first location was at Cherokee, where he remained until 1907, then going to Ingersoll, where he remained until 1911, and where he served one term as city treasurer in addition to carrying on his practice, and then in 1911 came to Elk City, which has continued to be his home. Here he is connected with the firm of Tedrowe, Tisdal & Palmer, owner of the Frances Hospital, one of the modern institutions in this part of the state. Doctor Palmer maintains offices on Main Street, and while his practice is general in its character it is perhaps as a specialist in diseases of the eye, ear, nose and throat, that he has gained his best reputation. Possessed in general measure of the qualities which make the personally popular as well as financially successful physician and surgeon, he has made a name as a careful, conscientious and thoroughly skilled devotee of his profession. He keeps in close touch with the professional brotherhood, belonging to the Beckham County Medical Society, the Oklahoma State Medical Society, the American Medical Association and the Southwestern Medical Society. His fraternal connections are with Elk City Lodge No. 182, Ancient Free and Accepted Masons, with the Knights Templar, and with the Benevolent and Protective Order of Elks, of Elk City. In politics he is a democrat.

Doctor Palmer was married in 1911, at Oklahoma City, to Miss Mary K. Spellman, of Hempstead, Long Island, New York. They have no children.

BENJAMIN D. WOODSON, M. D. Immediately after his graduation from Memphis Hospital College, Memphis, Tennessee, in 1890, Dr. Benjamin D. Woodson came to what was then Indian Territory and entered upon the practice of his profession at Monroe, and since that time has continued to follow his vocation in this section. Since 1912 he has been located at Poteau, where he is known as a skilled and successful practitioner, and in 1915 was appointed county superintendent of health for Le Flore County.

Doctor Woodson was born near Hartford, Sebastian County, Arkansas, March 6, 1868, and is a son of William G. and Nettie (Taner) Woodson. His father was a native of Virginia and a member of an old and highly respected family of Irish origin whose residence was in the vicinity of the City of Richmond. William G. Woodson was reared to manhood in Virginia, and when the Civil war came on joined one of the volunteer regiments from his state in the service of the Confederacy and fought valiantly as a soldier for the cause he deemed just. The war over, he moved to Arkansas, where he was married to Nettie Taner, a native of Texas, and they became the parents of five children, of whom Benjamin D. is the only survivor. A farmer by vocation, William G. Woodson's first location in Arkansas was in the vicinity of Greenwood, the county seat of Sebastian County, and later he moved to near Hartford, in the same county, that property continuing to be his home until 1882. At that time he came to a tract of land located near Monroe, in Indian Territory, where he died in 1883, aged about sixty years.

Benjamin D. Woodson was only about fifteen years of age when his father died, and he is accordingly greatly indebted to the late C. C. Matthews, of Wister, Oklahoma, for fatherly care and advice. He was reared as a farmer, but early determined upon a professional career, and after receiving his primary education in the public schools entered Buckner College, Witcherville, Arkansas, where he was graduated in 1884. For two years thereafter he was engaged in teaching school, thus earning the means wherewith to pursue his professional studies, and entered Memphis Hospital College, Memphis, Tennessee, where he was graduated with the degree of Doctor of Medicine in 1890. Returning to Monroe, Indian Territory, he opened a small office and hung out his shingle, and in the course of the next few years experienced the trials and disappointments through which every young physician is forced to pass before he can gain a foothold. However, he was persevering, and instead of showing his patience, cheerfully and industriously sought to impress himself favorably upon the community, so that practice was gradually attracted to him, and from that time forward his success was assured. In 1912, feeling that he had outgrown his community, he looked about for a broader scene for his activities and came to Poteau, where he has since built up an excellent general practice. On May 1, 1915, his abilities were recognized by his appointment to the office of county superintendent of health for Le Flore County. He keeps abreast of the progress made in his profession, and has taken two post-graduate courses, 1893 and 1900, at the Chicago Polyclinic, of Chicago, Illinois. He keeps likewise in touch with the medical brotherhood, and is a member of the Le Flore County Medical Society, the Oklahoma State Medical Society and the American Medical Association. Fraternally, he is a Royal Arch Mason, a Pythian and an Odd Fellow. His religious faith is that of the Methodist Episcopal Church, South.

Doctor Woodson was married in 1895 to Miss Lillie McClure, a native of Arkansas, and to this union there have been born five children.

ALMER SIDNEY NORVELL. About six years ago there came to Eastern Oklahoma a young attorney, who already had had considerable experience in handling cases before the courts of Arkansas and Tennessee, and in a year or so he had settled down to the enjoyment of a good practice at Wewoka. Then came official honors in the shape of the county judgeship, and he is now filling it for a second term and with such efficiency as to assure him of further promotions and public honors should he so desire.

A Tennessee man, Judge Norvell was born near Trenton in Gibson County, August 5, 1874, a son of Joseph S. and Margaret (Taylor) Norvell. Both parents were natives of Tennessee, where they spent their lives. The father, who was born August 21, 1841, died December 31, 1896, at the age of fifty-five and the mother, who was born October 13, 1850, died October 29, 1909, aged fifty-nine. Joseph S. Norvell was a farmer, and during the Civil war he served four years in a regiment of Tennessee Infantry, and was four times wounded. He was captured at the battle of Franklin and for several months was held a prisoner. He owned a good farm, gave it the best of attention and in that way and by its management provided well for his family. He also served for a number of years as justice of the peace, and was a lifelong democrat. He was deeply religious, was a deacon in the Baptist Church, and his wife also took an interest in church affairs. To their marriage were born six sons and four daughters, and four of the sons and three daughters are still living: Melville died at the age of nineteen; Walter died aged four; Dora lives at Trenton, Tennessee, widow of E. E. Strain; the fourth in age is Almer S. Norvell; John resides at Trenton, Tennessee; Hassie, deceased wife of J. M. McCord; Vannie married C. C. Sublet of Trenton; Zula married C. L. Ball of Rutherford, Tennessee; Spencer lives at Hoxey, Arkansas; and Vaughn is a resident of McKenzie, Tennessee.

Judge Norvell grew up in Gibson County, Tennessee, and lived there until 1898. In 1901 he graduated from the Normal School at Dickson, Tennessee. Three years of his young career were spent in teaching school. He studied law in the Cumberland University Law School at Lebanon, Tennessee, and on graduating LL. B. in 1904 began practice at Kenton, Tennessee. After three years there he moved to Arkansas City, Arkansas, in 1907, and thus with six years of practical experience he came in 1910 to Wewoka, Oklahoma. Here he practiced law actively until his first election in June, 1913, to the

office of county judge of Seminole County. He was re-elected and began his second term in 1915.

Judge Norvell is an active democrat and has exercised considerable influence in politics since he reached manhood. While in Arkansas he served by appointment as county examiner or superintendent of schools. Since coming to Oklahoma he has acquired some real estate and oil interests. He is a member of the Missionary Baptist Church and fraternally is a Mason.

In 1907 Judge Norvell married Ruby Patterson, who was born in Gibson County, Tennessee, in 1886, a daughter of Captain Patterson. To their marriage have been born two children: Albert Sidney and Grace Caroline.

C. M. MORGAN, M. D. Successfully identified with the medical profession at Chandler since 1909, Doctor Morgan represents the high class ability of the modern physician and surgeon, and furnishes a service of particular value to his home city in the Morgan Hospital, an institution which under his management has maintained the best standards of hospital equipment and operation. The hospital has its home in a substantial building, five private rooms, has all the modern facilities for comfort and for the appropriate care and treatment of its patients, and has skilled nurses in attendance.

Doctor Morgan was born in Vinton County, Ohio, February 4, 1873. His father was a farmer, H. M. Morgan, a native of Pennsylvania, and the Morgan family in Pennsylvania dates back as far as 1662. The maiden name of the mother was Margaret Hughes, a native of Ohio. She died in Ohio, leaving three children. The father is a democrat, and now lives at Oklahoma City.

Doctor Morgan was liberally educated, and was graduated M. D. in 1906 from the University Medical College at Kansas City, Missouri. He first located for practice at Davenport, Oklahoma, and about three years later moved to Chandler, where he now enjoys a large share of the better practice in the locality.

Doctor Morgan was married in 1913 to Harriet McLaury of this state. They have a daughter, Harriet Louella, now two years old. Doctor Morgan is a Knight Templar and thirty-second degree Mason, and the social qualities which have made him popular in that order have also made him a genial public spirited worker in his home community, where he is esteemed both for his professional standing and for his true work as a gentleman.

RICHARD WILKERSON. One of the successful and prosperous farmers of Washington County, whose entire life has been passed in agricultural pursuits, is Richard Wilkerson, a full-blooded Cherokee. He was born August 26, 1866, in the Choctaw Nation, and is a son of Thomas and Lizzie (Tenewey or Foster, the former the Indian name) Wilkerson.

The parents of Mr. Wilkerson, both full-blooded Cherokees, were born in Georgia and were children when brought to the Indian Territory by the United States Government. They resided there until the period of the Civil war, when Thomas Wilkerson, who was a minister of the Baptist Church, went to the South, leaving his family in the Choctaw Nation, whence he returned at the close of the war. He died when his son Richard, his only child by his last marriage, was about six months old. Mrs. Wilkerson survived until 1885, and died four miles west of Porum. By a previous marriage, Mrs. Wilkerson was the mother of two children: Eli and Ella, who are both deceased. The father had a son by a former marriage.

Richard Wilkerson was reared in the Canadian District of the Cherokee Nation, and as a youth entered the Male Seminary, at Tahlequah, which was conducted by the Cherokee Nation as a national school. He could not speak English when he entered that institution, but when he left, three years later, was well versed in the English tongue. He was brought up as a farmer, and remained in the Canadian District until he was twenty-four years of age, at which time he moved to the Cherokee Strip, and was living there at the time of the opening, in 1893, being at that time the owner of eighty acres. He was one of seventy families living there, and received his share from the sale of the land, amounting to $1.25 per acre. In 1895 Mr. Wilkerson came to his present location, three miles north of Dewey, where he and his children have an allotment, owning 450 acres here and ninety acres of cheap land. Mr. Wilkerson now has five oil wells on his property, while his son, Oliver C., who owns his own place of eighty acres, as well as twenty acres near Bartlesville, has seventeen producing oil wells. Mr. Wilkerson has been engaged in general farming all of his life and has made a success of his operations, being considered one of the well-to-do men of his locality. He is a democrat in political matters, is a faithful member of the Baptist Church at Sugar Mound, and is fraternally affiliated with Bartlesville Lodge, A. H. T. A., and is a Master Mason.

Mr. Wilkerson was married in March, 1891, to Anna Hendricks, a native of Tahlequah, Oklahoma, born October 10, 1870, a daughter of David and Martha (Manning) Hendricks, both full-blooded Cherokees. To this union there have been born eleven children: David, who died at the age of eight years; Lizzie, who died aged two years; Ella, who is the wife of Hope Teeke, of Washington County; Katie, who lives with her parents; Oliver C., a successful farmer and oil producer of Washington County; one child which died in infancy; William, who lives at home; Jessie, who died in infancy; Ernest and Earl, twins, the former of whom died aged four years; and Owen, who lives at home. Mr. Wilkerson also had an adopted child, Woodrow, who died February 19, 1915.

HARRY JAMES DRAY. The postmaster of Weatherford, Oklahoma, is Harry James Dray, a man of English birth and parentage, but a resident of America since he was five years old. He was born in Swansbrook, England, on January 12, 1868, and is the son of A. H. and Susan (Smith) Dray.

A. H. Dray was born in the vicinity of Swansbrook, where he was reared and married, and where his children were born. His birth occurred in 1844, and he died at Lincoln, Nebraska, in 1898. He came to America in 1873, and his family followed him ten months later. He was a blacksmith by trade, and when he came to America he made his way at once to Nebraska City, Nebraska, where he found work in the factory of the Breaking Plow Company. A little later, in 1874, he went to Essex, Iowa, the family having joined him in 1874, and in Essex the family settled down to the making of a home in a new land. The father worked at his trade there until 1887 when he moved to WaKeeney, in Western Kansas. His next move took the family to Plattsmouth, Nebraska, where he was employed in the Burlington Machine Shops, and he was by that company transferred to Lincoln, where he worked for the Burlington until his death in 1908.

Mr. Dray was democratic in his politics, and a member of the Episcopal Church. His wife, Susan Smith, was born in the same village that was his native place, in 1843, and she is now living in Black Lake, Idaho. They were the parents of a large family of fifteen children. A. H., Jr., lives in Stockton, California, where he is a blacksmith. Susan married Allen Voorhees, a farmer of Mullen, Idaho, where they have their home. J. P. is a barber of Ely, Nevada. Harry James was the fourth child. W. S. lives in Savannah, Missouri, where he is postmaster and the editor of a newspaper. Jennie married C. N. Cooley, pastor of the Congregational Church at Black Lake, Idaho. Nellie married Harry Cox, a merchant of Muskogee, Oklahoma. Richard died young, as did also Minnie, George, Edward and Irving. Frank is a resident of Black Lake, Idaho, where he is employed as a railroad machinist. He and his mother have a home there. Margaret married Morris Griffith, and they live in Livingston, Montana. The fifteenth child died in infancy.

Harry James Dray attended the public schools in Essex, Iowa, until 1887, when the family moved to WaKeeney, Kansas, and he entered a printing office there, following an apprenticeship in the printing business he had served in Essex, while still attending school. He spent three years in the office of The Tribune in WaKeeney, and in 1890 he went to Plattsmouth, Nebraska, as foreman of the Cass County Herald. He held that position until 1894, when he went to Auburn, Nebraska, and was foreman of the Herald there until 1903. In April, 1903, he came to Weatherford, Oklahoma, and entered the office of the Weatherford Republican as foreman, which position he filled for a year. He then bought the Weatherford Democrat, an opposition paper, and published it until April 1, 1915, when N. S. DeMotte bought an interest in the paper, and since then has been the editor of the paper. This is one of the foremost sheets in the county, and is an influence for good wherever it circulates. It is well managed and has a wide circulation in the county and state.

Mr. Dray is democratic in his convictions, and has served as clerk of the Weatherford School Board for seven years. In August, 1913, he was appointed postmaster of Weatherford by President Wilson, and is satisfactorily filling that office at the present time. He is a member of the Episcopal Church, and is a Mason with Ancient Free and Accepted Masonic affiliations. He is also a member of the Knights of Pythias No. 11, Auburn, Nebraska, and is past chancellor commander of that lodge. He is a member of the Modern Woodmen of America, the Royal Highlanders and the Court of Honor, and in all of them is popular and prominent, with an instinct for fraternalism and sociability that makes him welcome in whatever circles he frequents.

Mr. Dray was married in 1903 in Peru, Nebraska, to Miss Emma E. Randol, daughter of J. P. Randol, a retired farmer now living in Weatherford. They have four children: The first born, Rhea Ruth, died here at the age of nine years. Edith and Isabelle attend the public schools, while the youngest child, Margaret, is not yet of school age.

C. M. CADE. It is hardly necessary to make any point of introduction for this well known Oklahoma citizen, banker, pioneer, man of affairs and leader in the republican party. There are few men in the state better known for substantial activities and broad influence exerted continuously since the original opening of Oklahoma Territory to settlement.

Born in Noble County, Ohio, August 4, 1856, C. M. Cade represents an old American family. A short time after the Revolutionary war was concluded three brothers, William, Samuel and Moses Cade, emigrated from France to Virginia. Of these three brothers William was the grandfather of C. M. Cade. He was a planter in Virginia, and afterwards transferred his residence to a farm on Blennerhassett Island in the Ohio River, famous in history as the home of that unfortunate gentleman who became involved in the plots of Aaron Burr. William Cade spent the rest of his life in Ohio and died at Marietta, in that state.

Samuel Cade, father of C. M. Cade, was born at Natural Bridge, Virginia, in 1826, and died at Shawnee, Oklahoma, March 16, 1909. He was reared in Virginia but as a young man located at Marietta, Ohio. He was married in Monroe County, Ohio, a county from which Noble County was subsequently formed. In 1865 he established his home in Lawrence County, Ohio. From 1898 to 1900 he lived in Anthony, Kansas, and in 1900 moved to Kingfisher County, Oklahoma, where he was an early settler, and a farmer and stock raiser. He was a democrat in politics, and very active in the Baptist Church, in which he served as a deacon many years. Samuel Cade married Emeline Rowe, who was born in Guernsey County, Ohio, in 1822, and died at Anthony, Kansas, in 1900. Their children were: W. S. Cade, an attorney at Oklahoma City and for a number of years a United States marshal; B. M. Cade, who died in Lawrence County, Ohio, in 1881, also an attorney by profession and engaged in practice at Pomeroy, Ohio; Ceola Virginia, wife of Henry Shaw, a farmer and stock raiser at Burton, Nebraska; C. M. Cade; and Mary, wife of George E. Clark, who is in the railroad shops at Shawnee.

C. M. Cade grew up on his father's farm back in Ohio, spending the first sixteen years of his life in the wholesome atmosphere of the country and with such education as the local schools could supply. Afterwards he taught school in Lawrence County, Ohio, but in 1876 went West with the early pioneers of Nebraska, and became a farmer at Plum Creek in that state. In 1877 he went out to the Black Hills and spent a year in that famous mining region. From 1879 to 1884 he was a school teacher in Anthony, Kansas, and then took part as one of the founders of the flourishing little City of Coldwater, Kansas, and was secretary and treasurer of the Town Site Company from 1884 to 1889.

April 22, 1889, the opening day of the original Oklahoma Territory, he participated in the rush and landed in Kingfisher County. He was soon one of the leaders among the early settlers, and was elected and served as the first county clerk of Kingfisher county, holding that office a year and a half. Since 1895 Mr. Cade's home and activities have been largely centered at Shawnee. He was town site agent for the town, and until 1899 was in the employ of the old Choctaw, Oklahoma and Gulf Railroad, now part of the Rock Island System. On leaving the railway service he entered the First National Bank of Shawnee, and for one year was its vice president. He then resigned to become commercial agent for the Rock Island Railroad, and was also in the right of way department until 1902, in which year he helped to found the State National Bank of Shawnee, becoming its cashier, a position he still holds.

The State National Bank of Shawnee was established in 1902 by Willard Johnston, George E. McKinnis, Julius Greenlee, J. W. McLoud and Mr. Cade. It still keeps its original capitalization at $100,000. The bank is one of the commercial landmarks in Shawnee, situated at the corner of Main and Broadway. It now has a surplus of $20,000 and undivided profits of $8,000. The officers of the bank at this time are: Willard Johnston, president; George E. McKinnis and Frank Reed, vice presidents; C. M. Cade, cashier; Willard Barnett and N. S. Barnett, assistant cashiers. The bank is represented in the State and National Bankers Associations by its officers.

As a banker Mr. Cade's interests are somewhat widely extended. He is president of the Cimarron Valley

Bank, at Coyle; vice president of the Bank of Earlsboro; vice president of the Bank of Meeker; director in the First National Bank of Geary and in the First National Bank of Mounds, all of them Oklahoma institutions.

In republican politics Mr. Cade's name has long been familiar to the people of Oklahoma. From 1902 to 1904 he was state chairman of the State Central Committee, and from 1904 to 1912 was a National Committeeman from Oklahoma. He is an active member of the Shawnee Commercial Club, and fraternally is identified with Shawnee Lodge No. 657, Benevolent and Protective Order of Elks; Shawnee Lodge No. 107, Ancient Free and Accepted Masons; Shawnee Lodge of the Fraternal Order of Eagles, and of the Knights of Pythias.

On March 27, 1883, in Wellington, Kansas, he married Miss Helen Kitchen, daughter of F. H. Kitchen, who during his active lifetime was a farmer. Mrs. Cade died in Coldwater, Kansas, in 1884. The only child by her union is C. M. Cade, Jr., whose home is at Dale, Oklahoma, where he conducts a farm and raises stock, and he was also postmaster at Shawnee until April 1, 1915. On November 27, 1889, at Enid, Oklahoma, Mr. Cade married Miss Lizzie Hartz, daughter of Frank Hartz, who was a farmer. There is one child by this union, Leo Samuel, now a sophomore in the Shawnee High School.

DR. JAMES H. MILLER, whose appointment as representative of the Choctaw Nation in Washington, recently was made by Principal Chief Victor M. Locke, Jr., and confirmed by the Choctaw Senate, has for many years stood as one of the foremost intermarried citizens in the old Choctaw Nation, and has many interests as banker, merchant and stockman at Antlers and vicinity.

History is best translated and interpreted through the human actors engaged in making or witnessing it. Every human life helps to make or reflect the progress and experience of the age. It is the fundamental principle in the writing of history that "the life of a nation is at bottom only the life of a man."

The editor of this article believes there is no more illuminating chapter on the life, manners and customs of old Indian Territory, especially the old Choctaw Nation, than is found in the record of what Doctor Miller has witnessed and experienced. Hence this article is not so much a personal biography as a scroll of history as it has been unrolled and lived before the eyes of Doctor Miller.

In recalling happenings of nearly forty years ago in the Choctaw Nation, Doctor Miller remembers having attended a trial at Caddo in which several prominent men of the Indian Nation were tried for treason. Among these men were Col. James J. McAlester, a member of the first corporation commission of the state and more recently lieutenant governor. The late Tandy Walker, a half brother of Governor Douglas H. Johnston, of the Chickasaw Nation; James Thompson, then treasurer of the Choctaw Nation; and James Davis, an intermarried citizen. The first trial was held before District Judge Lorin Folsom, and had the jury found them guilty they would have been shot as the Indian law provided.

This trial occurred during the administration of Coleman Cole, principal chief of the Choctaw Nation. Cole was a character who deserves more than passing mention. He was a full-blood of the old Indian type and wore a blanket about his shoulders. Although he had a high regard for the white men of the nation who became his friends, his ambition was to hold the Choctaw estate intact as long as possible. Hence he had the Legislature enact a law providing that any person who should sell or attempt to sell any land of the Choctaw Nation should be guilty of treason.

About 1875 the Missouri, Kansas & Texas Railroad was projected south of Vinita toward the coal fields of McAlester and Lehigh, and the defendants in this notable case above referred to executed leases for coal mine purposes to certain Choctaw lands. Thereupon Cole had warrants issued for their arrest, charging them with treason, and they were indicted by a grand jury. Some of them fled into Arkansas, but later all surrendered. A special term of court in the Third Judicial District was convened at Caddo, and the men were tried and acquitted. Chief Cole attended the trial, as did also Doctor Miller, who meantime had become an intermarried citizen. The verdict incensed the chief and he arose in court and publicly rebuked Judge Folsom.

"Lorin Folsom," spoke the principal chief, "you are as much a traitor to our beloved nation as are these men you have acquitted, and you are not entitled to a seat on the Choctaw Bench. It was possible for you to have given the jury a charge that would have convicted these men." He then turned to the McAlester group and said: "Don't flatter yourselves that you are free." Then to Sheriff Joe Bryant he turned and commanded that they be rearrested and a new jury summoned. The chief then threw off his blanket and took the bench. Another trial proceeded and it too resulted in an acquittal.

To the jury the principal chief then addressed himself: "Gentlemen," he said, "by your act today you have driven the wedge to the hilt that will burst our country asunder. This is the beginning of the end. Who is to mine this coal? Not the Indian. Who lifts this coal? Not the Indian. You have opened the gates that will admit to our country white men like the leaves of the trees, without number. They will build houses and remain here and talk, as they did in Mississippi of old, of vested rights. The strong will rise and the weak will go down. There is nothing in common between the white man and the Indian. Like oil and water, they will not mix. Thank God, the sin is yours, not mine. I have done my full duty. Experience taught me much in Mississippi, and I don't want to live over again the days of the past. Your act probably won't seriously affect me or you, but your posterity will pay the penalty of your crime."

This event was near the close of the administration of Chief Cole and he was defeated for re-election. No governor of the Choctaws ever was such a czar, yet his acts on the whole were of benefit to his people. Neither was he averse to white men entering the nation if he were convinced that they were patriotic and would make the right sort of citizens.

When Doctor Miller, after attending lectures at Tulane University of New Orleans, established himself for the practice of medicine at Goodland in the Choctaw Nation, he found that a permit from the Choctaw Government was necessary. He boarded at the home of former Principal Chief B. L. LeFlore. When Governor LeFlore came home on a vacation from attending the Choctaw Council, he asked him to obtain a permit to practice medicine. So, when Governor LeFlore returned to Armstrong Academy, then the capitol of the Choctaw Nation, seeking out Chief Cole he said he had a young doctor at his home and that he wished to obtain a permit for him. Chief Cole said, "do you think he is qualified and all right?" LeFlore replied yes. Cole then turned to Joe Lawrence, who was permit collector, and said, "Joe, issue him a permit," which was done. Lawrence handed the permit to Cole, and the latter to LeFlore, saying: "Give him this with my compliments and tell him to make a good citizen, and if a Choctaw gets sick to go to see him whether he has money or not and that he will be rewarded."

As a slight token of this friendly act, Doctor Miller is now endeavoring to locate Cole's grave with the view of erecting a suitable monument to his memory. After entering Choctaw politics, Doctor Miller frequently opposed Chief Cole in policies vitally affecting the nation, but in later years he concluded that he was in error and that Cole was always right.

Before he lived in the Choctaw Nation two years Doctor Miller fell in love with an Indian girl, but was unable to marry her under Choctaw laws because he had not lived in the nation the required two years and could not get the required petition with ten signers testifying to his character. So he and Miss Ella J. Robuck crossed Red River and were married in the home of Captain Arthur, now on the site of the Village of Arthur City. Mrs. Miller is a daughter of Col. William Robuck, who filled the offices of auditor and attorney general in the Choctaw Government and was a member of the Senate when he died. Colonel Robuck, with Col. Dave Harkins and McGee King, constituted a commission that settled a boundary dispute on the eastern side of the nation, each receiving 5 per cent of the value of the territory recovered. Colonel Robuck died before the commission money was distributed and was succeeded by Campbell LeFlore, who paid to the Robuck estate its share of the fee. When Doctor Miller later was ambitious to enter Choctaw politics he complied with Choctaw laws and he and Mrs. Miller were married again under those laws. When the enrollment period came he was enrolled without question as a member of the Choctaw Tribe.

Doctor Miller's entrance into Choctaw politics made him an important factor in the campaign in which Principal Chief Wilson N. Jones was candidate for re-election, and so important were the doctor's activities that Governor Jones appointed him tribal collector in a section traversed by the Frisco Railroad. He was a member of the executive campaign committee in the campaign when Green McCurtain first ran for principal chief, and for twelve years was chairman of the campaign committee of his party, then known as the progressive party. In politics he has never lost a fight. He had for two terms the office of collector for the Third Judicial District, and he is the only white man ever confirmed by the Choctaw Council for a tribal office up to that time.

Doctor Miller speaks the Choctaw language and has been associated with the Indians in various capacities. He has known personally every principal chief since Coleman Cole and has attended nearly every session of the tribal legislature since that time. As a member of the Treaty Rights Association, he and Dr. T. P. Howell of Davis, and Edward B. Johnson of Norman, in 1913-14 represented the association in Washington to oppose measures that provided for the re-opening of the Choctaw rolls. This has been the greatest fight of recent years on the part of the Choctaws. Their tribal estate is worth many millions of dollars and about $7,000,000 in cash is now in the United States treasury to their credit. So long as this great estate remains in common and is held out as a bait, says Doctor Miller, all kinds of people will want to be Choctaws and get on the rolls, and money and influence almost without estimate will be used to break the seal put on the rolls years ago. Doctor Miller canvassed the Choctaw Nation in behalf of the Atoka Agreement and later in behalf of the Supplemental Agreement. The greatest feature of the Supplemental Agreement was its creation of a citizenship court which it made possible to review judgments that had been rendered by the Federal Court in the Indian Territory. The Choctaw Government was surprised and overawed by the vast number of appeals that were taken to this court. They were unprepared to make a defense and many thousand judgments were rendered by default, placing the names of what were known as court citizens on the roll. Through the efforts of Mansfield, McMurray and Cornish, who were employed by the two tribes to review these cases, some 3,600 names were expunged from the roll. A time limit was fixed for further enrollment of applicants and this limit is long expired. Doctor Miller is of the opinion that the citizenship question has long since been settled and that any effort to reopen the rolls is an invasion of the Choctaw-Chickasaw tribes' rights.

Doctor Miller witnessed at Goodland the execution of Wakum Evrin, charged with murdering his wife. John Wilson, deputy, under Sheriff Dave Gibson, fired the shot into the Indian's heart. Evrin had a voice of remarkable clearness and sweetness and was noted over the nation as one of the sweetest singers the tribe had produced. After the murder he fled the country where he committed the crime and located in Sansbois, Choctaw Nation. One night a few years later during church service the preacher Reverend Belinchey, a full blood Choctaw, recognized the voice of Evrin joining in the singing. He reported it to the sheriff and Evrin was arrested. Evrin sang beautifully and with a peculiar fervor while he was being prepared for the execution. He sang while a minister exhorted him about his soul's welfare and sang until the ball sped from the officer's gun. He ceased his song long enough, a half minute before the shot, to waive aside a medicine man who had come to paint a spot over his heart, and indicated with his own finger the target for the bullet.

Early one morning Doctor Miller was awakened by a call at the door. Sim Joe, a Choctaw, had come for him to visit Deupty Sheriff Wilson. The visit was made. The significance of the incident lies in the fact that Sim Joe was condemned to death at that time and yet had been selected by the sheriff as messenger to the doctor. There have been many Choctaws who exemplified similar reliability and in whom all faith and confidence could be placed.

James H. Miller was born in 1853 in Carroll County, Tennessee. His father died in 1858. In 1859 he and his mother started with his grandparents overland to Texas. His grandfather, however, located near what is now Prescott, Arkansas, and remained there until 1864. His mother died while living in Arkansas, and Doctor Miller came on to Paris, Texas, with his grandparents later. About 1866 the lad went back to Middle Tennessee and attended school in Giles County some three years. Returning to East Texas he was in the employ of his uncle in the lumber business for about a year, afterwards attended school three terms at Sulphur Springs in Hopkins County, Texas, and on finishing school entered the office of Dr. W. M. Clements, Paris, Texas, and began the study of medicine. He also attended lectures in New Orleans, and in October, 1875 came to Indian Territory and began the practice of medicine at Old Goodland, Kiamichi County, Choctaw Nation. About 1892 he moved his family to Paris, Texas, for educational and social purposes and remained there sixteen years, and from there moved to Antlers, Oklahoma, his present home.

Doctor Miller has valuable ranch interests on McGee Creek and Impson Valley. For twenty-five years he has dealt in cattle as his principal business. He was one of the organizers of the Hugo National Bank, is vice president of the Citizens National Bank of Antlers, owns stock in the American National Bank at Paris, Texas, has a general merchandise business at Grant and a general store at Kent. Eight miles south of Antlers he has one of the most modern and best equipped stock farms in Oklahoma. Among other features are a water plant and an electric light plant, large silos, a cotton gin and grist mill. Here are raised some of the finest stock in Southeastern Oklahoma and only the best methods of agriculture are employed.

It has recently become a matter of authentic knowledge that Mrs. Dr. Miller is a direct descendant of Pushmataha, the great war chief and governor of the Choctaws. Their relationship was outlined in a work published by S. J. Hotama, a witch killer and religious fanatic, who, having been convicted of murder because of his peculiar belief, was sentenced to life imprisonment in the Federal prison at Atlanta, where he died. When the fact of this relationship was known to the Council of the Nation, Senator Frank Folsom drafted a resolution providing that a large portrait of Pushmataha that hangs in the Council House at Tuskahoma should be presented to Doctor Miller. "Let Dr. Miller have the resolution," kindly remarked Principal Chief McCurtain to members of the Council, "but I am going to retain the portrait of Pushmataha." The resolution was not presented to the Council.

Doctor Miller has a fine family of five sons and two daughters. Edgar Poe Miller and S. G. Miller live in Antlers and are engaged principally in the livestock business. Mrs. W. T. Glenn, now deceased, was the wife of the present county judge of Choctaw County. W. W. Miller is in the livestock business and occupies the ranch his father established here many years ago. J. H. Miller Jr., who has lived for a number of years on old M Bar Ranch, is engaged in the livestock business in New Mexico. Mrs. Ruby C. McIntosh is the wife of W. R. McIntosh, mining trustee of the Choctaw Nation, and lives at McAlester. Miss Edith R. Miller is attending school at Denison, Texas. Frank Wright Miller, the youngest son, lives with his parents in Antlers.

RUFUS P. ROOPE. One of the best known and most honored citizens of Lincoln County is Rufus P. Roope, who is now serving as county treasurer and who previously has held the office of county clerk. He has been a resident of what is now the State of Oklahoma for nearly a quarter of a century, and may be termed with all consistency a pioneer, his original location having been in Lincoln County, which was then an integral part of Indian Territory. He has been closely and worthily identified with the development and upbuilding of Lincoln County and its attractive and thriving judicial center, the Village of Chandler, the while he has ever retained inviolable place in popular confidence and esteem, as indicated by his having been called to offices of signal public trust. Mr. Roope has shown much circumspection and executive ability as a public official, and his unfailing courtesy and consideration have gained to him the good will of all with whom he has come in contact in his official capacity as well as in the ordinary course of civic life. He was elected county treasurer in the autumn of 1914, as candidate on the republican ticket, and had served the preceding two years as county clerk. He is careful and methodical in his handling of all details of official work and Lincoln County has been favored in securing his services in connection with its governmental affairs.

Rufus P. Roope was born on a plantation in Franklin County, Tennessee, on the 13th of June, 1875, and is a son of Rev. Abner L. and Emarine (Protsman) Roope, both of whom were natives of Indiana and both of whom attained to the venerable age of eighty years before they were summoned to the life eternal. The father was a clergyman of the Methodist Episcopal Church and at the time of the Civil war he served as captain of the Eighty-second Indiana Volunteer Infantry, with which regiment he endured the full tension of the great conflict, having been with the commands of General Thomas and General Sherman in many sanguinary engagements on the battlefields of the South. In later years he perpetuated the memories of his military career through his membership in the Grand Army of the Republic, and he never faltered in his allegiance to the republican party. He labored with all of zeal and devotion for many years as a minister of the church of which both he and his wife were most devout members. Of their two children the subject of this review is the younger, the elder son, Charles, being deceased.

Passing the days of his boyhood and youth on the farm in Switzerland County, Indiana, Rufus P. Roope duly availed himself of the advantages of the public schools, this discipline having been supplemented by a course in a business college in Sedalia, Missouri.

Mr. Roope came to Indian Territory and established his residence in what is now Lincoln County in 1891. He was one of the early settlers in the Village of Meeker, where he engaged in farming and where he served five years as postmaster, besides which he was for a time a teacher in a school maintained for children of the Creek Indians. During the period of his effective service as a county official he has, as a matter of course, maintained his residence at Chandler, the judicial center of the county, and he has been progressive and public-spirited, a loyal supporter of the measures and enterprises that have furthered the social and industrial advancement and upbuilding of his home county and the Territory and State of Oklahoma. Mr. Roope gave careful attention to the study of law and is now a member of the Oklahoma bar; in the Masonic fraternity he has advanced to the thirty-second degree of the Ancient Accepted Scottish Rite; he is a stalwart republican in politics; and both he and his wife hold membership in the Presbyterian Church.

On the 4th of February, 1898, was solemnized the marriage of Mr. Roope to Miss Elizabeth McGee, who was born at Mexico, Missouri, where she acquired her rudimentary education. She was a young girl at the time of the family removal to Kansas, and at Iola, that state, she completed her educational discipline, after which she became a successful and popular teacher in the public schools. Among her schoolmates were the children of the Funston family, of which Gen. Fred Funston is a distinguished member. Mrs. Roope is a daughter of the late Albert L. McGee, who was a native of Indiana, and who later became a prosperous agriculturist and influential citizen in Audrain County, Missouri. Mr. and Mrs. Roope have two children—Frances Ruth and Marguerite Fern.

HARRY BROWN. There are turning points in every man's life called opportunity. Taken advantage of they mean ultimate success. The career of Harry Brown is a striking illustration of the latter statement. Diligent and ever alert for his chance of advancement, he has progressed steadily until he is recognized today as one of the foremost business men of Anadarko. Here he is held in high esteem by his fellow citizens, who honor him for his native ability and for his fair and straightforward career. Mr. Brown is the owner of a large lumber yard at Anadarko and in connection with his business sends supplies to various sections throughout Caddo County.

A native of the Emerald Isle, Harry Brown was born at St. Johnston, Donegal County, Ireland, September 30,

1861. His paternal grandfather was Henry Brown, who spent his entire life in Donegal County, Ireland, where he was keeper of a large landed estate. James Brown, father of Harry, was born at St. Johnston, Ireland, in 1845, and he emigrated to America in 1862, landing in Maryland, whence he journeyed west to Illinois and going thence to Carbondale, Kansas. He was a coal miner and followed his occupation in many states from the Atlantic to the Pacific. April 22, 1889, he settled permanently at Edmond, Oklahoma, and there he has since been most profitably engaged in the lumber and hardware business. Although seventy years of age he enjoys splendid health and his intellect is as keen as in the prime of life. In politics he is a loyal republican and he represented his district in the Oklahoma Legislature in 1893. He is a devout communicant of the Roman Catholic Church and is affiliated with the Knights of Columbus. He married Jane Britten, who was born in Paisley, Scotland, in 1845, and who died at Edmond, Oklahoma, in 1899. The following children were born to Mr. and Mrs. Brown: Harry is the subject of this sketch; Isabella married Dan Mooney, an oil man at Ponca City, this state; J. J. assists his father in the hardware business at Edmond, Oklahoma; Dennis T. has been lost track of; Catherine married Charles S. Pitman and they live at El Paso, Texas; she is a graduate of the Edmond Normal School; and Mayme, a graduate of the kindergarten department of the Edmond Normal School, is a stenographer and teacher and resides at home with her parents.

Harry Brown came to America with his mother in 1866, his father having come to this country five years earlier. As a result of the family moving so often, he was educated in the public schools of several states. April 22, 1889, he settled in Edmond, Oklahoma, and there was engaged in the mercantile business until 1894. He then accepted a position as traveling salesman for the Buford & George Manufacturing Company, selling farm implements for that concern in South Kansas and Oklahoma for the ensuing ten years. In 1904 he came to Anadarko among the pioneers and here engaged in the lumber business, continuing in that line of enterprise with marked success to the present time. His well equipped lumber yard is situated on the corner of East Broadway and Seventh Street and he ships large supplies of lumber to distant points throughout Caddo and neighboring counties. He is a republican in politics and has served on the school board in Anadarko for a number of years. He is a shrewd business man but is possessed of a kindly and genial personality that makes friends for him wherever he goes.

In Edmond, Oklahoma, in 1890, Mr. Brown married Miss Sarah McFadyen, a daughter of John McFadyen, who was a farmer near Edmond prior to his demise. Mr. and Mrs. Brown have two sons: Harry J. was graduated in the University of Oklahoma, in 1914, with the degree of Bachelor of Arts, and he is now pursuing a post-graduate course in that institution, making a specialty of mathematics and calisthenics, which subjects he expects to teach in the Durant Normal School next year; John D. is a junior in the University of Oklahoma. Both boys are fine examples of sturdy young American manhood and they have promising careers ahead of them.

The Brown family are communicants of the Roman Catholic Church, to whose good works they are liberal contributors of their time and means. Mrs. Brown is a woman of most gracious personality and she is popular with all who have had the pleasure of meeting her.

DR. J. MATT GORDON. Ten years ago Dr. J. Matt Gordon came to Weatherford and established himself in medical practice here. Since that time he has been a continuous resident here, and has a wide practice in the community and surrounding towns. He is a native son of Missouri, born at Bolivar, on November 14, 1865, and is a son of B. F. and Rebecca A. (Brown) Gordon.

B. F. Gordon was born in Kentucky in 1818, and he died near Bolivar, Missouri, in 1900. He came to Missouri in young manhood and engaged in the farming and stock raising business, in which he experienced a pleasing degree of success. He was a Baptist all his life and a deacon in the church. His wife was born in Kentucky in 1827, and she died near Bolivar, in 1892. Their children were six in number, and are briefly mentioned here as follows: Ruan married J. M. Mullis, and they live on a farm in Cameron, Missouri. Elizabeth married R. T. Ellis, and they live in Bolivar, Missouri. Thomas Benton is deceased. R. D. lives in Waynoka, Oklahoma, where he is a druggist. Naomi married W. E. Johnson and is now deceased. Dr. J. Matt Gordon was the sixth child.

Doctor Gordon as a boy attended the public schools at Bolivar, continuing his studies there until he was eighteen years old, when he turned his attention to school teaching. He taught several years in Polk County, Missouri, and then entered the state normal school at Warrensburg, Missouri, to further his training. He was graduated from that school in 1897, after which he was chosen to fill the position of superintendent of the Warrensburg Public Schools. He continued in that post from 1897 to 1902, when he entered the College of Physicians and Surgeons in Chicago, now the medical department of the University of Illinois, and he was graduated with the class of 1905, with the degree M. D. Since that time Doctor Gordon has taken the A. B. course in South-West Baptist College, Bolivar, Missouri, and post graduate courses in the Chicago Polyclinic in 1910 and 1912. Following his graduation Doctor Gordon came to Weatherford, and has been engaged in practice here ever since, with offices in the Weatherford Drug Store. He is at present serving as local health physician, and has in past years served as president of the school board, in which position he was especially well qualified to act, by reason of his previous wide experience in the educational fields. From 1909 to 1911 he was a member of the Board of Regents for the University of Oklahoma, at Norman. He has served as president of the Custer County Medical Society, and he also has membership in the State and American Medical Associations. At the present time he is president of the West Central Oklahoma Medical Society. He is local surgeon for the Rock Island Railroad, and is a member of the United States Pension Board, as well as local examining physician on that board. Doctor Gordon owns a splendid farm about three miles from Weatherford, and has a nice home in town.

Doctor Gordon was married in Bolivar, Missouri, in 1890, to Miss Pinnie E. Milliken, daughter of H. R. Milliken, now deceased. They have no living children.

In a fraternal way Doctor Gordon is especially popular in Weatherford. He is a Mason of high degree and is affiliated with Weatherford Lodge No. 138 Ancient Free and Accepted Masons, Weatherford Chapter No. 31, Royal Arch Masons, Weatherford Commandery No. 17, Knights Templar, and Indian Temple, Ancient Arabic Order Nobles of the Mystic Shrine, at Oklahoma City. He is also a member of the Independent Order of Odd Fellows, the Woodmen of the World, the Modern Woodmen of America.

ANDREW JACKSON BROWN, of Wewoka, has gained as much distinction in commercial affairs as his brother, John F. Brown, in the public life of the Seminole Nation. As a matter of fact, however, Andrew J. Brown and

John F. Brown have for many years been closely associated in business affairs, and these two brothers, with Mr. C. L. Long, own and control the two largest business institutions at Wewoka—the Wewoka Trading Company and the Wewoka Realty & Trust Company, which is incorporated with a capital of $100,000.

On other pages will be found a record of John F. Brown, the principal chief of the Seminole Nation. Governor Brown is about thirteen years older than Andrew Jackson Brown, who was born at Tahlequah, Oklahoma, March 3, 1856. He was fifth in a family of four sons and three daughters, and their parents were Dr. John F. and Lucy (Graybeard) Brown. Doctor Brown was a distinguished character in old Indian Territory and some of the more important details of the family record will be found in the sketch of Governor Brown.

When Andrew J. Brown was an infant his parents moved to that section of Indian Territory between Muskogee and the old Creek Agency, and in 1866 when he was ten years of age they moved to the old Seminole Agency in Pottawatomie County. He acquired his education by attending the day schools operated by the Government, was also a student at Sasakwa, the town founded by his brother, Governor Brown, and in 1873 completed a course in the Jones Commercial College at St. Louis.

He then returned to Indian Territory and from 1874 to 1880 took an active part in the management of the store at Sasakwa, operated under the name of John F. Brown & Brother. Andrew J. Brown has been a leader in business affairs at Wewoka since 1880. At that time there was one store and a blacksmith shop comprising all the commercial activities of the little village. Soon afterward C. L. Long entered the partnership, and for a number of years the firm conducted two stores, one at Wewoka and the other at Sasakwa. Later they organized the Wewoka Trading Company, and the store at Sasakwa was turned over to Governor Brown, who, however, still continued an active member of the partnership at Wewoka. The Wewoka Trading Company, not incorporated, operates the largest general department store in Seminole County and they also built the largest business house in the town, a two-story brick 90 by 100 feet, in addition to the old store, which occupies ground 80 by 40 feet. In this store are employed from six to twelve persons, and the trade extends all over Seminole County. The management of the business is in the hands of Andrew J. Brown and Mr. Long.

These three parties also own all the stock in the Wewoka Realty & Trust Company, of which Andrew J. Brown is president, John F. Brown vice president, and Mr. Long secretary and treasurer. Mr. Brown and family also have allotments of land in Seminole County and they control extensive stock and farming interests.

Andrew J. Brown for the last twenty years has been treasurer of the Seminole Nation, though that office since statehood has been of nominal importance only. For two terms, eight years, he was also superintendent of tribal schools. Like his brother, Governor Brown, he is a minister of the Gospel, of the Baptist faith, and was active in preaching and disseminating the Gospel truths for about fifteen years. He is pastor of the Buckeye Baptist Church on Little River. He was also one of the organizers and a leader in the building of that church.

In 1879 he married Miss Mamie Jacobs, who was born near Eufaula in 1861, a daughter of Frank Jacobs. Mrs. Brown is a half-blood Creek. They had one child, Clarence W. Brown, who was born January 24, 1880, and died June 9, 1911. This son married Rebecca Bell, and at his death he left three children who have their home with Mr. and Mrs. Andrew J. Brown. Their names are Lucy, Ruth and John.

H. V. FOSTER, as president of the Indian Territory Illuminating Oil Company of Bartlesville, and the directing head of the company that controls the famous Foster Lease in the Osage Nation, is easily one of the most conspicuous figures in the great oil industry of the Southwest. It was his honored father who negotiated the Foster Lease, but though a comparatively young man H. V. Foster has been the moving spirit in carrying out the plans and details of this great enterprise since 1902.

Born at Westerly, Washington County, Rhode Island, September 6, 1875, H. V. Foster is a son of Henry and Gertrude (Daniels) Foster, his father also a native of Westerly, while his mother was born at Paxton, Worcester County, Massachusetts. Henry Foster was one of the ablest financiers and oil operators of his generation. For many years he followed banking in Rhode Island, but about 1882 moved to Independence, Kansas, where he kept the center of his financial operations until his death on February 25, 1896, at the age of forty-seven. His name is closely associated with a great deal of important development work in the Southwest. He was the builder of the Missouri Pacific Railroad from Leroy to Coffeyville, Kansas, and was also interested in mining, constructed a number of waterworks plants in various parts of the Southwest, and owned or partly owned several ranches for cattle raising.

As already mentioned he secured the lease for the production of oil on the Osage Reservation, and died about the time the Government gave its final approval to the terms of that lease. His wife died at Independence, Kansas, about 1883 at the age of thirty-two. Their two children are: Annie G., a resident of New York City; and H. V. Foster.

H. V. Foster was specially equipped by education and native ability for the large business affairs which he has directed for a number of years. He is an engineer by profession, though most of his time has been devoted to the executive details of business. As a boy he attended public school in Rhode Island and Massachusetts, also at Independence, Kansas, and his parents being Quakers subsequently sent him to the Westtown Boarding School maintained by the Society of Friends at Westtown, Pennsylvania. Going abroad he entered University College of London, England, and graduated with his engineer's certificate in 1894. On his return to the United States he entered Columbia University at New York.

As an engineer his first work was on a drainage project comprising 60,000 acres in Wisconsin. In the meantime he became interested in oil development, and in 1902 removed to Bartlesville to take charge of the Osage Lease and becoming president of the Indian Territory Illuminating Oil Company. He has since devoted all his time and energy to this industry, and is a master of the business in every detail. Mr. Foster is also vice president and director of the Union National Bank, and his offices are in the Union National Bank Building.

Because of the active participation of the Foster family in the oil industry in Osage territory and because all matters affecting the Osage oil lands are subjects of historical interest in Oklahoma, a few quotations from a recent article that appeared in the Washington Star are properly presented at this point. "A modern industry represented by the huge oil derricks and pipe lines of Oklahoma," reads the article in question, "has brought at least one nation of Indians into its own as far as the individuals of its tribe are concerned in being the original landlords of that part of this continent in which they have made their home. The red man pictured in his feathered head-dress on the American penny is suggestive of the former wealth of the nation being held by the Indian. Today, when the white man's dollar has developed a part of the country upon which the Indians still live, the Osages have received such large oil and gas royalties that they have been declared the richest nation in the world. Had the white man never come to this continent these Indians would have undoubtedly been content in their original wild state, taking pleasure in their hunts and ceremonials, but since it is a fact that civilization has killed off their buffalo and so taken their livelihood from them, the Osage Nation may consider that the star of fortune rose about 1870.

"At that time the encroachment of settlers who were making their homes in Kansas was so evident to the Indian and to the Government that later Congress purchased the land upon which the Osages had been living and ceded them the territory they now occupy. By this deal the Indians unknowingly received lands worth millions of dollars on account of the oil lying beneath its surface. Today these resources are so extensive that the government in the capacity of guardian for the red man finds itself thrown in direct business relations with some of the greatest financial powers of the Nation. It gains through this particular management of affairs a clearer knowledge of the business of producing and marketing oil, the most potential wealth-making power of the present day.

"Nineteen years ago when James Bigheart was the principal chief of the Osage Nation, about one million five hundred thousand acres of land, or approximately two thousand square miles—a tract many times as large as the District of Columbia—was leased directly from the tribe, through the United States Government, to Edward B. Foster of New York City. The development of a large part of the territory was made by the sublessee, known as the Illuminating Company, engaged in producing oil. When the original blanket Foster lease and the subleases expired at the end of ten years they were renewed for another ten years, which will expire March 16, 1916. It was for this reason that in March, 1915, one year previous to the expiration of the lease of the vast stretch of oil lands, the oil interests of the world were assembled in a great conference with the government, hoping to receive a share of consideration when the time comes for Uncle Sam and the Osage Indians to say who shall obtain the right to produce oil in the Foster lease land in the future.

"The terms by which the Foster lease has been carried are that of payment of one-eighth royalty on all oil produced is made to the Indians. One twenty-fourth royalty is retained by the Foster interests for their management and extensive development of the land. In years past it has been a common cry that the Indians always came out at the little end of the horn when dealing with the white man. The story of the Osage, however, is a contradiction to such a plaint, for by the Foster lease alone the Osage Indians have to date gained more wealth than the real producers of the oil.

"As these red men have not allied themselves with modern civilization in being able to fill a place in the industrial world, and as their incomes from tribal trust funds and oil leases are more than sufficient to keep them in idleness, there is but one answer to the question of whether the Osages as a nation are better Indians because of their independence through wealth. In all there are about 2,230 citizens of the Osage tribe. From oil royalties alone they average per capita, including children, is nearly seven hundred dollars per year. A family with two children receives an average annual income of about twenty-seven hundred dollars from this one source, besides large sums from lands allotted to them, making the wealth of the people greater than that of any other nation in the world. * * * As a matter of record to date, the one-eighth royalty paid the Indians on the Foster lease contract exceeds the profit which the actual operators have made during the seventeen years on their five-sixths working interest. Nearly five million dollars have been paid to the Indians."

All this is interesting historical reading, and is especially suggestive of the important part played by Mr. Foster in the industrial affairs of this state. He is a splendid type of the modern American business man, and one who does big things always in a big generous way. While a republican, he has never sought public office and has preferred to confine his contributions to his adopted city's welfare by conscientiously performing the duties of good citizenship. He is a thirty-second degree Scottish Rite Mason and a Shriner, and is also a member of the local lodges of the Benevolent and Protective Order of Elks, the Knights of Pythias and the Modern Woodmen of America. In social and business circles he is known not only in Oklahoma but in most of the larger cities. He belongs to the Lotus and Republican clubs of New York; the Illinois Athletic Club of Chicago, the Misquamicut Golf and Country Club of Watch Hill, Rhode Island; the Colonial Club at Westerly, Rhode Island; and the Country Club of Bartlesville.

May 1, 1897, Mr. Foster married Miss Marie Dahlgren, who was born at Chicago, Illinois, a daughter of Carl John and Marie (Sierks) Dahlgren. Mr. and Mrs. Foster have two children: Ruth Daniels and Marie Dahlgren.

WALTER GRISWOLD BISBEE, M. D. Representing the first class ability and skill of his profession and enjoying a large general practice, Doctor Bisbee is one of the young physicians and surgeons of Oklahoma who have quickly taken front rank in their profession. Doctor Bisbee has a large general practice as a physician and surgeon in Chandler. He began practice with an excellent equipment and the test of real work found him qualified for this important service among the social professions. Doctor Bisbee is a graduate from the Dartmouth Medical College and Hospital of Philadelphia with the class of 1901.

Walter Griswold Bisbee was born at Dexter, Iowa, August 1, 1876. His father, Frank A. Bisbee, was one of the leading citizens of Dexter, and was born in Vermont of an old Vermont family, the ancestors having come from England to New England in the early days, and men of that name participated in all the early wars of the country, including the Revolution and the War of 1812. Frank A. Bisbee is now living at Chandler at the age of seventy-one, and his wife died at the age of seventy.

Doctor Bisbee, after some experience in the Post-Graduate and City Hospital of Philadelphia, came to Chandler and began active practice. He soon had all he could do, and the almost constant driving over the country, loss of sleep, and arduous devotion to his duty caused a breakdown in health. He then gave up his practice and spent two years in recuperating in San Antonio, Texas. While there he resumed practice, but soon afterwards returned to Chandler and now enjoys a reputation with the leading physicians and surgeons of Central Oklahoma.

Doctor Bisbee was married December 3, 1902, to Eleanor Carpenter. She comes from an old Tennessee family at Knoxville, where she was reared and educated. Her father was Maj. D. A. Carpenter, an officer in the Union army, with which he made a gallant record of service. Doctor Bisbee and wife have one son, Wallace, now seven years of age. Outside of his home and his profession Doctor Bisbee has few interests. With him medicine is not only a profession but also a hobby and enthusiasm, and he finds his chief interests in continued studies, and no doctor in the state keeps more closely in touch with the advance of knowledge in medical and surgical science than he.

JUDGE MARK L. BOZARTH. There comes no greater satisfaction to a man in public life than a practically unanimous election to an important post of responsibility. That was the experience of Judge Bozarth in 1914, when as a candidate for re-election as county judge of Okmulgee County he had no opposition either at the primaries or in the general election. Judge Bozarth is a thoroughly grounded and capable young lawyer, and has been in active practice of the law and a figure in public affairs at Okmulgee for the past fourteen years.

He is of fine stock of American ancestry, and his forebears of mingled French, German with an admixture of other early nationalities that figured in our Colonial era, were among the first settlers in the Trans-Allegheny District of Western Pennsylvania and Western Virginia. The first American of the name, who was probably Caleb Bozarth, came from France during the persecution of the Huguenots and about 1735 settled in New Jersey near Philadelphia. He had three sons, Isaac, Caleb and John, and the first two served under General Washington during the Revolution and afterwards were pioneers in Kentucky. These two Revolutionary soldiers became the ancestors of a very numerous group of descendants subsequently scattered over Kentucky, Illinois, Missouri and other middle western states. John Bozarth, who was born in 1743, a son of the immigrant ancestor, was about eleven or twelve years of age when General Braddock came over with the British regulars to fight the French and Indians on the western frontier, and John Bozarth drove one team and wagon and was present at the disastrous Battle of Braddock's Field. John Bozarth subsequently moved out to Western Pennsylvania and was a frontiersman during the Revolution. In his twenty-seventh year he married Jane Ivers, who was a native of Ireland. The Bozarths took a very prominent part in the frontier life of Western Pennsylvania in the early days, and one of the name Miss Rebecca Bozarth performed some exploits in defending her home against an attack of Indians which has been made the subject of a chapter in a book entitled "Daring Deeds of American Women."

George Bozarth, a son of the John Bozarth just mentioned, was born April 12, 1774, near the historic old Red Stone Fort in Western Pennsylvania and not far from the present City of Morganstown, West Virginia. At the age of seventeen he enlisted in a company of Rangers and did much service against the Indians and their British allies in patroling the country along the Ohio River and as far down as Kentucky. In March, 1795, George Bozarth married Mary Reger, who was of pure German extraction, spoke the German language fluently though after her marriage the English was constantly used in the household. George and Mary Reger Bozarth were the parents of fifteen children, six of whom died in infancy. Of those who reached maturity the names were Anna, Temperance, Mary, Jacob, Lot N., Gilbert, Jane and Ruanny. The descendants of these children became widely scattered in many of the states of the Middle West.

One of them, Jacob, who was born in September, 1810, was the grandfather of Judge Bozarth of Okmulgee. Jacob had three wives and five children. The three children of his first marriage were Elizabeth Ann, Amanda and Allen B. By the second wife there was a son named George Gilbert. By his third marriage, to Charlotte Warrington, there was a son Jacob, and thus Jacob Bozarth has for a number of years been a well known citizen and business man of Okmulgee.

Jacob Bozarth last mentioned was born in Starke County, Indiana, February 7, 1852, a son of Jacob and Charlotte (Warrington) Bozarth. Jacob Bozarth, Sr., was one of the pioneers of Starke County, and in 1850 had the honor of being elected the first county recorder after the organization of that county. He was married in Starke County to Miss Warrington, who was of a Delaware family. Jacob, Sr., died at Troy, Kansas, in 1880, and his wife died in Indiana, January 1, 1875. Jacob, Sr., had been a teacher in his early life.

Jacob Bozarth of Okmulgee had the distinction of being honored in 1882 with election to the same office which his father had filled more than twenty years earlier, county recorder of Starke County. He had grown up on the home farm in Indiana, was given a substantial education, but after being elected county recorder served in that office continuously for eight years. Afterwards he established himself in business at Knox, county seat of Starke County, and dealt in real estate, loans and abstracts and in 1891 was admitted to the bar, but confined his practice chiefly to real estate and title law. In 1900 he moved to Okmulgee, Indian Territory, and has since been a prominent factor in the upbuilding of that city, and has conducted a prosperous business in real estate, insurance and has also been a notary public. He built the Bozarth Hotel at Okmulgee and in many other ways has found opportunity to serve the public welfare as well as his own. He is an active democrat, a member of the Independent Order of Odd Fellows, and belongs to the Methodist Episcopal Church.

On October 4, 1874, Jacob Bozarth married in Starke County Phebe Westhaver, who was born in Ohio. To their marriage were born four children: Judge Mark L., Ernest LeGrande, who graduated from Valparaiso University in Indiana in 1902 and is now a druggist at Henryetta, Oklahoma; Mary, wife of B. W. Christian of Okmulgee; and Daisy, wife of H. L. Allen of Grass Range, Montana.

Judge Mark L. Bozarth was born at Knox, Indiana, August 17, 1875, and lived in Starke County until he came to Okmulgee, September 4, 1902. He was graduated in 1902 from Valparaiso University, then known as the Northern Indiana Law School, with the degree LL. B. In the meantime he had taken an active interest in local politics at Knox and served three years as city clerk. Along with a substantial practice he has combined an equal interest in public affairs since locating at Okmulgee. In November, 1912, he was elected county judge, and in 1914 was re-elected for a second term, in which he is still serving with admirable efficiency. He is one of the leading democrats of Okmulgee County and for four years was a member of the Territorial Democratic Executive Committee before statehood. He is a member of the Oklahoma State Bar Association and is affiliated with the Masonic Order, the Independent Order of Odd Fellows and the Benevolent and Protective Order of Elks.

On November 28, 1894, Judge Bozarth married Grace G. Garner, who was born in Indiana, daughter of J. A. Garner, now a resident of Okmulgee. Judge Bozarth and wife have three children: Mary Garner, born November 15, 1907; Helen, born in May, 1909, and died at the age of ten months; and Kathryn, born November 22, 1911.

J. W. WHITE. One of the leading grocery establishments of Edmond is conducted by the firm of White & O'Connor. Mr. White has for several years been one of that town's most influential citizens. He stands for high grade business principles, for good sanitation and good morals and is a leader in moral and educational affairs. Mr. White came West from Kentucky at the age of twenty-seven, in search of health, and soon afterwards turned his attention to ranching in Kansas. He established near Syracuse in that state, one of the best equipped ranches in that part of the country, and eventually reached a success which enabled him to take up another line of business that was less exciting and more suited to his talents.

J. W. White was born near Irvine, Kentucky, in 1860, a son of John Thomas and Mahala Jane (Barnett) White. His father, a native of Kentucky, was for many years one of the leading public school teachers of that state. The paternal grandfather was a native of Ireland and an early settler of Virginia, being a missionary Baptist preacher. The maternal grandparents were prosperous planters in Kentucky.

Mr. White had a liberal education, first in the public schools and later in the Edgar Institute at Paris, Kentucky. After finishing his course in the latter, he taught school for three years, but ill health compelled him to abandon that vocation. Thus at the age of twenty-seven he was beginning his career as a rancher at Syracuse, Kansas, and continued a resident of that locality until 1910, when he came to Edmond and engaged in the grocery trade. The junior member of the firm of White & O'Connor is M. J. O'Connor.

Mr. White was married in Kentucky in 1882 to Miss Sarah Elizabeth Barnett. They have two children: Miss Dula White, who was formerly principal of the public schools of Britton and is now a stenographer in Oklahoma City; and William Harrison White, aged fifteen, a student in the public schools of Edmond. Mr. White is a member of the Christian Church, has held several important chairs in the lodge of Odd Fellows, and is a member and chorister of the Men's Gospel Team of Edmond. One interesting direction in which his original mind has turned is as an inventor. He has patented an auto and vehicle wheel rim attachment, based on the coil spring principle, that promises to become an important substitute for pneumatic tires.

Mr. White has also been a useful citizen in the different localities where he has lived. In Kansas he held the office of township assessor and for a number of years was a member of the board of education in his school district. In March, 1915, he was nominated by the democrats for mayor of Edmond.

WILLIAM EZRA SEBA, M. D. One of the first medical men to locate and open an office at the new Town of Leedey was Dr. W. E. Seba, who during the past eight years has built up a large practice in the town and surrounding country, and is one of the best qualified physicians and surgeons in Dewey County, a fact that is readily attested by his high standing in the community and by his professional work here and elsewhere.

He comes of an old Southern Missouri family, and was born at Bland, in that state, January 15, 1884. His grandfather Seba came from Germany in 1853, located in Gasconade County, Missouri, on a farm, and died soon afterward. Doctor Seba's father is Dr. J. D. Seba, also a physician, who was born in Gasconade County, at Woollman, Missouri, in 1856. He is now living at Bland, where he has been in active practice as a physician since 1894. In that year he was graduated from the Beaumont College of Medicine at St. Louis. For a number of years before taking up medical practice he served as justice of the peace and is now editor of the Bland Courier. He has also been coroner of Gasconade County, and has filled all the chairs in the Gasconade County Medical Society and has served on several important committees in the Missouri State Medical Society. He is a member of the American Medical Association, of the Modern Woodmen of America, the Brotherhood of American Yeomen, is active in the Methodist Episcopal Church and in politics is a republican. Dr. J. D. Seba married Miss Katy Horstman, who was born in Osage County, Missouri, in 1857. Their children are: Henry F., a farmer at Feuersville, Missouri; John W., who has a draying business at Bland; Dr. William E.; Rosie L., wife of R. M. Stricklen, who is connected with the Swift Packing Company in East St. Louis; Fred L., who is manager and publisher of the Bland Courier, owned by himself and father jointly, and this republican paper has probably the largest circulation in Osage and Gasconade counties; and Louise, still at home with her parents.

William Ezra Seba attended the public schools in Bland, and by a course of study at home and under the direction of his father was well qualified to pass his examinations and receive his credentials when he entered medical school. He entered the Marion-Sims Medical College at St. Louis in 1900, took a two years' course, but at the end of that time was too young to graduate. He then employed his time in a drug store one year, entered the St. Louis College of Physicians and Surgeons, and was graduated there April 14, 1905, with the degree M. D. only a few months after his twenty-first birthday.

After a general practice at Bland, his old home town, for two years, Doctor Seba came to Oklahoma in 1907 and began practice at Leedey. His offices are in the Horr & Seba Building, of which he is one of the owners. Doctor Seba is president of the Dewey County Medical Society, and is a member of the State Society, the Southwestern Medical and the American Medical Association. He is a stockholder in the Leedey Oil & Gas Company, and has financial interests in various other enterprises. In politics he is a republican. He has served as deputy health officer at Leedey and also as a member of the town board. Fraternally he is affiliated with Leedey Lodge No. 369, I. O. O. F., being now Right Supporter to the Noble Grand; with Leedey Lodge No. 227, of the Knights of Pythias; with the Brotherhood of American Yeomen and the Modern Woodmen of America at Leedey, and with the Mutual Protective League.

On May 23, 1907, in Kansas City, Missouri, Doctor Seba married Miss Marie Telkamp of Sanborn, Iowa. Her parents, Mr. and Mrs. H. Telkamp are now living at Mitchell, South Dakota, where her father is a retired farmer and the owner of considerable property.

ALEX WILL CRAIN. The present tribal secretary of the Seminoles, and the oldest white resident of Seminole County, Alex Will Crain has an interesting career and personality not only for his prominent participation in Indian affairs but also because of the fact that he is descended from some of the oldest and most prominent American Colonial and Revolutionary stock. Among his forefathers were gallant soldiers and men of affairs who left their impress on different states and colonies of the

East. Mr. Crain is one of the two white men who received formal adoption into the Seminole tribe, and has been on the rolls of citizenship since 1883.

He was born in Cumberland County, Pennsylvania, March 10, 1847, a son of Dr. Joseph and Rebecca Gibson (Wills) Crain. His great-grandfather was Ambrose Crain, who as captain led a company to battle in the Revolutionary war, being part of a New Jersey regiment. Grandfather Richard M. Crain also had a prominent career. He was surveyor general or deputy surveyor general of Pennsylvania for about thirty years. He was also a member of one of the early Pennsylvania Legislatures when that body met at Lancaster. He served as a colonel of artillery during the War of 1812 and was at Fort Henry during the defense of Washington. Col. Richard M. Crain married Eleanor Whitehill. Her father, Robert Whitehill, was a member of the convention that drafted the Constitution of the United States and afterwards sat in Congress representing a Pennsylvania district for more than twenty years. Mr. Crain's father, Dr. Joseph Crain, was born at Lancaster, Pennsylvania, in 1808, spent his active career as a physician in Cumberland County and died there in 1876. His wife was born in Cumberland County and died when Alex W. Crain was three years of age. Two of their children died in infancy, and those who reached maturity were two daughters and three sons. Doctor Crain also had children by a second marriage, but all of them are now deceased. Mr. Crain's brother, Richard M., fought during a part of the Civil war as member of a New Jersey regiment, afterwards took up medicine, and he died while in the employ of the Government at the Sac and Fox Agency in Oklahoma.

The early life of Alex Will Crain was spent in Pennsylvania, attending the public schools, and he was also a student in the State College of Pennsylvania. In June, 1863, he left college to enlist from Center County as a member of Company D in Lutzinger's Battalion for three months' duty. In June, 1914, Mr. Crain visited Pennsylvania College, and at that time received a certificate of recognition for membership in the class of 1864, and of that class only fourteen were known to be living in 1914. Mr. Crain was promised by the college authorities in recognition of his services in leaving school to fight for his country a diploma, and this diploma was awarded at the commencement in June, 1916, at which time Mr. Crain returned to Pennsylvania to accept the honor.

For two years during his early youth he also worked on a Pennsylvania farm, and he spent two years on the plains of Nebraska, driving ox and mule teams and getting a taste of frontier existence which finally caused him to become a permanent resident of the Southwest. Returning East he spent another two years at home, and then went to Texas, where he was a cowboy for a year, and about 1872 he came into the Creek Nation. His services here for about twelve years were as teacher in the tribal schools, and he also clerked in a store about four years.

In 1883 he was adopted into the Seminole Nation and has ever since been a member of that tribe. He and the late E. J. Brown were the only white men ever formally adopted by this tribe. Mr. Crain served as assistant district Indian agent under the Department of Interior, but for the past eight years has been tribal secretary. From 1884 to 1909 he resided on his farm and applied himself successfully to the raising of cattle, horses and hogs, and in the early days the range for his livestock was unrestricted and his herds could wander for pasture where they would. Mr. Crain still has a farm in the northwestern part of Seminole County along the North Canadian River.

In politics he is a republican, though he was reared a democrat. He has a life membership in the Masonic order, having attained thirty-two degrees in the Scottish Rite, is a Royal Arch Mason and a member of the Mystic Shrine.

In 1880 at Sasakwa he married Lucy Brown, a half-blood Seminole and a sister of Governor John F. Brown, reference to whose career will be found on other pages. Mr. and Mrs. Crain have three children: Anna, wife of T. H. Oliver of Wewoka; Allen, of Sasakwa; and Ambrose, who lives on his allotment along the North Canadian River. Mr. Crain has one of the most interesting and attractive homes in Seminole County. All his life he has been a diligent reader, though his career on the whole has kept him in close touch with practical events. Some time ago during a general discussion of the question of state legal holidays for Oklahoma, Mr. Crain suggested that they make a ground-hog day of general observance, but he ceased to advocate this when the people apparently began to take his proposition seriously.

HON. JEREMIAH C. STRANG. Prior to coming to Guthrie, in 1893, Hon. Jeremiah C. Strang had established an enviable record in legal and judicial affairs in Kansas. There his distinguished talents had been early recognized by appointment and election to offices of grave responsibility, and when he came to Oklahoma he brought with him a reputation as one of the strong and forceful men of law of his day. In his new locality he soon took his merited place among the men directing legal and judicial machinery, and his subsequent activities have but served to add to and embellish his reputation gained in the Sunflower State.

Judge Strang was born December 31, 1854, in the Village of Trumbull Corners, Tompkins County, New York, and is a son of Daniel and Elizabeth (Case) Strang, natives and agricultural people of the Empire State. The public schools of his native locality furnished Judge Strang with his early education, following which he attended an academy at Ithaca, New York, and took a full course in the institution at Watkins, in that state. He was reared on his father's farm, it having been his intention to become an agriculturist, but one day, while operating a threshing machine, he met with an accident which cost him his right hand, and when he had recovered he realized the necessity of adopting a professional career. For two years Mr. Strang was engaged in teaching school in the country districts adjacent to his home, and during this time to apply himself to the study of law, to which he began to give his entire attention in 1869. In 1870 he removed from Ithaca, New York, to Westfield, Pennsylvania, and there completed his legal training under the preceptorship of Hon. Butler B. Strang, his cousin, and at that time a noted jurist. Judge Strang was admitted to practice in 1873, when but nineteen years of age, and for four years continued in the enjoyment of a large and representative legal patronage at Westfield, and during three years of that time served efficiently as district attorney.

In 1877 Judge Strang went to Kansas and entered upon a career that was destined to make his name known among the foremost men of his profession. Locating at Larned, in the same year he was elected county attorney of Pawnee County, and served in that capacity for two years. Up to this time he had been a stanch republican, and on going to Kansas had plunged energetically into political affairs. In 1880 he stumped the state in behalf of the successful prohibition constitutional amendment.

In that same year, without his solicitation, his party nominated him for state senator of his senatorial district, and he was subsequently elected by a large majority. He became the author of the bill putting into force the prohibition constitutional amendment, introduced and drafted many other important and successful measures, and was an active member of a number of important committees. He resigned after the first session of his four-year term in order to accept the appointment by Governor John P. St. John to the office of district judge of the Sixteenth Judicial District of Kansas. He served one year by appointment and two terms of four years by election in that important office, but declined a third nomination. In 1890 Governor Lyman U. Humphrey appointed Judge Strang a member of the Kansas State Supreme Court Commission, and in that connection he rendered a faithful and highly commendable service of three years.

In 1893 Judge Strang resigned and came to Oklahoma. Here he opened a law office at Guthrie and embarked upon an active practice, but he was not long allowed to act merely as a private citizen, for in 1895 he was petitioned by leading men of his community to make the race for the office of county attorney of Logan County on a law enforcement platform. To this he consented, was elected to the office, and fulfilled every pledge made to the voters, his record during his two years' of office being one that strengthened materially his place in the esteem and confidence of the people. In 1897 Governor Barnes, at the suggestion of the late President McKinley, one of Judge Strang's old and personal friends, appointed the judge to the office of attorney general of Oklahoma, a position which he held for two years and only resigned because of an attack of ill health. In 1905 he was nominated by acclamation and was elected probate judge of Logan County, an office which he retained for ten years and from which he then retired to give his entire attention to his private practice. Judge Strang seems to have assimilated the principles of jurisprudence and to be able to supply from his intellectual reservoir a correct solution to any new combination of details that will withstand the severest criticism. Before the court his mastery of legal principles, familiarity with precedents and power of logical and forcible argument make him well nigh invincible. As counsel his services have been in great demand, and he has been extensively retained in important and complicated litigation not alone in Oklahoma, but in various other states, before the highest tribunals.

Judge Strang has one daughter, Lulu, who is the wife of M. E. Trapp, lieutenant-governor of Oklahoma.

TEMPLE HOUSTON. In the history of the legal fraternity of Western Oklahoma there has appeared no more distinguished name than that of the late Temple Houston, who practiced at the Woodward bar from the time of the opening of the Cherokee Strip, in 1893, until his death, August 15, 1905. A son of the great Texas patriot, Gen. Sam Houston, his early career was marked by experiences of the most interesting character in the Lone Star State, and from early youth his achievements were notable in Texas jurisprudence.

Temple Houston was born August 12, 1860, in the Texas gubernatorial mansion at Austin, a son of Gen. Sam and Margaret (Lea) Houston. Samuel Houston was born in Rockbridge County, Virginia, March 2, 1793, and was of Scotch-Irish descent. In 1818 he began the study of law and in 1823 and 1825 was elected a member of Congress, and in 1827 governor of Tennessee. On his removal to Texas, in 1832, he was made a general of Texas troops, and in 1836 defeated the Mexicans at San Jacinto, which resulted in the independence of Texas, General Houston being elected president of the new republic. In 1845 Texas entered the Union and General Houston was chosen United States senator. He was elected governor of Texas in 1859, but in 1861 was deposed for adherence to the Union, and died at Huntsville, Texas, July 25, 1863. By his second wife, Margaret Lea, he was the father of four sons and four daughters: Samuel, deceased; Nancy, who is the wife of James Morrow, of Georgetown, Texas; Margaret, deceased; Mary, who is the widow of John Morrow, of Abilene, Texas; Nettie, the wife of Prof. James Bringhurst, of San Antonio, Texas; Andrew J., of Beaumont, Texas; William R., of Kemp, Texas; and Temple.

Left an orphan at the age of seven years, at the age of thirteen Temple Houston became a cowboy on the plains of his native state. With his first cattle outfit he went with a herd of stock to Bismark, North Dakota, where he engaged as a clerk on a steamer and went down the Mississippi River. He was then appointed to a position as page in the United States Senate and remained in that capacity at Washington, D. C., for three years, and while there began the study of the profession in which he was later to reach such a high position. On his return to Texas, at the age of seventeen years, he entered Bailey University, from which he was duly graduated, and when only nineteen years of age was admitted to the Texas bar. He soon attracted attention and a large practice in criminal law, and when but nineteen years old was elected county attorney of Brazoria County. He was district attorney of the Texas Panhandle District when he had just attained his majority, and at a time when to enter the courtroom unarmed was to take one's life in his hands, the young attorney made an exceptionally creditable record. Further honors awaited him. He was only twenty-four years old when elected to the Texas State Senate, a body in which he served with ability and distinction for eight years, but that service ended his life in Texas, for with the opening of the Cherokee Strip in 1893 he came to Oklahoma and opened an office at Woodward, this city continuing to be his home and the scene of his repeated successes until the time of his death.

Mr. Houston was married February 14, 1883, to Miss Laura Cross, who was born April 7, 1865, in Louisiana, and to this union there were born seven children: Temple; Louise and Laura, who are deceased; Sam; Richard; Lucile, who is deceased; and Mary. Mrs. Houston, who survives her husband and is a lady of many attainments, was appointed postmistress of Woodward, March 10, 1914. She has managed the affairs of this office in a highly creditable manner and in numerous ways has been able to improve the service.

DR. TIMOTHY JOSEPH BUTLER. The Butler family, represented in Weatherford by Dr. Timothy Joseph Butler, is distinctly southern in its habitat, and is of Scotch-Irish origin. Timothy Butler, grandshire of the subject, was the Irish emigrant ancestor. He came first to Canada, but his stay there was brief, and he died in Vicksburg, Mississippi, where he was a prosperous planter for years. Doctor Butler's maternal grandfather, Robert Marshall, came from Scotland to Cincinnati, Ohio, when he was a boy of three years, and he, too, died in the vicinity of Vicksburg, a well known planter of that place.

Dr. Timothy Joseph Butler was born in Vicksburg, Mississippi, on January 11, 1886, and is a son of T. J. Butler, also born in Vicksburg, the latter in the year 1854. He died on the family plantation, St. Elmo, Warren County, in 1889. He was Roman Catholic in his faith. His wife was Miss Emma Marshall, born in

Memphis, Tennessee, and she now makes her home with Doctor Butler, their only child.

Dr. Butler was graduated from the S. A. C., in Vicksburg, Mississippi, in 1902, with the equivalent of a high school education. In 1904 he was graduated from the C. H. A., in Port Gibson, Mississippi, his preparation for his professional studies being made there. He spent the years 1905 and 1906 in the medical department of the University of Virginia, and the next two years in Tulane University, in New Orleans. He was graduated from the University of the South, in Sewanee, Tennessee, with the class of 1909, when he received his M. D. degree.

In October, 1909, Doctor Butler began medical practice at Calvin, Oklahoma, and in 1911 he came to Weatherford, where he has since conducted a practice along general lines of medicine and surgery.

Dr. Butler is a democrat and a member of the Episcopal Church. His college fraternity is the Alpha Kappa Kappa, and in Masonry he is affiliated with the Weatherford Lodge No. 138, Ancient Free and Accepted Masons, Weatherford Chapter No. 31, Royal Arch Masons, and Weatherford Commandery No. 17, Knights Templar. He is a member of the County, State and American Medical societies, and the association of military surgeons, and holds a commission as first lieutenant in the Medical Reserve Corps, United States army.

In Vicksburg, Mississippi, 1910, was recorded the marriage of Doctor Butler to Miss Letitia Templeman Geiger, daughter of S. E. Geiger, of Charlottesville, Virginia, now deceased. Four children have been born to Doctor and Mrs. Butler: Emma M., Lily, Mildred and Marshall, all at home.

LOGAN AUTRAN WILHITE. A practical and experienced newspaper man and an expert follower of the old and honored trade of printing, Logan Autran Wilhite, foreman of the printing plant of the Daily Pioneer, at Alva, Oklahoma, has passed his entire life in this calling. He has followed his occupation in various places, and on several occasions has been the proprietor of newspapers, but since 1898 has made his home at Alva and is well known among newspaper men of Woods County.

Mr. Wilhite is a Missourian by nativity, born at Slater, Saline County, Missouri, September 30, 1875, a son of Daniel C. and Mary F. (Maupin) Wilhite. His father was born in that county, November 20, 1844, and was a mere lad when the Civil war came on, but enlisted in the Seventh Missouri Cavalry, and served therewith for 3½ years. He took part in numerous battles and had many escapes from death, on one occasion having his horse shot from under him, while later he was seriously wounded in the right leg. His military career finished, he returned to Saline County, Missouri, where he gradually drifted into building and contracting, vocations which he continued to follow throughout the remainder of his life. Mr. Wilhite prosecuted his activities at Slater until 1886, in which year he removed with his family to Wichita, Kansas, which city was then experiencing an extensive boom, and where he had his full share of the many building contracts that were being left. A number of the structures erected by him still stand as monuments to his skill and honest workmanship. In 1900, Mr. Wilhite removed to Alva, Oklahoma, where he purchased city property, and here continued to make his home until his death, which occurred July 6, 1906. Soon after coming to Alva, Mr. Wilhite became recognized as a progressive citizen, who stood for the strict enforcement of the law and took a keen interest in the town's advancement, and in 1903 and 1904 was elected police judge, a position in which he fully vindicated the trust and confidence reposed in him. He was a member of the Independent Order of Odd Fellows, as well as of the Grand Army of the Republic, and never lost interest in the welfare of his old army comrades. Throughout his life he remained true to the teachings of the Christian Church. Mr. Wilhite was married in 1864 to Mary F. Maupin, who was born October 20, 1843, in Virginia, and died at Alva, Oklahoma, December 25, 1908. She was an active worker in the movements of the Christian Church, was a woman of many excellencies of mind and heart, and her memory is still revered by those who knew her. Four daughters and three sons were born to Mr. and Mrs. Wilhite, namely: Fannie L., Paschal E., Ollie B., Hubert R., Logan A., Lilla M. and Bertha C.

Logan A. Wilhite was eight years of age when the family moved to Wichita, Kansas, and there, in the public schools, he completed his education. He was fifteen years of age at the time he began to learn the trade of printer, starting in the lowly position of "devil" in the office of the Hazelton Express, at Hazelton, Kansas, his brother-in-law, W. F. Hatfield, being the publisher of that newspaper. Since that time Mr. Wilhite has continued to devote his attention unreservedly to the same line of business, although in various localities. In 1895 he came to Oklahoma, locating at Taloga, Dewey County, where he became editor and owner of the Advocate, but after one year disposed of his interests therein and went to Higgins, Texas, where he became editor and owner of the Higgins News, which he published for two years. During one year of this time he also served in the capacity of postmaster at Higgins. Returning to Oklahoma in 1898, Mr. Wilhite located at Alva, where he again associated himself with his brother-in-law, Mr. Hatfield, who was publishing the Pioneer, Mr. Wilhite being made foreman of the plant and remaining as such until March 16, 1911, when he began the publication of the Morning Times, the first morning newspaper to be published at Alva. This was conducted by the firm of Eubank & Wilhite until 1914, when Mr. Wilhite disposed of his interests in it and returned to the Daily Pioneer, as foreman of the plant, this publication now being owned and edited by W. D. Wilkinson. Mr. Wilhite has had broad and varied experience in his work, and is considered a thorough master of the art of printing. He is a republican in his political views, but has never sought public office, with the exception of his year as postmaster in Texas, under the administration of the late President McKinley.

Mr. Wilhite was married April 22, 1897, to Miss Edna M. Elder, who was born June 16, 1878, at Slater, Missouri, daughter of A. J. and Elizabeth (McMahan) Elder, of that city. Mr. and Mrs. Wilhite have three children: Logan Errol, born July 6, 1898; Gerald A., born June 24, 1903; and Daniel Calvin, born June 4, 1908.

Mr. Wilhite is an active member of the Christian Church and graduated with a class of nine in Standard Bible work in 1916.

HON. JESSE ALBERT BAKER. While most of the early settlers of Oklahoma were young men, some left behind them the record of a successful experience in order to join their fortunes with the new frontier country. Among these was Jesse Albert Baker, who after fifteen years of influential membership in the Georgia bar identified himself with Oklahoma in 1893. As was to be expected he soon took a prominent part in the new territory, and has maintained a position of leadership down to the present time.

For a number of years Mr. Baker has been a resident of Wewoka, enjoys a large practice as a lawyer and has many business interests, and has been prominent in politics. He was a member of the Constitutional Convention from his section of old Indian Territory.

Representing an old and honored name in Georgia, he was born in Bartow County May 9, 1853, a son of Jesse and Parthenia (Moss) Baker. His grandfather, Charles Baker, a native of Virginia, served with gallantry in the war of the Revolution and was under the command of Thomas Marshall. He fought both at Cowpens and Kings Mountain in the southern campaign and was wounded at the Kings Mountain fight. He died in Cass, now Bartow County, Georgia, and was the only Revolutionary soldier buried in that county, and a few years ago the Daughters of the American Revolution marked his grave with a suitable memorial. He lived in South Carolina for some years, and in that state his son, Jesse, was born in 1800, but when quite young went to Georgia, where both Charles and Jesse Baker became prominent planters and slave owners. Jesse Baker died in Bartow County in 1871. His wife, Miss Moss, was born in Habersham County, Georgia, in 1809, and died in 1887. In their family were fourteen children, twelve of whom reached maturity, and three are now living: Fannie C., wife of James W. Rich of McCurtain, Oklahoma; Dr. Thomas H., of Cartersville, Bartow County, Georgia; and Jesse A., who was next to the youngest of the children.

Jesse A. Baker lived in his native County of Bartow, Georgia, until September, 1893, when he arrived at Guthrie, Oklahoma. He spent his early boyhood on a Georgia plantation, and in 1875 graduated A. B. from the University of Georgia, and then became a student in the law department of Cumberland University at Lebanon, Tennessee, where he finished his course in 1877. He was admitted to the bar in September, 1877, and the Supreme Court of Georgia admitted him to practice in all the state courts on November 27, 1878. During the next sixteen years he succeeded in building up a large practice in his home state and on moving to Guthrie in 1893 he practiced law with Dick T. Morgan and Judge J. L. Pancoast. He also acquired extensive farming interests in Pottawatomie County, and in 1901 he took part as a new settler in the southwestern district of Oklahoma, locating at Lawton, in Comanche County. There he practiced law for several years and on April 1, 1905, moved to Wewoka, which has since been his home.

His public career is worthy of special record. He has always been a loyal democrat. In 1882-83 he served as clerk of the Judiciary Committee of the Georgia State Senate. In 1897 he was assistant chief clerk of the Oklahoma Territorial Council, and had also served for a time as acting city attorney of Guthrie. In 1895 he made the race against Judge Hainer for city attorney of Guthrie, and in 1902 was a candidate against Jacob Hammond for city attorney of Lawton. In 1906 he was elected from District No. 81, comprising the Seminole Nation and a part of the Creek Nation, as a delegate to the Constitutional Convention. He was one of the influential men in the convention, and he has in his possession one of the historic documents pertaining to the work of that body. This is the original call for a democratic caucus to select a democratic candidate for president of the convention. This call was written by Mr. Baker himself, and is signed by nearly all the democratic delegates, including C. N. Haskell, who was the first governor of Oklahoma, and R. L. Williams, the present governor. In 1907 Mr. Baker was candidate for district judge at the primaries, that being the first primaries held after statehood. Out of a vote of 10,000 he lost the nomination by only 180. The district comprised the counties of Seminole, Pontotoc, Coal, Atoka and Johnson.

Mr. Baker now has a large amount of farming land which requires his supervision and, as already mentioned, in the early days he had a large farm in Pottawatomie County on the North Canadian River. He is a member of the Oklahoma Bar Association, and he and his family are Episcopalians. On June 5, 1878, he married Miss Jennie Bacon, who was born at LaGrange, Georgia, in 1858. Her father, Thomas J. Bacon, served as a captain in the Confederate army and was killed at the battle of Seven Pines. The Bacons are among the oldest and most prominent families of Georgia. Mr. and Mrs. Baker have two children. Lucy Bacon, who is now a student in the East Central State Normal at Ada; and George Merriweather, at home. They also have an adopted daughter, Beatrice, now the wife of J. V. Thomas of Canton, Georgia.

Miss Lucy Baker, the daughter, is a talented young poetess, and recently a paper read before a meeting of the United Daughters of the Confederacy contained some of her verses under the title "Not Forgotten," which deserve to be preserved in permanent form. These are:

They tell us to forget, they say
Our banner has been furled and put away,
Our cause is lost and all the strife,
The loss of home, the loss of life,
   They tell us to forget.

We know the North and South has been made one,
The tumult and the call to arms are done,
And now the Blue and Gray united stand,
To form one world-power, one beloved land,
   But why must we forget?

They do not know who tell us to forget
That blood of Southern sons flows in us yet,
That the old Blue is hallowed by the Gray,
That thoughts of those we lost make dear today,
   And we can not forget.

The Stars and Bars are furled but loved the same,
And through their bloody stains we love the name,
Of Stars and Stripes, our banner of today,
The old cause is not lost but laid away;
   So do not say "forget."

LESLIE GORDON NIBLACK. In the career of Leslie Gordon Niblack, of Guthrie, there is to be found much to instruct and encourage the youths who are forced to start out in life entirely on their own resources. When, more than twenty years ago, he first came to this city, he had little to aid him save a little experience in newspaper work, a willingness and ability to perform cheerfully and well whatever work came to his hands, and a consuming ambition to make a name and place for himself in the field of journalism. With these assets he started sturdily in to make his way, and through their possession he has advanced steadily to a leading position among Oklahoma newspaper men and in public and political life.

Mr. Niblack was born at Evansville, Indiana, October 1, 1876, and received his education in the public schools of Louisville, Kentucky, and Rockport, Indiana, and at the state university, at Bloomington, Indiana. As a lad of fifteen years he worked in vacation periods on the Louisville Courier-Journal, as a cub reporter, where his taste for journalism was whetted and where he determined upon this profession as his life work. Before he was eighteen years old he worked on newspapers at St Louis and Carthage, Missouri. Mr. Niblack located a

Guthrie in 1894 and began work as a reporter on the Daily Leader, which had been established two years before by politicians. Within one year he was in full charge of the paper, which for a number of years had hard sledding, it being a democratic paper in a strong republican city, the territorial capital. Mr. Niblack put all of his energy into his work. He labored night and day, often without pay, when the "ghost refused to walk." Little by little he acquired an interest in the Leader plant, which at that time was one of the most pretentious in the state. In 1902 he acquired full possession of the Leader property, the daily and weekly, the job department and the book bindery. As president of the Leader Printing Company he increased the equipment and business, bought the Leader Building, and did a large volume of business with the various counties of the territory.

During all this time Mr. Niblack was active in politics, serving successively as city and county chairman of the democratic central committees, as acting democratic national committeeman for the territory, and as delegate to the presidential conventions. In 1905 he served in the Oklahoma Senate and was minority leader of that body. Mr. Niblack's campaign for the Senate was the most sensational ever held in the territory. He elected the entire county and district democratic ticket and was himself elected by a majority of 614 in a district which two years before had been carried by a republican by 3,900 majority. On two occasions Mr. Niblack refused to become the democratic candidate for Congress, holding that a newspaper man should not run for office, but in 1912, reluctantly yielding to the importunities of his friends, ran for congressman at large in a field of fifteen candidates with three to be elected. He was the fourth man in the race, which he entered only three weeks before the primary election.

The Leader is the oldest democratic paper in Oklahoma and has been under one continuous management longer than any other daily in the state. It took the lead in the fight for statehood. When the Leader was made the official organ of the constitutional convention convened at Guthrie, in 1906, the Leader Printing Company did all the printing for the convention, the bill amounting to nearly $50,000. There was no appropriation to pay this by the government, and Mr. Niblack was forced to wait two years for his money or until the constitution had been carried and the first Legislature met. Mr. Niblack served on the state committee which waged the campaign for the adoption of the constitution, and the Leader did the printing for the first and second legislatures. One year after statehood Mr. Niblack was offered $175,000 for his plant at Guthrie.

Mr. Niblack has been identified with all the business, industrial and social interests of Guthrie and of the state. He is recognized as a forceful and successful newspaper man. On November 16, 1908, he administered the oath of office to the state's first governor, Hon. Charles N. Haskell, on the steps of the Carnegie Library at Guthrie. At the request of Governor-elect Haskell, Mr. Niblack took out a commission as notary public in order to administer the oath. He has served two terms as president of the Oklahoma Press Association, and has been also vice president of the National Editorial Association and a director of the Oklahoma State Historical Society. He is a Scottish Rite Mason of the thirty-second degree, K. C. C. H.; served two terms as exalted ruler of Guthrie Lodge No. 426, Benevolent and Protective Order of Elks, of which he is a life member; and holds membership in the Shrine, the Knights of Pythias Lodge, the Country Club the several other clubs and organizations of Guthrie and the state. With his wife he belongs to the Presbyterian Church. While Mr. Niblack has a beautiful and comfortable home at Guthrie, he believes in seeing how others live, and during three months of each year accompanies his family on long trips in this country and abroad.

Mr. Niblack was married March 31, 1909, to Miss Frances Haskell, daughter of Governor Charles N. Haskell, and to this union there has been born one child, a daughter, October 26, 1911. This marriage was an elaborate state affair, held in the capitol building, with all the state officials attending, and Chief Justice M. J. Kane officiating.

MANLY E. MICHAELSON is one of the successful younger lawyers of Bartlesville, where he has been in practice since 1910, and his business and professional interests have particularly identified him with the oil and gas industry in this section of the state.

He was born in Jackson County, Iowa, March 13, 1881, a son of George C. and Nancy Jane (Mann) Michaelson. His father was born in the Province of Schleswig-Holstein, Germany, in 1850, and was about eighteen years of age when he came to America. He made his way to Iowa, where he married Miss Mann, who was born in Jackson County, Iowa, in 1857. After their marriage they lived in that state until November, 1881, when they removed to Elk County, Kansas. George C. Michaelson became a quite successful farmer and stock raiser in Kansas, and he and his wife now reside at Baldwin, Kansas, enjoying the rewards of their former years of toil. They were the parents of four sons and one daughter.

The second in the family, Manly E. Michaelson was taken to Kansas when an infant, and he grew up on the old homestead near Moline in Elk County. The rural schools supplied his early education and in 1898 he graduated from the high school at Moline. Soon afterwards, at the age of seventeen, he enlisted as a private in Company F of the Twenty-first Kansas Volunteer Infantry for service in the Spanish-American war. He was with that regiment about seven months, being stationed at the Reserve Military Camp at Chickamauga Park and afterwards was in Kentucky and Kansas until receiving his honorable discharge.

Following this incident of his earlier career, he spent one year in the Kansas State Normal School at Emporia and for one term he taught school. He was a railway locomotive fireman until February, 1902, and with his savings from that work entered the law department of the University of Kansas at Lawrence, where he was graduated LL. B. in 1905. At intervals during his law course he had continued railroad work and even after his admission to the bar he followed such employment until 1907. In that year he set up in private practice at Beloit, Kansas, and from there in January, 1910, moved to Bartlesville, Oklahoma. For several years he was associated with the well known law firm of Brennan & Kane, but he is now alone in practice, and as attorney represents several of the larger oil and gas companies of the northern part of the state.

Politically he is a progressive, is a member of the Oklahoma State Bar Association, is affiliated with the Masonic Order, the Benevolent and Protective Order of Elks and with the Brotherhood of Locomotive Engineers. Mr. Michaelson is unmarried.

JOSEPH E. WHITENTON. Among the men contributed to the citizenship of Oklahoma by the State of Tennessee and who have won enviable and prominent positions in business and financial life, is found Joseph E. Whitenton, president of the Citizens Bank, of Henryetta, Okmulgee County. Mr. Whitenton's salient characteristics are determination, diligence and keen sagacity, and upon these he has builded his prosperity, and with them has won a high and well merited measure of success.

Mr. Whitenton was born in Madison County, Tennessee, January 21, 1882, and is a son of L. E. and Cordelia (Sammons) Whitenton. His father, a native of Madison County, Tennessee, where he was reared on a farm and educated. As a young man he engaged in a variety of pursuits, being for many years a farmer of Madison County, but eventually removed to Hardeman County, Tennessee, where he is now the proprietor of a hotel at Bolivar. They are stable, substantial people of their community, holding the respect and esteem of all who know them. Of their six children, five still survive.

Joseph E. Whitenton was granted the advantages to be secured in the log district school house during his youth, and later, for a time, attended high school. He was reared on his father's farm, was brought up to be industrious, honest and painstaking, and in 1900, deciding to seek his fortune in the West, came to Oklahoma. He first settled at Shawnee, where he secured employment as clerk and bookkeeper in a grocery store, and later transferred his services to a hardware store, where he acted in the same capacity. On January 1, 1907, he became a traveling representative of a wholesale hardware company, and for more than six years remained on the road, selling hardware in different parts of Oklahoma, but April 2, 1913, turned his attention to banking when he became the organizer and founder of the Guaranty State Bank of Henryetta, of which concern he acted as president. On January 1, 1915, this bank was consolidated with the Citizens Bank, of which Mr. Whitenton has since been president, the other officials being: W. L. Sullins, vice president; T. E. Keggin, cashier; and E. J. Kersting, assistant cashier. This is the only bank at Henryetta with a savings department, and its deposits are protected by the Depositors Guaranty Fund of the State of Oklahoma. A statement of its condition, as given March 7, 1916, follows:

Resources: Loans and discounts, $171,645.44; bonds and warrants, $19,251.41; overdrafts, $612.41; furniture and fixtures, $3,500; other real estate, $3,002.68; cash and sight exchange, $51,515.21; total, $249,527.15.

Liabilities: Capital, $25,000; surplus and undivided profits, $5,636.60; reserved for taxes, $618.78; deposits, $218,271.77; total, $249,527.15. The Citizens Bank now has a large patronage and is considered one of the sound and substantial institutions of this part of the state. Mr. Whitenton maintains a sound and conservative policy that has won public confidence, but at the same time his methods are progressive. He is also a director in the Guaranty State Bank of Muskogee. Aside from his banking connections Mr. Whitenton is largely interested in coal, oil and gas lands in Oklahoma. He is treasurer of the Henryetta & Western Railroad, an electric line which is being built to connect all the towns of this thriving mining community, and of which he was one of the organizers. He is a democrat in his political views, is chairman of the election board of Okmulgee County, and has served one term as a member of the council. Fraternally, he is a thirty-second degree Mason and a member of the Benevolent and Protective Order of Elks. A typical Oklahoman, wide awake, alert and enterprising, he has carried forward to successful completion whatever enterprise he has undertaken and has made opportunity for advancement if none has seemed to exist. Thus he has continued to work his way upward and already has attained a very creditable and enviable position in business and financial circles of Okmulgee County.

Mr. Whitenton was married in 1911 to Miss Fay Sacra, daughter of James Sacra, a cattleman of Texas and Oklahoma, Mrs. Whitenton being a native of the former state. They have one child: Peggy, aged three years.

IRA T. SMITH, M. D., a prominent physician and surgeon at LaKemp, was one of the pioneers of Oklahoma, having come to the state at the time of the opening of the Cherokee Strip, more than twenty years ago. For many years he has enjoyed a high standing in his profession and also in business affairs, and success has come to him as a reward for much earnest and hard labor during his younger years.

He was born November 3, 1868, in a log house on a farm in Sullivan County, Missouri. His parents were John E. and Nancy F. (Sipes) Smith. His father was born in Ireland, emigrated to America with his parents in 1829, the family locating in Pittsburg, Pennsylvania, and there as a young man he became a structural iron worker. He was born in 1827 and he died in Portland, Oregon, in 1904. He was one of the loyal natives of Ireland who fought for the integrity of the Union during the Civil war. He served as a private in Company E of an Iowa cavalry and went through the entire struggle with credit. His wife was born in 1830 in Pittsburg, Pennsylvania, and died at Vici, Oklahoma, in 1914. She was a lifelong member of the Methodist Episcopal Church. These worthy people became the parents of fourteen children, Robert, John S., Ephraim S., Margaret, Joseph G., Harriet Jane, James F. N., Daniel M., Nancy E., William T., Henry B., Ira T., Lena Belle, and Martha, the last two being now deceased.

The first temple of learning Doctor Smith attended was a log school house in Sullivan County, Missouri. This instruction was interspersed with such work as his strength permitted him to perform on his father's farm. Being one of a large family of children, he had the serious responsibilities of life early thrust upon him. In 1881 he left home and went out to Nebraska, which was then a frontier state, and from there in 1884 moved to Kiowa, Kansas. There he entered the drug business, studied pharmacy and also carried on his readings in medicine.

In 1893 Doctor Smith took part in the opening of the Cherokee Strip, and though failing to secure a claim in the strip he secured one in Dewey County in the old Cheyenne and Arapahoe country. For a number of years he devoted himself to his arduous duties as a country practitioner in Dewey and Ellis counties, but in 1913 removed to Beaver County and bought a drug store in the new town of LaKemp. He has a good business as a druggist, and also has a widely extended and profitable practice as a physician. Doctor Smith is a member of the Oklahoma Medical Society and the American Medical Association, and is a thirty-second degree Scottish Rite Mason, being a member of the Consistory No. 1 at Guthrie. He is a charter member and was the first noble grand of Fay Lodge, Independent Order of Odd Fellows, at Fay, Oklahoma. His church is the Presbyterian.

On December 24, 1889, in Sedgwick County, Kansas, Doctor Smith married Miss Minnie Adella Halsey, who was born in Kansas City, Missouri, September 16, 1869. To their marriage have been born five children, three daughters and two sons: Verga M., born November 18, 1892, now the wife of G. F. Partridge, a farmer at LaKemp; John Henry, born April 29, 1901; Lura Rose, born May 29, 1904; Georgia Lillian, born November 29, 1906; and Ira, born October 25, 1909.

KENNETH ROGERS. This is a name which will always have prominent association with that section of Osage

County where the Village of Wynona is now located. The land of the townsite was originally owned by Kenneth Rogers, who has spent all his life in the Osage country, and for a number of years has been looking after his extensive interests as a farmer, stock raiser, and fruit grower in that vicinity. He is a business man of judgment and enterprise, and his public spirit has been reflected in his varied activities and relations with the community where he now lives.

On a farm thirty miles east of the present Town of Wynona Kenneth Rogers was born November 10, 1879, a son of Antoine and Elizabeth (Carpenter) Rogers, both of whom were born in the Cherokee Nation. The mother was a white woman while in the veins of Antoine Rogers flows a mixture of Cherokee and Osage Indian blood, and also of French and English. After their marriage Antoine Rogers and wife moved to the Osage country about 1875, and have lived at Wynona for the past twenty-five years. He has extensive interests as a rancher and farmer, but has lived retired from active business for the past two years. Antoine Rogers married the widow of his twin brother, Joseph, who died leaving three children: Jasper, of Pawhuska; Minerva, who married Arthur Rogers, and both are now deceased, leaving five children; and Louis A., of Wynona. The six children of Antoine Rogers are: Eva, wife of Elmer Wheeler; Kenneth; Annie, wife of C. R. Clewein of Pawhuska; Ora, deceased wife of J. A. Owens; May, living at home with her parents; and Viola, wife of F. M. Watson, and they now live on the old Rogers homestead at Wynona.

While growing to manhood Kenneth Rogers acquired an education in the Osage schools, and from an early age has had abundant opportunity to test his ability and enterprise in the varied relations of farmer, stockman and fruit grower. He and his children own and control 1,800 acres of land in the vicinity of Wynona, and he has one of the best peach orchards in this section of the state, its crop in 1915 totaling about 3,000 bushels. It was in 1907 that Mr. Rogers sold a portion of his land for the townsite of Wynona, and in that year built the finest residence in the town for his own home. The year 1914 Mr. Rogers spent in California with his family.

In 1903 he married Miss Ida Murphy, who was born in St. Joseph, Missouri, December 9, 1879, lived there until eighteen, and then came to the Osage country with her parents, D. L. and Margaret (Campbell) Murphy. Her father was born in Richmond, Virginia, of Irish parentage, and he acquired his education in Yale University. He was a cattleman and later in life for a number of years an oil prospector, and died at the home of his daughter, Mrs. Rogers, in 1906, at the age of eighty-two. Her mother was a native of Richmond, Virginia, but of Irish parents, and she now lives part of the time in California and part of the time in Dakota. Mr. and Mrs. Rogers have two children: Helen, born December 9, 1903; and Antoine, Jr., born July 20, 1905, who is named for his Grandfather Rogers, being the only grandson. Mr. Rogers is a member of the Knights of Pythias lodge of Pawhuska.

ANDREW GREGG CURTIN BIERER. Since the first opening of Oklahoma, April 22, 1889, Andrew Gregg Curtin Bierer has been a strong and active member of the legal fraternity of the state, and during this time has been connected as counsel with some of the most important litigation brought before the state and federal courts. He has won substantial recognition of his fine legal talents, his fidelity to professional duties, and his careful conservation of all interests confided to his care, and on several occasions has been called to public offices of importance and trust.

Mr. Bierer is a Pennsylvanian by nativity, born at Uniontown, Fayette County, October 24, 1862, and is a son of Colonel Everard and Ellen (Smouse) Bierer, natives of the Keystone State and descendants of German ancestors who emigrated to this country at an early date in Pennsylvania's history and located in the German settlement of Fayette County. There Col. Everard Bierer was born in February, 1827. He was granted excellent educational advantages, and on graduating from college became a lawyer, and in 1848, when but twenty-one years of age, was elected the first district attorney of Fayette County. He continued to be actively engaged in the practice of law until the outbreak of the war between the states, at which time, an ardent Union sympathizer, he organized a company of which he served as captain. After being severely wounded in the fierce engagement at South Mountain he was transferred to the One Hundred and Seventy-first Regiment, Pennsylvania Veteran Reserve Corps, of which he became colonel, and during the later part of the war was placed in command of a division which participated in engagements in North Carolina. While still in the field Colonel Bierer was made one of the Lincoln electors from his home community in Pennsylvania. With an honorable record for gallant and faithful service he received his honorable discharge at the close of the war, and, after a short stay at home, in 1865 removed to Brown County, Kansas. There he not only became recognized as a thorough and resourceful lawyer, but as being made of legislative timber, and in 1867 he was sent to the Kansas State Legislature. In that body he was opposed to the fifteenth amendment, against which he voted, and urged Senator Ross to vote against the impeachment of President Johnson. With the close of his political and public services, he returned to his private practice, and continued to be engaged therein at Hiawatha, Kansas, until his death, which occurred December 26, 1910. Throughout his career Colonel Bierer's name continued to be connected with important events and large undertakings, and few men were better known or more highly esteemed in legal circles of Kansas. He was united in marriage in 1852 with Miss Ellen Smouse, who survived him several years and died May 7, 1913, at Hiawatha, Kansas, and they became the parents of six sons and two daughters, namely: Everard, Jr.; Anna; Samuel; Daniel; Andrew G. C.; Retta; William, who is deceased; and Bion B., who is now a captain in the United States navy.

Andrew G. C. Bierer received his early education in the public schools of Hiawatha, Kansas, following which he attended Georgetown University, at Washington, District of Columbia, where he was graduated in 1886 with the degree of Master of Law. In that same year he took up his residence and began practice at Garden City, Kansas, and while residing there served for two years in the capacity of city attorney. On April 22, 1889, at the first opening of Oklahoma, Mr. Bierer came to this state, having decided that the new community opened up better opportunities for the display of the young lawyer's abilities and talents, and from that time to the present, except when in the Supreme Court, he has carried on a large practice at Guthrie. On April 22, 1889, Mr. Bierer and H. B. Kelley were appointed the two members from Kansas on the initial committee, composed of two members from each state elected to initiate the organization of the provisional government, which was subsequently organized, laid out and governed the City of Guthrie until the organized act passed, May 2, 1889. The judge made a speech out of a wagon at the corner where the Guthrie Savings Bank now stands in the heart of city at that first meeting. He was not long in impressing the people of his adopted community with his abilities, and in 1891 was appointed city attorney, a position which he retained during that and part of the following year. On coming here he had formed a partnership with John H. Cotteral, under the firm style of Bierer & Cotteral, and this firm remained in business until Mr. Bierer was appointed on the Supreme bench. Mr. Cotteral at this time is serving as United States judge for the Western District of Oklahoma. On January 8, 1894, the late President Cleveland appointed Mr. Bierer to the office of associate justice of the Supreme Court of Oklahoma, upon which bench he served with high ability, dignity and distinction until February 28, 1898. He has since devoted himself unreservedly to the duties of his constantly increasing practice, and has earned the right to be numbered among the foremost men of his calling practicing at Guthrie.

Mr. Bierer is a thirty-second degree Mason, and has numerous friends in that fraternity. As a citizen he has taken an active and leading part in promoting and supporting movements for the public welfare and in encouraging enterprises for good citizenship and educational advancement. He was married, June 26, 1888, to Miss Nannie M. Stamper, daughter of Rev. J. N. Stamper, a well known divine of Meade, Kansas. They are the parents of two children: Margaretta Louise, born September 21, 1895; and Andrew Gregg Curtin, Jr., born December 1, 1899.

ROBERT L. LAWRENCE, the present city attorney of Anadarko, Oklahoma, has gained a position of distinctive priority as one of the representative members of the bar of Caddo County and he gave efficient service as deputy county attorney in 1913 and 1914. He has gained success and prestige through his own endeavors and thus the more honor is due him for his earnest labors in his exacting profession and for the precedence he has gained in his chosen vocation.

A son of John and Mary C. (Hale) Lawrence, Robert Lee Lawrence was born in Hamblin County, Tennessee, January 1, 1881. The founder of the Lawrence family in America was a native of Ireland and he settled in Virginia prior to the War of the Revolution. James Lawrence, grandfather of the subject of this sketch, was born in the Old Dominion commonwealth and died in Hamblin County, Tennessee, where he was killed by bushwhackers during the Civil war. John Lawrence was born in Virginia in 1834 and he removed to Tennessee as a young man and located on a farm in Hamblin County, where he was also engaged in stockraising. He was exceedingly well educated, having taken degrees both in law and as a divinity student. He was a graduate of old Newman College, now known as Carson & Newman College. He was active as an attorney and as a Baptist minister and his political affiliations were with the democratic party. He was summoned to the life eternal in Hamblin County, Tennessee, in 1890, aged fifty-six years. His wife, whose maiden name was Mary C. Hale, was born in Tennessee in 1858. After the death of her husband she removed, with her family, to Jefferson City, Tennessee, where she still maintains her home. The following children were born to Mr. and Mrs. Lawrence: John J., an attorney by profession and owner of a light and power company in his home city, is a resident of Jefferson City, Tennessee; Mabel V. is the wife of Rev. John F. Vines, pastor of the First Baptist Church of Richmond, Virginia; Robert Lee is the subject of this review; Maude E. died at the age of twenty-one years, unmarried; and Estelle is the wife of J. L. Wilhoite, manager of the Chattanooga Electric Light & Power Company, at Chattanooga, Tennessee.

After completing the high-school course in Jefferson City, Tennessee, Robert Lee Lawrence pursued an academic and business course in Carson & Newman College, finishing the latter course in 1904. He then farmed on the old homestead in Hamblin County, Tennessee, for three years, at the expiration of which he was matriculated as a student in Cumberland University, in the law department of which he was graduated, in 1909, with the degree of Bachelor of Laws. He was admitted to the bar in the Supreme Court of Tennessee January 29, 1909, and initiated the active practice of his profession in Jefferson City, Tennessee, remaining in that place for the ensuing nine months. He then went to Cisco, Eastland County, Texas, where he remained for three months, coming thence to Anadarko, Oklahoma, July 1, 1909. Here he has since maintained his home and here he has built up a large general, civil and criminal law practice. He was admitted to the Oklahoma bar in the fall of 1909. He was deputy county attorney in 1913 and 1914 and later was elected city attorney, his offices being in the city hall building. He is a member of the Commissioners of Insanity for Caddo County and in politics is a stalwart democrat. He is a Baptist in religious matters and since his collegiate days has been a member of the Sigma Alpha Epsilon Greek Letter Fraternity. He is broad minded in all matters pertaining to his profession and in private life is genial and popular among his fellow men.

Mr. Lawrence married Miss Bessie M. Bettis, a daughter of J. E. Bettis, a prominent physician and surgeon, whose home is in Cisco, Texas. This union has been prolific of two children: Mary Elizabeth, born May 21, 1910; and Robert, born December 6, 1913.

FRANK HALEY. The entire career of Frank Haley, of Henryetta, has been devoted to operations in mining. From the time he was twelve years old right up to the present he has been connected with one or another form of the industry, having visited many of the big fields in this country, and has steadily worked his way upward from an humble beginning to his present position as mine inspector for District No. 3 of the State of Oklahoma. His success speaks volumes for his energy, industry and steady perseverance, for each promotion has come because he has deserved and fairly won it, and not by reason of any favoring circumstance or monetary or other influence.

Mr. Haley was born in County Mayo, Ireland, October 12, 1872, and is a son of Frank and Winifred (O'Donahue) Haley, natives of the same county in Erin, where both families lived for more than 300 years, as testified by the inscriptions on tombstones, many of which are written in the Gaelic. When Frank Haley was eight years of age the family emigrated to the United States, first locating at Boston, Massachusetts, and later going to Scranton, Pennsylvania, where the youth secured his early education in the public schools. While residing there, as a lad of twelve years he secured employment in the mines, and continued to do a man's work as a miner until 1886, when the family changed their place of residence to the City of Marion, Ohio. There both of his parents died, the mother February 17, 1901, at sixty-three years of age, and the father in March, 1906, when he was seventy-eight years old. The father was a stone cutter by trade, a vocation which he followed during the greater part of his active life. There were five sons and five daughters in the family, and four children are now living.

After the family located at Marion, Ohio, Frank Haley of this review bettered his educational training by attendance at St. Mary's Convent School. He was nineteen years of age when he first came to the West, joining a party that took part in the rush to the Cripple Creek diggings in Colorado. After participation in the excitement there he went to Bridgeport, Texas, where for seven years he worked in the coal mines, and in 1902 came to Indian Territory and engaged in mining coal at Henryetta. This he followed until he was appointed mine inspector by Peter Hanretty, chief mine inspector of the state, and later he was elected inspector of Mine District No. 3. In 1914 he was reelected to this period for a term of four years. In his official capacity Mr. Haley is known as one of the most reliable men in this line of work in the state. He is aggressive, but popular, and has the friendship of many of the leading coal operators of Oklahoma.

Mr. Haley has been a lifelong democrat and is considered one of his party's influential men in this section. His fraternal connection is with the Benevolent and Protective Order of Elks, and since boyhood he has been a consistent communicant of the Roman Catholic Church. He is unmarried.

ED L. REED. While his time is now principally devoted to the real estate and timber business at Hugo, where he is head of the firm of Reed & Coffman, Ed L. Reed has had such variety of experience in the old Oklahoma Territory and in Indian Territory as to constitute him an authority on many matters connected with the development and political and social life of the country.

To start the story of his career when it first touched Oklahoma Mr. Reed made his first trip in 1893 as a participant in the run at the opening of the Cherokee Strip. He entered the Strip from Turkey Creek, a few miles west of Hennessey, and secured a homestead. That run demonstrated the fact that the Cayuse or cattle pony, had far the advantage of the blooded horse of the east for a service like that. Two extremes in methods of obtaining land are in the recollections of Mr. Reed. Near him in line, when thousands of men awaited the firing of the signal gun at the hour of noon, stood a negro, unmounted and perfectly composed, with a stick in hand. When the gun fired the negro chanced being killed by charging horses, and, remaining in his tracks, stooped forward and planted the end of his stick in the ground. He thereby became possessed of a valuable claim. On the other hand men slipped into the reserved territory before the opening, in spite of the United States troopers on duty around the border. When the actual runners passed they found these "sooners" calmly plowing their claims with oxen.

Something of the atmosphere of the unpeopled West of that day is in Mr. Reed's subsequent experiences. For instance, he spent the first night on the prairie with his saddle blanket for a bed and his saddle for a pillow. Next morning he got a meager breakfast and feed for his horse at the camp of claim holders nearby. His luncheon next day consisted of ginger snaps and apples in the frontier village of Hennessey. In the afternoon he set out on a long horseback journey back to Kingman, Kansas, his home. On the river near Pond Creek he met a man who had buried some bottles of cold beer in the wet sand. The heat of a September day suggested their value to the traveler and Reed paid for three bottles at the rate of $1 a bottle. His supper that evening was at Enid, where a hamburger, some bread and butter and a piece of pie cost him $1.50.

Three years later Mr. Reed entered the lumber business at Blackwell, which was becoming one of the leading and most prosperous towns of the new country. Kildare was the nearest railroad point and his lumber was freighted overland from there. Blackwell was the habitation then of seventeen saloon keepers and seventeen restaurant keepers, but could make no boast of having a hotel. The settlers brought money with them and all communities prospered. Many of them saved as they developed the region and had good bank accounts when Dennis Flynn, delegate to Congress from Oklahoma Territory, secured the passage of an act granting free homes to the settlers. Then these savings were invested in improvements. So rapidly were they spent that Mr. Reed sold forty-seven cars of lumber in forty-two days. Naturally these financial conditions brought a maximum of prosperity to the town of Blackwell, and Mr. Reed, during his residence there of 3½ years saw lots that at the outset could be bought for $10 sell for $10,000.

For a number of years now Mr. Reed's activities and home have been in the old Indian Territory section of Oklahoma. Making money with a stump puller has proved one of his fascinating occupations. Mr. Reed has not pulled stumps to rid agricultural lands of them, neither has he had any use for the average base of a tree that once helped to grace an eastern Oklahoma forest. Armed with modern forceps his men have traveled over the timber section and pulled the stumps of walnut trees exclusively. From the stumps the roots were cut and the stumps sawed into thin boards called flitches, and these have been sold by Mr. Reed for enough money to make the occupation not only an interesting one but highly profitable. The demand for walnut timber, of the variety that Oklahoma produces, created this novel industry, and it may be carried on indefinitely.

An idea of the value of Oklahoma walnut may be obtained from the fact that a few years ago a log 10 feet long and 43 inches in diameter was sold to an eastern veneering firm for $3,300. At that time walnut timber with a minimum of 26 inches and a maximum of 33 inches in diameter sold readily for an average of $240 for 1,000 feet.

Walnut has been one of the most valuable of Oklahoma timbers, but in recent years the demand for cottonwood and ash has increased the value of these varieties, and Mr. Reed as a timber dealer has turned his attention to them. His cottonwood and ash timber has been sold practically all over the world. Indeed, Hugo is the headquarters of the leading dealers of the world in these classes of timber.

Experiences of Mr. Reed and other timber dealers in Southeastern Oklahoma in the acquisition of timber would make an interesting volume. Some of them are unique among timber men of the United States because of the character and diversity of persons with whom it was necessary to deal. In earlier years, before Indian land was saleable, the Indian's interests were guarded by the United States Government and the Choctaw Tribal Government, and the dealer was constantly in danger of trespassing. These two governments also were not always in harmony. For instance, Secretary Garfield of the Interior Department, granted Mr. Reed the privilege of cutting timber from a tract of Indian land, and still another branch of the government removed him from that tract under charges of trespass.

There was always danger of making purchases where titles were not valid. Indians of the same name sold tracts that were not theirs, and some Indians made several sales of the same tract. There is on record a case in which one Indian sold the same body of land thirteen times. Errors in titles and departmental orders kept timber men on the move for several years. Mr. Reed and his associates established several sawmills, and some of these were moved about several times.

Mr. Reed was one of the first residents of Coweta, Indian Territory, and his lumber yard was one of the first established there. Difficulties beset the first residents because of a questionable title to the land on which the town was being built, and ten months elapsed before the question was finally settled. An intermarried citizen nearly created war by threatening to dynamite the Reed lumber yard. Mr. Reed also opened a timber and lumber business at Porter in the early days of the town's history. There he handled walnut timber successfully and in one and a half years shipped from that town eighty cars of walnut logs.

During his residence of fifteen years in former Indian Territory Mr. Reed has studied philosophically many of the fundamental phases of the Indian problem. His activities have taken him all over the Choctaw Nation and practically all of the Creek Nation. The Indian problem has not been solved and is the biggest problem in Oklahoma. Mr. Reed believes a solution might be found in the appointment of a commission of three men, two of them unfamiliar with Indian conditions in Oklahoma, to make a study of the various phases of the problem. The vital question would be the competency of Indians, and the commission should be instructed to remove all restrictions from competent Indians. This would result in the sale, and naturally the development of Indian lands, and all such lands, not now taxed, would be placed on the tax rolls of the state.

Ed L. Reed was born in Greenville, Illinois, August 17, 1873, a son of Perry and Marie (Rea) Reed. When he was a small boy his parents moved to Kingman County, Kansas, and there he grew up. The father, who has been a farmer and land owner, is now retired and lives in Kingman, at the age of eighty-two. Mr. Reed's mother is also living at the age of seventy-nine. Perry Reed is of English parentage and born at Ashtabula, Ohio.

Mr. Reed was married at Blackwell, in 1900, to Miss Jettie Tierney. In Mr. Reed's family are four brothers and two sisters: Mrs. Anna Griffing, wife of a pearl button manufacturer in Plainview, New York; Mrs. P. H. Parmenter, whose husband is at the head of a chain of retail stores, and they live in Kingman, Kansas; Andrew Reed, employed by the Peters Shoe Company in St. Louis; George B. Reed, a resident of Raven, Colorado; A. T. Reed, in the creamery business at Pratt, Kansas; John A. Reed, a retired merchant at Kingman. Mr. Reed is affiliated with the Masonic Lodge, and is also a well known member of the Oklahoma Lumber Dealers' Association.

FRED DRUMMOND. The late Fred Drummond was one of the foremost men who made commercial history in Osage County. He was one of the pioneer white men, and for a quarter of a century was a trader among the Osage Indians, and held a license from the Government until the system was abolished. He helped to build up Hominy as a commercial and population center, was active in banking and merchandising, and had begun to make farming and stock raising a specialty a short time before his death. While his material accomplishments were many, he is best remembered in that section for his sterling character, his thorough kindliness, and his ready acceptance of all the opportunities to benefit his fellow man. He always favored giving every man a chance, and frequently lent a helping hand to those who were struggling with difficulties.

A native of Scotland, Fred Drummond was born May 2, 1864, a son of Alexander and Henrietta (Henry) Drummond. He was the only member of the family in America except a brother, George H. Drummond, of Providence, Rhode Island. His mother died in 1911 at the age of seventy-five and his father passed away at the age of seventy-one. His father was a barrister or lawyer in the old country. Fred Drummond, who was one of eleven children, was the favorite son of his mother, who desired that he become a minister. At the age of eighteen his venturesome spirit and active nature got the better of these early influences, and he started out to see the world, having no special inclination toward the profession which his mother had chosen for him. He came to New York City and spent one year in business experience there, and then moved to Texas and for a year and a half tried ranching. He found that his early experiences in Scotland and New York had hardly prepared him for this industry, and he returned to St. Louis and took a position with a wholesale dry goods house. It was through his connection with this house that he finally came into the Osage Nation. John R. Skinner was for many years one of the big traders in the Osage country, and while in St. Louis on a buying trip induced Mr. Drummond to come out to the Osage country. Mr. Drummond was then twenty-two years of age, and arriving at Pawhuska found employment with Mr. Skinner and later with Emory Gibson, and finally became associated with R. E. Bird & Company in merchandising, being identified with some of the oldest Osage traders. In time Fred Drummond learned to speak the Osage language fluently and became one of the most popular and successful of the traders operating under Government license. At a later date he also took up ranching near Ponca City, but continued trading at Pawhuska until 1903, when he removed to Hominy and took a leading part in organizing the Hominy Trading Company, buying out the Price Mercantile Company as the basis of the business. Mr. Drummond continued actively as a member of the Trading Company until his death, which occurred August 22, 1913.

At the time of his death he was also president of the Farmers State Bank of Hominy, which had been organized a year or so before. His oldest son, Cecil, was his lieutenant in the ranching business, and together they operated a ranch of about 3,000 acres seven miles east of Hominy, and were extensively engaged in raising cattle. Mr. Drummond was in the Indian trading service until the white men began to come into the Osage country in large numbers, and then turned his trading post into a general mercantile business.

He was affiliated with the Guthrie Consistory of thirty-second degree Scottish Rite Masons, and his funeral service was conducted by members of that body. He was also a member of the Knights of Pythias and the Woodmen of the World, and of the Presbyterian Church. A public distinction that was very appropriate was his election as the first mayor of Hominy after its incorporation. In 1904 he also built the largest and finest home of the city, where his widow and some of his children now reside.

On July 6, 1890, Fred Drummond married Miss Addie Gentner at Coffeyville, Kansas. She was born in Kansas October 9, 1870, a daughter of Frederick and Blanche (Leonard) Gentner. Their children were: Blanche Henrietta, now wife of Oscar K. Petty, vice president of the Farmers State Bank of Hominy; Roy Cecil, manager of the large Drummond ranch seven miles east of Hominy; Frederick Gentner, who is a graduate of the Oklahoma Agricultural and Mechanical College at Stillwater, also took work in the commercial department of Harvard University, and is now an active partner in the Hominy Trading Company; Alfred Alexander, who is a graduate of the Oklahoma Agricultural and Mechanical College, and is now a student in the agricultural department of the Illinois State Uni-

versity; and Lois Hope, who is still at home with her mother.

REV. JOHN W. GARNER. An able and earnest worker in the evangelistic field, Mr. Garner has fought the good fight, has defended and upheld the faith and has been instrumental in bringing many souls as worthy sheaves in the harvest of the Divine Master whom he has served with all of devotion and consecrated zeal. He has not been lacking in the militant spirit of the church faith and in a secular way he did valiant military service as a soldier of the Union in the Civil war. He is one of the honored and loyal citizens of Payne County, is the owner of a well improved farm, was the organizer of the Christian Church at Perkins, of which he served four years as pastor and with which he is still actively identified, his work in the ministry having been largely along evangelistic lines since his retirement from the pastorate noted.

Mr. Garner was born in Wayne County, Kentucky, on the 14th of January, 1843, and is a son of Freeman and Rachel (Coyle) Garner, both likewise natives of Kentucky, where the former was born in 1806 and the latter in 1826, the respective families having been founded in the old Blue Grass State in the pioneer era of its history and both family names having been identified with American history since the colonial days. Freeman Garner was a stone cutter by trade and vocation and both he and his wife continued their residence in Kentucky until the time of their death, the subject of their review being the oldest of their five children; Henderson, the second son, is now a resident of the State of Washington, and he likewise is a veteran of the Civil war, in which he served the Union as a member of Company I, Sixth Kentucky Volunteer Cavalry, with which gallant command he remained at the front for a period of three years; Sarah is the widow of Lieut. Nathaniel Dobbs, who was a Union officer in the Civil war, and she still resides in Pulaski County, Kentucky; James P. is a prosperous farmer of Payne County, Oklahoma; and Martin died when young.

Rev. John W. Garner remained at the parental home until he felt the call of patriotism and subordinated all other interests to tender his aid in defense of the Union. On the 1st of January, 1863, about two weeks prior to his twentieth birthday anniversary, he enlisted in Company H, First Kentucky Cavalry, with which command he continued in active service until the close of the war. His regiment was a part of the Army of the Cumberland, and with it he participated in numerous engagements, taking part in the Atlanta campaign and in the memorable battle of Atlanta. From Georgia the regiment returned to Nashville, Tennessee, from which place Mr. Garner returned with his comrades to Kentucky, where he received his honorable discharge. He was mustered out as first sergeant of Company A, to which he had been transferred from Company H of his regiment. In later years he has vitalized his interest in his old comrades of the Civil war through his affiliation with the Grand Army of the Republic, in which he holds membership in W. T. Sherman Post No. 41 at Perkins, Oklahoma.

After the close of the war Mr. Garner continued to reside in Kentucky until 1872, when he removed to Mitchell County, Kansas, and became a pioneer farmer in the vicinity of Beloit, the county seat. He continued his residence in the Sunflower State until 1899, when he came to Oklahoma Territory and established his residence in Payne County, where he has since maintained his home on his well improved farm near the Village of Perkins, the place having been developed and admirably improved under his personal supervision.

Mr. Garner acquired his early education in the schools of his native state and in all the long intervening years he has continued to be a close and appreciative student and reader; with the result that he has broadened his mental ken to wide perspective and is a man of really liberal education and mature judgment. For the past thirty years he has served as a clergyman of the Christian Church, and his labors in the vineyard of the Master have been most zealous and effective, even as has his temporal work along practical lines of productive industry, through the medium of which he has won independence and definite prosperity. He finds much demand upon his services in the evangelistic field of ministerial work and when not thus engaged he gives careful supervision to the practical affairs of his fine farm, which is situated four miles west of Perkins. Mr. Garner is broad-minded, liberal and progressive in his civic attitude, is well fortified in his convictions concerning governmental and economic policies and is a stanch supporter of the principles of the republican party. Right living and right thinking have given to Mr. Garner superb physical powers and strong mental grasp, and his appearance is that of a man fully twenty years his junior, in fact many who meet him giving expression to doubt as to his having been a soldier in the Civil war, owing to the fact that he looks too young today to have been eligible by age for such service more than half a century ago. His devoted wife, who has been his cherished companion and helpmeet for nearly fifty years, has aided him in his service in behalf of his fellow men and has been unsparing in her zeal and earnestness as a member of the Christian Church.

On February 26, 1866, was solemnized the marriage of Mr. Garner to Miss Mary J. Friels, who was born in Morgan County, Tennessee, in 1849, a daughter of William and Martha (Hanks) Friels, and, on the maternal side, she is a third cousin of the great and martyred Abraham Lincoln. They celebrated their golden wedding February 26, 1916. No children have been born to Mr. and Mrs. Garner, but they are the friends of all children and the young folk have always found a gracious welcome in their home. They are well known in Payne County and their circle of friends is limited only by that of their acquaintances.

P. I. BROWN. After fifteen years of banking experience in Kansas P. I. Brown moved to Indian Territory in 1895, locating at Beggs in Okmulgee County and has since been one of the live factors in business enterprise in that section, and for a number of years has been president of the First National Bank of Beggs. The First National Bank is an institution with resources of over $200,000. It has capital and surplus of $37,500, and is one of the thoroughly stable institutions of Okmulgee County. The directors are P. I. Brown, Grover Moore, H. George, H. H. Johnson, L. B. Jackson and E. G. Kelley.

A native of Missouri, P. I. Brown was born in Johnson County January 1, 1853, a son of James and Martha (Harris) Brown. His father was born in Tennessee in 1812 and his mother in Johnson County, Missouri, in 1815. James Brown was brought to Missouri in childhood and spent the rest of his life there as a farmer and stock raiser. During the Civil war he served two years in a Missouri regiment of the Union army. He was a democrat and a member of the Presbyterian Church. He died in 1885 and his wife passed away two weeks later. There were seven children: Elizabeth, wife of Henry McElwee, living in Missouri; W. E. Brown, who for many years was head of the W. E. Brown & Company Livestock Commission House at Kansas City, Missouri, and is now living at Seattle, Washington; P. I. Brown, who is the second in age among the children; Marion, who is a farmer near Carthage, Missouri; Thomas, of Butler, Missouri; Mattie Woodruff, who died in Louisiana; and Edward, who died in Colorado.

P. I. Brown was reared and received his early education in Johnson County, Missouri, and lived on a farm there until 1876. He then went into Southwestern Kansas, establishing a stock ranch in Comanche County, and in 1881 moved to Elk County, Kansas, where he was in the grocery business for a time. In 1884 he organized the first bank in his town, The Farmers State Bank, which is still in existence and a flourishing institution.

In 1895 Mr. Brown brought his family to Indian Territory and located six miles northeast of where the Town of Beggs now stands, where he began operating as a farmer and cattle man. When the railroad was built and the Town of Beggs started he at once identified himself with its interests, and in 1901 organized the Beggs State Bank. In 1903 this was reorganized as the First National Bank. Mr. Brown has been its president since organization, and up to two years ago was very active in the management of its affairs. His business interests are extensive, comprising a large amount of town property and also ranch and cattle interests in the vicinity of Beggs.

Since casting his first vote more than forty years ago he has been an active democrat. Just before statehood in 1906-07 he served as a deputy United States marshal in Indian Territory. Mr. Brown is a charter member of Beggs Lodge No. 319, Ancient Free and Accepted Masons, and belongs to the Scottish Rite Consistory of the thirty-second degree at Macalester.

In December, 1872, he married in Johnson County, Missouri, Miss Hannah Jackson, daughter of Joel Jackson. They have two sons, W. E. Brown and Joel Ray.

W. E. Brown is a well known banker of Sapulpa. He was born in Elk County, Kansas, August 6, 1879, and after completing a business course at Quincy, Illinois, spent four years in the First National Bank at Beggs with his father. He was also connected with the First National Bank of Mounds, and since 1908 has been identified with the American National Bank of Sapulpa, having been cashier and one of its directors for the past four years. He is active in the Commercial Club, and in various civic and social organizations at Sapulpa, and by his marriage in 1900 to Miss Cora Lee Pendleton has three children: Naomi, W. E., Jr., and Maxine.

Joel Ray Brown is cashier of the Bank of Commerce at Wetumpka, and likewise has a capable record as an Oklahoma banker. He married Frances Jones of Warrensburg, Missouri, and has one son, Joel Ray, Jr.

H. C. FELLOWS first became identified with Henryetta as a coal operator, and managed for several years one of the largest companies operating at that time in this field. In recent years he has turned to the newspaper business and is now head of the Fellows Publishing and Printing Company and managing editor of the Henryetta Standard. His associates are his three talented young sons, all of whom have chosen journalism as a profession and there is probably no other paper in Oklahoma which has the distinction of being managed and edited by a single family group.

Born at Lincoln, Illinois, January 12, 1865, H. C. Fellows is a son of Dr. A. M. and Emily S. (Closson) Fellows. Both his parents were natives of Vermont, his father born in 1828 and his mother in 1832. Doctor Fellows acquired a medical education in New York, and then came to Illinois, where just before the war he married Miss Closson. After she had completed her education she taught in a girls' school in Virginia for a time before coming to Illinois. Early in the War of the Rebellion Doctor Fellows entered the service as a surgeon with an Illinois regiment and served during the greater part of the struggle. He was finally sent home from Mississippi ill with the fever. In 1872 he took his family to Parsons, Kansas, a town which had only recently been established, and engaged in practice there for many years. After retiring from practice in 1890 he lived in Kansas City, Missouri, until his death in 1895. He was for many years active in the republican party. His widow is still living in Kansas City with her son, and though eighty-three years of age writes most interesting letters in a clear legible hand. She has always been interested in educational and religious affairs and during her active life in Southern Kansas was known as a woman of superior culture and education. There are three children: H. C. Fellows, A. M. Fellows, a wholesale coal merchant at Kansas City; and Eva L., wife of W. H. Hoffstott of Kansas City.

H. C. Fellows was about seven years of age when the family removed to Parsons, Kansas, where he grew up and finished his education in the high school. In 1889 he went out to Pueblo, Colorado, and had charge of the fuel department of the Missouri Pacific Railroad. In 1894 he took charge of the coal business of the same railroad company at Kansas City, and in 1896 became president of the Trans-Missouri Coal Company at Omaha. Returning to Kansas City in 1897 he was sales manager for the Kansas & Texas Coal Company for a time, and when this corporation sold its business to the Central Coal and Coke Company Mr. Fellows moved to Springfield, Missouri, and became manager of the Crescent Iron Works for B. F. Hobart, then president of the company. In 1903 he went back to Kansas City as manager of the J. R. Crowe Coal & Mining Company, and this corporation sent him to Henryetta, Oklahoma, to open the mines of the Whitehead Mining Company. In 1906 Mr. Fellows was employed by the Randolph-Mason Coal Company, a New York corporation, to take charge of its mining operations in Missouri. After one year he returned to Oklahoma and again resumed charge of the Whitehead Coal Mining Company, with which he continued until 1910.

It was in 1910 that Mr. Fellows bought the Henryetta Standard and organized the Fellows Printing and Publishing Company, composed of himself and sons. Since then he has given most of his time and attention to the publication of the Standard, which is one of the influential weekly papers of Okmulgee County and is now in its sixth volume. In politics it is independently democratic. Mr. Fellows himself is managing editor, his sons Carl H. and Paul H. are editors, and Albert M. is assistant editor.

Since locating at Henryetta Mr. Fellows has been a vigorous factor in local progress and served several years as president of the Commercial Club. He is a thirty-second degree Scottish Rite Mason and a member of the Mystic Shrine and is also a charter member of the local lodge of Elks.

In 1891 he married Miss Lillian MacGowan, who is a graduate physician and one of the first women to take a regular M. D. degree from one of the larger institutions of the Middle West. She was born in Poweshiek County, Iowa, in 1867, but spent most of her girlhood in West Liberty in that state, where she finished the course of the high school. After teaching for a time she entered the medical department of the University of Michigan at Ann Arbor, and was graduated M. D. in 1890. She then went West and began practice at Pueblo, Colorado,

FRANK M. WATSON

where she met and married Mr. Fellows. Since her marriage she has made no serious attempt to practice medicine. Mrs. Fellows is well known in woman's club circles in Oklahoma, has been president of the Ladies Improvement Club at Henryetta, and has also been active in the federated club work of the state. She has also written a number of articles for newspapers. Her parents were Andrew and Eliza (Morgan) MacGowan, both of whom were born in the State of Ohio in 1826. The mother died in 1903 and her father in 1906 at West Liberty, Iowa, where he was for many years a farmer. The MacGowans were Quakers.

The three sons of Mr. and Mrs. Fellows are: Paul H., born in 1892; Carl H., born in 1894, and Albert M., born in 1898. Carl H., at this writing is attending the School of Journalism at the University of Missouri. Each one of the sons has his own particular bent and talent in the newspaper profession, and much may be expected of these young men in the future.

BENJAMIN FRANKLIN VAN DYKE. The emigrant ancestor of Benjamin Franklin Van Dyke was William Van Dyke, who came from Holland in company with Peter Stuyvesant and served as attorney general of the Colony of New Amsterdam under Governor Stuyvesant. From that day down to the present time men of the name have been leaders in their respective communities. Benjamin F. Van Dyke was born in Keokuk County, Iowa, August 6, 1862, and his parents were L. H. and Emily (Kinnick) Van Dyke. The father was of Indiana birth, born in 1826, and he died in Lawrence, Kansas, in 1909. To these people were born eight children: D. M. Van Dyke, the eldest, died in 1887 near Garden City, Kansas, at the age of forty-five, he had been a farmer. Louisa married W. H. Holland, a farmer, now deceased; she lives at Whatcheer, Iowa. James W. lives in Sacramento, California, and is the foreman of a large ranch in that vicinity. Mary L. married Albert Skinner, a farmer, of Peabody, Kansas. Anna died in infancy. John, who was a building contractor, died in Sacramento, California, in 1914. The seventh child was Benjamin F., of this review. Emma married J. V. Weidlein, and they live in Lawrence, Kansas, where he is employed in the express office of the Santa Fe Railroad.

Benjamin F. Van Dyke was brought up on his father's farm in Keokuk County, Iowa, and he had such schooling as was available in his community in those days. Nevertheless, it is reasonable to suppose that he was a student and that he made the best of such advantages as were to be found, for when he was twenty-one he began teaching in the country schools of the county, continuing through two terms. He then entered the Eastern Iowa Normal at Columbus Junction and in 1885 was graduated with the degree of B. S., upon which he was appointed to the principalship of the schools of Columbus City. This service was followed by a similar call to service in Hillsboro, Kansas, where he remained until 1888, and in that year he returned to Columbus Junction and read law in the offices of Senator C. A. Carpenter. Three years later, in 1891, Mr. Van Dyke was admitted to practice before the Supreme Court of Iowa.

For the next ten years Mr. Van Dyke conducted a law practice in Columbus Junction, and in 1901 he came to Granite, Oklahoma, where he has since been ably identified with the legal activities of the community. He has found friends here and has won to himself a following that is well worthy of his talents.

Mr. Van Dyke is a democrat since 1896, and is a member of the Masonic and Pythian orders. His Masonic affiliations are with Granite Lodge No. 164, Ancient Free and Accepted Masons. Other fraternal societies that claim him are the Modern Woodmen of America and the Woodmen of the World. In a professional way he is a member of the State Bar Association, and he is a member of the Sons of the American Revolution, an honorific membership to which he is eligible through his paternal grandfather, William Van Dyke, who gave valiant service as a soldier in the American Revolution from Somerset County, New Jersey.

In 1886 Mr. Van Dyke was married in Sigourney, Iowa, to Miss Fannie Fulton, daughter of C. M. Fulton, then postmaster of Columbus Junction. Two children were born to this marriage. Claire is married to Ray H. Arnett, superintendent of the water and light departments in Granite, where they live. Dorothy was graduated from Drury College in Springfield, Missouri, in 1914, with the degree of A. B., and in 1915 received an M. A. degree from the same school.

In March, 1903, Mrs. Van Dyke died, and in May, 1904, Mr. Van Dyke was married in Mangum, Oklahoma, to Miss Hattie Wright, daughter of T. E. Wright, a retired farmer of Missouri. There are no children of this later marriage.

FRANK M. WATSON. The title of biggest farmer in Osage County is rightly bestowed upon Frank M. Watson. His farm near Wynona is a splendid illustration of the methods and possibilities of "bonanza farming," and everything is conducted on a big scale. In his pastures are found hundreds of head of fine cattle, he plants and harvests hundreds of acres of wheat every year, and there are few business houses in Oklahoma which represent a larger investment of capital and employ more equipment and the services of more hands.

The head of this big agricultural industry is a young man thirty-one years old. However, he has lived in close touch with stock raising and agricultural matters in the Southwest since boyhood, and his father has for years been one of the well known cattle men of the Southwest. Frank M. Watson was born in Independence, Kansas, February 8, 1885, a son of William and Lannie (Lane) Watson, the former a native of Sherman, Texas, and the latter of Kentucky. The parents were married in Texas, and soon afterwards moved their home to Kansas. They were married at Gainsville, Texas, where William Watson was at that time engaged in his extensive ranching operations. He still owns two large ranches, and for twenty-five or thirty years has ranged his cattle herds over the states of Texas, Oklahoma and Kansas. Frank M. Watson is one of eight children, four sons and four daughters.

Most of his early life was spent in Kansas, chiefly in Montgomery County, though he also became acquainted with the Osage country of the Indian Territory through his practical association with his father's cattle business. For a number of years his father had a ranch on the Caney River near Bartlesville. In 1906 Mr. Watson went to Texas with his parents, but soon afterwards came to Wynona and that has since been his headquarters as a farmer and cattle raiser.

He now has the largest farming outfit in Osage County and has also earned the distinction of being the largest cattle man. He has 2,000 acres in his farm adjoining Wynona on the south, and it is all cultivated, with about 1,000 acres in wheat, 300 acres in oats, and the rest in feterita. It requires a big force of men to operate such an extensive farm, and his employes number from fifteen to thirty, depending upon the seasons. He keeps an average of about 1,500 head of cattle, and has had as high as 6,000 head. He also handles hogs on a large scale. Throughout this section of the country his place is known as the J. O. Ranch, his cattle brand being composed of those letters. Altogether Mr. Watson owns and controls 50,000 acres of land in Osage County. One of the noticeable features of his farm enterprise is the presence of three immense silos. He has also constructed an individual water system, the finest in the state, representing an investment of $1,500. In addition to the use of traction engines to draw his immense gang plows, he also requires about sixteen teams to perform the farm work. Instead of depending upon an itinerant threshing outfit he owns an equipment of that machinery of his own, and has several thousand dollars invested in all the machinery and appliances needed for the cultivation and harvesting of his crops.

Mr. Watson also keeps a pack of fourteen wolf hounds. These he employs for hunting, and they have proved an important factor in exterminating the wolves from this section of Oklahoma. During the first six months of 1915 he and his hounds have caught fifteen wolves. Mr. Watson is a member of the Masonic Order, the Benevolent and Protective Order of Elks, the Fraternal Order of Eagles and the Knights of Pythias. On March 21, 1908, he married Miss Viola E. Rogers, who was born in Osage County, a daughter of Antoine Rogers of Wynona. They have one daughter, Viola Camille.

IRA GILBERT MARKEE. Appreciative of the constructive business activities, the civic loyalty and progressiveness and the sterling character of Mr. Markee, the voters of the Village of Perkins, Payne County, consistently elected him to the office of president of the village board of trustees, a position of which he has been the incumbent since 1915, and in which he has given a most capable administration as chief executive of the municipal government. Mr. Markee has been a resident of Oklahoma since boyhood and is a representative of one of the sterling pioneer families of the state, his parents having here established their residence at the time of the opening to settlement of the Cherokee Strip, of which the present County of Payne was a part. He is one of the most influential business men of Perkins, where he operates a well equipped and thoroughly modern cotton gin and where he is general manager of the Farmers' Cotton Company, which is incorporated under the laws of the state.

Mr. Markee was born in Butler County, Kansas, on the 26th of October, 1880, and is a son of F. M. and Priscilla (Morgan) Markee, the former of whom was born in Illinois and the latter in North Carolina. J. M. Markee, grandfather of the subject of this review, was a loyal soldier of the Union in the Civil war, and the maternal grandfather, James Morgan, was in the same great conflict as a valiant soldier in the Confederate ranks, in which he served during virtually the entire period of the war. The marriage of the parents of Mr. Markee was solemnized in the State of Kansas, where they continued their residence until the opening to settlement of the Cherokee Strip of Oklahoma, in 1892, when they came to the territory and established their home on a pioneer farm in Payne County. They now reside at Stillwater, the county seat, where the father is living retired, after having contributed his share to the civic and material development and progress of this favored section of the state. Of the four children the mayor of the Village of Perkins is the eldest; May is the wife of Jesse Bennett, of Ripley, Payne County; J. Minard is identified with business interests at Stillwater; and Fay remains at the parental home.

Ira G. Markee acquired his early education in the public schools of Kansas and was about thirteen years of age at the time of the family removal to Payne County, Oklahoma, where he was reared to manhood on the pioneer farm and availed himself of the advantages of the local schools. He continued to be associated with his father in the work and management of the farm until 1904, when he engaged in the cotton business and established his headquarters in Stillwater, where he was associated with the Thompson Gin Company for four years and where he gained a thorough knowledge of all details of the cotton-ginning business. Upon leaving the county seat Mr. Markee established his home at Perkins, where he has since operated his modern gin and ably supervised the business of the Farmers' Cotton Company, of which he is general manager.

Mr. Markee is a stanch supporter of the cause of the democratic party and is a young man of invincible enterprise and public spirit, so that he is admirably fortified for the municipal office of which he is now the incumbent. He is affiliated with the Independent Order of Odd Fellows, in which he has passed the various officials chairs of his lodge, and both he and his wife hold membership in the Baptist Church at Perkins. In the State of Kansas, on the 12th of May, 1903, was solemnized the marriage of Mr. Markee to Miss Nora Rennick, who was born in that state on the 24th of May, 1886, being a daughter of John M. Rennick, a prosperous farmer of Dawson, Oklahoma. Mr. and Mrs. Markee have three children—Frances, Ruth and Bertha.

HON. WILLIAM JAMES LADD. A long and useful life, William J. Ladd has lived not without some of the more substantial honors paid to an upright and public spirited citizen. He is at the present time representing Creek County, his home locality, in the Oklahoma Legislature. He was a veteran of the Union army during the Civil war. He was a pioneer in Oklahoma at the original opening, and some twenty years ago came into the Creek Nation of Indian Territory, and has been very closely identified with the upbuilding and advancement of the little Town of Bristow, where he resides.

An Indiana man by birth, Mr. Ladd was born at Terre Haute June 29, 1843, a son of William D. and Sarah (Price) Ladd. His father was born near Cincinnati, Ohio, and his mother near Vincennes, Indiana. They were married in Vigo County, Indiana, spent many years of their lives there, but after the war moved to Vermillion County. Both parents died there, the mother aged eighty-four and the father at sixty-eight, his death having resulted from an accident. He was a farmer by occupation, and tilled the soil in the fertile valley of the Wabash River. In politics he was a republican and filled several county offices in the early days. He and his wife were active members of the Christian Church. There were four children in the family: Elizabeth, widow of William J. Morgan and living at Luther, Oklahoma; Amanda, who married M. D. Graves, died in Kansas as did also her husband; Leonard, now deceased; and William J.

William James Ladd grew up in his native county of Indiana, had the usual influences and circumstances of a rural Indiana boy, acquired a fair education, and was just coming into manhood when the war broke out. In 1862 he volunteered his services and enlisted in Company I of the Eighty-fifth Indiana Volunteer Infantry. From that time forward until the close of hostilities he was with his command in the various engagements and campaigns, and held the rank of non-commissioned officer. On July 20, 1864, he was wounded by a shell at Peach Tree Creek, Georgia, the site of that battlefield now being included in the City of Atlanta. After recovering from his wounds in the hospital he rejoined his regiment and continued until the Union arms were triumphant.

Following the war Mr. Ladd engaged in the milling business in Indiana, but in 1878 he transferred his activities to a newer country, locating in Montgomery

County along the southern line of Kansas. There he engaged in the shipping and dealing in live stock, and also conducted a ranch.

Mr. Ladd is one of the men who has many keen and interesting recollections of the opening of the original Oklahoma Territory in 1889. He secured a claim west of Edmond, lived upon it and proved it up, and one of the fine farms in that section of the state is the result of his enterprise and industry. In 1896 Mr. Ladd moved to the Creek Nation, locating in what is now Creek County, and was diligently engaged in looking after his ranching interests until the Town of Bristow was started. He was one of the men who promoted that village, and has had his home there ever since, and whenever possible has done what he could to advance its interests in the way of larger commercial outlook, better schools, churches, and all things that go to make up a good town. Until the last two years he engaged in buying cotton, but is now retired from active business.

Mr. Ladd is one of the oldest republicans in Oklahoma. He helped to organize the republican party in Indiana, and in the first Lincoln campaign in 1860 he was a member of one of those historic organizations known as "The Lincoln Wide-Awakes." He was also a delegate to the first territorial convention at Guthrie, Oklahoma, July 20, 1889. In the general election of 1914 he was a candidate on the republican ticket for the Lower House of the Oklahoma State Legislature, and was elected by a safe majority. He is now looking after the interests of his constituents and giving a studious attention to general legislation affecting the entire commonwealth. Outside of this position in the Legislature Mr. Ladd has never cared for official honors and never accepted any except some township offices. He is a member of the Christian Church, and is commander of Lawton Post No. 31 Grand Army of the Republic at Bristow.

At Paris, Illinois, September 27, 1866, not long after he had returned from the war Mr. Ladd married Miss Julia A. Cox. She was born in Edgar County, Illinois, September 15, 1845. For nearly half a century they traveled life's highway together, sharing in its joys and burdens. Mrs. Ladd died while on a visit to her old home on May 19, 1915. A large family of children were left to mourn her loss. There were ten born into their household altogether, but three boys died in infancy. A brief record of the remaining seven is as follows: Jane, who married William H. Mitchell and lives in Kansas City, Missouri; Alice, who married Harvey Gleason, is now living at home with her father; David lives in Creek County, where he is a prominent rancher; Thomas has been for the past thirteen years connected with the postoffice at Muskogee; Edgar lives in Colorado; Isaac E. lives in Creek County; Kate is the wife of Ernest Narjot of Los Angeles, California.

DANIEL PIERCE SPARKS. A veteran Confederate soldier, a man whose life has seen many of the vicissitudes and experiences of the past half century, Daniel P. Sparks is one of the old and honored citizens of Shawnee, where for several years he has filled with credit the office of justice of the peace. He came to Oklahoma in the early days from Texas, and for several years was engaged in business at Shawnee and elsewhere.

His birth occurred in the Parish of St. Mary's, near Franklin, Louisiana, April 3, 1845. The lives of himself and his father, who also bore the name of Daniel Pierce, cover practically the entire period of American national existence. The elder Sparks was born in 1787, the year the Federal Constitution was formulated. He was a native of South Carolina, and a son of Daniel Sparks. There were four brothers who came from England to Virginia about the outbreak of the American Revolution. Their names were Samuel, Charles, Harry and Daniel, the last being the grandfather of the Shawnee citizen. They were all soldiers in the American Revolution, and Harry, the youngest, was killed in battle. After the war the other brothers removed to South Carolina. Daniel P. Sparks, Sr., was reared in South Carolina, and when a young man went to St. Mary's Parish, Louisiana, where he married and where he became a sugar planter. He also maintained a residence in Greenville, South Carolina. His death occurred in New Orleans in 1867. Members of the Sparks family have been participants in practically every great war of the nation. While grandfather Daniel was a Revolutionary soldier, his son Daniel Pierce took part in the War of 1812, and Daniel Pierce, Jr., as already noted, was a Confederate soldier. Daniel Pierce Sparks, Sr., was an active member of the Baptist Church. He married Eliza Vinson, who was born in Tennessee and died at Houston, Texas.

The early education of Daniel Pierce Sparks was acquired chiefly in South Carolina, and he was pursuing his higher education in Furman University at Greenville when the war broke out. He was at that time just sixteen years of age. He left school at once and enlisted in Hampton's Legion of South Carolina Troops. His service covered a period of four years and three months, practically the entire duration of the war. He was promoted to second lieutenant in the cavalry attached to the Twenty-first South Carolina Regiment of Infantry, and when that organization was disbanded he returned to Hampton's Regiment and was one of its scouts. He was taken prisoner near Brentsville, Virginia, and was sent to the old Capital Prison in Washington, D. C., being exchanged after ninety days. While his own record as a soldier was most creditable, his brother, John Calhoun Sparks, came in for unusual distinction in the Confederate ranks. This brother was born in 1841, entered the army at the same time as Daniel P., and was made commander of Lee's Scouts in Virginia, having thirty picked and trusted men under his command. He was killed in 1863. Nearly fifty years after the war the Baptist Courier of Greenville, South Carolina, wrote of him as a daring soldier and scout, and speaks of him as "the fearless Sparks, who once was personally complimented by General Lee for his bravery." This article was ordered to be read in every camp of the United Confederate Veterans.

After the war Daniel Pierce Sparks returned to New Orleans, and in 1866 went to Houston, Texas. His first employment there was in Baldwin's book store, and for a little more than a year he was a messenger on the road in the employ of the old Texas Express Company. He then went to Hearne, Texas, as bookkeeper for the firm of Ledick & Reeves, and after nearly two years opened a mercantile establishment of his own at Hearne, and continued in business there two years. For a number of years Mr. Sparks' home was at Bellville, in Austin County, Texas. He bought and conducted a farm in that locality for three years, and then moved into Bellville, the county seat, and was engaged in the lumber business until 1880. While there he was again in the employ of the Texas Express Company as local agent. In 1880 Mr. Sparks moved to Greenville, Texas, where he conducted a restaurant and book store for more than fifteen years. Finally selling out, he came to Shawnee in 1897, and established a restaurant which had a large patronage and bore a splendid reputation among its customers for a number of years. In 1899 he also opened a similar business at

Oklahoma City, and conducted both establishments for two years, at the end of which time he sold the business at Oklahoma City.

As a result of an injury caused by his walking into an open gas ditch, Mr. Sparks was unable to prosecute his business affairs actively for some time, and one year of this he spent in New Mexico. Finally returning to Shawnee he entered politics and made an unsuccessful campaign for the office of register of deeds of Pottawatomie County. In 1912 he was elected justice of the peace, and that is his position of service at the present time.

Mr. Sparks is a democrat, a member of the Episcopal Church, and is affiliated with the Masonic Order, the Independent Order of Odd Fellows, and the Fraternal Order of Eagles. In the last named fraternity he has served as secretary for the past twenty years. He has been especially active in the United Confederate Veterans, and has served as commander of Camp No. 976, and as commander general of the Second Division.

In 1866, soon after the war, Mr. Sparks married Miss Lizzie Duncan of Greenville, South Carolina. She died in 1867, leaving one daughter, Lizzie Duncan, who is now the wife of W. T. Boyd, an employee of the Santa Fe Railroad Company, located at Albuquerque, New Mexico. In 1872, at Bellville, Texas, Mr. Sparks married Miss Josephine Haggerty. They are the parents of three children: John Calhoun is bookkeeper and head clerk for the firm of Phillips & Norris, cotton oil manufacturers, at Ada, Oklahoma; D. P. Sparks, Jr., is a foreman in the machine shops of the Rock Island Railroad Company, at Shawnee; Josephine is the wife of P. A. Norris, a cotton oil manufacturer at Ada, Oklahome.

WALTER R. WILSON. The list of the leading citizens of Henryetta includes the name of Walter R. Wilson, cashier and vice president of the First National Bank. While one of the younger representatives of financial interests, it would seem that his youth has been no bar to his progress, for his career has been one of steady advancement to a position which many older men might envy. Since his arrival at Henryetta he has been considered a factor in the development and progress of the city, and in his particular line is a man of recognized ability who carries to a successful completion the undertakings with which he identifies himself.

Mr. Wilson was born at Cissna Park, Iroquois County, Illinois, April 18, 1888, and is a son of Dr. Calvin C. and Anna H. (Brock) Wilson, the former a native of Indiana and the latter of Illinois. Dr. Calvin C. Wilson was a child when taken by his parents from Indiana to Illinois, and in the latter state received good educational advantages, for some years following the vocation of educator and being a teacher in high schols. Later he adopted the calling of medicine, and after graduation from the Ohio Medical College practiced for a number of years at various points in Illinois, but trouble with his hearing caused him to abandon his profession and in 1902 he brought his family to Henryetta. Here he became connected with the White Mercantile Company, and continued in the employ of this concern until the great fire of 1907, which practically wiped out Henryetta's business district and which destroyed the establishment with which Doctor Wilson was identified. Later he joined the First National Bank's clerical force, and still continues to be associated with this institution. He is one of the well known and highly esteemed citizens of the community, interested actively in its welfare, and for the past seven or eight years has acted in the capacity of city treasurer. He is a republican in politics. Doctor and Mrs. Wilson have two sons: Walter R.; and Charles L., a mechanical engineer and now professor of mechanical engineering at the Texas Agricultural and Mechanical College, at Bryan, or College Station, Texas.

Walter R. Wilson received a high school education at Chicago, Illinois, and Greencastle, Indiana, and was fourteen years of age when he accompanied his parents to Oklahoma. Here his first employment was as clerk in the postoffice at Henryetta, and later he received his introduction to banking with the Citizens Bank of Henryetta. In 1909 he became cashier of the First National Bank of Henryetta, and since then has also succeeded to the vice presidency of this institution, of which the other officials are: James M. Wise, president; Joe Hillman, vice president; and V. V. Kingsbury and O. D. Norred, assistant cashiers. The First National Bank has a capital and surplus of $60,000, and is accounted one of the strong and reliable banking houses of Okmulgee County. Mr. Wilson has an established place in the confidence of its patrons and depositors and has done much to make the institution a success. A young man, he possesses good business sagacity, keen discrimination and laudable ambition, and these are elements which have always had great force in the battle of life and the ultimate winning of success. In his political views he is a republican, believing that the principles of that party contain the best elements of good government. Fraternally he is a Knight Templar and Shriner Mason, and his religious affiliation is with the Presbyterian Church.

Mr. Wilson was married at Henryetta, in 1909, to Miss Mary M. Wise, a native of Missouri, and daughter of James Monroe Wise, president of the First National Bank and one of the pioneer coal operators of Henryetta. They have two children: Walter R., Jr., and Genevieve.

James Monroe Wise was born at Eugene, Vermilion County, Indiana, May 25, 1849, and is a son of Jacob and Mary (Taylor) Wise, the former born in Pennsylvania and the latter near Eugene. He came to Indiana at an early date, married near Eugene, and there he and the mother passed the greater part of their lives. After the close of the Civil war they moved to Paola, Kansas, where both passed away, the mother when about sixty years old and the father at the age of sixty-six years. He was a farmer and proprietor of a hotel and a stanch republican in his political views. There were five children in the family: H. G., of Dallas, Texas; James Monroe; Mary Margaret McCarthy, deceased; John F., of Joplin, Missouri; and Mrs. Margaret Johnson, a widow residing at Kirkwood, Missouri.

James M. Wise received his education in the public schools of Indiana, and soon after going to Kansas with his parents embarked upon his independent career. For two or three years he worked in a commission house at Paola, and through his energy, initiative and fidelity won a partnership in the firm of R. C. Crowell & Company, but after several years disposed of his interests in this concern and went to Colorado. For five or six years he followed the adventurous life of the freighter, and also established a grocery business at Leadville, in that state, but finally left Colorado, went to Rich Hill, Missouri, and became interested in coal operations, which have interested his attention to the present time. Mr. Wise came to Henryetta in 1902 and here started the first real coal mine, although there had been a small operator who had preceded him. He became the founder in that year of the Henryetta Coal and Mining Company, of which he has since been president, and which has been developed from a modest undertaking into a 700-ton mine. While the greater part of his attention and abilities have been given to the development of this industry,

he is also largely interested in oil companies, and since its organization has been the directing head of the First National Bank. As a citizen he has been foremost in the promotion of movements for the public welfare, and few men have in greater degree the respect and confidence of their fellow-citizens and business associates.

Mr. Wise was married in 1882 to Miss Hattie Scott, a native of Denver, Colorado, and to this union there have been born four daughters: Georgia, who is the wife of Frank Tutt, of St. Louis, Missouri; Mrs. Mildred Burress, who resides with her father; Mary Margaret, who is the wife of Walter R. Wilson, cashier and vice president of the First National Bank of Henryetta; and Miss Alice, who resides at home.

WILLIAM C. GROVE, who recently began his first term of service as one of the county commissioners of Osage County, is one of the oldest white residents of the Osage country, and as a rancher and cattleman is known among the prominent men of that industry throughout Kansas, Oklahoma and Texas, and it is doubtful if any one individual has handled more live stock in Osage County than Mr. Grove. He has had a varied career, beginning as a cowboy, later developed an independent business, and has come to occupy a place of such influence in his vicinity that it is proper to say that where he leads others follow.

His birth occurred at the little Village of Mirabile in Caldwell County, Missouri, June 8, 1872. His parents were John Harvey and Mary Ann (Frederick) Grove. His father and mother were both born near Canton, Ohio, were taken when children to Missouri, grew up in the same neighborhood, and after their marriage and when William C. Grove six years of age they moved to Franklin County, Kansas, where the mother died in the following year. John H. Grove died in Kansas March 30, 1912, and would have been seventy-three years of age on the following 19th of June. Most of his active career was spent as a rancher and he was well known among horse men, and made a specialty of handling fast horses, particularly trotting stock. He was well adapted for that business, and made it a life study. At one time he owned one of the noted trotters in the country, "Red Cloud." He owned a number of other fast horses and some fine stallions. Early in his career he served about three years with a Missouri regiment in the Civil war, and in the early days had experience as a freighter from St. Joseph, Missouri, over the old Santa Fe trail to Santa Fe, New Mexico. He made several of these trips, at first with ox teams and later with teams of mules, and through these varied activities gained a large acquaintance among frontiersmen. He was a republican, a Mason, and a member of the Christian Church. William C. Grove has one brother, Harvey Elmer, who is now in the oil business in Oklahoma.

After the death of his mother William C. Grove was sent back to live in the family of an uncle in Missouri for a year and a half, and then went to Kansas with another uncle, and practically grew up in the midst of the activities of the ranch and range. For five years he was employed on the Diamond X Ranch with his uncle, and his first acquaintance with Oklahoma began in 1886, when he accompanied a cattle outfit into the Cherokee Strip country. Later he was in Texas with the well known Gamble cattle organization, and from there came into the Osage Nation in 1892. With the exception of a season spent in New Mexico, another in Colorado, and one in Dakota, he has been continuously identified with the Osage country ever since. At an earlier time he had taken a large bunch of cattle over

Vol. V—12

one of the trails leading out from Texas through the intervening country to the northern pastures in Montana. He was still in the employ of the Gamble organization when he came to the Osage Nation, and was with that and other ranch outfits for a number of years.

After his marriage Mr. Grove located on a ranch 2½ miles west of Hominy. This comprises 1,700 acres under one fence, and is one of the largest and most valuable cattle ranches in Osage County. He combines farming with the live stock industry, and each season runs from 100 to 500 head of cattle. He has handled as high as 2,000 or 3,000 head of cattle in a single year. Mr. Grove is also an extensive hog raiser, of the Hampshire stock, and is a member of the National Hampshire Hog Association.

His success as a business man has naturally brought him into contact with local affairs, where his judgment and action are held in high esteem. In politics he is a lifelong democrat, has filled local offices as school director and road supervisor, as councilman at Hominy, and is now in his first term as county commissioner. Though a white man himself, he has taken a very active interest in the solution of the questions affecting the tribal affairs of the Osage people, and was a strong advocate of the present methods of handling the oil situation.

On October 12, 1900, Mr. Grove married at Independence, Kansas, Miss Agnes Herridge. She was born in South Dakota, April 27, 1883, and came with her parents to the Indian Territory about 1890. Her parents are Edward and Julia (Lessart) Herridge, her father a native of the State of New York, and now living near Gray Horse in Osage County, while the mother died at Pawhuska in 1906. Mrs. Grove's mother was the inheritor of Sioux blood on her mother's side and Osage blood through her father. Mrs. Grove's grandfather, Benjamin Lessart, who was part French and part Osage, founded a trading post at Denver, Colorado, in the early days, and was also a rancher and cattle man, operating in Dakota and over the Sioux Reservation.

Mr. and Mrs. Grove have four children: Muriel Wyoma, Mary Lutisha, Harry Leslie and Frederick Herridge. Mr. Grove in Masonry has taken thirty-two degrees in the Scottish Rite, is affiliated with the Lodge at Harmony and with the Consistory at Guthrie, and is also a member of the Knights of Pythias and the Benevolent and Protective Order of Elks at Pawhuska.

JOHN W. RICKETTS. Near the Cimarron River in the southern part of Payne County is situated the vigorous and attractive Village of Perkins, and that Mr. Ricketts is one of its popular and loyal citizens needs no further voucher than the statement that he is here serving in the office of postmaster.

Mr. Ricketts claims the old Blue Grass State as the place of his nativity and is a scion of stanch old Southern stock on the paternal side, his maternal ancestors having been pioneer settlers in the State of Ohio. Mr. Ricketts was born at Catlettsburg, Boyd County, Kentucky, on the 14th of February, 1854, and is a son of John W. and Jane (Johnston) Ricketts, the former of whom was born in the Shenandoah Valley of Virginia and the latter of whom was born in Ohio, where their marriage was solemnized. The parents of Mr. Ricketts passed most of their lives near the Ohio River, having resided for a time in Kentucky and having later located on the river in Southern Ohio, where the father died in 1900, when about seventy years of age, he having served as a pilot on the Ohio River in his young manhood and having later become a prosperous farmer. His widow still maintains her home in Ohio and celebrated in 1915 her ninety-fourth birthday anniversary, so that she is one of the most venerable women of her native state, even as she is a representative of a sterling pioneer family of the historic old Buckeye commonwealth. Of the children the eldest is Thomas C., who is now a resident of Texas; Mrs. Caroline Shattuck, the next in order of birth, is deceased; John W., of this review, is the third child; Mary died at the age of four years; Mrs. Nancy Baxter maintains her home in Ohio; and Mrs. Dora Johnston was a resident of Ohio at the time of her death, her husband having represented that state in the United States Congress.

John W. Ricketts was a child at the time when the family home was established in Lawrence County, Ohio, where he was reared to manhood and received the advantages of the public schools, the while he early began to assist in the work and management of the home farm. In 1886 he went to Minnesota, in which state he maintained his residence until Oklahoma Territory was thrown open to settlement, in 1889, when he came to the new territory, which was not formally organized until the following year, and numbered himself among the pioneer settlers of Payne County, where he secured Government land and reclaimed an excellent farm, his homestead place having been developed into one of the excellent farms of the county and the property being still in his possession. He served four years as carrier on a rural free delivery mail route from Perkins, and on the 5th of March, 1908, he was appointed postmaster at Perkins, the office being of the third class. He has since held this position and his continuous tenure of office indicates the popular estimate placed upon his administration.

Upon coming to Payne County, in 1889, Mr. Ricketts filed claim to the southwest quarter of section 1, township 17, range 2, east, and this is the well improved homestead which he still retains, the farm being eligibly situated one-half miles west of the Village of Perkins.

In politics Mr. Ricketts gives his allegiance to the republican party, and his civic loyalty and progressiveness have been manifested in his effective service in township offices and as a member of the school board of his district. He and his wife became charter members of the Congregational Church at Perkins, and he is a trustee of the same, besides which he contributed liberally to the erection of the church building. He is a Master Mason and maintains affiliation with the lodge at Perkins.

In Ohio, in 1872, Mr. Ricketts married Miss Sadie R. Ferguson, who was born and reared in that state, and who died on the home farm in Payne County, Oklahoma, about the year 1892. Of the three children of this union the eldest is William, who is a resident of the City of Minneapolis, Minnesota; Homer is now in Mexico; and Mrs. Mamie Banks is deceased. In 1901 was solemnized the marriage of Mr. Ricketts to Miss Christine B. Harpold, and no children have been born of this union.

MARTIN RYAN, D. D. S. Doctor Ryan has been a resident of Okmulgee County, Oklahoma, since 1906, and was engaged in the practice of his profession in the Village of Beggs, this county, until 1912, when he was elected county treasurer and removed to Okmulgee, the county seat, where he has since continued as the efficient and popular incumbent of this important fiscal office, in which he has given a most careful and acceptable administration and in which he is now serving his second term, through re-election in the autumn of 1914. His being called to this office offers the most effective evidence of the high place which is his in the confidence and esteem of the people of the county, and he is known as a loyal and progressive citizen of the state of his adoption.

Doctor Ryan was born in Outagamie County, Wisconsin, on the 30th of May, 1874, and is the youngest in a family of eight children, of whom three are living. He is a son of Daniel and Winifred (Powers) Ryan, both natives of Ireland, where the former was born in County Tyrone and the latter in County Clare. Daniel Ryan came to the United States in 1846 and his marriage was solemnized in the City of Boston, Massachusetts. In company with his young wife he soon made his way to the west and numbered himself among the pioneers of Outagamie County, Wisconsin, where he reclaimed and developed an excellent farm and where he and his wife passed the residue of their lives. Mrs. Ryan passed to the life eternal in 1903, at the age of seventy-two years, and Mr. Ryan died in 1905, at the venerable age of eighty-four years.

Doctor Ryan was reared to the sturdy discipline of the home farm and profited duly by the advantages afforded in the excellent public schools of his native state. In preparation for the profession of his choice he entered the Chicago College of Dental Surgery, in which institution he was graduated as a member of the class of 1895 and from which he received his well earned degree of Doctor of Dental Surgery. After his graduation he was engaged in the practice of his profession at Marion, Waupaca County, Wisconsin, until 1906, when he came to Oklahoma Territory and established himself in practice at Beggs, Okmulgee County, where, as previously stated, he continued his professional endeavors until his election to his present office, in 1912.

In politics Doctor Ryan accords unwavering allegiance to the democratic party and he has been one of its influential representatives in Okmulgee County. He was reared in the faith of the Catholic Church, of which he and his wife are communicants, and he is affiliated with the Knights of Columbus, the Benevolent and Protective Order of Elks and the Modern Woodmen of America.

In the year 1900 was solemnized the marriage of Doctor Ryan to Miss Anna Laura Donahue, who likewise was born and reared in Wisconsin, a daughter of Michael Donahue. The six children of this union are: Clement, Lucile, Martin, Jr., Earl, Carl and Mary.

R. B. F. HUMMER. The popular and energetic young city attorney of Henryetta, R. B. F. Hummer, has won his way to his present position and standing entirely through the medium of his own abilities and efforts. His career is notably illustrative of the opportunities offered by Oklahoma for advancement to the young and energetic men of other sections of the country, who are possessed of the ambition, initiative, determination and ability to win. He is a native of Pennsylvania, and was born at Penbrook, near the City of Harrisburg, Dauphin County, January 21, 1886, his parents being John W. and Alma (Yorty) Hummer, natives of Pennsylvania and still residents of Penbrook, where Mr. Hummer is engaged in business as a painting contractor. There were four sons and one daughter in the family.

After attending the public schools of Penbrook, R. B. F. Hummer went to the state normal school, at Millersville, Pennsylvania, and was graduated therefrom in 1909. Both before and after graduation he had engaged in teaching school, in order to pay his way through school, and in the meantime devoted his leisure hours to the study of law, having decided upon a career in that difficult profession. Eventually Mr. Hummer entered the law school of Georgetown University, at Washington, D. C., where he received the degree of Bachelor of Laws, in June, 1913. Not long thereafter he determined upon Oklahoma as the best field for the display of his abilities, and accordingly came to this state and in December, 1913, took the examination for admission to the bar. He passed second in the class of seventy-five applicants, being beaten for first place by H. H. Hagan, now of Oklahoma City, a former classmate at the Georgetown University Law School. Admitted to the bar at that time, Mr. Hummer formed a partnership with R. E. Simpson, the firm of Simpson & Hummer continuing in existence until the senior partner was elected county attorney, when he was forced to retire from the concern in order to give all his attention to the duties of his office. Mr. Hummer has since practiced alone and has been identified with much of the important litigation that has come before the courts in recent years. In the spring of 1915 he came before the people of Henryetta as the democratic candidate for the office of city attorney and was elected by a handsome majority, for a term of two years. His conduct in that office has shown that he possesses high executive talents. Mr. Hummer is secretary of the Roosterfood Oil Company of Henryetta, and is counsel for the Henryetta, Oklahoma & Western Railroad, the new electric transportation line which will connect all the towns of this thriving and prosperous mining community. He has always been a stanch and unswerving democrat and at this time stands high in the councils of his party in Okmulgee County. While he is a Lutheran in religious faith, owing to the fact that there is no church of that denomination at Henryetta, he is active in the Baptist Church and especially so in the Sunday school, in which he teaches a class of young men. Fraternally he is a thirty-second degree, Scottish Rite Mason and Shriner, a member of the Independent Order of Odd Fellows, secretary of the Loyal Order of the Moose, an Eagle at Henryetta, and a member of the Junior Order of American Mechanics at Penbrook, Pennsylvania. He is also a member of the Oklahoma Bar Association. Mr. Hummer is unmarried and one of the most popular young men in social circles of Henryetta.

In speaking of Mr. Hummer a contemporary newspaper recently said: "The voters of Henryetta have seen demonstrated in the official acts of our city attorney, R. B. F. Hummer, the wisdom they displayed in selecting Mr. Hummer for this position of trust and honor. Mr. Hummer's name is no misnomer, for in his official and private actions he is regarded as one of the hustlers. A man that to be contented must be occupied in some work or accomplishment. R. B. F. Hummer previous to his accepting the position of city attorney was recognized as one of the foremost successful young lawyers of this district, being of a studious nature, Mr. Hummer was always prepared when making a court appearance with the law and evidence in any way bearing upon an action in which he was interested. He is one of the attorneys who never failed in the service rendered a client to give them adequate service and sufficient study so that they had the advantage of a full knowledge of the law in every case undertaken by him.

"Mr. Hummer's acts as city attorney have added to his laurels as a successful practicing lawyer. He has contributed no little in his official position toward compelling a respect on the part of the criminally inclined to a due respect of the law, and in prosecuting the city cases he has shown himself a man and an attorney above reproach, being no respecter of classes. We unhesitatingly commend Mr. Hummer to our readers both as an official and an attorney, and close this short review with a hearty wish for his advancement and a long continuance of our present relations."

CHARLES K. CARY. Something like thirteen years of experience in the teaching profession was Charles K. Cary's before he lent his attention to the study of law. Such an experience is, of its very nature, bound to add something of value to the equipment of a conscientious man, and Mr. Cary may truthfully be said to have been the recipient of every benefit that could accrue to him in those years of faithful work. He began in 1888 with a country school under his guidance. His last connection with the profession was in 1901, when he concluded a four years term of service in the office of county superintendent of schools of Dewey County.

Mr. Cary was born in Livingston County, Missouri, on March 9, 1870, and is the son of Edward G. Cary, who was born in Northeastern Ohio, in the year 1846, and who died in the vicinity of Kanima, Haskell County, Oklahoma, in 1908.

Edward G. Cary was a preacher in the Methodist Episcopal Church for many years. As a boy he did not receive many advantages in an educational way, but he had a good home and his mother taught him much that could never be learned of books or schoolmasters. When he was a boy of about eight years the family moved to Iowa, locating in Decatur County, and there Mr. Cary lived for many years thereafter. In 1868 he moved with his family to Missouri, finally locating in Livingston County, where the subject of this sketch was born. He returned to Iowa in the fall of 1873, but two years later removed to Washington County, Kansas, for the purpose of entering government land. It was here that he entered the ministry, later becoming a member of the Northwest Kansas Conference of the Methodist Episcopal Church.

For many years he was a pioneer circuit rider of that part of the state, occupying the pulpit in many a rude hamlet which has since grown to be a thriving city. He later removed to Arkansas and still later to Haskell County, Oklahoma, where his death occurred in 1908. The many moves made by Reverend Cary was largely the result of the policy of his church, which for many years opposed long terms as pastor in one place.

Rev. Mr. Cary was a veteran of the Civil war, having served a year and a half in the Third Iowa Cavalry. He was in after years prominently identified with the Grand Army of the Republic. In 1866 he married Rebecca J. Exley, a native daughter of Iowa, born there in 1848. She survives him, and is now living in Smith County, Kansas.

To these worthy people were born seven children, briefly mentioned as follows: Ralph C., the oldest, is a resident of Western Nebraska. He is station agent for his town, and is also a farming man of some prominence in his community and the publisher of a thriving newspaper. The second child was Charles K., mentioned in greater detail in later paragraphs. John E. lives at Laramie, Wyoming. Bertha married John A. Fay, a clerk in the United States army, and they are now in Seattle, Washington, where Mr. Fay's regiment is stationed. Lillian Grace married John Oliver, and they live on his ranch in Western Nebraska. Leonard B. is a copper miner and lives at Bisbee, Arizona. The seventh and youngest child is Lila N., who married William H. Foster, a farming man, and they live in Smith County, Kansas.

Charles K. Cary was privileged to attend the country schools in Northern Kansas up to the age of seventeen, and in 1888 he began to teach school in his district. He was so occupied until 1896. Up to the year 1895 he had been filling positions in Northern Kansas, but in that year he came to Dewey County, Oklahoma, to take a homestead. He filed on a government homestead of 160 acres, following which he returned to Kansas and spent another winter in school teaching. Returning to Dewey county late in that year he located in a spot near where the Town of Cestos is now established, teaching a district school during the winter months. Mr. Cary's homestead claim was located ten miles west and three miles north of the Town of Taloga. He was careful to improve it in accordance with the demands of the land office, and in time was able to "prove up" on his claim. Soon after he did so he had an opportunity to sell to advantage, having lived on the place about a year and a half in all.

On January 1, 1897, Mr. Cary was elected to the office of superintendent of schools for Dewey County, and he served four years in that office, retiring on July 1, 1901, with a splendid record for efficiency and service in the office. During that time Mr. Cary succeeded in appreciably raising the standard of the schools of the county, never too high in a new and undeveloped district, and his efforts to that end were ably seconded by all who came.under his jurisdiction. As a builder of educational standards he carried out a work in those four years of service that will have a lasting effect on the public school system of Dewey County.

But it had been Mr. Cary's ambition for years to fit himself for the profession of law, and he felt then that he could not afford to defer his activities in that respect any longer. In 1901 he entered the law department of the University of Kansas, and in June, 1903, was graduated with the degree LL. B. He was admitted to practice in the Supreme Court of Kansas in the same month of his graduation, and almost immediately thereafter established himself in practice in Taloga, where he has since conducted a general civil and criminal practice. He has enjoyed a success that is well worthy of his efforts, and he has a splendid reputation in professional and other circles as a lawyer of ability, and a man with an assured future in his chosen field.

In 1907, at the statehood election, Mr. Cary was elected to the office of county attorney for Dewey County. He was a candidate on the republican ticket, though in earlier years he had given his vote to the populist forces. He served two full terms as county attorney, and retired on January 1, 1913, declining to stand for nomination a third time.

Mr. Cary has never ceased to manifest a healthy interest in local school affairs, and he is now serving the city as a member of its school board, in which position by reason of his former experience in the teaching profession he is able to render invaluable service to his community. He and his family are members of the Methodist Episcopal Church, and he is a member of its board of trustees. He is a Mason, and is a member of Taloga Lodge No. 179, Ancient Free and Accepted Masons, and Taloga Chapter No. 54, Royal Arch Masons.

On April 12, 1894, Mr. Cary was united in marriage in Smith County, Kansas, to Miss Lillian L. Sheddy, daughter of William B. Sheddy, a well known Kansan. One child has been born to the Cary family: Daphne L., now a student in Southwestern College at Winfield, Kansas.

STANLEY CUSHING TYLER. The exceptional climatic conditions in Western Oklahoma have been responsible for the presence here of many of the most energetic and enterprising citizens. Continued ill health back in his old homestead in Massachusetts, made it impossible for Stanley Cushing Tyler to successfully prosecute a business career, when about thirty-seven years ago he came west and became identified with the vast open range of the Texas Panhandle and No Man's Land of what is now the extreme western district of Oklahoma. Here he has since lived, a leading man of affairs, and now president of the First National Bank of Guymon, general manager of the Guymon & Hansford Telephone Company, and president of the Latham Dry Goods Company.

Born June 4, 1857, at Lowell, Massachusetts, Stanley Cushing Tyler is a son of Artemas S. and Angeline (Cushing) Tyler. His father was also a native of Lowell, Massachusetts, born November 2, 1824, of old New England stock, and spent all his active career as a banker. He died at Lowell, Massachusetts, October 14, 1901. He was at one time a member of the Massachusetts General Assembly, having been nominated and elected by both republicans and democrats. His first wife, Miss Angeline Cushing, died in 1860, leaving two children, Stanley Cushing and Artemas Lawrence, the latter now deceased. His second wife was Ethelinda Cushing, a sister of his first wife. There were two daughters by this union, both deceased.

In his native City of Lowell, Stanley C. Tyler was reared, and as his father was a man of affluence and prominence, he had all the advantages of a good home and the best of schooling. He attended the public schools and a private institution, and at the age of seventeen entered his father's bank. Ill health compelled him to make a change of scene and he next tried work in Boston with a wholesale drug house. He was finally obliged to give up employment in the East altogether, and in 1879 he went to Colorado, but in the same year came to the Panhandle of Texas. Here he took up the cattle business on the open range. It will be recalled that thirty-five years ago there was no railroad within hundreds of miles of the Texas Panhandle, the buffalo had not disappeared, and even the Indians were still occasionally troublesome. It was a great lonely land of adventure and hardship, but one eminently calculated to restore vigor to the constitution of any person who could endure its primitive hardships. Mr. Tyler regained not only rugged health but has prosecuted a flourishing business in this locality for many years. He has never given up the cattle industry, though years have compelled him to modify his efforts according to changing conditions. In the early days he raised his stock on the open range, and took it over the old cattle trails across country to Dodge City, Kansas. From the beginning his operations have included portions of No Man's Land, or the old Cimarron District of Oklahoma. He still owns a 5,000 acre ranch in Hansford County, Texas, forty-five miles south of Guymon, Oklahoma.

When the Rock Island Railroad was built through No Man's Land Mr. Tyler turned his attention to the development of Guymon, and local citizens say that he has done as much if not more than any other individual to place that city to the front in the way of business institutions and municipal improvement. He established the First National Bank of Guymon, organized the Guymon & Hansford Telephone Company, and became president and has remained in that office with each of these concerns. Subsequently he organized the Texas County Bank, which he subsequently sold. He also organized the Guymon Electric Light and Power Company, built the ice plant and installed Guymon's system of waterworks.

Mr. Tyler has had a happy home life, and for his wife he returned to his native state and was married at Boston, January 30, 1884, to Miss Mary Elizabeth Ayers of Boston, daughter of Oliver and Mary Ireland (Hooper) Ayers, both of whom were born in the State of New Hampshire of Mayflower stock. Mrs. Tyler was born September 18, 1860, in Boston, and was educated in private schools. To their marriage have been born five children, three daughters and two sons, namely: Mary Angeline, now the wife of Lewis E. Latham of Guymon; Stanley Cushing, Jr., who died in infancy; Ethel Maria,

now the wife of James Rutledge Henderson of Zulu, Texas; Oliver Stanley, now a cattle man in Baca County, Colorado; and Fanny Stanley, the wife of Samuel Alba of Liberal, Kansas.

As a republican Mr. Tyler has interested himself in political affairs, but more particularly with the practical welfare of every community where he has lived. He was at one time elected county judge in Hansford County, Texas. He and his family are members of the Episcopal Church. In Masonry he has attained the thirty-second degree of Scottish Rite, is also a Knight Templar and Shriner, and is district deputy grand master for the First District of Oklahoma, consisting of Beaver, Texas and Cimarron counties.

FRED L. WENNER. It was as a special correspondent for Eastern newspapers that Fred L. Wenner, now secretary-manager of the Guthrie Chamber of Commerce, first became identified with this state. His acquaintance and association with men of affairs in Oklahoma are based upon twenty-five years of experience as a newspaper man, public official, farmer and fruit grower and business man. While he now gives much of his time to the Guthrie Chamber of Commerce, he resides on his fruit farm outside the City of Guthrie and it is probable that he is the only active head of a city commercial organization who makes his home on a farm.

He is of German descent, his paternal grandparents and his maternal great-grandparents having come from Germany. Fred L. Wenner was born at Tiffin, Ohio, January 8, 1865, a son of Henry S. and Sarah (Kaull) Wenner, who went to Ohio from Eastern Pennsylvania. Henry S. Wenner was a pioneer carriage manufacturer in that state.

The morning after he graduated from the high school at Tiffin, Fred L. Wenner started out gathering news as a reporter for the Tiffin Daily Herald. Since then, for a period of more than thirty years, he has never been permanently dissociated from the newspaper profession, and while engaged in that work has also kept up writing for the press and for special purposes.

From reporter he became first city editor of the Tiffin Daily Herald and later filled the same position with the Tiffin Daily Tribune. In 1889 he was sent to Oklahoma as a special correspondent for the New York Herald, Cleveland Press and Chicago Times, and sent back for publication in these metropolitan journals a great many interesting articles that described the early rush and settlement of the original Oklahoma Territory. For a number of years he was employed as special correspondent for the papers just named and for other journals. For a year he was city editor of the Oklahoma Daily State Capital at Guthrie and for two years was editor and owner of the Kingfisher Free Press.

His work as a newspaper man naturally brought him into close touch with public affairs and public men. From 1897 to 1902 Mr. Wenner was secretary to the territorial governors of Oklahoma, serving under Governor C. M. Barnes, Governor William Jenkins and Governor T. B. Ferguson. From 1901 to 1903 he was secretary of the Oklahoma Commission to the St. Louis World's Fair, and from 1903 to 1908 served as secretary to the school land board for the Territory of Oklahoma.

On retiring from public office in 1908 Mr. Wenner moved to a fruit and stock farm, and for the next five years gave all his time to that business. In 1913 he was made secretary and manager of the Guthrie Chamber of Commerce, and now, as already stated, combines the duties of his civic position with his life and activities as a farmer and fruit raiser. For twenty-five years Mr. Wenner has been a director in the Guthrie Building & Loan Association. He is secretary of the Cimarron Valley Fair Association and the Logan County Fruit Growers' Association.

Politically his associations have always been with the republican party and for three years he was assistant secretary of the state committee. He is a Scottish Rite Mason and a member of the Knights of the Maccabees, but has held no chairs in these bodies. He is also a member of the Guthrie Country Club, and has been much interested in church work as a member of the Presbyterian Church, and in 1893 was one of the organizers of the Oklahoma Sunday School Association, in which for fifteen years he filled an office or was a member of the executive committee.

On January 18, 1885, at Bloomville, Ohio, Mr. Wenner married Ammy D. Myers, daughter of Rev. and Mrs. S. P. Myers. Her father, who was formerly a minister of the German Reformed Church, did pastoral work in Ohio, Indiana and Illinois, subsequently affiliated with the Presbyterian Church in Kansas and Oklahoma, and did much important service as a pioneer home missionary in Oklahoma. Mr. and Mrs. Wenner have five children: Robert M., Henry S., David J., Mary E. and Fanny I. All the children are living at home except David J., who is now a student in the State Agricultural and Mechanical College, and Henry S., who in 1912 married Louise Rouse, daughter of Dr. George Rouse of Charleston, South Carolina.

OSCAR C. WYBRANT. The legal fraternity of Woodward County numbers among its most able and thorough members Oscar C. Wybrant, ex-county attorney and the representative of large and important interests. Mr. Wybrant was born August 4, 1870, in a log house on a farm in Ralls County, Missouri, and is a son of William and Eliza (Heskett) Wybrant.

William Wybrant was born August 13, 1840, in Noble County, Ohio, a son of Hugh and Elmira Wybrant, the former a native of Scotland and the latter of Ireland. William Wybrant was reared on a farm in Ohio, and was engaged in farming when the Civil war broke out. He enlisted in an Ohio regiment of volunteers and served as a wagonmaster in the forces of General Thomas, and when the war was over returned to his Ohio home. In 1867 he was married in Ohio, and in that same year removed to Ralls County, Missouri, where he followed agricultural pursuits until 1903, then coming to Oklahoma and locating on Government land in Ellis County. His death occurred April 23, 1905. Mrs. Wybrant was born June 2, 1840, in Noble County, Ohio, a daughter of John B. Heskett, a native of Virginia. Her mother, who bore the maiden name of Cople, was born in Delaware, her parents being natives of the Netherlands. There were four sons and two daughters in the family, of whom two sons and one daughter died in infancy, while those surviving are: Oscar C.; Roy Cople, born September 18, 1878, a farmer of Ellis County, Oklahoma, married in 1906 Miss Minnie Whitehurst and has two children,—Paul and Fern; and Lucy, born October 9, 1880, was married in 1904 to Edward Bondurant, and has one child,—Viola.

After attending the public schools of Ralls County, Oscar C. Wybrant took a course in the Chillicothe (Missouri) Normal School, and at the age of seventeen years began teaching. His career as an educator covered a period of nine years, during which time he applied himself to the study of law, and in 1900 he was admitted to practice in the courts of Ralls County, Missouri. He came to Oklahoma in 1902, locating at Woodward, and here he has since built up a large and representative professional business, practicing in all the courts. In 1910 he was elected county attorney of Woodward County, on the law enforcement ticket, and his services during his first term were so satisfactory that he was re-elected to succeed himself in 1912, serving in all four years, with an excellent record for efficient performance of duty. Mr. Wybrant is a republican. He has served as a member of the school board, and at all times has been eager to contribute his abilities to the advancement of beneficial measures. He has been active also in the Christian Church, of which he and his family are members, and at present is superintendent of the Sunday school.

Mr. Wybrant was married June 16, 1903, at Mutual, Oklahoma, to Miss Margaret Frankie Roberts, who was born April 4, 1876, in Hardin County, Kentucky, the birthplace of Abraham Lincoln, daughter of David R. Roberts, a full review of whose life will be found on another page of this work in the sketch of Ed S. Roberts. David R. Roberts moved to Kansas in 1884 and to Mutual, Oklahoma, in 1894, and passed away at the latter place April 13, 1905. Mrs. Wybrant was one of the pioneer school teachers of Woodward County, and for ten years taught in the log schoolhouses which were the forerunners of Oklahoma's present excellent educational institutions. A woman of many attainments and accomplishments, she still continues active in educational, social and religious work, and was one of the organizers of the first church in Woodward County outside of those located in the towns. Mr. and Mrs. Wybrant are the parents of one daughter: Alma Joy, born at Woodward, March 25, 1904.

WILLIAM BUCK of Wetumka is one of the most highly successful fullblood Indians in Hughes County. He has spent his entire life in the old Creek Nation, and though he was twenty years of age before he could speak the English language, he has exercised such foresight and energy in managing his affairs that he is now one of the wealthy men of the county, and has made it all in farming and in judicial handling of real estate.

Mr. Buck is now about thirty-six years of age. He was born half a mile west of the present site of Wetumka, and his Indian name is Yekiche. His parents Daniel and Mary (Poyarfe) Buck were both born in the Creek Nation, were fullbloods, and neither could speak the English language as long as they lived. Both died on the farm where their son William was born, and the father passed away November 8, 1915, at the age of seventy-four, having spent his active career as a farmer and stock raiser. Their four children were: Joseph, now deceased; Tony, deceased; Roley, who gained his education in the Haskell Institute at Lawrence Kansas; and William.

William Buck as a boy attended the local schools, and finished his education in the boarding schools at Wetumka and Eufaula. He gave up his schooling as soon as he had learned to speak the English language and he soon afterwards started in business for himself as a farmer and real estate man. Mr. Buck now owns about 3,400 acres in the Creek Nation, and operates it all under his direct management. His prosperity is also represented by one of the finest homes of Wetumka, a residence which he built in 1913.

For a number of years before statehood he was a member of the Creek Council, and as a citizen of Oklahoma he votes the republican ticket and is alive and public spirited in relation to all public affairs. He is affiliated with the Woodmen of the World.

In 1907 Mr. Buck married Miss Lizzie Tiger, who was also born in the Creek Nation. They have two children: Lonnie, and Sapho, who died in 1909.

LEE DORROH, M. D. The quality of large-mindedness and resource required of the young man who would succeed in any of the learned professions in these days of severe competition and strenuous effort seems to be an integral part of the equipment of Dr. Lee Dorroh, the pioneer physician of Hammon, whence he came in April, 1909, shortly after the founding of the town. Doctor Dorroh was born at Fredonia, Caldwell County, Kentucky, June 28, 1872, and is a son of William W. and Mary (Easley) Dorroh. The family was founded in America by the great-grandfather of the doctor, who spelled his name O'Dorroh, a native of Ireland, who settled in North Carolina about the time of the war of the Revolution.

William W. Dorroh was born at Fredonia, Kentucky, February 22, 1827, and in 1875 removed to within four miles of Princeton, the county seat of Caldwell County, Kentucky, where he passed the remaining years of his life as a farmer and stock raiser and died in September, 1904. He was a staunch democrat and a consistent member of the Baptist Church. Mrs. Dorroh was born in Virginia, in 1830, and when nine years of age was taken by her parents to Fredonia, Kentucky, where she was reared, educated and married. She died at Princeton, in February, 1891. There were six children in the family, namely: Bobbie, who became the wife of Charles W. Guess, a farmer of Princeton, Kentucky; Frankie, who is the wife of J. J. Rorer, a farmer of Fredonia; William T., who is engaged in farming in Caldwell County; Annie, who is the wife of W. T. Hurst, a carpenter and mechanic of Hopkinsville, Kentucky; Dr. Henry C., a practicing physician and surgeon of Hammon, and graduate of the Louisville (Kentucky) Medical College, a sketch of whose career appears elsewhere in this work; and Doctor Lee, of this review.

Lee Dorroh grew up in the vicinity of Princeton, Kentucky, where he attended the district schools, and subsequently finished the teachers' course. In 1896, 1897 and 1898 he attended Bowling Green (Kentucky) Normal School, from which he was graduated in the latter year with the degree of Bachelor of Sciences, and in the meantime, in 1895, had become principal of schools of Caldwell County, acting in that capacity six months of each year until 1899. In the spring of 1899 Doctor Dorroh went to Angels Camp, California, where he was employed in the mining industry in connection with a quartz mill at that place, and continued to be thus engaged until January, 1902, when he began his medical studies as a student at the Louisville Hospital College of Medicine, at Louisville, Kentucky. Graduated from that institution in the class of 1906, with the degree of Doctor of Medicine, he first practiced for eighteen months at Fredonia, Kentucky, and then returned to Angels Camp, California, where he took charge of the hospital as surgeon for the Mica Mining Company for one year. In April, 1909, Doctor Dorroh came to Hammon, Oklahoma, shortly after the founding of the town, and here has carried on a general medical and surgical practice, his offices being located on Main Street. Since 1910 he has been physician for the Red Moon Indian Agency, and is also local surgeon for the Clinton, Oklahoma & Western Railway. His professional connections include membership in the Roger Mills County Medical Society, the Southwestern Medical Society, the Oklahoma Medical Society and the American Medical Association. He is the recipient of a patronage as financially remunerative as it is intellectually satisfying and encouraging, and notwithstanding his well known caution and respect for tradition is not afraid of untrod paths or independent, individual effort. Doctor Dorroh has interested himself variously in enterprises of a business nature and is vice president and a director of the Farmers National Bank of Ham-

George Riley Hall

The boy is Hugh, and the girl is Rebecca Kathryn who was the actual inspiration for the line "Here's to the daughters, as fair as the dawn." She is, to the author, the real Oklahoma "daughter" since she is his only daughter.

mon. A democrat in politics, he takes a lively interest in civic affairs, and has served as health officer, and is now a member of the school board. Fraternally, he belongs to Hammon Lodge No. 435, Ancient Free and Accepted Masons, of which he is treasurer.

Doctor Dorroh was married in October, 1906, at Bowling Green, Kentucky, to Miss Ophelia Alvis, daughter of Asa and Mabel Alvis, the former of whom, a farmer, is now deceased, while the latter still survives and resides at Salem, Kentucky. Doctor and Mrs. Dorroh have two children: Thelma Lee, born April 28, 1909; and Louise Camille, born December 14, 1910.

GEORGE RILEY HALL. About a year before the original Oklahoma opening there came into Indian Territory a green country boy in search of adventure and fortune. So far as known that kind of fortune represented by heaps of gilt-edged bank stock and securities has never been accumulated by George Riley Hall. He is nevertheless a very fortunate man, fortunate in his talents and attainments, in his long and varied experience, and in the warm and hearty friendship of many men whom it is an honor to know.

He has found in Oklahoma another resource than material wealth. This fortune is best described in words of his own, a poem known as "Land of My Dreaming," which has brought him recognition, not only in his home state, but throughout the country as a home-made poet with a gift of language and picturesque ideas such as men never acquire from books, but only from real life. It is a poem that has been widely read and frequently published, but it will not be superfluous to include it here:

Land of the mistletoe, smiling in splendor
Out from the borderland, mystic and old,
Sweet are the memories, precious and tender,
Linked with thy summers of azure and gold.

O! Oklahoma, fair land of my dreaming,
Land of the lover, the loved and the lost;
Cherish thy legends with tragedy teeming,
Legends where love reckoned not of the cost.

Land of Sequoyah, my heart's in thy keeping,
O, Tulledega, how can I forget!
Calm are thy vales where the silences sleeping,
Wake into melodies, tinged with regret.

Let the deep chorus of life's music throbbing,
Swell to full harmony born of the years;
Or for the loved and lost, tenderly sobbing,
Drop to that cadence that whispers of tears.

Land of the mistletoe, here's to thy glory!
Here's to thy daughters, as fair as the dawn!
Here's to thy pioneer sons, in whose story
Valor and love shall live endlessly on!

George Riley Hall was born at Rolla, Missouri, February 1, 1865, a son of George Riley and Rebecca (Reece) Hall. His mother was a daughter of Rev. Dr. Sherwood Reece of Tennessee, who moved into Southwest Missouri in 1851 and located in Lawrence County, where he continued his professional work as a Baptist clergyman and physician. Mr. Hall's grandfather, John Hall, was a native of Kentucky and moved to Sarcoxie, Missouri, also about 1851. George R. Hall, Sr., entered the Union army in the fall of 1864 as a member of Company C, Forty-eighth Missouri Infantry, served until the close of the struggle and came out of the army so broken in health that he soon afterwards died. He and his wife were married in Missouri in 1854 and she died in 1888. George R. Hall was a mechanic and farmer and had considerable artistic talent which came down to his son. Of the six children there are three now living, George R. and two daughters who live in Texas.

George Riley Hall had about three terms of district schooling. He is really self educated, and by much application to those lessons found in the course of his experience has attained a degree of culture such as many men with college degrees are not acquainted with. He became dependent upon his own exertions after his father's death, and after the death of his mother he and his brother, Samuel J., the latter now deceased, came into Indian Territory in 1888. He stopped on the Canadian River, near Eufaula, and for a time tried cotton raising, but without success. In the fall of 1890 he was appointed teacher in one of the neighborhood Indian schools, near the present site of Henryetta, having about a dozen wild Indian children under his supervision. He taught in neighborhood schools until 1895, and thereafter until 1900 was employed in the boarding and academic institutions among the Indians, and in 1897 became president of the Creek National Teachers' Normal School, in which he had previously served as vice president. This high position in the educational affairs of Indian Territory was a remarkable record for one who had not the advantages of liberal education, and had come here without special recommendations as a teacher and with practically no friends or other influence to promote him on his career. Mr. Hall, while teaching, acquired a considerable knowledge of the Creek language and there is perhaps no man in Eastern Oklahoma more favorably known among the Indians of the older generation.

On leaving the schoolroom in 1900 Mr. Hall leased a farm and for a time was actively identified with agriculture in Okmulgee County. Then, in 1902, he established the Free Lance at Henryetta, which is the oldest newspaper in the town and has become both a daily and weekly. He has published it continuously since then and has kept his home and plant on the same lot, at 211 South Fifth Street, one block south of Main Street. He conducts it as a republican paper, and in fourteen years he has made the Free Lance one of the most influential organs of public opinion in Eastern Oklahoma. He has never had the backing of wealthy men in this enterprise, and has always fought his own financial battles. He has conducted the Free Lance remarkably clean, and it has always stood high in the esteem of the other papers of the state.

Ever since coming to Indian Territory Mr. Hall has been a writer of poetry, and it was in 1906 that he produced the charming verses above quoted. This poem was widely published through the Associated Press, largely through the influence of Mr. Hall's friend, Alexander Posey. A great many favorable comments were passed upon the verses by papers throughout the United States. Mr. Hall is a natural poet and has found in literature and music his most satisfying pursuit. A few months ago he bought ten acres in the heart of the beautiful Tulledegan hills on the shore of the North Canadian River, and this place he has improved for a summer home and there he delights in the beauties of landscape and finds his greatest inspiration for writing.

In January, 1902, he married Miss Kathryn Harris of Fayetteville, Arkansas. She was a teacher in the Indian schools up to the time of her marriage. It is in his home and with his family that Mr. Hall spends all his spare time, and it may be truely said of him that he is in love with his family. He and his wife have four children. Rebecca Kathryn was the actual inspiration of the line above quoted, "Here's to thy daughters as fair as dawn," and she is to the author the real "Oklahoma daughter," since she is his only daughter. The three sons are: George Milton, who died at the age of seven weeks; Hugh; and Lawrence.

As a republican Mr. Hall served two terms as county chairman of the Republican Central Committee, and has also been active in state politics. He is past master and charter member of Tulledegan Lodge No. 201, Ancient, Free and Accepted Masons, at Henryetta, and he gave the name to this lodge in honor of the beautiful place which he had selected for his own summer home. He is also a Knight Templar and Shriner and he and his wife are members of the Christian Church. Mr. Hall is also known as an unerring marksman and "sure shot" with the rifle. Though he has spent more than a quarter of a century in the Indian Territory District of Oklahoma, and was here in the time marked by many scenes of violence and when "gun toting" was a regular custom, it has been his good fortune never to have his own hand stained by the shedding of human blood. He is a man strong, virile and wholesome, temperate in all his habits, and with all his varied experience has not a gray hair in his head.

HARRY LEE FOGG. The first county judge of Canadian County after statehood was Harry Lee Fogg. At the time of his election he was regarded as one of the rising young attorneys of the El Reno bar, and his position in the law is now regarded as one the highest in Western Oklahoma. While his chief ambition has always been within the limits of his profession, Judge Fogg has the qualities of a leader of men, and is prominent in the councils of the democratic party in the state.

Harry Lee Fogg is a native of Kentucky, born at Mt. Sterling, September 15, 1878, a son of Thomas L. and Kitty (Gillespie) Fogg. Both his parents were Kentuckians by birth and have spent their lives in that state. They now live in Montgomery County, where Thomas L. Fogg is still active as a farmer.

Judge Fogg grew up on a farm, received his early training in private schools, and before the completion of his literary education entered a law office at Mt. Sterling, where he trained himself in the law. He was admitted to the Kentucky bar in 1901 when twenty-three years of age.

His career as a practicing lawyer has all been passed at El Reno, where his services have been retained in some of the very important litigation before the local courts. In the office of county judge of Canadian County Mr. Fogg served with ability for three years. He has been much interested in democratic politics ever since coming to Oklahoma, and is now serving his second term as a member of the State Democratic Central Committee. His fraternal associations are with the Masonic Order and the Benevolent and Protective Order of Elks and his religious faith is that of the Christian Church.

In 1905 Judge Fogg was married at El Reno to Miss Blanche Fryberger, daughter of W. E. and Cora B. Fryberger. They are the parents of two children: William Lee and Rupert Metcalfe Fogg.

EDWIN FISHBACK. Among the older business men of Bartlesville mention should be made of Edwin Fishback, whose associations with that then small city began in 1904, and who for a number of years has been at the head of a large and prospering business as a plumbing contractor. Mr. Fishback is well known in Washington County, and his reputation for business ability and integrity is unassailable.

Born at Hall in Morgan County, Indiana, September 27, 1881, Edwin Fishback is a son of Edwin and Nancy Jane (Landfair) Fishback. His father was born in Taylorville, Kentucky, and his mother in Ohio, and they were married in Morgan County, Indiana. His father grew up in Kentucky and at the age of twenty-three removed to Indiana, and was a farmer in that state until his death in 1881. The widowed mother, left with two children, somewhat later married James A. Long, and they removed to Labette County, Kansas, when Edwin Fishback was ten years of age. Mr. Long died in 1913, and Mrs. Long is still living. Edwin Fishback has a brother Charles F., who lives at Edna, Kansas, and by the Long marriage there is a son A. L. of Edna.

Mr. Fishback lived with his mother until eleven years ago. He was graduated from the Labette County High School in 1903, and for a year found employment at Wichita, Kansas, with a hydro-carbon light company. In December, 1904, he arrived in Bartlesville, and the next three years were spent as a plumbing employe of W. T. Berentz. Since then he has been in independent work as a plumbing contractor and has executed some of the largest contracts installed in Washington County. He knows his trade in all its details and has a record of reliable and proficient performance which brings him all the business he and several employes can attend to. In 1911 Mr. Fishback built his shop on Chickasaw Avenue, and in 1913 erected a comfortable home on the same avenue.

In politics he is a republican, is a member of the Baptist Church, and is affiliated with the Masonic Order, the Independent Order of Odd Fellows and the Knights of Pythias. On December 28, 1908, he married Mrs. Jessie (Wood) Upham, widow of Anthony F. Upham, who by her first marriage has a son Stanley.

WILLIAM N. FAYANT. Probably no one citizen has exercised a more potent influence in the upbuilding of the little community of Dustin in Hughes County than William N. Fayant. Mr. Fayant came to Oklahoma about fifteen years ago after a broad and successful experience in business and civic life in South Dakota. He came South in search of a milder climate and was at El Reno in 1901 at the opening for settlement of the southwestern part of the present state.

In the next year he located at Spokogee, now Dustin, in Hughes County when that town was started and has participated actively in every enterprise of importance there since. His main business, to which he was trained in early youth, has been the cattle industry and the retail meat business. He has become extensively known all over this section of the state as a cattle man, both buying and shipping, and at the present time he has 200 head of stock, and at different times has owned much larger herds.

An important feature of his Oklahoma residence has been his public service in behalf of his home town. He was the first mayor of Dustin, and held the office three consecutive terms. He also organized the first school board, was elected its president, and was kept at the head of local school affairs until 1914, when he had decided that he had served long enough and that others should assume his share of the responsibilities. After retiring from the school board he was again elected mayor, but after one term declined further honors in that position. Politically Mr. Fayant is a democrat. The first state legislature appointed him one of the county commissioners of Hughes County, and he was one of the three first selected to that office and became chairman of the board, and was appointed by Governor Haskell to the first county election board and served as its president four years. This and nearly every other political honor came unsolicited. A few years ago Governor Cruce appointed him a delegate to the Southern Commercial Congress.

William N. Fayant was born at Tamaqua in Schuylkill County, Pennsylvania, December 10, 1850, a son of Bartoloma and Elizabeth (Baker) Fayant. His father was born in Alsace, France, in 1805, while the mother was born near the River Rhine in Germany in 1812. Both came when young to the United States during the '30s, and in 1839 they were married in Pennsylvania. In 1856 the family moved out to Wisconsin, and the father died in 1883 and the mother in 1898 at Muscoda, Grand County, Wisconsin. The father was a farmer and stockman, and in Wisconsin established a flourishing meat business which is one of the oldest institutions of its kind in that section of the state and is still conducted by members of the family. In earlier years he was also a contractor for the United States army, furnishing horses chiefly, and that business took him to all parts of the United States and the Territories. He also spent much time in Florida, where some of his children were born. His later years were passed in comparative retirement and ease. His children were: Margaret, wife of John Neff of Muscoda, Wisconsin; Victor, who now lives in Chicago; Josephine, wife of Frank Neff of Muscatine, Iowa; Francis, who was a member of the famous Iron Brigade, Company K, Seventh Wisconsin Regiment, served all through the Civil war, in one battle had a foot shot off and died largely as a result of his wounds two years after the war; Elizabeth, who became the wife of Joseph Seiger of La Crosse, Wisconsin, and both are now deceased; William N.; Mary, who died in 1900 as the wife of Jacob Huppler; and Theo of Iowa Falls, Iowa. Besides those named two other children died in infancy.

William N. Fayant lived with his parents until he was twenty-one years of age, and at that time his father turned over to him the meat business at Muscoda, Wisconsin. A little later when gold was discovered in the Black Hills of the Dakotas Mr. Fayant turned the business over to his brother Victor and went out to seek a fortune in that part of South Dakota. He was a miner there until stricken with the mountain fever, when he returned home, but later he moved out to Huron, South Dakota, and became a pioneer business man, establishing a meat market which he conducted successfully for a number of years. He was also a member of the town council at Huron and acquired a homestead there. In 1881 at Huron, South Dakota, Mr. Fayant married Miss Susie Shirt, who was born in Lancaster, Pennsylvania, in 1854. After his marriage Mr. Fayant continued to live at Huron until 1894, when on account of the cold climate he went South, spent several years at Houston, Texas, and then reached Oklahoma in 1901. During his residence in South Dakota he became well known all over the state not only as a buyer and shipper of cattle, but also in a civic way. He built one of the first houses at Huron, and on coming to Oklahoma he constructed the first stone house at Spokogee, now Dustin, and has since built three other stone business blocks on Main Street, and still owns them. He also has several farms near Dustin, owning outright 700 acres and having about 1,000 acres under lease. Fraternally he is affiliated with the Independent Order of Odd Fellows and his church is the Catholic.

Mr. and Mrs. Fayant have two children: Joseph W. who is still at home, and Benjamin, who died at the age of seventeen while a student in St. Joseph College at Muskogee. Mr. Fayant now has a partner in his local meat business at Dustin, Samuel A. Walker, and the firm is known as Fayant & Walker.

ALBERT A. BALLARD. About thirteen years ago Albert A. Ballard first identified himself with the newspaper business. Since that time he has advanced through all the stages from general office man in a business with which he was unfamiliar to his present post of publisher and editor of the leading newspaper of his town—the Seiling Messenger. Many vicissitudes beset his path in the years he has devoted to the upbuilding of his present enterprise, but he has won through them all in a manner that speaks of a sturdiness of character and an unswerving purpose, without which few really great successes have ever been realized.

Mr. Ballard was born in Barnard, Lincoln County, Kansas, on September 8, 1880, and he is the son of Isaac A. and Dicy A. (Beement) Ballard. The father was born in March, 1840, in Pulaski County, Kentucky. The mother, too, was a native daughter of the same place, and she was born on September 8, 1844.

The Ballard family is one that was established in Colonial days in old New York, and one line of the family pioneered it to Kentucky in the early days of settlement there. They established homes and became prominent in the affairs of the state, accumulated wealth and enjoyed a prosperity that is oft-times the portion of pioneer families. The Beements, too, were early settlers in New York, and with the Ballards settled in Kentucky.

After the marriage of Isaac A. Ballard to Dicy Beement, in Pulaski County, Kentucky, they moved to Illinois, and thence to Saline County, Kansas. In 1871, still unsettled, they went to Lincoln County, Kansas, and it was there the subject was born. The family continued in residence there for some years, and it was not until September 27, 1897, that they moved to Oklahoma, settling in Dewey County. Mr. Ballard, though well advanced in years, was a pioneer to the Dewey County district in the truest sense of the word, and he helped to establish the Town of Beement, and was largely instrumental in getting the postoffice for that town. Today he has his home five miles west of the Town of Cestos, on the site of the former Beement. He has a homestead farm, and though now in the seventy-eighth year of his life, he is active and energetic, and farms forty acres of his tract, which comprises the regular homestead allotment of 160 acres.

The children of Mr. and Mrs. Ballard were seven in number, and may be mentioned briefly at this point. The eldest, Sarah M., is deceased. She married O. B. Dryden, a farmer, who survives her and lives at Vici, Oklahoma. Martin O. is a farmer and lives at Silt, Colorado. The next-two, Edwin and Alfred, died young. The fifth child is Albert A., of this review. Kittie died in Fresno, California, September 21, 1914. She was the wife of John B. Vincent, a grocer now in business in Oakland, California. Grover C., a farmer and rural mail carrier, is located at Reason, Oklahoma.

Albert A. Ballard attended the country schools of Barnard, Lincoln County, Kansas, up to the age of sixteen years. His educational advantages, it will be seen, were not of the best, for the district school in any locality is apt to lack much that is desirable in the training of youth, and when he had finished that schooling he turned his attention to the farm, and for six years applied himself diligently to farm work under his father's direction. He was, therefore, twenty-two years old when he made his first attempt at anything beyond farm work, and he made the attempt in the office of a Geary, Oklahoma, publication. That was in November, 1902. In February, 1903, he went to Seiling, Oklahoma, where he soon became manager of the old Seiling Guide. He was in that position for two years, during which time W. G. Smith was editor of the paper. Mr. Ballard then went to Hitchcock and was employed in an important capacity on the Hitchcock Vanguard for a year. In February, 1906, the town was wiped out by a fire. Mr. Ballard saved enough equipment from the ruins of the plant to make it possible to bring out a news sheet on schedule, but the following month moved the remains of the plant to Seiling and joined in the work of producing the Seiling Messenger. The work was successful, but three years later it seemed expedient to consolidate with the Seiling Guide, the name of Messenger being retained, and Mr. Ballard is now editor and publisher of the paper.

He is the owner of the plant on Main Street, and also has a nice residence property in the town. The Messenger is an independent sheet, voicing no political sentiment, and circulates widely in Dewey and surrounding counties, with a good sized foreign list as well. It serves well the best interests of Seiling and its people, and is a clean, well managed and healthy publication, wielding an influence for good in those communities where it circulates.

Mr. Ballard is an independent republican. He has served as town clerk here, and has also been a member of the local school board. He is a member of the Methodist Episcopal Church, and is superintendent of its Sunday School. He is affiliated with the Oklahoma Press Association, and fraternally is identified with the Modern Woodmen of America, being clerk of Seiling Lodge No. 7345.

On May 7, 1901, Mr. Ballard was married in Woodward, Oklahoma, to Miss Sarah E. Hatfield, daughter of J. A. Hatfield, a well known contractor and builder in Bennington, Kansas. Mr. and Mrs. Ballard have one child, Sibyl Berenice, born October 3, 1907, and now attending the local schools.

PROF. JEFFERSON D. CAMPBELL. A man of fine intellectual attainments and of thorough executive ability, Professor Campbell has been a resident of Oklahoma since 1902. His career for many years has been identified with educational affairs, and to his work in Oklahoma he brought a long experience both as an educator and public official in his native State of Missouri. He has taught and supervised the instruction of a host of young people, many of whom have now grown to manhood and womanhood, and his position as an Oklahoma educator at the present time is in the important and exacting office of county superintendent of schools in Okmulgee County. He is now serving his second term and his administration has been characterized by a general raising of the standards of the schools of the county and the working out of effective systems for unity and symmetry in the school service.

Born near Paris, Monroe County, Missouri, January 11, 1863, Professor Campbell is a son of Morton and Mary (Northern) Campbell, both of whom were born and reared in Kentucky, where they married. They then came to Missouri, and the mother died there in 1874 when Professor Campbell was about eleven years old. His father, who died in 1885, had a long and unusually interesting career. He was one of the adventurous argonauts who crossed the plains and became pioneers in the gold fields in California in 1849. After a year he returned home, but later made a second trip to California by way of the Isthmus of Panama. Prior to that he had served in the Mexican war and for four years was in the Confederate army during the Civil war, becoming a non-commissioned officer. The papers granting him a Government pension as a veteran of the Mexican war came to him only a few days prior to his death. In a business way he was long numbered among the prosperous agriculturists and stock raisers of Vernon County, Missouri, was influential in community affairs and was an able and high-minded citizen. Politically he was identified with the democratic party and served many years in the office of justice of the peace. Incidentally it should be noted that his brother William was for many years on the bench of the District Court in their native State of Kentucky. Morton Campbell was the father of six sons and three daughters, and of the number three are still living.

After the death of his mother in 1874 the home was broken up, and Professor Campbell spent much of his early youth in the home of a devout English couple. When only twelve years of age he began working on a farm by the month and thereafter not only earned his own living but paid his way through school and college. He attended the public schools of Missouri and in 1892 graduated from the Missouri Normal School at Clarksburg. Later he attended the University of Missouri at Columbia. Thus by his own efforts and in the intervals of farm work and school teaching he gained a liberal education, and has long been recognized for his proficiency as a teacher and his ability to impart to others the knowledge and character which he himself possesses.

For about twenty years he was in successful work as a teacher in his native state, and in him the profession has been dignified and honored. For four years was county superintendent of schools in St. Clair County, Missouri. This and other offices were forced upon him by his friends and his party associates, and for four years he served as county clerk, and for another six years was a member of the county board of education. His service as county clerk of St. Clair County was at a peculiarly interesting period in the local history of that county. In the early days of railroad construction in Missouri, St. Clair County had bonded itself for a large sum to pay for a proposed railroad. The bonds were sold and the promoters of the enterprise used the funds without showing any net results in the way of a railroad, and with a deep sense of indignation at the swindle the people of St. Clair County thereafter persistently refused to pay the county bonds when they became due, and in consequence the county judges had to hold court in concealment, and every judge elected studiously kept out of the way of officers from the United States courts. Professor Campbell was one of such officials, and in those days the county officers held what was called "brush court," and he and the county attorney virtually conducted the entire business of St. Clair County, and with great credit to themselves.

When he came to Oklahoma in 1902 Professor Campbell assumed the position of principal of the high school at Mounds, Creek County. He was also for two years mayor of that town. From there he went to Beggs, in Okmulgee County, and became principal of the high school. His work as an educator in that county continued until 1912, at which time evidence of popular appreciation of his services was shown when he was elected county superintendent of schools. A still stronger testimonial to his ability was given him in 1914 when he was re-elected for a second term of two years. The county will always owe him a debt for the splendid service he has given in upbuilding its school system, which is not excelled by any other county in the state.

Politically Mr. Campbell has always been in line with the principles and policies of the democratic party. He is a member of the Masonic fraternity, and he and his wife are active in the Christian Church. They have a fine family, and move in the best social circles of the county. In 1884 Professor Campbell married Miss Fredonia May Teaney. A native of Tennessee she was a child when her family moved to Missouri, where she was reared and educated, being a daughter of James and Mary (Lambert) Teaney. Mrs. Campbell gave four

years of her early life to the work of the schoolroom. Mr. and Mrs. Campbell have six children: Lena Mabel, James M., Fannie L., William Clyde, Dorothy and Gordon L. Lena Mabel followed the example of her father and mother and was a popular teacher until the age of twenty, and is now the wife of Arthur M. Miller and they reside in Okmulgee County. James M. is serving as deputy county clerk of Okmulgee County, and Fannie L. is also a teacher in the county schools. The younger children are still at home.

FRANK W. BROOKS. The highly successful character of the commission form of government has been due in many cases to the efficient personnel of those selected by the citizens to take charge of their municipal affairs. A case in point is that of Frank W. Brooks, water commissioner of Enid, who, with the mayor and the commissioner of streets and alleys, constitute the governing body of the city. Enid has been under a commission form of government since 1908.

Mr. Brooks was made superintendent of waterworks at Enid April 12, 1907, and had charge of the local water plant as superintendent until his election in April, 1913, as water commissioner. Mr. Brooks has thus had supervision of this important public utility throughout the most important period of its development and extension.

Few cities in the Southwest have a better system of waterworks, either as to source of supply or system of distribution, than Enid. The source of supply is thirty-two deep wells, reaching down below the surface about fifty feet into an apparently inexhaustible underground stream flowing through gravel strata. Each well is connected directly with the main pipe line, leading from two great twin pumps. For 400 feet each way from the engine house the water is carried through a tunnel 5 feet wide and 6½ feet high, 31 feet below the surface. The wells are located 1½ miles northwest of the city. The cost of sinking the wells, constructing the tunnel and installing the engines at the main plant was $40,000.

This is an excellent example of municipal operation and ownership. Every one of the 15,000 inhabitants of Enid has an interest in the waterworks plant. The city was bonded for $240,000 in order to construct and equip the waterworks, and it is claimed that the enterprise is more than worth what it cost. In 1907 there were 431 meters in use, while at the present time the number has increased to 1,831. For the year ending in June, 1914, these consumers paid a total of over $18,000 for water service, and the expenses of running the plant for the same year were over $11,000. Thus the profit over operations was about $6,000, though that was not sufficient to pay the interest on the waterworks bond. The fourteen miles of water mains in 1907 have increased to thirty-one miles. During one year the extensions required twenty-two carloads of pipe. There are 159 fire hydrants, and service for these is supplied free, whereas under private ownership the charge would approximate probably $10 per hydrant. The water department has eight employes, six of them being engineers and firemen, with two others employed in the general water service.

Frank W. Brooks is a native of Ohio, and when nine years of age moved out to Nebraska in 1875 and grew up in what was then a raw western state. His education came from district schools, and his early life was spent on a farm. His first independent enterprise was as a liveryman at York, Nebraska, and for several years he was also a salesman in the hardware and agricultural implement trade. On September 16, 1893, in company with his brother Jerome, Mr. Brooks made the race into the Cherokee Strip. The brothers secured adjoining quarters in section 15, three miles southeast of Enid. Frank W. Brooks lived there and developed a farm until 1905, though for several years his chief business was as traveling salesman. His brother still owns and operates the farm near Enid. Mr. Brooks left the road to assume the superintendency of the waterworks plant at Enid, and his long and thorough experience in that department made his choice for the office of water commissioner one that was based upon the utmost consideration of fitness.

Mr. Brooks was married February 27, 1888, at York, Nebraska, to Miss Annie Bennett, a native of Illinois. They have a family of six children: Clarence L., who is employed by the Alton Mercantile Company at Enid; Lois M., a vocalist at York, Nebraska; Hazel, a stenographer in the Telephone Company at Enid; Laura, a vocal teacher; Bessie, a member of the high school class of 1915 at Enid; and Harold. Mr. Brooks is affiliated with the Independent Order of Odd Fellows and the Modern Woodmen of America, is secretary of the local chapter of the United Commercial Travelers at Enid, is a republican in politics, and a member of the official board of the Methodist Episcopal Church.

CHARLES W. GOREE. The unequivocal verdict of approbation passed upon Mr. Goree in the City and County of Okmulgee is shown forth most conclusively in his incumbency of the office of county clerk and in the fact that he is the only democrat who has been elected to this office in the history of the county. He is one of the appreciative and loyal citizens of Oklahoma, a man of marked public spirit, and is well entitled to specific recognition in this history.

Mr. Goree was born at Lumpkin, Stewart County, Georgia, on the 10th of November, 1867, and is a son of William A. and Louvisa (Hardie) Goree, the former of whom was born in Virginia, of Irish lineage, and the latter of whom was born in Georgia, her ancestry tracing back to staunch English origin. The Goree family was originally established in France, and from that country representatives of the name early immigrated to Ireland, with whose history the name has been identified for many generations. The paternal grandparents of the subject of this review immigrated from the Emerald Isle to the United States and established their home in Virginia, where they passed the residue of their lives.

He whose name initiates this review was a child at the time of his parents' immigration from Georgia to Navarro County, Texas, where he was reared and educated, his father being now a resident of Lubbock, that state, and his mother having died at Chillicothe, Hardeman County, Texas, in August, 1908, at which time she was sixty-seven years of age.

Charles W. Goree attended the public schools of the Lone Star State until he had profited duly by the advantages of the high school, and in the autumn of 1886 he entered the college at Summer Hill, Texas, in which he was graduated as a member of the class of 1890. Thereafter he was for thirteen years an ambitious and successful teacher in the schools of Texas, where he continued to maintain his home until 1904, when he came to Okmulgee County, Oklahoma, where he continued his effective services as a representative of the pedagogic profession for the ensuing four years. Thereafter he was engaged in the grocery business at Okmulgee until the autumn of 1912, when he was elected county clerk. His careful and efficient administration resulted in his re-election in the fall of 1914, and, as previously stated, he has the distinction of being the only democrat elected to this important office in Okmulgee County. In addition to giving most punctilious attention to his official duties Mr. Goree maintains a general supervision of his well improved dairy farm, eligibly situated a short distance west of the city. In honor of his collegiate alma mater he has named this well improved place Summer Hill Dairy. He is affiliated with the Independent Order of Odd Fellows and both he and his wife hold membership in the Baptist Church. Mr. Goree is the eldest in a family of eight children; Texanna, the next in order of birth, is the wife of Rev. John A. Jones, of Chillicothe, Texas; Mrs. Mary Lovett is deceased and is survived by three children; William H. has for the past fifteen years been in the employ of the great meatpacking firm of Armour & Company, at its establishment in the City of Forth Worth, Texas; Roland E. has the active management of the dairy farm of the subject of this sketch; Lena became the wife of Richard Rhyne and was a resident of Alvord, Texas, at the time of her death; Frederick E. has been associated with the building of the Government canal across the Isthmus of Panama, where he still remains in the employ of the Government, as a stenographer; and Orren C. is a resident of the City of Dallas, Texas.

At Corsicana, Texas, on the 10th of June, 1891, was solemnized the marriage of Charles W. Goree to Miss Mary Elizabeth Stroder, who was born and reared in Texas and who was a schoolmate of her husband when they were young. She is a daughter of Alexander and Catherine Stoder, who are still residents of Texas. To Mr. and Mrs. Goree have been born ten children, the first of whom, Katie, died at the age of 2½ years; Gladys is a popular teacher in the schools of Okmulgee County; Iona is deputy in the office of the county treasurer; Mattie and Thomas Bryan are, in 1916, students in the Okmulgee High School; and the younger children of the gracious home circle are Verna, John Gordon, Maggie May, Charles Stroder, and Sidney Frederick.

In 1904 Mr. Hodges came to Oklahoma and here his first service was in connection with a restaurant at Muskogee. He next became a solicitor for the Muskogee Democrat, and he continued his work in this capacity after the consolidation of the paper with the Muskogee Times. Since 1909 he has been manager of the Okmulgee Daily Democrat, and since January, 1915, he has been owner of a half-interest in the large and important publishing business in which his associate is James J. Moroney, of whom specific mention is made on other pages of this work, the firm publishing not only the Okmulgee Daily Democrat but also the Okmulgee Progress, the Mid-Continent Oil and Farm News, and the Morris News, at Morris, Okmulgee County. Mr. Hodges is also the owner of a half-interest in the Wagoner Democrat, published at the county seat of Wagoner County.

Mr. Hodges has been a most enthusiastic worker in behalf of the cause of the democratic party, and, as previously stated, is chairman of its central committee for Okmulgee County. He is affiliated with both the York and Scottish Rite bodies of the Masonic fraternity, and also with the Benevolent and Protective Order of Elks. He and his wife are earnest members of the Methodist Episcopal Church, South, at Okmulgee, and he is serving on its official board.

On the 28th of June, 1909, Mr. Hodges wedded Miss May Stinnett, who was born in Kentucky but reared and educated in Texas and Oklahoma, she being a daughter of P. B. Stinnett, who is still a resident of the Lone Star State. Mr. and Mrs. Hodges have a fine little son, Bert C., Jr.

HON. WILLIAM N. BARRY. One of the very capable members of the House of Representatives in the Fifth Oklahoma Legislature is William N. Barry of Okemah, Okfuskee County. Mr. Barry was elected in 1914 and had previously been closely identified with public affairs in his home county, where he is proprietor of a very successful business, The Okemah Hardware Company. While faithful to his constituency, Mr. Barry has brought a sound business judgment to the work of the Fifth Legislature, and has exercised an important influence on current legislation. In the House in the Fifth Legislature he has served as chairman of Committee on Elections and as a member of committees on public service corporations, municipal corporation, dentistry, enrolled and engrossed bills.

He is one of the younger members of the legislature, but is comparatively an old resident of his section of the state. He was born in Lafayette County, Mississippi, September 9, 1879, a son of Jesse R. and Ellen Elizabeth (Nichols) Barry. His father was born in South Carolina and his mother in Alabama, but they both came to Mississippi as children and in the house where they married they spent the rest of their days. The mother died in Lafayette County, Mississippi, August 12, 1906, at the age of fifty-seven, and the father on December 10, 1914, aged seventy-six. He spent all his active career as a farmer, but during the Civil war he was a private soldier in the Confederate army. He also held the office of county supervisor and exercised considerable influence in local politics. In the family were eight daughters and two sons.

After growing up on the old farm back in Mississippi and gaining a public school education, at the age of twenty he started out to make his fortune in a new country. In 1901 Mr. Barry went to Texas and for a year or so employed his energies on a farm, but in August, 1903, arrived at Okemah, Oklahoma, where he became clerk in a local hardware store and thus learned the business which he has since followed so successfully. From Okemah he went to Paden, another town in Okfuskee County, in 1907, and there engaged in the hardware business with John D. Richards as a partner. On January 1, 1911, he returned to Okemah and has since established and conducted a very large business under the name Okemah Hardware Company.

Always interested in public affairs, he was elected one of the first commissioners of Okfuskee County after statehood, representing District No. 1, and was reelected in 1910. He served two terms, or about five years after statehood. In 1914 he was elected to represent his home county in the House of Representatives.

Mr. Barry is a democrat, a member of the Masonic Order and the Knights of Pythias. On December 9, 1907, he married Eunice I. Busby, who was born in Mississippi and came to Oklahoma with her parents, Mr. and Mrs. J. D. Busby, who located at Okemah about the time the town was founded. To their marriage have been born three children, all of them natives of Okfuskee County. Their names are Eleanor E., Lois I. and William N. Jr.

JUDGE THOMAS LEWIS ROGERS. As the contents of these historical volumes will be esteemed by future generations in proportion as they include within their pages the records of men most closely identified with the old territory and the new state, it is especially suitable to the design of the publication to include a record of the late Thomas Lewis Rogers, who died at his home in Pawhuska, January 1, 1909, at the age of seventy-one years, four months and twenty-one days.

Judge Rogers was prominent both as the descendant of an eminent Cherokee-Osage family and in his own person as a successful farmer and stock raiser. For many years he lived at his home, seven miles southeast of Pawhuska. His relations to the Osage Nation were noteworthy and most commendable to both his head and his heart.

In the preliminary negotiations leading up to the acquirement of a permanent reservation for the Osages, Judge Rogers prominently participated as a member of the Osage council selected to treat with the Government and with the Cherokee Nation for the lands comprising the Osage Nation, as organized in 1872. For several terms he served on the Osage council and for many years was supreme judge of the nation itself. In Masonry he had attained the thirty-second degree, being a member of the Pawnee Chapter and Commandery, Guthrie Consistory and the Oklahoma City Shrine. His home lodge at Pawhuska participated officially in his burial, and his body was also followed to its last resting place by many friends and brothers in the Benevolent and Protective Order of Elks. The following is a tribute paid to him at that time: "He was a firm believer in fraternal orders and longed to see those who were near and dear to him under the benign protection of one of the great fraternal orders. In many ways he was a remarkable man. He was a man of great culture and refinement although reared under adverse circumstances. So genial was his hospitality and so rare his qualities of entertainment that he has often been called 'Prince of the Osages.' His friends were legion, and many a heart saddens at the news of his death. May his like increase; for it may be truly said of him, 'the world is better for his having lived.'"

The family of which Judge Rogers was so worthy a representative was founded in Indian Territory by Captain John Rogers, his grandfather, who came to the Cherokee Nation from his home in Georgia as early as 1829, being a member of what is known as the "Old Settlers," as distinguished from the emigrants who came in the early '30s. With his son, Thomas Lewis Rogers, Sr., he established the first salt industry west of the Mississippi River at the Rogers homestead on Spavinaw Creek. Without tools, machinery or equipment of any kind they dug their wells and built rude but practicable furnaces for boiling the water and extracting salt, selling their product in large quantities throughout Indian Territory, Missouri and Kansas. Among the pioneer enterprises of the Rogers, father and son, in this field was the plant which they established at Grand Saline, which was the forerunner of the extensive industry conducted at that point.

Thomas L. Rogers, Sr., married Ellen Lombard, a woman who was half French and half Osage Indian, and it is through her that Judge Rogers obtained his citizenship in the Osage Nation. Before the Civil war the Rogers homestead on the Spavinaw was a famous resort of the settlers for miles around, good cheer, comfort and old-time southern hospitality abounding in their most typical forms. Especially at Christmas and during the holiday season was the house "wide open" and warm with the best spirit of the day.

This homestead was located about four miles from the confluence of the Spavinaw with the Grand River, in what is now Mayes County, Oklahoma. In that homestead the late Judge Thomas L. Rogers was born, August 11, 1837. At the opening of the Civil war he was in the Confederate service as a member of Company G, commanded by Captain Butler, in General Stan Watie's Cherokee regiment. He spent most of his time as a scout on the frontier of the Indian Territory. He was also engaged in several severe battles, particularly the engagement at Big Cabin. The war so depreciated the value of his homestead and business properties that at the close he found employment as clerk in a large general store, being subsequently engaged in the more lucrative and independent occupation of buying and selling cattle. It is illustrative of the faithful and generous character of the late Judge Rogers that the profits of his business were not selfishly expended upon himself, but went toward the support of his widowed mother and the education of the younger members of the family.

In 1870 he married Miss Nancy Martin, member of one of the most prominent of the Cherokee families. In 1871 he located on the Big Caney, and in 1872 on Bird Creek in the northwestern part of the Cherokee Nation, adjoining the Osage Nation, soon after the lands in that locality were acquired for settlement by the Osages. Previously the lands had been leased from the Indians by white cattle raisers. Judge Rogers lived in that locality for fifteen years, then moved to Pawhuska, where he remained six years, and then went to the home southeast of Pawhuska, where he resided eighteen years, finally returning to Pawhuska a few years before his death. A tract of land southeast of Pawhuska became his regular homestead and remained so for many years and under his industry and skill was rated as one of the finest agricultural and stock farms for miles around. There he erected a splendid stone residence of ten rooms and provided every facility for conducting his large and varied operations. For several years he handled horses and cattle on an extensive scale and though still operating a farm he moved to Pawhuska, where he built another fine modern residence on East Main Street. During his first period of residence in Pawhuska he engaged successfully in general merchandising, at first in partnership with his kinsman, Hon. W. C. Rogers, the noted chief of the Cherokees, and later with John R. Skinner. His service in the negotiations by which the territorial limits of the Osage Nation were determined and the high post he filled in the legislative and judicial affairs of the nation have already been mentioned. Because of such activities his death marked the departure from the world of a man who had demonstrated not only unusual capacity, but the finest and warmest traits of heart and soul.

Mrs. Nancy (Martin) Rogers, his wife, was born on Cabin Creek, Cherokee Nation, October 30, 1848, a daughter of John and Martha (Chambers) Martin. Her father, John Martin, was a native of Georgia, born June 11, 1819, and was one of the emigrants to the Indian country of 1829. Both he and his wife were Indians to about a sixteenth degree. As a citizen of the Cherokee Nation he became one of its prominent men. John Martin's father, Jack Martin, served as first supreme judge of the nation. John Martin was a slave owner before the Civil war and served faithfully and bravely as a Confederate soldier. He died November 20, 1871. The mother of Mrs. Nancy Rogers was born in Georgia, a member of the Cherokee Nation. Her father, Jack Chambers, was of Irish and Cherokee stock, the father being an Irishman and the mother a fullblood Cherokee. The girlhood of Mrs. Rogers was spent in the Cherokee Nation as a daughter of one of its leading and prosperous citizens. After attaining a thorough education in its public schools she completed her schooling at Neosho Academy in Missouri, and was married to Judge Rogers, February 26, 1869.

The four children born to Judge and Mrs. Rogers were: Elnora, who died at the age of four years; Mrs. Bertha Leahy, wife of T. J. Leahy; Mrs. Martha Leahy, wife of William T. Leahy; and Thomas L. Rogers, Jr. Judge Rogers had been married previously in 1862 to Ellen Coody, and the only child of that marriage, Arthur Rogers, died about four years ago in Oklahoma. Mrs. Judge Rogers was married September 18, 1915, to D. A. Ware. Mr. Ware is one of the old settlers in this section of Oklahoma and has been a resident of the state for a quarter of a century.

GEORGE E. TINKER. To the white citizens who have spent practically all their lives among the Indian tribes of Oklahoma, George E. Tinker, a mixed blood Osage Indian, is a man of particular interest. He has lived among the Osages since his birth and has sustained some valuable relations to the city and country around Pawhuska. Even before he gained his majority he was active in politics, and has been one of the public spirited leaders of his people, and has also contributed a service as a newspaper man, is interested in local history in this part of the state, and it is doubtful if any citizen of Osage County is better known and more highly esteemed.

His birth occurred at the old Osage Mission in Kansas, September 24, 1868. His parents were George and Genevieve (Revard) Tinker. His father was a native of New England, but was reared in Humboldt, Ohio, and in the very early days made the trip across Kansas and on to California as a blacksmith with a large party who were journeying to the western gold fields with wagons and ox teams. Subsequently he returned to Kansas and located as a blacksmith among the Osage tribe in Neosho County. Mr. Tinker's mother also went out to California in 1850 and lost her first husband there, William Champlain. She had two children by that husband. In 1856 she returned to the states by way of the Isthmus of Panama and New York, and was married to Mr. Tinker at the Osage Mission in 1866. In 1870 they accompanied the tribe to the Osage country of Indian Territory, and spent the rest of their days in what is now Osage County. The father was for many years a Government blacksmith among the Indians and followed his trade all his active life. He died in June, 1880, at the age of sixty-seven, and his widow passed away in May, 1912, at the age of eighty-eight. George E. Tinker is the only child of his father and mother, but has three half-sisters living: Emeline, widow of Edward Revard of Pawhuska; Eliza A., widow of Julian Trumbley of Pawhuska; and Mary, widow of Thomas Leahy of Los Angeles, California.

Since he was two years of age George E. Tinker has always lived on the Osage Reservation or in what is now Osage County of Oklahoma. Through the first two grades he attended the Government Indian School maintained at Pawhuska and spent eight months during the winter of 1883-84 in the Osage Mission. Since reaching manhood he has been more or less actively interested in farming, and has a considerable property in and around Pawhuska.

The first weekly paper published in Pawhuska was the Wah-Shah-She News, which was founded and conducted by Mr. Tinker for two years. He also published the Osage Magazine. His interest in local history has led him to make researches and preserve a great many facts and data concerning the Osage people.

All his life he has been affiliated with the democratic party, and in the early days was keenly interested in Osage politics. He was the first chairman of the first democratic organization in Osage Reservation, and was a delegate to every territorial and state convention since the opening of the old Cherokee Strip in 1893. His first important distinction came to him when he was only nineteen years of age, in his election as prosecuting attorney for the Osage Nation, an office which he capably filled for two years. He was also for six years a member of the Osage Council.

Fraternally Mr. Tinker is a member of the Knights of Pythias in all its branches; is a charter member of Wah-Shah-She Lodge No. 110, Ancient, Free and Accepted Masons, at Pawhuska; has taken thirty-two degrees in the Scottish Rite, being a member of the consistory at Guthrie; is affiliated with the Temple of the Mystic Shrine at Oklahoma City, and is a member of both the Royal Arch Chapter and the Knights Templar Commandery at Pawhuska.

On January 1, 1886, Mr. Tinker married Sarah Ann Swigerty, who was born in Northeastern Kansas in 1867. They are the parents of a fine family of six children: Clarence L., who is now a lieutenant in the regular army of the United States and at present stationed at Honolulu; Genevieve, who is now Mrs. Leonard Dyer, married March 8, 1916; Anna, wife of Myer F. Ruffner of Osage County, and their two children are named Victoria and Leona; Nicholas A., who lives in Montana; George E., Jr., who attends college in Denver, Colorado, but is now at home; and Villa, at home and attending school.

G. R. GRIGGS, M. D. Successful and progressive small town and country doctors in Oklahoma are numerous. Some of them have taken post-graduate degrees, while the others keep abreast of modern things in the profession through reading, close observation and association with medical societies and other sources of learning. Typical of this class of doctors is Doctor Griggs, who grew up principally on a ranch in Texas, but whose ambition to take up and successfully follow a profession never abated. For eight years he has been engaged in practice as a physician and surgeon at Harrah, and these have been growing, prosperous years, and he enjoys a fine practice.

A Texan by birth, Doctor Griggs was born in Panola County, April 25, 1877, a son of William B. and Carrie (Roquemore) Griggs. His father, who now lives in Callahan County, Texas, is a native of Georgia, but has lived in Texas since the close of the Civil war. The mother, who was born and reared in Texas and is still living, is the daughter of Georgia parents who came to Texas prior to the Civil war.

As a boy Doctor Griggs attended the public school at May, Texas, for a few years, and then spent ten years of employment on farms and ranches. In 1903, largely with such means as he had himself supplied, he entered the Dallas Medical College at Dallas, and in 1907 graduated M. D. from the Southwestern Medical College of that city. He at once removed to Oklahoma and has since been established at Harrah.

In 1909, at Harrah, Doctor Griggs married Miss Minnie Martin, whose father was one of the pioneer farmers in that community. Their one daughter, Robbie Lee, is now three years of age. The brothers and sisters of Doctor Griggs are: Dr. R. L. Griggs, a successful physician and surgeon, specializing in surgery, at Baird, Texas; W. W. Griggs, who is fourteen years of age and lives with his father in Callahan County, Texas; Mrs. Odran Green, wife of a farmer near Baird, Texas; and Mrs. Lyns Ramsey, whose husband is a dentist at Cross Plains, Texas.

Doctor Griggs is a member of the Canadian Valley Medical Association, and fraternally is affiliated with the Independent Order of Odd Fellows and the Modern Woodmen of America, and is medical examiner for the camp of the latter at Harrah. He is also a member of the town board of trustees, and was an active and influential member of the Harrah Commercial Club before that organization ceased its activities. His progressive citizenship shows its many points, and he has worked untiringly and unselfishly to advance movements relating to the public schools, good roads and other needed facilities.

JAMES MONROE ADDLE. The average Oklahoman has had a greater range of experience and more opportunities

of adventure than the citizen of the older states. One expects something unusual and exceptional in the career of nearly everyone who claims this state as his home. But even among Oklahomans James M. Addle, who is well established as a lawyer at Bristow in Creek County, stands above the ordinary line of achievement and experience. Mr. Addle during the past forty years has been identified with almost every important section of the great developing work. He has been a miner, a pioneer in new countries, a soldier, and perhaps in Oklahoma where he has had his home for the last twelve years, he has enjoyed a quieter routine than befell his lot after he left his eastern home when a young man.

He was born at Meadville, Crawford County, Pennsylvania, October 8, 1851, a son of A. M. and Margaret (Shartle) Addle. His parents were of Dutch stock and both natives of Pennsylvania, where they spent all their lives. His father was a stone mason and brick layer by trade, and from his trade he developed a business as a contractor. There were two sons, William Henry and James M., and the former, now deceased, was also an attorney. James Monroe Addle spent the first twenty-one years of his life in his native City of Meadville. He acquired his education in the local schools and spent two years in that fine old institution of Meadville, Allegheny College. He took up the study of law with the firm of Farley & Hotchkiss at Meadville, and was admitted to the bar there April 10, 1872.

He soon afterwards started out on his life of adventure and wander. His first destination was San Antonio, Texas, from there he went to Wichita, Kansas, and it would be difficult to enumerate all the scenes and places of his activities and experience since then. He visited the states of California, Wyoming, Idaho and Montana, and from Shoshone County, Idaho, he came to Oklahoma in 1904. He was a prospector and miner in Idaho, California, Montana and New Mexico, also practiced law and has fared among many different peoples and in many out of the way places. Mr. Addle was a member of the rough rider regiment during the Spanish-American war.

In politics he is a democrat. On May 5, 1873, he married Clara O'Brien, who was born in Armstrong County, Pennsylvania. There were two children of the marriage, Maude, now lives at Meadville, Pennsylvania, and Kitty died in 1875.

JACOB SIMPSON BEARDEN. In many ways the agricultural, business and financial interests of Okfuskee County reflect the ability and enterprise of Jacob S. Bearden, who is one of the pioneers of this section of the state and was one of the first to take an interest in and supply capital and other resources to the starting of the new Town of Okemah. When he located in Okfuskee County about twenty years ago he engaged in merchandising, and around his store grew up a little village, which in his honor was named Bearden, and he has always been greatly concerned with the growth and improvement of this village. The town takes much pride in its fine school buildings, and is one of the flourishing smaller communities.

For a number of years Mr. Bearden has been best known as a banker, and for the past three years has been president of the First National Bank of Okemah. This bank has a capital of $25,000 and surplus of $5,000, and is one of the United States depositories in Oklahoma. By a statement issued in the closing months of 1915, the aggregate resources of this bank are shown to be upwards of $175,000, and deposits of over $100,000 reflect not only the integrity of the bank but also the prosperity of the surrounding community. The principal officers of the bank are: J. S. Bearden, president; E. R. Strain, vice president; O. P. Bearden, cashier; and G. E. Clowers, assistant cashier.

In many ways Jacob S. Bearden has had a remarkable career. He had few of the opportunities for culture which are usually given to modern boys, and he never mastered the rudimentary elements of learning, although he has apparently suffered no special handicap as a keen and vigorous business man. His success could be traced chiefly to hard work, the overcoming of difficulties and a steadfast honor and integrity in all of life's relations.

He was born in Marshall County, Alabama, May 5, 1858, a son of Jacob and Caroline (Hess) Bearden. His parents were born and were married in Georgia, and afterwards moved to Alabama where the father died when Jacob S. Bearden was four years of age. The mother spent her last days with her son Jacob S. in Tecumseh, Oklahoma, and died there in 1892 at the age of fifty-eight. In the family were three sons and three daughters.

Jacob S. Bearden grew up in Alabama, and at the age of twenty-two was married there in 1880 to Miss Norcenia King. Immediately after their marriage they moved to Pope County, Arkansas, where Mrs. Bearden died in the spring of 1882, without children. For his second wife Jacob S. Bearden married Mrs. Jodie (King) Bearden, a sister of his first wife and widow of his brother Richard.

Mr. Bearden came into Oklahoma and located at Tecumseh in 1890, and secured a claim at the opening of the Kickapoo Indian Reservation, but later sold out. His claim was 2½ miles from Shawnee. In 1893 he made the run to Perry at the opening of the Cherokee Strip. His second wife died at Tecumseh in 1893. Many years ago Mr. Bearden moved to Okfuskee County and established his store at Bearden. Up to that time he had followed farming, but soon proved a success as a merchant. In 1902 he located at Okemah at the beginning of that town and established a branch store there, but after a few years sold a two-third interest of the business at Bearden to the firm of Strain & Cowgill, which still continues the business there.

A number of years ago Mr. Bearden took stock in the Wewoka First National Bank, which was the first bank established there, and later opened the State Bank at Bearden, in which he owned most of the stock. At Okemah he acquired an interest in the Farmers & Merchants State Bank and after considerable negotiations, buying and selling, he consolidated that bank with the Citizens State Bank, and was its active manager until 1912, when he sold and bought the First National Bank, and for the past three years has been its president. In many ways Mr. Bearden has worked effectively to build up his little home City of Okemah. He is the owner of the Broadway Hotel there, a modern fifty-room hostelry which supplies adequate comforts to the traveling public. He is also owner of a cotton gin at Morris, and has approximately 500 acres of farming land in Okfuskee County. Mr. Bearden has been a lifelong democrat, though his interest in politics has usually extended only to local affairs. He is a Knight Templar Mason, is affiliated with the Woodmen of the World, and is a member of the Methodist Episcopal Church South.

At Wewoka on March 2, 1895, Mr. Bearden married for his present wife Mrs. Rose Langford Dunn. She was born in Parke County, Indiana, April 18, 1858, and when about seven years of age her parents removed to Moultrie County, Illinois, where she lived until her marriage to James K. Polk Taylor. He died seven years later, leaving one child, Quincy Taylor, who is now a resident of Bearden, Oklahoma. Mrs. Bearden married for her second husband Nathaniel Dunn at Sullivan, Illinois. They removed to Caney, Kansas, and from there into the Choctaw Nation of Indian Territory about 1910 where Mr. Dunn died. There were two children of that union: Roy Dunn of Bearden, and Opie, who has taken his stepfather's name and is known as O. P. Bearden, being cashier of the First National Bank of Okemah. Mr. and Mrs. Bearden are the parents of one daughter, Velva, and there was also a twin sister of Velva, Vera, who lived only three months. Mr. Bearden also has one daughter by his second marriage, Emeline, wife of H. L. Strain, of Bearden.

HON. ALPHEUS HENRY BROWN. Few men have been longer and more actively identified with the Osage country than Alpheus Henry Brown, with whose name is associated the distinction of having served as one of the principal chiefs or governor of the Osage Nation. Governor Brown knows Kansas, Oklahoma and Texas like an open book, having followed cattle herds all over this country in the early days, and is considered a walking encyclopedia of information concerning his own country and its people.

By the accident of birth Alpheus Henry Brown was born in the State of California December 11, 1859, but has spent the greater part of his life in old Indian Territory and Oklahoma. His parents were William Scipio and Mary Jane (Stratton) Brown. His mother was a one-eighth Osage Indian and also partly of French descent, and it was through her that the Brown family established their Osage citizenship.

His father was one of the conspicuous western frontiersmen, and at the time of his death at his home in Caney, Kansas, in June, 1905, it was said there was probably not another man in the State of Kansas who had had as varied a career as miner, merchant, stock grower and farmer or had seen more of the world than W. S. Brown, who was best known over this southwestern country as "Osage Brown." On account of his many prominent associations with the Osage country, it is appropriate that his life should be told somewhat in detail.

Born in Wyandotte County, Ohio, May 11, 1831, he was the son of Judge Henry Brown, a prominent citizen of Ohio. Against the wishes of his father and mother, at the age of seventeen he started West and began his career of adventure. He worked on a farm in Iowa two years, then bought some oxen and took a contract to break prairie on the reservations of the Crow Indians in Minnesota. After three seasons returning to his old home in Ohio, he was soon started again toward the West, this time for the California gold fields. He went around by the Isthmus route, and arriving on the Pacific side almost without money had to get on board a vessel going to San Francisco as a stowaway, and being discovered was compelled to work his passage by shoveling coal. Not long after he reached Sacramento, worked as a driver for a time, and then with a party engaged in mining on the Yuba River. This enterprise was cut short by a flood, but he had received as his share of the proceeds gold to the value of $4,000, which he deposited in a Sacramento Bank, which soon afterwards failed. Thereafter he had varied experience, making money in mining, buying cattle and horses in lower California and driving them to the mines, losing his property by the treachery of Indians and white people and other accidents and circumstances, and was again and again reduced to poverty and started out with renewed determination to build up. He also went with a party on a prospecting tour to Australia, and returning had various adventures in South America, crossing the Andes and descending the Amazon River, and returning to the Western Coast, and was finally back in California. In 1856 he bought an improved farm in Napa County, and the following year married Miss Mary J. Stratton. A few years later he opened a new ranch on Eel River, but the following winter his land was ruined by landslides and his cattle and horses driven off by Indians or starved by bad weather. His varied adventures and experiences in California would require too much space for detailed telling, and it will be necessary to pass over several years to 1864, when he sent his family back to Ohio with his sister and her husband. He remained behind to dispose of his property, and then started across the mountains on snow shoes, and arrived in Ohio just in time to be drafted for service in the Union Army. He hired a substitute, and was soon substantially settled as an Ohio farmer. At the end of three years he sold out, moved to Iowa, engaged in woolen manufacturing until a declining market set him back again, but having made considerable money in land speculation in 1869 he removed to Missouri and bought two farms in Bates County. He then removed to Baxter Springs in Kansas, and acquired a large herd of cattle in Texas. Unable to find a range for his stock, his wife then suggested a way out of the difficulty. She had been born on the Osage Indian Reserve, had attended the old school at Osage Mission, and these facts coupled with her small inheritance of Osage blood enabled her to secure a headright in the Osage lands. Mr. Brown then removed his family to the Osage Agency, and they were soon enrolled as members of the tribe. The Cherokees were at that time leaving the Osage lands, and Mr. Brown bought one of their claims, and thus having ample grazing lands he was soon prospering in the cattle business. About a year later he took his family out to California, where he bought a ranch, and was planning to make his permanent home there, when his wife was taken ill and died. This bereavement caused him to change his plans, and he took his children back to Ohio and left them with a deceased brother's widow, whom he subsequently married. In 1875 he moved to Texas, lived in that state four years, and then returned to Kansas and located a ranch on the Big Caney River in the Osage country. There he had a farm of 450 acres of improved land besides 30,000 acres of fenced pasture, and at times his cattle numbered as high as 5,000 head. For a time he had his home in Independence, Kansas, but finally removed to Caney, from which point he superintended his ranches in the Osage country, twelve miles southwest of that city. Thereafter he lived at Caney, being identified for many years with the cattle business, until the close of his career at the age of seventy-four. Concerning his character one of the papers at Caney said: "W. S. Brown was an excellent man. He possessed a big heart and a man in need found in him a true friend, so long as he did right. He was a member of the Presbyterian church," and surrounded by his family he passed away in communion with his Maker. His children, all by his first marriage, were: Alpheus H., Charles W., Edward S., Rosa, wife of John Cunningham, and Ernest E.

Of these children all now reside at Caney, Kansas, except Governor Brown. Some of the moves and experiences of his early boyhood have already been suggested in the sketch of his father. He completed his public school education at the age of fifteen, and afterwards spent two years in school at Lawrence, Kansas. After leaving school he became closely associated with his father in the cattle business, but in the memorable hard winter of the '80s, when the live stock industry all over the country was practically paralyzed, he and his brothers were compelled to shift for themselves. After that he spent about fifteen years of venturesome life in the Rocky Mountains, much of the time engaged in mining. He has thus evidently inherited many of the pioneer

qualities of his father, and has always lived as close to the frontier as the rapid development of modern times would permit. He has twice made the trip from the Middle West to the Pacific Coast by wagon, and endured many hardships in the West. At one time he was out of provisions for four days. He has been more or less closely identified with the Osage country for forty years, and after his marriage settled down permanently in what is now Osage County. Governor Brown has about 700 acres in fine farming land, the old homestead being about twenty miles southeast of Hominy, in which town his family reside.

A democrat in politics, Governor Brown was elected the first county commissioner after statehood. For about two years he was chief or governor of the Osage Nation, and held that office until he and the other members of the Osage Council were removed by the secretary of interior for refusing to sign the oil leases. The courageous stand taken by Governor Brown at that time reflected highly on his integrity and his sense of fairness and justice to the Indian people, and subsequent developments have proved the correctness of his course. Fraternally he is affiliated with the Independent Order of Odd Fellows.

On August 12, 1901, Mr. Brown married Miss Belle Cowen, who was born in Reno, Kansas, July 2, 1879, but was living in Arkansas at the time of her marriage. Her parents are John and Sarah (Ebright) Cowen, both natives of Pennsylvania. Her father came to Kansas in 1875, and was married in that state in 1877. He died at the home of Governor and Mrs. Brown October 8, 1914, at the age of seventy-six, while his widow is still living in the Brown home at Hominy. Mrs. Brown's father homesteaded a claim in Kansas in the early days, and for many years was engaged in the cattle business. Mr. and Mrs. Brown have two children: William Scipio and Frank Richard.

GEORGE E. McKINNIS. Since the Pottawatomie Reservation was opened for settlement twenty-five years ago, one of its most active and energetic citizens has been George E. McKinnis. In various directions Mr. McKinnis has been the real leader of progress in his home City of Shawnee, and if one went over the history of development in that section of the state very closely, he would find a great many things to credit to the public spirit and disinterested service of this genial business man.

So far as the future is concerned of Shawnee as an educational center, Mr. McKinnis was more than anyone else responsible for securing the location of the Oklahoma State Baptist University at Shawnee. Oftentimes alone in his fight he managed the campaign which brought that institution to the city in 1910, and he is now treasurer of the university. He is one of the charter members of this institution, its first secretary and treasurer, and has been a director of the board of trustees ever since the school was established.

In business circles Mr. McKinnis is known both as a banker and real estate operator. He was born in Wayne County, Missouri, November 23, 1869. His ancestors on the paternal side came originally from Scotland to North Carolina during colonial times. His great-grandfather, Alex McKinnnis, was one of the early settlers, going to North Carolina in 1770, and he served with distinction and honor in the Revolutionary war and the War of 1812. His father, J. A. McKinnis, a farmer and country preacher, was born in Tennessee, May 27, 1832, and had a long and active career. He died December 28, 1915, at Alvin, Texas. J. A. McKinnis was married in Macon County, Tennessee, to Miss Drucilla Donoho, who was born in Tennessee in 1838 and died in Major County, Oklahoma, in 1897. In 1859 the family removed to Wayne County, Missouri, but in 1872 went back to Macon County, Tennessee, and in 1884 J. A. McKinnis established his home among the early settlers of Kingman County, Kansas. In 1893 he again moved with the advancing tide of civilization into Western Oklahoma and established a home in Major County, then Woods County. By profession he was a minister of the Baptist faith and preached the gospel and helped to establish churches in many isolated communities during his active career. He took a homestead in Major County, Oklahoma, where he lived for about eleven years and employed himself mainly as a farmer. For the benefit of the coast climate he moved to Alvin, Texas, in 1908 and remained there until his death, December 28, 1915. In politics he was a republican. During the war between states he served three years in the Federal army. He was wounded in the great battle of Shiloh. In the Chickasaw Bayou, one of the important engagements in the Vicksburg campaign, he was captured, later was exchanged and rejoined his command and continued to serve until he was mustered out.

George E. McKinnis, his next to the youngest son, when an infant, removed with his parents to Macon County, Tennessee. Here he gained his first instruction in the public schools of that state and continued his education in the public schools of Kingman County, Kansas. He took a literary and public-speaking course in Ball's College at Harper, Kansas, having been a student there in 1889-1890. Early in life he gave some promise as a public speaker, and when only eighteen years old was elected lecturer of the Farmers Alliance in Kingman County, Kansas. The early part of his life was mainly devoted to farming and railroad work, working on the farm during the crop season, and on the railroad the time he could spare from the farm.

September 16, 1890, the opening day for Pottawatomie reserve, he went to Tecumseh, in Pottawatomie County, Oklahoma, and soon afterwards was employed as manager of the McKinnis & Beard Lumber Co. He served in this capacity until the company closed out its business at that point. Along with his ability as a practical man of affairs, Mr. McKinnis has associated service and qualification in various other lines. From his first business at Tecumseh he became principal of the public schools there, and served until 1895. He was a member of the first school board in Pottawatomie County, then known as County "B." He removed to Shawnee in the fall of 1895 and accepted principalship of the high school. He served two years as principal and one year as superintendent of the city schools. He did much to forward the cause of public education in the primitive period of about twenty years ago.

From his work as a schoolman Mr. McKinnis engaged in the real estate and loan business, and now for several years has conducted one of the oldest established and most reliable offices in that line in Central Oklahoma.

He was one of the organizers of the State National Bank of Shawnee, and has been director and vice president ever since its organization in 1902. At various times he has been associated with other banking interests and is now secretary of the Fidelity Building and Loan Association, which is one of the best institutions of its kind in the Southwest.

Another thing that should be remembered to his credit was his presidency of the Shawnee Commercial Club at the time the Missouri, Kansas and Texas and the Santa Fe railroads were brought into Shawnee. He is still an active and influential member of that organization of business men.

In the social and civic life of Shawnee, Mr. McKinnis has always taken an active and prominent part. He has donated liberally of his means and time to the move-

Vol. V—13

ments that stand for the elevation of his community. It was under his administration as chairman of the Park Commission of Shawnee that the system of street improvement organizations were launched, which did much to make Shawnee one of the most beautiful cities in Oklahoma. He was president and manager of the Chautauqua Association of Shawnee, 1902-1910-1916.

Politically, Mr. McKinnis is a republican. He has always been consistent and regular, and was elected delegate to the national convention at Chicago, 1916.

He served as postmaster of Shawnee from 1903 to 1907. Under his administration and through his efforts country rural free delivery service was established in Pottawatomie County. He was secretary of the first Republican Club in Pottawatomie County in 1891.

He was reared in the Baptist Church, of which his father was a devoted minister. He has several times been honored by the Baptist state conventions; he was elected and served three years as its auditor. As a Sunday-school worker Mr. McKinnis' ability is familiarly recognized. He has filled every important office of the interstate denominational work except that of secretary. He was its president in 1907-1908.

In 1897 Mr. McKinnis was married, at Shawnee, to Miss Mamie Dixon of Paris, Texas. Mrs. McKinnis is known throughout the state as one of Oklahoma's prominent club workers. She is now president of the Fifth District. They are the parents of one son, George E., Jr., born July 23, 1901, who is now attending the local high school.

THOMAS H. FLESHER, M. D. Many of the men in the medical profession today are devoting themselves in a large measure to the prevention of disease as well as its cure. In this way their efficiency as benefactors has extended much beyond the scope of the old-fashioned practice when the doctor was related to his patients only as an individual and in times of sickness. One of the prominent young physicians and surgeons of Oklahoma, Dr. Thomas H. Flesher has been largely distinguished for his work as a sanitarian at Edmond.

It is undeniable that without proper methods of sanitation and the conservation of health through proper safeguards and under the supervision of a scientific director, Edmond could not have gained the popularity it possesses as a college town. During the best period of its development, and when as many as 1,800 young men and women are spending their summers there in the Central State Normal School, Doctor Flesher has been city superintendent of health, and his recommendations to the city officials and the people forestalled disease to a wonderful degree. Besides being a successful practitioner and a town booster, this is one of the principal things that mark him as one of Edmond's leading citizens.

Dr. Thomas H. Flesher was born in Reedsville, Ohio, February 10, 1876, a son of Francis M. and Mary Frances (Thorn) Flesher. His father was for thirty years a steamboat engineer on the Ohio River, and during the Civil war was in the Government service in that capacity. He removed to Iowa in 1887 and died the following year. The maternal grandparents of Doctor Flesher were from West Virginia and early settlers of Ohio. Doctor Flesher has three brothers and three sisters: M. B. Flesher, a lawyer at Okemah, Oklahoma, and a graduate of the University of Michigan; Dr. W. E. Flesher, a dentist at Frederick, Oklahoma, and in 1915 president of the Oklahoma Dental Society; E. C. Flesher, engaged in the milling business at Edmond: Mrs. W. E. Edie, wife of a Methodist minister at Burr Oak, Iowa; Mrs. W. B. Bryant, wife of a merchant at Edmond; and Mrs. L. A. Bryant, wife of a farmer at Frederick, Oklahoma.

Left fatherless at the age of twelve years, Doctor Flesher was hampered by lack of funds in pursuing his education and much of his training in public schools was delayed by the necessity of work. He persevered and eventually acquired not only a liberal literary education, but a thorough training for his profession. In 1896 he graduated with a teacher's degree from the Central Normal University at Humeston, Iowa, and in 1901 received his degree Doctor of Medicine from the Keokuk, Iowa, Medical College and College of Physicians and Surgeons. Doctor Flesher began his practice of medicine in Edmond in 1901.

Besides his service as city superintendent of health, he was president of the Oklahoma County Medical Society in 1913, and at the present time is vice president for Oklahoma of the Southwestern Medical Association, an organization covering five states. He is a member of the Oklahoma State Medical Society and of the American Medical Association, and a life member of the Surgeons' Club of Rochester, Minnesota. Doctor Flesher has done post-graduate work in the Chicago Polyclinic and in the famous hospital clinics at Rochester, Minnesota. He is secretary of the Republican Club at Edmond, and a member of the Methodist Episcopal Church. In Masonry he is affiliated with Edmond Lodge No. 37, Ancient Free and Accepted Masons, the Scottish Rite Consistory of Guthrie and India Temple of the Mystic Shrine at Oklahoma City. He also belongs to the Modern Woodmen of America and the Yeomen at Edmond.

THOMAS LAFAYETTE MULLINS. The vocation of auctioneering in recent years has become more of a profession than a business, and the individual who would win success in this field must possess qualifications of a peculiar nature. He must in the first place be a good judge of values, and must be able to give an elaborate and intelligent description of the articles placed in his care. There are no references upon which he may rely, for every thought must be extemporaneous, and he must guide himself accordingly, and it is essential that he be able to intermingle comedy if the occasion demands. Among the men in Oklahoma who have made a success of this vocation because of the possession of the qualifications noted, is Thomas Lafayette Mullins, of Walters, ex-sheriff of Cotton County, who, before entering his present line of endeavor, had gained excellent results from his labors in the field of agriculture.

Mr. Mullins belongs to a family which originated in Ireland and probably came to America prior to the War of the Revolution, being pioneer settlers of Kentucky. He was born at Bear Creek, Cedar County, Missouri, April 25, 1872, and is a son of William and Susan (James) Mullins, the former born in Kentucky, in 1831, and the latter in Tennessee, in 1839. As a young man, William Mullins removed from Kentucky to Lawrence County, Missouri, where he took up a homestead, subsequently moved to Bear Creek, Cedar County, and finally to Dade County, in the same state, where he followed farming and stockraising until his death, in 1903, Mrs. Mullins having passed away in 1881, at Bear Creek. During the Civil war Mr. Mullins served as a member of the Home Guards, in the Union army. There were four children in the family: George, a farmer, whose death occurred in 1909, at Ash Grove, Green County, Missouri; Thomas Lafayette, of this review; Robert, who is an auctioneer, and resides at Geronimo, Oklahoma; and Louis, who is a farmer and agriculturist and resides at Temple, Oklahoma.

Thomas L. Mullins attended the public schools of Bear Creek and was reared on his father's farm until 1881, in which year his mother died and he went to live at the home of his uncle, R. F. Wetion, on whose farm he worked for three years. He then started out on his own account and for five or six years worked out among the agriculturists of Green County, Missouri. In 1890 he went to Marshall County, Kansas, where he continued his labors as a farm hand until 1901, and in that year came to Temple, Oklahoma, and drew a homestead at the opening. This he proved up and resided upon until 1905, when he removed to the Village of Temple, and started his work as an auctioneer. His advent in Walters occurred in 1912, and since that time he has successfully built up a large and profitable business in his chosen line, conducting large sales and handling all kinds of property for his clients. While he devotes his attention almost exclusively to this line of work, Mr. Mullins still has extensive farming interests, being the owner of 440 acres of land, on which his tenants do diversified farming and stockraising. Mr. Mullins is a republican and has been an active worker in his party. While a resident of Temple he served as constable and city marshal, and in 1912 became the candidate of his party for the office of sheriff of Cotton County, to which he was elected, and served two years in an entirely capable and satisfactory manner. With his family, he belongs to the Baptist Church. Mr. Mullins' fraternal connections include membership in Temple Lodge No. 210, Ancient Free and Accepted Masons, and Guthrie Consistory No. 1, of the thirty-second degree in Masonry; Temple Lodge of the Modern Woodmen of America; Walters Lodge of the Royal Neighbors of America, and the Temple lodges of the Independent Order of Odd Fellows and the Fraternal Order of Eagles.

Mr. Mullins was married at Marysville, Kansas, in 1896, to Miss Hattie McLeod, who was born in Marshall County, Kansas, daughter of the late Capt. Archie P. McLeod, who served in the Union army during the Civil war and subsequently became a Kansas farmer. Two children have been born to this union: Clarence, born July 19, 1903, who is attending the public schools at Walters; and Hattie Muriel, born August 26, 1913.

JAMES C. MENIFEE. No matter how dynamic the force of progress along all material lines of human endeavor, still agriculture and horticulture must ever figure as the base of industrial and general prosperity, and fortune is he whose ability and tastes enable him to achieve success in connection with any department of the great elemental art of husbandry. Though the natural resources of Oklahoma are varied and opulent, it is through agriculture and other utilization of the willing soil that civic and material development and upbuilding have mainly been compassed, and in Creek County it is pleasing to direct attention to Mr. Menifee as one of the prominent, substantial and representative exponents of such basic industry, though his activities have been of varied order and have marked him as a man of versatility in business, even as he is known as one of the loyal, appreciative and public-spirited citizens of Sapulpa, in the vicinity of which city he is giving special attention to fruit culture.

Mr. Menifee was born in Holt County, Missouri, on the 6th of September, 1860, and is a son of John M. and Eleanor M. (Scott) Menifee, the former of whom was born in Kentucky, a scion of an old and prominent Southern family, and the latter of whom was born in the State of Indiana, their marriage having been solemnized in Missouri, where the respective families settled in the early '50s.

John M. Menifee became a prosperous farmer and stock grower in Holt County, Missouri, and finally turned his attention more particularly to the propagation of fruit, of which line of enterprise he became one of the most prominent and successful exponents in that county, where he developed a fine fruit farm of 100 acres. When in advanced years he sold this valuable property and he and his devoted wife joined their son, James C., subject of this sketch, in Oklahoma, where both passed the remainder of their lives and where in death they were not long divided, Mr. Menifee having passed away on the 6th of June, 1910, at the age of seventy-five years, and his wife having died on the following day, at the age of seventy-one years, the memories of both being reverently cherished by all who came within the compass of their kindly and benignant influence. John C. Menifee was staunchly loyal to the Union during the climacteric period of the Civil war, though living in a state where the preponderating sympathy was for the cause of the Confederacy.. He did all in his power to uphold the Union arms but his physical condition was such that he was unable to enter military service. Both he and his wife were zealous members of the Presbyterian Church, earnest in support of temperance, and tolerant and considerate in their association with all with whom they came in contact in the various relations of life. Of their three children the subject of this sketch was the second in order of birth; Bettie W, the first born, became the wife of William Ward and is now deceased; and Robert L. is now a resident of the City of Fresno, California.

James C. Menifee was reared to adult age in Holt County, Missouri, where he early began to assist his father in the work of the home farm and where he gained thorough familiarity with the varied details of successful fruit culture. In the meanwhile he did not neglect to profit fully by the advantages afforded in the common schools of his native county, and he continued to reside at the parental home until his removal to what is now the State of Oklahoma, save that he passed one year in Montana, when eighteen years of age.

In 1892 Mr. Menifee came to Indian Territory and established his permanent residence at Sapulpa, the present metropolis and judicial center of Creek County, Oklahoma, and that he is distinctively entitled to pioneer honors is assured when it is stated that the now populous and metropolitan city was then represented by a railroad station, a general store and a few dwellings of primitive order. Mr. Menifee has always been a man of action, and thus, soon after his arrival in the embryonic city he here opened a general store, this being the second mercantile establishment of the diminutive but aspiring village. In 1893 he formed a partnership with P. B. France which continued for three years, when Mr. Menifee bought Mr. France's interests. With the development of the city and surrounding country the business of Mr. Menifee constantly expanded in scope and importance, though his trade in the earlier years was largely with the Indians, many of whom came from points as far as sixty miles distant to purchase goods, which they frequently carried away by the wagon load. At that time Sapulpa was the western terminus of the Frisco Railroad line and thus became a trading and shipping point of much importance, and the town was a place of interest and rendezvous on the part of many Indians who came to it to gain their first sight of a railway train. During the ten years that he was engaged in the mercantile business Mr. Menifee controlled a large and profitable trade and was recognized as one of the leading business men of Sapulpa, the while his fair dealings and impregnable integrity gained to him the unequivocal confidence and good will of both his white and Indian patrons and he became known to the white settlers and the Indians throughout a wide radius of country. After he had learned that Sapulpa was to be made a division headquarters for the Frisco Railroad Mr. Menifee showed his confidence in the future importance and growth of the town by making judicious investments in local real estate, and its appreciation in value eventually enabled him to realize large profit in the sale of much of the property thus acquired. Since his retirement from the mercantile business he has given his attention principally to the handling of real estate and agricultural enterprise, in both of which lines he has been definitely prospered. In Sapulpa he is the owner of valuable business and residence properties, and since 1912 he has maintained his residence on a fine rural estate one mile north of the city, where he has developed one of the excellent fruit farms of the county, his thorough knowledge of this line of enterprise having made him specially successful in exploiting this important line of enterprise, along which he is still continuing his effective development work, which is a definite lesson and incentive to others.

In politics Mr. Menifee does not consult expediency but votes in accord with his earnest convictions and is a staunch supporter of the cause of the prohibition party. He and his wife are zealous members of the Presbyterian Church, and he served as elder of the church of this denomination in Sapulpa until his removal to his farm.

It is worthy of special note that at the annual fair of the Creek County Agricultural Society in the autumn of 1915 Mr. Menifee captured second premium in the department of general exhibits from individual farm, and this is the more noteworthy in view of the fact that he had resided on and given his personal supervision to his farm for the brief period of somewhat less than three years.

In the year 1883 was solemnized the marriage of Mr. Menifee to Miss Alice S. Dulin, who like himself is a native of Holt County, Missouri, where she was born on the 13th of November, 1861, a daughter of Smith and Mary Elizabeth (Embree) Dulin, the former of whom was killed in an engagement at Helena, Arkansas, while serving as a soldier of the Confederacy in the Civil war, and the latter of whom now resides in the home of Mr. and Mrs. Menifee, who accord to her the deepest filial solicitude, as did they also to her mother, Mrs. Nancy Ann Embree, who passed her declining years in their home and who was summoned to the life eternal in June, 1915, about one month prior to the one hundredth anniversary of her birth. This venerable woman retained to the last wonderful control of her mental faculties, and her memory was such that she was able to give most graphic and interesting reminiscences of the years long past. Mr. and Mrs. Menifee became the parents of three children, of whom the first born, India, died at the age of three years; Miss Bettie W. remains at the parental home and is a popular factor in the social activities of the community; and Newell D. is engaged in the insurance and abstract business in the City of Sapulpa.

JOHN G. COPENHAVER. In those years now pleasantly distant when Northern Oklahoma was untouched by railroads, John G. Copenhaver gained his first acquaintance with what is now Osage County by work as a freighter, engaged in hauling goods from Kansas Point to some of the early trading posts in the Osage and Cherokee nations. For fully a quarter of a century he has been prominently identified with Osage County, is one of the enterprising men who have done much to stimulate and raise the standards of agriculture and stock raising in this section, and is now living retired in the enjoyment of a well earned prosperity with his home in Big Heart, Osage County. Mr. Copenhaver has taken much interest in political affairs, and is now serving as a justice of the peace.

An Indiana man by birth, he was born at Clinton on the Wabash River in Vermilion County, Indiana, in 1852. His parents were Thomas J. and Mary E. Gordon Copenhaver, both natives of Indiana, his mother being also born in Vermilion County. In 1869, when Mr. Copenhaver was seventeen years of age, the family moved out to Wilson County, Kansas, where his father took up a homestead, followed farming and stock raising for many years, and died in 1890 when about forty-five years old. The mother died February 19, 1916, at the old home which they took up as a government claim in 1869, when past eighty years of age. Thomas J. Copenhaver served for 4½ years as a Union soldier, enlisting at the beginning of the war in the Eighteeenth Indiana Regiment, subsequently veteranizing, and continuing until the close of hostilities in 1865. Most of his service was as regimental quartermaster. He was a stanch republican, and he and his wife active members of the Christian Church. All of their four sons and four daughters are still living, namely: John G.; Catherine, wife of George Woodard of Wilson County, Kansas; A. J., of Fall River, Kansas; Annie, wife of Alexander Nelson of Ramona, Oklahoma; M. S., who lives with his mother on the homestead; O. P., of Drumright, Oklahoma; Mrs. Eunice of Woodson County, Kansas; Mrs. Elsie Cooper, of Greenwood County, Kansas.

Though John G. Copenhaver resided with his parents until his marriage, he had already acquired an extensive experience as a farm boy, a student in local schools, and in employment in those occupations which are characteristic of a new state. On August 29, 1877, he married Miss Mary E. Scott, who was born in Illinois in 1856 and was brought to Kansas in 1871 with her parents.

After his marriage Mr. Copenhaver located on a farm in Wilson County, Kansas, and lived there until his removal to the vicinity of Pawhuska in 1890. He has been a resident of Osage County ever since, and most of his active career has been spent in farming. For the past six years he has lived retired. During his early manhood Mr. Copenhaver gained the experience already noted as a freighter. In 1872 he was employed by the Coy Brothers and Ogeese Captain, who operated an extensive trading post at Hominy Falls about seven miles north and west of Tulsa, and this firm had the first store built on the Osage Reservation. Mr. Copenhaver was employed chiefly in hauling goods to this trading post from Fort Leavenworth and later from Fort Scott, Kansas. The distance he had to cover between Fort Leavenworth and the trading post was fully 300 miles. In later years Mr. Copenhaver gained considerable note as a stock raiser, and at times had between 200 and 300 head of cattle and from forty to fifty head of horses. A pleasing distinction which is associated with his name is that he was the first to introduce Holstein cattle into Osage County. That was about twenty years ago.

Mr. Copenhaver was one of the organizers of the republican party in Osage County, and for more than twenty years has been identified with the Knights of Pythias fraternity. He and his wife are the parents of three children. Thomas J. lives in Independence, Kansas, and is married and has three children. William J. lives at Big Heart and is also married. Jacob resides at Independence and is married and has one child.

JUDGE CHARLES B. WILSON, JR. Deep and accurate knowledge of law, native shrewdness and ability, and unswerving integrity have made Judge Charles B. Wil-

son, Jr., of the Tenth Judicial District, an excellent lawyer and an admirable judge; high personal character, firm convictions of the right, a kind heart and strong sense of duty has made him a valuable citizen. A conscientious public servant, of high purpose and sincerity, he has long stood as one of the ablest representatives of the dignity of the law in Chandler and Lincoln County. The Tenth Judicial District of Oklahoma comprises the two counties of Lincoln and Pottawatomie.

Judge Wilson has long been known in Central Oklahoma as a successful lawyer and one of the strong and active figures of the democratic party. He was engaged in the active practice of law for sixteen years, and has lived in Oklahoma since the first opening in 1889. He was born in Clinton, Henry County, Missouri, August 2, 1872, and is a son of Charles B. Wilson, Sr., a pioneer lawyer of Chandler and a native of Missouri, where he was reared and educated. He is now retired from the active practice of law and belongs among the class of honored old-timers of the Southwest. The maiden name of the mother was Kate Thurston, who came of a family of Virginia people. Charles B. Wilson, Sr., and wife had two children: Charles B. Jr., and Ann Wilson, now of St. Joseph, Missouri. The father is a democrat, and is a member of the Methodist Episcopal Church South and a man honored and respected in all his relations.

Judge Wilson spent his early life in Clinton, Missouri, was educated in the Clinton high schools and was seventeen years of age when he became identified with Central Oklahoma. He studied law under the direction of his father at Chandler, and was admitted to the bar in that city in 1899. For several years he was junior member of the firm of Wilson & Wilson, and this was a firm which controlled a large and successful practice and in ability was ranked second to none in the Tenth District. Judge Wilson was formerly a member of the firm of Hoffman, Robinson & Wilson, and each of the three members have seen active service in judicial positions, either as county or district judges.

Judge Wilson has an eminently clean record in all his business and civic relations. One of his strongest characteristics is his faculty for making and retaining strong friendships. Judge Wilson has taken fourteen degrees in Scottish Rite Masonry and is also affiliated with Independent Order of Odd Fellows, the Knights of Pythias and the Modern Woodmen of America. He is a man of strong physical and mental address and his dignity and impartial conduct on the bench is matched by the strength and cordial manners of the lawyer and gentleman. In 1915 he was appointed a member of Division No. 5 of the Supreme Court Commission of the state appointed by the governor.

ROBERT DUNLOP. Ranked as one of the leading and most successful oil operators of Oklahoma, with properties scattered over all the important producing sections of the state, Robert Dunlop, of Newkirk, is also greatly interested in agricultural ventures, and during a long and active career has served his state in positions of responsibility and trust, in which he has demonstrated the possession of excellent executive powers as well as high ideals of public service.

Mr. Dunlop was born at Garnett, Anderson County, Kansas, September 6, 1869, and is a son of Alexander and Mary (Whitson) Dunlop, natives of Scotland, the former born at Dunlop Place, February 3, 1826, and the latter at Kelso, March 24, 1832. The parents were strict Scotch Presbyterians and were married in 1865 in Lawrence, Kansas, after the return of the father from his service in the Civil war, in which he fought as a private of the One Hundred and Forty-eighth Regiment, Illinois Volunteer Infantry. The parents of Mr. Dunlop's mother came to the United States in 1849 and her mother died in New York shortly afterward. In 1850 Mr. Dunlop moved to Quebec, Canada, and in 1856 to Fort Leavenworth, Kansas. The father of Mr. Dunlop settled first on the first homestead awarded to a white man in Howard County, Kansas, this being to George Hitchens, a late distinguished pioneer of that state. It is now occupied as the home of Mr. Dunlop's two brothers, George and James, and is located in the vicinity of Longton, Kansas.

Mr. Dunlop attended the public and high schools of Howard County, finishing a business education in the latter, and began life for himself in Oklahoma, working on the homestead of an uncle in Payne County. The next year, 1890, he did ranch work in the Osage Nation, and in 1891 entered the Iowa Indian country at its opening. He found no land that suited him there, however, and did not make any settlement. Having as a cowman traversed a large part of the territory embraced in the Cherokee Strip, he took part in the opening of that territory in 1893 and took a homestead in what is now Kay County. This in due time he patented and it became the nucleus of the 320 acre farm which now is one of his most valuable possessions. It is situated in the heart of one of the finest farming regions of the state, and the section of which it originally was a part ranks as the best in Oklahoma. On the land are successfully grown wheat, oats and alfalfa, and Mr. Dunlop for many years has had his men employ the best and most scientific methods of agriculture. As one of the leading and original settlers of the county he took an active part in a good roads movement that resulted in the establishment of a system of roads that were not surpassed in any of the original counties. In 1902 he was elected treasurer of Kay County and this position he held until 1907, the year of statehood, when he became a candidate on the democratic ticket for state treasurer, but was defeated for the nomination by James A. Menefee of Anadarko by 289 votes. He served during the administration of Governor C. N. Haskell as a member of the board of trustees of the Insane Asylum at Fort Supply, and sought to have an appropriation of $1,500,000 made early in the state's career for the proper care of the insane. He contended then and has since maintained that the new government should first make adequate provision for its unfortunate wards.

In 1910 Mr. Dunlop was elected state treasurer of Oklahoma, carrying, in the primary election over M. E. Trapp, of Guthrie, sixty-one of the seventy-six counties. His policy as state treasurer was a strict adherence to the rule established in other states that compels all departments of state government collecting money for the state to deposit the money immediately in the state treasury, but in this policy he was unsuccessful, owing to laws that permitted various departments to handle state moneys. The question of whether or not all state funds shall be deposited with the state treasurer has been an unsettled issue, due principally to the policy of administrations of maintaining the school land office as a separate state institution entrusted with the duty of handling school funds, and his views were virtually passed in 1915.

Mr. Dunlop's activities since retiring from office have been in furtherance of his agricultural and oil and gas interests. He has a farm in Kay County of 320 acres, with 300 acres in cultivation. In partnership with E. B. Howard, of Tulsa, he owns 600 acres of oil and gas bearing land in the eastern part of the state. He is a director in the Spreading Adder Oil and Gas Company, the Coleman Farms Oil and Gas Company, the Sipo Oil and Gas Company, the Kay Vernon Oil and Gas Co., the

Kay Wagoner Oil & Gas Co., the Flora Hope Oil & Gas Co., and the Dunlop Oil & Gas Co.

Mr. Dunlop was married in 1904, at Blackwell, Oklahoma, to Miss Flora Christian, of Blackwell, who was a native of Holden, Missouri, a graduate of the Emporia (Kansas) State Normal School, and a teacher for several years prior to her marriage. She died in the following year, leaving one daughter, Flora, aged ten years, who resides at Newkirk with her father. Fraternally Mr. Dunlop is a member of the Masonic Lodge, his Ancient Free and Accepted Masons membership being No. 57, at Tonkawa, Oklahoma; his Knight Templar membership being in Ben Hur Commandery, at Ponca City, Oklahoma; his chapter membership being with Hope No. 41, at Howard, Kansas, and his shrine membership being with Akdar Temple, Tulsa, Oklahoma. He is a member also of the Knights of Pythias, of the Country Club at Newkirk, and of the Capital City Gun Club of Oklahoma City.

Mr. Dunlop has been one of the state's most progressive citizens for many years. His success is compensation for the early day hardships he endured when, as a poor young man, he followed the herds of cattle over the raw prairies of the unsettled country and had visions of the establishment of a rich and resourceful commonwealth; and when, alone with his gun, he traveled over the wide and wild areas of the unsettled Cherokee Strip that now is one of the state's most prosperous regions.

STEVE DURHAM. Harper County has its livest and most progressive newspaper in the Buffalo Republican. This paper was the product of and was founded by L. R. H. Durham, but it is now the property and under the editorial management of his son, Steve Durham, whose history from the beginning to the present has been closely associated with printer's ink and newspaper work.

In fact, Steve Durham was born in a printing office. On June 9, 1888, he first saw the light of day in his father's print shop at Seward, Kansas. His parents are L. R. H. and Rebecca Jane (Warren) Durham. His father was born March 11, 1862, at Chandlersville, Illinois, a son of E. R. and Jane (McDaniel) Durham. The grandfather was born in Pennsylvania, but his wife was a native of Scotland.

When L. R. H. Durham was eleven years of age he was bound out as an apprentice in a printing office, and thus he, too, has had a long and active experience in the newspaper business. In 1876 he went to Stafford County, Kansas, and as one of the pioneers of that section established the Independent at Seward. He was editor and owner of this paper for two years. During that time his son Steve was born in a newspaper office, which was also the home of the family. In 1889 he removed to Colorado, and for six years conducted newspapers at Villa Grove and Saguache. Returning to Stafford County, Kansas in 1898 he established the Stafford Leader, remained at its head two years, conducted the Sun for one year at Sylvia, Kansas, and in 1901 removed to old Augusta, Oklahoma, where he published the Herald for a short time.

In 1902 the elder Mr. Durham established the Republican at Supply, Oklahoma, conducted it three years, and in 1910 he bought the Buffalo Republican, which is the pioneer newspaper of Harper County. He continued its active editor and owner until December 1, 1915, at which time he transferred its management to his son Steve.

On August 16, 1883, in Stafford County, Kansas, L. R. H. Durham married Miss Rebecca Jane Warren, daughter of James B. and Sarah (Caldwell) Warren. Her father was a native of Pennsylvania and her mother of Scotland, and thus Steve Durham from two sources has Scotch ancestors. Mrs. L. R. H. Durham was born July 10, 1863, at Plum Creek, Pennsylvania. She became the mother of three sons: William E., who was born May 20, 1884, and is now a farmer in Stafford County, Kansas; Albert L., who was born October 8, 1886, and is a farmer in Harper County, Oklahoma; and Steve Durham, whose birth date has already been given. The latter was educated in public schools, and practically grew up in a newspaper office, became familiar with the details of a printing office at an early age, in fact his earliest recollections are associated with such things, and he is a practical printer and newspaper man by experience as well as by vocation. The Buffalo Republican is his first venture on his own account and he is making it a very live and wholesome paper.

JOHN W. CORNELL. One of the well known figures in the journalistic world of Western Oklahoma is John W. Cornell, editor and manager of the Clinton News, of Clinton, one of the most alert, enterprising and interesting organs of the democratic party in Custer County. Mr. Cornell is a Kansan by nativity, born in Saline County, December 24, 1878, and is a son of Charles and Clara (Anderson) Cornell.

John Cornell, grandfather of John W. Cornell, was born in Sheffield, England, from whence he emigrated as a single man to the United States, and settled as a pioneer of Marshall County, Illinois, in the vicinity of the Town of Sparland. There he carried on agricultural pursuits throughout his life. He was married there to an Illinois girl and they became the parents of two sons: John, Jr., who died at the age of twenty-five years; and Charles. Charles Cornell was born on the home farm in Illinois, in 1850, and during the Civil war fought in an Illinois volunteer infantry regiment in the Union army. Shortly after the close of the war he removed to Saline County, Kansas, where he engaged in farming and stockraising and continued therein until 1907, when he went to Newton and secured employment in the storehouse department of the Santa Fe Railroad. He was residing at Newton at the time of his death, in 1911. Mr. Cornell was a member of the Independent Order of Odd Fellows, and a good and public-spirited citizen, and his known integrity and probity won him many friends and the high regard of a wide acquaintance. He married Miss Clara Anderson, who was born at Salina, Kansas, and who survives him and lives at Kansas City, Kansas. They became the parents of five children: John W.; James Robert, who is a commercial traveler out of San Francisco, California; Blanche E., who is the wife of Earl Bishop, engaged in the packing business at Kansas City, Missouri; R. E., who is connected with the Los Angeles Bank and Trust Company, at Los Angeles, California; and Ivan E., who is manager of the Harvey Restaurant, at Guthrie, Oklahoma.

John W. Cornell attended the public schools of Saline County, Kansas, and was graduated from the Gypsum (Kansas) High School with the class of 1899. His first position after leaving school was that of bookkeeper in the Gypsum Valley State Bank, where he remained one year, and in 1900 came to Oklahoma, locating at Cleo, as bookkeeper for the Cleo State Bank. He next continued his banking experiences as bookkeeper for the Watonga Bank, of Blaine County, Oklahoma, and in 1902 became the organizer of the Bank of Eagle City, Oklahoma, an institution of which he was cashier for a period of seven years. Mr. Cornell became one of the organizers of the Farmers State Bank, at Thomas, Oklahoma, in 1909, and continued to be identified with that concern for four years, but in 1913 resigned the cashiership to start editorial work as a member of the staff of the Thomas Tribune, a paper which retained his services

for two years. In March, 1915, he resigned and came to Clinton, where in partnership with S. R. Hawkes, the present postmaster of Clinton, he bought the Clinton News, of which he has since been editor and manager. The offices and plant are located in the Dipple Building, on Frisco Avenue, and are modern in every respect, not only including machinery of the latest manufacture for the printing of an up-to-the-minute newspaper, but for first class job work of all kinds as well. Under Mr. Cornell's editorship the News has won a reputation for veracity and reliability. While the paper is a democratic organ, an effort is made to place matter before the public in an impartial manner, and to print the whole news at all times. Mr. Cornell, himself an active and stalwart democrat, has held several positions of public trust, having served on the school board while a resident of Eagle City, and as mayor for two terms while living at Thomas. He is a Mason of high rank, belonging to Thomas Lodge No. 265, Ancient Free and Accepted Masons; Thomas Chapter No. 53, Royal Arch Masons; Weatherford Commander, Knights Templar; and India Temple, Ancient Arabic Order of Nobles of the Mystic Shrine, at Oklahoma City.

In 1904, at Gypsum, Kansas, Mr. Cornell was united in marriage with Miss Halle Whitmore, daughter of the late J. W. Whitmore, who was a cattleman, and to this union there have been born two children: Helen and William Kenneth, both of whom are attending the public schools of Clinton.

C. H. WESTGATE. For thirty years Dr. C. H. Westgate has been in the practice of his profession as veterinary surgeon, and has the largest and best equipped veterinary hospital in Kay County, Oklahoma, in the City of Blackwell. Doctor Westgate has lived in Blackwell since 1906, and was already well established and with a good reputation in professional circles when he came there. His faith in the future of Kay County led him to invest in farm and town property, and he is now one of the large tax payers of that section. His veterinary hospital is housed in a large building 24x50 feet, containing offices, store rooms, garage, operating facilities and everything needed for the care and treatment of domestic animals.

Dr. C. H. Westgate was born near Mendota in La Salle County, Illinois. His birthplace was the pioneer farm of La Salle County. It had been settled by his grandfather, Abner D. Westgate, ninety years ago, in 1826, and that part of Northern Illinois was still a wilderness and before the City of Chicago came into existence as a village. Abner D. Westgate was the first to improve a farm in La Salle County. David Westgate, Sr., was also born on that homestead and died there at the age of seventy-two. David, Sr., married Martha Gibbs, who now lives with her daughters at Aurora, Illinois. She was the mother of seven children. George H. is a horse dealer at York, Nebraska, and next to him comes Dr. Charles H. Letitia, who is a graduate physician from Rush Medical College at Chicago and is in practice of medicine at Aurora. Frank A. is a practical farmer and occupies the old homestead at Mendota. Frank A. lives in La Salle County.

Doctor Westgate was reared on the old farm, developed a good physique by farm work, and the schools at Mendota supplied him with a thorough education. For four years he served as chief of police at Mendota and made a record as a courageous officer.

In La Salle County, Illinois, August 6, 1888, Doctor Westgate married Jessie Wallace, whose grandmother, Elizabeth Wallace, lived to the remarkable age of one hundred and two years. Both Mrs. Westgate's parents are now deceased. Mrs. Westgate was one of twelve children, five sons and seven daughters. To their marriage have been born the following children: Lloyd A., a popular man in the United States postal mail service; Morth B. and David W. Doctor Westgate has an attractive modern eight-room residence, furnished in good taste and with everything needed for comfortable living. He owns three other good homes in Blackwell, and has two valuable farms in Kay County. Among the little possessions which he cherishes is the old deed written on parchment covering the title of the land in Illinois granted by the Government to his grandfather ninety years ago.

Doctor Westgate is a fine specimen of physical manhood, stands six feet in height and weighs 200 pounds and has the bearing and address of an army officer. He is interested in local manufacturing, and has a wide connection with men and affairs both in Oklahoma and elsewhere. He owns a fine automobile, and uses it both for business and for the recreation of himself and family.

H. T. HANSFORD. The manager of the Municipal Bath House at Guthrie, perhaps more widely known as the Guthrie Hercules Sanitarium, Mr. Hansford deserves the credit for making this splendid institution known far and wide and appreciated for the curative value of the waters and the efficiency of the service not only in Oklahoma but over the entire Middle West.

Mr. Hansford was a Kansas banker for many years, but in 1908 he moved to San Antonio, Texas, and became interested in lands in Southwest Texas and also in promotion and capitalistic affairs. It was while at San Antonio that he became familiar in a business way with mineral waters and the conduct of sanitariums. In 1913 he was attracted to Guthrie by the curative properties of the mineral waters at that point. During 1914 he made arrangements and secured a lease from the Park Board Commissioners, beginning January 1, 1915, for the Municipal Bathhouse and Sanitarium. His lease runs for a term of ten years, and since taking charge he has really been responsible for the growth and development of the institution. This is a very elaborate enterprise, and is recognized as the most complete in general equipment and service west of the Mississippi River.

It cost $100,000 to construct the fireproof building and install the splendid equipment. The building itself is one of the handsomest examples of architecture found anywhere in Oklahoma. Constructed on the mission style, its attractiveness is enhanced by its broad verandas and loggias, and the splendid expanse of glass, which indicates that sunlight and fresh air are combined with the curative properties of the waters which are supplied from five different mineral wells. There is a competent staff of attendants, and the building has facilities for furnishing thirty different types of baths. The equipment for hydrotherapeutics cannot be excelled by any institution in America. The building was erected by the City of Guthrie. The waters from these mineral wells are recognized as specifics in the treatment of a number of physical disorders, and are helpful agencies in assisting in the restoration to health of persons suffering from many ailments of the vital organs and nervous diseases.

Since Mr. Hansford took charge of the sanitarium its patronage has more than doubled, and its patients come from all parts of the United States, Mexico, Canada, and even from the Hawaiian Islands.

Mr. Hansford was born February 6, 1869, at Morrison, Whiteside County, Illinois, a son of Thomas J. and Lydia A. (Eads) Hansford, both of whom were natives of Kentucky. His mother was a relative of the famous engineer who designed and built the Eads Bridge at St. Louis. Thomas J. Hansford served in the Union army during the Civil war, and he died in 1875 from disease contracted during his military service. H. T. Hansford at that time was six years of age, and from boyhood he has relied upon his own efforts and enterprise to advance him through life. He came out to Kansas and finished his education in the college at Horton in that state, and also took a business course at Fort Scott. For several years he was in the insurance business, and was then elected cashier of the Kansas State Bank at Fort Scott, a position he filled until 1908, when he left for Texas, and his experiences there finally brought him to Guthrie.

Mr. Hansford is not only a man of great energy and enterprise but has a magnetic personality, has a host of friends and is recognized as a genial entertainer and one who shows a true Southern hospitality in all his relations. Fraternally he is a thirty-second degree Scottish Rite Mason.

TRUDO JONES WEBB. While one of the most difficult of professions, that of medicine is likewise one that brings the greatest service and value to humanity, and while its practitioners seldom occupy the conspicuous positions in the world they perform a work of more direct and greater value to individuals than can be claimed for any other calling. A young man of exceptional native qualifications and thorough training, Doctor Webb has already gained recognition and reputation for skill and successful work as a physician and surgeon, and after several years of practice in Northwest Texas has been located at Tipton, Oklahoma, since 1911.

He was born at Lockhart in Caldwell County, Texas, April 23, 1883. His grandfather James Webb was born in Tennessee, and while serving in a Tennessee regiment with the Confederate army was killed in the Civil war. He was a Tennessee farmer, and his family had settled in that state during the early days. F. M. Webb, father of Doctor Webb, was born at Winchester in Franklin County, Tennessee, in 1850. When he was a boy his parents removed to Southeastern Texas and he has lived in that state ever since, a farmer and stock raiser, and since 1890 has been established at Romney in Eastland County. He is an active member of the Methodist Episcopal Church and a democrat in politics. F. M. Webb married Alice McGinnis, a native of Texas. They have a large family of children, a brief record of them being as follows: Sophronia, wife of W. P. Grubbs, who owns several farms and lives at Carbon, Texas; Dr. Trudo J.; Brice, who is a farmer at Romney, Texas; Eva, wife of Iva Bostick, a farmer at Romney; Mack, a druggist at Tipton, Oklahoma; Elsie, wife of Mr. Elliott, a retail meat dealer at Sweetwater, Texas; Lou, who married A. Blackwell, now postmaster at Romney; Terry, Lillian and Beatrice, twins, and Bernard, all living at home and attending the public schools at Romney.

Doctor Webb was educated in the public schools at Romney, where he lived from the age of seven, and had the usual life and experiences of a farmer boy up to the age of eighteen. In preparation for his chosen profession he attended the medical department of the University of Nashville two years and spent three years at the Memphis Hospital College. He graduated M. D. April 29, 1904, and did his first practice at Hale Center, Texas, where he remained eight months. From 1905 till the fall of 1911 he was located at Texico, on the line between Texas and New Mexico, and in the fall of 1911 removed to Tipton, Oklahoma, where he has since acquired a profitable general medical and surgical practice. His offices are in the Tipton Drug Store and Postoffice Building on Main Street.

While living at Texico Doctor Webb served as health officer. He is a democrat, is affiliated with Tipton Lodge No. 417, Ancient Free and Accepted Masons, and with the Woodmen of the World at Tipton. On August 5, 1907, at Fort Worth, Texas, he married Miss Adelia Nichols, whose father is W. H. Nichols, of Texico, New Mexico.

AUGUSTUS WOOD HENDERSON. With the construction of the Midland Valley Railroad through Osage County and the laying out of the Townsite of Avant in 1909, one of the first settlers and business men to locate in the new community was Augustus Wood Henderson, who bought some lots and in the midst of a corn field erected the building in which the Bank of Avant has since been housed. Since then Mr. Henderson has been actively identified with local affairs chiefly as a real estate man, and is one of the local capitalists. Mr. Henderson is one of the characters of the Kansas-Oklahoma frontier, and has lived in close touch with the Indian peoples and the pioneer communities of the Southwest the greater part of his life. A distinction which will at once serve to identify him with early Oklahoma history is that he was a member of Payne's Colony of Oklahoma Boomers during the decade of the '80s, and several years before Oklahoma Territory was first opened to settlement.

He was born at Marion Center in Indiana County, Pennsylvania, December 21, 1850, a son of John McKinley and Elizabeth Black (Wood) Henderson, both of whom were natives of Pennsylvania, his father of Westmoreland County. John M. Henderson learned the trade of tailor at Punxsutawney, Pennsylvania, and was employed at his trade until 1856, when he removed to Henry County, Illinois, and was engaged in farming in that rich district of the Prairie State until 1865. He then moved to Eastern Kansas, settling on a farm seven miles from Olathe in Johnson County, where he continued to reside until his death in 1890. His first wife, and the mother of Augustus W. Henderson, had died in Illinois in 1863 while he was away in the army. He served in the One Hundred and Twelfth Illinois Mounted Infantry, was wounded at the Battle of Richmond, Kentucky, and after spending some time in the hospital was discharged in the fall of 1864. Not long afterward he returned to Pennsylvania and married for his second wife Miranda Brady. There were four children by the first wife and five by the second. The older son, William Henry Harrison Henderson, was wounded while fighting with the Union army, and died from the results after he returned home. Augustus W. Henderson is now the only one living of his mother's children, and there is one son by his father's second wife.

Since he was fifteen years of age Mr. A. W. Henderson has lived in the West and has witnessed almost the entire development of the states of Kansas and Oklahoma. Most of his education came from the country schools of Illinois, and his career of adventure began when he was eighteen years old, with his enlistment in 1868 in the Nineteenth Kansas Cavalry for service under General Custer against the Indians. He was with his command during the winter of 1868-69, and was discharged from the army in the spring of the latter year. In 1871 Mr. Henderson left home and the next three years were spent at Wichita, Kansas. He was married while living there to Cordelia C. Gillman, who was born near Monticello, Iowa, and died at Coffeyville, Kansas, in the spring of 1879. Her only child was Beulah L., who died at Alva, Oklahoma in 1901, after her marriage to W. C. Ferguson, by which union there was one child Carmalete.

After the death of his first wife Mr. Henderson, who had already gained an extensive experience on the cattle ranges of Central and Western Kansas, moved to the Sac and Fox Agency in Oklahoma, and was in the employ of the trader John Whistler during 1879-80. He continued in the cattle business until 1882, and it was during that time that he first became identified with the Payne Boomers. In 1882 he engaged in the saloon business at Honeywell, Kansas, but in the same fall removed his business to Kiowa. In the fall of 1893, with the opening of the Cherokee Strip, he took up a claim and about the same time established at Alva a saloon and cold storage plant, and he continued to be identified with that business until the admission of Oklahoma as a state in 1907 and the consequent closing of all the saloons throughout the territory. He soon afterwards moved to Osage County and has since been a factor in the upbuilding of Avant.

In 1900 at Oxford, Kansas, Mr. Henderson married Carrie A. McCann. She brought him one daughter, Edith L., who is now the wife of James L. Beeler, who is now conducting the bottling works at Alva which represents Mr. Henderson's original enterprise in that city. Mr. and Mrs. Henderson also have an adopted son, Fred Sweet Henderson, who is now a farmer in Major County, Oklahoma.

Among the interesting experiences of Mr. Henderson there should be recalled one which followed his entry into the Panhandle of Texas during the fall of 1887 while the Santa Fe Railroad was being built across that territory. He located at Miami, and was soon afterwards involved in the local struggle for the location of a county seat for Roberts County. For a time there were two sets of county officials in Roberts County, and owing to the fact that both of the nominal sheriffs appointed Mr. Henderson deputy sheriff, he was really the only legally constituted and qualified person in the county government. Politically Mr. Henderson is a democrat and has fraternal affiliations with the Knights of Pythias, the Fraternal Order of Eagles and the American Horse Thief Association. During his early days on the plains Mr. Henderson for about fifteen years allowed his hair to grow long until it fell over his shoulders like an Indian, and there is a photograph still extant which shows him in this picturesque costume. During the many years that Mr. Henderson conducted a saloon at Alva it is only a matter of justice to record that he never had a fight on his premises and no man was ever arrested at his bar.

STEVEN P. HANNIFIN. Among the enterprising and ambitious citizens of the enterprising and ambitious City of Devol, Oklahoma, none has labored more energetically in the interests of the community than has Steven P. Hannifin, proprietor and editor of the Devol Dispatch. During the two years that he has conducted this newspaper, he has developed it into one of the successful journalistic efforts of Cotton County, and at all times has given over its columns to a stanch support of Devol and its industries and institutions.

Mr. Hannifin was born at Waterloo, Wisconsin, July 23, 1895, and therefore is but twenty years of age, but it would seem in his case that youth has been no bar to his success. He comes of good old Irish stock, his grandfather, Steven Hannifin, for whom he was named, having been born in County Kerry, Ireland, in 1805. Shortly after his marriage, the grandfather emigrated to the United States, settling at Waterloo, Wisconsin; where he continued to be engaged in agricultural pursuits until his death, in 1902, when he was ninety-seven years of age. On the maternal side, Mr. Hannifin's grandfather was Patrick Griffin, a native of County Clare, who on his arrival in this country located at Waterloo, Wisconsin, but later moved to the City of Madison, in that state, and there died. He became a man of prominence and influence, and for several terms represented his district in the Wisconsin State Legislature.

D. L. Hannifin, the father of Steven P. Hannifin, was born on his father's farm in Wisconsin, June 12, 1863, and was brought up to agricultural pursuits, in which he was engaged in his native locality until 1907, being the owner of a handsome and valuable farm located one mile north of Waterloo. In the year mentioned he removed to Randlett, Oklahoma, where he established himself in the furniture and undertaking business, and continued at that place until 1913, when he added his name to the list of business men of Devol. Here he has continued in the same line to the present time, having a modern establishment and a large and representative patronage. In political matters a strong democrat, while a resident of Wisconsin Mr. Hannifin served in the legislature during the sessions of 1902 and 1904. Mr. Hannifin was married to Miss Etta Griffin, who was born in 1870, at Waterloo, Wisconsin, and they have had only one child: Steven P.

Steven P. Hannifin commenced his educational training in the public schools of Waterloo, Wisconsin, and was twelve years old when he accompanied his parents to Randlett, Oklahoma, where he graduated from the high school in the class of 1912. At that time he secured a position with the Bank of Randlett, where he worked for one year in the capacity of bookkeeper, but his inclinations indicated journalism as his field of effort, and in 1913 he came to Devol and purchased the Devol Dispatch, of which he has since been the proprietor and editor. This newspaper, a democratic organ, was established in 1909 by M. A. Forgy, and it was purchased by Mr. Hannifin in 1913. It circulates in Cotton and the surrounding counties and has also a respectable foreign list, its list of readers constantly growing because of the able management and clean policies of its owner. The plant, modern in every particular, with equipment for high class job printing, is located on Wichita Avenue. Mr. Hannifin has "made good" in his chosen field of effort, and is eminently deserving of the support which is being given him by his subscribers and advertisers.

Mr. Hannifin's political views make him a supporter of democratic principles. He is a member of the Woodmen of the World, at Devol, and his religious faith is that of the Roman Catholic Church. He is unmarried.

EDWARD L. CRUZAN. A resident of Oklahoma for more than a quarter of a century, Edward L. Cruzan has become widely known in a number of lines of endeavor, having been successively occupied as agriculturist, preacher, chiropractor and merchant. At the present time he is head of the prominent firm of Cruzan & Son Hardware Company, dealer in agricultural implements, wagons and vehicles and binder twine, a concern at Cushing which has been developed to large proportions by excellent management and honorable business methods.

Mr. Cruzan was born near the Town of West Union, in Adams County, Ohio, May 10, 1862, and is a son of Proverbs B. and Catherine (Blackburn) Cruzan, the former a native of Indiana and the latter of Ohio. He was a farmer by vocation and for a number of years carried on operations in Adams County, Ohio, but in 1882 moved to the West, settling on a farm in Chautauqua County, Kansas. That locality continued to be his home until 1889, when he moved with his son, Edward L., to Oklahoma, and here passed away near Cushing, at the age of sixty-five years. During the period of the Civil war, while living in Ohio, he attempted on three occasions to enlist for service in the Union army, but was each time rejected, owing to an injury he had received in youth and which made him ineligible for military duty. There were six children in the family, namely: Willie, who died in childhood; Mrs. Elizabeth McKee, who is deceased; Thomas J., who resides near Cushing; Edward L.; U. S. Grant, who lives on his farm five miles from Cushing; and Nora, who is the wife of Horve Custer, of Pauls Valley, Oklahoma.

Edward L. Cruzan was reared on his father's farm in Adams County, Ohio, and there received his education in the public schools. He was twenty years of age when he accompanied his parents to the West, and in the fall of 1889 came to Oklahoma, purchasing one-quarter section of land nine miles southwest of Stillwater, a property on which he resided until 1906, then disposing of his interests and moving to another tract on Euchee Creek, ten miles northeast of Cushing. Mr. Cruzan continued to be engaged in agricultural operations until the winter of 1914, when he retired from that line of endeavor, disposing of his interests therein and coming to Cushing, where he founded the present business of Cruzan & Son Hardware Company, succeeding the Cushing Trading Company. He has directed the affairs of this concern with judgment, acumen and foresight, and has attracted a large trade in shelf and heavy hardware, agricultural implements, wagons, binder twine and groceries, making a specialty of the Deere agricultural machinery. Aside from this business Mr. Cruzan has practiced during the past four years as a chiropractor, and has gained success and reputation as a devotee of the science of adjusting the joints, especially those of the spine, by hand, for the curing of disease. For about six years he was also a preacher of the Holiness faith, but in more recent years has been a member of the Presbyterian Church. Mr. Cruzan is a republican in his political views and at various times has been elected to public office, having been particularly active in educational affairs as a member of the school board. Since coming to Cushing he has been busily engaged with the establishment of his business, but has found time to take a lively and helpful interest in civic affairs.

Mr. Cruzan was married in 1887 to Miss Ida A. Stout, who was born July 17, 1866, in Indiana, daughter of Samuel and Eliza Stout, and they are the parents of five children: Virgil, who is a farmer; Carl B., who is his father's business associate in the firm of Cruzan & Son Hardware Company; and the Misses Golda Belle, Ethel and Naomi.

JOHN S. IRWIN, of Bartlesville, is one of the big men of Oklahoma. He deserves that reputation not on one count, but on many. He is a banker, a leader in oil development and operations, a big farmer, owning a large estate of farms and managing them under his personal supervision. Not only are his interests in a financial and material way of a large scope, but his mind and character are developed on an equally broad scale. His friends say that one of his dominating characteristics is his liberality. His business success can no doubt be attributed to the fact that he possesses a boundless energy and if he ever loses a minute no one has ever been found to convict him of the loss. He is readily approachable, affable, kindly and genial, yet those who seek him on business or for some other reason say that he is one of the hardest men to find in the state. He is seldom in his office, but is always where his services are most needed at the time, giving his personal supervision to every detail, and that is just as likely to be out on one of his farms as in his office.

He is Scotch-Irish, of the typical stock of Western Pennsylvania, and the fact that he has lived his life often in close touch with the hardships of circumstance as well as with prosperity has undoubtedly made him unusually sympathetic with misfortune. Those who know him best say that he thinks little of himself, but all for his family and his friends, and has helped many a struggling man over some of the hard rocks of the road.

He was born in Butler County, Pennsylvania, February 10, 1867, a son of Samuel and Martha J. (McCandless) Irwin. His parents were fine old Scotch-Irish people and spent most of their lives in Butler County, Pennsylvania, where his father died at the age of fifty-eight and his mother at sixty-four. Samuel Irwin was a gallant soldier in the Union army during the Civil war, and his period of service covered practically the entire period of struggle between the states of the North and the South. It was due to the hardships incurred during his military career with a Pennsylvania infantry regiment that his early death abbreviated his useful career. He and his wife were members of the United Brethren Church. There were four sons and four daughters in the family, and all the sons have been useful and successful men, though undoubtedly John S. Irwin has had the faculty of doing things and thinking quickly and acting energetically to a degree superior to them all. A brief record of these children is: Mary, wife of John G. McKissick of Oklahoma; John S.; Robert, a manufacturer of engines in the State of Oregon; Eva, wife of Loyal Aggs of Washington County, Oklahoma; James M., of Bartlesville; Samuel C., a resident of Copan, Washington County, Oklahoma; Carrie, wife of Clyde Wicks of Butler County, Pennsylvania; and Belle, of Pittsburgh, Pennsylvania.

Native judgment, common sense and the faculty of going ahead and doing things and profiting by experience have been the factors chiefly responsible for John S. Irwin's success. He had very little book learning, though during the first twenty-one years spent on the old homestead farm in Pennsylvania he attended the public schools about as regularly as most boys. A few months before he reached his majority, in 1867, he came west to Sumner County, Kansas, and from there went to Colorado, spending two seasons in the cattle business. Eventually he became associated with that group of stockmen whose operations extended from Southern Kansas by lease right from the Cherokee Indians into the old Cherokee Strip of Indian Territory. His individual operations were at a point south of the present Village of Caldwell. He was among the cattlemen affected by the ruling of the Government department to vacate the strip, and all his improvements were confiscated. Thus Mr. Irwin had two years of experience as a pioneer in one of the most prosperous sections of Oklahoma prior to its opening to settlement.

In 1892 Mr. Irwin married Miss Ollie H. Suddarth, and for the following two years was a Kansas farmer. He then returned with his family to Pennsylvania and turned to an entirely new vocation, the oil industry. In that as in other things he succeeded because of his temperamental courage and instinctive good judgment. He acquired a complete knowledge of all the technical details of oil development and from Pennsylvania went to West Virginia and was a factor in oil operations in that state until 1904. In that year he came to Oklahoma. His previous years had brought him alternate success and vicissitudes and when he arrived in Oklahoma he had practically nothing and in fact owed some debts. Some of his early associates in this state tell some very interesting stories that show Mr. Irwin's positive character and ability to convince others of his resourcefulness as a worker. It is said that he could get money from the banks when even men with much larger visible resources failed, and he did this not by any subterfuge or covering up the real circumstances of the case, but by explaining in a straightforward

John S. Irwin

manner that he had no money and did not know whether he would ever be able to repay the loan or not, but in some way he had the power of giving others the confidence which he seemed to feel in himself. He seldom encountered much difficulty in securing an outfit of rigs to start drilling in a new district, and such supplies were furnished him on credit as freely as they would have been given to others for cash. With eight years of experience in the oil business of Pennsylvania and West Virginia, he soon proved a factor in the oil development of Northern Oklahoma. For the past ten years he has been one of the most influential men in developing the oil and gas fields of Oklahoma, and in that time has drilled over 200 wells and more than 100 of them proved producing properties. At the present time he is president of the Matoaka Oil Company, which controls several producing wells in Washington County, and is also president of the Hester Oil Company, with wells in Greer County.

He is a stockholder in two of the national banks of Bartlesville, and since 1912 has been active in buying and improving Oklahoma lands, both as a farmer and stock raiser. One of his ranches comprises 1,700 acres and is situated at the head of Candy Creek in Osage County. He owns a fine farm six miles south of Bartlesville comprising 500 acres. In the vicinity of Oglesby, in Washington County, is another farm of 200 acres, and there are several other small farms owned by him. He goes at his farming and stock raising with the same energy that he takes into other business affairs, and never neglects a single detail. In 1915 he had 300 head of cattle and sixty head of horses, and it has been his ambition and his policy to bring the standard of his stock up to the highest possible excellence. Not only in the management of his extensive private affairs but also in the work of building and developing Bartlesville does he deserve special mention. He has done things himself and has been influential in getting things done that are of material benefit to this community. He was associated with William A. Smith in the erection of the fine store and office building on Third Street known as the Irwin-Brin Building, Mr. Smith having sold his interest to L. N. Brin. With two other progressive Bartlesville business men, Burlingame and Maire Bros., he was associated in the erection of the Empire Building, and also in the erection of the Maire Hotel, the Elks Building and the Bartlesville Country Club Building.

Politically he is a republican. Both he and his wife are very prominent in the Methodist Episcopal Church, of which his wife is a member, and only those in close touch with the church know the exact quantity of his liberality in supporting its various enterprises. He is affiliated with the Benevolent and Protective Order of Elks, is both a York and Scottish Rite Mason, having attained the thirty-second degree of Scottish Rite and is also a member of the Nobles of the Mystic Shrine and belongs to the Country Club. Mr. Irwin is proud of his family and the mainspring of his tremendous energy and working ability is found in his devotion to his home. He and his wife have four children, all of whom were born in Kansas except the youngest, who was born in West Virginia. Ima, the oldest, is the wife of Don Tyler of Bartlesville, and they have one child, Helen Louise. The three younger children, still at home, are Iva, Ivan and Ruth.

JOHN T. McWILLIAMS. The flourishing Town of Tipton in Tillman County was founded as the result of the enterprise of the late W. A. McWilliams and its present site, was originally comprised in the half section of land owned by that pioneer, and his son, J. T. John T. McWilliams has himself been identified with the town from its beginning, and is now one of the leading merchants and property owners and a vigorous and public spirited citizen.

The McWilliams family came over from Ireland many years ago, and were pioneer settlers in the State of Arkansas. In White County of the latter state John T. McWilliams was born October 6, 1876. His father, the late W. A. McWilliams, was born in Columbia County, Arkansas, in 1854, and died at Tinton, Oklahoma, October 3, 1911. He was a resident of White County, Arkansas, up to 1884, then removed to Hico, Texas, and in 1901 brought his family to what is now Tipton, where they were the first permanent settlers. At the opening of the Kiowa and Comanche reservation he brought a bunch of cattle to Lawton and in September, 1901, drove his stock to Tipton though at that time there was no village, no habitation, and nothing but a broad expanse of uncultivated and unoccupied wilderness. In Arkansas and Texas W. A. McWilliams was a substantial farmer, and continued farming and stock raising combined with merchandising at Tipton. He acquired the half section of land on which the town has been built. He was likewise influential in democratic politics, was a deacon in the Baptist Church, and was affiliated with the Woodmen of the World. His first wife was Frankie Manning who died in White County, Arkansas. She was the mother of John T. McWilliams and Lollie, who died at the age of fifteen. W. A. McWilliams married Lizzie E. Blackwell of White County, Arkansas. She is now a resident of Tipton, and is the wife of J. M. Baker. Mr. Baker owns a half section of land near Eldorado, Oklahoma, has an interest in a cotton gin, a drug store and other business interests, though he is now largely retired from active pursuits.

John T. McWilliams attended the public schools at Hico, Texas, grew up on his father's farm, and his previous training and native vigor enabled him to take an active part in affairs as soon as he came to Tipton. Here he was first engaged in farming, and was associated with his father in the diversified cultivation of the soil and in raising stock and also in merchandising. Before the town site had been regularly laid out his father established a general merchandise store, and the land surrounding that nucleus was sold in small parcels and lots to the new comers as they arrived, and thus gradually the town came into being and its growth has since continued until it is a populous and busy center. Mr. McWilliams now manages and owns most of the original business established by his father, his mother having a quarter interest. The store is situated on Main Street at the corner of Broadway, and its new building was erected in 1910. It is a prosperous trading center, drawing trade from Tillman and Jackson counties, and the farmers come in for a number of miles from every point of the compass to lay in their supplies at this old and reliable house.

Mr. McWilliams is also a director in the Farmers State Bank at Tipton, has served on the town council, and is an active democrat. Fraternally he is affiliated with the Masonic order, Tipton Lodge No. 417, Ancient Free and Accepted Masons, and with Tipton Camp of the Modern Woodmen of America. In 1898 at Hico, Texas, he married Miss Maudie Watson. Her father, J. W. Watson, now occupies his farm five miles southeast of Tipton. There are three children of their marriage: Oran, now in the eighth grade of the public schools; Ona, in the seventh grade; and Aaron, in the fourth grade.

PIRL B. MYERS, M. D., is of German descent, although his paternal great-grandfather was born and reared to maturity in Switzerland, whence he immigrated to the United States in the early part of the nineteenth century. Frederick Myers, grandfather of the doctor, was likewise born in Switzerland and he was a mere boy at the time of his parents' removal to this country. The family settled in the vicinity of Patton, Missouri, and there engaged in farming operations. Riley Myers, son of Frederick Myers, was born on his father's farm near Patton, in 1851, and he was summoned to the life eternal in July, 1914. At the age of thirty years Riley Myers located in Barton County, Missouri, and one year later he established his home at Edgewood, that state. In 1883, however, he was again farming near the old homestead at Patton and there he continued to reside during the remainder of his life. He was a republican in his political affiliations and he served his community as justice of the peace for a number of years. He was prominent in local affairs and was held in high esteem by all who knew him. He married Mary Sharrock, who was born at Patton, in 1855, and to them were born seven children: Marcella died at the age of twenty years; William C. is a farmer near Patton; Perry J. is an electrician for the interurban railway at Coffeyville, Kansas; Nick is a resident of Stillwell, Kansas, where he is telegraph operator and agent for the Missouri Pacific Railway Company; Emma is the wife of W. C. Evans, a merchant at Doe Run, Missouri; Pirl B. is the subject of this sketch; and Rayford R. is a teacher in the public schools of St. Louis, Missouri. Mrs. Myers survives her honored husband and now resides at Patton, where she is a member of the Methodist Episcopal Church.

At Patton, Missouri, August 5, 1887, occurred the birth of Dr. Pirl B. Myers. He passed his boyhood and youth on his father's farm and was educated in the public schools of Patton, where he graduated in high school in 1906. He then went to Coffeyville, Kansas, and there worked at the trade of carpenter for one year. In the spring of 1907 he came to Oklahoma and worked at the trade of boilermaker in the oil fields near Tulsa until fall, when he was matriculated as a student in Barnes University, at St. Louis. He was out of school during the year 1909-10 and during that time worked as carpenter at Garden City, Dodge City and Kingsley, all in Kansas. He then returned to college and June 17, 1912, was graduated with the degree of Doctor of Medicine, receiving the same from the American Medical College, which is combined with Barnes University. June 9, 10 and 11 he passed the state board medical examination for the State of Oklahoma and immediately entered upon the active practice of his profession at Bernice, where he remained for two months. He came to Lookeba, in Caddo County, October 29, 1912, and here he has since resided. He controls a large and lucrative medical practice and has been very successful in his work. His offices are located on Main Street. He is a member of Caddo County Medical Society and of the Oklahoma State Medical Society. In politics he is a democrat and in religious faith is a Methodist. Fraternally, he is affiliated with Lookeba Lodge, No. 456, Independent Order of Odd Fellows, of which he is past noble grand; Patton Lodge No. 10680, Modern Woodmen of America; Lookeba Camp, No. 919, Woodmen of the World; and with the Oklahoma National, an old life insurance company. Doctor Myers is popular with all classes of people and he is looked upon as one of the rising young physicians of this section of the state.

August 31, 1911, at Kinsley, Kansas, was celebrated the marriage of Doctor Myers to Miss Myrtle Smith, a daughter of O. E. Smith, who owns a section and a half of fine wheat land just south of Kinsley. Doctor and Mrs. Myers have one child, Neal, born December 25, 1912.

GEORGE M. TREDWAY. For practically twenty-five years Mr. Tredway has been intimately associated in a commercial way with the people and affairs of the old Osage Nation, and it is doubtful if any white man stands higher in the esteem of those citizens than Mr. Tredway. For a number of years he has been one of the leaders in commercial affairs at Hominy in Osage County, and is perhaps best known at the present time as cashier of the First National Bank of that city. The First National Bank is an organization now ten years old, and Mr. Tredway has been with it during most of its existence. As a bank it is a solid institution, well managed, and its officers are all conservative bankers. The president is Prentiss Price, and the vice president Daniel B. Maher, and these three men comprise a notable group in the handling of financial affairs in Osage County. The bank is capitalized at $25,000, has a surplus of $30,000, deposits of over $200,000, and its aggregate resources according to a recent statement shows more than $300,000.

How Mr. Tredway first came to be identified with this section of old Indian Territory is an interesting little story. He was born at Madison, Wisconsin, April 22, 1872, a son of William and Margaret (McLaughlin) Tredway, the former a native of New York and the latter of Pennsylvania. His father enlisted from New York and rose to the rank of an officer in the United States navy during the Civil war, and at the close of the war was married at Washington, D. C., and soon afterward went out to Wisconsin, where he followed farming until his death, and his widow still lives there. Of their three children, John D. is now living in Seattle, Washington, and Mary is the wife of Joseph W. Hanley of Roberts, Wisconsin.

After getting his education in the public schools of his native state, George M. Tredway went to visit a relative in St. Louis, and at the same time looked for a business opening. His uncle was at that time president and the active head of the wholesale grocery house of the Greeley-Burnham Grocer Co., and one of the valued customers at the time young Tredway was making his visit was Mr. Campbell of Nowata, Oklahoma. Mr. Campbell was asked as to the prospects for an opening in a business way in the Southwest for the nephew, and Campbell told the young man to go to Bartlesville, Oklahoma, and inquire for Colonel Bartles. Thus in 1890 he came into Indian Territory on the recommendation of Mr. Campbell, presented himself before Col. Jacob H. Bartles, and was almost immediately put to work. He was soon afterwards sent by Colonel Bartles to his branch store in Pawhuska, operated under the firm name of Barndollar, Bartles & Gibson. Young Tredway was also to give his assistance during the regular distribution of payment and rations among the Indians. He lived at Pawhuska and was connected with the mercantile business until 1895, and since then has had his home at Hominy. Here he was connected with Read & Bopst, Indian traders, until they sold out to W. C. Wood & Company, and he continued with the new firm until February, 1904. At that time he associated with Prentiss Price, Fred Drummond and Percy Dixon, formed the Hominy Trading Company, Incorporated, with Mr. Tredway as treasurer and one of the active managers. Several years later he sold his interests in the trading company, and then engaged in the real estate business and the leasing of Osage lands. He also became identified with the First National Bank as assistant cashier, and on the death of the late Howard M. Maher succeeded to his position as cashier. Mr. Tredway is also treasurer of the Osage Gin & Light Company. He and Mr. Price conducted a large business in the leasing of

farm lands in this part of Oklahoma, and has carried on extensive farming operations.

In politics Mr. Tredway is a democrat. He was elected the first treasurer of Black Dog Township and has always shown a vigorous and public spirited attitude in local affairs. He is a member of the Presbyterian Church, and in Masonry is affiliated with the Consistory of the thirty second degree Scottish Rite Masons and is a Knight Commander of the Court of Honor, was one of the charter members and the first master of Hominy Lodge, Ancient Free and Accepted Masons, is a member of the Knight Templar Commandery and the Temple of the Mystic Shrine. Through his intimate commercial relations with the Indians through the past twenty-five years he has acquired a fluent command of the Osage tongue. He prizes a large collection of Indian relics, and all the more for the fact that he has bought none of them, all of them being given to him as marks of appreciation and friendship by different members of the tribe.

In 1895 Mr. Tredway married Miss Sally B. Hughes, who was born in Missouri, a daughter of John B. Hughes of Sedalia, that state. They have two daughters, Margaret and Frances, both of whom were born at their home in Hominy.

MILTON B. COPE. The present postmaster of El Reno, Milton B. Cope, is a lawyer by profession, and is one of the men who can claim the honor and whose name will go down in history as members of the first State Legislature of Oklahoma. Mr. Cope has been identified with the Oklahoma bar nearly fifteen years and throughout his professional career has been more or less closely identified with public life.

Milton B. Cope was born in Wilkes Barre, Pennsylvania, March 3, 1877, a son of Chester and Permilla (Steele) Cope. On his father's side he is of Dutch descent, while his mother's family was Scotch-Irish. Both his parents were born in Pennsylvania, and when Milton B. was thirteen years of age they came west in 1890, first locating in Brooks County, Kansas. Ten years later, in 1900, they located in Canadian County, Oklahoma, but in 1902 removed to Gotebo, in Kiowa County, where they now reside. Chester Cope has always followed farming as his vocation.

It was on a farm that Milton B. Cope spent his boyhood and gained discipline for mind and body. His early education was acquired in the common schools, and in 1895 he was graduated from the Stockton Academy, now the Northwest Kansas Normal at Stockton. It was at Stockton that he began the study of law, in one of the law offices of that place, and in 1901 was admitted to the Oklahoma bar before the Supreme Court.

Mr. Cope served as deputy county attorney of Canadian County from 1901 to 1904, and in 1907 was elected a member of the first State Legislature. In the proceedings of that body which put into effect the organic constitution of the state, his name is frequently mentioned, and in many ways he left the impress of his influence on the first body of statutes of Oklahoma State. In 1908 he was re-elected to office, and served two terms in the Legislature. As a lawyer his practice has been of gratifying proportions almost from its beginning. From 1907 to 1913 he was associated in practice with James I. Phelps.

Mr. Cope was appointed postmaster of El Reno by President Wilson, May 22, 1913. Most of his time is now given to the affairs of an office which in extent of receipts and business transactions is one of the largest in Oklahoma. Mr. Cope has for a number of years been one of the democratic leaders and in 1912 was chairman of the Canadian County Democratic Central Committee.

Fraternally his membership is in the Masonic Order, the Independent Order of Odd Fellows and the Modern Woodmen of America. He is a member of the Christian Church.

In 1905 Mr. Cope married Miss Ethel Bradley of El Reno.

GEORGE W. CANFIELD. The men who have given of their energy, ability, enthusiasm and ambitious vigor in the development of a community are entitled to the gratitude and respect of their fellow citizens. In every undertaking there must be a beginning, and the individual who lays the foundations for what may in future years become a large, prosperous and flourishing city, must be possessed of the courage of his convictions, unlimited faith in the future of the community he selects as the scene of his activities, and the ability to direct the affairs thereof. When, in 1900, he purchased the townsite of Yale, George W. Canfield looked far beyond the narrow horizon of that day and in his mind's eye saw the possibilities of this rich and fertile section of country. His judgment has been vindicated, for today this is one of the most promising localities of Central Oklahoma, and he has prospered by his foresight and acumen, being the owner of some of the richest oil land in the world and the head of the Yale Wholesale Grocer Company, a concern which has been developed to splendid proportions under his personal direction.

Mr. Canfield was born at Mattoon, Illinois, February 1, 1863, and is a son of Jesse and Catherine (Bausman) Canfield. His father was born in Virginia and his mother in Pennsylvania and they were married in Ohio, following which they first moved to Indiana and later to Illinois. In 1869 they again turned their faces toward the West, following other pioneers to Cherokee County, Kansas, where Mr. Canfield secured a claim, subsequently becoming one of those to lay out the Town of Columbus. Later he returned to Carroll County, Arkansas, and then went to Madison County, in that state, where he died in 1888, at the age of forty-nine years. Mrs. Canfield survived her husband many years and passed away at Jennings, Oklahoma, at the age of sixty-nine. During the greater part of his life Mr. Canfield was an agriculturist, but he was also successfully engaged in the sawmill business and conducted a gristmill. He was a republican in politics. There were eight children in the family, as follows: W. E., who is engaged in business operations at Yale in partnership with his brother; Miss Ida, who lives at Yale; Anna C., who is deceased; George W.; Charles, of Fort Lauderdale, Florida; Laura Bradshaw, of Kingston, Arkansas; Jesse, of Fort Lauderdale, Florida; and Willis, a hardware merchant at Yale.

George W. Canfield received a country school education and remained with his parents until twenty-two years of age, at which time he left home and spent one year in cotton picking on the Arkansas River. Returning to Kingston, Arkansas, with a capital of $7.50, he started a grocery store in a small way, and subsequently added a modest stock of drugs. His business prospered and after three years he sold his store and came to Oklahoma, being first located at Soonersville, near Cushing, later at Jennings, and finally at Yale. In 1910, with others, he purchased the townsite of Yale, and two years later laid out the town in company with his brothers, W. E. and Willis Canfield, Dr. E. G. Newell, E. F. Knowlton and G. M. Weems. This community has since been his home and the scene of his almost phenomenal success. With his brother, W. E., he soon bought the State Bank of Yale and continued in the banking business for two years, and when he retired from that enterprise started the Yale Wholesale Grocer Company, of which he has been manager and president to the present time. A modest concern in 1907, in 1915 this company did a business amounting to $400,000, with a branch office at Drumright, Oklahoma, its statement of March 1, 1914, showing the following figures: Liabilities: Accounts payable, $40,223.48; bills payable, $11,339.83; cash on deposit, $703.72; capital stock, $75,000.00. Total, $127,-267.03. Assets: Inventory of stock on hand, $27,775.26; accounts receivable, $83,434.69; bills receivable, $4,-648.02; furniture, fixtures, etc., $769.30; real estate, $9,212.13; cash on hand, $1,427.63. Total, $127,267.03. In December, 1913, Mr. Canfield built his present business house, a structure erected of native stone, 50 by 124 feet, with basement under all, one of the finest buildings in this part of the county. The development of this great industry is a striking example of American enterprise and of western grit and initiative. Mr. Canfield is also the owner of some of the most valuable oil land in the world, and is interest in the Twin State Oil Company and the Sun Oil Company of Yale, as well as the Webster Refining Company of this place, of which he is president. He has large holdings also in the Yale State Bank and the Farmers National Bank of Yale. His brother, W. E. Canfield, is associated with him in the great number of his interests. Mr. Canfield was the owner of a town lot at Perry which he secured after making the run to the Cherokee Strip, September 16, 1893, and which later he disposed of, and also has a valuable claim north of Jennings, which he obtained shortly afterward. In politics a republican, he is ably discharging the duties of citizenship as a member of the Yale City Council. Fraternally he is a Mason and an Odd Fellow and has passed all the chairs in both lodges.

In 1893 Mr. Canfield was married to Miss Roxie Wright, who was born in Arkansas, a daughter of J. M. Wright, and six children have been born to this union: Jesse, Ralph, Roy, Teddy, Ira and Wright.

Mr. Canfield belongs to a family which can trace its ancestry back for generations in this country, pointing with pride to nine Canfield brothers who fought in the Revolutionary war. His success, however, has rested entirely upon himself, and has naught to do with ancestry, save as he may have inherited the sterling traits of sturdy ancestors. There may be a feeling of family pride when an individual points to lands and possessions which his forefathers have gained and given to him, but how much more gratifying it must be to realize that one is the builder of his own fortune and that the credit belongs to himself alone for obstacles overcome and successful results accomplished.

WILLIAM W. CHILDERS. About twenty-five years ago Mr. Childers began his career as a teacher, after obtaining the benefits of a school and college education, followed that profession in Mississippi, Tennessee and Texas, had a somewhat extensive business experience in the latter state, and since 1909 has been identified with the flourishing Town of Tipton in Tillman County, where he is now cashier of the Farmers State Bank. He was one of the organizers of this institution, and its capital stock is $12,000 with surplus and undivided profits of $6,000. The modern brick bank building was erected in 1911 at the corner of Broadway and Main Street, and contains the largest vault in Tillman County. The president of the bank is C. W. Howard of Frederick, while the other officers live at Tipton, including R. S. Carlile, vice president; Mr. Childers, cashier; and Miss Clara Childers, assistant cashier.

The Childers family originated in Ireland, and was established in one of the Carolinas during the colonial era. The grandfather of the Tipton banker was James Childers, a native of Tennessee, whence he removed to Mississippi, and was killed while a soldier on the Confederate side during the war between the states. William W. Childers was born at Corinth, Mississippi, March 14, 1874. His father, S. H. Childers, who was born in Tennessee in 1845, grew up on his father's plantation in Mississippi, and in 1861 enlisted and was a Confederate soldier throughout the course of the war. He was with a regiment of Mississippi cavalry under the command of the noted Bedford Forrest, and in one battle was wounded in the left arm. After the war he returned to Mississippi, and since 1875 has lived at Ripley with the exception of about three years spent in Corinth. He has been a farmer and stock raiser, and still occupies the old homestead at Ripley. He is an active member of the Baptist Church and in politics a democrat. The maiden name of his wife was Melinda Griffin, a native of Alabama. Their living children are: Etta who married John D. Wammack, a farmer near Ripley; Jennie, wife of R. E. Clark, also a farmer near Ripley; William W.; Luther M., who is cashier of Bank of Elmer, Elmer, Oklahoma, and owns a stock ranch in Texas; John Y., a merchant at Clarysville, near Ripley, Mississippi; Escar, a farmer and stock man in Mississippi; J. E., who is now a practicing physician in Natchez, Mississippi; Obie, who lives on the farm with his parents; and Clara, assistant cashier of The Farmers State Bank, Tipton, Oklahoma.

Beginning his education in the public schools at Ripley, Mississippi, William W. Childers continued in the high school at Chalybeate, Mississippi, and in 1894 graduated from the Southern Tennessee Normal School. In 1896 he graduated bachelor of science from the West Tennessee Christian College. With this thorough training he taught school in Tennessee two years, and in 1898 removed to Southwest Texas and continued his professional work there six years. From 1904 to 1908 he was in business at Lake Victor, Texas, and then spent one year in the real estate business at San Antonio. In 1909 Mr. Childers removed to Tipton, assisted in organizing the Farmers State Bank, and became its cashier. He is vice president of The Bank of Elmer, Elmer, Oklahoma.

In politics he is a staunch democrat of the old line school. He has served as city clerk at Tipton, was clerk of the local school board, is city treasurer, and for two years was a member of the village council. He is one of the strong supporters of church activities, is a steward in the Methodist Episcopal Church South and superintendent of the Sunday School. In the Tipton Lodge No. 417, Ancient Free and Accepted Masons, he is serving as senior warden, also belongs to Frederick Chapter No. 41, Royal Arch Masons, has membership in the lodge of Knights of Pythias at Burnet, Texas, and formerly was affiliated with the Independent Order of Odd Fellows in Tennessee.

In 1905 at Marble Falls, Texas, Mr. Childers married Susie Browning Parkhill, who died at San Antonio in 1909. The one daughter of that marriage is Ethel, now attending public schools at Tipton. At Tipton in 1912 Mr. Childers married Miss Mattie Reeves, who came from Mayfield, Kentucky.

JOHN SKELLEY. To say that John Skelley of Mineral, Cimarron County, has lived in the Panhandle district of Oklahoma for a period of thirty years is sufficient to classify him with the real old timers and pioneers. He has spent all his life in the Far West, and it was only a few years ago that civilization caught up with him. For years he lived and worked on the open range, when the country was innocent of settlers or civilization, except a scattered population of pioneers, and when towns, railroads, and the institutions of developed society were far and isolated.

He was about five years of age when brought to the western country from Montgomery County, New York, where he was born April 2, 1864. His parents were Michael and Louise (Bailey) Skelley, the former a native of Ireland and the latter of New York. Michael Skelley, who was born in Ireland in 1820 and came to America in infancy, had a career of exceedingly varied experience. In the early days he conducted a boat on the old Erie Canal in New York State. In 1869 he came out to Colorado and followed various occupations afterwards, principally ranching and running a wagon freighting train, in connection with his brother, from various points on the Kansas Pacific Railroad, hauling supplies to military posts and the settlements in New Mexico until the building of the Santa Fe Railroad through that territory in 1880. He was a well known man in his day. He died at Pueblo, Colorado, in 1890. His wife, Louise Bailey, was born in New York State in 1830, a daughter of George Bailey, a native of the same state. She died January 3, 1903, at Sheridan, Wyoming. There were eight children in the family, four sons and four daughters, five of them still living.

John Skelley came out to Trinidad, Colorado, with his parents in 1869. As a boy he attended the public schools in Trinidad, Colorado. When only fourteen he started out as a cowboy on a ranch. The next seven years were spent in the free and open life of the old time cattle man on the ranges of New Mexico and Wyoming. For one year during this period he was a government teamster with the quartermaster's department of the United States Army in Wyoming and the Black Hills of South Dakota, and he spent one year with a government surveying corps in northwestern Nebraska. After this, in 1885, a little more than thirty years ago, John Skelley directed his operations to what is now Cimarron County, Oklahoma, then described in the school geography as No Man's Land. His headquarters have been here ever since, except a period of two years, 1892 and 1893, when he went to Montana. He was first a teamster and cowboy, working for wages for different pioneers and ranch companies, but gradually his activities became his own, and for a number of years his operations have been such as to constitute him one of the leading ranchmen and citizens in this district of the Southwest. He now has a large ranch twenty-four miles northwest of Boise City at the old Mineral Postoffice in Cimarron County, comprising eight hundred acres of deeded land and eight thousand acres leased for ranch purposes. It is a ranch in size and equipment equal to the best still found in the ranching country. He has partly modern buildings, has set out a great many trees, and has considerable land under cultivation. The water for his ranch is furnished by both wells and stream. His home is noted for its hospitality, where the weary traveler gets both bed and board without question or price, should they need it.

For thirteen years Mr. Skelley conducted a general store at old Mineral City in No Man's Land, where he still resides, his postoffice address being Kenton, Oklahoma, and during that time his store was also the location of the postoffice, this office being established in 1888 and discontinued in 1911, and he served as postmaster thirteen years. In 1904 he was appointed United States Court Commissioner for the Western District of Oklahoma, and in 1907 was made a regular United States Commissioner, an office he filled for four years. He is a republican, though he has been too busy with practical affairs to seek office, and the few honors of that nature that have come to him came unsolicited. He is very popular with the native Mexican population of that part of Oklahoma and New Mexico, and he speaks the Mexican language like one of them and has their respect and confidence.

On April 25, 1895, Mr. Skelley married Miss Lucy Dacy, who was born in Kansas City, Missouri, October 12, 1871. She was a daughter of James Dacy, a pioneer who settled in No Man's Land in 1887 and who died in 1891. To their marriage have been born five children, two sons and three daughters: John Dacy, born December 27, 1896; Mary Catherine, born June 7, 1898, and died July 23, 1898; George Lewis, born May 23, 1899; Frances Louise, born April 5, 1902, and Lucy Elizabeth, born June 4, 1904.

P. R. WILLIAMS. When Mr. Williams started his business career fifteen years ago, in 1900, he had cash capital of less than $100. In Missouri and in Northeastern Oklahoma he has been steadily working upward, first as a merchant and subsequently as a banker, and is now the cashier of the First State Bank at Wynona and is a stockholder in four other banking institutions in this part of the state. He is one of the men who are providing the business leadership for Osage County.

Born in Lawrence County, Missouri, February 8, 1879, Mr. Williams is still a young man and his many friends predict a great deal for his future. His parents were Jesse A. and Eva (Ham) Williams, the former a native of North Carolina and the latter of Alabama. His mother came to Missouri with her parents, while his father removed to that state after he was grown, and was married in Lawrence County and both died on the homestead which he had acquired before his marriage. He passed away at the age of sixty-five, when his youngest son, P. R. Williams, was eight months of age, and the mother lived for a number of years and died at the age of fifty-nine. During the Civil war he was a soldier in the Union army with a Missouri regiment. The two oldest children are John, now living in California, and Jessie A., of Missouri.

P. R. Williams was reared on a farm, and in 1899 finished his education in the Collegiate Institute at Marionville in his native county. He soon afterwards became identified with merchandising at Verona, Missouri, and that was his home until he removed to Oklahoma in 1909. One year was spent at Mannsville, and he then came to Wynona, in Osage County. He and his brother-in-law, J. M. Browning, organized the First State Bank of Wynona in September, 1909, and Mr. Williams has since been its cashier. Mr. Browning has organized six different banks in this part of Oklahoma and Mr. Williams has an interest as a stockholder in five of them. The officers of the First State Bank are: J. M. Browning, president; J. A. Owens, vice president; P. R. Williams, cashier; and Mrs. Myrtle Williams, wife of Mr. Williams, assistant cashier. The bank has its deposits guaranteed by the Depositors Guaranty Fund of the State of Oklahoma.

Mr. Williams is active as a member of the Methodist Church, though he was reared a Presbyterian, and his wife is also active in the same denomination. In 1901 he married Myrtle Browning, who was born in Lawrence County, Missouri, a daughter of G. W. Browning. Mrs. Williams was graduated from the high school at Verona, Missouri.

JOHN S. BURGER. One of the dominating members of the Blackwell bar is John S. Burger, whose ability to render skillful service in the profession has brought him rapidly to a place of prominence in his section of the state. Mr. Burger is a former county attorney of Kay County, and is one of the pioneers of the old Cherokee Strip, having made the run to this country in September, 1893. He was at that time a young man, and for a number of years before taking up the law was a successful and popular teacher.

John S. Burger was born in Barry County, Missouri, February 25, 1871. The name is of German origin, but the family have been identified with this country for several generations. His grandfather was Rev. Jacob Burger, who became well known as a Methodist circuit rider both in Tennessee and in Missouri. He was one of the leaders in the abolition movement before the Civil war and preached and practiced that belief at a time when it was an exceedingly unpopular doctrine and exposed him to a great deal of personal danger and inconvenience. Rev. Jacob Burger died at Leavenworth, Kansas, in 1902, at the age of eighty-seven years. The father of the Blackwell lawyer was Lieut.-Col. George Burger, who was born in Tennessee, and he and his brother Samuel and their father were all soldiers in the Union army. Colonel Burger made a gallant record both as a soldier and officer. He was a mechanic and farmer, moved out to Fort Scott, Kansas, many years ago, and died in Noble County, Oklahoma, at the age of seventy-seven. He was a strong republican and a member of the Methodist Church. He was married in Bourbon County, Kansas, to Nancy Ellis, who was born in England, her family having come from that country and settled in Kansas. Colonel Burger and wife were the parents of five children. The daughter, Jennie, now lives in Grant County, Oklahoma; the next is John S.; W. F. is a railroad man living at Seattle, Washington; and Finis is an educator at Billings, Oklahoma.

John S. Burger was reared in the states of Missouri and Kansas, and largely through his own well directed efforts secured a liberal education. He is a man of fine physical frame and constitution and owes its development largely to the discipline of a Kansas farm while he was a boy. He attended the public schools at Winfield and Ureka, Kansas, was also a student in the State Normal, and spent five years in the active work of teaching. Some years after locating in a homestead in Clay County, Oklahoma, he returned to Kansas and entered the university at Lawrence, where he was graduated from the law department with the class of 1903. Since then he has been engaged in a successful practice at Blackwell. He was elected county attorney of Clay County in 1912, and the following two years gave a most effective administration to that office. He is a well read lawyer, and stands high in his profession. In politics he is a democrat.

Mr. Burger was married May 30, 1897, in Kansas, to Miss Carrie Barkly. Mrs. Burger was born in Illinois but was reared in the State of Kansas, and her father, J. S. Barkly, now lives at Tonkawa, Oklahoma. To this union have been born two sons and four daughters: Marietta, Altha, John S., Jr., Irena, William and Leonora. Mrs. Burger is a member of the Christian Church. He has taken much interest in Masonry, and is affiliated with the lodge, chapter and commandery, and is also a member of the India Temple of the Nobles of the Mystic Shrine at Oklahoma City. Mr. Burger, along with a fine knowledge of the law, has the ability of the forcible speaker, and these qualities, united with a frank and genial manner, have brought him hosts of friends, as well as a conspicuous position in his profession.

JAMES H. TOWNSEND. In the autumn of 1914 Mr. Townsend was elected sheriff of Payne County, whereupon he removed from the Village of Cushing to Stillwater, the county seat, and his alert and efficient administration is clearly proving that he is the right man in the right place and that the confidence of the electors of the county was fully justified when they called him to his present important and exacting office.

Sheriff Townsend was born at Sulphur Springs, the judicial center of Hopkins County, Texas, on the 22d of July, 1875, and is a son of William A. and Elizabeth (Perry) Townsend, the former of whom was born in Mississippi and the latter in Alabama, she having been fourteen years of age at the time of the family removal to Texas, prior to the Civil war, and having been reared and educated in the Lone Star State, where her marriage was solemnized. When the subject of this review was a child of six months his parents removed from his native place to Checota, Lamar County, Texas, where he received his early education in the public schools. The family then removed to Montague County, in the northern part of the state, and the present sheriff of Payne County, Oklahoma, was still a mere lad when he came with his parents to Indian Territory, about 1887. Mr. Townsend thus gained varied experience in connection with frontier life in old Indian Territory and is consistently to be designated as one of the pioneer citizens of Oklahoma, where he has kept step with the march of development and progress and has witnessed the upbuilding of a vigorous and prosperous commonwealth. The parents of Sheriff Townsend have maintained their home in Pontotoc County, Oklahoma, for nearly a score of years and the father has become one of the representative farmers and influential citizens of that county. Of the children Sheriff Townsend is the eldest; John is deceased; Joseph is now a resident of McNabb, Arkansas; and Jennie is the wife of Frederick W. Hutsey, of Oklahoma City.

The present sheriff of Payne County remained at the parental home until he had attained to the age of sixteen years. As a youth he was identified with the cattle industry on the ranges of Western Texas and the Indian Territory, and about 1891 his operations brought him into Indian Territory. He passed about two years in the Chickasaw region and then returned to Texas. He has maintained his permanent residence in what is now the State of Oklahoma since 1895. He resided in Pontotoc County until 1901 and then established his home at Sapulpa, Creek County, where he remained until May, 1913, when he became a resident of Cushing, Payne County. While a resident of Cushing Mr. Townsend was elected sheriff of the proposed County of Shaffer, but in the popular election the county failed of organization by a majority of sixty votes, so that the officers elected in anticipation of its establishment were not called upon to serve.

Mr. Townsend is a skilled mechanic, and as such has been prominently identified with railroad work, in which connection he has been employed in various railway shops in Oklahoma. While a resident of Sapulpa he served for some time as special agent for the St. Louis & San Francisco Railroad, and at the same place he was also called upon to serve as a member of the police force and as under-sheriff. His official service as a member of the constabulary of Creek County was initiated at the time of the opening of developments in the oil fields of that locality. In the autumn of 1914, as before noted, he was elected to the office of sheriff of Payne County, a position for which his previous experience and his general equipoise specially qualify him. The sheriff gives his allegiance to the democratic party and is identified with a number of fraternal and social organizations.

On the 18th of November, 1897, Sheriff Townsend wedded Miss Rosa Lee Solwell, who was born in Tarrant County, Texas, and who was reared to majority in Montague County, that state. Mr. and Mrs. Townsend have two children, Elmer Edwin, who was born March 13, 1904, and Horace Haskell, who was born November 8, 1907, and who was named in honor of the first governor of the new State of Oklahoma, which was admitted to the Union in that year.

FRANK GROVER PATTERSON. One of the youngest members of the newspaper fraternity in Western Oklahoma is Frank G. Patterson, proprietor and editor of the Davidson News. While a very young man in years, Mr. Patterson has had an extensive experience in the newspaper business, printing and allied arts, and for fully eight years has been identified with the papers of Tillman County.

He represents an old pioneer family of Livingston County, Missouri, and was born in the City of Chillicothe, in that county, May 31, 1889. The Patterson family originally came from England, was subsequently found both in Kentucky and Tennessee, and Mr. Patterson's grandfather Thomas Newton Patterson was born in Kentucky in 1816, shortly after his marriage moved to Chillicothe, Missouri, where he became one of the first farmers in Livingston County, and died at Waterloo, Oklahoma, in 1905. T. J. Patterson, father of the Davidson editor, was born at Chillicothe in 1863, and still lives in that city. In earlier years he was a teacher in the Chillicothe public schools, but eventually took up the business of contractor and builder, and has had a large business in that line at Chillicothe and vicinity, and has also carried out building contracts at El Reno and in other parts of Oklahoma. T. J. Patterson married Laura Belle Henderson, a native of Chillicothe. Their children are: Arthur, who lives at Louisville, Kentucky; Elizabeth, wife of Cam Fullerton, an elevator constructor at Kansas City, Missouri; Rae, who married Roy Berg, an electrician at Chillicothe; Frank G.; Harry, a linotype operator at Kansas City; Thomas, a senior in the Chillicothe High School; and Lena, also in high school.

The public schools of Chillicothe furnished Frank Grover Patterson his early training, but at an early age he entered the great university of a printing shop, serving an apprenticeship at Chillicothe. In 1907 he came to Southwestern Oklahoma and was employed first with the Frederick Enterprise. He managed the paper and subsequently other papers in Tillman County up to 1911, in which year he came to Davidson and bought the News from U. L. Jolly, and has since been its proprietor and editor. The News is democratic in politics, has a circulation throughout Tillman and neighboring counties, and its offices and plant are well equipped for newspaper and job printing.

Mr. Patterson himself is a democrat, and has made himself a factor in all public spirited movements undertaken at Davidson during recent years. He was married at Frederick, Oklahoma, in 1908 to Miss Elizabeth Pike, a daughter of B. M. Pike, who is proprietor of a hotel at Wichita Falls, Texas. Mr. Patterson and wife have two children: Lois born May 26, 1909, and Louise, born December 23, 1911.

JOHN RILEY THACKER. The life of a literary man seldom exhibits any of those striking incidents that seize upon public feeling and fix attention upon himself. His character, for the most part, is made up of the aggregate of the qualities and qualifications he may possess, as these may be elicited by the exercise of the duties of his vocation or the particular profession to which he may belong. However, it may be said that John Riley Thacker presents an exception to the general rule. His career has been passed largely in a literary atmosphere, for a major part of his activities have been spent in the schoolroom and in connection with journalistic work; yet he has also impressed himself and his character upon the people of the communities in which he has resided as a capable worker in other fields of endeavor, and his various achievements have raised his reputation greatly above that of the mediocre worker in the world of letters.
Vol. V—14

John Riley Thacker, proprietor and editor of the Eldorado Courier, was born at Randolph, Fannin County, Texas, December 5, 1869, and is a son of James Riley and Susanna Elizabeth (Patton) Thacker, and a member of a family of Scotch-Irish origin, whose original ancestor in America came to Virginia in the seventeenth century. Members of the family spread from that state to others of the South in early days, and a connection of the branch to which Mr. Thacker belongs was Daniel Boone, the great American frontiersman, explorer and colonizer. James Riley Thacker was born in Mississippi, March 16, 1833, and from that state removed with his parents to Louisiana and later to near Longview, Gregg County, Texas. About the time of the beginning of the Civil war Mr. Thacker went to the California gold fields, where he spent seven years in mining, and in 1867 returned to Collin County, Texas, from whence he went to Fannin County, in the same state, and there, October 30, 1868, was married to Susannah Elizabeth Patton, who was born at Randolph, Texas, December 30, 1844, where they still reside. Mr. Thacker has passed his entire life as a farmer and stockman, and has also been a local preacher of the Methodist Episcopal Church, South. He is a member of the Independent Order of Odd Fellows. There were nine children in the family of James R. and Susanna E. Thacker, as follows: John Riley; Martha Jane, who died in 1903 as the wife of Jacob Colvin, who now resides in Florida; Cora Anu, who married R. N. Davenport, a farmer of Harleton, Texas; Ida Catherine, who died at the age of eighteen years; Robert Oscar, formerly a railroad man for a number of years and now a farmer of Fannin County, Texas, residing at Randolph; Benjamin William, a barber of Denison, Texas; James Edwin, who died as a child; Elijah Otto, a farmer and school teacher of Randolph, Texas; and Miss Julia May, who is single and resides at the home of her parents.

John Riley Thacker attended the public schools at Randolph, and was graduated from Randolph High School in the class of 1889. He had shown himself a penmaster while at school and for a short time was engaged in teaching penmanship in Fannin and Williamson counties, Texas, and in 1892 received his introduction to journalistic work when he became connected with a printing office at Bonham, Texas, where was published the Farmers' Review. After one year with this paper and a like period spent in farming, Mr. Thacker became identified with the Leonard Graphic, at Leonard, Texas, a publication with which he was connected on and off until 1896, when he identified himself with a paper at Savoy, Texas, and about this time published a small book of poems entitled "Boyhood's Pencilings," which was received very favorably by both press and public. From that time forward Mr. Thacker was employed by various newspapers and wrote articles of a miscellaneous character until 1900, when he became district organizer in Montague County, Texas, for the Woodmen of the World, and after leaving that position attended Draughon's Business College, at Fort Worth, Texas. In 1901 he occupied a position with the Brownwood (Texas) Business College, teaching bookkeeping and penmanship, and in the same year went to San Angelo, Texas, where he occupied a like post. Returning to Fannin County in 1902, he was employed in a printing office there and at Whitewright for a time, and again, in 1903, took up his educational labors, teaching commercial branches at the East Texas Normal College. While thus engaged he was employed also as the college printer and took a literary course himself, being graduated in 1906 with the Bachelor of Arts degree. That year marked Mr. Thacker's advent at Eldorado, where for one year he taught a country school, and in February, 1908, went to Hollis, where he purchased the Hollis Post-Herald, which he edited for two years, and in 1909-1910 occupied the position of chief of the engrossing and enrolling department of the State Senate, a capacity in which he acted also in the year 1915. In 1910, when he accepted the position of adjuster for the Oklahoma State School Land Department, his duties were such that he was forced to sell his newspaper, but later in the same year he bought the Eldorado Courier, of which he has continued to be proprietor and editor. This paper is the combination of the Eldorado Light, founded in 1901, and the original Eldorado Courier, founded in 1902, and assumed its present form in the latter year. Originally a supporter of republican principles, since Mr. Thacker's ownership it has been a democratic organ, and exerts a strong influence in public and political affairs in Jackson, Harmon and the surrounding counties, where it enjoys a large circulation. The offices and plant are situated on Main Street, and have an equipment that equals any in the state in towns the size of Eldorado. The Courier is well printed and well edited, giving its readers the latest news, presented in an interesting and reliable manner, and its columns have always been open to matter supporting the civic welfare. It is considered a good advertising medium and is being given generous support by the business men of this and surrounding communities. Mr. Thacker is a stalwart democrat, but his activities in public life have been more as an influence than as a seeker for personal preferment. Fraternally he is an ex-member of the Knights of Pythias and the Prætorians, and a member of Eldorado Lodge No. 181, Ancient Free and Accepted Masons; Eldorado Chapter No. 56, Royal Arch Masons; Eldorado Council No. 19; Consistory No. 1, Valley of Guthrie, eighteenth degree of Masonry; Eldorado Chapter No. 178, Order of the Eastern Star; Mesquite Camp No. 69, Woodmen of the World, Eldorado; and Mesquite Grove No. 228, Woodmen Circle.

On February 6, 1910, at Erick, Oklahoma, Mr. Thacker was married to Miss Bertha Briley, daughter of John Briley, a retired farmer of Mangum, Oklahoma. One child has come to this union: James Glenn, born October 25, 1913, at Eldorado.

J. J. CLOUGHLEY. A little more than twenty years ago Mr. Cloughley was a messenger boy in the employ of the railroad company at Parsons, Kansas. He went through several grades of the railroad service, but for the last dozen years has been active in a similar progressive fashion in connection with Oklahoma and Indian Territory banking, and is now president of the First National Bank of Ringling. He is one of the able men in Oklahoma's banking fraternity, and his name and influence are respected all over the southern counties of the state.

The First National Bank of Ringling, in the establishment of which Mr. Cloughley was the principal factor, was founded May 23, 1914, and has occupied its new building on Main Street since December 15th of that year. The officers of the institution are: Mr. Cloughley, president; L. P. Anderson, vice president; A. A. Morris, cashier. Its capital stock is $50,000 and in a year's time its resources have shown a gratifying increase and its management has gained the confidence of the business community in and around Ringling.

John J. Cloughley is a native of Kansas, born in Parsons December 14, 1874. His parents, John and Margaret (Canada) Cloughley, were both natives of Liverpool, England, and in the family are mingled strains of both English and Scotch. John Cloughley, who was born in 1843, is now living at Parsons, Kansas. He came to this country in 1873, bringing his wife and three children, and for many years was an engineer employed by the Missouri, Kansas & Texas Railroad with headquarters at Parsons. He is now a retired railroad man. He is a staunch republican and a member of the Episcopal Church. He and his wife had eight children: Robert, who is a retired railroad engineer at Parsons; Maggie, who married Mr. Fuller and resides in Bellingham, Oregon; Nellie, wife of Frank Paragory, superintendent of a foundry at McAlester, Oklahoma; Isabelle, wife of L. C. Minkler, an engineer for the Southern Pacific Railway living at San Bernandino, California; John J.; William, who is secretary of the National Livestock Commission Company at Kansas City, Missouri; Anna, who lives at Sedalia, Missouri, her husband being a conductor on the Missouri, Kansas & Texas Railroad; and Susie, who lives at Wichita, Kansas, and whose husband is a contractor and builder.

J. J. Cloughley acquired his education in the public schools at Parsons. At the age of seventeen he found work as messenger boy for the Missouri, Kansas & Texas Railroad, and by 1892 had become proficient in telegraphy and for ten years was employed by the railroad as operator and train dispatcher. During that time his home was at Parsons. In 1902 Mr. Cloughley became assistant cashier of the State National Bank at South McAlester, Indian Territory. When that institution was sold to the American National Bank in 1903, he took the leading part in organizing the City National Bank of South McAlester, and was its cashier until 1904. He then organized the First National Bank of Cornish, Indian Territory, and was its president until it was reorganized as the Bank of Cornish, and continued as head of the new institution until 1914. Since then he has been president of the First National Bank of Ringling.

Mr. Cloughley is independent in politics, a member of the Episcopal Church, and takes an active interest in various Masonic bodies. He is a member and has served as secretary of Cornish Lodge No. 64, Ancient Free and Accepted Masons; belongs to McAlester Chapter, Royal Arch Masons; and has taken eighteen degrees in the Scottish Rite at the McAlester Consistory. In a business way he is also a director in the Newman-Harris Mercantile Company at Ringling.

At Vinita, Indian Territory, in 1893, Mr. Cloughley married Miss Sabra Harmon, daughter of J. H. Harmon, who is now deceased, and was for many years a cattleman at Seneca, Missouri. To their union have been born four children: Harmon, a sophomore in the Agricultural and Mechanical College at Stillwater, Oklahoma; Florence, a sophomore in St. Mary's Academy at Oklahoma City; Boone, and J. J., Jr., both in the public schools at Ringling.

JOHN W. RANDALL. The present postmaster of Blackwell, John W. Randall, is one of the pioneers of Kay County, and has supplied many of the resources of enterprise and business faith and hope which have accomplished so much in this section of the state during the past twenty years. Among his achievements was the development of a fine homestead in the vicinity of Blackwell. He has an important part in other business affairs, and received his appointment to the postoffice in February, 1908, taking charge on the 1st of April. The Blackwell office is second class, and has four rural carriers and two city carriers. The first assistant postmaster is John R. Camt, who has been connected with the Blackwell office for the past two years, and beginning with 1904 has served seven years in the railway mail service.

Mr. Randall made the run from the Kansas line into the Cherokee Strip in September, 1893, and was one of

the fortunate ones who staked out a valuable claim in the vicinity of Blackwell. John W. Randall was born at Gallatin, Missouri, September 22, 1859, but when an infant his parents removed to Green County, Wisconsin, where he grew up in the Town of Monroe. His father was Thomas Randall, a native of Tennessee, where he grew up, and his wife, Rachel Hodges, was a native of Indiana, but of Tennessee parents. In 1877 the Randall family left Wisconsin and removed to Kansas, locating at Winfield. The father was a prosperous farmer, and died in Scott County, Kansas, and the mother passed away at the age of seventy-eight. Their children were: Sarah, who lives in California; Alice, a resident at Belleville, Illinois; Mary Berkey, of Blackwell, Oklahoma, and Ella, of Spokane, Washington.

John W. Randall grew up at Monroe, Wisconsin, where he received his education in the public schools. His early life was spent on a farm, and he had a thorough training and discipline in the duties of farm work.

At Winfield, Kansas, July 16, 1882, Mr. Randall married Miss E. F. Freeland. Mrs. Randall has been a devoted wife and mother for thirty-three years, and is a woman of intelligence, high character, and with no little initiative. Before her marriage for several years she was a successful teacher. Her father, F. M. Freeland, was an Illinois man, and is now living in Oklahoma. Her mother died in 1913. Mr. and Mrs. Randall take pride in their family, comprising nine children, six sons and three daughters: Dwight B., who is a clerk in the local postoffice under his father; Gladys, a deaconess in the Methodist Episcopal Church and formerly a school teacher; Carl, who is secretary and treasurer of the Blackwell Brick Company; Laura; Paul and Beulah, twins; Glen; William, and Fred. The younger children are all attending the public schools, while the older ones are graduates of the high school.

Mr. Randall was for several years editor and proprietor of the Blackwell Times Record. For six years he served as United States commissioner at Blackwell, and made an excellent record in that office as he has in every other responsibility and business relation. While living in Kansas he served as postmaster at Floral for seven years. Fraternally he is a member of the lodge, chapter and commandery of Masonry and also belongs to the Temple of the Mystic Shrine at Tulsa. He finds his recreation in hunting and fishing, and is a man of splendid physical constitution, stands six feet high and weighs 185 pounds, and has always kept himself in sound health and vigor. Among other undertakings Mr. Randall was one of the active promoters of the Blackwell Oil & Gas Company, which is capitalized at $210,000 and has at the present time twelve wells in operation with a number of miles of pipe line. Mr. Randall has been one of the leaders in exploiting oil and gas resources in this section of Oklahoma.

JOHN H. BELLIS. At the time of the opening of the Cherokee Strip, September 16, 1893, John H. Bellis, then a young man of twenty-one years, rode his little Canadian horse seventeen miles in fifty-five minutes in an endeavor to secure a claim on the Black Bear Bottom west of Pawnee. In this endeavor he was unsuccessful, as when he got on the bottom he found men with families and some were plowing. He immediately went one-half mile north of Black Bear Creek, where he and his father secured the same claim, Mr. Bellis buying off another claimant and his father settling on the property. Following this John H. Bellis went on to Guthrie, but in his absence, on account of sickness, he lost his claim, and thus it was that he turned his attention to other enterprises and entered upon a career that has resulted in his becoming one of the foremost business men of Payne County, president of the Commonwealth Cotton Oil Company, an official in large and important industries, and the holder of extensive interests.

Mr. Bellis was born in Missouri, June 30, 1872, a son of David B. and Sarah (McReynolds) Bellis, natives of Indiana, a complete sketch of whose careers will be found on another page of this work. His parents were married in Indiana, following which they removed to Missouri, and in 1873 went to Abilene, Kansas, where they resided until the opening of the Cherokee Strip. Since that time David B. Bellis has been interested in farming and stock raising, although he is now practically retired from active life and is living at Cushing. He was a soldier for three years during the Civil war as a member of Company B, Sixty-fourth Regiment, Indiana Volunteer Infantry. There were six children in the family: James, who died at the age of six months; Mary, who is the wife of Edward Hunt of Guthrie; John H.; C. O., of Klamath County, Oregon; Etta M., the wife of W. L. Larmer, of Cushing; and Alice E., the wife of L. J. Martin of the Cushing State Bank. Mrs. Larmer was a teacher for seventeen years, and was elected the first county superintendent of schools of Shaffer County, but the election for this county did not carry by fifty-nine votes, so she had an office but no county to put it in.

John H. Bellis was reared on his father's farm near Abilene, in Dickinson County, Kansas, and there his early education was secured in the district schools. After coming to Oklahoma he assisted his father until determining upon a business career, and in 1899 was graduated from the Capitol City Business College at Guthrie. He was at that time employed by the firm of W. H. Coyle Company, at Guthrie, a cotton and grain concern, at a salary of $40 per month, but when he left that company seven years later he held the position of general manager. On March 1, 1907, he came to Cushing and superintended the building of the mill for the Commonwealth Cotton Oil Company, the first president of which was J. M. Aydelotte, P. A. Norris being the first secretary. These gentlemen continued with the concern until 1914, when Mr. Bellis, who had until that time been manager, bought their holdings and thus gaining a controlling interest became president of the industry. E. A. Smith, the present secretary and treasurer, came to Cushing from Shawnee in 1907 as bookkeeper for the company when it was organized and took his present position in 1914. In 1915 Mr. Bellis became the founder of the Bellis Furniture and Undertaking Company, of which he has since been president. He is also vice president of the Jones Oil and Gas Company of Cushing, and was the founder of the company and the builder of the plant of the Cushing Compress, which he subsequently sold to the Peoples Compress Company. He is owner of the Postoffice Building, Bellis Building and several other brick buildings, and in addition to his own home, one of the finest residences at Cushing, has erected about twenty dwellings, which are rented to tenants. He has two good farms and feeds from 1,500 to 2,000 cattle at the oil mill and has been one of the stanchest supporters of the agricultural interests of Payne and adjacent counties. While he does not hold membership in any religious denominations, he is a supporter of all the churches and his charitable benefactions are numerous. His fraternal connection is with the Masons, he being a member of the Shrine at Tulsa and a thirty-second degree Scottish Rite Mason.

As one of the leading industries of Oklahoma, a short history and description of the Commonwealth Cotton Oil Company may not be out of place in the sketch of Mr. Bellis, to whose enterprise, energy and business talent its success is due. The data is taken from a pamphlet recently prepared by local writers. The Commonwealth Cotton Oil Company at Cushing is one of the largest cotton oil companies in the state and is the fifth largest in the United States. Its yearly output will exceed $1,000,000. The company was organized in 1907 on a small scale. The business grew to wonderful proportions the first few years of the concern's existence and at once began to attract wide attention among the large interests of the East. Its products were the very finest that could be produced and the officers soon found a heavy demand for the plant's output. The business is now capitalized at $150,000. In 1914, 8,000 tons of cotton seed were pressed at the plant, the products of which amounted to more than $300,000 worth of business. More than 16,000 bales of cotton were handled by the company, which, with the cotton seed products, represent fully $1,000,000 in business. The company's plant is situated in the west part of Cushing near the Santa Fe Railroad tracks. The holdings consist of sixty acres of land and a number of brick structures for the different departments, the company's plant and property being valued at $150,000.

The crude cotton oil that is produced by the plant is sold in large quantities to some of the largest packing plants in the United States. A considerable amount of the company's output is sold to the manufacturers of Cottolene, Snowdrift, Crisco and numerous other preparations that in recent years have taken the place of pure lard for cooking purposes. Little do some of the Cushing people think that when they are using any of these standard brands that the contents are doubtless a portion of the output of one of their own home industries. The process by which the oil is taken from the seed is a most remarkable one. The seed is shipped to Cushing from the string of gins for a radius of fifty miles around after it has been separated from the cotton, and is then run through the delinters, large machines used to separate the lint that is left on the seed by the gins. The seed is then crushed and run through a system of shakers that are used to separate the hulls from the kernels. The kernels, or meat of the seed, are then ground into meal and formed into cakes by a machine called the cake former, the cakes then being passed into steel presses where enormous pressure is applied by a hydraulic ram that compresses and separates the oil from the meal. The oil thus produced or extracted is known as crude cotton oil and is disposed of to large corporations. The products produced by the mill and marketed are cotton seed meal, used for feed for live stock, and cotton seed hulls, also used for feed. These products are sold in large quantities to the stock yards at Kansas City and other large cities and to wholesale feed houses in Nebraska, Texas, Missouri, Oklahoma and Kansas.

John H. Bellis was married in 1902 to Miss Edith M. Bowdlear, who was at that time assistant postmistress at Ripley, Oklahoma, a native of Sioux City, Iowa, who was reared at Omaha, Nebraska, and came to Oklahoma with her sister, Mrs. John P. Hinkle. To this union there have been born four children: William H.; Nell; Lura May, who died at the age of two years; and Edith H.

FRED BOONE. The postoffice at Davidson is now under the efficient management of Fred Boone, one of the popular citizens of that community, and a man of broad and varied experience in the work and activities of the world.

His birth occurred at Table Rock, Nebraska, February 15, 1871, and he is a son of Ely T. and Eunice (Pepoon) Boone. His father was born in the same county in England where many generations before the father of the famous Daniel Boone was born. The mother's family is descended from that race of Pepins which furnished several of the great kings to the early French nation. Ely T. Boone, who died at Lincoln, Nebraska, in 1893, came to America in 1856, settling first in Illinois, from there moving out to Oregon, and from that state enlisted in a regiment of volunteer infantry during the Civil war, serving three years. After the war he removed to Nebraska, and was engaged in farming until his death. He was also a carpenter by trade. His wife was born in Ohio in 1841 and is now living at Twin Falls, Idaho. Their children are: Henry O., a resident of Twin Falls, Idaho; Gertrude, wife of Fred Leverett, a farmer at Lisbon, Iowa; Fred; Albert, Frank and Arthur, all farmers at Twin Falls, Idaho; and May, wife of Leslie Lewis, a clerk at Twin Falls.

Fred Boone attended the country schools in the vicinity of Table Rock, Nebraska, and finished his education with a course in a business college at Shenandoah, Iowa. His life to the age of twenty was spent on his father's farm, but during the last twenty or twenty-five years he has come into varied contact with the world. For two years he was a telegraph operator in the employ of the Chicago, Burlington & Quincy Railroad. Then six years were spent in fruit farming at Hardy, Arkansas. At Buffalo Center, Iowa, he conducted an electric power plant for three years. In 1903 he again came South and at Myrtle Springs, Texas, had charge of fifty acres of orchard up to 1906. During 1906 he was employed in sawmills and in electric light plants and for a short time served as commissary on a railroad. In 1907 he removed to Oklahoma City, and spent three years as news agent on trains. Then in 1910 came his removal to Vernon, Texas, where he was for two years engineer in the city waterworks. Mr. Boone removed to Davidson in 1912, and followed his business as engineer until his appointment on October 12, 1914, as postmaster. He received this appointment from President Wilson. Mr. Boone is a democrat and was formerly affiliated with the Modern Woodmen of America. He is unmarried.

BENJAMIN F. HARRISON. A man of fine intellectuality, wide experience and much executive ability, Hon. Benjamin F. Harrison, of Calvin, Hughes County, is consistently to be termed one of the honored and representative citizens of Oklahoma, and he has been a leader in conserving the interests and advancement of the Indians of the state, with just pride in his descent from the staunchest of Indian stock, his father having been a representative of the Choctaw and his mother of the Chickasaw tribe. Mr. Harrison has been the architect of his own fortunes and has been prominent and influential in public affairs in Oklahoma under both the territorial and state régimes. His ability and high civic ideals have not failed of recognition, as is evidenced by his having served as Secretary of State of Oklahoma and as a member of the State Legislature, he having been a member of the First Legislature after the admission of the state to the Union, and being the representative of Hughes County in the Fifth Legislature, that of 1915. A man of thought and action, a citizen of sterling worth, he well merits recognition in this history of the state within whose borders he has maintained his home from the time of his nativity. He is one of the substantial agriculturists and stock-growers of Hughes County, his well-improved farm, on which he maintains his residence, being situated in the South Canadian Valley and in close proximity to the Village of Calvin.

Mr. Harrison was born in the Choctaw Nation of Indian Territory, in the year 1875, and is a son of Hilburn and Sarah (Colbert) Harrison. Becoming practically dependent upon his own resources when a lad of fourteen years, Mr. Harrison made good use of the advantages afforded him in the public schools of the Choctaw Nation and was finally enabled to enter Trinity College, at Durham, North Carolina, in which institution he was graduated as a member of the class of 1897. In 1900 he established his residence on his present homestead farm, which he has developed into one of the best in Hughes County, and his progressiveness and marked success as an agriculturist and stock-grower have been a lesson and incentive to other residents of that section of the state. In 1906 Mr. Harrison was elected a member of the State Constitutional Convention, from the Eighty-eighth District, and he took a prominent part in the deliberations and work of the convention, in which he was assigned to a number of important committees, including those on public-service corporations, state and school lands, primary elections, and preamble and bill of rights. Upon the admission of the state to the Union, in 1907, Mr. Harrison was elected the floterial representative from Hughes and Pittsburg counties in the First Legislature, and in 1908 he was re-elected, as a member of the Second Legislature, in which he served as speaker pro tem. of the House of Representatives, as chairman of the Committee on Constitutional Amendments, and as a member of the Appropriation Committee. Further and distinguished honors were in store for Mr. Harrison in the gift of the voters of his native commonwealth, for in 1910 he was elected Secretary of State of Oklahoma, for the term of four years from January, 1911, until January, 1915. He gave a most careful and effective administration but resigned his position in November, 1914, in which month he was elected representative of Hughes County in the Fifth Legislature. He was made a candidate for the position of speaker of the House of Representatives of the Fifth General Assembly, but before the election he withdrew his candidacy, in the interest of harmony. He was made chairman of the Committee on Retrenchment and Reform, and a member of the following named committees also: Congressional Redistricting, Revenue and Taxation, State and School Lands, Public Roads and Highways, Constitutional Amendments, and Relation to the Five Civilized Tribes and Other Indians.

In the Fifth Legislature Mr. Harrison introduced a bill prescribing the qualifications for teachers in the public schools and other educational institutions of the state and defining causes for their removal, the purpose of the measure being to eliminate politics from educational affairs. Another bill introduced by him was that providing for a governor's council, consisting of all state officials, upon whom shall be conferred the powers now entrusted to the State Board of Affairs and the Board of Control of the state penal, charitable and educational institutions, except the power of selecting teachers. He made a careful survey of the subject and estimated that this measure would entail to the state a saving of $65,000 annually. Mr. Harrison was the author of the proposed constitutional amendment providing a mileage tax for the support of the state educational institutions,—a measure designed to relieve the Legislature of the responsibility of making appropriations for the support of these institutions. He was a co-author of a bill prescribing requirements for admission to the state insane asylums and providing that persons having property shall contribute to the support of relatives confined in such asylums. He not only showed much discrimination and ability in constructive legislation, but also opposed vigorously all proposed increases of appropriations for state institutions except such amounts as were actually necessary for maintenance.

In the Masonic fraternity Mr. Harrison has received the thirty-second degree of the Ancient Accepted Scottish Rite, besides being affiliated with the India Temple of the Ancient Arabic Order of the Nobles of the Mystic Shrine. He is prominently identified also with the Independent Order of Odd Fellows, in which he is past grand of the lodge at Calvin and also a member of the grand lodge of the state. He holds membership also in the Oklahoma Society of Eighty-niners, commemorating the organization of Oklahoma Territory and its opening to settlement.

In December, 1912, Mr. Harrison married Miss Grace Liegerot, daughter of Charles and Emma Liegerot, of Tonkawa, Kay County, this state. They have no children.

SAMUEL B. ELROD. The distinction of being the second youngest postmaster in the State of Oklahoma belongs to Samuel B. Elrod, who under the present democratic administration took charge of the postoffice at Hominy about a year ago. Mr. Elrod is one of the capable younger business men of Osage County, and his family has been identified with this state for a number of years.

He was born in Tennessee December 28, 1888, a son of B. F. and Annie E. (Milliken) Elrod, who were also natives of Tennessee, his father having been born in the same house as the son, and is now sixty-four, while his wife is aged sixty. The parents now reside 3½ miles north of Hominy. When Samuel B. was two years of age the parents moved to Texas, locating in Hill County, and lived there until 1903, when they removed to Southwestern Oklahoma. The father had been at El Reno at the opening of the Kiowa and Comanche Reservation in 1901. Samuel B. Elrod lived with his parents in Southwestern Oklahoma until 1911, when he came to Osage County, and was followed two years later by his parents. His father has been a farmer all his active career. Samuel B. Elrod is one of ten children, nine of whom are still living, and one having died at the age of five. He is the youngest of the six sons in the family, while two of the daughters are younger than he.

He lived with his parents until twenty-two and was then married to Miss Gertrude Harris, born in Bedford County, Tennessee, in 1893, and coming to Oklahoma about nine years ago with her grandparents, both her own parents having died when she was very young. Mr. Elrod was a practical farmer up to the time he removed to Hominy, and then worked a year in a meat market and for two years engaged in the ice and coal business. His appointment as postmaster at Hominy came on July 1, 1914. The Hominy postoffice is third class, and he is now giving all his attention to its management. He has been a democrat since casting his first ballot, and is one of the young leaders of the party in Osage County. He and his wife are members of the Baptist Church and his fraternal affiliations are with the Masonic Order and the Independent Order of Odd Fellows. Mr. and Mrs. Elrod have one son, Reynold Milton.

J. WILL MORSE. The Oklahoma Guaranty Bank of Blackwell, of which J. W. Morse is cashier, is in point of resources and stability one of the strongest financial institutions of Northeastern Oklahoma. A recent statement indicates total resources aggregating about $278,000. Its capital stock is $30,000, with surplus and profits of about $5,500, while the confidence of the community in its management is indicated by deposits approximating over $240,000.

Mr. J. W. Morse has been identified with Blackwell since 1897, and is a banker, business man, leader in community and church affairs, has been one of the men most directly responsible for the growth and improvement of his city during the past twenty years. Mr. Morse was born in

Christian County, Illinois, March 15, 1861. His father was W. L. Morse, long an active business man at Pana, Illinois. W. L. Morse was born at Worcester, Massachusetts, of an old Massachusetts family, and located in Christian County, Illinois, in 1856. W. L. Morse was married in Kentucky to Mary Jane Meteer, a woman of intelligence and good family, to whom her children owe much for their success in life. She was born in Kentucky, and two of her brothers, Thomas J. and John T., were soldiers in the Union army. She is still living at the old home in Illinois, at the age of seventy-seven. Both she and her husband were members of the Methodist Episcopal Church.

James W. Morse grew up in Illinois, and received his education by attending the public schools and by study at home. He has a sister, Sarah A., who is married and living at Champaign, Illinois. After leaving high school he went into business at Pana, and when he came to Oklahoma in 1897 he brought with him a broad and varied experience and was well qualified to take an active part in the upbuilding of the community at Blackwell.

In November, 1883, at Vincennes, Indiana, Mr. Morse married Miss Jessie M. Rice, who was born in Kentucky, a daughter of Rev. William G. Rice, who for many years was a successful minister of the gospel. He had also served as a soldier in the Confederate army, and spent the last days of his life in Kentucky. To the marriage of Mr. and Mrs. Morse have been born seven children. Irocu died in infancy, and Wilber died in childhood. Those living are: Florence, wife of C. D. Baily of Laurens, Iowa; C. E. Morse of Wichita, Kansas; Glyde, attending high school at Blackwell; Wilford and Evelyn, also in school. Mr. and Mrs. Morse have both been very prominent in the Presbyterian Church activities at Blackwell. He has served as superintendent of the Sunday-school and treasurer of the church board, and has always expressed himself positively and in terms of action in behalf of any movement for the improvement of churches, schools and general elevation of morality and temperance in his community. Mr. Morse is also prominent in the Masonic Order, a member of the Knights Templar, and belongs to Akdar Temple of the Mystic Shrine at Tulsa.

FRANKLIN J. SPRINGER. To grow old gracefully has been only one of many accomplishments associated with the career of Judge Springer of Cushing. Many men much younger are not so fortunate in carrying the weight of their years as Judge Springer, who is now close to four score. His is a pleasing retrospect and a consciousness of duty well performed and a long life of honorable service have undoubtedly been factors in enabling him to advance so easily toward a green old age.

From the time he was a hard-fighting soldier in the army of the Potomac during the Civil war until the present Judge Springer has employed much of his time and energy in the duties of citizenship. He was born in Northampton County, Pennsylvania, on a farm, May 18, 1837. He was the only child of his father, Louis Springer, who died before Judge Springer had any definite recollection of this parent. The mother's maiden name was Mary Kromer. Both were born in Pennsylvania and of German parentage. The mother spent all her life in that state. Up to the age of about ten years Judge Springer lived with his grandparents, and soon afterward started out to earn his own way in the world. Self-reliance, independence, faithful diligence, have been important factors in his career. For about six years he worked on a river boat on the Ohio River. In 1852 he went west to Cass County, Illinois, and lived on a farm there until the outbreak of the war. Returning to Pennsylvania he enlisted in July, 1861, as a private in Company B of the Forty-fifth Regiment of Pennsylvania Infantry, and was later in Company A, Twenty-first Pennsylvania Cavalry. He was continuously in service until 1865, the close of the war, having veteranized at the close of the first three years of his enlistment. He was mustered out by a special order taking effect May 15, 1865. In the meantime he had borne more than the ordinary duties and responsibilities of the soldier. Five days before the surrender of Lee he was taken prisoner at Amelia Springs, Virginia, and his regiment was mustered out two months later. From private his first promotion was to first sergeant, later to lieutenant, and for one year before his muster out he was captain of Company A of the Twenty-third Pennsylvania. This record is the more notable for the fact that he enlisted as a poor boy and a stranger among his comrades in Company A. He made no efforts to gain promotion, and every advance was on the basis of merit and efficiency and not by reason of personal influence. He took part in all the great battles in which the army of the Potomac was engaged from Antietam on to Appomattox. At Fredericksburg he was slightly wounded when a splinter from a gun carriage struck him in the forehead, leaving a scar which is still visible. While in the army he had three horses shot from under him, and his clothing was frequently struck by bullets, though he himself passed through practically unscathed.

After the war he lived in Pennsylvania for a time, was married there in 1866, and soon afterwards brought his bride to Illinois and to Cass County, where he had formerly lived, and engaged in farming. Five years later he moved to Iowa and was a resident of Lee County in that state until 1889. Judge Springer is an Oklahoma '89er. After participating in the great rush of colonists and home seekers on the 22d of April he secured a claim in Oklahoma County, and for a number of years gave his energy to its development. He has always been successful as a farmer, and has developed a large acreage since coming to Oklahoma. He was honored by election as one of the first county commissioners of Oklahoma County, helped to organize that district, and as the other members of the board of commissioners were city men and practically unacquainted with their duties, he bore a large share of the official responsibilities connected with that office. For about five years Captain Springer lived in Lincoln County, and about twelve years ago moved to Payne County, and for the past five years has lived retired in Cushing. The greater part of his career has been spent as a farmer, and he still owns considerable farming land in Oklahoma.

Politically he has had a part in politics only as a public spirited citizen, though frequently honored with official position. He is a republican, and in Cushing served as police judge until that office was abolished on the introduction of the commission form of government. Since then he has administered justice in the local courts as a justice of the peace. Judge Springer took an active part in the movement which brought about the organization of old Oklahoma Territory. Perhaps his chief interest since coming to Cushing has been the welfare of local schools. He has helped to establish school districts, has served many years on local school boards and his name should be definitely remembered for his help in founding the State Normal School at Edmond and the Agricultural College at Stillwater. Fraternally he is a member of the Masonic Order and also belongs to the Grand Army of the Republic.

In Pennsylvania, on March 1, 1866, Judge Springer married Emma Levan. She was born in Pennsylvania, June 13, 1845, a daughter of John and Catherine (Osterstock) Levan, both of whom spent all their lives in the Keystone State. Judge and Mrs. Springer are whole-

some people, always preserved good physical health, are still active in spite of their years, have reared a large family of children without the loss of a single one. Neither Judge Springer nor any of his sons have ever used tobacco or liquor in any form and he is as clean mentally and morally as he is physically. In religious matters he is somewhat liberal and prefers to analyze and study the scheme of the world and the problems beyond untrammeled by conventioned thought or dogma. A brief record of his ten children is as follows: Alice is the wife of Robert Yarbrough of Oklahoma City; Frank H. lives in Pawnee County; Hattie Belle is the wife of R. O. Pettigrew of Oklahoma City; Nora is the wife of S. W. King of Texas; Fred lives in Shawnee; Ida is the wife of Dusel Casto of Yukon; Lee lives in Texas; Albert lives in Payne County; John W. is a resident of Vinita; and Mamie is a teacher in the high school at Cushing.

THOMAS ANDREW GROSS. No individual in a community wields a stronger influence in the molding and shaping of character than the public instructor. The capable, conscientious teacher must needs assume heavy responsibilities, for on entering the schoolroom the child's mind is as plastic clay and is as readily made to take shape under guidance and instruction. That community is fortunate therefore that numbers among its citizens men and women of ability and high ideals, to whom the teaching of its future citizens is a trust not to be lightly assumed but to which thought, care and constant service must be rendered. In this category stands Thomas Andrew Gross, superintendent of schools of Frederick, Oklahoma, who has devoted himself to teaching almost from the time that he left college halls.

Mr. Gross was born in Birchwood, James County, Tennessee, in April, 1875, and is a son of A. J. and Harriet (Ziegler) Gross. The family originated in Germany, a number of generations ago, locating in Virginia in colonial times, and subsequently removed to Tennessee in the first settlement of that state. A. J. Gross was born at Birchwood, in the Big Bend State, in 1851, and for many years was engaged in farming there, but in 1910 moved to the vicinity of Dayton, Tennessee, where he now makes his home. He is a member of the Baptist Church and a democrat in politics, is interested in public and civic affairs, and has served as a member of the school board. Mrs. Gross, also a native of Birchwood, survives, and has been the mother of nine children, namely: J. F., who is identified with the Department of Indian Affairs at Washington, D. C.; Thomas Andrew, of this review; Tennessee, who resides with her parents at Dayton, Tennessee, and is unmarried; Lena, who married Mr. Jones, a ranchman of Ridge, Montana; Pearl, who married Mr. Brown, a civil engineer of Chapel, North Carolina; and Lilly, Lola, Blanche and Stella, who are unmarried and reside with their parents.

Thomas Andrew Gross first attended the Birchwood public schools and was graduated from Birchwood Academy in 1894. He next taught school for one year in James County, Tennessee, following which he enrolled as a student at Carson & Newman College, Jefferson, Tennessee, where he was graduated with the class of 1900, degree of Bachelor of Sciences, with the highest honors of his class. His college career was a notable one, in which he was a prominent figure in the Columbian Literary Society, in the work of the Young Men's Christian Association, in athletics and in the various musical organizations. Later, in 1908, he received the degree of Master of Arts from this institution.

In 1901 and 1902 Mr. Gross was engaged in editing a newspaper at Dayton, Tennessee, but following this venture entered upon his real career as principal of the Fairmount schools, at Hamilton, Tennessee, in 1903-4. The next three years he was principal of the County High School, at Hixon, Tennessee, and in 1907 he came to Weatherford, Oklahoma, as professor of English and Literature in the Southwestern State Normal School, a capacity in which he acted for four years. He was then head of the Department of English, Baptist University, Shawnee, Oklahoma, for one year; principal of the Okfuskee County High School, Okfuskee, Oklahoma, one year, and principal of the Frederick High School for one year, 1913-14, and in May of the latter year was elected superintendent of city schools of Frederick, a position in which he has since remained, and in which he has charge of four schools, twenty-five teachers and 800 scholars. Mr. Gross, aside from being a teacher possessed the happy and unusual faculty of instilling in the minds of others his own great store of knowledge, as well as an executive who is capable of looking after the business management of his charge, is a close student, and by constant study keeps abreast of his profession, for teaching, like other vocations, is progressive. He is a democrat in politics, is a member of the Baptist Church and superintendent of its Sunday School, and a director in the Carnegie Library at Frederick.

On May 1, 1901, at Talbot, Tennessee, Professor Gross was married to Miss Arrie M. Roberts, who at that time was living with her uncle, M. A. Roberts, but who came from Little Rock, Arkansas, her birthplace. Three children have come to this union, Marguerite, born in 1902; Ralph Franklin, born in 1906; and Byron Roberts, born in 1909.

The Roberts family is an old one in this country and traces its record back many generations in England, being originally from the family that gave to Great Britain its famous soldier, the late Lord Roberts. The great-grandfather of Mrs. Gross was a minister of the Methodist Episcopal faith, spent many years in Tennessee, and was identified prominently with the Indian history of his day and locality. Benjamin Roberts, the grandfather of Mrs. Gross, was born in North Carolina in 1808, and died at Dandridge, Tennessee, in 1892, having been a pioneer of East Tennessee where he was engaged as a merchant and farmer for many years. He was a republican in politics, but not a politician.

J. Newton Roberts, the father of Mrs. Gross, was born in Knox County, Tennessee, in 1839, and as a youth was taken by his parents to Jefferson County, Tennessee, and then to Little Rock, Arkansas, where he spent the remaining years of his life, being principally engaged as a contractor and builder. During the Civil war he served as a Confederate private for some time, and was stationed at Memphis, Tennessee. He was an active worker in the Methodist Episcopal Church, in which he was class leader, and in political affairs was a democrat. Five children were born to Mr. and Mrs. Roberts: Frank N., who is identified with a wholesale fruit company, at Little Rock, Arkansas; James Benjamin, bookkeeper for the Walker & Calef Ice Company, who died in 1900 at Little Rock, Arkansas; Laura C., who married Doctor Majors, a retired physician of Shiloh, Arkansas; George W., who is a merchant at Little Rock, Arkansas; and Arrie M., who is now Mrs. Gross. The mother of these children, who bore the maiden name of Ellen Davidson, was a native of Virginia, and died at Little Rock, Arkansas, in 1880.

Arrie M. Roberts attended the public schools of her native City of Little Rock, Arkansas, and after one year spent in the high school went to Cleburne County, Arkansas, both her parents having died. There she passed three years in teaching school, and attending the high school when she could find the time, and later taught at Heber Springs, Arkansas. Miss Roberts next went to

Maury Academy, Dandridge, Tennessee, where she passed one year, following which she became a student at Carson & Newman College, Jefferson, Tennessee, where she remained two and one-half years, and while there met Mr. Gross. She thereafter was engaged in teaching until her marriage, May 1, 1901. Mrs. Gross is well known in educational circles, is a lady of many attainments, and has a wide circle of appreciative friends living at Frederick and elsewhere.

WILLIAM A. CLUTE. A pioneer newspaper man of Oklahoma, having come here at the time of the first opening of lands for white settlement in 1889, William A. Clute has been connected with a number of publications in this state, but is now engaged as a traveling salesman. Mr. Clute was born September 22, 1859, in Livingston County, New York, and is a son of Andrew and Caroline Jane (Harris) Clute.

Andrew Clute was born in New York and when he entered upon his career took up farming in Livingston County, where he was living at the outbreak of the Civil war. He enlisted as a private and scout in Company F, 136th Regiment, New York Volunteer Infantry, and served three years with that organization, participating in thirty engagements, including Gettysburg, Lookout Mountain and Chattanooga and the battles incident to General Sherman's great march to the sea. Following the war he removed to Michigan and then to Nebraska, continuing his farming operations, and finally settled in Colorado, where he met his death in a railroad wreck in 1881. He was a member of the Masonic Fraternity. In 1855 Mr. Clute was married to Miss Caroline Jane Harris, who was born in 1848, the youngest of the eleven children of Isaac and Hanna (Howe) Harris. She died at Altus, December 9, 1915. There were four children in the family, namely: Andrew, born in 1856, and now a traveling man of Hastings, Nebraska; William A.; Francis M., born in 1859, who died in 1904; and Sidney E., born in 1873, a resident of Altus.

William A. Clute was educated in the schools of Michigan and Nebraska, and reared on the home farm. He later entered the service of the Chicago, Burlington & Quincy Railroad as agent for the townsite department in Nebraska and Colorado, and was subsequently agent and trustee for the townsite interests on the C. K. & N. Railroad in the latter state. He also spent five years in Mexico, as an exporter and, in 1889, when Indian Territory and Oklahoma Territory lands were thrown open to the public, came to El Reno, where he was given the first deed issued for a town lot. He also secured a claim two miles from the city of El Reno, paying the claimant for his relinquishment by the purchase of a pair of $5.00 boots. This land has since sold for $200 per acre. Mr. Clute took an active part in the organization of the town, being a member of the first city council under the Enabling Act, and in 1891 bought the El Reno Democrat, of which he was editor for two years. In the same year he was the nominee on the independent democratic ticket for the legislature, but was defeated after a close contest. He was also a member of the first grand jury ever impanelled in Canadian County, was president of the first democratic club organized in the county, was a delegate to the first state convention of his party, and was the organizer of the first independent company of state militia, Company A, of which he served as captain for several years. When the Cherokee' Strip was opened to settlement Mr. Clute made the race to Enid, at which place he edited the West-Side Democrat during the exciting period of the town's early history. In 1892, with his brother, Francis M., Mr. Clute established the Argus, at Arapaho, and conducted that paper for two years, and in 1894 bought from Lafe Merritt the El Reno Globe, being editor thereof for two years. Since disposing of his interests in that newspaper, Mr. Clute has devoted himself to traveling for wholesale houses as a salesman, having his headquarters and residence at points in the state as convenience demanded.

Mr. Clute has been an eye-witness to the wonderful development of this state, and still takes a keen and active interest in its institutions and industries. Few men contributed in greater degree to the advancement of Canadian County, the first history of which came from his pen. He is connected with various fraternal and social organizations and has a wide acquaintance all over the state, and has established enduring friendships with some of Oklahoma's most prominent and influential citizens.

THOMAS R. DUNLAP. One of the newest towns in Southern Oklahoma is Ringling, and though its annals are brief there has been no lack of enterprise and achievement. One of the men present when the first furrow was turned on the townsite is Thomas R. Dunlap, now serving as postmaster. Mr. Dunlap has had a long and active career, chiefly engaged in educational work, and many years ago was superintendent of schools at Ardmore.

Thomas R. Dunlap was born in Gibson County, Tennessee, February 11, 1853, a son of J. M. and Elizabeth (Carter) Dunlap. The Dunlaps came originally from Scotland prior to the Revolutionary war and settled in South Carolina. The Carters were likewise early in South Carolina and came from Holland. J. M. Dunlap was born in South Carolina in 1826 and died at Humboldt, Tennessee, in 1880, having been taken to Tennessee by his parents when he was a small boy. His life was spent as a farmer and he was a member of the Masonic fraternity. His wife was born in South Carolina in 1837 and died at Humboldt, Tennessee, in 1908. Their seven children were: Thomas R.; Sallie A., wife of Frank Craddock, a Tennessee farmer; Mary, wife of B. F. Rains, a horticulturist in Gibson County, Tennessee; Maggie, who died in 1910 as the wife of J. N. Jackson, who is a farmer in Tennessee; Amanda, who died at the age of six years, and Kendrick, a fruit grower in Crockett County, Tennessee.

Thomas R. Dunlap had the environment of a Tennessee farm during his youth, and began his education in the public schools of Gibson County. These advantages were improved by a course in the Southwestern Baptist University at Jackson, Tennessee, and in 1880 he graduated A. B. from Eminence College in Henry County, Kentucky. Educational work was his chosen vocation, and he served as superintendent of schools in several counties in Texas up to 1894, in which year he was elected superintendent of schools at Ardmore, Indian Territory. For four years he was principal of the Chickasha Collegiate Institute, and then returned to Texas and for four years had charge of the Jarvis Institute at Granbury, Texas. Subsequent service in the educational field comprised two years as president of Sulphur College at Sulphur, Kentucky, three years as professor of Latin at Wilson, North Carolina; one year in the Chair of Latin in the Virginia Christian College at Lynchburg, Virginia.

Mr. Dunlap came to Wilson, Oklahoma, in 1914, but in March of the same year identified himself with the new townsite at Ringling. He was made postmaster by Postmaster General Burleson and took the office July 17, 1915. On January 1, 1916, the office was made third class and Mr. Dunlap was made postmaster for a term of four years. He is a democrat in politics, an elder in

the Christian Church and has affiliations with Ardmore Circle of the Woodmen of the World.

At Florence, Alabama, in 1881, he married Miss Sallie F. Young, whose father was the late Thomas W. Young, a farmer at Florence. Their family comprises four children: Errett, who is in the land business with Mullen Bros., at Ardmore, Oklahoma; Allen Young, who was drowned at Fort Arbuckle, Oklahoma, June 29, 1897; Laurence, postmaster and merchant at Wilson, Oklahoma; and Mattie, a junior in Enid College.

VIRGIL A. WOOD, M. D. It is not only as a physician and surgeon, but as a citizen of varied usefulness and public spirit that Doctor Wood is identified with Blackwell and Kay County. He located in Blackwell in 1901, and since that year he has quietly and efficiently performed his services as a doctor in the city and surrounding country. He is a man of high standing in his profession, and has undoubtedly chosen wisely in devoting himself unselfishly and patriotically to the welfare of his fellow man, rather than concentrating his efforts towards the building up of a fortune. He enjoys the rewards of community esteem in a richer degree than some men perhaps more·fortunate in worldly wealth, and may well be content with his independence and his career of practical idealism.

Doctor Wood is a pioneer of Oklahoma, having come to the territory in 1889, the year of the first opening. He has practiced medicine upwards of thirty years, and by his skill and ability stands in the front rank of Oklahoma practitioners. Doctor Wood was born on a Georgia plantation August 12, 1849. His parents were James and Mary (Turner) Wood, the former a native of North Carolina and the latter of Georgia. His father gave service in behalf of the Southern cause during the war between the states. From Georgia the family subsequently removed to Texas, and later to Arkansas. James Wood followed farming all his active career and died at the age of eighty-two years, while his wife passed away at sixty. Both were members of the Baptist Church. Of their five children three are still living: Hon. R. E. Wood, a prominent citizen of Oklahoma City, assistant attorney-general of Oklahoma; O. M. Wood of Arkansas; and Dr. V. A. Wood.

Doctor Wood spent his early life on farms in Texas and Arkansas. This experience gave him a sound constitution and was a wholesome training for his later professional career. At the same time he attended public schools, studied at home, and also had the advantages of college. He began the study of medicine under a well known physician in Arkansas, and then entered the Louisville Medical College of Kentucky, where he was graduated M. D. in 1885.

Doctor Wood was married in 1874, in Arkansas, to Miss Sarah Robbins. They have now lived together as man and wife and in mutual confidence and esteem for more than forty years. Mrs. Wood is a member of a Georgia family and of old Southern antecedents. Doctor Wood and wife are proud of their family of nine children: Robert H., who is a geologist and is connected with the work of his profession in a Government position at Washington; Homa and Okla, twins, and both A. M. graduates from the University of Oklahoma, and Homa is an LL. D. of the same university; Virgil O.; Dudley; Beulah, of Shawnee; Minnie Rose, wife of a successful business man at Watonga; and Edna, wife of F. A. Smith of Fort Smith, Arkansas. All the children have received the best of educational advantages, and have been well prepared for their duties in life.

Doctor Wood, outside of his professional service, has interested himself above all in the advancement of the public schools of Blackwell and Kay County. For twelve years he has served as a member of the Blackwell School Board, and the people of that community readily give him credit for the splendid improvements which now give Blackwell rank among the first cities of Oklahoma in point of educational standards and equipment. He has worked assiduously and unselfishly to provide such opportunities to the growing generation and for many years to come his name will deserve recognition when the progress of the Blackwell schools is under discussion. Doctor Wood and wife are both active members of the Baptist Church, in which he is deacon, while Mrs. Wood is prominent in the church organizations. Both have been liberal supporters of the church, and Doctor Wood has probably accomplished as much as any other local physician in the direction of practical charity, giving his services without thought of remuneration to those requiring it, whether rich or poor. He has always believed in the golden rule, and has practiced it perhaps as acceptably as any man. While he has always enjoyed a high standing and a good practice as a physician, he has not accumulated wealth and has had little ambition to do so. Much of his income has gone in support of the manifold charities and causes in which he was interested, and in the community esteem which is paid him and in the wealth of his home and well trained children he has riches greater than could be measured by bank stocks or railroad bonds. Doctor Wood is a fine example of the old-time Southern gentleman, has proved himself trustworthy in all the relations of life, and greets hardship and ill fortune with the same kindly smile that he turns to his many friends.

WILLIAM R. JONES. Within the period of his residence in Oklahoma Judge Jones has proved a specially able representative of both the pedagogic and legal professions, and in the autumn of 1914 there came a well merited recognition of his eligibility and his high standing at the bar when he was elected to the bench of the County Court of Payne County, an exacting and responsible office in which he is giving a characteristically effective and popular administration. Prior to establishing his residence at Stillwater, the county seat, he had maintained his home at Cushing, this county, where he had been a successful teacher in the public schools and had also engaged in the practice of law.

Judge Jones was born on a farm in Wright County, Missouri, and the date of his nativity was December 18, 1877. He is a son of Thomas and Luvinia (Royster) Jones, who were born and reared in Tennessee and who were young folk at the time of the removal of the respective families to Missouri, just before the outbreak of the Civil war. In that state their marriage was solemnized and they still reside on their excellent homestead farm in Wright County, the subject of this review being the eldest of their eight surviving children.

Judge Jones acquired his early education in the schools of his native state and his initial experiences were those gained in connection with the activities of the home farm. He was an ambitious student and through his well directed application he acquired a liberal education along academic lines. Thus he admirably fortified himself for the pedagogic profession, of which he was a successful and popular representative for fourteen consecutive years, save for an interim of one year. His earlier work as a teacher was in schools of his native state, and he taught one year in Arkansas. In 1902 he came to Oklahoma Territory, and here he continued his efficient services as a teacher for a period of six years—until he turned his attention to the practice of law. During the first two years of his residence in the territory he taught in the schools of Oklahoma County, and he has been a resident of Payne County since 1908. While in Oklahoma

County Judge Jones further fortified himself by attending the State Normal School at Edmond, and later he continued his higher academic studies in the Oklahoma Agricultural & Mechanical College, at Stillwater. For three years he was principal of the public schools at Cushing, Payne County, and 1912 he was elected county superintendent of schools, an office which he held two years, and in which he did admirable work in systematizing and advancing the work of the schools of Payne County. While engaged in teaching he devoted close attention to the study of law and gained a comprehensive and practical knowledge of the science of jurisprudence, his admission to the Oklahoma bar having been granted in 1910. He removed to Stillwater upon assuming office as county superintendent of schools, and after his retirement from that responsible post he was here engaged in the active general practice of law until his election to his present office, that of county judge, in the autumn of 1914. He is a staunch and effective advocate of the principles and policies for which the democratic party stands sponsor and has rendered yeoman service in behalf of its cause during his residence in Oklahoma. He and his wife hold membership in the Christian Church and he is affiliated with the local lodge of Ancient Free and Accepted Masons.

In 1908 was solemnized the marriage of Judge Jones to Miss Naomi Howe, who was born in Kansas, and who is a daughter of Alexander C. and Harriet Howe, both of whom were born in Pennsylvania, whence they removed to Kansas in the pioneer period of its history. They remained in the Sunflower State until 1892, when they came to Oklahoma Territory and first located at Guthrie. Mr. Howe later became a prosperous farmer of Payne County, where his death occurred and where his widow still maintains her home. Judge and Mrs. Jones have three children: Lorene, Paul and Harold.

IRA EDWIN SNYDER. This young business man of Frederick where he is manager of the Southwestern Lumber Company, has shown an unusual ability to advance himself in the world, and immediately on finishing a high school course in Kansas started to learn the lumber business, and in a very few brief years has been advanced to responsibilities which make him an important factor in the Town of Frederick.

Born at Pleasanton, Kansas, February 11, 1889, he is a son of Edward Marcus Snyder, a grandson of Asa Snyder, and a great-grandson of an emigrant from Germany who spelled his name Schneider, who settled in Tennessee as a farmer and married a Miss Downey. Grandfather Asa Snyder removed his family from Tennessee to Kentucky, thence to Illinois, and finally to Kansas, and died near Pleasanton in the latter state. He combined the business of farming with his duties as a local Methodist Protestant minister. Edward Marcus Snyder, who was born near Danville, Vermilion County, Illinois, in 1853, was also a minister of the Methodist Protestant Church, and is now living at Centerville, Kansas. In that state he has had charge of churches at Centerville, Rose Hill, Battlefield, Whitewater, and other places, and for two years preached in the Congregational Church at Fredonia. His first wife was a Miss Perry, who died in Linn County, Kansas, the mother of three children, namely: Fred B., who is a machinist in the shingle mill at Blanchard, Washington; Lena May, who lives at Wichita, Kansas; and Clema Inez, wife of Frank Brooks, who is a farmer near Blue Mountain, Kansas. Edward M. Snyder married for his second wife Ella Ann Osborne, who was born at Uniontown, Pennsylvania. Their children are Ira Edwin Snyder and Charles Wilbur Snyder, the latter born October 31, 1890, and now manager of the Dascomb-Daniels Lumber Company at Frederick, Oklahoma.

His early training in the common schools Mr. Snyder acquired at Centerville, Rose Hill, Prairie Center, Kansas, and was graduated from the high school at Burns, Kansas, in 1909. On May 10th of the same year he placed his foot on the first round of the ladder of advancement by becoming yard man and bookkeeper in the lumber yard at Burns, and remained there until April, 1910. He was then sent to Westphalia, Kansas, as manager of the R. W. Long Lumber Company for 2½ years, and on October 5, 1912, arrived at Frederick, Oklahoma, where he has since had local management of the Southwestern Lumber Company. The headquarters of this company are at Kansas City and there are eleven branch yards maintained in Oklahoma. This company acts as sales and distributing agent for the East Oregon Lumber Company in the State of Oregon.

Mr. Snyder is independent in politics, a member of the Methodist Episcopal Church, is affiliated with Westphalia Lodge No. 305, Ancient Free and Accepted Masons, with Frederick Chapter No. 41, Royal Arch Masons, with the Brotherhood of American Yeomen, and belongs to the Business Men's Association of Frederick.

On December 31, 1912, at Westphalia, Kansas, he married Miss Violet Eagle, daughter of J. S. Eagle, who is now living retired at Westphalia. They have two daughters, Rose Marie and Eleanor Margaret.

THOMAS P. BRAIDWOOD. In 1887, about two years prior to the formal opening of Oklahoma Territory to white settlement, Mr. Braidwood came to the neutral strip of country then known as No Man's Land and became one of the influential figures in defining the government and instituting the development of this region that now includes a number of the most prosperous and progressive counties in the western part of the state. He established his residence in old Beaver City and there opened and conducted the first hardware store, operations having been continued in the original building until the same was destroyed by a cyclone that swept the locality on the 31st of March, 1892. In the year that marked his arrival in this new frontier region, Mr. Braidwood became one of the organizers of the Territory of Cimarron, and he served as a member of the Territorial Senate. In 1888 he was chosen territorial secretary, and of this office he continued the incumbent until the territorial organization was dissolved by the opening of Oklahoma Territory to settlement, as duly recorded in the direct historical department of this publication.

In 1890 when old Beaver County, including the present-day counties of Beaver, Texas and Cimarron, was organized, Mr. Braidwood was appointed county clerk by Hon. George W. Steele, then Governor of Oklahoma Territory. In the ensuing popular election, in 1891, he was duly chosen the incumbent of this office, in which he served two years. He then returned to his former home at Leavenworth, Kansas, where he remained until 1897, when he came again to Oklahoma and resumed his residence in Beaver County. In 1902 he was elected representative of Beaver and Woodward counties in the lower house of the Territorial Legislature, in which he served one term and did much to further the best interests of his constituent district, besides taking loyal and effective part in legislation for the benefit of the territory at large. In 1905 he served as journal clerk of the Legislature. In 1907, the year of the admission of Oklahoma as one of the sovereign states of the Union, Mr. Braidwood was appointed United States Commissioner for western Oklahoma, and of this Federal office he has since continued the efficient incumbent, his residence being maintained in the Village of Beaver, judicial center of the county of the same name. He has been foremost in all activities tending to promote the civic and material advancement of his home town and county, and in 1888 he served as mayor of old Beaver City, no other pioneer of this now opulent section of the state being better known or held in higher popular esteem. Mr. Braidwood has reclaimed and improved one of the large and valuable stock ranches of Beaver County, is still the owner of this property and on the same he maintained his residence for a period of eleven years. He has proved one of the strong, vigilant and resourceful pioneers and upbuilders of western Oklahoma and his name shall ever merit high place on the historical records of this section of the state.

Mr. Braidwood was born in the city of Albany, New York, on the 24th of March, 1855, and his father, Thomas L. Braidwood was born at Utica, that state, on the 3d of May, 1820, his death having occurred in Beaver County, Oklahoma, on the 1st of May, 1900, only two days prior to his eightieth birthday anniversary. Thomas L. Braidwood was reared and educated in the old Empire State, where he learned the trade of iron moulder and where he continued his residence until 1871, when he removed with his family to Kansas and became one of the pioneer settlers of Cowley County, where he entered claim to and settled upon a tract of government land. He instituted the development of this land and eventually perfected his title to the property. He continued to reside upon his pioneer homestead until 1875, when he removed to Leavenworth, that state, and became superintendent of a stove foundry. With this industrial enterprise he continued to be thus identified until 1889, when he came to Beaver County, Oklahoma, and resumed operations as an agriculturist and stock grower, with which lines of enterprise he here continued to be identified until his death, both he and his wife having been persons of superior intellectual powers and of sterling character, their worthy lives and worthy deeds having gained to them the good will and high esteem of all with whom they came in contact. In the State of New York was solemnized the marriage of Thomas L. Braidwood to Miss Marian Burgess, who was born in the City of Glasgow, Scotland, on the 11th of November, 1818, and who was thus an infant at the time of her parents' immigration to the United States, in 1820. She was reared and educated in the State of New York and survived her honored husband by exactly two years, she having been summoned to the life eternal on the 3d of May, 1902, in Beaver County, Oklahoma. The marriage of this loved pioneer couple was solemnized at West Troy, New York, on the 6th day of July, 1844, and after a period of nearly sixty years their devoted companionship was severed by the death of Mr. Braidwood. They became the parents of four sons and two daughters, concerning whom the following brief data are entered: James was born April 6, 1845, and died on the 15th of September of the following year. John Burgess was born September 5, 1846, and now resides in Albany, New York. He married Miss Caroline VanGuysling, on the 25th of December, 1870, and her death occurred in 1885, their surviving children being James A., born October 12, 1871, and John Burgess, Jr., born September 5, 1874. James Liddell was born September 25, 1848, and was drowned in the Arkansas River, at a point near Muskogee, Indian Territory, on the 10th of May, 1871. Marian E., who was born at Albany, New York, on the 10th of June, 1851, was married July 4, 1874, to Charles C. Black, and they became the parents of four children: Charlotte, Marian E., Francis and Charles B., all of whom are living except the first born. Thomas P., whose name introduces this article, was the next in order of birth. Anna J., who was born March 13, 1858, became, on the 31st of March, 1875, the wife of William M. Allison, and of their six children Howard and Robert died in infancy, as did also Nina, the three surviving being William A., born August 1, 1878; Marian, born in February, 1879, died in 1907; and Anna, born May 18, 1883. Mrs. Allison died July 6, 1892, at Chandler, Oklahoma, and her husband, who was a pioneer newspaper man, both in Southern Kansas and in Oklahoma, now resides at Snyder, Oklahoma, where he is serving as postmaster.

Thomas P. Braidwood acquired his early education in the public schools of his native city, the capital of the State of New York, and was a lad of about sixteen years when he accompanied his parents on their immigration to Kansas, in 1871. After his father assumed the superintendency of the stove foundry at Leavenworth, that state, Mr. Braidwood was employed twelve years as a moulder in the establishment, and he thus continued to be engaged until his removal to what is now the State of Oklahoma, in 1887, as noted in detail in former paragraphs of this article.

Mr. Braidwood is aligned as a stalwart advocate of the political principles and policies for which the republican party stands sponsor, has received the thirty-second degree of the Ancient Accepted Scottish Rite in the time-honored Masonic fraternity, and is affiliated also with the Knights of Pythias.

At Leavenworth, Kansas, on the 6th of June, 1877, was solemnized the marriage of Mr. Braidwood to Miss Josie A. Warner, who was born at Delavan, Tazewell County, Illinois, on the 10th day of July, 1855, a daughter of Alexander and Almira (Dossett) Warner, the former a native of England and the latter of Illinois. Mrs. Braidwood received a collegiate education and for three years prior to her marriage she was a successful teacher in the pioneer schools of Crawford County, Kansas. She died in the City of Leavenworth, that state, on the 12th of June, 1897, and of her two children the elder is living,—Thomas C., who was born at Leavenworth, Kansas, September 3, 1878, and resides at Beaver, Oklahoma. He married Miss Edith Hoover, a native of Kansas, on the 10th of April, 1913. Lottie, the younger of the two children of Thomas P. and Josie A. (Warner) Braidwood, was born November 26, 1880, and died in infancy.

LEWIS M. SPENCER. A well known citizen of Canadian County and an influential and honored resident of the thriving little City of Yukon, Mr. Spencer is specially entitled to recognition in this publication, as he figures as one of the founders and builders of the attractive town in which he maintains his home and in the original platting of which he was associated with his brother, A. N. Spencer.

Mr. Spencer reverts to the fine old Buckeye State as the place of his nativity and is a scion of one of its pioneer families. He was born at Wilmington, Clinton County, Ohio, on the 17th of April, 1842, and is one of the four sons born to Mahlon and Mary Ann (Little) Spencer, who removed from Ohio to Montgomery County, Illinois, in an early day and became pioneers of the latter state, where the father engaged in farming, both he and his wife having continued their residence in Illinois until the time of their death. He whose name initiates this review was a child at the time of the family removal to Illinois, and in Macoupin and Montgomery counties he was reared to maturity under the conditions and influences of the pioneer days, his early educational advantages having been limited to a somewhat desultory attendance of the winter sessions in a primitive log school-house of the type common to the locality and period. As a young man in 1860 he went to Baton Rouge, Louisiana, where Capt. W. Knott Little, a brother to his mother maintained his home. As a valiant soldier in the Confederate service he took part in the great conflict, and after the close of the war he made his way to Texas, where he gained practical experience in the herding of cattle on the great open ranges. From the Lone Star State he and his brother, A. N., who is now deceased, had occasion to drive cattle through what is now the State of Oklahoma, and in so doing they made their first visit in the vicinity of the present Town of Yukon, of which they were the founders. A. N. Spencer later became associated with the construction of the Choctaw Railroad, the line of which is now a part of the Chicago & Rock Island system, and on this early railway he became the founder of the Village of Yukon, in association with his brother Lewis M., of this sketch. The two brothers laid out the village and were the most influential factors in bringing about its development and upbuilding into one of the attractive and prosperous municipalities of the present State of Oklahoma. Lewis M. Spencer has maintained his home at Yukon since 1891, and is locally referred to, with all of appreciation, as the father of the town. He and his brother obtained four quarter-sections of land, and on this tract laid out the town, and built the railroad and to the development of which they vigorously applied themselves, their effective efforts having resulted in gaining to the new town an excellent class of enterprising citizens. Lewis M. Spencer has erected many houses in Yukon and has sold them on easy terms, thus enabling numerous families to obtain desirable homes. During all the years of his residence at Yukon he has here been a prominent and successful representative of the real-estate business, in the handling of both farm and town property, and with characteristic progressiveness and civic loyalty he has contributed liberally to the erection of church edifices and parsonages, and to the support of religious, educational and other agencies that ever conserve the best interests of the community. His success has been won by earnest and worthy effort, he has guided his course on a high plane of integrity and honor, and none of the sterling pioneers of Canadian County has more secure place in popular confidence and esteem than does this generous and public-spirited citizen.

Mr. Spencer has been closely identified with the development of the admirable agricultural resources of his home county, and at the Louisiana Purchase Exposition, in the City of St. Louis, he won a bronze medal for his exhibit of corn raised by him and pronounced the best exhibited at that great exposition. He has won also other prizes on corn and cotton exhibited by him at fairs conducted by both state and county agricultural societies. Yukon is located on a beautiful high site fifteen miles west of Oklahoma City, fourteen miles east of El Reno, three miles south of the North Canadian River and twelve miles north of the South Canadian River. It consists mostly of dark rich valley soil underlaid with oil and gas, and raises most any kind of produce in abundance. To the investor Yukon offers the largest revenue on the investment, the demand for houses at a good rental, with a low taxation and small capital invested, insures the investor a good net gain on his investment.

On September 13, 1874, was solemnized the marriage of Mr. Spencer to Miss Mary J. Siceluff, the only child of sterling German parents, and the one child of this union is Claudia, who is now the wife of Elmer E. Kirkpatrick, of Oklahoma City.

ROBERT C. WHINERY. Owner and editor of the Tonkawa News, Robert C. Whinery is one of the successful newspaper men of Oklahoma. To journalism he has brought the talents which would have enabled him to succeed in lines of business much more remunerative, and for many years has been through all the grades of service in the fourth estate, from printer and reporter to editor, and from a salaried position to independent publisher.

In many ways the Tonkawa News has a distinctive position in Oklahoma newspaperdom, and is acknowledged to be one of the brightest and most enterprising journals in the northern part of the state. It is now issuing the numbers of its eighteenth volume, and was established at Tonkawa in 1898 by Thomas Fry, now a resident of Wichita, Kansas. The paper is maintained independently so far as politics is concerned, and is first and last a strenuous advocate of everything that is good for Tonkawa and vicinity, whether in business, civic improvement, the elevation of schools and churches, or anything else that will make it a better town to live in. Mr. Whinery has a well equipped newspaper office and plant, with linotype, modern presses both for newspaper printing and job work, and is a man of broad experience both in the mechanical and editorial branches of his profession. For eleven years he has been identified with newspaper work in Oklahoma, having come to the territory in 1904. He brought the first linotype machines into Shawnee, Oklahoma, and for one year was connected with Charles Barrett on the Shawnee Herald. They conducted a live wire newspaper during the territorial days, and the Herald was a power both in politics and in general affairs. Mr. Whinery was associate editor with Mr. Barrett on the Herald. Later he removed to Tonkawa and bought the plant of the News, and has since developed this paper with a large circulation throughout Kay and adjoining counties.

Robert C. Whinery was born in Wilmington, Clinton County, Ohio, and is of Quaker parentage, a son of Isaiah and Hannah Whinery. His father is of Irish stock, and made a creditable record for himself and his descendants as a soldier in the Union army. He is now living at Pleasanton, Kansas, at the advanced age of eighty-four years. The mother died in 1906, aged sixty-eight. She was a native of Virginia, her parents being of the F. F. V. There were six children, four sons and two daughters.

Mr. Whinery received his early education in a little Quaker school in Ohio. His university career began with his entrance into a printing shop at the age of fifteen in the lowly capacity of a devil. He learned everything about printing and newspaper business that could be learned in the shop of the Pleasanton Observer, and then went to Kansas City, where he had a more metropolitan training and experience. For a time he was on Colonel Van Horn's republican paper, the Kansas City Journal, and also with the Kansas City Star under Colonel Nelson. One of the editors under whom he worked was the noted William Allen White, the great Emporia editor, author and statesman. He finally resigned and moved to Shawnee, Oklahoma, as already mentioned.

At Pleasanton, Kansas, in January, 1893, Mr. Whinery married Miss Mamie Latimer. Mrs. Whinery is a woman of education and culture, was educated in Park College in Missouri, and was a successful teacher before her marriage. Her parents were James and Elizabeth (Hartford) Latimer, her father having been a professor in Knox College in Illinois. Mr. and Mrs. Whinery have three children: Marie Elizabeth and Esther, students

at the State University at Norman; and Robert C., Jr., now nine years of age.

Mr. Whinery in politics has always been a republican. He has been honored with the office of mayor, and is a hard and independent worker for anything that will bring welfare to his community. His associates speak of him as a man of decided conviction, and always ready to take a firm stand on a platform of right and justice. He is a member of the Masonic Order, being a past master of the lodge, and of the Independent Order of Odd Fellows, and his family worship in the Presbyterian faith.

AARON DRUMRIGHT. Only to few men can come such distinction as that which has made Aaron Drumright the father of a city of fifteen thousand people, which bears his name, and which is now considered one of the greatest oil centers in the world. Drumright was worthily named. It was an honor fitly bestowed. Mr. Drumright was not only the fortunate possessor of a large acreage in Creek County which was underlaid by unusually rich deposits of oil and gas, but he had the public spirit, the business enterprise and the management which enabled him to make the best of these resources not only for himself but for the thousands of others who have since congregated around the site of his original homestead. The people of Drumright, both the old and new settlers, say that no one individual has done quite so much in a public spirited and liberal fashion for the upbuilding of the little city than the man for whom it was named.

It is also unusual to discover that Mr. Drumright is a very young man in spite of his wealth and position. He was born at West Plains, Howell County, Missouri, June 22, 1883. His parents were R. F. and Eliza Ann (Hatcher) Drumright, his father having been born in Tennessee in July, 1854, and his mother in Northern Missouri. The mother died at West Plains at the age of forty in May, 1896. The father spent about forty years on the old homestead at West Plains, but for the past five years has had his home in Oklahoma. In 1910 Aaron and his brother Otto traded their father's old place for a farm in Oklahoma. Aaron Drumright is one of a family of nine children, six of whom are still living, three sons and three daughters: Aletta, wife of Edward Sparks of Douglas County, Missouri; Viola May, wife of Preston Hesterly, and she is now deceased, while Mr. Hesterly was county clerk of Douglas County, Missouri, and later became a physician in Oklahoma; Otto is a farmer at Bristow, Oklahoma; Aaron is the fourth in order of age; Everett lives in Kansas; Arthur died at the age of three years; Lina married Henry Bridges of Kansas; Gertrude is the wife of Frank Nasworthy of Bristow, Oklahoma; and Eliza is now deceased.

The first sixteen years of his life Aaron Drumright spent on the old farm. His experiences have led him into Kansas, Oklahoma and Arkansas, and especially in earlier years he earned his bread by the sweat of his brow. He worked as a roustabout on railroads and with carpenter contractors until twenty-three, and then located near Cushing, Oklahoma, where in 1905 he married Miss Mary Ryan. She was born in Iowa, daughter of Dennis Ryan.

After his marriage Mr. Drumright began farming on leased Indian lands, and kept that up for five years. His efforts were successful, and at the end of five years he had twenty-eight hundred dollars to show for his work and management. He had begun with a minimum of capital, though he possessed the strength and industry and determination which enable a man to succeed in anything he undertakes. At the opening of the Cheyenne River and Standing Rock Indian Reservation in South Dakota he registered and drew Lot No. 1,750, which brought him a claim near Isabelle, South Dakota. He proved up and kept the claim for two years, then sold, and returning to Oklahoma located on the present site of Drumright in November, 1911. Here he bought 120 acres of land from B. B. Jones, paying fifteen dollars an acre or $1,800 for the entire tract. This has been his home and the scene of his fortunate operations down to the present time.

About the time Mr. Drumright bought his land B. B. Jones and T. B. Slick were drilling for oil two and a half miles northeast, at what is known as the old Tiger well. After the well was brought in it averaged a production of thirty-five barrels per day. There was no pipe line which could take the oil to market, and consequently the well was plugged. Other wells were brought in in that territory, and during 1912 Mr. C. B. Shafer put down the first well on Mr. Drumright's land, which struck oil in September, 1912. Then followed the great rush which has since made Drumright the largest active producing center for oil in the country. Nine wells were sunk on the 120 acres by C. B. Shafer, and one of them proved to be a gas well. Five of these wells averaged 250 barrels per day.

It was in July, 1912, that the first tent was set up on Mr. Drumright's farm at the southwest corner. It was used as a boarding camp, and quickly around it sprang up others, and in February, 1913, Mr. Drumright had the land surveyed and sold as lots. At the present time the entire farm of 120 acres is platted and nearly all of it sold. About one-third of the City of Drumright is on Mr. Drumright's old farm. As soon as the camp was formed a postoffice was required, and Mr. Drumright took a petition from one rig to another and secured sufficient signatures in order to get this branch of the service from the Federal Government. When it came to selecting a name for the office there was general suggestion and approval of the name of Mr. Drumright, and thus Drumright was put down in the directory of postoffices and as such the name will probably exist through all succeeding generations. It is interesting to note that the camp was first known as Fulkerson's Camp, because J. W. Fulkerson owned the south half of the town, but Mr. Drumright's interests and activities made him so popular a figure among the early comers that it was almost by unanimous choice that his name was selected for the name of the city.

In many ways he has been influential in helping forward every movement and institution in that locality. He was a member of the local school board in June, 1912, and served with the board until June, 1915. In that time he was largely responsible for the present splendid school system to be found in Drumright. At first the town had only one small building, with sixty pupils enrolled. Now there is a twelve-room stone building, a ten-room brick building, and a new high school building in course of construction that will cost $60,000. All this has been accomplished in about three years, and Drumright is not only a city of great natural commercial resources, but also a center of schools, churches, good homes and is rapidly progressing toward every other standard civic improvement. Mr. Drumright has also served as treasurer of the township board. He helped to organize the first bank, known as the Drumright State Bank, in 1914, and has since been its president. He gave his help toward organizing and maintaining the Commercial Club, of which he is treasurer. He is also city treasurer, and was president of the committee that secured the construction of a branch of the Santa Fe Railroad to Drumright. Thus the future historian will find not only the fact that the town was named for him, but that his activities went into and helped to vitalize every local movement and improvement. In polities he is a republican. He practically built the Methodist Episcopal Church of which he is an active member, and he is prominent in Masonry, being affiliated with the thirty-second degree Scottish Rite Consistory at Guthrie, and with the Mystic Shrine at Tulsa. He is also affiliated with the Independent Order of Odd Fellows, the Modern Woodmen of America and the Benevolent and Protective Order of Elks. Mr. and Mrs. Drumright are the parents of four children: Everett, aged nine; Bessie, aged seven; Irene, aged five; and Fred Haskell, aged three.

JOHN O. SHAW. When, in 1915, John O. Shaw was appointed principal of the Frederick High School, an individual was chosen for that position who is eminently fitted by education, training and experience to discharge its important duties. His entire career has been devoted to teaching and has been one of steady and well-won advancement, until today he is one of the best known and most popular educators in this part of Oklahoma, where his labors have been prosecuted for the past five years.

John O. Shaw was born at Harrisburg, Boone County, Missouri, September 26, 1880, and is a son of J. W. and Mildred French (Woods) Shaw, and a member of a family that originated in Ireland and settled in Virginia probably before the War of the Revolution. His grandfather, John Wesley Shaw, was born in the Old Dominion and was an infant when taken to Missouri, where the family located among the pioneers. The grandmother, Mrs. Elizabeth Shaw, still makes her home near Higbee, Missouri, in advanced years. J. W. Shaw was born near Harrisburg, Missouri, in 1856, was reared to agricultural pursuits and has been engaged in farming and raising stock all his life. He is an active member of the Baptist Church, as is his wife, and their children were reared in that faith. Mrs. Shaw was born in Harrisburg, and has been the mother of three children: John O., of this notice; W. A., who is engaged in banking at Columbia, Missouri; and Robert H., a farmer and the owner of a property located near the old homestead in Boone County.

John O. Shaw attended the public schools of Harrisburg, and in 1901 was graduated from Columbia Normal College, with the degree of Bachelor of Arts. He had been reared to agricultural pursuits, but had decided upon a career as an educator in preference to farming, and soon secured a school in the country district of Boone County, where he continued to teach for five years, there gaining much practical experience of a valuable nature. Realizing the need for further preparation, Mr. Shaw then took a course of three and one-half years in the University of Missouri, and in 1910 came to Watonga, Oklahoma, where he became principal of the high school. After two years he was made city superintendent of schools there, and continued to hold that position until 1915, when he received the appointment as principal of the Frederick High School. At the present time he has under his charge six teachers and 150 pupils. While Mr. Shaw has held his present office only for a short period he has already demonstrated that he is a man who can accomplish things, and he has under way a number of plans which will elevate the high school system here. The favorable impression which he has created among teachers, scholars and parents indicates that he will be one of the most popular principals Frederick has known. Professor Shaw is a member of the Baptist Church, and is a pledge member of the Nu Beta Rho, an honorary Greek letter teachers' fraternity.

In 1905, Mr. Shaw was united in marriage at Harrisburg, Missouri, with Miss Bessie Blakemore, daughter of Allen Blakemore, a hardware merchant of Harrisburg. To this union there have come two children, namely: Martha Vivian, who was born January 9, 1909; and Luda French, born June 26, 1912.

GEORGE H. HEALY. In point of continuous residence this honored member of the Beaver County Bar is to be consistently designated as the oldest citizen of the county, and in addition to this interesting feature of pioneer prestige he holds secure place as one of the representative members of the legal profession in this section of the state, and as a citizen whose influence and co-operation have been potent in connection with civic and material progress in western Oklahoma. He is engaged in the practice of his profession in the Town of Beaver, the county seat, has held various offices of distinctive public trust, including that of county judge, and became a resident of what is now the State of Oklahoma more than thirty years ago, so that he gained varied experience in connection with frontier life in old Indian Territory.

Judge Healy is a scion of a New England colonial family of English lineage and personally takes due pride in adverting to the old Pine Tree State as the place of his nativity. He was born in the Village of China, Kennebec County, Maine, on the 30th of May, 1857, and is a son of William H. and Ellen (Breck) Healy, both likewise natives of that state. Reared and educated in Maine, William H. Healy achieved success and prominence in New England as a tanner and an exporter and importer of leather and hides. He developed an extensive business, in connection with which he maintained tanneries and warehouses both in Boston and New York. His operations in this field of enterprise continued until 1875, when he removed with his family to Texas, where he engaged in the cattle business on a large scale, besides which, in line with his former business activities, he developed a prosperous business in the buying of furs from Indians and white trappers in Dakota Territory, his activities in this direction continuing from 1875 to 1879 and both of his business ventures in the West having proved very successful.

In 1878 William H. Healy established a cattle ranch in the western part of Indian Territory,—in the neutral strip commonly designated as No Man's Land and later included in Beaver County. He continued the handling of cattle upon an extensive scale on the great open ranges of Texas and Indian Territory until his death, which occurred in 1883, and he became widely known throughout the Southwest, both as a business man of great energy and ability and as a citizen of sterling character. His marriage to Miss Ellen Breck was solemnized in his young manhood, and his wife was summoned to eternal rest in 1867, while the family home was still maintained in the East. Of their six children the first born, a daughter, died in infancy. Caroline E., who was born in 1843, has never married and maintains her home in the City of Springfield, Massachusetts. William H., Jr., who was born in 1845, attained to distinction as one of the representative lawyers in the city of Boston and there his death occurred in 1897. Frank D., who was born in 1847, served as sheriff of Beaver County, Oklahoma Territory four years, his term having been initiated in 1894, and in 1897 he was appointed Register of the United States Land Office at Woodward, Oklahoma, a position which he retained until his death, in 1902. He established his residence in Indian Territory in 1878 and here was associated with his brother George H., of this review, in the cattle business in the early days. In 1866 he married Miss Frank B. Dow, likewise a native of China, Maine, and they are survived by three children, William, Charles and Dole. He became prominent in public affairs and political matters in

Oklahoma Territory, and was a stalwart advocate of the cause of the republican party. Nathaniel G., who was born in 1849 and who remains a bachelor, is now a resident of the City of Los Angeles, California.

George H. Healy, the youngest of the children, was graduated in an excellent private school in the city of Boston when he was seventeen years of age, and he accompanied his father on the removal to Texas, in 1875, so that virtually his entire mature life has been passed in the Southwest, where his memory links the pioneer past with the present-day era of opulent progress and prosperity, it having been his privilege to contribute a due quota to the march of advancement along both civic and industrial lines. Mr. Healy came to Indian Territory in 1880, and during the long intervening years he has maintained his home within the borders of what is now the vigorous young State of Oklahoma. He was early associated with his brother Frank in establishing a cattle ranch in the old Neutral strip in which the present Beaver County is included, and this ranch was situated on Beaver Creek, its operation having been continued by the brothers until the opening of Oklahoma Territory to settlement.

In 1890 Judge Healy was elected the first treasurer of old Beaver County, which then included also the present counties of Texas and Cimarron, and for eight years prior to the admission of Oklahoma to statehood he served as a member of the Republican Central Committee of the Territory, his vigorous and effective co-operation having been fruitful in the advancing of the party cause during the territorial days as well as under the later regime of state government. A man of broad intellectual keen and mature judgment, Judge Healy finally gave careful attention to the study of law until he had fortified himself well in accurate knowledge of the science of jurisprudence, and in 1900 he was admitted to the Oklahoma Bar. He soon afterward engaged in the practice of his profession at Beaver, his attention being given to his substantial law business until his election to the bench of the County Court of Beaver County, on which he served four consecutive years, 1910-14. Since his retirement from the bench Judge Healy has continued in the active work of his profession at Beaver, where he controls a large and representative law business and is known as one of the leading members of the bar of Beaver County.

In the City of Emporia, Kansas, on the 5th of November, 1890, was solemnized the marriage of Judge Healy to Miss Lydia Savage, who was born at Virginia, Cass County, Illinois, on the 23d of August, 1870, and who is a daughter of John W. and Caroline M. (Springer) Savage, the former of whom was born in Illinois, in 1838, and the latter in Pennsylvania, in the same year, she being now a resident of Beaver, Oklahoma, her husband having died at Emporia, Kansas, on the 20th of May, 1891. Judge and Mrs. Healy have but one child, Ledru Rollin, who was born in Beaver County, Oklahoma, on the 9th of August, 1891, and who was afforded the advantages of the Kansas State Agricultural College, at Manhattan, and of the Wesleyan Business College, at Saline, that state. He is now one of the representative young members of the bar of the City of El Paso, Texas.

P. L. BUCY. Since 1902 Mr. Bucy has been one of the active oil producers in the Kansas and Oklahoma Territory. For the past ten years he has lived at Bartlesville, and has not only been an operator in oil but is also the principal real estate man at Bartlesville, and head of the P. L. Bucy Realty & Investment Company. His active career began when he was still a boy, and he has lived in a number of the states of the Mississippi Basin.

P. L. Bucy was born at St. Mary's, West Virginia, September 3, 1878, a son of Alexander and Janet (Prunty) Bucy. His father was born in Steubenville, Ohio, February 4, 1833, and his mother at St. Mary's, West Virginia, in November, 1838. They were married at Steubenville, and the father died at Williamstown, West Virginia, November 4, 1908. The mother and one of her daughters now reside with Mr. Bucy at Bartlesville. The father was a soldier of the Union army, and at the beginning of the war enlisted in Company A of the Twenty-second Ohio Infantry, and after three years veteranized and continued until mustered out with an honorable discharge at the close of the war. He was engaged in coal mining until 1876, and thereafter was a farmer.

P. L. Bucy was the fifth in a family of nine children, and spent the first eighteen years of his life with his parents in West Virginia. After the age of fourteen he left school and became a worker, living at home but earning his own support. When eighteen he went to Steubenville, Ohio, and became a contractor. That was his business there until the age of twenty-two, and the following year he spent in the same business at St. Louis. Mr. Bucy then became identified with the Iron Mountain Railroad Company in construction work with headquarters at Pittsburg, Mississippi.

On April 5, 1902, he left Pittsburg and entered the oil business with headquarters at Pittsburg, Kansas. From there he came to Bartlesville in 1905, and has since done a great deal of drilling and producing in the Bartlesville field. He has organized a number of corporations under the laws of different states and has dealt extensively in real estate, farm lands, oil lands and city property in Ohio, West Virginia, Pennsylvania, Wisconsin, Kansas, Missouri and Oklahoma. The P. L. Bucy Realty & Investment Company is a co-partnership, and the largest concern of its kind in Bartlesville. It has extensive oil holdings in Oklahoma.

Mr. Bucy is a republican and was defeated by only thirty-three votes in the primary election of 1914 for the Legislature. He is a member of the First Baptist Church of Bartlesville and of the Benevolent and Protective Order of Elks. As a citizen he has worked effectively to prevent vicious legislation in land title laws, and has been engaged in considerable litigation. Some of his cases have been carried to the Supreme Court, and he is known as one of the most vigorous fighters for justice, but always contending for fair and honorable principles.

J. A. JONES, M. D. The senior member of the medical profession at Tonkawa is Dr. J. A. Jones, who has been in active practice there for the past fifteen years, and who in that time has seen many physicians come and go, and now, in point of continuous service, is the oldest doctor in that community. His success has been in proportion to his long residence, and he is known all over Kay County as a successful physician and a public-spirited man.

In 1900 Doctor Jones graduated from medical college, and in the same year moved from Northeastern Missouri to Oklahoma and began practice at Tonkawa. He was born in Northwestern Indiana on a farm near Valparaiso in January, 1874. His father, George W. Jones, was a substantial farmer and stockman, had made a record as a soldier in the Union army during the Civil war, and he now living retired at the age of seventy-seven in Tonkawa, Oklahoma. The mother, whose maiden name was Elizabeth Peterson, is now deceased.

One of a family of four children, Doctor Jones grew

up on a farm, and from his early experiences in the country gained the rugged constitution which has served him so well in his arduous practice as a physician. He attended public school in Valparaiso, also the Western College of La Belle, Missouri, and afterwards paid his way for several years as a teacher. His work as a teacher was done in Missouri, and in the meantime he took up the study of medicine and finally secured his degree from a medical college. Doctor Jones is a student all the time, keeps in close touch with advance in the medical profession by constant reading, association with other physicians, and possesses a fine library.

At Tonkawa, in 1902, he married Miss Myrtle Peppered. They have one daughter, Glayds, a bright girl of twelve years now attending school. Doctor Jones is a member of the County and State Medical societies, in Masonry has attained the thirty-second degree of the Scottish Rite, and is also an Odd Fellow. He has been prospered materially, resides in a comfortable seven-room cottage home at Tonkawa, furnished in excellent taste, and has considerable property both in the city and in Kay County. He has always manifested a public-spirited attitude toward local improvements, has performed his proportion of work in making Tonkawa a better place in which to live, and has contributed liberally to schools, churches and all local movements.

COL. A. H. NORWOOD. Forty-five years of residence and experience as a teacher, lawyer, newspaper man, merchant and in general business affairs and politics have given Colonel Norwood of Dewey many unique relations with the old Cherokee Nation and Northeastern Oklahoma. Among white men of prominence Colonel Norwood has lived in that section of Oklahoma longer than any other individual with the exception of N. F. Carr. Colonel Norwood is an authority on Cherokee history and has been both a witness and a participant in the progress and development of old Indian Territory from the time when there was not a railroad between Kansas and the Red River.

A. H. Norwood was born at Cleveland in East Tennessee, November 17, 1850. His parents were P. W. and Isabella Ann (Cowan) Norwood, both natives of East Tennessee, where they lived until 1876, and then removed to Texas, where they spent the rest of their lives. P. W. Norwood was a farmer and while a resident of Tennessee held several county and state offices, and during the war was a captain and served as provost marshal in the Union army. His wife was a first cousin to Sam Houston, the great Texas statesman, her mother being Hattie Houston. The maternal grandfather was Andrew Cowan, who served as an officer in the War of 1812. P. W. Norwood was descended from John Norwood, who settled at Lyons Mills near Baltimore, Maryland, and he and five of his sons were soldiers in the Revolutionary war. He came from the north of England and was a Scotchman. Colonel Norwood was the oldest in a family of eight children, six of whom reached maturity and five are now living. All the children accompanied their parents to Texas with the exception of Colonel Norwood.

The first twenty years of his life he spent at the old home in East Tennessee and received his education at Flint Springs Academy and at Cleveland. He studied law with a member of the bar at Chattanooga.

Colonel Norwood came to the Cherokee Nation of old Indian Territory in 1870, and for six years was a teacher, first at Fort Gibson and for three years was connected with the Orphan Asylum of the Cherokees. From Fort Gibson he went to the Coo Wes Scoo Wee district, and located on the site of the present City of Claremore, where he combined the practice of law with merchandising. He established the Claremore postoffice, at a time when mail was delivered only once a week and was carried by horseback. He was first postmaster, and gave the name to the office, since applied to the thriving little city. The name was given in honor of an old Osage chief. In 1881 Colonel Norwood became associated with Col. J. H. Bartles in the lumber and milling business, and they had common business relations more or less for fifteen years.

Soon after coming to Indian Territory Colonel Norwood became prominent among the Cherokees and for about twenty years was a member of the National Council of the Cherokee Nation. At different times he also served as secretary of both houses of the national Legislature and was one of the Cherokee officials that signed the patent for the lands now owned by the Osage tribes in Oklahoma. As a lawyer and representative of the Cherokee Nation he took an active part in the allotment of lands and has practiced largely before the interior department, a business which required his presence many times at Washington, D. C. He represented the Cherokees at Washington, and gave an active opposition to the bill for the original opening of Oklahoma Territory, and subsequently became a vigorous antagonist of the separate statehood movement, working ardently for the single statehood cause which finally prevailed. He was formerly active in tribal politics and in more recent years has been a democratic leader in his part of the state. In 1914 and 1915 he was secretary of the county central committee, and at the present writing is colonel on the governor's staff. Under appointment from the Federal Government he served as first mayor of Claremore, and by virtue of that office presided over the courts with jurisdiction similar to that of United States commissioner, and on account of that service has been long familiarly known as Judge Norwood. He was also the first mayor of Chelsea.

Colonel Norwood has long been in the newspaper business, published papers at Claremore and Chelsea, and is now the owner and editor of the Dewey Globe, which he established. Colonel Norwood is said to know more people in the Cherokee Nation than any other citizen. By his long residence and associations and also by study he has become familiar with both the Delaware and Cherokee tribes historically and personally, and has known all the chiefs and officials of the Cherokees since the time of John Ross.

Colonel Norwood was the first man to organize an oil company for operations in Oklahoma. This was the Cherokee Oil & Development Company, instituted in 1889 and incorporated under the laws of Illinois. A number of St. Louis men were associated with him in that enterprise, and they drilled their first wells at Chelsea. For ten years Colonel Norwood was the legal representative for Indian Territory of the Cudahy Oil Company, the first to develop the oil resources of Washington County and he secured many of the leases to the land on which they conducted their operations. During his residence at Claremore Colonel Norwood combined with his merchandising a business as buyer and shipper of stock. Along with his many other activities Colonel Norwood has constantly supported schools and churches and at different times has served on several local school boards and has helped to build several institutions in the old Cherokee Nation.

Colonel Norwood has been three times married. In 1872 Miss Alice R. Gourd became his wife. Her father was Judge Jackson R. Gourd, a prominent man in the Cherokee Nation. The mother and the one child of the union are both deceased. His second wife was Susie Love, a member of the Delaware tribe of Indians. She had an exceedingly fair skin, while Colonel Norwood's complexion is so dark that he would more readily have

A. H. NORWOOD

been taken for an Indian than his wife. There were two children by this union, and both are deceased, and their mother passed away in 1893. In 1904 Colonel Norwood married Ida M. Woodard, who was born in Indiana and was of Quaker parentage. Colonel Norwood can relate many interesting incidents in connection with Indian life, customs, religion and traditions. He speaks and understands to some extent the Cherokee language, and has some knowledge of the languages of the other tribes.

ANDREW HICKENLOOPER SMITH. By his enterprise Mr. Smith has contributed to the general commercial and business resources of the little City of Frederick, Oklahoma. He is now proprietor of the leading garage in that town, and for a number of years has been successful as a farmer and stock raiser in the same community. Though born at Winamac, Indiana, September 15, 1878, he belongs to an old Ohio family. The Smiths came originally from England, and his grandfather, Adolphus H. Smith, was born at Albany, New York, in 1809, and died on his farm at Enon, Ohio, in 1902, at the extreme age of ninety-three years. He was an early settler at Cincinnati, where he built up a large business as a distiller. He was at Indianapolis, Indiana, soon after the establishment of that town and was a trader there in skins and furs and other merchandise. Mr. A. H. Smith acquired his middle name from a prominent Cincinnati business man, General A. Hickenlooper, who married Maria Smith, a sister of William H. Smith, the father of Andrew H. Smith. General Hickenlooper gained his rank and title by service in the Civil war in the Engineers Corps, and later became president of the Cincinnati Gas & Electric Company. William H. Smith, the father, was born at Cincinnati, Ohio, in 1842, and died at Enon, Ohio, in 1901. He grew up on the farm at Enon, lived for a time at Winamac, Indiana, and in 1879 returned to Cincinnati. He was a democrat in politics, a member of the Episcopal Church, and was affiliated with the Masonic fraternity. He married Camilla A. Rees, who was born at Cincinnati in 1849 and died in the same city in 1911. Andrew H. Smith is their only surviving child, the daughter Laura having died in infancy.

After a high school education in Cincinnati, Andrew H. Smith took a course in Bartlett's Commercial College of that city in 1894, and for the next four years was a salesman in Cincinnati. Since then his time has been given almost entirely to farming and ranching in Ohio, Oklahoma and Arizona. He located at Frederick, Oklahoma, in 1906, and that has been his home with the exception of fourteen months during 1911-12 spent in Arizona. On coming to Southwestern Oklahoma he bought a farm nine miles southeast of Frederick comprising 160 acres, and on that land has demonstrated some of the possibilities of his section for diversified farming and stock raising. It was on February 1, 1915, that he bought the garage situated on South Tenth Street in Frederick, and thus became proprietor of a well equipped and prosperous enterprise. The garage was established by I. W. Yancey in 1913. The building is 32x140 feet, and furnishes storage for a number of cars, also facilities for repair work and the handling of automobile accessories, and Mr. Smith has the local agency for the Overland cars.

An interested member of the Masonic fraternity, he is affiliated with Lodge No. 222, Ancient Free and Accepted Masons, at Christiansburg, Ohio, and also with Frederick Chapter No. 41, Royal Arch Masons, with Frederick Commandery No. 19, Knights Templar, and with India Temple of the Nobles of the Mystic Shrine at Oklahoma City. He also belongs to Harmony Chapter of the Order of the Eastern Star at Wilcox, Arizona, and to the Junior Order of the United American

Vol. V—13

Mechanics at Hampton, Ohio. As a local business man he belongs to the Frederick Business Men's Association. At Northampton, Ohio, in 1901, Mr. Smith married Miss Lola M. Freeze, whose father William Freeze is a farmer at Frederick. Mrs. Smith is a member of Harmony Chapter of the Order of Eastern Star.

LEROY B. TOOKER. A popular and able young representative of the newspaper business in Western Oklahoma, Mr. Tooker is editor and manager of the Beaver Democrat, a well ordered weekly paper published at the county seat of Beaver County.

Mr. Tooker was born at Lawrence, McHenry County, Illinois, on the 12th of July, 1888, and is a son of Benjamin F. and Mary L. (Palmer) Tooker. His father was born in 1840, in the State of Wisconsin, where his parents were pioneer settlers, and for many years he was a successful building contractor, a vocation which he continued to follow until 1907, when he came to the newly-organized State of Oklahoma and obtained a tract of Government land in Beaver County. This homestead, which he has developed into one of the well-improved and valuable farms of the county, is situated twenty-four miles southwest of Beaver, the county seat, and there he and his wife still maintain their residence, their marriage having been solemnized, in 1879 and Mrs. Tooker having been born in Pennsylvania, on the 8th day of July, 1842, her parents likewise having been natives of the old Keystone State. They have three children, of whom the subject of this review is the youngest, as is he also the only son: Lynnia Belle, who was born February 20, 1880, at Lawrence, Illinois, was united in marriage in 1911, to Hugh N. Robertson, and they reside in Beaver County, Oklahoma, their two children being Linden and Lillian; Georgia May, who was born in 1882, became, in 1899, the wife of Charles L. Munger, their home being in Beaver County, and they have five children,—Vernon, Harlan, Adrian, Kenneth and Lila.

The public schools of his native place afforded to Leroy E. Tooker his early educational advantages and after completing the curriculum of the high school he pursued a higher course of study in the University of Illinois at Champaign. He left the university in 1909 and immediately came to Oklahoma, where his parents had established their home in the preceding year. Here he put his scholastic attainments to practical test and utilization by becoming a representative of the pedagogic profession. As such he devoted two years to teaching in the public schools of Beaver County, his successful work including a year of service as principal of the village schools of Beaver, in 1910-11.

On the 19th of June, 1911, Mr. Tooker purchased the plant and business of the Beaver County Democrat, and in the following year he founded the Forgan Enterprise, of both of which weekly papers he has since continued editor and publisher and both of which he has brought up to a high standard,—especially as purveyors of local news and as exponents of the general interests of Beaver County. Since assuming control of the Beaver County Democrat, which is the pioneer newspaper of the county, he has effected its absorption of the La Kemp Mirror, the Ivanhoe News and the Forgan Enterprise in the Beaver County villages of the names designated, and thus he had made the Beaver County Democrat a paper of specially wide circulation and dominating influence in the county, its political proclivities being indicated by its title. Both through his paper and in a personal way Mr. Tooker stands exemplar of civic progressiveness and spares neither time nor effort in his efforts to promote the social and material advancement and wellbeing of

Beaver County and its people. In the time-honored Masonic fraternity he has received the thirty-second degree of the Ancient Accepted Scottish Rite, and he is affiliated also with the Independent Order of Odd Fellows. He holds membership in the Presbyterian Church, of which his parents have been zealous members for many years. This energetic, wide-awake and progressive young journalist is still numbered among the eligible bachelors of western Oklahoma, and it is needless to say that this fact does not in the least militate against his popularity in social circles.

CHARLES S. BAXTER. When he was eighteen years old Charles S. Baxter began learning the printer's trade. His work as a printer and publisher and editor have been for nearly a quarter of a century identified with old Indian Territory, the Texas Panhandle and extreme Northwestern Oklahoma. He is now editor and owner of the Guymon Democrat, which is the official organ of Texas County and the City of Guymon. A democrat himself, he has not been without considerable influence in his party, and as a veteran Oklahoma editor is well known among his professional brethren all over the state.

He was born November 5, 1868, on a farm in Livingston County, Missouri, a son of W. H. H. and Nancy (England) Baxter. His father, a son of Richard Baxter, a native of Kentucky, was born in Mercer County, Kentucky, February 22, 1835, and in early boyhood went with the family to Missouri, where he was engaged in farming for many years. At one time he served as county judge of Polk County, Missouri. His death occurred at Bolivar, Missouri, January 7, 1902. He was married in 1850 at Lexington, Kentucky, to Miss Nancy England, who was born September 17, 1837, in Mercer County, Kentucky, a daughter of Mathew England, also a Kentuckian by birth. To Judge Baxter and wife were born nine children, four sons and five daughters, namely: John, who now lives in Springfield, Missouri; James R., a printer by trade living at Bolivar, Missouri; Charles S.; Frank, deceased; Mollie, wife of William Burton of Bolivar, Missouri; Nannie, wife of Harry Lightfoot of Bolivar, Missouri; Maggie, who is unmarried and living at Bolivar; Myrtle and Mattie, both deceased.

Charles S. Baxter acquired his early education in the public schools of Livingston and Polk counties, Missouri. Though reared on a farm he early conceived an ambition and aim to become a printer, and took up the trade at the age of eighteen. He has never deserted the printing shop for any length of time during the past thirty years. It was in 1891 that he moved to Indian Territory and located at old Rush Springs in the Chickasaw Nation, where he became one of the editors of the Landmark for three years. In 1895 he moved to Dalhart, Texas, and for a year was editor of the News at that place. In 1906 he came to Guymon, and has since been foreman, editor and owner of the Guymon Democrat, which was established in that year. This paper has a large circulation, and is a very flourishing concern as a business proposition. It has a modern equipped plant. Mr. Baxter is a thoroughly seasoned newspaper man, and has had fewer reverses to his credit than the average editor and publisher.

Fraternally he is identified with the Independent Order of Odd Fellows and is a member of the Christian Church. On August 21, 1901, at Bolivar, Missouri, he married Miss Ida Newport, a daughter of A. M. Newport, who was born in Dallas County, Missouri. Mrs. Baxter was born in Dallas County, September 21, 1868. To their marriage have been born five children, three sons and two daughters: Willie Lee, born September 21, 1902; Monroe, now deceased; Bertha, born October 9, 1905; Dorothy, born September 9, 1907; and Charles Louis Jr., born May 30, 1912.

REV. FRANK J. STOWE. The pastor of the Presbyterian Church at Blackwell is one of Oklahoma's ablest churchmen. He has the distinction of being one of the few ministers of the gospel who sat as a delegate in the constitutional convention of Oklahoma. As a teacher, preacher, church organizer and leader of movements for both personal and civic righteousness, his experience covers a large field and in many states.

Rev. Mr. Stowe took charge of the church at Blackwell in January, 1913. This church was organized in May, 1896, and was only a mission supplied by ministers resident of other places for some time. The first local pastor was Rev. J. R. E. Craighead from Pennsylvania. The formal organization of the church occurred on Thanksgiving Day in 1898. The first church building was brought to Blackwell from Arkansas City. It had been a mission church and constructed from funds supplied by New York. The old church building cost only $560, and is now used, since remodeling, as a manse. The second regular pastor in charge was the Rev. Thomas B. Barrier, who came in 1903 to serve four years. Under his pastorate a modern brick edifice was constructed at a cost of $8,000. It is well furnished and arranged for modern church work, containing a large audience room, a young men's room, with other rooms in the basement. The church is out of debt, and the business organization is unusually systematic and thorough, and all the bills, including the pastor's salary, are paid monthly. There is a fine Sunday-school with about 250 scholars enrolled, while the church membership numbers about 350. There are twelve elders and twelve on the business board. There are women's societies and missionary organizations and young people's societies. In 1907 Rev. T. H. Hawley began his ministry of two years, followed by Rev. B. Kuntz, who also served two years, and on January 20, 1913, Rev. Frank J. Stowe accepted the call to this church.

Frank J. Stowe was born in Lockport, Illinois, May 11, 1868. His father, William Stowe, who was a farmer and stockman, was born at Jamestown, New York, a son of Nathaniel Stowe, and a relative of Professor Stowe, husband of Harriet Beecher Stowe, author of Uncle Tom's Cabin. The Stowes were an old and prominent family of New York State. Rev. Mr. Stowe's mother was Laura Barnard, who was born at Ravenna, Ohio, and a sister of Capt. James Barnard, who served with a gallant record as an officer in an Ohio regiment during the Civil war. Rev. Mr. Stowe has a brother, H. B. Stowe, a railroad man at Streeter, Illinois. Both the parents are still living and now have their home at Lockport, Illinois.

Rev. Mr. Stowe spent his boyhood on a farm, with more or less regular attendance at the public schools. His education was continued in this wise until the age of seventeen, and after that he was employed in looking after the details of farm work on his father's place of 100 acres. His ambition was for an education and for a calling which would enable him to express his ability and character and service for humanity. He finally went to Boston, Massachusetts, and received $100 a year as salary while working as an apprentice in a wholesale jobbing house. He also attended school at Boston, paying his own way and taking special work in the Boston University, and the course at Emerson College where he was graduated in 1895. He then became a teacher of the college at Waynesburg, Pennsylvania. While in Boston he was also a worker in the mission and slums of that city. He continued his studies while

teaching, and finally entered the Cumberland University at Lebanon, Tennessee, where he remained as a student and teacher for eight years, completing his theological studies there and receiving the A. M. degree. His first regular pastorate was at Murfreesboro, Tennessee, on the site of the famous battle of Stone River. All the officers of the church board were former Confederate soldiers.

In 1907 Rev. Mr. Stowe removed to old Indian Territory, becoming pastor of the Presbyterian Church and president of Industrial College at Wynnewood. He was soon afterwards chosen a delegate to the constitutional convention, and took a very important part in its deliberations. He was a member of the liquor traffic and educational committees, and impressed his ideas and ideals on several important clauses of the organic law. After five years as a pastor at Wynnewood he took a church at Purcell for two years, and then accepted the call to Blackwell.

On August 4, 1898, at Barkyville, Pennsylvania, Mr. Stowe married Minerva Hunsberger. Mrs. Stowe is a woman of strong native intelligence and of thorough education and culture. She was born and reared at Barkyville, and is a graduate of Findlay College in Ohio, in music and art. For a time she was a teacher in the Waynesburg College of Pennsylvania, and while there formed her acquaintance with Mr. Stowe. Her parents were Abraham and Catherine (Barky) Hansberger. Her father was a well-to-do merchant, and a member of the Winebrennarian Church. He is now deceased, but his wife is living. Rev. Mr. Stowe is a member of the Masonic Order. He is an excellent speaker, a man of strong physique, and is an excellent leader in behalf of any cause which he espouses.

JOHN FOSTER. The name of John Foster will always be associated with the founding and development of the Town of Cushing. From the beginning of his residence there twenty-one years ago, when there was practically nothing to distinguish the townsite, Mr. Foster has made his own activities coincide with the best interests of the community, has exerted his influence and has expended time, energy and means in promoting everything that would give Cushing a proper prestige and standing among the towns of Northern Oklahoma. Cushing is today the center of one of the principal oil and gas fields in the state, and perhaps no town in Oklahoma has a more promising future. No small share of the credit for this accomplishment is due this banker, business man, and influential citizen. Mr. Foster organized and since the beginning has been cashier of the First National Bank of Cushing, and is also vice president of the First National Bank at Yale in Payne County.

A Missourian by birth, and for a quarter of a century a resident of Oklahoma, John Foster was born at Cape Girardeau in Southeastern Missouri June 19, 1864. His parents, T. C. and Eliza (Alton) Foster were born in the same locality, but nine years after the birth of their son, John, they moved to Independence, near Kansas City, Missouri, and ten years later went to Camden Point in Missouri. At the opening of the Sac and Fox reservation of Oklahoma the entire family settled there, and the father followed farming until he retired and he and his wife spent their last days with their son, John, in Cushing. The mother died about eight years ago and the father about five years ago.

The oldest of five children, John Foster spent his early life on a farm, gained from such surroundings a rugged physique and experience which has proved invaluable to him in his business career. He attended the common schools of Independence, Missouri, and was also given a thorough normal training in the State Normal School at Kirksville. As a part of his early record there should be mentioned eight terms of teaching in country schools. At the same time he carried on farming, and that was his vocation until he removed to Oklahoma in February following the opening of the Sac and Fox reservation. For a year and a half Mr. Foster ran his sawmill at Candler, also built a cotton gin and was connected for a time with the Sac and Fox Trading Company.

However, his most important achievements are found in the twenty-one years of his residence at Cushing. He and C. W. Carpenter, the two oldest residents of the town, have lived as close neighbors during all these years and have long been associated in the banking business. Mr. Foster was one of the five men who laid out what is known as the "South Addition" to the townsite of Cushing. That is now the heart of the town. Mr. Foster also used his influence in getting the Santa Fe Railroad Company to locate its right of way just where he wanted it and where it would be of the greatest advantage to the growing town. The South Addition to Cushing was a tract of 120 acres. Later Mr. Foster bought fifty acres on the east side, platted this into lots, and those lots are now practically covered with residences and homes. For several years Mr. Foster was engaged in merchandising in Cushing, and had stores at several other points in Payne County, and is still interested in a stock of merchandise at Quay.

His work as a banker and practical financier began in 1897, when he organized what was then a state bank, but which in 1903 took out a national charter and is now the First National Bank of Cushing. Mr. Foster has been cashier of the institution since it was organized in 1897. Some of the most prominent residents and business men of Cushing are identified with this institution as officers and stockholders. The president is C. W. Carpenter, Mr. Foster's old neighbor and associate. The vice president is N. Douglas, and the assistant cashier is Ernest Burford. With a capital stock of $25,000, the First National Bank has surplus and profits according to a recent statement of $13,500, total resources of over $633,000, and its deposits are well upward of $600,000.

Mr. Foster has been very active and prominent in making Cushing a center of the oil and gas development of this part of the state. At one time he owned seven quarter sections of land situated in the oil belt. He helped to organize the Home Gas Company, is a director in the company, which now has several producing wells and is prepared to furnish gas to local factories at the low rate of three cents per 1,000 feet. While Cushing has made much development in the past twenty years, its location close to an important gas field will undoubtedly bring it still greater prestige as a manufacturing and industrial center. Mr. Foster himself occupies one of the most attractive estates in Cushing, residing in a fine fourteen-room house surrounded with eleven acres of ground. Outside of business affairs his name is one of recognized influence in politics both in Payne County and over the state. For twenty years he has served as clerk of the board of education at Cushing, and under his personal supervision was constructed a handsome $20,000 high school which is now the pride of the town. There are also three modern ward school buildings of eight rooms each. Mr. Foster has also served on the city council. His office holding has been confined to those of unremunerative positions where the incumbent has opportunities for rendering much service, but without compensation. He is also a power in local democratic politics, and has served as secretary of two state conventions, one at Anadarko and the other at Oklahoma City. Mr. Foster helped to organize the Christian Church at Cushing. He served as president of the Commercial Club several years, and in Masonry is a thirty-second degree Scottish Rite.

In 1895 he married Miss Maggie Culbertson of Cambridge, Ohio. Their five children are: Margaret, who graduated from the Cushing High School in 1915; Lucile, Charles, John and T. C.

ZERAL ZENN ROGERS. One of the most prominent names in the history of Frederick since its establishment as a town following the opening of the Kiowa and Comanche country in 1901, has been Rogers. Mr. Z. Z. Rogers is a young business man of that city and at the present time is holding the office of mayor. His father was a pioneer settler and in many ways closely identified with the interests of the growing little city.

The Rogers family was established in colonial America by John Rogers, who came from England. Zeral Zenn Rogers was born in Clarksville, Arkansas, November 27, 1887, a son of the late William Wayne Rogers, whose death on August 28, 1913, was regarded in the light of a calamity to the community at Frederick.

William Wayne Rogers was born in Clarksville, Arkansas, in 1854, and in 1891 removed his family to Vernon, Texas, and in 1901 came to Frederick at the opening of the settlement. He was a dry goods merchant, and was prominent in church and fraternal affairs. He was president of the board of stewards, chairman of the board of trustees and chairman of the building committee when the Methodist Episcopal Church South erected its home at Frederick. He was also teacher of the Business Men's Bible Class, which at one time numbered 183 members. He stood high in both the Masonic and Odd Fellows fraternities. He was past master of Frederick Lodge No. 249, Ancient Free and Accepted Masons; past high priest of Frederick Chapter No. 41, Royal Arch Masons; past eminent commander of Frederick Commandery No. 19 of the Knights Templar; and was affiliated with the council, Royal and Select Masters, and with India Temple of the Nobles of the Mystic Shrine at Oklahoma City. In Odd Fellowship he belonged to Frederick Lodge No. 223, Independent Order of Odd Fellows, of which he was past grand. Associated with H. W. Leininger and A. S. J. Shaw he organized in 1907 the Southwest Odd Fellows Association, and became first president of that association. Mr. Shaw is now grand master of the State Lodge of Odd Fellows in Oklahoma. The Southwest Odd Fellows Association comprises the Odd Fellows lodges in Tillman, Jackson, Jefferson, Comanche and Cotton counties. Its object is to promote good fellowship and to hold contests to assure proficiency in the working of the degrees. The association held its last meeting at Lawton on April 26, 1915, and in 1914 Mr. Z. Z. Rogers was president. The late William W. Rogers was also a member of the first city council of Frederick, representing the First Ward, and on finishing that term served on the school board continuously until his death. He married Miss Addie Truscott, who was a native of Quincy, Illinois. Their children are: A. A. Rogers, who was the first county superintendent of schools of Tillman County, serving two terms, and is now county superintendent of schools at Wilson, Oklahoma; E. E. Rogers is a traveling salesman for Hutchison wholesale grocers, and resides at Hutchison, Kansas, and he drew the claim known as the Rogers Addition to Frederick, Oklahoma, the most desirable in the city. Vera is the wife of S. E. Patton, who has lived at Frederick since 1901 and has been continuously identified with the Oklahoma State Bank of that city as cashier; D. D., who is master mechanic in the machine shops at Wellington, Kansas; B. B. Rogers, who has a position with the government service at El Paso, Texas; Z. Z.; and J. J., who is now attending the Kansas City Dental College.

Mr. Z. Z. Rogers had just finished the high school course at Vernon, Texas, in 1901, when the southwestern section of Oklahoma was opened to settlement and in the same year he joined his father's family at Frederick. At that time he was still a boy in years, but soon took up the serious work of life as clerk in a grocery store. He was employed by the firm of Parker & McConnell, was with them nine years altogether, and was promoted from driver of a delivery wagon to keeping books in the office for the last four years. Early in 1911 came his first advancement in politics when elected city clerk, and he served two terms until 1913. His acceptable work in that position was his chief recommendation for election to the office of mayor of Frederick on April 6, 1915. He is now one of the youngest mayors of Oklahoma. The mayor's term runs for two years.

In July, 1915, Mr. Rogers engaged in the drug business with D. H. Hail as partner, and they have a well stocked store at the corner of North Grand Avenue and Ninth Street. Mr. Rogers is a democrat, a member of the Methodist Episcopal Church South and treasurer of its Sunday School and has fraternal affiliations with Frederick Lodge No. 249, Ancient Free and Accepted Masons; with Frederick Council, Royal and Select Masters; with Frederick Lodge No. 223, Independent Order of Foresters; with the Woodmen of the World, the Modern Woodmen of America, and the Praetorians. He is also associated with the Business Men's Association.

At Hobart, Oklahoma, in 1906, he married Miss Ana E. Hancock, daughter of Edward Hancock, who is a farmer at Grandfield, Oklahoma. Mr. and Mrs. Rogers have two children: Jim Jack, who was born January 23, 1908; and Trullus Truscott, born October 16, 1910.

ALBERT S. DICKSON. Coming in 1886 to that section of neutral strip in Indian Territory that was at the time commonly known as No Man's Land, Mr. Dickson established his residence at Neutral City, a true frontier town of period, where he remained until Oklahoma Territory was thrown open to settlement and formally organized, its prescribed confines including the former No Man's Land, when he removed to Beaver, which was made the judicial center of the county of the same name and which originally included also the present counties of Texas and Cimarron. In this now thriving and important town of western Oklahoma he has since continued in the active and successful practice of law, and he is junior member of the representative law firm of Dickson & Dickson, in which his coadjutor is his brother, Robert E. The firm controls a specially substantial and important practice in this section of the state and its high standing at the bar of Oklahoma determines the distinctive professional ability of its members and their secure place in popular confidence and good will.

On the paternal homestead farm in Andrew County, Missouri, a log house of the pioneer type figured as the stately domicile in which Albert S. Dickson was born and the date of his nativity was February 1, 1867. He is a son of Benjamin Franklin Dickson and Anna (Van Deventer) Dickson, whose marriage was solemnized in that state in the year 1860.

Benjamin F. Dickson was born in Boone County, Missouri, in 1826, his parents having been pioneers of that county, where they established their home on their emigration from their native State of Kentucky. He was reared to adult age in his home county and as a young man he removed to the northwestern part of Missouri, where he passed the remainder of his life as an energetic, progressive and duly successful farmer. He died in Andrew County in 1892, when about sixty-six years of age, and his wife survived him by a number of years. She was born in Missouri and was a daughter of Granville and Ursula (Clark) Van Deventer, her father having been a scion of the historic old Van Deventer family of Lee County, Virginia. Benjamin F. and Anna (Van Deventer) Dickson became the parents of three sons and two daughters, concerning whom the following brief record is given: Alexander Jackson, born in 1861, is now a prosperous agriculturist and stock-grower of Beaver County, Oklahoma. In 1886 he wedded Miss Belle Baker and they have one child, Anna. Robert, who was born in 1864, was afforded the advantage of Avalon College, at Avalon, Missouri, and is now senior member of the law firm of Dickson & Dickson, as previously noted. He was the first regularly elected county attorney of Beaver County and since his retirement from that office he has been associated with his brother Albert S. in the practice of law at Beaver. He whose name initiates this article, was the third in order of birth of the five children. Lucy D., who was born in 1869, was educated in the Missouri State Normal School at Strasburg and in 1896 became the wife of Godfrey Stegman, their home being in the City of St. Joseph, Missouri, and their only child being a daughter, Elsie. Bell, who was born in 1872, is the youngest of the children. In 1899 she became the wife of Hugh A. Ellingsworth and they now maintain their home at Helena, Missouri. They have one child, Everetta.

Albert S. Dickson passed the period of his childhood and early youth on the old homestead farm and is indebted to the public schools of Andrew County, Missouri, for his preliminary education, which was effectively supplemented by a course of higher study in Avalon College, at Avalon, that state. In the meanwhile he had given much attention to the reading of law, with the intention of eventually entering the legal profession. In August, 1886, Mr. Dickson came to the Indian Territory and, as previously stated, established his residence at Neutral City, in "No Man's Land," where he remained until 1890, when he removed to Beaver. In the following year he was admitted to the bar of Oklahoma Territory and since that time he has continued in the practice of his profession at Beaver, as one of the representative pioneer lawyers and a valued citizen of Beaver County. Though he takes a deep and loyal interest in public affairs and is a staunch advocate of the principles of the republican party, he has never sought or held political office, as he considers his profession worthy of his undivided allegiance. He is affiliated with the Knights of Pythias and both he and his wife hold membership in the Christian Church at Beaver.

At Liberal, Kansas, on the 29th of January, 1910, was solemnized the marriage of Mr. Dickson to Miss Edna Humphrey, who was born near Trenton, Missouri, on the 27th of September, 1884, and who is a daughter of Clark and Emma Humphrey, likewise natives of Missouri. Mr. and Mrs. Dickson have one child, Albert DeWitt, born September 24, 1913.

FRANK I. LEASURE. While not one of the largest papers and not published in one of the largest towns in the state, the Roosevelt Record at Roosevelt has a virility and vigor all of its own. Its editor and proprietor is Frank I. Leasure, well known in Oklahoma press circles, and whose experience as a practical printer and newspaper man cannot be measured entirely by the number of years since he reached his legal majority.

His birth occurred at Mount Auburn, Iowa, September 4, 1882. The Leasures are of French origin, and his great-grandfather, John Leasure, came to this country with two of his brothers, all of them settling in Pennsylvania. Mr. Leasure's father is H. E. Leasure, who was born in Ohio in 1852, and when a small boy was taken out to a farm in Iowa County, Iowa, where he grew up, but substituted railroading for agriculture as his regular career. He was a station agent at different places in Iowa and Kansas, but in 1899 left that business to become a jeweler at La Crosse, Kansas. He was afterwards in the same line at Independence, Kansas, spent several years in Missouri, and in 1904 located in Arkansas City, Kansas, where he is still in business as a jeweler. Politically H. E. Leasure is a socialist in belief, and has affiliations with the Independent Order of Odd Fellows, the Knights of Pythias, the Woodmen of the World and the Modern Woodmen of America. He married Arminta Dormer, who was born in North Missouri, in 1857. Their four children are: Carl C., who is a traveling salesman with home at Arkansas City, Kansas; Frank I.; Maude M., wife of P. T. Boyd, a telegraph operator residing at Texarkana, Texas; and Ernestine L., a teacher living with her parents.

Frank I. Leasure received his early education in the public schools of Iowa and Kansas and also attended a high school at Independence in the latter state, subsequently taking a business course at Rolla, Missouri. His independent work for himself began at the age of nineteen at Harrisonville, Missouri, as an apprentice in a drug store. Eighteen months later he left that employment for one which he liked better in a printing office at South Haven, Kansas. He spent two years at South Haven, and after that was employed as a journeyman on various newspapers in Kansas and Colorado until 1903, in which year he located in Kaw City, Kay County, Oklahoma, and spent one year with the Star at that place. After that he took a trip through Old Mexico, and then returned to Arkansas City, Kansas, and settled down to the daily routine of city editor of the daily paper there. He held that position from January, 1905, to January, 1912. In the month mentioned of the latter year he came to Roosevelt, Oklahoma, and bought the Roosevelt Record from E. F. Tennant, and has since been its capable proprietor and editor. The plant and offices are situated on Main Street in the Village of Roosevelt, and he has done much to build up its circulation and influence in Kiowa and surrounding counties since he took charge. It is a democratic paper, and was established in March, 1902, by G. H. Parker and E. M. Timber. In addition to its local circulation it now has a foreign list of more than a 150.

Mr. Leasure is himself a democrat in politics, and is affiliated with the Knights of Pythias at Hobart. He is well known in the Oklahoma Press Association, of which he is a member. In June, 1910, at Newkirk, Oklahoma, he married Miss Frances Cline, a daughter of Joseph Cline of Arkansas City. They have one son, Harold E., born February 4, 1913.

A. C. SMITH is editor of the Ponca City Democrat, of Ponca City, Oklahoma, a newspaper with an interesting history. The Democrat was born on the prairie in Northern Oklahoma at the opening of the Cherokee Strip in September, 1893. Mr. Smith is a veteran of the newspaper and printing business, and for a number of years conducted a paper in Southern Kansas, until he suddenly transferred his enterprise to the Cherokee Strip about twenty-three years ago and has guided the destiny of the democrats through all these years. The first issue of the Democrat was on Thursday, September 21, 1893, and with a magnificent development which has occurred in Oklahoma since that date the paper has likewise prospered, and now has a daily issue. Mr. Smith is also at the present time postmaster of Ponca City, having been appointed to that office in November, 1913, by President Wilson.

A. C. Smith was born at Bloomfield, Davis County, Iowa, October 25, 1865. His parents were neighbors and friends of Gen. James Weaver, who for many years was one of the notable figures in American politics and a great leader of the greenback party. His father was Berryman Smith, a native of Kentucky. From Kentucky he moved to Davis County, Iowa. Berryman Smith died at Bloomfield, Iowa, at the age of fifty-five, while his wife passed away in 1875. They were both active in the church and in politics he was a democrat. They were the parents of nine children, three sons and six daughters.

A. C. Smith grew up at Bloomfield, Iowa, attended the common and high schools, and when still a boy had his first practical experience and training as a newspaper man in the office of the Legal Tender, a greenback paper, the official organ of the greenback party. It was issued as a general newspaper, but particularly in support of General Weaver's position on money and other economic questions. Its editor was a man of no little ability as a writer and thinker, Crawford Davis, now deceased, who for a number of years was a zealous worker in the greenback cause. Mr. Smith had four years experience with the Legal Tender, and rose from the position of devil to that of city editor. He later moved to Arkansas City, Kansas, during the boom days of that locality, and was engaged in the newspaper business there until he made the run into Cherokee Strip on the opening day in September, 1893. His enterprise gave to the Cherokee Strip one of its first newspapers, and he has kept the paper up to a high standard of excellence through all these years.

Mr. Smith has been quite active in democratic politics, has served as delegate to various conventions both in territorial and statehood days, and through his paper and otherwise has effectually advocated good government and the general cause of morality, education and religion. He and his wife are active members of the Pentecostal Church of the Nazarene; he is a trustee and steward of the board and superintendent of the Sunday-school, having a school of about 200 scholars.

On December 25, 1889, Mr. Smith married Miss Nora Burrell of Arkansas City, Kansas. She was reared and educated there, a daughter of Capt. A. J. Burrell, now deceased, who came out of Indiana to Kansas. Mr. and Mrs. Smith have four children: Nadine, Juliet, Katherine and Allen. One daughter, Beatrice, died at the age of seven years. One daughter is now in charge of the Conservatory of Music at Bethany College, Oklahoma.

C. A. CONSTANTINE. In every corner of the wide world is found the Greek, everywhere plodding, patient, determined, steadfast, reliable, prosperous. The descendants of that sturdy race that once comprised the flower of civilization and culture in the ancient world are still active and indomitable, and though Greece is a small country, a little nation, yet the doings of the Greeks fill a large part in history and one of which they need not be ashamed when placed in comparison with any other people. Considering how widely dispersed are the members of this race, it is not strange that one of the important citizens of Oklahoma is from that race.

Pawhuska is the home town of Mr. C. A. Constantine, and there he is regarded as a benefactor. He was one of the first citizens to locate after the opening of the sale of the townsite and one of the most conspicuous semi-public buildings and institutions there is a monument to his public spirit and enterprise.

Mr. Constantine is truly a cosmopolitan. He has lived in nearly all quarters of the habitable globe and has had a fund of personal experiences and adventures such as many pages could hardly adequately describe. He is one of the most interesting as well as one of the most valuable citizens of the state which is notable for the cosmopolitan character of its citizenship.

He was born in the suburbs of Constantinople in March, 1866. His family is of Greek origin and his ancestry can be traced directly back to a Greek family that flourished in the Eastern Empire when Constantinople was the capital city for all the eastern half of Christendom prior to its conquest by the invading Turks in the middle of the fifteenth century. Mr. Constantine's father was a man of considerable prominence, serving in an office which would correspond with that of mayor or commissioner in one of the districts around Constantinople.

He was educated in the local schools up to the age of sixteen. His mother had died when he was twelve years of age. Three of his elder brothers were already employed, one of them taking charge of a city office, one of them in a maritime commercial exchange and the next older being also employed in a city office. After about a year Mr. Constantine became dissatisfied with his position as a subordinate, and at the age of seventeen ran away from home. He had no money, and after borrowing forty dollars from a friend took a young Greek companion with him and they shipped on a sailing vessel from Constantinople bound for Tripoli. After three months on the North African coast they returned to Constantinople, where the police acting under instruction from his father arrested young Constantine and returned him to the parental care. However, he soon secured his father's consent to leaving home, and next went to Athens, where he joined a cousin and for three years was employed in a store or in other lines of work. He left Athens suddenly, with only eighteen francs as capital, going to Alexandria, Egypt. At the end of three days he had only three francs left, and being without friends had to accept the first employment that offered. After a month he became better acquainted and secured a position as shipping clerk in a wholesale house, and spent one year in Alexandria. Greek was his native language and as a boy he had learned to speak the Turkish tongue, and while in Alexandria he also picked up some fluency in the Egyptian and Italian languages. This proficiency made him available for a position at Jedda, the seaport of Makha in Arabia, where he was given charge of a retail grocery concern and was paid wages double what he had received in Alexandria. However, after three months he found the climate did not agree with him, and he returned to Alexandria and was employed for a time in a money exchange. Soon afterwards he took charge of a grocery store at another place in Egypt, but while there contracted the smallpox and was shipped back to Alexandria consigned to the Greek Hospital. There was no room in the hospital, and he accordingly took his blankets and went to the woods resolved to die a quiet death. He was picked up by some Arabs, who reported his case to the Greek community, and he was cared for until he had recovered. While in Alexandria he and another Greek boy wandered out into the desert and were lost, and for fifteen days mingled with the Arabs. They told their captors many strange tales in order to preserve their lives, passing themselves off as dignitaries of the Sultan, and finally had themselves carried back into Alexandria. Three days later the historic massacre of whites in Alexandria, in 1881, began, and it was only after many desperate chances that Mr. Constantine escaped the general vengeance which fell upon thousands of the aliens living in that city. He left the country with many other refugees three days later, and was given free transportation by the Greek government to Piraeus, the seaport of Athens. His father learned of his condition and secured his return

to Constantinople. A few months later Mr. Constantine ran away again, taking passage on a sailing ship to the Black Sea and visiting several of the Russian ports. He next went to Marseilles, France, and after traveling in French vessels around the Mediterranean went on a French boat to Martinique in the French West Indies, returning on the same vessel. He again made the same trip, but on arriving at Martinique broke his contract and was put in jail for fifteen days and was released only on promise to leave the island at once. He shipped on an American vessel loaded with a cargo of sugar for New York. He worked his passage to New York, and thence took an English boat to Liverpool, where he was discharged. At Dublin he shipped on an American vessel bound on a cruise around Cape Horn to San Pedro, California, a voyage of six months and eighteen days without touching land. He landed from the boat ill and spent some time in a hospital at Los Angeles, and remained in Southern California altogether for two years. He found employment with the fruit packers and in that time picked up a good knowledge of the English language.

Up to that time most of his experiences had been in tropical or semi-tropical countries, but in 1889 he went north to Juneau, Alaska, but had little success in that quarter and returned as far as Seattle, afterwards through San Francisco, and was in the vicinity of Salt Lake until 1892. During the World's Columbian Exposition he was in the City of Chicago, and there his enterprises prospered so that he found himself with abundance of money and with this good fortune returned to Athens, Greece, where he was married in 1893 to a Greek girl named Alexandra Pakiadi, who was also born in Constantinople, the only child of her parents. After visiting his father Mr. Constantine sailed for the United States with his bride, landed in New York City, and for a time lived at Scranton, Pennsylvania. At Scranton was born his first child, a daughter, to whom was given the name Sappho. From there he removed to Atlanta, Georgia, and engaged in business as a grocer and proprietor of a refreshment parlor. In that city the second daughter was born into the household, and upon her was bestowed the name Antigone.

Mr. Constantine's experience in the northern latitude was renewed following the Klondike excitement. In August, 1896, he left his wife in charge of his business in Georgia and set out for Dawson City in Northwest Alaska, it requiring from August to the 3rd of November to make the trip. At San Francisco in obedience to the regulations it was necessary to lay in supplies of all kinds sufficient to last an entire year. On reaching the Yukon region it was necessary to make the trip down the river to Dawson City before the waters froze over, and he had to go into the woods and cut the timber to make a boat. Mr. Constantine was the first white man to shoot the White Horse Rapids with a loaded boat, and about four hundred people lined the banks to see him accomplish that notable feat. Never in all his life of varied experience had he received such a demonstration of popular applause as was given him by his fellow men as they stood on the banks and shores of the canyon and yelled their acclaim and fired off their pistols as he successfully navigated the rapids. It was not altogether a feat of reckless daring, since Mr. Constantine had been a teacher of swimming in California and had gained an expert skill in the handling of boats propelled by oars and paddles. Before reaching Dawson City on the 3rd of November the waters were frozen over and he had to chop through the ice for a considerable distance in order to land his boat. On the previous trip to Alaska in 1889 his partner had accidently struck Mr. Constantine with an axe, causing a severe injury to his leg. Again in 1896 he was injured and out of active employment for about three months. Starting another prospecting tour, at eleven o'clock at night when the thermometer was forty degrees below zero and he was twelve miles from Dawson City, he accidentally shot himself through the leg, and only after a struggle of two hours was finally rescued by a man with a sled. He spent two years in Klondike, with experiences of which those mentioned are only a sample, and made one trip back to San Francisco during the time. After that two years he returned to Atlanta, Georgia. Owing to the poor health of his wife he sent her back to Athens with their two children, and she died in Greece in 1903.

During 1904, at the Louisiana Purchase Exposition in St. Louis, Mr. Constantine again operated with considerable success, but after the close of the fair returned to Atlanta, and then started into the Southwest to look for a location, in 1906 establishing himself in Tulsa, Oklahoma. The Pawhuska townsite was opened in 1906, and he was present during the auction sale of lots, and has been identified with that thriving community of Northeastern Oklahoma ever since. He bought a few cheap lots during the sale and rented a bake shop, to which he added a confectionery. After one year in that location the business outgrew its quarters, and he then rented the store where his present conspicuous center of activities is located, and subsequently bought the ground and building. His location is now in the heart of the city, and he operates a confectionery and bakery, a candy and ice cream manufacturing establishment, and also conducts a hotel in connection.

In December, 1914, Mr. Constantine completed the theater that bears his name in Pawhuska. The Constantine Theater is regarded as the finest building of its kind in Oklahoma, and has the second largest stage of any theatrical house in the state. It represents the last word in every facility and equipment for comfort and enjoyment. It has a perfect system of heating, the fan system of ventilation, and the lighting and fire protection are of the latest design. No expense has been spared in making this theater the equal of any playhouse in the Southwest, and it stands as a splendid monument to the enterprise and public spirit of its builder. It also represents his own ideas, which were only expressed in solid material through his architect. One of the notable features of the playhouse is the convenience of its seating arrangement, the chairs being six inches wider than in all ordinary theaters. Mr. Constantine is the manager of the theater and has devoted the house to high class motion picture plays and the best obtainable legitimate drama. Adjoining the theater is his cafe, and both establishments are on the main street of the city.

It was not with an idea solely to profit that Mr. Constantine invested so heavily in this enterprise, but rather from the impulse of civic pride. It is the expression of his desire to give an entire community the benefit of his prosperity, and he has frequently turned over the theater free for school commencement exercises and religious assemblages.

Mr. Constantine stands high in Masonry having taken thirty-two degrees in the Scottish Rite, and having also completed the York Rite degrees. He is also affiliated with the Benevolent and Protective Order of Elks, the Knights of Pythias, and is a member of various insurance orders. His two daughters attended school in the Loretto Academy in one of the suburbs of Denver, Colorado and graduated from Pawhuska High School. The daughter Sappho is eighteen and Antigone is seventeen. Two more cultured and brilliant young women it would be difficult to find. Only recently Sappho was awarded a prize for work in domestic science, while Antigone received a state award as an appreciation of her musical talent, being an accomplished contralto singer. Both of these medals were awarded by the Oklahoma University at the interscholastic meet.

In connection with his theater and cafe and other business at Pawhuska, Mr. Constantine employs eighteen persons or more, some of whom are Greeks and some Americans, and he is everywhere known as a liberal employer, paying the highest standard of wages. His entire career in Pawhuska has been in consonance with the finest letter and spirit of American citizenship and he is one of the men of foreign birth who do credit to their adopted country.

PINKNEY R. AMOS. One of the real pioneers of the original Oklahoma now resides at Frederick, where he is engaged extensively in the real estate business, not only as a broker but also handling large quantities of land and other property of his own. Mr. Amos was one of the first men to sell goods at the present Oklahoma City in 1889, was likewise identified with the Cherokee Strip, and moved to Frederick about the time Tillman County was opened for settlement.

The Amos family has been identified with West Virginia for nearly a century, and both Mr. Amos and his father were born there when the country was only Western Virginia prior to the formation of a separate state. Pinkney R. Amos was born in Marion County at Fairview in what is now West Virginia March 12, 1852, a son of Peter Amos, who was born in the same state in 1813, and died at Fairview in 1892. Peter Amos was a man of prominence in his section, owned a number of farms, did business as a stock man, and was also a merchant. During the war between the states he sold supplies to the Confederate government and for that offence was arrested and was kept a prisoner in the Federal prison at Wheeling, West Virginia, for a number of months. His church was the Methodist Episcopal and in politics he was a democrat. Peter Amos married Mary Basnett, who was born in West Virginia in 1812, and died at Lampasas, Texas, in 1891. Their children, eight in number, were as follows: Elizabeth, who now resides at Clarksburg, West Virginia, is the widow of Dr. J. B. Conaway, who for a number of years was a practicing physician near Clarksburg; Catherine, who lives at Fairview, West Virginia, is the widow of George Brown, a farmer and trader; Philip B. lives at Fairview, where he has been a merchant for forty years and is now president of the First National Bank; Nannie C. lives at Fairview, the widow of Dave Ammons, who was a trader and cattle dealer; Charilla, who died in 1914, was the wife of A. E. Morgan, a farmer at Fairview; Luther J. is a minister of the Methodist Episcopal Church South in California; Pinkney R. is the seventh in age, and the youngest, Willie died at the age of five years.

Pinkney R. Amos received his education in the common schools of Marion County, West Virginia, up to the age of twenty, having in the meantime assisted his father and gained a practical acquaintance with business affairs. For a number of years he was associated with the elder Amos in the store, and also was an extensive stock shipper to Philadelphia, and owned a mill. He confined his attention to stock business from 1881 to 1889, and owned a large sheep and cattle ranch at Lampasas, Texas.

On April 22, 1889, Mr. Amos arrived at Oklahoma City, then only a tank station on the Santa Fe Railroad. In the city which sprang up there within a few days' time he established the first exclusive shoe store, which was the first establishment of its kind, not only in that city but in the entire territory. The store was located on Main Street. In 1893 Mr. Amos left Oklahoma City and moved his stock of goods to the newly opened district known as the Cherokee Strip, establishing a store at Perry. Then in 1901 he moved to Frederick, and here has followed the real estate business. His offices are in the Amos Building, which he owns. For the past fifteen years he has handled many thousands of acres of farm land in Southwestern Oklahoma, and handles city property, farm lands in Tillman County and other counties of Oklahoma and Texas, and probably has the chief business of its kind in Tillman County.

Mr. Amos is a democrat, attended the Methodist Episcopal Church, and is affiliated with Lodge No. 1217 of the Benevolent and Protective Order of Elks and with the Woodmen of the World. In his native state of West Virginia in 1875 he married Miss Alice D. Morgan, whose father was William Morgan, now deceased, a West Virginia farmer. They have two children: Frank, who has built up a large insurance business at Woodward, Oklahoma; and Fairie, who is the wife of D. S. Tant, an attorney living at Vernon, Texas.

WILLIAM F. CARSON. A prominent and successful representative of real estate and loan business in western Oklahoma is Mr. Carson, who maintains his residence at Beaver, judicial center of the county of the same name, where he is in charge of the office and business of the Renfrew Investment Company, the headquarters of which are in the City of Woodward. On other pages of this work is given a review of the career of the president of this important company, Rufus O. Renfrew, and to that article reference may be made for further information concerning the company and its extensive operations.

William Frank Carson, who has been a resident of Oklahoma since 1900, was born on his father's farm in Champaign County, Illinois, on the 23d of June, 1874, and is a son of William G. and Martha Jane (Bales) Carson. His father was born in Vermilion County, Indiana, in which state he was reared and educated and when, in 1855, he removed to Illinois and became one of the pioneer settlers of Champaign County, where he settled on a preëmption claim which he obtained from the Government. His entire active career, marked by consecutive industry and unpretentious worth of character, was one of close identification with the great and fundamental industry of agriculture, and through his well-directed endeavors he achieved independence and definite prosperity. He was a staunch democrat of the old school and though he was ever loyal and public-spirited as a citizen he never desired or held political office. Both he and his wife early became zealous members of the Universalist Church, and he exemplified his faith in his daily life, his death having occurred in the City of Champaign, Illinois, on the 10th of November, 1906, after he had been a resident of Champaign County for a full half century.

On the 22d of February, 1854, was solemnized the marriage of William G. Carson to Miss Martha Jane Bales, who likewise was born in Vermilion County, Indiana, the date of her nativity having been August 27, 1834, his birth having occurred in that county on the 29th of June, 1829,—dates that clearly denote that the respective families were founded in that section of the Hoosier State in the early pioneer days. Mrs. Carson, who still retains her home at Champaign, Illinois, is a daughter of Caleb and Emily (Spangler) Bales, natives of Virginia, and of her ten children—two sons and eight daughters—four daughters died in infancy,—Maria, Ella, Elizabeth and Laura. Emily Josephine, who was born December 20, 1858, became, in 1881, the wife of Eugene A. Ford, and they have four children,—Amos Carson, William Van Pelt, Martha Belle, and Eugene Bartholomew. Caleb W., who was born December 10, 1860, was reared and educated in Champaign County, Illinois, and in his native state he continued his residence until July 5, 1885, when he removed to Ashland, Kansas, where he accumulated a very large estate and where he was the largest individual taxpayer in Clark County at the time of his death, which occurred August 13, 1915. He served eight years as postmaster at Ashland, during both administrations of President Cleveland, and was a leader in the ranks of the democratic party in that section of the Sunflower State. He attained to the thirty-second degree in the Ancient Accepted Scottish Rite of the Masonic fraternity, besides being affiliated with the Mystic Shrine. In March, 1886, he wedded Miss Martha Congeleton, who survives him, as do also their four sons and one daughter,—Paul C., William G., Frank Lee, Caleb W., Jr., and Hazel Ellene. Ellen A. Carson was born August 11, 1864, was united in marriage on the 27th of February, 1890, to Hon. John I. Lee. Their only child, Irving Allen, died in infancy. Mr. Lee, who died at Cordell, Washita County, Oklahoma, on the 25th of December, 1914, was editor and publisher of the Clark County Clipper, at Ashland, Kansas, from 1885 to 1890, and thereafter served until 1892 as clerk of the District Court of that county. From 1894 to 1898 he was register of the United States Land Office at Dodge City, Kansas, and in 1901 he came to Oklahoma Territory and engaged in the lumber and coal business at Cordell, where he passed the residue of his life. He was influential in democratic political activities in Kansas and likewise after his removal to Oklahoma. Mary Marc Carson was born August 9, 1867, and on the 20th of August, 1886, she became the wife of Dr. David P. Sims, their only child being a son, Carson, and the family home being maintained at Philadelphia, Pennsylvania. Miss Luvilla B. Carson, who was born January 22, 1870, remains with her widowed mother.

William Frank Carson, the second son and youngest child in the above mentioned family, passed the period of his childhood and early youth upon the homestead farm which was the place of his birth, and after duly availing himself of the advantages of the public schools of Champaign County, Illinois, he pursued a higher course in what is now the great Valparaiso University, at Valparaiso, Indiana. He continued to be associated with the work and the management of his father's farm until 1899, when he removed to Ashland, Kansas, where he served as deputy clerk of Clark County. In that city he was thereafter associated with his only brother in the mercantile business for a period of two years, and upon coming to Oklahoma, in 1900, he established his home at Curtis, Woodward County, where he continued in the same line of enterprise four years. He had entered claim to a tract of Government land in that county and in 1904 he perfected his title to the property. In 1910-11 Mr. Carson held a clerical position in a mercantile establishment in the City of Woodward, and in 1912 he there assumed the position of bookkeeper in the head office of the Renfrew Investment Company. In October of the same year he was assigned to the management of the company's office at Beaver, where he has since continued the alert and efficient incumbent of this position, in which he has done much to extend the business controlled from this office.

Mr. Carson is found aligned as a staunch supporter of the cause of the democratic party, is affiliated with the Masonic fraternity, and both he and his wife are specially zealous and valued members of the Presbyterian Church at Beaver, in the Sunday School of which he has served three years as superintendent. It is worthy of incidental note that this is the oldest exclusively Presbyterian Church in the state, its organization having been effected in 1886, when Beaver County was still a part of the region commonly designated as No Man's Land,—prior to the creation of Oklahoma Territory. Mr. Carson is secretry of the Beaver Gospel Team, and also secretary of the Beaver County Sunday School Association.

At Reinbeck, Grundy County, Iowa, on the 14th of April, 1901, was solemnized the marriage of Mr. Carson to Miss Grace B. Klein, daughter of Herman E. and Katherine (Kline) Klein, both natives of Iowa, where their respective parents settled in the early pioneer days. Mrs. Carson was born on her father's homestead farm in Grundy County, Iowa, on the 4th of September, 1876, and in her youth she received excellent educational advantages, through the medium of which she prepared herself for service in the pedagogic profession. For eight years prior to her marriage she was a successful and popular teacher in the schools of her native state and in Kansas. Mr. and Mrs. Carson have five children, whose names and respective dates of birth are here noted: Francis Klein, March 26, 1902; Ellen Belva, June 1, 1905; Ernest Lee, September 1, 1906; Willis Spangler, July 26, 1910; and Luvilla Grace, July 22, 1912.

WILLIAM HENRY MILLER. To found a town and to exercise such a kindly and wholesome supervision over its welfare as to deserve the title of "town father" is an enviable distinction. That is only one phase of William Henry Miller's participation with the life and affairs of Oklahoma. He is one of the real pioneers, was out in "No Man's Land" in the primitive days of that country, and has participated in a number of the important land openings and as a homesteader, cattle raiser, civil engineer, teacher, business man, has played an unusual part in the development of this great state. His present home and activities are centered at Buffalo, which he founded.

He was born March 17, 1858, in a log house on a farm in Knox County, Missouri. At the age of three years left an orphan, he was reared by John Miller as his foster father and lived with that worthy Missouri gentleman the first twenty-seven years of his life. In the meantime he had made the best of his opportunities and had secured the equivalent of a liberal education. In 1881 he graduated from the Gem City Business College at Quincy, Illinois, and in 1884 he completed the work in the North Missouri State Normal at Kirksville, Missouri, near his old home. The following two years were spent as a teacher in Missouri.

It was in 1886 that Mr. Miller moved out to that portion of the present State of Oklahoma which then on the geography was marked as No Man's Land. There he followed the profession of civil engineer until 1891, in which year he resumed teaching. He taught the first public school in what is now Harper County, and was superintendent of city schools at Shawnee in 1896-97, and in 1898-99 superintendent of the city schools of Blackwell.

While in No Man's Land he was in the cattle business in 1886 and 1891, together with his work as a surveyor. He lived the thoroughly primitive life of the place and time. He ate buffalo meat when buffalo still contended for the prairies with domestic cattle, and he bore all the hardships of the frontier, including existence in sod houses. He was also a factor in that short-lived government known as the Territory of Cimarron, which was set up to furnish jurisdiction and competent local government for the narrow strip of land between the Texas Panhandle and Southern Kansas and Southern Colorado. He was elected to the senate of the provisional government and was the first territorial assessor in 1889-90.

As a civil engineer he surveyed nearly all the townsites of No Man's Land.

In 1891 Mr. Miller took part in the opening of the Cheyenne and Arapahoe Indian reservations. In 1893 he likewise participated in the opening of the Cherokee Strip, locating at Blackwell. In 1899, removing to old Woodward County, he secured a claim on Buffalo Creek. On a portion of that land he subsequently laid out the present Town of Buffalo, and gave to it the enterprise which started it as one of the flourishing town centers of Northwestern Oklahoma. In 1896 he was elected the first county surveyor of Harper County. In his own Town of Buffalo he erected some substantial buildings, and he has contributed generously to every public institution in the town. He owns a model farm of 280 acres adjoining the townsite, has a complete set of buildings, and also a modern home, and owns about 700 town lots. In politics he is a democrat, but has never had time for political work.

Mr. Miller has also distinguished himself in the field of invention. He is inventor of an ore separating machine on which he has a patent, and which has met the test of practical experience in the mines of Mexico. He is also patentee of a grain separator and thresher combined.

For much of what is best in his life's accomplishment Mr. Miller credits his able wife. On April 5, 1888, at Columbia, Missouri, he married Miss Fannie E. Turner. She was born in that university center on November 7, 1866, and she and her husband were school mates prior to their marriage. Mrs. Miller has been more or less closely identified with educational work since she was sixteen years of age. She now ranks as the leading authority on primary school work in Oklahoma. She and her husband are active members of the Christian Church and she has taken a specially active part in Sunday-school, having been secretary of the Oklahoma State Sunday School Association. She taught the first school in Blackwell and was connected with the schools there for seven years, while Mr. Miller conducted the first school in Harper County.

H. C. WALLACE, D. O. At Blackwell one of the physicians who can claim a patronage of exceptional numerical strength and value is Dr. H. C. Wallace, who is one of the leading representatives of the School of Osteopathy in Oklahoma, and has met with unanimous success during the fifteen years of his residence at Blackwell. Within twenty years the practice of osteopathy, starting in restricted localities and hampered by prejudice, has spread from coast to coast, and has won its place with older schools of medicine, and largely because of the work of Doctor Wallace the influence of the science is very apparent in Northern Oklahoma. Doctor Wallace is Resident Physician and Manager of the Southwestern Osteopathic Sanitarium of Blackwell, and the existence of this institution must be credited mostly to his untiring efforts to place his profession in the front rank, and provide suitable care for the adherents of the osteopathic system of treatment. Starting in 1912 with a small sixteen-room frame building, the institution has grown to its present dimensions. It has become one of the largest osteopathic institutions in existence, with one of the largest and finest hospital buildings and most complete and modern equipment of any hospital of any kind in the Southwest, having a capacity which can be utilized for about 100 patients, and beautiful grounds and park surrounding the building, and situated on the highest land in the city.

Miss Clara Powell, recent night superintendent of the Kirksville, Missouri, Hospital, is the Superintendent and assisting her is a corps of as efficient nurses as are to be found anywhere. Other physicians and surgeons associated with Doctor Wallace in this institution are Dr. George J. Conley of Kansas City, Missouri, the chief surgeon; Dr. L. S. Larimore, who has charge of the eye, ear, nose and throat and X-ray departments; and Dr. M. M. Estlack, both of Blackwell; Dr. Ernest Ewing of El Reno, Oklahoma; Doctors Mitchell and Mitchell, Dr. W. F. Nay and Dr. N. Triplett, all of Enid, Oklahoma; Dr. P. W. Gibbson of Winfield, Kansas; Dr. N. Howell of Wellington, Kansas; Dr. Fred Thompson of Caldwell, Kansas; Dr. L. Brenz of Arkansas City, Kansas; Doctor Calvert of Ponca City, Oklahoma; Dr. F. C. Davis of Tonkawa, Oklahoma; Dr. E. Hicks of Newkirk, Oklahoma; Dr. F. Barrows of Kingman, Kansas, and a number of others.

Doctor Wallace is a graduate of the American School of Osteopathy and a post-graduate of the Los Angeles College of Osteopathic Physicians and Surgeons.

A downtown office is maintained at Blackwell in the National Block, corner of Main and Blackwell Avenue.

Dr. H. C. Wallace was born near Juniata, on a farm in Adams County, Nebraska, January 21, 1882, and has lived in Blackwell since 1903. His father, John Wallace, was a native of Vermont, and during the Civil war made a record as a gallant soldier with the Fourth Iowa Cavalry. He came of Scotch ancestry, and for many generations the family has been noted for its integrity and vigor of citizenship. From Vermont John Wallace moved out to Iowa, and was one of the early settlers in Marshall County of that state. He married Ruth Ferguson, a native of Iowa, whose parents came from Pennsylvania. From Iowa the Wallace family moved out to Adams County, Nebraska, where they were among the early settlers. Later the father came to Blackwell in Kay County, Oklahoma, where he is now living at the age of eighty-eight years, being one of the oldest veteran soldiers in Kay County.

Dr. H. C. Wallace grew up in the states of Nebraska and Missouri, receiving his education and graduating from the high school at Grant City, Missouri, and then entered the American School of Osteopathy at Kirksville, where he finished in 1903. In the same year Doctor Wallace married Cora Roten, who prior to her marriage had been a successful teacher. Her father was John Roten of Albia, Iowa. They have two children: John Herbert and Velma Bernice.

H. H. BRENNER. While in a business way Mr. Brenner's chief distinction rests upon his work as a banker, he is also a splendid type of the business man and citizen who not only do things but get things done for the permanent welfare and prosperity of his community. His community can hardly be regarded as one town, since, though a resident of Pawhuska for many years, his interests extend all over Osage County, and his associations and friendships include many leading business men all over the country.

As a banker Mr. Brenner has been primarily identified with the First National Bank of Pawhuska, of which he is president. Some years ago, when he took charge of the bank, it was an institution with $25,000 capital, a surplus of $2,000, deposits of $34,000, and the books showed indebtedness at $10,000. At the present time its capital stock is $50,000, with surplus and undivided profits of $32,000, and a total of deposits amounting to over $500,000. The total resources of the First National in May, 1916, amounted to approximately $716,000.

In addition to being president of the First National Bank of Pawhuska, Mr. Brenner is president of the Pawhuska Oil & Gas Company; was formerly president of the Bank of Big Heart, an office which he resigned, thought still remaining a stockholder; was president of

the Foraker State Bank, now the First National Bank of Foraker, which he organized and managed four years, and at one time was identified with the National Reserve Bank of New York City.

The story of Mr. Brenner's career is one that illustrates the possibilities of accomplishment. In earlier life he lived in close touch with poverty and his independence and self-reliance have brought him to an enviable goal of prosperity and real success. He was born at Golding, in Courland, Russia, now Germany, June 15, 1852, a son of Benjamin and Gertrude (Nattison) Brenner. His parents spent all their lives in the old country, and his father in earlier life was a merchant. Mr. Brenner was the youngest of his mother's four children, two sons and two daughters, and by his second marriage his father had also four children, all of whom are living in this country except one. Two are in Memphis, Tennessee, and one in Brinkley, Arkansas. Mr. Brenner has a number of nephews and nieces in different parts of the United States.

He was seventeen years of age when he set out for the United States, making the journey alone, and arriving at Oxford, Mississippi, with neither money nor influential friends to help him. He lived at Oxford until 1886, having been connected with the mercantile firm of Meyers, Sichels & Company for twelve years. Afterwards he engaged in the mercantile business for himself, and in 1886 first came to Pawhuska, Indian Territory, under appointment from President Cleveland as post trader. Pawhuska was then one of the smallest posts in the Indian Territory. He remained as a trader there until 1890 and then returned to Mississippi, engaging in the merchandise business at Clarksdale. He also bought a large cotton plantation of 2,740 acres in the Yazoo Valley, but met with financial reverses in the management of his enterprise. In 1895 Mr. Brenner returned to Pawhuska, receiving a new appointment as post trader during Cleveland's second administration. Here he laid the solid foundation of his present prosperity. He was a merchant, and also engaged in the cattle business with Prentice Price of Hominy. It was as a merchant and cattle man that his chief interests were centered for twelve years. In 1903 Mr. Brenner came to the Bank of Pawhuska as president, and his success in raising that institution to one of the foremost in Northeastern Oklahoma has already been mentioned. During the past thirteen years he has devoted most of his time to banking and the oil and gas business. He owns extensive real estate interests at Pawhuska, and has effected much for local improvement.

In 1905 Mr. Brenner spent two months in Washington negotiating with Congress for the setting aside of various townsites in Osage County. As a result of his efforts 640 acres were set aside for the townsite of Pawhuska; 160 acres for Big Heart; and similar amounts for Hominy, Fairfax and Foraker. The setting aside of these townsites was a necessary preliminary to real development of towns that are now among the most important in Osage County.

In 1903 Mr. Brenner promoted the Pawhuska Oil & Gas Company, of which he is now president. At that time no oil or gas had been produced within twenty-five miles, but he proved his own faith and good judgment by investing his own resources, and now for a number of years this company has been one of the largest in the development of the local oil and gas fields. It is capitalized at $250,000. Throughout the state Mr. Brenner has interests in land, gas and oil leases.

The original oil and gas leases given by the Osages in 1896 expired in March, 1916. As the authority to lease all the Osage lands is vested in the Secretary of the Interior with the concurrence of the Indian Council, Mr. Brenner spent the preceding months of January and February in Washington, representing his company. There were many conflicting claims, all requiring careful investigation, and it was a difficult matter to do justice to all. The Pawhuska Oil and Gas Company was successful in securing 38,400 acres in the vicinity of the City of Pawhuska on terms which made it possible to offer gas to the consumers at reasonable prices. In fact, Pawhuska enjoys the distinction of possessing a larger gas field and cheaper rates than any other city in the United States.

Since getting his citizenship papers Mr. Brenner has been consistently a supporter of the democratic party. He was presidential elector from Oklahoma in 1912, and always active as a party man, and has served as a delegate to many state conventions both in Mississippi and Oklahoma. He has likewise contributed generously to the party treasury, though for himself he has never desired nor has he been willing to accept any honors in the way of office. Mr. Brenner has numbered among his personal friends many of the well known men in politics and business, but deems his most illustrious friendship as that which existed between him and the late Justice L. Q. C. Lamar of the United States Supreme Court. Mr. Brenner is a thirty-second degree Scottish Rite Mason, a member of the Mystic Shrine, an Elk and a Knight of Pythias, and belongs to a number of other social and civic orders. Though born of a Jewish family, in America he has always associated with Gentiles almost entirely, but shows his loyalty to his race by membership in the United Israelites and the B'Nai B'rith. He is also a member of both the State and National Bankers' Association and a member of the National Gas Association of America.

In January, 1899, Mr. Brenner married Mary Louisa Morris. She was born in New York State, and they were married at the City of Albany. Mrs. Brenner is one of the leading Pawhuska women in social and benevolent affairs. She was one of the founders of the Episcopal Church of Pawhuska, is a member of the Shakespeare Club and the Art Club, and spends much of her time in doing good in her community. While they have no children of their own Mr. Brenner is keenly interested in the welfare of his many younger relatives and has generously assisted a number to gain education and to fit themselves for usefulness in business and the professions. When Mr. Brenner came to the United States he had no knowledge of the English language. His mother tongue was German. He never attended school after coming to this country, and has acquired most of his education through close contact with men and affairs. Few men have lived their lives to better purpose than this Pawhuska banker.

GEORGE M. BURKHARDT. For a young man a little beyond thirty, George M. Burkhardt has had a long business experience and is well established as one of the proprietors and the active manager of the abstract company at Frederick in Tillman County.

Mr. Burkhardt represents the thrifty and substantial element of Texas citizenship that was introduced into that part of the Southwest from Germany. He was born at Round Top in Fayette County, Texas, December 3, 1884, a son of Louis G. and Bertha R. (Ullrich) Burkhardt. His grandfather Burkhardt was born and married in Germany, came over with his family, and was an early farmer settler in Fayette County, Texas. The grandfather Adam George Ullrich was born in Baden, Germany, and at the age of eighteen crossed the ocean and settled on a farm in Fayette County, Texas. He was employed by the owner of the farm, but later bought the place, and still lives on that farm, which is crossed by the line between Fayette and Washington counties, Texas. He was born in 1834, and is thus more than fourscore years of age. Louis G. Burkhardt was born in Fayette County, Texas, in 1853, and died near Round Top on his farm in 1887. He and his brother and a sister owned 270 acres near that village. He was a member of the Lutheran Church. His wife, Bertha R. Ullrich, was also born in Fayette County, and is now living in Washita County, Oklahoma. Their children were: Lina, the wife of Ernest Stein, farming people in Washita County, Oklahoma; Lizzie, wife of Gottlieb Stehr, a farmer in Custer County, Oklahoma; George M.; Amanda, who married Oscar Hoepfner, a farmer in Washita County, Oklahoma; and Katy, wife of Henry Funk, who lives in the Town of Bessie, Oklahoma. After the death of Louis G. Burkhardt his widow married C. H. Koch. He was born in Hesse, Germany, emigrated to Fayette County, Texas, and later to Washita County, Oklahoma, where he died in 1909. The children of this second marriage are: Justus Koch, who is a farmer in Washita County, Oklahoma; Otto Koch, also a farmer in the same county; Blandina, who is employed in the telephone office at Hobart in Kiowa County, Oklahoma; Christian, a farmer in Washita County; and Adam, a farmer in the same county.

George M. Burkhardt received more or less regular instruction in the public schools of Round Top up to the age of nine, at which time his mother removed to Copperas Cove, Texas, where he continued school attendance up to the age of fourteen. At that date he showed an indication of the reliance which has always characterized him by running away from home, and returning to his native Village of Round Top, continued his studies in the German language for two years. He then returned to Copperas Cove and was employed on his mother's farm up to the age of twenty. In 1904, realizing the need of better educational preparation, Mr. Burkhardt entered the Hills Business College at Waco, Texas, and after completing his course there engaged in the real estate business at Holland in Bell County, Texas, for two months. His next location was at Belton, the county seat of Bell County, where he was in the abstract business in the employ of A. M. Montieth up to the summer of 1907. At that time Mr. Burkhardt identified himself with Lawton, Oklahoma, but on the 18th of November of the same year entered the employ of the Moncrief Cook Company in the abstract business, and on February 28, 1909, came to Frederick to represent the same company. In 1910 E. J. Schowalter and Mr. Burkhardt bought the Moncrief Company's interests in the abstract business and Mr. Burkhardt has since had the sole management of this important concern, since Mr. Schowalter is vice president of the Chattanooga State Bank of Chattanooga, Oklahoma. Mr. Burkhardt's offices are in the rear of the First National Bank Building.

Up to the summer of 1912 Mr. Burkhardt was a regular republican, but has since been affiliated with the democratic party. He has served as councilman in Frederick from the Third Ward and is now secretary of the board of education. Fraternally his affiliations are with Belton Lodge No. 51 of the Knights of Pythias in Texas, with the Brotherhood of American Yeomen and his church is the German Lutheran.

On October 22, 1910, at Lawton, Oklahoma, Mr. Burkhardt married Miss Sadie S. Cory, daughter of W. H. Cory, who resides at Douglas, Arizona, where he and his son Walter C. Cory conduct a garage. Mr. and Mrs. Burkhardt have two children: Frances Blandina, born August 31, 1911; and Laureada Lavelle, born April 8, 1914.

GRANVILLE T. AYERS. In the year succeeding that in which Oklahoma was admitted to statehood Mr. Ayers became a teacher in the public schools of Beaver County, and during the intervening period he has continued as one of the prominent and influential figures in the educational affairs of this western section of the state, his broad pedagogic experience and his marked executive ability having met with consistent recognition when, in the autumn of 1914, he was elected county superintendent of schools, a position in which his administration is fully justifying the popular choice for the incumbent of this important office and is proving potent in advancing the standard of general school work in Beaver County. Mr. Ayers has been identified with educational work for virtually twenty years and has honored his chosen profession by his character, his scholarly attainments and his worthy achievement. As one of the representative citizens and valued officials of Beaver County he is specially entitled to specific recognition in this history of the state of his adoption.

In Wayne County, Illinois, Mr. Ayers was born on the 9th of April, 1874, and the place of his nativity was far from being one of sumptuous order, though it was a true home in which comfort and refinement were in evidence,—a log house of the pioneer type being at the time the parental domicile on one of the excellent farms of the county mentioned and the place being owned and operated by the father of the future Oklahoma pedagogue. Superintendent Ayers is a son of Robert S. and Samantha (Newman) Ayers, the former of whom was born in Gibson County, Indiana, in 1831, and the latter of whom was born in Kentucky, in 1841. Robert S. Ayers is a son of Christopher Ayers, who likewise was born in Indiana, where his parents settled in the earlier pioneer era in the history of that state. The entire active career of Robert S. Ayers has been marked by close association with the basic industries of agriculture and stock raising, in connection with which he continued his operations in Indiana until 1870, when he removed with his family to Wayne County, Illinois, where he developed and improved a valuable farm and where he is now living retired, in the city of Fairfield, the county seat, his eighty-fourth birthday anniversary having been celebrated in 1915. He was a personal friend of Abraham Lincoln, whom he accompanied on the latter's canvass during the historic Lincoln and Douglas campaign, in 1860. In 1855 was solemnized his marriage to Miss Samantha Newman, a daughter of Turner Newman, who was a native of Kentucky. Her grandfather, John Henry Newman, was a native of England and came to the United States in 1824 and settled on Duck River, Kentucky, where he purchased 2,000 acres of valley land, the original deed to this property being now in the possession of his great-grandson, Granville T. Ayers, subject of this review. Mrs. Samantha Ayers passed the closing period of her gentle and gracious life at Fairfield, Illinois, where she died in the year 1901. Of the five children the only son is he to whom this sketch is dedicated and who was the fourth in order of birth. Estella, who was born in 1856, is the wife of John McLain, and they have five children,—Homer, Lena, Orrin, Paul and Kathryn. Wilmoth, who was born in 1858, is the wife of Solon Hill and has three children,—Ayers, Earl and Katerine. Jesse May, born in 1860, is the wife of James Monroe and they have four children, Orilla, who was born in 1862, is the wife of Robert Lewis, of Louisville, Clay County, Illinois, and they have one child.

After duly availing himself of the advantages of the public schools of Wayne County, Illinois, Granville T. Ayers completed an effective course of higher study in Hayward College, at Fairfield, that county, and at the age of twenty-two years he initiated his pedagogic career as a teacher in the public schools of his native state, where he continued his labors as an educator for a period of twelve years, during two of which he was an instructor in the Illinois State Reform School, at Pontiac.

In 1908 Mr. Ayers came to Oklahoma and engaged in teaching in the schools of Beaver County, his services in this capacity having continued until he was elected to his present office, that of county superintendent of schools, in the autumn of 1914, since which time he has worked with characteristic zeal and efficiency in the broader field of educational activity. He is a stalwart supporter of the cause of the republican party, is affiliated with the Masonic fraternity, and both he and his wife hold membership in the Christian Church.

On the 22d of October, 1914, was solemnized the marriage of Mr. Ayers to Miss Mary White, who had been a popular teacher in the schools of Clay County, Illinois for eight years prior to her marriage. Mrs. Ayers was born in Posey County, Indiana, on the 20th of September, 1885, and in the same county were born her parents, Joseph and Mary (Montgomery) White. Mr. and Mrs. Ayers represent a distinct intellectual and moral force in their home community and also are zealous in the furtherance of high civic ideals and all things that make for the educational, moral and material welfare of their home city and county, where their circle of friends is coincident with that of their acquaintances, Mrs. Ayers being a leader in church and social activities at Beaver.

C. GUY CUTLIP. While Mr. Cutlip has for a number of years been successfully practicing law in Seminole County, with office and home at Wewoka, he is a pioneer white resident of old Oklahoma, and witnessed or participated in three different land openings. He was with his father at the beginning of settlement in the original Oklahoma, was at the opening of the Kickapoo, Sac and Fox reservations, the Cheyenne and Arapahoe Reservation, and the Cherokee Strip in 1893. He has interested himself in many of the important activities of Oklahoma during the last fifteen years, and though still young occupies a position of prominence in his section of the state.

He was born near Medicine Lodge, Kansas, April 6, 1881, a son of T. G. and Susan (Mills) Cutlip. His father was born near Parkersburg, West Virginia, and his mother in Tennessee. She was a daughter of Capt. William N. Mills, who was in the Confederate army under General Forrest, and after the war moved to Missouri and still later to Kansas. T. G. Cutlip went to Kansas in 1871 as a pioneer, was married near Medicine Lodge, and for some years was actively engaged in the cattle business in Western Kansas, until the destructive year 1886 brought about the loss of all his stock. He was a college graduate in law, and since then he has been in active practice in Oklahoma. From Medicine Lodge he moved to Kingfisher, Oklahoma, in 1889, the year of the original opening of Oklahoma, and in 1895 located at Tecumseh, where his wife died in 1902 at the age of forty-three. T. G. Cutlip is still living in Tecumseh and in the active practice of law. There were three children: C. Guy; William, who is secretary of the street railway at Muskogee and also at Shawnee; and Roy, of Medicine Lodge, Kansas.

C. Guy Cutlip lived at home with his parents until 1901. He had a common school education, later studied law privately, and he and his wife also took several courses in the University of Oklahoma. Mr. Cutlip has been a resident of Wewoka since 1901.

As a young man he learned stenography and served as court stenographer at Tecumseh for three years, serving under Judge J. D. F. Jennings, and then for a number of years was with the firm of Cutlip & Blakeney. He was admitted to the bar at Tecumseh and was later given a license by the Supreme Court to practice in all the courts of the territory and later of the state. He was formally admitted to the Oklahoma bar January 21, 1908, soon after statehood.

For several years after moving to Wewoka Mr. Cutlip was cashier of the Exchange Bank and was also in the abstract business. After statehood he was appointed deputy county attorney, a post he held until 1910, and since that year he has been handling a large private clientage as a lawyer. He also has some gas and oil interests, and was one of the original stockholders and helped secure the leaseholds of the Black Panther Oil & Gas Company. At the present time he owns farming lands, handles stock and controls the operation of nearly 1,000 acres. In politics he is a democrat and in Masonry was for three years deputy grand master.

On March 22, 1903, Mr. Cutlip married Amo Butts at Tecumseh, Oklahoma, a daughter of Judge A. W. Butts. They have one child, Maxine, who is now ten years of age. Mr. Cutlip is the possessor of one of the most extensive literary libraries in the state.

ROBERT B. BRETZ. In the year 1891, which marked the opening of the newly organized Territory of Oklahoma to settlement, by presidential proclamation, Robert B. Bretz, the present county treasurer of the important county designated by the name of Canadian, became one of its pioneer settlers, and he has been closely and worthily identified with the development and upbuilding of this section of the state, where he owns and has effected the excellent improvement of the fine tract of land which he obtained by "making the run" when the former district of the Cheyenne Nation was opened for colonization. He has been one of the alert, progressive and public-spirited citizens of Canadian County, has given his co-operation in the furtherance of measures and enterprises that have conserved civic and industrial advancement, and that he has gained impregnable place in popular esteem is shown by his having been called to serve in the important fiscal office of which he is the present incumbent and the duties of which he assumed in July, 1915.

Of stanch German and Irish lineage, Mr. Bretz is a scion of a family that was founded in Pennsylvania in the colonial era of our national history, though he himself is a native of the Province of Ontario, Canada, his birth having occurred in County Oxford on April 8, 1861. He is a son of Gerhardt and Elizabeth (Jacobs) Bretz, the former a native of the Province of Ontario, Canada, and the latter of whom was born in the State of New York, of Irish lineage. Of the five children of this union Annie and Eliza are deceased, and the three surviving are Robert B., Elizabeth and William, all of whom reside in the State of Oklahoma. The mother passed the closing years of her life in the Province of Ontario and years later the father came to Oklahoma, where he resided in the home of his son, William, until he, too, was called to eternal rest at a venerable age. Gerhardt Bretz was a son of Jacob Bretz, who likewise was born in the Province of Ontario and whose father, Jacob Bretz, Sr., a native of Lancaster County, Pennsylvania, was a member of a Mennonite colony that immigrated from the old Keystone State and settled in the Province of Ontario, Canada, in the pioneer days. The original progenitor of the Bretz family in America immigrated from Germany and settled in Pennsylvania prior to the war of the Revolution, and the German language was retained by the family until the fifth generation in America preceding that of which the subject of this review is a representative. Gerhardt Bretz was a carriage and wagon maker by trade and followed this vocation in the Province of Ontario for many years.

Robert B. Bretz received a good common school education in his native province, where also he completed a course and was graduated in the Guelph Business College. At the age of twenty-one years he assumed the position of bookkeeper in a hardware establishment in the City of Detroit, Michigan, but eighteen months later he resigned and joined a company of Canadian colonists who went to the State of Louisiana and settled on the old Stephanie Plantation, in St. Martin's Parish. In the purchase and operation of this plantation success failed to attend the colonists, and the property was finally sold to Kansas capitalists. Soon afterward, in 1891, Mr. Bretz came to the Territory of Oklahoma, where he was employed on the Mumford Johnston Ranch until the opening of the Cheyenne District to settlement, when he made the run and selected a homestead claim in what is now Canadian County. For a period of five years thereafter he was compelled to make a vigorous contest to retain his homestead, his claim to which was made a matter of prolonged litigation, but he was eventually able to perfect his title to the property, which he still owns and which he has developed into one of the valuable farms of the county, though he maintains his residence in the City of El Reno, the county seat, where he established his home prior to assuming his present county office.

Mr. Bretz has been active and influential in public affairs in Canadian County and is here a prominent and influential figure in the local councils and activities of the democratic party. In 1910 he was elected county clerk, and the appreciative estimate placed upon his administration of the affairs of this office was indicated in his re-election in 1912 for a second term of two years. His services as a public official were not permitted to terminate upon his retirement from this post, as in the election of 1914 he was chosen county treasurer. He met formidable opponents in this election but the voters of the county manifested their confidence and high regard by according to him a splendid majority at the polls, his assumption of office taking place in August, 1915, and the fiscal affairs of the county being assured of most careful and effective administration during his regime in this important office.

In the State of Louisiana, in 1910, was solemnized the marriage of Mr. Bretz to Miss Edith Sowers, whose parents were early settlers in Nebraska, whence they came as pioneers to Canadian County, Oklahoma. Mr. and Mrs. Bretz have two children—Daisy and William.

COL. JOHN W. JORDAN, of Cleveland, Oklahoma, is one of the distinguished representatives of the old Cherokee Nation. He has lived in what is now the State of Oklahoma more than seventy years. In the flush of young manhood he allied himself, like many of his people, with the Confederate cause and fought gallantly and bravely through the war. Since the close of that struggle has come a period of half a century of fruitful enterprise and as cattle man, oil producer, town builder and land owner, he is widely known all over the state.

Born December 9, 1843, his birthplace was six miles east of the old Cherokee capital Tahlequah. His parents were Levi and Malinda (Riley) Jordan. Levi Jordan was born in the State of Maine of Scotch-Irish ancestry. He was one of nine boys born to his parents, and it may be that he thought nine were too many for one household, since as a very young lad he ran away and made his way west to Illinois. He was still a boy when he enlisted in the regular army, becoming a member of the second regiment of United States Dragoons. This regiment was assigned to duty in Western Louisiana, along the border between what was then the United States and the country of Mexico. Soon afterward Texas undertook to win its independence from Mexican dominion and the company of which he was a member broke away from its command, enlisted in the service of the Texas Patriots, and took a part in the capture of Santa Ana and the winning of independence for the Lone Star Republic. After five years in the army Levi Jordan was honorably discharged with his regiment at Fort Gibson, Cherokee Nation, then one of the frontier posts in what is now Oklahoma. He remained in the Cherokee Nation after his discharge, took up work as a brick mason, and married there one of the Cherokee daughters. After two years she died, and Levi Jordan went abroad to Europe. After the close of the Civil war he returned to his native land, and died some place in the West. By his wife Malinda Riley he left one child, Col. John W. Jordan, who was reared by his maternal grandmother Riley. The Riley family came from the North of Ireland in colonial days and they intermarried with the Cherokees before the removal of the tribe west of the Mississippi.

Such were the circumstances of his birth and ancestry. John W. Jordan grew up in the Cherokee Nation, attended the Cherokee schools and learned both the English and Cherokee languages. He was just seventeen years of age when he enlisted in 1861 under the famous Gen. Stan Watie. With that contingent of Indian troops he served with the Confederacy until the close of the war. He saw much fighting from first to last, and did not escape unscathed. On July 17, 1863, at the battle of Honey Springs, southwest of Muskogee on Elk Creek, a minnie ball struck young Jordan in his belt and passed through his body. He still has the belt, with holes showing front and back. For two months a kindly woman cared for him, and he is firmly convinced that had he been taken to a field hospital his life could not have been saved. When he had been nursed back to comparative strength the young soldier returned to his regiment and was with it until the close of the war.

Since the war Colonel Jordan has taken a very prominent part in the United Confederate Veterans. At the time of statehood he was serving as major-general of the Indian Territory Division of the Confederate Veterans organization, and he took his division to Richmond at the unveiling of the Jefferson Davis monument during the Confederate reunion in that city.

After the war Colonel Jordan went to Texas and became extensively identified with the cattle business. Representing a number of wealthy Texans in the handling of their immense herds, he spent nine years on the free range, a life he loved so well. In 1878, returning to the Cherokee Nation, Colonel Jordan settled on a farm and since then has occupied himself independently as a cattle raiser. At the same time his service has been valuable to his people. He served as a Cherokee special agent in charge of the "outlet" or "strip" before its opening to settlement in 1893. In safeguarding the property rights of the Cherokees he carried a commission under Federal Judge I. C. Parker and also a United States Commission under Robert L. Owen, who was United States agent of the Five Civilized Tribes. He was the first settler on Cherokee land west of 96 I. M. in 1883, ten years before the strip or outlet was opened to settlement. Many legal battles were fought in an effort to remove Cherokee settlers from the land prior to the formal opening, but Judge Parker's ruling was favorable

Col John W Jordan

to those who entered that part of the domain before the Cherokees sold the strip to the United States.

Concerning Colonel Jordan's relations with what is known as "the triangle country," now part of Pawnee County, Oklahoma, a recent writer in Sturm's Oklahoma Magazine tells the story and some quotations should be made: "It was not until January, 1883, that any permanent settlement was made. At that time J. W. Jordan, a citizen of the Cherokee Nation, built the first permanent house in the triangle. He was the first Cherokee settler and his daughter Miss Dixie Jordan was the first Cherokee child born in the strip. This settlement had a greater significance than the mere fact that in the triangle was the first Cherokee settlement, for it also served as the hinge upon which hung greater events. It will be remembered that when David Payne organized his 'boomers' he first entered the Cherokee strip and was several times removed. Mr. Jordan at the time held a commission as special agent for the Cherokees, was deputy United States marshal, and a scout under the war department." The Cherokee Cattlemen's Association occupied the strip by lease, and when their case was brought to trial Judge Parker ruled that the lands were given to the Indians by patent in fee and that they had not abandoned them inasmuch as they were held through their agent, the cattlemen; furthermore, he said that they were not abandoned, because J. W. Jordan, a Cherokee citizen, was an actual resident of the strip or outlet.

The same article recounts many of Mr. Jordan's early experiences with the outlaws, particularly members of the Dalton gang, which in the early days infested the regions of Northern Oklahoma.

Up to the opening of the Cherokee strip there were few settlers, but after 1893 settlers came in rapidly and a number of towns quickly developed. Prior to the opening Dave Hendricks, a Cherokee, had a log cabin where the City of Cleveland now stands.

Colonel Jordan was one of a colony of seventy families receiving each an allotment of eighty acres by the payment of a nominal sum, amounting to $112 apiece. Colonel Jordan also bought from Dave Hendricks the latter's eighty acres for $1,200, and with Dr. G. W. Sutton and R. L. Dunlop laid out the original townsite of Cleveland. They formed the Cleveland Townsite Company, taking in sixteen members at $100 each. Thus Colonel Jordan was prominent in the founding and establishment of what is now one of the most thriving cities of Northeastern Oklahoma. He was purchasing agent for the Cherokee Townsite Company, and placed several allotments as townsites on the line of the Rock Island and Santa Fe railroads. Throughout his dealings with the Cherokees Colonel Jordan has managed their business not only with a high degree of skill but honorably and fairly safeguarding the interests of all concerned. He made five trips to Tampico, Mexico, securing ranch land, and came out after President Madero was assassinated.

At the present time Colonel Jordan owns a farm near Cleveland, and that farm has some producing oil wells. The first well struck in the vicinity was on the land of William Lavery, and the second on the Jordan place. At one time his farm contained five producing wells.

Though a lifelong democrat, Colonel Jordan has never held office except by commission. He and his wife are members of the Presbyterian Church, and he is a Knight of Pythias. In September, 1866, in Texas he married Sarah Thompson. She died near Muskogee, survived by three sons, Robert E. Lee, who is living in Vera, Oklahoma; Thomas Jackson and James Lang, both deceased. In July, 1882, Colonel Jordan married Tennessee Jane Riley, a distant relative. Mrs. Jordan also has Cherokee blood in her veins, the sixteenth degree. Into their home have come five children: Dixie, who married Charles Miller of Cleveland; John B., at home; Daisy Lee, who died at the age of ten years; Robert Owen and Winnie Davis, both at home, the daughter being named in honor of the daughter of Jefferson Davis.

THOMAS FRANKLIN SPURGEON, M. D. A successful physician and surgeon who has practiced long enough in Western Oklahoma to be considered a pioneer, Dr. Thomas F. Spurgeon was one of the first members of his profession to locate in the new town of Frederick in Tillman County as it is now, where he is recognized not only as a capable medical man but a high minded and useful citizen.

The Spurgeon family came from England during the seventeenth century and settled in Massachusetts, whence its descendants moved out in various directions, and are found in Tennessee, Virginia, and many other states. Doctor Spurgeon had ancestors who were soldiers on the American side in the Revolutionary war. Thomas Franklin Spurgeon was born in Gasconade County, Missouri, May 5, 1873. His father, W. M. Spurgeon, was born in Tennessee in 1842, and died at Coyle, Logan County, Oklahoma, in 1906. In 1852 at the age of ten he was taken to Iowa and in the following year to Missouri, and lived in that state as a prospering farmer up to 1906, when he moved to Coyle. He was a democrat, was a working member of the Baptist Church and had seen service as a member of the Missouri State Militia. W. M. Spurgeon married Miss C. C. Blevins, who was born in Missouri and is now living at Coyle, Oklahoma. Their children are: Allen, a retired farmer at Coyle; Cora, who lives at Frederick and is the widow of James Baxter, a blacksmith; Eliza, wife of James Nulty, a farmer at Frederick; Dr. Thomas F.; and G. M., a farmer at Frederick.

Doctor Spurgeon attended the public schools of Gasconade County, Missouri, and a high school in Crawford County of that state. Like many men who have made a success in other callings, his first vocation was that of teacher, and he taught five terms in Gasconade County before entering the Barnes Medical College at St. Louis. Doctor Spurgeon acquired his doctor of medicine degree at Barnes College with the class or 1897, and in 1908 took post-graduate courses in the St. Louis University. His practice began in Osage County, Missouri, in 1897, but after fifteen months he removed to Crawford County in the same state, and in December, 1898, identified himself with Western Oklahoma, practicing for eighteen months at Cimarron City. He was at the opening of the new Town of Coyle in 1899, and remained in practice there three years. In February, 1902, he located at Frederick, and has since built up a large general medical and surgical practice in that town and surrounding community. His offices are in the Guarantee Bank Building just north of Grand Avenue.

Always interested in local progress, Doctor Spurgeon for ten years has served as a member of the Tillman County School Board. He is a democrat, a member of the Baptist Church, and affiliates with the Modern Woodmen of America.

In 1896 in Dent County, Missouri, Doctor Spurgeon married Miss Fannie Vaughan, daughter of the late William Vaughan, who was a Baptist minister. Two children have been born to their marriage: Theron, living at home; and Thelma, now in the public schools at Frederick.

LEVI S. MUNSELL, M. D. The exacting and all important profession of medicine has found many able, loyal and zealous representatives in the various counties and communities of the vigorous young State of Oklahoma, and Beaver, the judicial center of Beaver County, is signally favored in having gained as a citizen a physician and surgeon of such distinctive technical attainments and such broad experience as are defined in the character and achievement of Doctor Munsell, who has here built up a large and representative practice and who holds high place as one of the leading members of his profession in Western Oklahoma.

In ascribing to Doctor Munsell special distinction of nativity the object is best attained by recalling the humorous paraphrase of a familiar quotation that was indulged in one of the famous post-graduate speeches of Hon. Chauncey M. Depew, when he said: "Some men are born great, some achieve greatness, and some are born in Ohio." Under the last clause Doctor Munsell is able to make classification, for he was born at Coldwater, Mercer County, Ohio, on the 21st of September, 1841. He is a son of William A. O. and Deborah (Gray) Munsell.

William A. O. Munsell was born near Fletcher, Miami County, Ohio, in the year 1812, and, as the date indicates was a representative of one of the very early pioneer families of the old Buckeye State, where his father, Levi Munsell, initated the reclamation of a farm from the wilderness prior to the War of 1812, the original American progenitors having come from England and settled in this country in the early colonial days. William A. O. Munsell was reared to manhood in Ohio, and though school facilities were very meager in the locality, and period, he provided advantages for himself, and his alert and receptive mentality enabled him to become a man of large intellectual force and broad mental ken. He became a representative farmer in his section of Ohio and also labored with consecrated devotion and zeal as a minister of the Methodist Episcopal Church, in which he was what was commonly designated as a "local preacher." During the climacteric period of the Civil war he served as a United States marshal for the Northwestern district of Ohio. In 1888 he removed to Missouri, and he died at Cameron, that state, in 1902, at the patriarchal age of ninety years. Early in his career he had been prominently identified with the promotion of railroad building in Ohio, and he was a man of marked business ability as well as one of exalted personal character.

In the year 1825 was solemnized the marriage of Rev. William A. O. Munsell to Miss Deborah Gray, who was born in 1818, a daughter of David and Sarah Gray, and who was summoned to the life eternal in 1849. Of this union were born two sons and two daughters, of whom Elmore Y. and Mary Elizabeth are deceased, Doctor Munsell, of this review, having been the third in order of birth, and the eldest of the children being Sarah L., who is the wife of Stephen Frank, a representative farmer near Cameron, Missouri.

The common schools of Ohio afforded to Dr. Levi S. Munsell his early educational advantages, and at the age of twenty-three years he was matriculated in the Ohio Wesleyan University, at Delaware, in which he completed his higher academic studies. In preparation for the profession of his choice he entered the medical department of the University of Ohio, at Columbus, and in this institution he was graduated as a member of the class of 1870, and with the well earned degree of Doctor of Medicine. Establishing his residence at Geneva, Adams County, Indiana, he there continued in the active practice of his profession nine years, and during the ensuing nine years he was engaged in practice at Rockport, judicial center of Atchison County, Missouri, where he was associated in practice with his brother, the late Dr. Elmore Y. Munsell. In 1886 he removed to Wichita, Kansas, where he built up a substantial practice and where he remained until the latter part of the year 1889, when he came to Indian Territory, and became one of the pioneer physicians in the Old Chickasaw Nation. When, in 1891, the present Town of Chickasha was founded, he became one of its first settlers, and there he maintained his professional headquarters two years. In 1897 he located at the old Town of Hardesty, Beaver County, where he remained until 1900, when he established his home at Beaver, the county seat, where he has since continued in active practice and where, in point of years, he holds prestige as the dean of his profession in this county. He has been an active practitioner for forty years, has kept in touch with the advances made in medical and surgical science, has honored his profession by his character and efficient services and is worthy of special consideration in this history as being one of the pioneer physicians and surgeons of Oklahoma. The Doctor has served as coroner and also as health officer of Beaver County and has in all things closely identified himself with community interests, as a broad-minded and progressive citizen. His political allegiance is given to the republican party, he has attained to the thirty-second degree in the Ancient Accepted Scottish Rite of the Masonic fraternity, as an affiliate of the consistory in the City of Guthrie, and is identified also with the Knights of Pythias and the Independent Order of Odd Fellows. He holds membership in the Methodist Episcopal Church, of which his wife was a lifelong and devoted adherent. He is a member of the Oklahoma State Medical Society and the American Medical Association.

At Coldwater, his native town in Ohio, the 1st of March, 1866, recorded the marriage of Doctor Munsell to Miss Elizabeth J. Young, daughter of Philip and Mary (Plummer) Young, who passed their entire lives in Ohio. Mrs. Munsell was born July 7, 1841, and the supreme loss and bereavement in the life of Doctor Munsell came when his cherished and devoted wife was summoned to eternal rest, at Fred, Oklahoma Territory, on the 2d of July, 1891, just five days prior to her fiftieth birthday anniversary. Of their seven children Paul and Fusia died young; Dayton is engaged in the banking business at El Reno, this state; Pearl E. is the wife of Thomas B. Carey, of Dallas, Texas; William O. is a resident of the City of Portland, Oregon; R. Netta is the wife of E. V. Roe, who maintains his residence at Caldwell, Kansas, and is in the railway postal service of the United States; and Grace A. is the wife of Robert Osborne, their home being now in the City of Detroit, Michigan.

W. M. ADELHELM. A prosperous farmer citizen of the Holdenville community, W. M. Adelhelm has lived there for the past fifteen years, and has busied himself with the care and cultivation of his Indian wife's allotment, comprising one of the fine farms of Hughes County.

His parents, Christian and Maggie (Reece) Adelhelm, were of German ancestry and were born in France. They first met and became acquainted while crossing the ocean to America and were married in Pennsylvania, where Christian Adelhelm for a time worked in the mines. He afterwards became an early settler at Burlington, Iowa, where his son, W. M. Adelhelm, was born July 15, 1863. The father died when this son was a small boy and the mother died later at Murray, Iowa. Their four children were: Rika, wife of Anton Schall of Murray, Iowa; W. M.; Tina, wife of Thomas Gore of Murray, Iowa; and Lizzie, who is married and lives in Oklahoma City.

Rosalie Avant

By the early death of his father W. M. Adelhelm was thrown upon his own resources and had only limited advantages in the way of an education. When most of his age were at home and in school he was accepting every legitimate means of earning his own livelihood, and constant industry has been the keynote of his success.

Coming to the Creek Nation in 1901, Mr. Adelhelm has lived on his present place near Holdenville since his marriage. The farm comprises his wife's allotment of 160 acres, and in the last fifteen years it has been improved in many ways and rendered highly valuable as a stock farm. Mr. Adelhelm raises some registered and high grade horses and a number of cattle. The farm is 3½ miles north of Holdenville.

On February 22, Washington's birthday, 1902, Mr. Adelhelm married Jennie Tuttle. She was born on the farm where she now resides, a daughter of Chester and Betsy Tuttle. Her father was a white man, while her mother was a fullblood Creek. Both died in what is now Hughes County. Mrs. Adelhelm by her first marriage to John McCaslin had four children, namely: Mrs. Mary Harris of Henryetta; Mrs. Nettie Palmer of Yeager, Hughes County; Mrs. Myrtle Long of Seminole; and Mrs. Jessie McBride of Henryetta. To the union of Mr. and Mrs. Adelhelm have been born four children, named Chester, Charles, Tina and Louis. The two older were born in time to receive allotments of Indian lands, but the two younger were not sharers in that distribution. Mrs. Adelhelm is a member of the Free Will Baptist Church and she was educated in the Tallahassee Mission.

FREDERICK EHLER. One of the leading business men of Kingfisher County, Frederick Ehler has the distinction of being the only merchant now in business at Hennessey who was here when the town was founded in 1889. While mercantile pursuits have claimed the major part of his attention, he has been interested also in other business, agricultural and financial enterprises, and in each direction has won well-earned success, in addition to conducting himself at all times as a practical, progressive, sound-minded and public-spirited citizen.

Mr. Ehler was born December 23, 1861, at West Alexandria, Ohio, and is a son of Harmon and Catherine (Schreel) Ehler. His father was born in Germany, in 1833, and was twenty-one years of age when he accompanied his mother to the United States, settling at West Alexandria, Ohio, where he continued to follow his trade of merchant tailor until his death, in November, 1900. He was married in 1858 to Catherine Schreel, a native of Ohio, born December 7, 1840, and they became the parents of four sons and two daughters, namely: Frederick, of this notice; George, born in 1863, who died in 1914; Mary, born in 1865, and now the wife of George Emerick, of Dayton, Ohio; Sallie, born in 1867, and now the wife of Lewis Herget, of Hennessey, Oklahoma; Joseph, born December 7, 1878; and Harry, born July 21, 1883.

Frederick Ehler received his education in the public schools of West Alexandria, Ohio, where he was graduated from the high school with the class of 1880, following which he enrolled as a student at the Ohio State University, Columbus, being graduated from that institution in 1884, with the degree of Bachelor of Arts. During the same year he went to Anderson, Indiana, where he became manager of a drug store, continuing in that capacity for six years and gaining much useful experience. However, Mr. Ehler felt that he was not advancing fast enough, and, believing that better opportunities awaited him in the West, he went to Kingman, Kansas, and secured employment as teller in the Kingman National Bank. This position Mr. Ehler held until 1889,

in which year he became a resident of Hennessey, here opening the first general store of the town. This was started in a modest and unassuming manner, but grew in strength and size with the growth and development of the city, and is now the most important department store in Kingfisher County, occupying a store 100 feet deep and with 100 feet front. This establishment, growing out of the needs of the community, has reached the proportions of a necessary commercial adjunct. Its success is due to the efforts and integrity of its proprietor, who has studied the wants of his patrons and supplied them with the best goods obtainable and at reasonable prices. He is also president of the Hennessey State Bank, one of the strong financial institutions of the county, is president of the Hennessey Electric Light Company, and has large farm holdings in Kingfisher County. In every possible way he has contributed to the upbuilding of the town and to the advancement of the general welfare. He has served as mayor of Hennessey, an office in which he secured a number of local improvements. Mr. Ehler is one of the best known Masons in Oklahoma, having been elected to the K. C. C. H. degree in 1905, and receiving the thirty-third honorary degree at Washington, District of Columbia, in October, 1907. He was one of the founders of the Scottish Rite Consistory of Oklahoma, organized at Guthrie, in 1900, and is a member of Indian Temple, Ancient Accepted Order of Nobles of the Mystic Shrine, of Oklahoma City.

Mr. Ehler was married at Hennessey, July 26, 1907, to Mrs. Annette B. Haskett, daughter of Joseph Blackburn. She was born in 1863, at Lawrenceville, Illinois, and after the death of her first husband, James Haskett, came as a widow to Oklahoma, in 1900, becoming principal of the Hennessey High School, a position which she held for four years. At the time of her marriage to Mr. Ehler she was acting in the capacity of editor of the Press-Democrat. Mrs. Ehler is prominent as a literary woman of marked talent, being the author of a book of poems entitled "The Fire Fly," and of a booklet relating to the early history of Hennessey and to the massacre of Pat Hennessey by Indians, in 1872, on the site where the town now stands and for whom it is named. Mrs. Ehler is likewise well known in club and fraternal circles, being chairman of the literary committee of the Oklahoma Women's Federated Clubs, and grand worthy matron for Oklahoma of the Order of the Eastern Star, in which organization she has filled all the chairs.

BEN F. AVANT. The name of this prominent farmer and cattle man of Osage County, who has conducted his operations in that vicinity of Oklahoma for the past twenty years, has a permanent memorial in the little Town of Avant, which was established as a station along the Midland Valley Railroad some years ago, and was given his name. The townsite comprises a part of the allotment of Mrs. Avant.

Through a period of more than thirty-five years Mr. Avant has been closely identified with the great cattle industry of the Southwest, both in Texas and in Oklahoma. He was born in Gonzales, Texas, January 6, 1868, a son of Abner and Letha (Elder) Avant. The Avant family is descended from French stock. Both parents were born in Tennessee, his father at Nashville, and they spent most of their lives in Texas. Abner Avant was in the Confederate army during the war, and the spring before he enlisted he branded 500 head of calves, but owing to the unsettled conditions and ravages resulting from the war this stock was all scattered or killed, and after his return from the army he had to begin his ranching operations with only a nucleus of about ten calves. Abner Avant spent all his career as a farmer and stock raiser, and lived in the vicinity of Gonzales until his death in 1901 at the age of seventy-two. His first wife and the mother of Ben Avant died when the latter was nine years of age. She was the mother of six children: Mamie, the wife of M. E. Lowry of Tishomingo, Oklahoma; A. M., who lives at Marfa, Texas; Ella, wife of John F. Laird of Wrightsboro, Texas; R. F., of Dilley, Texas; Ben; and Eula, wife of Charles Lory of Del Rio, Texas. The father married for his second wife Mattie Davis, and the one child of that union is Wallace M., now living at Jourdanton, Texas.

The early life of Ben Avant up to the year 1890 was spent in the vicinity of Gonzales, Texas. He acquired his education from local schools and has lived close to the activities of ranch and range all his life. In 1890 he went to Atascosa County, in the country south of San Antonio, and was employed as a cowboy. On June 1, 1892, he came into the Osage country with the cattle firm of Gussett, Brooks & Company, and remained in their employ until the fall of 1893. In 1894 he took the firm's herd of horses into Arkansas, where he sold them, and went back to Texas. In 1895 Mr. Avant returned to Osage County and has lived in this locality practically ever since. He was connected with the Skinner Cattle Company for a time, but in 1896 began independent operations as a cattleman and farmer. Like most men engaged in the business, met adversities, and several times has "gone broke," but has had the courage and persistence to begin over again and for a number of years has been prosperous and one of the substantial business men of Osage County. His home has been at Avant since 1895 with the exception of two years when he and his family resided in Tulsa in order that the children might have proper educational advantages. Mr. Avant has 200 acres of farming land, also owns 1,800 acres of grazing land, and keeps under lease about 1,200 acres more. He and his family reside in a modern home which was built in 1911 just outside the corporation limits of Avant.

When the Midland Valley Railroad was built through Osage County a postoffice was established and given the name of Avant, and as already stated, the townsite, where is now located a flourishing village, was originally a part of Mrs. Avant's allotment.

In 1895 Mr. Avant married Rosa Lee Rogers. She was born in Osage County July 8, 1877, a daughter of Lewis and Ellen (Ross) Rogers. Her mother is now deceased and her father resides at Pawhuska. Mrs. Avant's mother was a member of the Osage tribe, while her father was of Cherokee birth and extraction, but was adopted into the Osage tribe. Mr. and Mrs. Avant have two children: Theodore, born March 22, 1898; and Ethel, born February 16, 1901.

ADAM BERT FAIR, M. D. When the Kiowa and Comanche country was opened to settlement in 1901, among the thousands of new comers, including professional men of all classes, there was perhaps no better equipped physician who selected the new town of Lawton as his home than Dr. Adam B. Fair, who a few years later removed to Frederick, now in Tillman County, and has since developed not only a large professional practice as a physician and surgeon, but has also made himself a factor in the varied social life and enterprise of that community.

While Doctor Fair may be properly regarded as a pioneer of Southwestern Oklahoma, earlier generations of the same family earned similar distinctions in the territory and State of Iowa. Doctor Fair was born at Agency, Iowa, November 22, 1870. His father, E. D. Fair, was born in Maryland February 15, 1846, and has had his home at Agency almost continuously since he was ten years of age. The grandfather, John Fair, was a native of Pennsylvania, where the Fair family settled in colonial days on coming from Germany. John Fair was born about 1809, and after living in Pennsylvania a number of years took his family out to the new State of Iowa in 1856, and was one of the pioneer farmers in that locality, where he died at the age of eighty-three. E. D. Fair has been a bridge contractor, a manufacturer of iron bridges, and at one time operated a factory at Ottumwa, not far from Agency. He is now living retired in the latter city. The maiden name of his wife was Sarah E. Giltner, who was born near Agency in 1848. Her father, William Giltner, a native of Indiana, moved out to Iowa Territory about 1840, and was one of the first farmers in the vicinity of Agency. He was a prominent factor in that section of Iowa, known for his influential part in civil and political affairs, and reared a large family, his descendants being now scattered over that and other states. Doctor Fair was the oldest of the six children born to E. D. and Sarah E. Fair. His sister Loie is the wife of C. E. Adams, who is a stockholder and employee in the J. W. Edgerly Wholesale Drug Company at Ottumwa, Iowa, where they reside; Amy married O. E. Slafter, who lives in Fort Dodge, Iowa, where he is an assistant railroad superintendent; Jessie married Roy W. Johnston, an Ottumwa manufacturer, and the son of A. W. Johnston, who invented the Johnston Ruffler and other devices that have had an extensive manufacture and sale; Pearl is the wife of Dr. Benjamin Erb, a dentist at Anamosa, Iowa; William E., a resident of Cheyenne, Wyoming, is assistant bank examiner in Wyoming.

Adam Bert Fair grew up at Agency, attended the public schools there, graduating from the high school in 1887, and soon afterward entered the University of Iowa. In 1893 he was graduated Ph. B., having in the meantime pursued medical studies one year, and in 1895 was graduated M. D. from the medical department of the university. He took a prominent part in the student life of the university, was a member of the Irving Institute, a literary society, belonged to the University Band, was active in Young Men's Christian Association work, and also interested in athletics. In the past twenty years Doctor Fair has never abated his ambition for continued acquisition of scientific knowledge. He has taken several courses at the Chicago policlinic and one postgraduate course at the West Side Post-Graduate School in Chicago, where he specialized in diseases of the eye, ear, nose and throat.

His practice as a physician began at Danville, Iowa, in 1895, and he had a profitable business when he left there six years later. At the opening of the Southwestern Oklahoma country in 1901 he came to Lawton, but after three years in that city removed in 1904 to Frederick. The occasion of his location in that town was his appointment as health officer for what was then Southwest Comanche County, which was then being ravaged by an epidemic of smallpox. After strenuous efforts he succeeded in getting the plague well under control, and equal success has followed his efforts in building up a large general medical and surgical practice. He is a member of the County and State Medical societies and the American Medical Association, and in 1912 was honored with the position of vice president of the State Medical Society. He also served as censor of the Fifth District Society, comprising the counties of Kiowa, Tillman, Comanche, Stephens, Jefferson, Greer and Jackson. He has served as city health officer at Frederick.

Doctor Fair is independent in politics, and in his home church, the Methodist, has served as trustee and steward since the society built it and was president of the building committee. Doctor Fair is a stockholder in the Bank of Commerce at Frederick and has always allied himself with movements for local improvement. He was formerly a member of the Business Men's Association at Frederick. In Masonry he is a past master by service of Frederick Lodge No. 249, Ancient Free and Accepted Masons, and belongs to Frederick Chapter No. 41, Royal Arch Masons, and Frederick Commandery No. 19, Knight Templars, of which he is now recorder. Other affiliations are with the Modern Woodmen of America, the Knights and Ladies of Security, the Royal Neighbors, the Modern Brotherhood of America, and he was formerly a member of the Independent Order of Odd Fellows.

On June 24, 1896, at Iowa City, Iowa, Doctor Fair married Miss Clara R. Harvat, a graduate of the collegiate department of the State University of Iowa. She died October 22, 1911, leaving three children: Claude, Helen, and Robert, all of whom are attending school at Frederick. In September, 1912, Doctor Fair was married at Frederick to Miss Alma Boyd, daughter of J. M. Boyd, now a resident of Oklahoma City. Mrs. Fair was for several years a clerk in the Frederick postoffice, and is talented in vocal and instrumental music.

ROSCOE RIZLEY. Oklahoma is essentially a young and vigorous commonwealth, and in its field of professional and commercial activities, as well as in the domain of productive industrial enterprise, there are found enlisted a notably large number of progressive, energetic, able and loyal young men of high civic ideals and sterling attributes of character. Among such young men who are doing their part in upbuilding the high standard of the bar of the state Beaver County affords its due quota, and a prominent and popular younger member of the legal profession who has here found a desirable stage for his activities is Roscoe Rizley, who is engaged in active general practice at Beaver, the county seat. Further interest attaches to his career by reason of the fact that he is a native of this county and a scion of one of the sterling pioneer families of this section of the state.

Mr. Rizley can claim as the place of his nativity no sumptuous domicile, for he was ushered into the world in the little sod house, or dug-out, on the new homestead claim of his father, on Clear Creek, Beaver County, where he was born on the 5th of July, 1892. He takes just pride in reverting to the fact that he is thus a true representative of pioneer conditions in the state to which he pays high appreciation and unfaltering fealty, and the passing years will but add historic interest to the story he can tell relative to the conditions that compassed him at the time of his birth.

Mr. Rizley is a son of Robert M. and Belle (McCown) Rizley, and he doubly honors his parents for the courage and determination which they manifested in enduring the hardships and vicissitudes incidental to establishing a home in a new frontier country. His father was born in Washington County, Arkansas, on the 16th of November, 1861, at which time that state was the stage of much of the military conflict incidental to the early operations in the Civil war, his parents having removed from Tennessee to that state in an early day. Robert M. Rizley was reared and educated in Arkansas, with such advantages as could be given to him by parents in very moderate circumstances. In 1885, as a young man of about twenty-four years, he came to Indian Territory, four years prior to the opening of the new Territory of Oklahoma to settlement, and he made the neutral strip known as No Man's Land, in the western part of the territory, his destination. On land twelve miles south of the present thriving town of Beaver he located on a tract of land and turned his attention to farming and stock growing, the land duly coming into his possession and his title being perfected after the organization of Oklahoma Territory, in 1890. He has developed one of the well improved and valuable farms of Beaver County and still resides on his homestead, which is devoted to diversified agriculture and to the raising of live stock. He is a republican in politics and has been active and influential in public affairs in Beaver County, as shown by the fact that four years of effective service were given by him as a member of the board of county commissioners. His marriage to Miss Belle McCown was solemnized in the year 1882, his wife having been born in Illinois, in 1864, and her death having occurred June 8, 1902, in a hospital in Kansas City, Missouri, where she had been taken for treatment. She had been a devoted wife and mother, was a woman of abiding Christian faith and practice, and she had the warm esteem of all who came within the sphere of her influence. Of the three children the subject of this review was the second in order of birth and is the only son; Alta, who was born on the pioneer homestead in Beaver County, January 27, 1887, is the wife of Oscar Gardner, a farmer of Beaver County, to whom she was united in wedlock on the 20th of January, 1908, their two children being Velma and Bernard; the younger daughter, Verne Elizabeth, born August 13, 1896, remains with her father on the old homestead.

After having availed himself fully of the advantages of the public schools of Beaver County, Roscoe Rizley gained through his own well directed efforts and industry the financial reinforcement which made possible the attainment of his ambition. Through his own resources he defrayed the entire expense incidental to the prosecution of a full course in the Kansas City School of Law, where he applied himself with characteristic diligence and with that deeper appreciation that ever comes when desired objects have been gained through personal effort. In this institution he was graduated on the 7th of June, 1915, and after receiving his degree of Bachelor of Laws he immediately returned to his native county, where he was forthwith admitted to the Oklahoma bar and has since been in active and successful general practice at Beaver. He has already won his spurs and proved himself a careful and resourceful trial lawyer and well fortified counselor, so that his continued advancement in his profession is fully assured. Mr. Rizley subordinates all else to the work of his profession, but takes a lively interest in community affairs of a public nature, the while he is found arrayed as a staunch and effective advocate of the principles of the republican party, in the faith of which he was reared.

ROBERT H. RICHARDSON. Almost universal is a natural inclination toward some one line of effort, and in the lives of many individuals this becomes so compelling an impulse that it must be followed, thereby bringing inward satisfaction and contented existence. Other talents may bring success in a practical way, but no man feels entirely free until he can pursue the path that nature indicates. Thus, for a time, the law, civil engineering and honorable public service absorbed the time and attention of Robert H. Richardson, the present able editor of the Democrat at Erick, Oklahoma, but journalism was his secret ambition and the printing office training a coveted stepping-stone. He has shown himself a man of versatility and in the profession that now claims him he has displayed conspicuous ability.

Robert H. Richardson was born in Jackson County, Florida, December 18, 1869, and is a son of H. H. and Martha A. (Easterling) Richardson. The maternal ancestry may be traced to Scotland, but the Richardsons came to America from England and for many generations have left an impress on the best citizenship of many states of the Union.

H. H. Richardson was born in 1826, in Georgia, and died in 1871, at Campbelltown, Florida. Following his marriage to Martha A. Easterling, who was born at Social Center, Georgia, in 1834, he moved to Jackson County, Florida, where he engaged in farming and raising stock during the rest of his life. For many years he was identified with the Masonic fraternity. Of his children but three reached maturity, James N., Elizabeth B. and Robert H., the last named being the only survivor. The mother of the above family died in 1890, at Birmingham, Alabama.

Robert H. Richardson attended the public schools and in 1886 was graduated from the high school of Marianna, Florida, following which he applied himself to the study of law for eight months at Montgomery, Alabama, in the meanwhile giving attention to the study of civil engineering and making practical use of his knowledge along this line in Alabama, Texas and Iowa, until 1890, without determining to make this profession a life career. On the other hand circumstances so arranged his life that in that year he was able to enter a printing office at Cerrillos, New Mexico, and after becoming proficient in this trade he followed the same over New Mexico, Texas, Colorado and California. In 1898 he went into business for himself at Breckenridge, California, where he edited the Breckenridge Bulletin for one year.

In 1901 Mr. Richardson enlisted in the United States army and with his regiment went to the Phillipine Islands, serving three years, being attached to the adjutant-general's department. During this time his newspaper talent only slept and shortly after his return, in 1904, he became connected with a newspaper at Jackson, California, remaining there six months, and afterward, until 1907, worked on other papers in that state, and during two subsequent years worked on Texas papers, in 1909 buying the Kemp News, which journal he edited with vigor and ability for three years. In 1912 Mr. Richardson removed to Sweetwater, Texas, where he again invested, purchasing a one-third interest in the Sweetwater Reporter, which he retained for five months and then disposed of it and moved to Kaufman and for one year was associated there with the Kaufman Daily and Weekly Post.

Mr. Richardson then became interested elsewhere, conducting a newspaper at Winona, Texas, for six months, and for the same length of time, the Times at Chandler, Texas. In 1914 he came to Oklahoma and was connected with the Leader at Ryan until April 1, 1915, when he leased the Democrat at Erick and has had charge of all departments of the paper ever since. Democratic in politics, it has been established for eleven years, during which time its fortunes have fluctuated as have those of many other publications, but under Mr. Richardson's control and editing it has made rapid strides forward in public popularity and circulates all over Beckham County and also has a list of outside subscribers. Mr. Richardson recognizes the fact that he is conducting a modern newspaper, and realizing from a wide experience that the general intelligence of the present day demands much of a newspaper, it often being the single intellectual resource at hand, leaves no stone unturned to satisfy his readers.

In Jauary, 1909, Mr. Richardson was married, at Neches, Texas, to Miss Bertha E. Conerly, who is a daughter of O. F. Conerly. Mr. Conerly owns a valuable farm in Anderson County, Texas, but makes his home with Mr. and Mrs. Richardson. They have four children: Robert H., who was born January 26, 1910; Elizabeth, who was born May 20, 1911; Owen Lester, who was born September 11, 1913; and Wilson Ewing, who was born in March, 1915. Mr. Richardson and family are members of the Methodist Episcopal Church and he is superintendent of the Sunday-school.

Always a democrat in his political views, he has done yeoman work for his party in his newspapers, his trenchant pen loyally assisting his party's candidates. At the same time his editorial ability is exercised in other directions than political, and his advocacy of civic reforms, his calling attention to worthy charities and his appeals for educational and religious progress for the city have met with general approval. Fraternally Mr. Richardson is both a Knight of Pythias and an Odd Fellow. He is a member, in the former organization, of Kemp Lodge, of Kemp, Texas, of which he has served two terms as chancellor commander; and as an Odd Fellow belongs to the lodge at Erick and is past noble grand of the lodges at Kaufman and Chandler, Texas. He longs also to the Praetorians.

PHINEAS F. WRIGHT. The vital spirit that has animated those who have pushed forward the march of development and progress in America from the early colonial era through the stages that have marked the advance of civilization as the star of empire has led its westward course, has been distinctly shown in the character and achievement of Phineas Finch Wright, who became a settler of Oklahoma Territory in the year that the first section of the former Indian Territory was thrown open to white settlement and who has done well his part in connection with the marvelous civic and material development and upbuilding of a great and prosperous commonwealth. That he proved well equipped for such pioneer activities is specially interesting to note in view of the fact that he was reared under pioneer influences, his parents having established their home in the wilds of Wisconsin when that state was still under territorial government. Mr. Wright, who has but recently compassed the psalmist's span of three score years and ten, is senior member of the representative firm of P. F. Wright & Son, engaged in the hardware and agricultural implement business in the Village of Wakita, Grant County, and his valued co-adjutor in the control of the substantial and prosperous enterprise is his elder son, Fred C., who is an alert and progressive business man.

Mr. Wright was born at Potosi, Grant County, Wisconsin, on the 1st of April, 1845, and not until three years later was Wisconsin admitted as one of the sovereign states of the Union. He is a son of Phineas and Amanda (Finch) Wright, the former of whom was born in the State of New York and the latter in the Province of Ontario, Canada. The father of Mr. Wright became one of the influential pioneer settlers of Grant County, Wisconsin, where he obtained land and reclaimed the same to cultivation, besides which he identified himself also with other important lines of enterprise that tended to foster the development and prosperity of the community. He owned and operated a flour mill and was also concerned to a considerable extent with the lumber industry of Wisconsin in the pioneer days, both he and his wife having continued their residence in the Badger State until their death.

Phineas F. Wright, the immediate subject of this review, attended the common schools of his native county until he had attained to the age of fourteen years, and he early began to assist in the work of his father's flour mill. The great lumber industry was then at its height in Wisconsin and young Wright soon became identified with work in the timber forests and the operation of sawmills, with which line of enterprise he continued his association until he had attained to the age of twenty-

Henry Schmale and family

six years. Thereafter he was for a few years engaged in the general merchandise business at Whitehall, Trempealeau County, Wisconsin, and while a resident of that place he became active and influential in local politics and served two years as sheriff of the county, his allegiance having been given unreservedly to the republican party, to the cause of which he has given his stanch support during the long intervening years.

In 1881 Mr. Wright removed with his family to Winfield, Cowley County, Kansas, where he continued to be engaged in the mercantile business until 1885, when he became one of the founders of the Town of Bluff City, Harper County, that state, where he established himself in the general merchandise business and where he remained thus engaged until 1889, when he became one of those progressive and ambitious men who took advantage of the opening of Oklahoma Territory to settlement, the formal organization of the territory having occurred in the following year. Mr. Wright was one of those who "made the run" with the great throng that pushed forward into the new territory to enter claims for land on the memorable 22d of April, 1889, and he obtained a homestead claim 10½ miles southeast of Hennessey, in what is now Kingfisher County. He reclaimed and improved this land, perfected his title to the same, and after the lapse of two years he made an advantageous sale of the property. He then returned to Bluff City, Kansas, where he continued to be engaged in the hardware business until 1895, when he came again to Oklahoma Territory and became one of the pioneer settlers of the new Town of Wakita, Grant County. He erected the second business building in the town and became one of the first merchants of the place, so that all of pioneer honors are his in connection with this now thriving and enterprising village, which is the trading center for an extensive district of an important and prosperous farming community.

Mr. Wright has from the beginning been one of the most influential and honored citizens of Wakita, and his hold upon popular confidence and esteem is shown by the fact that he served for a long period as a member of the village council and thereafter gave a number of years to specially effective service in the office of mayor of the town. He has been liberal and public-spirited in giving his co-operation for the furtherance of all measures and enterprises that have tended to advance the social and material progress and prosperity of the village and county, and through his well ordered activities as a business man he has achieved substantial success. During virtually the entire period of his residence at Wakita Mr. Wright has here been actively engaged in the hardware and agricultural implement business, and in association with his older son he controls a trade that extends throughout the wide area of country normally tributary to Wakita.

In 1873 Mr. Wright wedded Miss Lottie Brush, who was born in Wisconsin, in the year 1855, a daughter of Benjamin and Mary Brush. Mrs. Wright was summoned to the life eternal, and is survived by two children, Florence and Fred C. Florence, who was born April 29, 1875, is now the wife of Dr. Charles W. Middleton, and they have one child, Jack Wright Middleton, who was born December 20, 1910.

Fred C. Wright was born at Whitehall, Trempealeau County, Wisconsin, on the 7th of November, 1878, and acquired his early education in the schools of Kansas, after which he completed a thorough course in a business university at St. Joseph, Missouri, in which institution he was graduated as a member of the class of 1895. As already noted, he is now junior member of the firm of P. F. Wright & Son, of Wakita, and in addition to being thus concerned with the hardware and implement business he is also the owner of the Wakita electric light plant, of which he has had control since 1913 and which he maintains at a high standard of efficiency. On the 12th of January, 1912, he married Miss Cora Palmer, of Lyndon, Osage County, Kansas, she being a young woman of exceptional talent and gracious personality. Mrs. Wright completed her musical education in the City of Berlin, Germany, and has fine ability as a pianist and vocalist. She is a daughter of Thomas J. Palmer, concerning whom specific mention is made on other pages of this work. Mr. and Mrs. Wright have two children—Lois Janet, who was born May 4, 1913, and Robert Hardy, who was born February 3, 1915.

The second marriage of Phineas P. Wright was solemnized at Anthony, Kansas, on the 23d of November, 1897, when Miss Kate Lewis became his wife. Mrs. Wright was born in the State of Ohio, on the 18th of May, 1874, and in the same state were born her parents, Elisha and Rachael (Chamberlain) Lewis, who removed to Kansas when she was a girl. Mr. and Mrs. Wright have three children—Ollie E., who was born March 27, 1899; Lewis Wayne, who was born August 30, 1901; and Geneva Ruth, who was born July 16, 1911.

HENRY SCHMALE. One of Pawnee County's most sterling, upright and honored citizens was the late Henry Schmale, who had lived in Oklahoma since 1893 and had gained a large amount of material prosperity and the esteem of hundreds of friends and business associates before death took him on May 12, 1916.

During his residence in Oklahoma he was primarily a farmer. In that occupation he showed the characteristic German industry, enterprise and good judgment. He had a long and active career, served as a young man in the Franco-Prussian war of 1870-71, but after coming to America more than forty years ago became one of the country's most loyal citizens, and was first and last devoted to the land of his adoption.

He was born in Hessen-Darmstadt, Germany, August 27, 1845, and was therefore in his seventy-first year when he died. His parents Henricus and Mary (Weifenbach) Schmale spent all their lives in Germany. On both sides the respective families had been German farmers for many generations. Henricus Schmale was one of the substantial tillers of the soil in Hessen-Darmstadt, now known as the Grand Duchy of Hesse.

The oldest of five children, the late Henry Schmale was the only one to come to America. His elder sister, Mrs. Maria Deling, is still living near the old German homestead, the wife of a prosperous farmer. The younger sister, Mrs. Sophia Stein, is also the wife of a German farmer. The son George resides upon the old farm and occupies the house in which the children were born and reared. Fred was a farmer in that district until his death.

The late Henry Schmale spent his first twenty-eight years on the old homestead with his parents. He attended the excellent schools of his native land up to the age of fourteen and as a youth served an apprenticeship at the trade of shoemaker in the City of Darmstadt. He became a skilled workman. In the meantime he was also called upon to serve his country in accordance with the laws of the Fatherland, and it was to his honor that he served faithfully and well in the German army during the Franco-Prussian war.

Mr. Schmale came to the United States in 1873. He soon went west and remained a few months in Muscatine, Iowa, but in June, 1874, returned to New York City. There he found employment as a journeyman at his trade for about five years. Industry was the keynote to his success in life, and he was pre-eminently a man of action, willing to get success only as a result of personal ability and well directed endeavor. He possessed a strong intellect and broad views and it is noteworthy that as a boy engaged in learning his trade he attended a medical school three years, taking up the study of this science chiefly during the evening hours.

Mr. Schmale was married in 1877 and as a bridal trip returned to Germany. They remained in that country a little more than a year, and on coming back to the United States Mr. Schmale established a shoe store on Fulton Street in the City of Brooklyn. Starting with a modest capital, he soon had a trade, and made a specialty of fine custom work in the manufacture of boots and shoes. He was one of Brooklyn's merchants until the late '80s. He then moved to the City of Chicago and established a shoe store on the west side of that city. He was in the shoe business until the spring of 1893.

At the opening of the Cherokee strip or outlet in September, 1893, Mr. Schmale made the run into the new territory and made his destination the present Town of Perry in Noble County. He did not enter a claim, but on the 23d of November the same year filed a claim to his homestead in Pawnee County. He at once settled down to the hard and practical life of a homesteader and in clearing up his land he found a great many Indian relics and assembled a very interesting collection of such.

In the course of years Mr. Schmale developed one of the model rural estates of Pawnee County. He endured in the meanwhile the responsibilities and burdens which fell to the lot of the pioneer, and it was well for him that he had a trade and could make use of it in providing for himself and family during the early years of stress and comparative poverty. The first two years he spent on his claim, he walked to and from his house to the City of Jennings, 3½ miles away, and made boots and shoes and repaired them in order to earn a living for his household. It is said that he arose at 4 o'clock in the morning, spent several hours working on his land, and then walked to the village and applied himself steadily to the work of his trade oftentimes until late in the evening. To such men success comes as a natural result and as a richly merited reward. Smiling prosperity crowned the efforts of Mr. Schmale long before his death.

Before his death he had about fifty acres of his land under cultivation, and all his farm under lease for oil development purposes. Hence he was in independent circumstances and was well able to retire, though his active spirit did not allow him to forego work altogether, and he spent much time in supervising his farm. For some years he had been a successful grower of Percheron draft horses, had sold a number of fine animals of that type, and a short time before his death owned a herd of about ten head. He also raised a number of mules on his farm. Another feature of his farm was dairying, and he kept for that purpose a herd of Jersey cattle. He was also known in Pawnee County as a successful poultryman, and for several years he had made a specialty of raising chickens and selling eggs. Each season he had two modern incubators employed for hatching.

After taking out his naturalization papers, Mr. Schmale began voting with the democratic party. After the campaign of 1876 he became a republican, but finally gravitated back into the ranks of the democratic party and to that gave his allegiance the rest of his days. While never a seeker for political office, he was several times given local offices of public trust and was a man who could be depended upon in every such position. Both he and his wife were members of the Lutheran Church.

In New York City in 1877 he married Miss Annie Reckert. Mrs. Schmale was born in Westphalia, Germany, June 22, 1856, and died at her home in Pawnee County, October 16, 1915, thus preceding her husband to the beyond about six months. She had come alone to the United States at the age of nineteen and found employment in New York City until her marriage. She was a devoted wife and mother, and was a loyal and effective aid to Mr. Schmale in his successful career. She was christened in the Lutheran Church as an infant and was confirmed at the age of fourteen.

The late Mr. and Mrs. Henry Schmale had five children. The oldest, Fred, died at Guthrie, Oklahoma, at the age of sixteen. The daughter Marie is the wife of Henry Rapp, and they reside at DeQueen, Sevier County, Arkansas. Henry Jr. now has the active supervision of the home farm and also leases an adjoining farm. The younger children, Frieda and Martha, are still at home and in school.

F. E. THURMAN was one of the alert and enterprising young men who were attracted to the southwestern oil fields at the beginning of exploration and exploitation, and for ten years has been a resident of Bartlesville. Formerly in the oil business, he now gives most of his attention to the insurance, surety bond and loan firm of McIlheny & Thurman. In insurance circles he is one of the most prominent men in Oklahoma, and has been officially identified with several organizations covering the activities of that business.

F. E. Thurman was born at West Union, Ohio, March 9, 1872, a son of J. M. and Mary Elizabeth (McCormick) Thurman, both natives of Ohio. His father died October 4, 1915, in West Union, while the mother died when F. E. Thurman was seven years old. J. M. Thurman has for the greater part of his active career been a banker at West Union and also for a long time has served as treasurer of Adams County. F. E. Thurman is the only survivor of two children, his brother William having died at the age of thirty-eight.

During the seventeen years that he lived at home he gained a substantial public school education, and his career was early directed to business affairs. His first practical experience was in the Cincinnati branch office of the Dun's Mercantile Agency, and he was soon afterwards sent out as traveling representative, spending seven years with that firm. At the beginning of the oil excitement he came to Neodesha, Kansas, and for two years was connected with the Prairie Oil & Gas Company in the producing department. Then for five years he was connected with the Barnsdall Oil Company, after which he entered business for himself in the general insurance, surety bond and loan field. This has been his principal activity since December, 1912.

Mr. Thurman is secretary of the People's Savings & Loan Association, and has held that office since the organization of the association. He is also president of the State Association of Local Fire Insurance Agents and president of the Local Fire Prevention Association. Since May, 1909, he has served as clerk of the board of education at Bartlesville, and can always be found among those working for the welfare of the city and state. His Masonic connections include the Blue Lodge of which he is a past master, the thirty-second degree consistory, the Mystic Shrine and the Eastern Star. He is also a member of the Benevolent and Protective Order of Elks. During the Spanish-American war he was in the Fourth Ohio Infantry as corporal, and saw some active campaigning in Porto Rico. During that experience he acted as correspondent for the Portsmouth Daily Blade. On October 31, 1904, Mr. Thurman married Miss Lucile Elizabeth Calvert, who was born in Kentucky and is a daughter of Isaac Calvert.

CHARLES FRENCH TWYFORD. Now serving as county attorney of Beaver County, Mr. Twyford has been known in different sections of Oklahoma both as a newspaper man and as a lawyer. He has made a splendid record both in his private practice and in the administration of his official duties since locating at Beaver. It is a matter of interest that Mrs. Twyford, his wife, is a graduate physician. The Twyford family has had many interesting associations with Oklahoma affairs ever since the year of the original opening. His father was one of Oklahoma's Eighty-Niners, while his mother has long been distinguished as having taught the first regular public school in Oklahoma Territory, and for her varied achievements and influence in both educational and missionary fields.

It was on a cotton plantation in Pontotoc County, Mississippi, that Charles French Twyford was born, December 1, 1875, a son of Samuel B. and Lucy E. (French) Twyford. His father was born April 1, 1843, at Terre Haute, Indiana, a son of Charles C. and Lucy (Belt) Twyford, who were natives of the State of Delaware and of Scotch ancestry. Samuel B. Twyford had a varied and active career. In early years he was a railroad man. At the outbreak of the Civil war he was living at Champaign, Illinois, and there enlisted with the Eleventh Illinois Volunteer Cavalry. After serving three months with that regiment he was transferred to Company M of the Fifth Missouri Cavalry, and was given scout duty with the rank and pay of a captain. He remained in active service until the close of the war. He then lived in Illinois for a few years, but in 1872 with an ox team wagon he drove from Illinois to Marion County, Kansas. There he was a grade contractor during the construction of the Atchison, Topeka & Santa Fe Railroad through that part of Kansas.

In 1873, two years before the birth of his son, Charles F., he removed to Pontotoc County, Mississippi, and engaged in cotton planting there until 1879. Returning to Kansas he resumed farming in Marion County, and lived in that state until 1889. In that year, which marked the opening of Oklahoma Territory, he joined in the rush, and was fortunate in locating a good tract of Government land near the present Town of Edmond. He was one of the best types of early Oklahoma settlers and was a progressive farmer and respected citizen of that locality until his death on March 28, 1898. He was an active member of the Methodist Episcopal Church all his life.

His wife, Lucy E. French, whom he married at Greenfield, Illinois, December 1, 1874, was born at Hamilton, Ohio, March 17, 1844, a daughter of John and Jane (French) French, who were natives of Hastings, England. Mrs. Twyford is a graduate of the Illinois State Normal School at Bloomington and took special work in the Illinois State University at Champaign. For five years she was a teacher in St. Louis and later did missionary work for ten years in Mississippi, organizing a number of churches and also conducting schools. In 1879, in addition to the burdens of her household and the care of her children, she began teaching in Kansas, and for nine years conducted schools at different points in that state. Soon after coming to Oklahoma with her family, in 1889, she organized and directed as teacher the first public school opened in the territory. The session began in September following the opening in April, and that was Edmond's first public school. It was conducted for a term of nine months, and this school graduated the first eighth grade class graduated in Oklahoma Territory or Oklahoma State. This class, all of whom were girls, and eleven in number, made up the first enrollment at the Central State Normal of Edmond. During the First Territorial Legislature Mrs. Twyford was one of the committee of five named by the governor to draft school laws and apportion school districts. In 1891 she took up church work under the auspices of the Congregational Church, and was engaged in organizing and building churches up to 1901. In the year that she retired from active responsibilities she had completed more than thirty years of active service in behalf of schools and religion. While in Oklahoma she was the prime factor in the erection of five rural churches in the vicinity of Edmond. She was regularly ordained to the ministry in 1891, and filled the pulpit in each of the churches which she organized. Since she retired in 1901 she has been regarded as one of the most useful women Oklahoma ever had. She now lives at 1015 North Kelly Street in Oklahoma City. To her marriage with Mr. Twyford were born five children: Charles French; Mary A., born August 5, 1877; Ethel, born June 20, 1879, and died in infancy; Theresa, born June 17, 1881; and James S., born June 5, 1882.

The atmosphere of culture and good ideals, every incentive to a life of integrity and honorable activity, were afforded Charles F. Twyford from childhood up. He obtained his education at the Central State Normal in Edmond and at Kingfisher College. He paid his way while in college by work as a printer, a trade which afforded him his livelihood for a number of years. Subsequently he became one of the editors and publishers of the Oklahoma Labor Signal and the Oklahoma Farmer. In 1903 he established the News at Bridgeport, conducted it twelve months, and then went to Topeka, Kansas, where he was employed at his trade as printer three years.

In 1909 Mr. Twyford entered the Epworth University School of Law at Oklahoma City, remained in attendance three years, and was admitted to practice June 12, 1911. In 1913 he located at Beaver, and has already secured a satisfying share of practice and his thorough qualifications were the basis for his successful candidacy as republican nominee for the office of county attorney of Beaver County in 1914. Fraternally he is a member of the Alva Lodge of Elks.

On September 17, 1913, at El Dorado, Oklahoma, Mr. Twyford married Miss May Drew, daughter of William H. and Ethelda (Wilson) Drew, who were natives of the State of Michigan. Mrs. Doctor Twyford was born in Greer County, Oklahoma, September 15, 1892, was educated at Fort Worth, Texas, in the university there, and with the class of 1913 graduated from the medical department of the University of Oklahoma and was awarded the degree Doctor of Medicine.

CLIFFORD G. MILLER. Having won a place among the progressive newspaper men of Western Oklahoma solely through the medium of his own efforts, Clifford G. Miller is eminently entitled to the confidence and esteem of his fellow men which he enjoys. Like the greater number of newspaper men in this part of the state, he has worked his way to the top from the most humble position, having commenced his career as a pressman's apprentice and being at this time proprietor and editor of a publication which has its acknowledged place among the journals of Beckham County—the Elk City Leader.

Mr. Miller belongs to a family which originated in France, and the American progenitor of which was his great-grandfather, David H. Miller, who was a pioneer of Missouri and homesteaded land on the present site of the City of St. Joseph. His son, Jonas Miller, was born on the Missouri farm, residing there until the period of the Civil war, when he went to Texas and became a pioneer of Grayson County, where he owned a gristmill and also followed the trade of blacksmith and wheelwright. Later he moved to Carroll County, Missouri, and there his death occurred about the year 1908, when he was sixty-one years of age.

J. W. Miller, son of Jonas Miller, and father of Clifford G. Miller, was born December 3, 1859, in Grayson County, Texas, and in 1865 was taken to Carroll County, Missouri, where he passed many years in agricultural pursuits. In 1898 he went to Buchanan County, Missouri, where he continued his farming and stock-raising operations until 1906, since which time he has been a resident of Elk City, employed in the construction department of a railroad. He is a member of the Independent Order of Odd Fellows at Elk City. Mr. Miller was married in 1883 to Miss Hattie E. Teter, of Dewitt, Carroll County, Missouri, who was born in that county in 1863. Four children have been born to this union: Clifford G.; Russell W., who is a general workman and resides at Elk City; and Jenevieve and Joe W., who reside with their parents.

Clifford G. Miller attended the public schools of Carroll County, Missouri, being graduated from the high school at Saxton Station, Buchanan County, in the class of 1904. In 1905 he attended Hill's Business College at St. Joseph, Missouri, but in the meantime, in the fall of 1903, had entered upon his business career as an employe in the general offices of the Burlington Railroad at St. Joseph, remaining there for about two years. Mr. Miller received his introduction to the printing business as an employe of the Combe Printing Company at St. Joseph, where he acted as pressman's apprentice from 1905 until October, 1906, when he came to Elk City, Oklahoma. He first worked at various jobs, accepting such honorable employment as came his way until he could gain a foothold, and in the spring of 1909 joined the Sayre Headlight, with which he was connected only for a short time. Later he was with the George Winn Printing Company until October 1, 1909, and then with J. W. McMurtry, printer, for two months, and December 3, 1909, went to Clinton, where he helped George Rhinehart start the Clinton Times. From Clinton Mr. Miller went to Arapaho, where for two years and two months he was connected with the Arapaho Bee, with J. W. Wagner, editor, and in November, 1914, returned to Elk City. Here, December 28, 1914, he bought a one-half interest in the Elk City Leader, and published the first edition January 7, 1915. Nine days after its appearance G. F. Stayton bought the other one-half interest, and the partners continued the publication of this sheet until August 3, 1915, when they sold out. On the 30th, however, Mr. Miller was given the opportunity of buying the paper again, and, the deal being consummated, he has continued to publish the Leader to the present time. The paper is independent in politics and circulates in Beckham and the surrounding counties, already having a respectable foreign list. The plant is situated on Jefferson Street and is modernly equipped for the publication of a neat, clear and attractive newspaper. The Leader has proven an excellent advertising medium, and under Mr. Miller's able management is daily growing in public favor and confidence.

Mr. Miller was married April 16, 1911, at Arapaho, Oklahoma, to Miss Dovie M. Miller, daughter of G. W. Miller, an extensive farm and ranch owner of Custer County, Oklahoma. They have no children.

ROBERT N. THOMAS. A member of the banking fraternity of Blaine County who has gained a substantial position in the confidence of the people of his community is Robert N. Thomas, cashier of the Greenfield State Bank of Greenfield, who became connected with this institution in 1909 as bookkeeper and after three months was promoted to his present capacity. Mr. Thomas belongs to the young and enthusiastic element which has been mainly instrumental in the development of the town, and has been a leading factor in educational affairs here, having been an instructor before entering upon his career as a banker.

Robert N. Thomas was born at Osage City, Osage County, Kansas, September 18, 1884, and is a son of Jesse and Hattie (Jones) Thomas, and a member of a family that, originating in Wales, emigrated to this country at an early day and became pioneers of Missouri. His father was born in 1833, near Springfield, Clark County, Ohio, and from his native state removed to Detroit, Dickinson County, Kansas, where he was married. After some years passed in agricultural pursuits there he removed to Osage City, Kansas, in 1882, and continued as a farmer and stock raiser until 1892, then coming to Oklahoma and taking up a homestead of 160 acres, 3½ miles northeast of Greenfield, in Blaine County, which still belongs to his estate, and on which he died in 1910. Mr. Thomas was a stanch democrat and good citizen, and was fraternally connected with the Masons. Mrs. Thomas was born in Wales in 1855, and when fourteen years of age came to this country with her parents, the family settling near Detroit, Kansas. She still survives and makes her home at Stillwater, Oklahoma. Mr. and Mrs. Thomas became the parents of seven children: Mary, who is the wife of Harry Ellenwood, of Williamstown, Vermont, formerly a contractor, but now an agriculturist; Alice, who is the wife of C. C. Walker, a farmer near Greenfield; Jesse R., a graduate of Stillwater (Oklahoma) Agricultural College, class of 1915, and now a demonstrator for that institution, with his residence at Medford, Oklahoma; Robert N.; John J., who died at Greenfield, aged seventeen years; Olive Branch, a senior at the Agricultural and Mechanical College, Stillwater; and Martha O., a member of the sophomore class at the same college.

The early education of Robert N. Thomas was secured in the public schools of Greenfield, following which he took a course in the Central Normal School, Edmond, Oklahoma. In 1908 he came to Greenfield as principal of the public school, but after one year gave up teaching to engage in banking, entering the Greenfield State Bank as bookkeeper. His abilities soon recognized, after three months he was made cashier of this institution, a position which he has retained to the present time, the other officials being: George M. Matlock, president; and E. G. Demunbrun, vice president. This bank was founded in 1909 as a state institution by I. E. Hemmingway and has grown steadily since its inception, being regarded as one of the safe and reliable concerns of Blaine County, managed in a conservative way by men whose fortunes and reputations are wrapped up in its success. It has a capital of $10,000, with a surplus of $5,000, and owns its own handsome bank building on Main Street, which was erected in 1906. It is a recognized factor in the business life of the community and is well patronized by the thrifty people of the county.

Mr. Thomas is a republican, but his activities in a political way are limited to an effort to secure good men and beneficial measures for his community. He is fraternally affiliated with Watonga Lodge No. 176, A. F. & A. M., in which he has made many friends, and is a member also of the Oklahoma State Bankers Association. He is unmarried.

JOHN A. WIMBERLEY. An Oklahoma eighty-niner, John A. Wimberley's name was found in the annals of some of the first political conventions held in the old territory of Oklahoma and he has been actively identified with the territory and state both in business and politics.

for more than a quarter of a century. For the past ten years Mr. Wimberley has lived at Pawhuska, and has extensive business interests in that locality.

A Tennessean, he was born in Henry County of that state April 20, 1865, and represents some fine old southern ancestry. His parents were Noah and Martha (Lee) Wimberley, who were married in Tennessee and in 1866 moved to Illinois. His father was a Union soldier, having served for four years and three months in the army. By occupation he was a farmer, was a member of the Methodist Church and a democrat in politics and his death occurred in Massac County, Illinois, in 1879. His wife, who was a member of the prominent Lee family of old Virginia, died in Massac County, Illinois, in 1870.

The youngest of five children, John A. Wimberley spent the first sixteen years of his life on an Illinois farm and during that time acquired all his school training. In every sense he is a self-made man. In 1882 he went out to Kansas and was engaged in farming with a brother in Kingman County until 1889. In that year, which marked the opening of the original Oklahoma territory, he located at Kingfisher and secured a Government homestead, whose cultivation he directed and on which he lived until 1900. After a short time at Pawnee he again participated in 1901 in a land opening, when the Kiowa and Comanche reservation was allotted to permanent settlers. For several years Mr. Wimberley lived at Anadarko, but in 1905 came to Pawhuska, which has since been his home. He has extensive interests as a farmer and stock raiser and for a number of years has also handled real estate, operating in lands not only in Osage but in several other counties of Oklahoma.

Though Mr. Wimberley can properly claim a diploma only from the post-graduate school of hard experience, he has seldom been unsuccessful in his business undertakings and has shown a great deal of enterprise and persistence in carrying out everything to which he directs his attention. This is a fine business trait, and it has been responsible not only for his success but for the useful part he has been able to play in local affairs and in politics in general. Throughout his career he has been identified with the republican party.

His public service makes his name notable in political annals of Oklahoma. He served as a member of the Territorial Legislature for two terms from 1891 to 1895, having taken his seat in the second year after the organization of the territory. The political history of Oklahoma during those trying first years after settlement should be read, as recounted on other pages of this publication, bearing the fact in mind that Mr. Wimberley was one of the most influential and active members of the State Legislature at the time. He was also a member of the board of regents at the Agricultural and Mechanical College from 1892 to 1894. During 1902-03 he was a member of the board of county commissioners in Caddo County. A fact that connects him especially with early political history is that he was a delegate to the first republican convention held in Oklahoma. This convention met at the old Town of Frisco in June, 1889, only a few weeks after the original opening. He was also chairman of the first republican convention ever held in Caddo County.

On January 1, 1890, he was married at Kingfisher to Miss Martha J. Gillam, who was born in Montgomery County, Indiana, in 1867, and was reared principally in that state. To their marriage have been born four children: Fern, who was born at Kingfisher June 18, 1892, is a graduate of the State Normal School at Edmond; Letha, born August 12, 1894, graduated from the Pawhuska High School and is now the wife of Frank Johnson of Oklahoma City; Jonnie Margaret, born in 1898, died in 1903; Martha Alice was born at Pawhuska in 1907 is still in school. Mr. Wimberley also has a grandson named John A. Wimberley Johnson.

J. F. McILHENY. Now one of Bartlesville's leading business men, Mr. McIlheny began his career many years ago as a telegraph operator. For about thirty years he was a private operator and secretary for the late Michael Cudahy, the Chicago packer and capitalist, and first came to Oklahoma as the representative of the Cudahy interests in the oil district about Bartlesville. Mr. McIlheny in recent years has been in business for himself and is now head of the firm of McIlheny & Thurman, insurance, surety bonds and loans.

J. F. McIlheny was born at Middletown, Ohio, December 15, 1854, a son of R. K. and Sarah (Monfort) McIlheny. His father was a native of Pennsylvania, and the mother was born in Ohio but was reared and married in Pennsylvania. They lived for a number of years after marriage in Ohio, and about 1880 moved to Chicago, and in October, 1903, came to Bartlesville, Oklahoma. J. F. McIlheny was their only child and his parents lived with him for many years. The father died at Bartlesville in April, 1904, and the mother on November 5, 1913. At his death he was eighty-two years of age and she was in her eighty-sixth year. While a resident of Ohio he had followed the grocery business.

Mr. McIlheny left school and took up practical work at the age of sixteen, when he learned telegraphy and was soon employed in the regular service. For several years he was train dispatcher on the Big Four Railway at Cincinnati, and then went to Chicago as a private operator for Michael Cudahy. The Cudahy interests sent him to Oklahoma as purchasing agent and later as local manager in the oil fields. He continued one of the active and trusted lieutenants of the Cudahy people in Oklahoma from 1903 to 1908, when the Cudahys sold their holdings to the National Refining Company. Mr. McIlheny was in the service of Mr. Cudahy for more than thirty years and finally retired, going into business for himself. Since 1908 he has been in business for himself as a general insurance man and loan agent. He was first associated with H. C. Moore, but since December, 1911, has been at the head of the firm of McIlheny & Thurman, his partner being F. E. Thurman.

Mr. McIlheny has been one of the men of affairs at Bartlesville since the early days, and served two terms on the city council when Bartlesville was a small town. During territorial days he was a member of the Republican County Central Committee. He stands high in Masonic circles being affiliated with the Blue Lodge, Royal Arch Chapter, Knights Templar Commandery, Eastern Star Chapter, and the Mystic Shrine, and is also a member of the Benevolent and Protective Order of Elks. On April 24, 1886, Mr. McIlheny married Miss Anna Sneed, of Rushville, Indiana.

CLAUDE TILDEN SMITH. A lawyer who now enjoys a lucrative private practice in Beaver County, Claude Tilden Smith also distinguished himself by a vigorous administration as county attorney for two years, and is the recognized leader of the democratic party in Beaver County.

He is of an old Southern family, long represented in the State of Maryland. He was born at Wakefield, Maryland, March 26, 1877, a son of James E. and Martha A. (Beach) Smith. His father was born July 17, 1850, at Warfieldsburg, Maryland, a son of James and Mary (Harmon) Smith, who were natives of Maryland. James E. Smith during his younger years was a very active democratic leader in Maryland, and held several state offices.

He is now living at Westminster, Maryland. He married, April 16, 1876, Miss Beach, who was born August 3, 1849, at Leesburg, Virginia, a daughter of James and Elizabeth (Higdon) Beach, both natives of Loudon County, Virginia, and of prominent Virginia stock. Claude Tilden Smith was the oldest of five sons. The others were: Rozier Gorman, born in 1879 and died in 1880; Grover Roberts, born in 1884 and died in 1885; John Ray, born in 1886, died in 1903; and James E., Jr., who was born in 1891, was married in 1915 to Beulah Ogle, and now lives with his father. That the family has been strongly democratic in politics will be observed from the fact that several of the sons were named for some of the great leaders in that party during the last three or four decades.

Claude Tilden Smith was given a liberal classical education at Western Maryland College in Westminster, where he graduated A. B. with the class of 1896. He took up the study of law at first under Judge James A. C. Bond and later under Reifsnider & Reifsnider at Westminster for three years. His preceptors subsequently filled places on the bench. He was admitted to practice before the Court of Appeals of Maryland on October 14, 1899. He soon had a promising law practice in his native state, and in 1903 was appointed examiner in equity causes for Carroll County, and in 1908 held office as city solicitor for Westminster. He resigned these positions June 26, 1909, on his removal to Beaver, Oklahoma.

At the present time Mr. Smith is state committeeman in the democratic organization from Beaver County. In 1910 he was the nominee of his party for county attorney, and in 1912 was again nominated and this time elected, leading his ticket. He remained in the office two years, but in his third campaign was defeated, largely on account of the fact that he had shown an unusual ability and fearlessness in the vigorous enforcement of all laws and the additional fact that Beaver County has a republican majority. Since leaving office he has looked after the interests of an extensive private practice. He is affiliated with the Independent Order of Odd Fellows and the Knights of Pythias.

On June 12, 1907, at Sparrow Point, Maryland, he married Miss Amelia E. Owings, who was born June 16, 1884, at Cockeysville, Maryland, a daughter of Perry Thomas and Margaret Stuart (Watson) Owings, the former a native of Baltimore County, Maryland, and the latter of England. Mrs. Smith is a descendant in the maternal line from the royal family of Stuarts of England and Scotland, and another branch of her ancestry was the fighting McKays of Scotland. Daniel Henry Stuart McKay, her grand-uncle, was the grand master of the Orange Society in the counties of Antrim and Londonderry, Ireland, for a number of years. Mr. and Mrs. Smith have four children, two sons and two daughters, namely: James Owings, born June 5, 1908; Claude Tilden, Jr., born September 22, 1909; Martha Amelia, born December 26, 1911; and Elizabeth Stuart, born December 1, 1913. The three youngest children were born in Beaver, Oklahoma.

While a resident of Maryland Mr. Smith took a very active part in military affairs. He was the organizer of Company H, First Maryland Infantry, Maryland National Guard, and he resigned from the office of captain when he came to Oklahoma.

VIRGIL F. CARLETON. Of the men who are lending practical encouragement to the industries and institutions of Custer County, few are contributing in more helpful degree to the general progress and advancement than is Virgil F. Carleton, who is engaged in the real estate and insurance business at Clinton. A resident of the county since 1897, and during a large part of this time engaged in farming operations, he is thoroughly conversant with values, and in several positions of public trust has evidenced the possession of traits which have made his reputation firm in the community.

Mr. Carleton was born on a farm in Ray County, Missouri, February 5, 1875, and is a son of L. M. and Frances M. (Tunnel) Carleton. His grandfather was G. M. Carleton, a native of England who emigrated to the United States and settled first at Haverhill, Massachusetts, subsequently moving as a pioneer to Ray County, Missouri, where he passed his remaining years in the pursuits of the husbandman. L. M. Carleton was born in 1826, at Haverhill, Massachusetts, and was twenty-three years of age when the news of the discovery of gold in California reached his New England home. Contracting a severe case of "gold fever," he packed his belongings, took a ship around the Horn, and joined the adventurous souls who were laboring to secure the precious metal. After about four years of indifferent success as a miner and prospector, Mr. Carleton returned to the East, but after a short stay migrated to Ray County, Missouri, where he preempted a homestead of 160 acres. There he continued to follow the pursuits of farming and stock raising until his death, in 1876, winning success through his industry, integrity and intelligent management. Mr. Carleton was a republican but not a politician. He married Miss Frances M. Tunnel, who was born near Knoxville, Ray County, Missouri, who survives her husband and resides near Elk City, in Custer County. They were the parents of four children, namely: Alpha, who married W. C. Cowherd and resides on a farm in Custer County; L. M., who conducts the Fay Mercantile Company at Fay, Oklahoma; Virgil F.; and G. M., who lives on the old homestead in Ray County, Missouri.

Virgil F. Carleton attended the public schools of Ray County, Missouri, while assisting in the work of the home farm, and in order to further prepare himself for a commercial career took a course in the Lexington (Missouri) Business College, where he was graduated in 1896. In that year he returned to Ray County and again resumed farming, but in February, 1897, came to Washita Township, Custer County, Oklahoma, and, settling near Elk City, filed on a homestead of 160 acres, a tract of land which he still owns. He resided on this farm until 1907, when he removed to Clinton, Oklahoma, and first engaged in the cattle business, in addition to holding an interest in a planing mill, and in 1909 was elected mayor of Clinton, in which office he served during that and the following year. At the close of his term of office he embarked in the real estate and insurance business, a line in which he has continued to be engaged to the present time, having offices in the Jeter Building. As an official Mr. Carleton gave Clinton one of the best administrations which it has known, and while a resident of Washita Township he rendered excellent service as a member of the school board. He is a democrat in his political views, but has not allowed party prejudices to interfere with the performance of the duties of citizenship. In business circles his name is an honored one, due to the straightforward and honorable manner in which his transactions have always been carried on. Mr. Carleton is well known fraternally, being a member of Clinton Lodge No. 339 of the Masonic Order; Clinton Lodge of the Independent Order of Odd Fellows; Elk City Lodge of the Benevolent and Protective Order of Elks; the Brotherhood of American Yeomen, and the Knights of the Maccabees.

Mr. Carleton was married in February, 1895, in Ray County, Missouri, to Miss Olga M. Smallwood, daughter of Dr. P. C. Smallwood, a practicing physician and surgeon of near Carpenter, Oklahoma. To this union there has been born one son, R. V., who is attending the public schools.

DAVID PRESTON PARKER is one of the acknowledged leaders of the Harper County bar, and for a young man has gone far in his profession, has accomplished a great deal in spite of difficulties and adversities which encumbered his early progress.

A North Carolina man by birth, he was born May 23, 1876, in a log house on a farm in Johnston County, a son of King Henry and Sarah Anne (Beasley) Parker. His father was of the Israel Putnam stock of New Englanders, but spent all his life in North Carolina. In 1905 he retired from his work as a farmer. He was born January 5, 1848, in Johnston County and died there March 27, 1911. In 1867 he married Sarah Anne Beasley, daughter of Enoch O. and Edith (Avery) Beasley, both natives of North Carolina. Mrs. Parker was born October 8, 1851, in Johnston County. To the parents were born a large family of fourteen children, eight sons and six daughters. Nancy Anne, born in 1869, died in 1873 as a result of severe burns; Sarah Anna, born September 28, 1871, was married in 1908 to David T. Lunceford; James Daniel, born March 23, 1874; David Preston who is the fourth in order of birth; Mary Ella, born July 23, 1878, married in 1904 N. G. Rand; the sixth in birth, a daughter, died in infancy; Joseph P., born September 1, 1881; Edith Ellen, born September 20, 1883, was married in 1911 to P. A. Putnam who died in 1915; Geneva, born December 23, 1885, married in 1909 Henry L. Graves; Mordecai, born June 5, 1887, died December 26, 1897; Ezra, born July 4, 1889; Henry Almond, born December 18, 1891; and the two youngest, Nehemiah and Horace Virgilius, both died in childhood.

David P. Parker spent his boyhood on a North Carolina farm. He grew up in a home of wholesome ideals but of limited comforts and few advantages except such as the members were able to secure for themselves. He attended the public schools in Johnston County, the Turlington Institute at Smithfield in that state, and was graduated with the class of 1900 and the degree A. B. from the State University of North Carolina at Chapel Hill. In 1901 he was given the degree of Master of Arts. He distinguished himself as an orator and debater while in university, and in 1900 won the Willie P. Mangum medal for oratory, and was also one of the successful North Carolina debaters in the interstate debating contest between North Carolina and Georgia. His scholarship standing while in university is well indicated by the fact that he is a Phi Beta Kappa, being a member of the Alpha Chapter of North Carolina. Though he was leader in school and university circles, he paid most of his way by teaching between terms. He was a teacher in the states of North Carolina and Texas from 1893 to 1909, held several superintendences in Texas and in 1907 was a member of the state board of summer normal examiners of Texas. In 1909 he removed to Oklahoma City, and on December 9, 1909, was admitted to practice by the Supreme Court at Guthrie.

In January, 1910, Mr. Parker located at Buffalo, Harper County, and the favorable impression he created soon brought him a paying and profitable practice. The same year he located there he was nominated on the republican ticket and elected county attorney of Harper County, and was re-elected to the office in 1912. His administration was characterized by exceptional vigor and impartiality, but after four years of service he declined a third nomination, and resumed the private practice of law, in which he is still engaged.

On July 30, 1905, Mr. Parker married at El Paso, Texas, Miss Mary Louise Potts, daughter of Charles B. and Elizabeth (Shirley) Potts. Her father was born in England and her mother in Mississippi. Mrs. Parker was born April 7, 1880, in Parker County, Texas. To their marriage have been born three children. David Preston, Jr., born September 20, 1907; Elizabeth Shirley, born May 27, 1911; and Annette, born October 25, 1914. Mr. Parker is affiliated with the Knights of Pythias, and he and his family are members of the Presbyterian Church, of which he is an elder. He has been president of the Harper County Sunday School Association continuously since 1911, and takes great interest in the work.

JOHN WILLIAMS DUKE, M. D. A widely known and prominent physician and surgeon of Guthrie, Dr. John W. Duke has practiced medicine in Oklahoma for many years and has been vitally identified with some of the larger movements connected with the public health of the state. He is also one of the most prominent Masons in the State of Oklahoma.

He was born at Scoby, Mississippi, June 5, 1868, and received his literary and professional education in his native state and in Tennessee and New York. In 1891 he graduated M. D. from the Memphis Hospital Medical College, and in 1893 received a diploma from the medical department of the University of New York. Since then he has been in active practice and most of his years have been spent in Oklahoma. He is a man of wide experience, of unusual natural gifts, and a natural leader in his profession.

From 1911 to 1915 Doctor Duke served as secretary of the Oklahoma State Board of Medical Examiners, and at the present time is state commissioner of health at Guthrie. He served that city as mayor from 1905 to 1907. For ten years he was surgeon-general of the Oklahoma National Guard.

Doctor Duke is a democrat. He took his first degrees in Masonry in Connecticut about 1896. In 1897 he became a Knight Templar in Shrine Commandery No. 8 at Middletown, Connecticut, and in 1900 completed the course of the thirty-two degrees of Scottish Rite at Guthrie. In 1909 he was honored with the supreme thirty-third degree in Scottish Rite Masonry at the House of the Temple in Washington, D. C.

On January 30, 1901, in the State of Connecticut, Doctor Duke married Isabelle Perkins, daughter of Doctor Edward Perkins, of Wallingford, Connecticut.

WILLIAM R. BARRY, M. D. A forcible illustration of pluck and determination leading a man to success is found in the career of Doctor Barry of Bradley, who after completing a course in the Agricultural and Mechanical College of Mississippi set out without means to make his way through a medical school and establish himself in a profession. Probably nine-tenths of the successful business men of Oklahoma have won their way through adversity from the beginning of their education. Doctor Barry earned every dollar of the money that was required to complete his medical education.

Born at Oxford, Mississippi, January 8, 1867, he is the son of James J. and Margaret E. (Nichols) Barry. His father, a native of South Carolina, settled in Mississippi in the early '30s, and in 1848, following the discovery of gold on the Pacific coast, went to the California mines, but returned before the outbreak of the Civil war to enter the Confederate army, in which he served three years, part of the time as a captain under General Forrest. Captain Barry was a successful farmer before and after the war, and a well known man in his state. The grandfather of Doctor Barry was a slave owner and a prosperous South Carolina planter before the war.

After completing a common school education in the public schools of Mississippi Doctor Barry entered the Agricultural and Mechanical College of that state, graduating with the degree A. B., July 6, 1887. Later for one term he was in the Memphis Hospital Medical College at Memphis, Tennessee, and then used his acquired knowledge and skill to practice medicine as a necessary means of earning the money required for the completion of his training. He was given the degree Doctor of Medicine at Memphis in 1889, and began his regular practice in his native state. He next removed to Campbell in Hunt County, Texas, remained there ten years, and in 1900 came to Bradley, Oklahoma, where he has since been in practice. Doctor Barry is a successful man from a professional standpoint, and his practice covers a large and fertile territory around Bradley. He is a member of the Grady County Medical Society, of the Oklahoma Medical Society, of the Southern Medical Society and the American Medical Association. He has held the office of township treasurer in his county and as chairman of the board of education in his school district.

Doctor Barry was married in Hunt County, Texas, to Miss Maggie M. Phillips. They are the parents of four children: Lucile, Merle, Louise and an infant as yet unnamed. The oldest daughter, aged thirteen, has completed the eighth grade in the Bradley public schools. A brother of Mrs. Barry is Ben F. Phillips, chief of police at Chickasha, Oklahoma. Doctor Barry is a member of the Presbyterian Church, and of the Masonic and Odd Fellows lodges, and is master of the former in Bradley. He is also a member of the Mutual Aid Society for Agriculture. Having been a factor in the promotion of such public enterprises and the establishment and betterment of public schools, highway building, town improvement, he ranks among the leading and most substantial men in the eastern part of Grady County.

CORREL C. DEGRAW. The present court clerk of Beaver County, one of the most popular residents of that section of the state, is an original Oklahoma eighty-niner, though he was only a child at the time. The DeGraw family settled in Kingfisher County, and its members have been closely associated with developments here for more than a quarter of a century. The DeGraw family came to Oklahoma from Kansas. Correl C. DeGraw was born in a stone house on a farm in Pottawatomie County, Kansas, July 26, 1879, a son of Byron and Anna (Bothsell) DeGraw. His father was born in 1847 in Iowa, a son of Joseph and Jane DeGraw, the former a native of Canada and the latter of Pennsylvania. Byron DeGraw has been a farmer all his life, combining that occupation with stock raising. He went from Iowa to Kansas in 1872, lived in Pottawatomie County a number of years, and in 1883 moved to Stafford County, where he was engaged in farming until the notable year of 1889. Though he was not a participant in the grand opening of Oklahoma, he arrived in August, about four months after the opening, and secured a tract of government land in Kingfisher County near the present City of Hennessey. That was his home for eight years, and he is now engaged in farming in Dewey County. Miss Anna Bothsell, whom he married in 1876, was born September 22, 1852, at Quincy, Illinois, a daughter of Joseph Bothsell, also a native of Illinois. Mrs. DeGraw died August 17, 1897, at Hennessey, Oklahoma. There were seven children, four sons and three daughters, mentioned briefly as follows: Correl C.; Joseph Parks, born January 10, 1881, now a farmer in Beaver County; Guy, born August 20, 1884, a farmer in Blaine County, Oklahoma; Flossie, born December 23, 1887, married in 1903 John Dugan, and they now live in Blaine County; Ionia, born December 23, 1889, and died January 23, 1890; Bessie, born March 3, 1893, who was married in 1914, and lived in Kansas City, Missouri; Rector, born March 15, 1895, and now engaged in farming in Dewey County.

Correl C. DeGraw was ten years of age when he came to Oklahoma with his parents. His subsequent education was obtained from the public schools of Hennessey, and his early youth was surrounded by the conditions typical of an Oklahoma farm during the decade of the '90s. In 1904 Mr. DeGraw took the Civil service examination the Indian school service, and soon afterward was appointed an industrial teacher at the Pierre Indian Schools in Pierre, South Dakota. He remained in that work in South Dakota for three years. In 1907, having returned to Oklahoma, he located at Beaver, and engaged in merchandising. In 1911 he bought a farm two miles north of Beaver, and that is where he now makes his home.

For a number of years he has taken an active part in republican politics, and it was on the republican ticket that he was chosen to his present office. In 1912 he was appointed clerk of the County Court of Beaver County, an office he held two years. In 1914 he was elected court clerk of the same county. He is a member of the Masonic Order and the Independent Order of Odd Fellows.

On August 1, 1900, at Watonga, Oklahoma, Mr. DeGraw married Miss Laura Boston, who was born September 21, 1882, in Johnson County, Missouri, a daughter of James W. and Eva (Thistle) Boston, both of them natives of St. Louis. Mr. and Mrs. De Graw are the parents of three children, two sons and one daughter, namely: Correl James, born May 14, 1901, at O'Keene, Oklahoma; Alva Byron, born September 11, 1904, at O'Keene; and Fern, born July 10, 1910, at Beaver.

GEORGE E. KERR, M. D. Now established in a successful practice as a physician and surgeon at Chattanooga, Doctor Kerr is one of the older physicians of Oklahoma, having begun practice in Grant County fifteen years ago. He was also one of the early settlers of Chattanooga, where he is well known not only for his skill and ability as a doctor but for his varied interests in the life and activities of the town.

A Canadian by birth, Dr. George E. Kerr was born at Tilbury, Ontario, February 3, 1867. His grandfather, James Kerr, spent his life in County Donegal, Ireland, where his business was that of fisherman. He rose to the rank of colonel in the English army under the great Duke of Wellington in the Napoleonic wars, and at the decisive battle of Waterloo was wounded. The son of this old soldier was George Kerr, who was born in County Donegal, Ireland, in 1803, and died at Tilbury, Canada, in 1886. He came to America when a young man and was a pioneer farmer and stock raiser at Tilbury. In politics he was a conservative. George Kerr married Julia Weldon, a native of County Monaghan, Ireland, whence she came to Tilbury when a young woman. She is now living at Deerfield, Michigan. She became the mother of five children: James, who is a collector of internal revenues at Windsor, Ontario; Elizabeth, whose first husband was Joseph Daniels, a farmer, now deceased, and who is now living with John Witt, a retired farmer at Deerfield; Mary, who married Jerry Vipond, a contractor and builder at Detroit, Michigan; the fourth child is a nurse in the Dearborn Hospital at Dearborn, Michigan, and the youngest is Doctor Kerr of Chattanooga.

The public schools of Tilbury, his birthplace, supplied

Doctor Kerr with his early education, and he graduated from the Chatham High School with the class of 1885. Four years later, in 1889, he finished the course of the Komoeo Seminary at Gault, Canada, and while there matriculated for a course in the Detroit College of Medicine, where he was given an excellent preparation for his chosen calling and was graduated M. D. with the class of 1894. For a year and a half Doctor Kerr had the many benefits gained by service as interne in St. Mary's Hospital, and in 1895 took up active practice at Deerfield, Michigan, where he remained until 1900. During the first seven years of his residence in Oklahoma Doctor Kerr was located in Grant County. In August, 1907, he moved to Chattanooga, where he was one of the first physicians and surgeons to locate, and is now well established in his business, having his offices in the Chattanooga State Bank Building. He is a member of the County and State Medical societies and the American Medical Association, and is now serving as deputy health officer.

Doctor Kerr was a member of the school board at Chattanooga up to 1915. He is a republican in politics, is past master of Chattanooga Lodge No. 349, Ancient, Free and Accepted Masons, a member of Chattanooga Chapter of the Eastern Star, of the Modern Woodmen of America, the Woodmen of the World, the Woodmen Circle and the Brotherhood of American Yeomen at Chattanooga and was formerly affiliated with the Independent Order of Odd Fellows.

In 1904, in Grant County, Oklahoma, Doctor Kerr married Miss Mary Kearney, who formerly lived in Illinois. Their four children are: Irene and Mabel, both attending the public schools at Chattanooga; George, who died in infancy, and James, the youngest.

W. B. TILTON, M. D. The roll of medical practitioners of Custer County includes the name of Dr. W. B. Tilton, of Clinton, a capable representative of his profession who has been engaged in practice since 1912. He came to Clinton in December, 1913, and since that time has been successful in building up a very satisfying practice in medicine and surgery and in winning the confidence of the people of his adopted field of labor.

Doctor Tilton belongs to a family which has been in America since colonial days, having been founded in Maine by an emigrant from England. He was born at Allendale, Missouri, June 3, 1884, and is a son of John L. and Margaret (McElvain) Tilton. John L. Tilton was born on a farm in Harrison County, Missouri, in 1861, and when a small boy was taken by his parents to the Town of Allendale, where he grew to manhood, secured a public school education, and established himself in business as a merchant. Later he also branched out into banking and became one of the prominent and influential men of Allendale, where he resided until 1896, in that year removing to his present home at Grant City. Here also he is well known in commercial and financial circles, being the proprietor of a store and interested in a banking concern. He is a member of the Baptist Church, is well known in Masonry, in which he has attained the thirty-second degree, and is also an Odd Fellow. At Allendale he was married to Miss Margaret McElvain, who was born in Worth County, Missouri, in 1863, and they have been the parents of four children, as follows: Dr. W. D.; Grace, who is the wife of Rev. W. A. Schullenberger, pastor of the Christian Church at Mexico, Missouri; Calvin, who resides with his parents at Grant City, Missouri; and Hale, who is a student at the Grant City High School.

Early in life W. B. Tilton decided upon a professional career, and with this end in view set about to fully prepare himself for his vocation. After attending the public schools, he entered the famous William Jewell College, at Liberty, Missouri, from which he was graduated in 1906, with the degree of Bachelor of Arts, and following this he attended the medical department of the University of Chicago for two terms. He was graduated from Northwestern University, Evanston, Illinois, in 1912, with the degree of Doctor of Medicine, and his first field of practice was the town of Freeport, Illinois, where he spent one year. In 1913 he first came to Oklahoma, as offering a better field for the display of his abilities and learning, and remained at Erick, Beckham County, until December of that year, which time marked his arrival at Clinton. Here he has well appointed offices in the Schaffer Building, equipped with all modern appliances. He is a constant student, a careful practitioner and a skilled surgeon, and holds membership in the Custer County Medical Society, the Oklahoma Medical Society and the American Medical Association. His religious connection is with the Baptist Church. Doctor Tilton is unmarried.

JAMES M. McCOMAS, M. D. Elk City, the metropolis of Beckham County, has been fortunate in gaining as one of the leading representatives of the medical profession in this county Dr. James Milton McComas, who has here been engaged in general practice as a physician and surgeon of marked ability and zeal since the spring of 1901, and whose character and achievement have lent dignity and distinction to his profession, the while he stands exponent of loyal and progressive citizenship and maintains lively and helpful interest in community affairs in general.

Doctor McComas is a scion of a sterling family that was founded in Virginia in the colonial era of our national history, and the lineage traces back to staunch Scottish origin. He himself is a native of Kentucky, and his father, Charles Lewis McComas, was born in Greenbrier County, Virginia, in 1795. In the colonial days two brothers of the name immigrated to America from the north of Ireland, one settling in Virginia and the other in Maryland, the Virginian figuring as the ancestor of him whose name introduces this article. Becoming a resident of Kentucky when young, Charles L. McComas was there married, in Morgan County, to Miss Clara Wells, who was born in that county in 1796, and from the old Bluegrass State they finally removed to Indiana, where Mr. McComas became a prosperous farmer. He later removed with his family to Illinois, where his wife died in 1856 and where he himself passed to the life eternal in 1860, both having been zealous and devout members of the Methodist Episcopal Church, and he having been for many years staunchly arrayed as an old-line whig in politics. He prepared himself for the legal profession and served for a protracted period in the office of justice of the peace. Of the children, the eldest was William Hamilton, who went to California in the early days, the other members of the family having eventually lost all trace of him; Sarah Ann, Frances Araminta, Elizabeth, Louisa, Clinton, and Albert S. are deceased; George met his death in a railroad accident; Charles Carroll resides in the City of Los Angeles, California, where he has long held prestige as a representative member of the bar and where he formerly served as prosecuting attorney of Los Angeles County; and Dr. James M., of this review, is the youngest of the number.

Doctor McComas was afforded in his youth the advantages of the common schools of the City of Louisville, Kentucky, and at Danville, that state, he was graduated in Central College as a member of the class of 1867. During this period he was also giving close attention to the study of medicine, under the effective preceptorship of leading physicians in his native state, besides which he availed himself of the advantages afforded in the city dispensary of Louisville. He has received the degree of Doctor of Medicine from each the medical department of the University of Pennsylvania, the Kentucky School of Medicine, the Kentucky Hospital College in Louisville, and the medical department of the University of Louisville, Kentucky. This statement shows his zeal in fortifying himself through the best available post-graduate courses, and his success in the practical work of his exacting profession has been on a parity with his recognized ability and unfaltering devotion to his chosen vocation.

Doctor McComas initiated the practice of his profession at Sturgeon, Boone County, Missouri, later practiced in St. Louis, and from 1888 to 1891 he was a successful practitioner in the City of Los Angeles, California. He then returned to St. Louis, Missouri, where he continued his professional labors until the autumn of 1900, when he came to Oklahoma Territory, his residence at Elk City having continued since April of the following year, where he holds precedence as a pioneer physician and surgeon as well as one of the leaders in the ranks of his profession in this section of the state. His offices are maintained in the Postoffice Building and he has at all times stood exemplar of the most advanced thought and most approved methods in medical and surgical science, with deep appreciation of the responsibilities of his chosen vocation and with insistent determination to uphold right loyally its unwritten ethical code, so that he has always commanded the respect and confidence of his confreres as well as of the public in general. In 1906 the doctor did effective post-graduate work in connection with the clinics at the great Augustana Hospital in the City of Chicago, and he has on several other occasions taken similar post-graduate work in leading institutions in that city and St. Louis. He was one of the foremost in effecting the organization of the Beckham County Medical Society, of which he was elected the first president—an office which he held consecutively until 1915, since which time he has not abated in the least his active zeal in the work of the society. He is identified also with the Oklahoma State Medical Society, the Southwestern Medical Society and the American Medical Association.

Doctor McComas is unwavering in his allegiance to the democratic party and though he has had no desire for public office his civic loyalty caused him to give most effective service during his incumbency of the position of member of the Elk City Board of Education. He is affiliated with Elk City Lodge No. 182, Ancient Free and Accepted Masons; Elk City Chapter No. 50, Royal Arch Masons; and Elk City Commandery, No. 15, Knights Templar.

Of the two children of the first marriage of Doctor McComas the elder is Arthur Rochford, who was graduated in the University of Missouri with the degree of Bachelor of Arts, after which he was graduated in the medical department of St. Louis University, with the degree of Doctor of Medicine. He is now engaged in the successful practice of his profession at Sturgeon, Missouri. The younger son, Judge Edwin Gaillard McComas, is now serving on the bench of the County Court of Beckham County, Oklahoma, and is individually mentioned on other pages of this work.

A. T. BROWN was in that great concourse of people who in Oklahoma are known as Eighty-niners. He developed a homestead in Canadian County. He was a pioneer of the Kiowa and Comanche Indian country, where other farms were developed. He became subsequently the leading merchant of the town of Bradley. These are the primary facts in the career of Mr. Brown in Oklahoma. He is now senior member of the firm of Brown & Stephens, dealers in general merchandise at Bradley. His success as a merchant is best attested by the fact that the firm has one of the largest stores handling general merchandise among any of the small towns of Oklahoma, and in addition operates three other stores in the same town, carrying flour, feed and furniture. The firm's trade is well distributed over a large section of the fertile valley of the Wachita River in one of the most productive and prosperous regions in the state.

A. T. Brown was born in Clermont County, Ohio, in 1875, a son of Adam and Catherine (Garland) Brown. His father is also a native of Ohio, and with his family came to Oklahoma at the time of the first opening in 1889, settling near Yukon in Canadian County, where he located a homestead and gained his title from the United States Government. He assisted in rebuilding the United States Government remount station at Fort Reno, and has done other important construction work in the state. A brother of Adam Brown is W. J. Brown, one of the best known pioneers of the original Oklahoma and an influential capitalist living at Kingfisher. A. T. Brown has four brothers and two sisters: G. S. Brown, who is associated with the National Livestock Commission Company at Oklahoma City; G. E. Brown, a farmer at Wynnewood, Oklahoma; W. O. Brown, a plumber in the employ of the National Stockyards Company at Oklahoma City; G. F. Brown, a farmer near Marlow; Mrs. E. J. Bailey, wife of a farmer near Rush Springs, Oklahoma; and Mrs. Wesley Armstrong, whose husband is a merchant at Marlow.

Mr. A. T. Brown received his public school education in Ohio, Kansas and Oklahoma, and began life for himself as a farmer in Canadian County. At the opening of the Kiowa and Comanche Indian country in 1901 he settled in Comanche County on a farm twelve miles west of Marlow. There he bought other land and successfully farmed and raised livestock until 1912, at which date he transferred his vocation from farming to mercantile lines. He came into Bradley and soon took the lead as a merchant. He was associated with J. F. Bell until the latter's retirement from business on March 1, 1915.

Mr. Brown was married in 1900 in Ohio to Miss Lorena Ball. Their three sons, Adam F., Loren B. and Truman, are all now attending public schools. Mr. Brown is president of the board of education at Bradley, and one of that town's most enthusiastic boosters. Besides his business he operates two fine farms in the western part of Grady County. It is interesting to note that his life in Oklahoma began under primitive conditions when Indian tepees were more frequent than houses and red men more numerous than white. Homes were far apart, and it was not unusual for the inhabitants to be frightened by rumors of Indian raids. Now he lives in a highly civilized and prosperous community, the result of transformations wrought by the last quarter of a century, and has a growing and happy family and is prospering.

CHARLES W. MORRISON, who has been a resident of Hinton, Oklahoma, since 1902, is a Baptist minister by profession and in addition to his work as a preacher he is serving most efficiently as town clerk of Hinton. He also owns and operates a finely improved farm of 160 acres just east of Hinton and he has ever been on the alert to forward all measures and enterprises projected for the good of the general welfare.

Of Scotch origin, Reverend Morrison is the grandson

of Tandy Morrison, who came from Scotland to Virginia with his parents when he was a mere child. As a young man Tandy Morrison removed from the Old Dominion commonwealth to Hancock County, Kentucky, where he was successfully engaged in farming until his demise. John A. Morrison, father of the subject of this sketch, was born in Hancock County, Kentucky, in 1835, and he is now living at Horse Branch, Kentucky, where he has followed agricultural pursuits all his life. He is a member of the Baptist Church and in politics gives his allegiance to the democratic party. He married, first, Basha Barnett, a native of Kentucky, where she was born in 1837 and where she died in 1860. This union was prolific of four children: Charles W. is the subject of this sketch; Edward M. is a printer and resides at Evansville, Indiana; and Mary C. and Aremus both died young. For his second wife Mr. Morrison married Bettie Stevens, who died in Kentucky and who is survived by one daughter, Ida.

Reverend Morrison was born at Owensboro, Davis County, Kentucky, November 1, 1856, and he was reared to maturity on his father's farm. He attended the public schools of Davis County and studied for the Baptist ministry. In 1884 he left Owensboro and located in Comanche County, Kansas, where he was engaged in agricultural pursuits until 1889. He then came to Oklahoma and was a pioneer Baptist minister in the vicinity of Oklahoma City. In 1892 he removed to Yukon, Oklahoma, preaching in a Baptist Church there for the ensuing eight years. From 1900 to 1902 he preached in Watonga, Blaine County, Oklahoma, and in the latter year he came to Hinton, where he has since maintained his home. He came to this section before the Town of Hinton was started and bought a farm of 160 acres right on the edge of the townsite. This farm is splendidly improved with modern buildings and cotton, oats and Kaffir corn are raised, in addition to which a specialty is made of livestock. Reverend Morrison is a democrat in politics and since 1907 he has been town clerk of Hinton. He still preaches and in this connection alternates at Greenfield and Laverty.

In Kentucky, in 1876, Reverend Morrison married Miss Annie Phillips, a daughter of J. B. Phillips, a farmer in Hancock County, Kentucky. Reverend and Mrs. Morrison have two children: Floy E. is assistant cashier in the Hinton State Bank; and Zada Belle is the wife of L. E. Brown, postmaster at Tuttle, Oklahoma.

Reverend Morrison is a man of fine mentality and broad human sympathy. He thoroughly enjoys home life and takes great pleasure in the society of his family and friends. He is always courteous, kindly and affable, and those who know him personally accord him the highest esteem. Mr. and Mrs. Morrison's lives have been exemplary in all respects and they have ever supported those interests which are calculated to uplift and benefit humanity, while their own high moral worth is deserving of the highest commendation.

LAWRENCE NILES HOUSTON. A pioneer attorney and one of the oldest members of the Enid bar, Lawrence Niles Houston has been much in public life, and probably no citizen of Enid has more stanch friends and well wishers. For about eight years Mr. Houston was register of the land office at Guthrie, and in that federal office he satisfied the predictions of his friends who had so many reasons to appreciate his public ability through his earlier work as city attorney at Enid.

Lawrence N. Houston was born in Manhattan, Kansas, July 9, 1858. His father, Samuel D. Houston, was prominent in the early days of "Bleeding Kansas," and had gone to that vexed territory in 1853 from Ohio. Samuel D. Houston was a cousin of the great Texas statesman, Sam Houston, and represented a family of Scotch-Irish ancestry, originally settled in Pennsylvania and furnishing many ministers and lawyers in the different generations. Samuel D. Houston was the first receiver of the land office at Junction City, Kansas, and for seventeen years gave a capable administration to that position. In 1859 he was a member of the Kansas Constitutional Convention, associated with John J. Ingalls, Gen. James G. Blunt, and other prominent Kansans at that time. He made himself a prominent figure in the political life of early Kansas, and was one of the best known residents of Manhattan. At the beginning of the war he abandoned his duties as receiver of the land office in order to enlist at Fort Leavenworth. Lincoln ordered him under arrest and sent him back to his official duties at Junction City under a guard of soldiers. The President believed his services were more important in that office than they would be in the army. Later in life he removed to Kingfisher and also lived at Enid for a time, but died at his old home city, Manhattan, at the age of ninety-two. Samuel D. Houston married an Ohio lady, a well educated woman, who in the early days taught school at Weston, Missouri. She was devoted to her home, reared a family of seven children, and was an active church worker.

L. N. Houston grew up in Kansas, attended the State Agricultural College at Manhattan, and at the age of twenty was admitted to the bar and began practice at Concordia. He was county clerk of Cloud County six years and assistant county attorney there for four years. While in that section of Kansas he made a name for himself both in the law and in politics, and lived there from 1877 to 1893. He had served as census enumerator and in other capacities became well known at Concordia.

Mr. Houston participated in the opening of the Cherokee strip on September 16, 1893. He came to Enid on a cattle train from Hennessey, and almost at once took up the practice of law, so that he is now one of the oldest attorneys in the city. For four years he was city attorney, a period in which the most important public improvements were inaugurated. An Enid paper recently called attention to the fact that he furnished the legal advice and drew up the contract by which the Frisco Railway got $25,000 of the waterworks funds in return for running the railway to Enid. For this service Mr. Houston received a salary of ten dollars a month, with no extras for clerk's hire or stenographer. The same paper gives an interesting account of how he came to occupy the office of register of the land office at Guthrie. In 1902 the republicans held a county convention in which Mr. Houston was chosen chairman of the county central committee. During the four years in that office he filled the court house with republicans, and in 1904 was chosen to manage the republican campaign, with the result that Bird McGuire was elected to congress. Congressman McGuire rewarded the services of Mr. Houston by securing his appointment as register of the Guthrie Land Office. President Roosevelt nominated him to that office in 1906, and he served as such until April, 1914. Though with two years more to serve he voluntarily resigned, and returned to his former home in Enid and has resumed the private practice of law. Mr. Houston is interested in the development of oil fields in Eastern Oklahoma, and has made his mark as a lawyer and public spirited citizen. Having lived in Oklahoma for more than twenty years he has sound reasons for his splendid faith in its great future.

In 1880 at Savannah, Missouri, Mr. Houston married Miss Alice Selecman. She was born in Kentucky, but received most of her education in Missouri, being a graduate of the University of Missouri. Mrs. Houston is active in the work of the Methodist Episcopal Church and in various charities. There are three children: Blanche, wife of John P. Cook, president of the Oklahoma State Bank of Enid; and Harold W. and Hazel K., the former a banker at Bisby, Oklahoma, and the latter of these twins being the wife of G. L. Levers, in the railway mail service with home at Tulsa.

MILO MELVILLE MACKELLAR, M. D. Nearly twenty years ago Doctor MacKellar was a regular graduate in medicine, but devoted nearly all the following four years to continued study and an experience which has greatly increased his qualifications for skillful and thorough practice. Doctor MacKellar has been in practice in Oklahoma for the past fifteen years, and is now the leading physician and surgeon at Loveland, in Tillman County. He is also a leader in educational movements and popular in social and fraternal life.

Born in Fayette County, Iowa, December 28, 1874, Doctor MacKellar is a son of Peter MacKellar, and grandson of Hugh MacKellar, who was born in Invery Castle, Scotland, emigrated to America and lived for a time in the village where is now found the great city of Chicago, and subsequently was a pioneer blacksmith and farmer in the State of Iowa. Peter MacKellar was born in the State of Ohio in 1842, when a young man moved out to Highland, Iowa, was a farmer and stock raiser all his active career, and quite recently moved from Highland to Elgin, Iowa, where he is now living retired. In politics he is a republican and an active member of the Presbyterian Church. The maiden name of his wife was Samantha Moore, who was born in Ohio in 1858, and died at Highland, Iowa, in 1894. Her ancestors came from Ireland prior to the American Revolution, and for many years lived in Ohio. The children of Peter MacKellar and wife were: Orville W., who was graduated from the medical department of the Iowa State University in 1885, and is now practicing as a surgeon in Chicago; L. W., a farmer at Elgin, Iowa; Hattie, who lives with her father; Dr. Milo Melville; John D., who graduated from the medical department of the University of Illinois in 1900, is now a physician in Chicago, and is secretary of the General Medical College in that city.

Milo Melville MacKellar attended the public schools in Fayette County, Iowa, grew up on a farm and in 1894 was graduated Bachelor of Science from the Upper Iowa University at Fayette. With this substantial literary training he entered the College of Physicians and Surgeons at Keokuk, Iowa, from which institution he obtained his Doctor of Medicine degree with the class of 1896. The years from 1896 to 1900 were spent in Chicago, where he practiced medicine and was also instructor of anatomy in the General Medical College, and almost continuously was pursuing post-graduate studies in the Chicago Policlinic.

From 1900 to 1903 Doctor MacKellar practiced at Cement, Oklahoma, was then at Tulsa, Oklahoma, up to 1907, and has since become established in a large practice, both in medicine and surgery, at Loveland. He is a member of the Loveland School Board, and that is now one of the most important positions in the community, since several districts have recently been consolidated and plans and preparations are being made for the erection of a handsome new schoolhouse to serve this consolidated district. He is thus a member of the first board of education of Consolidated School District No. 5 in Tillman County. Doctor MacKellar is a member of the county and state medical societies and the American Medical Association, is a republican in politics, is master of Loveland Lodge No. 392, Ancient Free and Accepted Masons, and a member of Frederick Chapter No. 41, Royal Arch Masons, and of Frederick Council, Royal and Select Masters. He was formerly a member of the Modern Woodmen of America, the Knights of Pythias, the Order of Praetorians, and the Fraternal Order of Eagles. He also belongs to the International Travelers' Association of Dallas, Texas. On June 3, 1914, at Wichita Falls, Texas, Doctor MacKellar married Miss Jennie Huggins. Her father was the late J. H. Huggins, who at the time of his death was serving as president of the Loveland Farmers and Merchants State Bank.

ROMNEY E. JOHNSTON, M. D. Other men's services to the people and the state can be measured by definite deeds, by dangers averted, by legislation secured, by institutions built, by commerce promoted. The work of a doctor is entirely estranged from these lines of enterprise, yet without his capable, health-giving assistance, all other accomplishment would count for naught. Man's greatest prize on earth is physical health and vigor: nothing deteriorates mental activity so quickly as prolonged sickness, hence the broad field for human helpfulness afforded in the medical profession. The successful doctor requires something more than mere technical training, he must be a man of broad human sympathy and genial kindliness, capable of inspiring hope and faith in the heart of his patient. Such a man is he whose name initiates this article.

Dr. Romney E. Johnston, who has been a resident of Bridgeport, Oklahoma, since 1908, was born at Harrodsburg, Indiana, January 22, 1884. He is a son of A. H. and Debbie Jones (Morgan) Johnston, both of whom were born in the vicinity of Harrodsburg, the former in 1861 and the latter in 1859. A. H. Johnston is a farmer and stockman in Monroe County, Indiana, and he is a deacon in the local Methodist Episcopal Church. He and his wife are the parents of eleven children, brief data concerning whom appears in the sketch of Judge C. R. Johnston, of Caddo County.

To the public schools of Harrodsburg and Danville, Indiana, Doctor Johnston is indebted for his early educational discipline. He attended the normal school at Valparaiso, Indiana, for one year, and in 1904 was matriculated as a student in the University of Louisville, in the medical department of which he was graduated in 1907, July receiving the degree of Doctor of Medicine. While in the university he belonged to the Students' Club, of which he was a charter member. Doctor Johnston entered upon the active practice of his profession at Harrodsburg, Indiana, and remained there until May, 1908, which date marks his advent in Bridgeport, Oklahoma. Here he has built up a splendid medical and surgical practice and in addition to his professional work he owns and conducts the only drug store in this city. The doctor is a democrat in politics and although elected health officer he declined to serve in that capacity. He has been a member of the Bridgeport School Board for the past five years and in religious faith is Methodist Episcopal. He affiliates with Bridgeport Lodge, No. 229, Ancient, Free & Accepted Masons, of which he is master, and he formerly belonged to the Harrodsburg Lodge of the Independent Order of Odd Fellows.

December 14, 1909, in Edinburg, Indiana, was solemnized the marriage of Doctor Johnston to Miss Helen Sanburn, a daughter of William Sanburn, now deceased, a painter and decorator at Bloomington, Indiana. Doctor and Mrs. Johnston have two children: Frank Woodrow born April 4, 1912; and Maxiene, born September 4, 1914.

WILLIAM TAYLOR. It has been but a matter of course that many of the older commonwealths of the Union have made valuable contribution to the citizenship of the

Mr. Taylor
AND FAMILY

vital new State of Oklahoma, and a representative farmer and progressive citizen of Pawnee County who claims the old Buckeye State as the place of his nativity and who is a scion of families early founded in the South, is William Taylor, the close of the year 1915 marking the twentieth year of his residence on his present well improved homestead, which is eligibly situated in the vicinity of the Village of Jennings, in section 10, township 20, the place having been well improved by him and his son George A., now having charge of the practical operations of the farm, the income from which has in recent years been augmented by the extending of leases for oil development on the property. Mr. Taylor further merits special consideration by reason of having served as a valiant soldier of the Union in the Civil war, and in all of the relations of citizenship he has shown the same loyal spirit that thus prompted him to go forth in defense of the nation's integrity.

William Taylor was born in Vinton County, Ohio, on the 21st of July, 1840, and though he is now venerable in years he retains much of his pristine physical and mental vigor and in the gracious evening of life enjoys the good health that marks the result of right living and right thinking. He is a son of Andrew and Sarah (Loving) Taylor, the former of whom was born in Greenbrier County, West Virginia, on the 4th of February, 1815, his native state having at that time been still an integral part of Virginia, and his wife having been born within the limits of the latter state as at present constituted. Both were young at the time of the immigration to Ohio, he having been a young man at the time and having severed the home ties to cast his lot with the pioneers of the Buckeye State, while his wife had removed with her parents to that commonwealth, their marriage having been solemnized in Vinton County. In the autumn of 1841 Andrew Taylor removed with his family to Sycamore County, Illinois, and in 1843, he became one of the pioneer settlers in Keokuk County, Iowa, a section then on the very frontier of civilization. He became one of the early representatives of the agricultural and live-stock industries in the Hawkeye State, where he continued his residence for nearly half a century. In 1884 he and his wife removed thence to Oregon, and they passed the closing years of their lives at Drain, Douglas County, that state. Andrew Taylor devoted his active life to farming and milling, and though he was blind during the last sixty years of his life he was able to attend to business affairs and to supervise practical details of farm work, even as he had no difficulty in driving about with a team and unaccompanied. He never swerved from his allegiance to the democratic party, and both he and his wife held membership in the Methodist Episcopal Church. Concerning their children who attained to maturity the following data are available: John is a resident of Oregon, in which state he established his home in 1862; the next in order of birth was William, subject of this review; Jame became the wife of Enos Rushton, and was a resident of Kansas at the time of her death; David died in the City of Los Angeles, California; Newton is a resident of Grand Junction, Colorado; and Mary Elizabeth is the wife of Mason E. Hindman, of Mount Idaho, in the State of Idaho.

William Taylor remained at the parental home until he had attained to his legal majority and in the meanwhile not only gave effective aid in the work and management of the home farm, but also made good use of the advantages afforded in the pioneer schools of Iowa, in which state he was reared to adult age.

At Fairfield, Jefferson County, Iowa, in September, 1861, Mr. Taylor wedded Miss Martha Ann Woodward, who was born in Indiana, as were also her parents, Silas and Sarah (Leonard) Woodward, who established their home in Iowa when she was still a child, her mother having died in that state and her father having been a resident of Kansas at the time of his death and having been a pioneer farmer in both Iowa and Kansas.

Shortly after his marriage Mr. Taylor subordinated all personal interests and left his grieving but loyal young wife to tender his aid in defense of the Union. On the 9th of August, 1862, he enlisted in Company B, Nineteenth Iowa Volunteer Infantry, Harry Jordan having been captain of the company, and he continued in active service with this gallant command until the close of the war, his honorable discharge having been received by him in July, 1865. He participated in all of the many engagements in which his regiment was involved. He took part in the battle at Prairie Grove, Arkansas, in December, 1862, and also in the siege of Vicksburg and the siege of Spanish Fort, besides many minor engagements. He held the office of corporal during all but the first year of his service in the ranks and proved himself a faithful and gallant soldier, his record having been such as to reflect lasting honor upon his name.

After the close of the war Mr. Taylor resumed farming operations in Wayne County, Iowa, until 1882, when he removed his family to Cloud County, Kansas, where he was a renter and where he continued successful operations as an agriculturist and stock-grower until the autumn of 1894, when he came to Oklahoma Territory and became one of the pioneer settlers of Pawnee County, where he has resided upon his present homestead since the spring of 1895, his energy and good judgment having been brought into effective play in the development and improving of the farm, which is now one of the valuable places of this section of the state.

Mr. Taylor has always exemplified the best type of loyal and public-spirited citizenship, is a stalwart democrat in his political proclivities, has been affiliated with the Independent Order of Odd Fellows for nearly half a century, and vitalized the more pleasing associations of his military career by his active affiliation with the Grand Army of the Republic, that noble organization whose ranks are being rapidly thinned by the one invincible foe, death. The first wife of Mr. Taylor did not long survive, as she was summoned to eternal rest in February, 1864, while he was still serving as a soldier of the Union. Their only child, William E., is now a resident of Minnesota.

On the 10th of September, 1865, was solemnized the marriage of Mr. Taylor to Mrs. Eliza R. Ryckman, who was born in Indiana, and whose death occurred in Wayne County, Iowa, on the 9th of August, 1871. Of the three children of this union Rosa became the wife of W. A. Robertson, and her death occurred in Iowa, she having been survived by three children; Eli, the second child, is a resident of the City of Lewiston, Idaho; and Alva maintains his home at Concordia, Kansas.

On the 9th of December, 1873, Mr. Taylor contracted a third marriage, when Miss Malinda C. Chapman became his wife, she having been born in the State of Iowa, where her parents settled in the pioneer days. Mr. and Mrs. Taylor became the parents of eight children, of whom Arthur and Rena died in infancy; Sarah C. is the wife of Bert Hart, of Custer County, Oklahoma; Cora is the wife of Daniel Hart, of Drumwright, Oklahoma; George A. has charge of the homestead farm of his parents; Eva is the wife of John Miller, of Ellis County, Oklahoma; Nellie married Jay Hart; and Fay is the wife of Lemuel Sugg, of Oklahoma. Mr. Taylor has twenty-nine grandchildren.

ORAN D. McCRAY, M. D., holds prestige as one of the most skilled young physicians and surgeons in Caddo County, where he has been engaged in a general medical practice for the past decade. He now resides at Binger and here controls a large and lucrative patronage. The McCrays are of Scotch-Irish descent and trace their ancestry to the wealthy and noted family of that name at Hedges, Scotland. The first McCrays in America came hither in the early colonial days of our national history and settled in Virginia.

Doctor McCray was born at Putnamville, Putnam County, Indiana, November 23, 1874, and he is a son of George S. McCray and Mary Alice (Sellers) McCray, the former of whom was born in the old Hoosier State in 1851 and the latter in the same place in 1855. In 1882, about ten years after his marriage, Mr. McCray established the family home in Saline County, Missouri, where he was a farmer and stockman until his demise, at Marshall, that county, in August, 1906. He was an elder in the Presbyterian Church, was affiliated with the time-honored Masonic fraternity and in politics was a stalwart democrat. His wife, whose maiden name was Mary Alice Sellers, survives him and maintains her home at Marshall, Missouri. Mr. and Mrs. McCray had but one child, namely, Oran D., of this notice.

After completing the curriculum of the public schools of Marshall, Missouri, Doctor McCray was matriculated as a student in the Missouri Valley College, in which excellent institution he was graduated in 1897. He then attended the University of Missouri, at Columbia, for two years, at the end of which he entered the University Medical College, at Kansas City, Missouri, being graduated in that institution in 1901, with the degree of Doctor of Medicine. Doctor McCray received his initial practice as a physician and surgeon at Carrolton, Missouri, where he maintained his professional headquarters for two years. In 1903 he came to Caddo County and for one year practiced at Anadarko, whence he removed to Binger, where he has since resided with the exception of one year spent in Clovis, New Mexico. His offices are on Elm Street and in connection with his life work he is a member of the Oklahoma State Medical Society, the Caddo County Medical Society and the American Medical Association. His political allegiance is given to the democratic party and in 1907 he was elected coroner of Caddo County and he held that office until it was abolished by the Legislature. He served for several years as health officer at Binger and in every way possible he contributes of his time and means to the general weal. He is a member of the Congregational Church and affiliates with Anadarko Lodge, Ancient, Free and Accepted Masons. He is an ex-member of the following organizations: Independent Order of Odd Fellows, Benevolent and Protective Order of Elks, Brotherhood of American Yeomen, and the Ancient Order of United Workmen.

At Binger, in 1906, Doctor McCray was married to Miss Florence Risch, a daughter of William Risch, a retired business man at Binger. This union has been prolific of two children: George, born January 19, 1909; and Kenneth, born January 6, 1912.

PORTER T. RAGLAND. The experiences of Mr. Ragland as a pioneer of Oklahoma are not only interesting and serve to throw light on early conditions in the territory, but are also instructive and encouraging to the ambitious youth of the present time. He lived in the territory under adverse and trying conditions but is the character of man who profits by experience and makes each obstacle only a stepping stone to higher and better things.

Born in Barren County, Kentucky, June 13, 1876, Porter T. Ragland when a small boy came west with his father, driving overland to Southwestern Kansas, where the family lived for six years. Before leaving Kentucky he had attended one term of school and spent three terms at Springfield, Kansas. The Ragland home in Kansas, established in 1884, was the first built in Seward County. In 1889 his father was one of the pioneers of the original Oklahoma Territory, and at the opening of public lands acquired town lots in Kingfisher. Later the family located on a farm immediately west of Oklahoma City, that farm being now included within the corporation limits. The elder Ragland later made the run into what was known as the Pottawotamie County, entering at Tecumseh, then into the Cheyenne and Arapaho Indian country through Cloud Chief, then into the Cherokee strip through Perry, and finally into the Kickapoo country. This probably establishes a record for entering public land areas opened to settlement such as few men in Oklahoma have equalled. Mr. Ragland's father is now living on a fine farm near the town of Harrah in Oklahoma County.

Porter T. Ragland, who was thirteen years old when he came to Oklahoma, attended one of the first public schools organized in Oklahoma County. It was taught by Mrs. B. F. Crozier in a ten by twelve room of her little home near Oklahoma City. There were no desks, and the pupils sat on rude benches. The next term of school he attended was taught by William Guernsey in his little home on the site of the present Washington School in Oklahoma City. The family then moved to a farm six miles northwest of the city, and while there he attended school two years more, equipping himself for teaching and receiving his first certificate at the age of seventeen. For a number of years Mr. Ragland followed teaching as a profession and there are many men and women in Oklahoma who sat under his instruction and have grateful memories of his schoolmastership. His first school was in the Pleasant Hill district six miles southeast of Edmond during the year 1894-95. The salary paid him, $28.00 a month, was the highest given to any teacher in the rural district at that time. Subsequently he taught two terms twenty miles east of Purcell in a log building. This building was 20 by 24 feet, there was no chinking between the bare logs, and humble and rude though its accommodations were the school had an enrollment of 114 pupils. O. G. McGehee, treasurer of the board of education of the district, was one of his pupils, and twenty of the scholars were older than the teacher. During the summer following the second term Mr. Ragland attended a business college in Oklahoma City, following which he taught three terms in the Star district of the former Kickapoo Indian country. This was followed by a term at Harmony and for three years he was superintendent of schools at Harrah. In 1904 Mr. Ragland was nominee of the republican party for county superintendent of schools, and was defeated by Laura Whistler, the democratic nominee, by 156 votes.

About that time he made up his mind to leave educational work and establish himself in some permanent business or profession. With that object in view in 1905 he entered the School of Pharmacy of the University of Oklahoma, and was graduated June 13, 1907. Four days later he found himself in the employ of the Carson Drug Company at Tecumseh. On June 17, 1909, Mr. Ragland, with his wife, his baby, fifty cents in money and a bull dog, entered the drug business in Harrah. Six years have passed, and in that time he has built up a profitable business. His is the only drug store in the town, and the stock is as large, varied and up to date as can be found in any other store in towns of the same size in Oklahoma. Mr. Ragland celebrated a quarter century's continued residence in Oklahoma in the Thanksgiving season of 1915, and during all that time he has never crossed the state borders. During his residence at Harrah he served four and a half years as postmaster, and in 1915 was honored by election to the office of mayor. While in Tecumseh he was for one term police judge. As a citizen of Harrah he has been energetic, public spirited and progressive, and partially due to his efforts the town has one of the most modern brick school buildings found in any of the small towns of the state, constructed at a cost of $10,000.

In Oklahoma City, January 27, 1897, Mr. Ragland married Miss Clare House. Their two children are Oscar, aged fifteen, and Marguerite, aged three. Mr. Ragland has three brothers and one sister: E. E. Ragland, a farmer living near Harrah; Neil Ragland, in the lumber and milling business at Arrow Springs, Colorado; E. M. Ragland, who lives with his father on the farm near Harrah; and Mrs. Ross Wood, of Oklahoma City. Mr. Ragland is a member of the Christian Church, is affiliated with Lodge No. 375, Ancient Free and Accepted Masons, at Harrah, with the Modern Woodmen of America, and belongs to the Oklahoma Pharmaceutical Association. He is also president of the board of education of Harrah, a position for which his long experience as a teacher has given him eminent qualifications.

C. A. FISHER. The career of C. A. Fisher is an expression of practical and diversified activity, and in its range has invaded the realms of education, business, finance and politics, all of which have profited by the breadth and conscientiousness which are distinctive characteristics of his character and labors. Mr. Fisher came to Oklahoma with the opening of the Cherokee Strip, in 1893, and for several years was engaged as an educator, following which he spent several years in Texas in a business venture. Since 1900 he has been identified with financial affairs in Oklahoma, and has been a factor in the development of one of the soundest institutions of Kiowa County, the First National Bank of Gotebo, of which he is cashier.

Mr. Fisher belongs to a family which came to America during the seventeenth century from England and settled in North Carolina, from whence its members spread to various states in the South and Middle West. His father, James A. Fisher, was born in Ohio in 1840, and as a young man removed to Pine Valley, Warren County, Indiana, where he was married to Anna H. Bradley, who was born in 1844 at Winchester, Virginia. After many years passed in agricultural pursuits in the Hoosier state, Mr. Fisher removed to Seward County, Kansas, where he located on a farm in the vicinity of the village of Liberal, and there continued to be engaged in farming and stock raising until his death, which occurred in 1893. Mrs. Fisher, who survives her husband, resides at Port Arthur, Texas, and is seventy-one years of age. During the Civil war, James A. Fisher joined the Union army, enlisting from Warren County, Indiana, in the 110th Regiment, Indiana Volunteer Infantry, with which he served three years, proving a faithful and valiant soldier. He was a lifelong member of the Methodist Episcopal Church, to which Mrs. Fisher still belongs. They became the parents of four children, as follows: C. A., of this review; Clinton, who was a stockman and farmer near Liberal, Kansas, and died at the age of twenty-seven years; L. B., who is a druggist and merchant at Port Arthur, Texas; and Mabel M., who is the wife of Eugene Davis, who is in the refining department of the Texas Refining Company, at Port Arthur.

C. A. Fisher was born at Pine Valley, Warren County, Indiana, January 1, 1865, and was reared on his father's farm, where he spent the summer months in assisting in its operation, while in the winter terms he attended the district schools. Later he supplemented this training by a course at Purdue University, Lafayette, Indiana, and on leaving that institution entered upon his career as an educator. For three years Mr. Fisher taught schools in various parts of Indiana, Missouri and Kansas, and in 1893, when the Cherokee Strip was thrown open, came to Enid, where he was appointed superintendent of schools. This office he retained for three years, as one of the popular and efficient instructors of the new country, but in 1896 he gave up the cap and gown of the educator to enter business life, as the proprietor of a real estate venture at Port Arthur, Texas, which he continued until 1900, when he became assistant cashier of the First National Bank. His promotion to the cashiership soon followed, he being the incumbent of that position from 1902 until 1908, and in the latter year he came to Gotebo, Kiowa County, Oklahoma, to accept the office of cashier of the Bank of Gotebo. In 1913, with other progressive business men and financiers of this place, Mr. Fisher founded and organized the First National Bank of Gotebo, which threw open its doors to the public in May of that year. This has grown consistently and is now one of the recognized institutions of the county and one which has won and retained the confidence and patronage of the people. The institution has a capital stock of $25,000, with $3,000 surplus, and its present officers are: president, M. F. Pierce, a leading farmer and stockman of Kiowa County, well known in Gotebo, where he has large interests; vice president, C. M. Haxton; cashier, C. A. Fisher, and assistant cashier, T. J. Howe. The modern bank building, a handsome and substantial structure, was completed in September, 1913, and in the building the postoffice also has quarters. Mr. Fisher is an experienced, capable and careful financier, who safely conserves the interests of the bank's depositors, and in whom they have learned to place the fullest trust. In addition to his duties at the bank, he is also looking after the people's financial interests in the capacity of city treasurer, an office to which he was elected on the republican ticket. His fraternal connections include membership in Gotebo Lodge No. 305, Ancient Free and Accepted Masons, and Lodge No. 881, Benevolent and Protective Order of Elks, of Hobart, in both of which he has numerous friends.

On April 3, 1888, at Lancaster, Missouri, where he was teaching school, Mr. Fisher was united in marriage with Miss A. M. Potter, daughter of the late W. S. Potter, a farm owner of Lancaster, now deceased. To this union one child, Helen, was born, March 6, 1909, she now being a student in the graded school at Gotebo.

BEN W. RILEY. While he has been successful in business throughout a period covering at least forty years in various southwestern states, Ben W. Riley has also been successful in politics, though not so much from the standpoint of elective offices as of influential participation in governmental affairs for the sake of the public welfare. Ben W. Riley is an eminent representative of that class of Americans who advocate playing the political game square. His success probably is best attested by the fact that in the four years he was secretary and chairman of the state election board there were few criticisms of his work and no contest, a record that brought him unsolicited an unqualified endorsement from Governor Cruce, under whom he served. Mr. Riley has lived in Oklahoma for about thirteen years, was formerly a resident of El Reno, and is now in Oklahoma City, his office being in the Mercantile Building and his home at 1501 West Thirty-first Street.

Ben W. Riley was born at Sutton, Worcester County,

Massachusetts. His mother's family were the Woodburys, who for generations have been prominent in New England affairs. Through his mother Mr. Riley is descended from the first settlers of Massachusetts. One of them was the first representative of the Massachusetts Bay Colony to England, and protected those charged with witchcraft at Salem and assisted them in reaching safety in the Roger Williams Colony in Rhode Island. Two of the ancestors were minute-men and participated in the first fight at Lexington and Concord. One was the first collector of port at Boston. The old Woodbury home, surrounded by eighty acres, granted by the Massachusetts Bay Colony, is still in possession of the family at Sutton, Massachusetts. Mr. Riley's sisters have taken an active interest in the Daughters of the American Revolution and Colonial Dames. One sister is the wife of C. A. Pratt, an active banker and business man at Little Rock, Arkansas, and for a number of years a director in the Iron Mountain Railway. Mr. Riley's father's family were early settlers of Rochester, New York, and materially assisted in the growth of that city.

When Mr. Riley was a baby his parents settled in Sandusky, Ohio. His father was an ardent supporter of Vallandingham, the Ohican who led the opposition to the prosecution of the Civil war in the North, and in consequence of this affiliation Mr. Riley's life in Sandusky was not in harmony with the people during the Civil war, and about the close of that struggle the family removed to Jefferson City, Missouri. The recollections of Ben W. Riley of Reconstruction days are not pleasant, owing to the bitter feeling that remained after the war between the adherents of both sides. In the meantime he had received his education in common schools, and during the late '70s he attended school at the University of Michigan in Ann Arbor for two years, and finished his education in Holy Cross College at Worcester, Massachusetts. Mr. Riley's father was a Catholic and his mother a Protestant, and though baptized and confirmed as a Catholic he has himself not been an active member of any church.

Mr. Riley studied law at Jefferson City, Missouri, but never entered formal practice, choosing a business career instead. He served a term as state librarian of Missouri and first became interested in politics in that state during the campaign for governor between Crittenden and Hockaday. He was a member of the convention which nominated Governor Crittenden, and represented that governor at the registration of voters in St. Louis during a trying political period. Later Mr. Riley became identified with the Gould railway system in the hotel and eating house business conducted along the lines, and was in the business through Kansas, Missouri, Arkansas and Texas.

He lived for a number of years at Little Rock, Arkansas, and was especially active in democratic politics while there. He served as a member of the city council and took part in the campaign that resulted in the election of United States Senator Clarke. While living in Texas he took an active part in the campaign that resulted in the nomination and election of "Buck" Killgore for Congress, and was also a persistent supporter of James Hogg in his campaign for attorney-general and for governor. He helped to organize and was first lieutenant of the Eagle Light Battery in Arkansas; and was a member of the Reagan Guards of Texas.

Mr. Riley came to Oklahoma in 1902, locating in El Reno and engaging in the hotel business. He was mayor of the city during the closing territorial days and during the first few years of statehood. During his administration the installation of the city's paving and sewer system was begun and practically completed. He was a member of the El Reno Board of Education and served a term as president of the Commercial Club. Mr. Riley took an active interest in all conventions in Oklahoma to bring about statehood. He supported the policy to make an individual state of old Oklahoma Territory. He has attended every democratic convention since statehood, and was temporary and permanent secretary of the convention which ratified Governor Cruce's nomination. He contributed much in money and influence towards Cruce's election in 1910, and was a member of the finance committee in that campaign. Governor Cruce after his inauguration appointed Mr. Riley secretary of the state election board, and towards the close of the administration he was made chairman of the board. The success he achieved in these positions was marked because of the opposition he encountered at the hands of the republican party and owing to his diplomatic and praiseworthy handling of the innumerable details involved in the appointment of county election boards and the conduct of many special elections. Mr. Riley has never been a candidate for any state office, and the only one he has filled was under Governor Cruce. For six years he served as chairman of the County Central Committee of Canadian County, and was an active member of the campaign committee both times that Senator Robert L. Owen was elected United States senator.

JOSEPH MOSIER. The Osage tribe has had few more prominent names among its citizens than that of Mosier. Several of the family are named in this publication and one of them requiring individual reference was Joseph Mosier.

Joseph Mosier was a son of Thomas Mosier, a Frenchman, who identified himself with the Osage people in the last century and worked as a blacksmith among the tribe. He married an Osage woman, Basille Ahsinkuh. In the early '50s they moved to Neosho County, Kansas.

It was in Neosho County, Kansas, that Joseph Mosier grew up. He received his early education in the Jesuit Mission of that county, and as a young man received one of the head-rights in the lands of Kansas. The Mosiers were one of twenty-five Osage families who were allotted land in that state by the government. Joseph Mosier and his two brothers, Thomas and John, all enlisted in the Union army, being members of the Ninth Kansas Cavalry, and they were in active service throughout the conflict along the Kansas-Missouri border and in Arkansas and Indian Territory. They were finally mustered out in 1865.

Joseph Mosier, who was born August 5, 1841, had a very brief though honorable career. His death occurred near the old Osage Mission in Southern Kansas, January 7, 1871. His home was attacked in the night time when twelve inches of snow covered the ground. Joseph dragged in his night clothes, the house was set on fire, and he and his wife, who carried her son William, then eighteen months of age, in her arms, walked five miles to the nearest house barefoot and scantily clad. Joseph Mosier never left his bed after that, and died of pneumonia. Due to exposure and internal injuries received his widow died nearly six years later, on October 31, 1876. She was born in 1848.

THOMAS MOSIER, who in his time was one of the most prominent members of the Osage tribe, and who died at Pawhuska, September 20, 1912, was one of the children of Thomas Mosier by his Osage wife, and was a brother of Joseph Mosier, mentioned elsewhere in these pages.

Born among the Osages in Southern Kansas, December 18, 1843, Thomas Mosier grew up there, received his education in the old Osage Mission, and was a youthful soldier with his brothers in the Ninth Kansas Cavalry

Joseph Mosier

of the Union army. After the war he returned to Southern Kansas and remained with his tribe until they gave up their lands there and moved across the line into Indian Territory in 1872.

His name is of particular importance because of his prominent activities as an Osage citizen. He filled many official positions such as delegate to Washington, as national secretary of the Osage Council, national interpreter, United States interpreter in the Federal courts of Topeka, Fort Smith and other court centers, and was also connected with the department in charge of the leasing of Osage lands at Pawhuska.

WILLIAM THOMAS MOSIER, who spent practically all his life in those various sections of country occupied by the Osages, both in Kansas and Oklahoma, has been primarily a merchant, for many years clerked in the agency store of the Osage country and latterly was engaged in merchandising on his own account, and is now one of the chief owners of improved real estate at Pawhuska.

He was born at Neosho County, Kansas, November 1, 1867, a son of Joseph and Nancy (Waller) Mosier, and a member of the prominent Mosier family elsewhere referred to. After the death of his parents he was reared in the home of his uncle, the late Thomas Mosier, until he was fourteen years of age. Since then he has made his own way in the world. He had some schooling in the Pawhuska Government School, and spent part of two terms, during 1883-84, in the old Osage Mission, now St. Paul, Kansas. On July 5, 1885, he located at Pawhuska, and during the summer was engaged in running a mowing machine, and secured work for the winter in a general merchandise store trading with the Osage Indians on the Osage Reservation. For ten years he was an employe in one store at Pawhuska, beginning with wages of eighteen dollars a month and board and finally being paid seventy-five dollars a month. He was hired on account of his ability to speak the Osage tongue, though otherwise he had no experience in mercantile life. In 1901 Mr. Mosier engaged in business for himself with two partners. He bought at the administrator's sale the stock of E. B. Gravelt. After six months in business he incorporated the firm of the Osage Mercantile Company, and was its vice president until he sold his interests in 1914. Mr. Mosier had been closely and actively identified with merchandising at Pawhuska for fifteen years up to 1914.

His present interests are of large scope and importance. He is vice president of the Mercantile Real Estate Company, which owns the Osage Mercantile Company Building, the best business structure at Pawhuska. This company also owns the postoffice or Oklahoma Building. Mr. Mosier is a director in the Pawhuska Oil and Gas Company. Individually he owns the Osage Agency Building at the corner of Main and Osage avenues. This is the chief landmark in the city, having been built by the government in 1872. It is a venerable stone structure, and within and around it are associated much of the history and life of the Osage people during the past forty years. Mr. Mosier also owns a substantial home at 133 Osage Avenue, in which he has lived for the past fifteen years. He and members of his family through allotment have 4,200 acres of Osage land. For four years he was a director in one of Pawhuska's banks.

In politics Mr. Mosier has been throughout most of his career a good democrat. He served on the first city council at Pawhuska and was one of the members that drafted the present charter providing for a commission form of government. During 1891-92-93 he was clerk of the Osage council and prior to that had been permit clerk. In earlier days he knew every person residing on the Osage reservation. Mr. Mosier was reared in the Catholic Church. He is now the second oldest living Mason among the Osage Indians. He was one of the charter members of Washesha Lodge No. 110, A. F. and A. M., at Pawhuska, and has also taken thirty-two degrees in the Scottish Rite, being affiliated with the Consistory at Guthrie, the Knight Templar Commandery at Pawhuska, and Akdar Temple of the Mystic Shrine at Tulsa. He was also one of the charter members of the local Elks lodge, but his since given up that affiliation.

On May 29, 1895, at Pawhuska Mr. Mosier married Louisa Prudom. She was born on the Caney River in Osage County in February, 1877, and is of Osage Indian blood mingled with French. Her parents were Charles N. and Lydia (Nowberry) Prudom, both of whom were born in Kansas and are now living in Texas. The children born to Mr. and Mrs. Mosier are enumerated as follows: Charles Prudom Mosier of Pawhuska married Louisa Plomondom, youngest daughter of Mr. and Mrs. Moses Plomondom. The other children are John Thomas, Edwin P., Luther P., Christeen A., James Russell, and the youngest, Margaret, died in infancy.

GEORGE WILLIAM FRASS. One of the interesting young men of half Indian blood in the western part of Oklahoma is George William Frass, whose operations as a stock man and farmer and whose good citizenship has made him an important factor in the community of Calumet. He represents one of the best families produced by the commingling of sturdy white stock and the native Indian, and while the members of the earlier generations were closely identified with the life of the plain and the frontier, the younger ones exhibit that combination of energy and culture which are the features of modern Oklahoma.

It was in an Indian camp on the Cheyenne and Arapahoe Indian Reservation that George William Frass was born October 29, 1878. His father, William Frass, who was born at San Antonio, Texas, in 1850 of German parentage, and who died at Kansas City, Missouri, April 24, 1909, was a picturesque character in the old Indian Territory. For a number of years he lived as a cowboy on ranch and range, and later became a military beef contractor at old Fort Supply, Fort Reno and the Cantonment. From about 1873 he engaged in the cattle business on the open range of Indian Territory, and his interests as a cattle man continued until his death. William Frass in 1874 married a northern Cheyenne Indian woman. She was the mother of three children: Emma, now the wife of A. Kinsley, who is of Winnebago Indian blood and is now in the United States Indian service at Cantonment, Oklahoma. Rosa is the wife of Isaac Seneca, who carries the blood of the New York tribe of Seneca Indians, and is now in the United States Indian service at Chilocco, Oklahoma; and George William Frass, who is the youngest and the only son. It should be noted that Isaac Seneca, who married Mr. Frass' sister, was a graduate of the Carlisle (Pennsylvania) Indian School, and is well remembered by devotees of inter-collegiate football since he was one of the strongest players of the Carlisle team and won a place on the All-American Football team.

George William Frass received his education in the Government Indian school at Carlisle, Pennsylvania, and the Haskell Institute at Lawrence, Kansas. He finished with a business course in Oklahoma City, and then returned to western Oklahoma and has since been active as a cattle man at Calumet, and owns some valuable farming interests in that section. He inherited from his

Indian forebears a natural expertness in all the vigorous sports of outdoors, and from youth up has been an expert horseman. For a number of years he traveled with a wild west show as a cowboy rough rider. Fraternally he is a member of the Masonic Order, and is very active in the Baptist Church, being a member of the Gospel team of that church. He married Miss Asie B. Lazzelle, of Oklahoma City.

HARTSON D. FILLMORE, M. D. Few members of the Oklahoma medical fraternity have a broader range of experience and training for their profession than Doctor Fillmore, who has practiced in this state nearly fifteen years, and is now the leading physician and surgeon at Martha, in Jackson County.

A few interesting facts should be recorded concerning his ancestry. The Fillmores are of Scotch-English descent, and have been in America since colonial days. Doctor Fillmore's great-grandfather was a cousin of Millard Fillmore, the Vice President who succeeded General Taylor in the presidential chair. The branch of the family to which Doctor Fillmore belongs has given a number of names of more than local reputation to musical circles. From the vicinity of Buffalo, New York, this branch of the Fillmores moved to Cincinnati, Ohio, where Doctor Fillmore's grandfather spent all his life. He was a mechanical engineer, and for many years served as tax assessor in the City of Cincinnati.

Doctor Fillmore himself was born at Newport, on the opposite side of the Ohio River, in Kentucky, April 25, 1877. His father, Ebenezer Fillmore, was born in Ohio in the early '50s, and died at Cincinnati in 1878, the year following Doctor Fillmore's birth. He was a steamboat captain, and had command of the steamboat Bostonia, which plied between Cincinnati and New Orleans, his headquarters being in the former city. Captain Fillmore was a member of the Methodist Church. He married Zuba Dustin, who was born near Lexington, Kentucky, in 1847, and now lives with her only son and child, Doctor Fillmore, at Martha.

In 1880 the widowed mother removed to Lawrence County, Tennessee, where Doctor Fillmore spent his youth and gained his early education, graduating from high school in 1895. Unlike most boys of that age, he had fully determined upon his future profession, and in order to secure the best possible advantages and at the same time pay his own way, he went to New York City and found a position in the city dispensary, in which he remained as an employee until 1897. In the meantime he attended lectures in the medical department of the University of New York, and on November 19, 1895, entered the City Hospital, from which he received a diploma May 19, 1897.

In April, 1898, at the beginning of the war against Spain, he sailed from New York in charge of the hospital on board the auxiliary cruiser Panther, with the First Marine Battalion. The Panther touched at Key West, and soon afterwards engaged in the bombardment of Matanzas and Cardenas, Cuba. The vessel then sailed to the Bay of Guantanamo, where the first actual land battle took place between the Americans and Spaniards, Colonel Eliott being in command of the First Marine Battalion. Throughout the entire course of actual warfare in Cuban waters Doctor Fillmore was connected with the United States Navy, and was then transferred under contract to the United States Hospital Ship Missouri, and remained in that service as long as the hospital was in commission.

His experience as a medical student in New York and in the hospital service there and in the navy department was of itself a broad and liberal equipment for professional work, but after being released from the navy he entered the University of Tennessee and was graduated from the medical department with his degree M. D. in 1901. Doctor Fillmore began practice at Lawrenceburg, in Lawrence County, Tennessee, in the spring of 1901, but in the same year moved out to Oklahoma, and became one of the pioneer physicians in Johnson County. He practiced in that section until 1911, and for the following two years was health officer in Coal County, Oklahoma, and during 1913 spent a short time in Ada, and since 1914 has been located at Martha, where he is already well established in a medical and surgical practice, his home and offices being on Main Street.

Doctor Fillmore is a democrat, is a member of the Methodist Episcopal Church, belongs to the county and state medical societies, and in fraternal matters is affiliated with Martha Lodge No. 278, Ancient Free and Accepted Masons, with McAlester Consistory of the thirty-second degree Scottish Rite, and with Martha Camp of the Woodmen of the World. On May 17, 1905, in Johnson County, Oklahoma, he married Miss Annie A. Hill, who came to this state from Arkansas. They are the parents of two children: Hartson William, born September 1, 1907; and Clyde Chastaine, born November 25, 1909.

JAMES A. UTTERBACK. The successful man in any walk of life is he whose vigilance enables him to recognize opportunity when she comes a-knocking to make the most advantageous circumstances. Mr. Utterback, through his persistence and determination to succeed, has built up a splendid business at Bridgeport, where he owns one of the largest and best general merchandise stores. He is interested in public affairs and at one time gave efficient service as city councilman.

At Riverton, Fremont County, Iowa, October 14, 1872, occurred the birth of James A. Utterback, whose ancestors were natives of Holland, whence they immigrated to America in the colonial times and located in Pennsylvania. He is a son of Harrison and Mary (Allison) Utterback, the former of whom was born in Illinois, in 1847, and the latter was born in Missouri. Harrison Utterback accompanied his parents to Riverton, Iowa, in 1853, at which time he was but six years of age. He has resided in the vicinity of Riverton during the major portion of his life thus far and has devoted his attention to farming and to conducting a general store. Although very young at the time, he served for four months in the Union army in the Civil war, just prior to its close. He is a democrat in politics and is deacon in the Christian Church at Riverton. He and his wife have seven children, concerning whom the following brief data are here incorporated: William resides at Binger, Oklahoma, being a farmer and banker; Jesse lives at Tulsa, this state; James A. is the subject of this sketch; Simpson conducts a telephone exchange at Imogene, Iowa; Emaline is the wife of George Zimmerman, a farmer near Riverton, Iowa; Mary is the wife of Hawes Yates, of Riverton; and Myrtle is married and resides on a farm in Iowa.

James A. Utterback passed his boyhood and youth on his father's farm and attended the public schools of Riverton, Iowa. After reaching his majority he operated his father's farm for seven years and in 1900 came to Oklahoma, taking up a claim at Colony, in Washita County. In 1903 he sold his claim and located in the vicinity of Bridgeport, where he farmed for two years, at the end of which he opened up a general store in this city, the same being located on Market Street. In recent years he has enlarged his place of business and he now has the distinction of conducting one of the best equipped and most modern general stores in this section.

He caters to a high-class trade in both Caddo and Blaine counties. In politics he is a stalwart democrat and he served as city councilman. He affiliates with Bridgeport Lodge, No. 229, Ancient, Free and Accepted Masons; and with the Valley of Guthrie Consistory, No. 1, being a thirty-second degree Mason. He is an ex-member of the Independent Order of Odd Fellows. Mr. Utterback is an up-to-date business man, thoroughly alive to every chance for advancement.

In Rockport, Missouri, in 1892, was celebrated the marriage of Mr. Utterback to Miss Ida Davis, a daughter of the late Benjamin Davis, formerly a farmer in Missouri. Mr. and Mrs. Utterback have two children: Leta is the wife of Francis Labounty, a merchant at Watseca, Illinois; and Cleo is at home with her parents.

GEORGE BARNETT has been closely associated with Oklahoma City's growth and development for nearly twenty-five years, having located in that prairie town about two years after the opening. As a merchant he conducted a business which made him familiar to thousands of local citizens, and since retiring from business he has given his time partly to the administration of public affairs as a county commissioner and also to his private investments in local real estate.

George Barnett was born in New Orleans, Louisiana, February 28, 1859, a son of Joseph and Theresa (Hart) Barnett, his father a native of Berlin, Germany, and his mother of Leeds, England. Joseph Barnett joined the Confederate Army during the Civil war, and saw two years of service under General Beauregard. Both before and after the war he was prominently identified with business affairs in New Orleans.

George Barnett finished his education in the Central Boys' High School in New Orleans, and at the age of eighteen entered the cotton business, following that two years. His business career has made him a cosmopolitan, and he is not only familiar with all the larger trade centers of America, but has spent much time abroad. This experience was gained largely during his work as a silk buyer in foreign countries. He imported large quantities of silk to the United States, and for several years was engaged in the business of selling silks to jobbers in the United States.

When George Barnett came to Oklahoma City in the spring of 1891 he found a raw western town, but one with a promise of splendid development, and it was with an eye to the future that he determined upon making it his permanent home. All the older citizens of Oklahoma City will recall his place of business as a wholesale and retail cigar dealer, which was first in the Grand Avenue Hotel, and later in the fine store at the corner of Grand and Broadway in the City Building. He was the active proprietor of that business until he sold out to its present owner in 1907. In the meantime Mr. Barnett had invested extensively all the capital he could command in real estate, and for many years has been a buyer and seller, and still owns some very handsome properties. Mr. Barnett still maintains a business office in the State National Bank Building.

In 1912 Mr. Barnett was nominated by the democratic party and elected a member of the board of county commissioners. This was an unusual distinction, since he was the first democrat ever elected to this office from the city district. His two years of service were marked with faithful and conscientious work for the reduction of tax burdens and the placing of the county's affairs on a purely business basis. Mr. Barnett claims and is given credit for reducing the assessment values from $129,612 to $94,928 in 1913 and from $118,322 to $92,771 in 1914. While this reduction was obviously in the interest of the tax payers, at the same time he directed his efforts to another phase of the county's fiscal affairs so that public administration did not thereby suffer. As a result of reforms brought about during his membership on the board the county warrants, which had for several years been circulating often a number of months after issue and bearing 6 per cent interest, were placed on a cash basis, which saved many thousand dollars of interest charges. In other ways expenses of the fiscal administration were reduced so as to approximate a savings to the tax payers of $500,000 during the two years Mr. Barnett was on the board.

At Little Rock, Arkansas, January 18, 1880, Mr. Barnett married Miss Corinne Winter, daughter of Moses and Sarah Winter of Fort Smith, Arkansas. Mrs. Barnett's father was born in Hungary, and her mother in Alsace-Lorraine, France. They have two sons: Joseph, born in 1890, and now in the State School Land Department of Oklahoma; and Louis, born in 1892, now in the county treasurer's office of Oklahoma County. While Mr. Barnett is not an orthodox in religion, he is a humanitarian in principle and action, and has done good wherever and whenever he could. Fraternally he is affiliated with the Benevolent and Protective Order of Elks and the Knights of Pythias. He and his family reside at 217 West Fifth Street.

JAMES A. EMMONS. On the Rural Route No. 3 out of Pawnee, on a beautiful country homestead known as Wildflower Farm, lives one of the most interesting characters in Oklahoma, a pioneer of the Cherokee Strip, and with a record of experience in the West such as few living men can now equal.

James A. Emmons was born December 29, 1845, at Guyandotte, Virginia, a son of James and Nancy Smith Emmons. He was the first in a family of nine children. Some of his maternal forebears were early settlers in New England, probably at Boston, since a family of the name has been identified with business affairs in that city for many years. Some of them moved to New Jersey and thence on to Philadelphia. Mr. Emmons' grandfather was a soldier under Washington in the Continental army, and after the close of the war took up his home in Philadelphia, where he learned the trade of cabinet or furniture maker. In a few years there opened a prospect for taking up his revolutionary land grant, and he started for the border. At that time the Indians were troublesome in the Ohio Territory, and in the meantime he awaited for quiet at Guyandotte, Virginia. There he married a Miss Holenbaugh, whose family had come from North Carolina for the same purpose, namely to settle in the Northwest. The fruit of this marriage was James A. Emmons, Martin Luther Emmons and a daughter Sarah Emmons, respectively the father, uncle and aunt of James A.

James Emmons was born at Guyandotte, Virginia, May 20, 1810, and died in the fall of 1888. He grew to manhood and at the age of thirty-five in 1844 married Miss Nancy Smith, who was born at Staunton, Virginia, and died at Tecumseh, Nebraska, in the fall of 1902. Miss Smith was a beautiful woman, with bright blue eyes and coal black hair and fair complexion. She was also of revolutionary stock.

In the brick home of these parents James A. Emmons first saw the light of the sun on a cold December morning in 1845. In 1853 his father succumbed to the wanderlust and started for the western frontier of Missouri. The family embarked on the little Ohio River steamer, Reveille, for Cincinnati, and there took passage on the Golden State for St. Louis. James A. Emmons recalls some of the incidents on landing in St. Louis, remembers the "runners" calling the name of Hotel Monroe and the Virginia House. He recalls the passage of the boat through the locks at Louisville. From St. Louis the family steamed away up the Mississippi and the Missouri on the boat St. Ange, under Captain Smith, for Hill's Landing in Carroll County, Missouri. There they lived four years, the father taking up the business of hemp, tobacco and grain shipping. While there James A. Emmons attended a subscription school. In the fall of 1856 the family were once more on the move, this time for Omaha, Nebraska. They arrived at nightfall at the site now occupied by that thriving city. There James A. Emmons first saw an Indian camp, with hundreds of fires gleaming from the woods that climbed up the hillsides above the river. As he lay awake with staring eyes in his stateroom he could hear the drums and tom-toms and the weird music of their chanted songs, and could see their strange dances around the camp fires. He finally fell asleep to dream of Pocahontas, Captain Smith and all the Indian characters he had read of. On the same evening he witnessed a ball held in the new City of Omaha, attended by all the pioneer settlers. He recalls the wonder and beauty of that scene to the present time, with the splendid figures of the happy young men and women, full of health and hope, the curtsies of the ladies, the grand march, the figures of the Virginia reel or the minuet. When he awoke the following morning the steamer was running rapidly down the muddy Missouri, his father having concluded to make Sonora Island his landing place. Sonora Island is an island in the Missouri River, included in what is now the State of Nebraska.

Arriving there the father bought a lumber and shingle machine, and set it up in the midst of a great forest of tall cottonwood trees. Mr. Emmons has many interesting recollections of that island, where he spent several of the formative years of his youth. He and the other boys of the country side enjoyed the very acme of happiness in hunting squirrels, turkey, deer and other small game, in fishing and in tracing the winged honey bee to his tree. When he and his companions would locate the home of the swarm, they would take their little axes and work for half a day in chopping the giant cottonwood. They would frequently secure as their booty a big tub and sometimes two tubfulls of white honey. In the woods could be found all kinds of fruit, plums, June berries and blackberries. In the fall they would gather the popcorn and the great sweet yellow pumpkins, and their capacity for enjoyment was vastly greater than that of the present pampered race of youth. During the winter he and his companions attended a school kept in a log building. Spelling was chiefly emphasized in such schools, and all the scholars learned spelling as one of their chief accomplishments. His father finally sold out his lumber mill and went on a farm, where the children again spent ideal days and years.

Upon this happy pioneer life there finally came a cloud. People began to talk of war, and in 1861 the great national tragedy opened in the conflict between the states. Mr. Emmons was then sixteen years of age. One day he called upon his father for a half dollar, the first requisition of that kind in his life. The older man looked upon his son with surprise, and inquired as to the use intended for such money. The boy promptly answered that it was to buy a copy of Hardee's Military Tactics in order to get ready to fight for Virginia, his native state. The half dollar was given, and the book was bought, and young Emmons soon had all the neighboring boys marking time, marching and standing guard, parading, and had organized a complete camp of aspiring young soldiers. But a mother's fears intervened to prevent the enthusiasm of the boy from enlisting and going away to the front. Like the wise woman she was, she did not actually forbid him carrying out his designs, but gave him an attractive substitute. She showed him how much better it would be to become a sailor an occupation which would require clean clothes, with low quartered shoes and a jacket of attractive blue. That idea took hold, and at the age of seventeen, with the blessing of his father and mother, and the precepts of the latter impressed on his heart that he should not drink whiskey nor gamble, should be for life, he broke home ties and started down the river on the packet Emily, which plied the river between St. Joseph, Missouri, and Omaha, Nebraska. His commander was Capt. S. P. Ray, and he was fortunately placed under the steward, Fred Harvey. His first duties were those of knife shiner, and he took care of all the silverware, counting and locking it up three times a day. Cabin work was not agreeable and seemed to offer little opportunity for learning navigation. In the following spring he went to the lower deck in order to climb up, and the climbing was rapid and apparently easy. He became the boy mate, then the boy captain, and pilot, and for twelve years was in the steamboat business on the Missouri and Mississippi rivers.

After giving up steamboating Captain Emmons went to Sioux City, Iowa, and bought a stock of merchandise and lumber, the latter to be used in the construction of a store building. He had made up his mind to locate at the crossing of the Northern Pacific over the Missouri River, far up and away from civilization. He embarked with his goods on a steamer, and after a voyage of a thousand miles landed in August, 1872, and there set up the first building on the location of what is now one of the important cities of the Northwest. While building his store Col. George W. Sweet came around and platted the town, naming it Edwinton, in honor of the deceased first chief engineer of the Northern Pacific Railway. On first locating there his goods had been seized on the ground that he was in Indian territory and had no government permission to trade. Later his property was restored to him by Major General Hancock.

He had hardly reached his new location before making up his mind that he could not get along without the presence of his sweetheart, who was then at Yankton, a thousand miles away. Soon afterward he steamed down the mighty river, and on the 18th of September on a beautiful moonlight night at the home of her brother-in-law, Dr. Franklin Wixon, the Reverend Doctor Ward in the presence of a company of friends read the ceremony that united the hearts and hands of Nina B. Burnham and James A. Emmons for a life partnership. At 10 o'clock on the same night the steamboat Miner, with the bride and groom and a large passenger list, started off up the river, with the first bride and groom to arrive at old Edwinton, now Bismarck, the capital of North Dakota. In passing it may be noted that the pioneer citizens to this day do not know who placed the hated name of Bismarck upon their town.

Mr. Emmons and wife remained in Bismarck up to 1885, and prospered until the great capitol boom collapsed through the greed of a dishonest governor, causing them a loss of the fortune which had required years of toil to accumulate. In 1873 Gen. Edwin S. McCook had come to select three commissioners to organize the County of Burleigh. Captain Emmons was selected as chairman of the board, he being a democrat, and all the other members republicans. He served as chairman of the county board for ten years, and in that time put up all the county buildings. He was then appointed by Judge Shannon as United States Court Commissioner, and in that office served three years. By a special act of the Territorial Legislature he was designated to organize the County of Emmons, which was named for him, and in that work as in every other public capacity he performed his duties with a strict fidelity to the public welfare. A few years after locating at Bismarck, when General Custer came to Fort Lincoln, he would allow no one else to act as his captain and pilot in transferring the troops, and Captain Emmons spoke the words of farewell to that noted general when he started out on the fatal expedition which ended with the Custer massacre. After that calamity it devolved upon Captain Emmons and Col. William Thompson, who had seen service under General Custer, to break the news to the family at Fort Lincoln, Mrs. Custer being the ranking lady at the fort they had to communicate their tragic intelligence to her first of all, and it was a most trying ordeal for all concerned.

In 1883 the citizens of the village of Edwinton, now Bismarck, raised a hundred thousand dollars in order to build the capitol. Governor Ordway caused these funds to be withdrawn from two reliable banks and deposited in a bank which he had established himself. As a result of this transfer and misuse of the funds, the citizens who had so generously donated their cash and credit were almost financially ruined. At that time Mr. Emmons was associated with the First National Bank and with William A. Hollenback in building a three-story brick block, the finest steam heated building at that time between the Mississippi and Missouri rivers. He had also been appointed by the Territorial Legislature as the commissioner to build a twenty-five thousand dollar public school house. Through the treachery of the governor this accumulation of responsibilities bore heavily upon Captain Emmons, and when he left Bismarck in May, 1885, having paid all his debts, he possessed only $400. At that time he had a trunk full of worthless deeds to town lots of land, which he never recorded until August, 1915.

Captain Emmons then brought his wife back to Nebraska, and leaving her on the old homestead went West to Leadville, Colorado, where he leased a mine twelve miles up the Arkansas River. A short time previously three men had been blown to pieces in a blasting explosion, and the cabin and all the equipment wrecked. He engaged in mining there until his capital had been depleted to $25, and then started back to Lincoln, Nebraska, arriving there with only $10 in his pocket.

Captain Emmons has had almost a veteran's share in the newspaper profession. In 1877 he bought the Bismarck Tribune, a weekly paper to support the campaign of Hon. Bartlett Tripp for Congress on the democratic ticket. He conducted the paper altogether for about six months, and at the close of the campaign sold it to Stanley Huntley and Marshall Jewell, on credit. After his mining ventures in Colorado, Captain Emmons again took up the newspaper business, establishing the Nebraska State Democrat, a weekly paper. This was in 1888. He set up the plant in a new bank building in Lincoln. Prior to the first issue he engaged a young lady to attend a meeting out in the country at a school house, where William Jennings Bryan, then unknown to fame, was to make his maiden speech. The young lady returned with an account of the meeting and a report of the speech, and it was published in the first issue of Mr. Emmons' paper. He continued in the newspaper business at Lincoln until 1892 and sold out and moved to Guthrie in Oklahoma Territory. Here he became connected with the West South, a populist newspaper, and was one of its editors until September, 1893.

On September 12, 1893, Captain Emmons set out for Stillwater to register for a homestead in the Cherokee Strip. Four days later, on the 16th of September, he was one of the great horde of homeseekers who entered the strip. He made the run on a very aged gray horse, and on the 20th located his homestead claim, now the nucleus of the beautiful Wildflower Farm, near Pawnee.

Captain Emmons has from the first taken a great interest in developing this country. He has developed the Egyptian wheat and Fetrita, a grain which Mr. Bryan has prophesied will become the future breadstuff of the world. In the organization of Pawnee County in the early part of 1894 Governor Renfrew appointed Captain Emmons one of the first board of commissioners, and he was made chairman of the board and took a very important part in organizing the county government. He served three months, supervised the planning of the court house and jail. His friend Charles E. Vandervoort then took up his plans, organized a building company, and constructed the court house and jail. This court house was the first in Oklahoma and did not cost the tax payers a single cent. Captain Emmons and his noble wife have been farming in Pawnee County for twenty-one years, and have never yet failed to raise a crop. They plant from early spring until July, and then with the help of the rains and the wonderful Oklahoma climate, bring in their bounteous harvest. Captain Emmons has for a number of years been a correspondent to some of the leading newspapers in the United States.

MRS. JAMES A. EMMONS is likewise a pioneer of the West, and her associations and experiences are such as to deserve an individual sketch.

Nina Barbara Cole was born at Philadelphia April 15, 1853, a daughter of Howard M. and Louise (Torbert) Cole. Her father, Howard M. Cole, served in the Mexican war, according to the official information given by the War Department, as a corporal in Company G of the First Pennsylvania Infantry. He was mustered into service December 17, 1846, was transferred to Company F in the same regiment June 23, 1847, and was honorably discharged July 28, 1848.

Howard M. Cole was a victim of the ill-fated steamer San Francisco, and the following information concerning that vessel is a close quotation from the Navy Department Record. The steamer San Francisco was chartered by the United States Quartermaster's Department October 15, 1853, to transport the officers and men of the Third United States Artillery from New York to Benicia, California, and also carried the families of some of the officers and other passengers. The vessel sailed from New York December 22, 1853. Two days later, when about three hundred miles from port, the engines gave out, a heavy sea washed over the steamer, carrying away the entire upper cabin and with it four officers, a number of enlisted men, the wife of Major Taylor, the son of Colonel Gates, commanding the regiment, and a number of the citizen passengers. For four days there was a constant succession of gales. On the 27th the bark Kilby hove in sight, and her commander Captain Lowe lay by the wrecked steamer until the 28th, when the sea having abated in a measure a hawser was used to attach the two vessels, and boats sent back and forth removed the women and children, citizen passengers, about fifty soldiers and some officers to the Kilby. Before the work was completed a sudden squall of wind separated the two vessels, the hawser parted and the vessels drifted apart. The Kilby being unable to render further aid tried to make an American port. She was picked up by the packet ship Lucy Thompson and taken into New York. On the 30th of December the ship Three Bells, Captain Creighton, hove in sight of the San Francisco, laid by her until January 3, 1854, by which time the waves had sufficiently subsided for those left on the wreck to be taken off. The next day the ship Antarctic, Captain Stouffer, came to their relief and assisted in the rescue of those for whom there was not room on the Three Bells. Captain Watkins, the commander of the San Francisco, was the last man to leave the steamer, and with his officers and crew was taken on board the Antarctic to Liverpool, whither she was bound. Before leaving, Captain Watson had the San Francisco scuttled, so she sank as he was leaving. The Three Bells sailed for New York, and largely owing to the hard work and self-sacrificing efforts of its commander, Captain Creighton, and his crew, the ship, though leaking badly, and with her pumps constantly manned, finally came into safety. The sufferings of the passengers on the Kilby were very great, they were reduced to a few handfuls of parched corn daily to each person, the water supply was limited to a wineglassful a day, adverse winds drove them back several times as they neared shore. The providential arrival of the Lucy Thompson January 13th prevented threatened mutiny on board the Kilby. To her the passengers from the San Francisco were transferred and reached New York January 14th. The Kilby eventually reached her port, Boston. The Three Bells arrived in New York January 13th, and though it brought grief to many was a great relief to those watching for news of the disaster, since news of the perilous condition of the San Francisco had come to New York some days before.

Miss Cole, at that time an infant, having lost her parents, was taken into the home of a relative, Mrs. Burnham, then living in Philadelphia. After the landing of the Three Bells in New York, in 1855, Jefferson Davis, at that time Secretary of War in the Pierce administration, appointed Mrs. Burnham a matron in the United States army. General Harney's expedition was organized to go to the far West, to the Upper Missouri River, to establish a military post for the protection of the frontier against the powerful tribes of the Sioux Indians. They took five steamers loaded with troops and supplies, and early in 1855 steamed up the Missouri River, making their first permanent landing at the village of Omaha. The commander of the troops called on Governor Izard of Nebraska, reporting an outbreak of cholera among the soldiers on the steamers. The governor promptly called Doctor Miller, a young physician, to take the post as surgeon of the expedition. His young and beautiful wife bravely faced the danger of cholera and accompanied her husband. After a long and tedious voyage the destination was reached, and Fort Pierre was established at the mouth of Bad River on the west side of the Missouri, opposite the present site of the City of Pierre, the capital of South Dakota. This location was abandoned the following spring and the great military post was established 300 miles down the river, as Fort Randall. Here about 1856 Mrs. Emmons' memory and consciousness began among the soldiers, the barracks, the camp fires and the Indians on the frontier. In 1857 her foster mother resigned her position in the army, and found a home in the embryo Sioux City. There Mrs. Emmons grew to womanhood, and it was there that she first met her future husband in May, 1870. Since then she has been his companion and the inspiration of his life. As a pioneer woman she has the honor of having her name in the Township of Burnham, in Pawnee County. Mrs. Emmons is a lovable character, and having grown up on the frontier has been accustomed from early girlhood to exert herself in those beneficent acts of kindness which are so characteristic of the old-fashioned people, and still continues her active interest in the welfare of all her neighbors in Oklahoma. After this sketch was compiled and after a long illness Nina B. Emmons on July 7, 1916, closed her eyes to all earthly scenes, and loving friends laid her to rest at Meramac, Oklahoma.

WILLIAM REED LEVERTON, M. D. The entire absence of competition at Cloud Chief cannot account for the success which has been obtained in his profession by Dr. William Reed Leverton, who, since his arrival in 1910, has gained a liberal patronage, the confidence of his fellow citizens who have elected him county superintendent of health, and the respect and esteem of his fellow-practitioners who have chosen him secretary of the Washita County Medical Society. Doctor Leverton was born at Bowie, Texas, August 20, 1882, and is a son of W. B. and Mary Agnes (Sandefer) Leverton. On his father's side he is descended from a family which originated in Germany and became pioneers of Georgia, while on his mother's side he is of Scotch-Irish descent.

W. B. Leverton was born in Georgia, March 19, 1844, removed to Arkansas when about eight years old, and from Arkansas state enlisted, at the age of sixteen years, in the Confederate army during the war between the South and the North, in which he served four years as a member of Parsons' Brigade. Following the war he went to Arkansas, and in 1874 removed to Bowie, Montague County, Texas, that community continuing to be his home until 1893. In that year he came to Oklahoma and located in Washita County, eleven miles west of Cordell, on a homestead of 160 acres, on which he resided and carried on operations until his death, in October, 1902. He was a man of sterling integrity of character, well meriting the esteem and regard in which he was held. In political matters he was a democrat, while fraternally he was affiliated with the Masons, having been the first worshipful master of Cordell Lodge No. 127, Ancient Free and Accepted Masons. Mr. Leverton married Miss Mary Agnes Sandefer, a native of Indiana, who now resides at Cordell. Nine children have been born to this union: John B., a cattleman, residing at Patterson, California; Fannie, who is the wife of J. W. Ferguson, a ranch and stockman of Alpine, Texas; Indiana, who is the wife of T. H. Armstrong, a farmer of Dill, Oklahoma; Matthew O. and A. C., who conduct a farm in the vicinity of Dill; Mattie, who is the wife of W. A. Albin, a farmer of Cross Plains, Texas; Dr. William Reed; Almedia, who is the wife of James Perman, a merchant at Cordell; and George Elmer, who is assistant cashier in the Farmers National Bank at Cordell.

William Reed Leverton was reared on the homestead farm in Washita County, Oklahoma, where he remained until he was twenty-one years of age, but it was no part of his plans to follow the life of a farmer. He had received a common and high school education at Cordell, and when he left the ranch took preparatory work in the University of Oklahoma, at Norman. He next pursued a two-year course in the medical department of the same university, and his junior and senior years in the study of his chosen vocation were passed in the medical department of Saint Louis University. He was graduated therefrom in the class of 1909, with the degree of Doctor of Medicine, and while a member of college was affiliated with the Alpha Kappa Greek letter medical fraternity. Doctor Leverton began the practice of medicine at Cordell, but in 1910 came to Cloud Chief, where he has offices on Main Street, and is the only physician here. He is known as a careful student, keeping fully abreast of the advancements made in the profession, and as a skilled and steady-handed surgeon. A democrat in politics, he is serving as county superintendent of health, and for three years was also a member of the school board of Cloud Chief. He is an elder in the Christian Church and has been active in the work of that denomination. Doctor Leverton is fraternally affiliated with Cordell Lodge No. 127, Ancient Free and Accepted Masons, of which he is a charter member. His abilities and respect for the ethics of the profession have been recognized by his election to the office of secretary of the Washita County Medical Society and he belongs also to the Oklahoma State Medical

Society and the American Medical Association. As a citizen he has withheld his support from no movement which has promised the advancement of the general welfare.

Doctor Leverton was married August 2, 1909, at Plainview, Texas, to Miss Lillian May Colwell, daughter of S. N. Colwell, a ranchman of Hamilton, Texas. Two children have been born to this union: Edith Forest, born November 17, 1913; and Wilfred Bailey, born May 2, 1915.

MOSES E. WOOD, PH. D. Among the highly educated men who in recent years have been raising the standard of instruction in the higher institutions of learning of Oklahoma, Dr. Moses E. Wood is easily one of the most noteworthy. He came to the state during the reorganization of the faculty of the Central Normal School, and in 1913 was elected head of the department of psychology and pedagogy. He brought that position a broad and thorough scholarship and a long and varied experience as a practical school man.

Professor Wood was born in Clermont County, Ohio, March 25, 1869, and is a son of Thomas H. and Clara E. (Dungan) Wood. The paternal ancestry was English, the first of the family settling in Virginia. The paternal great-grandfather settled at Jarrett Station, the present site of Cincinnati, Ohio, in 1779. The maternal grandfather was born in Baltimore and was descended from Col. William Dungan, a soldier in the days of James II, and descended from Irish earls of Kildare. Professor Wood's father was a native of Ohio and was a contractor and builder. Professor Wood has one brother, W. A. Wood, at the head of the machinery department of a manufacturing concern in Cincinnati.

Doctor Wood as a boy attended the public schools of Ohio and finished his high school course in Muncie, Indiana. He then entered the National Normal University at Lebanon, Ohio, from which he was graduated Bachelor of Arts in 1894. Several years later he was granted a special life diploma from the educational department of the University of Kentucky and special certificates from the Summer School of the South at Knoxville, Tennessee. His advanced university training was obtained in Clark University at Worcester, Massachusetts, from which he received his Master of Arts degree in 1911, and during 1911-12 was a senior fellow in psychology, pedagogy and history in Clark University. His Doctor of Philosophy degree comes from Clark University.

For five years he was superintendent of schools in Ohio and for two years president of Summerville College in Tennessee. His school work in Kentucky covered a period of fourteen years, as superintendent at Horse Cave, Hodgensville, Litchfield, Wickliffe and other places. For one year he was superintendent of schools at Skykomish, Washington, and came from that state to Oklahoma in 1913,

Doctor Wood was married in 1884 at Lebanon, Ohio, to Miss Ida Kirtley, who was a school principal. Since marriage she has remained in educational work, taking her A. M. and Ph. D. degrees with her husband at Clark University. She is a modern, progressive woman and takes an active interest in the leading subjects that are engaging the attention of federated club women. They have a son, Edwin K. Wood, who is a graduate of the high school at Worcester, Massachusetts, a post-graduate of the high school at Skykomish, Washington, and holds a life diploma from the Central State Normal School of Oklahoma. He expects to complete his education with a Ph. D. degree in Clark University.

Professor Wood is a member of the Christian Church and is affiliated with the Modern Woodmen of America. His name is well known in educational circles, not only as a teacher but also as an author. He is a member of the Oklahoma Educational Association, the Central Oklahoma Educational Association, and the National Educational Association, also the Washington Educational Association and the Massachusetts Psychological and Pedagogical Association. His name appears as author of a work entitled "History of Superintendency in the United States," and of "The Development of the South since 1860." He has a special talent for historical research, and in the course of a few years it is safe to predict that his labors will result in the publication of several historical volumes. Professor Wood is a live, active, practical educator, completely in love with his work, and possessed of a thorough sympathy and understanding of the needs of young men and young women with whom he is constantly associated.

HANS A. KROEGER. A somewhat eventful and varied career has been that of this representative member of the bar of Oklahoma City, and his advancement has been achieved entirely through his own ability and well ordered endeavors. Mr. Kroeger is recognized as a man of high professional attainments and controls a large and important general law business, in connection with which he is a representative of the legal department of the Oklahoma Railway.

Hans Adolph Kroeger was born on a farm near the Village of Watkins, Benton County, Iowa, on the 4th of February, 1872, and his parents, Martin and Amelia (Emke) Kroeger, were both born in Germany. Martin Kroeger gave signal manifestation of his loyalty to the land of his adoption by serving as a valiant soldier of the Union in the Civil war. In the City of St. Louis, Missouri, in 1861, he enlisted in a regiment of volunteer infantry, and he continued in active service during the entire period of the war. He was in the command of General Sherman in the memorable Atlanta campaign, but after the capitulation of Atlanta he was assigned to detached duty and sent to the North. He and his wife later became pioneer settlers of Iowa, where he became a prosperous farmer.

Hans A. Kroeger availed himself fully of the advantages of the public schools of his native state, where he continued his studies until he had completed the curriculum of the high school at Traer, Tama County. At the age of sixteen years he assumed a position as clerk in a dry goods establishment in the City of Des Moines, Iowa, where he continued to be thus employed until he had attained to his legal majority. He then took a course in a business college in that city, after which he returned to Traer, where he continued to be identified with the mercantile business for a year.

With the opening to settlement of the Cherokee Strip in Oklahoma Mr. Kroeger "made the run" from Caldwell, Kansas, and located a claim at Pond Creek, but this land later proved to be on a section reserved for the support of the territorial schools, and his claim being thus nullified he went to Enid, where he remained about two weeks, after which he visited also the towns of Kingfisher and El Reno, and finally remained for some time in Oklahoma City. In the meanwhile Mr. Kroeger had admirably fortified himself for the profession of which he is now a prominent representative in Oklahoma, as he had completed a thorough course in the law department of the great University of Michigan, in which he was graduated as a member of the class of 1896 and from which he received the degree of Bachelor of Laws. In 1899, after his sojourn in Oklahoma Territory, he returned to Des Moines, Iowa, where he was engaged in the practice of his profession about four years and where he was associated with George Wemback, one of the distinguished members of the bar of the Hawkeye State. In 1903 Mr. Kroeger returned to Oklahoma Territory and established his residence at Francis, Pontotoc County, where he effected the organization of the First State Bank, of which institution he served as cashier about four years. The bank building was destroyed by fire thirty days after the institution opened for business, but luckily none of the funds of the bank was destroyed, as no safe had been installed and the cashier safeguarded the money by carrying the same to his home at the close of business each night, the means of transfer having been an ordinary pail or bucket. Soon after the new building had been completed and a safe and time-lock installed, the bank was burglarized by two outlaws, Ed Cody and Dave Vaughn, and in this connection Mr. Kroeger and his wife met with a strenuous and exciting experience, as denoted by the following brief record:

The two highwaymen proceeded to the little home of Mr. Kroeger about bedtime, disarmed him and made him and his wife prisoners. Mrs. Kroeger succeeded in escaping from the house, hoping to alarm the neighbors, but when one of the bandits started in pursuit her husband called to her to return, which she did. After forcing Mr. and Mrs. Kroeger to sit quietly in their home about two hours, the two outlaws started to march them to the bank, but upon discovering that other persons were still on the streets they returned to the house, where they guarded their captives until midnight. Mr. and Mrs. Kroeger were then compelled to accompany their captors to the bank and a demand was made that he open the safe. He opened the outer doors of the vault and then informed the captors that the time lock prevented him from proceeding further, as neither he nor any other person could open the inner vault until about 8 o'clock in the morning, the time for which the clock had been set. After cursing for an hour or two and frequently threatening the life of Mr. Kroeger, the bandits finally abandoned hope of attaining their ends, and under these conditions they took their captives onto the street once more and ordered them to proceed quietly to their home. As Mr. and Mrs. Kroeger started to walk away, one of the men, enraged over the failure of the venture, said to his companion, "I've a h—l of a notion to shoot the top of his d—d head off anyway!" At this juncture was the only time during the entire experience that Mr. Kroeger really had any fear for his life.

During the period of Mr. Kroeger's identification with banking interests at Francis the merchants of that town were preyed upon by an organized band of thieves who were operating extensively in that section of the territory and who frequently set fire to store buildings after having sacked the same of a large amount of its contents. Several reputable business men were financially ruined in this manner, but Mr. Kroeger obtained the cooperation of other citizens and they finally ran down the gang and were able to avoid further havoc in the community, as they succeeded in sending twelve or more of the malefactors to the penitentiary for long terms, the headquarters and "fence" of these outlaws having been at Randolph, Johnston County.

In 1907, the year which marked the admission of Oklahoma to statehood, Mr. Kroeger returned to Oklahoma City, where he resumed the active practice of his profession. For four years he served as general attorney, secretary and auditor of the Patterson street car system, and when Mr. Patterson's interests were purchased by the Oklahoma Railway Company and the two systems were consolidated, Mr. Kroeger continued his service as a valued member of the legal department of the corporation, with which he has continued to be identified in this capacity, besides controlling a large and important general practice, extending into the various courts of the capital city and involving his appearance in a number of specially important litigations.

At Rockford, Iowa, on the 18th of August, 1901, was solemnized the marriage of Mr. Kroeger to Miss Marian Teape, who was born and reared in that state and who is a daughter of Theodeus S. and Emily (Montrose) Teape. The one child of this union is Earl, who was born on the 5th of September, 1905.

HON. RICHARD A. MITCHELL. In noting the qualities which have advanced Hon. Richard A. Mitchell to a position of prominence among the citizens of Roger Mills County one is forced to renewed appreciation of courage, moral strength, honesty in public and private life, and fidelity to business, political and social obligations. When he came here, in 1907, he entered the journalistic field as the editor and owner of the Roger Mills Sentinel, a newspaper which started in a modest manner but which under Mr. Mitchell's able management has grown to important proportions, being known as one of the strong democratic organs of Western Oklahoma. While he was succeeding as a journalist, Mr. Mitchell was also taking an active part in civic affairs, and finally, in 1914, was chosen by his fellow-citizens for the mayoralty of Cheyenne.

Mr. Mitchell was born in Clay County, Missouri, June 30, 1881, and is a son of G. W. and Josephine (Harris) Mitchell. The family originally came from Ireland, probably before the Revolution, settling first in Virginia and then removing to Kentucky, where the grandfather of Editor Mitchell was born. He was a farmer and merchant and as a young man moved to Ray County, Missouri, where he passed the remaining years of his life and died at the age of seventy years. G. W. Mitchell was born at Lexington, Missouri, in 1843, and has passed his entire life in his native state, at present being a resident of Excelsior Springs. He was educated for the law and in his younger years passed some time as an attorney, but later became a minister of the Christian Union Church, in which he became president of the general council and served as such for twenty years. He was a man of broad education, being a graduate of Lexington College with the degrees of Bachelor of Laws and Doctor of Divinity, and was president of Grand River College of Edinburg, Missouri, for twelve years. He is now living a retired life. Reverend Mitchell fought as a soldier in the Confederate army under the noted leader, General Price, during the war between the states. He is a democrat in his political affiliation and a member of the Masonic and Odd Fellows orders. Mrs. Mitchell, who was born in Kentucky, in 1845, also survives, and has been the mother of ten children, as follows: B. S., a newspaper editor of Shattuck, Oklahoma; G. W., Jr., who is engaged in the mercantile business at Excelsior Springs, Missouri; O. F., also a resident of that place, engaged in the real estate and farm loans business; H. S., a minister of the Methodist Episcopal Church, residing at Centerville, Iowa; E. B., superintendent of the Colorado Southwestern Railway, at Denver, Colorado; Iona, who is the wife of R. S. Yates, a druggist of Edinburg, Missouri; E. L., an attorney of Cheyenne, Oklahoma, and a member of the state senate; E. Daisy, who is the wife of Charles Helmandollar, of Edinburg, Missouri, a farmer; Richard A., of this notice; and Grace O., who is the wife of Charles Sanderson, a telegraph operator of Hardin, Missouri.

Richard A. Mitchell was graduated from the high school in the vicinity of his home in Clay County, Missouri, and at the age of nineteen years entered

Grand River College, Edinburg, Missouri. At that time he began his connection with newspaper work at Edinburg, and after one year came to Oklahoma and settled at Grand, where from 1903 until 1907 he was connected with the Canadian Valley Echo. In September, 1907, Mr. Mitchell came to Cheyenne, where he established the Roger Mills Sentinel, which has steadily grown to be one of the leading democratic organs of Western Oklahoma, with a large subscription list in this part of the state. Mr. Mitchell is the owner of the building, plant equipment and office, situated at the corner of Main Street and Broadway, and of his residence in the eastern part of the town, in addition to which he has invested in several other pieces of realty including a business building on Main Street. He has been active and energetic in support of every movement which has promised to benefit Cheyenne and Roger Mills county, contributing personally and through the columns of his paper to the general welfare. A stalwart democrat in politics, in 1914 he was chosen by the citizens as chief executive of Cheyenne, and is giving the community excellent service in this capacity, his administration having been made notable by several progressive enterprises for civic improvement. Editor Mitchell is a member of the Christian Union Church, and is fraternally affiliated with the Fraternal Order of Eagles, the Modern Woodmen of America and the Woodmen of the World.

In 1910, at Cheyenne, Editor Mitchell was united in marriage with Miss Myrtle Repass, daughter of E. S. Repass, a farmer of Grimes, Oklahoma. They are the parents of three children: Roger Mills, born March 29, 1911; Iona, born July 5, 1913; and Robert Agles, born September 28, 1915.

Mr. Mitchell has been a leader in the democratic party, has been a member of the democratic central committee of his county for ten years, and is at present state committeeman from his county.

On Friday morning, June 2, 1916, between the hours of 2 and 3 o'clock A. M. the Roger Mills Sentinel newspaper plant, building and library was destroyed by fire. The fire was of incendiary origin, Mr. Mitchell being a noted newspaper scrapper was strong in his fight against socialism. But not an issue of the paper was missed, for Mr. Mitchell ordered new equipment at once. The Roger Mills Sentinel is considered by all the leading citizens of the county as the county paper.

ROBERT F. MEADOWS. Pawnee County has enlisted in the development of its natural resources a due quota of energetic, reliable and progressive citizens, and worthy of designation as one of the representative farmers and stock-growers of the county is he whose name introduces this paragraph and whose well improved landed estate is situated in the vicinity of the Village of Jennings.

Mr. Meadows was born at Albany, Clinton County, Kentucky, on October 14, 1860, and on a farm in that county he was reared to the age of thirteen years, when he accompanied the family on their removal from the old Bluegrass State to Chautauqua County, Kansas, where his stepfather became a pioneer settler and where he reclaimed a productive farm. Mr. Meadows is a son of Robert and Mary Ann (Brown) Meadows, the former of whom was born in Germany and the latter of whom was born in Virginia, she, as an orphan girl, having accompanied her grandparents on their immigration from the historic Old Dominion to Kentucky, where she was reared to maturity and where her marriage was solemnized.

Robert Meadows was a boy at the time when his parents came to America and established their home in the State of Kentucky. There he grew to manhood and his loyalty to the land of his adoption was significantly shown when the Civil war was precipitated on a divided nation, for, in 1861, he tendered his services in defense of the Union. He enlisted in a Kentucky volunteer regiment, with which he proceeded to the front and with which he participated in numerous engagements. He was finally granted a furlough and after visiting his home was killed by Confederate soldiers, while on the way to rejoin his command. His widow later became the wife of Hezekiah Brown, and with him removed to Kansas, where they passed the residue of their lives, her death having occurred in Chautauqua County, that state, in 1886. Of the first marriage were born six children, concerning whom the following brief record is given: James is deceased; Eliza is the widow of William Neal and resides on her homestead farm, fourteen miles distant from Oklahoma City; Daniel is deceased, and Robert F., of this review, was the next in order of birth; Sarah is the widow of Edward Van Sant and maintains her home in the State of California; Emma is the wife of Marshal Martin, of Sedan, Kansas; and Emmett is a prosperous farmer at a point twelve miles distant from Sedan.

Robert F. Meadows was a child at the time of the family removal to Chautauqua County, Kansas, where he was reared to adult age on the pioneer farm and where his scholastic advantages were those afforded in the common schools of the period. In that county he continued his identification with agricultural pursuits until 1891, when, soon after the organization of Oklahoma Territory, he came to this new country and established his residence at Chandler, the present judicial center of Lincoln County, where he remained until the opening of the Cherokee Strip, when he here obtained his present homestead farm, his entire active career having been one of close association with the agricultural and stock-growing industries, so that his prolonged experience and broad practical knowledge naturally gives him prestige and has won him definite success as a representative farmer of Pawnee County, the while his civic loyalty and liberality have been shown in his ready support of measures and enterprises that have tended to advance the best interests of the community. In earlier years he was concerned with the handling of cattle on the great open range and had to do with extensive operations in this line. In politics Mr. Meadows is found aligned as a stanch supporter of the cause of the democratic party, though he has never manifested any desire for public office.

In the year 1879 was solemnized the marriage of Mr. Meadows to Miss May Rogers, who was born on May 1, 1862, a daughter of Hon. Richard W. and Selina (Billman) Rogers, concerning whom further mention is made on other pages of this work, in the sketch of the career of their son Joseph L. Rogers, a prominent citizen of Pawnee County.

Relative to the children of Mr. and Mrs. Meadows the following brief record is entered: Robert is identified with agricultural activities in Pawnee County; Austie became the wife of Charles Shipley and her death occurred in the year 1900; Earl is a resident of Centralia, Washington; Pearl is the wife of Ira Thompson and they reside in the State of South Dakota; Carl is living at Centralia, Washington; Sherman, Christopher and Zephyr remain at the parental home; Frank died at the age of four years; and Leo is the youngest member of the home circle.

ROY E. HUFFMAN. Among the men of the younger generation in Northwest Oklahoma who are winning success in the field of finance is found Roy E. Huffman, cashier of the Quinlan State Bank, of Woodward County.

Mr. Huffman has been the architect of his own fortunes as he came to Oklahoma as a stranger, without means or other favoring influences, content to accept such opportunities as were offered by a growing community. When his chance came he was not slow in grasping it, and the steady advance which he has made is indicative of higher honors to come.

Mr. Huffman is a native of Illinois, born at Mount Pulaski, Logan County, January 5, 1890, a son of Samuel M. and Addie L. (Fletcher) Huffman. His father was born June 5, 1856, in Kentucky, from which state he went as a lad of fifteen years to Illinois, and after many years passed in Logan County removed to Labette County, Kansas, in 1903. There he resided until 1907, when he came to Oklahoma, being now a retired resident of Alva. Throughout his active life Mr. Huffman was engaged in farming and stock raising, and through industry and good business management accumulated a very desirable property. He has been content to live the life of the farmer, never having been a seeker for political honors and engaging in few business enterprises aside from those immediately connected with the products of the soil. In 1883, at Mount Pulaski, Illinois, he was married to Miss Addie L. Fletcher, who was born at that place, December 25, 1860, a daughter of Thomas and Mary (Bowles) Fletcher, the former a native of Ohio, and the latter of New York. Mr. Fletcher was a pioneer of Logan County, Illinois, to which part of Central Illinois he drove an ox-team overland from his early home in the Buckeye state. He passed his active years as a farmer and breeder of stock and died in 1902, at Mount Pulaski, whence he had gone at the time of his retirement. He was the father of fourteen children. Mr. and Mrs. Huffman had two sons: Roy E., of this notice; and Shelton William, born March 25, 1894, at Mount Pulaski, Illinois, educated at the Oklahoma Northwestern Normal School of Alva, and now a resident of that place, with his parents.

Roy E. Huffman received his early education in the public schools of his native place and was thirteen years of age when he accompanied his parents to Labette County, Kansas. He was graduated from the Labette County High School, of Altamont, Kansas, in the class of 1907, and in that same year came to Oklahoma to enter upon his career as a teacher in the public schools. After one year thus spent in Woodward County, he went to a business college at Kansas City, Missouri, taking a one-year course, and in November, 1911, entered the Security State Bank of Moreland, Oklahoma, as bookkeeper. He displayed such ability in that capacity that after one year he was advanced to the position of cashier, and held that office until January 1, 1915, when he was elected cashier of the Quinlan State Bank of Quinlan, a position which he still retains. This institution was established in 1907 by J. G. Bailey, who is now president, and who has another bank at Harper, Kansas, where he spends the greater part of his time. The State Bank of Quinlan is a sound, conservative banking house which has won the confidence of the people of the community out of whose needs it grew. Its cashier has done much to make himself popular with the depositors, who come from all over this part of the county and whose business he transacts in a courteous, expeditious and entirely capable manner. Mr. Huffman is a Mason, fraternally, and his religious connection is with the Methodist Episcopal Church.

On September 15, 1913, at Alva, Oklahoma, Mr. Huffman was married to Miss Ollie J. Hampton, who was born at Rich Hill, Missouri, February 20, 1896, daughter of Thomas and Sadie Hampton, natives of Missouri. One daughter has been born to Mr. and Mrs. Huffman: Virginia Halycon.

BENJAMIN FRANKLIN HENNESSY. Few men have had a more active and beneficial relation with Oklahoma's general progress in educational and agricultural development during the past fifteen years than Benjamin F. Hennessy, who recently retired from his office as secretary of agriculture for the state and is now giving practically all his time to the management of a fine ranch at Ferguson, in Blaine County. However, Mr. Hennessy is as much at home on the lecture platform as in his fields and among his stock, and for a number of years his work has called for public appearance and the entertainment and instruction of people in groups. While he is a very popular entertainer, and is a master of the humorous anecdote, much of his accomplishment has been of a serious nature and for the training of Oklahoma people in particular to a better utilization of their resources and advantages. He has done a great deal of lecture work for the benefit of churches, lodges, library associations and other organizations.

During his four years of service from 1911 to 1915 as secretary of the State Board of Agriculture Mr. Hennessy was one of the leading figures in public life in Oklahoma. He injected an element of dignity into the activities of the board, and, being essentially a school man, furthered in every possible way the cause of industrial education among young men and women and practical farmers as well. He represented the board in important state and national conferences and was an active member of the Southern Commercial Congress, and is still a director from Oklahoma in that body. To the various affairs of the board he applied modern methods, taking an active and leading part in demonstration work and discriminating agricultural education through newspaper and bulletin articles and in speaking tours of college and railroad officials. As one of the important representatives of the state government he proved a favorite speaker before various clubs and societies, and as an after-dinner speaker he is regarded as one of the most pleasing in the entire state.

Benjamin Franklin Hennessy was born at Woodstock, Illinois, September 21, 1873, a son of Daniel and Katherine (Lynch) Hennessy. His father was born at Kilkenny and his mother at Tipperary, Ireland, and they were the parents of ten children, six boys and four girls.

Mr. Hennessy completed his education in the Central Normal College in Kansas, where he was awarded the degree of Bachelor of Science in June, 1898. At an earlier date he was teaching in the districts of McPherson County, Kansas, and in 1895 was elected to the chair of English and Expression of the Central Normal College and held that position while continuing the studies leading up to his collegiate degree. In 1897 he had been appointed vice president of the Central Normal College. In 1900 he was chosen superintendent of county schools of Barton County, Kansas, an office he held until 1902.

While living in Kansas he was one of the seven delegates sent by Governor Leedy in 1898 to St. Louis to discuss the advisability of holding a World's Fair to commemorate the Louisiana Purchase, and was elected secretary of the Kansas delegation and held that office two years. In 1905 he was presented with silver and gold medals by the president of the World's Fair at St. Louis and in 1906 the World's Fair board gave him a beautifully engraved diploma.

In 1903 Mr. Hennessy came to Oklahoma as teacher of English and Expression in the Logan County High School at Guthrie. In 1907 he was selected as official representative of Oklahoma at the Jamestown Exposition, and gave stereopticon lectures relating to the resources of Oklahoma at that fair. In the meantime he had spent parts of several years working as state

organizer of farmers institutes for Oklahoma. Altogether he was connected with the State Department of Agriculture for a period of seven years, and resigned his office as secretary of the board January 15, 1915.

Since leaving office Mr. Hennessy has taken up his residence on his ranch in Blaine County, where he owns several hundred acres and is happily and busily engaged in the raising of horses, mules, hogs and cattle. He is considered an expert polo player, and one department of his ranch industry is the raising and training of polo ponies for the eastern markets. He is a democrat and in Masonry a member of the thirty-second degree Consistory of the Scottish Rite.

JAMES E. BRESLIN has practiced law at Guymon for the past ten years. He is a very capable attorney, came to Oklahoma with a thorough training in his profession, and has built up a large and prosperous practice. His practice is not confined entirely to Texas County, but extends to courts in the adjacent states of Texas, Colorado, Kansas and New Mexico. Mr. Breslin has the best selected and largest law library in Texas County, and owns the modern office building in which he has his professional headquarters.

Though he has practiced in Oklahoma ever since he left law college Mr. Breslin is a northern man by birth and ancestry. He was born on a farm in St. Croix County, Wisconsin, January 16, 1882, a son of William and Julia Jeannette (Riley) Breslin. His father was born February 22, 1846, at Montreal, Canada, a son of James and Elizabeth Breslin, both natives of Ireland. At the age of eleven years William Breslin came to the United States, the family locating at Manistee, Michigan. For fourteen years he was engaged in the lumber business in the northern woods of Michigan and then removed to Wilson, Wisconsin, where he was a farmer until his death on January 22, 1907. He was married March 17, 1878, to Miss Riley, who was born March 16, 1860, at Alemont, Ontario, Canada, a daughter of Michael and Eliza (Fannan) Riley, both of whom were born in Ireland. Mrs. Breslin died October 23, 1905, at Wilson, Wisconsin. In the family were ten children, seven sons and three daughters, namely: Harry M. of St. Paul, Minnesota; James E.; William F., a resident at Wilson, Wisconsin; Thomas J. of Cloquette, Minnesota; P. J., a lawyer at Guymon, Oklahoma; Ellen, wife of M. J. Hirsh of Holabird, South Dakota; Clara Belle, who is married and living in Duluth; Anna Belle, deceased; Sylvester S. of Winnipeg, Canada; and Arthur S., who lives at Wilson, Wisconsin.

James E. Breslin grew up in Wisconsin, attended the local schools, but for his professional education went to St. Paul, Minnesota, where he was graduated from the St. Paul College of Law on June 5, 1905. It was only a few weeks after his graduation that he came to Oklahoma, was admitted to the bar, and began practice at Guymon. He is a member of the Benevolent and Protective Order of Elks at Delhart, Texas, Lodge No. 1159.

THOMAS RIDGWAY REID. A member of the El Reno bar for a period of twenty-one years, Thomas Ridgway Reid is one of the best known lawyers of that place, and since May, 1912, has served in the capacity of city attorney. Both as a private practitioner and as a city official he has displayed the possession of fine talents, so that he is justly accounted a reliable and progressive member of the bar, who stands high in professional ability and as a man of broad business and financial judgment.

Mr. Reid was born at Saline Mines, Gallatin County, Illinois, July 16, 1864, and is a son of Robert and Elizabeth (Campbell) Reid, natives of the shire of Renfrew, Scotland. They were reared in their native land, where they lived until about fifteen years of age, at which time they accompanied their respective parents to the United States. Here they met and were married. Robert Reid early became a minister of the Presbyterian faith, and some time during the '50s was given the parish of Saline Mines, where for a number of years previously he had been an operator of coal mines. As a minister he was earnest and zealous, laboring faithfully in the service of the church and winning the love and confidence of his parishioners, who found in him not only a spiritual adviser but a true and faithful friend. He spent a long, full and useful life, and was eighty-five years old when death claimed him.

The public schools of Saline Mines furnished Thomas R. Reid with his preliminary educational training, this being supplemented by a course in the Southern Illinois Normal University, at Carbondale, Illinois. He next accepted a position as a teacher in the country schools, being thus engaged for a period of three years, and in the meantime applied himself to the study of law, with the result that he successfully passed the examination and was admitted to the bar at Shawneetown, Illinois, in 1888. At that place Mr. Reid entered upon the practice of his profession, continuing there until 1894, and building up a large and representative practice. While there Mr. Reid also took an active part in political affairs, and became known as one of the party leaders of republicanism in that locality. In 1891 he became the republican candidate for representative to the Illinois State Legislature, to which he was elected and in which he served one term.

Mr. Reid changed his field of operations from Illinois to Oklahoma in 1894, in which year he opened an office at El Reno. He has had good reason to congratulate himself upon his change, for in this state he has advanced steadily to a high position in his vocation and has been successful in attracting to himself a lucrative professional business. Also, he has continued his activities in political matters, and has been frequently called upon to serve in offices of public trust. In 1894 he was elected county attorney for Canadian County, Oklahoma, in which position he served one term, and in 1899 and again in 1901 was elected a member of the Territorial Legislature of Oklahoma, and in his first term was speaker of the house. In 1901 Mr. Reid was appointed receiver of the United States Land Office, at El Reno, a capacity in which he acted efficiently for ten years. In May, 1912, Mr. Reid was elected city attorney of El Reno, and has continued to hold this office to the present time. In his various public capacities he has at all times demonstrated an earnest desire to be of use to his community, and few men are held in higher general confidence and esteem by the public. Mr. Reid is a prominent Mason, being a Knight Templar and Shriner, and belongs also to the Knights of Pythias, the Benevolent and Protective Order of Elks and the Fraternal Order of Eagles. He is a consistent member of the Presbyterian Church, and at present is serving on the board of trustees thereof.

Mr. Reid was married in Illinois, in 1908, to Miss Jessie Robinson.

SOLOMON REVARD. A considerable proportion of the families in Oklahoma bear traces of the influence and relationship of the early French traders who, going out from St. Louis as their general headquarters, and beginning back in the eighteenth century, carried the goods of civilized manufacture among these Indians, established trading posts and lived among them, and very frequently married Indian wives. There is now living retired in Fairfax in Osage County a descendant of these old traders, and one of the most interesting men in the Osage country. Solomon Revard has been a resident of the present Osage country more than forty years and until recently was a very successful farmer.

He was born in Jackson County, Missouri, at the present site of Kansas City, April 17, 1855, a son of Peter and Leonora (Roy) Revard. Both parents represent names of distinction among the Osage people. They were born in Missouri, his father in 1826 and his mother in 1828. The grandfather was Joseph Revard, who was of mixed Osage and French stock. Joseph Revard married a girl, whose first name was Frances, and who was of German and French stock. The Roy family came from France originally, and settled in Missouri, and a number of its representatives served as early traders and employees of the great American Fur Company. The Roy family has a number of important relations with different tribes of Indians, and the name and family stock are found among the Osages, the Kaws and the Sioux. The Revard family also furnished early employees to the American Fur Company. The parents of Solomon Revard continued to live in Missouri until 1872 when they joined the rest of the Osage people in their migration to their new homes in Indian Territory where they spent the rest of their lives. The mother died in Osage County in July, 1884, and the father in November, 1888. Before coming to Indian Territory he had served as a member of the police force at Kansas City for four or five years, and after coming to the reservation spent his time as a farmer. Peter Revard and wife had five sons and two daughters: Solomon, Charles, who now lives on the reservation near Elgin, Kansas; Alexander, of Osage County; Emily Allen, of Tulsa; William, of Pawhuska; Franklin, of Bartlesville; and Mary E. McGuire, of Tulsa.

When Solomon Revard came to Indian Territory with his parents in 1872 he was about seventeen years of age. The previous year he had spent in work in the Kansas City Stock Exchange. For eleven years he was employed by the United States Government at Pawhuska Agency in the shoe and harness department. His education was acquired in the public schools of Kansas City, followed by two years in the Osage Indian School at Pawhuska. After leaving the agency store Mr. Revard took up farming, and followed that industry prosperously and enterprisingly until about four years ago, when he retired from the active responsibilities of a well spent career and has since lived quietly in his substantial home at Fairfax. Mr. Revard still owns a nice estate of 445 acres.

Outside of his interests as a business man and farmer he has been frequently honored with positions of trust and responsibility in tribal affairs. His study and observation of political problems has inclined him to give his support to the socialist party. He was reared a Catholic, but has taken no part in church affairs for the past twenty years.

On February 4, 1880, Mr. Revard married Miss Anna Traylor. She was born in Illinois September 23, 1854, and grew up in the states of Missouri and Arkansas. Her parents were William and Elizabeth (Armstrong) Traylor, her mother having been twice married. Both her parents died in Indian Territory, her mother on the Caney River and her father at Grayhorse. He spent most of his life as a farmer. Mr. Revard has one daughter Leonora McCarty, who lives in Missouri, and her six children, grandchildren of Mr. Revard, are named: William Todd, Solomon, Charles Wesley, Edna, Elizabeth and Madeline. Among the public honors which Mr. Revard recalls with particular satisfaction was his service as a delegate to the county convention which

chose district delegates for the constitutional convention which framed the present organic law of Oklahoma.

JOHN COYLE. Rush Springs, in Grady County, is the home of one of the most interesting of Oklahoma's pioneers. John Coyle first became acquainted with the country now known as Oklahoma as a soldier in the regular army of the United States during the decade of the '50s. From that time to the present most of his life has been spent in this section of the Southwest, and for more than forty years he has been a resident of what is now Grady County. The events in which he has participated and which he has witnessed would, if narrated in detail, form an important portion of the history of Oklahoma's development and progress.

John Coyle is a native of Scotland, and was born in the City of Glasgow, in 1836, a son of Edward and Margaret (Moore) Coyle. At Glasgow he spent his youth, attended schools and learned the trade of stone cutter and stone mason, but at the age of seventeen, in 1853, took passage on a vessel bound for America, and landed in the City of Quebec, Canada, where he spent three months and then went to New York City to work at his trade. Owing to labor troubles he left there in the fall of 1855 and sought employment at Boston. Being unsuccessful, he accepted an employment which has appealed to a great many men out of work at different times. He enlisted November 10, 1855, in the United States Army, and was assigned to Company F of the First Regiment of United States Infantry. After being for a time on Governor's Island, in New York Harbor, his regiment was sent to Corpus Christi, Texas. At that time the present cities of Dallas, Waco and Austin were on the extreme frontier of settlement in Texas, and all the country to the north and west was still the domain of the Indians and buffalo. The Federal Government was endeavoring to maintain as a guard to the settlements a cordon of military posts extending from the Red River south and west across Texas. It was to one of the oldest and most noted of these posts that Mr. Coyle and his comrades marched from Corpus Christi and took station at Fort Chadbourne. While there fifty of the First Regiment, men from Company F and Company C, were detailed to accompany Captain Van Dorn to the Washita Mountains in Indian Territory. John Coyle was among those who participated in that noteworthy expedition, record of which is an important part of early Oklahoma history. The Second United States Cavalry was also a part of the expedition. They went to the post on Otter Creek, and remained there until the end of 1858. Mr. Coyle was then ordered to join his regiment at Fort Cobb, Indian Territory. His enlistment expired in November, 1860, and he chose to remain in the district where most of his service as a soldier had been. He was employed for a time by Colonel Leeper, the Indian agent at Washita, Indian Territory, and also by John Shirley, the Indian trader there.

With the outbreak of the Civil war most of the United States troops were withdrawn from the frontier post. Mr. Coyle and three companions then started north with the intention of enlisting in the Union army. Owing to the unsettled conditions, the presence of numerous Confederate troops and wild Indians, they had to make the journey at night, while during the day they remained securely hidden. They finally reached Fort Gibson. Orders had recently been given to fortify the place, and Mr. Coyle was induced to take charge of the masonry work on the fortifications, and stayed there one year. The rest of the war period was spent in Kansas, where he found plenty of work at his trade as stone mason. At Humboldt in Allen County he built the county jail and other buildings, and at times had as many as 125 men working under him.

When the Missouri, Kansas & Texas Railroad was built through Indian Territory to Texas, Mr. Coyle had the contract for all the stone work between the Red River and Denison, Texas. In 1871, when this railroad contract was finished, he returned to Indian Territory and located about six miles below Wynnewood, farmed there a year, and then went to the settlement known as Elm Springs, now Erin Springs, in Garvin County. In that locality he continued farming and stock raising, and in 1874 moved to Bailey on Rush Creek, lived there about ten years, and in 1884 located in the vicinity of Rush Springs, his present home. His occupation was farming and stock raising on land leased from the Indians, and with the opening of the country for settlement in 1893, he sold his stock and farming interests and moved into the town of Rush Springs to engage in the grocery trade. Several years later his store was burned out, and he lost everything, having no insurance. After that misfortune he once more resumed farming, but in recent years has lived quietly retired at Rush Springs.

The above is a mere outline of the career of Mr. Coyle. For many years he has been one of the most influential men in his section of the state. In 1896 he was a delegate to the National Republican Convention at St. Louis, and in that convention delivered the six votes from Indian Territory for the nomination of William McKinley as president. In 1906 President Roosevelt appointed him postmaster at Rush Springs, and by reappointment from President Taft he held that office and gave it most capable administration until 1913.

Mr. Coyle relates many interesting incidents connected with his life as a soldier and as an early settler in old Indian Territory. While with the United States Army he participated in a number of engagements with the Indians. While at old Fort Chadburn the Indians had killed the mail carrier, and about a month later, when a band of Indians appeared before the fort, he was one of a party of twenty-four detailed to capture them or shoot them down. They killed four and wounded many others. Because of this heavy reprisal the garrison daily expected an attack from the Comanches, and while such an attack was never made, the soldiers were forced on do considerable extra work in building a palisade around the fort. While under the command of Captain Van Dorn and stationed at Otter Creek in the Washita Mountains, Mr. Coyle was part of a company that participated in the battle against the Comanches fought three miles east of Rush Springs. In that engagement fifty-six Indians were killed. Another interesting fact in that connection is the prominence of some of the officers engaged. The second in command and captain of Company B was Kirby Smith, who rose to the rank of general in the Confederate army. The first lieutenant of Company D was Lieutenant, afterwards, in the Civil war, General Hood. The second lieutenant of the same company was Fitzhugh Lee, afterwards Governor of Virginia. While Robert E. Lee was not present at the fight, he was at that time lieutenant-colonel of the Second United States Cavalry, and Companies A and B from that regiment were engaged with the Indians.

During the Civil war, and while employed at the Washita agency, Mr. Coyle had a narrow escape. He left the agency one day to go to Arbuckle, ninety miles distant. During the same night the post was attacked by Shawnee and Delaware Indians from the north, armed with guns and pistols. As a result of their attack about one hundred and fifty Tonkawa Indians, who were friendly to the whites, and seventeen white men were killed, and the only whites that escaped the massacre were Colonel Leeper, Doctor Sturm and Mr. Jones.

Mr. Coyle is one of the pioneer Masons of Oklahoma, and one of the most prominent and veteran members of that Order in Oklahoma. He has always been a firm believer that "Masonry is the handmaiden of religion," and his activities in the order have brought him many distinctions, so that he is probably one of the best known members of the craft in the state. He took his first degrees in 1866 in Iola Lodge at Iola, Kansas. He is a charter member of Rush Springs Lodge No. 7, Ancient Free and Accepted Masons, which was organized in 1875 and chartered in 1876. In 1875 Mr. Coyle built a schoolhouse at Elm Springs (now Erin Springs) and arranged the upper floor for a lodge room, though it was a very small one. That was the first home of the Rush Springs Lodge, and it was organized there. The meeting of organization was held on a Saturday, and Mr. Coyle invited the Rev. Mr. Davis of Pauls Valley, then presiding elder of the Methodist Episcopal Church, to come to Rush Springs and hold services on the following Sunday, Mr. Coyle guaranteeing a congregation. Elder Davis accordingly came and found the audience so large that he preached to them in the open, standing in the doorway of the school. In consequence of that meeting he at once organized a church and Sunday school, and it has been in continuous existence ever since.

Mr. Coyle's affiliations with Masonry deserve particular mention. He was the first master of Rush Springs Lodge No. 7, Ancient Free and Accepted Masons, held the office of master thirteen years, and is still an active member. He belongs to Chickasha Chapter No. 17, Royal Arch Masons; Chickasha Council No. 4, Royal and Select Masters; DeMolai Commandery No. 7, Knights Templar; and India Temple of the Nobles of the Mystic Shrine. The honors paid him by the state body of Masons are also noteworthy. He is a past grand master of the State Lodge, Ancient Free and Accepted Masons; past grand high priest of the Royal Arch Chapter; past master of the Royal and Select Masters; and past grand commander of the Knights Templar. He also became a charter member of Rush Springs Lodge No. 226 of the Knights of Pythias, and is a past chancellor and representative to the Grand Lodge, and a member of the Knights of Kadosh.

In 1874 Mr. Coyle married Miss Margaret Bowen, and they have had a happy married companionship of more than forty years. Prior to her marriage Mrs. Coyle was a school teacher in Illinois. They are the parents of four children: Edward Coyle, who is married and has six children; John L. Coyle, who has two children; Charles R. Coyle, who is also married; and Mary Coyle, who like the other children, is living at Rush Springs.

SEYMOUR FOOSE. For twenty-four years Seymour Foose has attended strictly to his profession as a lawyer in Blaine County. He was one of the pioneer settlers, acquired a homestead on the opening, and though he was one of a number of representatives of the legal profession when he came he is now the only one who has continuously practiced law in Blaine County since it was established. His success has been in proportion to the years of his residence, and there is probably no name in Blaine County that is mentioned with more familiar association with the professional, civic and business affairs of that community than Seymour Foose.

In the paternal line he is of Prussian ancestry, his grandfather, William Foose, having come from Germany and settled in Ohio as one of the early farmers of that state. Through his mother Seymour Foose is of English and Irish stock. With such a heritage of ancestry, he was born in Meigs County, Ohio, November 11, 1862. His father, John W. Foose, is also well remembered in Oklahoma, where he was a pioneer. He was born in Trumbull County, Ohio, in 1838. When a young man he moved to Meigs County, but was married in Gallia County in the extreme southern part of the state. From Meigs County he went out to serve as a Union soldier during the Civil war. He was a member of the Seventh Ohio Cavalry, and was in the army three years and ten months. At Rogersville, Tennessee, he was wounded in the leg and taken prisoner, and thereafter spent fourteen months in some of the notorious prison pens of the South, at Libby, Belle Isle, Andersonville, Florence and Charleston. After being exchanged he rejoined his regiment in 1864 in Georgia, when the war was nearly over. Returning to Meigs County, Ohio, in 1871 he went to Illinois, living in Wayne County for a number of years, and in 1884 going to Shelby County in the same state. In the spring of 1887 he brought his family to Sedgwick County, Kansas. While for many years a farmer, he was also an ordained minister of the Cumberland Presbyterian Church, but later became affiliated with the Methodist Episcopal Church, and represented that denomination as a minister in several of the southern counties of Kansas, in Sumner, Harper and Barber counties. In 1893 John W. Foose homesteaded a claim in Grant County, Oklahoma, being identified with the opening of the Cherokee Strip. In 1902 he removed to Medford, and for several years he filled the position of territorial librarian, in the duties of which office he died at Guthrie May 7, 1907. He had first been appointed territorial librarian by Governor Ferguson, and was reappointed by Governor Frantz. Politically he was a staunch republican, and was a member of the Masonic fraternity. John W. Foose married Nancy E. Dickson, who was born in Virginia in January, 1844, and is now living, past seventy-two years old, with her son, Seymour, in Watonga. Seymour was the oldest of a family of six children. Addie F., the next in age, married Reber Homrighous, and is a very capable business woman, living in Chicago, and looking after extensive real estate interests in Gary, Indiana; Thomas D., also a resident of Chicago, has for the past fifteen years been superintendent of the Fay livery business in that City; Jennie married Leander Martin, who was at that time probate judge of Blaine County, Oklahoma, but they now reside in Portland, Oregon, where Mr. Martin is in the real estate and lumber business; Elias K. is the wanderer of the family, and his whereabouts have been unknown to his relatives since 1906; Carrie is the wife of C. L. Anderson, and they own and occupy a ranch on Shaw Island in the State of Washington.

As a boy in Wayne County, Illinois, Seymour Foose gained the equivalent of a high school education. For three years he attended the Southern Illinois College at Enfield, and for four years, during 1882-85, was a teacher in the country schools in Shelby County, Illinois. The next two years were spent in teaching in Nemaha County, Nebraska. In the spring of 1887 he made the journey with his parents to Sedgwick County, Kansas. They accomplished that migration in true pioneer style, driving overland with a four horse wagon. He lived at home, managing the farm during the summer season for five years and teaching school in the winter. In the meantime he took up the study of law, attended the law department of the Garfield University, now known as the Friends University, at Wichita, Kansas, and in 1891 was graduated LL. B. and admitted to the bar at that city in the same year. He had also spent one year in the law offices of Holmes, Haymaker & Holt at Wichita, and after graduation was for one year in the law offices of O. H. Bentley, who is now mayor of Wichita.

Leaving Kansas in 1892, Mr. Foose drove across country to what is now Watonga, and was present at the opening of the lands in Blaine County, and while making the run on foot he was fortune in securing a lot situated south of where the present courthouse stands. After proving up his claim he sold it, and later acquired a homestead of 160 acres one mile southwest of Watonga, but has since disposed of that property also.

It was on April 19, 1892, that Mr. Foose began his practice as a lawyer at Watonga. Since then for twenty-three years his reputation has been steadily growing and he has handled an increasing amount of the important civil and criminal practice in Blaine County. In the fall of 1892 he was appointed deputy county attorney, and at the same time became a candidate for the office and was regularly elected for a term of two years. He thus has the distinction of having been the first elected county attorney of Blaine County. His success as a lawyer is reflected in his extensive property holdings. He is the owner of three quarter sections and a farm of eighty acres, all in Blaine County, has considerable real estate at Watonga, has a three-fourth interest in Block 10 of that city, on which his residence is situated, at the corner of Noble and Prouty avenues.

In various ways Mr. Foose has been identified with the public life of Oklahoma. He is a republican, and was a delegate to the National Republican Convention that nominated Roosevelt in 1904. During the Spanish-American war he enlisted and in July, 1898, was mustered in as first sergeant of Company M, First Territorial Regiment of Volunteer Infantry. The captain of that company was F. L. Boynton, a well known attorney of Kingfisher. He was promoted and commissioned second lieutenant by Governor Barnes in January, 1899, and received an honorable discharge from the Volunteer army at Albany, Georgia, February 13, 1899. After returning to Oklahoma he was appointed by Governor Ferguson as a member of his staff, and held that position four years, and subsequently was on the staff of Governor Frantz, by whom he was promoted to the rank of major. He resigned this commission at the end of Governor Frantz's term. Fraternally Mr. Foose is affiliated with Watonga Lodge No. 176, Ancient Free and Accepted Masons; with Peaceful Valley Chapter, Royal Arch Masons, at Geary, Oklahoma; and with Consistory No. 1, thirty-second degree of Scottish Rite, Valley of Guthrie.

In August, 1893, at Wellington, Kansas, Mr. Foose married Miss Nora Gilbert. She died a few weeks later, in October, 1893. March 17, 1899, at Oklahoma City, he married Miss Minnie B. Beals. Her father, Dwight A. Beals, who died in July, 1914, was an Oklahoma pioneer and had been a veteran of the Union army during the Civil war. Mr. and Mrs. Foose have two children: John S., born in June, 1902, is now in the freshman class of the Watonga High School; and H. Theodore, born in September, 1904, is a student in the local public schools.

LUCIAN BULLOCK SNEED. One of the first citizens of Guymon, Oklahoma, both in point of time and prominence, is Lucian B. Sneed, the present postmaster. Ten years ago, when the town was incorporated, he was honored with one of the first city offices. Mr. Sneed represents one of the old families of Oklahoma, being a son of Col. Richard A. and Annie R. (Bullock) Sneed. Colonel Sneed is still one of the active men in Oklahoma's affairs and is widely known over the state at large.

It was in the home of his parents at Jackson, Tennessee, that Lucian Bullock Sneed was born January 4, 1878. He was educated in the public schools of Gainesville, Texas, where his father lived for some years, and also attended a private school at Paul's Valley in Indian Territory. From school he at once entered business life as salesman in a general merchandise house and remained in that business until 1904. In that year he came to Guymon and became identified with the real estate business. When the town was incorporated in 1905 he was elected the first city clerk. In 1907 he was chosen the first county clerk of Texas County on the democratic ticket. His present office as postmaster of Guymon was given him in 1914, and he is now very capably managing this branch of the federal service.

Mr. Sneed is also secretary of the Guymon Business Men's Association and fraternally is a member of the Masonic order. On December 23, 1909, at Guymon, Oklahoma, he married Miss Edna B. Crum, daughter of W. A. and Nannie (McHenry) Crum, who were natives of Kentucky and Illinois, respectively. Mrs. Sneed was born April 4, 1886, at Mattoon, Illinois, and is a graduate of the Eastern Illinois State Normal School at Charleston, Illinois. Prior to her marriage she spent five years as a teacher. Mr. and Mrs. Sneed are the parents of one child, Richard Bullock Sneed, born at Guymon, Oklahoma, November 14, 1910.

JAMES W. KERLEY, M. D. In such a new country as Oklahoma pioneers are often young men in spite of their experiences and services. A future generation will find much to admire in the arduous and faithful service of those who accepted the hardships and limitations of a life on the frontier partly from a desire to establish their own economic well being and partly to perform their proper tasks in the world. Though a physician and surgeon of only fifteen years active experience, Dr. James W. Kerley may properly claim the distinction of having been a pioneer doctor in at least two communities in Southwestern Oklahoma. He now has a most successful practice and enjoys business prosperity and the comforts of a good home and the honors of citizenship at Cordell.

Born at Mountain View, Arkansas, June 4, 1871, he is one of the seven children of James and Nancy (Meadows) Kerley. His father was born in Hardin County, Tennessee, in 1848 and his mother in Wayne County, Tennessee, in 1846. James Kerley when a young man went to Arkansas, was married there, and that state was his home until the death of his wife in 1907. He has since lived at Cordell, Oklahoma, where he is a farmer and stock man. The seven children were: Dr. William W., of Anadarko, the twin brother of Dr. James W.; Melissa A., wife of Joseph Smith, a druggist at Bessie, Oklahoma; P. A., a farmer and stock man at Oil City, Oklahoma; Albert M., a railroad man living at San Diego, California; Ollie, who lives in Arizona, the widow of Joseph Dodson, who was killed while in service as a United States marshal in Arkansas; and Joseph E., a railroad man at San Diego, California.

Dr. James W. Kerley grew up in his native state of Arkansas, attended the public schools there, and in 1888 removed from Mountain View to Baxter County, Arkansas, where he was graduated from the high school in 1894. Doctor Kerley early adopted the principle of self-help as a means of advancing himself in the world, and for several years performed some useful service and at the same time earned money necessary for his higher education by teaching school. This was his regular occupation from 1894 to 1896, though in the meantime he had started to read medical works. In 1896 he entered the university at Nashville, Tennessee, took an active part in student affairs while there, and graduated M. D. in 1900.

His first work as a physician was done at Burns, in Washita County, Oklahoma, where in 1900 he was one of the first physicians to attend the wants of a large surrounding country, only sparsely inhabited at the time. In 1904 he took up his permanent residence at Cordell, where he was likewise one of the first of his profession to open an office. He has since gained a splendid reputation, and has all the practice he can well attend to. Doctor Kerley is a man of progressive ideas, and has never been content to practice long without active contact with the great centers of medical learning. He took a general postgraduate course in the New York Policlinic in 1904 and in 1906 spent several months specializing in surgery in 1908 at the Postgraduate Medical School and Hospital in Chicago, and in March, 1914, took some courses in diseases of children at the New Orleans Polyclinic.

Doctor Kerley has deservedly prospered in material fortune. His offices are in the Kerley Building, a business structure at the corner of Main and College streets which he owns. He also owns his home on College Street, and has two farms of 320 acres in Elk Township of Washita County, the management of which is entrusted to tenants. Doctor Kerley served as county superintendent of public health in Washita County from statehood until quite recently. He is a democrat in politics, is a member of the county and state medical societies and the American Medical Association, and fraternally is identified with Cordell Lodge No. 137, A. F. & A. M., and Cordell Lodge No. 167, I. O. O. F.

On March 7, 1897, in Arkansas, while still a struggling student preparing for his profession, Doctor Kerley married Miss Zona Morrison, daughter of D. A. Morrison, who later became a farmer in Washita County, Oklahoma, but is now living retired in California. Mrs. Kerley died May 23, 1901, survived by two daughters: Myrtle, who died at the age of eleven years; and May, now a student in the public schools at Cordell. In October, 1904, in Washita County, Oklahoma, Doctor Kerley married Mrs. Alma (Mowery) Arnold. Her first husband was the late Samuel Houston Arnold, a rancher of Washita County. Her father is W. H. Mowrey, a Texas farmer. There are three children by this union: Edith and Arthur, twins, both now in the public schools at Cordell; and James W., Jr.

JOHN P. LYNN. About twenty-eight years ago a young man rode horseback into the country of the Osages, stopping in the vicinity of the present City of Pawhuska where he found employment as a farm hand in looking after the farm controlled by the sisters who have charge of the St. Louis Indian School. Three years later he married and ever since that time John P. Lynn has been identified with that part of Osage County, and in many interesting ways is related to the development and upbuilding of Pawhuska. He came into the country without money and with no immediate prospects, but is now one of the largest land holders and one of the most influential men in the locality.

A native of Illinois, John P. Lynn was born in LaSalle County August 3, 1861, a son of Patrick and Margaret (McNamara) Lynn, his father a native of north Ireland and his mother of southern Ireland. The father came to the United States when five years of age and was married in Philadelphia. The family moved to Illinois about 1860 and in 1869 the father located in the new country around the present City of Independence, Kansas, establishing his home and taking a claim among the Osage Indians, who about that time removed from Kansas into Indian Territory. That was a time of primitive conditions, when all travel was either by horseback or on foot, and the father developed a farm from the virgin prairie in the vicinity of Indepence and his wife died there when John P. Lynn was twenty-two years old. The father afterward married again, and took up a claim in old Oklahoma Territory. He died in Oklahoma City and was laid to rest by his wife in Independence, Kansas. By his first marriage there were three daughters and three sons and two of the sons and two daughters are still living. By the second marriage there were four boys and three girls.

John P. Lynn had to get his education by very limited attendance at local schools at Independence, Kansas. After coming into the Osage country as already related he spent three years as foreman on the farm near the St. Louis School. On March 19, 1895, he married Mary A. Rogers, who was born in Pawhuska or where that city now stands November 5, 1876, a daughter of Patrick and Constance (Canville) Rogers. Her father was born in Ireland and her mother in the United States, being French on her paternal side and Osage Indian through her mother. Mrs. Lynn's grandfather Canville belonged to the old French stock originally located in the vicinity of St. Louis, and from there moved West to where Kansas City now stands, and at one time owned forty acres of land covering the site of the old Union depot in that city. He was a French trader. Mrs. Lynn's father was a trader through the Osage country in the early days, and came to the Southwest from Decatur, Illinois, and both he and his wife died at Pawhuska and were laid to rest on the Cary River, twenty-five miles north of Pawhuska. Mr. and Mrs. Lynn have five children, named John, Joseph, Theresa, Patrick and William.

For many years Mr. Lynn has found full employment for his energies in ranching and stock raising. His wife and each of their five children have allotments of Indian lands, to the amount of a section for each person, and Mr. Lynn has charge of the operation of this large estate, and is also the individual owner of 1,400 acres which he has bought at different times. His home is in Pawhuska, and is a large and commodious residence at the east end of Main Street. He built the old part of this home soon after his marriage, but remodeled and added extensively two years ago. He has witnessed the entire development of the city, and some of the business and residence structures stand on land which he platted as the Lynn addition. Lynn Avenue was named for him, and he has a section of land along that thoroughfare at the east end of Main Street. Mr. Lynn has done considerable in improving the city, has built and sold several homes, but for the most part sells unimproved lots. In his home farm he has fifty acres of alfalfa, and keeps about 250 head of hogs in the fields. He is also a feeder of the black muley or Angus cattle. Other interests are as a stockholder in the Pawhuska Oil & Gas Company, the largest corporation in Osage County. Mr. Lynn is a democrat and a member of the Catholic Church.

When Mr. Lynn first came to the vicinity of Pawhuska and found employment with the sisters of the St. Louis School, there were no railroads through this section of country, and he frequently drove to Elgin and Cedarvale in Kansas, the nearest railroad stations, twenty-five and forty miles away. He made these trips on a number of occasions to meet the bishop or other missionaries, and the journeys were often made in bad weather, with no bridges over the swollen streams and the fords were not passed without some danger and inconvenience. At different times also in the early days Mr. Lynn drove hogs across the country to Elgin, the nearest place for shipment. These drives were also made in the cool winter seasons, and required three or four days. At night he would wrap his blanket around him and lie down among the hogs, and several times would get up in the morning with his blanket covered with snow. Another interesting fact in connection with the family record is that Mrs. Lynn's father in the early days had his corral on the site now occupied by the postoffice in the heart of the city at Pawhuska.

VERNON B. BROWNE is one of the youngest bankers in Oklahoma, and a few years ago organized and has since been cashier and chief executive of the May State Bank of May. This bank was established February 20, 1912, with a capital stock of $10,000. Its deposits on March 7, 1916, aggregated $87,684.92. While Mr. Browne is cashier and active manager the president is Charles H. Martin. The stockholders in the bank are largely local people, and it is a local institution and has thoroughly deserved the prosperity it has enjoyed.

Vernon B. Browne was born June 25, 1885, at Seneca, South Carolina, a son of A. C. and Anna M. (Hubbard) Browne, who were also natives of South Carolina. His father was born December 5, 1857, and his mother December 1, 1860, and they were married November 7, 1878. In 1888 the family removed to Texas, and in 1896 to Fargo, Oklahoma, where A. C. Browne is now engaged in the grain business. Of their five sons and four daughters only three are now living, Vernon, the son, and two daughters: T. Browne, was born June 27, 1889, and was married October 20, 1909, to J. W. McGinley, a farmer at Wheatland, Oklahoma, and their three children are: Onetia, Hugh and Vernon; and Anna M., born October 12, 1895, and still at home with her parents at Fargo.

Vernon Browne received his education in the public schools of Panhandle, Texas. At the age of twenty-one he took a business course at Oklahoma City, and in 1907 became bookkeeper in the Stock Exchange Bank of Fargo. On January 1, 1909, he was elected cashier of this institution, but resigned on January 1, 1912, in order to organize the May State Bank. He has been actively identified with that town in all its public spirited movements, and besides his interests as a banker he has extensive farm holdings.

Mr. Browne is a thirty-second degree Scottish Rite Mason, being a member of Consistory No. 1 at Guthrie, is also an Odd Fellow, and politically is a democrat, but without official aspirations. On August 5, 1914, at Cherryvale, Kansas, he married Miss Myrtle Williams, who was born November 24, 1887, in Kansas, a daughter of J. M. and Mollie (Laird) Williams. Mrs. Browne was a teacher for four years prior to her marriage in the city schools of Woodward, Oklahoma. They have one child, Eugene Vernon, born at May, October 24, 1915.

HON. ED BAKER. While it is in the office of county judge of Blaine County that Mr. Baker is best known to the general public, having administered that position with impartial ability and efficiency since 1912, he has for more than twenty years been identified with this section of Oklahoma, having come in as a pioneer, and has lived a life of usefulness and honor as a teacher, farmer, homesteader, and has been in the active practice of law at Watonga since 1901.

Of an old American family, the Bakers originally came from Germany and settled in Maryland prior to the Revolutionary war. Judge Baker was born in Creston, Iowa, September 23, 1866. His father, Britton Robert Baker, who was also a pioneer in Blaine County, was born in Maryland in 1827, and died on his homestead in Blaine County, Oklahoma, December 25, 1910. From Maryland he removed to Eastern Iowa, and was married near Burlington to Louisa Jane Anderson. She was born in 1832 in that portion of old Virginia now

West Virginia, and died at Watonga in October, 1911. After his marriage Britton R. Baker moved to Creston, Iowa, and in 1872 to Mount Ayr, Iowa, where he changed his vocation as a farmer to that of a merchant. He also lived in Nebraska and Kansas, and in 1887 went to Benton County, the center of the great fruit growing district of Northwestern Arkansas, and was a farmer there until 1893. In that year he joined the early colonists of Blaine County, Oklahoma, and bought a farm on which he lived until his death. As a young man he gave four years of active service in the Federal army during the Civil war, enlisting in the Twenty-ninth Regiment of Iowa Infantry. As a young man he had been an active worker in the Methodist Episcopal Church. The children were: Ulysses R., who was last heard of in 1880, and is thought to have been killed by the Indians in Arizona; Ida F., wife of William H. Boyce, a retired farmer living at Watonga; Ira L., a blacksmith at Colgate, Oklahoma; and Judge Ed Baker.

Judge Baker has been identified with the new West during most of his active life. He gained his education in the public schools of Mount Ayr, Iowa, up to the time he was fourteen. He helped his father in farming a Nebraska homestead in Knox County until 1885, and then went with the family to Ness County, Kansas, engaged in farming there two years, and after removing to Benton County, Arkansas, in 1887 taught school for three years. He continued his vocation as a school teacher for one term after going to Barber County, Kansas, in 1891, and from there came to Blaine County, Oklahoma, in August, 1892. Here he first identified himself with the primary work of developing homesteads, and secured for himself a claim of 160 acres in the north end of Blaine County. That was his home and the scene of his labors as an agriculturist for ten years. In the meantime he had taught a number of terms in the local schools, and while teaching diligently pursued his studies in the law, until admitted to the bar at Watonga in 1901. In 1902 Mr. Baker sold his farm and has since lived in Watonga. In that year he was elected county attorney, and the two years spent in that office were engaged in a creditable fulfillment of his public duties and also proved a valuable experience in his career as a lawyer. Judge Baker conducted a large general practice in civil and criminal law until 1912, in which year he was elected county judge of Blaine County, and in 1914 was re-elected for another term of two years. His offices are now in the courthouse at Watonga.

Judge Baker is a democrat, and fraternally is affiliated with Watonga Lodge No. 176, Ancient Free and Accepted Masons; Geary Chapter No. 59, Royal Arch Masons; Weatherford Commandery No. 17, Knights Templar; India Temple of the Nobles of the Mystic Shrine at Oklahoma City; with Watonga Camp of the Modern Woodmen of America; and with the Knights and Ladies of Security at Watonga. In Benton County, Arkansas, in 1891, Judge Baker married Miss Lula B. Locke, whose father, S. B. Locke, was a farmer in that part of Arkansas. Two children have been born to their marriage. Britton R., who graduated from the Watonga High School in 1913, spent the next year as a teacher in his home county, and is now a member of the freshman class of the University of Oklahoma in Norman. F. Locke, the second born, graduated from high school in 1915 and is now a teacher in the public schools of Hitchcock, Oklahoma.

JOHN FRANK STOTTS. During his early boyhood the horizon of J. F. Stotts was bounded by a Texas farm. He lived in a country where hard work was the rule and an education a difficult matter to obtain. He has earned his opportunities, and for the past thirteen years has been in the broader realm of business affairs, and is now a well known banker in Southern Oklahoma and cashier of the First State Bank of Ringling.

John Frank Stotts was born in Montague County, Texas, September 15, 1882, and his family originally came from Germany and settled in the State of Indiana. His father, J. M. Stotts, was born in Missouri in 1845 and died at Woolsey, Oklahoma, in December, 1903. He moved from Missouri to Texas and in 1891 to Woolsey, Indian Territory. He was a farmer and had a cotton gin at his place. As a boy he saw four years of service in the Confederate army, enlisting from Missouri in Price's army. He was three times taken prisoner, but effected his escape each time. He was a member of the Christian Church and for many years a deacon, and also affiliated with the Masonic fraternity. J. M. Stotts married Miss Anna Scott, who was born in 1855 and died at Loco, Oklahoma, in 1907. Their children were: Hattie, wife of W. J. Gossage, a farmer at Mangum, Oklahoma; Sim, a cattle man and deputy sheriff at Cornish, Oklahoma; John F.; Ida, wife of Clayton Durling, a painter and decorator at Comanche, Oklahoma; and Charles, who is assistant cashier of the First State Bank of Ringling.

John F. Stotts as a boy attended subscription schools maintained in log houses in the vicinity of Woolsey. His early life was spent on the farm and in assisting around the cotton gin, but in 1902 he graduated in a business course at Draughon's Practical Business College in Fort Worth, and from that time forward began making his ability and influence felt. In 1903 he entered the employ of the Chickasha Cotton Oil Company, and in 1904 became connected with J. M. Robberson's general mercantile house at Loco, Oklahoma, with which business he remained six years. He next became cashier of the State Bank of Loco, and continued in that office until May, 1914. He left Loco to organize the First State Bank of Ringling, of which he has been cashier, and has also served as vice president of the State Bank of Loco. The First State Bank of Ringling occupies a building constructed April, 1914, on Main Street, but a modern brick structure is now in course of construction, one block further west, and this will provide a splendid home for the institution, which has been growing rapidly. The officers of the bank are: J. M. Robberson of Loco, president; W. W. Woodworth, vice president; J. F. Stotts, cashier; and Charles Stotts, assistant cashier. The capital stock is $25,000, and a recent report already shows surplus and profits of $2,500.

Mr. Stotts is a democrat, and is affiliated with Loco Lodge No. 163, Independent Order of Odd Fellows, in which he is a past grand and a representative to the Grand Lodge two terms. He is past consul commander of Loco Camp No. 682 of the Woodmen of the World and was its representative to the head camp.

In 1906, at Loco, Mr. Stotts married Miss Lucy Wyatt of Montague County, Texas. Their children are: Orlando, born in 1908, and Maysel, born in 1910.

E. E. BREWER and NEATHA HOMER SEGER. The proprietor and editor of a newspaper occupies a certain ground of vantage from which he may make or mar the reputation of individual or community, build up or tear down a cause worthy of public approval or support. Not only the City of Geary, but Blaine County at large has reason for congratulation that the Geary Booster is in such safe, sagacious and clean hands. Founded in 1912, it is considered one of the best general newspapers published in this part of the state, as well as an outspoken, fair play exponent of the best elements of the republican party—in fact, it is in all respects worthy of the care and sound judgment displayed in its columns, and reflects credit upon its editors and publishers, Messrs. E. E. Brewer and Neatha Homer Seger

E. E. Brewer was born September 20, 1874, in Vermilion County, Illinois, and is a member of a family which originated in Holland, emigrated thence to New York in colonial times, and finally became pioneers of Ohio. His father, Rev. J. W. Brewer, was born in Sullivan County, Indiana, in 1831, and was there married and for some years followed preaching as a minister of the Methodist Episcopal Church. He then removed to Vermilion County, Illinois, where he followed contracting and building, and in 1875 removed to Sherman, Texas. Five years later he went to the Texas Pan Handle, in 1889 became a pioneer white settler of Oklahoma when he located at El Reno, and in 1901 came to Geary, Oklahoma, where he continued to be engaged in business as a contractor and builder until his death, June 24, 1913. He was a man of industrious and energetic habits, won friends through his many sterling qualities, and was considered a good and public-spirited citizen in whatever community he found himself located. He married Miss Emily Hawkins, who was also born in Sullivan County, Indiana, in 1835, and who died at Geary in 1904. They became the parents of four children, as follows: William A., who resides at Springfield, Missouri, and is a minister of the Methodist Episcopal Church; Estella, who married E. E. Carhart, a bank cashier and automobile dealer of Pan Handle, Texas; Jessie M., who is the wife of D. M. Young, a real estate dealer of Chicago, Illinois; and E. E.

E. E. Brewer attended the public schools of Pan Handle, Texas, and El Reno, Oklahoma, until reaching the age of fourteen years, at which time he engaged in newspaper work at Mobeetie, Wheeler County, Texas, on the Mobeetie News. There he remained nine months, receiving his initiation into the mysteries of journalism as represented in the office of a country newspaper, and in 1889 became a pioneer of Oklahoma when he came to El Reno and entered the employ of the El Reno News. From that time forward he was identified with various newspapers, always adding to his knowledge and capacity as a newspaper man, until 1901, when he came to Geary, Oklahoma, and after being with the Geary Bulletin for a time helped to establish the Geary Journal, in company with Mr. Stackhouse. After two years of operation the partners disposed of their interests and in 1912 Mr. Brewer became the founder of the Geary Booster, choosing as the name for his paper that word which must always hold a prominent position in the vocabulary of the industrial history of Oklahoma, as typical of what has caused its business, agricultural and general growth. Mr. Brewer continued as sole proprietor of this paper, until April 1, 1915, when he sold a half interest to Neatha Homer Seger, thus forming the firm of Brewer & Seger, which has since continued. The paper has republican policies and is considered as strong and influential among the people of Blaine and the surrounding counties where it has a large subscription list and secures its full share of advertising contracts. The plant and offices are on Main Street and are well equipped with newspaper and general printing machinery.

Mr. Brewer was married at Yukon, Oklahoma, in 1897, to Miss Ida Garrison, daughter of the late Oliver Garrison, who was a farmer, the ceremony being performed by Mr. Brewer's brother, the Rev. W. A. Brewer. Two children have been born to this union: LeRoy William and Lamara L., who are both members of the sophomore class at the Geary High School. Mr. and Mrs. Brewer are members of the Methodist Episcopal Church. He is independent in politics, and while not an office seeker has served four years as city clerk of Geary. His fraternal connection is with Geary Lodge No. 139, Ancient Free and Accepted Masons; Lodge No. 6976, Modern Woodmen of America; and Lodge No. 138, Independent Order of Odd Fellows. He is interested in several local industries and is a stockholder in the Oklahoma Oil Company.

Neatha Homer Seger, junior partner of the firm of Brewer & Seger, was born at Darlington, Canadian County, Oklahoma, December 2, 1876, and is a son of John H. Seger, of Colony, Oklahoma, in the sketch of whose career, elsewhere in this work, will be found a complete account of the family. Neatha H. Seger was educated in the district schools of Reno City, Canadian County, Oklahoma, following which he attended the Bryant Normal University, at Stromsburg, Nebraska, and was graduated from the business department of that institution in 1895. Following this Mr. Seger was engaged in teaching school for one term, when he turned his attention to the mercantile business at Colony and continued to be engaged therein in 1905. Removing at that time to Tuttle, Oklahoma, he continued in the same business for nearly four years and in 1909 returned to Colony, where he worked on a farm. In 1910 he received his introduction to newspaper life when he bought the Colony Courier, a publication which he edited at Colony until April 1, 1915, then coming to Geary and buying a half interest in the Geary Booster. While a resident of this place for only a comparatively short period, Mr. Seger has already established himself firmly in the confidence of the people, and has many friends in a wide acquaintance. Through the columns of the paper he is assisting Mr. Brewer in his efforts to advance the best interests of Geary and to encourage every movement for the making of better education, greater morality and a finer citizenship.

Mr. Seger was married December 30, 1903, at Colony, Oklahoma, to Miss Jessie Mattoon, daughter of the late William H. Mattoon, who was in the engineering department of the United States Government service. Two children have been born to this union: Genevieve Geraldine and Lloyd Francis, both of whom are attending the public school. Mr. Seger is a republican, and has served as a member of the school board of Colony and as justice of the peace for five years. He belongs to the Dutch Reformed Church, at Colony, and his fraternal connections are with Weatherford Lodge, Ancient Free and Accepted Masons, and the Modern Woodmen of America at Colony.

GILBERT W. DUKES. The name of Dukes is associated with the settlement of the Choctaw Nation from its earliest occupancy by the tribe, and one of its representatives has achieved the distinction of the governorship of the nation to which he belongs. The multifarious affairs of the nation developed and brought out the men of strength, and among them was Joseph Dukes, the founder of the pioneer family and the father of Gilbert W. Dukes.

Joseph Dukes and his family were of the first of the Choctaws to leave their Mississippi home in the early '40s and establish new homes in the wild country recently treated for in the Red River country of the Far West. He settled near Fort Towson and there became a man of prominence as a farmer and a minister of the Presbyterian Church. Among his children were Gilbert W., Charles, and Josephine, who married Benjamin Woods and died in the Choctaw Nation. The father and mother both passed away near Fort Towson, where they are buried.

Gilbert W. Dukes attained his majority in the vicinity

of Fort Towson and received a liberal education, joining the Confederate troops raised in the Choctaw Nation and in after years served his people in many civic positions. As sheriff and district judge his services marked him as a proper man for the safe and conservative conduct of the nation's affairs in the executive chair. He was a member of the Progressives, and in the deliberations looking toward final dissolution of tribal relations and the coming of statehood he showed his friendship for the movement and gave it his support. He was chosen governor and served two years. Since the advent of statehood he has espoused the principles of the republican party. Governor Dukes was married to Miss Angelina Wade, a daughter of Governor Wade, who also filled the gubernatorial chair. She died in 1893, the mother of Joseph A. and Henry Dukes, of Garvin, Oklahoma. For his second wife Governor Dukes married Mrs. Isabel Sexton, and their children were Minnie, Letta and Dee Dukes.

MATTHEW J. KANE. Justice Kane, of the state Supreme Court, is a native of the Empire State, born in Niagara County on the 28th of November, 1863. In 1887 he graduated in law from the Georgetown University, District of Columbia, with the regular degree of LL. B. He commenced the practice at Wichita, Kansas, in 1888, but upon the opening of Oklahoma to settlement, April 22, 1889, located at Kingfisher. In 1907 he served as a member of the Oklahoma Constitutional Convention, his first term as justice of the state Supreme Court commencing in September of that year. He was chief justice of that body in 1909-12. His present term expires in 1917. It is needless to say that he stands high in his profession. A further mark of his leadership was his selection, in 1904, as a delegate to the Universal Congress of Lawyers and Jurists, held at St. Louis in that year.

HENRY FRANKLIN BENSON. While the great metropolitan dailies, with their tremendously long lists of subscribers, exert a great influence in the country in molding public opinion, it is probable that their more modest and unassuming brethren of the fourth estate, the newspapers of the smaller cities and the country districts actually come into closer contact and are more in sympathy with their readers. Many of these latter are edited by men of journalistic capacity and broad knowledge, whose opinions are frequently quoted by the larger papers as indicative of the trend of public thought in their communities. An excellent representative of this type of alert and progressive newspaper, which has its recognized place and an important one in the scheme of things, is the Geary Journal, published at Geary, Blaine County. The proprietor and editor of this newspaper, Henry Franklin Benson, is still a young man, but his entire business career, covering half of his life, has been passed as a journalist, and he has already accomplished as much in his chosen vocation as many men attain after a lifetime of effort.

Mr. Benson was born on a farm six miles east of Marlow, Oklahoma, March 6, 1888, and is a son of James H. and Amanda (Squires) Benson, and belongs to a family which, originating in England, was founded in Colonial days in Massachusetts, from whence its members moved to Mississippi and later to Texas. James H. Benson was born in Burnett County, Texas, in 1855, and was but eight years of age when, with his father, James Benson, a pioneer ranchman of West Texas, he was attacked by a band of Comanche Indians, his father being killed. Young James H. was captured and held prisoner for two years, when the red men were rounded up and the lad's release was purchased by the United States Government. He grew to manhood in West Texas, where he became a cowboy during the days of the open range. Later he was married and with the coming of the agriculturists he settled down to farming, continuing to be engaged therein in Texas until 1887. In that year he came to Oklahoma and settled east of Marlow, and five years later became a pioneer in Roger Mills County, where he homesteaded 160 acres. He resided there until 1897 and then moved back to Marlow and engaged in the mercantile business until 1902, when he moved to Anadarko at the time of the opening. He remained there only two years, however, after which he came to Geary, where he has since been engaged in business as a carpenter and contractor. He has erected a number of the buildings of this city and is known as a skilled and reliable workman, a business man of the soundest integrity and a man faithful in the keeping of engagements. He is a stanch democrat, a supporter of progressive and beneficial movements, a consistent member of the Baptist Church, and a valued member of the Independent Order of Odd Fellows. Mr. Benson was married in West Texas to Miss Amanda Squires, who was born in the Lone Star State in 1864 and died at Marlow, Oklahoma, in 1899. Of their children, two are living: Henry Franklin, of this review; and Roy, born in Roger Mills County, Oklahoma, March 16, 1895, received a public school education in this state, began to work at the age of fourteen years in connection with newspapers, has followed that vocation at various places in Oklahoma, and is now associate editor of the Geary Journal.

Henry Franklin Benson attended the public schools of Roger Mills County for two years and completed the graded schools at Anadarko, Oklahoma. This training was subsequently supplemented by two years of attendance at the Geary High School, and when he was sixteen years of age he became an apprentice in the printing plant of the Geary Journal. One year later he went to Hinton, Oklahoma, where he entered the plant of the Hinton Record and soon won promotion to foreman, and later was made editorial manager, a position which he held until 1910. In that year he leased the Tuttle Standard, which he edited for six months and then spent one year at Oklahoma City, also in the newspaper business. Mr. Benson then became manager for W. B. Anthony's paper, the Marlow Review, and held that position for nearly a year while Mr. Anthony was acting as secretary to Governor Haskell. From that time forward, Mr. Benson worked on various papers in Oklahoma until 1912 when he came to Geary and became associated with E. E. Brewer in the founding of the Geary Booster, of which he was editor for 1½ years. With this thorough training and practical experience, Mr. Benson felt qualified to enter the newspaper field on his own account, and in April, 1914, purchased the Geary Journal, of which he has since continued as the editor and proprietor. The Geary Journal was founded in 1900 and is a supporter of the principles and candidates of the democratic party. It has an excellent subscription list in Blaine and the surrounding counties, and also has a number of subscribers outside of the state, while its prestige as an advertising medium has brought business of that character in constantly increasing volumes. The well equipped plant and offices are located on South Broadway. Mr. Benson is a supporter of good government, of progressive municipal measures and of the advancement of morality, religion and education, while his good citizenship has been displayed on numerous occasions. He is a democrat in his political views and is at present deputy court clerk of the Geary Division of the County Court.

In 1910 Mr. Benson was married in Oklahoma City to

Miss Grace Miller, daughter of F. W. Miller, a merchant of Hinton, Oklahoma. Mr. and Mrs. Benson have two children: Thelma, born November 20, 1910; and Frank, Jr., born August 31, 1912.

WILHELM WALTER MOORE. As an educator and minister of the Christian gospel Wilhelm Walter Moore has become well known in several communities of Oklahoma. He is now giving his entire time and attention to educational work and is principal of the Barnard School at Tecumseh.

Not yet thirty years of age, Professor Moore has laid the foundation of a career of great usefulness and is properly regarded as one of the able educators of the new State of Oklahoma. He was born at Casey, Illinois, July 27, 1888. His parents were Walter T. and Mary M. (Letner) Moore, both of whom were born in Illinois. The paternal great-grandfather Moore emigrated from Dublin, Ireland, in the early part of the nineteenth century and for a number of years was a slave-holding planter in the South. Grandfather Thomas Moore took up the profession of law and died at Charleston, Illinois, in 1858. Walter T. Moore, who was born in 1853, now resides at Marshall, Illinois. He began his career as a Baptist minister and preached in various towns in Illinois, and for three years lived at Geary, Oklahoma, where he also had charge of the Baptist Church. Just before leaving Geary he joined the Methodist Episcopal Conference, and has since been a regular minister of that denomination. With the exception of the three years spent in Geary, Oklahoma, he has lived practically all his life in Illinois. He is a democrat and a member of the Independent Order of Odd Fellows. His wife, Mary Letner, is the daughter of Louis Letner. The latter was born in 1818, has followed a career of farming, and is still living in Illinois only a few years short of a century. Louis Letner's father came from Germany and settled in Tennessee. Professor Moore was the youngest of three children. His sister Ella married Ed Marshall, a farmer living at Pawnee, Illinois. His only brother is L. Clarence, who finished his education in Shurtleff College at Albany, Illinois, leaving that institution in 1906, and is now pastor of the Central Christian Church at Waterloo, Iowa.

Wilhelm W. Moore in the winter of the year in which he was born went with his parents from Casey, Illinois, to Oakland in that state. He gained his early education in the public schools there, attended the preparatory department of old Shurtleff College at Albany, finishing in 1902, and then entered the regular collegiate department, where he remained lacking one term for the full four years' course, leaving school in 1906.

On leaving college his first employment was as passenger conductor on the I. T. S. Railroad, with home at Springfield. In that practical work he spent about two years. He then entered the ministry, as a member of the Illinois Conference of the Methodist Episcopal Church, and after having charge of the church at DeWitt, Illinois, for a time he was called to Stillwater, Oklahoma. In addition to preaching he also taught high school work. After six months at Stillwater he was transferred to Jet, Oklahoma, for a year and then joined the Christian Church. In 1913 Mr. Moore taught in the McLoud, Oklahoma, High School and at the same time filled the pulpit of the Christian Church at McLoud and Tecumseh, keeping his home in McLoud.

In June, 1914, Mr. Moore came to Tecumseh and has since been the capable man in charge as principal of the Barnard School. He has under his supervision ten teachers and a regular enrollment of 520 pupils. In June, 1916, he was granted the degree A. B. from the Teachers Professional College of Austin, Texas. In politics Professor Moore is a democrat.

On May 11, 1914, at Tecumseh, he married Miss Edith Fisbaugh. Her father, A. B. Fisbaugh, is a merchant at Jet, Oklahoma. Mrs. Moore was educated in the public schools, finishing the sophomore year in the Christian University at Enid, Oklahoma.

FRANK R. BUCHANAN, M. D. Among the younger members of the medical profession in Oklahoma, Dr. Frank R. Buchanan of Canton has the ability and skill which are guarantees of a permanent success, and has already gained a good practice in and about his home town in Blaine County.

The Buchanan family to which he belongs originated in Scotland and in colonial times was planted in the Province of Pennsylvania. Doctor Buchanan's grandparents, T. J. and Harriet Buchanan, were both born in the East. His grandfather, T. J. Buchanan, was born in Pennsylvania in 1829, was an early settler and farmer at Windsor, Missouri, where his wife died, and he afterwards moved to Kansas and in 1894 was one of the pioneers to settle in the vicinity of Thomas, where he homesteaded a claim of one hundred sixty acres. He is now living retired at the age of eighty-six in Thomas. During the Civil war he served on the Union side.

T. J. Buchanan, Jr., father of Doctor Buchanan, was born at Windsor, Missouri, in 1865, and when quite a young man entered the railroad service in the Southwest. He was married at Albuquerque, New Mexico, to Miss Martha Jane Hughes, who was born in Georgia in 1867. After that he followed railroading for a number of years, with home at Gallup, New Mexico, but in 1896 came to Thomas, Oklahoma, and buying a farm of 160 acres a quarter of a mile northwest of the town, developed his land and has since been one of the prosperous men engaged in diversified agriculture in this section. He is a member and trustee of the United Brethren Church, and is affiliated with the Brotherhood of American Yeomen. He and his wife are the parents of eight children: Harriet Nuel, wife of William C. Dodd, who is in the insurance business at Thomas, Oklahoma; James H., a railroad foreman at Bloomington, Illinois; Dr. Frank R.; Hazel Winona, a senior in the Thomas High School; Hobart Lawrence, in the freshman class of the Thomas High School; Lewis Edward and Wilhelmina, both students in the public schools; and Amy Oneta.

It was during the residence of his parents at Gallup, New Mexico, that Dr. Frank R. Buchanan was born, June 30, 1892. However, most of his life has been spent in Oklahoma, and he has been a witness to many transformations in the central part of the state. He attended public school at Thomas, but left high school before graduating, and in 1910 entered the University of Arkansas to take up the study of medicine. In 1911 he was granted a high school diploma before the Indiana State Board of Registration. After two years in the University of Arkansas he finished his education by two years in the College of Medicine and Surgery of Valparaiso University, from which he was graduated with the degree M. D. in the class of 1914.

Doctor Buchanan took up active practice at Thomas on June 1, 1914, in association with Dr. T. B. Hinson. While there he helped to establish the Thomas Hospital, and owned a half interest in that institution. A year later, on June 1, 1915, he removed to Canton, and has since conducted a general practice, though specializing largely in surgery. His offices are over the Bank of Canton.

He is a member of the state and county medical societies and the West Central Medical Society, is a

republican in politics, and is affiliated with Thomas Lodge No. 265, Ancient Free and Accepted Masons, and Thomas Chapter No. 53, Royal Arch Masons.

On September 10, 1914, at Osakis, Minnesota, Doctor Buchanan married Miss Carrie Hesse, daughter of the late George Hesse, who was a miller. They have one child, Hubert Ruel.

OREN V. DILLON. Since 1903 the cashier of the First National Bank of Geary, Oren V. Dillon has become well known in banking circles of Blaine County as a thoroughly capable and energetic business man and financier. Mr. Dillon, whose entire career has been passed in the banking business, was born at Scotttown, Ohio, November 19, 1883, and is a son of John H. and Josie (Mount) Dillon, natives of Lawrence County, Ohio.

Vincent Dillon, the great-grandfather of Oren V. Dillon, was born in Ireland and was brought to the United States when five years old by his parents, the family settling in Pennsylvania. He grew up in that state and became a pioneer homesteader in Ohio, from whence he drove large herds of cattle and hogs to New York and Boston, via Pittsburgh. His entire career was passed as a farmer and stockman and his death occurred in Lawrence County. Henry Dillon, the grandfather of Oren V. Dillon, was born in Pennsylvania in 1832 and as a lad was taken to Noble County, Ohio, and later to Lawrence County, where he grew up amid pioneer surroundings. Following in the footsteps of his father, he engaged in farming and the raising of live stock, and through industry, energy and good management became one of the substantial men of Lawrence County, where he died in 1896. He was married there to Miss Jane Reed, who was born in 1837, in Noble County, Ohio, and she survives him and resides on the old family homestead. Mr. Dillon was a republican in politics and a consistent member of the Methodist Episcopal Church, to which the grandmother still belongs. They were the parents of four children, namely: Mary, who married L. O. Enochs, and resides on the old homestead with her mother; John H.; Rose, who is the wife of John Ellsworth, the owner of a telephone exchange at Kenefic, Oklahoma; and Grant, who died at the age of nine years.

John H. Dillon was born in Lawrence County, June 12, 1859, and attended the public schools there as well as the normal school located at Lebanon, Ohio. Leaving school at the age of eighteen years, he continued to work on his father's farm until attaining his majority at which time he entered the general merchandise business at Scotttown, Ohio, and continued therein until 1886. In that year Mr. Dillon went to Colorado as manager for the Southern Colorado Townsite Company, a project in which he was interested for three years, and in 1889 came to Oklahoma and took up his residence at Kingfisher, where he was located during the opening of the Cheyenne-Arapaho Reservation. In 1892 he received the appointment as postmaster of Watonga, Oklahoma, and served in that capacity until March, 1893, when he was elected county treasurer of Blaine County, and served two terms, or four years, during which time he established an excellent record for faithful and efficient public performance of duty. In 1898 Mr. Dillon resigned his office and accepted the position of cashier of the First State Bank of Geary, of which he was one of the organizers, and in 1902 became president of the institution, a position which he has retained to the present time, the bank having received its national charter in 1904 and now being known as the First National Bank of Geary. Mr. Dillon has invested heavily in realty, owning farms in Blaine and Canadian counties, on which he carries on, through tenants, diversified farming and stock raising.

He owns also business houses at Geary and residential properties, as well as his own handsome modern residence, situated in the southwest part of the town. Mr. Dillon belongs to the Oklahoma State Bankers Association. He is a stalwart republican and is fraternally affiliated with Geary Lodge No. 138, Independent Order of Odd Fellows, and the Benevolent and Protective Order of Elks at El Reno.

In 1882, in Lawrence County, Ohio, Mr. Dillon was united in marriage with Miss Josie Mount, daughter of the late Sam Mount, who was a mechanic, and to this union there have been born six children: Oren V.; Mary, who is the wife of W. M. Gamble, of Oklahoma City, a traveling salesman for the Loose-Wiles Company, confectioners; Merrill, Mary's twin brother, who is a banker of Earlsboro, Oklahoma; Jack, who is an employe of the First National Bank of Geary; Miss Agnes, who resides with her parents; and Hobart, who is a freshman in the agricultural and mechanical college, at Stillwater, Oklahoma.

Oren V. Dillon received his education in the public schools of Kingfisher, Oklahoma, but at the age of seventeen years put aside his studies to begin to secure practical experience in banking, a career in which he had decided to engage. For two years he was connected with the Bank of Sayre, Oklahoma, in the capacity of cashier, and with this preparation came to Geary in 1903 as cashier of the Bank of Geary, which in the following year was nationalized. The bank occupies a structure on Main Street, corner of Broadway, which was built in 1898 for bank and office purposes, and the present officials of the institution are: John H. Dillon, president; Willard Johnston, vice president; Oren V. Dillon, cashier, and L. E. Troxel, assistant cashier. The capital of the First National Bank is $25,000, with a surplus of $5,000, and its depositors come from Blaine and the surrounding counties. It bears an excellent reputation in banking circles as a sound and conservative concern, ably and prudently managed.

Mr. Dillon is a republican, but has not been attracted by public life. He is well known in Masonic circles, belonging to Geary Lodge No. 139, Ancient Free and Accepted Masons; Peaceful Valley Chapter No. 59, Royal Arch Masons; Valley of Guthrie Consistory (thirty-second degree), No. 1, Royal and Select Masters, and India Temple, Ancient Arabic Order Nobles of the Mystic Shrine, of Oklahoma City. Mr. Dillon is unmarried.

CHARLES EVANS, B. S., M. A., LL. D. There can be no conjecture or other uncertainty in determining the value of the services of Doctor Evans in the domain of practical pedagogy, and to few of his age has it been given to wield larger or more benignant influence as an educator of high scholastic attainments and as a broad-minded and progressive executive. He has served since 1911 as president of the Oklahoma Central State Normal School, at Edmond, and prior to coming to Oklahoma he had attained to high reputation in educational circles in Kentucky, his earnest and effective services having given him in his chosen profession a reputation that, in fact, transcends all limitations of merely local order. Oklahoma is signally favored in having enlisted his co-operation and vital enthusiasm in carrying forward the work of popular education within her borders, and he is specially entitled to definite recognition in this publication, that at least a brief record of his service may be perpetuated in the history of this favored and vigorous young commonwealth.

Apropos of the work of Doctor Evans since assuming his present official position, there is consistency in offering in a preliminary way a few statements concerning the admirable state institution of which he is the executive head, and thus the following quotations are germane:

"Certain facts pertinent to the growth of the Central State Normal School during the four years that President Evans has been at its head are illustrative of the ability of the man as an educator and executive. By a unanimous vote of the State Board of Education he was called from the superintendency of the city schools of Ardmore, Carter county, to the presidency of the normal school at a time when the work of this important state institution was lagging and inadequate and when its spirit was at low ebb. The problem of conducting successfully a state normal school was to be solved in the new commonwealth, and Dr. Evans fortunately was the one called upon to make the solution,—a task that demanded vigorous policies, marked initiative and administrative ability, great circumspection, and no little constructive talent. He proved equal to all demands thus placed upon him and the results that he has achieved justify the application of the scriptural aphorism that 'By their fruits ye shall know them.' On the 1st of July, 1911, when Dr. Evans assumed charge of the Central Normal School its best enrollment record had been 1,154; the latest attendance figures are 2,981. The graduating class of the preceding year comprised only eighteen members; the graduating class of 1916 comprised 211 members. In 1911 the normal college department had an enrollment of sixty students; that department in 1916 had an enrollment of 1,210 students. Appropriation for the maintenance of the institution in 1911 was $52,500; the state appropriation for 1915, showing legislative appreciation of the work accomplished under the regime of President Evans, was $222,000. Within the four years an additional building for the schools has been erected and placed in commission. All of these statements are significant and bear their own lessons of incentive and inspiration."

In February, 1916, the trustees of Henry Kendall College, of Tulsa, Oklahoma, unanimously elected Doctor Evans to the presidency, carrying with it a tenure of five years and a salary of $5,000 a year. He accepted, and though urged by the State Board of Education and a great student body to remain with Central State Normal, he chose to serve, as he said, not only the schools, but school and church.

At Salem, Livingston County, Kentucky, Charles Evans was born on the 16th of August, 1870, and he is a son of Enoch E. and Frances E. (Dawson) Evans. His father was a village blacksmith at Salem, a man of strong individuality and sterling integrity, and a representative of an honored pioneer family of Tennessee. Enoch E. Evans was born in Montgomery County, Tennessee, where his father had served with efficiency as an early-day schoolmaster. The lineage of the Evans family, as the name indicates, traces back to Welsh origin, and that the American branch was founded in the Colonial era of our national history is evidenced by the fact that representatives of the name were found as valiant soldiers of the Continental Line in the war of the Revolution.

The preliminary educational discipline of Dr. Charles Evans was obtained in the village schools of his native county, and thereafter he attended the literary or academic department of the University of Kentucky until the close of his junior year. In 1891 he was graduated in the National Normal University, at Lebanon, Ohio, with the degree of Bachelor of Science, and from that time forward to the present has continued his services as an able and honored exponent of the pedagogic profession.

Doctor Evans' initial experience as a teacher was gained in his native Village of Salem, and for twelve years thereafter he was superintendent of the city schools of Marion, the judicial center of Crittenden County, Kentucky. Within this period of service he gained clear comprehension of the scope and details and the practical possibilities of the educational system that later became popular throughout the different states of the Union in the centralizing of school work in rural and semi-rural communities. He devised plans and methods through which he developed with marked success this community-center policy of educational work at Marion, to which place students were drawn from a wide radius of country, owing to the superior advantages thus possible of being afforded. Doctor Evans became known as one of the most successful pioneers of this admirable movement in the United States, and as his work became known he was frequently called upon for advice on the part of educators in Kentucky and other states. Year after year the Marion Board of Education re-elected him to the office of superintendent of schools, and when he finally announced his intention of removing to the West the board not only earnestly besought him to remain but also tendered to him a life tenure of the superintendency and a definite pension at the time when he became too old for further active service. Gratifying as were these overtures and deeply as he appreciated the same, Doctor Evans felt it expedient to adhere to his decision, and his field of labor in Oklahoma has given him such wide scope for achievement that he has found no cause to regret his decision. He became known as one of the most progressive and popular educators in his native State of Kentucky and was the first to serve throughout all sections of that commonwealth as an instructor in teachers' institutes, the while he was a most active and valued member of the Kentucky Teachers' Association, in the affairs and activities of which he was specially influential.

In 1905 Doctor Evans was elected superintendent of the public schools of the City of Ardmore, Oklahoma, at a salary of $1,200 a year, and the estimate placed upon his services is shown when it is stated that his salary at the time of his resignation, after a regime of six years, was $2,500, the greater part of this marked advancement in recompense having been made within a period of three years after he had assumed the superintendency. His splendid record in this incumbency marked him as a leader in educational circles of Oklahoma after the state was admitted to the Union and finally resulted in his election to the presidency of the Central State Normal School, in 1911, as previously noted in this context. In 1908 Doctor Evans was president of the Chickasaw Teachers' Association, an organization that had previously been formed in the Chickasaw Nation of the Indian Territory, and he has served also as president of the Oklahoma State Teachers' Association, as well as vice president of the National Educational Association. Not only in a direct and executive way has Doctor Evans been prominent in educational affairs, but he has also been the author of three valuable textbooks. In conjunction with Charles O. Bunn, of Oklahoma City, he prepared the work entitled "Oklahoma Civics," a textbook that has been adopted for general use in the public schools of the state and that has been thus employed since 1910. Doctor Evans is the author also of a work entitled "Oklahoma Civics and History;" and another entitled "Growing a Life," this being a treatise on pedagogy and psychology and one that has been adopted as a textbook in five different states of the Union, including his native State of Kentucky. In 1913, in recognition of his eminent services in his chosen profession and his high intellectual attainments, the University of Kentucky conferred upon him the honorary degree of Doctor of Laws. "He who serves is royal," and such mark of distinction signally applies to him whose life has been thus consecrated to high ideals and that has shown such large and worthy achievement as that of Doctor Evans, whose circle of friends and admirers is coincident with that of his acquaintances. Concerning him the following pertinent statements have been written and are worthy of perpetuation:

"As an educator Dr. Evans has emphasized the idea of usefulness,—in other words, he advocates and teaches that education should be vital and productive, an education that walks and talks and makes itself a factor in human activities. His practical exploiting of this idea gave birth to well matured plans for enhancing the civic and material attractiveness of Edmond, the seat of the Central Normal School, and the result is that the place has been reclaimed from a somewhat straggling and unkempt village into a modern little city of manifold attractions and great civic pride. As a member of the pedagogic profession Dr. Evans is one of its most forceful, well informed and pleasing public speakers in Oklahoma, and there is almost constant demand for his acceptance of engagements to address various representative associations of both public and private order. He is deeply interested in the work of the Young Men's Christian Association, is state committeeman from Oklahoma in the national organization, and both he and his wife are zealous and devoted members of the Presbyterian church."

In addition to his identification with Oklahoma State Teachers' Association and the National Educational Association, Doctor Evans holds membership in the North Central Council of Presidents of Normal Schools of the United States. He is president of the State Civic Association of Oklahoma, having aided in its organization and having from the beginning been one of its most active and enthusiastic workers. In the furtherance of civic beauty he is especially interested in promoting the cultivation of flowers, and his favorite in the floral kingdom is the chrysanthemum.

At Ardmore, this state, Doctor Evans is affiliated with the lodge of Ancient Free and Accepted Masons, and in this time-honored fraternity he has received, in the consistory at McAlester, Oklahoma, the thirty-second degree of the Ancient Accepted Scottish Rite, besides which he is affiliated with Ardmore Lodge, Benevolent and Protective Order of Elks, and with a lodge of Knights of Pythias at Marion, Kentucky. Doctor Evans has one brother and one sister,—Judge Thomas Evans, who is a resident of the City of Paducah, Kentucky, and who served twelve years on the bench of the County Court; and Dora, who is the wife of James A. Sherrill, a prosperous jewelery merchant at Stephansville, Texas.

At Marion, Kentucky, in 1897, was solemnized the marriage of Doctor Evans to Miss Martha Blue, daughter of Judge John W. Blue, a representative lawyer and jurist of the old Blue Grass State. Mrs. Evans is a woman of culture and gracious personality, representing the best of the gentle traditions concerning the women of her native state, and she has exceptional ability as an artist, her exhibits of drawing and china painting having been awarded prizes at the Louisiana Purchase Exposition, held in the City of St. Louis. Doctor and Mrs. Evans became the parents of two children, Charles and Edward, the latter of whom died in 1912, at the age of eight years. Charles, who was born in 1902, is now (1915) a student in the high school department of the Central Normal School of Oklahoma, of which his father is president.

EDD FITCH MILLIGAN, M. D. No physician of Blaine County has a better record for straightforward and high professional conduct, or for success gained through personal merit and effort, than has Dr. Edd Fitch Milligan, who since 1908 has been engaged in practice at Geary. Like a number of other prominent professional men of West Oklahoma, he is a native of the Buckeye State, born at Youngstown, October 11, 1875, a son of William John and Martha (Brownlee) Milligan.

The Milligan family was founded in the United States by William Milligan, a native of Ireland, who came from County Tyrone and settled in Ohio, being married at Canfield, where he subsequently enjoyed a long career as a successful attorney and died in advanced years before the birth of Doctor Milligan. On his grandmother's side, Doctor Milligan is related to the Professor McGuffey who was the author of the old McGuffey speller and reader so widely used in our schools several generations back. William John Milligan, father of Doctor Milligan, was born at Canfield, Ohio, in 1830, and as a young man removed to Youngstown, Ohio, where he passed the rest of his life as a stone contractor and died in 1907. He was a democrat, although not a politician, and was a member of the Presbyterian Church, to which Mrs. Milligan still belongs. She was born at Youngstown, Ohio, in 1840, and still makes her home there. There were eight children in the family as follows: N. R., who is a contractor and his father's successor in the business at Youngstown; W. R., who is a ranchman and resides at Denver, Colorado; McGuffey, who died at Youngstown, Ohio, at the age of forty years; Ada, who is the wife of O. E. Forsdick, a carpenter and builder at Cleveland, Ohio; J. T., who is a ranchman of Como, Colorado; Dr. Edd Fitch; Betsey B., who resides with her mother at the old home at Youngstown; and J. R., who is a contractor of that city.

Edd Fitch Milligan was educated in the public schools of Youngstown, and was graduated from the Reyen High School in the class of 1894. Following this he took a preparatory course at the Poland Seminary, being graduated in 1897, and matriculated in Northeastern University of Ohio, at Canfield, where he pursued a course and received his degree of Bachelor of Art in 1899. His medical studies were prosecuted in the medical department of Denver University, where he was graduated in 1905, with the degree of Doctor of Medicine, and while attending that institution became a member of the Alpha Kappa Kappa, a Greek letter medical fraternity, to which he still belongs. After receiving his degree, Doctor Milligan served one year as interne in St. Luke's Hospital, Denver, Colorado, and in 1906 entered upon the practice of his calling at Quenemo, Kansas, where he remained until coming to Geary, Oklahoma, October 1, 1908. Here he has since been successfully engaged in a general medical and surgical practice, with offices on Blaine Avenue. He has acquired a large and lucrative patronage and enjoys the respect and confidence of all classes, both at Geary and in the surrounding country, where he has numerous calls for his services. He keeps fully abreast of the various advancements being made in the profession, and holds membership in the organizations of his calling, thus keeping in close touch with the professional brotherhood. In 1915 Doctor Milligan completed his handsome new residence, in connection with which is his garage, where he keeps his two new model automobiles. Doctor Milligan is a republican, but has not mixed in public affairs save as an advocate of all measures promoted for the public welfare. He is a member of Golden Rule Lodge No. 87, Knights of Pythias, Quenemo, Kansas; past noble grand of Quenemo Lodge and a member of Geary Lodge No. 138, Independent Order of Odd Fellows, and is a thirty-second degree, Scottish Rite Mason, belonging to Geary Lodge No. 139, Ancient Free and Accepted Masons, of which he is past master; Peaceful Valley Chapter No. 59, Royal Arch Masons; Consistory No. 1, Topeka, Kansas; and Indian Temple, Ancient Arabic Order of Nobles of the Mystic Shrine, Oklahoma City. With Mrs. Milligan he attends the Presbyterian Church, of which both are members, and in which he is now serving as an elder.

Doctor Milligan was married September 30, 1908, at Fort Scott, Kansas, to Miss Myrtle J. Wright, of Eureka, Kansas, daughter of the late Edward Wright, who was in the insurance business. Doctor and Mrs. Milligan are the parents of one son: Donald Edd, who was born December 5, 1909.

FRANK BENCE, M. D. One of the early physicians and surgeons to establish themselves in practice in Pottawatomie and Cleveland counties is Dr. Frank Bence, whose home is now at Macomb. Doctor Bence is a practitioner of more than forty years active experience. He practiced in Ohio and Indiana before coming to Oklahoma, and at this date he is widely recognized for his ability and for his many associations with the profession and with public affairs.

He was born in Ashland County, Ohio, March 19, 1852. His father, William Bence, was drowned at sea soon after the birth of Doctor Bence and the mother had passed away a short time before. Doctor Bence grew up in the home of his maternal grandfather, Shriner, who was a native of Pennsylvania, in which state he was reared and married, and was an early settler in Ashland County, Ohio. Peter Shriner was also a physician, and combined that profession with farming. He had seen active service as a soldier in the Mexican war. From Ohio he moved to Indiana. At his death he was, it is said, one hundred fifteen years of age. He reared seventeen children to manhood and womanhood.

In the home of his grandfather Doctor Bence acquired his early training in Ashland County, Ohio. He studied medicine under his grandfather, and took his first case when only seventeen years of age. Some years later he entered the Physicians and Surgeons College in Chicago, from which he was graduated M. D. in June, 1889. His home and work as a physician were in Ashland County, Ohio, until 1890, in which year he removed to Talbott, Indiana. From there in 1897 he came to Oklahoma City, remained there about a year, and then went into Cleveland County, and has since been a prominent member of the medical fraternity in that and in Pottawatomie County with the exception of eighteen months spent at Rosedale, in McClain County.

Doctor Bence first located at Eteuwah in 1903, but from there a few months later moved to Tribbey and Old Burnett. In April, 1915, he re-established his practice and home at Macomb.

He was one of the charter members of the Oklahoma State Medical Society, and a member of the Pottawatomie County Society. In politics he is a republican and in earlier years took a very prominent part in political affairs. For six years he was a member of the school board in Old Burnett, and has served on the County Central Republican Committees of both Cleveland and Pottawatomie counties. Besides his large private practice he is examiner for the Kansas City Life Insurance Company, the Bankers' Life Insurance Company of Oklahoma, the Indianapolis Reserve and Loan Company, and the New York Life Insurance Company, and at one time was local surgeon for the Oklahoma Central Railroad. Doctor Bence was reared in the Episcopal faith. He is affiliated with the Independent Order of Odd Fellows and the Knights of Pythias in the lodges in Linwood, Kansas.

In Ashland County, Ohio, in 1874, he married Miss Mary Crull, who was born in Ohio in 1857. Her father was a Union soldier and was killed during the war. To their marriage have been born six children: Minnie, wife of William Slate, a farmer and stockman at Lindsay, Oklahoma; Walter, who is a motorman for the Street Railway Company at Shawnee; Leta, wife of Charles Sheppard, who is manager of the Central Telephone Exchange at Macomb; Pearl, wife of Willis Buggs, who resides in Leavenworth, Kansas; Vernon, in the livery business at Macomb; and Bertha, still at home with her parents.

STONEWALL JACKSON. That Mr. Jackson received his Christian or personal name in honor of one of the great and revered heroes and officers of the Confederate service in the Civil war and that his family name makes the appellation the more consistent finds further reinforcement through the fact that his father was a gallant soldier of the Confederacy during virtually the entire period of the war between the states of the North and the South, his service of four years having been rendered as a member of a Louisiana regiment and it having been his portion to participate in many spirited engagements, including a number of important battles. He was always found at the post of duty and in one engagement he received a severe wound.

Stonewall Jackson has been a resident of Cheyenne, judicial center of Roger Mills County, since 1902, and through his own executive ability, his circumspection as a financier and his impregnable integrity of purpose he has become an influential figure in connection with banking activities in the western part of the state. In his home town he is now president of the Cheyenne State Bank, of which office he has been the incumbent since 1912, and he is president also of the First State Bank of Strong City; vice president of the Crawford State Bank, of Crawford, Roger Mills County; and a director of the Guaranty State Bank of Texola, Beckham County. His prominence in financial circles is further indicated by his having served in 1913 as treasurer of the Oklahoma Bankers' Association, of which he continues an active and valued member.

Stonewall Jackson was born at Alto, Cherokee County, Texas, on the 2d of December, 1877, and is a son of William D. and Mary (Kendall) Jackson, both natives of Louisiana, the former having died at Mars Hill, Arkansas, in 1879, and the latter being now a resident of Magnum, Greer County, Oklahoma.

William D. Jackson was born in the year 1834, and was reared and educated in Louisiana, from which state he went forth as a valiant soldier of the Confederacy in the Civil war, as previously noted. In his native state his marriage was solemnized, and after the close of the war he removed to Arkansas, whence, about 1877, he went with his family to Texas, but about three years later he returned to Arkansas, where he passed the remainder of his life, his active career having found him successfully engaged as a contractor and also a representative of the live-stock industry. He was a scion of a sterling family that was founded in the state of Georgia in the colonial period of our national history, and it is to be presumed that the first representatives of the name in America settled in Virginia. Of his three children the eldest is Willie, who is the wife of William H. Thomason, a farmer in Beaver County, Oklahoma; Stonewall, of this review, was the next in order of birth; and Ida, whose death occurred at Magnum, Greer County, this state, was the wife of Rev. Charles

R. Roberts, who is still a resident of that place and who is a clergyman of the Baptist Church.

To the public schools of Arkansas and Texas Stonewall Jackson is indebted for his early educational discipline, and in 1901 he was graduated in the Sam Houston Normal School of Texas. He thereafter devoted his attention to teaching in the schools of the Lone Star State until June of the following year when he came to Oklahoma Territory and established his home at Cheyenne, where he assumed the position of cashier of the Cheyenne State Bank, with which he has since been actively identified and of which he has been president since 1912. The bank was established in 1898, by Thurmond Brothers, and it is one of the oldest and strongest financial institutions in this section of the state. Its operations are now based on a capital stock of $20,000, and its surplus fund is $2,500. The vice president of the institution is J. H. Kendall; G. B. Lovett is cashier, and J. L. Finch holds the position of assistant cashier.

Insistently progressive and public-spirited as a citizen, Mr. Jackson has taken a specially loyal interest in all that touches the civic and material welfare and advancement of his home town and county, and he is found aligned as a staunch supporter of the cause of the democratic party. He and his wife are zealous and influential members of the Baptist Church at Cheyenne, and he is giving effective service as teacher of the Bible class in its Sunday school. Mr. Jackson is affiliated with Cheyenne Lodge, Ancient Free and Accepted Masons, of which he is past master; with Cheyenne Chapter, Royal Arch Masons; with Elk City Commandery, Knights Templars, at the county seat of Beckham County; and with Indian Temple, Ancient Arabic Order of the Nobles of the Mystic Shrine, in Oklahoma City. In addition to these Masonic affiliations he holds membership in Cheyenne Lodge No. 237, Independent Order of Odd Fellows, and Cheyenne Camp, Modern Woodmen of America.

At Cheyenne the year 1904 recorded the marriage of Mr. Jackson to Miss Texia H. Hornbeak, daughter of Rev. James A. Hornbeak, who is a clergyman of the Presbyterian Church and who now resides in the City of Dallas, Texas, his brother, Dr. S. L. Hornbeak, being a member of the faculty of Trinity University, at Waxahachie, Texas, in which institution Mrs. Jackson was graduated. Mr. and Mrs. Jackson have one child, Marjorie, who was born July 8, 1907.

JAMES S. BARNETT, M. D. Of the contingent of able and successful physicians and surgeons who are well upholding the dignity and prestige of their profession in Blaine County, a prominent and popular representative is Doctor Barnett, who maintains his residence and professional headquarters in the vigorous and thriving Village of Hitchcock and who has built up an excellent general practice in that section of the county.

Doctor Barnett was born at Columbia, Boone County, Missouri, on the 31st of July, 1871, and is a son of Jesse E. and Mary A. (Butterton) Barnett, both likewise natives of Boone County, Missouri, where the former was born in 1843 and the latter in 1848, the respective families having been pioneers of that section of the state and prominently identified with its civic and industrial development. The lineage of the Barnett family traces back to staunch Scotch-Irish origin and its first representatives in America settled in Virginia, in the colonial period of our national history.

Jesse E. Barnett passed the major part of his long and useful life in his native county and his active career was given principally to agricultural pursuits and the livestock business. At the time of the Civil war he became one of the youthful and loyal soldiers of the Confederacy, his service covering a period of three years and he having been in the command of the gallant General Price. He took part in numerous engagements, in Missouri, Arkansas and Louisiana, and with his command surrendered at Shreveport, Louisiana, at the close of the war. He was a man of broad mental ken, earnest and steadfast in all of the relations of life, never desirous of notoriety or public office, but loyal to all civic duties. His allegiance was given to the democratic party, he was a deacon in the Christian Church, of which his widow has long been a devoted member, and was affiliated with the United Confederate Veterans. He continued his operations as a farmer and stock-grower in Boone County until 1889, when he removed to Columbia, the county seat, where he lived virtually retired until his death, which occurred in 1908, and where his widow still maintains her home. Of their children the firstborn, Pearl, died at the age of eighteen years; Dr. James S., of this review, was the next in order of birth; George H. was a resident of Columbia, Missouri, at the time of his death, when twenty-nine years of age, and thus was cut short a most prominent career, as he had been graduated in the law department of the University of Missouri and was prosecuting attorney in his native county at the time of his death; Lawrence died at the age of eight years; Edward, who was editor and publisher of a newspaper at Joplin, Missouri, at the time of his death, passed to the life eternal at the age of thirty-three years; Mary J. is a popular teacher in the high school at Columbia, Missouri; Bessie C. is superintendent of the telephone exchange in the same city; and Carrie is a teacher in the high school at Hannibal, Missouri.

To the public schools of his native city Dr. James S. Barnett is indebted for his preliminary educational discipline, which was supplemented by a four years' course in the academic department of the University of Missouri. In consonance with his ambition and well matured plans he then entered the medical department of the university, in which he completed the prescribed curriculum and was graduated as a member of the class of 1896, his reception of the degree of Doctor of Medicine having occurred on the 3rd of June of that year. The doctor wisely fortified himself in practical clinical experience by serving several months thereafter as interne in one of the leading hospitals in the City of St. Louis, and after leaving the metropolis of his native state he was engaged in practice one year in his home City of Columbia. Thereafter he continued his successful professional activities in Audrain County, Missouri, until 1901, when he came to Oklahoma Territory and engaged in practice at Geary, Blaine County. Two months later he transferred his residence and professional base of operations to the Town of Hitchcock, where he located in October, 1901, only a few weeks after the founding of the town. He is thus the pioneer physician and surgeon of this place and in addition to having given the best of his talents and powers to the exacting work of his profession during the entire period of his residence in Blaine County, he has been also one of the broad-minded and progressive citizens whose influence and co-operation has made possible the development and upbuilding of the fine little Town of Hitchcock. He is the only resident physician of the village and his practice extends throughout the wide section of country tributary to the town, his office being maintained in a building on Main Street. That Doctor Barnett is emphatically one of the representative physicians and surgeons of this section of the state and that he holds high place in the confidence and esteem of his confreres is shown by his having been called upon to serve as president of the Blaine County Medical Society, of which he continues an active and influential member, besides being identified also with the Oklahoma State Medical Society and the American Medical Association.

The doctor has pronounced himself an "old-school" democrat in politics, and though he has been importuned to become a candidate for political office he has invariably refused to consider such overtures, as he deems his profession worthy of his undivided time and attention. He and his wife hold membership in the Christian Church, and he is affiliated with Hitchcock Lodge, No. 191, Independent Order of Odd Fellows, of which he has served three different terms as noble grand, and he holds membership also in the local organizations of the Modern Woodmen of America, the Ancient Order of United Workmen, the Brotherhood of American Yeomen, and the Mutual Benefit Association.

At Mexico, Audrain County, Missouri, was solemnized the marriage of Doctor Barnett to Miss Lula B. Thomas, whose father, now deceased, was a representative farmer of that county. Doctor and Mrs. Barnett have four children, Ruth, Josephine, Lucille, and James Thomas.

L. A. WISMEYER. One of the oldest and best known Indian traders of the Osage County, it is likely that the name of L. A. Wismeyer will be chiefly remembered through future generations for his enterprise in founding the Town of Fairfax in Osage County. He took the lead in starting the town there when the railroad was constructed in 1903. Not long ago the editor of a local paper who was closely familiar with all Wismeyer's public spirited activities at the time described his part in the founding and upbuilding of the town in the following language: "He borned the town, nursed it in its infancy and paid the doctor's bill. He built the first schoolhouse and helped to build all the churches, and whether he belonged to any of them or all of them his name appears on the records of at least two as trustee or incorporator. In his townsite bill he secured for Fairfax ten acres of land for a cemetery, a gift from the department that no other town on the reservation received. He was the first merchant in Fairfax and established the first lumber yard. He was at the head of the Fairfax Grain Company that built the first elevator. He was one of the organizers of the First National Bank and served as president of that institution for a number of years and was one of three men that erected the bank's splendid quarters. In short, Mr. Wismeyer has been a public benefactor and in the long run Fairfax has been the greater beneficiary of his labors."

While Mr. Wismeyer has lived in the western states of Kansas and Oklahoma more than forty years, his boyhood recollections center about a home in the State of Ohio. He was born at Hamilton, Ohio, October 20, 1852, a son of Henry and Mary (Richter) Wismeyer, both of whom were of German parentage. His parents spent practically all their lives in Ohio, part of the time in Cleveland and at other locations in Northern Ohio, and were for many years at Hamilton. His father died at Hamilton about 1882 at the age of sixty-eight. He had conducted a malt house at Sandusky and later at Hamilton. The mother is still living with a daughter at Hamilton at the age of eighty-five. The five children were: L. A.; Henry of Emporia, Kansas; Emma, wife of Frank Cobaught of Connersville, Indiana; Carrie, wife of John A. Keller of Hamilton, Ohio; and John, who died in 1910 in Guadalajara, Mexico.

It was in the home of his parents that L. A. Wismeyer lived until 1873. In the meantime he had made the best of his advantages in the public schools, and for two years had gained a practical business training as clerk in a dry goods store, his salary beginning at $1.50 a week. In 1873 he went out to Kansas to join his uncle, Harry A. Richter, at Council Grove. His uncle was long prominent in Kansas politics, and served three terms as lieutenant governor of that state. Mr. Wismeyer remained with his uncle five years, employed in his drug store, and while there performed that various service required of pioneer druggists, not only in mixing and compounding medicines and pills, but also in prescribing in the role of a doctor, and he gained such confidence that he could prescribe anything from calomel and quinine to snake medicine for the customers of the store.

Leaving Kansas, Mr. Wismeyer arrived at the Osage Agency on the site of the present City of Pawhuska, June 18, 1878, becoming chief clerk in the agency. He continued the duties of that office until December, 1884. The Indian agent had many responsibilities, including the issue of rations to the Indians. The supplies furnished through the agency store included a large stock of general provisions as well as clothing of all kinds. The head of each Indian family had a ration check, and this was presented to the commissary clerk whenever rations were drawn. Every few days from forty to fifty head of beef cattle were killed for the benefit of the tribe living around the agency, and sometimes a hundred head of stock would be driven into the corral each week, and after the animals were shot down the Indians would go in and proceed to skin and cut up the carcasses. These cattle were the substitute for the buffaloes which had furnished most of the meat to the tribes before that noble animal of the plains was exterminated. The cash payments were made semi-annually, in May and December, and averaged $6.25 to each individual. A year or so after Mr. Wismeyer became connected with the agency, on account of the dissatisfaction which had arisen among the Indians over the ration distribution, that system was abolished, and thereafter the Indians were paid their entire share in cash. One of Mr. Wismeyer's experiences while chief clerk at the agency illustrates the attitude of the older full bloods toward the system of education which the Government was striving to introduce. The department had made a ruling that all Indians must have their children in school before they could draw their quarterly allowance. One day an old Indian demanded his money, and Mr. Wismeyer questioned him as to whether he had children in school. The Indian made a personal application of the school question to Mr. Wismeyer, who replied that he had attended school in order to learn reading and writing and to make a living, and that he held his job because of his education. The Indian retorted as follows: "You're a fool. I eat and wear clothes and don't have to hold down a job. If you hadn't went to school and got an education you wouldn't have to write, write, write all day and part of the night as you do here. White man heap fool. I want my money."

On December 1, 1884, Mr. Wismeyer secured a trader's license, and became associated with Dr. R. E. Bird, one of the old established Indian traders. They engaged in general merchandising at Pawhuska, as licensed traders, and in 1885 established a branch store at Gray Horse in Osage County. In 1889 Mr. Wismeyer moved to Gray Horse to manage that end of the business, and after 1890 became sole proprietor of the store there. He continued in business at Gray Horse until 1903. With the coming of the railroad he and the other traders at Gray Horse, in order to avoid freighting overland, determined to move their post to the railroad. Mr. Wismeyer finally succeeded in gaining the consent of the Government officials to locate a depot where the Village of Fairfax now stands. In arranging

for the townsite he had to go to Washington and came home with full instructions how to proceed in securing the use of lands for town purposes. He procured forty acres belonging to one of the Indians, and had it surveyed into lots, streets and alleys, and he took for his own purposes one of the chief corners in the new town for his store and lumber yard. The railroad company first named the depot Coda, but Mr. Wismeyer finally gained their consent to the name Fairfax, which was suggested to him by the old town of that name in Virginia. Owing to the fact that all the lots in the town could be used only by the right of occupancy the title to the land remaining with its Indian owners, Mr. Wismeyer spent almost the entire winter of 1904 at Washington, and finally secured a townsite bill which, while far from satisfactory, paved the way for a permanent town and the upbuilding of such institutions as churches, schools and business enterprises. For more than ten years Mr. Wismeyer, though a man of unobtrusive personality, has been one of the real leaders in the growth of the community, has invested freely and with faith in the ultimate outcome in the number of local business institutions, and has always given liberally to movements associated with the general welfare of the community. He has been identified with the mercantile interests of the town since it was founded, was president of the First National Bank until 1912, was in the lumber business for ten years, being the first lumber merchant there, and for about nine years was one of the interested principals in the operation of the first elevator.

Mr. Wismeyer speaks the Osage Indian language as fluently as the red men themselves, and also has a speaking knowledge of the language of the Kaws and Poncas. He has had continuous relations as an Indian trader for thirty-seven years. Politically he is a stanch republican, has been active in party affairs, but has never sought nor held an office. He is affiliated with the Benevolent and Protective Order of Elks at Pawhuska. While living at Council Grove, Kansas, Mr. Wismeyer became acquainted with one of the belles of local society, and in 1884 married Miss Aggie C. Huffaker. Mrs. Wismeyer was born in Council Grove, Kansas, November 1, 1857, a daughter of T. S. Huffaker, one of the pioneers in that section of Kansas. They have one daughter, Frances, still at home.

JAMES E. CRONKHITE. The Village of Hitchcock, one of the attractive and flourishing trade centers of Blaine County, claims among its progressive and substantial business men James Emmett Cronkhite, who here conducts a well established and prosperous hardware and implement business, as one of the representative exponents of this line of enterprise in the county. His sterling characteristics and personal popularity contribute a distinct commercial asset in his business, and he is known also for his loyalty and public spirit as a citizen.

Mr. Cronkhite was born at Melvern, Osage County, Kansas, on the 24th of February, 1873, and is a son of Benjamin and Marietta (High) Cronkhite, both natives of Iowa and representatives of sterling pioneer families of that state. Benjamin Cronkhite was born in the year 1842, and was reared and educated under the conditions and influences of the early pioneer era in the history of the Hawkeye State. After his marriage he removed to Osage County, Kansas, where he continued successful operations as a farmer and stock-grower. In the year 1898 he came to Oklahoma Territory and established his residence at Kiel, Kingfisher County, where he became a pioneer merchant, besides building up a successful business as a dealer in horses. In 1901 he became one of the first settlers of the newly founded town Hitchcock, Blaine County, and here he was associated with his son James E., of this review, in the general merchandise business until 1904. He continued his residence in this village until 1906, when he established his home on his farm, near Hitchcock, to the supervision of which property he gave his close attention until his removal to El Reno, when he practically retired from active business. He and his wife now maintain their home at Watonga, the judicial center of Blaine County, where they are enjoying the peace and prosperity that properly reward former years of earnest endeavor. At the time of the Civil war Mr. Cronkhite gave loyal and valiant service as a soldier of the Union. He was at the time residing in Iowa, but he enlisted in an Illinois regiment of volunteer cavalry, with which he continued in active service during virtually the entire period of the war. He is a democrat in politics and is affiliated with the Grand Army of the Republic. Of the family of six children James Emmett, of this sketch, was the fourth in order of birth; Frank, the eldest of the number, resides at Watonga and has valuable farm property in Blaine County; William resides on his homestead farm, eight miles west of Hitchcock; Lulu F. is the wife of Fred P. Higby, of El Reno, who is employed as a practical railroad man; Adell is the wife of Martin Truby, a jeweler at Coffeyville, Kansas; and John T. is engaged in the real-estate business at Watonga, Blaine County. The Cronkhite family removed to Florence, Kansas, in 1875, and in 1886 the home was established in the City of Emporia, that state, where the father remained until his removal to Oklahoma, as previously noted in this context.

James E. Cronkhite received his early education principally in the public schools of Florence and Emporia, Kansas, and he continued to be associated with his father in the latter's farming operations until 1896, after which he was engaged in the same line of enterprise in Kansas for two years in an independent way. In 1899 he came to Kiel, Oklahoma Territory, and two months later he returned to Kansas and disposed of his live stock, after which he came again to Kiel, where he was engaged in mercantile pursuits for one year. In 1901, as previously intimated, he became associated with his father in the general merchandise business in the new Town of Hitchcock, and in 1904 the business was divided and he assumed control of the hardware and implement stock and trade, which business he has since developed into the largest and most important of its kind in this section of Blaine County. The building which he uses for his business headquarters was erected by his father in 1906, shortly after the major part of the town had been destroyed by fire. The store is eligibly located on Main Street, has a floor space of 5,000 square feet, the establishment is kept up to high standard in both equipment and service and its trade is drawn from both Blaine and Kingfisher counties.

Mr. Cronkhite gives his allegiance to the democratic party and his civic loyalty has been shown by his effective service as counsel of Hitchcock, an office of which he was the incumbent one term, and also by his effective work as a member of the school board and his able administration in the office of treasurer of Lawton Township, a position which he is holding at the time of this writing, in 1915. In addition to his prosperous business at Hitchcock he is the owner of an improved farm of 160 acres, situated eight miles northwest of the village. He is affiliated with the Independent Order of Odd Fellows, the Modern Woodmen of America and the Mutual Benefit Association. It may well be noted that Mr. Cronkhite is a scion of American colonial stock, the original representatives of the name in this country having come from

Holland and settled in Dutchess County, New York, long prior to the War of the Revolution.

In 1894, in Kansas, was solemnized the marriage of Mr. Cronkhite to Miss Josie Gardner, a daughter of Thomas Gardner, who is a retired farmer now residing with his wife in a pleasant home in Hitchcock, Oklahoma. Mr. and Mrs. Cronkhite have four children: Hazel is the wife of Isaac Heibert and they maintain their home at Hitchcock, Mr. Heibert being a successful farmer near this village; Paul assists his father in the hardware and implement business; Clarence is in the eighth grade of the public schools in 1915; and Marion is the youngest of the children.

JESSE LEE JACKSON. Among the recent additions to the legal fraternity of Washita County, one who bids fair to gain a position of leadership by reason of inherent talent and thorough preparation is Jesse Lee Jackson. A member of an old and honored Southern family, Mr. Jackson came to Oklahoma in 1911 as an educator, but while practicing that vocation was preparing himself for the law, and after several years spent in practice at Cordell came to Sentinel in June, 1915, and has already attracted to himself a very desirable legal business.

Mr. Jackson was born January 6, 1884, at Middleton, Hardeman County, Tennessee, where the family had been pioneers, and is a son of J. S. and Edna (Bishop) Jackson. His father was born at Middleton in 1857 and there has passed his entire life as a planter and stockman and is known as one of the substantial agriculturists and public-spirited men of his locality. He is a member of the Christian Church, as was also Mrs. Jackson, who was born at Middleton in 1864 and died there in 1900. There were nine children in the family, as follows: Samuel, who is engaged in farming in the vicinity of Avoca, Texas; Sydney, who resides at Hobart, Oklahoma, and is employed as a machinist; Jesse Lee, of this notice; Prince, a graduate of Hall and Moody Institute, and of the Lebanon Law School, Lebanon, Tennessee, and now a practicing attorney of Woodford, Oklahoma; James, who is an employe of the Memphis (Tennessee) Street Railway Company; Gertrude, who is the wife of Estill Wynee, a farmer residing at Whiteville, Tennessee; Walter, who is engaged in farming in the vicinity of Middleton, Tennessee; Milton, who is engaged in teaching there; and Gracie, who is married and lives on a farm at Middleton.

The public schools of Middleton furnished Jesse Lee Jackson with his early educational preparation, following which he attended Hall and Moody Institute, at Martin, Tennessee, for one year. In 1910 and 1911 he was a student at the Southwestern State Normal School at Weatherford, Oklahoma, thus preparing himself for a career as an educator, and the school year of 1911-12 was passed as principal of schools at Texola, Oklahoma. In 1912-13 he was principal of schools at Gotebo, Oklahoma, and in the fall of 1914 entered the Oklahoma State University at Norman, where he remained until June, 1915. In the meantime Mr. Jackson had been admitted to the bar of Oklahoma, in 1913, and in that year opened an office and began practice at Cordell, where he remained until 1915, dividing his time between the practice of his profession and attending the university. In June, 1915, he changed his field of operation to the City of Sentinel, and here he has since devoted himself to a general and criminal practice. He has offices on Third Street, just off of Main Street.

Since coming to Sentinel, Mr. Jackson has lent dignity and stability to professional affairs and is accounted a young legist of decided promise. He is a broad-minded and progressive practitioner, a careful observer of the courtesies and amenities of his profession and at all times a seeker after its most intelligent and commendable compensations. He is a democrat in political matters, but has not found time to engage in public affairs, save as a supporter of movements for the general welfare. His religious connection is with the Christian Church, of which he is a consistent member, and his fraternal affiliations are with Cordell Camp of the Woodmen of the World and Cordell Lodge of the Praetorians. Mr. Jackson is not married.

WILEY BOOTHE MERRILL. Among the men whose opportunities along professional lines have been exceptional and who have made use of them in such a way as to make them important factors in the life of their communities, one who is deserving of mention is Wiley Boothe Merrill, who, since September, 1903, has been engaged in the practice of law at Elk City. A man of broad and comprehensive learning and legal talent of a high order, he has made a place for himself among the leaders of the Beckham County bar, where many of the leading cases of recent years have had the benefit of his capable services.

Mr. Merrill was born at Ladonia, Texas, November 17, 1881, a son of W. B. and Helen (Boothe) Merrill. He belongs to an old family of Virginia, founded there by John A. Merrill, who emigrated from England, engaged in planting in the Virginia Colony, became an adherent of the cause of the Patriots, and was finally murdered by the Tories of North Carolina. W. B. Merrill, the grandfather of Wiley B. Merrill, was born in Kentucky, in 1809, and in January, 1834, went to Texas. He returned to Kentucky for the rest of the family in 1835 and took them to Ladonia, Texas, where he became a pioneer ranchman. His name is connected with the military history of the Lone Star State as a lieutenant-colonel in the army of the Texas Republic, and his death occurred at Ladonia, in 1854. His son, also named W. B. Merrill, the father of Wiley B., was born at Ladonia, Texas, March 11, 1846, and has resided there all his life, being still engaged as a farmer and cattleman. He is a democrat in political matters and has been active in civic affairs, having held a number of offices within the gift of his fellow-citizens of the town and county. He is a steward in the Methodist Episcopal Church, South, having held that position for the past thirty years. At the age of sixteen years, he enlisted as a private in the Confederate army, as a member of Maxey's Texas regiment, and served during the last two years of the war between the states. He has never lost interest in the welfare of his old army comrades, and for many years has been commander of the United Confederate Veterans Camp at Ladonia. Mr. Merrill was married to Miss Helen Boothe, who was born at Rome, Georgia, December 4, 1847, and they became the parents of two children: O. L., who is a cotton broker residing at Ladonia, Texas; and Wiley Boothe.

Wiley Boothe Merrill attended the public schools of Ladonia, Texas, and was duly graduated from the high school there with the class of 1897. Following this, he took a course of three years in the academic department of the University of Texas, and then entered the legal department of the same institution, where he prosecuted his professional studies and was graduated in 1903, with the degree of Bachelor of Laws. While at the university he proved himself an assiduous and receptive scholar, applying himself closely to his studies, but found time to mingle freely with his fellows, with whom he was popular, being a member of the Sigma Alpha Epsilon Greek letter college fraternity. Mr Merrill entered upon the practice of his chosen profession at

Elk City, at that time in Roger Mills County, but now in Beckham County, and here his entire professional career has been passed in a general civil and criminal practice, his offices at this time being located in the First National Bank Building. Mr. Merrill has built up a decidedly satisfying practice, both from the viewpoint of its importance, as well as from its volume. Care and precision mark the preparation of all his cases of whatever nature, his thoroughness of preparation insuring a convincing and clear presentation of whatever subject comes before him for adjustment.

Mr. Merrill holds membership in the Beckham County Bar Association and the Oklahoma Bar Association. He is a democrat, although his activities in politics consist principally of the support of good men and progressive and beneficial measures. His fraternal connection is with Lodge No. 1144, Benevolent and Protective Order of Elks, of Elk City. Mr. Merrill has not married.

GEORGE H. LAING. One of the oldest public officials in Western Oklahoma is George H. Laing, for many years clerk of the District Court at Kingfisher. Two of the present judges now serving on this bench are Judge Cullison and Judge Roberts, both of Enid. Mr. Laing is an Oklahoma eighty-niner is a lawyer by profession, but his qualities and abilities have marked him out almost from the time of reaching the territory for official work, and he has been almost constantly in some office or another for twenty-five years.

George H. Laing was born in Edinburgh, Scotland, December 1, 1864, and has many prominent connections with old Scotch families. His grandfather, Alexander Andrew Laing, was born on the Isle of Skye, and was the owner of the Comely Bank Stock Farm three miles from Edinburgh noted as a breeding place of Galloway and Polled Angus cattle. Mr. Laing's father was Colonel George Alexander Laing, who was born in Edinburgh, and served in the Forty-second Highlanders during the Crimean war as captain of a company. He was awarded a Victoria cross for bravery at Inkermann and Alma. His death occurred at the stock farm near Edinburgh in 1873, about two years after the death of his wife. Her maiden name was Georgiana Isabel Brash, whose father was an Edinburgh architect and superintendent of construction. One son, John A. Laing, has long been in the British Army service, and was first lieutenant in the Seventeenth Punjar Light Infantry, in India.

George H. Laing was graduated from an Edinburgh academy at the age of seventeen. During 1878 he attended the Paris Exposition, and spent several months in travel over the continent. The following year he came to the United States, equipped with a good education, with special skill and proficiency as a penman and in accounting, and the following two years were spent as shipping clerk in a wholesale dry goods house at New York. Most of his active career, however, has been spent in the west. From 1882 he was for seven years engaged in operating a ranch on Platte River near Sidney, Nebraska. While there he introduced Polled Angus cattle into Western Nebraska and Wyoming.

Mr. Laing came to Oklahoma April 22, 1889. At that date, when a portion of the present Oklahoma was first opened to settlement, he secured a homestead claim one mile north of Kingfisher, and at once built a cabin to live in while proving up his land. In a few weeks he was called to other duties. In June, 1889, he was made contest clerk in the United States Land Office, and after fifteen months there became deputy district clerk at Oklahoma City under Judge Clark, then district judge. Resigning this office in the fall of 1892 Mr. Laing returned to Kingfisher, and resumed his work with the land office.

In January, 1893, he was admitted to the bar, and soon opened a law office at Kingfisher under the firm name Whiting & Laing. In the following September he opened an office at Enid, and in that town his practice was principally concentrated for four years. In 1897 he returned to Kingfisher and was soon called upon by Judge McAtee to become deputy district clerk. He was retained in the same capacity by Judge Irwin. Along with excellent penmanship Mr. Laing combined the valuable qualities of accuracy, painstaking care, and courteous and obliging attention to every duty, and these qualities have necessarily made him a very useful man in Oklahoma.

Mr. Laing still retains membership in the bar of Kingfisher County. He is an advocate of good schools, and as a member of the board of education has worked for their improvement, and always taken a prominent part for the upbuilding of Kingfisher and community. He was the first secretary of the Republican County Central Committee at Kingfisher, and was also its chairman at a later date, and has been active both during territorial and state periods in his section. He is affiliated with the Masonic Order and the Knights Templar, with the Caledonian Club, and with the St. Andrew Society of New York City. His church faith is that of the Episcopalian, and he takes an active part in church affairs.

On August 22, 1894, Mr. Laing married Miss Mina O. Menzies. She was born at Peterboro, Ontario, a daughter of Thomas and Isabelle (McIntyre) Menzies. Both parents were born in Perthshire, Scotland. Her father was a grandson of John Menzies, who was captain of the Seventy-ninth Highlanders under Sir Ralph Abercrombie at the Battle of the Nile in Egypt, when the British so thoroughly whipped the forces of the great Napoleon during his Egyptian campaign. Mrs. Laing's maternal grandfather, Donald McIntyre, was major in the Scotch Greys Cavalry at the Battle of Waterloo. Mr. and Mrs. Laing have three children: Ronald B., Christine I. and Louise M.

JOHN F. PALMER. A man of justice in all his relations with his fellows, is a tribute which no member of the Osage Nation deserves in a higher degree than John F. Palmer of Pawhuska. During the years since he was admitted to the full rights of citizenship in the Osage tribe he has stood steadfastly for the right as he sees it, and in a manner surpassing the abilities and opportunities of most men has succeeded in translating high ideals into terms of practical service and usefulness. In the ordinary aspect of his career Mr. Palmer was for many years an attorney, practicing both in the tribal courts and afterwards in the state and federal jurisdictions, and has likewise made his example stimulating to a large community as a farmer and farmer. But the interests and value of his career are chiefly due to his varied relations as a public leader, though seldom in official positions, among the Indian people in Northeastern Oklahoma whose heritage has made them the wealthiest people in the world, and no one man has fought more indefatigably, earnestly and unselfishly to safeguard that very heritage.

Though he is the son of a white man, his birth occurred on the wide open prairie in the far Northwest, hundreds of miles from the outposts of civilization, in what was then known vaguely as Dakota Territory, in 1862. The Palmers were prominent frontiersmen in Missouri and the western territories, and his grandfather was a physician of excellent ability and high standing. His father was an early owner of freighting outfits from Dakota to Oregon. He married a Sioux Indian woman, but the mother died at the birth of John F. Palmer. He was reared for the first few years of his life among

Indian relatives in Dakota Territory, but in 1869, when seven years of age, he was taken by his father to the latter's sister at Fort Scott, Kansas, and soon afterward his father placed him in the old Catholic school, known as the Osage Mission, at what is now St. Paul, Kansas. That school was conducted by the Jesuit Fathers, chief among whom was the noted priest of the Southwest, Rev. John Schoenmacher. Two or three years after he had been put in this school the news came that his father had been killed in Oregon, where he owned a cattle train. John F. Palmer remained at the school at Osage Mission until 1876, and was then adopted into the family of Samuel Bevinue, a member of the Osage Tribe. He accompanied his foster father to the Osage Reservation in what is now the State of Oklahoma, and they all settled on Salt Creek twenty-five miles west of the present City of Pawhuska, where they opened one of the first farms in that region.

His independent career outside of school and home influences may be said to have begun in 1881 when he went out as a cowboy in the employ of different outfits through the Chickasha Nation and Northern Texas. That was his regular occupation until 1887. His foster father, Samuel Bevinue, died in 1883, and in 1887 Mr. Palmer returned home to aid the family in managing the farm.

In the meantime Mr. Palmer had been formally adopted as a member of the Osage Tribe of Indians. This adoption required a procedure of an interesting and somewhat impressive character, including his appearance before the council of Osage chiefs and head men, prominent among whom were such men as Pawnee Numpahshe or Governor Joe and Black Dog, Wahtinkah, Strike Axe, Gus Strike Axe, Alvin Wood, Samuel Bevinue, Ogeese Captain, Cyprian Tayrien, and Ne-kah-wah-she-tan-kah, and others. All of these chiefs and headmen are now deceased excepting Cyprian Tayrien and Ne-kah-wah-she-tan-kah, prominent old residents near Gray Horse, Oklahoma.

On June 11, 1888, Mr. Palmer married Martha A. Plomondon, a member of the Osage Tribe. To their marriage were born six children: Mabel (Dot), John E., Mary E., Clementina, Martha M. and Marguerite. All of these children are living in Osage County except John E., who was drowned in Clear Creek when eleven years of age.

After his marriage Mr. Palmer engaged in the regular practice of law under the old Osage Tribal Government. In the meantime he had studied American law, and after the tribal form of government was abolished by department order, continued his studies in different offices, but chiefly in the office of W. S. Fitzpatrick of Sedan, Kansas, who formerly was a United States commissioner, located at Pawhuska, and is now serving as general counsel for the Prairie Oil & Gas Company of Kansas and Oklahoma. While in Mr. Fitzpatrick's office Mr. Palmer was admitted to the bar by Judge Aikman, then judge of District Court in Chautauqua and Elk counties, Kansas. For several years Mr. Palmer continued to practice law in the state and federal courts, but about 1912 discontinued this as a profession and has since given his entire time to his farming and stock raising interests. In fact, farming and stock raising has been his chief business for fully a quarter of a century.

Another distinction in the career of Mr. Palmer remains to be noted. In 1898 he enlisted as a volunteer private in Company K of the First Territorial Volunteer Infantry for service in the Spanish-American War. This famous regiment it will be recalled was recruited largely from the four territories of the United States at that time, Oklahoma, Indian Territory, Arizona and New Mexico. Mr. Palmer was the only volunteer from Osage County in this splendid regiment of frontiersmen and rough riders. Several others enlisted from the Osage Tribe and went into other regiments, but he was the only one in the First Territorial. He remained with the regiment in its arduous service during the actual period of hostilities, and received his honorable discharge February 9, 1899.

Mr. Palmer is a deep student of politics in the better sense of that word, and has always been particularly active and influential in public questions as they related to his own people. Though a democrat, he has never held office, but has served on various delegations. He was chairman of the first important statehood convention held at Oklahoma City. In practically every national, state and local campaign since 1896 he has been on the stump, both in Oklahoma and Kansas, and in this connection there may be stated another well earned distinction, that Mr. Palmer is known as the most eloquent Indian in Oklahoma. In the course of a speech at Pawhuska a few years ago, Senator Gore referred to Mr. Palmer as "the most eloquent Indian alive."

He served as the first master of Wah-Shah-She Lodge, No. 110, Ancient Free and Accepted Masons, at Pawhuska, and is also affiliated with the Royal Arch Chapter, has taken the various degrees in the Scottish Rite, and is a member of the Knights of Pythias. He was reared in the faith of the Catholic Church, and his wife and children are all members of that denomination.

Twenty-five years of his life have been spent in the active service of his chosen people. He probably would find it difficult to recall the number of times he has gone to Washington either individually or as a member of delegations during the past twenty-five years for the purpose of representing the Osage people in important matters under the jurisdiction of the department of Indian affairs or calling for a consultation with committees of Congress, or the President. In this time he has stood shoulder to shoulder with the public spirited men of the Osages in their fight on Indian traders, Indian agents, big cattle interests and the still bigger oil interests of recent times. He is even now engaged in what appears to be the final effort to wrest the richest oil and gas country in the world from the monopolistic control and domination of the Standard Oil Company and its various subsidiary corporations. Mr. Palmer has courageously fought a fight in the interests of all his fellow citizens to secure the full benefits of this marvelous aggregate of wealth, against which the plots of the most cunning and brilliant legal talent have been devised. Particular reference is made to the blanket lease which would include a territory of approximately 680,000 acres.

At the same time Mr. Palmer has for years favored the allotment in severalty of the Osage lands, believing that by such allotment individual initiative would be encouraged and a great impulse given to the actual development and improvement of the rich agricultural lands included in the Osage holdings. He has worked not only for raising the standards of agriculture, but also for the building of schools and churches, and has advocated the policy of inducing farmers from other states to come in and add their experience and enterprise to the Osage people in developing their lands. Several times he has appeared before the State Board of Agriculture in favor of the small farmer and stock man as against the big cattle interests, and has never failed to secure the object for which he was working. All of this service, it is perhaps needless to state, Mr. Palmer has given absolutely free to his people. He has never accepted a fee in return for any of his work as an attorney or advocate in behalf of the Osage country and its people as a whole, and hence it would be difficult to find, going through Oklahoma in all directions, a man of more fixed ideals of loyalty, of sturdy honesty, with more directness and simplicity of character and with finer natural abilities in mind and eloquence and in rare powers of judgment than John F. Palmer.

EDWARD S. MCCABE, the superintendent of the city schools of Kingfisher, is an educator of proved ability and long experience. Several things make his record one of interesting and distinctive character. The fourteen years he has been superintendent of the Kingfisher city schools constitute the longest term in the same superintendency in the State of Oklahoma. Another distinction is that he has been continuously in school work in Oklahoma since 1893, in just one county, Kingfisher County. He is a pioneer settler in the Cherokee Strip and in point of continuous service one of the oldest school men in the territory and state.

Edward S. McCabe was born at Newton County, Indiana, on September 11, 1870, and acquired his common school education in Gentry and Harrison counties in Northwest Missouri. His formal entrance into school work was preceded by a thorough course at the Chillicothe Normal School in Missouri, from which he graduated, and he had an experience of three terms in charge of country schools before coming to Oklahoma. In the spring of 1893 he accompanied his father, S. L. McCabe, to Kingfisher County, and in September of that year they participated in the opening of the Cherokee Strip, locating in Garfield County.

Mr. McCabe's first school work in Oklahoma was begun at Wandel, where he taught three terms. He then went to Kingfisher and had charge of the high school as principal but resigned at the close of the first year in order to enter the State University at Norman, where he continued higher studies for two years. He next took charge of the Hennessey public schools as superintendent, and during the four years there was largely instrumental in placing the school system of that city on a high plane of efficiency.

In the fall of 1902 Mr. McCabe was elected superintendent of the Kingfisher city schools, succeeding Charles H. Roberts, who had been elected to the chair of history at the Central State Normal at Edmond. His work at Kingfisher will probably constitute his best monument as an educator. A fine proof of his efficiency in directing the city school system is found in the unanimous support given him as to his work. At each recurring annual election since he was first made superintendent at Kingfisher he has received the entire vote of the Board of Education for superintendent, and though the board's personnel has frequently changed there has never been a member who has opposed his election.

Mr. McCabe has been a constant student and is as much in the van of educational progress in Oklahoma now as he was twenty years ago. He graduated from Kingfisher College in 1910, and during the past five years has done post-graduate work at the University of Chicago. He is well known in school circles all over the State of Oklahoma and has been vice president of the State Teachers' Association, and was twice elected secretary-treasurer and was twice on the executive committee of the association. He has also served as vice president of the Missouri Teachers' Club.

Mr. McCabe married at Hennessey in May, 1901, Miss Maude Binding, daughter of Charles and Kate Binding. They have two sons, Edward Earl and Charles Lafayette.

RUFUS LAFAYETTE SLAUGHTER. The present superintendent of schools at Macomb, though a young man of only thirty years, has been identified with educational work more or less for fully fourteen years. He did his first school work in Oklahoma in 1910, and is one of the highly competent educators of the state.

The family to which he belongs came from England to Virginia in colonial times. One of his ancestors was Philip Slaughter, who served in the Revolutionary war. Still another ancestor was a colonial governor in North Carolina. Professor Slaughter was born at Booneville, Arkansas, November 21, 1885. His father, W. L. Slaughter, who was born in Memphis, Tennessee, in 1857, is still living at Booneville. He spent his early career in Memphis, at Newport, Arkansas, but when still young established his home at Booneville, where he married and where for a number of years he has been successfully practicing as a lawyer. In politics he is a democrat and has filled the office of county judge. He is a member of the Missionary Baptist Church, the Masonic fraternity and the Independent Order of Odd Fellows. W. L. Slaughter married Dora Walker, who was born at Booneville, Arkansas, in 1866. Their children are: Frank L., a traveling salesman whose home is at Jonesboro, Arkansas; Robert N., a teacher at Jonesboro; Rufus L.; and H. S., who is a teacher at Saratago Arkansas.

Rufus L. Slaughter grew up in his native village of Booneville, attended the public schools there, graduating from high school in 1901. His first work as a teacher was as principal at Waldron, Arkansas, where he remained two years. For another year he was principal of the school at Cauthron, Arkansas. His higher education was continued in the Ouachita College at Arkadelphia, where he spent two years, finishing the sophomore course in the normal school. Leaving educational work for a time, from 1906 to 1910, Mr. Slaughter was in the railway mail service with a run between Memphis, Tennessee, and McAlester, Oklahoma.

In 1910 he came to Wilburton, Oklahoma, to take the principalship of the local schools for one year. During 1911-12 he was in charge of the schools at Heavener, Oklahoma, and after being out of school work again for a year became superintendent of schools at Asher during 1913-15, for two school years. In the fall of 1915 he became superintendent at Macomb.

In politics he is a democrat, is a member of the Christian Church, is affiliated with Logan Lodge No. 408, Ancient Free and Accepted Masons, is past high priest of Van Hoose Chapter No. 111, Royal Arch Masons; and is a member of the Independent Order of Odd Fellows and the Woodmen of the World. He is active and well known in educational organizations, a member of both the county and state teachers' associations, and was chairman of the Pottawatomie County Teachers' Association in 1913 and 1914. In 1912 at Fort Smith, Arkansas, Mr. Slaughter married Miss Eleanor Hull. Her father was the late H. W. Hull, who for a number of years was a machinist in the employ of the Kansas City Southern Railway on the Heavener division.

DANIEL K. CUNNINGHAM. In the settlement and development of Oklahoma thousands of men revealed their real character and ability. Probably much the greater part of those who came at the opening were unable to stand the testing and sifting processes, and have long since settled down into obscurity or have gone to other regions. Among the hosts of men who have had the opportunities of pioneers comparatively a handful can be classed as "men of light and leading," men who have been persistent in their ambitions, have worked steadily for the fulfillment of ideals, and from first to last have exercised a great force in the upbuilding of the territory and state. One of the most conspicuous of these lives at Kingfisher and is an attorney, one of the three still in practice out of the 150 or more who arrived at the town site within a few days of the opening in 1889. Daniel K. Cunningham secured and maintained against all opposition one of the first locations near the land office at Kingfisher. He has practiced law and represented hundreds of clients in the courts of the old territory and the new state. But perhaps his chief claim to distinction has been his broad public spirit, his vision of the future, and his untiring work in behalf of his home city. He is one of the men who has supplied faith and courage through all the years of prosperity and vicissitudes since Oklahoma first became the home of civilized men.

Daniel K. Cunningham is a Canadian by birth, born in County Kent on a farm in Ontario January 17, 1854. When he was seventeen years of age he went into Michigan, and for three years was identified with the lumber industry when that business was at its height in Western Michigan. He served as a lumber inspector at mills in Muskegon, Whitehall and other places. Those towns were then among the most important lumber centers in the world. Muskegon alone operated forty-five large mills, and all the country back of that city for miles was one vast pine forest. The panic of 1873 caused a severe decline in the industry, and about that time Mr. Cunningham returned to Canada and gave serious attention to the acquiring of a liberal education. He attended the high school and college at Gault and Hamilton, and spent five years in preparing for the legal profession in the Upper Canada Law Association at Toronto. He gave close attention to his studies in a private office, and passed the required annual examination conducted by the association above named, until his final examination in 1880 admitted him to Osgoode Hall at Toronto—a body corresponding to the famous Inns of Court in London. Thus he became a full-fledged attorney, solicitor and barrister. Much of the five years of study and experience had been in the office of Richard Baily, Q. C., of London, Ontario.

Mr. Cunningham began practice in his native county and remained there until 1885. He then removed to the United States, locating in McPherson County, Kansas, and was soon in possession of a promising practice. It was with little thought or desire to remain in Oklahoma that he responded to the persuasion of his friends to accompany them and take part in the long-looked for opening. He had just completed an arduous term of court, and being in need of a vacation he consented to accompany a party of friends, and while en route became infected with the prevailing fever which possessed the many thousands of emigrants to the new land of promise. On reaching the outskirts of the territory he decided to enter and secure if possible a homestead. The United States had designated the location of a land office at the present site of Kingfisher, and with this point in view he set his stake at a point about half a mile distant from the office. His reasoning was that he could thus secure a quarter section adjoining the town site. At this time no town site had been provided for by the Government. His stake was within a few paces of the northwest corner of his tract. He was one of the crowd of thousands of others who were congregated in the same locality, but the land office for filing of claims was not opened until April 23rd. At 2 o'clock in the morning Mr. Cunningham found four men on the steps of the land office, and a line was quickly formed. By 9 o'clock, when the office opened for the filing of the first claim, there were probably 4,000 men in line,

and about 15,000 people on or near the possible townsite. Mr. Cunningham's papers for filing were not at first received, and in fact not for about thirty days, until considerable correspondence had passed between the local authorities and Washington and instructions had issued from the central Government. Many others tried to secure this same land, and thus there ensued contests extending over a period of two years. Mr. Cunningham's claim was finally sustained. In the meantime he built a cabin and made it his home in order not to lose any rights of possession. At one time the contention became so bitter that a United States officer was secured to remove his house beyond the borders of the land. This act was subsequently repudiated by the Government, the deputy was dismissed, and the same man who had removed the house placed it back on its original site. A fence was also constructed for the purpose of shutting out this determined claimant, but with a knowledge of the location of survey lines, he subsequently built a far better residence, in fact, what was at that time the best house in the vicinity.

Mr. Cunningham has many interesting recollections of those pioneer days in and about Kingfisher. From the first he showed his public spirit and willingness to co-operate with and lead his fellow men to important improvements and undertakings. It was generally understood that the city blocks should be 300 feet square, and accordingly stakes were set as near the outer boundaries as could be determined. Naturally those stakes which were subsequently found to be in the street were thrown out and the claims thus instituted were lost. On the 23rd day of April public meetings were held which brought about the organization of two city governments. One was at the north and the other at the south of the land office. To one organization was given the name Kingfisher and to the other Lisbon. Each village chose boards of aldermen and mayor and other officials, and thus on one day two towns came into existence. The dual city continued for about two years until they were consolidated, and the name carried by the land office was made the title of the larger city. There was no law in Oklahoma Territory except such as emanated from the people themselves and from the rules of the Federal authorities until 1890, when the Government announced as a code a compilation from the statutes of Kansas, Nebraska and Indiana which should be applicable to the new country of Oklahoma. As is well known, all the later openings of Oklahoma Territory were much better systematized, town sites were established in advance, a system of registration and drawing was formulated, and in general these later openings were characterized by much less friction and bitterness.

In the very early days of Kingfisher about 150 attorneys did more or less law practice, and as already stated only three of these are still active members of the bar. Mr. Cunningham was also a leader in the movement when Kingfisher became an aspirant for the territorial capital location. He and two other men were a committee appointed to represent Kingfisher in the contest for the capital. They were in constant attendance at the Legislature from August until December, when after its second passage, the bill making Kingfisher the capital was finally vetoed by Governor George W. Steele.

Mr. Cunningham has added part of his land to the city in subdivisions and additions, and most of these lots have already been sold. He has made himself a factor in both local and state affairs during the development of Oklahoma, and has been one of the dominant influences in the progress of Kingfisher. Some of his ambitions have become realities, while other are still

John Collins

process of development. For years, both in season and out of season, Mr. Cunningham has labored for a railroad that would give direct communication from great grain and coal fields north and west of Kingfisher with the Gulf of Mexico. At times it seemed as if the project was in the way of direct fulfillment. Right of way over hundreds of miles had been secured, a charter worth a possible fortune was kept alive, and considerable grading done. However, opposition has developed from various sources, and some of this opposition has been apparently incomprehensible. An influence has been exerted even upon local men so as to make them stand against the enterprise, which clearly meant the greatest good to themselves and to their city. Kingfisher was for some years one of the world's greatest primary wheat markets. Grain fields for 100 miles to the west marketed their products at Kingfisher. Curiously enough, a number of local men argued, very shortsightedly, that if the proposed railroad should be built it would mean the establishment of a number of new towns along the line and closer to the sources of production. Thus for the sake of a temporary good they were willing to sacrifice the great price which would eventually bring permanent prosperity to the city. Other insidious influences have also operated to prevent the construction of the road. Financiers who had previously stated their approval of the plan and were apparently ready to finance the enterprise mysteriously and suddenly lost interest. With all these hindrances Mr. Cunningham still retains faith in having that line built, and it is his greatest ambition to make Kingfisher a great entrepot for the surrounding district even as it once was. Mr. Cunningham's name appears in perhaps more important cases than any other lawyer in the state.

EDWARD C. CAMPBELL. One of the youngest school superintendents of the state is Edward C. Campbell, at the head of the public schools at Asher. Mr. Campbell is only twenty-three years of age, but already has a record which shows his proficiency as a teacher and school executive.

Born in Dubois County, Indiana, March 11, 1893, Edward C. Campbell got his early education in the schools of his native county and was reared on a farm. From the district schools he went to the county seat at Jasper, and graduated from the high school there in 1912. After one year in the Indiana State Normal School at Terre Haute, he took charge of a school in Dubois County, and remained in active educational work there for three years. In the spring of 1915, with a view to identifying himself with educational work in the State of Oklahoma, Mr. Campbell entered the Central State Normal at Edmond. In September, 1913, he began his duties as principal of schools at Asher. Mr. Campbell is a democrat in politics and a member of the Christian Church.

His parents are Daniel and Rosa (Zehr) Campbell. The Campbells emigrated from Scotland to the Province of Ulster, Ireland, during Cromwell's time. From Northern Ireland they came to South Carolina, and one of the family commanded a brigade in the battle of King's Mountain during the Revolutionary war. Mr. Campbell's paternal grandfather, Horace Campbell, was born in North Carolina, became an early settler in Indiana, and died in Orange County of that state in 1897. By occupation he was a carpenter and farmer, and during the Civil war he was a Union volunteer and helped to repel Morgan's raids. The maternal grandfather, William Zehr, was born in Prussia, emigrated to America and settled at Cincinnati, and from there moved to Dubois County, Indiana, about 1859. He was born in 1837 and is still living in Indiana. While a young man in Prussia he had a thorough military training, and during the American Civil war he served four years in the Union army, being all through the campaign of Sherman into Tennessee and Georgia and following that great leader on his march to the sea.

Daniel Campbell, father of Edward C., was born in Washington County, Indiana, in 1855 and was quite young when the family moved to Dubois County. There he married, and has since followed farming and stock-raising. He is a democrat, and is a member and has served as trustee of the Christian Church and is affiliated with the Independent Order of Odd Fellows. His wife, Rosa Zehr, was born in Saxony, Germany, in 1858, but since infancy he has lived in this country. Their children are: Charles, a senior in the Central State Normal School at Edmond, Oklahoma; Sophia, who graduated from a business college at Louisville, Kentucky, in 1913, and is now a stenographer for the Falls City Bottling Works at Louisville; Edward C.; Frank, who lives on the farm with his parents back in Indiana; Clarence, a sophomore in the high school at Jasper, Indiana; and Emil, who is in the eighth grade of the public schools.

JOHN COLLINS. During the greater part of a lifetime of fifty-six years John Collins was identified with the country and people of the Osages. He was one of the pioneer farmers and stock men in the locality of Avant, and his years were spent with accomplishments not only from a business standpoint, but also in conferring a benefit upon the community in which he lived. He gave service as a member of the board of county commissioners, and in many other ways his name was well known throughout Osage County.

While a resident of Kansas and Northern Oklahoma from boyhood, John Collins was born in Cumberland, Guernsey County, Ohio, October 15, 1859. John and Nellie (Kelley) Collins, his parents, were born in County Galway, Ireland, were married there at the ages of seventeen and eighteen, respectively, and took their honeymoon on a sailing vessel bound for the United States. They landed after many weeks voyage, and for a number of years lived in Ohio. When John Collins was twelve years of age his parents removed to Independence, Kansas, and six years later they went along with the Osage people into the Osage Nation of Indian Territory, locating in the same general locality where John Collins lived until his death. His father died when about thirty-three years of age, and his mother passed away April 3, 1914, aged eighty-six. John Collins, the elder, was a soldier in the Civil war, enlisting in the One Hundred and Twenty-second Ohio Volunteer Infantry, and was twice wounded, though out of active service only a short time on that account, and was present with Grant's army at Lee's surrender at Appomattox. Outside of his military service his years were spent in farming and stock raising. He was a member of the Catholic Church and a democrat in politics. His six children are: Mrs. Mary Clark, who lives in Chicago; James, who died at the age of forty years, leaving a widow and one child; Ellen Shultz, who lives with her family in Illinois; Charles W., who died unmarried at the age of thirty; and Richard, who was killed while handling a horse at the age of twenty-six.

From the time he was eighteen years of age Mr. Collins lived in the present County of Osage. He grew up on a farm, had only fair opportunities to attend school, and gained a thorough training in the vocation which became his life work, that of farming and stock raising. His wife and two sons are both members of the old Osage tribe, and their allotments of land make a total of about 1,900 acres, all located within the vicinity of Avant. They reside in an excellent home, and have about 400 acres out of the three allotments under cultivation, the remainder being in pasture lands. Over this large estate Mr. Collins for many years until his death, on the 30th of November, 1915, supervised his farming and stock raising activities, and accomplished a more than ordinary success.

As to politics he was a republican voter from the time he came to his majority. For three years he was a member of the board of county commissioners after statehood, and from the time Oklahoma became a state was continuously a member of the local school board. On June 7, 1895, Mr. Collins married Lulu Payne. She was born in the Cherokee Nation, lost her parents when she was an infant and was reared in the home of her mother's brother, Judge T. L. Rogers, the distinguished citizen of the Osage tribe, of whom a sketch is published on other pages of this work. Two children were born to Mr. and Mrs. Collins: John W. and Roy W.

L. H. KERR. Since the establishment of the commission form of government at Enid in 1908 the local citizens have exercised a commendable discretion and discrimination in selecting men to fill the chief offices of responsibility. It has been the custom to choose men whose previous experience with business would give them special efficiency for their respective departments, and as a result of this care in selecting officials the City of Enid has probably gone forward as rapidly in general municipal development during the last ten years as any other community in the Southwest. It was due to this careful discrimination that L. H. Kerr was selected as commissioner of streets, alleys and public property in April, 1913. The capable manner in which Mr. Kerr has performed the duties of his office has proved the wisdom of his election, and he has made it a matter of pride as well as duty to keep up the affairs of his department at the highest point of efficiency.

Mr. Kerr took office on the first Monday of May following his election. In his department he has supervision of the city engineering department, the city health officer, the milk and dairy inspector, the building inspector, and inspector of dump grounds. Two men are kept constantly at street cleaning, and for a part of the year this force is increased by these additional men. Enid has 200 miles of streets, with sixteen miles of paving. With the exception of six blocks of brick, the paving is entirely of asphalt. The streets are laid out on the broad basis of 100 feet width, with paving about sixty feet wide.

L. H. Kerr was born in Marshall County, Illinois, near Sparland, a village on the west bank of the Illinois River not far from Lacon, the county seat, on September 24, 1873. His father located there in 1868. When Mr. Kerr was seven years of age his parents embarked in a typical prairie schooner and journeyed out to Greene County, Iowa. In March, 1901, the family came to Enid. The parents are Albert and Luana Kerr. Albert Kerr was a soldier in a Pennsylvania regiment during the Civil war. He became a prosperous farmer, and a number of years ago visited Oklahoma and was so pleased with the prospects that he determined to make it his home as soon as circumstances would permit. In Iowa he was a man of considerable prominence in public affairs, serving as county supervisor six years, the duties of that office including oversight of roads and bridge building and maintenance. Since coming to Enid he has devoted his energies mainly to carpenter and building work.

L. H. Kerr was associated with his father while the latter was supervisor in Iowa, and thus gained a practical experience in road construction, a knowledge that has served him well in his duties as street commissioner. Since coming to Enid he has worked as a carpenter, and for several years was foreman for the leading building contractor and has also been an independent contractor. Nearly all of the best homes in Enid and several of the churches were erected under his superintendence.

Mr. Kerr is a member of the Baptist Church. He has been specially prominent in the Independent Order of Odd Fellows, has been secretary of Enid Lodge No. 31 since 1911, has passed all the chairs in the subordinate lodge and encampment, and has represented both bodies in the grand lodges, being now grand marshal of the grand encampment. He is also affiliated with the Knights of Pythias. Outside of business he finds his chief pleasure in hunting, and takes one or two trips for that sport every year. April 2, 1898, in Greene County, Iowa, Mr. Kerr married Miss Bertha M. Newingham. They have a family of three sons: Frank, Keith and Carl.

WILLIAM T. HAWN, M. D., a successful young physician and surgeon at Binger, Oklahoma, is descended from fine old colonial stock, his ancestors having come to this country from Germany. The original progenitor of the name in America settled in North Carolina and subsequently members of the family removed to the Middle West, locating in Missouri, where John D. Hawn, father of the Doctor, was born in 1859. He lived in Bollinger County, Missouri, until 1913 when he came to Oklahoma and established his home at El Reno, there engaging in business as a merchant. In Missouri he farmed for a number of years, was hotel proprietor, and for several years served as county assessor of Bollinger County. He is a stalwart democrat in his political adherences and in religious matters is a devout member of the Methodist Episcopal Church, South. He married Miss Nancy Shell, who was born at Patton, Missouri, in 1863, and this union was prolific of three children, namely: Rayford, in business with his father at El Reno; Charles W., died in El Reno at the age of thirty years; and William T., subject of this review.

A native Missourian, Doctor Hawn was born at Patton, that state, February 1, 1885. He was educated in the public schools of Patton and graduated in the local high school in 1903. He then entered the Marvin Collegiate Institute, at Fredericktown, Missouri, and after completing his junior year there was matriculated as a student in Barnes University, at St. Louis, Missouri, in the medical department of which he was graduated as a member of the class of 1910, with the degree of Doctor of Medicine. His initial experience as a doctor was obtained at Glen Island, Missouri, where he remained for eight months, at the expiration of which he came to Caddo County, locating at Lookeba. After two years in the latter place he established his home and professional headquarters at Binger, and here he has since resided. He has built up a large general practice in Binger and in he country normally adjacent to this city and has met with unusual success in curing the sick. He is possessed of a genial disposition and his kind personality invariably inspires hope in the heart of his patient. His offices are on the north side of Main Street.

In politics Doctor Hawn is a democrat and in a fraternal way he is affiliated with Binger Lodge, Independent Order of Odd Fellows. In connection with his life work he is a valued and appreciative member of Caddo County Medical Society, the Oklahoma State Medical Society, and the American Medical Association, being vice president of the first mentioned.

In St. Louis, Missouri, in 1910, Doctor Hawn was united in marriage to Miss Opal F. Cander, a daughter of Fletcher Cander, a civil engineer who died in Cripple Creek, Colorado. Doctor and Mrs. Hawn have two children: Helen, born February 28, 1911; and Ruth, born July 1, 1914. The Doctor and his wife are members of the Congregational Church, to whose charities and good works they are liberal contributors.

JAMES WALLACE STEEN. One of the pioneer attorneys of the City of Enid, a participant in the opening of the strip in 1893, James Wallace Steen has been a prominent member of the Oklahoma bar for more than twenty years, and is specially remembered for his services as a district judge. He was appointed judge of the district including Enid by Governor Haskell, and served four and a half months, and also served three years and three months in the same office under appointment by Lieutenant Governor McAlester.

James Wallace Steen was born June 16, 1855, on a farm in Logan County, Ohio. Three weeks before his birth his father died, and his mother lived only nine days. An only child, he was reared in the home of his grandfather in Ohio until sixteen, spending these years on a farm near Huntsville. What he has accomplished in life is largely the product of his individual ambition and energy. In 1874 he entered the freshman class at Monmouth College in Monmouth, Illinois, and was graduated A. B. in 1877. Three years later that institution gave him the degree Master of Arts. He studied law at Bellefontaine, Ohio, in the office of Judge J. A. Price, and was admitted to the bar at Cleveland in September, 1879. Judge Steen practiced law at Cleveland and Bellefontaine until March 19, 1888, and then located in Kingman, Kansas. That was his home until the spring of 1893, when he removed to Kingfisher, Oklahoma, and on the date of the opening of the Cherokee Strip on September 16, 1893, was one of the many thousands who sought homes in the new country. He staked out a lot on the public square at Enid, but could not prove his claim and therefore was not among the lucky ones in gaining a piece of real estate. There were about 200 lawyers in the throng of homeseekers who arrived at Enid on that opening day, and Judge Steen is one of the few who still remain in active practice. Some of the others who were his contemporaries are W. E. Cogdal, H. J. Sturgis, L. N. Huston, C. H. Parker, John F. Curran, Jake Roberts, J. B. Cullison, and I. G. Conkling. Judge Steen in company with Judge L. M. Conkling and Mr. I. G. Conkling set up their first office in a tent on the public square, with a rough board sign on the outside announcing the firm of Conkling, Steen & Conkling, lawyers. A number of other lawyers and professional men likewise had their first offices in tents.

Judge Steen is a democrat in politics. He is a member of the Episcopal Church and when the first services of that church were held at Enid on September 17, 1893, by Bishop Brooks Mr. Steen was appointed the first senior warden of the newly organized congregation. As a lawyer Judge Steen has always enjoyed a liberal practice, and while on the bench proved himself a painstaking and impartial judge. One of his most important decisions was that upholding the rights of lessees of state school lands, and his decision sustaining the vote against the repeal of the anti-gambling law was also of far-reaching effect.

In 1887 at Bellefontaine, Ohio, Judge Steen married Miss Sallie Pate, who is of Virginia birth and parentage. Mrs. Steen is well known as a contributor of fiction under her own name to magazines. Among other public services Judge Steen was named by Governor Haskell as a member of the board of control of the Institute for the Feebleminded; and he served on that board while the buildings of the institution were in course of erection.

CHARLES BYRON HILL. It was the unusual qualifications and attainments demonstrated during fifteen years of practice at Guthrie that brought Dr. Charles B. Hill the appointment in the summer of 1915 as superintendent of the Oklahoma Hospital for the Insane at Supply. Doctor Hill has had an unusually broad and thorough experience in life. He earned his professional education, worked as a teacher and clerk for several years during his earlier career, and since gaining his title as a doctor of medicine has had unusual opportunities in professional lines.

Though most of his life was spent in Kansas up to the time he came to Oklahoma, Doctor Hill was born on a farm in Marshall County, Illinois, December 1, 1871, a son of Byron A. and Amanda (Leigh) Hill, his father and grandparents having been natives of Oneida County, New York. His father was born in 1829 and in 1850 moved to Marshall County, Illinois, worked for a few years as a carpenter, then bought land and during the rest of his life followed farming almost altogether. He moved out to Kansas in 1881, locating also in Marshall County of that state, and continued farming there until 1890. He then retired from farming, and for nine years served as postmaster of Stolzenbach, Kansas. In 1902 he came to Oklahoma, bought property in Guthrie, and lived retired in that city until his death on July 18, 1914. He was an active member of the Methodist Episcopal Church. He was married in 1852 to Miss Leigh, who was born in Illinois, in 1832. Her father was a native of England and her mother, whose first name was Elizabeth, was born in Virginia. Byron A. Hill and wife became parents of nine children, five sons and four daughters, mentioned briefly as follows: Rhoda, deceased; Alice, wife of J. C. Smith, a farmer at Great Bend, Kansas; Horace W., a farmer in South Dakota; Frank L., a dairy farmer at Norman, Oklahoma; Sherman S., who is a gold miner in California; Renette, who is unmarried and is superintendent of trained nurses in the State University Hospital at Oklahoma City; Dr. Charles B. who is seventh in order of birth; and Harry and Catherine, both of whom died in infancy.

When the family moved out to Kansas Dr. Charles B. Hill was ten years of age. He grew up on a farm, and in 1892 finished the course in the Marysville High School. After that came two years of work as a teacher in Marshall County, Kansas, followed by one year as a salesman in a bookstore at Marysville. Partly with the earnings of his work in these occupations he entered, in 1895, the University Medical School in Kansas City, and after four years of hard study earned his Doctor of Medicine degree in 1899. He was very fortunate in his next appointment to the position of assistant superintendent of the General Hospital for the Atchison, Topeka & Santa Fe Railroad at Topeka, Kansas. He remained in the railroad hospital until September 18, 1900, and on that date arrived in Guthrie and took up his general practice as a physician and surgeon. In a few years he came to be recognized as one of the leading medical men of Oklahoma, and it was entirely without solicitation on his part that he was appointed, August 1, 1915, as superintendent of the Oklahoma Hospital for the Insane at Supply.

Doctor Hill has long been interested in Masonry. In 1902 he attained the thirty-second degree of Scottish Rite, in 1912 was given the title K. C. C. H. and in 1914 received the supreme honorary thirty-third degree which was conferred upon him at Guthrie in 1915. His local affiliation is with Albert Pike Lodge No. 162, Ancient

Free and Accepted Masons, at Guthrie. He also retains membership in the Methodist Episcopal Church at Guthrie. For three years of his practice in that city he served as city physician.

On January 7, 1901, at Haddam, Kansas, Doctor Hill married Miss Florence Taylor, daughter of William H. and Mary Taylor, who were natives of Indiana. Mrs. Hill was born in Washington County, Kansas, August 7, 1876. To their marriage was born one child, Ruth, at Guthrie, July 3, 1909.

JOHN H. KANE is a member of the prominent Bartlesville law firm of Brennan, Kane & McCoy, and has been a factor in the prestige which this firm enjoys in Washington County and Northeastern Oklahoma. He is a lawyer of exceptional attainments, of great energy and resourcefulness, and has made his profession a medium of important public service since locating in Oklahoma twelve years ago.

Aside from his profession he has become interested in the Oklahoma oil industry as an individual operator and a stockholder in several different companies. In this connection it is a matter of interest to record that the place of his birth was an oil camp in Pennsylvania. This was at Fagundus, in Warren County, Pennsylvania, where John Henry Kane was born November 12, 1875, a son of James R. and Catharine (Strickler) Kane. Both parents were natives of Pennsylvania and his father was identified with the early petroleum industry of Pennsylvania until the early '80s, when he brought his family to the West and established a home in what is now Kiowa County, Kansas. There he was successfully identified with stock raising for many years.

The only son among four children, John H. Kane was seven years old when the family moved to Kansas and he grew up on his father's ranch in Kiowa County. Graduating from the high school at Greensburg, the county seat, he continued his education in the Kansas State Normal School at Emporia, where he was graduated in 1896 and from there entered the University of Kansas at Lawrence, where he graduated A. B. in 1899. With his liberal education as a foundation, Mr. Kane then entered the University of Kansas law department and took his degree LL. B. in 1900. He mixed his courses, thus taking both degrees within one year of each other. His preliminary service and experience as a lawyer was gained in Kansas City, Missouri, where he remained until 1904. In that year he came to Bartlesville, and his natural ability together with an untiring industry in working up his cases brought him a very active practice. For years he was associated with Frank Burford under the firm name of Kane & Burford. In 1907 Mr. Kane had the distinction of being chosen the first county attorney of Washington County under the state government. After one term he resumed his private practice and soon afterwards formed a partnership with Messrs. Brennan and McCoy. The firm of Brennan, Kane & McCoy has a splendid clientage, and most of their work is in corporation law.

Mr. Kane has attained the thirty-second degree of Scottish Rite Masonry, and also belongs to the Temple of the Mystic Shrine and the Benevolent and Protective Order of Elks. He has exercised an influential part in the Oklahoma State Bar Association and is now treasurer of the association. In 1907 he married Miss Louise Miller, who was born at Olathe, Johnson County, Kansas. Their two children are John and Robert.

BENJAMIN F. BUFFINGTON. A pioneer settler of Garfield County, one of the thousands who entered the strip on the opening day of September 16, 1893, Benjamin F. Buffington located upon a quarter section seven miles southwest of Enid. He moved to the City of Enid about twenty years ago, and has since been primarily identified with the abstract and conveyancing business. He is now one of the leading abstractors and conveyancers of Garfield County, has built up a valuable business, and has also connected himself in many ways with the public affairs of his city and county.

Benjamin F. Buffington was born in Clinton County, Ohio, near Martinsville, September 13, 1849. His father was a physician and dentist. The first twenty-five years of his life Mr. Buffington spent in Clinton and Highland counties of Ohio, and in the meantime had attended district schools and an academy at Salem, but for the greater part educated himself. For several years he taught country schools in Ohio, and in 1876 moved out to Van Meter, Iowa, taught there and at Dallas Center and Gowrie, and in the fall of 1878 moved on to Nebraska. He was principal of the schools at Schuyler two years, in April, 1880, moved to Osceola in Polk County, and in 1881 was elected superintendent of the county schools. He resigned that position to enter the Osceola Bank with which he was connected for ten years, the last five years as cashier.

In the fall of 1892 Mr. Buffington removed to Okarche in the Cheyenne Indian Country of Oklahoma. At Okarche he organized and conducted a bank in company with Julius Loosen, whose sons are still the chief bankers of Okarche. On September 16, 1893, Mr. Buffington made the race from the South into the Cherokee strip, and secured 160 acres six miles southwest of Enid. He lived on this claim until 1895 and then moved into the City of Enid. During the winter of 1895 he began the preparation of a set of abstracts for Garfield County and was the first to compile these records. Having been in the county from the beginning, he has continued in that line of work to this date, and through his office has offered a valuable service to all parties interested in lands of Garfield County.

In the fall of 1912 Mr. Buffington was elected a member of the Board of County Commissioners of Garfield County. His associates in that body being L. G. Gossett and H. H. Semke, who at once elected him as chairman of the board. During the past three years he has given much of his time and attention to the management of the county's fiscal and general administrative affairs. Though a republican, Mr. Buffington has been little of a politician, though a valuable man in local affairs and one who is animated by the strongest faith in Oklahoma's future destiny. In early life he was a member of the Congregational Church, but is now a Presbyterian, and is active in the Sunday school, teaching the young men's class. For forty years he has been affiliated with the Masonic fraternity, and has spent twenty years in Enid Lodge.

In Ohio in September, 1874, Mr. Buffington married Isabel Ellis, who also spent several years in work as a teacher. She is active in church and woman's club matters at Enid. Their one daughter, Ethel, is the wife of E. E. Cones, formerly of Enid and now connected with the City National Bank of Lawton, Oklahoma.

OKLAHOMA BAPTIST UNIVERSITY. In Sptember, 1915, came the formal opening of the Oklahoma Baptist University at Shawnee. This is an institution of which that city is particularly proud. Though its work has only begun, its plans have been so carefully laid, such high ideals and standards have been raised, and the institution has such magnificent backing not only in the local co-operation of Shawnee citizens but in the church as

a whole, that its future prestige and usefulness are practically assured.

The university originated in 1907 during the Baptist General Convention of Oklahoma while in annual session at Ardmore. The committee on location was appointed at this session and after three years of work finally located at Shawnee. The citizens of Shawnee deserve the highest credit for securing this institution and for laying the material foundation so liberally. While a number of men deserve credit, it was, by general consent, George E. McKinnis, who was primarily responsible for securing the location of the institution at Shawnee, and who almost single handed raised the fund for a beautiful administration building, the first of the large group of college structures which will eventually adorn the magnificent campus of sixty acres on a high rolling prairie a mile and a half north of the business center. The university is located on the high ground commanding a panoramic view of the Canadian River Valley.

The administration building was started in 1910 and completed in 1913 at a cost of approximately $100,000, all this money having been raised among the citizens of Shawnee. An attempt was made to start the scholastic work of the intsitution in 1911. Halls in the city were hired, and the work of the school begun under the presidency of J. M. Carroll of Texas with an enrollment of 200 pupils. However, in June, 1911, the school was closed until the administration building should be completed, since the hiring of halls proved to be of too great expense. At the meeting of the Baptist General Convention at Shawnee in November, 1914, it was definitely determined that the time had come to open the institution permanently. Rev. Frank M. Masters, then pastor of the Baptist Church at Ardmore was called to the president's chair. He took hold at once and under his vigorous management the administration building was completed and equipped and opened its doors for the first regular school year, which began September 14, 1915. There was an enrollment of 105 pupils at the start, and eight professors in the faculty.

The central building on the campus, known as the Administration Building, is one of the best structures of its kind in the country, considered from the standpoint of college administration and also architecturally. It is a modern adaptation of the classic school of architecture, and contains two stories and basement. The basement has been arranged for the science department of the institution, and also with gymnasiums and one or two class rooms. Besides the administration offices on the first floor there is a large auditorium with seating capacity for about 750, and six class rooms. The second story provides studios, society rooms and library, and additional class rooms. Additional dormitory buildings are one of the first needs to be provided and at least one will be erected in 1916. On May 2d ground was broken for the foundation of a hall for women, and an effort will be made to have it ready by September, 1916. Other buildings to be provided in the near future are a Science Hall and Library Building. The college already has the nucleus of a good library, and the Carnegie Library of Shawnee, open to the students, is one of the best in the state. In the session just closed 145 students were enrolled, and the session proved a very successful one. The institution is becoming thoroughly established in the hearts of its constituency.

The curriculum of the Baptist University, both in the academic and collegiate departments, has been prepared to meet all the requirements of the state law on accredited institutions. The members of the first faculty are men and women of mature scholarship and experience, and come from the leading university and colleges of the country.

The president, Rev. Frank M. Masters, was born in Franklin County, Texas, July 28, 1870, and comes of fine old American stock. His great-grandfather was a soldier in the Revolutionary war. The Masters family came originally from England and settled in Maryland near Washington, District of Columbia, in colonial times. His grandfather, Zachariah Masters, was a farmer and planter, and died in Cartersville, Georgia, at the age of ninety-two. President Masters' father was B. E. Masters, who was born in the Anderson District of South Carolina in 1842, but when quite young his parents removed to Georgia. He enlisted with a Georgia regiment in 1861 in the Civil war, and among other engagements was at the battle of Chickamauga, and was captured at Missionary Ridge in 1863 and spent the rest of the period of hostilities in the federal prison at Rock Island, Illinois. In 1865 he moved to Texas, became an early prominent stock raiser in that state, and lived for thirty-five years in Hunt County, where he died in March, 1913. He was a democrat and a member of the Baptist faith. B. E. Masters married Mary Ellen Penn, who was born in Alabama, and now lives on the old homestead in Celeste, Texas.

When President Masters was eleven years of age his parents moved to Hunt County, Texas, and there he continued his education in the common schools and the high school at Celeste. In 1892 he graduated A. B. from Calhoun College at Kingston, Texas, and for a time he was teacher in the preparatory department of that institution. In 1892-94 he was a teacher in Texas public schools, and in June, 1894, he was licensed to preach in the Kingston Baptist Church, and was regularly ordained to the ministry the following September. In October, 1894, he entered the Southern Baptist Theological Seminary at Louisville, Kentucky, where he was graduated Th. B. in 1896 and Th. M. in 1897. During 1897-98 he was a graduate student at the Southern Theological Seminary, and during 1896-98 was pastor of the Clifton Baptist Church of Louisville. Then followed an active pastoral career until he was called to the presidency of the Oklahoma Baptist University in December, 1914. In January, 1899, he became pastor of the First Baptist Church of San Angelo, Texas, and remained there until 1902. He was pastor of the First Baptist Church of Weatherford in 1902-05, of the College Avenue Baptist Church at Fort Worth from 1905 to 1910, and of the First Baptist Church of Ardmore, Oklahoma, from 1910 to 1915. In 1908 he was lecturer in the Mid-Winter Bible School at Howard Payne College in Texas; was lecturer in the Mid-Winter Bible School at Simmons College in 1909; a member of the State Mission Board, Baptist General Convention of Texas, in 1908-10; member of the State Mission Board, Baptist General Convention, Oklahoma, 1910-15; vice president Foreign Mission Board, Southern Baptist Convention of Oklahoma, 1913-14; president Baptist Pastors' Conference of Oklahoma, 1913-15. In politics Mr. Masters is a democrat.

On June 9, 1898, at Louisville, Kentucky, he married Miss Lillie R. Randolph, daughter of A. W. Randolph, who was a prominent citizen of Louisville, Kentucky, and for nineteen years before his death served as county surveyor of Jefferson County. Mr. and Mrs. Masters are the parents of five children: Catherine Chamberlin, now in the first year of the preparatory department of the Oklahoma Baptist University at Shawnee; E. Randolph, who is also in the preparatory department of the same university; C. Kerfoot, in the sixth grade of the public schools; Frank M. and Julian Penn, twins, who are in the fourth grade of the public schools.

The dean of the Oklahoma Baptist University is F. Erdman Smith, who is a graduate of the University of Toronto, of the Oklahoma Baptist College and the Temple

University. He was vice president during 1907-08 of ing a part of 1908, and again vice president from 1909 to 1911. He was appointed dean of the Oklahoma Baptist University in 1911, was dean of Burleson College in 1912-13, dean and professor of education at Howard Payne College in Texas from 1913 to 1915, and then returned to the Oklahoma University in 1915, where, in addition to his duties as dean, he is professor of education.

J. W. Jent, the university registrar and professor of philosophy and social science, is a man of unusual scholastic attainment. He pursued his studies successively in Pierce City Baptist College, in William Jewell College, in Baylor University, and in 1907 graduated Th. B. at the Southern Baptist Theological Seminary, and in 1908 took his degree Th. M. at Baylor University. Later he entered Yale University, where he graduated A. B. with general honors in 1911; was a graduate student there during 1912-14, securing his A. M. degree in 1914, and in 1912 he graduated Th. D. "Magna Cum Laude" from the Southwestern Baptist Theological Seminary. He has been connected as a teacher and in an official capacity with several of the institutions where he was a student, and came to the Oklahoma Baptist University in 1915.

W. D. Moorer holds the chair of Religious Education. He is a graduate A. B. from Furman University in South Carolina in 1892 and was pastor of a number of churches in South Carolina up to 1900, during the following five years was pastor of the First Baptist Church at Anadarko, Oklahoma, and from 1905 to 1915 was superintendent of Sunday-school work under the Baptist General Convention of Oklahoma. He was president of the board of trustees of Oklahoma Baptist College from 1906 to 1913, and was elected to his present office in June, 1915.

J. Louis Guthrie, who holds the chair of Greek and Latin, graduated A. M. from William Jewell College at Liberty, Missouri, was a professor in the Southwestern University at Jackson, Tennessee, two years, and was president of the Lane View College of Tennessee for about the same period.

W. T. Short, mathematics and science, did his first work as a teacher in the public schools of Oklahoma during 1902-04, was an instructor in mathematics in Oklahoma Baptist College from 1907 to 1911, graduated A. B. at the Oklahoma Baptist College in 1911, held the chair of mathematics in several collegiate institutions, and came to the Oklahoma Baptist University in June, 1915.

W. P. Powell, who has charge of English and modern languages, graduated A. B. from Richmond College in 1903, was a graduate student in the University of Virginia from 1907 to 1912, and in 1910 received the degree M. A. from that university, and in 1912 completed his residence work for the Th. D. degree. He was an instructor in the Texas A. & M. College and in Baylor University prior to coming to Shawnee.

Prof. E. O. Kaserman was recently elected as the head of the department of science. His early education was received in the public schools of Tennessee. Mr. Kaserman is an A. B. and A. M. graduate from the Winchester College, Winchester, Tennessee, and took his M. S. degree from Carson-Newman College, Jefferson City, Tennessee. He is also a Th. D. graduate from the Southern Baptist Seminary, though he is not a minister. For ten years Doctor Kaserman has been professor of science in the Carson-Newman College. He is one of the leading science teachers of the country.

Other members of the first faculty of the Oklahoma Baptist University are Joshua B. Lee, who has charge of public speaking, and Ola Gulledge, who is instructor in piano and voice, and is a product of the musical school of Baylor University and has also pursued her studies abroad in the Royal Conservatory of Music at Leipsic, Germany. Miss Inez Mazy Harris has recently been elected to the head of the voice department. Miss Harris has been trained under the best American talent, and has assisted in several of the most prominent choruses in the country. During the past two years she has taught voice in Howard Payne College.

GEORGE J. GENSMAN. One of the largest and most important mercantile enterprises in Oklahoma, with several unique features in the form of its organization and methods of doing business, is the Gensman Brothers & Company, wholesale and retail hardware, the central headquarters of which are in Enid. George J. Gensman was one of the founders and developers of this splendid business, and is now president and treasurer of the corporation, and is also vice president of the Central State Bank of Enid. His business and civic career is one of the most important to be considered in the history of Enid.

George J. Gensman was born in Washington County, Wisconsin, March 1, 1864, a son of Conrad and Margaret (Kellerman) Gensman. The former was a native of Prussia and the latter of Bavaria, and they came to Wisconsin with their parents aged respectively seventeen and four years. They were married in Wisconsin, where the father developed a farm from a heavy tract of timber, and lived on that one place for thirty-five years. In the meantime he had acquired extensive land interests in Sedgwick County, Kansas, and removed to the state to take their active management about 1891. There he developed a large farm of 480 acres. His death occurred at Enid in 1904 at the age of seventy-one, his wife having preceded him a year and a half before. He was a member of the Evangelical Lutheran while his wife was a strict Lutheran in religious belief. Of their seven children five are living in Oklahoma in or near Enid. George, Fred C. and William R. comprise the personnel of the old firm of Gensman Brothers. The daughter Bertha is the wife of C. W. Hackett, also connected with the Gensman Brothers & Company. Susie is the wife of D. B. Barnes, a farmer in Garfield County. The other two children are: Carrie, wife of Albert Thiel, living near the old Wisconsin home at Schleisengerville, Washington County; and Annie, wife of J. E. Jones, a manufacturer and foundryman at Richmond, Indiana.

George J. Gensman has had an active and progressive career since his boyhood on a Wisconsin farm. He attended common schools, and at the age of seventeen qualified as a teacher. His first school was near the old home place. He worked on a farm, taught, and for five different terms attended the Valparaiso Normal School, now the Valparaiso University in Indiana. In 1889, at the age of twenty-five, he removed to Sedgwick County, Kansas, where his father had invested in land, and gave some attention to its management for a year or two. At the same time he continued his work as an educator. He was principal of the Two-department School at Garden Plain, and while there acquired a farm of 160 acres near Wichita. This was unimproved land, and he developed it through renters. His work as principal at Garden Plain continued four years, after which he was principal at Andale in the same county two years, and then for three years was principal of the Four-department School at Mount Hope, one of the best towns in Sedgwick County.

In the meantime Mr. Gensman had married and there were children to be provided for. He and his brother Fred had taken counsel together and conceived the idea of opening in business in a new country. Fred had already acquired some land near Enid, Oklahoma, and that probably was the chief influence that brought them to the town. In March, 1898, the two brothers bought an interest with the H. E. Diehl & Company, a general hardware and farm implement house. The business was continued as H. E. Diehl & Company until January 1, 1901. At that date the three brothers, Fred, William and George, bought the Diehl interests, and established the firm of Gensman Brothers. In the meantime, under the impulse of the aggressive enterprise of the Gensmans, the business had grown to an annual volume of sales amounting to $50,000, about 3½ times what it was in 1898. Then came the chief calamity which this thriving business has known. In July, 1901, the entire plant was burned, causing a loss of $40,000 above insurance. There was not a moment of doubt or hesitation in the minds of the brothers about re-establishing the business. The plant was re-built, and the firm was accorded almost unlimited credit. They filled up their warehouses and shelves with a complete stock of goods on credit from the manufacturers, and in a short time had paid off every dollar of obligation, were discounting their bills regularly, and that record has since been maintained, only in increasing volume.

The greatest development and improvement in the business came about in 1914. At that time the house was selling goods aggregating a quarter of a million dollars annually. On January 1, 1912, the copartnership was replaced by an incorporation known as the Gensman Brothers & Company, and the capital was increased to $75,000. The business has since been modified and extended so as to afford the advantages of organization to practically all the trade territory surrounding Enid. In carrying out this plan branch retail stores have been established, two of them at Enid, one at Billings, one at Marshall, one at Salt Fork, one at Hunter, one at Goltry, one at Nash, and one at Jefferson. All these stores have ready access by railroad with Enid, and the manager of each branch store is a stockholder in the firm of Gensman Brothers & Company. At the present time about sixteen men are working stockholders and participants in the business. This original plan, though somewhat similar to the "chain of stores" idea, has reached a high degree of perfection in this particular case. A purpose always kept in mind is to give expert service to customers, and that principle has been emphasized in every particular. The two Enid retail stores employ from eighteen to twenty-five persons, and the entire business now represents a large capital, with several hundred people engaged. The results have fully justified all expectations. Goods are purchased in large quantities, and as a result local dealers whether within the chain of branch stores or not, have the advantages of low prices and large stocks. Gensman Brothers & Company have dealings with almost every hardware firm within the large territory comprising Garfield, Noble, Logan, Major, Alfalfa, Grant and part of Kay counties, all of which territory is accessible to Enid by the eleven lines of railroads centering there.

On May 1, 1913, Mr. Gensman became vice president at the organization of the Central State Bank of Enid. In two years time this bank has become the second largest in amount of resources and business in the State of Oklahoma.

The executive personnel of the Gensman Brothers & Company comprises George, president and treasurer; Fred C., secretary; and C. H. Hackett, vice president. The brother William was secretary of the company until his death by accident on January 20, 1913. At the time he was en route to the Santa Fe Station, intending to visit the branch store at Marshall. While driving his automobile he came into collision with the city fire truck, and after the accident never regained consciousness and died within a few hours.

George Gensman has also been an active factor in civic affairs at Enid. The city is now under an admirable plan of commission government. On April 27, 1902, a committee of twelve persons, two from each ward, was chosen to draw up a new charter. George Gensman was one of those representing the Fourth Ward. This charter was reported after six weeks of strenuous labor, was adopted at a popular election, received the approval of the courts, and is still in operation. Mr. Gensman is a member of the board of directors of the Chamber of Commerce and is usually found working in any movement for the general advancement.

On September 4, 1890, at Wichita, Kansas, he married Miss Dora Belle Osborn of Fort Scott, Kansas. They have three daughters. Mabel is the wife of G. P. Legg, who is connected with the Gensman Brothers & Company. The two younger daughters are Fay and Dorothy.

PROF. HARVEY LEMUEL ALLEN. The distinctions of good faithful work and successful accomplishment have come plentifully to Harvey L. Allen, not only in his regular vocation as a teacher and educator, but also in business and social and civic affairs. Professor Allen is now superintendent of the entire public school system of Tecumseh. He has been well known in educational circles in different parts of the state for several years.

Born in Bates County, Missouri, September 20, 1888, he is a son of Rev. H. W. and Mary B. (Warren) Allen, and comes of old American stock on both sides. The Allens were of Scotch-Irish descent, and included in one branch of the family the noted Ethan Allen of Revolutionary fame. The Warrens are direct descendants from the same ancestry as the brilliant General Warren, who fell at Bunker Hill.

Professor Allen and his ancestors have been prominently identified with the Masonic Order for generations, though his father never joined that order. His forefather, General Warren, was the first master of the lodge in America, serving one term and three years of a second term until he participated in that fateful battle of Bunker Hill and lost his life. In practically every generation since then there have been Allens and Warrens who have gained distinguished rank in Masonry.

Professor Allen's grandfather was William Allen, who was a pioneer of Oklahoma and died at Elk City in this state in 1911. He was born in Bradley County, Tennessee, in 1843. In 1852 his parents removed to Illinois, and when he was nineteen years of age he went to the young town of Kansas City, Jackson County, Missouri, although at that time Kansas City had hardly come into existence, certainly not as a city. William Allen was proprietor of a hotel in Kansas City and subsequently became a farmer. He served all through the Civil war under Joe Shelby in the Confederate Army, being a quarter master. After the war he removed to Bates County, Missouri, homesteaded a farm, lived there quietly and industriously until 1898 and then once more became a pioneer, this time in Canadian County, Oklahoma. He bought a relinquishment where the town of old Matthewson was later built. It was his distinction to have erected the first house in D County, now Dewey County, Oklahoma, and he became a general merchant. In 1909 he removed to Elk City and went into the lumber business, and that was his line of work until his death. The farm which he had in Dewey County he subsequently sold to the Leedey Townsite Company.

Rev. H. W. Allen, father of Professor Allen, was born in Bates County, Missouri, in 1869 and died at Weatherford, Oklahoma, February 9, 1913. His youth and early manhood were spent in Bates County until 1898. In that year he came to Oklahoma and filed a claim where the Town of Leedey stands. While he gave much attention to farming he was in reality first and last a minister, and was a pioneer missionary of the Church of God. He organized the first church of that denomination in that section of Oklahoma, and worked as a missionary under the national board both in Missouri and Oklahoma, being the highest salaried missionary of the Church of God in any state. In fact, he was at the head of this denomination in the State of Oklahoma. A democrat, he interested himself in politics not for personal advancement but for the good of the party and for good government. At one time he was president of the Democratic Club at Weatherford, and was twice given a nomination for office by his fellow citizens. He was a member of the Brotherhood of American Yeomen. Rev. Mr. Allen married Mary B. Warren, a native of Ohio, who is still living at Weatherford. Their children were: Harvey Lemuel; Eldon H., who died in Weatherford, Oklahoma, at the age of fifteen; and H. F. Allen, who is principal of the schools at Gotebo, Oklahoma.

As a boy Professor Allen attended country schools in Bates County, Missouri. He has allowed no opportunities for learning and self improvement to pass by. In 1905 he attended the Collegiate Institute at Fort Scott, Kansas, one year. He then entered the Southwestern Normal School at Weatherford, Oklahoma, graduating with the class of 1909, and has since received the degree Master of Pedagogy from the Teachers Professional College of Austin, Texas. During 1909-10 he was principal of the high school at Anadarko, then became superintendent of schools at Alderson, Oklahoma, for two years, and in the fall of 1912 entered Henry Kendall College for post-graduate work, and at the same time was an instructor in the institution. In 1913 he received his well earned degree of Bachelor of Arts. He has also taken a summer course of study in the University of Missouri. In the summers of 1914 and 1915 he took courses of instruction in the University of Oklahoma. Professor Allen is a member of the Kappa Delta Pi Greek Letter Honorary Educational Fraternity, the University of Oklahoma Chapter.

In the fall of 1913 Professor Allen accepted the position of dean of the Collegiate Institute at Fort Scott, Kansas. During the next year, 1914, he was superintendent of schools at Cleo Springs, and in the spring of 1915 he accepted the heavy responsibilities of superintendent of schools at Tecumseh. He now has under his supervision four public schools, with a staff of nineteen teachers, and a total enrollment of 733 scholars. He has been re-elected superintendent of schools of Tecumseh for 1916-17, and is assisting in erecting a splendid new high school building.

Politically he is a democrat, and is a member of the Church of God, the denomination in which his father was a minister. Fraternally he is almost by inheritance identified with Masonry. He has filled chairs in Anadarko Lodge No. 21, Ancient Free and Accepted Masons; is a member of Indian Consistory No. 2 of the thirty-second degree Scottish Rite at McAlester; a member of the Order of Eastern Star at Alderson; and is also a member and has served as chaplain of the Independent Order of Odd Fellows at Alderson. In educational circles his acquaintance is widespread, and he is an active member of the County and State Teachers' associations. At one time he was chairman of the Young Men's Democratic Club at Weatherford. The wide scope of his interests is shown by the fact that for three years he was a member of Company B of the Second Missouri Militia. He is also a stockholder in the Farmers State Bank at Weatherford.

In 1912 Professor Allen was married at Mounds, Oklahoma, to Miss Neva Young. Her father, A. J. Young, is a Union veteran of the Civil war, a republican in politics, and has long been a farmer, and now resides at Quincy, Missouri. Mr. and Mrs. Allen have one child, Geraldine, born October 22, 1914.

REDMOND SELECMAN COLE. The achievement of such a position as that occupied by Redmond Selecman Cole in legal circles of Oklahoma, when attained by one still so young in years, is typical of American grit and the true western spirit of enterprise. A resident of Pawnee since 1909, he has attracted to himself a wide and influential clientele, and at the same time has become one of the democratic leaders of Pawnee County.

Mr. Cole was born east of Savannah, in Andrew County, Missouri, August 22, 1881, and is a son of James Buchanan and Virginia Lee (Bedford) Cole, and on both sides of the family traces his ancestry back through generations of distinguished men and gentle women, prominent in the professions and arts, in business, society and politics, and in military and civil life. His grandparents on the paternal side were Capt. James L. and Eliza (Patterson) Cole, of Washington County, Virginia; his great-grandparents, Peleg and Mary (Williams) Cole; his great-great-grandfather, John Cole, and his great-great-great-grandfather, Joseph Cole, who settled on the Holston River, in southwestern Virginia, in 1774, and was captain of a company of Patriots at King's Mountain during the War of the Revolution. On the maternal side, Mr. Cole's grandparents were Lieut. Alexander Marshall and Mary (Selecman) Bedford, his great-grandparents John and Elizabeth Rich (Howard) Bedford, his great-great-grandparents, John and Mary Ann (Marshall) Bedford, his great-great-great-grandparents, Thomas and Mary Ligon (Coleman) Bedford, and his great-great-great-great-grandfather, Stephen Bedford, who died in Charlotte County, Virginia, in 1758. Thomas Bedford was selected a member of the Committee of Safety for Charlotte County, Virginia, January 13, 1777. The grandfathers of Mr. Cole, Capt. James L. Cole and Lieut. Alexander M. Bedford, secured their titles as officers of the Confederacy during the Civil war. On the Selecman side, Mr. Cole's grandparents were Henry W. and Mary (Simpson) Selecman, his great-grandparents, George and Jane (Davis) Selecman, and his great-great-grandparents, Henry and Margaret (Harmon) Selecman, who emigrated to America from Germany shortly before the War of the Revolution and settled below Washington on Occoquan River, in Virginia. Redmond Selecman Cole is the namesake of Redmond Selecman, who served in the Confederate army with the rank of lieutenant.

Redmond S. Cole passed his boyhood days in Andrew County, Missouri, where he secured a common school education, this being supplemented by attendance at the Kirksville (Missouri) Normal School from 1899 until 1901. He spent eight years, from 1901 until 1909, at the Missouri University, Columbia, and his college career was one that was replete with brilliant achievements and well-earned honors. As editor of the college paper, the Independent, from 1905 until 1907, he gave the student body a well-edited journal; in 1909 he acted as colonel of cadets at the Missouri University Military School; at various times he represented his college in debates with the Universities of Texas, Kansas and Oklahoma, in which his oratorical powers and skillful and forceful logic did much to uphold the prestige of his alma mater. He received the degree of Fellow in Economics, 1905-9, the Bachelor of Arts degree in 1905 and the Master of Arts degree in 1906, and following this studied in the law school for two years. In fraternity circles he was always popular, and still retains membership in the Delta Tau Delta, Delta Sigma Rho (honorary debating) and Phi Alpha Delta (honorary law) societies.

In 1908 Mr. Cole became associate editor of the Columbia, Missouri, Sentinel, but in the same year resigned that position to accept that of editor of the Herald, a daily and weekly publication, issued at the same place, and continued as its editor until entering upon the practice of his profession. Admitted to the bar in Missouri, in January, 1909, on April 26th of that year he came to Pawnee, Oklahoma, where he became associated in practice with George E. Merritt, under the firm style of Merritt & Cole. On February 8, 1910, he was appointed county attorney of Pawnee County, to fill a vacancy, and in November, 1910, was elected to succeed himself, his popularity and the recognition of his ability being indicated by the fact that he ran 300 votes ahead of the democratic candidate for governor. He was re-elected to succeed himself in November, 1912, but January 4, 1915, retired from office to devote his attention to his rapidly growing law practice, although he has continued to maintain his interest in politics, and is accounted a democratic party leader in Pawnee County. Mr. Cole fraternizes with the Independent Order of Odd Fellows and the Modern Woodmen of America. While a student at the University of Missouri, he acquired a fondness for history and research work, and has continued to indulge his taste for these interesting labors, being at present a member of the state historical societies of Missouri, Iowa, Illinois, Wisconsin, Kansas and Oklahoma, of which last three named he is a life member. He is now engaged in the preparation of a comprehensive history of Pawnee County.

On June 11, 1905, Mr. Cole was married at Columbia, Missouri, to Miss Mary Thompson Cross, who was born at Ladonia, Missouri, October 22, 1884, daughter of John Newton and Olivia McClure (Harris) Cross, now of Keyes, California, granddaughter of William Blythe and Mary Jane (Shores) Cross, great-granddaughter of John and Sally (Blythe) Cross, great-great-granddaughter of William and Sarah (McGowan) Cross, and great-great-great-granddaughter of James Cross, who came from England in 1773 to fight with General Braddock and who later fought in the Patriot army in the Revolutionary war. On the maternal side, Mrs. Cole is the granddaughter of Thomas Banks and Margaret Dun (Thompson) Harris, and great-granddaughter of William and Margaret (Downing) Harris, and of Morgan N. and Elizabeth (Williams) Thompson. Mrs. Cole graduated from the Mexico (Missouri) High School in 1902, and in 1908 received the degree of Bachelor of Sciences from Missouri University. Mr. and Mrs. Cole are members of the Methodist Episcopal Church. They are the parents of one child, Olivia Harris Cole, born at Pawnee, Oklahoma, June 27, 1915.

WILLIAM H. HILLS. In the field of corporation law one of the ablest attorneys in Western Oklahoma is William H. Hills, who has been identified with the Enid bar since 1902. Mr. Hills has had a varied experience during his career, and gained his law education while working for the Armour Packing Company in Kansas City, studying at night. As a lawyer he has since handled many important cases, involving large values and grave principles, and has likewise taken a leading part in politics, church and social affairs.

William H. Hills was born in Crawfordsville, Indiana, October 6, 1869. His father, Captain Francis E. Hills, who is a pioneer of the Cherokee Strip, was born in Xenia, Ohio, went to Indiana as a boy, and at the outbreak of the Civil war enlisted as a private in the famous Indiana Zouaves commanded by Colonel, late General Lew Wallace, the noted soldier-author of Crawfordsville, Indiana. Few men had a longer or more active service. He was in the army four years and eight months, and was with Grant at Belmont, Missouri, at the beginning of the great campaign for the wresting of the Mississippi Valley from the Confederacy, and was under that leader at Richmond, at the end of the war. He participated at Fort Donelson, Shiloh, Vicksburg, where he was wounded, in the Atlanta campaign, was with Sheridan in the Shenandoah Valley, and thence in the final operations leading up to the fall of Richmond. He went into the army as a private, and was discharged with the rank of captain of Company I of the Eleventh Indiana Infantry. From 1870 he lived in Iowa for about six years, and then removed to the vicinity of Kansas City, Missouri, in 1876. In 1893 at the opening of the Cherokee Strip he made the race into the new country, secured a farm in McHenry Township twenty miles northwest of Enid, and has lived there ever since. He is recognized as one of the best farmers of the county, and has also made himself an influence in politics. He is a republican, served as chairman of the County Central Committee, and has been a member of the school board of his locality for twenty years or more.

William H. Hills lived at Kansas City from 1876 until June, 1902. His common school education was acquired at Liberty, Missouri, and he also took a classical course in the William Jewell College at Liberty, graduating in 1893. He attended the Kansas City School of Law, and received his degree from that institution in 1900. For thirteen years off and on he was in the employ of the Armour Packing Company at Kansas City, most of the time as superintendent of the lard department.

In 1902 Mr. Hills removed to Enid and has since been in a general practice. For six years, however, he has specialized in corporation cases, and now handles business in all the courts. In several important cases he has appeared before the United States Circuit Court of Appeals at St. Paul. A varied corporation practice has come to him, and he is entrusted with the arguing and handling of cases involving banking and other important matters. As a citizen Mr. Hills served on the city council one term, and also on the board of education. Under the auspices of the county and state committee he has been an active campaigner in the interests of the republican ticket, and has served as a delegate to various local and state conventions. He has also attended national conventions of both parties as a spectator, and heard Bryan make his great speech in the old Chicago Coliseum in 1896. Mr. Hills is a Mason and is well known in the Benevolent and Protective Order of Elks, being a past exalted ruler of his lodge and having sat in the supreme lodge.

In church affairs Mr. Hills is a Presbyterian. Under the influence of a celebrated evangelist he was converted about six years ago, and it being his nature to enlist himself with a whole heart in every cause, he became an enthusiastic Christian worker, believing that the greatest happiness to self and humanity comes as a result of the Christian life. He served as president of the Union Churchmen's League, an organization which developed its strength to 600 members.

Mr. Hills was married at Kansas City, Missouri, in January, 1896, to Miss Elsie C. Lindgren, of Rockford, Illinois. She graduated from the Kansas City High School, and became the mother of one daughter, Florence E., who is now a student in the Scarritt School at Kansas City. Mrs. Hills died November 22, 1914, and is buried at Kansas City beside her mother.

JOHN W. BROWNING, M. D. Among the leading members of the Blaine County medical fraternity is found Dr. John W. Browning, in whose long and uniformly progressive career several personal traits are noticeable, these including versatility of talents combined with thoroughness of preparation and depth of medical and surgical knowledge. A man of broad education and experience, of high personal character, courteous and capable, he is justly accounted one of Geary's foremost citizens.

Doctor Browning is a member of a family which was founded in America by three brothers of the name who immigrated from England and settled during colonial days, one in Virginia, one in Maryland and one in Pennsylvania, Doctor Browning being descended from either the Virginia or Maryland branches. He was born at Limestone, Washington County, Tennessee, December 23, 1869, his parents being William A. and Betty (Carr) Browning. William A. Browning was born at Boone's Creek, Tennessee, in 1846, and was reared to agricultural pursuits, in which he was engaged at the outbreak between the states. He enlisted in a Tennessee volunteer cavalry regiment, in which he served during the war. Since the close of the struggle he has devoted his energies to general farming, and is now a resident of Washington College Station, Tennessee. He is a republican in his political belief, and a consistent member of the United Brethren Church. Mrs. Browning was a Dunkard. She was born in Tennessee in 1839 and died in January, 1915, the mother of seven children, as follows: Anna, who is the wife of H. H. Diveley, of Guthrie, and she is a teacher in the Methodist Episcopal College at that place; Dr. John W. Browning; Bertha, who died at Limestone, Tennessee, at the age of ten years; Dora, who resides on the home farm with her father; Rev. Samuel, who is a minister of the Methodist Episcopal Church South at Knoxville, Tennessee; Rev. William E., also a minister of the Methodist Episcopal Church South, with a charge in Tennessee; and Maggie, who died in infancy.

John W. Browning laid the foundation for his education in the public schools of Limestone, Tennessee, and afterward pursued a business course at Washington College in his native state. He next turned his attention to the study of medicine, and after some preparation in the Baltimore Medical College of Baltimore, Maryland, he entered. Barnes Medical College, St. Louis, Missouri, from which he was graduated in 1899 with the degree of Doctor of Medicine. While he began practice at that time he did not cease his studies, for he has always been a close student and has taken several post-graduate courses, one at the Chicago Polyclinic in 1903, and he attended the New York Post-Graduate School in 1908. At the time of securing his degree in May, 1899, Doctor Browning came to Geary, Oklahoma, and here his entire professional career has been passed. He devotes his learning, skill and energies to a general medical and surgical practice and has offices in the Gillespie Building, where his many patients find conveniences and equipment for the handling of the most delicate and complicated cases. His ability has been recognized by his professional brethren, who elected him president of the Blaine County Medical Society, of which he is still a member, as he is also of the Oklahoma Medical Society and the American Medical Association. Fraternally the doctor is a member of the Masonic Order, and his political affiliation is with the republican party.

In 1899, at Wilson, Texas, Doctor Browning was married to Miss Ida E. Clarke, a daughter of the late Preston J. Clarke. Mr. Clarke, a man of broad education, was a justice of the peace in his native State of Georgia, and later became postmaster at Wilson, Texas, where he was a leading democrat and influential citizen. Four children have been born to Doctor and Mrs. Browning: Vanda, who is a member of the sophomore class at the Geary High School; Margaret, a pupil in the eighth grade of the public schools; Grace, in the seventh grade; and Verona, attending the second grade.

HENRY J. STURGIS. Before coming to Enid at the opening of the Strip in 1893, Henry J. Sturgis was already a well seasoned lawyer and for seven years had practiced in Kansas. Mr. Sturgis is one of the prominent men of Western Oklahoma, with recognized ability and attainments in the law, and has made himself an influential figure in politics and social life.

Henry J. Sturgis was born in Fayette County, Pennsylvania, March 5, 1862, a son of respected and substantial farming people. His early life until twenty-one was spent on a farm, with such education as the district schools and the neighboring academy afforded. Having resolved to study law, he entered the law department of the University of West Virginia at Morgantown, and was graduated with his class in 1885. He was admitted by examination before three circuit judges, and in 1886 came out to a comparatively new country to begin practice. His location was at Great Bend, Kansas, which was then a frontier town.

On September 16, 1893, Mr. Sturgis made the run at the opening of the Cherokee Strip, and arrived in Enid by train from Hennessey. From the day of his arrival he made himself known as a lawyer and has been identified with a substantial general practice for many years. A high tribute to his ability as a lawyer came when he was nominated by the republican party as candidate for justice of the Supreme Court in 1914.

His public service has been of varied and responsible character. From 1903 to 1905 he served as county attorney of Garfield County. He was chairman of the Republican County Central Committee in 1906 and in 1907 during the statehood election. From 1907 to 1912 he served as federal referee in bankruptcy. He has been a delegate to numerous state and local conventions, and is noted as a forceful campaigner.

Mr. Sturgis was honored by election as the first president of the Garfield County Bar Association upon the reorganization of that association in 1908 following statehood. He did much to promote the welfare and membership of the organization, and continued to preside over its meetings for two years. Each year the annual banquet is held on Lincoln's birthday. He is also a member of the State Bar Association. For many years he has been identified with the Benevolent and Protective Order of Elks, and was the first exalted ruler of the lodge at Enid, and has attended two grand conventions, one at Los Angeles and the other at Buffalo.

At Great Bend, Kansas, in 1890 Mr. Sturgis married Miss Lulu Luttrell, who was born in Illinois. Their one daughter, Roqua, completed her education in St. Joseph's Institute at Enid.

DAVID B. BELLIS. Prominent among the retired citizens of Cushing, Oklahoma, is found David B. Bellis, who has resided in this state since the opening of the Cherokee Strip. During the more than twenty years of his residence here he has been interested in farming and stock raising and kindred enterprises, and now, in the evening of life, is resting from his labors, having accumulated a satisfying property.

Mr. Bellis was born in Posey County, Indiana, near the Town of Cynthiana, December 25, 1843, and is a son of Charles H. and Mary (Benson) Bellis, natives of Indiana, the father born July 4, 1818, and the mother about 1827. She died about 1860, when thirty-three

years of age, and in 1863 Charles H. Bellis was again married, being united with Jane Alcon. Two years later, with David B. Bellis and his wife, they moved to Kansas, and there the father was engaged in agricultural pursuits until his death in 1885, which was caused by a fall when he was sixty-seven years of age. Charles H. Bellis was the father of six children: David B.; Elizabeth, who died as the wife of Charles Shultice; Jane, who is the widow of Mark Benson, of New Mexico; Euphemia, deceased, who was the wife of Peter Gursch, deceased; Mary, deceased, who was the wife of John Calhoun; and William, a resident of Kansas.

David B. Bellis was educated in the district schools of Posey County, Indiana, and grew up on the home farm, where he was residing at the outbreak of the Civil war. He was eighteen years of age when he enlisted in the Union army as a private in Company B, Sixtieth Regiment, Indiana Volunteer Infantry, with which organization he served for eleven months and ten days, at the end of that time receiving his honorable discharge on account of disability. Returning to his home, he again took up farming with his father, with whom he continued operations until his marriage, October 5, 1865, to Miss Sarah J. McReynolds, who was born in Warrick County, Indiana, July 18, 1847, a daughter of J. B. and Matilda (Carnahan) McReynolds, natives of Indiana, the former of whom died in Kansas and the latter in California.

Shortly after his marriage Mr. Bellis and his wife started on their wedding tour, a journey which lasted seven weeks and five days. During this time they traveled in a covered wagon across the country, and finally reached their destination in Ottawa County, Kansas, where they lived for twenty-three years. In 1868, during the Indian raids, they moved to Missouri, but after about four years returned to Kansas. At the time of their arrival they found hardships and difficulties facing them. Railroads there were none, or schools or school districts; even ordinary highways were few and far between; labor was to be secured at not less than $5 a day, and even the barest necessities of life were correspondingly high. Mrs. Bellis organized a subscription school in their home during the latter '60s, and soon had a class of twenty pupils. Money was scarce at that time and she received remuneration for her labors in various ways, one family paying her in buffalo meat, while another neighbor, anxious to educate her children, paid off his debt in breaking a tract of prairie for the Bellis family. Mr. Bellis, who devoted his time to breaking his land and putting it under cultivation, also found the leisure to serve as the first postmaster at Coal Creek, Kansas, Mrs. Bellis looking after the postoffice. As the years passed he was able to develop a good farm and resided thereon until the opening of the Cherokee Strip, in 1893, attracted him to Oklahoma. He first secured a claim twelve miles south of Guthrie, on which he resided until coming to Payne County, and four years later retired from active pursuits and took up his residence at Cushing, where he now lives, one of his community's highly respected and substantial citizens. Mr. Bellis is a republican in politics. The religious faith of himself and wife is that of the Presbyterian Church, and the only order with which he is connected is the Grand Army of the Republic.

Mr. and Mrs. Bellis have been the parents of five children: Mary Matilda, who is the wife of E. N. Hunt, of Guthrie; John H., president of the Commonwealth Cotton Oil Company, and one of the foremost business men of Cushing, a sketch of whose career appears elsewhere in this work; Etta M., for seventeen years a teacher in the schools of Oklahoma, and now the wife of W. L. Lormer, of Cushing; C. Oliver, who is a resident of Klamath County, Oregon; and Alice, who was also a teacher for several years, is the wife of L. J. Martin, of Cushing.

HON. OLIVER C. DALE. A willingness to face hardships in the working out of a well defined plan of action, a perseverance which declined to accept defeat, a faith in self which buoyed him up under discouragement and disappointment, and a preparedness to grasp opportunity when it finally presented itself, combined to place Oliver C. Dale, now mayor of Yale and one of the leading oil men of Oklahoma, on the high road to fortune and position.

He and his family are now reckoned among the wealthiest people of Oklahoma. Their wealth is not only due to the fact that their land holdings are a part of the great Cushing oil field, but also to the splendid ability with which Mr. Dale has handled the suddenly increased responsibilities thrust upon him after the discovery of oil. When he came to Red Fork in the Creek Nation in 1901, he had experienced a set back in his individual fortunes that would have terminated the efforts of one less determined in nature, but Mr. Dale would not admit failure. He had the courage of his convictions—implicit confidence in his own judgment. Perseveringly and along a straight line of action he worked out his own salvation and his career is well worthy a place among the annals of men of Oklahoma who have lived and labored to purpose.

Oliver C. Dale was born in Jasper County, Missouri, December 23, 1871, a son of Henry C. and Emma J. (Barker) Dale. He belongs to a family which traces its ancestry in America back to Sir Thomas Dale, the founder of the family in this country, and the first governor of Virginia. Rev. George Dale, his great-great-grandfather, was a missionary Baptist preacher in Virginia and a man of great physique, weighing nearly 400 pounds. Elijah Dale, his great-grandfather, was born in 1794 in Virginia, was captured by the Indians at the battle of Tippecanoe while fighting under General Harrison, was subsequently exchanged and fought through the War of 1812. When still a young man he went to Kentucky and married there Frances Shelton. They went to Boone County, Missouri, then to Jasper County, and later to Moniteau County, where Elijah Dale died at the age of seventy-four. His wife passed away in Jasper County when eighty-eight years of age. They had eight children: Alfred, Robert J., James M., Phielden, Meadley, Mrs. Malinda Griffith, Mrs. Mary Sunday and Mrs. Rebecca Martin.

Robert J. Dale, the grandfather of Oliver C. Dale, was born in Kentucky in 1820 and was eighteen years of age when he located with his parents in Jasper County, Missouri. There he married Olive Cox, who was born in 1822 in Tennessee and was brought to Missouri by her parents about the same time as her husband arrived. With the exception of seven years from 1863 until 1870, when they lived in Moniteau County, they passed the remaining years of their lives in Jasper County and both died at Carthage, Missouri, Robert J. at the age of ninety and his wife when about eighty. He was a farmer, trader and stock dealer, was clerk in the Baptist Church for a long period and throughout his life supported the principles of the democratic party. Robert J. and Olive Dale had seven children as follows: George F., of Moniteau County, Missouri; Mrs. Mary M. Hughes, deceased; Henry C.; Mrs. Ann F. Wise, of Carthage, Missouri; Mrs. Permelia B. Howard of Cooper County, Missouri; Mrs. Martha J. Johnson of Carl Junction, Jasper County, Missouri; and Mrs. Canzada Hind, deceased.

Henry C. Dale, father of Oliver C. Dale, was educated in the public schools of Missouri and until reaching the age of twenty-three resided with his parents. He then attended school for six months and for six years thereafter was occupied as an educator in the country districts, at the end of that time turning his attention once more to farming, in which he was occupied for sixteen years. Next he went to Galena, Cherokee County, Kansas, where he followed mining for a short time and the real estate business for two years, and then again resumed the vocation of agriculture. He was one of the prominent men of his community and served as justice of the peace for twelve years, resigning that office when he came to Yale, Oklahoma, February 14, 1915. He still lives at Yale and has assisted his son Oliver in the latter's extensive business affairs. A democrat all his life, he is a devout member of the Missionary Baptist Church. Henry Dale at one time owned a farm in Jasper County, Missouri, which had been homesteaded from the Government by a man named Hammer. Hammer sold it to Robert J. Dale for $500. Robert sold it to his son Henry for $600. Henry disposed of the land to M. L. Reed for $1,600, who in turn received $2,200 for it from Tom Pete Moss. This farm has always been an object of special association and affection in the Dale family. In 1915 Oliver C. Dale went to Missouri and bought the land for $17,800. He now has a corps of experts engaged in making a thorough test of the property, prospecting for lead and zinc deposits. The property contains 220 acres.

On December 11, 1870, Henry C. Dale married Miss Emma J. Barker, who was born November 19, 1851, in Moniteau County, Missouri, daughter of Charles L. and Delilah (Eads) Barker. Of this union there were eight children: Oliver C.; Charley, who resides at Galena, Kansas; Arthur, deceased; Mrs. Maggie Lewman and Mrs. Canzada Jarrett, both deceased; Henry Clay, principal of the high school at Columbus, Kansas; Gordon, who is manager of the O. C. Dale Department Store at Yale; and Mrs. Willa Anna Pettit, of Yale.

Oliver C. Dale received a public school education and worked with his father on the home farm, and while the family was living at Galena, Kansas, worked in the mines there and at Joplin, Missouri, for about three years. On May 6, 1896, at Galena, Kansas, he married Miss Izora E. Miller, who was born in Luzerne County, Pennsylvania, February 28, 1879, and at five years of age came to Indian Territory with her parents, Charles H. and Cevilla (Mowery) Miller. Charles H. Miller, who was a prominent ranchman, died at the home of Mayor Dale in 1912, while Mrs. Miller still survives and resides on a farm in Creek County, Oklahoma. Charles Miller was a very prominent man in the Creek Nation in the early days. He was a quarter-blood Cherokee and was an adopted citizen of the Creek tribe. It was his Indian citizenship which brought to the Dale family the heritage of land which by a happy turn of fortune have converted his descendants to the wealthiest people in their section of Oklahoma. In an illustrated article which was published in the magazine section of the St. Louis Post-Dispatch in August, 1915, something is said about Charlie Miller and the part he played in the early days of Oklahoma. He was one of the men who stood for law and order in a country where lawless conditions largely prevailed. He rendered special service as member of a band of vigilantes which expelled two of the most notorious bands of outlaws ever known in Eastern Oklahoma, one of them being the Buck gang and the other led by "Narrow-Gauged Kid," one of the most infamous cattle rustlers in the territory. Charlie Miller himself had some exciting battles with these marauders. Due to this and his otherwise prominent activities he was adopted into the Creek tribe.

After his marriage Oliver C. Dale made a trip to the Indian country but failed to establish himself with any degree of success and then returned to Kansas. In 1901 he came to Red Fork in the Creek Nation, where he helped to unload and set up the rig of the party that made the first oil strike in Indian Territory. Subsequently he came to the lands of his wife in Creek County, nine miles southeast of Yale. Mrs. Dale and her children had participated in the allotment of lands in that section, she and her two daughters receiving 150 acres each. On this land Mr. Dale spent part of his time hunting and fishing. At that time the Dale farm was thirty miles from any railroad. He and his family experienced all the hardships that are a part of the life of the pioneer, and he drove on several occasions sixty miles for the purpose of spending $2 for provisions. In the Post-Dispatch article already mentioned there is illustrated the old log house in which the Dale family lived while on the farm. After four years he removed from the farm to Yale in 1905, and worked for one year in a store. Later for three years he ran an engine in a cotton gin, which was put up originally for the big blacksmith shop in this end of the state. Mr. Dale in fact supported his family by work at the anvil, and comparatively little attention was given to the family land. Then came the great oil strike which brought the Cushing oil field into existence. The Dale lands were in the very center of this new oil district, and the allotment of the older daughter, Vida, soon was yielding 100,000 barrels a month, while the land of her sister Mabel developed about fourteen producing wells and was almost equally productive.

About the beginning of the Cushing oil field Mr. Dale gave up his work as a blacksmith and began trading in oil leases. He proved a very shrewd trader, and in two years built up a fortune on his own account. His oil interests and his many other affairs now occupy his entire attention. He is identified with the Twin State Oil Company, the Producers Oil Company, the McMann Oil Company and the Shaffer Oil Company. In the interests of these concerns he travels all over Oklahoma and adjoining states. He is the owner in his own right of 700 acres of oil land in Ada, and his holdings total 2,000 acres in Oklahoma, 900 acres in Missouri and 1,000 acres in Kansas. In the spring of 1915 Mr. Dale became the owner by purchase of the O. C. Dale department store, which is now under the management of his brother Gordon. He has contributed materially to the upbuilding of Yale, his latest contribution in this line being his own residence, Fern Dale, erected in 1915 at a cost of $14,000. This is a seventeen room house on F Street, located on an elevation overlooking Yale and three other towns, and is not only the costliest home in Yale but one of the finest in the state. It has every modern convenience, is finished in mahogany with white maple floors, every room is hand decorated and this last item alone cost $1,600. Mr. Dale has also erected a number of other residences in Yale and at present owns five valuable homes. He is interested in the Farmers National Bank and in various other enterprises which contribute to Yale's business importance and prestige.

A stalwart democrat in politics, in 1912 he was made a Wilson delegate to the National Convention at Baltimore. He was one of the original Wilson men in Oklahoma, and has been a strong supporter of his administration. He has also had experience as a delegate to county and state conventions of his party, and spent six years on the school board. He was on the board when the district was consolidated, this being the first consolidated district in the state.

In the spring of 1915 he was elected mayor of Yale without opposition, and is proving himself as able an executive as he has shown himself a business man. The office means to him not only a distinctive honor but also a responsibility. It is said that he has spent many times his salary on public improvements which he considers the town should have, and is working constantly for the best interests of the entire community. In fact the welfare of Yale has first place in his thoughts, in spite of the fact that his enormous business interests might well require his entire time. He has been one of the community's most liberal supporters of movements making for religious, social, educational or civic benefit.

Mr. and Mrs. Dale are the parents of six children: Vida May, who married Arthur I. Tull of Yale and has a son named Arthur; Mabel, now about fifteen years of age; and Charles Henry, Dare D., Georgia and Del Val. All the younger children still reside in the magnificent home of their parents. The two older daughters are now said to be the richest girls in Oklahoma, and on that account have received much attention from the press and the public generally. It is an interesting fact that wealth has left them unspoiled. Vida, the older daughter, did not allow her sudden wealth to interfere with the continuance of her happy courtship with Arthur Tull, and the younger daughter Mabel has continued to be a friend to her child playmates in Yale without special regard for the distinctions that wealth have surrounded her with.

HARRY E. ALTON. The Alton Mercantile Company of Enid is almost in a class by itself among the wholesale grocery houses of the Southwest. It is a business with more than twenty-five years of development, and has behind it a remarkable wealth of experience and personal ability. "The Alton Goods" are distributed among the retail merchants all over Western Oklahoma and the City of Enid takes special pride in this magnificent enterprise. The president of the corporation is S. T. Alton, who was formerly a traveling salesman, and founded a small business at Arkansas, Kansas, during the '80s, and is now practically retired. The vice president is T. C. Smallwood, and the secretary and treasurer and active manager is Harry E. Alton, a son of the president.

The business was established at Enid in 1903 as a branch of the main house at Oklahoma City. S. T. Alton engaged in the wholesale grocery business at Oklahoma City in 1897, and that city was headquarters until 1905. In the latter year the business was concentrated at Enid, and in the past ten years there has been a constant expansion. In 1905 $100,000 approximately was invested in the business. This has since been increased to an aggregate of more than $250,000, including the value of the buildings. The main building has 30,000 square feet of floor space, and an additional building containing 20,000 square feet of warehouse space, with convenient railroad connections, was erected in 1915. The trade of the company extends all over Western and Southern Oklahoma, the Panhandle of Texas and Southern Kansas. There are twelve traveling representatives, who are constantly on the road visiting the 1,500 or more retail customers. About fifty persons are employed in the local establishment at Enid. The growth in the ten years since locating at Enid has been very satisfactory, and the limits of expansion are not yet in sight.

S. T. Alton was in the wholesale business at Arkansas City, Kansas, from 1889, and the house which he established there is still flourishing. He finally sold to his partner, J. A. Ranney, who is now deceased, but whose sons continue the business. Though Mr. S. T. Alton is still president and the principal owner, he has lived at Los Angeles since 1910. For fifteen years he was a traveling salesman representing the Chicago soap manufacturing house of James S. Kirk & Company, and covered the Western States. With this thorough experience and acquaintance with the trade, he established a business of his own with a very modest capital at Arkansas City. Throughout his career of residence in Oklahoma he has been in the wholesale grocery business.

The Alton Mercantile Company, as importers, wholesale grocers and coffee roasters, now have annual sales aggregating $1,000,000. From time to time the company has taken advantage of developing trade and transportation conditions. When S. T. Alton moved from Arkansas City to Oklahoma City, it was to take advantage of distribution conditions, and the same factor was prominent in establishing the branch at Enid. At Oklahoma City the house already had other competitors, but there was no wholesale house at Enid. The company roasts its own brand of coffee, and a graduate chemist from the State University of Oklahoma is at the head of this department. The roasting is done in the most scientific manner, and a very superior grade of coffee is sold as one of the features of the Alton goods. The company also packs grocers' sundries, spices, and other commodities, and this feature is not usually found in ordinary jobbing houses.

Harry E. Alton, secretary, treasurer and general manager of the company, has had the full responsibility of management since 1910. He practically grew up in the Arkansas City house, and the details of the business were ground into him from the start. In 1908 he went to Enid as the active representative of the firm in the branch house, and has filled important positions in a progressive scale until he is now carrying the chief responsibilities.

Mr. Alton was born in Chicago in 1880, and was educated in the public schools of Arkansas City and the military school at Salina, Kansas. He is a clear-headed, genial merchant, with ability to grasp the salient points in whatever situation confronts him, has great skill as a manager and is an aggressive worker in planning and carrying out business campaigns. He has also made himself a factor in good citizenship at Enid. He has served on the city council, and has always worked to keep Enid up to the high mark of its opportunities. He has the faculty of co-operation highly developed, and his business friends find him a most valuable confrère. He is a director of the Chamber of Commerce, and the future greatness of Enid is a subject upon which he readily becomes eloquent. Mr. Alton serves on the vestry of the Episcopal Church. In 1914 he married Miss Lucile Mullett of Kansas City, Missouri.

CHARLES B. SWARTOUT, president of the Oklahoma State Bank of Cushing, has been a resident of Oklahoma since 1889 and of his present home in Payne County since the opening of the Sac and Fox lands. During this long period he has been engaged in farming, in building as a contractor and in financial enterprises, and in each avenue of endeavor has gained a satisfying and well-merited success. He is one of the men contributed by the Empire State for the upbuilding of the great commonwealth of Oklahoma, having been born at Watkins, Schuyler County, New York, September 30, 1856, and is a son of Heman C. and Sarah A. (Monroe) Swartout.

The parents of Mr. Swartout, who passed their entire lives in New York and died at Watkins, were agricultural people and natives of the state, the father being born in Yates County and the mother near Watertown, Jefferson County. Of their ten children, three died young and one after reaching years of maturity, and six are still living. Charles B. Swartout received a good common school education in his youth, grew up on his father's farm and as a young man learned the trade of carpenter. By the time he had reached his twenty-fourth year he was engaged in business as a building contractor, a vocation which he followed in New York until 1889, in that year coming West to take advantage of the original opening of Oklahoma lands. At the time he made his second run the horse which he was riding fell, and the crowd was so dense about him that he was unable to jump either to the right or left, but was compelled to leap straight over his horse's head. Luckily he was uninjured, was able to remount, and was eventually successful in securing lots in Guthrie. In that city he made his home for two years, and then again took part in a run for land, at the opening of the Sac and Fox country, when he secured a claim in the southwest one-quarter of section 3, township 17, range 5 east, on which he has resided ever since. He has a well cultivated, valuable and productive property, thirty acres of which is included within the corporation limits of Cushing, while his residence adjoins the limits. For many years, in connection with his agricultural operations, he was engaged in contracting and building, but retired from that vocation in 1913. He was one of the founders of the Oklahoma State Bank of Cushing, of which he has been president for several years, a strong and substantial institution of Payne County which has grown and developed steadily under his capable and far-sighted direction. Politically a democrat, he is not an office seeker but has shown an interest in his party's success in Oklahoma. His progressive ideas of citizenship have led him to support movements for the welfare of his community.

In 1887 Mr. Swartout was married to Miss Edna M. Purdy, who was born in 1867, March 6, in Shiawassee County, Michigan, daughter of Nelson F. and Harriet N. (Smith) Purdy, the former of whom died in Michigan, while the latter still survives and resides at Kansas City, Missouri. Two children have been born to Mr. and Mrs. Swartout: Bessie, who is the wife of Henry Oursler, who is an attorney in Cushing, and has two children—Henry Charles and Dorothy Edna; and Annie, who is the wife of Earl K. Odom, of Cushing.

JAMES W. TYLER. The position of the educator was never so valuable nor so full of intimate significance in the life of the country as today. One of the men whose qualifications for the heavy responsibilities of directing the public system of education are unquestioned and who has to a large degree realized some of the best ideals for which the public school stands is the present county superintendent of schools in Garfield County, James W. Tyler. In noting the work which Mr. Tyler has accomplished it is clear that he is impressed with the value of the principle that to educate the plain people for life is more important than to educate a cultured class, and some of the best results of his work in Garfield County have been in the better and greater diffusion of the advantages of the public schools among all the people.

This Oklahoma educator was born at Cairo in Randolph County, Missouri, July 21, 1874, and spent his life on a farm up to the age of thirty. He attended the country schools and also a village high school, had two years of teaching experience when a young man, and finished his education in the Northeastern Missouri Normal at Kirksville. Since coming to Enid he has received the degrees A. B. and A. M. at Phillips University of that city.

For two years following his attendance at Kirksville Normal he was principal of the public schools at Atlanta, Missouri. In 1901 Mr. Tyler came to Enid, and has since been identified with the schools in that section of the state. For two years he was in the village schools of Fairmont, and for five years was superintendent of Waukomis, with seven teachers under his direction, and his work in that position was so satisfactory as to be commended with an appreciable increase of salary. For the following five years Mr. Tyler was principal of the Garfield Ward School at Enid, and in the fall of 1912 was elected superintendent of the county school system, taking up the duties of his office on July 1, 1913.

Outside of Enid there are in Garfield County 124 schools with 175 teachers, and the total scholastic enrolment is 9,326. In 1915 there are fourteen high schools in the county, four having been added since Mr. Tyler began his administration. In 1913 less than 48 per cent of the county's teachers had high school or better training, and this percentage has now been increased to 63. Mr. Tyler has the rare gift of imparting his enthusiasm to his subordinates and associates, and the large body of Garfield County teachers have enthusiastically endorsed and adopted his educational ideas and ideals.

He has been particularly interested in securing a larger school attendance. In 1914 900 pupils in the county received certificates of perfect attendance, while 1,500 had a perfect score from three to five months. He has also introduced a valuable feature in securing records for home work, and this has brought about a notable increase in the efficiency, attendance and interest on the part of both pupils and parents. The home work which is made a matter of record is not merely study of books, but any task which is essentially useful and best adapted to the needs and ability of the individual pupil. Thus the records include such duties as housework, sewing, performance of chores, etc. One backward girl pupil, mentioned in particular by Mr. Tyler, had on her report card the record of milking eight cows twice daily. Mr. Tyler has organized the county schools for athletic and literary work, securing a beneficent rivalry by contests. The county has been divided into eight districts containing fifteen schools each, and there are at different times contests held between the various schools in each district, and the winners of the district contests meet for an annual general exhibition, which attracts large crowds and great interest, and appropriate awards are given to the winners in athletics, debating and other features. At the beginning some of the teachers held aloof, saying that such contests were mere nonsense, but in time nearly all have become convinced of the value of such features of school work. Every possible effort has been made to induce the country pupils to advance to the high schools, with a natural increase in high school attendance.

During 1913 124 teachers in Garfield County attended the Normal Institute and eight took summer school instruction. In 1914 the number who took the work of the Normal Institute rose to 148 while forty-one teachers took summer school instruction. It costs about $75 to attend the summer schools, and in order that those availing themselves of such instruction, probably at the cost of much self sacrifice, might be properly rewarded, Mr. Tyler has induced the school board to pay $5 a month above the averages wages to teachers who have secured this superior training. As a result, many of the boards now show a decided preference for the better trained and experienced teachers. On the whole, during the past two or three years, the general average of wages paid to the school teachers in Garfield County has increased between 20 and 50 per cent, and some schools are paying $25 a month more to their teachers than in 1913. Mr. Tyler is also directing his efforts toward raising the standard of school instruction by the process of consolidating small individual schools into one central district, and by establishing central schools that can offer a thoroughly graded

Preston A. Shinn,

and organized course, including also the first year of the regular high school work.

Mr. Tyler since beginning his work as a teacher has been a student of educational methods and keeps himself thoroughly abreast of educational ideas. At the present time he is president of the State Association of County Superintendents. In 1907 Mr. Tyler married Beulah Benton Goodding of Atlanta, Missouri. Mrs. Tyler was also educated in the Kirksville Normal and was a teacher before her marriage. Their two sons are Donald Jett and Gerald Goodding. Mr. Tyler is a member of the Christian Church, has been president of the church board twelve years, while Mrs. Tyler is a Presbyterian.

S. R. STATON. Among the men who came to Oklahoma at the time the Cheyenne and Arapaho lands, consisting of 3,000,000 acres, were thrown open to white settlement in April, 1892, is S. R. Staton, the present postmaster of Cushing. Like many others, he was at that time possessed of little save ambition and determination, qualities which he combined with youthful enthusiasm and energy to such good effect that he was able to establish himself firmly and to lay the foundation for what has since become a satisfying success. His activities in Oklahoma have invaded the fields of agriculture, business and public service, and in each he has acquitted himself commendably, so that he may lay claim to being one of the builders of the commonwealth.

Mr. Staton was born in Dade County, Illinois, November 18, 1869, and is a son of John W. and Eliza (Eaton) Staton, natives of Illinois. In the Prairie State the parents were farming people, and on moving to Missouri followed the pursuits of the soil, first in Dade County and later in Worth County, in the northwestern part of the state, where the father died in 1879, at the age of forty-four years, the mother surviving until 1885 and passing away in Gentry County, Missouri, when aged sixty-three years. There were five children in the family: William, now a resident of Albany, Missouri; Lucy, who is the wife of Ed Hymer, of Belle Plaine, Kansas; Pierce, of Darlington, Missouri; Charles, of DeKalb, Missouri; and S. R.

S. R. Staton was five years of age when his father died and only sixteen when he was left an orphan by the death of his mother. He had received a public school education, and worked with his brother at Darlington, Missouri, in a lumber yard and as an employe of the postoffice during President Cleveland's first administration. He continued to make his home with his brother, Charles, until his marriage, in 1889, to Miss Eva M. Garman, a native of Missouri and a daughter of Epaphras Garman, shortly after which he came with his bride to Oklahoma and secured a claim in Custer County. His land at that time was sixty-five miles from the nearest town, but the country soon began to build up, and, with the organization of the Town of Thomas, near his property, Mr. Staton was appointed assessor, serving in that capacity during the first two terms of the existence of that office. He continued to reside on his Custer County farm until 1907, in which year he moved to Cushing, Payne County, and here established himself in business at the postoffice as the proprietor of a news stand and soda water fountain, an enterprise which he continued with some success for two years. His next venture was in buying cream for the Continental people, and he was so engaged at the time of his appointment to the postmastership, May 20, 1913. He entered upon his duties July 1st of that year and has since devoted his entire time and attention thereto. During his administration the office has advanced from a third to a second class office and through his intelligent and energetic management the service has been greatly improved. His unfailing courtesy and expeditious handling of the mail has gained him both the friendship and the confidence of the people who have business at the postoffice, and his conscientious labors have been generally appreciated by business houses and individuals. Mr. Staton has been a lifelong democrat. During a quarter of a century he has been a member of the Methodist Episcopal Church, and his fraternal connections are with the local lodges of the Woodmen of the World and the Knights of Pythias. Mr. and Mrs. Staton are the parents of three daughters: Carrie, Epaphra and Levana.

PRESTON A. SHINN. For the past ten years Mr. Shinn has been one of the leading members of the bar at Pawhuska. After locating there his ability was soon recognized in his appointment as tribal attorney for the Osages, one of the best paid positions in the Indian service, and his handling of the many intricate questions submitted to him in his official capacity won many favorable comments from the Interior Department and from the leading members of the tribe, and this experience served to advance him to his present high standing in the Oklahoma bar. Mr. Shinn has worked to a place of high esteem in his profession, and at the same time has proved his usefulness and influence as a member of the community.

It is not without due pride that Mr. Shinn refers to that period of his early life which was marked by a combination of hard circumstances and manual toil. For a number of years he was a coal miner back in Illinois, and gained his education largely through the fruits of his labors underground. He was born at Mattoon, Illinois, September 13, 1875. His parents were William and Sarah (Cole) Shinn. His father, who died when Preston was nine years of age, was born in North Carolina, while the mother, who is now living at Odin, Illinois, was born near the famous battlefield of Lookout Mountain April 10, 1843. The parents moved to Illinois, where the father followed farming most of his career. There were three sons and one daughter: Frank, who is a miner at Odin, Illinois; William, who died at the age of sixteen; Ina, wife of J. J. Murphy of Odin, Illinois.

The second in age among these children, Preston A. Shinn grew up at Odin, Illinois, and not long after the death of his father realized that his future depended upon his own exertions. At the age of twelve he started working in the coal mines, and for several years spent most of the summer season in this vocation, while he attended school in the winter. His record as a miner really extends from the time he was twelve years of age until he was twenty-five. During 1899, in the last year of his mining work, he was recording secretary of the local union of the United Mine Workers of America at Odin. During the many months spent by Mr. Shinn in the hard toil of the coal mines, he was constantly inspired by an ambition for higher and better things, and was utilizing all his savings to advance his education. From his wages as a miner he paid his way through the higher schools and law school. For one year he was a student in law offices, and spent two years in the Northern Illinois College of Law at Dixon. On examination before the State Bar Association of Illinois he stood second in a class of 242 applicants, and was admitted to practice in that state in 1901. Besides his work as a miner Mr. Shinn was for several years a practical railroader. For four months he was conductor on a street car in St. Louis. For two years he was train auditor on the Wabash, with a run between Detroit and Buffalo, and also worked for one year with the Missouri, Kansas & Texas Railroad.

After being admitted to the bar Mr. Shinn was in

practice at Centralia, Illinois, one year, and in 1905 moved to Pawhuska. Here he at once identified himself with everything that would benefit the condition of the people and it was not long before his ability as a lawyer brought him favorable distinction and preferment. For four years he served as assistant tribal attorney for the Osages and for three years was tribal attorney. He held this office under a contract with the tribe subject to approval from the Department of the Interior. His term expired in April, 1914, and he has since devoted himself without interruption to his large general practice.

In 1907 Mr. Shinn was republican candidate for the office of county attorney. Politically he is to be classified as an independent republican. He is also affiliated with the Masonic Lodge and with the Modern Woodmen of America, and is a member of the Episcopal Church.

In April, 1905, he married Miss Nellie Taplin of Oswego, New York. Mrs. Shinn was formerly a trained nurse and was engaged in that profession at Detroit when she met Mr. Shinn. Without children of their own, they are rearing in their home in Pawhuska two of Mrs. Shinn's brother's children.

M. M. CALLAWAY. As a business center Enid has many distinctions. The fact that it has become a great market for horses and mules is largely due to the vigorous enterprise of the firm of Callaway & Son, whose operations have not only directed to that point the attention of hundreds of stock raisers in Western Oklahoma, but have also noticeably improved the quality and general standard of horses and mules raised in that district.

M. M. Callaway, the head of the firm, is one of the original citizens of Enid, having come in at the opening on September 16, 1893. He secured a homestead three miles west of Enid, but proved up on it as soon as possible in order to concentrate his attention to the handling of stock, a line of industry which he has followed for forty years. For many years Mr. Callaway was a general stock buyer and shipper in Missouri, but transferred the headquarters of his business from there to Wichita, Kansas, and was active at that point for several years before the opening of the Cherokee Strip. For the past eighteen years Mr. Callaway has concentrated on horses and mules. Few if any men in Oklahoma are better known as an expert judge of horses and a liberal dealer who recognizes that trade must have mutual advantages to both parties concerned. In company with his son, Ben, he has done an extensive business, and not infrequently handled 1,500 animals each year, with aggregate value of sales reaching more than $400,000. Since the outbreak of the European war all records have been broken in the horse and mule market, and this firm has been busily engaged in gathering, selecting and shipping hundreds of horses and mules to be used abroad.

The operations of the firm of Callaway & Son cover a wide area, though the bulk of the stock is purchased within a radius of fifty miles about Enid. As already mentioned, probably no other man has done so much to encourage the breeding and growing of improved classes of stock in this district. It is now acknowledged that a superior class of both horses and mules is produced in this section of Oklahoma. Several years ago Mr. Callaway erected a large and specially equipped horse barn at an expense of $14,000. The barn at present is occupied by the Aaron Produce Company. In addition to his stock business Mr. Callaway has been a farmer to such an extent as to justify his prominence in that industry were it the only occupation which he followed.

He owns several hundred acres of land, and has made wheat growing his specialty. In 1914 he had 350 acres in the crop, with a yield of about thirty bushels per acre. Thus he had about 10,000 bushels ready for market at a time when wheat was soaring above $1 a bushel.

M. M. Callaway was born near Springfield, Missouri, in 1847. His parents had located in that section about 1840, his father coming from North Carolina and his mother from Tennessee. Mr. Callaway has been a democratic voter since early manhood, but has never sought public distinction. His ability as a business man and integrity as a citizen caused the people of Garfield County to choose him as one of the county commissioners, in which office he served from 1904 to 1910. It was during that period that the courthouse was erected at a cost of $100,000. So skilfully were the county finances managed that within four years the entire obligation caused by this improvement was liquidated. At the same time the tax rate, instead of being increased, was actually lessened. While his associates on the board, H. C. Davis and C. P. Epley, were both republicans, in most matters the board worked in absolute harmony and efficiency. The only important exception was Mr. Callaway's decided preference for locating the courthouse on the site of the old building at the north end of the public square.

Mr. Callaway was married at Marshfield, Missouri, where he lived during the severe cyclone which demolished that town, to Elizabeth Buford. To their union have been born a family of five children. Two daughters live at Springfield, Missouri. The son, Charles, is operating one of the farms owned by his father, while Ben is associated in the horse and mule business. The daughter, Lillie, is still at home.

ASA DONALDSON. It is with a comfortable sense of duty well performed and many responsibilities capably fulfilled that Asa Donaldson now enjoys the privileges of a retired life in Cushing. When a very young man Mr. Donaldson served in one of the concluding campaigns of the Union armies during the Civil war. Preliminary to his introduction to Oklahoma he lived in Kansas and had his share of the early struggles that were the lot of the early farmers in that state. He became a pioneer of the Sac and Fox country at its opening, and has been identified with this section ever since.

In the early days of Cushing before railroads had been constructed, Mr. Donaldson did a great deal of business as a freighter. For eight years he hauled goods back and forth across the country between Cushing and Sapulpa and Cushing and Guthrie. Those larger cities were the nearest railroad points, and it was forty-five miles to either place. The roads were little better than prairie trails, there were no bridges across the streams, and Mr. Donaldson usually spent from four to six days in making a round trip. He was paid 40 cents a hundred for hauling goods, but the limit of capacity for his wagon was one ton.

Asa Donaldson was born at Lexington, LaGrange County, Indiana, April 21, 1846, a son of George and Nancy (Norton) Donaldson. His father was born in Scotland, while the mother was a native of Connecticut. When a child George Donaldson came to America with his parents, who settled in West Virginia, but as a young man he went out to Northern Indiana and secured a homestead of eighty acres one mile east of the Town of Lexington, where he lived as a farmer and blacksmith until about 1859. He then removed to Crawford County, Illinois, where he was engaged in the same occupation until about 1862. Returning then to Lexington, Indiana, he remained there until his death, when about seventy years of age. The mother died in Crawford County, Illinois, when ninety-two years of age.

There were nine children altogether in the family and only three are now living. Asa's older brother, Charles, two years his senior, enlisted in the Ninth Michigan Cavalry early in the Civil war and was accidentally killed while returning home in June, 1865, after having passed safely through the various campaigns under General Sherman. Asa Donaldson was about fourteen years of age when the war broke out, and his early life was spent on a farm in Northern Indiana, with such advantages as the common schools of that district afforded. On August 9, 1864, he likewise enlisted for service in the Union army, and at Sturgis, Michigan, went out with the Ninth Michigan Infantry. He served until the close of the war, and was in the army commanded by General Thomas. On returning home to LaGrange County, Indiana, he was married a little later, on July 1, 1866, to Miss Lavina Culler. She was born near Canton in Stark County, Ohio, in April, 1847, lost her father when she was one year of age, and at the age of eleven came to Koscinsko County, Indiana, with her widowed mother.

After his marriage Mr. Donaldson lived on a farm in LaGrange County, Indiana, for a number of years, but finally moved west and identified himself with the pioneer district of Harvey County, Kansas. He was a farmer there for six years, and then at the opening of the Sac and Fox Reservation made his entry into Oklahoma. Up to that time he had not greatly prospered, and it adds to the interest of his present standing as a business man to note that he came into Oklahoma driving two teams and two cows, and without a pair of shoes to cover his own feet. He secured a claim three miles north of Cushing, and that was the scene of his industrious endeavors for a number of years. He cleared up the land, developed a good homestead, and lived there until 1909, at which time he moved into the Town of Cushing and sold his farm. He then spent six months in touring the Pacific Coast, and returning to Oklahoma bought a tract of forty acres half a mile south of Cushing, and has since introduced many improvements in that little farm. For six years he has been a resident of Cushing, and for two years was in the furniture business, but now has no interests outside of his private affairs and the management of his city property.

Mr. Donaldson is a republican in politics, and for eight years held the position of justice of the peace. He is a member of the Grand Army of the Republic, the Masonic Order, and belongs to the Christian Church. The active responsibilities and burdens of life are now carried forward by his children. Mr. Donaldson became the father of six. The oldest, Charles, died in Kansas at the age of twenty-one. Orsena, who died at the age of thirty, married Frank Faulls. Maude married Leon High, and she died at the age of twenty-nine, leaving two sons, William Ray and Lawrence, who are now living with their grandfather, Mr. Donaldson, and with their own father, who is proprietor of a grocery store at Cushing. George, the fourth child, died at the age of fourteen. Arbie is a farmer near Cushing, and by his marriage to Etta Cotterman has the following children: Irwin; Floyd, deceased; Edna; Lloyd; Fern; Truman; and one that died in infancy. The youngest of Mr. Donaldson's children is William, a farmer in Payne County; he married Hattie Brooks, and their children are Bessie, Leland, Lavina, Henry (deceased), Ora and Goldie.

JOHN N. INNIS. There is probably no better known or more picturesque figure in Western Oklahoma than "Jack" Innis, now settled down to the routine of business affairs as manager of the York-Key Lumber Company of Supply. The varied incidents and exciting scenes of the frontier are indelibly impressed as pictures upon Mr. Innis' mind, since he was in this country nearly thirty years ago, followed the range and trail over No Man's Land for several years, was connected with the Government service in the different forts of Western Oklahoma, particularly at Fort Supply, and was at the founding of the modern Town of Supply and gave the community one of its first stores.

As his family were pioneers before him, and moved successively to different points as civilization advanced toward the West, he was well fitted by birth and environment for the accomplishments of his own career. John N. Innis was born in a log cabin in Ripley County, Indiana, September 1, 1863, a son of James Innis. There is another member of the family well known in Western Oklahoma, Joseph A. Innis, also a son of James, and a more particular sketch of the earlier generations will be found under the former name. John N. Innis when three years of age was taken by his parents to Bates County, Missouri, grew up there on a farm and a sufficient amount of education was given him for all practical purposes in the public schools of that section of Missouri.

He was twenty-three years of age when in 1886 he came into Old Indian Territory. It was three years before the first great opening of the Indian lands was made, and his first adventures were as a cowboy on the cattle ranch of Col. C. W. Peary in No Man's Land, as it was then designated in the school geography, and perhaps better known to the present generation as the Oklahoma Panhandle. He followed the trail in that country for four years, and in that time became acquainted with nearly all the picturesque characters, both whites and Indians, who inhabited the extreme western part of Oklahoma. In 1891 he entered the employ of the United States army as a teamster in the quartermaster's department. The headquarters were at Fort Supply, and he is one of the few men who have witnessed the transformation of that noted old military post into a modern city. Subsequently he was corral boss, and worked in that capacity both at Fort Supply and at Fort Sill altogether for four years. Still later he proved up on a claim in Harper County, Oklahoma, but when the new Town of Supply was founded in 1901 he established there the first general store. He conducted that successfully and sold goods to all his old friends in that vicinity and to hundreds of the new settlers. When he disposed of his mercantile stock in 1905 he accepted the post of manager for the York-Key Lumber Company at Supply, and has contributed not a little to the business of this large lumber corporation in Oklahoma. At the same time he has made himself a factor in local improvements, is one of the stanchest friends of Supply as a town, and prospective city, and he can always be depended upon for an intelligent and enlightened interest in its welfare. Fraternally Mr. Innis is affiliated with the Modern Woodmen of America.

At Woodward, Oklahoma, December 27, 1897, he married Miss Margaret Valker. She was born at old Fort Supply, Indian Territory, December 1, 1874, a daughter of Philip Valker, who was at that time serving as an enlisted soldier in the United States army. Her mother, now Mrs. L. Mason, came to Fort Supply with her parents in 1868 at the time the fort was established. Mrs. Innis was educated in a Catholic school at Purcell, Indian Territory. To their marriage were born seven children, four sons and three daughters: John P., born January 31, 1899; Robert Vinton, born February 20, 1901, and died March 30, 1901; Joseph Everett, born

July 19, 1903; Archie Ward, born September 28, 1905; Josephine May, born May 20, 1907; Bessie, born December 30, 1910; and Mary Ellen, born February 19, 1912.

COL. OLIVER R. LILLEY. Always will there be a glamor of romance about those interesting adventurers who participated in the first opening of the Oklahoma lands. Few men took part in more of these openings and endured more of the inconveniences and hardships connected therewith than Col. Oliver R. Lilley, who for a number of years has been a prominent citizen of Cushing in Payne County. Colonel Lilley has seen a great deal of western life during his career, has been in most of the states west of the Mississippi River, and has been hardy, fearless, enterprising and a ready fighter for any cause he believed to be just and right. While he has been identified with other affairs, Colonel Lilley is perhaps best known among most people as an auctioneer, a profession he has followed since early youth.

Born in Whiteside County, Illinois, November 23, 1861, he was taken in the same fall out to Kansas by his parents, Joseph John and Anna (Cross) Lilley, who were pioneers in Kansas at the beginning of the Civil war. His father, who was born in Pennsylvania, died in 1880 at the age of fifty on his old homestead in Riley County, Kansas, twenty miles north of Manhattan. He had located on that home in the fall of 1861. By occupation he was a farmer and stock raiser. The mother was born in West Virginia, and is now living at the old home in Kansas at the age of eighty-six. She became the mother of four sons and one daughter, and the father had children by a previous marriage.

Up to the age of ten Oliver R. Lilley lived at home and the next six years were spent in the same locality of Kansas, until the spirit of adventure led him entirely away from home surroundings and out to California. He spent 3½ years in that state, earning his way at any employment which he could secure. He did his first work as an auctioneer at the age of eighteen, and has since officiated at sales and has sold all manner of goods, live stock, household possessions, land and other property, and his operations have been carried on in Kansas, Missouri, Texas and elsewhere.

Colonel Lilley arrived in Oklahoma June 22, 1890. After that he took part in all the important land openings. At some of these openings he has paid as high as 10 cents a glass for drinking water. He lay for hours at a time in the thick dust along the line which marked the limit of the land for which thousands were striving to gain possession. At the opening of the Sac and Fox Reservation he had a fortunate number, No. 370, secured a claim, and lived there and improved it for fifteen years. For several years he lived at Ripley, and his home has been at Cushing since 1907. Here he has spent most of his time as an auctioneer.

Colonel Lilley is credited with many public spirited movements and enterprises in Payne County. He built and still owns the Lilley Hotel, a thirty-nine-room modern hostelry, and managed it himself for three years, and has since leased it. He also has other real estate in Cushing. Up to 1912 he was a republican, and has since been identified with the progressive policies. Colonel Lilley was for two years mayor at Cushing during the great boom following the discoveries of the oil fields. At that time the town was unable to provide accommodations for the hosts of people who flocked to this center, and hundreds of persons lived in tents. Colonel Lilley has always stood for a clean town, has lead the fight against the illegal liquor traffic, and has done much to keep that element of danger out of the local life. For twenty years he has been a member of the Christian Church, is affiliated with the Scottish Rite Consistory of Masonry at Guthrie, and with the Temple of the Mystic Shrine at Oklahoma City. He also belongs to the Eastern Star, the Knights and Ladies of Security, and many other fraternal orders.

On September 22, 1889, Colonel Lilley married Miss Emma A. Hetherington. She was born at Racine, Newton County, Missouri, February 16, 1872, and died at Stillwater, Oklahoma, April 3, 1915. Their four children, all born in Oklahoma, are named Lenna A., Jessie O., John H. and Oliver L.

CHIEF JAMES BIGHEART. Of all the characters in the history of the Osage tribe undoubtedly the greatest, so far as individual influence and forcefulness in politics and all economic measures affecting the tribe are concerned, was the late Chief James Bigheart, who died in October, 1908.

At the time of his death he was eighty-two years old. He was a fullblood Osage Indian, and it is conceded that he was the brainiest member of that tribe during the last century and was one of the keenest and shrewdest Indians ever known.

He had a long and active career. When a young man he served in the Union army during the Civil war and for many years his name was on the pension list. During the greater part of his lifetime Indian lands were held in common, and it was rather as a worker and a handler in cattle and other transactions that he gained his fortune. Until a few years before his death he was regarded as the richest man in the wealthiest tribe of Indians in the country.

It was due to many other things besides his extensive possessions of land that his name formed so important a feature of Osage life. The flourishing Town of Bigheart is only a small but significant tribute to his life and career.

He held nearly every office among the Osages, including the position as chieftain, and it is said that he was the most respected and the most dreaded man in the tribe. Though many honors were given him, he showed no tendency toward pompous display. He wore ordinary clothes, was quiet and thoughtful in appearance, and spoke fluently both the English and Osage languages. His name is destined to be long remembered as that of a great man and one whose life was devoted to what he believed the best interests of the fullblood Indian.

It is said that for many years he had more influence in the Interior Department than any other living Indian. For fully twenty years he was a controlling factor in his tribe, and his word was practically law among the fullbloods. About two years before his death he was stricken with paralysis but up to that time the affairs of the tribe were largely a reflex of his action and influence. He was constantly consulted and the tribe would practically refuse to act on any important matter until his advice could be obtained. In 1896 Chief Bigheart advocated the investigation of the citizenship rolls, and though defeated at first he persistently and doggedly kept up the work until a second investigation was ordered by Congress. He was bitterly opposed to the allotment of the Osage lands, and many say that he delayed that event for at least ten years. No doubt his dominant characteristic was an unflinching courage and a determination that knew no defeat. When he undertook anything, he persisted in it until it was finished to his satisfaction. While many of the definite details of Chief Bigheart's career can not be obtained it is only proper that the history of Oklahoma should give at least this brief character sketch of one of the foremost among its fullblooded Indian citizens.

Chief Bigheart married Alice McIntosh, a Cherokee Indian, and of a prominent old family of Oklahoma

CHIEF JAMES BIGHEART

To Mr. and Mrs. Bigheart were born seven children. Four of them are still living. The daughter Mary married Tom Clendenning, and they have two sons named James and Jack. Rosa married Sherman Heal, and became the mother of five children named Francis, Oliva, Julia, Roselay and Josephine. Lillian married W. C. Spurrier, referred to on other pages of this work. Isabel lives at home with her mother. On February 26, 1910, Mrs. Chief Bigheart, who is still living, married Mr. J. C. McGraw. Mrs. McGraw was married both times very close to the locality where she was born. She is a woman of unusual intelligence and ability, and her character is well reflected in the lives of her children. Mr. McGraw is one of the leading citizens of the Town of Bigheart, has prospered as a cattle man and farmer, and is filling a place of usefulness and honor in the Osage country. Mr. and Mrs. McGraw are the parents of three children: Blanche, Leo and Sylvester.

CHRIS E. HERSCHBERGER. There is a reason for Mr. Herschberger's successful work as an editor and newspaper owner, being proprietor of The Supply Republican at Supply, and there is also ground to expect much from him in the future, judged by what he has done in the past. Mr. Herschberger educated himself, has been a worker ever since early boyhood, and has found in teaching, printing and publishing congenial tasks which have furnished a solid foundation upon which to rear a superstructure of important accomplishment. Born May 23, 1888, on the farm in McPherson County, Kansas, he is a son of Moses C. and Mary (Bontrager) Herschberger. Originally the family was undoubtedly German, but several generations or more of the Herschbergers have lived in America. Moses C. Herschberger was born in the State of Indiana October 17, 1860, while his parents before him were natives of Ohio. Farming has always been his vocation since he reached mature years, and in 1881 he ventured into what was then an unproved country, Kansas, buying land in McPherson County. That was his home until 1889, after which he spent three years in the State of Missouri, but then returned to Kansas. In 1899 the family came to Oklahoma, locating on a farm near Jet in Alfalfa County until 1906. Moses C. Herschberger is now in the grain business at Blackwell. He and his wife were married at McPherson in 1882, and the latter was a daughter of John C. and Elizabeth (Miller) Bontrager, who were natives of Pennsylvania. She was born October 21, 1864, in Holmes County, Ohio. They are the parents of six children, three sons and three daughters, namely: John Carl, born March 28, 1886; Chris Earl; Clarence Austin, born June 25, 1891; Mabel E., born September 24, 1893; Susana Grace, born July 21, 1896; and Alta Mae, born August 20, 1901.

When Chris E. Herschberger came to Oklahoma with his parents in 1899 he was only eleven years of age. In the meantime he had profited by such opportunities as were afforded him to attend the public schools of southern Kansas. After coming to Oklahoma he worked three years in a general store at Jet. Then in 1902 began his experience as a printer's apprentice in the office of U. Finch. He learned the printing trade, and developed no little talent for artistic job work and also a tendency to the broader field of newspaper work. During 1906-07, in order to remedy some of the deficiencies of his early education, he attended the Woods County High School and during 1907-08 was a student in Goshen College at Goshen, Indiana, where he took the business course. Then with the equivalent of a substantial education, he took the post of editor of the Jet Visitor for two years, but in 1911 bought the Fort Supply Republican at Supply, Oklahoma, and has been identified with the progress and success of that journal ever since. He conducts an excellent paper, bright, newsy, a good medium for local advertising, and a vigorous supporter of all public improvements. Mr. Herschberger is popular as a citizen and in 1915 was elected city clerk at Supply. In the spring of 1916 he was also selected as chairman of the Executive Committee, having charge of the Tri-County Farm Products Exhibit, which has done much during the past few years in encouraging the farmers of Harper, Ellis and Woodward counties in producing better live stock, more and better crops, etc.

On September 22, 1909, about the time he moved to Supply he was married at Cherokee, Oklahoma, to Miss Rhea McDaniel, daughter of George W. and Rachel McDaniel, who were natives of Indiana. Mrs. Herschberger was born May 4, 1889, at Anthony, Kansas, and gained her education in Oklahoma, where she attended the Northwestern Normal at Alva, and prior to her marriage spent two years as teacher in Alfalfa County. To their union have been born two children: Max C., born July 4, 1910; and George Glenn, born April 5, 1913. Mr. and Mrs. Herschberger are members of the Christian Church.

CHARLES EDWIN FOY. A service record which will always make his life one of interest and esteem to his family and descendants was that portion of his early manhood which Charles E. Foy spent as a soldier in the Civil war. Since then, for a period of more than a half century, he has been successively identified with farming enterprise in various states, Illinois, Iowa, Nebraska and Oklahoma. Mr. Foy, as a result of good business management and long continued industry, is now comfortably situated, owns both farm and city property, and is living retired at Cushing.

Born on a farm in Hancock County, Illinois, January 28, 1844, he is a son of George and Nancy (Jones) Foy. His father was born in New York State and his mother in Kentucky. George Foy at the age of eighteen came west to Illinois, was married in Hancock County, and two years after the birth of his son, Charles E., moved to Whiteside County. He lived there nearly all the rest of his life, and finally went to Missouri, where he died shortly afterwards on April 10, 1896, at the age of seventy-seven. His wife passed away in Whiteside County, Illinois, in 1899, aged seventy-seven. George Foy was a farmer all his active career, exercised unusual thrift and intelligence in the management of his affairs, and came to be regarded as one of the most prosperous citizens of Whiteside County. He was a great reader of current literature, always kept himself informed on public affairs, was a republican voter and a member of the Methodist Episcopal Church. In the family of eleven children Charles E. was the oldest, four of the children died very young, and the others are briefly mentioned as follows: Mary, wife of George Klock of Bureau County, Illinois; Augusta, wife of Hubert Bonker of Denver, Colorado; Elmira, deceased wife of Edward Forward; Wilber, deceased; Edgar, deceased, who was a physician; and Freeman, who lives in Bureau County, Illinois.

The early life of Charles E. Foy was spent on a farm in Illinois, and he gained such education as the local schools had to bestow. When he was about nineteen years of age, on January 1, 1863, he enlisted in Whiteside County and went out with the Union army as a member of Company B in the Thirty-fourth Illinois Infantry. His service continued until the close of the war. He was with Sherman in the Atlanta campaign, on the march to the sea, in the campaign through the Carolinas, and finally took part in the glorious review of the victorious troops at Washington. While at Atlanta he suffered a flesh wound in the left leg as a result of an exploding shell, and was in the hospital two weeks. While on a foraging expedition in North Carolina he was captured, but was held a prisoner only about three hours until the Union cavalry came to his rescue and released him.

After the war Mr. Foy lived in Whiteside County on the old farm for a year. In 1866 he married Miss Adelia Arnold, who was born in Illinois and died in Nebraska in 1890. For several years after his marriage Mr. Foy followed farming in his native state, and in 1874 settled near Hastings in Adams County, Nebraska. He secured a homestead there and practically all the country was undeveloped, and most of the people lived in sod houses and had to fight all the plagues which assailed agricultural efforts in Nebraska during those years, including grasshoppers and many successive droughts. He continued a Nebraska farmer until the death of his wife, and then lived for a time in Kansas City, Missouri. The year following the opening of the Sac and Fox Reservation he came to Oklahoma and bought a quarter of section of land six miles west of Cushing. He developed a farm out of what had been for centuries a wilderness, and was quietly and industriously occupied with the farming interests there until he sold out in 1905. His next purchase was a farm two miles south of Drumright. Three years later he retired to Cushing, but still owns the farm of 160 acres near Drumright. Mr. Foy also has fourteen lots on East Broadway in Cushing, and has part of this developed, owning three residences. At the present time his farm, which is situated in the oil belt, is leased for productive operation. Politically he is a republican and has an honored membership in the Grand Army of the Republic.

By his first marriage there were six children, two of these died in infancy and the four still living are: Charles Edmund, who lives in Seattle, Washington; Arthur Elberton, also of Seattle; George, of Seattle; and Edgar, whose home is in Logan County, Colorado. In 1895 Mr. Foy married for his second wife at Guthrie, Oklahoma, Mrs. Anna (Kilmer) Parker. She was born in Van Buren County, Iowa, a daughter of Chandler Kilmer, and her first husband was Thomas Parker. Mr. and Mrs. Foy have one child, Hazel Fern, who is the wife of Luther Toalson of Cushing, and by this union Mr. Foy has a grandchild, Marlin Lucile.

BENJAMAN ELLIOTT ADAMS JR. Now proprietor and editor of the Okeene Leader, Mr. Adams is an Oklahoma pioneer by virtue of the fact that he came with the family to this territory as early as 1892. His trade and profession as printer and newspaper man were learned in Kansas, and while most of his active career has been spent in that line of work, he has also been identified with local affairs and business interests, and is a former postmaster of Okeene. The Okeene Leader is now one of the most influential newspapers in Blaine County, has a large circulation both in that and in Major and neighboring counties. Mr. Adams owns the plant, which is situated on Fifth Street near Main Street. The Leader was established July 12, 1906, as a democratic paper, but under Mr. Adams' management reflects republican sentiments.

Born at Grafton, Chautauqua County, Kansas, December 16, 1874, Benjaman Elliott Adams Jr. is a son of Benjaman Elliott Adams Sr., who carries in his veins a mixture of both English and Cherokee Indian stock. The original Burns of the Adams family came to Virginia from England in Colonial times. The senior Mr. Adams was born in Johnson County, Missouri, in 1846, and now lives on a ranch in Ellis County, Oklahoma, with his son Edgar A. He was one of the men who helped to develop the rich land of Chautauqua County, Kansas, for agricultural purposes, having removed to that section in 1870 from Missouri. In 1880 he went to Sedan, Kansas, and served as undersheriff for twelve years. In 1892 he came to Blaine County, Oklahoma, and made the run at the opening of the Cheyenne and Arapahoe reservation, obtaining a homestead of one hundred and sixty acres two miles south of Watonga. He lived on that place and developed it as a fine farm for ten years, and on selling out went to Ellis County, where he is still living. He is a member of the Masonic fraternity. The senior Mr. Adams married Miss Hattie Narron, who is of German stock. Their children are: Oliver J., who died in Artesia, New Mexico, in February, 1915, at the age of forty-five; Benjaman E. Jr.; Edgar Allen, who is a rancher in Ellis County, Oklahoma; Maude, wife of D. D. DeLancy, who is assistant cashier of the First National Bank of Taloga, Oklahoma; Otto, an electrician living at Whittier, California.

Benjaman E. Adams Jr. spent all his early youth in Kansas, completing a high school education at Sedan. On leaving school in 1890 he spent two years in learning the printing trade in the office of the Sedan Republican, which at that time was under the editorial management of former Governor T. B. Ferguson. In 1892 he came with his father to Blaine County, and for several years handled a plow and other implements in subduing the virgin soil of his father's homestead claim. He then allied himself again with T. B. Ferguson on the Watonga Republican, and continued that work off and on until 1900. Then going to Homestead, Oklahoma, he took charge of the Homestead News for W. W. Waterman, and in 1901 bought the paper and it was continued under his effective editorial control until the spring of 1907. Selling out he then removed to Okeene, and had charge of the Okeene Eagle during the statehood campaign. For several years after that Mr. Adams was not actively identified with newspaper work. For two years he was a director and assistant cashier of the Farmers and Merchants Bank of Okeene, and in 1910 President Taft appointed him postmaster, an office to which he devoted his time and attention until August 25, 1914. In April, 1915, he bought the Okeene Leader, and is making that one of the very successful newspapers in his district.

Politically Mr. Adams is a republican, and for three years served as trustee of Homestead Township and for two years was constable of Watonga Township. He is affiliated with Homestead Lodge No. 224, Ancient Free and Accepted Masons, and with the Brotherhood of American Yeomen at Okeene. On December 25, Christmas Day, 1900, in Watonga, he married Miss Anna Marie Howry. Her father, J. C. Howry, lives on a farm southwest of Watonga, where he homesteaded in 1892. To their marriage have been born three children: Lucile Frances, born in September 1904; Robert Howry, born in February, 1906; and Marguerite, born in February, 1913.

JOHN P. HICKAM. One of the strong, resourceful, versatile and loyal citizens whose influence has been potent in connection with governmental and general civic affairs in Oklahoma since the early territorial era in the history of this commonwealth and whose high ideals and downright sincerity have made him a leader in the furtherance of the interests of the people of the state of his adoption, is the honored member of the bar whose name introduces this paragraph. Mr. Hickam has been engaged in the practice of his profession at Stillwater, judicial center of Payne County, since the spring of 1897, and is one of the representative pioneer members of the bar of this section of the state. He has been a recognized leader in political activities in Oklahoma, and that he has been one of the foremost figures in the ranks of the progressive party in this state needs no further voucher than the statement that in the election of 1914 he was the progressive party's candidate for the office of governor of Oklahoma. Who knows the man can not fail to have lively appreciation of his ability, his unfaltering integrity of purpose, his admirable equipment for leadership in sentiment and action, and his invincible courage in upholding the rights and interests of the people as against the domination of capitalistic and corrupt political forces.

It is but consistent that in a preliminary way be given an outline of the political activities and public service of Mr. Hickam within the period of his residence in Oklahoma, and such a résumé is afforded in the following quotations from an article published at the time when he was in the midst of his campaign for governor of the state, in 1914:

"In 1902 Mr. Hickam was elected to the Territorial Senate, from the Payne-Pawnee district. He was renominated for the Senate in 1904 and after one of the bitterest fights ever waged against any candidate in Oklahoma by the old Territorial carpet-bag, stand-pat bunch of Federal officeholders, his majority was four times what it was in 1902. A prominent citizen of his own county said a short time ago: 'Hickam has no enemies in this county except those he has made in fighting crooked politics and machine politicians, and we love him for the enemies he has made.'

"Hickam is in tune with the times. He has kept step with the rapid march of human progress. He believes that political platforms are made for fulfillment instead of to catch votes. In that way he is distinguished from scheming politicians who are brokers in offices. He believes that the Progressive party must remain firm to its principles and hold above all else its opportunity for patriotic service, must hold itself unfettered for the service of the great mass of the people who are looking to it for all that is best and fairest and greatest in the political and governmental activities. He believes that, politically, evasion and indecision are at an end and that the Progressive party has made its choice. The making of that choice was no slight matter. It is no child's play to defy the power of entrenched party machines drawn by the lure of Federal and State offices whose victims will do the bidding of their masters.

"Hickam made the first fight ever made against lobbyists west of the Mississippi river. In his speech in the senate defying the lobbyists he said: 'Why all this delay, Mr. President, over the important legislation now pending? Bills are held up in committees until it is too late to pass matters of great interest to the people. The fact is that the capital since the first day we met has been full of lobbyists—a set of grafters, sir, who have tried in every way to defeat honest legislation in this body. These parasites have flocked about this chamber like buzzards over a carcass.' After Hickam had made this fight the Kansas City Star, in reviewing the conditions around the Oklahoma Legislature, said: 'Several members of the lobby lost their nerve yesterday and could not be found when the senate sergeant-at-arms went after them. Some are thought to have gone to Texas and others to Kansas. Their whereabouts are unknown and requisitions will be required to bring them back if they can be located.'

"The Stillwater Advance, in speaking of Hickam's fight at that time, said: 'Hickam stands stalwart, colossal, contending for the rights and interests of the great common people—the farmer, the small cattleraiser, the honest business man, as against the combined and powerful interests of the great cattle kings, the railroads, the oil mills, who have kept the cloak-rooms and hotel lobbies filled with the shrewdest and smartest men available to defeat good legislation. But Hickam has proved equal to the occasion and has denounced the lobbyists in unmeasured terms. He has earned the eternal gratitude and the confidence of the people in the splendid and able fight he has made in their behalf and for their interests. Senator Hickam is an able and strong man in every way. His fight against the lobbyists demonstrates the fact that he is unquestionably the strongest member of the Senate.'

"At the close of Mr. Hickam's second term in the Territorial Senate the Stillwater Gazette had this to say: 'Senator Hickam returns to his constituency—the people of Payne and Pawnee counties—with a consciousness that his labors fulfilled the promises he made to the people in his last campaign, that he would at all times care for their interests and fight the corrupt lobbyists, which he did as far as human power could do. He never missed a roll call, was ready to throw harpoon into all kinds of corrupt legislation. For a fearless legislator he had not a peer in the Senate, and he comes home with a clean page and can frankly say, "I did all I could for the interests of my people at home and in the Territory at large."'

In view of the statements quoted above it may well be understood that Mr. Hickam was recognized as the most available candidate to be put forth by the progressive party for the office of governor of Oklahoma, and though he made a characteristically vigorous and effective campaign and made a powerful impression upon the people of all sections of the state, he encountered the adverse political exigencies that compassed his defeat, though this defeat was not lacking in the better elements of victory.

John P. Hickam was born in Madison County, North Carolina, on the 2d of December, 1870, and is a son of Robert B. and Jane (Plemmens) Hickam, both of whom were born in the year 1844, the father having been a native of Virginia and the mother having been born in North Carolina, where their marriage was solemnized. Robert B. Hickam was a youth when he accompanied his parents on their removal from Virginia to North Carolina, in the '50s, and there he was reared to manhood. When the Civil war was precipitated on the nation Robert B. Hickam enlisted in the Second North Carolina Infantry, in the Confederate service, and with this gallant command he continued in service during virtually the entire period of the war. He participated in many engagements, including a number of important battles, and made a record for able and gallant service. His father, Jacob Hickam, who was a native of Virginia and who attained to the patriarchal age of ninety-seven years, was an old-line whig in politics and was vigorously opposed to the secession of the Southern States, so that his sympathies were with the Union when the Civil war became imminent. His sons, however, were loyal to the institutions and cause of the South and tendered their aid in defense of the Confederacy, though John, the elder of the two sons, had first decided to enlist in the Union army, but was deflected from this course largely on account of his kinsmen in appreciable number having enlisted in the Confederate ranks. Both sons served until the close of the war, and upon their return to the parental home the most amicable relations again obtained, the venerable father offering no criticism of the course of his sons and both of the latter having remained on their respective portions of the old homestead estate for nearly a quarter of a century after the war.

In 1885, when the subject of this review was a lad of eleven years, he accompanied his parents on their removal from North Carolina to Sevier County, Tennessee, and there his father passed the residue of his long and worthy life, his active career having been one of close identification with the basic industry of agriculture and his death having occurred on his homestead farm in Sevier County in 1914, his widow still remaining with one of her sons on the old home place, which is endeared to her by the memories and associations of many years. Robert B. Hickam achieved independence and definite prosperity through his operations as a farmer and was a man of strong mentality and inviolable integrity, he having held the office of deacon in the Baptist Church for fifty-five years prior to his death, and his widow likewise having been for many years a devoted adherent of the same religious organization. He was a stanch supporter of the cause of the republican party, but never sought or held political office. His great-grandfather, Jacob Hickam, was a native of Ireland and came to America in the colonial days, as indicated by the fact that he was enrolled as a patriot soldier in the Continental line in the war of the Revolution. Richard Hickam, grandfather of Robert B., was born and reared in Virginia, became a prosperous planter in that state and attained to the remarkable age of one hundred and four years. The father of Robert B. Hickam was a gallant soldier in the Mexican war, and from the brief data here given it may well be seen that the history of the family in America has been one of interesting order, typifying loyal and worthy citizenship as one generation has followed another on to the stage of life's activities.

John P. Hickam was the fifth in order of birth in a family of eleven children, eight of whom are living, and he acquired his rudimentary education in North Carolina. As previously noted, he was eleven years of age at the time of the family removal to Sevier County, Tennessee, where he was reared to maturity under the invigorating discipline of the home farm and where he made good use of the advantages afforded in the public schools, as shown by the fact that when seventeen years of age he proved himself eligible for pedagogic honors, three years having been given by him to successful work as a teacher in the schools of Tennessee. Thereafter he completed a four years' course in Carson & Newman College, at Jefferson City, that state. He simultaneously gave careful attention to the study of law, under effective preceptorship, and in the spring of 1896 he was admitted to the Tennessee bar. In the following autumn he came to Oklahoma Territory, and he remained in Oklahoma City until the spring of 1897, when he established his permanent residence in Payne County. During the first four years he maintained his home in the Village of Perkins, where he was a teacher in the public schools, besides serving as assistant editor of the Perkins Journal, which had been established in 1889. Upon leaving Perkins he removed to Stillwater, the county seat, where he has since been engaged in the successful practice of his profession and where he has gained definite priority as one of the leading members of the bar of this section of the state. He served two terms as a member of the Territorial Senate, as noted in preceding paragraphs, and was elected on the republican ticket. During the entire period of his residence in Oklahoma Mr. Hickam has shown a lively interest in political affairs and he continued a prominent representative of the republican party in Payne County until the organization of the progressive party, in 1912, when he transferred his allegiance to the same and became one of its most influential exponents in Oklahoma, as shown by the fact that he became its candidate for representative of his district in the United States Congress in the national election of 1912, and in 1914 was the progressive candidate for governor of the state, adequate mention having already been made of his political activities.

In a fraternal way Mr. Hickam is a Master Mason, and both he and his wife are zealous members of the Baptist Church in their home city.

In 1899 was solemnized the marriage of Mr. Hickam to Miss Flavilla Duck, who was born in Iowa and who was a child at the time of her parents' removal to Payne County, Oklahoma, where she was reared to maturity and was afforded the advantages of the Oklahoma Agricultural & Mechanical College at Stillwater. She was thereafter a popular teacher in the schools of Payne County until the time of her marriage. Her father, John W. Duck, was a gallant soldier of the Union in the Civil war, in which he served as a member of an Iowa regiment. Mr. and Mrs. Hickam have three children— Elmer, Horace and Eunice.

WESLEY M. DIAL. Probably the most influential white man in the Osage country is Wesley M. Dial, owner and proprietor of the beautiful Mount Dial homestead north of Pawhuska. His father was an Oklahoma eighty-niner, and that brought Mr. Dial into contact with Oklahoma affairs when he was still a boy. Something over twenty years ago he was a plain cowboy in the Chickasaw Nation, and one of the early achievements which is mentioned to his credit was establishing a townsite and postoffice out in Payne County. His marriage about twenty years ago with an Osage woman brought him into tribal relations with that people, and it is said that he has enjoyed more of the confidence and distinctions of tribal honors and responsibilities than any other white man. For years he was employed as one of the principal agents in handling the vast wealth of the Osage tribes in the negotiations between the people and the General Government at Washington, and there has never been one of his acts which could be properly construed as reflecting upon his absolute integrity and honesty in all the aggregate of his relations as an intermediary between his people and the controlling Government.

The career of this most interesting citizen of Oklahoma began at Jasper, Newton County, Arkansas, August 14, 1871, when he was born to Samuel and Susan (Stallion) Dial. His father was born in Maysville, Kentucky, September 13, 1834, and his mother was born near Nashville, Tennessee, November 22, 1843. Both his father and mother had been previously married, and she had two sons and he had one son by their previous unions. The two sons of his mother were: Witt and John Penn, while his father's first son was Edward Dial who died in 1879. By their second union the parents had four sons and three daughters: Emma, now deceased; Clemmie Kirk, of Ripley, Oklahoma; Wesley M. Clayton, deceased; Samuel R., who lives in California; Arthur, of Foraker, Osage County; Mattie, wife of Jacob Martin of Yale, Oklahoma. The mother of these children died in Yellville, Arkansas, in 1907, and the father now resides with his son Wesley at Pawhuska.

Mr. Dial spent the first ten years of his life at Harrison, Arkansas, and his father, who was a farmer and stock man, then removed to Taney County, Missouri. In 1889 the family came into Oklahoma at the original opening, and secured a claim at Clayton in Payne County. Wesley M. Dial was then eighteen years of age. His regular schooling aggregated only four months in different district schools, and he has gained his education by self study and by practical experience with men and affairs. At the age of twenty-one he went to the vicinity of Denison, Texas, and was employed as a farm hand. In the spring of 1891 he went into the

western part of the Chickasaw Nation near Minco, and was soon riding herd as a cow puncher.

His first real experience as an Oklahoma City citizen came in September, 1893, at the opening of the Cherokee Strip, when he secured a farm near Glencoe in Payne County, and established a postoffice and store named West Point. In 1895 he sold out and removed to Northwestern Kansas and for a time was engaged in the hay business. Again coming into what is now the State of Oklahoma, he was married on September 7, 1897, in Osage County, to Eliza Penn, a widow with four children. These children are: Dora, wife of Sid Dalic of Osage County; Augustus M. of Arkansas City, Kansas; Rosa E., who lives with Mr. Dial; and Robert E., who died in 1901.

Mrs. Dial has tribal rights in the Osage country, and since his marriage Mr. Dial has always had his home in the vicinity of Pawhuska. He and his family have eighty acres adjoining the corporation limits on the north and another eighty acres on the east. His home, known throughout the county as Mount Dial, is located on the eighty acres north of the city. Mount Dial is situated on an elevation which is 1,000 feet above sea level and 185 feet above the grade of Main Street, and from the Dial home is secured one of the finest views of surrounding country to be found anywhere in the state. On the south is the City of Pawhuska, and on all other sides for a distance of seven miles or more the eye sweeps over a panorama of hills and valleys comprising a landscape such as is unusual even in Northeastern Oklahoma. Mr. Dial and his family control in the aggregate about 6,000 acres of land in Osage County. Since these lands were allotted in severalty, Mr. Dial has spent about $35,000 in improvements. One of the finest farms in Northeastern Oklahoma is 1,000 acres under the Dial ownership, cultivated to the full extent of its fertile soil, and situated near Foraker.

For a number of years Mr. Dial has been in the land business at Pawhuska and has long been considered an expert authority on land values. He is the first and only white man who has ever been elected by the tribal meeting of Osage citizens as an official representative to handle tribal matters relating to the oil and gas interests. Every one in Oklahoma and a great many people outside the state know how vastly important and valuable these interests are. Mr. Dial represented the tribal interests in that capacity several months and drew up a report which was submitted to the tribal council, and which in turn the council forwarded to the Secretary of the Interior at Washington. That report was the basis for the subsequent negotiations which have brought about the disposal of the oil and gas interests in the Osage territory. In 1905 Mr. Dial was also a delegate from the Osage people to Washington to defend claims being prosecuted against the Osage tribe to the sum of $230,000 by the heirs of Van and Adair, and he appeared in both the House and the Senate committees of Congress and largely through his arguments and effective testimony brought about the defeat of the claims. No other citizen with intermarried rights in the tribe has figured so conspicuously in tribal affairs. He also assisted in defending the Glenn oil lease before committees of Congress, and for the past fifteen years has made from one to two trips to Washington annually, appearing before the various committees of Congress on department matters. At the present time Mr. Dial is the business representative for the Uncle Sam Oil Company in Osage County, and this is one of the most responsible and most profitable business positions in the state.

In politics Mr. Dial is a republican, and has helped to make some interesting political history in Oklahoma. Under the Enabling Act of Congress providing for statehood he was appointed an election commissioner of Osage County. He established the voting places, appointed the election judges and clerks, canvassed the returns, and with that sturdy regard for public opinion which is characteristic of the man, when the returns showed a democratic majority, issued his proclamation of the result with a judicial impartiality which was in entire consonance with every other transaction by which he has been known to the people of the state. For several years he was a member of the State Republican Committee, and was president of the Oklahoma State Organization of Republican Clubs in 1908.

In Masonry Mr. Dial has taken thirty-two degrees in the Scottish Rite and has also taken the various degrees in the York Rite, and is a member of the Nobles of the Mystic Shrine, and is affiliated with the Benevolent and Protective Order of Elks. By his marriage to Mrs. Penn he has three children: Cora E., Eva and Charles P. The two daughters are now students in the Loretto Academy at Kansas City, Missouri.

Probably no man in Northeastern Oklahoma has handled larger financial sums and more important business transactions than Mr. Dial. He, was chiefly instrumental in securing a lease through the Osage Council for 230,000 acres of oil and gas lands. It should also be noted as a matter of history that he was one of the ten men who were tried in the Federal courts of Oklahoma City during the months of May and June, 1914, for conspiracy in an alleged attempt to defraud the Government in matters connected with the Osage oil and gas lands. While the trial and the argument of the case required many weeks, it required the jury only ten minutes to give him a complete acquittal and exoneration from all the charges of the indictment.

HENRY C. CHAPMAN. A veteran of the newspaper profession, and proprietor and editor of the Okeene Eagle, which he founded more than twenty years ago, Henry C. Chapman has lived a life of intensive activity and experience for more than half a century. He was a soldier in the Civil war on the Union side, gained admittance to the bar about the close of the war, spent many years with the metropolitan press in New York and other cities in the East, and for the last thirty-five years has lived in the western states and has been chiefly identified with the management and editorial direction of various newspapers.

The family to which he belongs came from England to Holyoke, Massachusetts, during Colonial times. His father, John S. Chapman, was born in Holyoke, Massachusetts, in 1812, started West as a youth and found a location in northern Indiana in LaPorte County, where he was a pioneer farmer, one who cleared out a portion of the wilderness and developed it for purposes of cultivation, and exercised his business ability in the buying and selling of extensive farm lands in that region. He died in LaPorte County in 1847. He was married there to Lucinda Atkins, who was born in Washington County, New York, in 1814, and died in LaPorte County in August, 1844. Henry C. Chapman was the older of their two children. His brother Francis M., who died in LaPorte County in 1881, built up an extensive business in the buying of scrap metal.

Born in LaPorte County, Indiana, September 6, 1842, H. C. Chapman knew little of his parents, since his mother died when he was two years old and his father when he was five. He was also reared in a pioneer district and among pioneer surroundings. He attended country schools in LaPorte County, but most of his education came from hard study directed only by his strong, intellectual curiosity and ambition to amount to something in the world. Many nights he lay before the open fireplace in northern Indiana and studied every good book he could get his hands upon. By diligent application he acquired a practical education, and at the age of seventeen emerged from a farm in the woods and spent one term in a village school at Laporte. Following that he was a farmer and taught school for two terms, but in 1862 answered the call of patriotism by enlisting in the Twenty-First Battery of Indiana Light Artillery. His service continued for nine months, and in the several engagements in which he participated he received severe injuries to shoulder and elbow and was mustered out and given an honorable discharge.

After returning from the war he continued teaching and reading law in Indiana, and in the law department of the University of Michigan gained his degree LL. B. with the class of 1865. He remained in Indiana until 1868 and then identified himself with the trade of newspaper man, which practically ever since has been his real career.

Going to New York City in 1872, he did reportorial work with practically all the great papers of the metropolis. He was under Horace Greeley on the Tribune, was also for a time in Orange County, New York, and reported for the New York Herald, the Times and the Sun, and was at one time a member of the staff working under the direction of the firm of Raymond & Bennett. After about eight years of metropolitan experience, he removed to Iowa in 1880, and in that state combined newspaper work and school teaching until 1890. From there he went to Nebraska, later to Kansas, and in Logan County of the latter state served as probate judge for four years, three months.

Mr. Chapman's identification with Oklahoma began in April, 1894, and in September of the same year he located at Okeene, where he was one of the pioneers. He started the Okeene Eagle, the first issue of which was on September 26, 1894. He remained in active charge of this newspaper until 1902, when he removed to Muskogee County, and was connected with the Council Hill Times and also edited the Boynton Eagle. Returning to Okeene in 1910, he bought back the Okeene Eagle, and has since been its proprietor and editor. The Eagle reflects the essential principles of the republican party for which Mr. Chapman has always stood, and it has a large circulation over Blaine and surrounding counties.

Mr. Chapman is a member of the Oklahoma State Press Association, and is affiliated with Excelsior Lodge No. 191, Ancient Free and Accepted Masons, back in his native district of Laporte, Indiana. On August 23, 1865, at West Brookville, New York, Mr. Chapman married Miss Augusta Collard. Her father, Henry Collard, was a farmer in Sullivan and Orange counties, New York. Mr. Chapman's son, Loran H., is a jeweler at Okeene. His daughter, Hattie J., is the wife of Dr. J. A. Norris, who established himself in 1896 as a pioneer physician at Okeene, but is now retired from active practice and assists Mr. Chapman in publishing the Okeene Eagle.

JAMES B. MURPHY, M. D. Stillwater, the judicial center of Payne County, is the place of residence of Doctor Murphy, who is consistently to be designated as one of the leading representatives of his profession in this part of the state, his high attainments, insistent loyalty and devotion to his exacting vocation, and his sterling attributes of character having not only proved potent in the furtherance of his professional success but having also given him inviolable place in popular confidence and esteem. He maintains his well appointed offices in the First National Bank Building, and his definite prestige is indicated by his incumbency of the positions here noted: Local surgeon for the Atchison, Topeka & Santa Fe Railroad; county superintendent of public health; city health officer; county physician; the vice president of the Atchison, Topeka & Santa Fe Hospital Association; and secretary and treasurer of the Payne County Medical Society.

At New Albany, the judicial center of Floyd County, Indiana, a place situated on the Ohio River a few miles below the City of Louisville, Kentucky, Dr. James B. Murphy was born on the 30th of November, 1856, and he is a scion of one of the honored pioneer families of that section of the fine old Hoosier commonwealth. The doctor is a son of John and Serrilda (Clipp) Murphy, and his father was born at Harper's Ferry, Virginia, in 1815; the mother of the doctor was born in Indiana in 1833.

John Murphy was reared and educated in his native place, which eventually became a town in the segregated State of West Virginia, and as a young man he came to Indiana, where he continued his residence in Floyd County until his death, at the age of sixty-nine years. For many years he followed the trade of carpenter, but the closing period of his active life was passed on his farm, he having been one of the prosperous agriculturists of Floyd County at the time of his death. Six sons were born of his first marriage—Hiram, who still resides in Indiana, and all the others died in that state. Hiram was a distinguished soldier of the Union during the entire period of the Civil war, in which he rose to the office of adjutant general of an Indiana regiment, his enlistment having occurred at the time of President Lincoln's first call for volunteers. Of the children of the second marriage—four sons and six daughters—Doctor Murphy is the only surviving son, and four of his sisters are living, one being a resident of Texas and the other three still maintaining their residence in Indiana.

Doctor Murphy left the parental home when he was a lad of fourteen years and through his own exertions he provided the means for gaining his higher academic education as well as that of professional order. For eight years he was a successful and popular teacher in the public schools of his native state, and in consonance with his ambitious purpose he was finally matriculated in the medical department of the University of Louisville, Kentucky, in which he was graduated as a member of the class of 1881 and from which he received his well earned degree of Medicine. In the same year was solemnized his marriage to Miss Anna K. Smith, likewise a native of Indiana, her father, George W. Smith, having been a well known citizen of Floyd County. In 1882 Doctor Murphy came to the West and established his residence at Milan, Sumner County, Kansas, where he continued in the work of his profession until 1889, when he went to the western part of that state, but in July of that year, 1889, he came to Oklahoma, about three months after the territory had been thrown open to settlement, and established his residence at Stillwater, where he is the pioneer physician and surgeon of Payne County, and where he has long controlled an extensive and representative general practice. His professional labors here were of most arduous order in the early years, when he was called upon to minister to families throughout a wide section of sparsely settled country, his zeal and unselfish devotion being such that he never hesitated to go forth on his work of succor, no matter what might be the adverse conditions of roads, weather, etc., or the dangers incidental to his lonely trips by night. Thus it is but natural that he hold the affectionate esteem of the many families to whom he has ministered with all of efficiency, kindliness and unselfishness during the years of a signally active professional career in the now vigorous young state of his adoption, and in the midst of the manifold cares and exactions of his large practice he has found time and opportunity to keep abreast of the advances made in medical and surgical science, so that he well merits his high reputation as one of the able and representative physicians and surgeons of Oklahoma.

Doctor Murphy has been loyal and progressive as a citizen, has shown a lively interest in all things touching the welfare of his home town and county, and has not denied his service in public offices having direct relation to his profession. He served as coroner of Payne County for ten years, has been county health officer since 1907, the year that marked the admission of Oklahoma to statehood; and he has been city health officer of Stillwater since 1911, besides which he has in a private way done all in his power to conserve sanitary improvements and to maintain the best possible conditions for the preserving of public health. The doctor was prominently concerned in the organization of the Payne County Medical Society, has served as president of the same and is at the present time its secretary and treasurer. He is identified also with the Oklahoma State Medical Society and the American Medical Association.

Doctor Murphy and his wife were among those who "made the run" at the opening to settlement of the now historic Cherokee Strip, and through their lively action on this occasion they fortified themselves for permanent residence in this section of the state, though their original run had Pawnee County as its objective point. In early days the doctor served as a member of the city council of Stillwater, and his loyal civic activities included also effective service as mayor and as city clerk. While the incumbent of the office of county coroner he was for a short time acting sheriff of the county, and he served as first assistant postmaster during the incumbency of Postmaster Robert A. Lowry, with whom he was associated also in conducting the first drug store at Stillwater, the doctor having been the first registered pharmacist in Payne County and still retaining his prerogatives along this line.

Doctor Murphy is a Knights Templar Mason, holds membership in the Benevolent and Protective Order of Elks, and has been actively affiliated with the Independent Order of Odd Fellows since his twenty-first birthday anniversary. He aided in the organization of the Oklahoma Grand Lodge of the Independent Order of Odd Fellows, and later was honored by being made a life member of the same, he having been specially active and influential in the affairs of this fraternal order.

Doctor and Mrs. Murphy became the parents of three children—May, who is the wife of George B. Gulder, of Stillwater, has two children, George B., Jr., and Katherine; Edward Palmer Murphy, who married Miss Edna Gilges, is identified with business enterprises at Stillwater; and Nellie Bly, the youngest of the children, died at the age of one year.

WILLIAM T. KEYS. Eligibility of definite order and marked personal popularity were the contributing causes that led to the election of Mr. Keys to the office of county clerk of Payne County, and he assumed the administration of the multifarious and responsible duties of this position on the 1st of January, 1915, his first year of service having clearly demonstrated the wisdom shown by the voters of the county in selecting him as the incumbent of one of the most important executive officers of the local government.

Mr. Keys was born in the City of Pittsburgh, Pennsylvania, on the 2d of October, 1873, and is a son of Hugh and Lida (West) Keys, both likewise natives of the old Keystone State, where the mother died when the subject of this review was a child of three years. About the year 1880 Hugh Keys removed with his family to Edgar County, Illinois, where he continued in the practice of his profession, that of dentist, until the time of his death, in 1889, William T., the youngest of his children, having been a lad of about sixteen years when thus doubly orphaned. All of the six children were sons and of the number the subject of this review, the youngest, is now the only survivor.

Upon the removal of his father to Illinois, William T. Keys, because of the death of his mother, was there received into the home of one of his uncles, with whom he remained two years. He was then sent to the home of another uncle, in Linn County, Missouri, where he lived under these conditions until he had attained to the age of thirteen years, when he became dependent upon his own resources. In the meanwhile he had duly availed himself of the advantages of the public schools of Illinois and Missouri, but his broader education has been that gained under the direction of that wisest of all headmasters, experience.

Mr. Keys continued his residence in Missouri until the spring of 1890, when, at the age of seventeen years, he came to the new Territory of Oklahoma, which was organized in that year, and established his residence in Payne County. Here he was employed by the month at farm work until 1896, when he wedded Miss Ella Grindstaff, who was born in Missouri and whose parents, Alexander and Elizabeth (James) Grindstaff, came to Oklahoma in 1891 and became pioneer settlers of Payne County, where they passed the remainder of their lives and where both died in the early part of the present decade. After his marriage Mr. Keys engaged in farming in an independent way, near the Town of Cushing. He rented land for a period of about six years and then purchased a tract of eighty acres, which he later traded for a farm of 160 acres four miles east of Stillwater. He made excellent improvements on this property and developed the same into one of the valuable farms of Payne County. He still owns this homestead, where he continued his residence until his election to the office of county clerk, when he removed with his family to Stillwater, the county seat, where he now gives his entire time and attention to his official duties, of which he is giving a most efficient and acceptable administration. Mr. Keys is found aligned as one of Payne County's stanch and active supporters of the cause of the democratic party, and he has been influential in its councils and activities in this county. He and his wife are held in high esteem in the community that has long represented their home, and they have two children—Ona and Chester.

N. H. HIGH. The life of N. H. High, ex-deputy United States marshal, and now a farmer of Payne County, has been one in which he has passed through experiences of a thrilling character, from the days of the last great buffalo hunt on the plains to the more recent excitement of the opening of the various Indian reservations. It has been his privilege to have participated personally in bringing civilization to Oklahoma, and his energetic, courageous and faithful service as a government official during the early days had its part in changing the old spirit of lawlessness into a condition in which the industries and institutions of modern life have thrived and prospered.

Mr. High was born at Madison, Wisconsin, December 17, 1855, a son of James H. and Margaret Ann (Stuart) High, the former a native of Seneca Flats, Seneca County, New York, and the latter of Cork, Ireland. The mother was two years of age when brought by her parents to the

United States, and was reared in New York, where she was married to George R. Ford, with whom she went to St. Louis, Missouri, and later to Illinois. In that state Mr. Ford died, leaving his widow with four sons. James H. High was a young man when he went to the West, settling in Illinois, where, as a contemporary of Abraham Lincoln, he was a riverman on the Mississippi. Later he engaged in railroading in that state, being engaged in construction work, and while thus employed met Mrs. Ford at Davenport, Iowa. They were married and subsequently went to Wisconsin, where Mr. High engaged in the lumber business, and in 1857 went to Michigan, where both parents died, the father at Ovid and the mother at Grass Lake. They were the parents of two sons: N. H. and Hiram, the latter of whom is deceased.

N. H. High resided in Michigan with his parents until he was eleven years of age, at which time he joined his grandfather, Nathan H. High, who had settled on a farm in Montgomery County, Kansas, and who later died in Michigan. Mr. High remained with his grandfather for eight years, teaching school during the winter terms and working as a farmer during the summer months, but in 1881 went to Michigan, where he was married on October 17th of that year to Miss Alice Perkins, who was born at Ovid, Michigan, October 26, 1864, a daughter of Josiah and Eunice (Tower) Perkins. Mr. Perkins, a native of New York, died in Oklahoma, while Mrs. Perkins, a native of Michigan, passed away in New Mexico. After his marriage Mr. High went to New Mexico, where he entered upon a railroad career that covered a period of fourteen years, the greater part of this time having been passed in construction work. He had had previous experience in the West, when, in the winter of 1872-3, he joined a party of fourteen hunters and went to Western Kansas and Colorado, participating in the last great hunt that practically exterminated the great American bison. During this trip the men traveled and slept in covered wagons and grazed their horses, the accepted method of living on the plains. It was about this time also, that Mr. High saw the great Indian chief Geronimo, who was then on the warpath.

After about four years in New Mexico, during which time he had charge of the construction material for the work on the Santa Fe, Mr. High returned to Kansas and engaged in farming for a short time. He later went back to New Mexico, however, and remained there until the opening of the Sac and Fox Indian reservation, when he was appointed a United States deputy marshal and as such came to Oklahoma. At the same time, in company with Fred Curtley, he established a store on Euchre Creek, under the name of Curtley & Company, and engaged in this business for six years. Later he was for eight years a merchant at Cushing. During the time Mr. High was in the Government service, he was present at the opening of the Kickapoo, Cheyenne and Arapaho country, and at one time was the only deputy marshal allowed therein. At the opening here he had the north one-half of the reservation and his service was crowded with thrilling experiences in which his courage was tested to the utmost and not found wanting. When he came he had secured a claim and obtained a deed to a tract on Big Creek, six miles west of Cushing, but disposed of his interest therein. For one and one-half years Mr. High was also engaged in the transfer business with his son-in-law, but since selling his share therein has devoted his energies to the cultivation of his forty-acre farm which adjoins the corporation on the northwest. At the time he sold his claim on Big Creek, Mr. High went to Guthrie, where he spent six years, and during that time was a member of the police department and also contracted for excavation work. He is a republican in political matters and has served as a delegate to numerous conventions. Fraternally he is connected with the Masons, the Independent Order of Odd Fellows and the Knights of Pythias, and is the oldest member in point of membership in Oklahoma of the Ancient Order of United Workmen.

Mr. and Mrs. High have been the parents of eight children, as follows: James L., born in New Mexico, now a successful merchant of Cushing; LeRoy Marion, born in Kansas, a merchant at Stroud, Oklahoma; Alie Lew, born in New Mexico; Ena Belle, born in Kansas, who died at the age of nineteen years; Jessie May, born in Oklahoma, who died at the age of nineteen months; Charles Leslie, born in Oklahoma, who resides with his parents at Cushing; Fred Lloyd, born in Oklahoma, who died in infancy; and Margaret Ann, born in Oklahoma, who lives at home.

WILLIAM J. BROCKMAN. A representative of the class of men who are maintaining the high standards of stock-raising in Payne County is found in the person of William J. Brockman, of Yale, who has been a progressive and energetic breeder of stock since his arrival here in 1890. During his quarter of a century of residence here he has seen the marvelous development of the community and the replacing of pioneer conditions by civilization. Mr. Brockman is an Illinoisan by nativity, and was born at Hillsboro, Montgomery County, August 25, 1849, a son of Samuel and Charlotta (Brown) Brockman.

The parents of Mr. Brockman were born in Adair County, Kentucky, and there married, and migrated to Illinois in early days with the eldest of their children, a baby boy, John, who died in the winter of 1914 at the age of eighty-six years. The parents settled in Montgomery County and there passed the remainder of their lives on a farm, the mother dying in 1861 at the age of sixty-five years, and the father surviving until 1885, when he passed away at the age of eighty-five years. They were the parents of the following children: John, Walter, Boone, Hiram and Mrs. Betsy Armstrong, all of whom are deceased; Mrs. Artemesia Joice, who lives on the old homestead place in Montgomery County, Illinois; and William J. The parents of these children were honest, God-fearing people, who worked industriously to make a home and who reared their children to lives of integrity and useful endeavor.

William J. Brockman was brought up amid pioneer surroundings and practically his entire career has been passed in advance of the rush of civilization. His boyhood was filled with the hard work of cultivating a prairie farm and reclaiming the land from the wilderness, but it was the type of existence that builds sturdy bodies and inures their owners to conditions which may be found anywhere on the frontier. He well remembers seeing deer in large numbers around his Illinois home, while the wild geese and ducks were so numerous that it was necessary to keep a constant lookout for them to prevent them from destroying the growing grain in the fields. Mr. Brockman's education came from the district schools of his home vicinity, where he resided and engaged in farming until the death of his father, in 1885 in which year he went West to Lane County, Kansas, and took up a claim. While there he followed the pursuits of stock-raising and farming, and also found time for public service, acting as turnkey and deputy sheriff positions which he had held in Illinois, for eight years, and finally being elected sheriff of Lane County for two terms, being the only democrat elected to county office there up to that time. In 1890 he disposed of his Kansas holdings and came to Indian Territory, locating first at Stillwater and subsequently buying a farm in Payne County, where he has since continued to be inter

ested extensively in the stock business, now leasing 1,000 acres of land. On September 16, 1893, when the Cherokee Strip was opened for white settlement he made the race for land and secured a valuable piece of property at Pawnee, which he still owns. He also made the run at the opening of the Cheyenne and Arapaho country and the Sac and Fox reservation, but not with an equal measure of success. In the Indian Territory Mr. Brockman's former experience, gained in Illinois and Kansas, stood him in good stead and he was able to compete with conditions in a much more successful way than could many who had not had his advantages. He was a witness to much of the lawlessness which swept over this part of the country, was personally acquainted with several of the bad men of his district, and was an eye-witness to the shooting of three United States marshals at Ingalls. At one time he made the race for sheriff of Payne County, on the democratic ticket, but although he ran 285 votes ahead of his party, met with defeat. In 1902 Mr. Brockman came to Yale, which at that time was a hamlet with but one house. He has contributed to the upbuilding of this flourishing community by the erection of several structures, including the two fine business places which he built in 1915 to replace the two, valued at $10,000, which he lost by fire in April of that year. In the same year he erected a handsome residence at Yale. He is a Master Mason and a member of the Independent Order of Odd Fellows, the Knights of Pythias and the Woodmen of the World. As a citizen he has discharged every obligation which has devolved upon him, and in commercial circles his reputation is that of a man of the strictest integrity.

On February 25, 1873, Mr. Brockman was married to Miss Susan C. Blackburn, who was born in Montgomery County, Illinois, October 22, 1847, daughter of George Blackburn, and to this union there have been born three children: Arthur, of Raton, New Mexico; Oscar, who is employed on a ranch in Payne County, Oklahoma; and Versa, who is the wife of S. W. Binnie, a resident of Kiowa, Kansas.

JOHN R. SPURRIER. A special distinction that belongs to John R. Spurrier of Big Heart, Osage County, is that he is one of the native sons of the original Oklahoma Territory, being one of the few men now active in affairs who were born after the first land opening in 1889. Mr. Spurrier has had an active and successful business career in various localities and states and is now engaged in handling a large ranch at Big Heart. Mrs. Spurrier, his wife, is a daughter of the noted Chief Bigheart, of the Osage tribe.

The birth of John R. Spurrier occurred on a homestead ten miles from Oklahoma City June 30, 1891. His parents were John and Louise (James) Spurrier. His father was born in Virginia July 27, 1857. His mother was born in Millville, Arkansas, in 1870, and spent the first nineteen years of her life in her native state. The father resided in Virginia until the age of fifteen, then moved to Missouri, and for a time was engaged in teaching school. After his marriage in Arkansas he went west to Wyoming, and for a number of years was foreman of a lumber company, and spent all his active life as a lumberman, cattle man and farmer. He was one of the original settlers in Oklahoma in 1889, and for about seven years conducted a large ranch as a stock farmer near Oklahoma City. He and his wife are still living in Oklahoma and are the parents of three children: John R.; Smead, who is proprietor of a garage and machine shop at Millville, Arkansas; and Guy, living at home.

The independent career of John R. Spurrier may be said to have begun when he was only twelve years of age. In the meantime he had attended the local schools in Oklahoma City and at that early age left home and assisted Wess Hilton in taking a great herd of some 2,800 head of cattle from Wyoming to Buenos Ayres in South America. After his return from this long voyage he was employed in a garage in Denver, Colorado, and for several years was engaged in making extended trips in automobiles. For two years he was a special detective in the employ of the Denver & Rio Grande Railroad and for two years after coming to Pawhuska was in the secret service. Since his marriage he has been engaged in ranching and is now owner of 640 acres in his home place and has several hundred acres under lease. Mr. Spurrier has recently completed the finest ranch home in his section of Osage County, it being located on his ranch close to Big Heart.

In December, 1914, he married Sarah L. Bigheart, who was born on the old Big Heart homestead in Osage County August 20, 1898. Her father, the late Chief James Bigheart of the Osage tribe, died in 1908 when about eighty-seven years of age. All his life had been spent among the Osage tribe and he was one of its most distinguished members, and held high rank not only as a business man but as a wise statesman in tribal affairs. Prior to the allotment of the Indian lands he had several thousand acres under fence, and at the allotment received the same share as other members of the tribe. For many years one of the most notable ranches in Osage County is that known as the Big Heart Ranch, and the Town of Big Heart was named for this notable Indian. In a business way he was identified with several banks in his part of the state and had merchandise store interests. About 1885 Chief Bigheart married Alice Butler, who was born in the Cherokee Nation and was a seven-eighths Cherokee in blood. She is now living on the Big Heart homestead. Chief Bigheart and his wife had seven children: Mary, wife of Thomas Clendenning of Broken Arrow; Louis, deceased; Rose Lee, wife of Sherman Deal of Pawhuska; William, deceased; Josephine, deceased; Mrs. Spurrier; and Belle, at home with her mother. By a previous marriage Chief Bigheart had one child, Maggie Oberlee, now deceased. The story of Chief Bigheart's marriage reveals an interesting Indian romance. Having found the young woman of his choice, he made the usual arrangements for the marriage with the girl's mother and in the marriage settlement gave a wagon, a team, an old cow and two pigs. However, the Cherokee people objected to his taking away the Indian maiden, and after he was well started on his way with his bride to the Osage country the Cherokees assembled and started after the runaways with guns and determined to restore the bride to her people. Chief Bigheart barely succeeded in crossing the Osage line with his wife in time to escape his pursuers. Once among his own people he was safe, since the Osages were as ready to defend him as the Cherokees were to attack him. In contrast with this experience of his wife's parents, Mr. Spurrier took his bride to their new home in an automobile, over roads that were made almost impassable by heavy rains. Their interesting romance and marriage occurred while Mr. Spurrier was in the secret service, stationed at Big Heart, and engaged in driving a car. There he met the little Indian princess, Miss Lillian Bigheart, now his wife, Mrs. John R. Spurrier, and then their romance started. As several months had passed they decided not to leave each other as long as the grass grew and the water run, and then they began to plan their long journey across the Osage hills and canyons to Pawnee to get married. They had planned this trip to Pawnee several times but something would prevail until finally one afternoon in December they had planned to start for Pawnee their third time and about 5 p. m. they were off, Mr. Spurrier running his automobile as fast as the roads and car would permit. About half way from Big Heart to Pawnee it began raining and sleeting. Everything seemed against this young couple, but in their hearts they were determined to reach Pawnee before morning. They got lost off of the roads and as all of the ranchers and cowboys had retired it was difficult to arouse them at that late hour by holloing, so Mr. Spurrier used his .45 six-shooter to warn them that there was some one at the road wanting them. They would respond immediately to the reports of his .45 and then would direct him the road to Pawnee which they finally reached at a late hour that night. They were married and back to Big Heart at 5 p. m. the following morning, the car being covered with ice and snow. The little Indian bride got out of the car to go to one of her friends, where she was to spend that night. She bid her squaw man (Mr. Spurrier) good night, and upon arriving at a livery stable, where Mr. Spurrier kept his car he was frozen to the steering wheel of his machine and had to have the assistance of the livery stable man to help him from his car, and it was three weeks before he could hardly use his hands and feet, but he is now enjoying the life of a squaw man and rancher on their magnificent estate near Big Heart, Oklahoma. A daughter, Alice Floreine, was born to Mr. and Mrs. Spurrier on the 8th of September, 1915.

HENRY C. DALE. A recent addition to the citizenship of Yale, Oklahoma, Henry C. Dale was formerly for many years a resident of Kansas, where he was well known in public and business affairs. He was born in Jasper County, Missouri, April 6, 1848, and is a son of Robert J. and Olive (Cox) Dale. The Dale family in America traces its ancestry back to Sir Thomas Dale, the first governor of Virginia.

The great-grandfather of Henry C. Dale, Rev. George Dale, was a Missionary Baptist preacher who passed his entire life in Virginia, and who is remembered chiefly for his large physique, he weighing in the neighborhood of 400 pounds. His son, Elijah Dale, was born in 1794, in Virginia, and as a young man fought in the American army during the War of 1812-14. He was captured by the Indians at the battle of Tippecanoe, November 7, 1811, but after being made to run the gauntlet was exchanged for two blankets and four pounds of beads. Subsequently he moved to Kentucky, and was there married to Frances Shelton, with whom he moved to Boone County, Missouri, and later to Moniteau County in that state, where he died at the age of seventy-four years, Mrs. Dale surviving him for some time and passing away in Jasper County, aged eighty-eight years. They were the parents of the following children: Alfred, Robert J., James M., Pheldin, Meadley, Mrs. Malinda Griffith, Mrs. Mary Sunday and Mrs. Rebecca Martin.

Robert J. Dale, father of Henry C. Dale, was born in Kentucky in 1820, and in 1838 located with his parents in Jasper County, Missouri, where he was married to Oliver Cox, who was born in 1822 in Tennessee and had come to Missouri about the same time as her husband. With the exception of seven years, from 1863 until 1870, when they lived in Moniteau County, they passed the remaining years of their lives in Jasper County, and both died at Carthage, the father when ninety years of age and the mother aged about eighty. He was a farmer, trader and stock dealer, was clerk in the Baptist Church for many years, and in politics was a stanch democrat. They were the parents of two sons and five daughters: George F., of Moniteau County, Missouri; Mary M. Hughes, deceased; Henry C.; Ann F. Wise, of Carthage, Missouri; Permelia B. Howard, of Cooper County, Missouri; Martha J. Johnson, of Carl Junction, Jasper County, Missouri; and Canada Hind, deceased.

Henry C. Dale received his early education in the public schools of Missouri and resided on the home farm with his parents until twenty-three years of age. At that time he further prepared himself by attending school for six months, and for six years thereafter was engaged in teaching in the country schools. He next followed farming for sixteen years, and then took up mining at Galena, Cherokee County, Kansas, but after several years gave up that occupation to engage in the real estate business, which he followed two years. He became the owner of a valuable farming property, which he later sold, and was one of the substantial and highly respected citizens of his community. He was elected justice of the peace of Galena, Kansas, and served in that capacity for twelve years, resigning when he had twenty-two months to serve. On February 14, 1915, he came to Yale, Oklahoma, where he has since been assisting his son, Oliver C. Dale, in his extensive and important business operations. Mr. Dale has been a lifelong democrat, and his religious faith is that of the Missionary Baptist Church.

On December 11, 1870, Mr. Dale was married to Miss Emma J. Barker, who was born November 19, 1851, in Moniteau County, Missouri, daughter of Charles L. and Delilah (Eads) Barker. To this union there were born eight children, as follows: Oliver C., mayor of Yale, and one of the leading business men and oil producers of this part of the state, a sketch of whose remarkable career appears elsewhere in this work; Charley, who resides at Galena, Kansas; Arthur, who is deceased; Maggie Lewman, who is deceased; Canzada Jarrett, also deceased; Henry Clay, principal of the high school at Columbus, Kansas; Gordon, who is manager of the O. C. Dale department store, at Yale; and Willa Anna Pettit, of Yale.

MILTON THOMPSON. When it is said that Milton Thompson is the largest property owner and tax payer in that rich and populous County of Payne, it is evident that he has not lived his forty years since birth without a great deal of practical accomplishment and successful enterprise. In Payne County his name is synonymous with push and vigor, and few men in the state started with less and have gained more in the course of a comparatively brief space of time. When he was eighteen years of age he left home with only $85.00 as his capital. He came as a pioneer to the Sac and Fox Indian reservation in Oklahoma, and has long been identified with farming, cattle raising, with merchandising, and more recently with the oil and gas development in the Cushing field. It is noteworthy that Mr. Thompson has had few partners during his business career. He himself says that his one best partner and chief assistant both at home and in business has been his wife.

Representing a family of Kansas pioneers, Milton Thompson was born at Atchison, April 6, 1876, a son of Marion and Nancy (Southridge) Thompson. His father was born near Chicago, Illinois, and his mother at St. Joseph, Missouri, but they were brought as children by their respective parents to Atchison, Kansas, at the time Kansas Territory was opened for settlement early in the decade of the '50s. The parents were married at Atchison and the mother died there twenty-eight years ago. Marion Thompson came to Oklahoma a year after the opening of the Sac and Fox reservation, has been a farmer and stock man, and for the past twenty years has lived at Avery. He made a record as Union soldier during the Civil war, serving in the

Fourteenth Kansas, and was out for more than four years.

The sixth son in a family of nine boys and one girl, Milton Thompson has lived in close touch with practical affairs since early boyhood. After getting into independent work for himself, he supplemented the few advantages which he had received in the common schools as a boy, by a course in the business college at Shawnee, Oklahoma, where he was graduated in 1896. He was with his father in the cattle business up to the age of twenty-one, and has since been working independently. Up to 1905 his home was in the vicinity of Avery, and for the past ten years he has been in Cushing. He still has ranching and cattle interests, but has also carried on merchandising at Cushing for a number of years, and still has two stores, one carrying a general stock and the other an exclusive shoe store, but no longer gives his personal supervision to either of these enterprises. In 1913 Mr. Thompson organized the Oklahoma State Bank at Cushing, and was its president until he sold his stock on January 1, 1915.

As soon as Cushing came into prominence as a center of the oil and gas business, Mr. Thompson was identified with the movement, beginning in March, 1912. He has handled many leases and is individual owner of much land which has produced both oil and gas. It is now his unique distinction to be the owner of the largest rock pressure gas well in the world, known as Thompson Well No. 1, situated two miles east and two miles north of Cushing. The gas from this well is sold to one of the pipe line companies, and brings in a revenue of four thousand dollars a month. Mr. Thompson owns fifteen different farms in and about Cushing and in Payne County, and also has a large acreage under lease. In 1913 he built the Thompson Hotel, a modern 100-room hotel at the corner of Cleveland and Broadway in Cushing, and the first up to date house of public entertainment in the growing young city. For some time he was president of the First National Bank of Terlton, Oklahoma, but resigned that office when the institution was changed to a state bank.

Mr. Thompson's comfortable ten-room house in Cushing, where he and his wife reside, was originally the principal building improvement on a tract of fifty acres, which has since been laid out as the Thompson & Highland Addition, and this part of the city is now well built up with homes. Politically Mr. Thompson is a democrat, though only a voter and in no sense a politician. He is affiliated with the local lodge of Masons, with the Scottish Rite Consistory at Guthrie and the Temple of the Mystic Shrine at Oklahoma City.

On May 2, 1898, Mr. Thompson married Miss Maude Ickes. She was born in West Virginia, but was reared in Kansas, a daughter of J. M. and Elizabeth A. (Smith) Ickes. Her mother is now living at Wellington, Kansas. Her father, who died in the Thompson home at Cushing, April 20, 1912, was a Methodist Episcopal preacher and spent four years as a soldier in the Twenty-second Ohio Regiment during the Civil war. Mrs. Thompson is an active worker in the Methodist Episcopal Church. She has like her husband been identified with Oklahoma for many years, and finished her education in the State Normal at Edmond. She was one of the first school teachers in Lincoln County, and her first school was held in a log building without a floor. She possesses almost unique ability as a business woman, and Mr. Thompson gives her full credit for his great success in business affairs. She was his bookkeeper in the stores as long as he gave his personal supervision to that branch of his business.

FREEMAN E. MILLER. Fortunate it is for the weary and workaday world that there are those whose lives are attuned to deep human sympathy and appreciation, who find time and opportunity to touch upon and glorify the common things of life, who in realm of fancy and gracious ideality of thought come near to the castles of their dreams and who trail the beatitudes in their train. Such a man is Prof. Freeman E. Miller, who is a native of Indiana and worthy to be classed among the foremost in the galaxy of Hoosier stars in the literary firmament. His dreams have crystallized into deeds of kindness and into inspiring thoughts and sentiments that have offered lesson and incentive to all who have read or heard. Professor Miller has played a large part in bringing the manifold attractions and advantages of Oklahoma before the reading and thinking people of the Union, and his reputation as a poet, author, editor, lawyer, legislator and educator has far transcended local limitations. He has been consistently designated the poet laureate of Oklahoma, and he is now the incumbent of the chair of English in the Oklahoma Agricultural and Mechanical College, at Stillwater, Payne County, a position which he had previously filled when the institution was in the initial stage of its development. Oklahoma shall ever owe much to Professor Miller, and this publication can not be consistent with itself if there is failure to pay to him a measure of appreciative tribute. So admirable is the estimate written by C. M. Sarchet and published in Daily Oklahoman of Sunday, August 29, 1915, that it is a pleasing privilege to incorporate at this juncture certain quotations from the article, though minor paraphrase and certain elimination must necessarily be indulged in the reproduction:

"Freeman E. Miller, of Stillwater, Oklahoma's poet laureate, criminal lawyer and newspaper man, has been showing up the bright side of life and of things in general to the people of Oklahoma for so many years that his writings are proving to be a prolonged 'journey in contentment' for the many who have followed him—and that means thousands. For the man or woman who reads Miller's 'Oklahoma Sunshine,' which has been appearing in the Daily Oklahoman for the past ten years, his daily little sermons, cotton-patch philosophy, sayings by the way, and from the short-grass country, can not help be benefitted. They put a song in the heart of men, lighten the labors, brighten the daily life and keep dull care far in the background. Miller is constantly directing his pen that others may be happier. He preaches individual effort as the best method of dispelling sorrow and dissatisfaction—declaring that the man who is busy at honest labor is the happiest man of the human race. 'When a man whistles at his work,' writes Miller, 'the angels come down to boss the job.' And again he writes: 'Dis ole worl' am all de time ehtuhning debright side up, so break up dem dahrk specs on youah eyes an' grab a hoe.' and another time— 'there may be more devotion in tears than in laughter, but I'll tie up with the latter and take the risk.'

"Miller is a Hoosier by birth; perhaps that's one of the main reasons that he is a poet. He came to Oklahoma when President Harrison, also a Hoosier, issued the proclamation that opened this country to white settlement, in 1889, and he located in Stillwater. He was a newspaper man, owned and edited a weekly paper, and he has returned to the pastepot and shears several times since. He has always found it difficult, although a successful criminal lawyer, to keep away from a newspaper office, and his friends are never surprised when he breaks over the traces again.

"There are numerous sweet singers developing throughout Oklahoma, but the newspaper men have always liked Miller, not only because he is one of them but also because he has a way of saying things that appeals to the average reader. There is no parent that can not appreciate his 'Santa Claus Boy.'

"It was as editor of a country weekly that Miller first won fame throughout the Southwest as a poet, when Oklahoma was still young. His paper always contained some verses by the editor, but his distinction as Oklahoma's poet laureate was when he composed the poem read when the Oklahoma building at the St. Louis exposition was dedicated. That was 'Oklahoma.' In his Stillwater Advance and later in his Stillwater Progress there appeared 'The Opening of Oklahoma,' 'The Ballad of the Alamo,' 'The Plaint of the Tenderfoot,' 'The Faith Cure,' and other poems. When statehood came he was ready with 'The Birth of the State,' and when the constitutional convention assembled in Guthrie, late in 1906, it was opened by the clerk's reading of Miller's poem, 'The Builders':

"'Oh Builders, called forth of the people!
Not only for us is your toil!
For tribes that shall follow through shadows the paths of the stars and the soil,
Through seed-time and harvest forever, whatever ye fashion or frame
Shall live till the land is legend and time is a meaningless name!'

"Things that happen in Oklahoma and that are told about in the news columns of the papers, the current events, are promptly made use of by Miller. When a Territory election was over, a number of years ago, and the democrats were overwhelmingly defeated in Oklahoma and also in the nation at large—Miller is a democrat—he comforted his party comrades with a resignation that caused the verses to be the most widely copied of all of his productions up to that time. All of his verses have been free-will offerings. They appeared originally in his paper, 'without money and without price,' but they increased the paper's circulation just the same. And for ten years past they have been appearing regularly in the Sunday issues of the Daily Oklahoman, ever carrying their sermon of contentment:

"'Needn't talk to me of sorrow,
Needn't tell of Sorrow Town,
For the blossoms heap the highways
Till they hold the brambles down.'

"He preached contentment and happiness in his 'Birth of the State,' outlining that the state that is wealthy is not the best unless the character of its men and women is high and its people are happy:

"'Glory and peace and power, but greater than all of these
Is the smile of a happy people and the laugh of a land at ease,
And the states that are rich and mighty are poor and helpless yet,
If the lips of its men are ashen and the eyes of its women wet!'

"'So fashion the state in glory, but build it wise and good,
And build it strong for the weak ones and rich for the peasant's brood;
And fashion it all with justice, till the joys of the people's mirth
Shall conquer the ancient sorrows and gladden the sad of earth.'

"For a long time Miller has had his weekly grist of 'little sermons' for the readers, and they contain many good, pithy sayings:

"' 'No one except Christ ever called the devil Satan to his face; and then they went up into a high mountain and into a private place where no one else could hear the muss.'

"' 'All that Joy asks is a place to eat and sleep and fairly good company; but when you bring Old Trouble into the kitchen and go to introducing him to the family, right then Joy tells you goodbye.'

"It is necessary in treating of Miller to give him due credit for being the first member of an Oklahoma Legislature to introduce a 'Jim Crow' or separate-coach law. Many have claimed this distinction, but to Miller it belongs. He represented his County of Payne in the old Oklahoma Territorial senate on several occasions, and in 1901, six years prior to statehood, he fathered a bill that sought to compel all railroads in the territory to furnish separate coaches for negroes. Later his idea was enacted into a statute of the state. Miller has always been a prominent figure in politics, but never a partisan. An Indiana democrat, he has frequently returned to his native state to campaign it for his party's nominees, and he has been on the ticket in Oklahoma on several occasions. He was twice the nominee for district judge, but on both occasions in a district that was decidedly republican in its voting.

"'In the near future the people of Oklahoma are to see Freeman E. Miller in a new role to many of them but an old role to the first-day people of old Oklahoma Territory—that of instructor in English in the Oklahoma Agricultural and Mechanical College, at Stillwater. He held the chair of English when that institution was first opened, in the early '90s, but later retired to go back to newspaper work. Now, after many years, he is to return and be in charge of the English department. It was a deserved honor and his selection will give a distinction to the school. If the young men who attend the college will get close to Miller, and it will not be the fault if they do not, they will find him a fine, entertaining gentleman, an ever-ready friend; and if they will heed his sermons in contentment they will find life pathways have been smoothed down in their journeying to 'Happy Town':

"' 'Folks are always apt and able all their hearts' desires to crown,
If they journey to the sunrise at the gates of Happy Town.
They are always finding blossoms in the glories of the dew,
That will crown their dearest longings and their royal robes renew.' "

It may be further stated at this juncture that Professor Miller's ode entitled "Oklahoma" was read on Oklahoma Day, July 19, 1915, at the Oklahoma Building, Panama-Pacific International Exposition, San Francisco, California, and that the beautiful and appreciative poem is reproduced in full on other pages of this publication.

Freeman E. Miller was born in Fountain County, Indiana, on the 19th of May, 1864, and is a son of Louis W. and Amanda (Rynearson) Miller, both likewise natives of Fountain County and representatives of honored pioneer families of that section of the Hoosier State. The father, now of patriarchal age, still resides on his old homestead farm, and there the devoted wife and mother was summoned to the life eternal on the 9th of October, 1911, at the age of seventy years, the subject of this review being the only child. The boyhood days of Professor Miller were compassed by the benignant influences and discipline of the home farm, and he continued to look upon the parental domicile as the place of ultimate refuge and content until the time his marriage, though he passed but irregular intervals at home after he had attained to the age of sixteen years. He acquired his preliminary education in the public schools of his native state and supplemented this by a full classical course in DePauw University, at Greencastle, Indiana, in which institution he was graduated as a member of the class of 1887 and from which he received his degree of Bachelor of Arts, his alma mater conferring upon him in 1890 the degree of Master of Arts. He defrayed the major part of the expenses of his collegiate course through his service as a teacher in the district schools.

In the year of his graduation in DePauw University, Professor Miller, then a young man of twenty-three years, made his way to the Panhandle of Texas, and when Oklahoma Territory was thrown open to settlement he was one of the ambitious young men who cast in his lot with this new country. In 1890 he established his residence at Stillwater, now the thriving judicial center of Payne County, and here he engaged in the practice of law, his preparation for this profession having been compassed while he was still in his native state, and his admission to the Indiana bar having been granted in 1886. He became one of the pioneer lawyers of Payne County and also a pioneer in the local newspaper field. He had practiced law in Indiana, where he had also been editor and publisher of a weekly paper at Veedersburg, one of the principal towns of his native county.

In 1894 the versatile young lawyer and journalist was elected to the chair of English in the newly established Oklahoma Agricultural and Mechanical College, and he retained this incumbency until 1898, his service having been most effective during this formative period in the history of the college. Upon resigning his position as a member of the faculty of the college he resumed the practice of law, and in time he gained special prestige as one of the able and resourceful criminal lawyers of the territory. In 1900 he was elected representative of his district in the council or senate of the Territorial Legislature, and in 1902 he was a candidate for re-election, but was defeated by a small majority. In 1905 he became editor and publisher of the Stillwater Advance-Democrat, and in the following year he assumed the editorial charge of the Stillwater People's Progress, each of these weekly papers having gained high standing in the Oklahoma field of journalism under his administration. In 1910 Professor Miller was the democratic candidate for the office of judge of the District Court, but was unable to overcome the large and normal republican majority in the district. In 1915 he was again elected to the chair of English in the Oklahoma Agricultural and Mechanical College, and he has entered upon his service in this capacity with characteristic earnestness and enthusiasm, with matured powers and with specially high reputation in the domain of literature, so that the institution gains to its faculty a most valuable member and one whose benignant influence can not but be far reaching. He is by nature buoyant and optimistic, and thus is by very birthright the apostle of contentment and good cheer. He recognizes the well-springs of human thought and motive, is kindly and tolerant in judgment and finds his chiefest pleasure in trying to make others happy and contented—a higher mission than which no man could ask.

As a lawyer Professor Miller had charge of the legal fight made in the territorial days to eliminate the liquor traffic in Payne County, and as a result of his efforts, which were ably supported by the temperance people of the county, the desired end was achieved in the county six months before the territory cast its popular vote on the question of prohibition. It is pleasing to record that many of the poetical productions of Professor Miller have been collected and issued in book form. In 1895 was published his volume of verses entitled "Oklahoma, and Other Poems;" in 1898 his "Songs from the Southwest Country" was issued; and in 1906 was published a volume of his prose and verse, under the title of "Oklahoma Sunshine."

Professor Miller is affiliated with the Masonic fraternity and is identified with the Oklahoma State Bar Association and the Oklahoma Newspaper Association. Both he and his wife hold membership in the Methodist Episcopal Church, as did also his first wife.

On the 22d of March, 1886, Professor Miller wedded Miss Estelle Shroyer, and she was called to eternal rest on the 24th of September, 1912, one child, Roy F., surviving her and remaining at the parental home, in Stillwater. On the 2d of August, 1914, was solemnized the marriage of Professor Miller to Mrs. Ada M. Kelly, who is the gracious and popular chatelaine of their pleasant home in Stillwater.

COL. GEORGE W. LEWIS. Oklahoma can claim no pioneer citizen whose career has been one of more interesting order, whose genealogical history has touched more worthily and prominently the history of America, or whose personal popularity is more secure than Colonel Lewis, who has been one of the most honored and influential citizens of Payne County since the year that Oklahoma Territory was thrown open to settlement and whose fine farmstead home lies contiguous to Stillwater, the county seat, his residence being one of the most modern and attractive in this section of the state and being worthy of its owner as well as a matter of pride to him and the community in general. The Lewis family was founded in America in the colonial era of our national history and representatives of the same have been found arrayed as gallant soldiers in every war in which the nation has been involved, Colonel Lewis himself having been a valiant soldier of the Union in the Civil war, and after its close having served with distinction as an officer of the State Militia of Kansas. As a pioneer of Kansas he participated in early Indian wars, and he was given the title and rank of colonel before he had attained to his legal majority. A broad-minded, loyal and honored citizen and representative pioneer, he is entitled to special consideration in this history of the state of his adoption.

Col. George Washington Lewis was born in Yadkin County, North Carolina, on the 16th of April, 1846, and is a son of William and Catherine (Pinix) Lewis, the former a native of Virginia and the latter of North Carolina. William Lewis was about fifty-five years of age at the time of his death, when the subject of this review was a child of two years, and his widow passed the closing years of her life in Douglas County, Kansas, where her death occurred in 1886.

The founders of the Lewis family in America came from England in the colonial days and established their residence in the beautiful Shenandoah Valley of Virginia. Both the paternal and maternal grandfathers of Colonel Lewis were loyal soldiers of the Continental line in the war of the Revolution. His maternal grandfather, Capt. Overton Pinix, was a member of the military staff of General Washington, and after the close of the Revolution he served many years on the bench of the Supreme Court of North Carolina. The father of Colonel Lewis was a soldier in the War of 1812, and his father, William Lewis, was an officer in a Virginia regiment in the war of the Revolution. He was with the patriot forces at Valley Forge and was present at the surrender of Lord Cornwallis.

Colonel Lewis is the youngest and only surviving member of a family of eleven children, and his father was a farmer and miller in North Carolina at the time of his death. Alexander D. Lewis, eldest brother of the subject of this review, was a captain in the United States army and as such participated in the Mexican war as a member of a cavalry regiment. He continued his service as a member of the United States army during the greater part of his adult life, and he died at Fort Scott, Kansas, in 1903, at a venerable age.

Col. George W. Lewis was a lad of about thirteen years when the family home was established at Iola, Allen County, Kansas, in 1859, two of his brothers, Irving G. and Albert C., having removed to that state in the preceding year and having platted the town site of Iola, the present county seat. Both of these brothers, as well as the brothers, William B., Columbus and George W., all enlisted from Kansas as Union soldiers in the Civil war, and all went forth as privates in the ranks. He whose name initiates this sketch was but fifteen years of age at the inception of the war, and he remained at home until his brothers had seen three years of military service in defense of the Union. When it became possible for them to return home and assume the care of the widowed mother, George W. himself found opportunity to give rein to his spirit of loyalty and patriotism. In 1864 he enlisted in Company K, Sixteenth Kansas Volunteer Cavalry, all of his brothers likewise having been in the cavalry arm of the service, a fact which has left him to make the statement that a Lewis has invariably been too lazy to walk, this fact being fortified by the cavalry service given by Colonel Lewis and his brothers. His personal service was entirely with the Western army, in the region west of the Mississippi River, and he continued in the ranks until the close of the war, when he received his honorable discharge, and, like his brothers, resumed active association with agricultural pursuits in Kansas. He took part in the Indian wars in Kansas in the late '60s, and in this connection participated in the fights with the forces of the celebrated Indian chief, Sitting Bull. He served about two years as senior major of Kansas volunteers in these conflicts with the Indians, and in the winter of 1866, when twenty years of age, he was elected colonel of the Twentieth Kansas Regiment of the State Militia, this election representing the unanimous vote of the regiment, and the young colonel having been a sturdy youth of 175 pounds, which has represented his average weight in later years. Colonel Lewis gained wide and varied experience in connection with Indian warfare on the frontier, and traversed the western plains when buffalo were still to be seen in great numbers, he having killed a number of these animals within the period of his pioneer experiences. He was a member of the military forces that made the first exploration in the Powder River Country and traversed a considerable part of the Yellowstone National Park, as now constituted. Many incidents of these experiences were of interesting order, but he and his companions endured also numerous hardships and privations. On one occasion, when the command was far from civilization, its stock of provisions was exhausted and it became necessary to kill the poorest of the mules to provide food, one of the party having made a mistake and killed the horse of one of the lieutenants, the meat from this animal having proved the most palatable of all, and the appreciation of the men having perhaps justified the questionable mistake that sacrificed the horse.

Colonel Lewis became one of the representative agriculturists and influential citizens of Allen County, Kansas, and for a time was engaged in the mercantile business at Iola. He continued his residence in that county until 1889, when he came to Oklahoma and, on the 22d of April, participated in the historic opening of the territory to settlement, the formal organization of the new territory having not been completed until the following year. At that time the colonel entered claim to his present homestead, which adjoins Stillwater on the west. His attractive residence commands an excellent view of the city and also of the grounds and buildings of the Oklahoma Agricultural and Mechanical College. The colonel has been one of the most zealous and influential factors in the development and upbuilding of his home county and its judicial center, and his active co-operation has been given in every normal movement and enterprise making for civic and material progress. About fifty-one acres of his farm are platted into village lots and constitute the Lewis Addition to the City of Stillwater. Many of the lots have been sold and building operations have been carried forward to the point of making this one of the attractive residence sections of the county seat. In 1914 Colonel Lewis completed the erection of his present fine residence, which is a modern house of ten rooms, with the most approved appointments and facilities, and the same is recognized as one of the finest residence properties in Payne County, even as it is known as a center of gracious hospitality.

Like all other male representatives of the family, Colonel Lewis has not deviated from the line of strict allegiance to the democratic party, and he has been called upon to serve in various local offices of public trust within the period of his residence in Oklahoma. He is at the present time chairman of the board of county commissioners of Payne County, and has been four times elected a member of this board, on which he has served since the year 1907, which marked the admission of Oklahoma as one of the sovereign states of the Union. On one occasion he was the only democratic candidate elected in the county, and at another election he was one of the two democrats elected. In the territorial days he served as township trustee for a number of terms.

Since 1866 Colonel Lewis has held membership in the Baptist Church, and he and his wife are the only two persons who have maintained continuous membership in the church of this denomination at Stillwater from the time of its organization, in 1872, to the present time, he having contributed liberally to the erection of the present church edifice. His continued interest in his old comrades of the Civil war is indicated by his affiliation with the Grand Army of the Republic. In influence and financial support no one citizen of Payne County did as much to obtain for Stillwater the Oklahoma Agricultural and Mechanical College as did Colonel Lewis, the city having voted bonds for $10,000 to secure this important state institution, and Colonel Lewis, though not a resident within the corporate limits of the city, having been glad to make liberal contribution to the cause, besides which he made two trips to the state capitol to further the interests of Stillwater before the Legislature at the time when the question of locating the college was under consideration.

In the year 1873 was solemnized the marriage of Colonel Lewis to Miss Vessa Moore, who was born in Franklin County, Kansas, on the 16th of February, 1850, her parents, Silas and Anna (Martin) Moore, having removed from Indiana to Kansas in 1854 and having been numbered among the very early settlers of Franklin County, the remainder of their lives having been passed in the Sunflower State. In the concluding paragraph of this article is entered brief record concerning the children of Colonel and Mrs. Lewis: Capt. E. G., who is now a representative business man in the City of Tulsa, was educated in the Oklahoma Agricultural and Mechanical College, where he was captain and drill master of the military organization of the institution, and he served

Mrs. N. M. Bartles.

later as a captain in the Oklahoma National Guard. Anna is the wife of Frederick Fields and they reside in the State of Colorado. George H. is a successful farmer in the vicinity of Stillwater. Albert E. is president of the Liberty National Bank in the City of Tulsa, and is prominently identified also with oil development in the fields of that part of the state. Flossie B. is the wife of William L. Burleson, who is a member of the faculty of the University of Illinois, at Champaign. William L. is cashier of the Liberty National Bank at Tulsa. Myrtle I. is the wife of Stephen B. Johnson, who is a professor in the University of Arizona, at Tucson. Earl and Velma remain at the parental home; and Cecil died when about one year of age.

COL. JACOB H. BARTLES. The people of Oklahoma have been rarely called upon to mourn the loss of a distinguished citizen whose death occasioned as widespread sorrow as did that of Col. Jacob H. Bartles. It has been the privilege of but few men in this, or any other, community to become the center of as wide a circle of personal friends or to attach to themselves, by the indissoluble chains of affectionate esteem, so many men and women of widely varying fortune and social rank. The founder of both the cities of Bartlesville and Dewey his unceasing labors, his great power of organization, his ability to instill into other men the great energy which he always himself possessed, and his great good judgment, foresight and acumen, won him the title of "An Empire Builder." As gallant soldier of the Civil war, as a pioneer of Kansas and Eastern Oklahoma, as a successful merchant and promoter, and as a useful and public-spirited citizen, Colonel Bartles stood as one of the most prominent figures of his day and locality, and in his death his community lost one whose place has not yet been filled.

Jacob H. Bartles was born at Chester, Morris County, New Jersey, June 11, 1842, a son of Joseph A. and Phoebe Helene Bartles. His father, a native of New York, put up the first telegraph wires in New York City, and subsequently moved to New Jersey, where, in Chester County, he was the owner of a farm that is now the property of Childs, the famous New York restaurateur, and from which come the supplies for the restaurants bearing his name. In 1857 Mr. Bartles removed to Wyandotte County, Kansas, where he was engaged in farming and stock raising, and also was the proprietor of a butcher business at Quindaro. There both he and Mrs. Bartles spent the remaining years of their lives. They were the parents of three children: Louise, who is the widow of Alfred Brown, of Chester, New Jersey, and now resides in New York City with her daughter, Mrs. Sadie Reynolds; Theodore, who is deceased; and Jacob H.

The early education of Jacob H. Bartles was secured in the public schools of his native place, and at the age of fifteen years started for the West with his parents. The family embarked on a steamer at Pittsburgh, coming as far as St. Louis, Missouri, where they took another boat for Quindaro, Kansas, the historic spot seven miles west of the present site of Kansas City, which they reached May 2, 1857. During the next three years young Bartles made that place his home, and was engaged in steamboating on the Missouri River, between Omaha and St. Louis, and at the end of that time moved to a farm near Quindaro, which he occupied and assisted in clearing of its heavy timber. When the Civil war came on, Jacob H. Bartles was found as one of his community's patriotic sons, and in that memorable strife had a conspicuous part and one marked with zeal, courage and faithfulness from beginning to end. A record of his activities in the war, as prepared by himself in 1896, is here given:

"In company with seventeen Wyandotte boys and Captain Veale, I went to Fort Leavenworth in the early part of June, 1861. We organized a company, with Veale as captain, and remained there about two weeks before they could arm us. Then we were ordered to Kansas City and south to Little Santa Fe, where we were compelled to put half the company on guard at a time. The second morning the old guard were ordered to discharge their arms, which were old Belgian muskets with the barrels cut off to make cavalry guns. When the guns were discharged all the men fell backwards as if shot by the enemy, and when they had fairly recovered and found out the cause of the disaster they gathered up their Belgian muskets, as also did the boys in camp, piled them all on a fire and burned them up.

"There we were, left without any arms whatever except a few sabres and Colt's revolvers. Captain Veale sent a message to the commanding officer at Fort Leavenworth that if he wanted us to go further to send arms. In two weeks they sent us some Sharp's carbines and we carried them through the war. We went south next and were at the battles of Big Blue, Lone Jack, Dry Wood, Lincoln, West Point, Morristown, Osceola, two engagements at Eutonia, the Jim Lane expedition to Springfield, leaving Kansas City October 1st and returning December 8th.

"On July 3, 1862, under the command of Col. Bill Wier, we captured a part of Stan Watie's regiment, including Colonel Adair in command. Camped at Wolf Creek, on the Military Road, July 4th, and on the 6th Colonel Ross came in and surrendered with 600 men. Returned to Fort Scott about August 13th and took a trip up through Missouri, through Spring River and Sarcoxie, which latter place we left October 3rd and traveled all night, routing the enemy on the 6th. We went to Bentonville on the 21st, and had a fight with Cooper's command at Maysville or Fort Wayne on the 22nd, taking four pieces of artillery; went on a scout to Cincinnati and Cane Hill, had a fight November 28th at the latter place, and camped at Rae's Mills on the 29th; moved the train and had a fight at Prairie Grove, December 6th; moved the train from Fayetteville back to Rae's Mills on the 9th, and started on the Van Buren expedition on the 27th. We next had a fight and routed the First Texas Regiment at Dripping Springs, on the 28th, running them to and through Van Buren. At Van Buren I climbed the flagstaff, hauled down the Confederate flag and hoisted our company's 'Old Glory.'

"We next went on a scout down the Arkansas River on the 29th, but returned to Rae's Mills on the 31st; camped at Cross Hollow, January 12, 1863, camped on White River on the 20th, and swam the White River on the 24th with sabre, pistols and overcoat on. Returning to Fort Scott March 10, we camped at Rolla June 7, and July 1, 1863, came back to Fort Scott. On August 6th we camped at Fort Gibson, and on the 26th had a fight with Cooper's command at Perryville, then returning to the Arkansas River and camping at Fort Davis on the 21st. We next moved to Camp Smith and camped on the north bank of the Arkansas River, March 26, 1864, starting on the Camden expedition from that place. We formed a junction with Steele's command on the Little Missouri River, April 9, and this command formed a line of battle and skirmished with the Confederates on the following day. Our division and Steele's formed a line and laid on our arms during the day and night of the 11th and on the morning of the 12th the army was ordered forward in solid column, the Confederates retreating and our army moving to the left. General

Thayer's division had a fight in the rear with Price's division, driving the latter two miles. We marched all night on the 13th, camped at Camden on the 16th, sent out a foraging trip of 440 wagons on the 17th, the Confederates attacking and capturing the same and taking also our two 12-pound Howitzers, which were the pets of the regiment. On the 19th Steele sent out a train to Pine Bluff, of about 500 six-mule teams which were also captured by the Southerners. We then moved one mile northeast of Camden, where the enemy fired on our pickets on the 16th of April, and we then moved across Washita River, cut up eighty-three wagons, burned most of our camp equipment, and marched five miles on the 26th. On the 27th we marched thirteen miles and camped at Princeton, and on the 28th marched seventeen miles. The Confederates had fought with the rear guard on the 26th, and we then moved the train, artillery and cavalry across the Saline River on a rubber pontoon bridge, the infantry remaining on the west side. We had a hard fight with Kirby Smith and Price and drove them back with heavy loss, the Second Colored Infantry capturing two pieces of artillery. We moved five miles and secured something to eat, crossed at Jenkins Ferry April 30, 1864, moved thirty miles and buried the balance of our train May 1st, reached Little Rock on the 3rd, crossed the Arkansas River at Little Rock on the 8th, and arrived at Fort Smith, May 17th. We then marched six miles south of that place and camped on the south side of Mazard's Prairie on the 29th, and had a review and went to a dance on the 9th of July. Gano's Confederates, about 1900 strong, attacked our camp of about 200 men on July 22nd at 7 o'clock, A. M., and killed about thirteen of us, wounded twenty and took 125 prisoners, but my mule 'Chaney' (the best animal on earth) took me out safe. We moved the camp to Fort Smith on the 27th and when the Confederates drove in our pickets, the Sixth Kansas went out with Colonel Judson in command and scrimmaged a little, the colonel getting hit in the leg with grape shot. We were then reenforced by two pieces of Smith's battery and dismounted one of the Confederate guns, driving them out of the woods on the 31st. On October 13th we camped at Fort Gibson, and at Baxter Springs on the 21st, and marched up Cow Creek, where the enemy captured and burnt the train, on the 23rd. We reached Fort Scott on that same day, and two days later Generals Marmaduke and Cable were taken prisoners with 448 men from Price's army, twelve miles northeast of Fort Scott. We reached Kansas City October 13, 1864. I never lost a day's duty or took a dose of medicine, was never wounded, and was discharged in January, 1865. The above is merely an outline of the many incidents which occurred during the service of myself and comrades in the old Sixth Kansas Volunteer Cavalry.''

After the close of his military services, Mr. Bartles returned to the home of his father, and continued to be associated with him until his marriage in 1868, at which time he located on his wife's farm in Wyandotte County, Kansas, remaining there until 1873. In that year, at Silver Lake, a point six miles southeast of the present location of Bartlesville, and in a log house, Mr. Bartles commenced his career as a merchant. In 1874 he built a better building and moved his stock there, and in 1877 built the first flour mill in Indian Territory, on Caney River, northeast of where Bartlesville now stands. In 1878 he built a two-story frame building, 25 by 100 feet, near the mill, for a storeroom and residence and moved to it. In 1878 he planted the first wheat grown on Caney River and the followng year furnished seed to other farmers in order to increase wheat growing, an industry in which he continued to be engaged for a number of years, raising his banner crop of 45,000 bushels in the early '90s. During the same period Mr. Bartles engaged in the cattle raising business, in the walnut log and lumber business at various places in the Cherokee Nation, and in the mercantile business at Alluwee, Pawhuska, Claremore, Milltown, Nowata and Old Bartlesville. Mr. Bartles also built what is now the Santa Fe Railroad from Caney, Kansas, to Collinsville, Oklahoma, in 1898-1899, and moved to Dewey in the following year.

The Turkey Creek store and residence, in which his son, Joseph A. Bartles, was born, was moved to the mill at Old Bartlesville, and there used as a furniture and cabinet shop and later was moved to Dewey and is now the home of the Dewey World. The two-story frame store and residence erected at the mill was made of black walnut and was the best building in the Cherokee Nation when erected with the exception of the capitol building at Tahlequah. This building was also moved to Dewey, stood across the street from the First National Bank, and now stands opposite the Hotel Dewey, which Mr. Bartles built in 1889 and which always continued to be his home.

Mr. Bartles always referred with pride to the fact that during his early business career in Indian Territory, he had in his employ J. F. Campbell of Nowata, John Bullet of Claymore, George B. Keeler, William Johnstone, N. T. Carr and Frank Overlees of Bartlesville, A. H. Gibson of Pawhuska and H. M. Brent of Dewey. He added that these men, many of whom are now leading citizens of Oklahoma, were all faithful employes and that it was very gratifying to him to know that they had become prosperous, prominent business men of the communities in which they made their homes.

On October 1, 1868, at Leavenworth, Kansas, Mr. Bartles was married to Mrs. Nannie M. (Journeycake) Pratt, who was born August 28, 1843, a daughter of the Rev. Charles and Jane (Sancia) Journeycake. They moved to the Cherokee Nation in 1873 and there were remarried according to the laws and customs of the Cherokee Nation. Rev. Charles Journeycake was a chief of the Delawares and an ordained Baptist clergyman and did missionary work all through the territory, never accepting one cent for his services, but making his own living by farming. He was the organizer of the Baptist Church at Alluwee. He died in 1894 and Mrs. Journeycake in 1893. Their children were as follows: Mary E., deceased, who married Charles H. Armstrong; Rachel, deceased, who was the wife of N. J. Tanner; Nannie M., who is the widow of Colonel Bartles; Lucy Jane, deceased, who was the wife of Henry Armstrong; Baron Stowe, who died at the age of three years; Emeline, who is the wife of J. E. Campbell of Nowata; Adeline, deceased, who was the wife of Samuel Love; Anna, deceased, who married Henry Armstrong, the widower of her sister Lucy; Cora Lee, deceased, who was the wife of William Carey, and an infant daughter, deceased.

Mrs. Bartles was given excellent educational advantages, attending the Delaware Baptist Mission at Dennison, Kansas, and spending one year in the Baptist College, at Granville, Ohio. She was the first Christian woman along the Caney River, and on one occasion conducted the funeral services over an infant, there being no minister near. She has always been an active religious worker, organized the Baptist Church at Dewey, and has held all offices in the church and Sunday school, having been church clerk until 1913. In 1904 Mrs. Bartles conceived the idea of building a monument to the memory of her father, and also of aiding the Baptist Church work in the Town of Dewey. The present beautiful memorial Baptist Church of Dewey is the outgrowth of that idea, the church being completed at a cost of $5,000, and is known as The Journeycake Memorial Baptist Church of Dewey. The dedicatory services were held Sunday, November 25, 1906, when Rev. J. S. Murrow, a venerable Indian missionary of Atoka, Indian Territory, conducted the services.

Mrs. Bartles was married first to L. B. Pratt, who was first engaged in the lumber business at Leavenworth but turned his attention to farming when his health failed. He went from Shurtleff to Denison, and graduated from the latter institution. His death occurred in 1865, he having been the father of three children: Nonie, born March 2, 1861, who married J. J. Barndollar, of Coffeyville, Kansas, and has one son, Pratt; Ella May, born May 14, 1863, who married Frank Neilson, of Coffeyville, Kansas, and has one daughter, Nonie; and Ida F., born November 7, 1865, who married A. H. Gibson, of Coffeyville, Kansas, and has one daughter, Mary Ella. Mr. and Mrs. Bartles were the parents of two children: Charles, born August 13, 1869, who died September 6, 1870; and Joseph A., born December 15, 1873, who now resides at Dewey.

Colonel Bartles always took the greatest interest in the Grand Army of the Republic, and it is with a large degree of satisfaction that the members of his family reflect upon the great pleasure which came to him when he entertained the survivors of his regiment, the Sixth Kansas Cavalry, in a three days' reunion at Dewey, in September, 1908. A very sick man at the time he was still able to attend most of the campfires and those present will never forget his beaming countenance as he beat time to the campaign songs. A short account, as copied from one of the local newspapers, is herewith given: "Dressed in gala attire, with flags, bunting, pennants and streamers flying from every available pole and building around the square, Dewey is this week assisting Uncle 'Jake' Bartles in the entertainment of his guests, the survivors of the Sixth Kansas Cavalry. This is the twenty-fourth annual reunion of the famous old regiment and all of the survivors, who are in attendance, are the guests at the Dewey Hotel of J. H. Bartles. The illness of the latter, who is confined to his cot on the veranda of the hotel, serves to mar the pleasure of the occasion. Mr. Bartles is able, however, to sit up and converse with his guests who are coming to the entertainment on every incoming train. In connection with the entertainment of his old regiment, which will last three days, Mr. Bartles has arranged for a general reunion which will be attended by the old soldiers of all regiments. This is the first day of the entertainment and it is starting with a swing that promises to make it a notable event. The crowds began gathering late yesterday and today the people are coming from all points of the compass. Dewey threatens to be taxed to the extreme in caring for her guests, but the people have determined to render all assistance they can to make the visit of 'Uncle Jake's' guests as pleasant as possible. The Commercial Club is taking a leading part in the entertainment. The old cannon brought from Washington by Mr. Bartles was brought down from Sedan, a band has been secured for the three days and nights and excursions have been arranged on the Cement company's road and the interurban to Bartlesville.''

It was not long after the foregoing was written that Colonel Bartles passed away, at 6 o'clock, A. M., October 18, 1908. His death, which was due to Bright's disease, occurred at the Bartles Hotel, Dewey, it being about four years from the time that the disease had first manifested itself. With his old spirit and energy, he valiantly battled against it, and the courage and pluck which had characterized his entire life probably added a year or more to it. It will not be inappropriate to close this all too inadequate a review of one of Oklahoma's builders and benefactors, to quote from an article which appeared in the Dewey Sentinel, June 9, 1911, and which was written by Judge Andrew H. Norwood, a lifelong friend of Colonel Bartles, and himself a pioneer of this country and familiar with its development during the past half a century. The article referred to says in part:

"In 1872 Capt. J. H. Bartles with his family located at Silver Lake, a few miles south of Dewey, and opened a store and at the same time put in a sawmill on the Verdigris River, some twenty-five miles east, the mill being the first institution of the kind ever seen in this section of the country. After two or three years he moved his store and residence to Whiteturkey Creek and continued business there for several years and at the same time opened a big farm just west of this city and used every means within his power to promote agricultural development and achieved great success in that direction.

"Then he began the construction of the big flouring mill that still stands a monument to his energy and enterprise on the bank of the Caney, some three miles south of the city. He entered upon this undertaking against the strenuous advice of his family and friends, whose opposition was of such a character as would have discouraged a less sturdy and determined man. In a few years he had induced many farmers to locate throughout the surrounding country and develop wheat lands, furnished them seed and implements on long credit and in other substantial ways helping them to get a start, until eventually he demonstrated that this valley was one of the greatest wheat producing sections of the world, and his mill and store became one of the greatest distributing points in the Southwest. At the same time he was extensively engaged in the cattle business and many other enterprises all of which proved successful.

"This industrialism and enormous productiveness was hampered by the primitive methods of transportation prevailing at that time and to overcome this disadvantage Colonel Bartles conceived the idea of building a railroad and telegraph and telephone lines and thus to get in closer touch with the outside world. He organized a company and became its president and general manager and at his own expense began at once the construction from Caney, Kansas, south of what is now the Atchison, Topeka & Santa Fe Railroad, and when graded from Caney to Collinsville, he sold it to the company under whose name it is now operated. Desiring a more suitable location than the one on the river and one better adapted to all his pursuits and varied interests, he came up on to the high rolling prairie about four miles north and laid out and platted a townsite, and commemorative of the world-famed hero whose marvelous exploit in Manila Bay just at that time had stirred the civilized world and fired the hearts of his countrymen with a military ardor almost beyond conception—Admiral George Dewey—he gave to the future city the name of Dewey. This was accomplished in 1898 and Colonel Bartles proceeded to move his holdings on the river to the new town, the most healthful, beautiful and accessible point on the line of his new railroad and away from floods, marshes, swamps, impure water, and in every way superior to his former location on the river or what is now the city of Bartlesville.

"It has been charged that Colonel Bartles founded Dewey in a spirit of selfishness and self aggrandizement, prompted by a desire to obliterate the growing settlement of Bartlesville that had sprung into existence at his former location on the river, the fact of its growth bringing into existence interests competitive with his own. The statement is unfounded in fact and conceived in fiction and refuted by the footprints along the trail of his indefatigable efforts to develop a new country, every change he made being inspired by advancing conditions of the development he sought and an ambition to conserve to the utmost the rapidly growing commercial and community interests of the wonderful new country he loved and whose future greatness was revealed to this remarkable man and pioneer almost with the eye of prophecy.

"In passing from the story of the birth of Dewey to Col. J. H. Bartles, its founder, a tribute is due. He was the pioneer merchant, miller and farmer and was the first man to establish in the state electric light and waterworks plant; was always the first and foremost and the most liberal in promoting educational, moral and all public utilities and in all these undertakings was generous to a fault. In founding and building Dewey he was prompted and governed by the same spirit and judgment that had directed his actions throughout the whole of his busy and successful life. In 1908 he died after laying down his manifold interests and with the happy reflection that Dewey was on the high road to a realization of his ambitions of a splendid city, and time and the future will reveal that there was nothing chimerical in his scheme to meet the demands of a new and magnificent commonwealth, and this city will remain for all time a monument to his genius and magnanimity."

ARCHIBALD W. TURNER. At Alexandria, the judicial center of Rapides County, Louisiana, July 9, 1869, recorded the birth of the present county attorney of Payne County, Oklahoma, and in the vital young state of his adoption he has gained secure place as one of the able and successful members of its bar; his place of residence has been City of Stillwater, the county seat, since 1911.

Mr. Turner is a scion of one of the patrician old French families that was founded in New Orleans, Louisiana, when that state was still a province, and the original orthography of the family name was Tournaire. Mr. Turner is a son of Squire Turner and Sally (Stone) Turner, and his father was born in Louisiana, where he was reared and educated, and where he continued to maintain his home until 1872, when, immediately after his marriage, he removed to Missouri, his father, Archibald Tournaire, having been a native of France and having come to America soon after the battle of Waterloo brought disaster to the imperial forces of the great Napoleon, under whom he had served as a soldier in a cavalry command. Upon coming to America he established his residence in Louisiana, and he was the owner of a fine plantation near Alexandria, Rapides Parish, that state, at the time of his death. The mother of the subject of this review was born at Richmond, Kentucky, and she now passes her time in the homes of her children, who accord to her the deepest filial love and solicitude, she having celebrated in 1915 the seventy-second anniversary of her birth, and her honored husband having died at Columbia, Boone County, Missouri, in 1906, at the age of seventy-two years. Mrs. Turner is of staunch Scotch lineage, her ancestors having settled in Maryland in the colonial era of our national history, and representatives of the family having been valiant soldiers of the Continental line in the war of the Revolution, and one of her ancestors, Thomas Stone, having been a signer of the Declaration of Independence. He whose name initiates this article is the eldest in a family of three children: Mary Hood is the wife of Edward W. Hinton, who is head of the chair of evidence and pleading in the law department of the great University of Chicago; and Catherine Elizabeth is the wife of Judge Oliver M. Spencer, who resides in St. Joe, Missouri, and who is now chief counsel of the Chicago, Burlington & Quincy Railroad Company for the territory west of the Mississippi River.

Archibald W. Turner was about three years old at the time of the family removal to Columbia, Boone County, Missouri, where he was reared to maturity, and where he acquired his early education in the public schools. There he was graduated in the law department of the University of Missouri, as a member of the class of 1892, and after thus receiving his degree of Bachelor of Laws he continued to be engaged in the practice of his profession at Columbia until 1908, when he came to the newly organized State of Oklahoma and engaged in practice at Altus, county seat of Jackson County. About one year later he removed to Hobart, judicial center of Kiowa County, and in 1911 he established his permanent home at Stillwater, the thriving capital of Payne County, where he has since continued in the successful general practice of law and has built up a substantial and representative business, in connection with which he has appeared in much of the important litigation in the courts of this section of the state. He served two terms as city attorney of Columbia, Missouri, and in 1914 he was elected county attorney of Payne County, an office in which he is giving a most vigorous and effective administration. Mr. Turner is a stalwart in the local camp of the democratic party, is a loyal and progressive citizen, and in a fraternal way he is affiliated with the lodge of the Benevolent and Protective Order of Elks at Hobart.

In 1910 was solemnized the marriage of Mr. Turner to Mrs. Clara Farley, whose first husband is survived by one son, Max, a sturdy boy who gives cheer to the home circle, no children having been born to Mr. and Mrs. Turner.

Mr. Turner's paternal and maternal ancestors were slave holders, and both families were earnest supporters of the Confederate cause during the period of the Civil war. It is thus but natural that Mr. Turner himself should retain a full sympathy with the principles for which the Southern States contended as their inherent right, though his loyalty to the now undivided nation of his birth is of the most insistent order.

HON. WILBERFORCE JONES. Among the leaders of the Payne County bar, no name is held in higher esteem than that of Hon. Wilberforce Jones, a thorough, learned and talented legist, a practical citizen of public-spirited views and a courteous, finished gentleman of the old school. He has been engaged in practice at Cushing since January 1, 1913, and during this time has added to the reputation which he gained first in Missouri and later in Lincoln County, Oklahoma. Mr. Jones was born in Cass County, Michigan, April 27, 1846, and is a son of William H. and Catherine (Messike) Jones.

The great-grandfather of Wilberforce Jones was the original settler of the family in America, coming from Wales and locating in Virginia as early as 1792. Later he became a pioneer of Madison County, Indiana, settling on virgin land in the vicinity of what is now Pendleton, where he passed the remaining years of his life in clearing the timber and brush, draining the swamps, and making a home for his family. His death occurred in 1835. His son, Smith Jones, was born in Virginia and accompanied his parents to Indiana, where his early years were passed amid pioneer surroundings. He was an industrious and energetic man and through years of hard work managed to accumulate a satisfying property. His death occurred in 1834, in Indiana, and there the grandmother also died.

William H. Jones was born near Pendleton, Madison County, Indiana, in 1818, and after a number of years spent in farming there went to Cass County, Michigan. In the spring of 1853 he started from Michigan in an ox-team, traveling slowly across the country and finally arriving at his destination in Brown County, Kansas, in November of that year, and locating in the vicinity of what is now Hiawatha. He was an abolitionist and became a squatter under the Abolition Aid Society. This was at a time when the slavery and abolition parties were engaged in a series of conflicts, which continued for several years, fights taking place, towns being burned, and illegal voting freely indulged in. In these contests William H. Jones was a frequent participant. In 1855 there came to Kansas John Brown, who afterward frequently made his headquarters at the home of Mr. Jones, but the latter, while a warm friend of this impulsive opponent of slavery, endeavored in every way to keep him from going to Virginia, trying to impress upon him the fact that his act would be looked upon as one of treason. Wilberforce Jones still retains a vivid memory of John Brown, who, as is known, went to Virginia, surprised and captured the arsenal at Harper's Ferry, October 16, 1859, but on the following day was wounded and captured and taken a prisoner by the Virginia militia, and was tried and executed at Charlestown, December 2, 1859. Mr. Jones remembers that his father traveled with Brown through Kansas, that they would talk for hours, and that for one whole day Brown pleaded with the elder Jones to become one of the party in the journey to Virginia that resulted so disastrously.

During the Civil war William H. Jones served the Union cause as captain of Company B, First United States Colored Infantry, and at the close of the struggle returned to Kansas, where for a short time he resumed his agricultural operations. In 1866 he removed with his family to Jasper County, Missouri, and that state continued to be his home until his retirement from active participation in farming and stock raising, when he removed to San Benito County, California. There he died in 1893. Mr. Jones was married at Pendleton, Indiana, to Catherine Messike, who was born in Hardin County, Kentucky, and reared in Indiana, and whose death occurred in San Benito County, California, in 1899, when she was seventy-six years of age. They were the parents of four sons: Chester G., who served in Company A, Ninth Kansas Cavalry, for 4½ years during the Civil war period, and died at Hiawatha, Kansas, in 1905; D. C., of Newton County, Missouri, who served 1½ years as a member of the Thirteenth Kansas Infantry during the Civil war; Wilberforce; and James M., whose death occurred in a runaway accident at San Francisco, California, in 1912.

Wilberforce Jones was a lad of seven years when he accompanied his parents in the long overland journey from Michigan to Kansas, and his boyhood was passed amid the turbulent scenes that preceded secession. He was only ten years of age when he began to show his allegiance to the republican party by carrying a banner ratifying the nomination of Fremont in a republican parade, and from that time to the present has been a stalwart supporter of the Grand Old Party. On February 26, 1863, when not yet seventeen years of age, he enlisted in Company C, Seventh Kansas Cavalry, with which he served until receiving his honorable discharge at Leavenworth, September 29, 1865, participating in a number of engagements, and, despite his youth, displaying courage and faithfulness to duty at all times. In November, 1864, under special act of Congress allowing soldiers in the field to vote, he cast his first ballot, in support of Abraham Lincoln. His vote was challenged, as he was under age, but Adjt. Maj. John Utt, who was one of the judges of election, demanded that he be permitted his franchise on his military record.

After the war Mr. Jones went with his family to Missouri, but soon left home for the western plains, where he spent five years in the hard and exciting life of the cowboy. When he returned to Missouri he began the study of law, after some years spent in farming, and was admitted to the bar at West Plains, Missouri, in 1887, with permission to practice in the state and federal courts. He soon gained an important and satisfying practice and took an active part in public affairs, and in 1899 was elected to the Fortieth General Assembly of Missouri, a body in which he discharged his duties capably and energetically. He remained in Missouri until 1906, when he came to Oklahoma and settled in Lincoln County, where for one term, 1910 to 1912, he served in the capacity of county attorney. Since January 1, 1913, his field of practice has been the City of Cushing, where he is recognized as one of Payne County's most able practitioners. Mr. Jones has maintained his interest in his old army comrades and is a valued and popular member of the local post of the Grand Army of the Republic, and was department commander of the Grand Army of the Republic of Oklahoma in 1912. With his family he attends the Christian Church.

In 1887 Mr. Jones was married to Miss Laura Roberts, who was born in 1867, in Illinois, and to this union there have been born four children: Anna Fay, who is the wife of Fred D. Riddle, of Cushing; George W., a telegraph operator for the Prairie Oil and Gas Company at Independence, Oklahoma; Lottie, who is the wife of Jesse Jones, a telephone operator for the Magnum Oil Company; and Walter Wilberforce, who is attending high school at Cushing, Oklahoma.

ADAM FOCHT. The world looks on with peculiar satisfaction and pleasure when a career of struggle and adversity meets an overflowing and abundant prosperity. None could justly begrudge Adam Focht and wife the fortune that has rewarded their later years. Mr. Focht was one of the early settlers in Payne County, resides at Stillwater, has been a farmer there for a quarter of a century, but is rapidly being made wealthy through a foresighted investment he made a few years ago in Creek County, where he owns land in one of the richest oil fields of the world.

About forty years ago Mr. and Mrs. Focht were combating with grim determination and industry the vicissitudes of life on the western prairies. Both had been reared in Iowa when that state was almost on the frontier. They married and started life poor. After renting for a time they went out to Gage County, Nebraska, in 1875, at the time the Otoe Indian Reservation was opened for settlement. Adam Focht was the ninth white settler to locate on that reservation. People of the present time have difficulty in understanding what difficulties and hardships the early settlers of Nebraska endured. There was a long chain of evils, dry weather, grasshoppers, hot winds, uncertain crops, lack of markets, dugouts and sod houses, and hardly was one obstacle overcome before another even greater sprung up.

Mr. and Mrs. Focht struggled along, both of them hiring out at times in order to make a little money to pay household expenses. At one time it seemed that their cup of misfortune was full and running over. Without money in the house, they lost their only cow, and one of their team of horses was crippled. Mr. Focht wanted to sell his claim then, but his wife said no, stick and we will get along some way. Persistence has its reward. They remained, developed a good farm, and with better times they had some money when they came to Oklahoma, the year after it was opened to settlement. In Payne

County they took another stake in a new country, and there gradually developed a good farm, and from the proceeds Mr. Focht was able to buy a tract of cheap land in Creek County, but which today is situated in the midst of the great oil fields around Shamrock. At the present writing Mr. Focht has twelve producing oil wells, the first one brought in on December 23, 1915, and the last one only a few days before this is being written. In the five months and eight days from December 23, 1915, to June 12, 1916, his royalties from all amounted to $35,213.85. There is still room for more wells on his farm and it would be impossible to estimate the ultimate value of his property. Considering all they went through in the early years, certainly Mr. and Mrs. Focht deserve a bright fortune to illuminate their closing years. Their thought now is chiefly of their children, and the wealth which is coming in from the royalties is being chiefly invested in farms for his sons.

Adam Focht was born in Auglaize County, Ohio, April 27, 1847, a son of Lewis and Martha (Balyliff) Focht. His father was born in Schuylkill County, Pennsylvania, of German ancestry. The mother was born probably in Philadelphia, of English parentage, and she was reared a Quaker. They were married in Ohio, and the mother died there at the age of thirty-two. Later the father, who was a farmer, moved to Fremont County, Iowa, and bought a farm where he spent the rest of his days, dying at the age of seventy-five. He was a democrat.

Adam Focht was about seven or eight years of age when his father moved out to Iowa. He grew up on the home farm, and received a limited education in the graded schools. When about seventeen his own career of adventure began. During 1862-63 he crossed the plains, driving a team with provisions to Julesburg, Colorado, and subsequently taking provisions to Fort Laramie, Wyoming. That was a time when the Indians were on the warpath, and he witnessed much of the exciting scenes of the period. He witnessed a massacre in 1863 in which thirty-five white men were killed by the Indians near Poll Creek. Returning home, he rented one of his father's farms for three years, then operated the home place two years, and in the meantime having married he set out in 1875 for the recently opened Indian reservation in Gage County, Nebraska. He and his good wife lived there for thirteen years.

In 1890 he came to Oklahoma and took up a homestead in Payne County. He proved up his claim, and has lived there ever since, though he also has a residence in Stillwater and lived there for the purpose of educating his children in the local schools. While his family were in town he spent most of his time on the farm.

It was in 1911 that Mr. Focht went to Creek County and bought 200 acres near where the Town of Shamrock now stands. In 1912 he moved to this land, cleared some of it, and in the following year rented it to his son. Then in the fall of 1915 it was included in the rich strike of oil, and one of his twelve wells now produced 2,500 barrels. He has leased the property to the Gipey Oil Company and receives an eighth royalty. He sold an interest in part of his land, but what he still owns is a fortune.

On New Year's day, in 1872, Mr. Focht married Miss Addie Fletcher. She was born in Fremont County, Iowa, August 29, 1856, a daughter of Vardaman and Drusilla (Shaw) Fletcher. Her father was a native of Indiana and her mother of Tennessee, and they were married in Buchanan County, Missouri, and from there moved to Fremont County, Iowa. Vardaman Fletcher was the second white settler in Fremont County and was there at such an early time that once or twice he was driven out by hostile Indians. He spent many years in Fremont and Mills counties and was a very successful farmer.

In 1875 he also went out to Nebraska and improved land in that state, and in the year that Oklahoma was first opened to settlement he again took up pioneering, though then well advanced in years, and secured a homestead in Payne County, which after improving he sold. For a time he was engaged in the grocery business at Perkins, and then made his home with his children until he died, in 1898, when about seventy-five years of age. His wife had died in Nebraska in 1891 at the age of sixty-four. He was a member of the Methodist Church.

Mrs. Focht remained in the old home until her marriage, and then she, too, showed her dauntless spirit by becoming a pioneer with her husband, and by her exhibition of nerve in the face of adverse conditions she deserves a great share of the credit for the prosperity that has since come to them. Mrs. Focht is a member of the Methodist Church and of the Ladies' Aid Society. On July 6, 1916, Mr. Focht rounds out forty years of active membership in the Independent Order of Odd Fellows.

Through all their days of struggle they were encouraged by the thought that what they were doing was for the benefit of their children. Into their home came thirteen children, five of whom died in childhood, but the other eight are still living. James W. is a farmer in Payne County; Emma E., now living at St. Joseph, Missouri, is the widow of Dennis Johnson; Jessie is the wife of George Webb of Ripley, Oklahoma; Russell C., Lewis Lloyd, Ralph L. and Charles G. are all farmers in Payne County, Charles living with his parents. The youngest is Myrtle May Clendening, at home.

HON. WALTER R. EATON. Few of Oklahoma's citizens have been engaged in equally as many business enterprises as has Walter R. Eaton, of Muskogee, member of the State Legislature from Muskogee County, and probably none has accomplished more important things. Since shortly before the advent of statehood, his name has appeared as an officer or director of nearly a hundred corporations, among them railroads, interurbans, oil and gas developing companies and other large enterprises. A conservationist of scientific thought, his motives have been tinged with a hue for the public weal, while out of his projects at the same time he has prospered individually.

Walter R. Eaton was born at Bucyrus, Crawford County, Ohio, in 1874, and is a son of Reason B. and Margaret (Hayes) Eaton. His father, a native of Ohio, was a farmer of repute, who unselfishly gave considerable of his time to politics for the public good. Mr. Eaton's mother, a native of Pennsylvania, was a cousin of President Rutherford B. Hayes. In the family there were five sons and two daughters: Walter R., of this review; Mrs. Ethel Richie, who is the wife of a practicing attorney of Lima, Ohio; Mrs. Walter B. Richie, who is also the wife of a Lima lawyer; Horace P., who is engaged in the manufacturing business at Kalamazoo, Michigan; J. H., who is a merchant at Bucyrus, Ohio; John A., who is a Kansas City lawyer; and Reason B., who resides some place in the West.

Walter R. Eaton acquired his rudimentary education in the public schools, and in 1898 passed the bar examination for entrance to the University of Michigan, at Ann Arbor, but did not enter that institution as he was forced into politics. Prior to that time, in 1894, he had been appointed private secretary to Walter B. Richie, of Lima, Ohio, supreme chancellor of the Knights of Pythias, and served in that capacity two years, at the end of that period succeeding himself as private secretary to the successor of Mr. Richie, Philip T. Colgrove, of Hastings, Michigan, the latter term of two years expiring in 1898. In 1886 his parents had removed to Winfield, Kansas,

and there Mr. Eaton made his home until going to Lima in 1894. In 1898 he began the practice of law at Hastings, Michigan, and continued there until 1901 when he moved to Oklahoma and settled at Muskogee, this being but a few years before the advent of statehood and the conditions being therefore favorable for profitable promotion of industries. Mr. Eaton became associated with C. N. Haskell of Muskogee, who afterwards was governor of the state, in various business ventures, and during the next few years was a moving spirit in no less than 100 important undertakings in the eastern part of the state. He has been engaged in the building of railroads, the sale of real estate, the establishment of townsites and the development of. oil and gas properties. As president of the park board of the City of Muskogee he supervised the laying out and beautifying of parks until no other city in the Southwest has an equally modern and beautiful park system. Mr. Eaton has evolved a modern park and civic improvement plan which he intends to publish and it will probably be adopted by the State Civic Improvement Association, of which he is a member. His theory deals with the utilization of ground for reasons of thrift rather than of beauty, although he is a lover of the beautiful in park architecture.

Mr. Eaton is the author of the work entitled "Eaton's Method of Pheasantry," which has been adopted as a text for the propagation and rearing of pheasants in all parts of the country. For fifteen years he has made a study of game breeding and is one of the best informed men in the country on the subject. His ideas depart from those of sportsmen who advocate propagation, and he preaches rather the doctrine of game creation as fundamental in dealing with the game problem. His game breeder's bill, introduced in the State Legislature, in 1915, is said to be one of the most advanced in the United States. Among his latest achievements may be mentioned the establishment of the Town of Oilton, in the heart of one of the leading oil and gas regions of the state. Eaton & Dunn promoted and have the sale of the townsites of Oilton, Shamrock and Pemeta, all in the oil belt.

Mr. Eaton was elected to the Oklahoma Legislature, on the democratic ticket, in 1914, leading the ticket in both the primary and general elections. He was made chairman of the committee on revenue and taxation and a member of the committees on public buildings, public roads and highways, code, impeachment and removal from office, oil and gas and fish and game. He was the author of a bill changing the method of making tax assessments and issuing tax receipts, a measure he estimated, if adopted, would save taxpayers $150,000 annually. He was the author also of a bill providing for the removal of necessity for notice before property advertised for delinquent taxes should be shorn of penalty if paid before October 1st; a bill providing means of breeding game and fur-bearing animals; a bill accepting the authority conferred by Congress on county courts with reference to Indian matters; a bill providing for appeal from county courts in taxation matters; a bill creating a county excise board, and a bill providing for the establishment of school and municipal playgrounds. He was joint author of a bill providing the establishment of a Pasteur Institute for the treatment of hydrophobia and of the bill providing for a tax on the gross production of oil and gas. He is a candidate for re-election in the fall of 1916.

Mr. Eaton was married in December, 1911, to Miss Lillian Pittman, daughter of Judge L. P. Pittman, of Shawnee, Oklahoma, one of the most widely known lawyers and legislators of his day in Oklahoma. By a former wife Mr. Eaton has two children: Marquis, aged sixteen years, who is a student at Wentworth Military Academy, Lexington, Missouri; and Richie, who lives with his parents and attends school at Muskogee.

Mr. Eaton is a member of the Episcopal Church. He is fraternally identified with the Knights of Pythias, in which he has filled all the chairs, and the Dramatic Order of Knights of Khorassan, of which he has been royal vizier and is now royal prince. Mr. Eaton also holds membership in the Muskogee Chamber of Commerce and the Muskogee Rotary Club.

EARL W. SINCLAIR of Tulsa is president of the Exchange National Bank, the largest bank in Oklahoma and one of the largest financial institutions in the Southwest. He is interested in the Sinclair Oil and Refining Corporation, which owns refineries and producing properties all over the Mid-Continent field.

During the greater part of his active business career he has been identified with banking and other interests at Independence, Kansas, but about three years ago transferred his home to Tulsa, Oklahoma. Mr. Sinclair is a man who has come up from the ranks relying on his keen intelligence and steady industry to promote himself to favor and position in affairs.

He was born at Wheeling, West Virginia, May 15, 1874, a son of John and Phoebe (Simmons) Sinclair. His father was born at Woodsfield, Ohio, and died April 1, 1896, at the age of fifty-one. His mother was born in Wheeling, West Virginia, and is now living at the age of sixty-two. Both the sons, Earl W. and Harry F., are well known and prominent men at Tulsa. John Sinclair was in the quartermaster's department of the Union army during the Civil war. After the war he engaged in the drug business at Wheeling, and in 1884 removed to Independence, Kansas, where he continued in the same business until his death. In politics he was first a democrat and later a republican, and both he and his wife were members of the Congregational Church.

Earl W. Sinclair finished his public school education at Independence, then attended the Northern Indiana Normal School at Valparaiso. His first business experience came as clerk in the freight department of the Chicago, Burlington & Quincy Railway at Chicago, and after about five years there he moved to St. Louis and spent about four years with a lumber company. It was at Independence, Kansas, that he received a solid position in business affairs. After locating there he was agent for the Independence Gas Company for a time, until the plant was taken over by the Kansas Natural Gas Company, with which he continued as agent for several years.

On January 6, 1907, he helped organize the State Bank of Commerce at Independence, and became its cashier. Consolidated with and became vice president of the First National Bank of Independence on January 17, 1910. On January 14, 1913, Mr. Sinclair came to Tulsa and became vice president of the Exchange National Bank of this city, and in January, 1916, was elected president of the bank succeeding P. J. White.

Some of his important business interests and relations are thus described by The Oil and Gas Journal: "When the Sinclair Oil & Refining Corporation took over the Milliken, Chanute and other properties in Oklahoma, making it the largest oil producing and refining company in business in Oklahoma outside of the Standard Oil Company, Earl Sinclair was unanimously chosen secretary and treasurer. After three months' service he found the duties of the office too onerous and resigned the treasurership but is still secretary and a director of the company. In addition to his banking interests in Tulsa, he is one of the directors of the State National

Bank at Oklahoma City, and is a large stock holder in several Kansas City and New York financial institutions. He has devoted himself almost exclusively to banking during the last ten years."

Mr. Sinclair is a member of all the bodies of Masonry, including Wichita Consistory of the thirty-second degree and Akdar Temple of the Mystic Shrine. He belongs to the Benevolent and Protective Order of Elks, the Tulsa Commercial Club and the Country Club, and in politics is a republican. On May 20, 1902, he married Miss Blanche Stich of Independence, Kansas. They have two children. Besides his beautiful home in Tulsa Mr. Sinclair has a summer home on Buzzard Bay, Massachusetts.

PROF. C. E. TOPE. The superintendent of the Chandler public schools is one of the leading educators of Central Oklahoma, is a man whose experience in educational work began when he was a boy, and has shown exceptional ability in all phases of school work. Under his administration the Chandler schools have reached a standard hardly second to any in Oklahoma. The Central School Building was erected in 1900 at a cost of about $15,000, with eight rooms and a corps of seven teachers. In 1903 another building was erected of four rooms, with four teachers. The colored schools of the city are in charge of three teachers. In the white schools there is an enrollment of nearly 500 pupils, and 110 are in the high school proper. The Chandler schools are conducted for nine months in the year, and it has been the pride of local citizens and those officially connected with the schools to keep them up to the highest standards in equipment and efficiency of instruction.

C. E. Tope was born at Gallipolis on the Ohio River in the State of Ohio, February 6, 1885. His father, Richard Tope. was a native of Ohio, and his ancestors had settled on the Chesapeake Bay, Maryland, during colonial times. The family have contributed farmers, mechanics, teachers and members of the various professions. Grandfather Tope was a carpenter. Richard Tope married Rebecca Irvin, also a native of Ohio, but representing early English settlers in Pennsylvania. When Professor Tope was about one year old, the mother died, leaving three children.

C. E. Tope grew up on a farm, developed his body as well as his mind, received training in the public schools, and began his career as a teacher at the age of sixteen. He taught in the schools of his native county, and during intervals of teaching attended the Oak Hill and Rio Grande colleges of Ohio, from which he was graduated in 1905. He continued teaching in Ohio until 1907 and then moved to Oklahoma and was superintendent of the public schools at Mulhall for two years. Professor Tope has been identified with the Chandler public schools since 1909, and it is a reflection of credit upon him to say that the local schools have enjoyed their greatest period of improvement and advancement in all lines since he took charge.

At Mulhall, Oklahoma, in 1908, Mr. Tope married Rosa McCall, a woman of thorough education and culture, who was also born in Ohio, a daughter of James McCall. Professor Tope is active in Masonic circles, having affiliation with Lodge No. 58, Ancient Free and Accepted Masons; with the Royal Arch Chapter, No. 51; the Knight Templar Commandery, No. 4, and Consistory of Guthrie, Oklahoma. He has held chairs in the local lodge and has been high priest of the chapter and is also a member of the Scottish Rite team at Guthrie. He and his wife take much part in the Presbyterian Church in which he is teacher of a class of thirty men. He possesses the broad sympathy, the thorough understanding of young people, so necessary to the equipment of the educator, and possesses the faculty of imparting not only information but the more valuable one of inspiring his pupils to work for themselves.

JULIAN TRUMBLY. The City of Pawhuska honored one of the most distinguished men of the old Osage Nation by naming for him one of its beautiful streets, Trumbly Avenue. The Trumbly family have their home at 119 North Trumbly Avenue. The late Julian Trumbly, while identified with Pawhuska from its beginning, spent the greater part of his active lifetime on his farm near the Kansas line, and died there May 20, 1912.

He was not only one of the pioneers and active members of the Osage Nation but a citizen whose interests extended in many directions, including large business affairs, and he was frequently delegated for official duties in connection with the tribal government and every position of honor and trust was well bestowed in his case.

Inheriting his Osage citizenship through his mother, Julian Trumbly was born at Kansas City, Kansas, September 13, 1850, a son of Francis Louis and Lorene Trumbly. His father was of French ancestry and his mother partly French and a quarter blood Osage. They were regularly enrolled among the tribe in Neosho County, Kansas, and both died at St. Paul in that state. They were survived by three sons: Francis, Julian and John Baptiste, all of whom are now deceased.

In the late '60s Julian Trumbly accompanied the other members of the Osage tribe to Indian Territory and in company with the venerable Indian agent of that time, Isaac Gibson, assisted in locating the old agency at what is now Pawhuska. He was employed in a store for several years until after his marriage, and in 1875 moved to a farm near the state line in the Caney Valley, and for forty years that farm was his home and the center of his extended activities in business.

In 1906 Mr. Trumbly served as an Osage townsite commissioner, and helped to lay out all the towns in Osage County, including Pawhuska. He was prominent in tribal affairs from the early days and made many trips to Washington as an Osage delegate. He spent one entire winter, four months, in Washington acting for the Osage people in company with William T. Leahy. For many years he was a member of the Osage Council, and at one time declined the high honor of election as chief of the nation. In a business way the late Mr. Trumbly was interested in the Southern Kansas Supply Company of Elgin, was identified with the First National Bank of Pawhuska and had interests in three other banks, was a stockholder in the Pawhuska Oil & Gas Company and the Pawhuska-Cleveland Oil & Gas Company. For many years he gave active supervision to the large landed interests of his family, their aggregate allotment comprising about twelve sections of land. In politics Mr. Trumbly was a democrat, and was reared in and was always faithful to the Catholic Church.

On February 10, 1873, he married Miss Eliza Ann Tinker, who was born in Neosho County, Kansas, September 11, 1854, and came to Indian Territory with the removal of the Osages from Southern Kansas. Her parents were George and Lucretia (La Shappel) Tinker, and through her mother she inherits one-fourth French blood and three-quarters Osage. The Tinker family has long been prominent in the Osage country, and further information concerning its members will be found on other pages. Mrs. Trumbly is still living at the old family residence in Pawhuska. She was the mother of nine children. George Francis is a farmer in Osage County. Mary E. is the wife of A. J. McClintock of Osage County. Maude C is the wife of Bruce Todd of Osage County. Clarence A is a merchant at Elgin, Kansas. Oliver W. lives on the old homestead in the northern part of Osage County

Henry is also a farmer in that county. Augusta is the wife of Bruce Hendricks, a farmer in the Caney Valley of Osage County. Charles was married February 14, 1915, to Minna A. Chambers, and they live in Pawhuska. Theresa, the youngest child, is still at home with her mother.

WALDO E. MORRIS, a prominent young attorney of Harper County, now filling the office of county attorney, has been identified with that section of the state for the past fifteen years, was a homesteader and farmer, then took up the law, and a few years ago gravitated into journalism, and is now editor and manager of the May Record at May.

He was eighteen years old when his family came to Oklahoma. Mr. Morris was born in a log house on a farm in Jasper County, Illinois, March 25, 1883, his parents being James and Ora J. (Melton) Morris. His father was born April 9, 1854, in Ohio, and has spent his active career as a farmer and merchant. In 1901 he brought his family to Oklahoma, and he is now in the hotel business at May. In 1879 he married Miss Melton, who was born in 1860, a daughter of John Melton, a native of Illinois, and her death occurred February 14, 1890. She is survived by five children, four sons and one daughter, as follows: Clinton, born in 1881 and a farmer in Ellis County, Oklahoma; Waldo E.; Emmons Gray, born December 20, 1884; Verna Valeria, born September 20, 1887, was married in 1906 to Robert V. Patton, a farmer of Ellis County; and John Israel, born August 31, 1889, and a farmer in Ellis County.

Waldo E. Morris received his public school education in Jasper County, Illinois. When he came to Oklahoma in 1901 he located a claim of Government land in Woodward County, and vigorously followed up his business as a practical farmer and homesteader until 1909. With such money as he had been able to acquire and save he entered Washburn College at Topeka, Kansas, and was graduated LL. B. from the law class in 1912. In that year he began practice at May, and has done very well in his profession.

In 1914 he was elected county attorney of Harper County. His election came on the Socialist ticket and for several years he has been a recognized leader in that party in Oklahoma. In 1914 he bought the May Record and has made it a vigorous exponent of the principles of socialism, and has not only extended its circulation throughout Harper County, but to many remote points in the state. Individually and through his paper he has constantly espoused the cause of political reform. Mr. Morris deserves the credit of having inaugurated a state usury league, and this league brought about the passage of new usury measures through the State Legislature.

On February 20, 1909, Mr. Morris married Miss Lilly Frances Getz, who was born in Effingham County, Illinois, September 20, 1889, a daughter of William and Elizabeth Getz, who were also natives of Illinois. Mr. and Mrs. Morris have four children: Lillian Elizabeth, born November 6, 1909; Theodore Earl, born December 20, 1911; Thera May, born April 29, 1913; and Erma Catherine, born February 20, 1915.

CLYDE MUSGROVE. Though for a number of years his principle work has been in the postoffice at El Reno, where he is now senior clerk under the civil service rules, Clyde Musgrove is a well known newspaper man and writer, and as cartoonist, correspondent, editor and publisher was identified with several of the prominent early papers in the western section of the state.

He was born December 11, 1874, at South Haven, Kansas, son of Jacob R. and Isabella C. (Graham) Musgrove. The late Jacob R. Musgrove was prominent as a pioneer both in Kansas and Oklahoma. He was born in Jackson County, Ohio, of which state his parents were also natives, and of Scotch stock. Reared on a farm, Jacob R. Musgrove served full four years as a private in Company E of the Twenty-second Ohio Volunteer Infantry. He was with his regiment in all its battles and campaigns, followed Sherman on his march from Atlanta to the sea, and was finally mustered out at Washington, D. C.

In 1870, some years after the close of the war, he moved into the sparsely settled and undeveloped districts of Southern Kansas, acquiring a tract of Government land in Pottawatomie County. In 1872 he opened one of the first stores at Winfield, Kansas. In 1873 he founded the Town of South Haven in Sumner County. For a number of years he was one of the leading merchants along the South Kansas border, erecting stores at old Salt City, Guelph and South Haven. He was the first and for many years was postmaster at South Haven. His stores along the border of Indian Territory were conducted largely as Indian trading posts. In the early days he organized and maintained an ox wagon freighting train for the hauling of supplies to the Fort Reno and Darlington agency.

In 1889 the late Jacob R. Musgrove participated in the original Oklahoma opening, and located at old Reno City. The railroad avoided that town, and he moved and identified himself with the new railroad station at the present City of El Reno, having acquired a homestead right near the town. This homestead is still a part of his estate, and is situated a mile east of El Reno. Jacob R. Musgrove was a prominent republican, and took part in the organization of Canadian County. He was a member of the Masonic order and of the Grand Army of the Republic. His death occurred at South Haven, Kansas, July 28, 1899.

Jacob R. Musgrove and wife were married January 27, 1874. They were the parents of two sons and two daughters, namely: Clyde; Birdie, deceased; Carl, a resident of Oklahoma City; and Edith, deceased.

Clyde Musgrove acquired his early education in the public schools of Winfield, Kansas, and also attended the Southwestern Methodist College at Winfield. When eighteen years of age he entered a printing office and learned the trade. In time he became versed in all the phases of the printer's trade and the newspaper profession, and in 1896 he established and for five years was editor of the News at El Reno, now the El Reno American. He made this one of the most influential newspapers of old Oklahoma Territory, and as a political cartoonist his work received recognition and appreciation over the state. He served as city editor of the Oklahoma City Star during its existence, and in 1901 founded the News at Lawton, soon after the opening of that section of the state.

After his father's death Mr. Musgrove returned to El Reno and accepted a clerkship in the postoffice under civil service, and is now senior clerk.

On August 19, 1905, at Girard, Kansas, he married Miss Alice E. Firmin. She was born in London, England, September 20, 1875, a daughter of John T. Firmin, also a native of England. Mr. Musgrove has made himself a considerable factor in El Reno affairs and since 1910 has been a member and is now president of the board of directors of the Carnegie Library.

NAT EMMONS LIGON. That integrity and ability, as combined with untiring industry and good judgment, will not lack recognition and appreciation has been significantly shown in the meteoric career of Mr. Ligon, who is now serving as counsel for the Mid-Co. Petroleum Company and Mid-Co. Gasoline Company, two of the largest independent oil producing and oil refining companies operating in the great mid-continent field, with offices in the City of Tulsa, Tulsa County, Oklahoma.

Having already served for two years as assistant prosecuting attorney for Tulsa County, from which office he was elevated to that of United States Probate Attorney for the Creek Indians, and, later, at the age of twenty-six years, employed as chief legal representative of two large corporations whose combined property holdings aggregate millions of dollars in value, and whom he represents both as legal adviser and in litigation involving hundreds of thousands of dollars worth of property, Mr. Ligon bears the distinction of being the youngest corporation lawyer in the state.

Fine personal address, buoyant and optimistic nature and unbounded kindliness and geniality have gained to Mr. Ligon a wide circle of friends in the state of his adoption, and all rejoice in his success, for the same has been won entirely through his own ability and earnest endeavors. His brilliant achievements have placed him foremost in the ranks of the younger generation of professional men, and it is gratifying to accord him recognition in this history.

A scion of staunch old Southern stock, Mr. Ligon was born at Gloster, Amite County, Mississippi, on the first day of September, 1888, and he is the son of William O. Ligon and Jennie D. (Faust) Ligon, the former of whom was one of the earliest settlers of Amite County, and the latter of whom was born at Liberty, Mississippi, their present home being at Gloster, Mississippi. William O. Ligon served for twelve years as Deputy United States Marshal and for three years as United States Marshal in the Southern Judicial District of Mississippi, with official headquarters in the cities of Vicksburg and Jackson, respectively. In early life he was a prosperous planter and merchant, and during the Civil war he served the Confederacy under General Wirt Adams of Mississippi. He resigned from the office of United States Marshal in July, 1914, and returned to Gloster where he is now living, virtually retired.

Nat Emmons Ligon (universally known and referred to as Nat Ligon), the youngest in a family of six sons, acquired his early education in the public schools of his native state and thereafter entered the University of Mississippi at Oxford. For two years he was a student in the academic or literary department of the university and later entered the university law school. On account of financial reverses which came to his parents, Mr. Ligon remained in the university only through endurance of untold difficulties and hardships. For a time he earned his own expenses by directing the university band and orchestra, for which the authorities allowed him board and tuition. While thus engaged he, as president of the sophomore class, was largely instrumental in organizing the Students Self Help Bureau, which has since enabled hundreds of worthy young men of limited resources to be self-sustaining while pursuing their course of study. He took an active interest in debating and public speaking and his present effectiveness as a trial lawyer is due largely to his forensic ability. He won two class medals for oratory, represented his alma mater in a collegiate state oratorical contest and in a collegiate inter-state debating contest and was undefeated during his scholastic career. Financial difficulties and ill health finally forced him to withdraw from the law school three months prior to the graduation of his class, and he came direct from Oxford to Tulsa, Oklahoma, where he arrived on the 8th day of March, 1911.

With his finances at the lowest possible ebb and without an acquaintance in the city, he was not discouraged but turning his face toward the dawn of a new day for him, he sought employment that would enable him to provide the necessities of life and, at the same time, continue his study of the law. He was received as a clerk in the first office to which he applied for admission, that of Davidson & Williams, attorneys, where he remained and eked out a scanty subsistence for the first year of his residence in the new and growing city. At night he vigorously continued his study of the science of jurisprudence and in the following June he was admitted to practice in the courts of Oklahoma—the same week in which his class in the law department of the University of Mississippi was graduated.

In June, 1912, Mr. Ligon was employed by the city authorities of Tulsa to revise and codify the municipal ordinance, and this work demanded his attention for three months. In August, 1912, with his work for the city scarcely begun, he was appointed to the position of assistant prosecuting attorney of Tulsa County under Pat Malloy. Only a few weeks after his appointment to this office Mr. Ligon gained prominence for himself and drew words of lavish praise from the press in Oklahoma, and throughout the country, for his masterful efforts in the prosecution of Mrs. Laura T. Renter, and her co-conspirators, for the murder of her husband, Charles T. Renter, a prominent attorney of Tulsa. In three successive trials of the different defendants in this famous case, Mr. Ligon made the opening address for the prosecution to the jury. In speaking of his argument in the first of these trials, the Tulsa Daily World of October 30, 1912, used, in part, the following language:

"Probably never before in the history of criminal practice has a better argument been made by an attorney with so few years on his shoulders than that of the young assistant prosecutor who has just passed his twenty-fourth birthday. It was his second appeal to a jury and it happens that the first appeal was also in a murder case. Old attorneys who listened for two hours and a half while Ligon reviewed the evidence and made a strong plea for the maximum penalty, death, were unanimous in their opinion that his effort was worthy of a man years older, both in age and experience."

In February, 1914, Mr. Ligon resigned as assistant prosecuting attorney to accept an appointment as United States Probate Attorney for the Creek Indians, with official headquarters in the City of Sapulpa, Creek County.

The United States Government spends the sum of $85,000.00 annually in the employment of probate attorneys, one in each of the counties inhabited by citizens of the Five Civilized Tribes in Oklahoma, whose duty it is to guard the interests of minor and incompetent Indian allottees against the inroads made on their estates by corrupt guardians and designing persons. During the first twelve months that he held this office, Mr. Ligon saved and recovered for the estates of minors and incompetents in Creek County alone, more than $90,000.00, or more than the entire annual appropriation of Congress for the salaries and expenses of twenty other probate attorneys in Oklahoma.

In September, 1915, while serving as probate attorney further professional distinction was conferred upon Mr. Ligon, when he was elected special judge to preside in the trial of an important murder case in the District Court of Creek County. The youngest jurist who ever presided in the trial of a murder case in Oklahoma, he thus occupied the position on the bench for three days and his rulings bore the stamp of true judicial wisdom and a broad and accurate knowledge of the law.

Mr. Ligon is a Royal Arch Mason, a member of th

Benevolent and Protective Order of Elks, and holds membership in the secret order of Kappa Alpha, a Greek letter college fraternity. He is a member of the First Baptist Church at Tulsa.

On January 20, 1916, Mr. Ligon was happily married at Sapulpa, Oklahoma, to Miss Zula Lee Nash, formerly of Austin, Texas. Mrs. Ligon was born in Bastrop County, Texas, and is the daughter of Horace Nash and Lillian L. (Billingsley) Nash, both of Bastrop County, Texas. The forefathers of her mother (the Billingsleys) are well known in Texas history, having been active in establishing the independence of Texas. Long before this time, however, her ancestors had won fame in the struggle for the American Independence and their deeds of virtue engraved on the tablets of American history. Her ancestry dates back to the tenth century, she being the direct descendant of the historic Puleston family in England, and of Edward I of England and Ferdinand, King of Spain.

The proud descendant of a family with a long list of noble achievements, one of the Southland's fairest daughters and a typically American woman, Mrs. Ligon represents the crowning success of her husband's many brilliant attainments.

CAMPBELL RUSSELL. Coming to Indian Territory as a youth of seventeen years, Senator Russell has had a broad and varied experience in pioneer life on the frontier and has been a prominent and influential force in connection with the civic and industrial development of what is now the State of Oklahoma. He has shown himself a man of resourcefulness and decisive action, and stands today as one of the vigorous and successful representatives of the agricultural and live-stock interests of this commonwealth, the while his civic loyalty and public spirit are indicated in the fact that he was a member of the first State Senate after the admission of Oklahoma to the Union and that he is at the present time a member of that body, as representative of the Twenty-seventh senatorial district. The senator's liberality and progressiveness have been of noteworthy order and have inured greatly to the march of development and advancement in the vital young commonwealth within which he has maintained his residence for more than thirty years.

Campbell Russell was born in Northern Alabama, on the 22d of October, 1863, and is a son of Thomas and Margaret (Stringer) Russell, the former a native of North Carolina and the latter of Kentucky, in which state her father was a pioneer settler. Thomas Russell, as a young man, established his home in the northern part of the State of Alabama, where he became a pioneer teacher in the common schools and where he was long a prosperous agriculturist and influential citizen. Both he and his wife continued their residence in Alabama until their death, the former having passed away in 1895 and the latter in 1901.

After availing himself of the advantages of the common schools of his native state Senator Russell completed, in 1881, a course in the business college of the University of Lexington, in the metropolis of Kentucky. In the same year he immigrated to Indian Territory and found employment on the Three Bar Ranch, which was at that time the largest cattle ranch in the Cherokee Nation and which was situated twelve miles distant from Muskogee. This great ranch was owned and controlled by Gen. Pleasant Porter and C. W. Turner, the former of whom was the principal chief of the Creek tribe. Eventually Senator Russell engaged in farming and stock-growing on his own account, and in 1895 he handled 14,000 head of cattle, this representing the largest herd that up to that time had ever been assembled in Indian Territory. His ranch was in Younger's Bend on the Canadian River, this bend having been named for the well known bandits, the Younger Brothers, of Missouri, who there maintained a rendezvous during their days of outlawry on the frontier, the locality having likewise been a headquarters for Belle Starr, a woman known throughout the Southwest as an accomplice and associate of the Younger Brothers.

In that historic district Senator Russell cleared and improved a ranch of 400 acres, and there he established the first free school for white children within the entire confines of Indian Territory, the schoolhouse having been erected by him at his own expense and he having defrayed individually also the expense of employing a teacher in the school each summer for a period of five years. As one of the most enterprising and energetic of pioneers, the senator made his constructive influence felt in many other avenues of progress. After his removal to Warner, his present home, he individually graded at his own expense sixteen miles of public road besides which he erected a schoolhouse, at a cost of $5,300, and donated the same to the township. Such is the spirit of liberality and unselfish devotion to the public weal that has animated him and that has made an honored and influential citizen of the state of which he may consistently be termed one of the founders and builders.

After initiating the development of his ranch in the vicinity of the Village of Warner Senator Russell directed his attention definitely to the breeding of registered cattle, from select stock which he purchased in the northern states. He raised principally Shorthorn and Hereford cattle, and later he made disposition of much of his stock product in various years by means of public sales in Alabama, Florida, Louisiana, Arkansas, Texas and Oklahoma, the proceeds of each of several of these sales was above $30,000. At the Louisiana Purchase Exposition, in the City of St. Louis, in 1904, Senator Russell won twenty-seven premiums on his exhibit of Hereford cattle and also a diploma as the champion breeder of Herefords in the sub-quarantine (or southern) division of the country. It may well be understood that he had done much to advance the standards of live-stock and agricultural industry in Oklahoma, and a detailed record of his progressive activities would make a context sufficient for an entire published volume.

As a resident of the domain of the Five Tribes, Senator Russell cast his first vote for Joel Mayes for chief of the Cherokees, and his next vote was for Green McCurtain for chief of the Choctaws. Having by marriage a "right" in both of these nations, he traveled on horse-back forty miles from outside of the Cherokee Nation to vote in a Cherokee election, and traveled sixty miles to exercise a similar function in a Choctaw election. The senator served three years as a member of the executive committee of the Farmers' Educational & Cooperative Union of Oklahoma; one term as president of the state union; and three terms as secretary of the board of directors of the national union. Upon his retirement from the latter office, on the 5th of September, 1911, the board of directors presented him with a handsome gold medal, on which were inscribed the words, "Weighed in the balance and not found found wanting," a most consonant expression touching his character and services during the long years of his residence in what is now the State of Oklahoma. In 1896 the senator effected the organization of the Canadian District Protective Association, which later was merged with the Indian Territory division of the Anti-Horse-Thief Association. Of this latter and more comprehensive organization he served three years as president, one year as vice president, and has since continued a member of its executive committee. During one year he captured nine men charged with the theft of horses and cattle, and he succeeded also in recovering during that year ten horses that had been stolen.

Senator Russell was a member of the first state senate of Oklahoma and in the initial session of the Legislature he came into special prominence as the chief champion of what became known as the "New Jerusalem" capital scheme, a measure that provided for the establishment of the capital of the new commonwealth near the geographical center of the state and which was carried at a popular election held in 1908. In the first session of the Legislature Senator Russell was chairman of the senate committee on roads and highways and at succeeding sessions his membership in the senate having been continuous, he has served as chairman of the committee on agriculture. In the Second Legislature three of the first five bills passed in the senate were introduced and championed by him, and one of them authorized the establishing of county agricultural demonstration farms; another prevented married minors from selling inherited real estate. In this session also he obtained in the senate the passage of a bill providing for the carrying out of the provisions of the "New Jerusalem" measure, but the bill failed to pass the House of Representatives. A constitutional amendment, of which he was the author, providing for per capita distribution of tax paid by public-service corporations for school purposes, was five times given enactive approval by the senate, but three times the resolution was killed in the house, and twice it was submitted to the people. In the first popular election it received more than two-thirds of the votes but it was defeated by reason of not having met the requirement of receiving a majority of all votes cast in that election. In a special session of the Legislature, in 1913, the proposition was again submitted and carried by a substantial majority.

In the Fourth Legislature Senator Russell introduced a measure providing for congressional representation of Oklahoma upon the basis of the relative strength of the various political parties, but this bill failed enactment. He also succeeded in securing the passage of an act providing for a 2 per cent gross production tax on oil and gas. In this session he secured the passage of a provision recalling the state board of agriculture. This board was twice recalled inside of twelve months; first by initiative petition, and second by provision submitted by the Legislature. In the Fifth Legislature Senator Russell was author of a rural credits bill which was enacted without a dissenting vote, and also of a proposed constitutional amendment fixing a graduated land tax which was defeated in the house. In the First Legislature he had put through a similar measure, but five years later this was declared by the Supreme Court to be unconstitutional. He passed another bill for the same purpose in the Fourth Legislature, which was invalidated by the court on account of premature adjournment of the Legislature. He was the author of graduated tax upon net income, which is now being successfully applied in Oklahoma, also of the 3 per cent gross production tax upon oil and gas, which is still being contested in the court.

In 1910 Senator Russell was defeated for the democratic nomination of representative of the third district in the United States Congress, by Hon. James Davenport; and in the newly created second district he was again defeated for congressional nomination in 1914, his successful opponent in the primaries having been Hon. William W. Hastings, of Tahlequah. Senator Russell is a member of the Christian Church, is affiliated with the lodge of the Ancient Free and Accepted Masons in his home Village of Warner and with the chapter of Royal Arch Masons at Muskogee; with the Independent Order of Odd Fellows at Warner, and with the local organization at Warner of the National Farmers' Educational and Cooperative Union. He has one sister, Mrs. Nannie Windes, of Tempe, Arizona, and one brother, James E., who is a resident of Texas.

On the 25th of December, 1890, Senator Russell married Martha Shinn, who was of Cherokee Indian blood, and she died a few years later, leaving no children. In November, 1896, was solemnized the marriage of the Senator to Mamie Overstreet, who is of Choctaw descent. Concerning the children of these unions brief data is given in conclusion of this article: Connie is engaged in business at Warner; Carl is a teacher in the Oklahoma Secondary Agricultural School at Helena; Christopher is a student in the law department of the University of Oklahoma; Mary is a teacher; Margaret is a student in the Oklahoma Agricultural and Mechanical College at Stillwater; and Clayton and Martha remain at the parental home.

FRANK D. NORTHUP. Incidental to the individual career and ancestral history of Mr. Northup there are many points of distinctive interest, and even this necessarily epitomized record can not fail measurably to denote the consistency of the above statement. Personally he is to be designated as a pioneer in each of two counties in the present State of Oklahoma; he was one of the early and valued members of the faculty of the Oklahoma Agricultural and Mechanical College at Stillwater; he has been specially prominent and influential in connection with the development of the agricultural and live-stock industries in this state; and is at the present time one of the interested principals and efficient executives of the company publishing the Oklahoma Farm Journal, the leading agricultural periodical of the Southwest, besides being secretary and business manager of the Times Publishing Company, which publishes the Oklahoma City Times, one of the most important daily papers of the state. Apropos of the genealogical history of this well known and honored citizen it may be stated that the original progenitors of the Northup family in America immigrated from England in first decade of the seventeenth century, and settled at New Providence, Rhode Island. In 1735 an ancestor of the subject of this review became one of the pioneer settlers of Berkshire County, Massachusetts, and the family name has long stood representative of prominence and influence in the annals of that picturesque section of the old Bay State.

Frank D. Northup was born on a farm near the city of Pittsfield, Berkshire County, Massachusetts, on the 14th of July, 1870, and is a son of Langham D. and Addie M. (Baird) Northup, the former a native of Massachusetts and the latter of Ohio. In 1874 the family removed from Massachusetts to the West and the father became a pioneer farmer in Kansas; he developed a fine farm in that state, and continued a prominent and honored citizen of that section of Kansas until his death, in 1904, his widow being now a resident of Oklahoma City.

He whose name initiates this review was about four years old at the time of the family removal to Kansas, where he was reared to adult age under the invigorating discipline of the home farm and where he was afforded the advantages of the excellent public schools. In the Sunflower State he also gained practical experience in the printing and newspaper business, and in April, 1892, about three months prior to his twenty-second birthday anniversary, he came to the newly organized Territory of Oklahoma and became one of the pioneer settlers of Taloga, Dewey County. There he continued as editor and publisher of the Taloga Occident, a weekly paper, until May of the following year, when he removed to Stillwater, and thus became likewise a pioneer of Payne County. In September, 1893, when the famous Cherokee strip, or outlet, was thrown open to settlement, Mr. Northup was among those who made the historic "run" to obtain land in the new district, and he secured a tract of 160 acres, eligibly situated nine miles from Stillwater. He reclaimed this land to cultivation and perfected his title to the property, of which he is still the owner. On the 1st of March, 1899, Mr. Northup became a member of the faculty of the Oklahoma Agricultural and Mechanical College at Stillwater, in which institution he became superintendent of the department of printing. Of this office he continued the incumbent until the 1st of May, 1901, when he resigned and assumed that of editor and publisher of the Stockman-Farmer, at Stillwater. While still identified with the affairs of the college he had served for a time as editor of the Stillwater Gazette, and after publishing the Stockman-Farmer one year he became associated, in 1902, with John Fields in the purchase of the Oklahoma Farm Journal, the publication of which paper they continued at Stillwater until the 1st of October, 1906, when they removed the plant to Oklahoma City, which in the following year became the capital of the new State of Oklahoma. In this city the Oklahoma Farm Journal has since continued to be published, and with constantly expanding influence, its progressive business and editorial policies have made it the leading farm publication of the state and its circulation now extending into virtually all agricultural sections of the Southwest. In January, 1915, Mr. Northup and his associates purchased also the stock of the Times Publishing Company, publishers of the Oklahoma City Times, the issuing of which daily paper is continued in connection with the publishing of the Farm Journal. Mr. Northup is secretary and advertising manager of the Oklahoma Farm Journal Company and secretary and business manager of the Times Publishing Company.

In politics Mr. Northup has ever given unwavering allegiance to the republican party. In 1898 he enlisted for service in the Spanish-American war, as a member of the First Territorial Volunteer Infantry, and with this command he held the rank of corporal during the period of active military operations in Cuba, though his regiment was not called to the front. Mr. Northup is past commander of Oklahoma City Post of the United Spanish-American War Veterans, and since 1910 he has been secretary of the Oklahoma State Historical Society, a fact that indicates his deep and abiding interest in all that touches the history and advancement of the state of which he is a pioneer and in which his circle of friends is coincident with that of his acquaintances. He is past chancellor of Stillwater Lodge No. 8, Knights of Pythias, and both he and his wife hold membership in the Methodist Episcopal Church.

December 25, 1895, Mr. Northup wedded Miss Myrtle A. Hutto, daughter of Isaac N. Hutto, of Stillwater, and her death occurred in June, 1897. On the 27th of June, 1900, was solemnized the marriage of Mr. Northup to Miss Elsie M. Parker, daughter of H. Parker, of Claiborne, this state, and the two children of this union are Dorothy Elizabeth and Carolyn Duane. The family residence is at 424 East Park Street, Oklahoma City, and the business offices of Mr. Northup are at 220 West Second Street.

WARREN ZIMMERMAN. Since 1907 Mr. Zimmerman has been the capable editor and owner of the Guymon Herald at Guymon. Since reaching manhood Mr. Zimmerman has always worked at the printer's trade or in newspaper business, and has been identified with Oklahoma journalism for ten years. He has more than succeeded in keeping the Guymon Herald at the high place it deserves by reason of a quarter century's existence in this district of Western Oklahoma.

The primitive conditions of western pioneer life surrounded Warren Zimmerman at his birth. He was born January 8, 1880, in a sod house on a farm in Osborne County, Kansas. His parents were Benjamin Franklin Grush and Phoebe (Smiley) Zimmerman. His father was born in Perry County, Pennsylvania, September 14, 1844, a son of William Zimmerman, also a native of Pennsylvania. The father spent all his active career as a farmer. During the Civil war he enlisted in the One Hundred and Forty-fourth Regiment of Pennsylvania Infantry, but was out only six months, being discharged on account of illness. A few years after the war, in 1871, he moved out to Kansas, locating on Government land in Osborne County. Like many of the early settlers there he was a man of limited means and he put up the kind of house which was typical of that district then and for many years afterwards. He and his family lived in the sod dugout, enduring hardships and privations, and for several years practically all the meat that was consumed in the family came from buffaloes, which were still numerous on the Kansas prairies. In politics he was a republican, but had no aspirations to official position, although he was one of the organizers of Osborne County. His death occurred at Porter, Kansas, January 15, 1910. He was a member of the Methodist Episcopal Church, and was active in Grand Army circles. In 1874, at Waterville, Kansas, Benjamin F. Zimmerman married Mrs. Phoebe (Smiley) Kistler. She was born in Pennsylvania, September 17, 1846, and in 1868 she married William Kistler. There was one child by this union, Lillian, now the wife of Bert Long of Liberal, Kansas. Mr. Kistler died in 1870. By her second union she became the mother of five children, two sons and three daughters, namely: Gertrude, who was the first born, was born June 6, 1875, and died in 1881; William Luther, born February 8, 1876; Warren; Mary Smiley, born November 17, 1882; and Winifred, born May 3, 1884, now the wife of John Hahn of Osborne, Kansas.

Warren Zimmerman came to manhood with the equivalent of a liberal education. He attended the public schools in Osborne and the Kansas Wesleyan College at Salina. In 1901, at the age of twenty-one, he entered the office of the Osborne County Farmer at Osborne, and there learned the printer's trade and many details of practical newspaper management. In 1903 he was made editor and manager of the Osborne News, directed that paper for two years, and then in 1905 came to Oklahoma and bought an interest in the Chandler News. He remained at Chandler two years, and then in 1907 bought the Guymon Herald at Guymon.

Since taking charge of the Herald Mr. Zimmerman has introduced many changes and improvements in the interests of a modern newspaper plant. In towns of the size there are few newspaper plants in the state that equal the Herald office. The Herald is a republican paper, has a large and influential circulation, and is a credit to the large district it serves as the chief medium for news, opinion and advertising. It was established in 1890 and was the pioneer paper of Texas County.

On January 22, 1906, at Fort Worth, Texas, Mr. Zimmerman married Martha Edgemon. She was born

January 22, 1883, at Athens, Tennessee, where her parents were also born. To their union has been born one child, Richard Grush, born February 4, 1909, at Guymon. Mr. Zimmerman and wife are members of the Methodist Episcopal Church, and fraternally he is a Knight Templar Mason.

COL. S. A. MCGINNIS. One of the most prominent lawyers and citizens of Kay County is Colonel McGinnis of Newkirk. Colonel McGinnis has been identified with Oklahoma as a lawyer and man of affairs since 1893, and for twenty-two years has made his help and service count for value and progress in the Southwest.

S. A. McGinnis was born in Coffey County, Kansas, November 10, 1867. His father, Dr. J. A. McGinnis, was a native of West Virginia and an early settler in Kansas. He was a soldier in the Union Army during the Civil war, and was the son of a soldier in the Mexican war, while his great-grandfather has served in the War of 1812, and a great-grandfather was a soldier of the Revolution. Thus there has been a strong tendency to military life in every successive generation, and Colonel McGinnis of Newkirk has his title as a result of active participation in the National Guards of both Kansas and Oklahoma. Dr. J. A. McGinnis was a successful physician and well known factor in Coffey and Butler counties, Kansas. He had moved from the East to Indiana, later to Illinois, and finally to Kansas, being identified for varying lengths of time with all these states.

Col. S. A. McGinnis was married in 1890 to Laura Laughlin, a woman of culture and intelligence and belonging to a family of noted educators. Her father, George H. Laughlin, was at one time president of Hiram College in Ohio, the insitution over which James A. Garfield at one time presided, and a strong and intimate friendship existed between Mr. Garfield and Professor Laughlin. The children born to Colonel and Mrs. McGinnis are: Harold, who has served four years in the United States navy as an electrician, and has visited every important part of the Globe; Eilene; Ward A.; Grant; and Arthur.

Colonel McGinnis rose to the rank of colonel in the Second Regiment of Kansas troops in the National Guards, and has also served as captain of Troop I, First United States Volunteer Cavalry, "Roosevelt Rough Riders," of Oklahoma. He was attorney to the Dawes Commission in Indian Territory for eighteen months, and has also served in many other legal capacities. He was attorney for Butler County, Kansas, and has also served as county attorney in Oklahoma. He is a man of most pleasing address and manner, is a splendid speaker and is a large man both physically and mentally.

LOUIS ROGERS, SR., is one of the men who have known Pawhuska in all its growth and development from an Indian agency to a thriving and flourishing city. Mr. Rogers has himself been a part of that development and growth. His is a name synonymous with integrity, good business ability, and all the sterling qualities of citizenship.

Though most of his life has been spent in Oklahoma, he was born in Georgia, March 15, 1843. His parents were Nelson and Rosa (West) Rogers, both of whom were natives of Georgia, where they married. They were the parents of two sons and two daughters. The oldest and the youngest of the family are still living. Nelson Rogers and his wife came to Indian Territory in the early days, and he was successfully identified with general farming and the cattle business.

For many years Louis Rogers was a successful farmer near Avant, Oklahoma, and conducted ranching on a small scale. After the death of his first wife he sold his farm in that locality and has since had his home at Pawhuska. In his long and active career Mr. Rogers has also acquired military experience. He served three years in the war between the states and is one of the honored veterans of that great struggle. All his life he has been a democrat, and for twenty years has been affiliated with the Knights of Pythias. While he himself has no church affiliations, his wife is a Methodist.

About forty years ago Mr. Rogers married Miss Helen Ross, a daughter of Louis Ross, a prominent name among the early Indian families of Indian Territory. Louis Ross brought his family to Oklahoma from Georgia. Mr. Rogers by his first marriage had five children. Three are now deceased. His daughter is the wife of Ben Avant, reference to whom is found on other pages of this work. Mr. Rogers' son lives near Avant. For his second wife Mr. Rogers married Mrs. Hood, a white woman from Fort Smith, Arkansas.

ROBERT LEE FLYNN. Perhaps no one class of men more thoroughly appreciate the fact that Oklahoma is a new state than those upon whom are thrust the responsibilities of county offices. In the older states it is customary for each distinct set of duties to be performed by a special official. As a matter of economy and on account of the great expense involved in organizing and establishing county government all over the state, it is not unusual to find in Oklahoma one official filling what is in reality half a dozen offices at once.

This state of affairs is well illustrated in the person of Robert Lee Flynn of Shawnee, whose official designation is court clerk. He has his offices both in the City Hall at Shawnee and in the County Courthouse at Tecumseh. He is clerk of the District Court of Pottawatomie and Lincoln counties; is clerk of the Superior Court located at Shawnee, with jurisdiction over Pottawatomie County; and is also clerk of the Pottawatomie County Court at Tecumseh. Robert E. Flynn is a Missourian and was born in Howard County, April 4, 1885. His father, Stephen A. Flynn, was born in Ireland in 1839, came to America about 1855 when little more than a boy, and after living for a time in New York State and in Ohio came out to Missouri, where he married and soon afterward established his home in Howard County. He was one of the pioneer settlers in Oklahoma, having located in Lincoln County in 1892, not long after the opening opening of lands in that district. In 1899 he removed to Keokuk Falls in Pottawatomie County, and homesteaded a claim. He was not only a farmer but also a school teacher. He also rendered service to his adopted country during the dark days of the Civil war as a Union soldier for three years. In one battle he was severely wounded, but recovered in time to join his comrades and served the full term of three years. He was a member of the Masonic fraternity. The death of this old Oklahoma settler occurred at Keokuk Falls in June 1904. The maiden name of his wife was Sarah C. Lowden, who was born in Missouri and now lives at Seminole Oklahoma. Their family comprised nine children, noted briefly as follows: Mrs. Maggie Buck, who lives at Anadarko and whose husband is a farmer; Maud, who married L. Tribble, who is a harness maker and merchant at Seminole City, Oklahoma; William H., who is now filling the office of sheriff in Lubbock County, Texas; Ivan L., who is a minister in the Nazarene Church in Seminole City; Thomas S., whose home is at Drumright, Oklahoma; Robert Lee, who comes next in order of birth; Joseph S., who is an employee in the United States Navy Yard at San Francisco; James W., a farmer at Anadarko; and May, wife of James Embree, a carpenter and builder at Perry, Oklahoma.

As will be noted Robert L. Flynn was only about seven years of age when his parents came to Oklahoma. During their residence in Lincoln County he attended public school at Ardmore. Still later he was sent to school at Whitewater, Wisconsin, and was graduated from the high school of that city in 1904. During 1905 he attended the Indianola Business College at Tecumseh, where he took a course in bookkeeping, and in 1906 learned stenography in the New State Business College at Shawnee.

From 1907 to 1911 Mr. Flynn was a stenographer in the law offices of Standard, Wahl & Ennis at Shawnee, and left that work to accept the position of deputy in the district clerk's office of Pottawatomie County. He continued as deputy until January 4, 1915, when he assumed his present onerous duties, having been elected to the office of court clerk in the preceding November. Mr. Flynn resides at 513 Louisa Street in Shawnee. He is a stockholder in the Fidelity Loan Company of that city, and is affiliated with the Knights of Pythias at Shawnee and Camp No. 7781 of the Modern Woodmen of America. In politics he is a democrat. In 1909 he became identified with the Oklahoma National Guard at Shawnee and is now lieutenant of the company.

On December 24, 1912, he was married at Shawnee to Miss Winnie McColgan of Shawnee. They have one daughter, Glorya Louise, born January 20, 1914.

W. R. KELLY, M. D. A man to whom may be consistently ascribed much versatility of talent, but the genius of whose success has been well ordered personal effort, is the sterling pioneer citizen whose name initiates this paragraph and who was one of the host of ambitious men who came into Oklahoma Territory at the time when the historic Cherokee Strip was thrown open to settlement. He has had the prescience and judgment to make good use of the manifold opportunities afforded in the state of his adoption and has become one of the substantial capitalists of Oklahoma, with large and varied interests. He still gives a considerable attention to the work of his profession, is the editor and publisher of the Watonga Herald, has been largely concerned with the real estate business and with banking interests, and has been one of the foremost in the development and upbuilding of the thriving Town of Watonga, the judicial center of Blaine County, where his property interests are large and valuable and where he maintains his residence, as one of the honored and influential citizens of that section of the state. Of him it has been properly said that "He is a type of the men of genius and courage who established civilized communities upon the prairies where only Indians had previously held sway, and who have contributed greately to the civic advancement and material wealth of the new state." The doctor is the owner of one of the largest and most effectively improved farms in Blaine County, and is the owner of a large number of properties in Watonga, including business and residence buildings to the number of thirty or more.

Doctor Kelly was born in the City of Fond du Lac, Wisconsin, in 1864, and is a representative of a sterling pioneer family of the fine old Badger State, where his father settled in 1848, soon after his immigration from Ireland. The doctor was one of a family of six sons and six daughters, and the mental alertness of the family is indicated by the fact that all of the sons and daughters eventually became successful teachers, the parents, Anthony and Abbie (Malley) Kelly, both of stanch old Irish stock, having continued their residence in Wisconsin until the time of their death. The six sisters of Doctor Kelly are still living, and concerning them the following brief record is consistently entered: Mrs. R. H. Murphy is a widow and resides in the City of Los Angeles, California, her husband having become known as the king of wheat farmers in North Dakota many years prior to his death; Mrs. B. A. Kindergan is the wife of a successful contractor in Sioux City, Iowa; Mrs. J. M. Rider resides in the same city and is a widow, her husband having been a prosperous farmer; Mrs. Frank Malley is the wife of a prominent real estate dealer in Sioux City; Miss Mary E. is a popular teacher in the high school in the City of Milwaukee, Wisconsin; and Mrs. T. J. Conley is the wife of a retired farmer, their home being now in Oklahoma City.

After duly availing himself of the advantages of the excellent public schools of his native state Doctor Kelly attended the Wisconsin State Normal School at Oshkosh from 1880 to 1884, and after the completing of his effective normal course he turned his attention to the pedagogic profession, of which he became a successful and popular representative as a teacher in the public schools of Wisconsin and later those of North Dakota. After devoting three years to this vocation the doctor was for a time engaged in farming in North Dakota, and then, in consonance with his ambition and well matured plans, he began the work of preparing himself for his chosen profession. He entered the celebrated Rush Medical College in the City of Chicago, in which he was graduated in 1892, with the degree of Doctor of Medicine. He forthwith entered upon a post-graduate course in the medical department of the University of Illinois, and in 1893 this institution likewise conferred upon him the degree of Doctor of Medicine. In the latter year he engaged in the practice of medicine at Watonga, Oklahoma Territory, and in the pioneer community he soon built up a substantial practice that marked him as one of the representative physicians and surgeons of the territory. He early became identified with other lines of productive activity in connection with which he resided for a time at Geary, Blaine County, and Weatherford, Custer County. In 1900 Doctor Kelly effected the organization of the First National Bank of Watonga, and of this institution he served six years as president. In 1894 he passed an examination before the territorial pharmaceutical board and then opened a drug store at Watonga, the same having been conducted in connection with his medical practice. Retiring from the banking business in 1906, he engaged in the real estate business, in connection with which he built up a large and important enterprise in the handling of both town and farm property. In the meanwhile he had become a stockholder in the company that published the Watonga Herald, and to protect his interest he was finally compelled to assume control of the newspaper plant and business, the result being that he has become well known also as one of the successful newspaper men of Oklahoma. He is still the owner and publisher of the Watonga Herald, of the editorial department of which he maintains personal supervision, and for a time he was the owner also of the Geary Bulletin and the Okeene Leader, in two other of the prosperous towns of Blaine County. The doctor is a member of the Oklahoma Press Association, the Oklahoma State Medical Association, the Blaine County Medical Society, the Oklahoma Pharmaceutical Association, the American Medical Association and the Oklahoma Telephone Association, besides which he was formerly an active member of the Oklahoma Bankers' Association. He is serving as health officer of Blaine County and as a member of the board of United States pension examiners for the county, besides being local surgeon at Watonga for the Chicago & Rock Island

Railroad. For the past ten years he has been president of the Watonga Commercial Club and has been a valued leader in the furtherance of its progressive civic policies and ideals, with special influence in giving to this thriving little city its excellent municipal waterworks and electric lighting systems and other public utilities. Under the energetic and capable direction of Doctor Kelly was constructed the first mile of modern improved road in Oklahoma, and he has been one of the liberal and zealous supporters of the good roads movement. Most of the brick buildings in Watonga were erected by this progressive and public-spirited citizen, and he is still the owner of fully thirty buildings in the town, including business structures and houses. He had also the distinction of being the prime factor in the movement to effect the erection of a suitable county courthouse at Watonga, and he is looked to for leadership and decisive action in every progressive measure advanced for the social and material benefit of his home city and county.

In the time-honored Masonic fraternity Doctor Kelly has received the thirty-second degree of the Ancient Accepted Scottish Rite, as a member of the Consistory in the City of Guthrie; his ancient craft affiliation is with Watonga Lodge No. 176, Ancient Free and Accepted Masons; and at Oklahoma City he holds membership in the Temple of the Ancient Arabic Order of Nobles of the Mystic Shrine. He is past master of the Masonic lodge in his home city, and is identified also with the Knights of Pythias, the Modern Woodmen of America, and the Ancient Order of United Workmen.

In 1896, at Watonga, was solemnized the marriage of Doctor Kelly to Miss Iva Carpenter, and she was summoned to the life eternal in July, 1911, being survived by two children, Cleo, who is a graduate of the Watonga High School and is one of the popular young women in the social activities of her home city, and William C., who was twelve years of age in 1915 and who is still attending the public schools.

BERT SMITH. On the basis of his record, Bert Smith is undoubtedly the most popular man in Garfield County politics. As everyone acquainted with things political in Oklahoma knows, Garfield County has long been one of the republican strongholds of the state, and yet Mr. Smith, as a democrat, has succeeded in overcoming the opposition forces on several occasions, and at the present time is holding the dual office of county clerk and register of deeds.

Bert Smith was born in Crawfordsville, Indiana, November 28, 1871, and in 1880, at the age of nine years, went with his parents to Reno County, Kansas, growing up on a farm in that section of the Sunflower State. From the farm he entered an office of the Rock Island Railway and learned telegraphy, was a telegraph operator at McPherson, Kansas, and in 1895 was transferred by the Rock Island Company to El Reno, Oklahoma. In 1897, leaving the railway service, Mr. Smith removed to Enid, and the following two years was engaged in farming seven miles west of that city. For ten years he sold nursery stock all over the state. He was also in business as a merchant at LaHoma for two years.

In 1912 Mr. Smith was elected register of deeds of Garfield County, and while he was in that office by act of the Legislature the duties of a register of deeds were combined with those of county clerk, and in November, 1914, Mr. Smith was elected to the combined office. In that campaign he had a strong contest with the former county clerk, a republican, who had not only the prestige attaching to him on the ground of his previous service, but also the backing of a normal republican majority in the county of 600. In 1912 Mr. Smith had carried the county with the largest majority ever given to any democrat, going into office with a margin of 731 votes. In 1914 he carried the county by a majority of sixty-nine. His duties as county clerk and register of deeds began on January 1, 1915, and he now gives all his time to this office, having three deputies.

Mr. Smith is affiliated with the Masonic and Odd Fellows fraternities. He married Miss Thirza I. Willis of Kirksville, Missouri. They have one daughter, Julia Pauline.

JESSE M. ROBBERSON. Farmer, banker and one of the old-timers of the Chickasaw Nation, Jesse M. Robberson lives at Loco in Stephens County, but his interests in farming lands and financial affairs are so extended as to make him one of the leading business figures in the state.

Jesse M. Robberson was born in Cedar County, Missouri, August 4, 1855, and there spent the first six years of his life, after which he went to Dade County, Missouri, in company with his parents, Richard Allen and Maria H. (Mitchell) Robberson. Several generations back the Robberson family were among the pioneer settlers of Middle Tennessee. Mr. Robberson's grandfather, William Robberson, was a Methodist preacher, and lived at Ebenezer, near Springfield, Missouri, and probably died there. Robberson Prairie, near Springfield, was named in his honor. The maternal grandfather, Jesse Mitchell, was also a minister of the Methodist Church and spent his last years at Brighton in Polk County, Missouri. In 1865 Richard A. Robberson took his family to Polk County, Missouri, renting a farm near Brighton. While the family lived there Jesse M. Robberson found plenty of work on the farm, after which he spent two years at Pleasant Hope or Pinhook. The father then removed his family to a tract of 160 acres of unimproved timber land, and the son helped to clear and reduce that to cultivation. Finally selling the farm, Richard A. Robberson removed to Paul's Valley, Indian Territory, in November, 1874. Several years later he went on a journey to Bellevue in Cooke County, Texas, to make arrangements to secure the benefit of the schools of that place for his children, and finally went on to Sherman, Texas, to procure lumber for the building of a home for his family in Bellevue. While in Sherman he was taken ill and died there September 28, 1878, and was buried in Sherman. His widow died March 4, 1884, and is also buried at Sherman. Their children, nine in number, are enumerated briefly as follows: Jesse M.; W. F., twin brother of Jesse, who is now a farmer near Edna in Jackson County, Texas; James W., who owned a livery stable at Wynnewood, Oklahoma, where he died in 1901; Newton S., who is a retired farmer at Davenport, Oklahoma; Lillian, who died at the age of two years; B. W., who is a farmer near Perry, Oklahoma; Dora, whose clothing caught fire and was burned to death at Paul's Valley, Oklahoma, in February, 1880, she being at that time the wife of John T. Hill, a Paul's Valley farmer, who died in 1914; Allen G., a well known business man of Loco, of whom there is individual mention in following paragraphs; and Annie, twin sister of Albert, now the wife of Henry Smith, a farmer and stock raiser at Clarendon, Texas.

Jesse M. Robberson continued to aid in the operation of the home farm until 1874, when he removed to Paul's Valley in the Indian Territory and for a year continued at home helping his father. For five years following 1875 he was afflicted almost to the point of being a cripple by rheumatism and a malady of the eyes. He was employed with the firm of Miller & Green, Paul's

Valley merchants, until September, 1878, and then went to Cooke County, Texas, with the intention of attending school, but changed his plans and went out to Hall County, Texas, with a bunch of 3,500 head of cattle, he and his mother and brother owning ninety-six head of that lot. There he was engaged in the care and raising of the cattle until 1883, when he sold out for $6,500, giving his mother a third of the proceeds.

His next location was at Fort Arbuckle, where he was employed for wages in the winter of 1883. In the spring of 1884 he and his brother went to Hall County, where they obtained thirteen saddle horses, and at Ganesville bought 337 head of yearlings, which they drove to the Grant and Beeler's Ranch, where Chickasha, Oklahoma, is now located. In this venture they were in partnership with their brother, W. F. Robberson. After holding the cattle until they were three years old they sold but realized no profit on the investment. Jesse Robberson was afterward employed by Ed Huntley in the cattle business until the succeeding fall, when they went to Belcher, Texas, and purchased 350 two-year-old steers, driving them to the Polk Ranch on Mud Creek, owned by Florence Hall. The next July the cattle were sold at a profit for $1,500. Mr. Robberson then took a trip on horseback to Belcher, Henrietta and to Stephens County on a cattle-buying expedition. After returning home they went to Quanah, Texas, and bought 251 head of three- and four-year-old steers, rounded them up and had them driven to Hamilton, that state. Jesse M. Robberson took charge of a cattle drove to Mud Creek, where he sold 177 head to McCaughey Brothers for "feeders," and eighty to his brothers, A. G. and B. W., and including the remainder, which he sold the following June, he realized a profit of $1,500.

In the spring of 1899 he dissolved partnership with his brother and went to Gainesville, Texas, where he purchased 350 head of yearlings, which he drove to Mud Creek, continuing in the cattle business at that place until the fall of 1900, when he sold out for $25,000. On January 13, 1891, with his brother, A. G., he engaged in the mercantile business at Dixie, Oklahoma, under the name of J. M. Robberson, and they continued this as a successful enterprise until selling out on January 13, 1908. In 1893 Mr. Robberson also opened a store at Loco, which he sold to his brother, A. G., in February, 1912. In 1897, in connection with A. S. Hathaway, he erected the cotton gin in Loco, and sold his interest in that enterprise in 1909. For many years he has been extensively interested in raising mules, horses and hogs.

Mr. Robberson is the largest individual taxpayer in Stephens County. He owns 2,500 acres in Stephens, Jefferson, Carter, Grady and Garvin counties, Oklahoma, and also in Texas. He is a stockholder and director in the Oklahoma National Life Insurance Company of Oklahoma City and is president of the First State Bank of Ringling, having organized that bank in April, 1914, and opening it for business on May 11, 1914. He is also president of the State Bank of Loco. This was established as a private bank by Mr. Robberson in 1903, M. M. Bowman being bookkeeper. It became a state bank in 1907, Mr. Bowman resigning at that time. The present officers of this bank at Loco are: J. M. Robberson, who has been president since its organization; J. F. Stotts of Ringling, vice president; Percy W. Newton, cashier; Miss Lulu Cain, assistant cashier. The bank has capital stock of $10,000 dollars, and its present surplus amounts to $2,500.

Mr. Robberson is a democrat and for a number of years during territorial days served as a member of the school board of Loco. He is affiliated with the Masonic and Odd Fellows orders. On March 21, 1898, he married at Grand View, Texas, Miss Nora Conner, daughter of Dr. L. H. Conner, of that place. Their first child, Jesse, was born June 30, 1900, and died October 12th of the same year. They now have a daughter, Gracie Jurhee, who was born February 5, 1902, and is a student in the seventh grade of the public schools at Loco.

ALLEN G. ROBBERSON. A young brother of Jesse M. Robberson, whose career as a business man and whose family history has been detailed in preceding paragraphs, Allen Green Robberson was for a number of years associated with his brother in their business undertakings and is one of the leading merchants, farmers and citizens of Stephens County.

He was born in Polk County, Missouri, July 16, 1866, a son of Richard A. and Maria H. (Mitchell) Robberson, concerning whom information is given above. In 1874 the family removed to the Chickasha Nation, locating at Paul's Valley, and Allen G. Robberson completed his education in Cooke County, Texas, in private schools. At the age of fifteen he left school and went to the cattle range of the Texas Panhandle and spent six years in the exciting and arduous experience of cowboy. In 1887 he located on Beef Creek, near the Washita River in Indian Territory, and was for three years engaged in general farming. During 1890 he was for three months a clerk under his brother, W. F. Robberson, at Robberson near Honey Creek in Indian Territory. On January 13, 1891, he and his brother, Jesse M., bought out a general store at Dixie, and he was actively identified with the management of that successful concern for seventeen years, until January 13, 1908, when the business was closed out. He then removed to Loco, and after four years spent in trading and collection, in 1912 bought the large general store which had been established many years before by his brother, Jesse, and is now the proprietor of this establishment, which, though located in one of the small towns of Southern Oklahoma, has an immense volume of trade, drawn from Stephens, Carter and Jefferson counties. The store occupies 30 by 97 feet of ground and is located on Main and Broadway streets in Loco. His attention, however, is divided between the management of this mercantile concern and his extensive farming and stock interests. He is the owner of 1,100 acres of land situated in the northeast corner of Jefferson County, six miles north of Ringling. He cultivates 200 acres of this himself, while tenants handle the rest.

For many years Mr. Robberson has been one of the hard-working, shrewd and intelligent business men and citizens of the old Chickasaw Nation. He is a democrat, has helped to provide good schools for Loco as a member of the school board and was county representative in the organization of the state. He is affiliated with Loco Lodge No. 361 of the Independent Order of Odd Fellows and Camp No. 682 of the Woodmen of the World at Loco.

On June 18, 1900, at Bettina, Oklahoma, he married Miss Pearl Price, daughter of William P. Price, who up to his death was a farmer and stock man at Bettina. To their marriage have been born four children: Price A., born January 29, 1901, and now a freshman in the Loco High School; Annabett, born in 1903 and in the sixth grade of the public school; Lucile, born in 1905 and in the fifth grade; and Hylagene, born January 28, 1912.

CHARLES NAPOLEON PRUDOM. The fact that one of the streets of Pawhuska is named Prudom is a small but lasting tribute to the services of an Osage citizen who has lived in that community since early boyhood and who has identified himself public spiritedly with nearly everything of importance that has been a part of the general progress and upbuilding of this section of Oklahoma.

A casual acquaintance with Mr. Prudom does not reveal the depths of his character and the great sources of his ability. He has that quiet efficiency which accomplishes a great deal with very little noise and no confusion. He has a mind which comprehends large things, and his energy makes every plan a definite result. He is truly a self made man, and has not only pulled his own weight in the world, but has borne heavy responsibilities for others.

His has been an interesting as well as a fruitful career. Born near Topeka, Kansas, January 8, 1856, he takes justifiable pride in his ancestry and the blood that flows in his veins. His father, Peter Prudom, was born in Missouri and was a Frenchman with a quarter blood of the New York Indian stock that was part of the seven great tribes around the Great Lakes. His mother, Mary B. Revlett, also a native of Missouri, was of French ancestry, and a one-eighth blood Osage Indian. Peter Prudom, who was a farmer and cattle man, died in 1870 a few months after he and his family had settled in the Osage Nation. Among the seven children in the family Charles Napoleon was the oldest, and after his father's death the care of the household and outside affairs devolved largely upon his youthful shoulders. It is said that he practically reared all the other members of the family, four of whom reached maturity. Most of his early schooling came from the old Mission School in Neosho County, Kansas.

Coming to the Osage Nation when a boy of fourteen and losing his father a few months later and his mother in March, 1875, Mr. Prudom showed an unusual responsiveness to those duties which early became his lot. He started life with a meager education. Poor, with industry as his chief asset, he became one of the pioneer farmers and cattle raisers along the Caney River just south of the Kansas line in the Osage Nation. With those operations he was identified until 1883.

If any man can say that he has seen Pawhuska rise from the wilderness into a thriving city it is Mr. Prudom. His first visit to the town was in 1872, when he was a boy of sixteen. At that time the only structure of importance on the site was a little building used for the Indian Agency, whose quarters were in one end, while the other end was a shoe shop. Since 1883 Mr. Prudom has been continuously identified with the town, which then however was only a small Indian village. In that year he bought a ranch just below Pawhuska and engaged extensively in the cattle and horse business until about three years ago, when he sold his stock and most of his land and retired to a town home in Pawhuska.

In these thirty or more years Mr. Prudom's means and enterprise have gone liberally to the upbuilding of his home locality. Those who are in a position to know say that he has done as much if not more to promote the material interests of the city as any other man. He still owns several brick blocks that he built, besides residences and other pieces of property, and has handled and developed much real estate in the city. His capital has been used almost wholesale in the development of the town, and on every hand might be pointed out some conspicuous building which was erected directly by him or with his financial support.

On retiring from his country home he bought a beautiful place on a hill overlooking the city and commanding an extensive view of the surrounding landscape for many miles. There he erected a home designed to satisfy all the cultured tastes of the family and provide every modern comfort. It is a large and ample mansion, complete even down to the smallest detail, including sleeping porches.

His name has been associated with every public enterprise of importance at Pawhuska. He assisted in organizing and establishing nearly every church, gave financial assistance to building their edifices, and has been a factor in various fraternity organizations. He is a Knight Templar Mason, is a charter member of the Lodge at Pawhuska, and also a charter member of the Knights of Pythias.

Ever since Bryan came out for free silver he has voted the republican ticket. During territorial days he was a member of the Osage council six or seven times, was a member of the committee called to allot the land of the Osages, and performed several missions for his people in Washington. In fact during the last generation every affair of importance concerning the Osage Indians has been impressed with the advice and ability of Mr. Prudom.

He was one of the first men to find gas in Osage County and is a stockholder in the Pawhuska Oil and Gas Company. He is a director and stockholder in the First National Bank, an old and stable institution that is the outgrowth of a little bank started in pioneer times. Mr. Prudom was one of those who bought and reorganized the bank as the First National. He is also president and the largest stockholder of the Prue State Bank and is a stockholder in the Midland Continental Life Insurance Company.

Through all these years since he reached his majority he has enjoyed a happy home life. He is properly proud of his family, and his children and grandchildren give him the affection and respect paid to the patriarchs of old. To his wife he gives credit for a loyal and faithful co-operation with him through adversity and success. She has never failed him and her influence has been a factor in his material prosperity as well as in the successful training of their children. On March 28, 1875, he married Anna Eliza Norbury. Mrs. Prudom, who was born in Iowa, is of German and English descent. Of the ten children of their marriage six died in infancy. The four still living are daughters. Three of these are married and Mr. Prudom finds great satisfaction in his sons-in-law, who are capable business men in and around Pawhuska, and Mr. Prudom has been associated with them in varied enterprises. The daughter Lula married Thomas Mosier, of the well known family mentioned on other pages of this publication. Maud is the wife of Henry Prue, a large rancher near Pawhuska. Norine lives at home with her parents. Nettie is Mrs. A. W. Lohmann, whose husband is a rancher near Pawhuska. Mrs. Prudom is an active member of the Catholic Church, which Mr. Prudom generously supports, and she reared her children in the same faith. Mr. and Mrs. Prudom have a number of grandchildren and as they take great pride in these members of the younger generation, and as some of them are now working for Mr. Prudom, it is but proper that their names should be appended to this article. The names of the grandchildren are: Chas. Prudom Mosier, Thomas Mosier, Jr., Edwin Mosier, Christina Mosier, Luther Mosier, James Mosier. Hattie M. Prue, Charles Franklin Prue, Everett H. Prue, Floyd B. Prue, Annabell Prue, Annetta Lohmann, and August W. Lohmann.

THE ELK CITY LIBRARY. The definite need for a Carnegie library in Elk City, the metropolis of Beckham County, had for many years been a matter of discussion on the part of individual citizens and civic organizations, but to achieve the desired end no distinctive movement was made until the 24th of February, 1912, when a committee of six ladies from the Presbyterian Church called a meeting of the ladies of Elk City to consider the possibility of establishing a public library. As a matter of historic record it should be noted that the six women comprising this original and public-spirited committee from the Presbyterian Church of Elk City were Mesdames S. L. Neely, George Dramer, Samuel Orr, W. E. Allen, O. H. Young and Mrs. Florence Brown.

By the 1st of March, 1912, permanent organization had been made, and constitution and by-laws were adopted by which all executive power was vested in a board of twelve members. The ladies elected to the board at that time—with the exception of those who have removed from Elk City—have since served faithfully and effectively, the personnel of the sterling corps who have thus labored so earnestly for the achievement of a noble public service being as here noted: Mesdames S. L. Neely, Fried Mayer, A. G. Low, George F. Sisson, D. A. Mayer, E. C. Willison, O. H. Cafky, W. E. Allen, Jodie Burnett, Charles Durie and John G. Scott. Those who have been added to fill vacancies are Mesdames Guy McClung, H. C. Powell, John Forsythe, John Maupin and W. A. Wright.

The library was started with 250 volumes, which were donated by townspeople, and from this nucleus has been evolved a collection that at the close of the year 1915 includes 850 volumes. The business men of the town were solicited for monthly subscription to defray running expenses, such as rent for the room occupied and the paying of the salary of the librarian. Many other methods were used to obtain funds with which to purchase books.

On the 22d of February, 1914, at a "Colonial Banquet," the Elk City Library Association asked the Commercial Club to assist in securing for the library a Carnegie building. It was through the co-operation thus effected that lots were purchased and final arrangements made for the building, which was completed in the autumn of 1915, its dedication having been made, with most consistent ceremony and other observances, in October of that year.

The board appointed by the city council to direct the affairs of the Carnegie Library of Elk City has the following personnel: Judge R. E. Echols, W. C. Thomas, O. F. Tesmar, John G. Scott, Mrs. O. H. Cafky, Mrs. W. E. Allen and Mrs. John G. Scott.

R. B. BUTLER. The Tribune Press, publishing the Evening and Weekly Tribune, at Blackwell, of which R. B. Butler is editor and proprietor, is one of the most enterprising younger journals of Northern Oklahoma. Established three years ago, it has already forged to the front among the county papers and has fulfilled the essential purposes of a new organ in publishing the news in an attractive manner, in furnishing an excellent medium for business and advertising, and in advocating through its columns every movement for righteousness, clean-mindedness, wholesome civic standards, temperance, education and religion. It practices the precepts of home first and world afterwards. The Tribune has a large support both in the city and county and goes regularly to subscribers living in every state in the Union. It is published from a strictly modern plant, equipped with a Mergenthaler linotype and with all the facilities for high class printing and press work. The office also makes a specialty of high grade job and book printing. The paper was established in Blackwell in the fall of 1912 and Mr. Butler has shown a rare degree of enterprise and success in bringing it so quickly to favor and influence.

R. B. Butler was born at Huntingdon, Tennessee, November 26, 1882, and for a young man still under thirty-five has accomplished a great deal of excellent work in the world, both as a newspaper man and as a minister of the gospel. He comes of an old Tennessee family, whose ancestors were hardy pioneers and noted for the courage of their convictions. Mr. Butler's father, Garvin B. Butler, is a native Tennesseean and is one of the leading stock breeders of the west half of the state. The mother's maiden name was Mary E. Chambers. Both parents are members of the Baptist Church and the father is affiliated with the Independent Order of Odd Fellows. There are five children and both the sons, R. B. and A. C., are connected with the Tribune Press at Blackwell.

Mr. Butler grew up on a farm in Tennessee where he learned the meaning of honest toil. His early education was received in the public schools, after which he attended Union University at Jackson, Tennessee, and finally graduated from Hall-Moody Baptist College at Martin, Tennessee. He was ordained to the ministry in 1906, the year after graduation, since which time he has been actively engaged in that work. He held several pastorates in Oklahoma prior to entering into the newspaper business and is still active in church work, preaching regularly. He is a member of the Independent Order of Odd Fellows and served two years as a member of the Tennessee State Militia.

On July 14, 1906, Mr. Butler was married to Miss Maude White, daughter of A. B. White of Enid, Oklahoma. To their union have been born two daughters: Mary Virginia and Marguritte. He is a republican in politics and with his wife holds membership in the Baptist Church.

CLARENCE B. LEEDY. The first county attorney of Ellis County after its organization and statehood was Clarence B. Leedy. His father some year before had been the first postmaster of one of the new towns in Dewey County, and the town was named in his honor, Leedey, with only a slight modification of the name. These two facts indicate that members of the Leedy family have been exceptionally active in that section of Oklahoma, and they have been a fine type of those worthy characters who in future years will be credited as empire builders. Clarence B. Leedy is one of the most successful lawyers of Ellis County, lives at Arnett, and has been quite a man of affairs for a number of years.

Though he is still on the lee side of middle age, he came into close touch with pioneer conditions at his birth, since his birthplace was a log house on a farm in Fulton County, Indiana. There he first saw the light of day September 9, 1875. His parents were Amos and Sarah C. (Hunter) Leedy. Amos Leedy was born June 6, 1850, near Akron, Ohio, a son of Abraham A. and Elizabeth E. (Leedy) Leedy, both of whom were natives of Pennsylvania. Abraham was born in 1819 and died in 1901, and his wife was born March 25, 1826, and is now living at Tiosa, Indiana.

In 1859 Amos Leedy moved to Fulton County, Indiana, and in 1882 took his family to Illinois, and from there came on to Oklahoma in 1898. While not one of the earliest pioneers of the original Oklahoma, he was one of the most active of the early settlers in Dewey County, where he established his home on Government land. A part of that land has since been covered by the thriving Town of Leedey and his name was fitly accepted as the name of the incipient village. As already stated, he was the first postmaster when the office was established in 1899 and held that position until 1902. He is now living quietly retired at Leedey and the major part of his activities as a business man have been performed as a farmer. In 1873 Amos Leedy married Miss Sarah C. Hunter, daughter of Jacob Hunter, who was a native of New York. She was born March 20, 1854, in Marshall County, Indiana, and died in Piatt County, Illinois, October 20, 1895. She was a very religious woman, an active member of the German Baptist Church, and divided her time and interests between her home and family and her church duties. She became the mother of ten children, five sons and five daughters, namely: Clarence B.; Tempy Ann; Ira, deceased; Harley G.; Aaron A.; Charles A.; Dora; Hassie; Elizabeth E.; and a daughter, the fifth in age, who died in infancy. On January 20, '1905, at Independence, Kansas, Amos Leedy married his present wife. She was born in Kansas. In 1883 Mr. Amos Leedy was regularly ordained a minister of the German Baptist Church, and for a great many years has performed the part of a leader in church work.

Clarence B. Leedy was about seven years old when the family moved to Illinois, and he acquired his early education in Piatt County of that state. He attended college at the Central Normal College in Danville, Indiana, where he took a course in law and graduated in 1898. On May 12, 1898, Mr. Leedy enlisted in Company A of the Sixteenth United States Infantry for service in the Spanish-American war, which had broken out only a few weeks previous. He was sent to Cuba and took part in the noted battle of San Juan Hill on July 1, 1898. In that historic engagement he was wounded though not seriously. He was discharged with a record of "excellent" in character and conduct.

During the years 1899-1900 Mr. Leedy was a traveling representative for the Chicago Journal and Herald. In June, 1900, he joined his family in Oklahoma, and his first venture here was to locate a claim near Leedey in old Day County. He served as deputy county attorney of Day County one term. In 1904 he was appointed assistant county attorney of old Day County, and located for private practice at Grand.

In September, 1907, Mr. Leedy was elected county attorney of Ellis County on the republican ticket. The county had been created by the constitutional convention, and he was the first to fill that important office in the local civil government. He filled it for 3½ years and since his term of office as county attorney has expired he has refused to accept any office, and has enjoyed the largest law practice of any attorney in Western Oklahoma. Mr. Leedy is said to have the largest law library in Ellis County, and is a thoroughly informed and skillful attorney. He is active as a republican, and has been a member of the central and state committees since 1901. Fraternally he is identified with the Independent Order of Odd Fellows and has passed all the chairs in his home lodge.

On February 2, 1902, at Leedey, he married Miss Mabel Ann Foster, daughter of Alexander W. and Clara (Sharp) Foster. Her parents were both born in Cass County, Missouri, and that was also her birthplace on July 4, 1882. Mr. and Mrs. Leedy have a fine family of eight children, five sons and three daughters, namely: Mabel Ethel, born March 16, 1903, and died January 4, 1905; Charles B., born November 24, 1904; Eva, born July 16, 1906; Raymond, born February 18, 1908; Darwin, born February 16, 1910; Clara, born September 30, 1912; Frank, born June 12, 1914; and Eldon Leedy, born February 26, 1916.

WILLIAM DAVID ATKINS. While he is one of the more recent recruits to the field of commercial endeavor, the success which has already attended the efforts of William David Atkins gives promise of his becoming one of the leading merchants of Garfield County, as he is now the proprietor of the principal store at Kremlin. Mr. Atkins is pre-eminently an excellent example of the self-made man, having worked his own way through college, and prior to entering mercantile lines taught school, his capital for his business having been saved from his earnings as an educator.

Mr. Atkins is a product of the agricultural community of Lyon County, Kansas, where he was born on his father's farm, July 27, 1883, a son of Albert W. and Margaret Jane (Wyrick) Atkins. The family is of English origin, and was founded in the United States by the grandparents of William D. Atkins, William and Anna Atkins, natives of the mother country, who emigrated here in 1831 and passed the remaining years of their lives in Will County, Illinois. Albert W. Atkins was born at Joliet, Illinois, February 10, 1852, was reared amid agricultural surroundings, adopted the vocation of a farmer when he reached years of maturity, and has passed the entire period of his active life in pastoral pursuits. He was educated in the public schools of Illinois, but when eighteen years of age went to Kansas and purchased land in Lyon County, continuing to carry on his operations there until 1899. At this time there came the only break in his agricultural career, when he became the proprietor of a meat market at Drummond, but after one year's experience in this line he disposed of his interests therein and in 1900 located on a claim in Woods County. In 1913 he removed to Kremlin, and is now retired from active pursuits. He has a successful career in a material way, and in the evening of life is able to enjoy the fruits of his years of labor. Mr. Atkins was married at Emporia, Kansas, March 15, 1879, to Miss Margaret Jane Wyrick, a daughter of David and Jemima (Brown) Wyrick, who were natives of Indiana. She was born December 14, 1862, in Marion County, Indiana, and became the mother of three daughters and seven sons, as follows: Anna Elizabeth, born December 15, 1881, who is now a teacher in the public schools of Oklahoma; William David, of this review; Albert Pearl, born December 6, 1884; Nellie and Nettie, twins, born December 24, 1886; Lawrence LeRoy, born December 29, 1888; James Oliver, born April 22, 1890; Walter, who died in infancy; Orlando, born July 9, 1899; and Ivan Guy, born May 20, 1904, who died May 20, 1906.

William David Atkins was sixteen years of age when he accompanied his parents to Oklahoma. He had secured a common school education in Lyon County, Kansas, but was ambitious for a better and more advanced training, and accordingly resolved to work his own way through school. Enrolling as a student at the Oklahoma Northwestern Normal School, he solicited such honorable employment as might be found about the institution, to which he devoted himself during the hours he was not engaged in study, and thus, through industry and the strictest economy, he was enabled to work his way through and to graduate with the class that left the Alva institution in 1907. In 1909, 1910, 1911 and 1912, with this equipment, Mr. Atkins was superintendent of city schools of Cleo, Oklahoma, and in 1912 came to Kremlin in the same capacity. During the two years that he acted as superintendent of schools he became widely and favorably known among the people of this locality, and when the opportunity presented itself he decided to enter business affairs, and accordingly embarked in mercantile lines. It is illustrative of his ability to state that he doffed the cap and gown of the educator and donned the apron of the merchant without trouble, and that in his new field of endeavor he is making

prodigious strides toward success. He carries a general stock, selected after a careful study of the needs and wants of the community, well arranged, moderately priced and attractively displayed. His establishment has taken its place as the leading store at Kremlin.

Mr. Atkins was married at Alva, Oklahoma, June 2, 1909, to Miss Mary Elizabeth Else, who was born at Weeping Water, Nebraska, November 22, 1886, a daughter of John and Mary (Evans) Else, the former a native of England and the latter of Illinois. Mrs. Atkins is a graduate of Oklahoma Northwestern Normal School, class of 1907, having been president of her class during her senior year. After her graduation she began to teach school, was married to Mr. Atkins two years later, and continued to teach for two years more. She now devotes herself to the duties of her household, and to her children, of whom there are four: Leah May, born March 11, 1910; George William, born October 1, 1911; Bessie, born November 23, 1913; and John Ivan, born August 20, 1915. Mr. Atkins is a member of the Masonic fraternity, in which, as elsewhere, he has numerous friends. With his family he belongs to the Baptist Church.

ROBERT DRAKELEY ROOD, M. D., D. S. One must occupy a very high elevation to observe and follow with any degree of sanity the intricate meshes of state, national and international life. Especially is this true in these days when strong men move with difficulty through subtle threatening entanglements induced by the great labor problems and the European war.

Perhaps the newer states in our Union offer the most pronounced example of these intricate conditions with their admixture of material from the oldest families, financiers, adventurers, foreign and native element. To trace a pathway through such, requires deliberate judgment, persistent individualism, tact to live against and to respect multitudinous views of so-called right standards. Such a course is an interpretation of character, strong to meet mutation, adjustment and emergency with alertness and a demonstration of the best scholarship in life, which knows and searches for the heart of man, finds and holds it whilst hewing definitely to a finalé of results. Some men appear to be especially gifted in these qualities which make for the successes in life. As a representative of this class, he whose name heads this sketch is most worthy of honorable mention.

The subject of this biography, Robert Drakeley Rood, was born October 20, 1863, at Stevens Point, Wisconsin. He is the second son of Galen Gear Rood, M. D., and Nancy Jane Sylvester.

The early ancestors were of the Puritans of New England and belonged to the oldest families in the United States. Charles Sumner, the great statesman; Caroline Hazard, former president of Wellesley College; Senator Gear of Iowa, Ogden N. Rood, one of the founders of Columbia, are familiar names in the family record.

His father, a much loved man, is still living at the age of eighty-seven years. He was graduated from the Ohio Medical College at Cincinnati, Ohio, in the spring of 1856. The same season he opened an office at Stevens Point, Wisconsin, which has never been closed. His mother, who shared equally the love of the community in which they lived, was an extraction of the French through the Gerard family of Paris. She passed away in 1906 at the age of seventy-two, much mourned by her family and all who knew her. She was a most consistent Christian and worker in the Presbyterian Church. All phases of her energy seemed tireless in direct effort for all that was uplifting. The other members of Dr. Robert Rood's family were two brothers, Myron Galen Rood, M. D.; Price Walton Rood, D. S., and a sister, Katharine Abagail Rood, who after graduation from the University of Wisconsin chose music as a profession.

Dr. Robert Rood's boyhood was not unusual in its educational advantages of city graded and high school courses. The summer times of camping, fishing and athletic sports with some business ventures and adventures introduced at times, were arrow points showing the trend of the man. Few have found and enjoyed more varied and adventurous experiments. His failures were not met with the best good nature, and his successes, always shared with his friends, were many times due not to luck but to the vim that comes of well weathered experience. Later he was given every opportunity to find his own bearings through the higher educational institutions of Lake Forest and the Northwestern universities, and to choose either the professional or business career, both of which were elements in his mental inheritance. After an elective course of two years, he decided to matriculate at the Ohio College of Dental Surgery, from which he was graduated with the class of 1887. The following year he entered Rush Medical College, Chicago. He successfully practiced his profession in his home town for some years, during which time he was married, December 11, 1895, to Ethel Kirwan, also a native of Stevens Point, Wisconsin.

At this time he was appointed by Governor LaFollette of Wisconsin secretary of the World's Fair Commission for the State of Wisconsin. Though a professional man he was keenly alive to the trend of business thought, and was quick to sense a possible advantage in the opening of the mid-continent oil fields. In the fall of 1903 he moved with his family to Bartlesville, Oklahoma, and in a phenomenally short time proved himself one of the energetic factors which made, what was then the old Indian Territory, the national center of oil activity.

Doctor Rood brought in the first large well in Indian Territory. In his business he has been associated with the Indian Territory Illuminating Oil Company, the Stevens Point Oil Company, Waukesha Oil Company, Plover Drilling Company, etc. He is orthodox in his religion, a member of the Masonic order, being a Thirty-second Degree Mason, a generous citizen interested in all civic betterment, and in close sympathy always with a progressive city and state.

Three children—Esther, a graduate from the Emma Willard School at Troy, New York; Katharine Abagail, and Robert Drakeley, Jr.—make a very happy home. Mrs. Rood is the eldest daughter of Frank Grahame Kirwan and Elizabeth Wadleigh Kirwan, representative Maryland and New England families whose ancestors include the Fletchers, Pooles, Evans, Harveys, Pierces, Travers and Smallwoods. Mrs. Rood has been identified with the early growth and development of her adopted home city and state in all that pertains to the highest welfare of its citizens. A graduate of the best schools and instructors, Mrs. Rood has won professionally, both in her native state, Wisconsin and Oklahoma, innumerable laurels in vocal art, and has done a great deal to stimulate and promote music and art by organizing the Musical Research Society. Mrs. Rood has been secretary of the library board since its inception; officer and member of Musical and Women's State and National Federated clubs, and of other organizations both state and national, and has effectively co-operated with the State Dental Board in promoting oral hygiene in the public schools. Throughout this pioneer period of Oklahoma, Mrs. Rood has kept abreast of the times and her interests by frequent studies in Chicago, Baltimore and Kansas City. Mrs. Rood holds a court of the choicest social life around a hearth second to none in its delightful hospitality.

Written September 6, 1916.

CHARLES ROBINSON HUME, M. D. During his twenty-five years of residence in Oklahoma Doctor Hume has acquired many interesting associations and useful relations with the state. His home throughout that period has been on practically the same section of land. For eleven years he served as physician to the United States Indian Agency of Anadarko, and for the past fourteen years has been engaged in general practice as a physician and surgeon in the City of Anadarko. Both the old Indian agency and the present city are identical so far as location is concerned, and the modern city is the outgrowth of the old agency headquarters.

The oldest child of his parents, Charles Robinson Hume was born October 21, 1847, at Riga, Monroe County, New York. Both he and his father were born on the same farm. His parents were Roderick R. and Ruth Ann (Payne) Hume. The farm in New York on which his father was born was settled by Moses Hume, who emigrated from Massachusetts in 1811.

Doctor Hume's ancestors have all been in America for more than two hundred years, and were identified with the colonies of Massachusetts and Connecticut. He is fifth in descent from Nicholas Hume, who was married in Boston in 1714 and probably was from the Wedderburn Humes of Scotland. All four of Doctor Hume's great-grandfathers had a record of service in the Revolutionary war, and another distant ancestor whose record is of special interest was Capt. John Gallup, who fought in the first naval battle of the American colonies during the Pequot Indian war of 1636. By virtue of these several ancestors who were patriots during the war for independence, Doctor Hume is a member of the Sons of the American Revolution. His mother, Ruth Ann Payne, was born and reared in the same locality of New York state as her husband, and her parents had come from Berkshire County, Massachusetts.

In 1854 the Hume family, including Charles R., who was then seven years old, moved out to Medina in Lenawee County, Michigan. The farm which the father bought there was the family homestead for a period of forty years. It was in that region of Southern Michigan that Doctor Hume grew to manhood. He attended the common schools and also acquired an academic course in the Oak Grove Academy in Medina, where he finished in 1870. He continued his education in the University of Michigan, where he was graduated M. D. in 1874.

Thus more than forty years have passed since he began to render service to humanity in the capacity of physician and surgeon. In earlier years before taking up active practice he followed farming and teaching and paid the expenses of his university course through his own earnings. Reared on a farm, and a practical farmer before he became a physician, Doctor Hume has always kept up his interest in agricultural affairs and has owned farms in connection with his professional business. However, he has allowed nothing to interfere with the studious and active devotion to his real calling.

In 1874 after leaving the University of Michigan he began practice at Perrysburg in Wood County, Ohio. Later he was at Tontogany in the same Ohio county, and from there went out in 1881 to Caldwell in Sumner County, Kansas. He was one of the early physicians in that then sparsely settled district of Kansas, and remained there, growing up with the country and enjoying a large practice for ten years.

In 1890 Doctor Hume came to the Indian Agency of Anadarko as agency physician. He continued in the United States Indian service from December 1, 1890, to February 28, 1902, as resident physician for the Kiowa and Comanche Agency, and performed all the services connected with that office until after the opening to white settlement of the Kiowa and Comanche country. He then opened an office for general practice, and is now the dean of the medical fraternity of Anadarko. For years the demands upon his professional time and energy have been all that he could satisfy.

For the past seventeen years Doctor Hume has been local surgeon for the Chicago, Rock Island & Pacific Railway Company; from 1901 to 1914 was president of the Board of Pension Examiners of Caddo County; was superintendent of public health of Caddo County from 1901 to 1907, was district councillor of the State Medical Society five years; was vice president of the State Medical Society in 1914; and in May, 1916, was elected president of the State Medical Society. While living in Kansas he became a director of the Citizens Bank of Caldwell in 1887. In politics he is a republican and is a member of the Presbyterian Church.

At Perrysburg in Wood County, Ohio, December 27, 1876, Doctor Hume married Annette Ross. She was born in Perrysburg on March 8, 1858, daughter of James White and Catherine (Darling) Ross. Her father was a prominent factor in local affairs in Wood County, Ohio. Mrs. Hume has been a home maker and a social leader, has served as president and secretary of the Woman's Missionary Society of the Presbyterian Church in Oklahoma and recently retired from the office of president of the Oklahoma State Federation of Women's Clubs. To their marriage were born five children, three of whom died in infancy. C. Ross Hume, one of the surviving sons, married Verne Gossard, and has a family of one son and two daughters; Raymond R. Hume, the other son, is unmarried. The older son is an attorney, has served for four years as county judge of Caddo County, while the other is a practicing physician and is located at Minco, Oklahoma. Both sons are graduates of the Oklahoma State University and took their professional degrees in the University of Kansas and the University Medical School of Kansas City, respectively.

OSMAN A. GILBERT. Perhaps no family in Pawnee County, Oklahoma, has a more historic ancestry than has the family represented by Osman A. Gilbert, successful druggist and former postmaster of Cleveland. They are in the direct line of descent from Sir Humphrey Gilbert, well known in English history, and Sir Walter Raleigh, equally prominent in history and literature. On the mother's side there is known relationship to General Grant, whose tomb on Riverside Drive is one of the most interesting objects in New York City. The family came to New York in Colonial days, and Rev. Joseph O. Gilbert, grandsire of the subject, was a well known circuit rider of the Methodist Church in his day.

Osman A. Gilbert is one of nine children born to his parents, Osman A. and Fannie E. Gilbert. The father was born in Italy, New York, and died on January 6, 1899, near Geneseo, Illinois, at the age of seventy. His widow survived until 1905, and died near Geneseo, Illinois, when she was sixty-three years old. The senior Gilbert came to Michigan with his parents when he was two years old, and later when he was sixteen, they moved to Illinois. They were farming people practically all of their lives and the father owned the farm on which he died for a period of fifty-two years. He was a prominent citizen in his part of Illinois, and was active politically, though he never cared to hold office. He was twice married, and the subject of this review was th oldest child of the second marriage. Until he was twenty-three years old Osman A. Gilbert, Jr., lived at home with his parents and assisted his father as he grew to manhood in his extensive farming interests and cheese manufactory, which his father established at Cleveland, Illinois.

He secured a very good education, following his high-school training with two years at a normal school, and when he was twenty-three years old he came to Oklahoma on April 22, 1889. He first settled on a government claim near Edmond, which he held for two and a half years and then sold, and went to work in the drug store of Moore and Howard at Edmond. He was with that firm for eight months, when he entered into a partnership with them and purchased a drug store at Stillwater. He continued there for a year and a half, sold out his interest in the business and came to Cleveland on April 4, 1894, just five years after coming to the state. He opened his present establishment, which he has continuously operated since that time, with commendable success.

Mr. Gilbert is vice president and a director of the First National Bank since it was nationalized in 1900, and is interested in a number of oil projects in the county, as well as extensive farming interests. He was one of a company of three who organized the Cleveland telephone exchange, which the organizing company later sold to the Pioneer Telephone Company. For eight years Mr. Gilbert was postmaster during the McKinley and Roosevelt administrations, and has twice served as mayor of Cleveland. He is a member of and one of the official board of the Christian Church at Cleveland, and is fraternally associated with the Knights of Pythias and the Masons.

On June 29, 1893, Mr. Gilbert was married to Miss Evie A. Powell at Edmond, Oklahoma. She was born at Vandalia, Michigan, and is the only daughter of Jason A. and Barbara A. Powell. She is of Welsh-English and German descent. On the paternal side she is directly descended from John Hart, one of the signers of the Declaration of Independence. Her husband smiles and says she is a consistent relative of her ancestor. Her father's people moved to Michigan in an early day from the State of New York and the relatives there claim Revolutionary fame. On the maternal side her grandmother came from Germany when she was thirteen years old. Her parents afterward lived in Kansas, where she was educated, and in 1889 she came with her parents to Edmond, Oklahoma. Her father was for many years engaged in the market and stock business. In 1900 her parents moved to Cleveland to be near their daughter and purchased property in that town and vicinity. Jason A. Powell died in Cleveland in 1910 at sixty-seven years of age. His wife still survives him.

Mr. and Mrs. Gilbert have no children. For fourteen years she assisted her husband in his store, was his assistant pharmacist and was his assistant postmistress during his incumbency of the postoffice. During the past few years Mrs. Gilbert has been a leader in Maccabee circles in Oklahoma, and has served on state and national delegations. The Ladies Review, the official paper of the Maccabee order, published at Port Huron, Michigan, in the October, 1913, number says: "Mrs. Gilbert is not only an excellent Officer but upon many occasions of Maccabee Rallies has shown herself a brilliant and able orator." In addition to the standing she has in the Maccabee order she holds an official position in the Grand Temple of the Order of Pythian Sisters in Oklahoma, and has received commendatory mention as a fluent speaker and a thoughtful woman, in the leading newspapers of the state.

She is at present grand chief of the Pythian Sisters of the Grand Jurisdiction of Oklahoma; and had the honor of delivering the state address for that order at the joint public convocation of the lodges of that order at Convention Hall, Tulsa, Oklahoma, May, 1916.

Mrs. Gilbert is a member of the Christian Church, and has been an active worker in her home city, having been a teacher of a young ladies' class for several years, and for a number of years had charge of the choir, being an accomplished musician. During the last few years other duties which took her often from home have caused her to give up much of the local work.

Together with her father she did much to secure the building of the first church erected in Cleveland, and was a charter member of the board of trustees and the first clerk of the church. Mrs. Gilbert is the possessor of a one hundred and sixty acre farm located three miles from Cleveland, purchased with her own earnings, and says she is prouder of this than of any other achievement. Mr. and Mrs. Gilbert are pioneers in the State of Oklahoma and have been en rapport with the activities of the state from the beginning.

Mr. Gilbert who was present at the famous opening of the "strip" in 1893, tells many interesting stories of the rush at that time and of the early days of Oklahoma. He was one of sixty who made the race from Stillwater to the location of the present Town of Pawnee, a distance of thirteen miles, and of that company only eight arrived, he being one of them. This distance was covered in thirty-nine minutes.

EDWARD ANDREW ROWLAND, M. D. Two members of the Rowland family have gained a secure place in medical circles in Oklahoma, and both for a time were located at Shawnee. Dr. Edward A. Rowland is now the leading physician and surgeon at Maud, and his older brother still resides and enjoys a large practice at Shawnee.

The Rowlands are a Mississippi family. The great-grandfather of Doctor Rowland immigrated from Wales and settled in Georgia shortly after the Revolutionary war. He became a farmer and planter. There were two brothers who came with him from Liverpool and one of them settled in New York State and one subsequently went to Illinois. Dr. Edward Andrew Rowland was born at Falkner, Mississippi, January 5, 1884.

His father, A. J. Rowland, was born in Mississippi in 1846 and now resides at Mobile, Alabama. He was reared and married in his native state and during the last year of the Civil war served on the Union side. Following the war he removed to Falkner, Mississippi, engaged in merchandising, and in 1888 went to Pontotoc, Mississippi, and became identified with the railway postal service. In 1907 he removed to Mobile and is now transfer clerk in the railway mail service. In politics he is republican and at one time served as tax assessor of Tippah County, Mississippi. He is a member of the Christian Church and the Masonic fraternity. A. J. Rowland married Martha Annie Northcross, who was born in Mississippi in 1847. Their children are Dr. T. D. Rowland of Shawnee; C. W. Rowland, a farmer at Haskell, Texas; R. E. Rowland, who conducts a cotton compress and ice factory at New Albany, Mississippi; and Dr. Edward A.

Dr. Taswell D. Rowland, the oldest of the brothers, was born at Ripley, Tippah County, Mississippi, November 3, 1870. He attended public schools in his native locality, graduated from high school at Salisbury, Tennessee, in 1889, and for two years was a teacher in Tippah County. He then entered the railway mail service, the same line which his father has followed for so many years, and continued in that work for ten years. In the meantime he had been looking ahead and planning upon a professional career. In 1899 having left the railway postal service, he entered the Medical College at Memphis, Tennessee, and was graduated M. D. with the class of 1903. He subsequently took post-graduate work in the same college in 1906 and 1910, and did post-graduate work at Tulane University, New Orleans, in 1907 and 1913. In May, 1903, he located at Shawnee, Oklahoma, and since then has enjoyed a large and profitable general medical and surgical practice, his offices being in the Mammoth Building. He is a deacon in the Christian Church, is affiliated with the Knights of Pythias and the Knights of the Maccabees, and has served as president of the Pottawatomie Medical Society and is a member of the State Society and the American Medical Association. He has been a vigorous citizen at Shawnee, and his name is usually found associated with any movement for the public welfare. In politics he is a republican.

At Jackson, Tennessee, Dr. T. D. Rowland married Miss Hattie Barnett, a daughter of the late Sam B. Barnett, who was court clerk of Madison County, Tennessee, for many years. Doctor Rowland and wife have four children: Barnett, who graduated from the Shawnee High School in 1913 and is now taking special courses in commercial art in Chicago; Annie, who graduated from the Shawnee High School in 1914, is a freshman in the State University at Norman; Elizabeth, who is in the fourth grade of the public schools; and Louise, who has not yet reached school age.

Edward Andrew Rowland, whose successful work as a physician is being done at Maud in Pottawatomie County, received his early education in the public schools of Pontotoc, Mississippi, and graduated from high school there in 1902. For a time he was employed in the superintendent's office of the M. J. & K. T. Railroad at New Albany, Mississippi, and was from there transferred to Mobile, Alabama, in the employ of the same railroad. That was his line of work up to 1907 at which time he invested his savings in a professional education, entering the Medical Department of the University of Aabama, from which he was graduated M. D. with the class of 1910. He is an alert student, and has accepted every opportunity to fit himself for proficient and skillful work. From January to May, 1915, he took post-graduate work at Tulane University in New Orleans and also at the University of Alabama at Mobile. He is a member of the Phi Beta Pi College Fraternity.

In 1910 Doctor Rowland located at Shawnee, where his brother had been established in practice for a number of years, but after one year he returned to Mobile, Alabama, remained there a short time, practiced a year at Creola, Alabama, and in April, 1913, established himself permanently at Maud, Oklahoma, where he now has a promising medical and surgical practice, with offices in the Tribbey Drug Store Building. In politics Doctor Rowland is a republican, is a member of the Christian Church, and is a member of the county and state medical societies. The only fraternity to which he belongs is the Modern Woodmen of America.

CHIEF CHARLES JOURNEYCAKE. In the annals of the Delaware tribe of Indians there is no name more conspicuous than that of Chief Journeycake. He was not only a political leader of his people but also one of their spiritual pastors, and some years ago when the Federal Government published one of its important reports on the five civilized tribes in Indian Territory the portrait of Rev. Charles Journeycake, chief of the Delawares, was given an appropriate place of honor in that portion of the bulletin devoted to the Delaware people.

Chief Journeycake was the first person baptized in what is now the State of Kansas, where he lived with his people for many years, the Delawares moving into Indian Territory after 1868. His life of splendid integrity and Christian virtue gained him the highest respect of all who came in contact with him, and his memory is reverenced by all his people. He was their guide as well as their pastor, and was chiefly instrumental in converting the Delawares to the Christian religion. He was a master of the various Indian dialects, including the Shawnee, Wyandotte, Seneca, Ottawa as well as the Delaware dialect. It is said that during the Civil war when 80 per cent of his men had enlisted, it was his statesmanship that held the tribe together. He led the Delawares from Kansas into Indian Territory, and throughout he was the master spirit of his people. As an ordained Baptist clergyman he did missionary work all over Indian Territory, but never accepted one cent for his services, making his own living by farming.

Chief Journeycake died in 1894, and his wife, Jane (Sancia) Journeycake, passed away in 1893. A brief record of their children is as follows: Mary E., deceased, who married Charles H. Armstrong; Rachel, the deceased wife of N. J. Tanner; Nannie M., widow of the late Col. Jacob H. Bartles of Bartlesville; Lucy Jane, deceased, who married Henry Armstrong; Baron Stowe, who died when three years old; Emeline, wife of J. E. Campbell of Nowata; Adeline, deceased wife of Samuel Love; Anna, who also married Henry Armstrong and is now deceased; Cora Lee, who died after her marriage to William Carey; and one that died in infancy.

DAVID RATNER. Ten years ago David Ratner came to Cleveland, Oklahoma, and established a mercantile business in which he has since continued successfully. He has carried his activities into the adjacent Town of Yale in recent years, and since 1914 has operated a general store there with the same success he has enjoyed in Cleveland.

Mr. Ratner was born in Russia in 1863, September 11th being the day of his birth. He is a son of Mose and Esther (Ullman) Ratner, who came to America in 1884, bringing their family with them and settling in Kansas. For about four years these people lived on a farm and then moved to the Town of Wichita which move was followed no longer by their removal to Oklahoma about the time the famous "strip" was opened in 1893. They had their home at Blackwel. Moses Ratner died in Wichita when he was in th sixty-third year of his life, and his widow survive him until 1912, when she died in Cleveland, Oklahom: aged seventy years. They were the parents of thre sons and four daughters, all of whom are living at th time. They all lived under the paternal roof until th passing of the father, and the mother was living wit her son, David, when she passed away.

David Ratner was the first to leave Wichita and g to the new territory when it was opened in 1893. H father and others of the family joined him there soc after and they launched a small mercantile busines continuing therein for two years, when the fath retired and returned to Wichita, Kansas. David Ra ner went then to Blackwell, Oklahoma, and there too charge of a store which he operated for a year a then disposed of. His next venture was on his ov responsibility, and the business he established the he continued to run for about two years, when he so out and came to Cleveland in 1905. Since then he h conducted a general store here with good success, a

CHARLES JOURNEYCAKE

In 1914, in the month of October, he opened a general store in Yale. He has prospered in both these ventures, and in addition to his mercantile activities, has become the owner of a section of land in Jackson County.

Mr. Ratner, who is a democrat, was a presidential elector for his district in 1912, and has served on many important political committees in the years of his residence here. He is a Mason of high degree, a member of the Benevolent and Protective Order of Elks and the Knights of Pythias. He is unmarried, and has his home with his sisters in Cleveland. His brothers are Sam and Harry, the former a resident of Kansas City, and Harry a traveling salesman. Anna, the eldest sister of the subject, is a widow and makes her home with him. Rosa married Frank Stephens of Wichita, Kansas. Elizabeth lives with her brother David.

S. WELDON MORRISON. In September, 1915, Mr. Morrison began his duties as superintendent of schools at Byars. With that work he entered upon his eleventh consecutive year as an Oklahoma educator. He has been connected with a number of schools in different parts of the state and the record of his efficient service has been impressed upon a number of communities where the people regard him with especial esteem.

Professor Morrison is still a young man. He was born at Hazlehurst, Mississippi, April 17, 1884. His Scotch-Irish ancestors came to South Carolina during colonial times. His father, R. S. Morrison, who was born in Alabama in 1857, and when a young man went to Hazlehurst, Mississipipi, where he married; eventually became a pioneer in North Texas, locating at Vernon in the Red River Valley in 1888. By profession he is an attorney, and has practiced in several of the large circuits in North and Northwest Texas. In 1898 he located at Warren, Oklahoma, but in 1907 returned to Texas and established his home and profession at Archer City, where he now resides. He is now serving as county attorney of Archer County. In politics he is a democrat, is an active member and deacon of the Baptist Church, and is affiliated with the Masonic fraternity and the Independent Order of Odd Fellows. He also belongs to County, State and American Bar Associations. R. S. Morrison married Miss Nettie Wheeler who was born in Mississippi in 1867. Their children are: Professor Morrison; Mary Bell, who died at the age of five years; a daughter who died in infancy; Rubie, wife of Dave Anders, a farmer at Hobart, Oklahoma; Thomas, in the railroad service at Archer City, Texas; John, a railroad man at Orth, Texas; Ethel, who is living at home and employed in one of the stores at Archer City; Emma Joda, a junior in the high school at Archer City; Claud, Hazel, Percy and Maggie, all of them attending public school at Archer City.

S. Weldon Morrison completed the eighth grade of the public schools at Vernon, Texas, in 1901. During 1902 he attended the Agricultural and Mechanical College at Stillwater, Oklahoma, and the years 1903, 1904 and 1905 were spent as a farmer in Kiowa County of this state. He was just twenty-one when he began his career as an Oklahoma educator. His first school year 1905-06, was spent as principal of schools at Duke in Jackson County. His successive locations and terms of service have been: 1906-07, principal of schools at Cottage Hill, Jackson County; 1907-09, principal at South Greer, Oklahoma; 1909-11, principal of Centerview School; 1911-14, principal at Tipton, three years; 1914-15, principal of the Washington schools in McClain County; and in the fall of 1915 he became superintendent of schools at Byars. During all these years Mr. Morrison has been attending the Central State Normal School at Edmond during the summer sessions and also for two fall terms and for two spring terms. He is now a member of the senior class in that institution.

He has also identified himself with the work and interests of the County and State Teachers' Association. In politics he is a democrat, is a member of the Christian Church, and is affiliated with Tipton Lodge No. 417, Ancient Free and Accepted Masons. At Warren, Oklahoma, in 1905, Mr. Morrison married Miss Ethel Byrd. Her father, Thomas Byrd, who now lives at Edmond, Oklahoma, is a mechanic in the employ of the Santa Fe Railroad. Three children were born to their union: Orion and Harold, both in school; and Waldo.

EDWARD KARL ALLIS, M. D. Oklahoma has benefited by the coming to this state of many young and highly trained professional men. One of these is Dr. Edward K. Allis, who after acquiring all the advantages of northern and eastern schools and a general preliminary experience as a physician and surgeon, came to Wanette about six years ago, and has since made his service of great value to that community. That it has been appreciated is shown in the fact that he now enjoys a large practice, and is the owner of considerable property and has varied interests in the community.

A native of Indiana, Edward Karl Allis was born at Arcadia in that state May 1, 1881. The Allis family came originally from England, and Doctor Allis' great-grandfather after crossing the ocean established a home in Illinois, became a manufacturer there, and died in that state. The grandfather, W. B. Allis, was born in Switzerland County, Indiana, in 1817, and died at Sheridan, Indiana, in 1887. He too was a physician and surgeon.

W. D. Allis, father of Doctor Allis, was born in Switzerland County, Indiana, in 1850, and is still living at Arcadia in that state. His home has been in Indiana practically all his life, and his business has been that of contractor and builder. He also owns a fruit farm near Hanford, California. He is affiliated with the Independent Order of Odd Fellows and is a member and deacon in the Christian Church. W. D. Allis married Julia Teal, a native of Indiana. Dr. Allis is the older of their two sons, and the younger is Harlan Isaac, who now has charge of his father's fruit farm near Hanford, California.

As a boy Doctor Allis attended the public schools in Arcadia, graduated from high school in 1900, and he soon afterward entered the Hahnemann Medical College in Chicago, where he was graduated M. D. with the class of 1905. In choosing a location for practice he began at Hanford, West Virginia, where he remained during two years, 1905-07. During 1908 he took postgraduate courses in medicine at the University of Indiana Medical Department.

Thus with a liberal equipment for the duties of his profession he arrived in Wanette, Oklahoma, in March, 1909. His offices are in the First National Bank Building. Doctor Allis owns a farm of sixty acres just west of Wanette and owns his residence in the northern part of the village. He is also a director in the Lone Tree Oil Company. His professional relations are with the County and State Medical societies and the American Medical Association. Fraternally he is identified with Wanette Lodge No. 171, Ancient Free and Accepted Masons, and with Shawnee Lodge No. 657, Benevolent and Protective Order of Elks. He is a member of the Christian Church and in politics is a democrat.

At Wanette in 1911 Doctor Allis married Miss Stella Kidd. Her father was the later N. A. Kidd, a farmer and stockman. To their marriage have been born two children: Wilber Karl, born July 18, 1913; and Rita Lorine, born September 30, 1914.

GEORGE WILSON. Due largely to the individual efforts and enthusiasm of George Wilson, head of the Department of Agriculture for Schools in the State Agricultural and Mechanical College at Stillwater, agriculture as a subject of instruction has advanced during the last two years to much higher standing in school and college curriculums in Oklahoma. The state schools of agriculture have been creditably efficient but prior to 1914 there was little serious effort to have agriculture taught in the high schools. Indeed, until that time the state normal school curriculum provided for the teaching of agriculture during only one term, or part of a year, as a prescribed portion of the course leading to graduation. It was discovered that the graduate teachers turned out of the state normals took home with them the notion that the state did not consider the teaching of agriculture very important. It was to overcome this condition and build up agricultural education in the public schools that the department of agriculture for schools was created in the Oklahoma Agricultural and Mechanical College. Mr. Wilson had taught in district and city schools, state normal schools and the Agricultural and Mechanical College and the board of agriculture found him especially qualified for the work. His duties required that he visit high schools and normal schools and establish departments of agriculture, deliver addresses on the work of the department, and assist in making the practical and scientific study of agriculture an important feature of the school curriculum.

Born in Grayson County, Kentucky, in 1870, George Wilson is a son of James F. and Ellen (Craig) Wilson, who are now living a retired life at Hennessey, Oklahoma. John Craig, his mother's father, was for forty years one of the best known public school teachers of Kentucky. Mr. Wilson has three brothers and two sisters: Cord Wilson, a farmer at Cashion, Oklahoma; Clyde Wilson, a teacher in Oregon; Roy Wilson, living with his parents at Hennessey; Mrs. Nannie Cross, wife of a farmer at Glencoe, Oklahoma; Mrs. Donna Campbell, whose husband is a farmer at LeGrande, Oregon.

Work in the tobacco fields and illness interfered with the early education of Mr. Wilson in Kentucky, and it was not until after he reached manhood that he was able to satisfy his ambition for a thorough, practical, well rounded schooling, and he still retained the fire of youth when, after a few years of well directed study, he completed the highest course in the Central State Normal School of Oklahoma, which is recognized as one of the leading normal schools of the country. When he was still a boy his father had removed to Western Kansas in 1884. The country was new and sparsely settled, and educational advantages were meager. It was three years before the son was able to continue his primary training. Then in two years, with a few months of school each year and home study, he prepared himself for teaching in the common schools, and thereafter for two years taught in Kansas. In 1891, at the age of twenty-one, he came into the original Oklahoma Territory and in Kingfisher County continued his professional work and from every possible source sought a more complete education for himself. During 1903-04 he was a teacher in Comanche County, and from there entered the Central State Normal School, where after three years he completed a course and received his diploma in 1907. The following year he was elected superintendent of schools at Guymon, one of the leading towns of the Oklahoma Panhandle. In 1908 he was elected assistant teacher in the history department of the Northwestern State Normal School at Alva, and remained in that position until the history department was discontinued because of lack of appropriation. The year of 1908-09 he spent as a teacher in the Agricultural and Mechanical College at Stillwater, and the following year he returned to the Northwestern State Normal as head of the history department. The next year he was superintendent of city schools at Okemah, and the following year was elected by the state board of agriculture as head of the extension department of the Agricultural and Mechanical College. In 1914 he was promoted by the board to the head of the department of agriculture for schools.

This department under Mr. Wilson's management has become vastly more important than formerly. He raised the standards to such an extent that the Legislature of 1915, on advice and counsel of himself and Robert H. Wilson, state superintendent of public instruction, enacted a law providing that there shall be one year of agricultural work in every high school curriculum of the state. Mr. Wilson is emphasizing the practical side of agriculture, and he believes that in many instances the subject should take precedence over classical studies in the high schools and normal schools. His theory is that the high school is a community-serving institution and should develop the minds of pupils in the channels toward which they are bent.

In 1898 at Kingfisher Mr. Wilson married Miss Ella Brown, who died March 2, 1900. In 1908 Miss Mary Reece became his wife. Mrs. Wilson is a graduate of the fine old college of Tehuacana, Texas. They are the parents of two children: Wilbur, aged five, and Eugenia, now one year of age. Mr. Wilson is a prominent member of the Oklahoma Educational Association, and for years has been a participant in county and district teachers' associations. Throughout the state he is recognized as a practical and thorough educator, ranking high in the profession. He claims both Oklahoma City and Stillwater as his home, though his regular office and headquarters for mail are at Stillwater.

CARL E. MOHRBACHER. One of the rising young attorneys of Shawnee, Carl E. Mohrbacher who is a graduate of the law department of the state university is already established in a successful practice and has shown such ability that his future high rank in legal circles is practically assured. His office is in the Elks Building at Shawnee.

Born at Scott City, Kansas, March 24, 1888, he is a son of Fred W. and Louisa (Rouse) Mohrbacher. His father was born in Wisconsin, a son of German parents who were farmers in that state and died there during the '80s. Fred W. Mohrbacher moved out to Kansas in 1883 and in 1890 went to Nebraska, where he was successfully engaged in the grocery and real estate and loan business up to 1904. Since then for more than ten years he has lived at Shawnee, and from 1906 to 1914 was city treasurer, serving three times in that office. He is now substantially identified with the banking interests of the city.

Carl E. Mohrbacher acquired his early schooling in Nebraska, and in 1909 graduated from the Shawnee High School. In September, 1909, he entered the law department of the University of Oklahoma, being the first to enroll in the law school for the three year course. He was graduated LL. B. in June, 1912. There occurred an incident of his college career which should be mentioned. In the early part of 1912 he was formally accused of connection with an anonymous letter sent to members of the Legislature with reference to the state university building. He was tried before the State bar commission, his attorney being Moman Pruitt, and was completely exonerated of the charge and thus relieved of what might have been a serious handicap to his career at the outset.

Immediately after graduation and admission to the bar he began practice with Hon. William N. Maben in Shawnee, and has been associated with that attorney ever since. While engaged in a general practice he makes a specialty of personal injury cases, and has shown somewhat remarkable ability in handling this class of litigation. Mr. Mohrbacher is unmarried and resides at 644 North Louisa Street in Shawnee. He is a member of the county and state bar associations, belongs to the Alpha Psi Omega fraternity, is affiliated with the Fraternal Order of Eagles and belongs to the Presbyterian Church.

JAMES B. SCOTT. One of the staunch and ably conducted financial institutions of Blaine County is the First State Bank of Hitchcock, and as the chief practical executive of this bank Mr. Scott has served from the time of its organization, its inception having, in fact, been due to his efforts, and he having efficiently directed its affairs, in the capacity of cashier, since 1901. He established his residence at Hitchcock in that year and has been prominent and influential in business activities and also in the civic affairs of the community, as a progressive and public-spirited citizen whose popularity is of unequivocal order.

James Bryant Scott was born in the City of Emporia, Kansas, on the 12th of August, 1875, and is a scion of sterling Scotch ancestry, his grandfather, James Scott, having been born near the City of Edinburgh, Scotland, in 1802, and having come to the United States with his wife and children when he was still comparatively a young man. He established his home in New York City, where he continued to be identified with business activities for many years, and he was a resident of the State of Kansas at the time of his death, which occurred in 1890, so that he had attained to the patriarchal age of nearly ninety years. He achieved success in connection with his business activities after coming to America and was a man of steadfast rectitude and strong mental powers.

He whose name introduces this article is a son of W. W. and Annie (Bryant) Scott, the former of whom was born in Scotland, in 1842, and the latter of whom was born at Bridgewater, Massachusetts, in 1849, a representative of a prominent colonial family of New England. In 1843, the year succeeding that of his birth, W. W. Scott was brought by his parents to the United States, and he was reared to adult age in New York City, where he received the best of educational advantages. He was finally graduated in what is now the law department of historic old Columbia University, and as a young man he removed to Minnesota, becoming one of the pioneer members of the bar of that state and there continuing in the practice of his profession until 1873, when he removed to Emporia, Kansas, where he became one of the leading lawyers of that section of the Sunflower State and where he continued in active practice until virtually the time of his death, which occurred in 1890. He achieved specially high reputation as a versatile trial lawyer and was identified with many important litigations in the various courts of Kansas, besides which he was prominently identified with the Kansas State Bar Association and the American Bar Association. He was a republican in his political proclivities and was affiliated with the Masonic fraternity. His venerable widow still survives him and now maintains her home in the City of Topeka, Kansas. Of the children the first-born is Helen, who is the wife of Prof. William H. Johnson, a member of the faculty of the University of Kansas, at Lawrence; Mabel is the wife of William L. Gardner, of Topeka, Kansas, where Mr. Johnson is state agent for the National Fire Insurance Company; James B., of this review, was the next in order of birth and is the youngest of the children.

In the public schools of his native city of Emporia, Kansas, James B. Scott acquired his early educational discipline, and he was about fifteen years of age at the time of the death of his honored father. During the years 1893 and 1894 his widowed mother maintained the family home at Lawrence, Kansas, and there James continued his studies in the high school. He soon afterward returned to Emporia, where he completed a two years' course in the Kansas State Normal School. Upon leaving this institution, in 1895, Mr. Scott assumed the position of collector for the First National Bank of Emporia, and shortly afterward won promotion to the post of bookkeeper. He continued his association with this institution until 1898, and thereafter served as bookkeeper for the Citizens National Bank of Emporia until 1900.

In the year last mentioned Mr. Scott came to Oklahoma Territory and became identified with the Bank of Kiel, at Kiel, Kingfisher County. He served as cashier of this new institution for one year, and in August, 1901, he removed to the newly founded town of Hitchcock, in the adjoining County of Blaine, where he effected the organization of the First Bank of Hitchcock, of which he has since served as cashier and the affairs of which he has directed with the utmost circumspection and efficiency. The bank has been an important factor in facilitating general business activities in the town and surrounding country and has also aided in the furtherance of the civic and material development and progress of Hitchcock, the while its cashier has become one of the representative business man and loyal and valued citizens of the community. The bank building is eligibly located at the corner of Main Street and Broadway, and the officers of the institution are as here noted: B. Cronkhite, president; J. A. Overstreet, vice president; James B. Scott, cashier; and Van Bee Higby, assistant cashier. The bank bases its operations on a capital stock of $10,000 and has a surplus fund of $5,000.

Mr. Scott accords staunch allegiance to the republican party, is a member of the Oklahoma State Bankers' Association, is a valued member of the board of education of Hitchcock, and both he and his wife hold membership in the Christian Church in their home village, where also they take leading part in the representative social activities of the community. At the county seat Mr. Scott is affiliated with Watonga Lodge, No. 176, Ancient Free and Accepted Masons, and he has received the thirty-second degree in the Ancient Accepted Scottish Rite of Masonry, in which connection he is affiliated with Consistory No. 1, Valley of Guthrie, besides which he holds membership in India Temple, Ancient Arabic Order of the Nobles of the Mystic Shrine, in Oklahoma City. In his home village he holds membership in the lodge of the Independent Order of Odd Fellows and the camp of the Modern Woodmen of America.

At Emporia, Kansas, in the year 1902, was solemnized the marriage of Mr. Scott to Miss Mary I. Wiley, who, like himself, was born and reared in the Sunflower State. They have two children, Helen and James Bryant, Jr.

JAMES WIDENER, retired farmer and Civil war veteran, has been a resident of Cleveland and its neighborhood since the autumn of 1893, when he came into possession of 160 acres of land on the opening of the strip. In 1910 he withdrew from ranch life and settled in the City of Cleveland, where he is now living, in the seventy-second year of his life. Mr. Widener has had a varied career. The pioneer instinct was ever strong within him, and many a new and virgin territory has he entered, subdued to civilization and wholly conquered.

Born in Sandusky, Ohio, on March 10, 1843, James Widener is the son of Samuel and Jane (McGown) Widener, both natives of Ohio. Jane McGown's father was of Irish birth and ancestry and her mother was of a German family. Michael Widener, grandsire of the subject, was a native of the State of Virginia, and a pioneer to Ohio in young manhood. He spent many years among the native Indians of the state, and was well known to them as their faithful friend through many years. After Samuel Widener's marriage to Jane McGown, and when their son, James, of this review, was about two years old, they, in company with Michael Widener, James' grandsire, moved from Ohio to Indiana and located in Noble County. The white settlers were widely scattered, and the Indians were friendly for the most part, though they gave some trouble to the straggling white families. James Widener tells today with pride of the time when a famous Indian chief came to visit them and spent a week as their guest. There ever existed between them and the Indians a warm and true friendship, and they learned from their red brothers of the forest many of their secrets, such as the treatment of snake bite, etc. The grandfather died in Indiana, and after his second marriage, the son, Samuel, moved to Genesee County, Michigan, in the autumn of Buchanan's election to the presidency. Later they moved into Illinois, and still later to Missouri, James being a boy of sixteen at that time. While there, the father and sons worked for the railroad company, and young Widener helped to haul material for a bridge across the Sheridan River on the Hannibal and St. Joe Railroad. He spent three years in the construction department of this road in Indiana, Illinois and Missouri.

The next location of the family was at Brunswick, Missouri, where they spent a short time and moved on to Iowa and settling near Millersburg. The father died in Illinois about the year 1899. He had been three times married, and there were children of each union. James Widener was the eldest of the three children born to his mother, and she died when he was seven years old. The others were Michael and John. The former enlisted in Company C, Twenty-eighth Iowa Infantry, in 1862, and served until the close of the war. John also served as a member of the Thirty-seventh Illinois Regiment, enlisting in 1862 for the remainder of the war. He died in Granola, Kansas, in 1894.

Like his brothers, James Widener gave service to the Union during the war. He enlisted in 1861 at the first call. He was for three years a member of Company F, Tenth Iowa Infantry, and served three years and twenty-one days. He participated in many of the hottest engagements of the war in that time, including Farmington, Corinth, the siege of Vicksburg, being in both famous charges on the 22d day of May, as well as Missionary Ridge, and many minor engagements. He was never off duty except for a few weeks' illness as a victim of pneumonia.

After the war Mr. Widener returned to Iowa and worked at the carpenter's trade, in which he had been trained while in service with the construction crew of the Hannibal and St. Joe. He kept at that work for a while, then turned his attention to farm life. He remained in Iowa County, Iowa, then went to Kansas and settled in Shawnee County, and from there to Sumner County, Kansas. He came to Oklahoma before the opening of the Cherokee Strip in the fall of 1893, and in the race for land secured a quarter section located five miles south of the present Town of Cleveland. He farmed there until 1910, when he gave up active life and moved into town, where he has since lived.

On September 10, 1866, Mr. Widener was first married to Miss Wealthy. Ann Kine, born in Seneca County, Ohio, in 1848, became his wife, and she bore him seven children. She died in Cleveland on April 10, 1909. Rosanna, the first born, is the widow of P. J. Gallagher, of this city. John is a resident of Cleveland. Amanda is the wife of C. B. Lewis, a farmer in the community. Lettie married Paul Wheeler, of Pawhuska. James B. lives in Oilton, Oklahoma. Ethel is the wife of W. S. Estep of Cleveland. Clarence also lives in Cleveland.

On February 2, 1914, Mr. Widener married Mrs. Minnie B. Green. They have no children.

Mr. Widener may be regarded as one of the independently wealthy men of the town, for he has on his farm fourteen producing oil wells, with much unexplored territory. At one time he ran a harness shop in town, but has no interests of that nature to look after now. He owns two business buildings in the city.

Mr. Widener is a republican, a member of the Presbyterian Church, a thirty-second degree Mason and a member of the Grand Army of the Republic. His wife was born in Pennsylvania, though she was reared for the most part in Illinois and Missouri. She was married first in Missouri to James A. Green, a Civil war veteran, who died in 1900, near Springfield, Missouri. She came to Cleveland in 1902. She had four children by her first marriage. Roy; Mabel, the wife of Clarence Barnes of Pawnee; Okie Enid and Una Waive. All have had excellent educations. Mrs. Widener is a member of the Women's Relief Corps, and active in its worthy work. She was a Methodist for thirty-two years, and since her marriage to Mr. Widener has become a member of the Presbyterian Church.

HAYS HAMILTON is one of the pioneer citizens who has done much to further the civic and material development and upbuilding of Payne County and its judicial center, the thriving little City of Stillwater, where he is vice president of the Sater Abstract Company, which has assembled and has control of the only complete record of real estate titles in this county.

Mr. Hamilton was born at San Jose, California, on the 30th of September, 1863, and is a son of James G. and Cornelia (Bernard) Hamilton, both natives of Augusta County, Virginia, of which Staunton is the county seat, the father having been born about the year 1816 and the mother about 1820. Both were young at the time of the removal of the respective families to Callaway County, Missouri, in 1833, where they were reared to maturity under the conditions of the pioneer days and where their marriage was solemnized in 1844. Soon afterward they removed to Westport, Missouri, the village that was the nucleus of the present metropolis of Kansas City, and there James G. Hamilton engaged in the merchandise and shipping business, with which lines of enterprise he continued to be identified during the remainder of his active career, though in the meanwhile the family home was maintained for a short time in the State of California. He died in 1869, and his widow survived him by nearly half a century, she having been in her ninety-first year at the time of her death, in February, 1913, and having passed the closing period of her life in the home of one of her daughters in Colorado.

Hays Hamilton was reared to adult age in Kansas City, Missouri, and in 1882 he came to the Osage Indian Agency of Indian Territory. For four years he was employed by his elder brother, John B., who was an Indian trader and who maintained headquarters at Pawhuska, the present judicial center of Osage County, Oklahoma. Within this period of frontier experience Mr. Hamilton learned to speak the Osage language with considerable fluency, and at the expiration of the period noted he returned to Kansas City, where he continued his residence until 1889, when Oklahoma Territory was thrown open to settlement. He was among the sturdy pioneers who here established a residence at that time and he made Stillwater his abiding place at that early period in the history of Oklahoma. Here he has maintained his home during the intervening period of nearly thirty years, and the only other citizens of Payne County who came at the same time and who still reside here are Robert A. Lowery, William A. and Ambrose Swiles, and John Barnes.

Soon after thus becoming a pioneer settler at Stillwater Mr. Hamilton engaged in the grocery and general feed-supply business, and with this line of enterprise he continued to be actively identified a number of years. He was prominently concerned in the development of grape propagation and wine manufacturing in this section of the state, and for a number of years raised grapes and manufactured wine upon a somewhat extensive scale, his efforts at all times having been zealously directed to the advancement of measures and enterprises that have tended to foster the social and industrial development of the territory and state of his adoption.

As one of the interested principals and vice president of the Sater Abstract Company, Mr. Hamilton gives much of his attention to its business, and the abstracts owned by the company are the only complete records of titles in the county, as the public records were destroyed by fire in 1894. Mr. Hamilton is progressive as a citizen and his political allegiance is given to the democratic party.

Mr. Hamilton first passed through Payne County at the time when Captain Hatch, U. S. A., was making his effort to drive out the professional "Boomers," led by Captain Couch, and missed seeing the final expulsion of the boomers from the Stillwater Valley by only a few minutes, after having been attracted to this locality principally by a curiosity to witness the generally expected battle between the contending forces. He was concerned with the better element of citizenship in the establishing of the general democracy which here held sway until the laws for proper government could be formulated and brought into force, and he has viewed with satisfaction the effective popular activity and controlling interest in governmental affairs in Payne County, all citizens of standing having worked together with unity of interest to further the well-being of the county in general.

Mr. Hamilton has taken the deepest interest in the history of Oklahoma and has personally taken the pains to gather a large amount of interesting and valuable historical data. He had completed a most valuable record of Payne County history, and after this valuable manuscript was destroyed by fire he renewed his efforts and has to a large extent made good the data, his facilities for gathering historical material having been

advanced through his connection with the abstract business. His civic pride and loyalty have been shown through his earnest work for the advancement of his home city and making it an attractive and desirable place of residence. He was one of those specially influential in securing to Stillwater the Oklahoma Agricultural and Mechanical College, and he aided in raising the fund through which a representative citizen was sent to Washington to appear before the members of Congress and make possible the enlarging of Payne County by the addition of a portion of the Cherokee Strip when the latter was thrown open to settlement.

Mr. Hamilton is a devotee of hunting and fishing and has found in this section of the state opportunities for proving his prowess in both of these lines of outdoor sport. He is a member of the Stillwater Country Club, which has provided a fine artificial lake and stocked the same with the best varieties of fish. He is a member also of the Redlands Club and the Stillwater Commercial Club, of which latter he is a director. He has taken much interest in the advancement of the standards of agricultural and horticultural industry in this section, and is the owner of two well improved farms in Payne County, one of the same being in close proximity to Stillwater and the other being several miles distant.

In the year 1891 Mr. Hamilton wedded Miss Margaret J. Harper, who was born in the State of Kentucky, and their only child, Fern, was graduated in the Oklahoma Agricultural and Mechanical College, as a member of the class of 1913, she being a popular figure in the representative social activities of her home community.

E. L. GAY. The pioneer newspaper enterprise at Pawhuska was the establishment of the Osage Journal of which E. L. Gay became editor in 1904, when Pawhuska had very little claim to the business activities and improvements of a town or city. Not only in the newspaper field but in other affairs Mr. Gay's life has been one of varied and interesting experience. He is one of the original Oklahomans, and in fact can claim membership in that goodly company of enterprising men who were denominated as "sooners." He and his family had many interesting associations with frontier life in the Southwest, and there are few who possess in their memory a greater fund of information concerning Oklahoma history than this Pawhuska editor.

Born in Hillsdale County, Michigan, October 12, 1862, E. L. Gay is one of a family of six sons and two daughters, all of whom grew up and are all living except one. He was the fifth in order of age. His parents were Charles H. and Catherine (Fulton) Gay. His grandfather was William H. Gay, who was born in Scotland and was brought to America when a child. About 1830 he settled in Michigan, and in 1852 was appointed United States Indian agent for the Wyandotte tribe at the Wyandotte Agency located near where Kansas City, Kansas, now stands. He held that post until 1856. In that year he and his son James were making a trip from the Indian agency to Fort Leavenworth. While going up the river they were halted by a band of horsemen, and were questioned as to their attitude toward the then critical question of whether Kansas should be admitted as a slave or free state. William H. Gay, it should be remembered, was a Scotchman, and possessed all the courage of his convictions. He expressed himself decisively in favor of making a free state of Kansas, and the words were hardly out of his mouth when he was shot down and killed, while his son was severely wounded. William H. Gay was a real frontier character, and in the early days had made a couple of trips to Texas in the interests of the government, and while there formed a great friendship with Governor Houston. Charles H. Gay, who was born in New York State in 1825, was one of three children, two sons and a daughter, his brother being James H. Gay, already mentioned as the companion of their father at the time of the latter's death. Charles H. Gay spent most of his active career in Southern Michigan and Northern Ohio. He was a millwright by trade in early life but in later years took up the profession of law and became one of the noted young jurists of that section. He married Catherine Fulton, who was of the same family as the noted inventor, Robert Fulton. She died at Pioneer, Ohio, in 1884. At their home in the same place and in the same house Charles H. Gay passed away in 1903.

The early life of E. L. Gay brought him into close touch with the actualities of existence, and he had a hard struggle to gain the education which his ambition craved. He lost his mother in the spring of 1884, when he was twenty-two years of age, and up to that time he had kept quite close to the old homestead. He attended high school at Pioneer, Ohio, and for one year was a student in the Valparaiso Normal School in Indiana. In order to pay his way through school he taught, beginning when he was seventeen years of age, and continued alternately as a teacher and student for five years. His practice was to teach the short winter terms and attend school himself the rest of the year. In 1884, after the death of his mother Mr. Gay went to Kansas City, Kansas, and taught in the Wyandotte County public schools one year, but from there went to Western Kansas and identified himself with the exciting incidents of the frontier. He was also in Texas and for a time was in that region described in the old geographies as "No Man's Land" of Indian Territory. In the spring of 1887 he was in the Panhandle of Texas, looking after a herd of cattle. From there he returned to No Man's Land and in 1889 began the publication of the Tribune at Beaver City. Mr. Gay was closely identified with that movement which is an important chapter in any history of Oklahoma for the erection of a local government in the Panhandle of Oklahoma, and was a member of the first provisional council that adopted a plan of government for "provisional territory of Cimarron." He was also elected to one of the proposed territorial officers as district attorney. Mr. Gay published the Tribune at Beaver City for about a year. In the meantime he had received an appointment as chief clerk in the first Territorial Legislature of Oklahoma, and spent five months at Guthrie, the capital, during that session. After leaving Beaver City he moved to El Reno and bought the Oklahoma Democrat in that city, which had just been started. He conducted this journal as a partnership for two or three years, and in the meantime had participated in the opening of the Cheyenne and Arapaho lands. Subsequently for one year Mr. Gay conducted the Evening News at Shawnee, and during the boom times that followed railroad construction identified himself with Holdenville. He also lived at Tulsa for a time, and in 1904 came to Pawhuska for the definite purpose of establishing a paper. He was one of the organizers of the Osage Journal Company, and has edited this prominent and influential weekly democratic paper ever since. When Mr. Gay first came to Pawhuska there was not a foot of sidewalk in the town, and not a single brick building. He has used the influence of his paper and has worked as an individual citizen for everything tending to the betterment of his town and has been one of the real factors in its advancement.

In politics he has been a lifelong democrat. He was not only clerk in the first but also in the second Territorial Legislature of Oklahoma. In the early days and while a resident of No Man's Land he held a commission as Deputy United States Marshal under J. J. Dickerson when the federal court of the second Texas District was supposed to have jurisdiction over that country. As such officer he was instrumental in bringing to trial the participants in the Wild Horse Lake massacre which occurred in the central part of that country.

Fraternally he is affiliated with the Benevolent and Protective Order of Elks, the Ancient Order of United Workmen, the Homesteaders and the Independent Order of Odd Fellows.

While engaged in the newspaper business at El Reno he was married to Alice Crawmer at Wichita, Kansas, on November 26, 1891. Four children have been born to their union, one of them, Eugene Fenton, dying in infancy. Those living are: Leah Frances, Elgin Crawmer and Allen G. Thurman.

WILLIAM H. EDMISTEN. A resident of Indian Territory since 1886, William H. Edmisten has been an eyewitness of the growth and development of this wonderful country from the days when it was almost entirely inhabited by the red man to the present era of business and agricultural prosperity and advanced civilization. During this period he has been engaged principally in pursuits connected with farming and the raising of stock, but at present is living a retired life at Cleveland, although he has some valuable holdings, particularly on Turkey Island, on which one oil well has been drilled.

Mr. Edmisten was born at Neosho, Newton County, Missouri, February 26, 1857, and is a son of Richard and Eliza C. (Rhodes) Edmisten. His father, a native of either Kentucky or Tennessee, came to the West with his parents in 1830 and settled in Newton County, Missouri, where he passed the remaining years of his life as a farmer and stock-raiser. The mother, also a native of the South, located in Missouri about the same time as her husband and now makes her home at Goodman, in that state. They were the parents of eleven children, as follows: Daniel, who is deceased; William H.; Mary Ellen, of Seattle, Washington, the wife of Lewis D. Stone; John D., a resident of Missouri; Florence, who is the wife of Charles Barnes, of Missouri; Rosa Lee, who is the wife of John Stites, of Missouri; Richard and Eliza, twins, both of whom died young; Maggie, the wife of William Foster, of Joplin, Missouri; Matt, cashier of the Goodman State Bank of Goodman, Missouri; and Theo, who is the wife of William Cornelison, of Kansas.

William H. Edmisten was educated in the schools of Newton County, Missouri, and grew up as a farmer and stock-raiser. Feeling that he could better his fortune further to the West, in 1886 he came to Indian Territory and for about fifteen or sixteen years was engaged in the stock business, a line in which he won well merited success. In the winter of 1901 he came to Pawnee County, settling on a farm on the Arkansas River, six miles southeast of Cleveland, a tract of 16 acres, which he still owns and which consists of good bottom land. There he continued to make his home until January 1, 1914, at which time he came to Cleveland. Mr. Edmisten's farm is a part of Turkey Island, and at the present time this property is in litigation, in regard to riparian rights. If Mr. Edmisten wins his suit he will have 275 acres, but it is not the quantity of land that makes this case an important one, but the oil that has been discovered there. There have been a number of wells drilled on his land, shallow sand wells, yielding from twenty to sixty barrels.

Mr. Edmisten has had many and varied experiences since coming to the West, many of which center around the Indians. At one period in his career he was farming 1,100 acres, twelve miles east of Vinita, at the head of Duck and Shawnee creeks, where he operated four farms, worked twenty mules, and kept two jacks in his stud. He bought and shipped much stock during that time and did much dealing with the Indians, with whom he managed to keep on friendly terms.

As an incident showing the turn that fortune may take at some time and that a man's judgment and foresight cannot always be infallible, the following may be related: On September 16, 1893, Mr. Edmisten was standing at the elbow of the man who fired the gun announcing the opening of the Cherokee Strip, at Stillwater. It was noon, and he was off with the shot, mounted on a good horse which took him over twenty miles to Pawnee in one and one-half hours, and there he secured several lots which now form the property on which the high school stands. Mr. Edmisten, however, figured that this was an undesirable part of the country, that it would likely never amount to anything, and accordingly gave his lots away and rode to another locality. A sight which impressed itself upon his mind on that same day occurred at Stillwater. It was hot and dusty, water was at a premium, and the anxious homeseekers were gathered in hordes. Some enterprising citizen started selling water melons, soon others followed suit, and before all had registered the water melon rinds lay two feet deep on the ground for a space covering nearly a half a mile! While Mr. Edmisten has been a permanent resident of Cleveland for only a comparativey short time, he may be said to have been one of the town's earliest arrivals, having come here before the place was started, and buying groceries for himself and feed for his horses three days after the town opened. He has always been a progressive promoter of beneficial movements, lending encouragement and support to any enterprise that has promised to make for the betterment of his locality or its people. As a business man, he has built up a substantial reputation for integrity and honorable dealing, while his good citizenship has never been doubted.

Mr. Edmisten was married in 1876 to Miss Samantha C. Stark, who was born in Washington County, Indiana, January 16, 1856, and brought to Missouri when twelve years of age by her parents, Vinyard and Susan (Kester) Stark, natives of Indiana, the former of whom, a farmer, died in Missouri, and the latter in Kansas. Eleven children have been born to Mr. and Mrs. Edmisten, as follows: Harlington Lafayette, who spent a number of years in Idaho and Montana but is now engaged in operating one of his father's farms; Ada Belle, who is the wife of Andrew McCaffrey, of Afton, Oklahoma; Jack E., of Goldboro, Washington; Daniel Horace, of Cleveland, an oil man connected with the Prairie Oil and Gas Company; Alta Lee, the wife of F. C. Larabee, of Los Vegas, New Mexico; Walter W., of Cleveland, engaged in oil production; Orville Harrison, who for six years has been connected with the relay office of the Santa Fe Railroad, at Topeka, Kansas; Myrtle, who is the wife of J. O. Martin, of Waxahachie, Texas; Lillian, who resides with her parents; Richard, an oil man of Cleveland; and Goldie, who resides at home. Mr. and Mrs. Edmisten have never lost a child and have sixteen living grandchildren. Their first seven children were born in Missouri and the rest in this state, and all have been well educated and trained admirably for the positions in life to which they have been called.

ALBERT D. BROWN. Until he became proprietor and editor of the Observer at McLoud in Pottawatomie County, Albert D. Brown had been for a number of years identified with educational work in Oklahoma. Mr. Brown comes from a family of educators and churchmen, and he is himself an ordained minister of the Baptist Church and has preached in several localities in this state. His father before him was a minister and also his grandfather.

In August, 1915, Mr. Brown came to McLoud and bought the Observer from B. McGlathey. The Observer was established in 1902 as a democratic paper and is now independent in politics. The plant is well equipped and the office is situated on the main street of the village. It is a paper with much influence and has a circulation over Pottawatomie County and Oklahoma County and also goes in considerable numbers outside the state.

Albert D. Brown was born in Henry County, Missouri, August 23, 1877. The Brown family came from Scotland originally, and were pioneers in Kentucky. The grandfather was a minister of the Presbyterian Church in Kentucky and moved from that state about 1837, to Missouri where he was one of the early settlers in Henry County. Elder Peter Brown, father of Albert D., was born in Washington County, Kentucky, in 1835, and was thirteen years of age when the family moved to Missouri, where he grew to manhood. He was largely self educated, and in younger years practiced medicine for a time. At the age of twenty-one he began active work as a Baptist preacher, and in spite of the early handicaps in the way of an education he was for a number of years considered the best Greek Bible-scholar in the state. His life work as a Baptist minister was confined to Missouri, though his influence and activities were in various other spheres as well. As a democrat he was once nominated for the State Legislature. During the Civil war he was on the Confederate side as a soldier. He was a member of the Masonic fraternity. Elder Peter Brown married Elizabeth Shanks who was born in Pettis County, Missouri, in 1835. She now lives at Hatfield, Arkansas. Elder Peter Brown died a few years ago in the Baptist Sanitarium at St. Louis. Their children were: Catherine, wife of Ellis Tuttle, a brick manufacturer in Butler, Missouri; Peter, who is an architect at Hatfield, Arkansas; George, a farmer in Roger Mills County, Oklahoma; Benjamin Franklin, a farmer at Hatfield, Arkansas; Lucy, wife of U. G. Roberts, a farmer in Wyandotte, Oklahoma; Stephen, a farmer and stock raiser in Missouri; and Albert D.

The youngest in this large family, Albert D. Brown was eight years of age when his parents moved in 1885 to St. Clair County, Missouri. He attended the public school there, and afterwards attended the Wiliam Jewell College at Liberty, Missouri, where he took two years of academic work and two years in the regular collegiate department. He finished the Sophomore course in 1906. While in college he was a member of the Philomathic Literary Society, and took first prize in competition for an essay and tied for honor in oratory. He also won several honors in prose and poetry contests.

On leaving college Mr. Brown came into Oklahoma in 1906 and began teaching school in Roger Mills County. He was principal of schools in that county until 1914 and then for a year taught at Harrah in this state. As an ordained minister of the Baptist Church Mr. Brown also filled pulpits in several parishes in Roger Mills County and elsewhere, but several years ago lost his voice and had to retire from the ministry. In politics he is a democrat, and is affiliated with the Independent Order of Odd Fellows and the Woodmen of the World.

In 1909 in Navarro County, Texas, he married Miss Minnie Meredith. Her father was the late Doctor Meredith, a physician and surgeon at Navarro County. Two children were born to this union. Mattie Ellen, born October 14, 1911, and Byron Addison, born April 30, 1914.

Mr. Brown has gained no little distinction as a writer of poetry. He rarely edits an edition of his paper without featuring some poetry of his own composition. He possesses a rare knowledge of rhythm and verse and his poetry is as scholarly and correct in technic as it is elevated in sentiment and feeling. As an example of his style and diction there is quoted herewith a poem which he dedicated to his mother and which Mr. Brown himself considers his best composition.

TO MY MOTHER
(By A. D. Brown)

The world's at the morning in sweet mother's love
Like sweet roses sparkle with dew from above
My mother directs me and watches my way
And keeps me from evil wherever I stray.
Ofttimes I remember when temptations arise
The precepts which mother brought down from the skies.
And when in my strength all my vows I fulfill
My sweet mother, smiling, approves of me still.
I see her dear face wheresoever I roam.
It strengthens the ties and affections of home.

Purest, sweet mother! A shrine I will make
And worship thine image, and never forsake
Thy faithful instruction. Thy tears I will heed,
Regard all thy prayers, for when I'm in need
Of strong resolution, and determined will,
I need to remember what thou didst instill.
I can't compensate thee for what thou hast done,
But please take this tribute from thy grateful son.

For what thou hast suffered, what thou underwent
For thy watching o'er me, the wakeful nights spent,
The pains and the pangs and the griefs that thou bore
I don't understand, but I reverence the more.
Thou gavest thy strength and thy blood and thy bone.
Thou gavest thy life for me, thou, thou alone.
Thou'st done this and more for me, Mother, and now
A halo of glory I place on thy brow.

The times that I worried thee, disobeyed thee,
For when I was truant thou tried to save me
When I was ungrateful and cruel and bad
And mean and deceitful, it makes my heart sad
To think for thy goodness, I rendered thee woe.
For when I went places thou begged me not go,
I lied to thee sometimes regarding my ways.
Forgive me sweet Mother, accept of my praise.

For all thy instruction, thy good moral laws
Thy discipline sweet, and thy life without flaws,
Thy love and compassion, thy pity in shame,
Sometimes thou approved me when I was to blame.
I cannot undo what's been done to my shame
I always shall love thee and honor thy name.

Thy life and thy love, like a book, has been read,
And shall be remembered long after thou'rt dead
I know of thy purity, piety, truth,
Thou art my sweet angel, my guardian in youth,
My ideal in manhood, my idol in age,
My most sober worship, my best thoughts engage.
And when thou art glorified, raised upon high,
I know I shall see thee, for souls cannot die,
The Christ that thou lovest will also love me
Forgive all my failings and take me to thee.

GEORGE BRENTNALL. Among the men who have assisted in the agricultural and commercial development of Pawnee County during the past two decades, one who is well and widely known is George Brentnall, of Cleveland, the owner of a seventy-eight-acre farm in the county, who during the past seven years has also carried on a hardware and furniture business in the city. He was born at Pomeroy, Meigs County, Ohio, December 12, 1861, and is a son of George and Elizabeth (Edwards) Brentnall, the former a native of England and the latter of Wales.

In his native land the father of Mr. Brentnall was employed as a laborer in the coal mines, and on emigrating to the United States, in his youth, found employment in the coal fields of Pittsburgh, Pennsylvania. He was married in England and after the birth of one child they came to America. In 1848 he removed to Kittanning, Pennsylvania, where he spent one year. He next moved to Meigs County, Ohio, locating at Pomeroy, and while there, during the Civil war, was one of the men who turned the Southern raider Morgan, although Mr. Brentnall was at that time too old for active service at the front. In April, 1866, he moved with his family to Macon County, Missouri, where he invested his life's savings in a farm, and continued to pass the remaining years of his life there, dying December 25, 1880. Mrs. Brentnall passed away in March, 1894, the mother of seven children, namely: Samuel, of Topeka, Kansas; Robert, of Ness City, Kansas; Margaret Ellen Davenport, who died in Missouri, in 1898; Susan, the wife of William Appal, of Hannibal, Missouri; Mary, who is the wife of Wesley Cherington and resides near the old home, in Jackson County, Ohio; George; and Elizabeth, who is the wife of Al Robinette, of Mountain Grove, Missouri.

George Brentnall was reared on the home farm and received his education in the public schools. He remained under the parental roof until reaching the age of twenty-seven years, or until the time of his marriage, having taken care of his aged mother after his father's death. On December 2, 1887, he was married to Miss Zora Bodenhammer, a native of Iowa, and in 1888 they took a trip to Australia to join Mr. Brentnall's uncle, Samuel Brentnall, a cattleman there. Mrs. Brentnall died in that country in 1890, leaving one child, Grace, who is now the wife of Lucius Peek, of Vinita, Oklahoma. Mr. Brentnall was in Australia at the time of his uncle's death in 1893, when he returned to Missouri, but in the following year came to Pawnee County, Oklahoma, taking up a homestead nine miles southeast of Cleveland. This he improved and cultivated until his children grew old enough to need better educational advantages than the country afforded, when he changed his residence to Cleveland. He still owns seventy-eight acres of good land, improved with large and substantial buildings, adjoining Cleveland, and there carries on operations on an extensive scale, being engaged in both general farming and in the raising of stock and meeting with success in both departments. On his homestead nine miles southeast of Cleveland are located nine producing oil wells, which contribute materially to his income. Mr. Brentnall bears an excellent reputation in commercial circles, and as a citizen has gained and maintained a position of standing. He is a republican, but while he takes an interest in the success of his party is not what is generally known as a politician. With his family, he belongs to the Christian Church.

Mr. Brentnall was married the second time, October 18, 1896, to Miss Ida Sharp, of Kansas, born September 21, 1874, and they are the parents of five children, all residing at home: Mabel, Blanche, Opal, Robert and Gerald.

O. B. KIZER. The life of O. B. Kizer, a well known resident of Jennings, is an illustration of the possible control over early limitations and of the wise utilization of ordinary opportunities. His career has been identified with Oklahoma since the opening of the Cherokee Strip, in 1893, and the substantial property which allows him to live in comfortable retirement at Jennings has been accumulated through wise investment in farming land and other real estate and careful management of his large interests.

Born November 28, 1858, in Edgar County, Illinois, Mr. Kizer is a son of Sebastian and Mary Elizabeth (Aye) Kizer. His father, a native of Pennsylvania, ventured into Illinois as a young man and was there married and engaged in agricultural pursuits for some years, but in 1864 again turned his face to the West and journeyed to Kansas, where he also followed farming and stock raising. In his later life, after spending a few years in Colorado, he came to Jennings, Oklahoma, and here died at the home of his son, O. B., in 1906, when eighty-four years of age. He was a hard and industrious worker and was content to pass his life in the peaceful pursuits of the soil, not caring for public office or the doubtful honors of political life. By his first wife he had two children, and after her death he was married to Mary Elizabeth Aye, who was born in Illinois and whose death occurred in Kansas in 1874. They were the parents of seven children, while by a third marriage Mr. Kizer became the father of three children.

O. B. Kizer was first sent to the district schools of Edgar County, Illinois, but when eight years of age accompanied his parents to Kansas and there his education was completed. He remained at home until twenty-four years of age, dividing his time between assisting his father and working out among the neighboring farmers, but at the time of his marriage, in 1883, decided to embark upon a career of his own. For two years he resided at Chautauqua Springs, Kansas, where he was variously employed, and at the end of that time came to the Osage Nation. He had resided here for five years when the announcement was made of the proposed opening of the Cherokee Strip, and Mr. Kizer went to Arkansas City, Kansas, from whence he made the run, September 16, 1893. He was unsuccessful, however, in obtaining a homestead and settled instead at Jennings, where for twelve years he was commercially occupied. Business conditions there at the end of that time caused him to leave the city and move to a leased property in Creek County, on which he was engaged in farming for a period of eight years, and then rented his land and moved to Jennings, where he has continued to live in retirement to the present time. He has 160 acres in the tract mentioned, as well as another tract of like size one-half mile south and one-half mile west of Jennings. Both places are oil leased and are yielding Mr. Kizer a substantial income. In addition to these properties, Mr. Kizer is the owner of some valuable and desirable Jennings realty and is engaged in the real estate business as an occupation to keep his energetic mind satisfied. Politically he is a democrat, but political life has never appealed to him. He may always be counted upon to support those movements which make for the welfare of his community.

Mr. Kizer was married in 1883, while a resident of Kansas, to Miss Mary Potter, who was born in Kentucky, September 15, 1861. As a small child she was taken to Illinois, and in 1871, when ten years old was removed with her parents to Kansas, where she was reared and educated and where she met and married Mr. Kizer. Eight children have been born to Mr. and Mrs. Kizer, namely: Claude, who is a resident and farmer of Pawnee County, Oklahoma; Fay, who lives in Kansas; Pearl, who is the wife of E. D. Fudge, of Creek County, Oklahoma; Bruce, who lives with his parents; O. B., Jr., also at home; Glenn, who met an accidental death at the age of twelve years when killed by a horse; and Irene and Hazel, who reside at home and are attending school.

GEORGE H. SCHROEDER. As history is reckoned in Oklahoma thirty years includes the extremes of frontier life and twentieth century existence. The lure of land to be obtained for a mere pittance brought men from all over the country in search of homes where they might make themselves independent, but it was only the courageous who came, and to know a pioneer of the '80s is to know a man possessed of virile and purposeful traits of character. Such a man is George H. Schroeder, who came to Indian Territory in 1885, and who is now living in comfortable retirement at Jennings. He is not only the possessor of a large property, gained through his own efforts and industry, but has also the confidence of his fellow-citizens, as witnessed by the fact that he is now serving his second term in the office of county commissioner of Pawnee County.

Mr. Schroeder was born on a farm in Jersey County, Illinois, February 16, 1855, and is a son of Joseph B. and Priscilla C. (Patterson) Schroeder. His father, a direct descendant of Jane Brown, who came to America on the Mayflower, was born at Portsmouth, New Hampshire, and was reared in the City of Philadelphia, Pennsylvania, where he learned the trade of wagon maker and carriage trimmer. In 1844 he migrated to the prairies of Illinois, settling on a farm in Jersey County, where he passed the remaining years of his life in agricultural pursuits and died in 1892. He married a Jersey County girl, Priscilla C. Patterson, who passed her life there and died in 1875. They were the parents of four children: Nellie S., who married L. L. Hereford, and is now deceased; Gersham F., a resident of Ponca City, Oklahoma; George H.; and Mary Kate, who is the wife of George Miller, of Vinita, Oklahoma.

George H. Schroeder was reared in Jersey County, where he received the advantages of a district school education. On attaining his majority he moved to a farm of his own in the same county and resided there until July, 1881, when he moved to Vernon, Missouri, and established himself in the grocery business. This enterprise occupied his attention and activities until 1885, when he moved to Bartlesville, Indian Territory, and in April, 1893, went to Guthrie, where he awaited the opening of the Cherokee Strip, September 16th. At that time he succeeded in securing a homestead west of Ponca City, Kay County, and there carried on operations until May, 1902, when he came to Pawnee County. In 1812, when his wife died, Mr. Schroeder moved to Jennings, and here he has just completed a handsome modern home. Mr. Schroeder is still the owner of two farms, each comprising a quarter of a section, one located 1½ miles south of Jennings, and the other five miles northwest of this place, on Ranch Creek, and all of this land, with the exception of forty acres, is under oil lease. He carried on general farming during his residence in Oklahoma, and also was interested extensively in the raising of thoroughbred horses, cattle and hogs, and in all of his ventures gained a full measure of success by his strict adherence to honorable business methods and his close application to his work. His entire life has been passed in agricultural and stock raising pursuits, with the exception of three years in the grocery business at Vernon, Missouri, and nine years in the monument and tombstone business at Bartlesville. He has always been a supporter of public-spirited movements for the public welfare and bears an excellent reputation as a citizen. A democrat in politics, Mr. Schroeder has supported his party faithfully, but never held public office until 1912, when he was elected a county commissioner of Pawnee County, a position in which he served so capably and faithfully that he was reelected in 1914. Since his twenty-first year he has been a member of the A. H. T. A.

On March 30, 1880, Mr. Schroeder was united in marriage with Miss Ida J. Brown, who was born in Jersey County, Illinois, within a mile of her husband's birthplace, July 24, 1862. Mr. and Mrs. Schroeder grew up together, and during the long years of their married life she proved him a willing, devoted and faithful helpmeet. Her death, which occurred October 2, 1912, was not only a shock to her immediate family and friends, but to a wide circle of acquaintances who had come to know and appreciate her many lovable traits of mind and heart. She was also a descendant of one of the passengers of the little ship Mayflower. Five children were born to Mr. and Mrs. Schroeder, namely: Neddie, who died at the age of five years at Bartlesville; Nellie Fay, who is the wife of Hurley McDaniel of Jennings, and the mother of one child, Wanda Rose; Ethel C., who is the wife of L. C. Harper, of Tulsa; Fern, a son, who died in infancy; and Joseph Brown, named for his grandfather and great-grandfather, who resides with his father.

CHARLEY MELCHOR FOIL. The postmaster of the thriving and prosperous little City of Jennings, Charley Melchor Foil, has been a resident of this place for fifteen years, during which period he has been connected with several commercial houses and has won the confidence of his fellow-citizens by a strict adherence to high ideals of citizenship. In his official capacity he is proving one of the most efficient and popular postmasters Jennings has known, and through his earnest and conscientious efforts is doing much to improve the service.

Mr. Foil comes of Holland Dutch ancestry, and was born at Mount Pleasant, Cabarrus County, North Carolina, July 17, 1871, a son of Alexander and Amelia Louise (Melcher) Foil, natives of that state where the father was born in 1834 and the mother in 1835. Alexander Foil was a merchant at Concord, North Carolina, where the family moved after the birth of Charley M., and was also a well known and influential factor in public and political life, serving as county commissioner and sheriff of Cabarrus County and being sent to the State Legislature. He was a democrat and stood high in the councils of his party. During the Civil war he saw service as a soldier, being stationed at Fort Fisher. Mr. Foil died at Concord in 1890, the mother surviving him two years. They were the parents of three children: Lizzie, who is the wife of W. S. Bingham, of Concord, North Carolina; Thomas Alexander, a resident of Salisbury, North Carolina; and Charley Melchor.

Charley M. Foil was reared at Concord, where he attended the public schools, but felt that there was a better future awaiting him in the West, and at the age of nineteen years, in 1890, migrated to Kansas, where he spent six months. He then came to Indian Territory and secured work as a farm hand, and in February, 1893, moved to a farm south of Jennings, which he worked on a lease. On first coming to Jennings, in 1900, he became bookkeeper for the firm of Todd & Bishop, general merchants, and continued to be connected with that concern for a period of ten years, then entering the employ of the Treese Cotton Company in the same capacity. Subsequently he was placed in charge of their cotton gin here, which he has continued to manage. In August, 1914, after a civil service examination, Mr. Foil was appointed postmaster at Jennings, which is a first class office. He is alert, energetic and capable in the discharge of his duties, and his courtesy and geniality have made him decidedly popular with the public. Mr. Foil is a democrat in politics and a dependable party worker. He is prominent fraternally, being a member of the Independent Order of Odd Fellows, the Modern Woodmen of America, the Knights of the Maccabees and the Masons, and in the last-named order has reached the thirty-second degree, belonging to the Blue Lodge at Jennings, the Chapter at Pawnee, and the Consistory at Guthrie. He belongs likewise to the Encampment of Odd Fellows at Yale.

Mr. Foil was married August 8, 1893, to Miss Emma Pearl Whitehead, a native of Kansas, and daughter of Edmund and Malinda J. Whitehead. Her father is deceased, while her mother still survives and is a resident of Jennings. Mr. and Mrs. Foil have no children.

CLYDE H. MORRIS. During a period of five years Clyde H. Morris has become well and favorably known to the people of Mooreland, Oklahoma, through his connection with the postoffice. Formerly postmaster and now assistant, his capable and energetic handling of the mails and the courteous manner in which he transacts business with those with whom he comes into contact have made him one of the most popular public officials of this part of Woodward County. Mr. Morris is a type of the class of which the West is proud, the type that came here without means and here worked out a success. He is an Indianan by nativity, having been born at Mace, Montgomery County, April 18, 1874, a son of John A. and Mary S. (Hale) Morris, both Hoosiers by birth.

John A. Morris was born at Mace, Indiana, in 1830, and has never left the state. In his early life he was engaged in mercantile pursuits for some years, but subsequently turned his attention to farming, and through a life of industry and well-directed effort has won a competence, so that he is now living in comfortable retirement. In 1873 he was united in marriage with Miss Mary S. Hale, who was born in 1852, in Indiana, a daughter of Nathan and Mary (Noftzger) Hale. She was a woman of many virtues and Christian character, who lived her Christianity every day. She died in 1882, at the early age of thirty years, having been the mother of only one child, Clyde H., of this review.

Clyde H. Morris was born in a village, but when his mother died he was sent to live with an uncle, Tillman Hale, who was the owner of a large Indiana farm. There the lad worked from his eighth to his sixteenth year, receiving his education in the district school as well as the schools of hard work and experience, and when he reached the latter age he left Indiana for the West. On his arrival at his destination, in Franklin County, Kansas, he began working on a farm, and his subsequent labors carried him to various parts of that state. In 1898 he came to Oklahoma and settled on government land, two miles east of the present side of Mooreland, where he proved up after five years and continued to carry on operations until coming to the town. From the time of attaining his majority, he had been an active and enthusiastic republican, and, after taking some active part in the success of his party in Woodward County, he was, in 1910, appointed postmaster of Mooreland by President Taft. He discharged the duties of this office in a creditable and satisfactory manner, but with the change of the national administration came a change in postmasters. When Mr. Morris was succeeded as postmaster by Omer Schnoebelen, a democrat, in 1914, he was retained as assistant postmaster, and as such is in practical charge of the postoffice affairs. He is a member of the Knights of Pythias, in which, as in other avenues of activity, he has numerous friends. He is one of the men who may be accredited with the growth and development of Mooreland, for its industries and institutions have ever received his unqualified and unswerving support.

Mr. Morris was married November 3, 1905, in Woodward County, Oklahoma, to Miss Nellye C. Renfrow, who was born in 1883 in Comanche County, Kansas, daughter of Edward and Amy (Ray) Renfrow, natives of Kansas and pioneer settlers of Woodward County. Mr. Renfrow, who throughout his life was engaged in agricultural pursuits, died in 1899, while his widow still survives and makes her home in this county. Mr. and Mrs. Morris are the parents of two sons and one daughter: Arthur Newell, born May 20, 1907; Hilma Inez, born in May, 1909; and Homer Lewis, born May 20, 1911. Mr. and Mrs. Morris are members of the Methodist Episcopal Church and have been active in its work.

ROBERT T. WRAY has had a life of varied experience and accomplishment. He has been a merchant, a manufacturer, inventor and founder and builder of towns, and his career has been closely identified with Oklahoma since he came at the opening of the Cherokee Strip twenty-three years ago. His name is closely associated with the history of several thriving towns, and he is now in the real estate business and as a loan and insurance broker at Tyrone, in Texas County.

His birth occurred in a log house on a farm in Armstrong County, Pennsylvania, May 4, 1853. His parents were John M. and Anna Margaret (Townsend) Wray, his father being a native Pennsylvanian of Scotch-Irish stock. He was a farmer and merchant all his life and died in Pennsylvania in 1902. His wife was also a native of the same state and of German and English stock. She died in 1905. Their eight children, two sons and six daughters, were: Harriet M., deceased; Clara E.; Abigail, deceased; Hiram H.; Anna Margaret; Robert T.; Emma, deceased; and Mary A.

Reared in Armstrong County, with the advantages of the public schools, Robert T. Wray also attended the academy at Eldridge Ridge. He spent the first twenty-five years of his life on the old home farm. Then came business experience in mercantile lines at Parker City, Pennsylvania. For several years he was in the coal and coke business at Dunbar, Pennsylvania.

In 1884 Mr. Wray came West and located at Kansas City, Missouri. There he began the manufacture of composition roofing, a material which was then just being introduced to popular use. Mr. Wray was himself the patentee of a machine for making this new style of roofing and his original genius has been exercised in a number of other important devices which he has patented. For eleven years he lived in Kansas City engaged in manufacturing and other lines.

Then in 1893 came the opening of the Cherokee Strip. He was a participant, and locating at Ponca City he dug the first well on the townsite, erected a hotel, and was also proprietor of one of the first stores. He was active in the early life of the town, serving as a member of the first town board.

In 1898 he became one of the founders of the town of Bliss, where he opened the first store and was the first postmaster, an office he filled for three years. In 1904 came another change of scene and activity. In that year he homesteaded a claim in Texas County five miles from Tyrone, and remained on the same five years in order to prove up. In 1915 Mr. Wray erected the first brick mercantile building in Tyrone, and since then has been very closely identified with both the public and commercial life of the little town. He is serving as a justice of the peace. Mr. Wray belongs to the Presbyterian Church. On April 20, 1898, Mr. Wray married Miss Ida Regnier who was born at Coffeyville, Kansas. They are the parents of four children, two sons and two daughters: Emma E., born January 1, 1900; John M., born May 20, 1902; George E., born May 20, 1904; and Adaline, born May 20, 1906.

ORAN J. LOGAN. One of the pioneers in the southwestern quarter of Oklahoma, a resident of Hobart since 1901, Oran J. Logan is a lawyer by profession and acquired his first political experience and did his first legal practice in the State of Texas. He has been a factor in local affairs in Kiowa County since its organization, and is now a member of the State Senate from the Sixth Senatorial District.

Oran J. Logan was born at Morganton, Fannin County, Georgia, March 19, 1870. His father, John Calhoun Logan, was a Confederate soldier, and a native of Tennessee, representing one of the pioneer families of that state. Senator Logan, like many successful men, had an early environment of comparative poverty. His parents were too poor to send him to college, and his education while a boy was acquired in the common schools. In 1883 his parents removed to Erath County, Texas, locating on a farm. That part of Texas was then almost on the western frontier, and Oran J. Logan has seen much of the rough and active life of the old range country and his mind and character are impressed with the freedom and movement of the western prairies. He worked as a farmer in Erath County until 1887, and then found a position with the Texas Express Company, which operated over the Santa Fe lines. After one year he left the railroad and went to work on a ranch in west Texas. This experience was gained chiefly in Fisher County, far out on the western plains, and he became a typical cowboy possessing the vigilance and the hardy qualities so often associated with plainsmen, and acquired some note as a "broncho buster." For three years beginning in 1889 Mr. Logan was employed at Alvarado, Texas, by D. T. Lyon Lumber Company, and afterward was with the Alvarado Cotton Company.

In 1894 he was selected as deputy county clerk of Johnson County, serving under Samuel P. Ramsey, of the prominent Ramsey family of Texas. While living at Cleburne, he was elected justice of the peace in 1896, and having in the meantime taken up the study of law was admitted to the Texas bar in 1898. After several years in practice in Texas Mr. Logan was drawn to Oklahoma by one of those several historic events known as "openings," and thus was on the ground at Hobart when the Kiowa and Comanche Indian Reservation was opened to settlement in 1901.

On November 17, 1901, Senator Logan married Margaret Falkenburg, of Cleburne, Texas. They have one child, Oran Beulah, now twelve years of age. Mr. Logan is a member of the Methodist Episcopal Church South, and has affiliations with the Masonic, the Modern Woodmen and the Ancient Order of United Workmen lodges. In his own career he has exhibited some of the hardy qualities for which his ancestors were noted. The Logans in the early days were merchantmen and traders who traveled over the hills of the Carolinas with their freight wagons and long teams, years before the introduction of railroads and other modern methods of transportation.

His first actual experience in politics was in Texas in

1892, when he espoused the cause of James S. Hogg for governor during the famous Hogg-Clark campaign. After coming to Oklahoma he was the first chairman of the Democratic County Central Committee of Kiowa County, after the organization of that county. In 1904 he acquired his first legislative experience as a member of the Territorial Legislature, representing Kiowa County. In 1910 he was elected a member of third State Legislature, and in 1914 was elected to the Senate from the Sixth Senatorial District, which includes several counties in the southwestern part of the state. During the extraordinary session of the third Legislature he was chairman of a committee on capitol location, and as a result of the labors of that committee and of the Legislature the capitol was removed from Guthrie to Oklahoma City. Senator Logan's legislative record also includes authorship of a law during the third session which brought an end to the apparently much abused privilege of county division. Since taking his seat in the Senate Mr. Logan has been chairman of the committees on commerce and labor and a member of the committee on code revision, revenue and taxation, public service corporations, roads and highways, education, insurance, oil and gas, Indian affairs, and drugs and pure foods. It should also be recalled that Senator Logan was a conspicuous figure in the noted fight in the Territorial Legislature in 1905, during the consideration of the proposed fellow servant law. Two members of the committee of the House that were favorable to the bill were sent to Fort Supply as members of a committee to investigate the feasibility of the territory taking the buildings at the fort for an insane asylum. During their absence lobbyists against the bill thought to kill it. The plan and hope of the lobbyists was that in the absence of these two members it would be possible to muster a majority vote against the proposition. Logan, as a member of the House, who was favorable to the bill and sensed what was going on, took the floor in debate on the measure and held it for four hours. At the conclusion of his speech supporters of the bill had enough strength to postpone a vote until the two committee members could return from Fort Supply.

Senator Logan's father, James Calhoun Logan, was born in Rutherford County, North Carolina, August 21, 1828, a son of J. J. and Mary (Withrow) Logan. The Logan family is of Scotch origin, and was established in America many generations ago. The great-great-grandfather of Senator Logan, a native of South Carolina, served throughout the war of Independence, and afterward became a pioneer in Rutherford County of North Carolina. James Logan, the great-grandfather of Senator Logan, lived a quietly active career on the old homestead in North Carolina and at that place was born J. J. Logan. Mary Ann Withrow, who married J. J. Logan, was also born in North Carolina, a daughter of John Withrow whose father, Capt. James Withrow, won his title by service in the Revolutionary army and afterward represented his home county in the State Legislature for thirty successive years. J. J. Logan, Senator Logan's grandfather, was a farmer and lived in Rutherford County, North Carolina, until 1832. He then took his family to the Cherokee Nation in Northern Georgia. In 1834 he went still further west, becoming a resident of Gibson County, Tennessee, where his first wife died in 1840. She was the mother of six children, and four of the sons reached a good old age. J. J. Logan married again and had five children. He died at the age of ninety years in 1893.

James C. Logan was reared on a frontier farm, and had very limited opportunities to gain an education. He lived with his father until he was twenty-two, and in 1851 he married Nancy E. King, whose father was a citizen of Cherokee County, North Carolina. Soon afterward Mr. and Mrs. Logan left North Carolina and started for California, making the journey by way of the Isthmus of Panama and spending eighty-eight days en route. After trying the mines in California he went north to the Klamath River, and for six years was a miner and prospector in that region. He then returned to his native county, followed farming and the business of tanning until his removal to Texas. In 1883 James C. Logan brought his family out to Erath County, Texas, and he purchased a tract of wild land at Morgan Mill. He developed a farm, but in 1889 he sold out and established a drug store at Morgan Mill, and thenceforward was one of the leading merchants and most influential citizens of that locality. His affiliations are those of a democrat, a Mason and member of the Methodist Episcopal Church South.

In the summer of 1862 James C. Logan enlisted in the Confederate army as a member of Company B, Georgia Cavalry, under Col. John R. Hart. The command went to Tennessee and accompanied Kirby Smith into Kentucky and afterward was with Bragg at Chickamauga and with J. E. Johnston at Atlanta and with Hood in Tennessee, where he participated in the battles of Franklin and Nashville. Mr. Logan surrendered with his company to General Sherman at Greensboro, North Carolina, April 25, 1865, being then a part of General Johnston's army.

The ten children of James C. Logan and wife were named as follows: J. D., who became a minister of the Methodist Episcopal Church; Jennie, who married Mr. Davidson, who is now deceased; Josa, wife of W. S. Dobbs of Georgia; Emma, who married A. J. Davis; Della, widow of J. M. Taylor; Dr. M. H.; Dr. W. H.; Mark, who took up the law as his profession; Oran J.; and John M. The mother of these children died in 1882 at the age of fifty-two. She was survived by her husband and ten children, and her death was the first in the family in a period of forty-five years.

L. C. HEADLEY. The editor of the Ponca City Courier, L. C. Headley is now dean of Oklahoma journalism and has been identified with Ponca City since the famous rush of September, 1893. He is a newspaper man of broad and varied experience, both in Kansas and Oklahoma, and through the daily and weekly issues of the Courier has a valuable influence throughout Kay County and Northeastern Oklahoma. The Ponca City Courier was first published and edited by Mr. Hoyt of Lyons, Kansas, and Mr. Headley bought out the plant in 1901. He and his sons now look after the general editorial and business management of the Courier. It is a republican paper and has always stood strong in support of original republican principles. Mr. L. C. Headley has been identified more or less actively with newspaper business for fifty years. He is a practical printer of the old school and wields a trenchant pen as an editor. The circulation of the Courier has reached 3,000. The paper advocates every material improvement, and stands not only for business progress, but for a better diffusion of prosperity, means of intelligence, and general enlightenment throughout Kay County.

Mr. L. C. Headley was born at Columbus, Ohio, June 25, 1848. His father, David Headley, was a member of the same family of the noted historian Headley, author of Headley's History of the Civil war. Davis Headley was born in New Jersey, and saw service as a soldier during the war with Mexico. Two of his sons were soldiers in the Civil war. Edward G. Headley was in the Third Iowa Battery until his death, while Alfred

Headley was killed in the battle of Pea Ridge, Arkansas. Davis Headley married Sally Williams, who was born in New Jersey, daughter of William Williams and of Welsh ancestors. Davis Headley and wife moved out to Mitchell County, Kansas, locating on a homestead near Beloit. He died there at the age of sixty-nine, while his wife passed away in Smith County, Kansas, at the age of eighty. In politics he was first a whig and later a staunch republican, and the church affiliation of the family is Methodist.

L. C. Headley was educated in the public schools and acquired his better education as an early apprentice and worker in a printing shop. He also took up a homestead in Mitchell County, Kansas, near Beloit, and for a time was employed on the Beloit Democrat, when that paper was first established. Later he went to Gaylord, Kansas, and was a publisher and editor there for twenty-five years. He next came to Ponca City, Oklahoma, and he and his sons have since brought the Courier to a condition of splendid prosperity.

Mr. Headley was married at the age of twenty-three in Waterloo, Iowa, to Eliza W. Davis, who was born and reared and educated in Illinois, afterwards going to Iowa with her father, Joshua Davis, who was one of the early settlers and one of the business leaders in Waterloo. To Mr. and Mrs. Headley have been born the following children: Edward, a member of the firm of Headley & Sons, proprietors of the Ponca City Courier; Henry, who for three and a half years was postmaster at Ponca, and also was one of the leading members of the House of Representatives; William, another member of the firm of publishers; Bert, who edits the Smith County Pioneer at Smith Center, Kansas; one daughter is now deceased, leaving a son Paul, a bright boy of four years who lives at home with his grandparents at Ponca; another daughter, whose home is in Bucklin, Kansas; and Mildred, a graduate trained nurse at Kansas City, who has practiced her profession in all the leading hospitals and in many of the towns and larger cities of the Southwest. Mr. Headley and family are members of the Methodist Church, and his fraternal affiliations are with the Masons, the Knights of Pythias, and the Independent Order of Odd Fellows.

D. A. MILLER. In the practice of medicine and surgery one of the best known firms in Oklahoma is Dr. D. A. Miller and his wife, who is also a capable physician. They located at Blackwell, April 11, 1901, and their practice is now one not circumscribed by territory, but extending pretty well over all Northern Oklahoma. Dr. D. A. Miller is a specialist in diseases of the eye and ear. He is a graduate from the Hahnemann College of Medicine with the class of 1901, and during 1904 was a post-graduate student in the medical department of the College of New York, one of the oldest medical schools in the country. He also took special work in the Philadelphia Medical and Surgical College, where he was associated with the well known surgeon, Doctor Knapp. Doctor Miller is one of the few medical men of Oklahoma who have been honored by election to the American College of Surgeons, an honor bestowed only for special merit in the field of surgery, and thus giving a special distinction apart from the possession of the usual degree Doctor of Medicine. Doctor Miller and wife have a fine suite of offices in Blackwell and one of the best medical libraries to be found in the state. He also has an office at Ponca City, where he has a large clientage.

Doctor Miller first became acquainted with Northern Oklahoma during the rush for homes in September, 1893. He rode into the state on the opening day, looking for a homestead, and though failing to secure one, he spent a week or more in touring about the country, and was so pleased with the soil, climate and future possibilities that he then and there gained a definite direction as to his future home.

Dr. D. A. Miller was born in Brown County, Kansas, on the old homestead of his father, a few miles southeast of Hiawatha, on April 23, 1867. The Miller family is numbered among the prominent pioneers in the settlement of Northeastern Kansas. His father was Charles Miller, Jr., who was born in Germany, and was brought to the United States when a child. Charles Miller, Sr., was a pioneer settler in Wisconsin, later in Illinois, and eventually took up a homestead in Northeastern Kansas, where subsequently about 2,000 acres were under the ownership of this one family. Charles Miller, Jr., was born in Germany in 1838, and died in 1909. He came of a Lutheran family. The wife of Charles Miller is still living, and has her home at Blackwell. Charles Miller, Jr., was a prosperous farmer and stockman, and in the early days did a great amount of freighting across the plains, much of the time in the employ of the United States Government, engaged in carrying supplies to the Government forts. He made a number of trips through the West to Salt Lake and Denver and other points. In his business relations he was noted for his honesty and upright character, and in every way was a man above reproach. Charles Miller, Jr., married Sarah Miller, of the same name, but not related. Her father was Dan Miller. Charles and Sarah Miller were the parents of five sons and one daughter.

Dr. D. A. Miller spent his early life on a farm, and there developed the physical constitution which has stood him in such good stead during the strain of a professional career. He attended public schools and was also a pupil of the Pardee Institute under Professor Reid, the famous educator, whose daughter he subsequently married. For eight years Doctor Miller was a teacher, and five years of this time had charge of the school in his home district in Brown County. Doctor Miller's father had two brothers who were soldiers during the Civil war. One of them was William Miller, in the Confederate army, while Fred Miller was on the opposite side of the conflict. Doctor Miller has an interesting ancestor on his maternal side, a young woman of sixteen who risked her life to carry dispatches to one of the American leaders during the Revolutionary war.

Doctor Miller was married January 1, 1902, at Eureka, Kansas, to Miss Ethel Reid. Mrs. Miller is one of the best known women physicians in Northern Oklahoma, and comes of a family noted for its attainments in intellectual and professional life. Her father was Prof. John M. Reid, A. M. and M. D., of Eureka, Kansas. An interesting fact about the marriage of Doctor Miller is that the minister who performed the ceremony was Rev. C. E. Hastings, of Effingham, Kansas, a son-in-law of Rev. Pardee Butler, the famous abolitionist and early pioneer of Kansas, who was associated with John Brown in the memorable contest during the free state movement following the Kansas-Nebraska Bill of 1854. John M. Reid was born in Kenton, Ohio, November 4, 1847, and grew up in Columbiana County of that state. His father, Isaiah Reid, was born July 20, 1820, a son of Manly Reid, who served as a soldier in the War of 1812, and was in turn a son of Capt. John Reid, a minute-man of the Revolution. The Reids were one of the best families of Ohio, where they were settled in the early days. The mother of Prof. John M. Reid was Eliza Houser, a daughter of John H. and Barbara Houser, who had settled in Hardin County, Ohio, as early as 1828. Professor Reid was educated in Ohio, and began teaching school at the age of seventeen. He had a long and varied experience as an educator, and in 1876 took charge of the Pardee Seminary in Kansas. Practically his entire life was given to the training of young men and women. He was honored by the attainments of his pupils, all of whom regarded him with special affection and credited his influence as being one of the most powerful factors in their lives. Many men successful in the professions might be mentioned, several of them prominent in Oklahoma, who were at one time students under Professor Reid. Professor Reid was also a graduate physician, from the Hahnemann College, and several others of the family were likewise physicians, including Mrs. Miller. Her brother is Dr. John L. Reid, a successful physician at Portales, New Mexico. Mrs. Miller began the study of medicine under the direction of her father when she was only sixteen years of age. She graduated from the Kansas City Homeopathic College with the degree M. D. on March 28, 1901, and previously her classical studies had brought her the degree A. B.

Doctor Miller and wife are prominent in the Christian Church. He is superintendent of the Bible school class, and both have devoted their time so far as professional engagements would allow to the cause of church and practical charity. Doctor Miller has risen high in the Masonic order, belongs to the Lodge, Chapter and Knight Templar Commandery at Blackwell, has served as eminent commander of the Knights Templar and also belongs to the Tulsa Temple of the Mystic Shrine. He and his wife have had much of the examination work in connection with several fraternal orders.

J. C. COX, D. V. S. An important service has been rendered by Doctor Cox to the farming and stock raising community around Tonkawa in the capacity of veterinary surgeon and as proprietor of the Cox Veterinary Hospital at Tonkawa. Doctor Cox located in Tonkawa in 1913 in the month of May. He brought with him a thorough skill as a practitioner, and that ability quickly brought him a reputation and practice, and he has done much to extend it through his frank and genial manner, his undoubted qualifications, and his readiness to work alongside and shoulder to shoulder with other citizens in promoting the local welfare.

He is a graduate of one of the best veterinary schools in the Southwest, the Kansas City Veterinary College, and in the class of 1912 with which he graduated stood among the first in the class. Doctor Cox is about thirty-six years of age. He was born near Carthage in Jasper County, Missouri, and his father was a well known farmer and stock raiser there, J. C. Cox, who is now deceased. The father was born at Ashland, Ohio, and during the Civil war served in the Second Ohio Cavalry, and made an excellent war record. He died in Kansas City, Missouri, at the age of seventy-seven, and his wife passed away in the same city, aged seventy-five. Doctor Cox was one of three children, and his two sisters are Mrs. E. Wait of Kansas City, and Mrs. Ober of Haleyville, Oklahoma.

Like the other children, Doctor Cox received a substantial education during his youth. When he was a child his parents removed to Champaign, Illinois, and when he was six years of age they took up their home on a farm in Wilson County, Kansas. It was on that farm that he grew up, was taught the value of honesty and industry, and developed a physique that has furnished him strength for the varied occupations to which he has turned his attention. On leaving the farm Doctor Cox went to Kansas City, Missouri, and for several years was an employee in the Kansas City post-office, and for ten years was a fireman on the Kansas City and Fort Scott Railroad. He made good in both occupations, was diligent and faithful to duty, but finally turned his attention to the study of veterinary surgery and now has a permanent profession.

At Neodesha, Kansas, Doctor Cox married Everlo Ditto, who was born in Iowa, a daughter of John Ditto, who also made a soldier's record in the Union army and is now deceased. Doctor Cox and wife have two children: Agnes and Curtiss.

In politics Doctor Cox is a republican. He is a thirty-second degree Scottish Rite Mason. Physically he stands six feet high, has an excellent physique, a strong mind, and is a man of broad and progressive views. He makes and retains friends, and being thoroughly versed in his profession, is already one of the successful citizens of Tonkawa.

HARRY WALKER, M. D. It is doubtful if any one family has contributed more distinguished services to the medical profession of Oklahoma than that of Walker. Dr. Harry Walker of Pawhuska is a son of the late Delos Walker, who from the opening of the original Oklahoma Territory in April, 1889, until his death in 1910, was one of the ablest physicians and most public spirited citizens of Oklahoma City. Representatives of three successive generations of this family have practiced medicine and surgery in Oklahoma, since only a year or two elapsed after the death of Dr. Delos Walker before his grandson, a son of Doctor Harry, began his work as a surgeon in Pawhuska.

Dr. Delos Walker, who deserves a foremost place in any record of Oklahoma physicians, was born October 19, 1837. At that time his parents, William and Sally (Fisher) Walker, were living in Crawford County, Pennsylvania. William Walker was a native of Washington County, Pennsylvania, and William Walker's father was born in Lancaster County, Pennsylvania, and saw service in the early Indian wars under General St. Clair. In 1866 the parents of Dr. Delos Walker moved to Anderson County, Kansas, where they located at a time when that section was on the frontier.

Reared on a farm, Delos Walker gained his education in local schools and at Conneautville Academy, and in 1858 began the study of medicine at that village with Dr. James L. Dunn. He had not yet completed his studies when, on April 22, 1861, a few days after the firing on Fort Sumter, he enlisted as orderly sergeant in Company B of McLean's Regiment at Conneautville. After his first term he was mustered out in 1862, and then entered the medical department of the University of Michigan. Again he left his studies and as captain of Company B of the One Hundred and Thirty-seventh Pennsylvania Volunteers, was in the battles of South Mountain, Antietam, Chancellorsville and other engagements of the campaign through Maryland and Virginia. He rose to rank of major in his regiment in 1863, but soon afterward returned to the University of Michigan, where he was graduated M. D. in 1864. After a brief private practice, he went back to Pennsylvania to become surgeon for the Twentieth Provost District. At Harrisburg he co-operated with Adjutant General Russell and organized eight companies, which were formed as the One Hundred and Third Pennsylvania Infantry, with which he served as lieutenant colonel during the spring and early summer of 1865. For a time after the close of the war Dr. Delos Walker practiced at Conneautville, Pennsylvania, and in Union City of the same state, and at the latter place was surgeon for the Philadelphia and Erie Railroad. In 1867 he joined his parents in Anderson County, Kansas, and fo the next twenty-two years was surgeon in a successful practice at Greeley.

It was almost a matter of chance and circumstance that Dr. Delos Walker became permanently identified with the destinies of the young City of Oklahoma at the time of its founding. He took part in the rush into the district on April 22, 1889, and something in the enthusiasm and excitement and the promise of future opportunities caused him to decide to remain as one of the first citizens of Oklahoma City. His long experience and recognized ability soon brought him distinction as one of the first physicians, and he was also prominent in many other activities which were closely related with the upbuilding of that community. He helped organize the first public schools and became the first president of the school board of Oklahoma City. For five years he was health superintendent of Oklahoma County and was the first president of the board of health of Oklahoma City, holding that office five years. He was also one of the organizers and the first president of the Oklahoma Medical Society. He also served as president of the pioneer association known as Oklahoma Eighty-Niners. Dr. Delos Walker was married in Pennsylvania to Miss Emeret Greenfield. Their only daughter, Maud, died at the age of nineteen. Mrs. Delos Walker was born in 1842 and died in 1905.

Dr. Harry Walker, whose individual attainments have brought him such distinction that he does not stand in the shadow of his father's eminence, was born at Coneautville, Pennsylvania, May 10, 1861. He also attended the University of Michigan, where he was both a literary and medical student, and in 1884 was graduated M. D. from the Bellevue Hospital Medical College of New York City. He also had the benefit during his earlier career of almost constant association with his father, and they were together in practice both at Greeley, Kansas, and at Oklahoma City. In 1900 Dr. Harry Walker accepted appointment as Government surgeon for the Osage Indian Agency at Pawhuska. After leaving that service he continued in private practice at Pawhuska, and in point of residence is one of the oldest physicians in Osage County, and easily one of the ablest in this part of the state.

Doctor Walker is a member of the Osage County and Oklahoma State Medical societies and the American Medical Association. While devoted to his profession, he has also acquired many interests on the outside and for years has been a student of Indian customs and lore. His interesting articles on the romantic features of Osage Indian history have appeared in a number of papers, particularly the Kansas City Star. He has helped to preserve in permanent form some of the time honored records in connection with the Roy family of Osages and also has written of the famous Chouteau family of St. Louis regarding its transactions as traders with the Osage tribe.

In politics Doctor Walker is a republican. He has affiliations with the Masonic order, the Knights of Pythias, the Modern Woodmen of America and the Woodmen of the World. His wife before her marriage was Miss Villa McFadden. She was born in Illinois. Their three sons are Roscoe, Joseph and Delos, Jr. Doctor Roscoe is now associated in practice with his father at Pawhuska, and is a young surgeon of brilliant promise. He was born at Greeley, Kansas, in 1885, graduated Bachelor of Science from the University of Oklahoma in 1909, then entered Columbia University at New York City, where he took his degree of medicine in 1911, and after two years as surgical interne in the Post-graduate Hospital of New York, returned to Pawhuska to begin practice with his father. The son Joseph, born at Greeley, Kansas, in 1888, completed his education in the Oklahoma City High School and is now at home. The younger son, Delos, born in 1892, attended the Pawhuska High School, spent three years in the State University, and is now a newspaper man, being a reporter on the Denver Express.

C. K. TEMPLETON was born in Magoffin County, Kentucky, May 10, 1877. He was the third son of Dr. James E. and Julia Q. Templeton. The family consisted of six boys: L. C., who lives in Morgan County, Kentucky; J. W., of Scott County, Virginia; C. K., of Pawhuska, Osage County, Oklahoma; T. O. and R. C., both of Scott County, Virginia; and O. F., of Washington, D. C. His father and mother were native Virginians, his mother having died when he was eleven years old. His father was a Confederate soldier, and served throughout the Civil war under Lee and Jackson, and when the war ended he returned to his home in Scott County, Virginia, and resumed the practice of medicine, which he has continued to the present day. C. K. attended the public free schools of Kentucky until sixteen years of age, when he started out as a teacher in that state, and from there went to Virginia, where he taught school for several years, and in 1898 graduated from Shoemaker College at Gate City, Virginia, having specialized in history and science. He continued to teach and study law, and in 1901 he entered the University at Valparaiso, in Indiana, where he was able to work his way through school, and completed the law class of nearly seventy, making a general average for the two years of a fraction over 98 per cent, and received the degree of LL. B. He was admitted to the bar in both Kentucky and Indiana, and went back to Virginia and taught school and studied law in the office of Hon. W. S. Cox, then commonwealth attorney, at Gate City. Coming to Oklahoma Territory in April, 1905, he located at Pawhuska, worked in the "Old Red Store," for C. M. Hirt, until he was able to get acquainted and get into the practice of his profession. He worked in the store for about eleven months and has since been engaged in the practice of law. He was elected prosecuting attorney in the fall of 1910, on the democratic ticket by a large majority. His majority in the City of Pawhuska, in both the primary and general elections, was about seventy more than that of his opponents in the whole county, though they all lived in Pawhuska. He lost but few precincts in the county at either the primary or general election. He believed in and followed a strict enforcement of the laws. At the expiration of his term of office he formed a partnership with John W. Tillman, who was his assistant, and that partnership continued until Mr. Tillman was elected to the same office in the fall of 1914, and he is now assistant under Mr. Tillman. He also has a large civil practice which extends to Kansas, Missouri, Indiana and Texas, and is local attorney for the Atchison, Topeka & Santa Fe Railway Company, and Wells Fargo & Company Express. He has been a democratic worker and speaker since the presidential election of 1906, and is at this time secretary of the Osage County Democratic Central Committee. He is also a member of his local bar, and treasurer of the Oklahoma State Bar Association and is rated among the best attorneys of the state.

Mr. Templeton is a great lover of Freemasonry. He was made a Master Mason when twenty-one years of age at Fort Blackmore Lodge No. 87, Ancient Free and Accepted Masons, Fort Blackmore, Virginia, and was master of that lodge when he left Virginia for his law course, in September, 1901. He is now a member of Wah-Shah-She Lodge No. 110, Ancient Free and Accepted

Masons, Pawhuska, Oklahoma; Gate City Chapter No. 35, Royal Arch Masons, Gate City, Virginia; Palestine Commandery No. 35, Knights Templar, Pawhuska, Oklahoma; Oklahoma Consistory No. 1, Ancient and Accepted Scottish Rite of Freemasonry (thirty-second degree), Guthrie, Oklahoma; Akdar Temple, Ancient Arabic Order Nobles of the Mystic Shrine, of Tulsa, Oklahoma, and Chapter No. 63, Order of the Eastern Star, Pawhuska, Oklahoma. And he is also a Knight of Pythias, and member of White Hair Lodge No. 11, at Pawhuska, Oklahoma, being now (May, 1916) chancellor commander of that lodge. He married Miss Nellie Roberts, the daughter of Rush Roberts, then one of the council and head men of the Pawnee tribe of Indians, at Pawnee, Oklahoma. Mr. and Mrs. Templeton were married at Pawnee, Oklahoma, July, 1908. To their marriage have been born three children: Lena Myrtle; James E. R., and C. K., Jr.

JAMES ALBERT McCOLLUM. Among the men who have risen to prominence in the law in Oklahoma during recent years, one of the younger generation whose abilities have gained him professional success and public honors is James Albert McCollum, county attorney of Pawnee County. His achievements have not been the result of happy chance, but have been fairly earned, for from the start of his career Mr. McCollum has depended upon his own resources and has fitted his talents to his opportunities.

Mr. McCollum was born in Berry County, Missouri, October 26, 1883, and is a son of William Wallace and Mary Ann (Fawver) McCollum. On the paternal side he belongs to an old family of Scotch-Irish origin, while his maternal grandfather was a native of Germany, and although the latter married a woman of American birth she was of German lineage. William Wallace McCollum was born in Tennessee, in 1849, and was three years of age when taken by his parents to Berry County, Missouri, where as a young man he followed school-teaching as a vocation. There he was married to Mary Ann Fawver, who had been born in Virginia, in 1853, and after their marriage they settled on a Berry County farm, where the father has since continued to be engaged in farming and raising stock. He has been active in democratic politics, and he and Mrs. McCollum have been lifelong members of the Methodist Church. Of their nine children, two died in infancy, the survivors being: Emma, who is the wife of G. W. Roller, of Wichita, Kansas; Etta, who is the wife of Frank Major, of Wheaton, Missouri; Jenna, who is the wife of E. M. Peter, of Boulder, Colorado; Augusta, who is the wife of Elliott Roller, of Rocky Comfort, Missouri; James Albert; Claude C., a practicing attorney of Pawnee, Oklahoma; and Earl C., who is in Boulder, Colorado, in the hardware business.

James Albert McCollum resided on the home farm until twenty-one years of age, receiving his education in the country schools and Marionville Collegiate Institute, at Marionville, Missouri, where he spent three profitable years. After his graduation, in 1905, he went to Western Kansas, where he remained three years, proving up on a homestead, and in the meantime taught one term of school. He had had former experience in the latter line, as when he was a youth he had taught three terms of school in order to gain the means with which to complete his studies at the institute. In the fall of 1908 Mr. McCollum returned to Missouri and entered the law school of the University of Missouri, where he was graduated in 1911 with the degree of Doctor of Laws, and in July of that year came to Pawnee and opened an office for the practice of his profession. Not long afterward, he formed a law partnership with V. H. Biddison, and the firm of Biddison & McCollum continued in existence one year, when the senior member disposed of his interest to Mr. McCollum's brother, Claude C. McCollum, at which time the concern of McCollum & McCollum was founded. This subsequently became one of the formidable combinations of Pawnee, and continued as such until the fall of 1914, when James A. McCollum was elected county attorney for Pawnee County. Mr. McCollum is the only republican in his family, and it is worthy of note that, in a democratic county, he was elected by a majority of 643 votes, thus demonstrating his popularity, as well as showing that his talents were recognized and appreciated. He has established an excellent record in office, has acquitted himself ably and honorably in a number of important cases, and has won and held the full confidence of the people who elected him to his important position. While a student at the University of Missouri, he was a member of the Athenaeum Society, organized in 1841, and the oldest student organization west of the Mississippi River. He also showed himself a master of debate, taking part in numerous interstate contests, and won high honors therein, never losing a contest, a record that has never been equalled in that institution. In the year 1910 the State Republican Committee of Missouri employed four university men to stump the state during the campaign, of whom Mr. McCollum was one, and during the thirty days that he was so engaged, he made two speeches each day. He is considered one of the ablest orators of Pawnee County, and his services are in constant demand during the campaigns of his party, of which he is a leader in this part of Oklahoma. Mr. McCollum is a Mason. With his family, he belongs to the Methodist Episcopal Church.

Mr. McCollum was married July 23, 1911, to Miss Lillian McCann, born in Berry County, Missouri, in 1887, daughter of Frank McCann, and to this union there have been born two children: Mary and Mildred.

J. L. HUDSON. In the First National Bank of Fairfax, which is the oldest and most substantial institution of its kind in that flourishing town of Osage County, J. L. Hudson has filled the office of cashier for the past three years. The other officers of the bank are J. C. Stribling, president, and J. H. Ward, vice president, all well known business men in that section of Oklahoma. Though Mr. Hudson has been a resident of Fairfax as a town only a few years, he formerly operated as a cattle man and rancher over the very site now occupied by Fairfax.

A native of Southern Texas, J. L. Hudson was born in Fayette County, January 1, 1875, a son of D. W. and Eugenia (Loman) Hudson. His father was born in Tennessee, and at the age of three years was brought to Texas by his parents, who located at Rutersville, one of the old educational centers of Southern Texas. Mr. Hudson's mother was born in Fayette County in 1854, a daughter of Upton Loman, who had come as a pioneer from Illinois to Texas, and was extensively engaged in the cattle industry until his death. Mr. Hudson's mother died June 24, 1914, and his father is now residing at Fairfax, having retired from an active career as a cattleman and farmer. For eighteen years D. W. Hudson lived on one ranch in Llano County, Texas. J. L. Hudson is the older of two sons, and his brother W. M. Hudson, has for the past seven or eight years been located at Tampico, Mexico, where he has a large ranch, and is also engaged in the oil and real estate business.

Reared in Texas, J. L. Hudson attended the public schools there, and in 1896 was graduated from the scientific course in the National Normal University

Lebanon, Ohio. Thus equipped for life's duties he took up teaching, and spent two years in that vocation in Gonzales County, Texas. Afterwards he worked as bookkeeper and as cashier in the First National Bank at Flatonia, Texas, for two years, and for a similar period was cashier of the First National Bank at Moulton in that state. In 1901 he transferred his home to the Osage Nation of Indian Territory, and was engaged in the cattle industry and farming in the vicinity now occupied by the Town of Fairfax. He left this locality in the spring of 1903, about the time the railroad was constructed and Fairfax was founded, and returned to Texas and spent four years in the oil business at Beaumont, and for three years combined the rice cultivation and the cattle business in Matagorda County. For about four or five years he gave his attention chiefly to the telephone business at Llano, Texas, and then came to the Town of Fairfax in September, 1912, and has since been identified with the First National Bank. Mr. Hudson has many other interests that make him one of the leaders in business affairs in Osage County. He owns about 1,000 head of cattle, and has also built up a successful business in the cattle and cattle loan business, furnishing the resources to a number of small cattle men in this part of the state.

In politics he is a democrat, is affiliated with the Masonic Order in the Lodge, the Royal Arch Chapter, the Council and the Knight Templar Commandery, and belongs to the Methodist Episcopal Church. On June 30, 1909, he married Miss Louise Fowler, who was born in Llano, Texas, and lived there until her marriage. Her father is J. W. Fowler, a prominent cattleman and farmer. To their marriage has been born one son, Wilson Lane.

L. H. WINBORN, M. D. When he was seventeen years old Doctor Winborn, now successfully established in his profession as physician and surgeon at Tuttle in Grady County, was drawn by a vision of opportunities for young men in the Southwest, and leaving his home in Mississippi sought employment in the Choctaw Nation of Indian Territory. There, while working for the Choctaw Coal and Mining Company and for other firms and individuals, he developed his ambition for a professional career. A young man of earnest purpose and energy usually gets what he wants. With the savings from his earnings he matriculated in the Louisville Hospital Medical College at Louisville, Kentucky, and remained there as long as his funds permitted. He then returned to the Indian country and began the practice of medicine. Settlements were few and sparse in those days, and the majority of his patients were Indians. Hospital facilities were practically unknown, and the young doctor faced conditions as primitive almost as did the missionary doctors who came into the Indian country thirty years before. Under such conditions his practice was not lucrative and the outlook for the future was not encouraging. He had a surplus of about $150, and one day confided to a friend his disappointment at not being able to finish his medical training. This friend was Robert Brewer, son of Dr. T. F. Brewer, of Wagoner. Without solicitation Brewer advanced the necessary money, and on July 30, 1908, the young physician left the Louisville Hospital Medical College carrying a diploma which entitled him to the degree Doctor of Medicine. He settled at Quinton, Indian Territory, and continued his practice among the Indians. He became family physician for Hon. Green McCurtain, principal chief of the Choctaw Nation, and his practice was among many of the old and noted families of the Choctaw Tribe. He lived there until 1911, when he removed to Tuttle, where he now has a handsome home and enjoys a substantial and profitable practice.

Doctor Winborn was born in Hernando, Mississippi, June 25, 1873, a son of Francis Marion and Amorette (Doyle) Winborn. His father was a graduate of the medical department of the University of Alabama, and for thirty-five years did a successful practice in Mississippi and Arkansas, and during the Civil war was a Confederate soldier. Doctor Winborn's grandfather was a successful planter in Mississippi. Doctor Winborn has two brothers and a sister: R. L. and Doctor Winborn, both of whom are farmers and stock men at Farris, Oklahoma; and Mrs. Ollie Smith, wife of a farmer at Bristow.

After finishing his education in the public schools of Mississippi, Doctor Winborn studied mechanical engineering, a vocation which he followed after coming to Indian Territory. His first course in medicine enabled him to pass the federal examination for practice in the Indian Territory. As already explained he was in very humble financial circumstances at the outset of his career, and has made his own way to standing and prosperity in the profession. While living in the mountains of the old Choctaw Nation he became a fast friend of some of the noted men of the tribe. Among them was Richard Locke, Sr., father of the present principal chief of the Choctaw Nation. He was with the elder Locke in a historic fight that took place at Antlers, the present county seat of Pushmataha County. The present Chief Locke was then a boy in knee trousers.

Doctor Winborn was married October 1, 1901, to Miss Mary Heck of Denison, Texas. Her father was a pioneer contractor and builder who helped to found and build the Town of Colbert, Oklahoma, and also had the distinction of erecting the first house on the site of Denison, Texas, when that became the terminus of the Missouri, Kansas & Texas Railway during the early '70s. He was a man of prominence in the country about Denison and in the southern part of the Choctaw Nation, where he had lived prior to the building of the Missouri, Kansas & Texas, which was the first railroad that traversed the Indian Territory.

Doctor Winborn is a member of the Christian Church and has fraternal affiliations with the Masons, the Independent Order of Odd Fellows, the Modern Woodmen of America and the Woodmen of the World. In Masonry he has attained the thirty-second degree of Scottish Rite, and his Blue Lodge is at Quinton, and he is a member of the Consistory at McAlester. He has occupied head positions in local lodges and at present is consul commander of the Woodmen of the World. He is examining physician for fourteen life insurance companies and is assistant county health officer of Grady County. Professionally he is a member of the Grady County Medical Society, the Oklahoma Medical Society and the Tri-State Medical Association and the American Medical Association. No sketch of Doctor Winborn would be complete without reference to his civic enthusiasm and leadership. He is a member of the Tuttle Commercial Club, and has been one of the leading workers in behalf of a project for building a section of the proposed state highway between Oklahoma City and Fort Sill. This project involves the erection of a bridge over the South Canadian River near Tuttle at a cost of approximately $100,000. Doctor Winborn is a liberal contributor of time and money in carrying out all plans for the commercial, industrial, educational and social upbuilding of his locality.

MICHAEL J. FOLEY. One of the best hotels in a town of its size in Oklahoma is the Hotel Ponton at Fairfax, of which Michael J. Foley has been proprietor and manager for the past eight years. Mr. Foley is an old-timer in the hotel business, having formerly been identified with the first business enterprise and hotel at Ralston in Pawnee County. Many years ago, long before Indian Territory was merged into the State of Oklahoma, he was identified with the Osage Nation, and it was a return to old friends and earlier associations when he sold out his business in Ralston in August, 1907, and on the 15th of October following moved to Fairfax in Osage County and bought the Hotel Ponton. This is the only commercial hotel of the town, and he has extensively remodeled the building and has brought its service up to a high standard.

Since early boyhood the career of Michael J. Foley has been one of varied activities and experiences. He was born in Ireland, April 29, 1849, and when two years of age came to America with his parents, Cornelius and Julia (Lynch) Foley. The family lived in Rochester, New York, for two or three years, and then settled in Kalamazoo, Michigan. Cornelius Foley enlisted with the Seventh Michigan Volunteer Infantry during the Civil war and served as a soldier from 1863 to 1865. Michael J. was the fourth in a family of eight children, as follows: Julia Madigan, deceased; Mary Madigan, of Kalamazoo; Ellen, who died at the age of sixteen; Daniel, who died when four years old; Michael J.; Cornelius, of Kalamazoo; Patrick, who died in Kalamazoo in 1913; and Kate, of Mill City, Oregon.

With only the rudiments of a common school education, Michael J. Foley as a boy left home and removed to Chicago, where he learned the trade of plasterer. The great fire of 1871 in that city furnished abundant employment in all branches of the building trade, and for several months after the fire he was employed by the city in a relief corps. For two years he was in the employ of his brother, engaged in the liquor business on Canal Street in Chicago, and subsequently engaged in the railroad service, a work to which he gave his time for a number of years, though not continuously. His first eighteen months of that work was as brakeman, and then for three years he was a conductor on one of the eastern railroads leading out of Chicago. While in charge of his train he met with an accident, and after returning to the service was put in charge of a local freight between Cleveland and Toledo on the Lake Shore and Michigan Southern. For a year he conducted his father's farm near Kalamazoo, after which he returned to railroading on the Pan Handle route of the Pennsylvania lines in Ohio, working as a conductor for eighteen months. Returning to Chicago in 1879, Mr. Foley was again employed by his brother for a year and a half, and then found work in the construction of the West Side Waterworks of that city. It is also interesting to note that he assisted in erecting the old Panorama Building on Wabash Avenue in Chicago, a place known to many thousands of Chicago visitors during the decade of the '90s for the panorama of the battle of Gettysburg which was exhibited there. The building afterwards had a varied history of uses, and is still standing. Later Mr. Foley was employed in the construction of an addition to Asylum No. 2 at St. Joseph, Missouri, and continued the work of his trade in Coffeyville, Kansas, and also in the locality of the present Bartlesville, Oklahoma. Thus he became introduced to the Indian country of the Osage Nation, and was not long in gaining a familiarity with the language of those Indians, and also won the good will of several of the influential chiefs. At Pawhuska he was employed for a time in butchering cattle allotted to the red men, but in the spring of the following year made a practical demonstration to the Indians of the use and wisdom of plastering their houses, and as this improvement was quickly taken up by one after another he found abundant employment for his skill.

In 1892 Mr. Foley returned to Chicago, and in the spring of the following year his father died at Kalamazoo. The mother had passed away about twelve years before. Not long afterwards Mr. Foley came again to the Osage country of Indian Territory, locating at Gray Horse, and soon afterward prepared to make the race at the opening of the Cherokee Strip. He did not succeed in acquiring a claim, but in March, 1894, removed to Talston in Pawnee County, and soon afterward laid the foundation for the first building erected on that town site. He bought a lot, put up a small building, and on the 4th of July celebrated Independence Day by opening his restaurant, which in time was supplemented by a large hotel covering three lots. As the pioneer hotel man and business man of Ralston he was in successful business there until he sold out thirteen years later and identified himself with the community of Fairfax.

On March 28, 1893, Mr. Foley married Miss Maggie Bennett, a daughter of Mathew and Frances Bennett. Mrs. Foley was born in Indiana, but was reared in Kansas. She died December 27, 1913, at the age of forty-three, leaving three children: Cornelius, Emmett and Ruth. Mr. Foley is a democrat in politics, and while a resident of Ralston served as a justice of the peace a number of years. His church is the Catholic.

JASPER NEWTON TODD. Among the men who have contributed to the commercial upbuilding of the City of Jennings, one who established a record for business acumen and founded an establishment which still bears his name was the late Jasper Newton Todd. Coming here in 1896 in moderate circumstances, he embarked in mercantile affairs and directed his operations so wisely and well that at the time of his death, August 17, 1913, he was not only one of the substantial men of his adopted community but had established a firm reputation as a man of the highest business honor.

Mr. Todd was a native of Missouri, born June 17, 1859, a son of Owen and Elizabeth (Reynolds) Todd. His parents were born in Kentucky, and went to Missouri, where they settled on a farm and passed the remaining years of their lives in agricultural operations. There were thirteen children in the family, and Jasper N., one of the younger members, was given a country school education. He had only ordinary advantages in his youth, but early showed himself possessed of qualities of industry and energy that augured well for his future. He grew up as a farmer in the vicinity of Versailles, the county seat of Morgan County, Missouri, where he continued to make his home with his parents for a number of years. About 1890 he went to Walla Walla, in Washington Territory, where he began his experience as a merchant, continuing there and at another town in the same territory for three or four years. His advent in Oklahoma occurred in May, 1894, when he located on a leased farm in Creek County, but after two years his health failed and he was compelled to seek other employment. Disposing of his interests he gathered together about $1,700, with which he came to Jennings, and engaged in business with J. L. Bishop under the firm name of Todd & Bishop. The partners were successful in building up an excellent trade in general merchandise and the association continued satisfactorily until the combination was broken, after several years, by the death of Mr. Bishop. Subsequently Mr. Todd's brother-in-law, C. M. Foil, was admitted to partnership and the firm of Todd & Foil continued in business for about two years, when Mr. Todd bought his partner's interest and continued the business under

JASPER N. TODD

his own name until his death. He was a man of excellent business and executive abilities, sagacious and farsighted, and by his earnest desire to please his customers and his courteous treatment and fair dealing secured the liberal patronage of which he was deserving. Since his death the business has been continued by his widow and son, under the style of the J. N. Todd Estate. The present store, a stone structure, 25 by 100 feet, two stories in height, was erected in 1902 during the life of the firm of Todd & Bishop, and here is still carried a full line of first-class general merchandise of all kinds. The building is located on Main Street, in the heart of the business district, and trade is attracted not only from all over Jennings, but from the surrounding countryside. Mr. Todd was a democrat in his political views and always gave his party loyal support. As a citizen the best interests of the community found in him a stanch friend, and he withheld his co-operation from no worthy undertaking calculated to promote the general welfare. He was a devout member of the Methodist Episcopal Church, and was fraternally connected with the local lodges of the Independent Order of Odd Fellows and the Knights of the Maccabees in which he had many sincere friends. Mr. Todd was vice president of the Jennings State Bank, but the greater part of his attention was devoted to the business which still stands as a monument to his industry and business ability.

Mr. Todd was married in Missouri to Miss Anna Collier, who died in that state, leaving one daughter: Gorda May, who is the wife of T. O. Ham, of Jennings, and has two children, Earl and Mabel. In 1892, Mr. Todd was married in Washington to Miss Alice Whitehead, who was born November 27, 1874, at Sedalia, Missouri, and was reared in that state. They became the parents of three children: Edmond Jasper, one of the enterprising young business men of Jennings, engaged with his mother in conducting the business, who married Miss Nell McLain, of Tryon, Oklahoma, a former teacher in the public schools; and Zoe and Flo, who reside with their mother. Mrs. Todd is a devout member of the Methodist Episcopal Church, in the work of which she has been active, as she is also in the Ladies of the Maccabees. The late Mr. Todd, when he could leave the cares of business, enjoyed nothing more than a hunting trip. He kept several hounds and had something more than a local reputation as a deer hunter, seldom returning from a trip without some noble trophy of the chase.

CARL I. HUFFAKER. On other pages of this publication will be found an ample sketch of the prominent Huffaker family, which for many years has been closely identified not only with the history of Kansas but also of Oklahoma. Several active representatives of this family are now found in Northeastern Oklahoma, and one of them is Carl I. Huffaker, who until recently was postmaster of Fairfax in Osage County and has been more or less closely identified with affairs in that section for the past ten years.

A son of Hon. Thomas Sears and Eliza A. (Baker) Huffaker, he was born at Council Grove, Kansas, January 24, 1880. He grew up in the old Kansas town where his family have helped to make history since territorial days, and lived there until 1904. In 1899 he graduated from the Council Grove High School, and for the following 3½ years was employed in the Council Grove waterworks and electric light plant. He first came to Fairfax, Oklahoma, in 1904, where he became identified with the Santa Fe Railroad Company. He was with the Santa Fe five years, a part of that time in the general offices at Topeka. The rest of the period, eighteen months, he was connected with the offices of the Cudahy Packing Company, and during this time he was transferred from one place to another in Oklahoma, Colorado, Missouri and Kansas.

In 1910 Mr. Huffaker returned to Fairfax and in the following year was appointed postmaster. Fairfax has a third class office and Mr. Huffaker gave to the service a most capable and painstaking administration. His term of office expired in the fall of 1915, and he is now the owner of the electric light and power plant at Fairfax, which he began to install before leaving the postoffice.

In politics Mr. Huffaker has been a republican ever since casting his first vote. He is a member of the Methodist Church and in the Masonic fraternity is affiliated with the lodge, Royal Arch Chapter, Knight Templar Commandery and the Mystic Shrine. He is unmarried. Mr. Huffaker also owns a half interest in the Fairfax Drug Company.

JOSEPH L. ROGERS. At the time, in 1889, when the present State of Oklahoma had the first portion of its territory thrown open to settlement, just prior to the formal organization of the territory, Mr. Rogers became one of the progressive citizens of Chandler, the present judicial center of Lincoln County, and as one of the pioneers of this commonwealth he has played well his part in aiding the march of development and progress along both civic and industrial lines. Like many others he has met with reverses at certain stages in his career, but he has not been daunted or discouraged, but has pressed forward with ambition and determined purpose, with the result that he now holds place as one of the substantial representatives of the agricultural interests of Pawnee County, where his well improved farm is situated about five miles distant from the Village of Jennings, his landed estate comprising 320 acres. He is one of the substantial farmers and vigorous and public-spirited citizens of Pawnee County, commands secure place in the confidence and good will of the community and is fully entitled to recognition in this history of the state of his adoption.

Mr. Rogers was born at Red Oak, Montgomery County, Iowa, on the 12th of November, 1852, and is a son of Richard W. and Salina (Billman) Rogers, the former of whom was born in Kentucky and the latter in Indiana, Illinois. The father passed the closing period of his life in the home of his son, Joseph L., of this review, and thus his death occurred in Pawnee County, Oklahoma Territory, where he passed away on the 10th of March, 1905, at which time he was seventy-five years and four months old; his widow now resides in the home of her youngest daughter, at Centralia, Washington.

Richard W. Rogers removed from Illinois and became one of the pioneer settlers in Montgomery County, Iowa. He assisted in the erection of the first three houses in that county and there became a substantial farmer and honored and influential citizen. He represented the county several terms in the Lower House of the Iowa Legislature and was called upon to serve also in various local offices of public trust. His entire active career was one of close identification with the basic industry of agriculture, and he reclaimed and improved one of the excellent farms of Montgomery County, Iowa. This sterling citizen showed his intrinsic loyalty and patriotism through his valiant service as a soldier in the Mexican war, and he went forth also as a soldier of the Union in the Civil war, his widow now receiving a pension in recognition of his services in the Mexican war. He was a stanch supporter of the cause of the democratic party and many years ago both he and his wife became zealous members of the Missionary Baptist Church, in which he served as a deacon for a very prolonged period and virtually until the time of his death. Of the eight children the subject of this sketch was the second in order of birth, the eldest being William, who maintains his home in the State of New Mexico; Alice is the wife of Ves. S. Hibbins, of Lincoln, Illinois; Isaac is a resident of Prescott, Arizona; May is the wife of Frank Meadows, of Pawnee County, Oklahoma; Richard met an accidental death, having been killed by a fall from a bridge near the City of Albuquerque, New Mexico, he having been a bridge-builder by occupation at the time; Ida Belle is the widow of George Fiske and resides at Chandler, Oklahoma; and Artie is the wife of Edward A. Bacon, of Centralia, Washington.

In his native county Joseph L. Rogers was reared to the age of fourteen years and there he acquired his early education in the district schools. At the age noted he accompanied his parents on their removal to Cherokee County, Kansas, where his father repeated his experiences as a pioneer farmer, the family home being there established for many years. He continued to attend school at such times as his services were not demanded in connection with the work of the home farm, and when twenty years of age he went to Chautauqua County, Kansas, where he continued his identification with agricultural pursuits until 1889, when he became one of the pioneers in Oklahoma Territory, as previously stated. At Chandler he engaged in the grocery and feed business, and there he continued operations until the Cherokee Strip was thrown open to settlement, in 1893, when he made the run into this new country and filed claim to his present homestead, which he has developed into one of the excellent farms of Pawnee County, the revenues from the same being materially augmented by the leases which he had made in connection with the oil development work in this section. There is one producing oil well on the farm at the present time, and in addition to his general farm industry Mr. Rogers operates each season his two modern threshing outfits, with which he covers a wide area of country and does a profitable business. At Cleveland, Pawnee County, Mr. Rogers operated a cotton gin and corn mill until the line of the Atchison, Topeka and Santa Fe Railroad was extended through that place, when the railroad company condemned his property for its use and purchased the same. Mr. Rogers has devoted one year to railroad contract work since he established his residence on his present homestead, which he now gives over largely to the raising of excellent grades of live stock. He was associated with the Canfield brothers in the organization of the Jennings State Bank and was its first president. This was the first bank in the village and he assisted materially in its development and upbuilding, though he has since disposed of his interest in the same. Mr. Rogers has served in various township offices since he established his residence in Pawnee County, and is one of the influential representatives of the democratic party in this county.

On the 25th of December, 1878, Mr. Rogers married Miss Marian M. Rawlings, who was born in Jackson County, Illinois, on the 4th of March, 1859, a daughter of David and Sarah (Carr) Rawlings, both of whom were born in the State of Tennessee, their marriage having been solemnized in Illinois, and the closing period of their lives having been passed in Ripley County, Missouri. Mr. and Mrs. Rogers became the parents of four children, of whom only the firstborn is living, William M., who resides upon and has practical charge of the homestead farm of his father. He wedded Miss Laura Will and they have six children, Manila, Chelsea, Robert, Iris, Laura May, and Leon. Bertha, the second child of Mr. and Mrs. Rogers, died at the age of eighteen months; Pollie died at the age of four months; and Callahan died at the age of four years.

W. B. ALLEN of Bartlesville has practiced law in Washington County for the past fifteen years, though a part of that time was spent in school work and he is well known in Northern Oklahoma in educational circles and still keeps an active interest in that department of public affairs. His own education was secured only through hard and constant labor and sacrifice, and it is probable that his remembrance of his own early struggles has been the cause of devoting himself so zealously to higher standards of public school training. He is one of the prominent and capable members of the Washington County bar and has handled a very high class and important practice.

He was born in Franklin County, Kansas, May 20, 1868, a son of William J. and Charlotte (Stith) Allen, both of whom are natives of Tennessee, but were married at Petersburg, Illinois. In 1862 William J. Allen enlisted in the One Hundred and Fourteenth Regiment of Illinois Infantry, took part in the Vicksburg campaign, and in 1864 was in the expedition sent after General Forrest. At Guntown, Mississippi, he was wounded, his hip bone being broken, and falling into the hands of the enemy he was confined in Cahaba Prison until the close of the war, when he returned to Illinois. The next year he removed to Kansas, located on a farm in Franklin County, went from there in 1872 to Chautauqua County, and continued farming until his death in 1895 at the age of sixty-one. His family were whigs in early American politics, and he gave his constant and loyal support to the republican organization. His wife, who was born in 1841, died at the age of fifty years. Of their six sons and four daughters, three sons and one daughter are now deceased, and W. B. Allen was fourth in order of birth.

With an early training on the home farm and in the district schools of Kansas W. B. Allen at the age of twenty entered upon his career as teacher. Most of his education in the meantime had come from study during spare times between farm duties, and when he became a teacher he entered upon his work with an enthusiasm and understanding that brought a high appreciation to his service. He taught for ten years in the country schools, then for five years was a salesman for a wholesale house on the road, and with the means he had thus accumulated he took up the study of law at Fort Scott, Kansas, in the office of Judge J. D. Hill. Admitted to the bar in 1899, after two years of practice at Fort Scott Mr. Allen located at Dewey, Oklahoma, in 1901. During 1901-02 he was superintendent of schools at Dewey and for the following year taught and served as superintendent at Pryor. Then came two years in the Town of Talala, but in 1905 he returned to Dewey and resumed practice. In 1914, in order the better to attend to his large clientage, Mr. Allen moved to Bartlesville. He is a constant student, keeps fully abreast of the advancements made in his calling, and holds membership in the leading legal organizations.

Politically he was a republican until the campaign of 1912, when he became a progressive. He is less a party man than a public spirited citizen working for the best interests of his home county and state. While at Dewey he spent three years as a member of the school board and was an influential factor in bringing about the erection of a new high school building at a cost of $40,000, and when this was destroyed by fire another structure was erected costing $75,000. The movement for a new courthouse in Washington County had twice suffered defeat when Mr. Allen was made chairman of the committee. He brought the plan and proposition so forcibly before the people that at the next election an overwhelming majority was given for the new courthouse, fully 80 per cent of the votes being in favor of the measure. As city attorney, an office he filled several years, Mr. Allen was fought constantly by the worst element, but stood unflinchingly for a strict enforcement of the law. His own private life has been exemplary. He has never touched liquor nor tobacco, has never gambled, and since early manhood has applied himself unceasingly to the service and duties which have been his lot. He finds his greatest pleasure in his home, and his leisure is usually spent there surrounded by his books and papers. He is also a man of genial fellowship, and is a member of the Masonic fraternity.

In 1897 Mr. Allen married Miss Susie Keefer, who was born at Van Buren, Arkansas, in 1876. Her father, Louis Keefer, now a resident of Bartlesville, was born in Alsace, France, and during the American Civil war served in the Third Wisconsin Cavalry. They are the parents of two children: Ida Grace, born in 1902; and Wendell B., born in 1904.

STRINGER W. FENTON. A small, quiet, unassuming man, with a keen eye, a quick wit, an alert body, muscles of steel and a nerve of iron, such, at a glance, is the chief of police of Cleveland, Oklahoma, the hero of a hundred battles with desperate outlaws, the man whom his friends claim to be the best detective in the United States, Stringer W. Fenton. The criminal history of Oklahoma is one which is crowded with the deeds and achievements of men of courage and daring, officers of the law who have repeatedly taken their lives in their hands in their endeavors to rid one of the country's most fertile, wealthy and beautiful states of its criminal element; but in the entire record there is found no one man whose achievements have overshadowed those of Chief Fenton.

Born June 15, 1865, near Lexington, Rockbridge County, Virginia, Chief Fenton comes of fighting stock, his father, Stephen J. Fenton, having been a lieutenant in the famous "Stonewall Brigade," under that intrepid southern leader, Gen. Thomas J. Jackson, during the Civil war. Lieutenant Fenton was born at Baltimore, Maryland, and early in life engaged in contracting and building, his work taking him to Virginia, where he was married to Mary E. Enroe, a native of Rockbridge County. In the early '70s he took his family to Columbia, Boone County, Missouri, where his death occurred about 1875, when he was sixty years of age. The mother survived until August, 1899, and died at Slater, Saline County, Missouri, aged seventy years. In the family there were seven sons and four daughters, as follows: John, who enlisted with his father in a Virginia regiment and fought in General Jackson's division, now a resident of Howard County, Missouri; G. S., who served three years during the Civil war under General Gordon, subsequently became a pioneer farmer of Oklahoma, was appointed the first sheriff of Kay County by Governor Renfro, and died at Newkirk, Oklahoma; J. H., holding an official position at Pawhuska, farmed in Missouri until 1900, when he became a pioneer agriculturist of Oklahoma; Mary, who died as the wife of the late Jacob Cromwell, of Saline County, Missouri; Mattie, who is the wife of D. P. Mong, of Marshall, Saline County, Missouri; William, a resident of Elk, New Mexico, where he was a pioneer; Jennie, who is the wife of William Tobson, of Kingman, Kansas; R. T. who for the past fourteen years has been connected with the United States Enforcement Department of Indian Service; Stringer W., of this notice; S. P., who is engaged in merchandising at Pawhuska; and Sallie, deceased, who was the wife of J. H. Jones.

Stringer W. Fenton was a child when taken to Missouri, and there he grew to young manhood, attending the district schools and working in a store at Slater during the winter months and spending his summers in working on the farm. When eighteen years of age he went to Kingman, Kansas, where he was subsequently employed by C. D. Hutchings, George F. Berry & Company and Gillette & Company. At the age of twenty-one years he returned to Missouri for a short time, but returned to Kingman, and remained there, employed as stated, until the opening of the Oklahoma country in 1893, when he decided to try his fortunes in the new commonwealth. First locating at Newkirk, he subsequently went to Pawhuska, and after eight years came to Cleveland, in 1903, this city since having been his home.

On his arrival in Oklahoma Mr. Fenton gave his attention to farming pursuits, but it was not long before his courage, strength and alertness attracted attention and he was drawn into police work. He became a government official in Osage County (then Osage Reservation) and continued as a deputy United States marshal until the close of Abernathy's administration. At the time of the attainment of statehood, he was appointed by Governor Haskell a member of the body of men forming the State Enforcement Officers, and continued to hold that position for four years, when he became special agent for the Missouri, Kansas & Texas Railroad. He resigned in December, 1912, to go to Mexico, where he passed the winter in viewing the insurrection, and on his return to Cleveland was elected chief of police, an office to which he was reelected in 1915.

During his long and exciting career, Chief Fenton has passed through many interesting and dangerous experiences, of which but a few can be mentioned in this article. The Martins and Simons, notorious bank and train robbers, had his skill and courage to thank for their capture. One of his notable achievements was the capture of Henry Starr, the bank robber, a feat which illustrates the swiftness with which Chief Fenton works, in that, leaving Bartlesville May 5, 1910, he caught his man at Bouse, Arizona, took him back to Phoenix, in the same state, then to Lamar, Colorado, and arrived in Oklahoma again on the 25th. Another noted capture was that of C. Henry, wanted for the murder of two men, who it was said had five murders behind him, and who, until Chief Fenton got on his trail, had eluded the officers of the law for two years. He has been particularly active and successful in running down bootleggers and confiscating many carloads of whiskey, an extremely dangerous and difficult work, entailing detective ability of no small order and clear headed courage to offset the criminal desperation of bad men made doubly bad by the alcohol which they have freely sampled while bringing their illegal cargo into the state. It was this indefatigable western Vidocq who rounded up the train robbers at South Coffeyville, and who killed the notorious Elmer McUrday, who held up the Missouri, Kansas & Texas train and robbed it at Okesa, Oklahoma.

In the line of his duty, Chief Fenton has been compelled to shoot a number of men, but only in self defense, for it has always been his aim to capture his man alive. On three occasions he has been shot from ambush by criminals who have feared and hated him, but his worst wound was received while in a battle with a desperado whom he was compelled to kill. On December 26, 1914, Al Crain, criminal and bad man, was holding up twenty-five men in a pool room and relieving them of their money and valuables. Word was taken to Chief Fenton, who decided to try to take him without killing him, but Crain grazed him with three shots and then sent a bullet through his leg. The chief's shot went true, as his shots have a habit of doing, and Oklahoma was rid of another criminal.

While Chief Fenton is best known for his work as a police and government official, he has also engaged at various times in business ventures, having been the founder of the Cleveland Leader, a weekly newspaper, his interest in which, however, he has since sold. He also had holdings in farm land and is engaged in agricultural ventures, but it may be said that his official work has his sympathy and affection. A democrat in politics, he was a delegate to the El Reno convention, in 1900, from the Osage Reservation, his associates being William Murdoch, John Palmer and Sylvester Saldina. He has been a Woodman at Pawhuska for fifteen years, and is prominent in Masonry, belonging to the Blue Lodge and Chapter at Cleveland, the Consistory at Guthrie and the Commandery at Pawnee.

On February 1, 1905, Chief Fenton was married to Miss Nellie Rice, a native of Missouri, and daughter of Q. A. Rice. They have an adopted daughter: Edith.

MORRIS L. WARDELL, now principal of the Guymon High School, has lived in Oklahoma fifteen years, completed his education in the state schools, and is one of the young and enthusiastic men who carry into their work in the schoolroom a wide range of practical knowledge and a capable experience in the agricultural industry which is at the basis of permanent prosperity in his section of the state.

Mr. Wardell was born on a farm in Lawrence County, Illinois, June 19, 1889, a son of William and Melissa (Shinn) Wardell. His father was born in the same county and state December 12, 1849, a son of Anthony and Susan (Pinkstaff) Wardell, who were of Scotch parentage. William Wardell has spent his active career as a farmer and in 1903 sold out his holdings in Illinois, and moving to Oklahoma bought land ten miles east of Alva in what was then Woods County but is now Alfalfa County. In that locality he has lived for the past thirteen years and has gone in for the raising of alfalfa and blooded horses on a large scale. When he was about forty years of age he became a member of the United Brethren Church, and has since been very active in its cause. On September 7, 1871, William Wardell married Miss Melissa Shinn, who was born in Ohio, November 23, 1851, a daughter of Aaron and Emily (Hughes) Shinn, the father a native of Virginia and the mother of Ohio. William Wardell and wife had eight children: Charles, born August 9, 1874, is now a minister of the United Brethren Church. In 1903 he married Eva Cunningham, and their one child, Gertrude, was born September 22, 1905. Elmer, the second child, born January 20, 1876, died September 15, 1876. An infant girl, born June 5, 1877, died the same day. Mary, a twin sister of Mattie, born August 17, 1878, died March 1, 1879. Mattie, born August 17, 1878, is unmarried and living with her parents. Jessie, born February 2, 1881, died February 8, 1881. Chester, born May 23, 1882, was married in 1904 to Myrtle Mills, and they live in Colorado Springs, Colorado.

The eighth and youngest of the family, Morris L. Wardell, spent the first fourteen years of his life on his father's farm in Lawrence County, Illinois. While there he attended the public schools. Coming with the family to Oklahoma, he continued his education during 1905-06 in the Stella Friends Academy at Ingersoll. In 1906 he entered the Oklahoma Northwestern State Normal at Alva, where he was graduated with the class of 1912. In the meantime he had taught several terms of school, actually paying a large part of his expenses in college. Mr. Wardell gained a reputation in several diverse lines of college activities. For two years he was a member of the state debating team. He was also for two years associate and editor of the college paper, The Northwestern. He did much in the Students' League work and was also one of the athletes of the college.

During 1912-13 Mr. Wardell was principal of the high school at Geary, Oklahoma. In 1914-15 he was a teacher in the Panhandle Agricultural Institute at Goodwell, Oklahoma. In the meantime he had filed on Government land in Texas County, and still owns 480 acres which he is rapidly developing as a farm and ranch. In 1914 he was republican nominee for county superintendent of public instruction of Texas County, and lost the election by only thirty-eight votes. Since September 1, 1915, he has been principal of the Guymon High School. Mr. Wardell is a member of the United Brethren Church.

WILLIAM LEWIS DETWILER is a veteran westerner, having lived in several of the states beyond the Mississippi for forty years. His early career was that of a railroad man, and he was in the railroad service during the Civil war. He was one of the early settlers and homesteaders in the Oklahoma Panhandle country and is now engaged in the real estate and loan business at Knowles in Beaver County.

His birth occurred at Pottstown, Pennsylvania, October 1, 1844. His parents, William H. and Mary (Longabaugh) Detwiler, were born in Pennsylvania of German stock. William L. was the first of their five children. John Barton is now deceased; Mary Jane is the wife of Joseph Perkins; Laura is the wife of Rev. John Gallagher; Josephine is the wife of Fred Clinton.

The early life of W. L. Detwiler was spent in Wheeling, West Virginia, where he attended the local schools. That was before West Virginia was a state. At the age of seventeen he took up railroading, entering the service of that pioneer railroad, the Baltimore & Ohio, and during the Civil war was advanced to the position of a conductor. He followed railroading actively both in the East and West for twenty years. His home has been in the West since 1876, and in that year he conducted the first passenger train running west of Lincoln, Nebraska, over the Burlington Railroad. For a number of years he also followed prospecting for gold in the Rocky Mountains.

Mr. Detwiler came to Oklahoma in 1900, locating on a tract of Government land in Beaver County. That land is still in his possession and has been greatly improved from the condition in which he first found it. He has employed his energies and capital in cattle raising, farming and also in selling real estate, and his operations as a real estate man included participation in the founding of the Town of Knowles, where he now has his office. A democrat in politics, he has never been a candidate for office, though he has done much in the way of local betterment in his home town. Mr. Detwiler is a thirty second degree Scottish Rite Mason and a Mystic Shriner and also belongs to the Knights of Pythias.

In 1886, at Linneus, Missouri, he married Miss Martha A. Dail, a native of Linn County, Missouri. Mr. and Mrs. Detwiler have no children of their own, but adopted a son, Chester, who was born in 1898.

CHARLES F. TALIAFERRO, M. D. In states older than Oklahoma it has been many years since men traveled toward a destination in a bee-line direction without having to turn right-angled corners caused by section-line roads. It has been but ten years in that section of

Oklahoma that formerly was Indian Territory since an individual might travel indefinitely in any diagonal direction with hindrances only of rough banked streams or wire pasture fences. That he might drive ten miles northwest without square turns and mile-long stretches was an interesting thought to a doctor on a dark night in winter. It was not always interesting, however, to contemplate swollen streams or dangerous gullies on an unsurveyed road made public only by common usage.

These general statements give an idea of conditions in the vicinity of Bennington ten years ago, as well as of the experiences of Dr. Charles F. Taliaferro as a pioneer physician of that section. The "northwest" direction mentioned illustratively is significant, for it is in that direction that the doctor has traveled for several years to reach the ranch of John Kirk and the kennels of the doctor's blooded hounds kept there by Mr. Kirk for fox and wolf hunting purposes. The sporting blood of more than one generation is in Doctor Taliaferro's veins, and it calls him out into the forests and mountains every fall and winter. The hounds are of as good blood as Tennessee produces, and he imported them here for the revival of a sport that nearly became extinct with the passing of the big Indian reservations. Doctor Taliaferro is a broad and liberal minded man, enthusiastic for his community's uplift and progress; but he has taken a position in the ranks of the social and municipal activities in order that he may remain a general in the woods.

There is no name more familiar to the various generations of national and particularly Southern history than that of Taliaferro, which has produced soldiers, statesmen, and people famous in all the professions and vocations. Charles F. Taliaferro was born in 1870 in Tennessee, a son of William H. and Martha (Franklin) Taliaferro. His father, a native of Tennessee, fought as a member of Company B, First Tennessee Cavalry, in the Confederate army during the war between the states. The grandfather also fought for the Confederacy, and after the war declined to vote because of the enfranchisement of the negro. Doctor Taliaferro's granduncle, Harden Taliaferro, a native of Virginia, became the founder of the famous female institute at Muskogee, Alabama, and as a minister of the Baptist faith edited for several years one of the leading religious papers of the South, known as the Southwestern Baptist. Doctor Taliaferro's mother was descended from a prominent family of North Carolina which produced Colonel Franklin, a hero of the American Revolution, and Governor Jesse Franklin of North Carolina. Both Colonel Franklin and Col. Richard Taliaferro, the latter a prominent member in the early generations of the Taliaferros, fought with those gallant North Carolina troops and rangers in the war of the revolution. In the bloody hand to hand fight with the British of Tarleton's Cavalry at Guilford Court House, Col. Richard Taliaferro was slain, was buried at the battlefield, and a monument has since been erected to his memory.

Doctor Taliaferro's early education was acquired in the public schools of Tennessee, and later he took an academic course at Mount Airy, North Carolina, where he was a schoolmate of the girl who subsequently became his wife. He was graduated in medicine from the Tennessee Medical College at Knoxville in 1895, and in that same year became associated with Dr. C. M. Drake, chief surgeon for the East Tennessee, Virginia and Georgia Railway Company. Later for twelve years Doctor Taliaferro practiced in James County, Tennessee, during which time he supplemented his early medical education with post-graduate courses.

On January 5, 1907, he located at Bennington, Oklahoma, a town which was a typical non-progressive village of the Indian country, but destined to grow to a population of 1,500 in less than ten years. There were but two miles of improved highway in the community, and the country was largely of virgin soil and almost totally unsettled. The doctor's practice for a few years was scattered over a wide area, and he traveled both in a buggy and on horseback as the occasion demanded.

In January, 1896, Doctor Taliaferro married Miss Ida Virginia Boleyjack, a daughter of Nat and Victoria (Bunker) Boleyjack. Her maternal grandfather was Chang Bunker, who was one of the noted "Siamese Twins" of Mount Airy, North Carolina. Doctor Taliaferro is a member of the Odd Fellows and Masonic lodges and of the Bryan County Medical Society, the Oklahoma State Medical Society and the American Medical Association. He has acquired some of the best farming lands of that notably fertile region of the east side of Bryan County and is developing it along modern lines. Excursions to his farm are nearly always likely to lead him on to the haunts of the red fox hounds, which, reminding him of the fox hunting days of his earlier years in Tennessee, make him one of the stanchest advocates in Oklahoma of the segregation of forest and mountain regions and the propagation and protection of wild life.

MARCUS L. LOCKWOOD, who for a number of years had lived at Tulsa, was a conspicuous figure not alone in Oklahoma but all over the nation as a pioneer oil operator and for many years as president and one of the most vigorous fighters in the American Anti-Trust League. In Oklahoma Mr. Lockwood was perhaps best known as president of the Sabine Oil and Marketing Company of Oklahoma, the headquarters of which organization were in Tulsa.

In every way he proved himself one of the world's productive workers, and though at the time of his death, he had passed the psalmist's span of three score and ten, he had not abated his vital interest in and association with practical affairs of life. If his biography were written in complete detail it would present almost a history of the great American petroleum industry from its pioneer beginnings in Western Pennsylvania until the second decade of the twentieth century. He began operations in the oil fields of Pennsylvania and then extended them into many other states, and was especially concerned in development work. He was long recognized as an authority on subjects of petroleum production, but he perhaps received his widest reputation as president of the American Anti-Trust League, of which he was one of the organizers. From first to last he was implacable in his opposition to monopolistic and predatory trust organizations.

A year or so before his death Mr. Lockwood addressed an appeal to President Woodrow Wilson for a Government owned and operated pipe line from the mid-continent oil fields to the Gulf of Mexico. This letter was widely published and circulated in countless form, and one of the newspapers that published it serially said of the writer: "There lives in Tulsa a man known to as many of the men prominent in the management of the affairs of this government as anyone in Oklahoma; a man who has done as much as almost any man in the United States to bring about the great reform now being accomplished at Washington. That man is M. L. Lockwood, who for many years was president of the American Anti-Trust League—a man who has made and spent more than one fortune, and much of this having been expended in this fight for better government for the people."

For many years before his death Mr. Lockwood's name was familiarly mentioned in the American press in connection with his efforts to regulate and curb the trusts, and naturally enough Oklahoma was proud to claim him as a citizen.

Marcus L. Lockwood was born in East Hamburg, Erie County, New York, December 5, 1844, a son of Philo B. and Polly (Utley) Lockwood, the former a native of Dutchess County, New York, and the latter of Vermont. Philo B. Lockwood died at the age of sixty-two and his widow survived a number of years, passing away at the age of sixty-three. Of their eight children the only one now living is George Lockwood of Buffalo, New York. Philo B. Lockwood was a successful farmer in New York, and both he and his wife were birthright members of the Society of Friends, in which organization he served as a preacher. The lineage of the Lockwood family in America goes back to Robert Lockwood, who came from England in 1630 and settled at Winthrop, Massachusetts. The paternal grandfather of Marcus L. Lockwood was a patriot soldier in the War of the Revolution, and subsequently became a pioneer in Western New York State.

It was with a common school education that Marcus L. Lockwood began his early career. He was fourteen when his father died and that necessarily threw upon his young shoulders responsibilities beyond his age. He helped manfully in the cultivation and operation of the old homestead farm in Erie County, New York, until 1865. At the age of twenty, having gained the consent of his devoted mother, he went into the oil fields of Pennsylvania. The petroleum industry was then in its infancy. His first experience was in dressing the tools used in the operation of the oil wells in the Cherry Creek district and near the old Humboldt Oil Refinery. Later he started out as an independent oil producer, a member of the firm of Patterson & Lockwood. In 1888 Mr. Lockwood was one of the organizers of the Pure Oil Company, a Pennsylvania corporation of which he later became a trustee. He was also one of the organizers of the Sabine Oil and Marketing Company of Pennsylvania, and subsequently of the Sabine Oil and Marketing Company of Oklahoma in 1891. The date of the organization of the latter company in Oklahoma shows that it was one of the pioneer concerns for the development of the oil fields of Oklahoma. In fact, during the next decade very little oil was produced in the Oklahoma fields.

However, though some of his early ventures were failures, Mr. Lockwood truly led the way in the development of the petroleum interests of the Middle West and Southwest. In 1887 he put down a well near Ottumwa in Wapello County, Iowa, and in the following year drove another well at Ackley, in Hardin County of the same state. He first came into Indian Territory in 1888, and on the opening of Oklahoma to settlement in the following year he took a claim to the northwest quarter of the section of land on which Oklahoma City now stands.

He was naturally attracted to Beaumont, Texas, when the Spindletop gusher brought fame to that hitherto obscure city. He obtained oil and gas leases on 2,800 acres of land, though development results proved unsatisfactory. He next bought a producing well in the Spindletop field, and provided tanking facilities for the accommodation of 750,000 barrels. To fill these tanks required 253,000 feet of lumber. Mr. Lockwood then purchased forty acres of land six miles distant from Spindletop, paying $100 an acre. A pipe line was constructed from his well to the storage tank, and as a contract operator he arranged for the taking over of 11,700,000 barrels of crude oil, though his actual receipts did not exceed 400,000 barrels. He contracted for the product at the rate of 30 cents a barrel, and sold the oil to the Standard Oil and independent companies for from 50 to 82 cents a barrel.

After leaving Texas Mr. Lockwood was identified with development operations and oil production at Independence and other points in the State of Kansas. In 1905 he established his home at Tulsa, Oklahoma, and was a resident of that great oil center until his death. He acquired the ownership of 20,000 acres of land in Southeastern Oklahoma and was one of the most important factors in the independent oil production of the state.

In 1897 the late Mr. Lockwood was one of the organizers of the American Anti-Trust League, and later was elected its president. Thenceforward for fifteen years or more he labored in season and out for bringing about the substantial reforms and the ideals which were fundamentally proclaimed by this league. The league has had its headquarters in Washington, and some idea of its purposes and results might be obtained from the following quotation which is found in an address issued by the executive committee of the league signed by Mr. Lockwood as president and others: "By virtue of the action of the Anti-Trust League there assembled in the city of Chicago, February 12, 1900, a national anti-trust conference, composed of many hundreds of representative citizens, from thirty-one states of the Union, one territory and the District of Columbia. This conference was non-partisan and was participated in by earnest men and women affiliated with the different political parties and by independent citizens who saw the danger to the people living and those yet to be born, in those rising industrial combinations commonly known as trusts. It lasted three days, and after full discussion and deliberation it adopted a platform and issued an address to the people, and instituted a systematic and organized warfare upon the criminal trusts. This warfare has been continuous, widespread and persistent ever since. The people became aroused, and as they learned more and more of the criminal character of these combinations and the outrageous wrongs inflicted, their indignation was such that the political parties were compelled to take up the question, declare their hostility to the trusts and promise their destruction." Every well informed person knows what a vastly different attitude is now maintained toward criminal trust organizations by not only the Government but by the general public, and in giving credit for this remarkable change which has occurred in the past fifteen years mention should be made at the very first of the Anti-Trust League, of which Mr. Lockwood was president.

Politically Mr. Lockwood was always a true democrat. From 1876 to 1880 he served as a member of the State Senate of Pennsylvania. In 1900 he was a democratic candidate for representative in Congress from one of the strong republican districts in that state, and by his strong hold upon the confidence and esteem of the people he reduced the normal republican majority by fully 2,000 votes, so that the campaign was a gratifying tribute to the man and his work for the people. Both he and his wife were active members of the Presbyterian Church.

On October 11, 1871, Mr. Lockwood married Miss Lydia H. Tompkins, only daughter of Robert Tompkins of East Hamburg, Erie County, New York. After a happy companionship of more than forty years Mrs. Lockwood passed away February 1, 1914. She and her husband were schoolmates as children, and their married life was ideal. Of their ten children, three died in infancy. The daughter, Clara, is the wife of Howard W. Alling of Jamestown, New York, and they have three children; Jennie T. is the wife of Harold Helm, also residents of New York State; Mabel is the wife of Roy

Porter of Guthrie, Oklahoma, and they have one child; Martha is the wife of Schuyler S. French of Tulsa, and they have one child; Robert Ralph, who graduated from Yale University and from the law department of Harvard University, is now practicing law at Tulsa; Kate is the wife of Elton Everett of Ottawa, Kansas, and they have two children; Philo D., who was associated with his father in business until his tragic death in an automobile accident in October, 1914, is survived by his widow, Mrs. Delia (Tyner) Lockwood, and their only daughter.

ANDREW J. LOVETT. By the high standard of its equipment and the efficiency of its school work the public school system of Blackwell can be compared on terms of favorable equality with any in the State of Oklahoma. The citizens of Blackwell are not loath to give credit for this achievement to Prof. Andrew J. Lovett, who has been superintendent of the public schools in that city for the past nine years, and has worked indefatigably as an organizer, director and teacher. He brought to his position a long and thorough experience in the schoolroom both as an instructor and as a superintendent, and the results obtained by him at Blackwell are most creditable.

The main feature of the Blackwell school system is the high school which was constructed in 1910-11 at a cost of $75,000. It is one of the very modern school buildings in Oklahoma. It contains twenty-one rooms, and there are twenty teachers in the building. The principal of the high school is Harry Huston. Four of the teachers are men. The rooms are all well arranged, equipped with modern furniture. There is a gymnasium, a fine laboratory for scientific work, one of the best libraries in the state and in many ways the school has become a central feature in the life of Blackwell. The high school building stands on grounds comprising an entire block. The high school contains 266 pupils. The total number in the building is 600. There were forty-four graduates from the high school in the class of 1916. In another part of the city is a ward school, containing eight rooms and a third building of four rooms, besides these buildings, it has been necessary to construct several single room buildings in order to take care of the large number of pupils. The total enrollment of the school at Blackwell numbers more than 1,200. The schools are kept up for nine months in the year, and one fact that indicates the interest in education in the city is that the enrollment is more than 100 per cent of the school enumeration.

Mr. Lovett during his nine years as superintendent has brought these schools up to modern standards, and his reputation as a school man and organizer has extended over the entire state. He was born in Kentucky. His father, Rev. Martin V. Lovett, was a well known Methodist minister. His mother, Rosanah Vaught, was of Scotch ancestry. They were the parents of five children, two sons and three daughters. Professor Lovett has a brother, William G., who has been one of the leading members of the Board of Education of Neodesha, Kansas, for several years. The mother died at the age of forty-one, but the father is still living at the age of eighty-one. From Kentucky the family removed to Oakland City, Indiana, where Professor Lovett received his common school and high school education. After gradusting from college he came to Kansas in 1884. Since then he has been identified with the teaching profession continuously. He spent fourteen years as superintendent of schools in Kansas and in 1908 accepted the superintendency of the schools at Blackwell. Mr. Lovett has been a member of the National Education Association for many years, and attends the annual meetings of the Department of Superintendence.

On December 26, 1886, he was married to Miss Estella Brundidge, of Fredonia, Kansas. Mr. and Mrs. Lovett are the parents of four children, three of whom are still at home. In politics, Mr. Lovett has always been a republican, and he and his wife are members of the Methodist Episcopal Church, and he has been teacher of the men's Bible class in that church for several years. Fraternally his connections are with the Masonic Order in the Blue Lodge, Chapter and Commandery and with India Temple of the Mystic Shrine at Oklahoma City. He is also a member of the Knights of Pythias and the Modern Woodmen of America.

JAMES J. QUARLES. Cashier of the Osage Bank at Fairfax, James J. Quarles has been identified with that community since its founding, having moved to the town with L. A. Wismeyer, who is honored with the distinction of being the father of Fairfax. Mr. Quarles is a Mississippi man, gained his early experience as a merchant and farmer in his native state, but has been identified with the Osage country of Indian Territory and Oklahoma for more than twenty years. Outside of his connection with business affairs he is also well known over the state through his efforts and influence in a public capacity, and was a member of the Oklahoma Constitutional Convention and has served on several of the important commissions in the state.

Born in Lafayette County, Mississippi, May 5, 1862, he is a son of James J. and Sarah E. (Buford) Quarles. The first American settler of this name was Francis Quarles, who came from England, and it is claimed that the Quarles ancestry can be traced back as far in English history as that of any other family. On the maternal side the Bufords were also English people, and the name was originally spelled Beaufort. One of the family in England was Margaret Beaufort, who was a granddaughter of King Edward III. The members of the family that came to America subsequently changed their name to the spelling Buford. Mr. Quarles' father was born in South Carolina in 1828, and in early youth moved to Lafayette County, Mississippi. The seat of the State University of Mississippi is located at Oxford in Lafayette County, and the elder James J. Quarles was one of the honored graduates in the first class in that institution in 1849. He was married in 1850 to Miss Buford, who was born in Tennessee in 1833, and had been brought as a child to Lafayette County. James J. Quarles, Sr., was a school teacher for a number of years, and also owned a plantation in Lafayette County. Early in the war he enlisted in the Confederate army, and died in a Confederate Hospital at Atlanta in 1863. He was survived many years by his widow, who died at Oxford, Mississippi, in 1911. There were five children: Robert W., who is a dentist at Van Buren, Arkansas; Lillie, widow of Mr. Hurt, living in Lafayette County; Olivia, who died in infancy; Francis, who died at the age of twenty-eight; and James J. Jr., who was only about a year old when his father died. His home was in Mississippi until 1892, and while there he received the advantages of the common schools, and grew up and was trained to farming. He also had several years of merchandising experience, and since moving to the Osage Nation in 1892 has been principally identified with merchandising and banking. Since 1905, two years after the founding of Fairfax, he has been cashier of the Osage Bank. The other officers of this bank are W. T. Carroll, president; and E. B. Glover, vice president. Mr. Quarles also has farming and live stock interests in Osage County, and also founded the Quarles Hardware

Company, the management of which is now entrusted to his sons who are partners in the company.

As a Mississippian and a son of a Confederate veteran Mr. Quarles has naturally been identified with the democratic party all his active career. He and T. J. Leahy were the only two delegates from the Fifty-sixth District in the Constitutional Convention of Oklahoma. Since statehood he has been quite active in Oklahoma affairs. During 1910 he was a member of the State Board of Public Affairs, and was president of the Board of Regents of the University Preparatory School during 1908-09. He was also a member of the commission for the advancement of the constitutional amendment for election of United States senators by direct vote of the people. These various commission offices were all received under appointment from Governor Haskell. While a member of these bodies he came into close relations with a number of the prominent men of the state, and in addition to the opportunity these places gave him for rendering public spirited service he naturally prizes the association by which he was brought into close touch with the state government and with men prominent in Oklahoma affairs. He has been a member of the school board in Osage County a number of years, and was identified with the management of the schools before statehood, when all the white schools were supported by subscription, there being no free public schools. He is active in the prohibition movement and in the equal suffrage cause, and is a member of the Presbyterian Church and the Knights of Pythias Order.

In 1884 Mr. Quarles married Miss Jimmie Orr. She was born in his native state, and died in 1902. The four children born to their marriage are: Frank O. and James J., Jr., both now associated with their father in the hardware business; Laura Gray, who died at the age of four years; and Mary Alleen. The son Frank married Anna Chapman. In 1905 Mr. Quarles married Ella Todd Gravett, who was born in Iowa. By her former marriage she has two daughters, Gertrude and Jean.

J. A. LOPEMAN. A business institution of Enid which is notable both for its importance in the material development of that part of Oklahoma, and for the personal and business character of the man behind it is the Enid Nursery, which is probably the highest grade establishment of its kind in the entire state. This business represents years of practical experience, the overcoming of difficulties, and the persistent testing and working out of plans which would adapt fruit bearing trees to soil, climate and other local conditions.

J. A. Lopeman was born in Crawford County near Oil City, Pennsylvania, about sixty years ago. The farm which his father owned there was sold when Mr. Lopeman was five years of age, and later oil was discovered upon it which made its subsequent owners millionaires. From Pennsylvania the family moved to the vicinity of Bradford, Iowa, and in 1859, to Pleasant Hill in Cass County, Missouri. The father of Mr. Lopeman was a pronounced Union man, and soon found the climate too warm in Missouri during early war times, and accordingly removed to Kansas. Mr. Lopeman arrived at manhood at Leavenworth in that state. His father enlisted in the Union army from Kansas, and a year later died while still a soldier.

Such education as Mr. Lopeman had from schools was acquired while assisting in the support of his mother and family. He qualified as a teacher, and for six years was engaged in that work. For four years he had experience in a store at Milo, Iowa, and in 1884 found the field for which his talents were best adapted. At that time he became a grower of nursery stock at Red Cloud, Nebraska, and his experience in that line has thus been continuous for thirty-one years.

At the opening of the Cherokee Strip on September 16, 1893, Mr. Lopeman was one of the homeseekers, and secured a claim of 160 acres six miles north of Enid. That land he still owns, and it is famous over that part of the country for its splendid orchard of forty acres. This has been profitable, particularly that portion devoted to the growing of berries and cherries. His cherry orchard of 2,000 trees has yielded handsome returns. Mr. Lopeman came to Oklahoma with the idea that a business might be developed for the supplying of new settlers with young trees. He knew that every American settler would as soon as possible set out a variety of fruit, shade and ornamental trees around his home, and therefore in the spring of 1894 he leased three or four acres at the north edge of Enid, and started what promised to be a lucrative business. Enemies, of which his experience at Fillmore, Nebraska, had given him no intimation, came and he found it an uphill, slow and hazardous enterprise. The new country abounded with rabbits, which were probably the most serious plague he had to contend with. These pests were accustomed to the bark of the tenacious native plum, hackberry, elm and bolsd'arc, and consequently the tender rind of the young fruit trees offered an especially attractive morsel for these animals. Several times his stock was almost annihilated. He fought with this and other obstacles for eight years, and then secured a tract of land in South Enid, where his present residence, office and packing house are located.

There he took a fresh hold. Studying the needs in Oklahoma, considering climate, moisture, winds and live pests, he studied to supply what would prove profitable. Many promising varieties of fruits after a test covering a few years would be abandoned, but he continued his trials and experiments and succeeded in the end in selecting and acclimating the stock most suitable to soil and climate. Since then his business has had a continued and constant expansion.

Mr. Lopeman soon bought 160 acres at a mile and a half distant, of which 140 acres are now devoted to the growing of fruit and shade trees, also shrubs, roses and other miscellaneous plants. He sells both wholesale and retail, and the latter feature is handled by about fifty salesmen. Orchards from the Lopeman nursery are now found in every section of Oklahoma, also in the Panhandle and other parts of Texas, in Southern Kansas, and New Mexico. From ten to forty men are kept employed under the immediate supervision of Mr. Lopeman's son, J. A., Jr., and about $6,000 are paid out annually for the matter of labor alone. Annual sales of his nursery stock approximate $75,000. This business gives its proprietor a solid satisfaction since it is the proof of his patient and indefatigable working out of fundamental plans. His thorough knowledge comes from actual experience, failure as well as success, and the fruits of his work have extended to practically every fruit bearing district in the Southwest. He is prominent and well known in all nurserymen's associations, both district and national, and his success is to be measured not only by its material profits but also by the splendid principles which he has kept fundamental from the beginning to the end. It has been his desire and determination to deal squarely with every customer. Knowing the hazards of producing a good orchard when climatic conditions are so strenuous, he has made specially liberal terms to replace stock that does not attain fruit bearing age, no matter what the cause of loss may be. He has of course suffered bitter experience as a result of malicious misrepresentation or failure on the part of someone to act in accord with instructions, and this has caused him temporary financial losses. Nevertheless, he has adhered strictly to the rule to deal openly and above board with every man, and in the end has gained a continued and extending business. With a disposition to be frank and outspoken, and with personal relations characterized by a hearty greeting and welcome clasp of the hand, few men in Enid or in Oklahoma have now a more extended or loyal circle of personal friends. A less outspoken manner and more diplomatic ways might have carried him to the same financial heights in less time, but no one who learns the honesty of heart and elements of good will back of his brusque nature has not also learned to respect and honor this man, whose qualities as a man and citizen are unsurpassed.

In 1893 Mr. Lopeman married Miss Catherine McClellan, who died in July, 1909. She was a splendid companion to him, devoted to her home, took a great interest in the development of his interests, and had a large circle of warm friends. She left two children: J. A., Jr., who is closely associated with his father in business; and Laura E., wife of Charles Musser of Bristow, Oklahoma.

HOMER HUFFAKER. One of the pioneer white men in the Osage country, identified with the thriving Town of Fairfax since its beginning, now the head of one of the largest mercantile concerns there, and also one of the present county commissioners of Osage County, Homer Huffaker is one of the men who have made their influence count for improvement and development in this section of the state.

He belongs to one of the oldest and most prominent pioneer families of the State of Kansas. Homer Huffaker was born at Council Grove, Kansas, March 1, 1875, a son of the late Thomas S. and Eliza A. (Baker) Huffaker. In addition to the many honorable distinctions associated with his father's name in Kansas, Judge Huffaker's activities also extend into what is now Oklahoma. About 1870 he established a trading store at Pond Creek, Oklahoma, and conducted it a number of years. It was an important supply point for the Indians of that vicinity, and also for both the white men and the Indians during the high tide of the industry of buffalo hunting on the plains.

When Judge Thomas Sears Huffaker died at his old home in Council Grove, July 10, 1910, that event closed the career of one of the most remarkable of early Kansans. He was born in Clay County, Missouri, March 30, 1825, of a pioneer family in Northwest Missouri, and moving to Kansas in 1849, five years before the organization of the territory, his subsequent career was such that he was called "the grand old man of Kansas" first in Indian affairs and then in politics and public matters. He went to Kansas as a missionary teacher at the Manual Training School in Johnson County, but about two years later, in 1850, moved to Council Grove, where he was given charge of the Kaw Indians, who had recently been transferred to their reservation in the Neosho Valley. At Council Grove he founded a mission school, and the building is still one of the picturesque landmarks on the banks of the Neosho. It was built under the supervision of Mr. Huffaker in 1850, and was large enough to furnish quarters not only for school but also for the residence of the teacher and his family. The school was opened in 1851, but the enterprise was not successful, since few of the Indians would allow their children to attend, and after a few years the school was abandoned. However, Judge Huffaker remained and soon became a man of importance in the community. He was one of the three incorporators of the City of Council Grove in 1858, was appointed the first postmaster, and soon afterward Territorial Governor Reeder appointed him president of the county commissioners. He was next elected probate judge of Wise County, his jurisdiction extending over portions of several adjacent counties of the present time. He later served two terms in the Kansas Legislature. Judge Huffaker was a Missouri slaveholder, and took his slaves with him to Kansas, but after the Kansas troubles had eventuated in the Civil war he took the side of the Union, and during the last forty years of his life was a stanch republican. He had come into Kansas as a missionary under the auspices of the Methodist Episcopal Church South, and the old Kaw Mission School was founded jointly by that church and the United States Government. He was also a member of the Masonic Order. At the time of his death Judge Morehouse of Topeka described his personality in these words: "He was stately of bearing—like a judge. The Indians regarded him as 'father,' accepting his decrees without murmur. Called to settle the many difficulties of the early days, he always was careful to learn both sides, and so advised as to make no enemies. He was rewarded by the love of all."

The widow of Judge Huffaker and the mother of the Fairfax merchant is still living at her old home in Council Grove. She was born at Salem, Illinois, in 1836, and is one of the splendid pioneer women of Kansas. A year or so before the death of Judge Huffaker her career was chosen as the subject for a beautiful article by a Kansas writer, who wove her story into a collection of articles describing notable Kansas women. A few sentences are taken from that interesting sketch before introducing the career of the Fairfax business man, who has so many reasons to honor the memory and character of his noble mother: "On May 6, 1852, there was a wedding in the stone schoolhouse at Council Grove. The bride was a girl of sixteen. By her picture of the day she must have been a pretty girl, for her face is handsome at seventy. Her maiden name was Eliza A. Baker, and one of her brothers, Jesse Baker, was one of the victims of the border ruffian days in Morris County, Kansas. She was born in Illinois in 1836. She had lived in Iowa, where her father was blacksmith for the Sac and Fox Indians, and now at the age when our girls are beginning to talk of sophomore class parties, she became the wife of a frontiersman in the trackless Indian country. A missionary on his way to Mexico, a Rev. Mr. Nicholson, performed the ceremony. The duties of a home keeper, always strenuous on the frontier, were multiplied for Mrs. Huffaker. In the old stone house her children were born, and there a school for white children was soon opened. Council Grove, at first a mere trading point on the Santa Fe trail, had grown to be the trading point, then a village and later a city and county seat in the center of a rich productive valley. The old stone house began to serve other purposes. Travelers, explorers, missionaries and state officials slept under its roof when they came hither. The Civil war came and passed and then came fifteen years of fear of the plains Indians. The old schoolhouse became by turns council house, school building, church and fort. It was a refuge for the defenceless, where women and children fled to the stronghold for protection. Lost in the duties of wife and mother, housekeeper and teacher, friend and neighbor, Mrs. Huffaker's years ran by. In all the stirring days of border strife and Civil war and the Indian peril, she bore her part. In the old stone house where she became a bride one May day, she lived through the scenes of territorial and state making. Children grew up in that home and went out to make homes for themselves. There are no great deeds to be set in bold faced type against Mrs. Huffaker's name. Her's was the silent story that is written in good deeds and measureless influence, and yet her name was one of the very first to suggest itself to me when I conceived the idea of gathering together the names of the women of the State whose stories appealed to me."

At the death of Judge Huffaker six children survived him: Mrs. J. H. Simcock of St. Louis; Mrs. Louis Wismeyer of Fairfax, Oklahoma; Mrs. Fred B. Carpenter of Topeka; Homer Huffaker; and George and Carl Huffaker.

In Council Grove Homer Huffaker spent his youthful days until 1892, then a boy of seventeen, he came to the Osage Reservation with his brother-in-law, L. A. Wismeyer. He had attended the local schools and had grown up in a home which inspired in him the best qualities of manhood. He became an assistant at Gray Horse in the Osage Nation to L. A. Wismeyer in the trading store, and remained in that locality until 1903, when he joined in the business exodus from Gray Horse to the new railroad town founded by Mr. Wismeyer and named Fairfax. For two years Mr. Huffaker was assistant cashier in the Osage Bank of Fairfax. When the Wismeyer Mercantile Company was formed and incorporated he became its secretary and treasurer, and was identified with the concern in that capacity for ten years. In 1913 he organized the Big Hill Trading Company of Fairfax, and is now its president. This firm carries a large stock of general merchandise, and has extensive trade relations both with the white and Indian population around Fairfax. In many ways Mr. Huffaker has been identified with the business and civic upbuilding of Fairfax since it was founded. In 1907 he added to the improvement of the town by the erection of the fine home in which he and his family now reside. He has also acquired farming and stock raising interests in that locality.

In politics he has been a republican voter for twenty years. In 1912 he was elected county commissioner of Osage county, served as chairman of the board during his first term, and was re-elected in 1914. He was also chairman of the first delegation which chose a representative for Congress from the Osage country, and assisted in nominating former Congressman Bird S. McGuire. Mr. Huffaker is a thirty-second degree Scottish Rite Mason, belongs to the Nobles of the Mystic Shrine, and is also a member of the Elks Lodge of Pawhuska.

In 1905 he married Miss Erma Robins Bates. She was born in Tupelo, Mississippi, September 29, 1879, was partly reared in Cairo, Illinois, and at the age of six years went with her parents to Council Grove, Kansas. Later her parents removed to Kansas City, Missouri, where she lived until her marriage. Her parents are W. T. and Mary (Hall) Bates, who are still residents of Kansas City. Her father is a railroad man. Mr. and Mrs. Huffaker are the parents of three sons: Thomas Bates, born June 23, 1906; Homer Hall, born October 22, 1908; and Darwin S., born August 10, 1912. Mr. Huffaker is a master of the Osage language, and readily acquired fluency in that tongue within a short time after coming to the Osage country.

GEORGE M. BERRY. The citizens of Pawnee County know George M. Berry as a successful farmer and banker. He has lived in this part of the old Cherokee Strip for thirty-six years. Some of the old-timers know of his early struggles and the perseverance and industry which put him on the road to success.

The keynote of his character and success is perhaps to be found in a little incident of his earlier career.

When he was nineteen years of age, being out of employment, he took work on a ranch. He remained with his employer there nine years. All that time he was getting his board and keep but was never drawing a cent of wages. As a matter of fact he did not know for what wages he was working, or what he was to receive at the end of his term. When the nine years were up the old Oklahoma was opened for settlers, and the ranch was accordingly closed out. In settling up the accounts Mr. Berry was paid $5,400 as a reward for the nine years of patient work he had put in there. It was possibly no more than he was worth, but the point of the story is his willingness to work for work's sake and to go diligently about his business without any particular concern about the financial rewards.

Mr. Berry is a Kentuckian. He was born in the southeastern part of the state December 1, 1858, a son of T. N. and Sophia J. (King) Berry. His father was born in Whitley County, Kentucky, and died there January 31, 1868, when his son George was ten years of age. The widowed mother subsequently brought her family to Arkansas City, Kansas, in the fall of 1877, and she died at Ashland, Kansas, April 19, 1886. Her nine children were: W. E. of Stillwater, Oklahoma; I. K., formerly a rancher in Oklahoma and now living in Mexico; Nan, a resident of Cushing, Oklahoma, and widow of Lycurgus Laughlin; T. E., formerly an Indian trader, who died at Norman, Oklahoma; A. A., who was a licensed Indian trader and conducted a ranch for nine years before the opening of Pawnee County, and is now a resident of Norman; Eliza Earley, who died in Texas; George M.; Susie, who married J. W. Arthur of Oklahoma City; and R. C., a merchant at Norman.

After the death of his father George M. Berry lived much with his older brothers, who looked after him, and for two years he attended the public schools of Arkansas City, Kansas. It was in 1879 when he came to Pawnee, where his brothers, I. K., T. E. and A. A. Berry were licensed Indian traders. For a time he was also in the service of the United States Government engaged to teach the Indians how to break the prairie sod and raise crops. After a course in a business college at Lawrence, Kansas, he worked in a store and on a ranch from 1880 until the opening of Oklahoma in 1889.

In 1889 he settled on a claim in Lincoln County. After three years he returned to Pawnee, and for eight years gave his time to farming. Since then he has lived in the City of Pawnee, but still owns a large amount of farm lands, including three improved farms, and is an extensive grower of grain and stock.

In 1894 Mr. Berry assisted in organizing the Bank of Pawnee. Since 1899 this has been the First National Bank, and is the oldest bank of Pawnee County. Mr. Berry has been its vice president since it was incorporated as a national bank. The other officers are: C. J. Shapard, president; S. Thornton, cashier; and John W. Wilson, assistant cashier. The bank has a capital of $50,000, surplus of $10,000, and its total resources are more than $400,000. The deposits average about $300,000.

Among other interests Mr. Berry has some oil holdings in the Cleveland field at the east end of Pawnee County. He has long been active in political and public life and is a loyal democrat. At Pawnee he served on the city council several years, and was mayor of the town for two terms before statehood. For many years he was also treasurer of the school board. Mr. Berry represented the eighteenth district in the Constitutional Convention, and was an influential member of several important committees. He was elected a delegate to the Constitutional Convention by 200 votes, although the district was normally republican by 300. It is evidence of his popularity and ability, as well as the value of his public service, that he has never been defeated for any office for which he has been a candidate. During statehood he has been state committeeman from Pawnee County, a delegate to a number of state conventions, and secretary of the county election board. In public life, as in business and private affairs, he has a large circle of friends, and men place implicit trust in his integrity as well as his ability. Again and again he has sacrificed his own interests in order to do good to the community. Oklahoma has a warm place in his affection. He first saw the country when he rode horseback from Arkansas City to Pawnee, before the building of railroads. In the early days he received mail for the Pawnee country. The mail was brought from Coffeyville, Kansas, by way of Pawhuska and when high waters did not interfere with the schedule it was delivered twice a week. Mr. Berry and his family are members of the Methodist Church.

At Perth, Kansas, in February, 1887, he married Miss Nellie Dowis. She is a native of Missouri. They have nine children: Roy, Jennie, Ethel, Elida, Everett, Margaret, Lesta, Catherine and Robert. The three older children are graduates of the Pawnee High School and also attended the University of Missouri at Columbia, and Elida is now a student in the Oklahoma State University at Norman. The son, Roy, lives at Pawnee, while Jennie is the wife of E. A. Holden of Clinton, Oklahoma.

HON. THOMAS S. JONES. This veteran lawyer of Guthrie has had a long and interesting career of experience in many fields. He was a boy soldier in the war between the states, rising to the rank of lieutenant in the Confederate army. He went out to Kansas in pioneer times, had a brilliant career as a lawyer and in politics in that state, and was one of the first members of his profession to arrive in the Town of Guthrie at the original opening of Oklahoma in 1889. He has known all the leading figures in Oklahoma affairs from the beginning of white settlement and is himself one of the conspicuous features among the old timers of the state.

He was born in a log house which stood on a farm near Richmond, Virginia, on August 17, 1838. His parents were Meredith and Julia (Coleman) Jones, both natives of Virginia and of Welsh stock. When Judge Jones was six months old he lost both his parents by death, and he was afterwards reared and attended school while living with his grandfather, Stephen Coleman. His preparatory education was acquired in the State Masonic Institute at Germantown, North Carolina. When only fourteen years of age he qualified and entered as a student the University of Virginia at Charlottesville, where he remained to complete his course in the law department. He was admitted to the bar by the Supreme Court of Virginia.

He had hardly begun practice when the Civil war broke out with all its fury, and almost at the first he enlisted in the Confederate army as a private, and one year later was promoted to lieutenant. He also served as an inspector on the staff of General Wise, and he made a brilliant record while with his gallant Virginia regiment.

In 1865 at the close of the war Mr. Jones came West and was one of the early settlers at Cottonwood Falls, Kansas. There he set up in practice as a pioneer lawyer, and soon found himself busied with his practice and with politics. His home was in Chase County, known at that time as a republican stronghold. In spite of that fact the young Virginia lawyer overcame all normal obstacles and was elected in 1867 county attorney. Another test of his personal popularity and his influence came a few years later when he was elected by the people of Chase County to represent them one term in the state Legislature. While in the Legislature he served as a member of a number of important committees including the judiciary committee.

Judge Jones in the course of the last forty years has seen much of the pioneer experiences. In fact he seems to have had a fondness for the frontier rather than for the settled districts of civilization, and this was indicated in 1873 when he moved out to a center of some of the wildest life of the West, Dodge City, Kansas. He came well recommended as a lawyer, and in a short time became a recognized leader in that community. He was much admired for his personal courage as well as his efficiency in the profession, and though a democrat he was elected prosecuting attorney of Ford County. He was elected on the law-enforcement platform, and the enunciation of such a policy in Dodge City forty years ago meant a great deal, and as he had been elected for the purpose of enforcing the law and clearing the city of its disorderly element, he never hesitated a moment to do all that his office and duty demanded.

After a number of years of practice at Dodge City, Judge Jones in 1889 participated in the first opening of Oklahoma Territory and established his home in Guthrie. Here he was made one of the first judges of the provisional court of Guthrie and was the first county attorney of Logan County to hold that post by election. For the past twenty years or more he has been in active practice at Guthrie, and still enjoys a large clientage. Judge Jones is an active member of the Masonic Order.

In 1865 he married Miss Mary G. West, who was born in Virginia. They are the parents of two children. Judge Jones' daughter Mary is the wife of Harmon Doolittle, a banker of Strong City, Kansas, and his grandson, Dudley Doolittle, has already made a distinguished record and is the present congressman from the fourth district of Kansas. Judge Jones' only son was Edgar W. Jones, now deceased. He took a prominent part in the early history of Oklahoma, served as private secretary to Governor W. C. Renfrow, was librarian of the State Supreme Court and also served four years as prosecuting attorney of Logan County and was a member of the Territorial Legislature. Edgar W. Jones attained the thirty-second degree in Scottish Rite Masonry.

EUGENE F. SCOTT. For nearly fifteen years Eugene F. Scott has been a practicing member of the Oklahoma bar. With a large private practice at Pawhuska, he also looks after the interests of several large corporations in that part of the state, and outside of his profession he has become distinguished as one of the most influential leaders in the democratic party.

A son of W. G. Scott, whose career as an old time Oklahoman has been sketched on other pages, Eugene F. Scott was born at Ocheltree in Johnston County, Kansas, May 4, 1881. From the age of four until 1901 his home was at Arkansas City, where he gained his early education graduating from the high school in 1898. He pursued his law studies at Arkansas City under the direction of Charles L. Brown, a prominent railroad attorney there, and was admitted to the bar in the District Court of Cowley County, Kansas, in 1901. Soon after his admission to the bar Mr. Scott moved to Cleveland, Oklahoma, and soon afterward came to Pawhuska. He was a partner with T. J. Leahy at Pawhuska until 1908, and from that year until 1913 was a member of the firm of Grimstead & Scott. Since the latter year he has been in practice alone. Mr. Scott is attorney in Osage County for the Midland Valley and the Missouri, Kansas & Texas railroads. His work as a lawyer is largely in civil practice.

As a democrat he was chairman of the first Democratic County Committee when Osage County was organized and managed the first campaign of the party. He was also the first chairman of the city committee, and conducted several of the local campaigns. For eight years he was a valued member of the State Democratic Committee from Osage County, up to 1914. The only office in which he has consented to serve was as president of the city council of Pawhuska for three years. Mr. Scott also assisted in organizing as a charter member the Pawhuska Lodge of Elks and has served as exalted ruler of that order. He is a member of the general council of the State Bar Association, and president of the Osage County Bar Association.

In 1904 he married Miss Dolly Johnson, who died in 1907, leaving two children, William J. and Violet. In 1913 he married Miss Roxie James of Boonville, Missouri.

WILLIAM S. HEWITT. Twenty years of purposeful participation in business affairs has marked the career of William S. Hewitt in Oklahoma. Since his arrival here, in 1895, he has been variously engaged, his activities having included operations in freighting, agriculture and merchandise, and connection with various enterprises of a business and financial nature, and in each line of effort he has shown himself capable, energetic and trustworthy. Mr. Hewitt is the grandson of a preacher of the Latter Day Saints, who was twice married and traveled all over the Southwest, living at different times in Missouri, Kansas, Indian Territory and Texas. His death occurred in Indian Territory, while the grandmother of Mr. Hewitt died in Kansas.

Richard H. Hewitt, the father of William S. Hewitt, was born in Illinois, January 7, 1844, and was reared on the frontier, his entire life being passed amid exciting scenes and marked with many interesting incidents. His first venture on his own account was the operation of a ranch in Nebraska, where his property was destroyed by a roving band of Pawnee Indians, and in 1863, with his brother William, they began general freighting for themselves from Marysville, Kansas, to their ranch twenty-eight miles east of Fort Carney. About the year 1867 he went to Marshall County, Kansas, where he filed on a tract of eighty acres of land, which he continued to cultivate until 1894, and for seven years also engaged in merchandising and in conducting a hotel. This latter property was destroyed by fire in 1876 and he returned to his farm in Marshall County, but about the year 1893 moved to Blue Rapids, Kansas, where he made his home for two years. On April 19, 1895, he and his son, William S., filed on their present farm in Pawnee County, a tract of 120 acres in the southwest quarter of section 28, adjoining Jennings on the East. But the father bought out the man who was on this farm. On first coming here Richard H. Hewitt was engaged for several years in freighting. The farm is now conducted by the son, William S. Mr. Hewitt, Sr., was married in September, 1868, to Miss Nancy J. Strange, who was born in Missouri in 1850, and to this union there have been born two children: William S.; and Hettie, who is the wife of William Dexter, of Marshall County, Kansas.

William S. Hewitt was born on his father's farm in Marshall County, Kansas, July 23, 1869, and was there reared to farming pursuits and educated in the district schools. From the time of his arrival in Oklahoma until his marriage, a period of about three years, he was engaged in freighting from Sapulpa and Perry to Jennings and following this again engaged in farming, and stock raising. On coming to Jennings he became a clerk in the general store of Todd & Bishop, but after a few months resigned and entered the employ of A. E. Ansley, a general merchant and hardware and implement dealer. He was with Mr. Ansley on and off for about five years, and during this time was also employed as a clerk in the postoffice for several months, as well as in a bank and drug store for a short time. In 1907 Mr. Hewitt was made manager of Spurrie's Lumber Yards and held that position until May, 1915. His chief contribution to the upbuilding of Jennings has been the laying out and development of the Hewitt Addition, a tract of seven acres which is almost entirely built up. Every enterprise of any importance has received his support, and he is considered one of the energetic and capable men of the community who has been a factor in the life of Jennings since his arrival. Mr. Hewitt is a republican, while his fraternal connections are with the local lodge of the Independent Order of Odd Fellows, the Knights of the Maccabees, the Modern Woodmen of America and the Blue Lodge.

On July 31, 1898, Mr. Hewitt was united in marriage with Miss Lillie Belle Wharton, who was born February 13, 1887, in Jefferson County, Kansas, daughter of A. E. and Sarah (Butcher) Wharton, who are now residents of Hallett, Oklahoma. Mr. and Mrs. Hewitt have been the parents of three children: Harry Glenn; Ralph W., who died when 2½ years old; and Ruth.

GEORGE G. LAMOTTE. One of the most interesting as well as one of the most efficient business partnerships in Oklahoma is that of LaMotte & LaMotte, the constituent members of which are Mr. and Mrs. George G. LaMotte of Pawhuska. Since their marriage and in the course of five years on a partnership basis they have engaged in the leasing of Osage lands for farming and grazing purposes, and they probable handle as much land under one ownership as any other one firm or individual in the state. Their holdings under lease run to more than 400,000 acres each year, and with such a vast pasturage it is easy to understand that they are among the largest producers of cattle and other livestock for the market in the state. Mr. LaMotte is a young business man well known through his relations with the public service and in other affairs, and Mrs. LaMotte is undoubtedly one of the business women in the Southwest. She has a talent for getting large things accomplished in a large way, and is equally at home in the handling of business and in the brilliant social circles of the national capital, where she spent several years with her former husband, Congressman McGuire.

Mr. LaMotte was born at Hayward, at that time one of the lumber centers of Northern Wisconsin, on March 13, 1880, a son of Frank and Elizabeth (Limry) LaMotte. His father was born near Montreal, Canada, of French parentage. He grew up in that locality, became identified with the lumber industry, and followed the call of the lumber woods into Wisconsin and Minnesota. He died when his son was about twelve years of age. The mother was born at Green Bay, Wisconsin, spent all her life in that state, and died at Hayward in 1902. Through her Mr. LaMotte has a portion of Chippewa Indian blood in his veins. He was the oldest of four sons, his brother James being a resident of Wisconsin, Edward of Oklahoma, and Lloyd in Kansas.

His early boyhood was spent at Hayward, Wisconsin, where he attended the public schools, a Government school at Tomah, Wisconsin, and also the high school there. Mr. LaMotte gained his higher education and business training in the Haskell Indian School at Lawrence,

Kansas, where he spent four years. During that time he was prominent both in the social and athletic life of the college, was a member of the noted Haskell Indian football team, and also served as secretary of the superintendent, H. P. Peavis of the Haskell School. He spent portions of two seasons on the road with the Wheelock Indian Band, playing the bass solo instrument. After the activities of his college career, he was for one year in the offices of the Santa Fe Railroad at Topeka, and was then with the Rock Island at Kansas City. A part of the time was spent on the road with different musical organizations, and this and other activities account for the fact that though still a young man Mr. LaMotte has seen perhaps as much of the people and cities of America as anyone. From Kansas City he moved to Pawhuska in 1905, and here became identified with the Osage Townsite Commission. He entered the Civil Service, and up to 1910 was identified with the Osage Agency.

Mr. LaMotte was first married in 1904 to Louise Bayhylle, who died in 1908, leaving one child, Georgia. In 1910 Mr. LaMotte married Mrs. Anna (Marx) McGuire. They soon afterwards started their unique business partnership of LaMotte & LaMotte. Mr. LaMotte is a democrat in politics, and takes much interest in party affairs, though he is essentially a business man and his large and varied interests demand his entire attention.

Mrs. LaMotte is a native of Illinois, but was reared and educated in Southern Kansas and from an early age has been remarkable for her intense activity and vigor of mind and charm and social character. When a girl she held the responsibilities of postmaster at Sedan, Kansas. She went into Oklahoma at Pawnee about the time the strip was opened, and not only displayed a keen ability in competition with men and business affairs, but was from the start an attractive figure in social circles. He has a large acquaintance over this and other states, and when she went to Washington she quickly proved her ability as a social leader.

JUDGE JOHN M. HAYES. The Hayes family, of which Judge John M. of this review is the local representative, had its origin in Ireland, and the first of the name to come to America was William Hayes, great-grandfather of the subject. He was a surveyor in his native land, and coming to America settled in New Hampshire, the family home being near historic Concord then and for many years thereafter. He was occupied in his profession when the Revolutionary fires, long smouldering in the hearts of the Colonials, burst out vigorously, and he was soon fighting in the ranks of the Colonial army with the rank of colonel. His record was a brilliant one throughout the long struggle for American independence, and many tales are told of his nerve and daring in encounters with the enemy.

The son of Colonel Hayes was also named William and was the father of the subject of this sketch. He was born in New Hampshire, and was educated at Dartmouth. He was a man of considerable talent in a literary way, and was long prominent in governmental affairs of his native state. He served thirty-six years as a member of the New Hampshire Legislature, and was a life-long democrat. He served through the War of 1812 with the rank of colonel, and in 1850 left his native state and came to Illinois, where he bought and operated a large farm for some years.

Dr. A. W. Hayes was born in New Hampshire, and like his father, had his education at Dartmouth College. He came to Illinois with his father in 1850, and they located at Buda, Berrian County. When the Civil war came on he enlisted in a New Hampshire regiment in the capacity of an army surgeon, passing through the conflict until November, 1864. The young surgeon, then but thirty-two years old, died suddenly as a result of illness, and his wife survived him only a few hours. Both were interred in the same grave, and their burial place is at Buda, Illinois. His wife was Sarah M. Webb, also of New Hampshire birth, and she left one child John M. Hayes, then an infant.

Judge Hayes was reared on his grandfather's farm in Illinois, and was graduated from the Buda High School in 1879. He entered a law school later and in 1883 was graduated with the degree LL.B. He established himself in practice in Coles County, Illinois, continuing there until 1901, and winning various professional and political honors in the time of his service there. In 1901 he came to Oklahoma, settled on a farm in Karva County and practiced law at the same time. For some time he owned and edited the Sulphur Democrat. During the first years of Oklahoma's statehood he was an attorney in the land department, and in 1911 he came to Cleveland and settled down to the practice of his profession. Judge Hayes has been a democrat all his life.

In 1886 Judge Hayes was married to May Shepherd, a native of Burrage County, Illinois, and the daughter of a Buda (Illinois) merchant. She had her higher education in the Geneseo Normal School of Illinois and for some years was occupied as a teacher in her native state. She is prominent in the social activities of Cleveland, and is president of the Mothers' Club of the city. To Judge and Mrs. Hayes have been born three children: Harold, Ophelia, and John M. Jr.

HON. SCOTT FERRIS. The representative of the Fifth Congressional District of Oklahoma in the United States Congress, Hon. Scott Ferris, is also known as one of the leading legal lights of Lawton, Oklahoma, his home city, and as an agriculturist has been identified with the development of Comanche County during the past decade. In each capacity he has shown himself capable, painstaking and thoroughly informed, and although he is still a comparatively young man he is generally accounted as one of Lawton's leading citizens.

Mr. Ferris was born November 3, 1877, at Neosho, Missouri, and is a son of the late Scott and Anna M. (Thorp) Ferris, and a member of a family which, originating in England, emigrated to the United States and settled first in Delaware and later in New York. Scott Ferris, the father of Congressman Ferris, was born in 1842, at Mount Morris, near Rochester, New York, and as a young man came to the West, locating at Neosho, Missouri, in 1866. There he followed agricultural pursuits with success until 1902, in which year he took up his residence at Walter, Oklahoma, where he died two years later. He was an active democrat in his political views, and fraternally was connected with the Masons and the Ancient Order of United Workmen. Mrs. Ferris, who was born at Mount Morris, New York, in 1847, died at Walter, Oklahoma, in 1905. They were the parents of three children, namely: Thomas, who is in the Government Indian Service and resides at Lame Deer, Montana; Scott, of this review; and Anne, who makes her home with her brother at Lawton.

Scott Ferris received his early education in the public schools of Neosho, Missouri, where he was graduated from the high school in 1897, and following this attended the University of Missouri for one year. He then enrolled as a student in the Kansas City School of Law, being graduated therefrom in 1901, with the degree of Bachelor of Laws, and almost immediately took up his residence at Lawton, where he has continued in active practice, his law office being located at 406 D Avenue.

As a lawyer he early attracted to himself an excellent professional business, and in the meantime became actively interested in democratic politics, being elected a member of the last Territorial Legislature of 1905-06. In 1907 he became the candidate of his party for Congress, as representative of the Fifth Congressional District of Oklahoma, and was sent to that body, where he immediately demonstrated his fitness for public service of an exalted character. His excellent services gained him repeated re-elections, and at the present time he is serving his fifth consecutive term. In this time, Mr. Ferris has served on many important committees, and the work that he has accomplished for the benefit of his constituents has been of a nature to give him prestige as one of Oklahoma's most helpful public servants. At the present time Mr. Ferris is chairman of the important Public Lands Commission. In 1911 he was appointed by Speaker Champ Clark as one of the two members of Congress chosen as members of the Board of Regents of the Smithsonian Institute.

Fraternally, Mr. Ferris is affiliated with Lawton Lodge No. 183, Ancient Free and Accepted Masons; Lawton Chapter No. 44, Royal Arch Masons; Lodge No. 1056, Benevolent and Protective Order of Elks, of Lawton, and the Modern Woodmen of America. He is a working member of the Lawton Chamber of Commerce and has done much to accelerate its undertakings. As a farmer, Mr. Ferris is the owner of two valuable properties, one of 126 acres adjoining Lawton and one of 160 acres located 1½ miles from the city, in Comanche County. He has specialized in alfalfa and has met with excellent success in his agricultural ventures.

On June 23, 1906, at Neosho, Missouri, Mr. Ferris was united in marriage with Miss Grace Hubbert, daughter of George Hubbert, a prominent attorney of that city. They have no children.

J. C. BYERS. Long a cattle man in Oklahoma, in the days before it was opened, J. C. Byers has lived the life of the open through a good many years. In more recent years he has devoted himself to the operating of a general merchandise store in Cleveland. He is a pioneer in this section of the country, and is identified with numerous branches of industry, including farming, oil production, real estate and insurance. Mr. Byers was born in Fairfield, Iowa, on August 14, 1861, and he is a son of H. H. and Mary E. (Laughlin) Byers.

H. H. Byers was born on April 13, 1838, and his wife on June 9th of the same year, in Ohio and Pennsylvania, respectively. He was a son of John and Mary (Hunter) Byers, and they came from Virginia to Ohio in the early pioneer days of that state, and John Byers was killed by the Indians when in middle life. They had two sons, H. H., father of the subject, and John H. Mary Hunter, his wife, was a sister of General Hunter, a Union general in the Civil war, and one of their brothers was a member of Jeff Davis' cabinet.

When H. H. Byers was sixteen years of age the family came to Iowa, and he and his brother were still in their early twenties when they enlisted in Company H, Second Iowa Infantry in 1861. Both served through a three year period, and they were stationed at Beaconsville, Texas, when the war was closed. H. H. finished his service with the rank of second lieutenant. He was at Pikes Peak, Colorado, when the war broke out, but lost no time in getting back to his native state so that he might enlist for service. He was at the front when his son, J. E., of this review, was born. In 1869 H. H. Byers came to the Osage Nation, near Old Hickory Fort. He thought he was on the Kansas side, but when the survey was made discovered that he was mistaken, so he moved across the line into Kansas and settled on a farm on the state line. When the Cherokee strip was opened in 1893 he came to Oklahoma, and he died here, in Cleveland, in 1898. All his life he was a cattleman and farmer, and he enjoyed a generous measure of success.

Of his marriage with Mary E. Laughlin, five sons were born. J. E. is the eldest. W. L. is a resident of Osage County. Fred L. lives near Cleveland. Emmor also lives in Cleveland, and Rolla lives in Cushing.

J. E. Byers spent his early life as his father's assistant, and he was very young when he familiarized himself with the details of the cattle business. He was eight years old when the family moved to the Osage Nation, where the father had contracts for supplying the Indians with beef, and the boy was not slow to learn the Osage language. When he first left his father young Byers went to Texas and there was employed by cattle men. He drove cattle over the trail from Texas to Emporia, Kansas, in 1872, and later made many trips over the same trail. It may properly be said that he has been a cattle man all his life, for he began in 1869 when he was only eight years old.

On coming to Cleveland Mr. Byers established a mercantile business. He ran a general store here and at Horning until 1897, when he moved on a ranch in Osage County and continued there for three years. He then became assistant cashier in the Cleveland National Bank, and a little later went into the oil business. Prior to that time, however, he had been interested in the oil activities of the district, and had operated to some extent, so that he may properly be called one of the pioneer oil men of the state. In fact, he was one of those who discovered the oil deposits in Oklahoma. Today he is the owner of extensive oil lands. Mr. Byers owns considerable farm land in the county, and has a one-fourth interest in the second addition to the Town of Cleveland. He has a real estate and insurance office in the National Bank Building, where his interests are handled. Another enterprise that has had his attention is the zinc industry in Arkansas, where he has some valuable properties.

Mr. Byers is a member of the progressive party, and with his family has membership in the Presbyterian Church, of which he is a trustee. He is a Master Mason and a Pythian Knight.

On June 2, 1897, Mr. Byers was married to Florence Powell, of Independence, Kansas. They have three sons: Harold C., Dale and Lewis.

MILTON CLARK WARE. One of the prominent families of the old Osage tribe is that household of which Milton C. Ware is the head, residents of Pawhuska. For many years the Ware family lived on a large ranch and farm in Osage County, but moved to Pawhuska some years ago in order that the children might secure better educational advantages.

Mr. Ware himself is an intermarried citizen of the Osages. He was born in Collin County, Texas, October 11, 1856, a son of James and Nancy (Howell) Ware. His father was born in Lawrence County, Arkansas, and his mother in Illinois, but they spent most of their lives in Collin County, Texas, where his father was a farmer and stock raiser and also one of the pioneer settlers. That section of Northern Texas had a very scant population until after the close of the Civil war. In their family are five sons and one daughter still living.

Milton Clark Ware grew up on the old Texas farm, gained his education in the common schools of that country and lived there as a farmer and stock man until coming to Osage County in 1890. After his marriage he located on a large farm five miles south of Pawhuska, and that was his home until six years ago when he moved his family to Pawhuska in order that his children might be close to good schools. He keeps a home in town and also lives at the ranch, and still operates the farm and has some very extensive interests as a farmer and stock man. His wife and children have shared in the allotment of Indian lands, and there are seven individual participants in this allotment among his own family, each one having more than a section of land.

Mr. Ware is affiliated with the Independent Order of Odd Fellows, and he and his family belong to the Christian Church. October 3, 1891, he married Agnes Martin. She was born near Tahlequah in the Cherokee Nation September 13, 1870, and she is of Cherokee and Osage blood. She lost her mother when she was fourteen months old, and soon afterward her father brought her to the Osage Nation. Her parents were Alexander and Rachel (Sanders) Martin. Her father was born near Pryor Creek in the Cherokee Nation, and her mother near Talequah. Both were half blood Indians, her father being of the Osage and her mother of the Cherokee blood. Her father died December 17, 1915, his home having been on Eighth Street, Pawhuska. He married for his third wife Minnie Denton. By the first marriage there were two children and Mrs. Ware's sister is Julia, the wife of William Edwards of Wynona.

Mr. and Mrs. Ware have eight children: Julia, wife of Gordon Wells, living near Bartlesville; Nancy, wife of Edward German of Ponca City; Beulah May, Rose Lee, Henry, Davis, Marie and James, at home.

EBEN SODERSTROM. This is one of the few men who can claim lifelong residence at Pawhuska, though until recent years there was no city specially worthy of the name in that locality. The milling industry in this section of Oklahoma owes more to the enterprise of the Soderstroms, father and son, than to any other individual. It has been with milling and the grain business that Eben Soderstrom has been identified all his active career, and his father before him was one of the prominent millers in the early days of old Indian Territory.

Born at Pawhuska November 3, 1879, Eben Soderstrom is a son of John and Laura (Coffey) Soderstrom. His father was born in Sweden in 1853, and died at Pawhuska in 1905. When nineteen years of age he came to America, having learned the trade of millwright in the old country, and from Chicago, where he first located, worked at different points until he came to Indian Territory in 1878. He was at that time and for a number of years in the employ of the United States Government, and it was under Government auspices that he built two mills in this part of Oklahoma, one at Kaw Agency and another at the Osage Agency at what is now Pawhuska. When the Government sold this latter mill at auction he and W. S. Mathews secured the property, and following this purchase he continued its operation until his death. His early death was the result of drowning in Bird Creek, while putting up ice. While he followed the milling industry all his life, and built a number of mills in different parts of the country, he was also for a number of years in the cattle business, operating a large ranch near Pawhuska. In politics he was a republican, but contented himself merely with voting, and was not an active party man. He was affiliated with the Masonic order and the Independent Order of Odd Fellows. John Soderstrom was married soon after coming to Indian Territory in the spring of 1878 to Miss Laura Coffey, who is still living at Pawhuska. Special interest attaches to her because of the fact that she is one of the daughters of Colonel Coffey, the founder of the City of Coffeyville, Kansas, where she was born in 1863. Of their six children Eben is the oldest; Della is the wife of Ben Parsons of Pawhuska; J. W. lives at Pawhuska; Hannah is the wife of John Renfrew, also of Pawhuska; and Carl and Floyd are likewise residents of that city.

After his education in local schools up to the age of sixteen, Eben Soderstrom found a place in his father's mill, and under the latter's direction learned all the details of the milling business. He was associated with the elder Soderstrom until his death, and then in partnership with J. E. Scarborough bought the old stone mill on Bird Creek which his father had built and operated. Three years later this landmark of early industry burned. Then with his own capital Mr. Soderstrom built the present grain elevator and seed mill located near the Midland Valley Railroad station in Pawhuska. The elevator has a capacity of 10,000 bushels of grain, and he also does a business of custom grinding for the farmers of that community. He is wholesale flour agent in this part of Oklahoma for the Globe Flour Mills. In his business Mr. Soderstrom employs three men, and is one of the live and enterprising citizens of Pawhuska. Fraternally he is affiliated with the Masonic Order and the Independent Order of Odd Fellows. In 1914 occurred his marriage to Naomi Conley, who was born at Arkansas City, Kansas, in 1886, a daughter of Joseph Conley. They have a son, John, who is one year old at this writing and named in honor of his grandfather.

LORIS E. BRYANT. One of the progressive young men who have fully availed themselves of the opportunities afforded in the vital young State of Oklahoma is Hon. Loris E. Bryant, who was elected representative of Osage County in the Fifth Legislature of this commonwealth and who is a prominent and successful merchant and agriculturist of that county, his home and mercantile establishment being in the thriving and ambitious Village of Bigheart.

Mr. Bryant was born at Chautauqua Springs, Chautauqua County, Kansas, on the 15th of October, 1884, and is a son of Thomas A. and Sarah (Davenport) Bryant, the former a native of Bates County, Missouri, and the latter of Cass County, that state, her father having been a valiant soldier of the Union in the Civil war. Thomas A. Bryant was a pioneer of where he eventually became a substantial agriculturist and stock grower. Shortly after the close of the Civil war he removed from Missouri to Chase County, Kansas, where he settled near Cottonwood Falls. He endured the full tension of the turbulent period attended by the operations of the jayhawkers and bushwhackers in the Sunflower State after the close of the war and served as a member of the home guard, a militia organization established to defend the settlers against the depredations of these lawless elements. He became one of the honored and well known citizens of Chautauqua County and served at one time as mayor of Chautauqua Springs, where his death occurred on the 6th of July, 1914. He was seventy-one years of age when he passed away, his devoted wife having been summoned to the life eternal on the 26th of April, 1907, at the age of sixty years, and both having been persons of sterling character as well as of deep and abiding Christian faith and effective practice.

Relative to the formative period in the life of Loris E. Bryant the following significant statements have been made: "Mr. Bryant's early training was exemplary and benignant, his parents having been devoted Christians, and when, at the age of thirteen years, he faced the world alone and set forth to make his own way, he was fortified by conscientious honesty and integrity, from the course of which he has never wavered during the later years of earnest and successful endeavor." Between the ages of eight and eighteen years Mr. Bryant had attended school for a total period of only nineteen months, but his alert mentality and self-reliance have enabled him effectually to make good this handicap of earlier years. He was still a boy at the time of his parents' removal from Kansas to the territory of the Osage Nation in Oklahoma, where they made settlement on a farm. The financial resources of his parents were extremely limited, but Mr. Brown determined to acquire through his own exertions the means for further education. It will thus be seen that his ambition was one of action, and by zealous application to farm work before and after entering the institution, he was enabled to defray the expenses of a three years' course in the Oklahoma Agricultural & Mechanical College at Stillwater. He left college in his junior year and came forth well fortified in both academic and scientific knowledge, as he had applied himself with all diligence and earnestness. He returned to the home farm and later he became associated with one of his brothers in the operation of a ranch near Pawhuska, the present judicial center of Osage County. After a time this property was sold by the brothers and Loris E. Bryant then engaged in the general merchandise business at Kiefer, Creek County. There he contracted typhoid fever and in his period of convalescence it was found imperative for him to seek a change of climate. Accordingly he passed a year in Tampico, Mexico, where he held the position of managing editor of the Tampico Post, the only paper there published in the English language. After his return to Oklahoma he passed another year at Kiefer and then engaged in the mercantile business at Pawhuska, Osage County. Later he and his brother established a general store at Bigheart, this county, where they built up a prosperous business, under the firm name of Bryant Brothers. The subject of this review finally sold his interest in this enterprise and purchased stock in the Bank of Bigheart, of which he was assistant cashier until 1912, when he there resumed his association with the mercantile business, with which he is still actively and successfully identified, besides being the owner of valuable farm property in the northern part of the county. It is his purpose to devote eventually his entire attention to scientific agriculture and stock growing, and his experience and technical knowledge assure to him large and worthy success in this important field of industrial enterprise. Mr. Bryant has served as city clerk of Bigheart, as clerk of the board of education of the village, and as clerk of the Osage County Association of Boards of Education. He is progressive and energetic in his efforts to raise the standard of these lines of enterprise in his section of the state and is a close student of the scientific and practical matters pertaining thereto. Mr. Bryant is a young man of sterling character and high civic ideals. He has shown a lively concern in political and religious affairs and assisted in the organization of the Young Men's Christian Association at the Oklahoma Agricultural & Mechanical College at Stilwell, representing the same at the meeting of the Western Division of the Students' Young Men's Christian Association at Lake Geneva, Wisconsin, in 1903, while he was still a student in the college mentioned.

In the autumn of 1914 Mr. Bryant was elected representative of Osage County in the Oklahoma Legislature, as candidate on the Democratic ticket. He received a plurality of 322 votes, though the largest previous plurality accorded to a Democratic candidate for this office in the county had been but seventy votes. In the Fifth General Assembly Mr. Bryant was assigned to membership on a number of important house committees, namely: General agriculture, oil and gas, insurance, county and township organization and government, relations to the Five Civilized Tribes and other Indians, and enrolled and engrossed bills. He was the author of a bill providing for the free distribution of dyphtheria antitoxin; a bill establishing a Pasteur station for the prevention and treatment of hydrophobia, this having the strong approval of the administration; a bill providing for the election of county commissioners for a term of six years, with the term of one of the commissioners to expire every two years; a bill providing regulations for the sanitary operation of bottling works; a bill abolishing township government in Osage county; and a bill creating county courts at Hominy and Fairfax, that county. Mr. Bryant proved a far-sighted, careful and practical member of the legislative body and manifested specially active interest in measures relating to good roads, education, home ownership, and workmen's compensation.

As may be inferred, Mr. Bryant is a stalwart advocate of the principles and policies of the Democratic party and is one of its influential representatives in Osage county. In his home village of Bigheart he is affiliated with the organizations of the Independent Order of Odd Fellows and the Modern Woodmen of America, and at Pawhuska, the county seat, he is identified with the fraternal association known as the Homesteaders. He has been liberal in the support of measures and enterprises tending to advance the general welfare of his home village and county and is vice-president of the Bigheart Telephone Company. He has two brothers—Charles A., who is engaged in business at Pawhuska, and Thomas Edward, who conducts a general merchandise business at that place.

At Pawhuska, on the 29th of December, 1909, was solemnized the marriage of Mr. Bryant to Miss Mary Jessie Tinker, whose father possesses a strain of Osage Indian blood. Mrs. Bryant was educated in the Ursline Academy at Paola, Kansas, is a young woman of refinement and gracious presence, and is active in religious and social affairs at Bigheart. The two children of Mr. and Mrs. Bryant are Harold T. and Velma, the former having been born in 1911 and the latter in 1913.

FRANCIS T. NORBURY was a man most prominent and influential in founding the town of Hooker in Texas County. The creation and upbuilding of that center of population and trade are the facts which give Mr. Norbury a special place in Oklahoma City.

By profession he is a lawyer, has been in practice in Oklahoma in connection with his large business interests, and is also a real estate and loan broker.

An Englishman by birth, he was born February 16, 1857, at Worcestershire, was educated in Cheltenham College, beginning with the age of nineteen and took up the law in his native country. In 1889 he came to America and practiced in Wisconsin and Illinois and for a few years was a member of the Chicago bar.

It was in 1903 that he came to Oklahoma with Captain A. R. Cobb. They bought the site and started the town of Hooker and Mr. Norbury erected the first house in that town. He also opened the first law office and was soon appointed a justice of the peace. Everything vitally concerning the welfare and upbuilding of the town has had his earnest support. He organized the first Christian church, and was ordained a deacon and has been especially prominent in its affairs. Since becoming an American citizen he has been aligned with the republican party, and in Oklahoma has served as chairman of the township committee and for four years was clerk of the town of Hooker.

While living in England Mr. Norbury married and has eight children, three daughters and five sons, all of whom live in England and the boys are now fighting with the British army. On February 14, 1893, in Oconto County, Wisconsin, he married Miss Clara Anderson, who was also a native of England. They have no children of their own, but adopted a son Lionel, who was born September 10, 1912.

THOMAS E. WILLIS, a lawyer at Fairview in Major County, is an Oklahoma pioneer. His early years in this state were spent as a teacher, and he has been an active member of the bar since 1897.

Mr. Willis represents an old and honorable line of American ancestry. His forbears were patriots, and all of them for several generations had military records. His great-grandfather Colonel Nathaniel Willis served with that rank in the army of General Washington during the Revolution. Colonel Samuel Willis, the grandfather, saw active service at the head of a regiment in the War of 1812, being under the command of General Andrew Jackson.

Captain William R. Willis, father of the Oklahoma lawyer, was born April 6, 1834, in Grayson County, Kentucky. Though a Kentuckian he was a strong Union man, and commanded a company in the army of General Sherman during the Civil war. He also came to Oklahoma, where he spent his last years and died at Canton April 6, 1906. In 1865 Captain Willis married Harriet L. Brown, who was born in Grayson County, Kentucky, in 1842 and died at Enid, Oklahoma, in 1901. Her parents Jacob H. and Sarah (Anderson) Brown were natives of Tennessee. Captain Willis and wife were members of the Christian Church. They were the parents of eleven children, eight sons and three daughters, namely: Thomas E., H. Clay, Jacob H., Oliver P., Sarah Viola, William E., Eugene, Phelegmon, (deceased), Albert R., Laura and Myrtle.

In the same log house in Grayson County, Kentucky, where his father was born, Thomas E. Willis also saw the light of day September 15, 1865. His early years were spent on his father's farm. He attended the public schools until he was nineteen, and graduated from the Litchfield Academy of Litchfield, Kentucky. Mr. Willis came west in 1885, locating in Kansas with his parents. In Comanche County of that state he proved up a claim of land, and for six years was also a locomotive engineer. In 1892 Mr. Willis came to Oklahoma, identified himself with Kingfisher County, and was one of the early school teachers in that locality. While teaching he also pursued his studies of law, and in 1897 was admitted to the territorial bar. In the same year he was elected on a fusion ticket to the fifth session of the territorial legislature, representing Kingfisher County. He took an active apart in the deliberations of that body and was chairman of the Committee on Education. In this capacity he became author of the first bill providing for free school text books that was ever introduced in Oklahoma. He was also author of the fee and salary law which found a place on the statute books.

Since 1910 Mr. Willis has been in active practice at Fairview in Major County. He is one of the leading democrats of the state, served as state committeeman, and has given his time generously to the public welfare. He is recognized as one of the ablest lawyers of his county. Mr. Willis has been an active member of the Independent Order of Odd Fellows since 1890.

On May 12, 1893, in Comanche County, Kansas, he married Miss Josephine L. Bratcher. She was born in Kentucky November 9, 1872. To their union have been born three children: Mabel O., born July 22, 1896; Roland Emmet, born June 1, 1898, and died June 1, 1899; Jessie Lillian, born November 16, 1900.

DEE RODMAN is one of the successful newspaper men of Oklahoma, entered the profession through the ranks of a printer, and is now editor and publisher of the Fairview Enterprise at Fairview in Major County.

Mr. Rodman is a young man, and has spent most of his years in Oklahoma. He was born March 6, 1884, on a farm in Erath County, Texas, a son of John B. and Nancy Jane (Kimbro) Rodman, the former a native of Kentucky and the latter of Arkansas. John B. Rodman was born December 17, 1860, at Paducah, Kentucky, followed farming and stone masonry for his active career, and is still farming in Beaver County, Oklahoma. He was married in 1880 and his wife was born May 22, 1861, in Hope County, Arkansas, daughter of Thomas W. and Clementine Kimbro, both of whom are natives of Tennessee. John B. Rodman and wife have the following children: Arthur, born August 3, 1882; Dee; Ella, who was born December 19, 1886, and was married in 1902 to L. R. Houx, and they live in Colorado; Fred L. born February 14, 1888; John J., born June 21, 1891; Ila Belle born December 28, 1894; Daisy, born December 21, 1896; and Hugh B., born June 30, 1901.

The first sixteen years of his life Dee Rodman spent on his father's farms in Erath and Ellis counties, Texas. His parents then moved to Oklahoma, locating in Cheyenne, and there he continued his education in the public schools. Mr. Rodman also had the benefit of a two years' business course in the University of Oklahoma at Norman. In 1903 at the age of nineteen he entered the office of the Beacon at Cordell, Oklahoma, and learned by practical experience the printer's trade. In 1905 he came to Fairview and followed his trade as a journeyman printer until 1914. In that year he bought the plant of the Enterprise at Ames, Oklahoma, removed it to Fairview and has since published the Fairview Enterprise, one of the leading papers of Major County. Politically Mr. Rodman is a republican, and he and his wife are members of the Christian Church.

On March 12, 1910, at Fairview he married Miss Vie Morse. Mrs. Rodman was born at Girard, Kansas, November 20, 1891, a daughter of J. E. and Sadie (Nunally) Morse. To their marriage was born one child, Roberta Marian, born May 28, 1914.

THE CITY NATIONAL BANK, of Lawton, Oklahoma, the pioneer bank of Comanche County, was organized March 23, 1901, as the First National Bank of Fort Sill, with a capital of $25,000, authorized to do business by the comptroller of the currency as No. 5753. It was the first bank organized to do business in the Kiowa, Comanche and Apache Reservation, comprising the country now included in Comanche, Kiowa, Caddo and Tillman counties, as well as part of the counties of Stephens, Jefferson and Grady.

When this country was opened for settlement, and the City of Lawton entered upon its career, the name of this institution was changed to the City National Bank, of Lawton, and doors thrown open for business at nine o'clock, A. M., August 6, 1901. From that time to the present this bank has prospered and developed, growing with the needs of the country and contributing to the growth of that country and the wealth and welfare of its citizens. The first home of the City National Bank was in a small frame structure, located on a lot adjoining the United States Land Office property, but this was soon found to be too small, although the institution continued to have its residence there until its new brick building, the second brick building in the City of Lawton, was ready for occupancy, July 1, 1902. The bank's continued prosperity and growing business has compelled its present removal to still larger and better quarters.

On April 16, 1906, the capital of the City National Bank was doubled out of its earnings, and at the present time its capital, surplus and profits approximate nearly $100,000, while its deposits average in the neighborhood of $500,000. The City National was designated as a depositary of the United States by the Treasury Department, July 19, 1906, and since that time this institution has handled millions of dollars of the moneys of the United States Government.

The success and growth of this bank may be ascribed to the judgment, acumen, foresight and ability of its officers, all well known business men of Lawton, whose well known integrity has inspired confidence in depositors and has naturally attracted business. They are: Frank M. English, president; Samuel M. King, vice president; Edwin E. Shipley, cashier, and Charles W. Crabtree, assistant cashier.

DR. TOLBERT BARTON HINSON. The Hinson family was long established in Tennessee before one of its number migrated in a westerly direction and located in Arkansas. It was in that state that Dr. Tolbert Barton Hinson was born, and his father before him, one A. J. Hinson, was also born there, in the vicinity of Cave City, on May 25, 1855. He died there on July 16, 1915, having spent his entire life in that community, barring a period of one year's time spent in Walden, Arkansas, and a brief time in Philadelphia, Arkansas, sometime in the early eighties. It was in Walden that Doctor Hinson was born, on February 8, 1882.

A. J. Hinson was a farmer and stockman, prosperous and progressive, and he was a lifelong member of the Presbyterian Church. He married Elizabeth McGee, who was born in Arkansas in 1858, and who died in Oxford, Arkansas, in November, 1890. Their children were six in number, and are briefly mentioned as follows: George Franklin, the eldest, is living in Newport, Arkansas, where he is a dealer in marble; Doctor Hinson was the second born; W. E. resides at Fort Smith, Arkansas, where he has charge of a cut glass and china store; Parkie Elmore is a farmer and lives in Day, Arkansas; Lily married William Hood, a farmer of Day; and Sturling Alexander is a farmer and lives near Thomas, Oklahoma.

Doctor Hinson had his early education in the public schools of Arkansas. His ambition was toward the medical profession, however, and he entered the Hospital Medical College, in Louisville, Kentucky, and for four years pursued a rigid course of study. He was graduated in the class of 1905 with the degree M. D., since which time he has taken post graduate work in Chicago in 1913 and 1915. In June, 1908, Doctor Hinson located in Thomas, which place was the center of his professional activities until 1915, when he located in Enid, forming a partnership with Doctor Boyle and buying a half interest in the Enid Springs Sanitarium and Hospital with Doctor Boyle. Enid Springs Sanitarium and Bath House was established by Dr. Boyle on September 1, 1814. This institution filled a long felt want and is the only institution in the state combining the three features of sanitarium, hospital and bath house. It has an ideal location within a half block of Enid's famous Mineral Springs. Its house physicians are Doctors Boyle and Hinson. Doctor Hinson was the founder of the Thomas Hospital. He is a member of the Presbyterian Church, and is a Mason of high degree. His Masonic affiliations are with Enid Lodge No. 80, Ancient Free and Accepted Masons, Enid Chapter No. 27, Royal Arch Masons, Enid Commandery No. 13, Knights Templar, Council No. 35, Guthrie Consistory No. 1, and Akdar, Ancient Arabic Order of the Noble Mystic Shrine, of Tulsa Oklahoma.

In Salem, Arkansas, in the year 1901, was recorded the marriage of Doctor Hinson to Miss Docia Gault, daughter of J. H. Gault, now living retired in Day, Arkansas. They have three children: Amy, born November 15, 1902; Bruce Ratliff, born August 4, 1906; and Kirk, born May 7, 1909.

NATHAN A. ROBERTSON. Among the men of Oklahoma who have been connected with financial enterprises, few are more widely known than Nathan A. Robertson, of Lawton. While his activities are centered in this city, his connections are of such an extensive nature that they include this entire part of the state. Mr. Robertson was born in Appanoose County, Iowa, January 30, 1855, and is a son of Moses C. and Elizabeth Jane (Streepey) Robertson. The Robertson family originated in England, and Mr. Robertson's great-grandfather was a participant in the Revolutionary War, while his great-uncle was the founder of the City of Nashville, Tennessee.

Moses C. Robertson was born in Tennessee, in 1811, and at twelve years of age removed to Indiana, where he engaged in farming. He was a pioneer of Appanoose County, Iowa, in 1851, a strong Presbyterian and elder in the church, and a stalwart abolitionist. He died at Cincinnati, Iowa, in 1889. Mr. Robertson was married first to Mildred Pringle, who died in Indiana. His second wife was Elizabeth Jane Streepey, who was born in Indiana, in 1826, and died at Cincinnati, Iowa, in 1863, and they became the parents of five children, namely: Edward, deceased, was a farmer and stockman of Cincinnati, Ohio; Nathan A., of this review; J. H., who was formerly a large farmer and stockman of Montana, and is now living retired at Butte, that state; M. M., who is a ranchman in Montana; and Charles Sumner, of Des Moines, Iowa, who was formerly a merchant and traveling salesman, but is now engaged in the real estate and insurance business. Moses C. Robertson was married a third time, his wife being a Miss Sheppard, who died at Cincinnati, Iowa.

The early education of Nathan A. Robertson was secured in the public schools at Cincinnati, Iowa, where he completed the high school course in 1871. At that time he became a grain buyer for a concern of that place, continuing as such until the year 1875, when he went to Promise City, Iowa, and established himself in the grain and stock business, with which he was connected until 1910, when he disposed of his interests there. As early as 1882 Mr. Robertson became interested in financial matters, when he established a private banking business at Promise City, and from that time to the present he has been an important figure in the financial world of Oklahoma and Iowa. In 1895 he incorporated his bank at Promise City into the Farmers State Bank, continuing as its president until coming to Lawton, Oklahoma, in 1910. In the meantime, in 1903, he had opened the Farmers and Commercial Bank at Cincinnati, of which he is still president. At the present time he is a stockholder in the National Bank at Walter, Oklahoma, president of the National Bank of Waurika, Oklahoma, and president of the National Bank of Hastings, Oklahoma, a position which he has held since 1901. On coming to Lawton, in 1910, he became interested in the First National Bank, and in that same year purchased the Oklahoma State Bank, which was consolidated, December 31, 1912, with the First National Bank, of which Mr. Robertson has been president since January, 1913. He is also president of the Citizens State Bank, of Geronimo, Oklahoma, a director in the Bank of Tuttle, Oklahoma, and president of the J. J. Brown Cotton Company, of Lawton. There is probably no name in this part of Oklahoma that stands in greater degree for integrity, probity, honorable dealing and devotion to the highest ethics of business life than that borne by Mr. Robertson. He has been deeply interested in every movement which has tended to secure the best interests of his community, and with this end in view has been a hearty worker in all elevating undertakings. With his family, Mr. Robertson is a member of the Methodist Episcopal Church. He belongs to Lawton Lodge No. 183, Ancient Free and Accepted Masons, of which he is past master; Centerville (Iowa) Chapter, Royal Arch Masons; Centerville Commandery, Knights Templar, and Za-Ga-Ziz Temple, Ancient Arabic Order of the Nobles of the Mystic Shrine, and also holds membership in the Knights of Pythias and the Independent Order of Odd Fellows. He is a member and active worker of the Chamber of Commerce, and in political matters is a republican, although not a politician.

Mr. Robertson was married at Cincinnati, Iowa, to Miss Emma Lesney, daughter of the late Jonathan Lesney, a hardware merchant. Nine children were born to this union, as follows: R. L., who attended Drake University for three terms, a graduate of Parson's College, Fairfield, Iowa, with the degree of Bachelor of Arts, and now engaged in the real estate business at Lawton; Guy C., a graduate of C. C. C. College, Des Moines, Iowa, and now cashier of the First National Bank of Lawton; Cecile, a graduate of Des Moines Conservatory of Music, who died at the age of twenty years; Lela J., who lives at home; Mabel, a graduate of elocution at Drake University, a talented speaker and much in demand at entertainments and public gatherings of various kinds; Pansy I., residing at home, a graduate of Drake University, in music, who also took a four-year course at Howard Hall; James B., residing with his parents; Nathan Ray, educated in the high school at El Paso, Texas, and now cashier of the Citizens State Bank of Geronimo, Oklahoma, and Rex Wayne, also educated in the El Paso High School, who is now secretary and treasurer of the J. J. Brown Cotton Company, at Lawton.

HARRIS L. DANNER, of the law firm of Shirk & Danner, although still so young a man, has already attained an enviable degree of prominence among the legal fraternity of Oklahoma City. He has fairly earned the right to bear the honorable title of self-made man, for from the time he was fourteen years of age he has made his own way in the world, educationg himself and making his own opportunities. He was born at Astoria, Fulton County, Illinois, February 13, 1888, and is a son of A. B. and Melissa (Moore) Danner, the father being of German descent and for many years an agriculturist in the fertile fields of the Prairie state.

Reared amid rural surroundings, Harris L. Danner received his early education in the country schools, while his vacation periods were spent in the work of the farm. He became self-supporting at the age of fourteen years, and when he had graduated from Rushville Normal School, Rushville, Illinois, at the age of seventeen years, began teaching school in Schuyler County, that state. During the next three years, in addition to discharging his duties in the school room, he accepted whatever honorable outside employment presented itself, and also found time to devote to the study of law, finally being enabled to enter the law department of the University of Indiana, at Valparaiso, from which he was graduated with the class of 1909 with the degree of Bachelor of Law and was immediately admitted to the bar of Indiana, and in the same year came to Oklahoma and was here admitted by the Supreme Court, taking up his residence and practice at Oklahoma City. Shortly after his arrival, Mr. Danner formed a partnership with John Shirk, under the firm style of Shirk & Danner, and this combination has continued to the present time, offices being maintained at 604-610 Security Building. The firm carries on a general practice, which has steadily increased in volume and importance.

Mr. Danner is unmarried and resides at No. 1210 North Broadway, Oklahoma City.

CHESTER C. CLARK. In education circles of Southern Oklahoma, Chester C. Clark has, within recent years, become known as a young man of energetic spirit, whose zeal is leading him toward an elevation of educational standards and whose abilities and talents undoubtedly will bring him to a realization of his ambitions. Himself an earnest, conscientious and untiring scholar, he is possessed of the happy faculty of being able to imbue others with his own ideals, and the period of his incumbency of the position of superintendent of schools of Pauls Valley has been characterized by marked advancement in system and efficiency.

Mr. Clark is a Kansan by nativity, born at Mayetta, Jackson County, December 30, 1885, a son of Charles C. and Alice (Morrow) Clark. His branch of the Clark family originated in England and its early members in this country were pioneers of Ohio. The Morrows were of Scotch-Irish origin and early settlers of Tennessee. Charles C. Clark was born in Southern Ohio in 1852, and as a lad of five years accompanied his parents to Leavenworth, Kansas, where he was reared, educated and married. In 1884 he removed to Mayetta, six years later went to Holton, in the same state, and in 1899 took up his residence at Lawrence, Kansas, from whence he came in 1901, to his present home at Comanche, Oklahoma. He has devoted his energies to agricultural work and at the present time is the owner of a tract of 160 acres of valuable land lying six miles west of Comanche on which he does stockraising and diversified farming. Mr. Clark is a republican and fraternizes with the Masons. He married Alice Morrow, a native of Southern Missouri, and they have had five children: Chester C., of this notice; Glenn, a graduate of the Oklahoma State University at Norman, where he was captain of the varsity football team, and now head of the mathematical department of the State Normal School at Ada, Oklahoma; Hazel, who died aged one year; William, a graduate of the Oklahoma State Normal University, at Norman, where, like his brother, he captained the football team, and now a teacher in the Shawnee High School; and Grace a graduate of the State Normal School at Edmond, Oklahoma, now a teacher in the Pauls Valley schools.

After attending the school at Holton, Kansas, through the eighth grade, Chester C. spent two years in the Lawrence (Kansas) High School, then returning to the farm, where he assisted his father for four years, or until 1905. He then resumed his studies as a student at the Norman preparatory department of the State University, being graduated from the university proper in 1910, with the degree of Bachelor of Arts. Many of the wiseacres are inclined to make us believe that athletics and intellectual attainments cannot be formed into a happy combination, but in refutation of this idea we may state that the name of Clark is one idelibly inscribed upon the athletic annals of the university, while the brothers bearing this name have all shown rare

Vol. V—25

worth and ability in the field of education. Like his brothers, Chester C. Clark showed a wholesome desire for athletics and his prowess upon the gridiron won him a place in the hearts of students and faculty alike. He played with the varsity team, and not only won his full share of honors in the strenuous game of football, but proved himself a valuable man in track events. During the school year of 1910-11 he was principal of Cordell (Oklahoma) High School, and in the summer of the latter joined the United States Geological Survey, gaining valuable experience during the four and one-half months he spent in the service in Montana and North Dakota. To further prepare himself, in October, 1911, he entered Columbia University, New York, where for three months he specialized in geology. The school year 1912-13 found him principal of Tishomingo (Oklahoma) High School, and during the summer of the latter year he was an instructor at the Ada State Normal School. In the fall of 1913 he left this position to become principal of the Pauls Valley High School, where his work attracted such favorable notice that in September, 1914, he was made superintendent of schools of Pauls Valley, a position in which he has under his supervision three schools, twenty-two teachers and 900 scholars. In the summer of 1914 Mr. Clark took post-graduate work at Chicago University, and in the summer of 1915 again attended that institution, taking a course in educational work. He is in line to receive the degree of Master of Arts, in 1916. Popular, capable, and possessed of much executive ability, Mr. Clark is undoubtedly doing great things for the Pauls Valley schools, and, naturally, for the future welfare and advancement of the community.

Mr. Clark is on the Garvin County Examining Board for Teachers, and belongs to the Garvin County Teachers' Association and the Oklahoma State Teachers' Association. He is a democrat, a Methodist by religious faith and a member of Valley Lodge No. 6, Ancient Free and Accepted Masons, of Pauls Valley. He is unmarried.

D. C. MAHER. One of the men of real business leadership in Osage County is D. C. Maher, who has been cashier of the Fairfax National Bank since its organization. Mr. Maher has spent all his years since early childhood in this part of Oklahoma and in point of residence is one of the oldest white citizens among the Osage people.

He was born in St. Lawrence County, New York, October 29, 1877, a son of John B. and Amelia (McEwen) Maher. On both sides his grandparents came from Ireland. His parents were both born in northern New York, and his father died at the home of his son in Fairfax November 10, 1913, aged seventy-three. The mother died at Pawhuska November 20, 1904, at the age of fifty-nine. The family lived in New York until 1885, when they moved to Indian Territory, and for about twenty-five years the father managed the Leland Hotel at Pawhuska. His later years were spent in practically total blindness, and in spite of this affliction he knew all the people around him by the sound of their voices and their footsteps. He possessed a wonderful memory, and was one of the kindly and loved characters of Pawhuska. While living in the East he performed clerical work and was a cattle buyer. D. C. Maher was the fifth in a family of six children, record of the others being as follows: Alice, wife of H. L. Cox of Cedarvale; Ransom J. of Pawhuska; Daniel B. of Pawhuska; Howard M., who died October 5, 1912, at the age of thirty-eight; and Bertha, wife of N. D. Sanders of Phoenix, Arizona.

When the family removed to Indian Territory in 1885 D. C. Maher was eight years of age. He grew up in Pawhuska, attended the subscription school there, and the high school at Cedar Vale, Kansas, two years, but since boyhood his life has been one of independent venture and of increasing commercial experience. At 17 years of age he went to work at Hominy, and was employed by the old Indian traders Read & Bopst for about three years until that firm went out of business. The following three years he worked for Prentice Price in mercantile business. It was during these associations that Mr. Maher gained his fluency and command of the Osage language and for years he has spoken it like a native. Mr. Maher in association with Mr. Price and R. J. Inge bought a store at Cleveland and Maher & Inge conducted this establishment for six years. They sold it during the oil boom. For a time Mr. Maher was connected with the oil industry.

In 1905 he came to Fairfax and soon afterward organized the Fairfax National Bank, which opened its doors to business May 12, 1906. He has since been its cashier and has much to do with the solid prosperity of this institution. The bank was first housed in a frame building, but since 1910 has been in its fireproof and modern bank home. The Fairfax National Bank is a strong institution for a town of the size. Its total resources in June, 1916, according to the official statement at the time, were $154,491.02. It has capital stock of $25,000, surplus of $5,000, undivided profits of $2,411.11. The deposits at that time were upwards of a hundred thousand dollars. The officers of the bank are: G. M. Carpenter, president; J. L. Bird, vice president; D. C. Maher, cashier.

Outside of banking Mr. Maher is also interested in farming and stock raising and owns a well improved ranch on Dago Creek with about three hundred head of cattle. He is a breeder of thoroughbred Herefords. He is also secretary and one of the directors of the Big Hill Trading Company, Incorporated.

Politically his actions have always been in harmony with republican policies and principles. He is a thirty-second degree Scottish Rite Mason, a member of the Mystic Shrine, and is also affiliated with the Benevolent and Protective Order of Elks, August 10, 1904, Mr. Maher married Miss Genevieve Elwell. She was born in Leonardville, Kansas, December 24, 1885, a daughter of Samuel Elwell. At their happy home in Fairfax they have four children: Madalene, Dyke C., Jr., Don Elwell and John P.

CHARLES D. WEBBER, now sheriff of Pawnee County has had a career of many experiences, pleasant and otherwise, but all of an interesting character, both in the line of his official duties and as a traveling salesman for large business houses. He first came to Oklahoma in 1898, and with the exception of about three years has continued to make his home in this territory and state with headquarters in the larger cities, but since 190_ has lived at Pawnee.

Born on a farm near Warsaw, Gallatin County, Kentucky, February 14, 1870, Sheriff Webber is a son of Virginians and Sally (Ellis) Webber. The family is of Scotch origin and for many years has been prominently represented in Gallatin County, Kentucky. His grandfather Phillip Webber was an early settler there, owned extensive tracts of land and many slaves, was prominent in public affairs, and was the first county clerk of the county and held other offices besides. Phillip Webber was a man of unusual education for the times, particularly in the line of mathematics, and completed an arithmetic which was widely used as a text book during his day in the public schools. Otherwise he was a quiet, unassuming man with no desire for publicity, and ma...

it a rule never to accept remuneration for his official services. He and his wife had six children.

Virginius Webber was born on the homestead farm in Gallatin County, Kentucky, and spent his entire active career as a farmer. He is now living in quiet retirement in his native county. His wife died in 1909. She was active in the Baptist Church, of which her husband is also a member. During the Civil war Virginius Webber spent two years in the Union army. He is a republican in politics, and a man of substantial reputation in his community, where his sterling integrity and probity of character has won him the regard of his fellow citizens. He and his wife were the parents of eight daughters and five sons.

One of this large family of children, Charles D. Webber found his early life one of mingled duty and pleasure, and his first twenty-one years were spent on the old Kentucky homestead. In the meantime he attended the public schools and on starting out independently went to Illinois where he began work as a traveling salesman. From Illinois he came to Oklahoma in 1898, locating at El Reno. At that time he was district manager for the Singer Sewing Machine Company and had a number of men under him. With this force he covered the north half of Oklahoma and part of Indian Territory, selling machines and making collections, and he or his men visited practically every Indian tribe in this section of the country. It was a difficult as well as interesting experience. In many localities railroads had not yet been built, and there Mr. Webber made his journeys in a wagon. He slept under the wagonbed at night, and was more than once exposed to danger as well as hardship. At the same time he gained an intimate knowledge of the country, which has since been useful to him, and also became familiar with the habits and customs of the Indians, among whom he made many friends. While pursuing that business Mr. Webber had his home at various places, including El Reno, South McAlester and Guthrie. Later he moved to Salina, Kansas, from there to St. Joseph, Missouri, and in 1909 took up his permanent residence in Pawnee. Here he became traveling representative for a wholesale grocery concern. A man of great popularity on the road and among business men, he also gained the confidence and friendship of the people of his home city, and in December, 1914 was elected to the office of sheriff of Pawnee County. After his election he at once gave up his work on the road and began the duties of his office January 4, 1915. As sheriff he has shown himself an efficient and fearless officer, and has come through several desperate struggles with desperadoes and bad men with great personal credit. In one of these fights a deputy, Robert Moore, was shot through the heart.

A republican, Mr. Webber is one of the stalwart wheel horses of his party in Pawnee County. He is an elder in the Christian Church, of which his wife is also a member, and she is very active in its work. Fraternally he is a member of the Masonic Order, the Independent Order of Odd Fellows, and the United Commercial Travelers. A number of years ago while traveling over the wild district of the southwest, Sheriff Webber acquired a fondness for hunting, and he still takes great delight in getting into the country with his gun and hounds, rarely returning without some fine specimens to show for his skill and prowess as a marksman.

Sheriff Webber was married February 15, 1891, in Gallatin County, Kentucky, to Miss Florence A. Roberts, who was born in that county October 8, 1862, a daughter of John Samuel and Mary E. (Taylor) Roberts. Both her parents died in Illinois, where they had spent the last few years of their lives. Mr. and Mrs. Webber had five children. Maude, who graduated from the St. Joseph High School in Missouri, spent one year in a college at Hopkinsville, Kentucky, and then taught school four years, two years at Pawnee, was married June 1, 1915, to Forest Ryan, and they now reside near Glencoe in Payne County, Oklahoma. Ira Earl, the second child, is a graduate of the Pawnee High School and is now a student in Phillips University at Enid, Oklahoma, preparing for the ministry of the Christian Church. Florence Fern, is a graduate of the Pawnee High School and is now teaching at Terlton, Oklahoma. Margaret Esther is also a graduate of the Pawnee High School and is a student in the Phillips University. Harry E., the youngest, is still pursuing his studies in the Pawnee High School.

HON. MILTON M. RYAN. It was with a long experience as an educator and civil engineer that Milton M. Ryan was so highly qualified for the honor he received from the Twenty-first Senatorial District in election to the Oklahoma Senate in 1914. In contributing to the material growth of his town, in championing and defending measures of interest or organized labor, and in participating in the passage of laws affecting farmers and other land owners, Senator Ryan proved himself both a useful and patriotic Oklahoman.

A brief sketch of his career will indicate how well he has utilized his opportunities. He was born in Whitley County, Kentucky, June 6, 1860, a son of Joel and Jennie (Creekmore) Ryan. The Ryan ancestry goes back beyond the days of the American Revolution, is of Irish stock, and members of the family were among the colonists who traveled with Daniel Boone into Kentucky. Joel Ryan was a native of Virginia, an early settler in Southeastern Kentucky, a farmer and stock man, and widely known as an advocate of free schools in a section of Kentucky where education was backward for many years. He died at the age of seventy-seven. The mother of Senator Ryan was a native of Kentucky, descended from a sturdy stock of farmers and stockmen, and died at the age of eighty-four in Missouri, her body being returned to the family burying grounds in Kentucky. Senator Ryan has a sister and three brothers: Mrs. Louisa Beard, the wife of a farmer in Crawford County, Arkansas; James, a former police judge and real estate dealer of Claremore, Oklahoma; J. C., superintendent of schools at Portland, Oregon; and S. S., a farmer and teacher in Benton County, Arkansas.

Senator Ryan was educated in the Kentucky public schools, in 1879 entered the London Academy of that state, was there one year, and for two years in the Cumberland Academy at Williamsburg, Kentucky. Then followed several years of teaching, and among his students at that period was Charles Findlay, afterwards secretary of state of Kentucky. While teaching in the Cumberland Academy he also continued his academic courses, and finished the work in mathematics, German and French and lacked six months of completing the course in Latin. After leaving school he took up the profession of civil engineering, but after a year abandoned it in favor of educational work, and was teacher for twenty-five years, of which were in Kentucky, thirteen in Arkansas and eight in Oklahoma. Mr. Ryan located in Le Flore County, Oklahoma, in 1893, and his last school work was as principal of the public schools at Spiro. Senator Ryan is also a lawyer, having studied law at home between the ages of twenty-one and twenty-eight, and for a short time was in practice at Alma, Arkansas. After giving up school work definitely at Spiro, Mr. Ryan resumed his profession as engineer and was the first elected county surveyor of Le Flore County.

Later for three years he was county assessor, refusing the nomination for continued service at the end of his last term. For a number of years he has been a municipal and county leader in affairs, served as a member of the board of trustees at Spiro, and in 1910 led a campaign that resulted in the town voting $50,000 in bonds to establish a municipal water and light system. Spiro has a population of about 1,000, and the fight for the bonds was won against the opposition of some of its most influential citizens.

As a defender of labor issues, Senator Ryan made an aggressive campaign for the national democratic ticket in 1912, and gained a reputation over this part of the state as a forcible and effective speaker. In 1914 he was elected to the senate by a plurality of 771 over his republican and socialist opponent, and was gratified by receiving a larger vote than was cast for the state ticket. In the senate he was made chairman of the Committee of Fees and Salaries, and a member of committees on Code Revision, Roads and Highways, Education, Public Buildings, Oil and Gas, Drugs and Pure Foods, Fish and Game and State and County affairs. In several of these committees his own work and experience has made him an invaluable member. He joined with Senator Campbell Russell in preparing and securing the passage of the graduated land tax measure and was author of a bill pensioning Confederate soldiers, and, jointly with Representative Council, prepared a bill rearranging a system of taxation and providing that tax assessors should meet tax payers at stated times for the returning of their assessable property. He was a supporter of the rural credits bill, and of other measures of interest to the farming and laboring class.

Senator Ryan is now a resident of Poteau. He was married June 24, 1883, in Crawford County, Arkansas, to Miss Laura E. Ford. They have nine children living: Wendell M., a printer in Poteau; Mrs. Hazel G. Adams, wife of a bookkeeper and salesman of Pittsburg, Kansas; Leonard G., in Alaska; Flora A., a teacher in Poteau; and Robert W., Louis M., Reba J., Berkley B., and Lucy A., all at home with their parents. Senator Ryan is a member of the Baptist Church and of the Woodmen of the World, and belongs to the Oklahoma Association of County Tax Assessors. His career as a teacher has been especially gratifying in that a large number of his pupils profited by his example and instruction and are filling honorable and lucrative financial and professional positions.

GEORGE H. MONTGOMERY. There is much of romance and considerable of tragedy contained in the history of a large region of the Chickasaw Nation of which the Washington ranch at Marietta was the center. Here for nearly forty years Bill and Jerry Washington had their activities among the leading live stock men of the Southwest. Near their ranches grew the little Town of Marietta that prospered and reached the proportions of a city of the first class between the years of the building of the Santa Fe Railroad and the entrance of the territories into statehood. The history of the Washingtons and of Marietta is another story, but a fragment of that history is contained in the activities of George H. Montgomery, of Valliant.

Mr. Montgomery was the first lawyer at Marietta, whence he went in April, 1904, the year in which a federal court was established there, and his practice in federal courts for a few years was before Judge Hosea Townsend and Judge J. T. Dickerson, who were assigned consecutively to the Southern District of Indian Territory. After statehood, in 1907, Mr. Montgomery was elected the first county judge of Love County, of which Marietta had become the county seat, and which obtained its name from Sobe Love, an Indian of parts and much wealth, and a picturesque character into whose family Jerry Washington married. Before he became county judge Mr. Montgomery was asked to write the will of Jerry Washington, which he declined because he feared that later the will would come before him as county judge, in which belief he was correct. J. R. McCalla, of Marietta, who was a member of the First State Legislature, wrote the will, which, during the term of office of Mr. Montgomery as county judge, was contested by certain of the children of Jerry Washington, unsuccessfully, however, and the estate of nearly $200,000 was divided as Jerry Washington had willed it.

Mr. Montgomery was born near Bells, Grayson County, Texas, in 1873, and is a son of George H. and Martha (Pritchett) Montgomery. His father, who was a native of Tennessee, settled in Grayson County, Texas, near the close of the Mexican war, in which two brothers who preceded him to the Lone Star State, Purris and Atwood Montgomery enlisted as soldiers and with General Scott went to the City of Mexico. Prior to the Civil war, George H. Montgomery, Sr., was a United States ranger in Texas and later received a pension as reward for his service in that capacity. His health did not permit him to fight for the Confederacy and during the war his time was largely given to the care of the wives and children of those who were at the front. He lived in Grayson County thirty-two years, and died in Hall County in 1906. The mother of George H. Montgomery, Jr., was descended from a Virginia family from which several educators of note came, among them Dr. Henry Pritchett, and Professor Pritchett, former state superintendent of education in Texas and president of the Sam Houston State Normal School.

Most of the education received by George H. Montgomery was as a student of a private college conducted by Prof. R. R. Halsell, now of Durant, Oklahoma, located at Savoy, Texas. When he completed his education there he became a teacher and taught for a number of years in Texas and Oklahoma, and for two years was in charge of the school at Supply, Oklahoma, near the historic old post of Fort Supply. He taught also at Texline, Texas, for two years, and while thus engaged applied himself so steadfastly to the study of law that he was admitted to the bar, and later was elected prosecuting attorney of Dallam County. Mr. Montgomery recalls that when he located at Dalhart there were but thirty-five voters in the county, whereas two years later the vote exceeded 1,200. He moved to Marietta, Indian Territory, in 1904 and after completing his term as county judge there, in January, 1911, moved to Valliant, where he has since lived. Here he has served as city attorney, and is in the enjoyment of a large, important and lucrative professional business.

Mr. Montgomery was married December 25, 1897, at Memphis, Texas, to Miss Pearl Pritchett, and they are the parents of five children: Maude, who is seventeen years of age; Joel, born in 1900; George H., Jr., born in 1903; William, aged ten years; and Rebecca Elizabeth, who is one year old. Mr. and Mrs. Montgomery and their children are members of the Presbyterian Church. He belongs to the McCurtain County Bar Association and the Oklahoma State Bar Association, and his fraternal affiliation is with the local lodge of the Knights of Pythias.

J. P. MARTIN. In 1893 J. P. Martin came to Cleveland, Oklahoma, and here started the first store that was operated in the city. It was a grocery in the beginning and later, in response to the incessant demand for a d goods establishment of some sort, he added that end of the business. Five years after the business was first established Mr. Martin built his present store, adding many facilities for the successful handling of his continually growing trade, and today six clerks are required to handle the business, with his supervision. The building is a one-story affair, with a floor space of 25x125 feet, and is adequate to the proper display of the stocks they handle. Mr. Martin has been successful, and has made a name and a position for himself in the town to which he came in its early days, and his prosperity is the just reward of his business integrity and energy.

Mr. Martin was born in St. James, Maries County, Missouri, on February 28, 1863, and he is a son of J. T. and Clementine (Underwood) Martin. The father was born in St. Louis County, Missouri, on December 25, 1814, and died in Cleveland at the home of his son in 1906, when he was ninety-two years old. He came of a family noted for its longevity, many of the men of his name having reached that fine old age. His wife, the mother of the subject, died when J. P. Martin was one month old, so that he was forever deprived of the love and care that should have been his in childhood. J. T. Martin was a farmer all his active life, carrying on his business in Missouri, his native state. Horse and mule buying and trading formed an important part of his lifework. He bought and sold in Missouri and Texas, driving his purchases from one point to another, for his greatest activity in that line was carried on prior to the days when railroads made transportation a simple problem. Before the war this thrifty Missourian sold goods on his farm, conducting a primitive sort of general store at his farm, and so adding much to the material comforts of the farming people in his section, as well as adding something to his legitimate profits and prosperity. When the war came on he disposed of that end of the business, but still carried on his buying and trading.

This native Missourian had two wives. There were nine children born of the first union, and three of the second. J. P. Martin of this review was the last of the nine.

Until he was eighteen years J. P. Martin lived at home with his father, obtaining what education he might in the primitive schools of that period, and helping on the home farm. When he was eighteen he went to Fort Smith, Arkansas, in company with his father and a brother, and they farmed there until 1888, when the subject went to Arizona and was there for two years, being engaged in operating the Arizona Ore Works at Prescott. In 1893 he was induced to come for the opening of the Cherokee Strip, and located in Cleveland, Oklahoma, and he was so impressed with the possibilities for the future that he established himself in business, as has already been set forth in the opening paragraph.

Other activities than merchandising have had a share in Mr. Martin's attention, and he is president of the Fidelity State Bank of Cleveland since its organization in 1912. In fact, he organized the bank and has since served as a member of its directorate, as well as being president of the concern. Mr. Martin has given a good deal of attention to gas and oil interests in this section of the state, and has located several paying properties, which he has disposed of from time to time after getting them in shape.

Politically Mr. Martin is a democrat and he is a member of the Cleveland Presbyterian Church. His fraternal affiliations are confined to the Knights of Pythias.

In 1897 Mr. Martin was married to Miss Gertrude Diem, who was born in Pennsylvania in 1874, and came to Kansas with her parents when a child of about five years. Two children have been born to the Martins. They are James Parvin, Jr., and Gertrude Maxime.

Mr. Martin is conducting the oldest mercantile establishment in Pawnee County, having started to carry on business in a tent on September 16, 1893, when the Cherokee Strip was first opened.

Among a number of family relics which Mr. Martin has in his possession is the old Bible used by Thomas R. Musick, a brother of his maternal grandmother. This pioneer Missourian was a well known circuit rider in the early days of Missouri and he organized and built the Fee Fee Church in 1801, which was the first church built in the Louisiana purchase, and is still standing on the old rock road near St. Louis, Missouri. He is a devout Christian and he spent his life in a labor of love that was productive of such results as no man can estimate in these later days.

ROBERT E. EDMISSON has had a long and favorable business experience in Western Oklahoma, particularly in Beaver County, was in the grain and elevator industry for some years, but now has an office at Gate, for the handling of real estate and farm loans.

He was born November 11, 1883, at Conway, Missouri, a son of George T. and Amanda M. (Stafford) Edmisson, and a grandson of John George Edmisson, a native of Kentucky. George T. Edmisson was born October 11, 1834, in a log house on a farm in Dallas County, Missouri. Early in life he was a teacher, gained admission to the bar at the age of twenty-four and at thirty-two was representing as attorney in Missouri the St. Louis and San Francisco Railway Company. He became one of the leading lawyers of the state. He also served two terms as county attorney of Dallas County, and was the founder of the Town of Conway. He rose to the distinction of the 33rd and Supreme Degree in Scottish Rite Masonry. He took that degree at a time when candidates for the honor were required to go to Scotland to receive the work. He was also a factor in democratic state politics in Missouri. His death occurred at Buffalo in that state August 3, 1909. In 1872 George T. Edmisson married Miss Stafford, whose father was Nathaniel Stafford, a native of Kentucky. She was born in Dallas County, Missouri, April 28, 1856. To their union were born ten children, nine sons and one daughter. Those now living are: Felix C., born October 28, 1876, and a merchant at Centralia, Washington; George I., born April 14, 1880, and a farmer and stockman in Harper County, Oklahoma; Robert E.; Albert P., born November 8, 1886, engaged in merchandising at Larned, Kansas; and Clarence R., born April 2, 1889, and a merchant at Gate, Oklahoma.

Robert E. Edmisson spent his early youth at Buffalo, Missouri. He attended public school there but at the age of twelve went out to live with a brother in Colorado Springs, Colorado, where he was graduated from the high school in 1907. He then removed to Englewood, Kansas, where for two years he was in mercantile pursuits and then with four brothers he engaged in the grain business under the name Edmisson Brothers. This firm had an elevator at Englewood, Kansas, and other elevators and shipping points at Knowles, Gate, Rosston and LaVerne, Oklahoma.

Mr. Edmisson sold out his business in the grain business in 1912, and since then has devoted his time successfully to the real estate and loan business. Fraternally he is a Mason. On October 2, 1907, at Englewood, Kansas, he married Miss Minnie Edith Walden, daughter of William and Emma Walden. Mrs. Edmisson claims Oklahoma as her native state. She was born January 1, 1891, in a sod ranch house owned by her father and located on Kiowa Creek at a point now in Beaver County. Her birth occurred nearly three years before the opening of the Cherokee Strip to settlement. Mrs. Edmisson spent most of her early life in Kansas, and graduated from the Englewood High School. They have one child, Francis Albert, born May 15, 1911, at Red Cliff, Colorado.

CAPT. GEORGE W. SUTTON, veteran of the Civil war, long a practicing physician in Cleveland, Oklahoma, for several terms a member of the Kansas and Oklahoma State legislatures and a banker of prominence in Cleveland and Bartlesville, has had a varied and interesting career, amply deserving of mention in this work.

Captain Sutton was born in Rising Sun, Indiana, August 5, 1843, and is a son of Joshua and Sarah (Wells) Sutton, natives of Pennsylvania and Ohio, respectively.

Joshua Sutton, be it said, was a young man when he left Pittsburg and sailed down the Ohio River seeking adventure and a new home. He was still young when he met and married Sarah Wells at Rising Sun, and they lived there until 1868. In that year they moved to Kansas, settling near Emporia, and there they passed their remaining years. He was a farmer all his life, and enjoyed a fair measure of success in that field. They were the parents of seven children, four sons and three daughters, three of whom are now living. Calvin, the eldest, a farmer all his days, is deceased. Mary Ann married first W. McIntyre, and second, B. Bodine and is deceased. Lucy is deceased. Candice also died young. The fifth child was George W., of this review. Rachel married Mr. Ridland and lives in Gardner, Kansas. Louis W. is a resident of Americus, Kansas. He served in the Civil war, a member of Company H, One Hundred and Forty-sixth Regiment Indiana Volunteer Infantry.

George W. Sutton lived with his parents on the home farm until he enlisted in 1862 in Company E., Fiftieth Indiana Volunteer Infantry. He served two years in that regiment, and later was a member of Company I, One Hundred and Thirty-ninth Indiana Volunteer Infantry, going out as a captain and serving until the close of the war. He was in action at the battles of Mills Springs, Kentucky, Shiloh, Three Days, and many other important engagements, acquitting himself creditably on all occasions.

Returning to pursuits of peace, the young captain turned his attention to the study of medicine. He studied first at Rising Sun and later at Cincinnati College of Medicine and Surgery, receiving his M. D. degree in 1867.

Captain Sutton, or Doctor Sutton, as he was then called, began medical practice in Americus, Kansas, and was there two years. He then went to Hartford, in the same county and continued in practice there until the year 1889. In 1881 he was elected to the state legislature of Kansas and served from 1881 to 1884, four successive terms in all. In the year 1889 he was appointed Government physician and served the Comanche, Wichita and Osage tribes in that capacity from 1889 to 1893.

Following that period of public service, Doctor Sutton resumed the practice of his profession; and he was thus engaged in Cleveland until a few years ago, when he withdrew from that field of labor and since has devoted himself to banking activities.

In 1900 he organized the First National Bank in Cleveland and the First National Bank in Bartlesville. He has been president of each bank since organization, and is now a member of their respective directorates. The First National Bank of Cleveland has a capital stock of $50,000, with deposits of more than $522,000, and a surplus and undivided profits aggregating $40,449.50. The officers and directors of the bank are men of high local standing, and the Bartlesville institution is run according to the same high standard that is one of the essentials of the Cleveland bank. Both banks have fine homes, the Bartlesville concern bearing the reputation of being the best housed bank in the state.

Doctor Sutton has been a lifelong republican, and has done excellent party work wherever he has been found. Since coming to Oklahoma he served one term in the Territorial Legislature in the years 1893-4 and he has served four terms as mayor of Cleveland. He was one of those who layed out the townsite of Cleveland in 1893, and from then until now has been a leading spirit in the affairs of the community city. He was regent of the State University and president of the Board of Regents for seven years, and has ever been the friend of the schools and colleges of the state. He has been financially interested in the Caney Valley Oil Company, and assisted in its organization. He is president of the Coronado Oil Company of Cleveland, capitalized at $50,000.

Doctor Sutton is a Mason since 1870, and has all degrees known to Masonry. He organized and was Master for six years of Hebron Lodge, Ancient Free and Accepted Masons of Cleveland. He also is a member of Grand Army of the Republic Post McPherson.

Doctor Sutton was married in Kansas in 1871 to Kate King, and they have three children. Birdie is the wife of Frank Boucher, cashier of the First National Bank of Bartlesville. Dr. F. R. Sutton is a practicing physician in Bartlesville. Leila is the wife of W. H. Boles, assistant cashier of the First National Bank of Cleveland.

The family have membership in the Methodist Episcopal Church. Mrs. Sutton is a prominent club woman, and is now president of the Mistletoe Club, and has been its president for ten years. She is also active in Eastern Star work.

RICHARD T. HOPE. Born in Wisconsin and reared and educated in Kansas, Mr. Hope has been a resident of Oklahoma since 1892 and is now one of the successful and highly esteemed representatives of the agricultural interests of Pawnee County, where he owns a well improved landed estate of 160 acres, in section 24, township 20, range 16, east, he being the only white man who has occupied the place and having purchased the property from the man who had filed claim to the same when this section was thrown open to settlement.

Richard Thomas Hope was born in Racine County, Wisconsin, on a farm near the City of Racine, which was then a mere village, and the date of his nativity was March 6, 1856. He is a son of Thomas and Mary Ann (Turner) Hope, both of whom were born and reared in Gloucestershire, England, where their marriage was solemnized and whence they immigrated to the United States in 1849. They remained in the State of New York about two years and in 1851 they numbered themselves among the pioneers of Racine County, Wisconsin, where the father was engaged in farming for several years. He then removed with his family to Missouri, where he remained one year, and in November, 1858, he set forth for Linn County, Kansas, the devoted wife and mother dying while enroute and being laid to rest in the cemetery at Rose Hill, St. Louis County, Missouri. Proceeding to his destination, Thomas Hope became a pioneer settler in Linn County, Kansas, where he took up Government land and instituted the reclamation of a farm, this homestead continuing to be his place of residence until his death; he died at the age of eighty-four.

In his native land he had succeeded his father in the local public office of road builder, and there he also followed for some time the trade of stone mason, his activities in this trade having continued also after he came to the United States. He and his wife were reared in the faith of the Church of England, but about 1860 he became identified with the Spiritualist organization, to the tenets of which he held zealously during the remainder of his life. Prior to his marriage, in 1843, he had made a trip to America and passed two years in the Dominion of Canada, where he taught in the common schools and also in Sunday school. He was a man of strong conviction, alert mentality and impregnable integrity in all of the relations of life. He was earnest in the support of the cause of temperance and his gentle and appreciative ideals were shown in his surpassing love of Nature and especially of flowers. Of his children the eldest is John, who still resides in Linn County, Kansas; Edwin is a resident of Colorado, and these two children were born in England. Sarah, the first to be born after the immigration to the United States, died in infancy, as did also the next child, a son; Elizabeth is the wife of Martin Van Buren Donley, of Pendleton, Oregon; Richard T., of this sketch, was the next in order of birth; and George died at the age of four years.

Richard T. Hope was about two years of age at the time of the family removal to Linn County, Kansas, where he was reared to manhood on the old homestead farm, in the work and management of which he continued to be associated with his father until he had attained to the age of thirty-two years, when he engaged in independent operations as a farmer in the same vicinity. There he became a prosperous farmer and there he continued his residence until the autumn of 1892, when he came to Oklahoma Territory and established himself as a farmer in Lincoln County. In 1893 he "made the run" at the opening of the Cherokee Strip, but failed to obtain a claim, and in the spring of 1894 he purchased the claim which constitutes his present homestead farm, all of the improvements on which have been made by him. He gives his attention to diversified agriculture and stock raising, and has extended oil leases on his land. He takes loyal interest in all that touches the welfare of the community, though never a seeker of public office, and in politics he is an ardent socialist.

In 1888 Mr. Hope wedded Miss Kate Witchey, who was born at Lanark, Carroll County, Illinois, on the 26th of June, 1867, and whose parents removed to Kansas in the autumn of the following year. She is a daughter of Jacob and Mary (Fox) Witchey, both natives of Germany. Mr. Witchey died in Kansas in 1880 at the age of seventy, and his widow still resides in Linn County, that state, he having been one of the pioneer farmers of that county. Mr. and Mrs. Hope became the parents of six children, of whom two are deceased: Byron, who died at the age of sixteen months, and Elston, who passed away at the age of three years. The surviving children are: Viola, Stanley, Harvey and Edna. Miss Viola has been a successful and popular teacher in the public schools of Pawnee County since 1911, and the family is one of special prominence and popularity in connection with the social activities of the community.

ELBERT I. HAWORTH, now editor and owner of the Gate Valley Star at Gate, has been closely identified with this section of Western Oklahoma for a number of years and before taking up the newspaper business was a successful teacher. He is succeeding in making his newspaper an organ of influential journalism in Beaver County, and has all the qualifications for the successful journalist.

Mr. Haworth was born February 12, 1889, on a farm in Republic County, Kansas, a son of John H. and Harriet (Baker) Haworth, both of whom were natives of Iowa and were married in 1881. John Haworth was born October 15, 1855, on a farm in Warren County, Iowa, and has spent his life as a farmer and as a minister of the Society of Friends. He is still active as a farmer and minister and lives in Beaver County, Oklahoma. His wife, who was born in Iowa, March 27, 1858, a daughter of John S. and Sarah (George) Baker, was a teacher for a number of years prior to her marriage, and she is also a devout Quaker in religion. They became the parents of four children, three sons and one daughter, namely: Ralph C., born December 27, 1882, now engaged in farming in Lipscomb County in the Texas Panhandle; Floyd C., born June 5, 1887, is now a member of the regular United States army and is employed in recruiting service; Elbert I.; and Cora E., born April 1, 1893, and married April 13, 1910, M. J. Keck, a farmer in Wood County, Oklahoma, and they have a child Zola born February 11, 1911.

Reared in the wholesome atmosphere of a Quaker family, Elbert I. Haworth finished his education in the Friends Academy at Ingersoll, Oklahoma. Prior to 1916 he taught seven terms in Beaver County, and during 1912-13 was a member of the County Examining Board for Teachers. In 1913 he bought the Gate Valley Star and is now giving all his time to its management both in the editorial and business department. Mr. Haworth is a member of the Society of Friends. On April 3, 1910, in Beaver County he married Miss Zela DeGroodt, daughter of John W. and Ella (Sharp) DeGroodt, natives of Iowa. Mrs. Haworth was born August 1, 1893, in Lynn County, Kansas. To their union have been born two children: Elver H., born February 5, 1911; and Pauline De, born December 13, 1914.

THOMPSON B. FERGUSON. It has been given to Hon. Thompson B. Ferguson to play a large and benignant part in the annals of Oklahoma history, and his loyal services found their apotheosis during the period of his admirable administration as governor of the territory, within the borders of which he established his residence in 1890, the year that marked the organization of Oklahoma Territory, so that, aside from his activities in public affairs, his is the honor of being a pioneer of this vigorous young commonwealth. His being called to the office of governor constitutes in itself ample voucher for his ability, his civic loyalty and public spirit and his strong hold upon popular confidence and esteem. In 1892, at the judicial center and now thriving metropolis of Blaine County, he founded the Watonga Republican, of which he has since continued the editor and publisher and which he has made one of the representative newspapers of the state, with wide influence in political and general public affairs and with the best of service in the exploiting of local interests and in formulating and directing popular sentiment and action.

On a pioneer farm in Polk County, Iowa, Mr. Ferguson was born on the 17th of March, 1857, and in the agnatic line he is a scion of fine old Scottish ancestry, being a descendant of James Ferguson, who in company with two of his brothers, immigrated from Scotland to America in the colonial period of our national history, representatives of the name in later generations having been conspicuous in connection with the development and civic and material progress of various of the younger states of the Union.

Mr. Ferguson is a son of Abner and Hannah (Atkinson) Ferguson, the former of whom was born in Mahoning County, Ohio, in 1823, a member of a sterling pioneer family of that section of the Buckeye State, and the latter of whom was a representative of a family early founded in Indiana, in which state she was born in 1831, her death having occurred in Kansas, in 1861, and her husband, who contracted a second marriage ultimately, having survived her by nearly forty years, his death having occurred at Emporia, Kansas, in 1900.

Abner Ferguson, a man possessed of the strong mentality and sterling character typical of the sturdy race from which he was sprung, was reared and educated in his native state, under the conditions and influences of the pioneer epoch in Ohio history, and as a young man he went to Henry County, Indiana, where his marriage was solemnized. He continued his residence in the Hoosier State until his removal to Iowa. He became one of the pioneer settlers in Polk County, where he obtained government land and engaged in farming and stock growing. In 1860 he removed with his family to Emporia, Kansas, and shortly afterward he engaged in agricultural pursuits and stock raising in that vicinity. He was later identified with the same basic industries in other parts of the Sunflower State, but he passed the closing period of his life in the City of Emporia, as previously noted in this context. In 1889, when Oklahoma was first thrown open to settlement, he came to the new territory, where he remained only a short time. He came again to the territory in 1891, but in 1893 he returned to Kansas, where he passed the residue of his long and worthy life. He was a resident of Kansas at the inception of the Civil war, and he represented that state as one of the loyal and gallant soldiers of the Union, his service, as a member of the Sixteenth Kansas Volunteer Infantry, having covered a period of nearly three years, within which he took part in numerous engagements marking the progress of the great conflict through which the integrity of the nation was preserved. After the close of the war, in 1866, he took part in an engagement with hostile Indians, on Powder River, Kansas, and his fortune it was to be wounded at this time, though he had escaped severe wounds during his prior and prolonged military service in the Civil war. Abner Ferguson was aligned as an uncompromising advocate of the principles of the republican party, was affiliated with the Grand Army of the Republic, the Masonic fraternity, and the Independent Order of Odd Fellows, his religious faith having been that of the Methodist Episcopal Church, of which he was a member for many years, the wife of his youth and younger manhood having likewise been a devout member of this church. They became the parents of five children: Emeline is the wife of Harry Butler, of Cleveland, Pawnee County, Oklahoma, and her husband is a prosperous farmer and dairyman of that locality; Isaac, who became one of the substantial agriculturists of Oklahoma, died at Skiatook, Tulsa County, at the age of fifty-five years; Ruth is the wife of Enoch Childers, a retired farmer, and they maintain their home in the City of Emporia, Kansas, where Mr. Childers continues his activities in the handling of blooded livestock; the former governor of Oklahoma, Thompson B., of this review, was the next in order of birth; and Mary, who became the wife of Charles Herron, died at Sherman, Cherokee County, Kansas, Mr. Herron being now a resident of Crawford County, that state, where he is a substantial farmer.

Thompson B. Ferguson gained the major part of his early educational discipline in the public schools of Emporia, Kansas, where he received the virtual equivalent of a high school course, and thereafter he completed his academic education in the Kansas State Normal School at Emporia, in which he was graduated as a member of the class of 1884. He put his scholastic acquirements to practical test and use by turning his attention to the pedagogic profession, of which he became a successful and popular representative as a teacher in the public schools of Wauneta and other places in Chautauqua County, Kansas. He also did effective service as an instructor at the teachers' institute held at Sedan, the judicial center of that county. He continued his pedagogic activities in the Sunflower State until 1890, when he identified himself fully and loyally with the newly organized Territory of Oklahoma, with no thought that here he would eventually be called upon to serve as chief executive of a great and prosperous commonwealth of the Union. In the preceding year, which had marked the opening of the territory to settlement, he had come here and obtained a claim of 160 acres, on Deep Fork, about eight miles distant from Oklahoma City. This claim he gave to his father, and in the spring of 1892 he established his permanent home at Watonga, the judicial center of Blaine County. He has been essentially and emphatically one of the founders and builders of this now prosperous and progressive little city, and here, on the 18th of October, 1892, he established the Watonga Republican, of which he has since continued editor and publisher. He has today one of the well equipped newspaper and job printing plants of Oklahoma, and the Republican has prestige and influence as one of the strong pioneer papers of Western Oklahoma, its circulation being of representative order throughout Blaine and surrounding counties, besides which its general excellence and its strong editorial utterances have given it also a very appreciable state circulation of general order and its friends and supporters have caused its list of subscribers outside of Oklahoma to reach proportions by no means insignificant. It is needless to say, by reason of its name and the marked prominence of its proprietor in the domain of Oklahoma politics, that the policy of the Republican is fundamentally that of furthering the cause of the republican party, of which Mr. Ferguson has been and continues one of the most prominent and influential representatives in the state.

During the entire period of his residence in Oklahoma Mr. Ferguson has shown a vital interest in all that has touched or tended to further the civic and industrial development and progress of the state—both under the territorial regime and since its admission to the Union. He has been personally and through the columns of his paper a leader in popular thought and action in this vigorous young commonwealth, and his influence has always been guided by the highest loyalty, by broad and well fortified convictions concerning governmental affairs and general public polity, and by an insistent desire to bring the state up to the highest possible standard in all things that make for a splendid and prosperous commonwealth. From 1895 to 1897 Mr. Ferguson was an active and prominent member of the Oklahoma Territorial Historical Society. In 1900 he was elected governor of the territory, his inauguration as chief executive taking place in the spring of 1901, and his retirement from office occurring on the 15th of January, 1906, so that he was the last of the territorial governors of Oklahoma, his admirable administration having become an integral part of the history of the state, with due record concerning the same, so that it is unnecessary in this connection to enter into details concerning his regime as governor. For nearly three years, under the administration of Governor Cruce, Mr. Ferguson was the republican member of the state election board. While a resident of Chautauqua County, Kansas, he served four years as a member of the board of teachers' examiners for the county, and in 1899 he held a similar position in Blaine County, Oklahoma. He attends and gives liberal support to the Methodist Episcopal Church at Watonga, of which his wife is a zealous member.

At Wauneta, Chautauqua County, Kansas, in June, 1885, was solemnized the marriage of Mr. Ferguson to Miss Elva Shartel, a daughter of the late David E. Shartel, who was a representative farmer of that county and who also served as county superintendent of schools. In conclusion is entered brief record concerning the children of Mr. and Mrs. Ferguson: Walter Scott, who was graduated in the military academy at Wentworth, Missouri, and who afterward completed a three years' course in the University of Oklahoma, is now editor and publisher of the Cherokee Republican, at the county seat of Alfalfa County, and is well upholding the journalistic prestige of the family name; Rowena died at the age of fifteen months, the family home at the time having been at Wauneta, Kansas; Tom Shartel, who was graduated in the Watonga High School and thereafter continued his studies for one year in the Methodist University at Guthrie, is now his father's valued assistant in the office of the Watonga Republican; Norna died at Sedan, Kansas, when two years of age; and Effie was 3½ years old at the time of her death, which occurred at Watonga, in 1899.

JOHN SCRUGHAN. An educator like every other professional man must be judged by the results of his work. For a city of its size Tonkawa has about as complete a school system and as perfect an organization for the efficient training of young citizens as can be found in the State of Oklahoma. This high standard of scholastic organization has frequently been attributed to the work of John Scrughan, who has been superintendent of the public schools of that city since 1910. The home of the schools and the center of his activities is a handsome $25,000 building, containing ten rooms, and with a teaching staff of ten instructors, presided over by Mr. Scrughan. The total enrollment of pupils is 425, and there is a well organized high school and in 1914 there were thirty-six graduates, Superintendent Scrughan having watched over this class from its entrance into high school until its graduation. Mr. Scrughan has vitalized the work of the school and has gathered about him a splendid corps of teachers. Mr. Scrughan succeeded as superintendent of the Tonkawa schools R. L. Johnson.

John Scrughan has had a long record as an educator beginning in country schools back in Illinois, where he was born on a farm in Richland County, January 4, 1864. His parents were George and Nancy Scrughan, substantial farmers and stock raisers in the Prairie State. They occupied the same homestead in Richland County for fifty-three years, and in that old home reared their five children, four sons and one daughter, all of whom are living in Illinois except John.

His early life was divided between the farm and country school, and he learned the lessons of industry and honor at home in addition to the instruction of a formal nature given in the schools. He studied at home and completed his education in the Valparaiso University in Indiana. His career as a teacher began in country schools, and later he was in the city schools in Clay County, Illinois, and in 1907 came to Oklahoma as one of the teachers at Coalgate. Three years later he came to Tonkawa to accept the superintendency and for the past five years has largely built up the school system to its present admirable condition.

In Clay County, Illinois, June 20, 1888, Mr. Scrughan married Olive L. Speers, a woman of education and culture, who has been a capable assistant to him in his work and also an admirable home maker. Her parents were B. R. and Emma Speers. Mr. and Mrs. Scrughan have three children: Bertha May, who is now a teacher in the public schools at Newkirk, Oklahoma; Mabel Agnes, a senior in the University of Oklahoma at Norman; and Raymond, still in the public schools. Mr. Scrughan is a republican in politics, affiliates with the Independent Order of Odd Fellows and is a member of the board of trustees of the Methodist Episcopal Church.

ISAAC S. DRUMMOND. The subject of this sketch was born in Jefferson County, Ohio, April 28, 1836. He is of Scotch-Irish stock, his father having been born in Ireland. His parents died when "Ike" was very young, and he was left to "rustle" for himself, having neither home nor guardian. He lived among the farmer folk in Harrison County, Ohio, earning his "keep" by doing chores and any sort of work that a boy between eight and eleven years of age could do.

A month before he was eleven years old he apprenticed himself to Alexander Hall, of the Village of Great Western, in Belmont County, Ohio, to learn the printing trade. Mr. Hall was a very prominent preacher in the Christian Church, a writer of distinction, and a noted debator of religious subjects. He was not yet thirty years old, but had written several books, and was the author of "Universalism Against Itself," a book that did much to curb the belief in universal salvation, regardless of the kind of life a man had lived.

Young Drummond served his apprenticeship of five years with Hall, who was at that time (1848) publishing a monthly religious magazine named The Gospel Proclamation. The printing office was well equipped for that age. There were but few of the modern conveniences, such as are found in almost all offices in these days, but a boy had to graduate in every branch of the art, from rolling the forms and making the rollers, to composition, proofreading, advertising and job work, stereotyping and wood letter cutting. Until he could show good grades in all departments he was not considered a printer. There were no power presses or rotary job presses in those days.

All the education young Drummond received until after the end of his apprenticeship he "dug" out of Mr. Hall's library. Mr. Hall owned a fine, big library, and he kindly granted the boy the use of it, and sometimes gave him some guidance in his reading. After his apprentice days were over he tried for further education at two or three advanced schools, or academies, paying good prices for all the instruction he received. There were no free schools in those days.

After he got his free papers he traveled to larger towns and worked in other offices to complete his trade, as was the rule in that age.

At the age of twenty-four years he married Miss Rebecca White, at Brighton, Iowa. From that time on, Drummond's life was very like that of the average American. He served in the Union army during the Civil war of '61 to '65. After the war he worked in various book and newspaper offices owned by other men; was editor, compositor, job and ad man; then bought and run newspapers and job offices in Iowa, Kansas, Texas and Oklahoma.

In his newspaper work Mr. Drummond has mostly been on the frontier, and did much to help settle the great Southwest. He has not done much writing during the past five years, except on special subjects for newspapers and magazines. However, his work is not yet done, even if he is more than four score years old.

His beloved wife died suddenly some ten years ago, but he has six children living, namely: Franz S. Drummond, editorial writer and printer, now located in the State of Washington; A. L. (Link) Drummond, ex-newspaper man, Christian minister and lawyer, Norton, Kansas; W. I. Drummond, chairman of the Board of Governors of the International Farm Congress, Enid, Oklahoma; George L. Drummond, editor and proprietor of The Glendale News, Glendale, Oregon; Mrs. Clara Smith, teacher of music, Beaver, Oklahoma; Mrs. Mary L. Keith, music teacher, Protection, Kansas. All of the children learned the printers' trade, the girls being expert compositors.

FRANK M. WHEELER. In the wonderful oil country of Creek County, Oklahoma, now conceded to be the biggest producing field in the world, one of the pioneers was Frank M. Wheeler, on whose property, now a part of Drumright, the first well was drilled. Mr. Wheeler is a self-made man, having spent the early years of his life at the stonecutter's trade prior to taking up agriculture and securing the land upon which oil was discovered solely through his own efforts. While he still maintains his office at Drumright, he makes his home at Stillwater, where he is connected with a number of interests and takes an active part in civic affairs.

Mr. Wheeler was born in Ross County, Ohio, June 22, 1857, and is a son of A. J. and Elizabeth (Smith) Wheeler. His father was a native of Ohio, and was married in that state, the mother having been born in Virginia and taken by her parents to Ohio as a child. After their marriage Mr. and Mrs. Wheeler moved to Pike County, Illinois, in 1865, and there Mrs. Wheeler died in 1870, when her son, Frank M., was thirteen years old. Subsequently the father went to Texas, where he engaged in farming, and died at Worth, in that state, when seventy-nine years of age. Of the seven children in the family, five were reared to maturity: John B., who is deceased; Frank M.; Everett, a resident of Kansas City, Missouri; Ollie White, who died at the age of twenty-two years, leaving one child; and Susie, who is the wife of Charles Wampler, of Kansas City, Missouri.

Frank M. Wheeler was educated in the public schools of Ohio and Illinois, and after the death of his mother learned the trade of stonecutter. In the winter of 1874-5 he went to Kansas, and following that worked all over Kansas, Colorado, Utah and Arkansas, following his trade. In 1891 he secured a claim in the Sac and Fox country, now in Lincoln County, Oklahoma, but continued to work at his vocation for several years more, in 1894 turning his attention to farming and stockraising. He continued to operate his Lincoln County property until the railroad was built through, when he disposed of his land at a profit, and this now comprises the present townsite of Agra. At that time he bought another property two miles north, on which he lived for eight years, and March 16, 1910, purchased a quarter section of land in Creek County, which now forms a part of Drumright. The lease on his farm was the first in the Cushing oil field, there was drilled the first well, and this was made payable to Mr. Wheeler when oil began running. The new sand taken from this well was named in his honor, and Wheeler sand has since become famous. Mr. Wheeler now has fourteen wells on this quarter section of land, and at times has produced as much as 3,500 barrels daily. In recent years he platted forty acres, known as Wheeler's First Addition to Drumright, a locality which is now almost entirely built up. He is the owner of a stock ranch of 1,200 acres, near Foraker, in Osage County, and owns also farm and residence properties in five counties of Oklahoma. In August, 1912, Mr. Wheeler came to Stillwater to make his home, and his residence, at No. 232 Duncan Street, is the finest in the city. Politically a democrat, he has not been an office seeker, but has at all times shown an interest in the welfare of his city and its institutions. He is a firm believer in the value of education, and his children have been given the best advantages available.

Mr. Wheeler was married in 1881 to Miss Hannah E. Fritch, a native of Indiana and a daughter of B. Fritch, and to this union there have been born nine children: Luella May, who is the wife of Arthur Pratt, of Pottawatomie County, Oklahoma; Carrie, the wife of Bert Evans, who is superintending the operations on Mr. Wheeler's ranch in Osage County; Josie, the wife of Robert Spartman, of Pottawatomie County; Maude, who is the wife of James Weaver, of Creek County, Oklahoma; Frank, who is employed on the Osage County ranch; Pearl, Blanche and Birdie, who are all attending the Agricultural and Mechanical College, at Stillwater; and Babe.

SHIRLEY CHAPMAN. A veteran Oklahoma newspaper man, Shirley Chapman, now of Oklahoma City, is associated with the Oklahoma Publishing Company, publishers of the Oklahoman, the Times and the Farmer-Stockman. He has been connected with a number of different newspapers in Western Oklahoma, and has the distinction of having helped publish and bring out the first paper ever issued in the Cherokee Strip.

He was born February 3, 1874, at Pleasant Hill, Missouri, the youngest of the four children of Benjamin Franklin and Alma W. (Welch) Chapman. His father was born September 27, 1832, in Vermont, was a contractor and builder, and followed that business in a number of different localities until 1889, when he joined the first rush of settlers in Oklahoma. Going to El Reno, he secured a claim three miles south of the city and soon became prominent and well known in local affairs. During the early days there he served as a justice of the peace. His wife, Alma W. Welch, was born in Russelltown, Canada, November 25, 1836. Of their children the three besides Shirley were: Hermione L., who has for many years been a successful teacher in Missouri, Kansas and Oklahoma, and is still living unmarried with his parents at El Reno; Alma is the wife of David T. Slatten, a farmer of Bethany, Missouri; and Leonora, who died in infancy.

Shirley Chapman obtained most of his education in the public schools of Sedalia, Missouri. When fourteen years of age he began learning the printing trade at Wichita, Kansas, and in the following year, when he came with his parents to El Reno, this experience opened for him an opportunity at employment on some of the first papers established in that city.

In 1893, with the opening of the Cherokee Strip, he and Frank L. Grove established and printed the first newspaper ever issued in the Cherokee Strip after the opening. It was the Daily Enterprise of Enid. The first copies of the Enterprise came from the press on Monday, September 18th, two days after the opening. After settlement there Mr. Chapman became editor and publisher of the Waukomis Wizard at Waukomis, but at the end of two years he sold that paper and returned to his old home at El Reno. Here he was editor of the Daily Star and Weekly Herald until 1902, and beginning in 1905 was for four years city editor of the El Reno Daily American. In 1915 he came to Oklahoma City, where he has since been associated with the Oklahoma Publishing Company. He is active in newspaper circles, has a wide acquaintance with newspaper men all over the state, and is one of the honored figures in Oklahoma journalism.

Mr. Chapman is also well known for his activities in a musical way. For a number of years he was instructor and leader of a band and orchestra at El Reno, and has done much to organize and promote musical entertainment in El Reno and several other cities of the state. He is unmarried, is a charter member of El Reno Lodge, No. 743, Benevolent Protective Order of Elks, and is a member of the Episcopal Church.

HENRY CLAY. One of the oldest residents of the vicinity of Bartlesville, where for many years he was engaged in a blacksmithing and general repair business, Henry Clay is now engaged in farming on a leased Osage allotment, located 2½ miles northwest of the city. He came to this part of the country practically without means, and through industry and constant effort has advanced himself steadily to a position of financial independence and a place of esteem in the minds of his fellow citizens. His career is illustrative of the rewards to be gained through honest labor and fidelity to the engagements of life.

Mr. Clay is a native of the Empire State, born in Erie County, February 24, 1854, a son of John and Sarah (Crispin) Clay, natives of Lincolnshire, England. The father was born March 18, 1819, and the mother January 7, 1820, and not long after their marriage they emigrated to the United States, locating first at Buffalo, New York, in 1846. Seeking the better opportunities offered by the West, in 1854 John Clay, who was a farmer, took his family to the State of Iowa, where he lived for sixteen years. In 1870 he moved on to Kansas, locating in the vicinity of Coffeyville, where he settled on a farm and continued to be engaged in agricultural pursuits during the remaining years of his life, his death occurring in July, 1882. Mrs. Clay survived him until September, 1905, and died at Bartlesville, Oklahoma. They were the parents of four children, as follows: Elizabeth, deceased, who was the wife of Mr. Paxon and was born in England; Anna, born in New York, married Millett, and is now a resident of Kansas City, Missouri; Henry, of this notice, and William, a resident of Lenapah, Oklahoma.

Henry Clay was an infant when taken by his parents to Iowa, and there his education was secured in the public schools. He remained under the parental roof until about the year 1875, when he started learning the blacksmith trade, a vocation which he subsequently followed for upwards of thirty years, at Coffeyville, Kansas, and Bartlesville, Oklahoma. In partnership with A. I. Morgan, a sketch of whose career will be found on another page of this work, he founded the firm of Morgan & Clay, which was at the time of its founding and for many years afterward the only blacksmith and general repair shop on the south side of the Carney River, there being only one store on that side of the river at that time. Mr. Morgan was skilled in woodworking, and accordingly took charge of the work that came to the firm in that direction, while to Mr. Clay fell the task of upholding the blacksmithing end of the firm's business. This enterprise, started in a modest way, gradually grew and developed, attracting trade from all over this part of the county because of the excellent manner in which work was done and the dependable manner in which the partners lived up to all contracts. The partnership continued successfully and congenially until 1913, when, by mutual consent, it was dissolved and the business, after its long and prosperous career, was sold. In January, 1915, Mr. Clay leased his present home, an Osage allotment on Bartles Creek, 2½ miles north of the City of Bartlesville. Here he is operating 180 acres of land, on which he has good improvements, and carries on diversified farming and stock raising. He is using the most modern approved methods in his work, and is making the same success in his agricultural ventures that he attained as a blacksmith. In addition to farming, Mr. Clay continues to engage in selling farm implements, an occupation which he has carried on as a side line for ten years. In political matters a republican, he has long taken a keen interest in civic affairs, and has an excellent record as a public official in the offices of councilman and mayor of Bartlesville. He is a charter member of the Woodmen of the World, the first lodge organized at Bartlesville, and also holds membership in the local lodge of the Independent Order of Odd Fellows, of which he is a charter member, and the Rebekahs of Bartlesville. During his entire career at Coffeyville and Bartlesville he has enjoyed the esteem of his fellow-citizens, and at the present time he has a large number of friends who wish him success in his new venture.

On November 6, 1893, Mr. Clay was married to Miss Emma Foster, who was born in 1864, in Macon, Illinois, and was fourteen years of age when taken to Kansas by her parents, John and Jane (Gassaway) Foster, the former born in Kentucky, April 11, 1841, and the latter in Ohio, September 30, 1841. They were married at Springfield, Illinois, and in 1878 moved to Coffeyville, in the vicinity of which city Mr. Foster was engaged in farming. He later moved to Havensville, Kansas, where he died September 16, 1892. Mrs. Foster still survives and makes her home with her daughter, Mrs. Alice Skinner, at Caney, Kansas. They were the parents of three daughters and four sons who are now living, Mrs. Clay being the second child in order of birth. To Mr. and Mrs. Clay there have been born two children: Hattie, the wife of G. S. Hill, an attorney of Bartlesville, who has three children, Lillian, Ruth and George J.; and Sadie, the wife of Ross Spick, has one child, Emma.

HON. NEAL WILTBANK EVANS. While it is usual to speak of the pioneers of Oklahoma as the men who settled here about the time of the first opening in 1889, such a distinction is hardly adequate to describe the long residence and business, official and civic standing of such men as the late Judge Evans of El Reno. For nearly half a century he was identified with the west half of old Indian Territory and with the Territory and State of Oklahoma. He was one of the hardy and courageous men who chose the activities of the western frontier when a cordon of military forts and establishments were necessary to protect the advancing tide of civilization and settlement. He knew and was actively identified with the country around El Reno since the establishment of the military post of Fort Reno. From the year of statehood he gave a capable service as police judge of the City of El Reno.

Neal Wiltbank Evans was born at Lewis, Sussex County, Delaware, May 20, 1844, a son of William and Hettie (Cullen) Evans. His father was born at Baltimore Hundred, Delaware, and his mother at Berlin, Maryland. The Evans family, long established in Delaware, is of Welsh origin, while the Cullens were English. William Evans was a Methodist minister by profession, and lived and died in his native state. He was the father of four daughters and eight sons.

At the age of ten years Judge Evans, after a brief schooling, went to Philadelphia and had a thorough apprenticeship in the dry goods business. The persistency of his character is well illustrated in the fact that he was in the employ of one merchant in that city fourteen years. Eventually his fidelity was rewarded by promotion to a partnership.

It was in the year 1867 that Mr. Evans came West with his brother Jack and with John Fisher. Under the firm name of Evans and Fisher his brother and partner became general merchants with stores known as post or Indian traders' stores at Forts Gibson, Arbuckle and Sill in the old Indian Territory. With this firm Judge Evans was identified until 1876, and in that year was appointed post or Indian trader at Fort Reno. Fort Reno, it should be explained, is distinct from El Reno, the city. Fort Reno has been a military post since 1876, and is still in existence as a military reservation, being a remount station. It lies five miles west of the City of El Reno. The City of El Reno came into existence in 1889 after the opening of the original Oklahoma Territory.

As post or Indian trader at Fort Reno Judge Evans remained for about fourteen years. With the opening of Oklahoma to settlement and the establishment of El Reno, Mr. Evans as an old timer and man of ability at once became a leading citizen of the new community, and thenceforward held a conspicuous place in the development of the city. For several years he was proprietor of a "racket store" at El Reno, and gave up this business when seriously injured in a runaway accident.

He was one of the original councilmen of El Reno and in 1907 became police judge of the city, a position in which his service was both prompt and efficient and in which he continued until stricken with paralysis, resulting in his death on November 11, 1915. In the early days of Canadian County he held for two terms of two years each the position of county treasurer. Judge Evans was always a republican in politics.

Probably no man was held in higher esteem in El Reno and Canadian County. He had been identified with Oklahoma nearly fifty years, and in that time had come in contact with all the classes of its population and with many of its most prominent characters. He became intimately acquainted with many of the men who were commanding officers of the various frontier posts, such as Sheridan, McKenzie and Lawton, whose confidence he always enjoyed, and he was likewise a friend of those old scouts Cody, Stillwell, Clark, Morrison and Horace P. Jones. He possessed a rare fund of information as to incidents and history of the territory and state and its people, and was one of the last survivors of the early pioneers. In church faith Judge Evans was a Presbyterian. He was one of the oldest Masons of Oklahoma, having taken the Master's degrees in early life, and being a life member of the lodge back in his native state. He was a Knight Templar and also a member of the Mystic Shrine.

In 1868 Judge Evans married Miss Sallie Hague, who was born in Philadelphia. She possessed many excellent qualities of heart and mind and as his helpmate gave him a courage sufficient to surmount the many obstacles in their pioneer life in Oklahoma. Mrs. Evans died in 1894, and her death was an irreparable loss to her husband and two surviving daughters. Two of the children died in childhood, and the daughters now living are: Hettie, wife of Judge W. A. Maurer of El Reno; and Mary, wife of Rev. Archibald Cardle, D. D., pastor of the First Presbyterian Church of Burlington, Iowa.

HON. GUSTAVUS ADOLPHUS RAMSEY. Representative in the fifth legislature from Bryan County, Gustavus Adolphus Ramsey is one of the older American citizens in Oklahoma, and has been prominent as a farmer and stockman in the old Choctaw country for many years. He became a factor in politics before the success of the statehood movement, and has represented both his party and the people in various commissions and offices. His home is at Colbert. Having come from Texas into the Choctaw Nation in early days, Mr. Ramsey brought many ideas on agriculture and stock raising that were of value to the natives, and during the twenty-eight years of his residence there has been one of the most conspicuous in the upbuilding of that region.

Gustavus Adolphus Ramsey was born in Pittsylvania County, Virginia, July 24, 1857, a son of John C. and Judie Ramsey. His father was descended from natives of Scotland who settled in Pennsylvania before the Revolution and later participated in that war as residents of Virginia. John C. Ramsey brought his family out from Virginia to Northern Texas in 1866, making the journey with wagon and team, and from Fannin County, the place of his first settlement, subsequently removed to Grayson County. Gustavus A. Ramsey was nine years of age when he came to Texas, and on account of the disturbed conditions of society in the South during war times and the years immediately following had little opportunity to go to school, and acquired the most satisfactory part of his early training while in Grayson County. At the age of twenty-one he went to Fort Sill, Oklahoma, then a post on the frontier, and spent two years as a freighter. In 1886 he crossed the Red River and located in what is now Bryan County, Oklahoma, and thenceforth identified himself with farming and stock raising. In recent years Mr. Ramsey has specialized in Duroc hogs, and has taken some premiums on his animals.

His first noteworthy participation in politics was in 1905 when selected as a member of the executive committee of fourteen by the Statehood Convention to assist in getting legislation from Congress admitting Indian and Oklahoma territories to statehood. He sat as a delegate in the convention at Ardmore that selected the first democratic national committeeman for Indian Territory. For some time he has been president of the Democratic Club at Colbert and manager for his precinct in behalf of prohibition in campaigns involving that subject. Governor Lee Cruce appointed him a member of the State Board of Agriculture that was created in 1913, as a result of an initiatory act submitted to the people. Mr. Ramsey represented the State Board of Agriculture at the National Farmers Congress in Washington in November, 1913. He resigned his seat on the board January 6, 1915, to take his place as representative in the fifth legislature, following his election in November, 1914. In the legislature Mr. Ramsey served as chairman of the Committee on Charities and Corrections, and a member of committees on education, insurance, relation to the Five Civilized and other Indian tribes, and general agriculture. His interests were chiefly in measures affecting agriculture, and it was his thorough and long experience in that subject that has given his service special value to the law making body. He was author of a bill prohibiting the operation of pool and billiard halls for hire, and of a bill accepting the provisions of the Smith-Lever law enacted by Congress relating to co-operation with the National Government by the state in farm demonstration and extension work.

Mr. Ramsey married, December 24, 1891, Miss Amanda Potts, granddaughter of Benjamin Love, one of the prominent Choctaws who once represented his tribe before the department in Washington. Mrs. Ramsey is related to the Choctaw family of Colbert, that have long been conspicuous in the old Choctaw Nation. Mr. and Mrs. Ramsey have a daughter, Mabel, aged sixteen, now finishing her second year in the literary department of Baylor College at Belton, Texas.

Mr. Ramsey is a member of the Baptist Church, and clerk, deacon and Sunday school superintendent, and was a member of the first Baptist general convention of old Indian Territory. He is affiliated with Lodge No. 80, Ancient Free and Accepted Masons at Colbert, having filled the chair of master, and is also affiliated with Lodge No. 75, Independent Order of Odd Fellows, at Colbert, and has been officially honored in that order, and has been representative from the Colbert lodges in the grand lodges of both the Masons and Odd Fellows. Mr. Ramsey is a member of the Farmers Institute of Bryan County, and of the National Farmers Educational and Co-operative Union. He was the first president of the First National Bank of Colbert. Mr. Ramsey was appointed a member of the reception committee to receive President Wilson at Muskogee, in April, 1915, during the Southern Commercial Congress.

K. L. COLLEY, M. D. The leading representative of the medical and surgical profession in the community of Big Heart since 1907 has been Doctor Colley. Doctor Colley is an eastern man of old Virginia colonial family, and came to Oklahoma after a thorough training and with a generous equipment for his chosen vocation. Doctor Colley has securely established himself in the esteem of the people of Osage County, has a large and profitable practice, and has that faculty which enables him to make friends wherever he goes.

Born at Birchleaf, Virginia, September 14, 1877, Doctor Colley is a son of Richard J. and Mary E. (Hill) Colley, both of whom were born in the Old Dominion State. His father died in 1913 at the age of sixty-nine at the old home at Birchleaf, where the mother still lives. The Colleys were of Scotch-Irish stock, and the family was settled in Virginia before the Revolution. Richard J. Colley spent his life as a farmer, and during the war between the states was in the Confederate army, and many of his relatives gave up their lives in the struggle. One of a family of nine children, four sons and five daughters, all of whom are still living, Doctor Colley grew up in Dickenson County, Virginia, had the environments and influences of a Virginia farm, and was educated in the local schools. He finally went to Kentucky and entered the University School of Medicine at Louisville, from which he was graduated M. D. in 1907. Soon after his graduation he moved to the new State of Oklahoma, and has since been in active practice at Big Heart. Doctor Colley has a special diploma representing his study and experience in the treatment of diseases of children, but spends his time in the general practice of medicine and surgery. Doctor Colley rendered notable service at Big Heart during the cyclone of 1911, when he was the only medical man capable of assuming the sudden responsibilities devolving upon him as a result of that calamity. Three persons were killed during the storm, and sixty wounded, and he was the first to bring medical aid to the sufferers, and carried thirty-nine of the wounded and injured to the Tulsa Hospital on a special train.

Politically Doctor Colley is also well known in his home community and state, and is now a member from Osage County of the State Democratic Committee. He belongs to the County and State Medical societies, and is affiliated with the Masonic Order, the Knights of Pythias and the Benevolent and Protective Order of Elks.

On July 18, 1912, he married Miss Ertle Swift. Mrs. Colley was born in Oklahoma, and her father, James A. Swift, was one of the pioneer settlers. To their marriage have been born two children: Elander and Beatrice.

HENRY W. SITTON. Elected representative of Stephens County in the State Legislature, Mr. Sitton proved a most zealous and efficient member of the lower house during the fifth general assembly, in which he introduced and ably championed a number of wise and important measures. He is engaged in the practice of law at Duncan, the judicial center of Stephens County and through his sterling attributes and effective services he has gained secure place as one of the representative members of the bar of the southern part of the state.

Mr. Sitton was born near Houston, Texas County, Missouri, on the 12th of May, 1874, and is a son of James and Sarah R. Sitton, the former a representative of an old and influential family of the South, where his father and grandfather were prominently identified with the iron industry at Birmingham, Alabama. James Sitton removed from Alabama to Missouri at the time of the Civil war, and later he removed with his family to Northern Arkansas. His wife is a native of Georgia. Her maiden name was Wilson and she is a descendant of the early settlers of Virginia. Of the children of James and Sarah R. Sitton Henry W. was the youngest in order of birth; George W. is a farmer in the vicinity of St. Joe, Arkansas; Cicero is engaged in the mercantile business at Pyote, Texas; William is a successful farmer and stock grower in Stephens County, Oklahoma, and resides near Comanche; James P. is a farmer in Okfuskee County, this state; Mrs. Nancy McClain resides near Calico Rock, Arkansas, her husband being a farmer by vocation; and Mrs. Mary Russell is the wife of a prosperous farmer residing near St. Joe, Arkansas.

Henry W. Sitton was a child at the time of the family removal to Arkansas and as his parents were in very modest financial circumstances he became dependent upon his own resources in acquiring his liberal education. He was enabled to attend, with more or less regularity, the public schools of Northern Arkansas until he had attained to the age of thirteen years, and later he provided the means necessary to defray the expenses incidental to the completion of a course in high school. He left the Harrison School in 1891 and for the ensuing three years was a student in the Valley Springs Academy in Boone County, Arkansas, where he finally received a scholarship that admitted him to Hendrix College, at Conway, Arkansas. In this institution he prosecuted higher academic studies during the years 1894 and 1895, and thereafter he entered Mountain Home College, at Mountain Home, that state, in which institution he was graduated in June, 1897, and from which he received the degree of Bachelor of Science. In the same year he was elected president of Big Flat Academy, at Big Flat, Arkansas, and he continued the executive head of this institution four years. In 1900 Mr. Sitton was appointed county examiner of Baxter County, whereupon he returned to Mountain Home. While incumbent of this office he held also a position as member of the faculty of Mountain Home College, where he served in turn in the chairs of higher English and higher mathematics.

In 1904 Mr. Sitton established his residence at Comanche, Indian Territory, where he engaged in the practice of law, for which work he had prepared himself through private study of assiduous order and through technical reading in the office and under the preceptorship of the law firm of Horton & Smith, at Mountain Home, Arkansas, where he was admitted to the bar in 1901. He continued his residence at Comanche until the admission of Oklahoma to statehood, in 1907, and on the 15th of May, 1908, he was appointed deputy county attorney of Stephens County, this preferment leading to his removal to Duncan, the county seat, where he has since maintained his residence. In 1910 Mr. Sitton was elected county attorney and was re-elected to that position in 1912, and in the last election there came to him a most gratifying evidence of popular confidence and approval, in that he received the largest majority ever given to any candidate for county office in that county—1,624 votes out of a total voting strength of approximately 1,800, and his opponent having been D. A. Bridges, who was also his opponent in the 1910 election. Concerning his administration as county attorney the following consistent estimate has been given: "He was among the most active officials of the State in conserving the suppression of crime, especially in the enforcement of the prohibition law, and he succeeded in breaking up one of the most obnoxious and thoroughly organized bands of horse thieves that had ever infested that section of the state. He was punctilious and indomitable in his efforts to foster law and order, and malefactors in Stephens County gained a wholesome fear of him."

In the primary election of 1914 Mr. Sitton was nominated by a plurality of 1,000 votes, in a strongly contested election, and as candidate for representative of his county in the State Legislature the ensuing popular election gave to him a most gratifying and significant majority, his political allegiance being given to the democratic party. In the fifth legislature Mr. Sitton was chairman of the committee on criminal jurisprudence, and a member of each of the following named committees also: Legal advisory, appropriations, congressional redistricting, public-service corporations, public buildings, constitutional amendments, retrenchment and reform, revenue and taxation, and state capitol. He urgently championed amendments to the judicial code in the matter of avoiding useless litigations; he introduced an amendment in repeal of the law requiring county treasurers to notify taxpayers of the impending delinquency of their taxes, this action being based on the Supreme Court ruling which made such an amendment virtually imperative; he introduced a bill providing that in all civil cases in which a jury is demanded, the demand shall be made within three days after the issues at law are joined, thus eliminating the holding of jurymen during the trial of cases not demanding a jury and enabling the judge to so arrange his docket that all jury cases shall be tried at the beginning of the term and the venire then be discharged. Mr. Sitton manifested also a lively interest in the deliberations relative to amendments to the primary election law and the matter of preferential primaries. A distinguished honor was conferred on him by the fifth legislature before adjournment, in that he was unanimously selected to aid the house managers in the impeachment trials of A. P. Watson, corporation commissioner, and A. L. Welch, insurance commissioner.

In his home city of Duncan Mr. Sitton is past chancellor commander of Mistletoe Lodge, No. 117, Knights of Pythias; is master of Duncan Lodge, No. 60, Ancient Free and Accepted Masons; and affiliated with Duncan Chapter, No. 20, Royal Arch Masons. He is a member of the Duncan Commercial Club, holds membership in the Stephens County Bar Association and the Oklahoma State Bar Association, and both he and his wife are zealous members of the Christian Church.

At Mountain Home, Arkansas, on the 12th of November, 1903, was solemnized the marriage of Mr. Sitton to Miss Stacye Baker, daughter of John T. Baker, a representative merchant of that place. Mrs. Sitton was graduated in the department of elocution and expression in Mountain Home College and later was a teacher of elocution in Big Flat Academy, at the time when her husband was principal of that institution. Mr. and Mrs. Sitton have four children: Frances Elizabeth, Mary Louise, Ellen Virginia, and Rebecca Jean.

DAVID S. SCHUBER. Few men have lent more practical encouragement to the agricultural and grain interests of Alfalfa County than has David S. Schuber, of Byron, general manager of the Byron Alfalfa Mill and Elevator Company. Coming here in 1913, he bought his present business and since that time has been identified with the commercial, industrial and civic interests of his adopted community, and has proven himself a valuable and helpful citizen. Mr. Schuber is a man of industry and enterprise; otherwise, he could not have gained his present standing in the business world, for his father died when he was still a lad, and he has always been compelled to depend upon his own resources to gain for him the things that he has wanted in life.

By birth a Russian, Mr. Schuber was born January 3, 1871, a son of David and Lizzie (Eckhart) Schuber, who were born in Russia of German parents. The family came to the United States in 1878, when David S. was seven years of age, and located on a farm in Kansas, where the father continued to be engaged in agricultural operations until his death, which was caused by the explosion of a lamp at his home in Russell County, Kansas, in 1883. The mother survived until 1903 and died on a farm in Marion County, Kansas, to which she had removed following the death of her husband. Mr. and Mrs. Schuber were the parents of four sons and three daughters, namely: Adam, who is deceased; David S.; Mollie; Henry; Mary; Annie, who is deceased; and Samuel.

David S. Schuber was reared on the family farms in Russell and Marion counties, Kansas, was brought up to industry and honorable dealing, and reared to appreciate the value of hard work and thrift. In the meantime he attended the public schools, his education being limited to the branches offered by the country schools, but being a lad of retentive memory and an apt scholar he obtained a good training, which has since been added to by observation, reading and coming into contact with men and affairs. In 1892 Mr. Schuber left Kansas for Oklahoma, being one of those who sought land in the opening of the Cheyenne and Arapahoe Reservation, April 21st. He was successful in securing a homestead, locating on Government land in Blaine County, and there proved up on his tract and developed a good farm, with substantial buildings and many improvements. Of this he was able to dispose at a good figure in 1901, when he decided to try his fortunes in a mercantile venture, at Ferguson, Oklahoma. While this enterprise proved satisfactory, he saw a broader field in the grain business, and accordingly disposed of his interests in the store to enter upon a career as a miller, continuing in the same line at Ferguson until 1913, when he came to Byron, which has since been his place of residence and the scene of his business success. When he came here Mr. Schuber purchased the plant of the Byron Alfalfa Milling Company, and here he has been engaged in the manufacture of alfalfa meal and other products. He has since established an elevator, in connection with which he purchases and handles grain of all kinds, but principally wheat, on a large scale, shipping to all points. The extent of his operations may be seen in the fact that he has already shipped more than 40,000 bushels of grain in a year from Byron, thereby contributing in no small way to the business importance and prestige of this thriving little Oklahoma community. Mr. Schuber is also the owner of the only hotel at Byron, the Commercial Hotel, which is managed by Mrs. Schuber, who has built up a large business and won the patronage of the traveling public by the homelike manner in which the hostelry is arranged and the many comforts prepared for the guests.

Mr. Schuber was married December 8, 1892, in Marion

County, Kansas, to Miss Lizzie Adler, who was born in Russia, September 20, 1876, and came with her parents to the United States in 1884, they being Jacob and Lizzie (Schlotthauer) Adler, now residents of Marion County, Kansas. Six children have been born to this union: Hanna, Emanuel, Lida, Elsie, Jacob and Evelyn. Mr. Schuber is a popular member of the local lodge of the Independent Order of Odd Fellows. A republican in politics, he has been too closely devoted to business affairs to engage actively in the public arena, but has never refused his support to any movement which would advance the welfare of his community or the civic, moral or educational betterment of its people.

GEORGE E. ELLISON has the distinction of having opened the first merchandise store at Guymon, Oklahoma. He is now manager of the Star Mercantile Company there. In many ways during the last fifteen years his name and activities have been closely identified and associated with the growth and prosperity of that community. As a merchant he has made his business a reliable service to a constantly growing circle of patronage, while as a citizen his part has been equally public spirited and nothing affecting the welfare of Guymon has passed without his consideration and helpful support.

He was born February 7, 1878, at Coatsburg, Illinois, a son of Henry and Irene (Guymon) Ellison. He was one of two sons, and his brother Arthur E. was born at the same place in Illinois May 17, 1880.

In 1879 the family moved to Kansas, and he completed his education in the public schools of Topeka and Liberal. While living at Liberal he had his first experience in merchandising, and was also the first cashier of the First National Bank of that town.

Mr. Ellison was just twenty years of age when the Spanish-American war broke out. He enlisted in the famous Twentieth Kansas Regiment, commanded by Colonel, now General, Fred Funston. He went out as principal musician, and was with the regiment in its Philippine campaign. Mr. Ellison had marked talent for music as a boy, and has always been extremely interested in musical affairs.

It was in 1901 that he located at Guymon, Oklahoma, opened the first store there, and has kept at the forefront in the progress of the community. While an active republican, and liberally supporting the party, he has never sought any office for himself. Mr. Ellison is a thirty-second degree Scottish Rite Mason and a member of the Mystic Shrine.

On June 25, 1902, in Texas County, Oklahoma, he married Miss Carrie Lee Cain, daughter of Zach and Thena (Smith) Cain. Mrs. Ellison was born in Virginia May 25, 1882. They have four children, all daughters: Irene, born August 17, 1903; Helen, born July 5, 1904; and Gaynette and Dolores, twins, born July 8, 1908.

ROBERT LONG. After a varied experience in the states of Texas, Kansas and Missouri, Mr. Long came to Oklahoma in 1892 and became one of the pioneers in the present Pawnee County at the time when the Cherokee Strip was thrown open to settlement, in the following year. He here obtained a homestead claim and from a beginning of most modest order he has pressed forward in worthy achievement until he has gained secure status as one of the representative agriculturists and stock growers of the county, his well improved landed estate being situated in the vicinity of the Village of Jennings, which is his postoffice address. His life has been one of consecutive application and he has so availed himself of opportunities afforded in connection with industrial enterprise in Oklahoma that he has gained substantial prosperity, the while he is significantly appreciative of and loyal to the state of his adoption.

Mr. Long was born in the State of Tennessee, on the 5th of May, 1845, and is a son of John E. and Catherine (Hawser) Long, both natives of Pennsylvania and both of sterling German ancestry, the respective families having been founded in the old Keystone State in an early day, and both the paternal and maternal grandparents of the subject of this review having used the German language exclusively. The parents of Mr. Long were children at the time of the removal of the respective families to Tennessee, where they were reared to maturity and where their marriage was solemnized. In 1850 they removed from that state to Jersey County, Illinois, in which state the father devoted his attention very effectively to agricultural pursuits. He was born on the 10th of October, 1819, and attained to venerable age, the closing period of his life having been passed in Carroll County, Missouri, to which state he removed about the year 1884, his death having there occurred in July, 1907. In Tennessee he had followed the trade of shoemaker and after his removal to Illinois he not only became a farmer but also worked at the carpenter's trade. His wife, who was born in 1822, died in Illinois, on the 12th of November, 1862. Of their children the eldest is Mrs. Jane Rankin, who maintains her home at Carrollton, Missouri; Mrs. Sarah E. Dampkey is a widow and resides in Madison County, Illinois; Robert, subject of this sketch, was the next in order of birth; Jonathan H., who was born November 18, 1847, was a resident of the city of East St. Louis, Illinois, at the time of his death, on the 15th of August, 1910; Mrs. Catherine McCanney died in the State of Kansas; Mary J. is the wife of Louis Tigner, of Madison County, Illinois; William H. is a resident of Edwardsville, that county; and Joseph maintains his home in Montgomery County, that state.

Robert Long was a lad of five years at the time of the family removal from Tennessee to Illinois, where he was reared to adult age under the sturdy discipline of the farm. He availed himself of the advantages of the common schools of Jersey County and when he was sixteen years of age the family removed thence to Montgomery County, where he grew to manhood and where he cast his first presidential vote. As a lad he was a great admirer of the distinguished Illinois statesman, Hon. Stephen A. Douglas, and he was a lad of about fifteen years when the "little giant" was made the independent democratic candidate for President of the United States, in 1860.

Mr. Long continued his association with agricultural industry in Illinois until 1879, when he made his way to Texas and established his residence in Parker County, where he had the distinction of being the first to plant cotton and thus initiate a profitable line of enterprise in that section, though he did not remain to witness the advancement made, as he returned to Illinois in the following year. There he remained until 1882, when he located in Carroll County, Missouri, where he raised one farm crop and then removed to Stoddard County, that state, where he remained during one summer. For the ensuing six years he was engaged in farming and stock growing in Cherokee County, Kansas, in which state he continued to maintain his home until 1892, when he came to Oklahoma Territory and made ready to avail himself of the opportunity offered for securing government land at the opening to settlement of the Cherokee Strip. On the 8th day of March, 1894, he established his residence on his present homestead farm, which comprises 160 acres of excellent land and which is eligibly situated at a point 4½ miles distant from the Village of Jennings. He has reclaimed the major part of his farm to cultivation, has made excellent improvements of a permanent order and is one of the successful agriculturists and stock raisers of Pawnee County, even as he is a citizen who has secure place in popular confidence and esteem.

Mr. Long was aligned as a supporter of the cause of the democratic party until the national election of 1876, since which time he has been a staunch advocate of the principles and policies for which the republican party stands sponsor, though he has in later years manifested a distinctive appreciation of certain of the tenets of the socialist party. When Mr. Long established his home on his present farm his tangible assets in initiating operations were represented in two cows, and in the early period of his residence in the new country he encountered a full share of pioneer hardships, his success eventually having been specially advanced through the negotiating of oil leases on his land.

In the year 1867, in Madison County, Illinois, was solemnized the marriage of Mr. Long to Miss Catherine Judson, who was born in that county, on the 9th of May, 1846, the great loss and bereavement of the life of Mr. Long having come when his devoted wife and helpmeet was summoned to the life eternal, her death having occurred on his present homestead farm, on the 2d of November, 1905. Of the children the eldest is Charles M., who has the active management of his father's farm, the maiden name of his wife having been Bertha Marple, and their one child being a son, Myrle Wilson. Mary Jeannette is the wife of William W. Sims, of Mannford, Creek County, Oklahoma, and they have three children: Creta May, Emma and Gilford. Albert is a successful representative of agricultural industry in Pawnee County. He wedded Miss Emma Bell and they have four children: Clifford, Philip, Robert and Otis. John, the fourth child of the subject of this sketch, died on the 25th of December, 1908, at the age of twenty-six years, and James died at the age of seven years, in Missouri.

RAYMOND A. GRADDY. The year 1915 finds the thriving little City of Watonga, judicial center of Blaine county, signally favored in having as the superintendent of its public schools so able an instructor as the popular young citizen whose name introduces this paragraph and who was elected to his present position in the autumn of 1914, his effective administration assuring his continuation in service so long, practically, as he will consent to retain the incumbency.

Mr. Graddy was born in Franklin County, Illinois, on the 31st of December, 1889, and is a son of George W. and Emma (Whiffen) Graddy, the former of whom was born in the State of Indiana, in 1851, and the latter of whom was born in White County, Illinois, in 1852. The parents passed the closing years of their lives in Franklin County, Illinois, and in death their devoted companionship was not long severed, the father having passed away in 1891, and the mother having been summoned to the life eternal in the preceding year. George W. Graddy was reared and educated in the old Hoosier State and as a young man he established his residence in Franklin County, Illinois, where he became a prosperous farmer and stock grower, where his marriage was solemnized and where he and his wife passed the residue of their lives, both having been earnest members of the Baptist Church, and he having been a republican in his political proclivities, the while he was affiliated with the Masonic fraternity and the Independent Order of Odd Fellows. Of the children the eldest is Nora E., who resides at Canyon City, Colo., the widow of Virgil Hayes, who was a farmer by vocation; Lolle is the wife of William J. Thorpe, and they reside in the City of Des Moines, Iowa, where Mr. Thorpe is local manager for the Rumeley Company, the extensive manufacturers of farm machinery; Thomas is a prosperous farmer in Posey County, Ind.; Susie died at New Haven, that state, when nineteen years of age; Clinton is engaged in the lumber business at Dudley, Missouri; and Raymond A., of this review, is the youngest of the number.

The original American progenitors of the Graddy family immigrated to the new world, from Ireland, in the colonial era of our national history, and became pioneers of Kentucky, from which historic old commonwealth went the early representatives of the name in Indiana.

Raymond A. Graddy found the period of his childhood and early youth compassed by the benignant conditions and influences of the home farm, and after availing himself of the advantages of the local schools of his native county he entered the high school at Marion, Williamson County, Illinois, in which he was graduated in 1905. Thereafter he completed a two years' course in the Illinois State Normal School at Normal, Ill., and his ambition for higher academic training was not satisfied until he had continued his studies two years in Valparaiso University, Indiana, and one year in the Southern Illinois College, at Carmi, Ill., in which institution he was graduated as a member of the class of 1912 and from which he received the degree of Bachelor of Arts. Since that time he has taken effective post graduate work in the great University of Chicago.

During the school year of 1911-12 Mr. Graddy was principal of the high school at Marlow, Stephens County, Oklahoma, to which state he had come prior to his graduation in the college mentioned above. During the autumn of 1912 and the ensuing spring he served as principal of the high school at Cleveland, Pawnee County; and the school year of 1913-14 found him the successful and popular principal of the high school at Norman, Cleveland County. Since the autumn of 1914 he has retained the superintendency of the public schools at Watonga, Blaine County, and it may consistently be said that his career as a teacher in the Oklahoma schools has been marked by consecutive advancement and by such scholastic and executive ability as to give him prestige as one of the representative figures in the educational circles of the state, the while his personal popularity in each of the fields in which he has labored has been of unequivocal order. At Watonga he has under his supervision three school houses and a corps of eighteen teachers, the enrollment of pupils showing an aggregate of 800.

Mr. Graddy is found aligned as a staunch supporter of the cause of the republican party, and he is essentially progressive and public-spirited in his civic attitude, with specially deep interest in all that pertains to the educational affairs of the state of his adoption. Both he and his wife hold membership in the Christian Church, in which he holds the office of deacon, and he is affiliated with the Watonga lodge of the Independent Order of Odd Fellows, as well as with the Delta Sigma Phi college fraternity. He has identified himself fully with Oklahoma, with the intention of here maintaining his permanent home, and he was formerly treasurer of a company identified with the oil industry in this state.

At Oklahoma City, Oklahoma, in 1914, was solemnized the marriage of Mr. Graddy to Miss Ina Rose Hastings, daughter of Albert W. Hastings, a well known citizen of Oklahoma City. Mr. and Mrs. Graddy are popular factors in the leading social life of Watonga, and both are zealous in connection with the affairs of the local Christian Church.

EDWARD SWENGEL, superintendent of the Mekusukey Academy located near Seminole, Oklahoma, was born at Neoga, Cumberland County, Illinois, March 4, 1873. His parents, George and Sarah Swengel, came from Indiana to Neoga, Illinois, about 1866. His father was a progressive and prosperous farmer and both parents were very much interested in churches and schools and the upbuilding of the community in which they lived. They were members of the United Brethren Church and were very careful to see that their five sons had educational advantages and Christian influences. George Swengel died when his son Edward was thirteen years of age.

The latter had his early training in the public schools of Illinois, and also had the advantage of courses in the United Brethren College at Westfield, Illinois, and Austin College at Effingham, Illinois. His early years were divided between teaching in the rural schools of Illinois and working a farm. He was elected principal of the schools at Dieterich in his native state, and as editor and owner of the Dieterich Gazette got a taste of newspaper work which was repeated after he came to Oklahoma.

When he arrived in Tulsa in the spring of 1902 he found the town just beginning to grow, and with a population of not more than 2,000 people. In the following September he was appointed principal teacher in the Wealaka Indian Boarding School near Tulsa, and was soon afterwards made superintendent of that school. After two years at Wealaka he was promoted to the superintendency of the National Boarding School at Wetumka, a capacity in which he served three years. While superintendent at Wetumka Mr. Swengel bought the land adjoining the site of the school and several years later when the school was discontinued he bought the school land and buildings. This land now comprises one of the fine farms in the Canadian River bottom, and in point of fertility and improvement it is one of the best farms in Eastern Oklahoma. Mr. Swengel also bought a half interest in the Wetumka Gazette and filled the chair of editor for some time. His interest in the raising of Poland China hogs and Hereford cattle on his farm required so much time and attention that he sold his interest in the paper. After five years of practical farming he accepted the principalship of the Capitol Heights School at Holdenville, Oklahoma, and later was promoted to the principalship of the Central School in the same city. In September, 1914, he was tendered the principalship of Armstrong Male Academy at Academy, Oklahoma, and from that place was promoted to superintendent of the Mekusukey Academy December 16, 1915.

Both Mr. and Mrs. Swengel are deeply interested in the education of Indian children. He is now beginning his eighth year in the Indian service. Mekusukey Academy, of which he is superintendent, has a capacity of 100 Indian children with fifteen employees. This school is conducted like a big home for children, and they remain there nine months of the year. All the pupils are required to take the literary course, while the girls are instructed in domestic science and art and the boys in agriculture and manual training. Every effort is made to make these students useful men and women. The school is situated on a farm of 320 acres on one of the most beautiful and picturesque spots in Eastern Oklahoma. No other one factor has done so much for the uplift and welfare of the Seminole Indians as the Mekusukey Academy.

For several years prior to his entering the Indian services in 1914, Mr. Swengel was secretary of the Hughes County Farmers Institute, and in that capacity and as a practical farmer and far-seeing educator has devoted much time and money to the encouragement of a better system of farming, better livestock and better seeds for this section of Oklahoma. Upon the advent of statehood he was elected representative of Hughes County in the first State Legislature. In that session he gave particular attention to laws concerning agriculture, public schools and taxation. Mr. Swengel is a lifelong democrat and though a man of positive ideas on political questions is tolerant and liberal with people who hold different views. His influence has been worthily directed to maintain the purity and integrity of official administration, and he has ever declined to support any man for office he thought incompetent or unworthy. It is a part of his creed that the future success of the party depends upon the uprightness of its leaders.

Mr. Swengel is a Master Mason, and was trustee of Wetumka Lodge when its hall was built, and he assisted in the supervision of that work. For many years he has been affiliated with the Modern Woodmen of America and was clerk of his camp several years at Dieterich, Illinois. Mr. and Mrs. Swengel are active members of the Methodist Episcopal Church.

In ancestry Mr. Swengel is of German stock on his father's side, while from his mother he received the qualities of Scotch-Irish. On September 10, 1893, at Paradise, Illinois, he married Lula B. Morrison, daughter of G. C. and P. A. Morrison. Her father was a successful stock buyer and farmer near Neoga, Illinois. Mrs. Swengel has been not only the guardian of the destinies of the home but also a factor of constant encouragement and inspiration to Mr. Swengel in his career. She is a woman of fine education, and in addition to the public schools of Illinois which she attended she was a student in the United Brethren College at Westfield and Austin College at Effingham, the same institutions which Mr. Swengel attended. They have one bright and attractive daughter, Ruth Louise, now six years of age.

OSCAR K. PETTY, vice president and active manager of the Farmers State Bank of Hominy, Mr. Petty has for several years been closely identified with the general commercial enterprise of Hominy. The successful position of the bank is in a considerable degree due to his personality and ability as financial manager, and he has furthermore shown a ready interest and public spirit in promoting every enterprise for the upbuilding and development of his section. The Farmers State Bank of Hominy was chartered and opened for business March 18, 1912, and on May 10, 1913, occurred a reorganization by the present owners. W. S. Crowe is president, Mr. Petty is vice president, O. L. Barlow, cashier, and the other directors are Percy Dixon and Mrs. Addie Drummond. The capital stock is $25,000, surplus and profits $4,000, and its aggregate resources now place it among the leading institutions of the kind in Northeastern Oklahoma.

The vice president of this bank comes of a fine old Tennessee family, and was born at Hamburg in that state March 6, 1884, a son of William G. and Margaret A. (Perkins) Petty, both of whom were natives of McNairy County, Tennessee, his father born September 6, 1841, and his mother in 1866. They are still living at Hamburg. His father has been a farmer, physician, merchant and banker, is now president of the Planters and Merchants Bank of Hamburg, and gives most of his time to the handling of his extensive financial interests. He was graduated from the Kentucky School of Medicine and took post-graduate work in the New York schools, but for several years has been retired from his profession.

One of a family of thirteen children and the oldest of the nine still living, Oscar K. Petty grew up in Tennessee, graduated from a local collegiate institution in 1901, and then became associated with his father in merchandising up to 1904. After attending a college in St. Louis for a time, he first came to Hominy in 1905, where he served as an expert accountant for M. F. Fraley.

In 1907 Mr. Petty married Miss Blanche Henrietta Drummond, daughter of the late Fred Drummond, one of the pioneer traders of the Osage country and an active factor in the Farmers State Bank at the time of his death. The life of Fred Drummond, who was one of Hominy's leading citizens, is sketched on other pages. After his marriage Mr. Petty returned with his bride to Tennessee, and spent two years with the Hamburg Mercantile Company. Returning to Hominy in 1909, he became actively identified with the Hominy Trading Company, and was with that concern until 1913, when he took part in the reorganization of the Farmers State Bank and has since been its vice president and active manager.

Mr. Petty is a thirty-second degree Scottish Rite Mason, has been a member of the Mystic Shrine since 1906, and is also affiliated with the Eastern Star, the Benevolent and Protective Order of Elks and the Knights of Pythias and the Independent Order of Odd Fellows. He is active in the Christian Church and is now superintendent of its Sunday school. His politics are democratic. He served three years on the local school board and was a member of the city council two years. Mr. and Mrs. Petty have four children: Drummond, Helen Claire, Blanche and Margaret. The oldest was born in Tennessee, while the three other children claim Hominy as the place of their nativity.

I. O. DIGGS, Stillwater, Oklahoma, has been editor and publisher of The Advance-Democrat since 1900, and postmaster at Stillwater since February, 1914. As postmaster of this important office of the second class, Mr. Diggs has been eminently effective and universally satisfactory. But it is as editor of The Advance-Democrat that Mr. Diggs has made his impression on the people of Oklahoma and especially of Payne County.

The location of the A. & M. College at Stillwater makes that city the center of considerable interest in Oklahoma, and in the intellectual life of that college community a very significant part has always been played by The Advance-Democrat and its editor, Mr. Diggs. In fact he has made The Advance-Democrat known and respected as a fine, strong, clean exponent of all that is best in community welfare.

Mr. Diggs is a recognized leader in the councils of the democratic party in Payne County and in Oklahoma. He has served as chairman of the county organization and been repeatedly elected as state committeeman. His paper has always been a virile exponent of the principles of the democratic party.

Irvin Owings Diggs was born at Arrow Rock, Saline County, Missouri, June 5, 1873, and is a son of William Bailey Diggs and Cynthia Emeline (Morris) Diggs.

William Bailey Diggs was born at Yorktown, Virginia, June 9, 1827, and Cynthia E. Morris was born at Danville, Missouri, August 11, 1836. William Bailey Diggs came to Missouri as a young man established his residence in St. Louis and there attended school. He was married to Cynthia E. Morris in Montgomery County, Missouri, where she had been born and reared. Thereafter they lived for many years in Saline County where he was a very successful farmer.

William Bailey Diggs died at Arrow Rock, Saline County, Missouri, November 2, 1912, at the hale old age of eighty-five years. He was ever public spirited. He was a member of the Southern Methodist Church, lived a hearty and a noble life and spent time and money for the upbuilding of the church and the betterment of humanity. He was a staunch democrat, influential in local affairs, and commanded the respect and esteem of his fellow men. His wife Cynthia Emeline still survives him (in 1916) and is hale and hearty at the age of eighty years. Of their nine children all but one attained to years of maturity and seven of them are now living (1916). The names of the children of William Bailey Diggs are: Wirtley Marvin, Nora Jane, Esther Catherine, Laura, William Thomas, Bascom, Watson, Irvin Owings, Seth Morris.

I. O. Diggs is descended from a fine old Virginia family which can trace its ancestry back to good blood in England. The name now spelled Diggs was spelled Degge (Digges). William Bailey Diggs, the father of I. O. Diggs, was a son of Jesse Diggs who served in the War of 1812. Jesse Diggs was the son of Augustine Degge, the son of Simon Degge, the son of Capt. John Degge, who according to the William and Mary Quarterly is directly descended from Sir Simon Degge of England, who was justice for Staffordshire of the inner temple at London, one of His Majesty's council.

The Virginia family which began with Capt. John Degge still holds a very ancient coat of arms described in Burke's General Armory. The names of important persons called "Headrights" are given at the foot of land patents, and the name of Capt. John Degge is found in the land office records at Richmond as one who got a patent in 1678 for 1,800 acres for importing thirty-six persons.

I. O. Diggs got his early training on the home farm and in the public schools of his native county. After finishing the public school he pursued higher academic studies in The McMahan Institute at Arrow Rock, Missouri, and in the state normal at Warrensburg, Missouri. At twenty-four years of age he began his career as a newspaper man, by purchasing, in partnership with his brother, Bascom Diggs, the Arrow Rock Statesman, of which his brother is still the editor and publisher. In 1898 I. O. Diggs sold his interest in this paper and for the two following years he was engaged in publishing a weekly paper at Hartville, Missouri. He then went to Arizona for some months, and from Arizona he returned for a time to his old home in Missouri.

In 1900 Mr. Diggs came to Stillwater, Oklahoma Territory and engaged in the newspaper business, to which he has given his talent until he added the duties of postmaster in February, 1914.

Mr. Diggs was married to Miss Malinda Blanche Wise June 24, 1903. Mrs. Diggs had been reared and educated in Oklahoma where her parents had established their home when she was a child and where they spent the rest of their lives meriting enduring appreciation and respect for their honored part among the pioneers of the state.

Mrs. Diggs' father, Levi Wise, was born August 2, 1833, near Louisville, Kentucky, and died February 27, 1908. Mrs. Diggs' mother, Alice (Wheeler) Wise, was born January 3, 1853, at Liberty, Missouri, and died June 14, 1908, at Stillwater, Oklahoma.

Mrs. Diggs graduated from the Oklahoma A. & M. College in the third graduating class of that institution, in 1898. She was a successful and popular teacher in the public schools of Oklahoma until the time of her marriage.

Mrs. Diggs has unusual talent and typical southern culture. She is gifted and trained in public speaking and won the entire series of Demorest medal contests, silver medal, gold medal, grand gold medal, and diamond medal, which entitled her to a diploma for proficiency in oratory. Mr. and Mrs. Diggs have one daughter, Cynthalice Io, born April 20, 1910. Both Mr. and Mrs. Diggs are members of the Methodist Episcopal Church, South, of which he has always been an official member and a most helpful supporter, and in which she has been

always a spiritual helper. Mrs. Diggs is also strong and active in the social organizations and public spirited agencies of the community.

Mr. Diggs' most important social service has been through the high moral tone and excellent quality of his paper and through the things that he has stood for in the life of the community and the state. His paper has always been an able exponent of the principles of the democratic party. He has also used his pen always for the ideals which promise the largest measure of human welfare. Whatever is evil he has opposed fearlessly. Whatever is good he has advocated at whatever cost. His courage and his devotion to human welfare was nobly and heroically manifested when before the state had a law prohibiting the liquor traffic he through his own efforts and self sacrifice and great material loss gave to his own county effective prohibition. For that sacrificial service and for an ideal life of absolute integrity many will praise and appreciate him always as a fine, strong, noble, manly man.

WILLIAM JOURDAN WHITEMAN. A conspicuous figure in business and civic affairs in the old Choctaw Nation and in later years around Goodwater and Idabel has been William Jourdan Whiteman, a resident of Oklahoma since 1893.

He was born in Red River County, Texas, three and a half miles northeast of Clarksville on November 3, 1869, a son of David C. and Mary E. Whiteman, who now have their home at Haworth, Oklahoma, aged respectively seventy-nine and seventy-five years.

His first business experience was gained as clerk for his father at the age of eleven years in 1880. For schooling he attended Whiteman's Chapel and the Annona schools and later took a course in the Little Rock Commercial College at Little Rock, Arkansas. His diploma from that school is dated June 3, 1890.

Coming to the old Choctaw Nation of Indian Territory in 1893, the following year he began his independent commercial career at Goodwater, his home ever since, and where he is now president of the Whiteman Mercantile Company, dealers in general merchandise.

With a genius for merchandising and general lines of business, Mr. Whiteman has acquired numerous influential interests in his section of the state. He is identified with stores at Goodwater, Jadie and Haworth, with cotton gins at Goodwater and Haworth, owns farming interests in different parts of McCurtain County, has been a director since organization of the First National Bank of Idabel, and is director and president of the First National Bank of Haworth. He is also a member of the Haworth Mercantile Company, the Haworth Publishing Company, the Southern Oklahoma Abstract Company of Idabel, and of several other concerns.

On December 19, 1894, he was appointed postmaster at Goodwater, and has filled that office continuously to the present time, a period of twenty-two years. At one time Mr. Whiteman was a member of the Red River Rifles, a volunteer company of the Texas militia, and with it he attended annual encampments at San Antonio and Austin.

Mr. Whiteman was a member of the first grand jury of McCurtain County after statehood. He has served as a member of the school board and is now president of the McCurtain County School Board Association, which was recently organized. Politically he is a republican and is now republican nominee for representative from McCurtain County.

He was also actively identified with Choctaw national politics.. He drew up the bill which was presented by Gov. Greene McCurtain to the Choctaw Legislation in 1898, forbidding citizens of that nation to sell pine timber from their reserve lands. He thus became an active ally in the movement for the conservation of the natural resources by the Choctaw people. In 1904 he was a delegate to the notable convention at Tuskahoma that nominated Thomas Hunter for governor of the nation. This brought on the famous feud between the Hunter and McCurtain factions, finally ending when the military authorities compelled the Hunter people to vacate the national capital in favor of McCurtain. Mr. Whiteman lived during that most interesting period of Oklahoma history when the tribe passed from their old forms of government to those set up by the new state, a period in Indian annals of equal importance to the migration of the tribes to the Indian Territory. When Mr. Whiteman came to Goodwater in 1893, though it was one of the oldest Indian settlements, very few white men lived in that region. It was due to Mr. Whiteman's influence that a postoffice was established there, and he was the first and only incumbent to date of the office of postmaster.

Mr. Whiteman is prominent in Masonry, having filled nearly all the offices and having been worshipful master for five years of Goodwater Lodge No. 148, Ancient Free and Accepted Masons, and its secretary for seven or eight years; is also a member of Garvin Chapter of the Royal Arch Masons; belongs to Indian Consistory of the thirty-second degree Scottish Rite at McAlester, and to the Bedouin Temple of the Mystic Shrine at Muskogee. His church is the Methodist Protestant.

On August 2, 1896, at the residence of Judge H. C. Harris in Bokhoma County in the Choctaw Nation, he married Mattie J. Harris, daughter of Judge Henry C. and Margarette E. Harris. Judge Henry C. Harris was a member of the Choctaw tribe of Indians and one of the most distinguished figures for many years. He had founded the Harris ferry on Red River, one of the oldest and most historic crossings of that stream, had been sheriff of his county, royalty collector and senator, and as a member of the Legislature was author of the bill creating Wheelock Academy in what is now McCurtain County. At the time of his death he was serving as supreme judge of the Choctaw Nation. Judge Harris was a nephew of Peter P. Pytchlin, who was once a governor of the Choctaws and assisted in making the Choctaw treaty with the United States Government. Judge Harris was also related to the Garland and Fulsom families, prominent in Choctaw affairs. President Grover Cleveland married a member of one branch of the Fulsom family.

Mr. and Mrs. Whiteman are the parents of seven children: Magie E., who married W. L. Barrick; Mary L., who married Carl S. Prewett; Henry A.; Beatrice, David C., W. J., Jr. and Bessie A., all of whom are still unmarried.

HON. JOSEPH JEROME JONES. In a long, active and varied career, Joseph Jerome Jones has carried on activities in various states of the Union and has invaded the fields of law, real estate, farming and politics, in all of which he has won success and reputation. Of recent years agriculture has received the greater part of his attention, aside from his labors of a public character, and during fifteen years his home has been at or near Sapulpa.

Mr. Jones was born April 3, 1864, at Cowden, Shelby County, Illinois, and is a son of Samuel and Martha (Rhodes) Jones. He traces his ancestry back in a direct line to the year 1192, and in this country to 1631, when the founder of the family, a native of England and an uncle of John Locke, the great English philosopher, settled at Woburn, Massachusetts. Mrs. Martha (Rhodes) Jones was a direct descendant of Rev. George

Whitefield, who was born in Gloucester, England, in 1714, in youth joined the Wesleys, was ordained preacher in 1736 and in 1738 came to the American settlement of Georgia. He became chaplain of the first colony of Georgia, was one of the greatest evangelists the world has known, founded the Calvinistic Methodists, and died in 1770 at Newburyport, Massachusetts. Joseph Jerome Jones is also a blood relative of two American presidents, John Adams and John Quincy Adams. Samuel Jones was born in Knox County, Ohio, in 1834, and as a young man went to Shelby County, Illinois, where he was married, his wife having been born there in 1837. They passed the remaining years of their lives on a farm in Shelby County, the father dying in 1881 and the mother in 1905. They were the parents of five children, of whom four are living, a daughter being deceased.

Joseph Jerome Jones attended the public and high schools of Cowden, Illinois, and at the age of seventeen years left the homestead farm and went to Valparaiso (Indiana) University, where he spent three years. His education was so far advanced, however, that, while continuing his studies, he taught school at intervals for four years in Illinois. His law studies also overlapped his career as a teacher, and he was finally admitted to the bar in 1890, in his native state. During the next ten years Mr. Jones practice in the courts of Illinois, Nebraska, Iowa, Utah and Oklahoma, residing at various points in those states, and in 1900 located at Sapulpa, where he carried on a successful practice until the time of statehood, when he gave up his practice to give his attention to real estate and investments, in which he had become largely interested. Still later he embarked in farming, and at the present time he has large and valuable landed holdings in Creek County. In January, 1916, he located at Tulsa, where he is engaged in the abstract business, being president of the Oklahoma Abstract Company.

Mr. Jones was a republican until 1912, in which year he cast his fortunes with the newly-organized progressive party. His public service has been of great practical value to his constituents, and his fearless independence, both of speech and political action, has sometimes brought him into conflict with certain leaders, while decidedly raising him in public estimation. He served as mayor of Sapulpa, until his resignation, and was also city attorney, from which position he likewise resigned. In 1910 he was elected to the State Senate and served one term of four years. In this capacity, he was known as one of the most serviceable members of the upper house of the Legislature, ready and logical in debate and at the same time alive to all the practical demands of his district and industrious in pushing forward all needful legislation. He still holds membership in the Creek County Bar Association, and for twenty-five years has been a member of the Independent Order of Odd Fellows.

Mr. Jones was married in 1894 to Miss Charlotte M. Paxton, who was born near Tama, Tama County, Iowa, where she resided until her marriage, daughter of Thomas Paxton, whose neighbor for forty-two years was Hon. James Wilson, ex-secretary of agriculture. Four children have been born to Mr. and Mrs. Jones, namely: Jerald J., born October 9, 1895, who is now a student at Notre Dame University, South Bend, Indiana; Quelma, born January 4, 1900; Xerma, born December 24, 1902; and X, born January 21, 1905.

BION F. COLE. To the material success and broad industrial influence of the Live Stock Daily News, one of the most valuable and important of the progressive publications of the State of Oklahoma, Mr. Cole has contributed much through his effective policies and services in the capacity of advertising manager, and he is consistently to be designated as one of the representative figures in the domain of newspaper enterprise in this favored commonwealth.

Bion Franklin Cole was born at Liberty Mills, Wabash County, Indiana, on the 1st of May, 1857, and when he was three years of age the family removed to North Manchester, in the same county, where the home was established at the time of the inception of the Civil war. The father, George E. Cole, manifested his patriotism by promptly enlisting in defense of the Union. He became a second lieutenant in the Forty-seventh Indiana Volunteer Infantry, and sacrificed his life in the cause. He was killed in the final engagement at Champion's Hill, Mississippi, and his body was taken by the Confederates, who believed it to have been that of one of their own officers and who gave it burial as such, the location of the grave never having been discovered by the members of his family. Lieutenant Cole's parents were born in England and upon coming to the United States established their home in Pennsylvania. In the old Keystone State was solemnized the marriage of Lieut. George E. Cole to Miss Mary E. Raper, in 1843, his wife being a daughter of Adam Raper, a descendant of one of the sterling old German families of Pennsylvania, and finally they removed to Indiana, where the venerable wife and mother still resides, her home being in the fine little City of Goshen, Elkhart County, and her mental and physical powers being remarkable, in view of the fact that she is nearing the age of four score years and ten. Of the six children Bion F., of this review, was the fourth in order of birth, and all save one of the number are still living.

The devoted and widowed mother was left to care for her five young children and soon after the war had closed it became practically imperative for the older sons to contribute their quota to the support of the family. Bion F. Cole, when a lad of nine years, was taken to the home of a farmer in Wabash County, Indiana, his compensation being comprised in his reception of his board and clothing. Concerning this unduly strenuous period of his life the following pertinent statements have been written and are worthy of perpetuation, as indicating the conditions and influences under which a strong and resourceful character was developed:

"This foster-father proved anything but a kind employer, the boy being assigned to such work as cutting large logs by handling one end of a cross-cut saw, plowing new ground, husking corn, chopping wood, etc., and in the meanwhile being afforded no school privileges. At the end of two years family friends took action and brought about a dissolution of the agreement under which the boy was bound, and he was returned to his mother's home at North Manchester, where he was able to attend school one year. When his mother contracted a second marriage and removed to Albion, Noble County, Indiana, young Cole was hired out to a kinsman of his stepfather, but here his lot proved even less favorable than under former conditions. He was compelled to work early and late and when weather was unpropitious or there was nothing else for him to do he was set to clearing off dead timber and other work more onerous than he had done for the farmer to whom he was originally bound out. From Albion he accompanied his mother and stepfather on their removal to Goshen, Indiana, and after working for a time in a manufacturing establishment he was there able to enter upon an apprenticeship in the office of the Goshen Times, owned and published by William Star. He completed a four years' apprenticeship and the discipline in this connection justified the statement that the service of this order in a newspaper and printing office is equal to a liberal education. Young Cole had an alert mind, was ambitious and persevering and made rapid advancement in acquiring knowledge of the intricacies and mysteries of the 'art preservative of all arts.' In those days the 'printer's devil' was the common pack-horse of the office and his duties comprised everything from sawing four-foot cord wood to standing at a press during the daylight hours, after which he carried the papers to subscribers in the evening."

At the completion of his apprenticeship of four years, within which his maximum salary was $3.50 a week, Mr. Cole obtained a position with the great Chicago firm of Rand, McNally & Company, then one of the greatest publishing concerns in railway maps and schedules in the United States and still one of the most important publishing houses in the City of Chicago. Here the reception of a stipend of $12 a week while working under instructions seemed to the young printer a wondrous financial stride, but in the meanwhile he had developed a distinct appreciation of and liking for newspaper work, and through the influence of representative business men of Chicago he was enabled to make advancement in this field of enterprise. By the well-known publisher of the Chicago Times, the late Wilber F. Story, he was sent to Springfield, the capital city of Illinois, where he profited much through observing the various details of the state governmental work and where he edited for the Chicago Times a column under the heading of "Rambling Musings." When he left Springfield Mr. Story gave him a command or admonition which he has ever retained as his guide in newspaper work. Story said to him: "We want news, not a story. To illustrate, in case of a big fire give us simple facts—the cause, the loss, the amount of insurance if any, the owners of the property. Make it brief." The policies thus implied made Wilber F. Story one of the foremost newspaper men in the United States, and his counsel has been immeasurably valued by Mr. Cole, who recalls that eccentric personality with much of appreciation.

Apropos of the further advancement of Mr. Cole in his chosen field of endeavor the following succinct account has been given:

"On his return trip from Springfield to Chicago Mr. Cole stopped at Bloomington, Illinois. The place appealed to him especially on account of its beautiful homes and stirring business. There he met H. R. Persinger, who had just started a society paper called the Bloomington Eye, and he joined Mr. Persinger in the new venture, which was virtually the initiatory step in society journalism west of New York. The enterprise had proved so promising and successful in its early stages that Mr. Cole was offered a position on its editorial staff, and his technical knowledge likewise came into effective play through his serving as compositor and makeup man. From this experience young Cole was inspired to continue his association with society publications, and after an interval of two years he went to Burlington, Iowa, where he assumed a position with the celebrated Burlington Hawkeye, of which the editor was at that time Hon. Frank Hatton, who later served as postmaster general of the United States. In this connection Mr. Cole formed the acquaintance of the late Robert J. Burdette, one of the greatest paragraphers and humorists of the West at that time and at the time of his recent death a clergyman in California. Leaving Burlington in the winter of 1883-4, Mr. Cole accepted a position on the Rocky Mountain News, the leading daily paper of Denver, Colorado. Being an allround man he was soon assigned to detached duty as makeup on the city and state directories for Denver, Pueblo, Leadville, and Colorado Springs, and within a short time thereafter, at the suggestion of John Arkins, owner of the News, he was assigned to service in the mining camps of Colorado, to report for the mining page of the Sunday editions of the Rocky Mountain News, the silver-mining excitement and operations having then been at their zenith in that state. In those days the present mode of illustrating newspaper articles was unknown, but young Cole injected illustrations of the various mining fields in connection with his articles, and these attracted attention throughout the entire country.

"Returning to Denver after six months passed in the mining camps of the mountain fastnesses, Mr. Cole found awaiting him a position on the Denver Republican, where he formed the acquaintanceship of the illustrious and loved Eugene Field, later with the Chicago Daily News, and of such satirists as O. H. Rothiker, Will Vicher and others of the world's greatest newspaper writers."

Mr. Cole remained in Denver until going to Des Moines, Iowa, where he again became associated with Persinger, whom he assisted in the establishing of the Des Moines Mail and Times. With this paper he continued to be identified seven years and he then purchased the Grand Island Times, at Grand Island, Nebraska, and in connection with the editing and publishing of this paper he first became actively concerned with political affairs. He made his paper a success and a power in politics in Nebraska. Through his paper and personal influence he opposed the nomination and candidacy for the United States Senate of Hon. George W. E. Dorsey, one of the strongest republicans in the state, and supported the populist nominee, Senator Kemm, who was victorious at the polls and who defeated Dorsey by an appreciable majority. Mr. Cole had been a delegate to the republican state convention and the article which he wrote for his paper upon returning from the convention was entitled "Dorsey's Money Did It," this leading editorial having become the slogan of those opposing Dorsey in the succeeding campaign, which was a most spirited one.

In 1891 Mr. Cole assumed the position of traveling representative and salesman for the Western Newspaper Union, with the service of which he continued to be identified fourteen years, during the last four of which he was manager and made a record for being the best producer of business the organization ever had upon the road. He introduced the business of this corporation in Oklahoma and never thereafter lost a paper among the hundreds that were established within the period directly succeeding the opening of the territory to settlement. He assisted William Jennings Bryan in the establishing and launching of The Commoner, and his wide and varied experience had definite influence in furthering the phenomenal and almost instant success of this noteworthy paper.

In July, 1909, Mr. Cole established his residence in Oklahoma City, where he assumed control of a syndicate of ten county papers designated as the Suburban List, and founded also the Live Stock Exchange, a weekly paper. He made the ventures definitely successful and after disposing of his interests in the same he became the valued incumbent of his present responsible position, that of advertising manager of the Oklahoma Daily Live Stock News, which has a wide circulation throughout the state and the broad usefulness and value of which have been significantly fostered through the effective methods and policies which he has evolved. Mr. Cole is consistently to be considered one of the leading newspaper men of the West, his acquaintanceship is specially large and his manifold activities and broad mental ken have made him a person of great versatility and resourcefulness, the while his steadfastness and genial individuality have gained to him troops of friends in both business and social circles.

In the City of Denver, on the 14th of June, 1882, Mr. Cole wedded Miss Jessie F. Miller, daughter of Samuel P. and Emily W. (Swan) Miller, formerly of Des Moines, Iowa. Mrs. Cole was summoned to the life eternal on the 10th of January, 1900, and is survived by her only child, Holland Ralph Cole, who was born October 28, 1884. At Lincoln, Nebraska, on the 4th of June, 1903, was solemnized the second marriage of Mr. Cole, when Mrs. Ida (Vanstrum) Dillon, of that city became his wife. They have no children.

GREENWOOD McCURTAIN. Of the names that have figured most conspicuously in the history of the Choctaw Nation from its removal to Indian Territory until the tribal relations were dissolved and the nation was merged into the State of Oklahoma, none has enjoyed more of the worthy distinctions of private and public honor than McCurtain. One of the finest counties in the southeastern part of the state bears the name of the family as a permanent tribute to their valued citizenship, and it was the lasting distinction of the late Greenwood McCurtain to have been elected the last principal chief or governor of the nation, and was the executive head in winding up its tribal affairs, and he continued to enjoy the honorary title after statehood until his death. He was a leader among the Tuskahoma or progressive party in Indian politics.

In the early years of Indian Territory the home of the McCurtains was near Fort Smith, Arkansas, in what is now LeFlore County, Oklahoma. Greenwood McCurtain was born in that locality in November, 1848, but for many years had his home in what is now Haskell County, and in that county at the Sans Bois Cemetery he was laid to rest after his death on December 27, 1910.

The name McCurtain is of Scotch or Irish origin, though Governor McCurtain was almost a fullblood Choctaw. His father Cornelius McCurtain was born in Mississippi and was a member of the Choctaw tribe and married a fullblood Choctaw woman, Miss Belvin.

Green McCurtain, as he was most familiarly known, grew up on the frontier, a part of his youthful experience coinciding with that desolating period of the Civil war. In a business way he was chiefly successful as a stock raiser, and he was also identified to some extent with mercantile and trading interests.

However, it was in his public relations that he most thoroughly impressed his influence upon the life of the Choctaw Nation. One of the greatest services he rendered in behalf of his people, and in which he attracted the attention of the United States Government, was in the office of Choctaw National Treasurer. He served two terms of four years each as treasurer of the Choctaw Nation and during that time the Federal Government paid through him $2,000,000 to the Choctaws. He distributed this vast sum to his tribesmen, the Government requiring no bond of him as its agent. He was twice chosen to represent the Choctaw tribe as its delegate at Washington, but resigned during his second term.

Mr. McCurtain's first position of importance was as a member of the national board of education from his, the first, district. He was ever a friend and ardent supporter of education among his people. He was later elected to the position of district attorney, wherein he distinguished himself as a public prosecutor and an official who vigorously enforced the law.

In 1896 he was elected governor of chief of the Choctaw Nation, and two years later was re-elected to that high office. Under the law he was not eligible to election a third time, so he retired after four years of careful and conscientious administration of the national affairs. In 1902 Governor McCurtain was again elected principal chief after a spirited contest in which he was opposed by an anti-statehood candidate, who was aided by the national republican party. Two years later he was elected governor for the fourth time, and thereafter he was retained in the office by Congress and the general government until his death. His service of twelve years constituted the longest individual service in that office, and only death severed his official relations with his people.

Above all else, his fidelity to his people should be longest remembered and most closely associated with his name and character. It was said of him that he was "first an Indian and then a democrat, but there came a time when he believed the democratic delegation in Congress was unfriendly to his people, and then he became, and died, a republican in politics."

In religious matters he was a Baptist and he died in that faith at his home at Kinta, at the age of sixty-two. Governor McCurtain was twice married. By his first wife he was the father of one child, D. C. McCurtain, a lawyer and now a resident of Spiro. By his second marriage there were four daughters and one son.

DAVID CORNELIUS McCURTAIN. One of the important phases of the statehood movement in Oklahoma and Indian Territory was the convention of August, 1905, at Muskogee, which met for the purpose of providing for a government of the Indian country and for drafting a constitution for a single state comprising approximately what was then Indian Territory. As a result of the labors of this convention there was adopted what will always be known in history as "The Sequoyah Constitution." The temporary chairman of this convention was D. C. McCurtain, a son of Governor McCurtain of the Choctaw Nation, and at that time as now a prominent leader among his people and one of the able lawyers of the state.

This representative of the Choctaw Nation was born at old Scullyville near Spiro, Oklahoma, January 29, 1873. He was the son of Greenwood and Martha A. (Ainsworth) McCurtain. His mother was a white woman and a native of Mississippi.

After getting his primary education in the national school near his father's home, he continued his education at Roanoke College in Virginia, and in 1895 graduated from the Kemper Military School at Boonville, Missouri. Taking up the study of law, he first entered the University of Missouri and finished his legal studies at Columbian University in Washington, D. C. On returning to Indian Territory he forthwith began the practice of law and took his place as a leader among his people. In 1898 he was elected district attorney for the First District of the Choctaw Nation, and re-elected in 1900, but resigned to accept his appointment as clerk of the Citizenship Commission. After one year he resigned as clerk, and in 1901 was chosen a delegate to represent the Choctaw Nation at Washington. For this post his ability and training as a lawyer and his intimate knowledge of the Choctaw people and their needs proved exceptional qualifications. He continued as the Choctaw delegate at Washington until 1904, when he returned to Indian Territory and became probate attorney for the Choctaws. In 1906 he resigned that office to become again a delegate in the interest of the Choctaws at Washington, and represented his people before the national government until statehood.

In October, 1907, James R. Garfield, then secretary of the interior under Roosevelt, tendered him the position of attorney for the Choctaws, and he remained in that position, together with his associate in the practice of the law, until 1912.

Mr. McCurtain was a resident of McAlester from 1900 to 1914, and in December of the latter year removed to Poteau, and later to Spiro, where he is now living, engaged in the practice of law independently. While a resident of McAlester he filled out an unexpired term, by appointment, as mayor of that city. He is a democrat, a thirty-second degree Mason of the Scottish Rite, a member of the Benevolent and Protective Order of Elks, and belongs to the Presbyterian Church.

In 1896 he married Miss Katherine N. Mitchell, a Choctaw woman. They have four living children: Ewart Preston, Greenwood Mitchell, Jackson Haskell and Martha Elizabeth McCurtain.

E. B. BREWINGTON, D. O. The leading representative of the school of osteopathy in Kay County is Doctor Brewington, who has conducted a very successful practice at Tonkawa for the past fifteen years. He is one of the men who has brought osteopathy to an equal standing among the older schools of medicine, and is himself a graduate of the pioneer school of osteopathy, the Doctor Still Institute at Kirksville, Missouri.

A resident of Oklahoma since 1901, Doctor Brewington was graduated in osteopathy in 1899, standing among the first in his class. He was born near Monticello, Missouri, September 23, 1861, and was the son of a farmer and stock man, Capt. David Brewington, now deceased. His father made an excellent record as a soldier in the Union army during the Civil war, and died at the age of fifty-seven. He was a citizen who commanded the high respect of all who knew him, and possessed many splendid qualities of heart and mind. The mother, whose maiden name was Miss E. Smith, a daughter of Rice Smith, is now living at Caddo, Oklahoma. His father was a republican in politics, and a very active member of the Methodist Episcopal Church, and was also affiliated with the Masonic fraternity. There are five sons: E. M., a farmer and stock man at Caddo; Dr. E. B.; C. M., of Caddo; Dr. O. M., now well established in practice at Wichita, Kansas; and M. R., a farmer and stock man at Caddo.

Doctor Brewington spent the early years of his life on a farm, gained an education in the public schools, and has been an industrious and energetic citizen since early youth. For several years he was engaged in business in Kansas, and finally gave up merchandising in order to enter the school of osteopathy at Kirksville founded by the eminent Doctor Still, an institution which more than any other fact has made Kirksville known all over the country as a medical center. In 1901 Doctor Brewington came to Oklahoma to assist his brother, Dr. O. M., who was at that time living in Grant County, and from there moved to Tonkawa, where he has since been the chief representative of his particular school in medical circles.

In 1884 in Ellis County, Kansas, Doctor Brewington married Miss Daisy Lowe. Four children have been born to their union. Doctor Brewington is affiliated with the Independent Order of Odd Fellows. As a citizen as well as a physician he has supported all those movements planned for the benefit of his community, and is always mentioned among the leading citizens of that town.

RICHARD S. BURNS. Varied activities as an early homesteader, a farmer and citizen in Dewey and Blaine counties, have served to make the name of Richard S. Burns well known and highly respected in this section of the state, and at the present time he is identified with public service as postmaster at Canton. Mr. Burns has spent the greater part of his active career in the West, is thoroughly familiar with the conditions in this section of country, and has always been a man of hope and enthusiasm concerning the future development and prosperity of Oklahoma in particular.

The Burns family to which he belongs originated in Germany, and settled among the pioneers of the old State of Kentucky. His grandfather, Jacob Burns, was born in the year 1799, and probably in Washington County, Kentucky. Anyhow, that county was his home when he was very young. He died there in 1881. As a boy he had given some active service as a soldier in the War of 1812, while the rest of his long life was spent as a farmer.

Richard S. Burns, the Canton postmaster, was born April 21, 1861, at Willisburg, Washington County, Kentucky. His father, S. N. Burns, was born in the same county in 1832 and died there in 1877. His life was spent as a farmer and he belonged to the Baptist church and the Masonic fraternity. He married Mary A. Cheatham, who was born in Washington County in 1836 and died there in 1881. There were three children: L. H. lives at Decatur, Illinois; the second is Richard S.; and Elizabeth, now deceased, married Jerome Trent, who is a merchant in Washington County, Kentucky.

From the time he was sixteen years of age Richard S. Burns has taken care of his own fortunes in the world. In the meantime he had attended public schools in Washington County, and at Perryville, Kentucky, received the equivalent of a modern high school education. On starting out for himself he made a living for several years by teaching school. In 1888 he moved West and spent a year on a farm near Hutchinson, Kansas, and thus combined the vocation of teaching with that of farming for several years. From Kansas Mr. Burns moved to Oklahoma in March, 1897, and acquired a homestead of 160 acres near Fountain in Dewey County. That farm has been his home ever since, though his activities and interests are well diversified. His homestead is located a half a mile south and ten miles west of Canton, in Dewey County.

During 1907 Mr. Burns served on the State Board of Agriculture for Oklahoma. On September 16, 1914, he was appointed postmaster at Canton, and has since given his principal time and attention to the duties of this office. His farm is in Little Robe Township, and he has been a member of the school board of that township. Mr. Burns is a democrat, a member of the Baptist Church, and can always be found as a supporter of all public spirited movements in his community.

While living in Kentucky in 1884 he married Miss Mattie Sale, whose father, the Rev. R. Sale, was a Baptist minister. To their marriage have been born five children: Mary A. is the wife of L. L. Murray, and they live on their farm in Dewey County, Oklahoma; Lucy L. married W. F. Bussing and they have a farm at Fonda, Oklahoma; R. S. is a pharmacist at Dumright, Oklahoma; R. H. is the active manager of his father's farm; and Ernest is assistant postmaster at Canton.

CLARENCE W. KERFOOT is an Oklahoma pioneer and during the twenty-five years spent in this state has touched with his enterprise a great variety of undertakings. He helped to start things in a business way in several localities at the successive openings of the old Oklahoma Territory. He was a homesteader in the Cherokee Strip. In the past fifteen years his home and activities have been centered at Shawnee, where he is now at the head of one of the largest real estate offices and has been a prime factor in developing Shawnee real estate.

Mr. Kerfoot is of Kentucky and Virginia lineage. Back in the old Shenandoah Valley of Virginia, where his ancestors lived, the old family estate is still known as the Kerfoot homestead. His great-grandfather was Samuel Kerfoot, who with two brothers, John and William, came over from Dublin, Ireland, in 1777, and reached American shores in time to participate with the patriots in the war of the Revolution. All three of these brothers were in Washington's army in the final campaign against Cornwallis and were present at the surrender at Yorktown. Afterwards these brothers were associated with some surveying and western land proposition of General Washington, and in return for their services they received grants of land in the beautiful Shenandoah Valley. Samuel Kerfoot died in that valley. The grandfather was also named Samuel Kerfoot and was born in the Shenandoah Valley of Virginia and died in Hardin County, Kentucky, before Clarence W. Kerfoot was born. He was an early settler in Hardin County, owned a large farm, one of the finest in the state, at Long Grove, Kentucky.

It was in Hardin County, Kentucky, that Clarence W. Kerfoot was born September 9, 1866, and his father Jesse L. Kerfoot was born in the same county in 1835, and is still living there at the venerable age of eighty years. It has been his home all his life, and besides his work as a farmer he has loyally served as a minister of the Methodist Episcopal Church, South. He is now retired. He is a member of the Masonic fraternity and in politics a democrat. Jesse L. Kerfoot married Mattie Williams, who was born in Hardin County in 1845 and died there in 1899. The four children are: Annie, who lives at Louisville, Kentucky, is the widow of R. C. Crist, a contractor and builder; Clarence W.; Melvin H., who is a farmer and stock man in Hardin County; and Clitus, who graduated M. D. from the Louisville Medical College and is now practicing medicine at Prague, Oklahoma.

Growing up on the old Hardin County homestead, Clarence W. Kerfoot had liberal advantages both at home and in school. He attended the common schools, a private school at Millerstown, Kentucky, and in 1885 finished his senior year in the high school at Horse Cave, Kentucky. The first twenty-three years of his life were spent on his father's farm.

In 1888 he went out on his own account and bought a farm of 100 acres in Hardin County, and after cultivating it for two years sold out. Then on October 10, 1890, he arrived at El Reno, Oklahoma, in the second year after the original opening. At El Reno he remained as clerk in a grocery store until 1892. With the opening of the Cheyenne and Arapahoe reservations he made the run and established one of the first grocery stores at Cloud Chief. However, he soon sold out, and returning to El Reno was again connected with a local grocery establishment till September, 1893. With the opening of the Cherokee Strip he went in as a homestead claimant, and secured 160 acres twelve miles east of Enid. He made this the scene of his activities for six months and then sold out to advantage.

Since that experience Mr. Kerfoot's activities have embraced a wider and more general scope. With his cousins, George and John Kerfoot, each of whom put in $1,100, he helped establish a wholesale dry goods business at El Reno. He was identified with that establishment until he sold out in 1899. In March, 1900, he came to Shawnee, and since then his influence has been a potent factor in the upbuilding of this central city of Oklahoma. He and his cousins, George H. and M. M. Kerfoot, bought the Mammoth general dry goods store, situated at the corner of Main and Bell streets. George H. Kerfoot is now manager of this large emporium, one of the best dry goods stores in the state. At the close of 1900 Clarence W. Kerfoot sold his interest in this store, and then opened the Kerfoot-Wayland wholesale grocery, with which he was actively identified until 1906. This is now a branch of the Williamson, Halsell, Frazier Wholesale Grocery Company, in which Mr. Kerfoot is still a stockholder.

In recent years Mr. Kerfoot has bought and sold a number of merchandise stocks, but primarily has been in the real estate business as a developer and property owner on his own account. His offices are in a building which he owns at 112 East Main Street. On Ninth and Union streets he owns a block of land 100x140 feet, on which are three substantial buildings, one of them recently completed. He also owns a comfortable home at 327 North Union Street, and a number of city lots. As a farmer he is proprietor of 120 acres one mile from Maud, but has sold all the other farm property which at different times he has owned in this state.

In politics Mr. Kerfoot is a democrat, is a member of the Methodist Episcopal Church, South, and is affiliated with Shawnee Lodge No. 657, Benevolent and Protective Order of Elks. On October 28, 1898, at El Reno, he married Miss Anna Richardson. Her father is David Richardson, a farmer in Mead County, Kentucky. Mr. and Mrs. Kerfoot have two interesting children. Mary Weldon, who was born October 21, 1900, has shown brilliant scholarship, and is now combining the junior and senior years of work in the Shawnee High School, and will complete the regular four-year course in less than three years. She is especially proficient in history. C. W., Jr., born September 30, 1909, is now in the first grade of the public schools.

T. S. CHAMBERS. One of the pioneers of the Cherokee country, T. S. Chambers has for more than twenty years been actively identified with Kay County, was one of the builders of the first railway line in that section of the state, and is now giving an excellent administration to the duties of postmaster at Tonkawa. He received his appointment to this office during the Wilson administration on August 18, 1913. Tonkawa is one of the thriving little cities of Northern Oklahoma, has a population of about 2,000, and was first settled in 1896. The postoffice is third class, and the personnel of its official staff are: T. S. Chambers, postmaster; R. K. Ferguson, assistant postmaster; and three rural carriers, P. J. Devore, R. L. Johnson and H. S. Chambers.

T. S. Chambers was born in Clay County, Indiana, October 31, 1868, and has had a life filled with activities, from school teacher to postmaster. He is a man of great breadth of mind, vigorous in the handling of business affairs, and has been a constructive factor in the life of Kay County. His father, T. Chambers, was born in Ohio, and was a successful farmer. He married Sarah Eckert, also a native of Ohio. Her father died at the age of seventy-two and the mother at seventy-one. They were the parents of the following children: L. P., a resident of California; O. L., a farmer; T. S.; F. G., a farmer; H. N.; Anna Ballinger, a widow living at Ponca City; H. S., in the service of the postoffice at Tonkawa; Edna V. Thomas of Tonkawa; and Dennis D., of Junction City, Kansas.

T. S. Chambers spent his early youth on an Iowa farm, and acquired a substantial education. For about ten years he was engaged in the work of teaching school, largely in Sumner County, Kansas. He received part of his education in Guthrie Center, Iowa, and also attended a college.

Mr. Chambers made the run into the Cherokee Strip in September, 1893, and succeeded in staking out a claim for himself. He then took the lead in securing better transportation facilities for the county, and was secretary and treasurer of the old Southwestern Railroad Company, which constructed the first railway line in the county.

This road was subsequently sold to and is now a part of the Frisco System. It was Mr. Chambers who went to New York and succeeded in interesting capitalists, who took the bonds of the proposed road, and he also secured a large part of the right of way. For four years Mr. Chambers was an active factor in the development of the oil and gas resources about Tulsa.

At Perry, Oklahoma, in October, 1906, he married Miss Edith Ferguson. Mrs. Chambers has spent most of her life in Oklahoma, and completed her education in Norman. Her father, D. K. Ferguson, is now assistant postmaster at Tonkawa. To their marriage have been born two children: Roland S. and Robert Glen. Mr. Chambers is a thirty-second degree Scottish Rite Mason and also a Knight Templar and Shriner. In politics he has long been an influence in the democratic party in his section of the state, and in 1912 was a delegate to the Baltimore Convention which nominated the great statesman and scholar, Woodrow Wilson, and is one of the enthusiastic supporters of that President, whose administration bids fair to take rank as one of the most notable in the country's history.

J. BERT FOSTER. The position of J. Bert Foster in the City of Chandler is one both of prominence and influence. He is city clerk and superintendent of waterworks, and is also president of the state firemen's association of Oklahoma. During the twenty years he has lived in the town no one has been more actively and public spiritedly useful in boosting the resources and development of that thriving Oklahoma city. His popularity is as great as his usefulness, and he has that excellent faculty of making and retaining strong friendships. In both his private business and in public affairs he has shown intelligence, hard common sense, and an ability to meet all the exigencies that come up during the routine of responsibility.

J. Bert Foster has lived in Lincoln County twenty-three years, having come to Oklahoma from DesMoines, Iowa. He was born in Decatur, Illinois, July 18, 1872, of a family noted for honesty and integrity. His father was Sam T. Foster, a native of Ohio, and of Scotch-Irish ancestry. He was married in Illinois to Jane Stevenson, who was born in Pennsylvania of an old family of that state. Sam T. Foster died at the age of fifty-three, after an active career as a farmer. In politics he was a democrat, and once served as sheriff of Moultrie County, Illinois. He was affiliated with the Independent Order of Odd Fellows.

J. Bert Foster, who was one of two children, was reared and educated in Illinois and at Des Moines, Iowa, and as a young man learned the cigar maker's trade. He followed that occupation as a workman until removing to Chandler, when he founded one of the first cigar factories in this part of Oklahoma. Mr. Foster was married in Chandler to Miss Ella Mills, who has spent most of her life in Oklahoma and received her education in the Sac and Fox schools. They are the parents of one son, J. Bert, Jr. Mr. Foster is affiliated with the Independent Order of Odd Fellows and the Modern Woodmen of America and has passed the different chairs in these lodges. He is affable, courteous, and everyone who has business at the office of the city clerk or with the superintendent of the waterworks plant is impressed both with his efficiency and his genial manner.

HON. MAXWELL SLOAN BLASSINGAME. By patient and conscientious work and consistent study during the first half of his term as a member of the State Senate, Senator Blassingame established himself in the esteem and confidence of his colleagues, thereby laying the foundation for the honor that was conferred upon him at the beginning of the regular session of the Fifth Legislature. With little or no opposition he was chosen chairman of the Senate Democratic Caucus, by virtue of which position he was majority leader of that body in the Fifth Legislature. The first half of his senatorial career was filled with efforts toward constructive legislation and party harmony, and the experience gained qualified him for both legislative and political leadership in the second half. Senator Blassingame has spent many years in Oklahoma Territory and State, and in his home town of Sallisaw was a prominent newspaper editor and publisher.

Maxwell Sloan Blassingame was born March 29, 1874, in Murray County, Georgia, and represents some fine old southern stock. His parents were W. G. and Margaret (Anthony) Blassingame. His father, now living, at the age of seventy-seven, with his son in Sallisaw, is a veteran of the Confederate army, in which he served with distinction as a lieutenant. He was born in Georgia and descended from ancestors who were among the earliest settlers of the Carolinas. The Blassingame family left South Carolina and removed to Georgia in 1870. On his mother's side Senator Blassingame is descended from Germans in Saxony who became pioneer Americans in Pennsylvania and later in the Carolinas. The various generations of the Blassingames in America have been among the foremost people of their communities in political, social, church and military life. Dr. William Fields, a cousin of W. G. Blassingame, and Thomas Bowen, a nephew, represented Pickens County in the convention that framed the present constitution of South Carolina. Doctor Fields was one of the few democratic members of the House during "reconstruction days" in that state, and later of the Senate, during which time Thomas Bowen served in the House. The Bowens were among the leading families of the state during more than one generation, and now have distinguished representatives in South Carolina and Texas. Samuel E. Fields, a double cousin of Doctor Fields and another cousin of Senator Blassingame's father, once served as state senator from the Forty-third Senatorial District of Georgia.

Senator Blassingame has been largely the architect of his own fortune, and has had few favors in life which he did not earn. As a boy he attended the short-term rural schools of his home county, later was a student in the Coosawatee Institute at Decora, Georgia, in the Fairmount College at Fairmount, and also in the N. G. A. College at Dahlonega, Georgia. In 1893, in order to earn money to complete his college education, he came out to McGregor, Texas, and by the sweat of his brow in cotton fields labored early and late until his savings were sufficient for his ambitious purpose. He then returned to Georgia, entered Fairmount College as a student under George S. Fulton, one of the ablest, best-known and most loved professors of his day, and subsequently attended the N. G. A. College.

About sixteen years ago Senator Blassingame came out to Oklahoma, locating in Washita County. There he taught in the public schools, and for four years was a member of the county board of examiners, during the administration of County Superintendent J. S. Norton. While teaching a subsequent term at Spiro he purchased the Sallisaw Gazette, and when school was out took charge of the paper and plant. That year, 1906, he organized the Democrat Publishing Company at Sallisaw, which bought and consolidated the papers and plant of the Gazette and the Star. He continued in charge of the new publication, the Star-Gazette, until 1912, when he sold it to Alexander & Hentzel.

Senator Blassingame's activity in politics began in his early youth, and in Oklahoma with statehood, and reveals many of the interesting facts in local political annals since that time. He was secretary of the first democratic central committee of Sequoyah County, which was created by the constitutional convention in 1907, and for two years was a member of the democratic state central committee from Sequoyah County. Many times he has represented his county in state conventions of the democratic party and when delegates were selected to attend the Baltimore convention which nominated Woodrow Wilson, now President, he was chosen, by acclamation, secretary of the convention, perhaps the largest and most representative body of democrats ever assembled in the state. In the City of Sallisaw he has served as a member of the city council and the board of education. His election to the State Senate came in 1912. In the Fourth Legislature Senator Blassingame was chosen chairman of the senate committee on printing. During that session he had the honor of nominating Robert L. Owen to succeed himself in the United States Senate. With that nomination one function of the State Legislature was probably abolished for all time, since Senator Owen was the last of Federal senators to be elected by the Oklahoma Legislature. The honor was especially gratifying to Senator Blassingame in view of the fact that Mrs. Owen is a niece of George S. Fulton, the beloved tutor of Senator Blassingame in Georgia. Besides the chairmanship of the printing committee, Senator Blassingame in the fourth session was a member of the committee on banks and banking, and had much to do with the preparation and passage of the banking act which inaugurated a new era in financial affairs in the state. He was co-author with Senator Pugh of Anadarko of a law compelling public officials and their employes to file with their claims against the public treasury receipts received for the money spent. During the session he also labored assiduously as a pronounced supporter of the administration of Governor Cruce, opposing some of the notable and wholly unnecessary investigations of that period and seeking to prevent prolonged legislative sessions.

In the Fifth Legislature Senator Blassingame was chairman of the democratic caucus, and proved himself a worthy and commendable leader of his party.

For his success in life Senator Blassingame bestowed much credit upon his wife, a woman of distinctive culture and leadership in woman's affairs in her home city, and representing a prominent southern family. Before their marriage, which occurred July 10, 1902, Mrs. Blassingame was Miss Judith Bertena Byrd, of Fairmount, Georgia. The Byrd family has been prominent in many important undertakings for several generations in Georgia, in Virginia and in Oklahoma. William Byrd, of whom Mrs. Blassingame is a lineal descendant, the most prominent of the family, was a member of the King's Council in Virginia in colonial days, and some of his conspicuous achievements were the laying out of the principal cities of Virginia, including Richmond, and establishing the boundary line between Virginia and North Carolina. He is said to have possessed the largest library and was one of the most learned men in all the colonies. Mrs. Blassingame is an active leader in church and social circles, and possesses a genuine affability and an ever-present desire for service that has won her esteem among all classes, and among her elders in particular. Senator and Mrs. Blassingame have two children: Ruth Fern, aged thirteen; and Maxwell Sloan, Jr., aged eleven. Another son, William Byrd, died at the age of seven months. Six brothers and sisters of Senator Blassingame live in various states of the South, Southwest and Middle West.

Senator Blassingame is a member of the Baptist Church at Sallisaw, is affiliated with the Masonic lodge and the Knights of Pythias lodge in that town, being a past chancellor in the latter. He is a member of the Sigma Nu college fraternity, No. 7, at Dahlonega, Georgia, which was one of the original chapters of that fraternity in the United States. Senator Blassingame is a member of the Sallisaw Hunting and Fishing Club, of the Sallisaw Commercial Club, of the Oklahoma Press Association, and of the Oklahoma Board of the National Red Cross Society, an honor conferred upon him by the governor of the state.

JACOB JOHNSON, who became closely identified both in business and marriage with the Indian tribes of Kansas and Oklahoma, was born in Washington, District of Columbia, March 2, 1823, and died May 8, 1911, on his wife's allotment 2½ miles west of Shawnee, Oklahoma. One of his children is Mrs. Emma D. Goulette of Shawnee.

William Johnson, his father, was born in England in 1771. From about the age of twelve he followed the sea until he retired as captain at sixty-five. His death occurred in Washington, District of Columbia, in 1859. He was a man of excellent education, and was a communicant of the Episcopal faith. He made his home in Frederick County, Maryland, till about 1815 when he removed to Washington. He was mayor of the national capital, sometime between the years 1824 and 1859.

Barbara Miller, who became the wife of William Johnson, was born in Ohio April 21, 1782, but her home for many years was at Middletown, Frederick County, Maryland, where many of her blood connections are still found. In the early days of Washington Barbara Miller conducted a dairy whose products supplied the homes of Washington people for a number of years.

Though his early home and training were in the East, the real life of Jacob Johnson was identified with the western frontier and its people. His literary education was acquired in Washington schools. At the age of nineteen he was earning his own way, being first employed in the District of Columbia navy yards, with his brothers, unloading produce and freighting by boat from the Carolinas.

The turning point of his life came in 1849 when he went to the California gold fields with a Government caravan, though not in the Government employ. After prospecting a year, he sold his mines and came home for a short visit. On going back to California he learned that the purchaser of his property had struck gold, had sold out and had left the fields wealthy.

On this second trip to California Jacob Johnson established a general store. His stock of groceries, mining implements, etc., were freighted from Omaha, Nebraska, in caravans, each trip requiring three to four months. Flour then sold from thirty to forty dollars a barrel; granulated sugar was a distinct luxury, maple sugar being the staple, while whiskey was the only article that was cheap. While freighting Mr. Johnson gave and sold produce to the Indians, and in that way he laid the foundation of a strong friendship which ever afterward existed between him and the red men. After conducting his store and wagon trains three or four years, he made his second visit home, going to his twin brother Henry in Baltimore, where many of his relatives now live.

His next experience in the West was a trip to Washington and Oregon, following the Lewis and Clark trail most of the way. His occupation of fishing and trapping acquainted him with these territories as few white men ever came to know them. With his trapping products he made three or four annual trips to New York.

Next he was one of the engineering party that surveyed the present boundary line from the Rio Grande to the Gulf of California, after the new treaty establishing the line was made with Mexico in 1853. This concluded, he came to Kansas, still a territory, and with his youngest brother as cook conducted a very successful restaurant at Indianola.

It was at Indianola that his destiny became linked by marriage with the Pottawatomie tribe, and a number of years later his family was among the 1,400 who separated from the prairie band of the Pottawatomies in Kansas and located on the thirty mile square in Oklahoma in 1872. At Indianola Mr. Johnson met and in 1856 married his Indian-French wife, Sophia Jarveau (Shovo), who had just returned from school at St. Mary's, Kansas.

Sophia Johnson, a three-quarter blood Pottawatomie, whose given Indian name is "So-pe," was born at Council Bluffs, Iowa, in 1840. Her paternal grandfather Jarveau came direct from France, and his father, and then he, for years engaged in the fur trade for the Indians with the Hudson Bay Company. Her maternal grandfather Ches-haw-gan and wife were fullbloods and prominent members of the Menominee tribe. Her paternal grandmother was a fullblood Pottawatomic Indian from Michigan. All her ancestors were among those Indians, to whom our United States Government treated then ceded to them what is known in history as the Northwest Territory, created by the Ordinance of 1787.

Her father, Louis Jarveau, whose name the "Great White Father" changed to Vieux on his rolls, was a half-breed Pottawatomie of Michigan who met and married Sha-note (Charlotte), daughter of Ches-haw-gan while in Michigan. After their marriage, about 1830, they, with Ches-haw-gan, wife and son Po-mom-ke-tuck or "Peter the Great" moved to what is now Milwaukee, Wisconsin. Here Madaline and Jake were born to the young couple. Louis and family left Milwaukee about 1834, going to Council Bluffs, Iowa, where he was elected tribal chief of the Pottawatomies. The family lived there between eighteen and twenty years. During that time Ellen, Margaret, Rachel, Sophia and Louis were born.

The next move was to Indianola, Kansas, near Topeka. Here Sophia's grandfather and family lived about six miles from them, in bark wigwams, till they saw how houses were built. At Indianola, in addition to his extensive farming and stock raising, Louis "Vieux" continued helping the Indians in their business affairs and in their times of sickness and need, generally. This kind of home life was excellent training for Sophia and the other six children, as each child was required in turn to assist in every line of work from the cooking, sewing and care of the smaller children, to milking and maple tree tapping. A good old negro, "Uncle Charlie," not a slave, lived in Jarveau's family for years, cooking for both hired hands and the family, also helping with the housework generally.

From Indianola Sophia was taken in a wagon to St. Mary's, Kansas, to attend school. While here her eyes became weak so she was compelled to discontinue her studies at the age of thirteen. Thus she had only four or five years of literary training. While she always lived the life of the citizen Indian, her mother Charlotte lived the camp life until her marriage to Louis Jarveau. Measured by the standards of the time, the Jarveaus were wealthy folk. Sophia often tells about her mother's silk and broadcloth Indian dresses, furs, the hired servants, etc. The Indian dress waist those days was what is known as the middy blouse now.

Upon her return from St. Mary's, Sophia met Jacob Johnson, a white American restaurant proprietor, whom she married three years later. The next year, 1857, her mother Charlotte Jarveau died. The father then moved to Vermillion and kept the toll bridge over the Kansas River. Louis "Vieux" married again while here, then moved to Louisville, Kansas, where he lived and farmed until his death in 1872. His death was deeply mourned by hundreds, and to this date his descendants are never without welcome or friends when among those who knew him.

Now to resume the career of Jacob Johnson. After the death of his brother, Andrew, at Indianola, he removed to Vermillion, where he was toll bridge collector for his father-in-law. From Vermillion the family moved in 1861 to Rossville, Kansas, not far from Louisville, where Louis Vieux had his home. There Jacob Johnson spent eleven years engaged in farming, raising corn, wheat, cattle and hogs. He had gone to Oklahoma a short time before his father-in-law died.

After locating temporarily at Sacred Heart, Oklahoma, Mr. Johnson's family moved to Pleasant Prairie, now Beyers, about 1873. There he owned a general store. Not long afterward his large herd of cattle was stolen in a bunch. This, with his generous western disposition for assisting his fellow men by the too generous extension of credit, ruined him financially. He returned to Sacred Heart in 1876. Eighteen seventy-eight found the family at Salt Creek near Sacred Heart. Here he built a small temporary log house where he expected to wait until it was decided where the Pottawatomies would take their allotments of land. This year at Salt Creek favored Mr. Johnson financially. He and his boys farmed, raising corn, hogs and cattle principally.

Better home comforts were found in the roomy rented house, splendid orchard and stock accommodations at Greenhead in 1879, on the Pettifer's place, where the older boys did the farming. The chief crops were corn, cotton and beans. Had the wild deer, hogs, turkeys, quail and prairie chickens not been so plentiful, the family would have been in hard straits for meat that year, since negroes stole most of the large drove of domestic hogs.

While at Greenhead the oldest son, Richard, left home to become mail carrier between Sac and Fox and Red Fork, now known as Sapulpa. There being no bridges, he often risked his life swimming the swollen streams of Deep Fork. The oldest daughter Rachel found employment at the Friends Mission, which was located near the now Shawnee, Pottawatomie and Kickapoo Indian School near Shawnee. The next older boy Lawrence remained home, while the next three in age, James, Sarah Ann and Andrew, entered the Friends Mission as pupils. Here James died.

In 1883 the family moved to Kickapoo near what is now McLoud, until a two-roomed log house was built on the wife's present allotment. This house remained there until 1913 when the site was covered with a new barn. Mrs. Sophia Johnson in her declining years, on her allotment 2½ miles west of Shawnee, resides in a neat five-room frame cottage, built and originally furnished by her educated children.

Mr. Johnson joined the Friends Church at old Shawneetown when Franklin Elliott and wife were missionaries from 1879 to 1884. His wife, baptized and raised a Catholic, united with the Friends Church also, but returned to her original faith after his death. "Grandpa and Grandma Johnson," as they were affectionately called, made a wide circle of acquaintances and friends in their locality, and business men knew them as people of the highest honesty and integrity. In his earlier days Jacob Johnson belonged to the Masonic lodge, but pioneer life forbade a continued active relationship.

Twelve children were born to Mr. and Mrs. Johnson. The first two, Seraphine and Jacob, died at Vermillion, Kansas, Seraphine at the age of four and Jacob when an infant. Richard, born at Vermillion, Kansas, February 26, 1860, died a bachelor January 22, 1889.

Rachel, whose allotment home is at Norman, was born at Rossville, Kansas, May 2, 1863, and married in 1881 John Wall (white) and about 1892 married Jim Hale (white). Loren, born at Rossville, January 31, 1866, married December, 1896, Florence Wooford (white), and has his home near Shawnee. James, born at Rossville in 1868, died in 1884. Sarah Ann, born at Rossville March 14, 1870, married April 7, 1896, J. D. Goulette (Indian), and she died at Shawnee November 2, 1909, her allotment being at McLoud. Andrew, born at Rossville August 11, 1872, is single, and has his allotment at McLoud. Ida, born at Pleasant Prairie, now Beyers, Oklahoma, April 29, 1874, has her allotment at Tecumseh, and married Ben Bollman (white). Emma, born at Sacred Heart, Indian Territory, March 31, 1876, married January 28, 1912, J. D. Goulette, and has allotment at Tecumseh. David, born at Salt Creek, Indian Territory, November 16, 1878, has his allotment at Tecumseh, and married Kate Fansler (white). Katherine, born at Greenhead January 19, 1882, married Charles Craig (white), her allotment being at Shawnee.

JOHN T. HAYS. Among the men who composed the early bar of Kiowa County were several who brought to their practice an experience and ability gained by a number of years of court and office practice in other states, and of these John T. Hays, who located at Hobart in 1903, has continuously maintained the reputation to which his previous training entitled him. Mr. Hays had practiced a number of years in Kentucky before moving to Oklahoma and is one of the best known members of the Oklahoma State Bar Association.

Born in Knox County, Kentucky, in February, 1861, John T. Hays is descended from an Irish family of that name which established its home in Virginia prior to the War of 1812, and one or more of the name participated on the American side in that conflict. His father, Joseph C. Hays, was born in Knox County, Kentucky, in 1834, and died at Winchester in that state October 30, 1902. He was a farmer and stock raiser and in 1890 moved from Knox County, Kentucky, to Boone County, Missouri, and that was his home the rest of his life, his death having occurred while on a visit to Winchester, Kentucky. During the war between the states he was a Confederate soldier under General Morgan one year, but made his escape. He was a member of the Christian Church, and a democrat in politics. Joseph C. Hays married Minerva N. Bain, who was born in Knox County, Kentucky, in 1837, and is now living at Columbia, Missouri. Their children were: Alexander, who died in infancy; John T.; Arah, who died at the age of thirty-five, the wife of Thomas Gilbert, who is now a farmer at Lawton, Oklahoma; J. Smith, an attorney at Winchester, Kentucky; James M., also an attorney, practicing at Okmulgee, Oklahoma; Thomas B., a farmer at Hobart; William, who was a physician and surgeon and died at Highlands, North Carolina, at the age of thirty-five; Ora, who married F. A. Henninger, a jeweler at Columbia, Missouri; and Mrs. Mary Elizabeth Spillman, wife of a farmer at Harris, Kentucky.

John T. Hays grew up in his native county in Kentucky, where he attended the public schools and spent the first eighteen years of his life on his father's farm. He had a varied experience of self help and effort for a number of years before gaining admittance to the legal profession. Three years were spent as a teacher at Barbersville, Kentucky, where he was principal of the public schools, and one year at Williamsburg, Kentucky. For nearly four years he was a student in the Agricultural and Mechanical College at Lexington, and during 1888 was a student in the law department of Vanderbilt University at Nashville, Tennessee. He had already pursued a private course of study in the law, and was admitted to the bar at Franklin, Kentucky, September 9, 1888. Thus Mr. Hays has had an active career as a lawyer for more than a quarter of a century. His first practice was at Barbersville in Knox County, Kentucky, and his practice, continued from 1888 to 1903, brought him into relations with not only the local but the state and federal courts. In 1903 he came to Hobart, Oklahoma, about two years after the opening of the Kiowa and Comanche reservation and has since enjoyed an increasing civil and criminal practice.

A service which has brought his name into prominence among legal circles throughout the state was as a member of the State Code Commission, which revised, annotated and codified the laws of Oklahoma. He is a member of the County, State and American Bar Associations, and in 1910 was a member of the council of the state association and is now a member of its committee on uniformity of laws.

His law offices are in the Starns Building on Fourth Street in Hobart. For several years he has served as a member of the Hobart School Board and has thus assisted in the construction of the school buildings and has promoted the general advancement of local educational facilities. He is a member of the Christian Church, is a democrat in politics, is affiliated with Lodge No. 108, Ancient Free and Accepted Masons, at Barbersville, Kentucky, and also with Barbersville Chapter, Royal Arch Masons.

In 1897 at Barbersville Mr. Hays married Miss Lucy J. Tye. She is a daughter of the late George W. Tye, a farmer at Barbersville. To their marriage have been born four children: Howard Homer, who died when six years of age; Howell Edmond, now in the freshman class of the Hobart High School; Russell Randolph and Helen Hortense, both students in the grammar schools.

PROVIDENCE MOUNTS. One of the oldest lawyers in point of continuous service at Frederick is Providence Mounts, who was an attorney of mature experience and well tried ability when he located there more than ten years ago, and has since developed a profitable business as a lawyer and has made himself a factor in the growth and development of the town.

A Texan by birth, Providence Mounts was born at Denton, Denton County, February 25, 1872. The Mounts family came originally from France, settled in Virginia, moved at a later date to Kentucky, and the grandfather, Providence Mounts, was born in Virginia about 1804, went as a pioneer to Texas and died at Denton about 1876. William H. Mounts, father of the Frederick lawyer, was born in Virginia in 1832 and died at Denton, Texas, in 1889. He went out to the latter state about 1850 and became identified with the farming, stock raising and mercantile interests of North Texas from pioneer times onward. As a democrat he took much interest in the party and in local affairs, and the family has always been one of prominence in Denton County. He served as an elder in the Presbyterian Church and his family were reared in the same faith. During the early days along the Texas frontier he participated in several engagements with the Indians. William H. Mounts married Miss Mattie Haynes, who was born in Mississippi in 1838 and died at Denton, Texas, in January, 1914. Their children were: R. M., who is a stock raiser at Hereford, Texas; Emma, who lives at Denton, and is the widow of Dr. C. Lipscomb; Ena, who married Frank A. Tompkins, in the real estate and insurance business at Corpus Christi, Texas; Providence; John H., a merchant at Frederick, Oklahoma; Sena, wife of W. W. Wright, a farmer and stock man at

Denton; and Alice, wife of Clarence Cockrell, who is in the electrical business at Dallas, Texas.

Providence Mounts obtained his education from the public schools of Denton, and was a student for a time in the high school, and spent one year at the Agricultural and Mechanical College at Bryan, Texas, before entering the law department of the State University. In 1893 he was graduated LL. B., and was thus equipped for practice in a profession at the age of twenty-one. Returning to his old home town of Denton for the next eleven years he was marked as one of the rising attorneys of the Denton County bar, and during that time served both as city attorney and county attorney. Since 1904 he has looked after a growing general civil and criminal practice with home at Frederick, Oklahoma. His offices are in the Stinson-Mounts Building on Grand Avenue, of which he is a part owner.

In politics he belongs to the dominant party in Oklahoma, is a member of the Presbyterian Church, and was formerly identified with the fraternal orders of the Knights of Pythias, the Independent Order of Odd Fellows, the Woodmen of the World and the Mystic Circle. At Denton in 1896 he married Miss May Matlock, daughter of the late Dr. W. R. Matlock, a well known Denton physician. They have one daughter, Barbara Lee, who was born at Denton July 25, 1905.

HON. FRANK CARPENTER. So far as known Representative Frank Carpenter is the only member of the Legislature who participated in three successive land openings of the original Oklahoma. Mr. Carpenter has been identified either with the State of Kansas or with Oklahoma more than thirty years, and for nearly fifteen years has been one of the most progressive and successful farmers in what originally was the Kiowa and Comanche Indian country. He was sent to the Legislature as representative from Caddo County, and his home is at Bridgeport.

Frank Carpenter was born in Erie County, New York, in 1852, and in his pioneering followed the example of his ancestors, who in that relation were identified with several zones of settlement beginning with the early Atlantic coast. His parents were William and Julia (Foote) Carpenter. His father was at one time mayor of the City of Buffalo, New York. The ancestry goes back to the first settlement on Sherman Isle, now Prince Edward Island, the title to which is believed to be in the Carpenter family to this day, although the papers that would establish such a claim were lost by one of the Carpenters in Lake Erie. Mr. Carpenter's mother is a member of the historic Foote family, from which came Commodore Foote, one of America's naval heroes, and Dr. Luman Foote, a noted pioneer minister of the Episcopal Church in Michigan. In the earlier lines of the family one of the most prominent connections was Governor Bradford, the first executive of the Massachusetts Colony.

When Frank Carpenter was sixteen years of age his father moved to Michigan, and for his common school education he attended the schools both of New York and Michigan, and began making his own way in the world as clerk in a wholesale and retail grocery house in Charlotte, Michigan. He remained with that firm for seven years, then became identified with farming and lumbering in Michigan. In 1882 the family removed to Marion County, Kansas, where he took up farming and also engaged in stock raising.

As a resident of the neighboring State of Kansas the opening of the original Oklahoma appealed with special strength to Frank Carpenter, who was a member of the great throng of people who on April 22, 1889, awaited the signal fired at high noon and made the great rush into Oklahoma to get public lands. He was on horseback, and rode for forty miles until reaching a homestead in what is now Deer Creek Township of Oklahoma County. Mr. Carpenter remained two years to prove up his claim, and then returned to Kansas, where in the meantime he had kept his former farm and livestock. The Oklahoma homestead was relinquished to his brother Henry. In 1893 Mr. Carpenter joined the second throng of people seeking public land in Oklahoma, making the run into the Cherokee Strip. Having already held a claim in Oklahoma, he assisted his sister and an uncle in obtaining land, and they settled in Payne County. Mr. Carpenter remained there four years, and again returned to his Kansas farm. When the Kiowa and Comanche Indian reservation was opened in 1901, he went a third time among the land seekers, but this time instead of the race and physical contest engaged in the lottery by registering for claims at El Reno. He was unsuccessful in the drawing but bought land in what afterwards was known as Caddo County. There he established his first permanent home in Oklahoma, and has been identified with that locality ever since.

The first office through which Frank Carpenter served the people of Oklahoma was as county assessor of Caddo County, to which he was appointed by Governor Cruce in 1912. At the end of the same year he was elected to the office for a two year term. In 1914 he was elected a member of the Legislature, and at the beginning of the fifth session was appointed chairman of the Committee on State and School Lands and a member of committees on Appropriations, Public Roads and Highways, Practice of Medicine and Mines and Mining. He was one of the authors of a bill making an appropriation for rewards for bank burglars and was a joint author of a bill correcting the practice of false statements made to merchants by their patrons. He was chairman of the Farmers Caucus in the Legislature and interested in legislation particularly tending to improve farm conditions. Mr. Carpenter has proved a stimulating factor in the Legislature, and has favored a short and busy session, has opposed his influence to the introduction of many useless bills, and has cared little for changes in legislation save those that were vital to the commercial and industrial welfare of the state. He was a supporter of most of the policies of Governor Williams, but avoided being an extremist on economy.

Mr. Carpenter was married at Florence, Kansas, in 1883, to Miss Annie Arnold, who died nine months after the wedding. January 15, 1893, he married Miss Flora Wagner of Florence, Kansas, who died in April, 1908. The three children of this marriage are: Charles, a graduate of the Bridgeport High School and now completing his junior year in the Agricultural and Mechanical College at Stillwater; Edward, completing his freshman year in the Agricultural and Mechanical College; and Mrs. Eris Shacklin, a graduate of the Bridgeport High School and wife of a farmer near Bridgeport. Mr. Carpenter was married January 22, 1913, to Mrs. Annie L. Sharp, whose home was in the State of Washington and whose father was a Polish count in banishment in America. Mr. Carpenter has three brothers and two sisters: Henry lives on the original Carpenter homestead in Oklahoma County; Edward is a farmer at Muskogee; W. H. was for a number of years prosecuting attorney of Marion County, Kansas, and now one of the leading land owners of that state; Mrs. H. S. McDonald is the wife of a retired druggist and capitalist of Kansas City; Miss Emma Carpenter lives with her brother at Bridgeport.

Mr. Carpenter is not a member of church, lodges, clubs or associations, and instead of such associations has devoted himself to improving his farm and livestock and properly rearing his family. Liberal but conservative, he is one of the leading citizens of his county. He has never used tobacco or liquor in any form, and his sons are following his example in that respect.

C. O. WHITE. When Mr. White first became identified with the community of Wynona in Osage County about five years ago, it was in the capacity of a teacher. He was already a well qualified lawyer, and in a short time his practice demanded his entire attention, and as the only local attorney in that part of the county he has proved himself master of the situation and has handled an extensive practice, particularly the settling of estates and in questions affecting the land titles both in Osage and adjoining counties.

An Ohio man, Mr. White was born at Montpelier in Williams County May 30, 1877, a son of I. M. and Lavina (Weitz) White, the former a native of Williams County and the latter of Lucas County, Ohio. Mr. White's maternal grandfather, Adam Weitz, was born in Germany, came when a young man to Pennsylvania, and was married there to Miss Yager, after which he became an early settler on a farm in Williams County, Ohio, where both he and his wife died. Adam Weitz in earlier years was a stone cutter by trade. The paternal grandfather was Joseph White, also a native of Pennsylvania, and he married Miss Barclaw of that state, but of Welsh parentage. Joseph White was a cabinet maker by trade but spent most of his active life as a farmer in Williams County. I. M. White and wife are still living at Montpelier, Ohio, being retired from the farm. Their three children are: Alice, wife of George W. Farlee of Williams County; Myrtle, wife of Alva Shankster of Williams County; and C. O.

C. O. White lived at home with his parents in Northwestern Ohio until he was about twenty-two years of age. In the meantime he had graduated from the Montpelier High School, and prepared for work as a teacher in the Tri-State Normal at Angola, Indiana. His services were employed in several schools in Ohio, and he paid most of his expenses through law school and university either by teaching or by traveling on the road during vacation. In 1902 he entered the law department of the Ohio State University at Columbus, and was graduated in law in 1908. In June, 1909, Mr. White arrived in Oklahoma, and spent a few weeks in normal training at Bartlesville until getting a certificate as an Oklahoma teacher. For three years both he and his wife taught school at Wynona, and he then engaged in practice of the law, but interrupted that to take charge of a school at Osage, but after four months resigned his position and returned to his law office in Wynona. His business as a lawyer developed rapidly after he opened his office, and it was owing to the demands upon his personal attention that he was obliged to resign school work at Osage. In addition to his large practice as the only attorney at Wynona, Mr. White is owner and manager of the Wynona Telephone Exchange and is secretary and attorney for the Wynona Realty Company and handles considerable real estate on his own account. He has been interested in every local enterprise since he established his home at Wynona, and has effected a number of important oil leases in this district.

In politics he is a republican, and took an active interest in politics even during his minority. He is a member of the Methodist Church. In June, 1908, Mr. White married Miss Ida Backus at Hillsdale, Michigan. Mrs. White was born in Kansas May 13, 1885, but when about four years of age her parents returned to Ohio, and she was afterwards sent as a student to Hillsdale College in Michigan, of which institution she is a graduate. She was engaged in teaching school part of the time with her husband, until four years after her marriage. Mr. and Mrs. White have two sons, John Henry Isaiah, born at Wynona May 19, 1914, and Wesley Leonard, born at Wynona June 17, 1916.

E. B. WOOD. As superintendent of the public schools of Newkirk, Professor Wood occupies one of the most responsible posts in the educational system of the state. He has an enviable record as an educator, having spent about thirteen years in the schools of Kay County. He has been identified with the schools at Newkirk for the past four years, and his administration must be given credit for the construction of the splendid new building for the schools in 1914, costing for building and furniture about $50,000. It is one of the most modern and best adapted buildings for school purposes in the state. On the first floor are five classrooms and a gymnasium, with seven rooms on the second floor. The staff of teachers includes twelve in number, with four in the high school which is a highly organized department and sends its graduates direct into the colleges and the universities. The principal of the high school is A. J. Walter. The enrollment in the high school is about 115, and altogether there are 382 pupils. During his four years at Newkirk Mr. Wood has built up the schools in a highly creditable manner, and judged by results alone his position is among the first of Oklahoma school managers.

E. B. Wood was born on a farm near Winfield, Kansas, August 14, 1873. His father, Warren Wood, was a New York State man and during the Civil war served as a soldier in the Union army. He married in Norton County, Kansas, Jennie Hatcher. She was born, reared and educated in Kansas. There were four children, three sons and one daughter.

Professor Wood was reared in Kansas, had the discipline of a farm as well as the advantages of public schools, and after attending country schools entered the Winfield High School and in 1898 was graduated from St. John's College in Kansas. For the past thirteen years he has been connected with the public schools of Kay County. He spent two years at Kildare, and two years in the Tonkawa schools, two years in the Newkirk grade and four years as principal of the high school, before accepting his present post as superintendent of the schools of the entire city.

Mr. Wood was married June 5, 1901, to Effie Burke, a young woman of cultured mind and many happy social qualities. Her father was William Burke. They have two sons: Warren and Harold. Professor Wood is a republican in politics, and is affiliated with the Knights of Pythias.

RALPH P. STANION has been connected with the United States Indian Service continuously for seventeen years, and in this long period is contained a service that for usefulness and faithful discharge of duty is rarely surpassed. His effective labors in connection with the Government's wards have been of a nature which have made him one of the most valued men in the service, and at the present time he occupies one of the most responsible positions therein, the superintendency of the Pawnee Indian Agency.

Mr. Stanion was born at Ithaca, Tompkins County, New York, May 12, 1875, and is a son of James H. and Harriet L. (Parsons) Stanion. His father was born in England, October 30, 1839, and as a youth of eighteen years emigrated to the United States, settling at Ithaca, New York, where he was married to his first wife, who died leaving two children. Later he married Harriet L.

Parsons, who was born in Connecticut, June 21, 1845, and they became the parents of four children. When the Civil war came on, Mr. Stanion, who had become a loyal citizen of his adopted country, enlisted in Company D, One Hundred and Thirty-seventh Regiment, New York Volunteer Infantry, with which organization he later veteranized, serving throughout the period of the war and receiving his honorable discharge at its close with the rank of orderly sergeant. He was in numerous important engagements and at the sanguine battle of Kenesaw Mountain received a wound which incapacitated him for several months. He always maintained his interest in his old army comrades, and until the close of his life was active in the Grand Army of the Republic. As a business man Mr. Stanion was engaged in the manufacture of carriages, wagons and buggies, and won gratifying success through industry and honorable business methods. An Episcopalian, he was observant of church obligations, and reared his children to respect their religious duties. Politically he was a republican, and served several terms as tax collector of this city. His death occurred at Ithaca, August 25, 1914, Mrs. Stanion having passed away there February 11, 1908.

Ralph P. Stanion was a resident of Ithaca until 1898. He secured his early education in the public schools of that city, following this by attendance at Georgetown University, from which he was graduated in law in 1905, with the degree of Bachelor of Laws, and two years later was admitted to practice in the courts of Oklahoma, but has never followed his profession as a calling. In the meantime, in 1898, Mr. Stanion had successfully passed the Civil Service examination for the position of teacher in the Indian Service, and began his duties at Pine Ridge, South Dakota. Subsequently, he was sent to the Fort Shaw (Montana) Indian School, in 1903, and in 1904 went to the General Land Office at Washington, District of Columbia, as clerk, and it was while thus engaged that he pursued his college course. Later he was sent to Darlington, Oklahoma, as superintendent of the Rapahan Indian School, then to the Rosebud Indian School in South Dakota, as superintendent, and in 1909 to Otoe, Oklahoma, as superintendent of the agency. There he remained until 1914, when he came to Pawnee as superintendent of the Pawnee Indian Agency. Mr. Stanion is a republican, stands high in Masonry, being a Shriner and a member of the Consistory at Guthrie, and is an adherent of the faith of the Episcopal Church, in which he was reared.

On January 31, 1900, Mr. Stanion was married to Miss Lillian Carter, who was born at Syracuse, New York, and to this union there have come four children: Elizabeth Lillian, born at Pine Ridge, South Dakota; Ralph Carter, born at Rochester, New York; James Henry, born at Washington, District of Columbia; and Charles Parsons, born at Rosebud, South Dakota.

EDWARD MILTON WASHINGTON. In the local campaign for the election of county officers in Hughes County, in 1914, Mr. E. M. Washington supplied much spice and vigor in his candidacy for the newly-created office of court clerk. Mr. Washington at that time was clerk of the County Court, but by an act of the Legislature in 1913, the offices of county clerk and clerk of the District Court were to be consolidated, resulting in a new office, known as court clerk, the incumbent of which should perform the duties of clerk of both the County Court and the District Court.

The actual qualifications of Mr. Washington for the position to which he aspired were unquestionable. He had been a resident of the county for many years, had a successful business record, and had proved capable and efficient in every position of trust to which he had been called. Especially convincing to the voters was the fiscal record of his administration as county clerk. This record showed that from receipts of something more than $7,000, all the expenses of the office, including salaries, were paid, and a surplus turned over to the county treasurer of over $3,000.

With all these solid facts behind him he could well afford to introduce some of the amenities into the campaign, and one of these which attracted special attention was a speech in which he said that the people of the United States had elected George Washington the first President of the United States, and consequently why should not the people of Hughes County elect E. M. Washington the first court clerk. The people answered this question by electing him by a substantial majority, and he has justified their confidence and so far in his administration has been able to realize the ideal expressed in his promise to the people that he would do his full duty, would assume the responsibilities of the office without delegating them to a deputy, and would do all in an official capacity that any one man should reasonably be expected to do.

Edward Milton Washington is a native of Missouri and was born near Portland, Callaway County, October 5, 1875, a son of Lewis E. and Marian (Bryan) Washington. His father was born at Lexington, Kentucky, August 12, 1835, and was a son of Edward S. Washington, a native of Virginia, who came to Missouri in 1849, and followed farming and stock-raising in Callaway County until his death at the age of seventy-seven. The Virginia branch of the family was closely related to the Washingtons of whom the most conspicuous representative was President George Washington. Lewis E. Washington spent most of his life in Missouri as a farmer and merchant, was for four years county clerk in that state, and he died at the home of his son in Holdenville, Oklahoma, February 3, 1914. He was an active democrat in politics. His wife was born December 10, 1855, near Portland, Missouri, in the same house in which E. M. Washington first saw the light of day, and she died there in July, 1909. Her family was related to the Bryan of which William Jennings Bryan is the most notable representative. E. M. Washington was the first of six children, the others being: Lottie L., of Tulsa; W. D. Washington of Ashfork, Arizona; Vera A., wife of R. B. Williams of Stigler, Oklahoma; Lewis E., Jr., of Tulsa; and Bettie M., who died in infancy.

Edward M. Washington spent the first eighteen years of his life on the old farm in Callaway County, Missouri. He finished his education in that well-known institution of higher training, Westminster College at Fulton, Missouri. A little more than twenty years ago, in 1894, he came to Indian Territory and located at Eufaula in August of that year, and for ten years applied himself assiduously to his duties as a druggist and for three years was bookkeeper in the Eufaula National Bank. In 1907 Mr. Washington came to the east side of Hughes County and at Lamar was engaged in the mercantile business for five years.

On January 1, 1913, he was appointed clerk of the County Court and from that office he entered upon his duties in 1914 as the first court clerk of Hughes County. He has been a democrat all his life and among other positions was city treasurer of Eufaula three years and city recorder two years. He is active in the Methodist Episcopal Chuch South, is a thirty-second degree Scottish Rite Mason, being affiliated with the Indian Consistory No. 2 at McAlester and with the Lodge and Royal Arch Chapter at Holdenville. He is also a member of the Modern Woodmen of America.

On October 19, 1898, Mr. Washington married Miss Catherine Simpson. Mrs. Washington was born at

Eufaula, Oklahoma, August 3, 1878, a daughter of John D. Simpson, an Oklahoma pioneer from Kentucky, who was married in Oklahoma to Susan A. Crabtree Morris, a widow. Mrs. Washington has a little Indian blood in her veins, being a one-sixty-fourth blood Creek. Mr. and Mrs. Washington have four children: Marion M., Sue, E. M., Jr., and George.

JOHN H. BRENNAN, of Bartlesville, is a prominent lawyer of Oklahoma. As attorney for many of the great oil and gas companies operating in the state he has handled a great volume of litigation.

Mr. Brennan is the general counsel for the great natural gas pipe-line interests and oil interests of the allied companies known as the Wichita Natural Gas Company, Wichita Pipe Line Company, Quapaw Gas Company, Empire Gas & Fuel Company and Indian Territory Illuminating Oil Company, operating in the several states of the Southwest.

These interests are known as the Doherty & Company interests.

Mr. Brennan was born at Oshkosh, Wisconsin, in September, 1861. Largely by his own efforts he gained a liberal education, attending the Wisconsin Normal School and the University of Wisconsin. Admitted to the bar in 1884, he was engaged in general practice in Wisconsin for a number of years. While a resident of Wisconsin he was retained by the Foster Estate of Rhode Island to look after its interests involved in the Foster lease on the Osage Reservation in Indian Territory, which he handled from Wisconsin from 1902 to 1906, when he came to Oklahoma to be more closely identified with it.

HON. CHARLES MARTIN, who in 1915 took the post of mayor of Hominy, has long been identified with business affairs in the Southwest, is a civil engineer by profession who helped construct several of the railroads penetrating Oklahoma, and in the handling of large tracts of land and the improvement of real estate has performed a notable service in Osage County.

Born in the rugged mineral section of Southern Missouri, at Pilot Knob, April 18, 1868, he is a son of D. F. and Emily (Franks) Martin, the former a native of Tennessee and the latter of Missouri. His father was long prominent in public affairs in Missouri, served as a major in a Missouri regiment with the Confederate army throughout the war, later became sheriff and tax collector in Iron County, and was also Circuit Court and Probate judge of Howell County. He died at Piedmont in Wayne County, Missouri, in October, 1901, at the age of sixty-nine. His wife, who was reared at Arcadia, Missouri, died at Elkhart, Indiana, in 1913, at the age of sixty-nine. The father was a democrat and while living in Howell County gained the public offices already mentioned against a normal republican majority, and in all his political life was stronger than his local party. There were five children: George, who died at St. Louis in June, 1914; Charles; May, wife of George J. Williams of Elkhart, Indiana; Virginia, wife of T. M. Polk of Wayne County, Missouri; and Jessie, wife of J. W. Story, who is a presiding elder of the Methodist Episcopal Church South, living at Claude, Texas.

Charles Martin was reared in the counties of Iron, Wayne and Howell, in his native state, and obtained his education by self-efforts, though he attended district schools for a time and was also under the instruction of W. D. Vandiver of St. Louis, for two years. He left home at the age of fourteen, and his first regular employment was in the train service of the Iron Mountain & Kansas City Road, now a part of the Frisco System. He was an active railroad man from the ages of nineteen to twenty-eight, and then engaged in merchandising.

At the age of twenty-eight he was married at Siloam Springs, Missouri, to Miss Hallie R. Goodin, who was born in Missouri. Mr. Martin soon afterwards engaged in railroad construction work as a civil engineer, and in that capacity was connected with the building of several lines in the Southwestern country. His last work was as assistant engineer in locating the route of the Missouri, Kansas & Texas from Coffeyville, Kansas, to Oklahoma City, which was finished in 1902. In that year he located in Hominy, spent two years with the Osage Allotment Commission, and for six months was with the Townsite Commission. This commission platted five towns in Osage County. Since then Mr. Martin has been largely engaged in the leasing of pasture lands for Texas cattle men. In 1911 he assisted in organizing the Farmers State Bank at Hominy and later became its vice president. His business is now largely general real estate and townsite promotion, with John L. Freeman as partner, under the firm name of Martin & Freeman. They leased 40,000 acres of land from William Blair of Tulsa each year. In a public way Mr. Martin has been active for a number of years, being an independent democrat. For several years he served as police judge, and in 1915 was elected to his present dignity as mayor. In Masonry he has taken thirty-two degrees of the Scottish Rite and is a member of the Mystic Shrine, is a member of the Presbyterian Church. In association with Mr. Freeman he has constructed a number of fine residences at Hominy, and his own home is one of the attractive bungalows of the town. He has built most of the homes on Price Avenue and several blocks along the west side.

MRS. ELIZABETH PERKINS, of Pawhuska, is a member of the celebrated Chouteau family, which so far as historical records go was the first white family to locate in what is now the State of Oklahoma. Thus Mrs. Perkins, who carried in her veins the blood of those enterprising French traders whose names are so intimately linked with the early history of the City of St. Louis as well as with Oklahoma, and also of members of the Osage Tribe, is one of the most interesting women of the state.

Quite recently in an article that appeared in local papers the editor of this standard history of Oklahoma called attention to the fact that Salina is the site of the first white settlement in Oklahoma. In 1796 a trading post was established by the Chouteaus of St. Louis. The Chouteau brothers were mere lads when they were brought to St. Louis at the time of the first settlement in 1764. They had grown up in the Indian trade and for many years had a practical monopoly of that of the Osage Tribe, the members of which were several times as numerous as they are now.

In 1795 Manual Lisa, a Creole Spaniard, secured from the Spanish governor general of the Province of Louisiana an exclusive concession or monopoly of trading with the Indians of the valley of the Missouri and those of all its tributaries. As the Osage Indians spent most of their time in the valley of the Osage River and as the Osage River was a tributary of the Missouri, it followed that the Chouteaus would lose the lucrative business which they had built up among the Osages. However, there was nothing to prevent the Chouteaus from trading with the Osages at any place outside the watershed of the Missouri. Accordingly the members of this enterprising firm busied themselves in inducing a large part of the Osages to move over and settle in the valleys of the Neosho (or Grand) and Verdigris rivers in Southern Kansas and Northern Oklahoma. The establishment of the trading post in the valley of the Grand River, in

Mayes County, on the present site of the Town of Salina, followed shortly afterward. The selection of this site was doubtless influenced by its proximity to the Saline Springs which made the manufacture of salt possible.

The establishment of a trading post in this remote wilderness brought a retinue of hunters, trappers, traders, clerks and other employees to live there. Probably most of these were Creole French, from Canada, Louisiana and the French settlements in Illinois, Missouri and Arkansas, but there were doubtless several who were of Spanish or Anglo-American antecedents. In common with the customs of the time many if not most of these contracted matrimonial alliances with women of the Osage Tribe. So it is not improbable that there were several families who were prominent residents of the post from the date of its establishment. Prior to 1820 a number of the half blood French Osage offsprings of this community at the Chouteau trading post settled a few miles lower down the valley on the opposite side of the Grand River in the vicinity of the mouth of Chouteau Creek. The location of this French-Osage settlement was probably the consideration which most influenced Rev. Epaphras Chapman in selecting the site for the establishment of the Union Mission, located about seven miles southeast of the Town of Chouteau in 1820.

At some time subsequent to 1815 the Chouteau trading post passed into the possession of Col. Auguste P. Chouteau and his brother Paul. Colonel Chouteau continued to make his home at this place until his death, which occurred in the winter of 1838-39, though a large part of his trading operations had been transferred to other points after steam navigation was introduced upon the Upper Arkansas as far as Fort Gibson. Washington Irving visited Colonel Chouteau here in the fall of 1832, having brought letters of introduction from the kinsmen of the latter in St. Louis.

Shortly after the death of Colonel Chouteau the body of the Cherokee Tribe of Indians migrated to the Indian Territory and the site of the Chouteau trading post having been included within the limits of the Cherokee Nation, the property passed into the hands of Lewis Ross, a brother of Chief John Ross. After the death of Lewis Ross it was acquired by the Cherokee tribal government and it then became the seat of the Cherokee Orphan Asylum. The last of the log buildings of the Chouteau trading post was said to have been destroyed during the Civil war. No vestige of any of them remains now, though several uneven places in the ground are still noticeable, together with a few fragments of rock which were probably left when the remains of ruined fireplaces and chimneys were carted away. The site was on the edge of the second bottom just north of the original road to the ferry. It was in a thicket until the building of the Missouri, Oklahoma & Gulf Railroad in the year of 1912. One noticeable feature was the fact that several ailanthus trees were growing where the post had stood. This species is not a native one in Oklahoma and there are no other specimens growing in the surrounding country. Another noteworthy fact was that prior to the building of the railroad the fleur-de-lis was growing wild in and about the thicket, a mute reminder of the loyalty of the French people of the western frontier to la belle France. As already stated, the railroad right of way occupies a part of the site of the Chouteau trading post. Fortunately, the rest of it is included in the south end of the block reserved for park purposes when the town site was platted and opposite which is the depot location. This will afford an opportunity for the people of Oklahoma to place a monument or marker upon the site of the old trading post.

It was in the locality of the old trading post that Mrs.

Perkins' father, Legess Chouteau, spent many of his years. He was born in Missouri, but was educated at the old Hominy Mission. Legess Chouteau's mother was a full blood Osage, while his father was one of the French traders of that name. The elder Chouteau had been appointed a United States Indian agent in 1826, and died on the Grand River in the home that, as already stated, subsequently became the orphanage for the Cherokee Indians.

Legess Chouteau died at Pawhuska when about sixty years of age. For many years he served as a Government interpreter for the Osage Tribe. He also accompanied the nine full blooded Osage scouts who were engaged by General Custer to trail "Sitting Bull" and his band in the Northwest, and for six months he acted as interpreter between the scouts and the general. He had become an interpreter soon after leaving school, being first employed in that capacity by the American Fur Company in Missouri. While the Osages were living in Southern Kansas Legess Chouteau helped to hew the logs for the building of the first Catholic Mission, now St. Paul, Kansas.

Legess Chouteau was twice married, having eight children by his first wife and two by the second. The children of the first mariage were: Mary Ellen Foraker; Joseph; Charles; Augusta Donavan, who is still living in Osage County; Lewis; Elizabeth, now Mrs. Perkins; Gesso; and Palisia. All these are now deceased except Mrs. Donavan and Mrs. Perkins. The two children of the second marriage were: Mrs. Lena Robinson, who lived at Adamson, Oklahoma; and Henry, of Pawnee County.

Mrs. Perkins grew up among the Osage Tribe and has many interesting associations with this section of Oklahoma. She first married John Ross. By that union there were four children, both sons dying young, while her two daughters still living are: Emma, wife of Clement de Noya of Osage County, and Ella, wife of C. C Haven of Osage County. Mrs. Perkins for her second husband married John Kilbie. There are also two children of this marriage: Coene, wife of William Leesey of Osage County; and Earl, of Chautauqua Springs, Kansas.

In September, 1895, Mrs. Kilbie became the wife of Dr. S. W. Perkins. Doctor Perkins was born near Van Buren, Arkansas, March 1, 1858. After the war his parents located in the Cherokee Nation, and he grew up in Northern Oklahoma and Southern Kansas, but since 1884 has been a resident of Osage County. In 1886 he graduated from the dental department of the University of Michigan, and soon afterwards began practice in the Osage country, and continued the active work of his profession until 1900. Since then he has employed his time in looking after his extensive ranching and real estate interests. Doctor and Mrs. Perkins have a fine farm of 480 acres five miles west of Pawhuska.

JOHN McMULLEN. In the office of municipal commission of highways and public improvements in the City of Bartlesville, the metropolis and judicial center of Washington County, Mr. McMullen has found ample scope for the effective manifestation of his progressiveness and public spirit and he is one of the valued and popular officials of this vigorous and important city. He has been prominently identified with operations in the oil fields of this section of the state and has been connected with this line of enterprise since his youth, his experience having been wide and varied and having touched various states in the Union.

Mr. McMullen was born at Batavia, Genesee County, New York, on the 31st of July, 1871, and is a son of Maurice and Catherine (Canbell) McMullen, both likewise natives of the old Empire State, where the former was born in Niagara County and the latter in Wyoming County. The father died at Arcade, Wyoming County, in 1907, at the age of sixty-five years, and his widow still resides at that place, in which her birth occurred. Maurice McMullen was prominently concerned with oil operations in the fields of Pennsylvania for a number of years and his activities in this line likewise extended into his native state. He was an energetic and duly successful business man and resided for varying intervals at different places in the State of New York, including Olean, Batavia and Arcade. He represented his native commonwealth as a gallant soldier of the Union in the Civil war, in which he served as a member of Company L, Eighth New York Heavy Artillery. He was with this command about two years, participated in a number of important battles, and his regiment was a part of the Second Army Corps under General Hancock, being in front of Petersburg at the time of the surrender of General Lee. Mr. McMullen participated in the Grand Review of the victorious but jaded troops in the City of Washington at the close of the war and in later years he perpetuated his interest in his old comrades through his active affiliation with the Grand Army of the Republic. His political allegiance was given unreservedly to the democratic party and he was a man who commanded the respect and esteem of all who knew him. Of the four children the subject of this review is the eldest: Maurice J. is a resident of Drumright, Creek County, Oklahoma; Elizabeth is deceased; Mary Jane is the wife of Walter J. McCormack, a farmer near North Java, Wyoming County, New York.

John McMullen acquired his early education in the public schools of New York and Pennsylvania, his parents having removed to Butler County in the latter state when he was a child and his father having become a prominent figure in oil operations in that district. As a youth Mr. McMullen was thus enabled to acquire practical experience in connection with the oil-producing business, and in 1893 he went to the oil fields of Indiana, where he became associated with his uncle, Frank Campbell, and others in the oil-producing enterprise. In October, 1898, he went to Los Angeles, California, and after being identified for some time with oil operations in that section of the Golden State he made his way to the oil fields of Wyoming and became associated with the American Consolidated Oil Company. In 1903 he was identified with the same line of enterprise at Chanute and other points in Kansas, and the following year recorded his arrival at Bartlesville, Oklahoma, where he found requisition for his services as an expert in the oil fields of this locality, his activities having extended also into the celebrated oil fields of Texas. He has thus kept in close touch with the development of the various new fields of the West and may well be considered an authority in practical details of oil production.

Mr. McMullen has never deviated from the line of strict allegiance to the cause of the democratic party and has been an active worker in its ranks. In 1913 he was elected to his present responsible office of commissioner of highways and public improvements in the City of Bartlesville, of which he has been indefatigable and circumspect in the discharge of his executive functions. Prior to assuming this office he has served two years as deputy sheriff of Washington County.

Mr. McMullen is a prominent representative in Oklahoma of the time honored Masonic fraternity, in which he has received the thirty-second degree of the Ancient Accepted Scottish Rite. His ancient craft affiliation is with Bartlesville Lodge, No. 284, Ancient Free & Accepted Masons, of which he is past master, and he is past patron of Bartlesville Chapter, Order of the Eastern Star, with which his wife likewise is affiliated. He has been specially active in the affairs of the York Rite bodies with which he is identified and is at the present time, 1915, representative of the same before the Connecticut Grand Lodge.

In October, 1905, was solemnized the marriage of Mr. McMullen to Mrs. Nettie Adkins, who was born in Indiana and who is a daughter of Nathan and Octavia Lounsbury. Mr. and Mrs. McMullen have no children but Mrs. McMullen has one daughter by her previous marriage, Octavia Adkins, who is a member of the home circle.

GEORGE C. PRIESTLEY. One of the best known and influential men in all Oklahoma is George C. Priestley, whose home since 1904 has been in Bartlesville. Mr. Priestley is primarily an oil man, an industry with which he became acquainted in Western Pennsylvania while growing to manhood. His mature years have brought many distinctions and achievements. A few years ago he was regarded as the largest individual oil operator in Oklahoma, and possibly the largest in the United States. He has helped to build and operate many miles of electric railway lines in the Southwest, and has recently concluded improvements and extensions which make the system of waterworks at Bartlesville the best in the state for a city of the size. His financial and business connections are numerous, and his name is one of national prominence in politics. He became identified with the progressive movement in the summer of 1912, and was made chairman of the finance committee of the national progressive party.

George C. Priestley was born at Houlton, Maine, June 10, 1862. He is of Scotch ancestry. His grandfather, George Calvin Priestley, was born in Scotland in 1802, was a graduate of the University of Edinburg, and came to America late in the '20s. He was an engineer by profession, and was a prominent man both in Maine and other sections of the United States. During the threatened war around the Maine-Canada boundary he was employed to locate many of the defenses erected by the United States near the boundary. The trouble was finally settled by arbitration. He became identified with the lumber business, and during the '60s was in the service of Jay Cook in the construction of the Union Pacific Railway, and lost heavily in the memorable "Black Friday" of 1873. He was also engaged in trading with the Indians along the western frontier, and spent his last years in Minnesota, where he died in 1884, and was buried at Brainerd in that state. He was the father of one son and two daughters.

George C. Priestley is a son of George C. and Mattie (Pollock) Priestley, both of whom were born in the State of Maine. His father lived in Maine until the Civil war and then entered the service of the Union army as a private in the Fifteenth Maine Regiment and continued a soldier until the close of the war. He then moved to the oil fields in Western Pennsylvania, and became prominent in the oil well supply business during the early history of that industry. In 1873 he suffered a fracture of his skull and was practically an invalid for many years and died from the effects of the accident in 1892 at Pleasantville, Venango County, Pennsylvania. His widow continued to live in Pennsylvania until her death in 1911. She was the mother of five sons and three daughters, George C. being the oldest child.

Mr. Priestley spent his early life in Pennsylvania, and left school when a mere boy to take up practical affairs. He was employed in a store at Pleasantville, and one of his first employers was the late Sam Q. Brown, at one time president of the Tidewater Oil Company, a subsidiary organization of the Standard Oil. Mr. Priestley soon got into the oil business, and oil has been a study with him for many years, and he is familiar with all phases, producing, refining and marketing. From

Pennsylvania he moved to Bartlesville in 1904, about the time the Oklahoma oil fields were coming into prominence, and operated on an extensive scale until 1909, when he sold some of his most valuable holdings to an English syndicate. However, he has continued to be interested in the industry, though many other concerns have taken much of his time. Mr. Priestley bought and reconstructed the waterworks system of Bartlesville, and during the past eighteen months has spent $100,000 in improvements. The Bartlesville Waterworks Plant represents an investment of $250,000. Mr. Priestley was also president of the local stock company which constructed the Maire Hotel at Bartlesville, at a cost of $135,000, a handsome five-story hotel building that would be a credit to a city twice the size. This hotel was constructed by local citizens for the good of the town and not as an investment. Mr. Priestley has also been a director of the Union National Bank at Bartlesville since its reorganization. This bank has total resources, according to a statement of March, 1915, of nearly $1,200,000, and its deposits aggregate more than $1,000,000. M. F. Stillwell is president, and all the other officers and directors are well known and substantial men in southwestern financial affairs. Mr. Priestley acquired a majority of the stock in this institution, and brought about the reorganization.

He is also president of the Union Traction Company of Kansas. This company has fully 100 miles of electric lines in operation, connecting Coffeyville, Independence, Cherryvale and Parsons. These roads were built by Mr. Priestley associated with eastern capitalists. Mr. Priestley has been a power for good at Bartlesville in connection with various local betterments, particularly the upbuilding of schools and churches. He is chairman of the board of trustees of the Presbyterian Church. Fraternally he is a Mason, and a member of a number of clubs, societies and civic organizations. The only political office he ever held was that of treasurer of Warren County, Pennsylvania. He is one of the largest realty holders in Oklahoma and Texas. During the Spanish-American war he very materially assisted General Wood.

Mr. Priestley's political career has been one of disinterested service. He is a practical and successful business man, and has always believed in the square deal in political life. He came into national prominence during the campaign of 1912, when he upset the republican machine in Oklahoma and gave Roosevelt his first delegate to the national convention. Colonel Roosevelt's remark, "Oklahoma turned the trick," gives Mr. Priestley credit for starting the movement which resulted in the practical disorganization of the republican party at its convention of that year. Mr. Priestley entered that convention as a republican of the progressive type, and later was one of the many who repudiated the actions of the convention leaders and brought about the organization of a new party. Mr. Priestley resigned as national committeeman of the republican party for Oklahoma on August 1st, and soon afterwards was made national committeeman of the progressive party, and became a member of its executive committee and was then made chairman of the finance committee.

Mr. Priestley was married in 1885 to Miss Ruland of Pennsylvania. They are the parents of five children: Willis B., who is associated with his father in business; Hazel, wife of Paul R. Johnson of Bartlesville; Bessie, at home; George C., Jr., connected with the Union Oil Company of Tulsa; and Helen, at home.

B. W. KEY. If there is one firm name that means more than any other to the old timers of Western Oklahoma as well as to the present generation, it is the York-Key Mercantile Company. In the days when this organization sold supplies to ranches and cattle men all over the Southwest, the company had a highly developed organization for supplying goods to all points, whether on the railroad or not. In later years the company's business is almost entirely confined to lumber and building material. The present headquarters of the York-Key Mercantile Company are at Woodward, Oklahoma, but the company maintains a number of branch yards all over the Southwest.

The junior member of this firm is B. W. Key, who was born in Alabama and has been associated with this firm for thirty years. He first became identified with the firm of York-Parker-Draper Mercantile Company. Under this title the company carried on an exceedingly extensive business, handling supplies for cattle men and ranchers and maintained several branches in Western and Southern Kansas, during which time he came to know all of the old ranchers and cattle men in the Panhandle of Texas and Western Kansas and Oklahoma. In a few years Mr. Key had risen to a partnership in this firm. He was a very business-like and astute young man, a hard worker, could be relied upon to make every promise good, and for many years the people of Oklahoma as well as elsewhere have looked upon him as one of the foremost business men. After the deaths of Messrs. Parker and Draper, he became a full partner to F. B. York and the present firm style of York-Key Mercantile Company was originated. It has been a very successful business, and has done a great deal to develop many of the towns of the Southwest. Although Mr. York died December 19, 1915, he, too, like Mr. Key, will always be remembered for his many notable achievements and as a grand, good man—and this is said by the writer of this sketch who knew him well for almost half a century and knew him to stand the acid test in the different walks of life.

In 1893, at the opening of the Cherokee Strip, Mr. Key went to Woodward and opened for his firm the first mercantile house in the town. The Key Building and the Post Office Building are two of the most modern business blocks in Woodward or in Western Oklahoma, and that is only two of the many monuments to Mr. Key's personal enterprise and public spirit. His company were among the first to operate a general store and line of lumber yards in this section of Western Oklahoma, and in neary every live and bustling Oklahoma town is to be found tangible evidence of the influence and enterprise of this company. A few years ago the company closed out its mercantile stores and is now confining the business to a line of lumber yards.

Thus, for more than twenty years, Mr. Key has through his individual enterprise and through the company of which he is the active head, been closely identified with the welfare and benefit of Western Oklahoma.

Those who have observed his activities and influence most closely are positive in their assertions and belief that no one has done more to promote the welfare of the Town of Woodward and the schools of Woodward, or the town and school interests of any other place in Northwestern Oklahoma, where one of the York-Key Lumber Yards is located, than Mr. Key himself. It is said that he has always instructed his men to vote for any measure for the permanent advancement of the town and especially the schools and county roads. He has done this notwithstanding the fact that he had no children of his own to educate and realized that voting for such measure would increase the taxes on his property. That is the quality of public spirit such as few business men can exemplify.

Mr. Key is now living retired in a comfortable home in Galveston, Texas. He is connected with some of the chief financial interests of that city, and is president of the Security Trust Company of Galveston, a three hundred thousand dollar corporation; is president of the Gulf Lumber Company of Galveston; vice president of the City National Bank of Galveston; and a director of the American National Insurance Company of Galveston.

SAMUEL ECKER. A great many citizens of Texas County know Samuel Ecker only in his capacity of United States Commissioner and through his active relations as a citizen of Guymon and with the real estate and loan business there. However, he has had many other experiences, and has traveled about the western world a great deal, has been in many of the most noted mining districts of both North and Central and Southern America, and for two years he was a United States soldier in the Philippine Islands. In fact, he comes of a military family, and his father gained the rank of colonel in the Confederate army during the war between the states.

He was born June 27, 1872, at 3036 Lucas Avenue in St. Louis, Missouri, a son of Samuel and Margaret (Gerbig) Ecker. His father, who was born in 1837, in France, came along to America at the age of twelve years, locating at New Orleans.. From there he went up the river by steamer to St. Louis, but at the outbreak of the Civil war returned to the South and enlisted in the Confederate army with a Louisiana regiment. He was in active service until the close of hostilities, and was mustered out with the rank of colonel. After the war he returned to St. Louis, and became a hotel man. It was in the hotel business that he was actively engaged until he retired, and many thousands of travelers have known him as a genial and successful boniface. From St. Louis in 1888 he moved to El Paso, Texas, and was at the head of a hotel there until it burned in 1892. From there he went to Denver, Colorado, conducted a hotel until 1900, and has since lived retired, his home being now in Chicago. In 1865 Samuel Ecker, Sr., married Miss Margaret Gerbig, who was born in Germany November 20, 1845. Six children were born to their union, two sons and four daughters, namely: Emma Margaret, born February 9, 1886, is now the wife of Major James E. Normoyle of the United States Army and they have one child named Margaret; Anna Laura, born February 12, 1868, is the wife of Eugene C. Morton of Chicago and their one child is named Eugene Ecker; Samuel, Jr.; Helen Marie, born February 17, 1876, is unmarried and living with her parents in Chicago; Jessie Dorothy, born February 20, 1878, is also at home with her parents; Eugene Chester, born December 20, 1880, recently retired from the United States regular army with the rank of second lieutenant.

Samuel Ecker, Jr., was reared and educated in his native city of St. Louis, and completed his education in the Christian Brothers College. After that he spent four years in Mexico, in the gold mines of that country. He continued his adventurous life in the Latin American Republic by a prospecting tour through Central and South America, but finally returned to the States and was living at Pueblo, Colorado, at the outbreak of the Spanish-American war. At the first call for volunteers he enlisted in Company A of the First Colorado Regiment, United States Volunteer Infantry. He was mustered in May 1, 1898, the day of Dewey's great victory in Manila Bay, and soon afterwards sailed as a private on June 15th for the Philippine Islands. He was gone two years, and participated in many of the campaigns which finally brought about the subjugation of the Filipinos and eventually returned with his command to San Francisco, where he was mustered out in September, 1900. At that time he was regimental sergeant major.

After leaving the army Mr. Ecker engaged in the real estate and oil business in Indiana for three years. In 1903 he came to Oklahoma, was at Oklahoma City for several years, and during 1905-06 was an assistant secretary to the secretary of the State School Land Commission. In 1907 he located at Guymon, and with that city he has since been closely identified not only as a business man but as an upbuilder of the town. In 1910 he was appointed United States Commissioner for the Western District of Oklahoma. Politically he has always been active as republican, and for six years has been chairman of the Texas County Central Committee. Fraternally he is a thirty-second degree Scottish Rite Mason and Shriner and also a member of the Benevolent and Protective Order of Elks. He and his family are members of the Methodist Episcopal Church.

On December 25, 1907, at Guthrie, Oklahoma, Mr. Ecker married Miss Joan Massey. She was born in Marshall County, Kansas, August 14, 1883, a daughter of John and Said (Allen) Massey, the former a native of Ireland and the latter of Illinois. Her parents came to Logan County, Oklahoma, at the original opening on April 22, 1889, and her father and mother are now living retired in Guthrie. Mr. and Mrs. Ecker have one child, Helen Marie, who was born at Guymon, March 4, 1909.

WILLIAM H. LEWIS, of Laverne has been a participant in the pioneer activities of two states, Kansas and Oklahoma. He came to Oklahoma with the opening of the Cherokee strip in 1893, and for many years was a factor in business and public affairs in old Woods County. He moved to Laverne with the opening of that town, as is now proprietor of the Laverne Electric Light, Ice and Power Company.

Still a comparatively young man, with all the vigor of his prime, he was born August 22, 1870, at New Waterford, Ohio, a son of Stephen and Mary (Schrum) Lewis. His father, who is now living retired at Alva, Oklahoma, is a veteran of the Civil war, having been for three years a member of the Twelfth Ohio Infantry under the late President William McKinley, who was a major in that regiment. Stephen Lewis was born in Indiana April 5, 1836, and in 1859 was married in Mahoning County, Ohio, to Miss Mary Ann Schrum. She was born in Mahoning County, Ohio, April 10, 1838, a daughter of Joseph Schrum, a native of Germany. She died at Alva, Oklahoma, September 14, 1900. Through practically all her years she was a devoted member of the Christian Church. There were ten children, six sons and four daughters namely: Myron, now deceased; Ollie, the wife of Henry Moore, of Ellsworth, Kansas; Rhoda, wife of W. S. Kessler, a retired farmer at Guthrie; William H.; Ida, wife of John G. Smith of Alva, Oklahoma; Frank J., farmer at Waynoka, Oklahoma; Charles F. of Beaver, Oklahoma; Elmira, wife of Christopher Webber, a merchant at Alva; Clark and Arthur, both of whom are merchants at Canadian, Texas.

In 1876, when William H. Lewis was six years old, his parents removed to Russell County, Kansas, where his father took up a tract of Government land. Later they went to Fort Kit Carson, Colorado, where at the age of twelve years William participated in a buffalo hunt. About the same time he made a 300 mile horseback ride back to civilization in Kansas. The first school he ever attended was at Bunker Hill, Kansas, where he entered as a student at the age of fourteen. After attending there one year he entered the law office as office boy of Judge James Lewis, an uncle, at Scotia, Nebraska. Having read law three years he was admitted to the Nebraska bar, but has never followed the law as a profession.

With all these varied activities and experiences William H. Lewis lived the first twenty-three years of his life, and was about that age when in 1893 he participated in the opening of the Cherokee strip in Oklahoma. He secured a claim in the southwest portion of Woods County, and remained there to develop a good farm and cultivate it for ten years. During the following three years he conducted a real estate business, and also had a grocery store at Alva, of which city he was a resident until 1912. Then with the opening of the new townsite of Laverne he joined his fortunes with a new community, and took an active part in one of Oklahoma's leading agricultural industries by buying and shipping broom corn on a large scale. In 1915 he secured a franchise for an electric system in Laverne, built the plant, and gave that town the first electric light service in that section of the state. In 1915 Mr. Lewis increased his public utility by the erection of a modern building in which he installed an eight ton ice plant. The business is now conducted under the firm name of W. H. Lewis & Son. Fraternally Mr. Lewis is an Odd Fellow.

On March 18, 1894, at Alva, Oklahoma, he married Miss Marcie Keith, who was born in Kentucky in 1878, a daughter of Rev. E. R. Keith of Courtland, Kansas, also a native of Kentucky, and Mrs. Lewis is a niece of the late Governor Gobel of Kentucky. The one son of their union is Elmer Reed Lewis, who was born at Alva November 3, 1896, was educated in the Alva public schools, graduating from high school at the age of sixteen, and is now actively associated with his father in business.

JAMES GEORGE WRIGHT. Peculiar qualities are demanded in those dealing with the Government wards, the Indians. Not only must a man be capable, but he has to understand the Indian character and while proving himself their friend, impress upon them the dignity of the government. J. George Wright, formerly commissioner of the Five Civilized Tribes at Muskogee, Oklahoma, and later superintendent of the Osage Indian Agency at Pawhuska, Oklahoma, is one of the most efficient of the Government's trusted officers.

Mr. Wright was born at Naperville, DuPage County, Illinois, January 8, 1860, being the son of the late James G. Wright and Almira (Van Osdel) Wright, pioneers of Naperville. The father a farmer and banker, a strong republican, was postmaster under President Lincoln and served six terms in the State Assembly of Illinois and later as United States Indian Agent at the Rosebud Reservation in Dakota.

J. George Wright attended the public school and the Northwestern College at Naperville, Illinois. In 1883 he was appointed clerk of the Rosebud Indian Agency, in Dakota, where his father was Indian agent, and later was made agent in charge. Showing marked ability and tact in handling these Sioux Indians, he was in 1889 appointed United States Indian agent of the agency by President Harrison upon the recommendation of Gen. George Crook and others, and though a republican he was reappointed by President Cleveland. In 1896 he was appointed United States Indian inspector by President Cleveland, reappointed by President McKinley and President Roosevelt, serving in such capacity until 1907, and during most of this period he had the superintendency of Indian matters in Indian Territory with the exception of the allotments of land.

In 1907 he was appointed as commissioner of the Five Civilized Tribes in Oklahoma. In 1914, by an act of Congress, this office was abolished by its consolidation with the office of superintendent and Mr. Wright was appointed to his present position as superintendent of the Osage agency and assumed its duties in February, 1915, with headquarters at Pawhuska.

A man of marked ability, thoroughly conversant with all matters pertaining to the care and supervision of the Indians, Mr. Wright has served the Government faithfully and acceptably for a period of thirty-three years.

WILLIAM S. MATHEWS. Among the prominent men of the Osage Tribe during the last half century probably none was more distinguished for his personal individuality and his varied service in business and public affairs than William Shirley Mathews, who died at his home in Pawhuska March 15, 1915, at the age of sixty-six years and six months. To the modern City of Pawhuska Judge Mathews was perhaps best known as a banker, but during his long residence in the Osage country had filled nearly all the important posts of honor and responsibility in the tribal government, and possessed that strength of character, judgment and ability which made him a natural leader of his people.

The mother of Judge Mathews was a half-blood Osage Indian, and this fact accounts for his membership in the tribe and also his primary qualification for the various honors which he received at the hands of his people. William Shirley Mathews was born near the old Creek Agency near Muskogee September 15, 1848. His father was born in Kentucky but in the early days moved to Indian Territory, and was long identified with the Osage tribe, at first in Kansas near Oswego, and later in the Indian Territory. The ancestry of this branch of the Mathews family extends back to Judge Mathews' great-great-grandfather, John Mathews, who served as a sergeant in General Washington's army during the Revolution. Judge Mathews' mother was also of prominent stock. She was a daughter of William Shirley Williams, of Vermont, who discovered and named Williams' Peak in the moutains of Colorado.

Up to the beginning of the Civil war the Mathews family resided near Oswego, Kansas, and Judge Mathews gained his early education at the hands of the Jesuits in charge of the old Osage Mission where the present town of St. Paul, Kansas, is located. During the war the family removed to Texas, but after its close Judge Mathews came to Indian Territory and worked as a cattle herder in the Cherokee Nation. He was employed by a number of the big cattle outfits of Texas, and frequently took cattle over the trails through Indian Territory to Kansas, his most frequent route being the old military trail that passed through Fort Gibson.

From 1874 until his death Judge Mathews was a resident of Pawhuska, the old capital of the Osage Indian. It should be remembered that Pawhuska was in no sense a city at that time nor for many years afterwards, since the real municipal history of that community covers hardly more than ten years. The first two years he spent at Pawhuska was in the employ of Isaac T. Gibson, the old Indian agent. He was also interested in cattle ranching until an injury resulting from a fall and causing the injury of one leg caused him to give up ranching and he finally turned his energies almost altogether to banking. He was one of the original founders of the Osage Mercantile Company, and also helped organize the First National Bank at Pawhuska, but subsequently sold his stock in that institution. He was one of the organizers of the First State Bank at Hominy and the bank at Grayhorse, but disposed of his interests in those towns when he organized what is now the Citizens National Bank at Pawhuska. This was organized in August, 1905, and he became its first president. After the reorganization of the bank in 1909, Judge Mathews remained one of its directors until his death.

Pawhuska had no more public spirited and enterprising citizen in promoting its general upbuilding than Judge Mathews. He was always generous of his time and means to forward improvements in which he believed, and was also willing to serve in public offices that meant only work and neither compensation nor any special honor. For two terms he was a member of the city council, and at the time of his death was serving as a member of the board of education. Earlier, in the Osage tribe, he filled the office of national treasurer from 1882 to 1886. From 1890 to 1892 he was chief justice of the Osage Nation, and from 1894 to 1896 was national attorney. He was also a member of the national council several times before allotment and twice afterward. The tribe frequently chose him to look after the interests of the nation in Washington. He was a man of strict and rigid integrity, and commanded the respect of all who knew him or had business relations with him. Judge Mathews was deeply interested in Osage history and tribal affairs, and was regarded as one of the authorities whose knowledge of Osage annals was almost encyclopedic.

Judge Mathews was affiliated with Pawhuska Lodge No. 31, Ancient Free and Accepted Masons, and his family were members of the Catholic Church. At his funeral the service was preached by the pastor of the local Catholic Church, and as a tribute to his long and useful life the public schools and various business houses closed their doors. Judge Mathews was married April 11, 1887, to Miss Eugenia Girard. Mrs. Mathews, who is still living at Pawhuska, was born in Missouri and is of French ancestry. Her five children are also still living, namely: Sarah Josephine, John Joseph, Marie Imogene, Lillian Bernard and Florence Julia.

RALPH E. CAMPBELL, whose commission as United States district judge for the eastern district of Oklahoma commenced in November, 1907, was born in Butler County, Pennsylvania, May 9, 1867. His parents were Washington and Ann Eliza Campbell. Judge Campbell received his degrees of B. S. from the Indiana Normal University in 1891, A. B. from the same institution in 1892, and LL. B. from the University of Kansas, in 1894. For several years he had a leading connection with the legal department of the Colorado, Oklahoma and Gulf Railroad, being its assistant general solicitor at South McAlester, Indian Territory, and at Little Rock, Arkansas, from 1895-1901, and general solicitor of that corporation in Oklahoma Territory during 1901-03. From 1905 to 1907 he was engaged in general practice at South McAlester, in the fall of that year being appointed to the Federal bench, his commission dating from the following January and his headquarters being Muskogee.

FRANK DALE. One of the leading lawyers and jurists of the Southwest, Frank Dale, of Guthrie, is a native of Illinois, born in DeKalb County, November 26, 1849. He laid the basis of his education in the public schools of Leland, Illinois, and settled at Wichita, Kansas, in 1872. Four years later he was admitted to the bar in that city and in 1880-85 served as prosecuting attorney for Wichita and Sedgwick counties. Judge Dale was appointed register of the United States land office at Wichita, 1885, and held the position until 1889, when he moved to Guthrie, Oklahoma. He then and there resumed practice; from May to September, 1893, was associate justice of the Territorial Supreme Court and chief justice, from 1893-98. At the conclusion of his judicial term, he continued the practice of his profession, being a member of the law firm, Dale & Bierer, of Guthrie.

JESSE J. DUNN. Although comparatively a young man during his activities in Oklahoma, Judge Dunn made a decided impress upon both the territory and the state. He was born in Channahon, Illinois, October 2, 1867, the son of James McCann and Alta F. (Lewis) Dunn. Judge Dunn obtained his higher education at the Illinois State Normal School, the Garden City (Kansas) Business College and the University of Kansas, graduating from the last named in 1893 with the degree of LL. B. He served as county attorney of Woods County, Oklahoma Territory from 1896-1900; was chairman of the democratic territorial committee in 1904, and as chairman of the democratic state committee in 1906 conducted the campaign for the election of delegates to the constitutional convention and wrote the platform on which the contest was waged. His term as associate justice of the state Supreme Court commenced in 1907 and concluded in 1913. He resigned as chief justice in 1908. After his retirement from the Supreme bench Judge Dunn moved to Oakland, California, where he is now practicing his profession.

ROBERT MCINTYRE. The late Robert McIntyre, Methodist Episcopal bishop of Oklahoma, was born at Selkirk, Scotland, November 20, 1851. He graduated from Vanderbilt University, Tennessee, in 1877, and received his D. D. degree from the University of Denver. In 1878 Bishop McIntyre was ordained to the Methodist ministry and served as pastor of churches at Easton, Marshall, Charleston, Urbana and Chicago, Illinois; at Denver, Colorado, and Los Angeles, California. His active ministry was concluded in 1908, when he was elected bishop of Oklahoma. From that time virtually until his death at Chicago, August 31, 1914, he ably served the church in that capacity, with headquarters at Oklahoma City. Bishop McIntyre was an able writer, as well as preacher and administrator of church affairs. Among his literary productions he was the author of the poems "At Early Candle Light" (1899) and "A Modern Apollos" (1900).

TAMS BIXBY. Although preferring to be known simply as a "newspaper man," Tams Bixby has left a decided impress on both Indian Territory and Oklahoma State. He is a Virginian, born at Staunton, December 12, 1855, but was educated in the public schools of Red Wing, Minnesota. Mr. Bixby entered the newspaper field early in life, and became a leading republican of the state. In 1888-9 he served as secretary of the railroad and warehouse commission of Minnesota and has acted as private secretary of three governors—William R. Merriam, in 1889-92; Knute Nelson, in 1892-6; and David M. Clough, in 1896-7. Throughout these periods, he had been acquiring leadership in the field of journalism and in 1896 became editor and proprietor of the Red Wing (daily) Republican. In 1888-9, or the year previous to becoming the gubernatorial secretary, Mr. Bixby served as secretary of the railroad and warehouse commission of Minnesota, and at various times was chairman of the republican county committee, secretary of the state republican league and secretary and chairman of the republican state central committee of Minnesota.

Mr. Bixby's record as a factor in the development of the southwestern county commenced in 1897 when he was appointed a member of the commission of the Five Civilized Tribes of the Indian Territory. He served as chairman of that body from the year named until 1905 and was a member of the commission for two years thereafter. He was general manager of the Pioneer Press Company of St. Paul in 1907-9, and since the latter year has been editor and proprietor of the Daily Phoenix, at Muskogee.

CHARLES D. CARTER. The congressman from the third Oklahoma district was long identified with the governmental and educational affairs of the Chickasaw Nation before he entered national politics. He was born near Boggy depot, at the old fort in the Choctaw Nation, Indian Territory, August 16, 1868, and is the son of Winsor and Serena Josephine (Guy) Carter. Mr. Carter was educated in the district schools and at the Chickasaw Manual Labor Academy, Tishomingo, Indian Territory, and in December, 1891, married Miss Gertrude Wilson, of Ardmore, who died in January, 1901. Until 1892 he worked on a ranch and clerked in a store, and in the year named became auditor of public accounts of the Chickasaw Nation, holding that office for two years. From 1894 to 1896 he served as superintendent of schools for the Indian Territory; was a member of the Chickasaw Council in 1897, and in 1900-04 mining trustee of the territory. From June to December, 1906, he was secretary of the first democratic executive committee for the proposed State of Oklahoma, and in 1907 commenced his terms of service as congressman from the third district which will cover the sixtieth to the sixty-fourth congresses, inclusive, and conclude with the year 1917. Since 1905 he has been a member of the Carter & Cannen Fire Insurance Company, Ardmore, and is a director of the City National Bank of that place. He is a leading Methodist and identified with Masonry and the order of Elks, having served as exalted ruler in the latter organization.

THOMAS H. DOYLE. Judge Doyle, who presides over the Oklahoma Court of Appeals, is a man of active middle age, born in Worcester County, Massachusetts, December 21, 1863. He obtained the bulk of his education in the public schools, and was admitted to practice at the Kansas bar in 1887. Judge Doyle served in the House of Representatives of Oklahoma Territory in 1897-1901, and during the former year was speaker of that body. From the Fifty-seventh to the Fifty-ninth congresses, inclusive (1901-07), he was a non-partisan delegate at Washington in the cause of joint statehood; in 1908 served as delegate-at-large and chairman of the Oklahoma delegation to the democratic national convention held at Denver, Colorado, and in 1912 was honorary vice chairman of the delegation which represented Oklahoma in the democratic national convention which assembled at Baltimore in 1912. In January, 1908, he had been chosen associate justice of the Oklahoma Court of Appeals and has been presiding judge since January, 1915. His term expires in January, 1917.

CHARLES HODGE MILLER. One of the fine old pioneers of Eastern Oklahoma was the late Charles Hodge Miller, who died at Yale, Oklahoma, February 12, 1910, aged sixty-six years. His had been a varied and eventful career, one of many experiences and vicissitudes, but through it all he carried the character of an upright and generous hearted gentleman, and left a large circle of friends to cherish his manhood and the honorable part he played during a lifetime.

He was born in the Cherokee Nation of Georgia, a son of Jacob and Sarah (Fields) Miller. After the discovery of gold on the Pacific coast the father set out for California, and was never heard of again by members of his family. Thus Charles H. Miller grew up with scanty advantages of school but with the practical training that comes to every pioneer youth, and with a discipline in the manliness and honor that count most in the world. He attended school at Coweta Mission and Greenfield, Missouri.

When a mere boy he left school to enlist in the Northern Army in Company H of the Fourteenth Missouri Volunteer Cavalry. He served throughout the war, and after leaving the Missouri regiment he enlisted in Company G of the Fifth Regiment, United States Artillery. At the close of his period of enlistment he was honorably discharged from the service at Little Rock, Arkansas, November 4, 1868, being recommended as a good soldier in both the volunteers and the regulars.

After his army career he went East and for a time ran a steamboat on the St. Lawrence River. From there he removed to Pennsylvania, and was connected with the powder mills at Wapwallopen in that state. He held various positions of trust in Pennsylvania, and from there he came to Eastern Oklahoma thirty-two years ago. He arrived at Muskogee in October of that year and thence came to Red Fork near Tulsa, where for a number of years he was proprietor of a hotel. Eventually he acquired considerable interest as a ranch owner and stockman in the old Creek Nation, and it was with those interests he was chiefly busy during his later years. When not looking after his stock and land he made his home for the last two years of his life with his daughter, Mrs. O. C. Dale, in Yale, Oklahoma.

Because of his long and honorable service in the army, four years in the volunteers and three years in the regulars, Mr. Miller always enjoyed a special place of honor among the Grand Army Veterans, and his old comrades as well as hundreds of friends and fellow citizens attended his funeral and paid the proper tribute of respect when he was buried at Yale.

In politics he was a republican, though most of his people were democrats. At Wapwallopen, Pennsylvania, Charles H. Miller married Civilla Mowery, daughter of Philip and Lydia Mowery. There were three children: Izora Miller, now the wife of Oliver C. Dale, president of the Yale Oil and Gas Company at Tulsa; Ambrose Miller, who is treasurer of the Yale Oil and Gas Company, and married Miss Alice Tage; and Chester Arthur Miller, who died in Pennsylvania, when about four years of age. Mr. Miller was also survived by his sister, Mrs. Lizzie Montgall, of Okmulgee. The late Mr. Miller was on the ground during the original opening of Oklahoma Territory, being one of the first men in Guthrie, though he did not homestead any land.

THOMAS P. GORE. United States Senator Gore is a Mississippian, born in Webster County, December 10, 1870. Although he lost the sight of both eyes, by accidents, before he was twelve years of age, he made rapid progress in his studies, and in 1890 graduated from the Normal School at Walthall, his native state. In 1892 Cumberland University, Tennessee, conferred the degree of B. L. upon him, and in the same year he was admitted to the bar. While pursuing his law studies he also taught school for about a year.

In 1895 Mr. Gore moved to Texas and at once became prominent in independent political movements. He served as delegate to the populist national convention of 1896, which met in St. Louis, and in 1898 became the congressional nominee of the people's party for the sixth district, but was defeated in the election. Joining the democracy in 1899, during the following year he was an active campaigner in South Dakota, and also served his party in that capacity in Illinois, Ohio, New York and Indiana, during the year 1904.

Mr. Gore had moved to Oklahoma in 1901, and in the following year was elected to the Territorial Council, serving in that body until 1905. He commenced his senatorial career in November, 1907, and in 1909 was elected for the full six years' term. He was re-elected in 1915 for the term ending 1921. In 1912 Senator Gore served as a member of the executive committee of the democratic national committee, and is an acknowledged leader in the upper house of Congress.

CHARLES WEST. A leading member of the bar and for eight years attorney general of the state, Charles West is a native of Savannah, Georgia, born March 16, 1872. He graduated from Johns Hopkins University, Baltimore, in 1891, with the degree A. B., and in 1892-4 pursued post-graduate work at the University of Leipzig and his alma mater. Mr. West was admitted to the bar of Oklahoma Territory in 1895 and practiced for a number of years at Pound Creek and Enid. In 1907 he was elected attorney general of the state, and at the conclusion of his term, in 1915, located for the resumption of private practice at Oklahoma City. At present he is the senior member of the firm of West, Hull & Hagan.

Mr. West has served as president of the Attorney Generals' Association (1911-12); is a lecturer on law at the State University; is a member of the National Tax Association, and in 1898-1910 was especially active in national guard matters. In the latter year he retired with the rank of lieutenant colonel.

JOSEPH A. GILL, ex-United States district judge of Indian Territory, has been an active factor in the bench and bar of the West for over thirty years. He was born in Wheeling, West Virginia, February 17, 1854, and received his scholastic education in the public schools of Springfield, Illinois, and the Illinois Industrial University at Champaign. After teaching school and studying law for several years, in 1880 he was admitted to the bar at Springfield, and practiced in that city until 1883. Since the latter year he has been a resident of the West. From 1883-7 he practiced his profession at Astoria, Oregon, and from 1887-99 at Colby, Kansas. He was appointed United States district judge for the Northern district of Indian Territory in 1899, and occupied that bench until 1908. Judge Gill also served as one of the three commissioners charged with the organization of Indian Territory as part of the State of Oklahoma. Since his retirement from the bench, in 1908, he has been engaged in practice at Vinita. The judge is a member of the Missionary Baptist Church and a leading Mason (thirty-second degree Shriner).

ROBERT L. WILLIAMS. The present incumbent of the gubernatorial chair, Robert L. Williams, was born at Brundige, Alabama, December 20, 1868. He received his higher education at the Southern University of Alabama, which conferred upon him the degree of M. A. in 1894. He was admitted to the bar in 1891, and first practiced at Troy, Alabama. In 1896 he became a resident of Atoka, Indian Territory, and six months later moved to Durant. He served as city attorney of that place in 1899; was a member of the Indian Territory Democratic Committee in 1902-4 and of the democratic national committee in 1904-8. In 1906 he had been sent as a delegate to the Oklahoma Constitutional Convention, and in the following year became chief justice of the state Supreme Court. He served, by re-election, until his resignation from the bench in March, 1915. In the latter year he was elected governor of Oklahoma for the term ending 1919. Although his official residence is at Oklahoma City, his home is still at Durant.

COL. SIDNEY SUGGS. Since early territorial days the name of Sidney Suggs has figured prominently in many varied business activities and in the civic life of Southern Oklahoma, particularly the country around Ardmore. His ability to handle large affairs has always meant more than a private fortune. In many ways his prosperity has been reflected in the growth and improvement of every community which he has touched. Particularly in recent years has Colonel Suggs given his advocacy and influence to the improvement of Oklahoma highways, and the good roads movement has no stronger and more effectual friend than this Ardmore citizen. To him belongs the distinction of having originated the idea of the "Educational Mile of Road" and of having demonstrated its feasibility by having actually constructed a mile of highway in Seminole County, October 12, 1914. The idea has been adopted by several counties in Oklahoma and in one county seventy-five miles of road were built in one year. Under this plan school boys construct the road while the girls of the school set out trees and shrubbery along the highway to shade and beautify it.

A native of Mississippi, Sidney Suggs was born in 1853 and is of old and prominent American stock. His parents were Dr. Isaac T. and Jane (Fullwood) Suggs. The name was originally spelled Sugg, but his great-grandfather sometime before the Revolutionary war added an s, and that method of spelling has been followed by all his descendants. George Suggs was an officer in the American army during the Revolution, and afterwards established a home on the boundary line between North and South Carolina. He married Miss Catherine Sanders. One of their sons was Laban Suggs, grandfather of Colonel Suggs. When eighteen years of age Laban Suggs married Ione Hood, who was then sixteen. Her father, Capt. John Hood, a native of Ireland, came to America about the time the Revolution started, joined a cavalry company of which he became captain, and in the course of one of his campaigns he stopped with his men for a meal at the house of a family named Wallace. The meal was cooked by little Mary Wallace, then twelve years of age, and on leaving the house Captain Hood told her he would return after the war, and he did so and she became his wife. She was Irish or Scotch and of a noble family. She was one of the heroines of the Revolution. One time about fifteen Tories came to her father's house and demanded dinner, and finding some apple brandy they became very drunk. The daughter ran away while they were engaged in eating and drinking and informed a band of Whigs of their presence. The patriots made a rush on the place and captured the entire number of Tories, two of whom they hanged for murder. Captain Hood was a zealous patriot. After the war, hearing a man express his loyalty to King George, the captain seized the Tory by the hair, jerked him down and with a handsaw commenced to saw off his head. The fellow begged and pleaded for mercy, and finally took the oath never to mention the name of King George again. His neck was badly injured, but the patriotic assailant nursed him well again and the man became a good neighbor. Captain Hood built the first cotton gin in the York district of South Carolina.

Dr. Isaac T. Suggs, who was one of the family of fourteen children born to Laban and Ione Suggs, spent his early life in South Carolina and near Yorkville married Miss Jane Fullwood. Her ancestors came from Holland, and her father, Robert Fullwood, was a man of considerable prominence in South Carolina. Doctor Suggs took his family to Mississippi soon after his marriage in 1838, and in 1866 moved to Texas, locating at Mount Pleasant, where he lived until his death in September, 1887, at the age of seventy-four. His wife died at the age of seventy-one in January, 1891. During the war Doctor Suggs served as post surgeon in charge of the hospital at Tupelo, Mississippi.

Col. Sidney Suggs was fourteen years of age when he came with his parents to Texas, and he continued his education in the common schools in the eastern part of that state.. For fifteen years of his early career he represented the Tompkins Machinery & Implement Company of Dallas. When the firm failed he was appointed sole adjuster, and in the course of five years he cleared up and collected a large share of the accounts left by the firm, amounting to upwards of four hundred thousand dollars. In 1877 Col. Sidney Suggs formed a copartenership with his brother Hugh, and for many years they were closely associated in all their varied business undertakings and on terms of such mutual confidence as seldom exist even among brothers. Neither party ever thought it necessary to ask for an accounting of the other, each was interested in every venture, and the profits from every enterprise whether individual or partnership was turned into a common fund for the equal benefit of both. These brothers established and conducted cotton gins, corn and flour mills, sawmills, lumber yard, and were also extensively connected with the cattle industry. Two towns in particular benefited from their enterprise, Ardmore and Berwyn.

Colonel Suggs has long been a notable figure in business circles at Ardmore, and in 1897 he became proprietor of the Ardmorite, and soon made it the leading newspaper in that section of Indian Territory.

At the age of twelve years Colonel Suggs became a member of the old school Presbyterian Church, and has always been true to the Christian teachings' of his youth and active in membership as well as in support of the church and benevolent activities. He is a Mason, having affiliation with the Blue Lodge, Chapter, Commandery and Mystic Shrine, and is affiliated with the various branches of the Independent Order of Odd Fellows, the Woodmen of the World, and other organizations.

In 1876 Colonel Suggs married Miss Dixie Barnhart, who died June 6, 1891, the mother of six children named Edna, Ella, Stella, Sidney, Velie Charles and Kate. On September 20, 1892, Colonel Suggs married Miss Minnie Murray, of North Carolina. She survived only two months and seven days after her marriage. On June 26, 1895, Colonel Suggs married the widow of Judge Olive, an attorney of Texas, and who was the mother of three children: Zoe, Vera and John.

OS M. STEVENS. Education and financial assistance are very important factors in achieving success in the business world of today, where every faculty must be brought into play, but they are not the main elements. Persistence and determination figure much more prominently and a man possessed of these qualities is bound to win a fair amount of success. Os M. Stevens, whose name forms the caption for this article, practically earned his own education and he enjoys the unique experience of stepping from a cattle-ranch saddle into the ink-stained interior of a printshop. The success he has accomplished, culminating in his present office as editor and manager of one of the leading weekly newspapers of Oklahoma, is proof that hard and consistent work in the printshop is more profitable and gives better compensation for education and character than does the cattle range.

A native of the Old Dominion State, Mr. Stevens was born in Virginia in 1877. His parents were both honored descendants of families that sent warriors to the front in the days of the Revolution. Through his ancestors Mr. Stevens is related to Henry Ward Beecher and to the noted Hitt and Brace families of Virginia. The Stevens family consists of six children, concerning whom the following brief data are here inserted: E. P. is a viaduct builder and inventor in Chicago; Mattie Griffith is a widow and makes her home in Chicago; Laura is the wife of Mr. Hantz, of Scott Center, Kansas; Mrs. C. M. Worter, of Chicago; Mrs. E. C. Dowd, of Guthrie, Oklahoma; and Os M. is the subject of this sketch.

After a common-school education in the public schools of Kansas, Mr. Stevens was for a number of years employed on a cattle ranch. He then decided to learn the art of printing and after an apprenticeship in a newspaper office in Kansas, he located at Lexington, Oklahoma, where he became one of the well known editors and publishers of the equally well known weekly Youall's Doin's, a publication that attracted unusual attention throughout the entire state by reason of its bizarre name and unusual contents. In 1901 he located at Coalgate and became associated with Michael B. Hickman in the publication of the Courier. When Mr. Hickman became owner of the Record-Register, Mr. Stevens became editor of that paper. His editorial attitude has always been toward high morals and one of his principal achievements in Coal County has been that of conducting his paper as a leader in a campaign for prohibition and law enforcement. In addition to being editor of the Record-Register Mr. Stevens is manager of the Coalgate Publishing Company, a corporation of which M. B. Hickman is president; Arthur Jones, of Lehigh, vice president; A. T. West, of Coalgate, secretary; and J. I. Murray, of Coalgate, treasurer. Mr. Stevens is doing efficient work as county probation officer of Coal County and in politics he is a stalwart democrat.

June 22, 1900, at Lexington, Oklahoma, Mr. Stevens married Miss Willia B. Hickman and to them have been born three children, whose names and dates of birth are here incorporated: Laur, 1901; Edna, 1903; and Ruth, 1906. Mr. and Mrs. Stevens are devout members of the Methodist Episcopal Church and he is affiliated with the Knights of Pythias, in which he holds the rank of past chancellor and past district deputy grand chancellor of the state.

MORRIS HANDVERKER. Among the men of Lawton, Oklahoma, who have attained business success and prominence through the medium of hard work, business sagacity and indomitable perseverance, Harris and Morris Handverker, father and son, stand in a foremost position. In their careers, and particularly in that of the father, are to be found lessons which prove the value of persistence in the face of difficulties and discouragements which cannot fail to be of value to the rising generation, while the incidents of their lives must prove of interest to all who admire the characteristics which make up self-made manhood.

Harris Handverker was born in Poland, Russia, July 8, 1861, a son of Philip and Helen (Jaxobowitz) Handverker, the former born in 1819 and died in 1892. He was a well-to-do tanner, a man of some influence in his community, and well versed in the Jewish Ritual. There were seven children in the family: Cirvis, who was married and died in Russia; Augusta, who married David Bernstein, now retired, of Poland; Celia, who is the wife of Jacob Hoffman, a butcher of Poland; Harris; Leah, who was married and died in Poland; Irle, who is the wife of Jacob Cincinnati, a tailor of Poland; and Wilhelm, a newspaper publisher of Poland, and as such one of the most prominent men of his locality.

Harris Handverker was educated in his native land, and as a young man of twenty-one years decided to try his fortunes in the United States. Arriving in New

York City, he found employment at his trade, that of lathe turner, at which he worked for two years, and in 1884 went back to his native place where he remained for two years. In 1886 he returned to New York City and began to work at the cloakmaker's trade, but after one year went back to Russia and remained one year. Again he came to New York City, and again, in 1890, he went back to Poland, but in 1891 he came again to the United States, this time to remain. After ten months here, he sent for his wife and children, and continued to work in New York City for one year, accumulating enough money through hard and faithful work to take his family to Colton, California, where he began his career as a peddler in a modest way. He spent one year at Colton, two years at San Bernardino and three years at Los Angeles, and then went to San Diego, California, where he continued peddling for one year and then established himself in the hide business. Having accumulated some small means, Mr. Handverker came to Oklahoma and located in Oklahoma City, one year before the opening of that place. He worked as a retail clothing salesman for one year, and at the opening of the reservation became a pioneer of Lawton, August 4, 1901, and purchased a business and residence lot, all that was allowed by law. For about three years he continued to work for wages in the clothing business, and then established an enterprise of his own in the same line. He was capable, thoroughly informed, energetic and courteous, and his business soon began to prosper and to grow to large proportions, but the panic of 1907 came on, and, with other able business men, he failed and lost the fortune that he had so laboriously accumulated. This misfortune would have entirely discouraged and beaten the great majority of men, but Mr. Handverker was made of sterner stuff. He failed to acknowledge defeat, and although the blow had been a heavy one he at once set to work to recuperate his lost prosperity. He was content to follow general work for two years and to accept whatever honorable employment fell to his lot. Mrs. Handverker owned three building properties and in the fall of 1909 these were sold and Mr. Handverker again engaged in business on his own account, opening a small store on C Avenue. Again his enterprise, business judgment and tireless energy brought him success, and in 1911 he was compelled to open larger quarters. These sufficed until 1915, when his business had grown to such large proportions that he was again compelled to seek more extensive space, and on April 1st of that year he moved into his present establishment, at 327-329 D Avenue, where he occupies the ground floor and a floor space of 50 by 120 feet, one of the largest stores of Lawton. Here he has a model modern department store, stocked with the finest of goods of every variety. His business attracts its trade from Comanche, Cotton, Jefferson, Tillman, Kiowa, Caddo and even more distant counties, and no better testimonial of Mr. Handverker's honorable dealings can be found than the fact that the customers who deal with him once remain as his patrons afterward. In business circles, Mr. Handverker bears the highest reputation, for he has been found faithful in his engagements and a man in whom his associates may place the utmost confidence. In addition to his store on D Avenue, he owns a business property on C Avenue, his residence in Lawton and other valuable realty. He has not been found wanting in public spirit when civic movements are started, and is one of the active and working members of the Lawton Chamber of Commerce. Fraternally, he is connected with the Woodmen of the World, the Modern Woodmen of America No. 10,256 and the Woodmen's Circle, and his political support is given to the republican party. Mr. Handverker is a member of the Jewish Church, and is widely known for his proficiency in the Jewish Ritual.

Harris Handverker was married in Poland, in 1880, to Miss Minnie Eckstein, who was born in Poland in 1861, daughter of the late David Eckstein, who was a tailor. Seven children have been born to this union, namely: Herman, who died in Russia at the age of three years; Leah, who also died there when three years old; Samuel, who died at Kingfisher, Oklahoma, at the age of eight years; Morris; Frank, who died while the family was moving from Oklahoma City to Lawton, aged fourteen years; Helen, who is attending the Lawton High School; and Everett, born November 11, 1900, who entered high school in September, 1915.

Morris Handverker was born November 12, 1891, in New York City, and was given good educational advantages, attending the public schools of Lawton and the Lawton Business College, from which he was graduated in 1908. He first became a stenographer in a law office, where he remained a short time and then secured a like position in the government service, following which he became a public court stenographer. In 1909 he entered his father's business, and in 1913 was admitted to partnership. He has inherited many of his father's excellent business qualities, is a young man of energy, enterprise and progressive spirit, and as a courteous and genial gentleman has done much to attract trade to the business. He is also a member of the Chamber of Commerce and a republican in politics, and was reared in the faith of the Jewish Church, to which he belongs. His fraternal connections include membership in the Woodmen of the World and in the Masons, in which he has reached the Rose Cross (Eighteenth) degree, being a member of Lawton Lodge No. 183, Ancient Free and Accepted Masons, and Valley of Guthrie Consistory No. 1. Mr. Handverker is not married.

HENRY N. GREIS. Junior member of the firm of Ross & Greis, which controls an important business in the drilling of oil and gas wells in the Oklahoma fields, and with other noteworthy connection with the oil and gas industry, Mr. Greis is recognized as one of the substantial, straightforward and progressive business men of the younger generation in the City of Tulsa, and in addition to the business associated noted above he is also president of the Wyoming Torpedo Company and vice president of the Central Torpedo Company, both of which are engaged in the manufacturing of torpedoes used in connection with the sinking of wells in oil and gas districts.

Mr. Greis was born in the City of Buffalo, New York, on the 5th of July, 1880, the eldest in a family of five children, all but one of whom are living. He is a son of Jacob M. and Amelia (Nauert) Greis, both of whom were born and reared in Erie County, New York, and both are living, the father at the age of fifty-eight years and the mother at the age of fifty-six. The political allegiance of Mr. Greis is given to the republican party. He whose name initiates this article acquired his early education in the public schools and Central High School of his native city, and there he initiated his business career as bookkeeper and clerical assistant in the German Bank of Buffalo, with which institution he continued to be identified four years and in which, through effective and faithful service, he won promotion to the responsible office of cashier. On severing this association Mr. Greis became bookkeeper in the Marine National Bank of Buffalo. but within a comparatively brief time he resigned his office and made his first independent venture, and that in connection with the important industry with which he is now identified. As a contractor he engaged in the construction of oil pipe lines from points in the oil fields of West Virginia and Maryland, and the first contract with which he became thus associated was for the building of a pipe line from the western part of West Virginia to Cumberland, Maryland. He was for six months assistant to the superintendent of this work, and he then returned to Buffalo. There his marriage was solemnized in October, 1907, and shortly afterward he came to the newly created State of Oklahoma, and established his residence at Bartlesville, the present judicial center of Washington County. There he engaged in the invention and manufacturing of gas meters for natural gas and in general construction work in connection with the oil and gas operations in that section of the state. Later he established a branch business at Chanute, Kansas, where he maintained his residence about two years, since which time he has given his attention principally to oil and gas development operations, in the drilling of wells and the supplying of incidental appurtenances and accessories. He has been a resident of Tulsa since 1910 and here his associated and able coadjutor in the firm of Ross & Greis is Edward A. Ross, the office of the firm being at 304 Drew Building.

Mr. Greis has gained secure place as one of the alert and ambitious young business men of the state of his adoption and is liberal and progressive in his civic attitude, his political allegiance being given to the democratic party. He is prominently identified with the time-honored Masonic fraternity, in which he became and entered apprentice and was finally raised to the degree of Master Mason in Dupew Lodge, No. 823, Ancient Free & Accepted Masons, in the City of Buffalo, New York. From this lodge he received his dimit and became a member of Delta Lodge, No. 425, at Tulsa. From Mount Sinai Chapter, No. 293, Royal Arch Masons, at Buffalo, New York, and from Wichita Commandery, Knights Templars, in the City of Wichita, Kansas, he received dimit to Trinity Commandery, No. 20, at Tulsa. In Indian Consistory, Ancient Accepted Scottish Rite, in the City of McAlester, he has received the thirty-second degree, and to form his present affiliation with Akdar Temple of the Ancient Arabic Order of the Nobles of the Mystic Shrine, in his home City of Tulsa, he received dimission from Abdalla Temple in the City of Leavenworth, Kansas. He is a popular member also of Tulsa Lodge, No. 946, Benevolent & Protective Order of Elks.

On the 1st of October, 1907, was solemnized the marriage of Mr. Greis to Miss Bertha DeLace Westcott, who was born at Rochester, New York, and they have one daughter, Elizabeth.

JAMES J. MORONEY. By inherent predilection and early discipline Mr. Moroney acquired in his youth a practical experience in the domain of newspaper publishing, and since the year that marked the admission of Oklahoma to the Union he has held secure prestige as one of the representative newspaper men of this state. Since that year, 1907, he has been editor in chief of the Okmulgee Democrat, which is now published in both daily and weekly editions, and which he has brought into special prominence and influence as an exponent of the oil-producing industry in Oklahoma, besides making it an effective force in exploiting the general interests of the city and state in which it is published. In connection with oil and gas operations, the paper has a reputation and circulation which far transcend local limitations, and both its daily and weekly editions have numerous subscribers in the leading centers of the oil business in other states of the Union. In the publishing of this important and influential Oklahoma paper Mr. Moroney now has as his valued coadjutor Bert C. Hodges, concerning whom individual mention is made on other pages of this volume.

James J. Moroney was born in the beautiful collegiate City of Oberlin, Lorain County, Ohio, on the 22d of January, 1868, and is a son of James P. and Mary (Shields) Moroney, the former of whom was born in the City of London, England, in 1838, and the latter of whom was born in County Galway, Ireland, in 1840, she having thus been a girl of about seven years at the time of her parents' immigration to the United States, in 1847, and her future husband having come to America with his parents in 1851, when he was about thirteen years old. James P. Moroney was a man of most alert and vigorous mentality, was afforded good educational advantages as a youth, but his more liberal education was that which he acquired through self-discipline and through his long and effective association with the newspaper business. At Oberlin, Ohio, on the 30th of November, 1865, was solemnized his marriage to Miss Mary Shields, and they passed the remainder of their lives in the old Buckeye State, where both were called to eternal rest in the year 1898.

James P. Moroney early served an apprenticeship to the trade of printer, and as a journeyman he went to Ohio and engaged in the work of his trade. At Bucyrus he founded eventually the Crawford County Democrat, and prior to this he had been associated intimately with the distinguished founder of the Toledo Blade, David Locke. When the Civil war was precipitated Mr. Moroney promptly showed his loyalty to his adopted country, by tendering his service in defense of the Union. In 1861 he enlisted as a member of Company I, Forty-first Ohio Volunteer Infantry, with which gallant command he proceeded to the front and with which he participated in a number of important engagements, besides many of minor order. At the Battle of Chickamauga he was so severely wounded as to become incapacitated for further service in the field, and thus was accorded an honorable discharge. After recuperating from his injury he re-enlisted, and thereafter he continued in active service with his original command until the regiment was mustered out, at the close of the war. Mr. Moroney was a skilled printer of the old-school regime and developed much ability as an editor and publisher, virtually his entire active life as a farmer having been marked by quite close identification with the newspaper business and by friendships with numbers engaged in it. He was an influential and effective exponent of the principles and policies of the democratic party, and prior to the Civil war he had been a staunch Union man though not an abolitionist. Of his twelve children all are living except one and six of the number are residents of Oklahoma, the subject of this review having been the second in order of birth. P. H. is engaged in the practice of law at Tulsa, this state; Nora C. is society editor of the Okmulgee Democrat; J. D. resides at Tulsa and is actively identified with the oil industry in that section of Oklahoma; M. F. is mayor of Okmulgee and interested in oil and real estate projects; T. M. is connected with the pipe line business at Bartlesville, this state; Ellen resides in Arizona; William resides at Kingman, Arizona, is engaged in the practice of law and was serving, at statehood, as county attorney of Mohave County; S. F. resides in the State of California; Margaret is the wife of G. C. Conrad, of Norwalk, Ohio; Alice is the wife of George C. Wilcox, of Toledo, Ohio; and Mary died in Ohio at the age of thirty years, as the wife of P. J. Murray.

James J. Moroney attended the public schools of Ohio

until he had completed the curriculum of the high school, and later he pursued higher studies in the Ohio Normal School at Lebanon, Warren County. As a youth he became associated with the oil industry in his native state, and in the eastern fields he continued his association with this line of enterprise principally in salaried positions. He resided in the City of Toledo, Ohio, about seven years and maintained his home at Marietta, that state, for five years. In the meanwhile he had gained as a boy a taste and ambition for his father's early life business and profession. In 1907 he came to Oklahoma and associated himself with Dr. O. A. Lambert in the purchase of the plant and business of the Okmulgee Democrat, of which he has continued the editor in chief since that time and which he has made one of the leading papers of the state, with broad influence and remarkably large circulation. In 1915 he, with his other partner, B. C. Hodges, purchased Doctor Lambert's interest in the business. Mr. Hodges owns a half interest and is business manager of the substantial and prosperous newspaper and job-printing enterprise. The firm issues three independent publications: The Okmulgee Daily Democrat, The Mid-Continent Oil and Farm News, and the Weekly Progress, besides which the firm also publishes the Morris News, of Morris, Okmulgee County.

Mr. Moroney has been a zealous and effective worker in advancing the cause of the democratic party and is one of its leading and most influential representatives in the eastern part of the state. He is identified with independent movements in connection with the oil industry and has made his paper, the Mid-Continent Oil and Farm News, a potent influence in connection with both the oil and agricultural industries in Oklahoma, besides which the paper has gained a wide circulation in the oil regions of other states. He is a broad-minded, liberal and progressive citizen and is one of the strong and valued citizens of Oklahoma. Both he and his wife are zealous communicants of St. Anthony's Church, Roman Catholic, in Okmulgee.

In the year 1893 was solemnized the marriage of Mr. Moroney to Miss Mary Boland, of Toledo, Ohio, and they are the parents of six children,—James P., William J., Francis, Vincent, Bernard and Anna. James P. is a member of the class of 1917 in the school of journalism of Missouri University; and William J. is a member of the reportorial staff of the papers of which his father is publisher, having a university course in view.

BERT C. HODGES. Holding prestige as half-owner and manager of the Okmulgee Daily Democrat, at the judicial center of Okmulgee County, Mr. Hodges is not only one of the prominent representatives of the newspaper business in Oklahoma but is also a specially influential figure in the local councils and campaign activities of the democratic party, as indicated by the fact that he has served as chairman of the Okmulgee County Democratic Central Committee since 1913 and has wielded much influence in the successful maneuvering of political forces in this section of the state.

Mr. Hodges was born at Calico Rock, Izard County, Arkansas, on the 1st of November, 1883, and is a son of Ferd T. and Anna Elizabeth (Stark) Hodges, the former of whom was born at Paducah, Kentucky, and the latter near the City of Nashville, Tennessee. The father of Mr. Hodges served throughout the Civil war as a valiant soldier of the Confederacy, having been in the command of General Beauregard and having taken part in many sanguinary battles, including those of Shiloh and Gettysburg. He was assigned to duty as a spy, was captured by the enemy and was sentenced to be shot, but he was saved through his affiliation with the Masonic fraternity.

He entered the Confederate service when but sixteen years of age and was three times wounded in action. After his marriage he established his residence in Arkansas, and he and his wife now reside at Branch, Franklin County, that state. Mr. Hodges was a railroad contractor in the earlier period of his independent business career and later was successfully identified with the lumber industry in Arkansas, as the owner and operator of saw mills. He is now living retired,—a man of broad mental ken and sterling character and a citizen who commands unqualified popular esteem. He is a stalwart democrat in his political allegiance and is affiliated with the United Confederate Veterans. Of the ten children seven are now living, and the subject of this sketch was the seventh in order of birth.

Bert C. Hodges remained at the parental home until he had attained to the age of twenty years, and in the meanwhile his principal experience had been that gained in connection with the work of his father's farm. He continued his studies in the public schools until he had finished the curriculum of the high school, and after leaving the farm he was employed in a general store for two years.

In 1904 Mr. Hodges came to Oklahoma and here his first service was in connection with a restaurant at Muskogee. He next became a solicitor for the Muskogee Democrat, and he continued his work in this capacity after the consolidation of the paper with the Muskogee Times. Since 1909 he has been manager of the Okmulgee Daily Democrat, and since January, 1915, has been owner of a half-interest in the large and important publishing business in which his associate is James J. Moroney, of whom specific mention is made on other pages of this work, the firm publishing not only the Okmulgee Daily Democrat but also the Okmulgee Progress, the Mid-Continent Oil and Farm News, and the Morris News, at Morris, Okmulgee County. Mr. Hodges is also the owner of a half-interest in the Wagoner Democrat, published at the county seat of Wagoner County.

Mr. Hodges has been a most enthusiastic worker in behalf of the cause of the democratic party, and, as previously stated, is chairman of its central committee for Okmulgee County. He is affiliated with both the York and Scottish Rite bodies of the Masonic fraternity and also with the Benevolent and Protective Order of Elks. He and his wife are earnest members of the Methodist Episcopal Church, South, at Okmulgee, and he is serving on its official board.

On the 28th of June, 1909, Mr. Hodges wedded Miss May Stinnett, who was born in Kentucky but reared and educated in Texas and Oklahoma, she being a daughter of P. B. Stinnett, who is still a resident of the Lone Star State. Mr. and Mrs. Hodges have a fine little son, Bert C., Jr.

ISAAC T. GIBSON, who died September 20, 1915, while visiting relatives near his former home in Iowa, had endeared himself and his memory to the Osage people by many years of honest, constructive labor in behalf of their welfare, and justly earned a high place in Oklahoma history. Affectionately known among both the Indians and the whites as "Father Gibson," he helped make early history during the years when the Osage people were being settled in Indian Territory. In his declining years he returned to live among the people for whom he so patiently labored forty or forty-five years ago.

He was born near Xenia in Greene County, Ohio, May 11, 1831, a son of Montelian and Sarah (Embree) Gibson, the former a native of Fairfax County, Virginia, and the latter born near Jonesboro, Tennessee.

The father when a boy was indentured to a milling firm in Virginia, and thus learned the trade of millwright and miller. In 1805 he came to Ohio, and was engaged at his trade by Thomas Embree, a prominent land owner and miller in the Miami Valley, whose daughter he subsequently married. Thomas Embree had secured a military land warrant covering 1,000 acres of land and including a number of valuable mill sites along the Miami River in Southwestern Ohio. He divided this land among his children and Montelian Gibson and wife made a good farm out of their portion and also had a mill on the Little Miami River three miles north of Xenia.

Isaac T. Gibson was the last survivor of a family of nine children. His parents both died at Salem, in Henry County, Iowa. When Isaac was five years of age his parents removed to Morgan County, Indiana, and at the age of eighteen he accompanied his mother to Salem, Iowa, where two of his sisters lived at that time. Mr. Gibson considered the State of Iowa his home until 1906, though many years were spent in other states.

As a boy he had a limited education, since he was practically reared on the frontier, and largely educated himself. He had not only a thorough knowledge of men and affairs, but also read extensively and was a most interesting conversationalist. His early years were spent on a farm and after going to Iowa he was employed as clerk in a store at $11 a month, paying his own board. Afterwards he engaged in business for himself, and was a merchant for ten years, but after his marriage returned to farming. On October 20, 1858, he married Miss Anna Mary Hiatt, who was born in that noted Quaker community of Grant County, Indiana, February 3, 1835, and who died in Salem, Iowa, September 16, 1906.

For a few months after leaving the farm in Iowa Mr. Gibson was employed in the commission business in Chicago, but about the close of the war was appointed at the yearly meeting of the Society of Friends for the purpose of looking after the educational and material welfare of the colored freedmen in the State of Missouri. This was a work which required not only a sincere interest in the welfare of the colored people, so recently freed from slavery, but also a splendid moral courage in carrying out a work which was met with strenuous opposition by most of the white people in the southern states. On that mission Mr. Gibson established colored schools in nearly all of the principal towns that were located along railway lines in Missouri, and was also influential in inducing the school board of St. Louis to establish schools for the instruction of colored children in that city. It was not only difficult to get money appropriated for such schools, but almost impossible to secure competent white teachers in the southern states, and this deficiency was met by the Friends Society in agreeing to furnish teachers for the colored people. He was one of the men who endeavored to secure the proper expenditure of the thousands of dollars raised by the Society of Friends for the education of the colored people in the South. He spent nearly two years in the work, and almost every day had to proceed to his duty in the face of threats on the part of the white people, who entertained strong prejudices against the entire freedmen movement. While in St. Louis he discovered that the school board was wasting funds which had been set aside for the colored schools, and the colored people in addition to paying taxes on $1,000,000 worth of property in the city were also supporting half a dozen colored schools by private subscription. Mr. Gibson found his most difficult work in St. Louis, where the school board raised every possible argument against the advantage of educating the negroes, but under his courageous direction and with the support of his Quaker teachers he finally aroused and created a different sentiment, and one which favored colored education.

After the conclusion of this work Mr. Gibson was engaged in farming in Iowa until the fall of 1869. He was then appointed United States Indian agent for the Osage Indians and other tribes. On taking up his duties he found the temporary agency for the Osages located four miles east of Independence, Kansas. The Osage Reservation at that time included a tract of country fifty miles wide and 300 miles long, including about a fifth of the present State of Kansas, and bordering the north line of Indian Territory. In the previous year, 1868, these Indians had been compelled to sign a treaty with a railroad company sacrificing their land at 18 cents per acre. They were forced to accept this price, the threat being made that they would get nothing at all in case they refused to accept the treaty. Through the intervention of President Grant agents were appointed to the Indians by various religious bodies, and Mr. Gibson was selected for these duties by the Society of Friends. When he first came among the Osages they were people still existing in a semi-barbarous condition, and lived on buffalo meat nearly altogether. He assisted Enoch Hoag, the superintendent of Indian Affairs in the central superintendency, in investigating the affairs of the Indians, and helped to demonstrate how the Indians had been swindled out of their lands, and it was the Hoag report which caused President Grant to withdraw the treaty already mentioned from the United States Senate. Later Mr. Gibson went to Washington and assisted in securing legislation by which the Indian Reservation might be surveyed and sold and the Indians transferred to another reservation in Indian Territory. This was in line with the Government policy at that time to concentrate all the Indian tribes possible within the borders of Indian Territory. Mr. Gibson was the sole representative of the Osages in Washington for several years, and was instrumental in securing the sale of the Osage lands at a price aggregating $1.25 per acre. The proceeds from this sale were placed in the United States treasury at 5 per cent interest, and it was that fund, growing from year to year that made the Osages the wealthiest body of people in the world.

While acting as Indian agent Mr. Gibson moved the agency to Silver Lake, a few miles south of where Bartlesville now stands. Then, as a result of further legislation and re-arrangement of boundaries, he moved the agency to its present location. He selected this site, where the city of Pawhuska now stands, on May 1, 1872, and moved his quarters to that point on the 15th of May. It was then a beautiful location, in the midst of a fine valley, with the Osage hills almost enclosing it, and with a landscape which could not but please and charm. Mr. Gibson also established the Indian school at Pawhuska and erected the buildings. Out of the $50,000 fund appropriated for the removal of Indians to their new reservation, Mr. Gibson did not use a single dollar, and that is only one illustration out of many to prove his absolute disinterestedness and honesty in all his dealings with the Indians. He was appointed local agent October 1, 1869, and was succeeded in the office on February 22, 1876.

In that time he had performed a great deal of constructive work of improvement among the Osages. In three years time he had converted them from a wild roving tribe into peaceful and permanent settlers, interested in the upbuilding of homes and in the arts and pursuits of agriculture and civilization. He induced his wards to split many thousands of rails, to erect permanent homes, and to till the soil. When he first came among them the Osages had a bad reputation, and he had the satisfaction of seeing that yield to a reputation for honesty and quiet law abiding industry. Among these people he won close friends, and all of them admired him for his thorough honesty. While he had opportunities to make a fortune he actually left the agency poorer in dollars and cents than when he had come. This is certainly a record which makes his experience notable in the Indian country. After the Osages moved to Indian territory Mr. Gibson laid out a white man's road and announced publicly to the Indians that for those who wished to take the white man's way he would secure allotments of land and get it recorded and thus established them severally in independent homes of their own. He helped them in clearing up the land, in securing appropriate, implements for them to carry on their simple agriculture, and also .induced several Indian missionaries to come and assist the women in learning the fundamentals of housekeeping. During the first year he induced more than fifty families to remain and continue the work of splitting rails and effecting other permanent improvements, and during that winter these families got out over 80,000 rails instead of going on the annual hunt. In the next season a still larger number remained behind and kept up their fence building and other farm improvements. In the year 1875 those who had not accepted his plan of permanent settlement went away to the plains for hunting, but in the meantime the buffalo had been practically exterminated, and the hunters soon returned disheartened and quite willing to accept the circumstances of civilized life.

Some other points in the work of this Oklahoma missionary are brought out in the following quotation from a letter written by his son:

"It might be of interest to add that Father Gibson was one of fourteen 'Quaker' Indian agents appointed under President Grant's so-called 'church policy' with the wild tribes of Indians. The writer has in his possession a group photograph of eleven of them including Lawrie Tatum, agent for the Kiowas and Comanches; Brinton Darlington for the Cheyennes and Arapahoes; Mahlon Stubbs for the Kaws; John D. Miles, Dr. Richards, and others, all of whom have doubtless had honorable mention in your historical work, since these men were among the first authorized white settlers of the Indian Territory, as they were the first Indian Agents to live with the tribes under their charge. This fact was appreciated by the Indians themselves who stated in speeches in Council —'Heretofore our govenment agents have visited us about once a year bringing us a few presents, but you have shown enough interest in our welfare to bring your families and live with us, showing us the white man's road and his religion.'

"An examination of their reports and letters to the Commissioner of Indian Affairs at Washington, D..C., will indicate how largely instrumental these devoted men were in reconciling these wild, roving, thieving, murderous bands of Indians to their reservations in the Indian Territory, and the changed conditions of living so at variance with their previous customs, habits and traditions. Verily their works do live after them."

In 1876 Mr. Gibson returned to Iowa and was engaged in farming in that state until the death of his wife. He then lived with his sons in Kansas and Oklahoma. His older son is Allen H. of Coffeyville, Kansas, and the other is Thomas Embree, of Big Heart, Oklahoma. Mr. and Mrs. Gibson had seven children, but four of them died in infancy, and the daughter, Mary Elma, died at the age of twenty-eight.

REV. JOSEPH S. MURROW. It is impossible to characterize fitly the life and service of this venerable and dignified minister of the Gospel whose name is known and revered by many thousands of Oklahoma people. No measure of gold or mundane success could be applied to his career. Yet on the life of two generations of people, especially the old Indian tribes of Oklahoma, he has exercised an influence beyond all estimates and reckonings. And it is noteworthy that even now, when others can perceive the widespread fruits of his ministry and when he is rounding out a lifetime in his eighties, Reverend Mr. Murrow is inclined to depreciate and undervalue the effectiveness of his life work. Such is the essential modesty, simplicity of the man, who has no disposition to crave the fame of men and leaves to a higher power any judgment of his achievements.

As to those facts which are usually considered in a biography, Joseph Samuel Murrow was born in Jefferson County, Georgia, June 7, 1835. His grandfather, William Murrow, was one of the followers of General Francis Marion in the War of the Revolution. His father, John Murrow, married Mary Amelia Badger, and this couple had six children.

He received a meager education in the public schools of his native community, and a better training in the Springfield Academy in Effingham County. Later he was a student in Mercer University, one of the leading Baptist schools in Georgia. From early childhood he was possessed of an earnest desire to become a minister, and this desire, augmented by the teachings of a noble father already in the work, was a great help to the ambitious youth.

At the age of nineteen in 1854 he united with the Green Fork Baptist Church and the following year was licensed to preach. It was after that time, in 1856, that he matriculated as a student in Mercer University.

Ordained to the ministry in September, 1857, at Macon, Georgia, he was appointed by the Domestic and Indian Mission Board of the Southern Baptist Convention and supported by the Rehoboth Association as a missionary to the Indians in the West. On November 13, 1857, he arrived at old North Fork town, now Eufaula. At that time there were no railroads west of the Mississippi River. He spent five weeks making the trip.

Some years ago Reverend Mr. Murrow furnished an interview to a correspondent who wrote up the substance of the interview under the title "Reminiscences of a Missionary Among South-West Wild Indians." In that article Mr. Murrow was quoted as saying: "I was one of the earliest of the Baptist missionaries to come among the Indians of the Indian Territory in the Southwest. Preceding me were Rev. Evan Jones who came out with the Cherokees in 1832 and remained with them until after the war, when he died, still in the service. Later his work was taken up by his son John B. Jones. Their work was exclusively among the Cherokees. Another was Rev. H. F. Buckner, who came out from Kentucky in 1849 and for thirty-one years did noble work among the Creeks. He too died in the service. I knew them both well and was quite intimately associated with Rev. Mr. Buckner. Rev. Ramsay Potts came among the Choctaws in 1832 and Rev. Joseph Smedley came in 1835. They had both retired from the work before I came. All of these men were noble ambassadors of God and no words of praise are too strong in commendation of their good work among these people.

"My work has been among all of the Five Civilized Tribes and among the blanket or wild Indians as well. Of all the missionaries representing several church organizations in the early days of this work I alone remain to tell in person anything of the trials, hardships, joys and successes and failures of those pioneer days."

On coming to Indian Territory Reverend Mr. Murrow and his wife settled in a little log cabin in old North Fork town in the Creek Nation. His wife died there ten months later. He aided Mr. Buckner in his work, traveling on his pony all over the Creek, Seminole and Choctaw Nations. In 1859 he married Miss Clara Burns, daughter of Rev. Willis Burns, who came to the territory as a missionary in 1858. Of this union four children were born; one only is still living, a daughter, Mrs. W. A. McBride, of Atoka. After his marriage Mr. Murrow immediately moved to the Seminole Nation and established the mission work in that tribe.

As to the conditions among the Indians in 1861 Reverend Mr. Murrow is quoted as saying: "At the breaking out of the Civil war the Five Tribes were in a desperately agitated state Great pressure, persuasion, cajoling, bribing, coaxing, threatening and every conceivable influence was brought to bear upon them from both the Union and the Confederacy in attempts to persuade them to cast their lot with either side. The chiefs and old men of the tribes and, for the most part the women, were against taking sides at all, preferring to remain absolutely neutral. This was undoubtedly the wise policy, but continued persuasion and pressure so wrought upon the young men that in the end all of the tribes took up arms for one side or the other, being used mostly as scouts or else were organized into bands of raiders, the Indian character not being adaptable to the rigorous restrictions of regular army life. The Creeks, the Cherokees and the Seminoles divided in their allegiance, about one half of each tribe going to either side. The Choctaws and Chickasaws, these tribes being allied and located in the southern part of the territory, went solidly with the Confederacy. During the war the country was devastated by raiders and skirmishes, and immediately following the close of hostilities it became a rendezvous for a horde of outlaws of the worst kind. Had the tribes all remained neutral much of this suffering and privation would have been avoided and the Indian people would have advanced far more rapidly in Christianity and education.

"In 1862 at the request of the Seminole Council, I was appointed Confederate States Indian Agent for that tribe. The following year I received additional powers, including the purchase and distribution of supplies and provisions to the women, children and old men of several tribes, including Creeks, Osages, Comanches, Wichitas and others, whose able bodied men had enlisted with the Confederate army. These Comanches mostly belonged to To-sho-way's band and the Osages to Black Dog's band. They were all very wild and savage. They had never heard of the Christian religion. So I continued to be a missionary for Christ as well as a representative of the Confederate Government, and endeavored as best I could to feed their souls with spiritual food as well as to care for their temporal wants. Like all agents similarly placed I was often called upon to withstand temptation in the shape of bribes offered by contractors for supplies, such as accepting poor and diseased beef for good and dividing the profit with the contractor, but I thank God that I was able, through His spirit, to conquer and keep my hands clean and free of the contamination of bribery in any form. My reports were always made out to the last cent. Sometimes I paid out great sums of money. Once I received over forty thousand dollars as a single payment of 'head money' to members of the tribes. These sums were not always all Confederate money but sometimes included sums of gold.

"After the war I returned to my missionary work among the Five Tribes and was busy most of the time in reorganizing the demoralized churches in the Choctaw and Creek tribes. My wife died in 1868. In 1870 I suffered from a severe disease of the eyes brought on by excessive labor and neglect, and was compelled to return to my home in Georgia, where friends placed me in a hospital for the blind in the City of Atlanta. I was absent from my mission work for six months. During this time I had ample time to look over the Indian field of work and I became impressed with the thought that something should be done for the wild Indians of the western part of the Indian Territory."

As a result of the plans thus formulated and his exertions a mission was commenced among these wild or blanket Indians in 1874, and it has continued to the present time.

After four years of work among the Creeks and four years with the Seminoles, Doctor Murrow came to the Choctaw Nation and in 1867 located at what is now the City of Atoka, a place to which he gave the name and of which he will always be regarded as the founder. When he located there only two white families were living anywhere in that locality. As the location was on the direct trail and mail route of the Government, Mr. Murrow determined to have a postoffice established there and after writing the petition and the necessary correspondence was successful and the postoffice was named Atoka.

In July, 1872, Reverend Mr. Murrow issued a call to the churches of the Choctaw and Chickasaw Nations to meet in Atoka for the purpose of organizing the Choctaw and Chickasaw Baptist Association. Sixteen churches responded. The organization thus established did much for the two nations and sent from its ranks many of the present strong Baptist bodies of the old territory and the new state. In 1876 he introduced a preamble and resolution in the annual meeting of the Choctaw and Chickasaw Association, looking to the immediate organization of all the Baptist associations of the territory into a general convention. This was done for the purpose of breaking up tribal walls in religious work, bringing about a more fraternal feeling and a broader acquaintance between the workers in the field and to secure a more active co-operation and interest in the support and maintenance of mission work among the blanket Indians and other needy fields. This was not effected until 1881, when the Baptist Missionary and Educational Convention was organized and rapidly grew into a great power for good. Mr. Murrow was for seventeen years president of this convention, giving much of his time, means and prayers to its work.

In 1879 in the same association he introduced a resolution recommending the establishment of a Bible School for the instruction of native preachers in Bible doctrine and Baptist faith and practice. Further conferences with Rev. A. C. Bacone and Rev. Daniel Rogers led to the establishment of Indian University at Bacone, Indian Territory, which has also been a potent factor for good in Oklahoma.

For many years Reverend Mr. Murrow's missionary work was done under the auspices of the mission board of the Southern Baptist Church. In 1889 he changed his relationship to the Baptist Home Mission Society of New York, and for fourteen years had general supervision of all Indian missionary work for the Baptist Church in Oklahoma and Indian Territory. His work during these years of trying circumstances and self sacrifices was arduous and difficult, but was none the less effective. He organized more than seventy-five Baptist churches in the Indian Territory, and assisted with his own hands and money in the building of nearly that many houses of worship. He assisted in, the ordination of more than seventy preachers, mostly Indians, and baptized not less than 2,000 people, most of whom were also Indians.

In 1887, largely due to Reverend Mr. Murrow's leadership, the Atoka Baptist Church successfully inaugurated the Atoka Baptist Academy. This splendid school was conducted under the auspices of the American Baptist Home Mission Society for eighteen years, and was then merged into or absorbed by the Murrow Indian Orphans Home. The founding of this home has been considered by Mr. Murrow as his last and best effort for the assistance of the people to whom he has given nearly sixty years of service.

His work in connection with the Orphans Home has been practically continuous since January 1, 1903. He secured as a permanent site a large farm located in the Choctaw Nation. He has been indefatigable in the practical work of the school and in securing support for it from over the country. He enlisted the sympathy of President Roosevelt and many foremost Americans, and in the years before Oklahoma statehood had secured contributions of about $20,000 for the buying of property and making improvements suitable to the work and the purposes of the home.

On June 26, 1888, at Bacone College at Muskogee, Reverend Mr. Murrow married Kathrina Lois Ellett, who was born near Cleveland, Ohio. She was a zealous Christian worker in behalf of the Indians before her marriage, and since then has loyally aided and abetted Reverend Mr. Murrow in his continued efforts in behalf of the uplift and betterment of the Indian people in Oklahoma.

Reverend Mr. Murrow is one of the oldest and most distinguished Masons of Oklahoma. He organized the first Masonic Lodge in the territory after the war, locating it at Boggy Depot. For more than thirty years he was grand secretary of the Blue Lodge of the territory, and he assisted in organizing and at one time was secretary of the Grand Lodge and the Grand Chapter and grand recorder of the Grand Commandery of the Grand Council. He also organized the first council of Royal and Select Masters in Oklahoma and served as grand master of the Grand Council until April, 1912. In the Scottish Rite he attained the very great distinction of the thirty-third degree.

W. A. SMITH, of Bartlesville, who has been extensively indentified with the oil development of Oklahoma for more than ten years, has a well earned reputation of a man who does things in a large way, and whose activities are a matter of public interest because they are so closely connected with the public welfare.

His success and prosperity are the result of hard experience and practical work in the oil regions of many diverse sections. He has used his means liberally and elsewhere and he is well known both in Oklahoma and in other states.

His birth occurred at Buffalo, New York, October 31, 1869. His parents, Herbert G. and Rosalie (Clark) Smith, were natives of Erie County, New York, and his father for the past eight years has been a citizen of Bartlesville. Herbert G. Smith was born in Erie County, New York, on a farm, February 2, 1850, and lived there until twenty-two years of age. His parents, William and Rachel (Healy) Smith, also natives of New York State, were early residents and farmers of Erie County, and William Smith died in 1870 and his wife in 1885. Their seven children were: Chester, who was killed in the battle of Gettysburg; Myra, deceased; Albert, deceased; Herbert G.; Chloe, deceased; Annie, deceased; and William, who died in infancy. Herbert G. Smith at the age of twenty-two located on a farm in the State of Michigan, afterwards returned to New York and lived on the home farm three years, and next engaged in the oil business at Bradford, Pennsylvania, following which his operations took him into Ohio, Indiana, West Virginia, out to Kansas, and since 1907 his home and headquarters have been in Bartlesville. He is a republican voter but has never been active in politics, and is a member of the Order of the Maccabees, while his wife is a Presbyterian. His wife, whose maiden name was Rosalie Clark, was born in Erie County, New York, February 2, 1851, a daughter of Amos and Louisa (Fuller) Clark, also a native of New York State. Her mother died in 1859 and her father in 1902, and their four children were: Ellen, deceased; Etta, wife of Alonzo Wilkinson of Montgomery County, Missouri; Adelbert, who died in infancy; and Mrs. H. G. Smith.

The only child of his parents, W. A. Smith grew up in Western New York and also in Western Pennsylvania. At the age of sixteen he left school and became associated with his father in the oil business in Pennsylvania and Indiana. Thus for more than thirty years his activities have been concentrated along the line of oil development, and there is no man in Oklahoma of broader and more active experience in this industry. More than ordinary responsibilities came to him at an early age. While in Indiana he took the position of general superintendent for the West Indian Oil Syndicate, operating in the Barbadoes and on the coast of Venezuela. He remained in South America about three years and was also identified to some extent with placer mining. Returning to the United States he was for about three years in the oil fields of West Virginia, and then went out to Kansas. He is a man of cosmopolitan experience and training, has known all sorts and conditions of men, and he has the bearing and address of the man who has traveled widely and has seen much of the world and of life.

Since 1905 he has operated with Bartlesville as his headquarters. In the subsequent decade he has been among the foremost in several lines of development and Washington County in particular owes much to his enterprise. He was one of the promoters in building the street railway and the interurban line at Bartlesville, and was treasurer of the company and a director until the plant was sold to a syndicate of New York capitalists. The directors of the company had raised among themselves the money necessary to build these lines, and the business was always a paying proposition.

Mr. Smith and John Irwin built at Bartlesville the fine Smith-Irwin Block, but Mr. Smith has since sold his interest and it is now known as the Brin-Irwin Building. His interests as an oil man are widely extended, not only in the region surrounding Bartlesville but also in Okmulgee County, Oklahoma, in Texas and even in California. He has the distinction of having opened the Copan Oil & Gas Company, drilled the first well and brought in one of the best oil pools in the country. He is the owner also of a large orange grove in the San Joaquin Valley of California.

Mr. Smith is a republican, a member of the Masonic Order and the Benevolent and Protective Order of Elks, and also of the Bartlesville Country Club.

His first wife was Eva Miller of Claysville, Pennsylvania. The only child of that union, Herbert Leman, was born at Pennville, Indiana, July 6, 1894, and was reared by his grandparents, Herbert G. Smith and wife. Mrs. Smith died July 15, 1894, a few days after the birth of her son.

On November 28, 1903, Mr. Smith married Mrs. Sarah Rebecca (Cole) Cook. Both as a home maker and in social affairs Mrs. Smith has been well known in Bartlesville for the past ten years. She represents an old and quite prominent American family. She was born January 14, 1871, a daughter of Alfred H. and Dorcas M. (Reynolds) Cole, natives of Ohio and West Virginia, respectively. Her father was born at Powhattan Point, Ohio, October 9, 1842, and is now living retired at Parkerville, West Virginia. His wife was born March 6, 1846, at St. Mary's, West Virginia. The old Cole homestead is still owned by a member of the family and a piece of rock blasted from the famous Plymouth Rock in Massachusetts is lying at the foot of what is known as Cole's Hill. The nine children of the Cole family were: Charles, Cora, Mrs. Smith, Lillian, Walter, Sylvia, Martha, Chester, and one that died in infancy. Mrs. Smith was first married September 29, 1887, to James H. Cook, and her children by that union are Louis Alfred and Calvin Cole Cook. Louis Alfred was born February 14, 1889, in Findlay, Ohio, now lives in Okmulgee County, Oklahoma, and married Ethel Saunders of Lexington, Missouri. Calvin C. Cook, born January 10, 1891, in Parkersburg, West Virginia, now lives in the San Joaquin Valley of California and married Lula Brooks.

JAMES A. WEISELOGEL. In these days when revelations of political corruption are so common as to occasion no surprise, and to be a politician, is, in the minds of many very respectable but undiscriminating people, to be a suspicious character, it is pleasing to find a man brave enough and strong enough to enter the political field, not for purposes of self-aggrandizement, but in order to abolish old abuses and establish better and cleaner conditions in municipal government. And when such a one, by sheer force of character, wins a clean cut victory against a strong opposition entrenched in the very seat of government, honest citizens may well feel hopeful for the future. The election of James A. Wieselogel as mayor of Pawhuska, Osage County, Oklahoma, which occurred in the spring of the year, 1915, was a step in the right direction and an encouragement to the friends of law and order in this county. As this was a notable achievement, a few words in regard to Mayor Weiselogel's personality and previous career will be of interest to the readers of this volume.

James A. Weiselogel was born at Linn Creek, Camden County, Missouri, October 21, 1886, the son of Michael and Laura E. (McIntyre) Weiselogel. The father, born in Baden, Germany, in 1852, at the age of twenty-one years came to the United States, landing at New York. After awhile he removed to Missouri, where he married, residing for a number of years in Camden County. About 1893 he made another change of location, this time going to Newkirk, Oklahoma, of which place he has since been a resident, being now a retired merchant there. His wife, mother of the subject of this sketch, was born in Indiana in 1858 and subsequently moved to Missouri, where, as already intimated, she became the wife of Michael Weiselogel. They became the parents of five children, all of whom are now living, namely D. W., a resident of Tulsa, Oklahoma; Effie, wife of Elner Gearhart; James A., the direct subject of this biography; J. M., who is proprietor of the Eagle Cafe in Pawhuska; and Clara, who resides at home with her parents.

James A. Weiselogel resided with his parents until reaching the age of twenty years, at which time he came to Oklahoma. He acquired his elementary education in the common schools, afterwards attended the high school for awhile and then finished his studies by attendance for one year at the Presbyterian Academy at Newkirk. His father being a merchant, he began industrial life in his store and thus acquired a practical knowledge of mercantile affairs and general business methods, of which he subsequently availed himself, working as clerk in stores in various places for several years. He then returned home for a visit with his parents, remaining with them for some time. Returning to Oklahoma, he located in Fairfax, where, in company with O. C. Miller, he engaged in the restaurant business, which they conducted together successfully for about a year. At the end of that time Mr. Weiselogel sold out his interest and went to Oklahoma City, where, for a few months he was employed as a clerk. He then accepted a position as travelling man for the Great Western Sales Company, his headquarters being with the company's office at Omaha, Nebraska. Subsequently he was transferred to Wichita, Kansas, from which point he worked for the same company until the summer of 1911. In June of that year he made his advent in Pawhuska, Oklahoma, finding employment in a restaurant, where he remained for eighteen months. In August, 1912, he bought a restaurant and conducted it successfully until the spring of 1915. During this time he had made a wide acquaintance and impressed his personality upon many of the leading citizens of the town, taking an interest in public affairs and discussing the political situation, especially with those citizens who desired to see a reform movement inaugurated. The greatest obstacle to such a movement was the liquor interest, which held the city in its grip and was supported by many citizens who were either its open friends, or who were not farsighted enough to see that a "wide open" town kept away the more reputable class of settlers and was inimical to the city's future progress, as well as to its present prosperity. Indeed, the situation was rendered more acute from the fact that the Department of the Interior demands that the towns in the state keep "dry" under the warning that if they do not the department will remove the Indians elsewhere, which would naturally work a great injury to legitimate trade. On the advice of his friends, therefore, Mr. Weiselogel declared himself a candidate for mayor at the election to be held April 6, 1915. He made his own canvass chiefly and was so successful in impressing the voters with the necessity of having a clean town, uncontaminated by the liquor trade, that he was triumphantly elected on the republican ticket, having a majority of thirty-two votes. This result was the more impressive, as Pawhuska has a usual democratic majority of about 200. Taking office May 3, 1915, Mayor Weiselogel at once set about his duties in a progressive spirit and, although little more than a month has elapsed (at this writing) since he assumed the chair as presiding officer of the city government, the hostile forces have been obliged to capitulate and Pawhuska is now one of the "driest" towns of its size in Oklahoma. The beneficial results are already observable. The police force has been reformed and the city is now in a much more clean and orderly condition than it was under the old regime. Something yet remains to be done, but Mr. Weiselogel is not the man to falter or turn his hand from the work until the highest degree of efficiency in every department of the city government, which is a commission government, has been attained. And when attained, it may safely be said, it will be maintained. Mayor Weiselogel is unmarried, but as he is still a young man, that fault, if it be one, may be remedied in the future. He has advanced in the Masonic order as far as the Chapter, and belongs also to the Eastern Star, the Benevolent and Protective Order of Elks, the Knights of Pythias and the society known as Homesteaders, of all of which he is a useful and active member. To be anything else would be foreign to his nature, which is essentially progressive and wedded to high ideals of life and duty.

BENJAMIN F. BURWELL. The late Judge Burwell, who served as an associate justice of the Supreme Court of Oklahoma for a decade, 1898-1908, was a Pennsylvanian, born in Armstrong County, April 15, 1866, a son of Joseph Yarenton and Maxia (Lanham) Burwell. He was educated in the public and normal schools of West Virginia. The earlier years of his manhood were spent in Kansas, and in 1888 he married Miss Agnes J. Carnahan, of Hope, that state. Mr. Burwell was admitted to the bar in 1890, practiced at Gypsum City, Kansas, for about a year thereafter, and in 1891 moved to Oklahoma City, where he afterward engaged in practice and in the performance of his judicial duties. In 1892 he was an unsuccessful candidate for probate judge, and after his retirement from the Supreme bench of Oklahoma in 1908 continued in active practice of his profession until the time of his death, April 2, 1916.

CLINTON A. GALBRAITH. Judge Galbraith has a substantial record both as a jurist and as lawyer, although he has never occupied the bench in Oklahoma. He was born in Hartsville, Indiana, on March 6, 1860, and graduated from the college at that place in 1883. For the remainder of that year and a portion of 1884 he was a law student at the University of Michigan and afterward studied alone and under private tutorship. Judge Galbraith was admitted to the bar in 1888; served as attorney general of Oklahoma Territory from 1893-7, and in April, 1898, located at Hilo, Hawaiian Islands. He was associate justice of the Hawaiian Supreme Court from 1900-4, and in the latter year returned to Oklahoma for the practice of his profession, fixing his residence at Ada. In September, 1913, Judge Galbraith was appointed a Supreme Court Commissioner; was reappointed in March, 1915, and is now presiding judge of Division No. 2. Although his official residence is Oklahoma City his home is still Ada.

JOSEPH B. THOBURN was born at Bellaire, Ohio, August 8, 1866, the son of Maj. Thomas C. and Mary Eleanor (Crozier) Thoburn. His parents migrated to Kansas in March, 1871, settling on a homestead in Marion County. His early life was spent on the farm. Subsequently he learned the printer's trade. He graduated from the Kansas Agricultural College in 1893. In 1894 he was married to Miss Callie Conwell, of Manhattan, Kansas. They have two daughters, Mary Eleanor and Jeanne Isabel.

Mr. Thoburn located at Oklahoma City in 1899, where he was engaged in printing and newspaper writing for several years. In 1902 he assumed the duties of the secretaryship of the local commercial club, which position he filled until March 1, 1903, a reorganization being effected during that interval. In the meantime, in December, 1902, he had been chosen as the secretary of the Territorial Board of Agriculture—being the first to fill that position and serving in that capacity until July, 1905.

During the past ten years Mr. Thoburn's time and attention have been devoted almost exclusively to the work or research and writing along the lines of local and western history. In 1913, he was elected a member of the faculty of the University of Oklahoma, where his work has been more nearly that of a curator than an instructor, his field of effort being widened to include American archaeology and ethnology as well as local history. He has been one of the most active members of the board of trustees of the Oklahoma Historical Society for many years past.

Mr. Thoburn is a member of the Methodist Episcopal Church, a Mason and a Modern Woodman. He is also a member of the Oklahoma Society of the Sons of the American Revolution. As the work incident to the collection of the material and writing the text of the Standard History of Oklahoma required all of his time for a year, he has been on leave of absence from his regular duties at the university during the scholastic year 1915-6.

Printed in the USA
CPSIA information can be obtained
at www.ICGtesting.com
LVHW012137181023
761521LV00038B/739

9 781015 154612